ABOUT THE EDITOR

NORMAN LEWIS, author, editor and teacher, has been active in the fields of language improvement and lexicography for over twenty years. This is his thirteenth published book. He has had over five hundred articles or word tests printed in national magazines such as *Ladies' Home Journal, Cosmopolitan, The Saturday Evening Post, Good Housekeeping, Coronet, Harper's,* etc.

His book *30 Days to a More Powerful Vocabulary,* written with Wilfred Funk, is the best-selling paper-bound book on vocabulary building ever published; over three and a half million copies have been sold (Pocket Books, 75414, 75¢). Over a million copies have been sold of the paper-bound edition of his book *Word Power Made Easy* (Pocket CARDINAL 75295, 75¢).

❄ ❄ ❄

This book is a specially prepared and shorter version of *The New Roget's Thesaurus in Dictionary Form,* published in a hard-bound edition by G. P. Putnam's Sons.

THE NEW POCKET

ROGET'S THESAURUS

IN DICTIONARY FORM

EDITED BY

NORMAN LEWIS

ADJUNCT ASSISTANT PROFESSOR OF ENGLISH,

DIVISION OF GENERAL EDUCATION,

NEW YORK UNIVERSITY

BASED ON C. O. SYLVESTER MAWSON'S
ALPHABETICAL ARRANGEMENT OF THE
FAMOUS ROGET SYSTEM OF WORD
CLASSIFICATION.

WSP

WASHINGTON SQUARE PRESS   •   NEW YORK

THE NEW POCKET ROGET'S THESAURUS
IN DICTIONARY FORM

A *Washington Square Press* edition

1st printing........................March, 1961
34th printing........................June, 1970

This Washington Square Press edition is a somewhat abridged version of *The New Roget's Thesaurus of the English Language in Dictionary Form*, published January, 1961, by G. P. Putnam's Sons and simultaneously by Garden City Books by special arrangement with G. P. Putnam's Sons. Copyright, ©, 1961, by G. P. Putnam's Sons.

Both the plan of this book and the application of the dictionary idea to *Roget's Thesaurus* are original and must not be imitated.

PATENT APPLIED FOR

L

Published by Washington Square Press,
a division of Simon & Schuster, Inc., 630 Fifth Avenue, New York, N.Y.

WASHINGTON SQUARE PRESS editions are distributed in the U.S. by Simon & Schuster, Inc., 630 Fifth Avenue, New York, N.Y. 10020 and in Canada by Simon & Schuster of Canada, Ltd., Richmond Hill, Ontario, Canada.

FOR

MARY, MARGIE, DEBRA

PREFACE TO THE FIRST EDITION

Roget's Thesaurus has been the stand-by of writers for almost three generations. Edition after edition has been published; revisions and enlargements have enhanced its usefulness, but the form has remained the same: classification according to ideas, followed by a colossal index.

A Roget dictionary is an innovation. Users of the Thesaurus well know that the excellence of the book is heavily discounted by the time required to find a word. As in any other academic treatise, it is always necessary to look in two places: the index and the chapter or category. From the viewpoint of the actual user, the strength of the Thesaurus constitutes its essential weakness. Separation into watertight compartments makes neither for speed nor convenience. In substance, the arrangement is: one word, one sense. Thus, under *greenness*, the color alone is treated (and rightly so according to the original plan); for other senses, the index refers us to nine different categories. *Softness* (including *soften* and *soft*) likewise deals only with the literal meaning; for others, the index sends us hunting through no less than twenty categories. And so it goes. We do not mean that a man must necessarily consult this number to find the particular word he has in mind, for the index does briefly suggest the general character of the references. But if a reader is not very clear as to the meaning; if, as frequently happens, the senses of a word shade off into each other; above all, if he is in a hurry; then his search will be a tedious one.

Imagine a dictionary built on these lines. Suppose you turned to a common word and found only one meaning given, obliging you to look under several generalized headings for the other senses. However logically such a system might be worked out, it would be unwieldy, unworkmanlike, and unalluring.

The present volume retains the practical advantages of the standardized Thesaurus without the disadvantages. It was fashioned with a two-fold aim: to provide ready synonyms for the time-pressed worker and to give a richer list—thought expressing and thought provoking—to the more leisured writer, the scholar, and the stylist. There is an abundance of plain fare for the plain man; there is besides a discriminate and bounteous provision—a Lucullan feast—for the literary epicure.

About 1910, I made my first revision of Roget and, twelve years later, a still more elaborate version. This was the *International Thesaurus*. But though various improvements in arrangement and format were devised, the general plan was the same—increasing the size but adding to the complexity. Further progress could be made only by cutting loose from tradition.

The severance has at last been made and this dictionary is the result. Virtually, it is a dictionary within a dictionary. The old Roget lists are here, modernized, refurbished, and rearranged. The categories are no longer mere exemplifications of a philosophical treatment but are self-contained lists of classified synonyms, reflecting every phase of meaning and every shade of thought. It is a true dictionary, not of words and their meanings but of words and their synonyms.

Simplicity is the keynote, the convenience of the consulter being always kept in mind. The hyphen-and-dash devices, adopted by Roget for saving space, have been abolished. They were a source of confusion to the uninitiated and often threw into juxtaposition words in no way allied. Clarity was sacrificed to formula. Space has now been gained by other methods, typographical and editorial.

The outstanding characteristics of this volume may be briefly summarized:

1. The dictionary method is followed throughout, all entries being listed in alphabetical order and in one vocabulary.

2. Synonyms, grouped according to meaning, immediately follow each entry, so that reference to other parts of the book is not absolutely essential.

3. The reconstructed Roget categories are incorporated in the general alphabet.

4. The Roget plan of giving nouns, verbs, adjectives, adverbs, and interjections under each main head has been retained; but whereas Roget made his "adverbs" an olla-podrida of adverbs, prepositions, conjunctions, and sometimes of non-adverbial phrases, such terms are now separately classified.

5. Under these main heads, each meaning of a synonymized word is clearly distinguished, a key word giving the general sense of each subdivision.

6. Reference to the major subjects is made from the ordinary entries in the vocabulary, which entries take the place of the former index.

7. All special words have been characterized so that the writer may select his synonyms with greater sureness. If he wishes to use a scientific or technical term, a colloquial or slang expression, an Americanism or a Briticism, or some word peculiar to another country, he can do so knowingly and with precision.

8. Plurals are recorded in every case of irregularity and wherever the consulter might be in doubt.

9. Phrases are given freely. This was one of Roget's most valuable contributions to the subject. It is just as important, and difficult, to find a substitute phrase as a synonymous word: moreover, a phrase is often the only alternative for a word that has no true synonym. Yet most books of synonyms omit phrases entirely.

10. Obsolete words have been discarded. This is a dictionary of living words only.

11. New words have been added—thousands of them—to bring the work abreast of modern scholarship and usage. Our language has been enriched in recent years with many terms contributed by aeronautics, radio, the moving-picture industry, meteorology, psychology—in fact, by practically every branch of knowledge and every technical calling. Side by side with these recruited terms are many older words that have taken to themselves new meanings. The synonym book, like the ordinary dictionary, must keep pace with these additions and changes.

12. The Roget Dictionary is at once a vade mecum for the

busy man and a complete thesaurus for the exacting writer who lives with words and by them.

In these days, when worth is often measured by magnitude, it may be pointed out that this book not only contains more synonyms than any previous edition of Roget, but is more comprehensive than any other book of synonyms whatever. Size alone, however, is a poor criterion of merit. A work of reference must stand or fall by its accuracy and authority.

The authority of this work rests on almost a lifetime of practical experience in the making of dictionaries. This experience included association with great lexicographers such as Sir James Murray of the Oxford Dictionary and Benjamin E. Smith of the Century, while several years were spent on the permanent staff of Webster. Those years were an invaluable preparation for this undertaking, for on such dictionaries accuracy and scholarship are appraised at their full value. This book has been made under the stimulus of that great tradition. Three years have been spent in its actual construction, but behind this period is the accumulated store of a quarter of a century.

—C. O. S. M.

Wellesley, Massachusetts

WHAT THIS BOOK CAN DO FOR YOU

The New Pocket Roget's Thesaurus in Dictionary Form is designed to help you find the words with which to express yourself more clearly, more effectively, more precisely.

It offers you immediate, practical, and invaluable assistance whenever you are in trouble.

Do you want a few quick synonyms for a word you have been overusing?

Do you need the one particular word or phrase that will most successfully convey to your reader the subtle shading of thought or emotion you wish to get across to him?

Do you feel that your language lacks freshness or vigor because some of the words in which you are couching your ideas are drab, weak, vague, or overly general?

Do you ever find yourself laboring over phraseology because the words that can make your writing come alive continue tantalizingly to elude you no matter how desperately you search for them in the recesses of your mind?

Then this book is tailor-made for your needs.

This book is as simple to use as a dictionary—no elaborate index to thumb through, no time-consuming hopping from page to page, before you can start tracking down a particular word or a specific shade of meaning.

EXCLUSIVE FEATURES OF
THE NEW POCKET
ROGET'S THESAURUS IN DICTIONARY FORM

1. Over 17,000 individual entries
Any word for which you are ever likely to require a syno-

nym can be found within seconds under the simple alphabetical system that characterizes the book.

Do you need another way of saying *adulterate?* Turning to the *A*'s, you find: **adulterate,** *v.* contaminate, debase, pollute (IMPURITY).

Do you want a substitute expression for *journey?* Under the *J*'s: **journey,** *n.* travel, trip, tour (TRAVELING).

Are you not quite satisfied with the adjective *unbeatable,* possibly because it doesn't fit the rhythm of your sentence or fails, in some subtle way, to achieve the exact effect you are striving for? Under the *U*'s: **unbeatable,** *adj.* undefeatable, indomitable, invincible (SUCCESS).

Are you a little doubtful whether the verb *censure* expresses what you have in mind, even though you can't, for the moment, think of a better word? Under the *C*'s: **censure,** *v.* chide, exprobrate, lecture, reprehend (DISAPPROVAL, SCOLDING).

2. More than 1,000 major categories

Each category explores an idea in depth, offering a veritable cornucopia of words and phrases catalogued both by parts of speech and by logically associated facets of meaning.

The categories cover such broad concepts as ABILITY, BURIAL, CHANGE, DEATH, HUNGER, LIFE, RIDICULE, SEX, UNCERTAINTY, YOUTH, etc., etc.

3. Every individual entry followed by a reference to one or more major categories

If you want *all* the possible synonyms for a word you are looking up, or if you decide to investigate more fully the general idea behind your word, you turn to the major category indicated in parentheses following each entry.

The category IMPURITY, for example, not only suggests seven more verbs related to *adulterate,* but in addition spreads before you a wealth of nouns and adjectives revolving around the concept of *adulteration.*

The category TRAVELING similarly enriches your thinking in respect to *journey.* Here you may first be interested in the score of further synonyms for the word. But you will find, as well, an abundance of nouns signifying kinds of journeying, motives for journeying, people who journey, etc.; twenty-eight different ways of saying *to make a journey;* and all the adjectives that describe journeys or journeyers.

4. Synonyms grouped according to the varying senses of a word

Brief, to take a simple example, may be understood as a description either of shortness or of impermanence. This division of meaning is clearly shown in the entry, each of the two series of synonyms directly followed by the category reference that contains further information: **brief,** *adj.* concise, terse, succinct (SHORTNESS); short-lived, momentary, meteoric (IMPERMANENCE).

For another example, the adjective *forced* may show either unwillingness or lack of sincere feeling; notice again how clearly this division is indicated: **forced,** *adj.* grudging, begrudging, involuntary (UNWILLINGNESS); artificial, constrained, contrived (UNNATURALNESS).

5. Major categories fully cross-referenced

If you wish to research further aspects of a concept, you are referred, at the end of each category, to synonymous or related areas of meaning.

For example, APPROVAL is cross-referenced to ACCEPTANCE, FLATTERY, LOVE, PRAISE, PRIDE, RESPECT, and WORSHIP, in any of which you will discover fresh and colorful ways of expressing an idea you may be developing. Similarly, DEFIANCE is cross-referenced to COURAGE, DISAGREEMENT, DISOBEDIENCE, and THREAT; GOD to CHURCH, HEAVEN, RELIGION, SUPERNATURAL BEINGS, and WORSHIP; SADNESS to DEJECTION, GLOOM, HOPELESSNESS, REGRET, and WEEPING.

Category cross-references also indicate where you will find a wide range of *antonyms.* Under INCREASE, for example, you are directed, for opposed or contrasting concepts, to DECREASE and DEDUCTION; under OSTENTATION, to MODESTY and SIMPLICITY; under RAIN, to DRYNESS; under SIN, to ACQUITTAL and INNOCENCE; under SLEEP, to ACTION, ACTIVITY, and WAKEFULNESS.

The random examples detailed above highlight the infinite richness, tight efficiency, and clear-cut organization of the book. With a single word as a point of departure, you can, within minutes, unlock a vast treasury of colorful, exciting phraseology that will stimulate your thinking, sharpen your powers of communication, and add freshness and punch to your writing.

THE NEW POCKET

ROGET'S THESAURUS

IN DICTIONARY FORM

ABBREVIATIONS USED IN THIS BOOK

abbr. .... abbreviation
adj. .... adjective
adv. .... adverb
aero. .... aeronautics
Am. or *Amer.*..America, American
anat. .... anatomy
antiq. .... antiquities
anthropol. .... anthropology
Ar. .... Arabic
arch. .... architecture
archæol. .... archæology
arith. .... arithmetic
astrol. .... astrology
astron. .... astronomy
Bib. .... Biblical
biol. .... biology
bot. .... botany
Brit. .... British
cf. .... confer (L., compare)
chem. .... chemistry
Ch. of Eng. .... Church of England
colloq. .... colloquial
comp. .... comparative
conj. .... conjunction
derog. .... derogatory
dial. .... dialect, dialectal
dim. .... diminutive
E. .... East
eccl. .... ecclesiastical
econ. .... economics
elec. .... electricity
embryol. .... embryology
Eng. .... English, England
entom. .... entomology
esp. .... especially
ethnol. .... ethnology
F. .... French
fem. .... feminine
fig. .... figurative, figuratively
G. or *Ger.* .... German
geol. .... geology
geom. .... geometry
Gr. .... Greek
gram. .... grammar
Gr. Brit. .... Great Britain
Heb. .... Hebrew
Hind. .... Hindustani
hist. .... history, historical
hort. .... horticulture

interj. .... interjection
It. .... Italian
Jap. .... Japanese
L. .... Latin
lit. .... literal, literally
masc. .... masculine
math. .... mathematics
mech. ....mechanics
med. .... medicine
metal. .... metallurgy
meteorol. .... meteorology
mil. .... military
Moham. .... Mohammedan
mus. .... music
myth. .... mythology
N. .... North
n. .... noun
naut. .... nautical
Per. .... Persian
Pg. .... Portuguese
pharm. .... pharmacy
philol. .... philology
philos. .... philosophy
physiol. .... physiology
pl. .... plural
polit. .... political
prep. .... preposition
pros. .... prosody
psychoanal. .... psychoanalysis
psychol. .... psychology
R.C.Ch......Roman Catholic Church
relig. .... religion
rhet. .... rhetoric, rhetorical
Russ. .... Russian
S. .... South
Scot. .... Scottish
sculp. .... sculpture
sing. .... singular
Skr. ....Sanskrit
Sp. .... Spanish
superl. .... superlative
tech. .... technical
theat. .... theatrical
theol. .... theology
typog. .... typography
Univ. .... University
U.S. .... United States
v. .... verb
W. .... West
Zool. .... Zoology

A

abandon, *n.* wantonness, libertinism, unconstraint (FREEDOM).

abandon, *v.* quit, forsake, leave (DESERTION); surrender, forfeit, sacrifice (RELINQUISHMENT).

abandoned, *adj.* deserted, vacant, unoccupied (ABSENCE); forsaken, left, marooned (DESERTION); wild, rampant, riotous (FREEDOM); corrupt, Augean, base (IMMORALITY); depraved, perverted, unnatural (WICKEDNESS); incorrigible, irredeemable, irreclaimable, unreformable (LOSS); loose, immoral, wanton (SEX).

abate, *v.* alleviate, mitigate, slacken, lessen, dwindle, taper, slack off (WEAKNESS, DECREASE, MODERATENESS).

abbey, *n.* cloister, priory, monastery (RELIGIOUS COMMUNITY).

abbreviate, *v.* take in, abridge, shorten (SHORTNESS).

abdicate, *v.* resign, secede, retire (DEPARTURE); renounce, quit, abandon (RELINQUISHMENT).

abdomen, *n.* pelvis, paunch, stomach (BELLY).

abduct, *v.* kidnap, shanghai, carry off, spirit away (TAKING, THIEVERY).

aberration, *n.* abnormality, aberrance, perversion; freak, heteroclite (UNNATURALNESS, UNUSUALNESS); mental disorder, derangement, delirium (INSANITY).

abet, *v.* connive with, collude with, assist (AID).

abeyance, *n.* subsidence, suspension, discontinuance (CESSATION, INACTION).

abhor, *v.* hate, abominate, detest, loathe, abhorrence (HATRED).

abide, *v.* stop, roost, visit (INHABITANT); endure, last, remain (CONTINUATION); suffer, submit to, tolerate, stomach (SUPPORT).

ABILITY—*N.* ability, aptitude, caliber, appetency, habilitation, bent, turn, knack, flair, faculty, talent, gift, forte, endowment, verve.

competence, efficiency, know-how (*slang*), facility, proficiency, adequacy, qualification, workmanship, technique; capability, capacity, compass, initiative.

genius, brilliance, prowess, superability.

cleverness, artifice, ingenuity, craft, strategy.

skill, art, artistry, address, felicity, mastery, wizardry, virtuosity, versatility.

tact, diplomacy, diplomatism, statesmanship, delicacy, discretion, finesse, *savoir-faire* (*F.*); strategy, management, execution.

expert, ace, authority, specialist, master, past master, wizard, crackerjack (*slang*), shark, whiz (*colloq.*).

skillful person, adept, artist, craftsman, master workman, virtuoso; diplomat, diplomatist, statesman, strategist, maneuverer, politician, tactician, technician, genius, prodigy.

achievement, accomplishment, attainment, acquirement; exploit, deed, feat, stunt (*colloq.*).

V. enable, empower, capacitate, verse, qualify, train; make efficient, streamline.

be able, etc. (see *Adj.*); qualify, suffice, do; master, excel in.

Adj. able, competent, efficient, proficient; adequate, equal, qualified, trained, capable, sciential; accomplished, finished, brilliant, expert, *au fait* (*F.*), top-flight, top-drawer (*both slang*), masterly, crack; apt, gifted, endowed, talented; delicate, diplomatic, discreet, resourceful, tactful, statesmanlike.

skillful, skilled, practiced, adroit, adept, apt, artistic, felicitous, facile; clever, cunning, artful, crafty, canny, ingenious; master, masterly, neat, consummate, versatile, many-sided; handy, adroit, deft, dexterous, nimble, nimble-fingered, light-fingered, light-handed, ambidextrous; well-handled; workmanlike; tricky, tender, ticklish, tactical, strategic; lambent.

See also CLEVERNESS, EASE, IMAGINATION, INTELLIGENCE, POWER. *Antonyms*—See CLUMSINESS, DISABLEMENT.

abject, *adj.* contemptible, beggarly, cheap (CONTEMPT); wretched, spiritless, vaporish (DEJECTION); slavish, servile, subservient (SLAVERY).

ablaze, *adj.* afire, aflame, fired, on

fire (EXCITEMENT); bright, shiny, aglow (LIGHT).

able, *adj.* competent, efficient, proficient, skillful (ABILITY).

able-bodied, *adj.* brawny, muscular, athletic, burly (STRENGTH).

abnormal, *adj.* grotesque, monstrous, freakish, perverted (UNNATURALNESS); irregular, anomalous, atypical (UNUSUALNESS).

abnormality, *n.* aberrance, aberration, perversion (UNNATURALNESS); freak, heteroclite, abnormity (UNUSUALNESS).

abode, *n.* haunt, living quarters, dwelling (HABITATION).

abolish, *v.* do away with, abrogate, exterminate (ELIMINATION); put an end to, make an end of, destroy (END).

abominable, *adj.* hateful, abhorrent, detestable, despicable (HATRED); bad, atrocious, awful, dreadful, horrible (INFERIORITY).

aboriginal, *adj.* native, indigenous, original (INHABITANT).

abortion, *n.* miscarriage, stillbirth, curettage, feticide, aborticide (BIRTH, PREGNANCY); misfire, fiasco, failure (FAILURE); arrested development, hypoplasty (*med.*), arrest (SLOWNESS).

abortive, *adj.* unsuccessful, unavailing, futile, vain (FAILURE); premature, stillborn (BIRTH); undeveloped, embryonic, latent (IMMATURITY).

abound, *v.* be numerous, exuberate, pullulate (MULTITUDE); be prevalent, prevail, obtain (PRESENCE); teem, superabound, overabound (SUFFICIENCY).

about, *adv.* around, on every side, on all sides (ENVIRONMENT); nearly, approximately, *circa* (*L.*), almost (NEARNESS).

about, *prep.* in respect to, in reference to, in connection with (RELATIONSHIP).

about-face, *n.* *volte-face* (*F.*), change of heart (REVERSION).

above, *adj.* said, above-mentioned, above-stated (PRECEDENCE); higher, greater, upper (SUPERIORITY).

above, *adv.* upward, overhead, aloft, on high (HEIGHT).

aboveboard, *adj.* straightforward, truthful, veracious, frank (HONESTY).

abracadabra, *n.* hocus-pocus, mumbo jumbo, open-sesame (MAGIC).

abrasion, *n.* bruise, blemish, wale, mouse (HARM); pulverization, detrition, trituration (POWDERINESS); excoriation, chafe, friction (RUBBING).

abrasive, *adj.* corrosive, erosive, caustic (DESTRUCTION).

abrasive, *n.* pumice, triturator, grater (RUBBING).

abreast, *adj.* side-by-side, collateral, juxtaposed (SIDE); familiar, informed, apprised (KNOWLEDGE).

abridge, *v.* condense, compact, reduce (SHORTNESS).

abridgment, *n.* brief, abstract, digest; abbreviation, curtailment, contraction (SHORTNESS).

abrupt, *adj.* brusque, unceremonious, curt (BLUNTNESS, DISCOURTESY); hilly, steep, declivitous (HEIGHT, SLOPE); hasty, hurried, precipitate (SPEED); sudden, unexpected, swift, impetuous (SUDDENNESS, SURPRISE).

abscess, *n.* pus sore, ulcer, phagedena (UNCLEANNESS).

abscond, *v.* decamp, take flight, steal away (DEPARTURE, ABSENCE).

ABSENCE—N. absence, nonexistence: nonattendance, nonpresence, nonappearance, absentation; absence without leave, French leave, cut (*colloq.*).

absenteeism, hooky, truancy, truantism.

furlough, leave, leave of absence, liberty (*naval*), sabbatical.

absentee, truant, hooky player, nonattender; no-show (*plane travel*).

lack, want, need, requirement, deficiency, scarcity, dearth, paucity, insufficiency, scantness.

emptiness, vacancy, vacuity, inanity, inanition, vacuum, void.

[*empty space*] blank, gap, hiatus, interstice, lacuna, hollow, infinite, infinity, void, inane.

V. be absent, keep away, keep out of the way, truant, play truant, absent oneself, stay away, hold aloof; abscond, decamp, skip, skip town, cut class, jump bail; not show up, not turn up, make oneself scarce (*colloq.*).

withdraw, retreat, retire, quit, vacate, go away.

lack, want, be empty of, be without, not have.

empty, deplete, exhaust, drain, void, vacate, clear, strip, sweep off, discharge, evacuate; unload, unship, unlade; disembogue; draw off, tap, broach, decant.

Adj. absent, absentee, not present, away, elsewhere, A.W.O.L. (*mil.*), truant, nonattendant; gone, missing, lost, omitted, left out.

empty, bare, barren, void, vacant, vacuous, blank, clear; deserted, abandoned, forsaken, desolate, waste, untenanted, unoccupied, uninhabited, tenantless; flatulent, hollow, inane.

lacking, wanting, devoid, destitute, scarce, scant.

Prep., prepositional phrases. in the absence of, *in absentia* (*L.*): in default of, without, less, minus, *sans* (*F.*); deprived of, free from, for lack of, lacking in, in want of.

See also AVOIDANCE, DEPARTURE, INATTENTION, INSUFFICIENCY, INTERVAL, NONEXISTENCE. *Antonyms*—See EXISTENCE, FULLNESS, PRESENCE, SUFFICIENCY.

absent-minded, *adj.* preoccupied, abstracted, distracted, heedless (INATTENTION).

absolute, *adj.* blank, blanket, sheer, utter (COMPLETENESS); positive, unqualified, downright (FLATNESS); assured, cocksure, confident (CERTAINTY); plenary, complete, thorough (FULLNESS); perfect, consummate, ideal (PERFECTION); despotic, autocratic, absolutistic (POWER).

absolution, *n.* acquittal, exoneration, purgation (ACQUITTAL); pardon, remission, dispensation (FORGIVENESS).

absolve, *v.* exonerate, clear, exculpate, purge (ACQUITTAL); forgive, pardon (FORGIVENESS).

absorb, *v.* take in, assimilate, soak up, devour (INTAKE); interest, fascinate, enthrall (INTERESTINGNESS); ingest, drink in, imbibe (RECEIVING); pull in, suck, resorb (TRACTION).

absorbed, *adj.* intent, rapt, engrossed, preoccupied (ATTENTION, THOUGHT).

abstain, *v.* refrain, keep from, not do (AVOIDANCE); avoid, desist, forbear (INACTION); be temperate, go on the water wagon (*slang*), not indulge (SOBRIETY).

abstemious, *adj.* temperate, moderate, sober (SOBRIETY); abstinent, abstentious, self-denying (UNSELFISHNESS); ascetic, austere (ASCETICISM).

abstention, *n.* abstinence, temperance, self-restraint (AVOIDANCE).

abstinence, *n.* abstention, temperance, self-restraint (AVOIDANCE); teetotalism, total abstinence, asceticism (SOBRIETY).

abstinent, *adj.* abstemious, austere, ascetic (UNSELFISHNESS); teetotal, dry, anti-saloon (SOBRIETY); continent, virginal, chaste (CELIBACY).

abstract, *adj.* abstruse, intangible, impalpable (MYSTERY); impractical, quixotic, theoretical (IMAGINATION).

abstract, *n.* brief, condensation, digest (SHORTNESS); essence, distillation, juice (EXTRACTION).

abstract, *v.* withdraw, remove, take away (REMOVAL, TAKING); appropriate, loot, rifle (THIEVERY); abridge, digest, epitomize (SHORTNESS).

abstraction, *n.* concept, conception, thought (IDEA); absent-mindedness, preoccupation, dreaminess (INATTENTION, THOUGHT); withdrawal, appropriation, confiscation (REMOVAL, TAKING); theft, stealing, filchery (THIEVERY).

abstractionist, *n.* nonobjective painter, dadaist, surrealist (ARTIST).

abstruse, *adj.* scholarly, erudite, learned (LEARNING); abstract, intangible, impalpable (MYSTERY); oversubtle, metaphysical, Jesuitic (SOPHISTRY).

ABSURDITY—*N.* absurdity, comicality, *bêtise* (*F.*), paradox, inconsistency, futility, imbecility, idiocy, stupidity, *reductio ad absurdum* (*L.*).

antic, apery, folly, zanyism; drollery, rib tickler, the ridiculous, scream (*colloq.*), slapstick.

farce, burlesque, travesty, parody, caricature, amphigory, farrago, extravagance.

nonsense, poppycock, claptrap, bunk (*slang*), hot air (*slang*), bull (*slang*), bosh, buncombe, tommyrot, moonshine, pap, tripe (*colloq.*), trash, rubbish.

[*nonsensical talk*] babble, jargon, jabber, gibberish, gabble, balderdash, bilge, drivel, blather, cackle, flapdoodle (*colloq.*), twaddle, slush, slaver, prattle, ravings; mumbo jumbo, rigmarole, hocuspocus, abracadabra, double-talk.

nonsensicality, asininity, lunacy, irrationality, unreason, inanity, fatuity, vacuity, vapidity, simplicity.

tomfoolery, mummery, buffoonery, harlequinade, antics.

V. be absurd, play the fool, frisk, caper, joke, fool, clown, mountebank, fool around, play practical jokes.

talk nonsense, make no sense, cackle, drivel, twaddle, blather, babble, blat, burble, gibber, jabber, gabble, jargon, prate, prattle, rattle on, rave, slaver, rant.

Adj. absurd, preposterous, screwy (*slang*), unreasonable, inconsistent, ridiculous, extravagant, self-contradictory, paradoxical; foolish, ludicrous, laughable, ribtickling, hilarious, amusing, droll, comical, risible, mirthful, slapstick, sidesplitting; asinine, silly, stupid, idiotic, imbecilic, amphigoric, fantastic, farcical, burlesque, incredible, incongruous.

nonsensical, balmy, barmy, brainless, mad, lunatic, zany, crazy, daft, dizzy (*colloq.*); fatuitous, fatuous, witless, simple, simple-minded, vapid.

meaningless, senseless, pointless, inane, empty, vacuous, skimble-skamble, irrational, without rhyme or reason.

See also FOLLY, IMPOSSIBILITY, IMPROBABILITY, STUPIDITY, WITTINESS. *Antonyms*—See INTELLIGENCE, MEANING, REASONABLENESS, REASONING, THOUGHT, WISDOM.

abundance, *n.* affluence, flood, deluge (MULTITUDE, WEALTH); plenty, profusion, shower (SUFFICIENCY); extravagance, munificence, lavishness (UNSELFISHNESS); accumulation, hoard, stock, store (STORE, QUANTITY).

abundant, *adj.* ample, copious, profuse, rich (SUFFICIENCY); bountiful, bounteous, lavish (UNSELFISHNESS).

abuse, *n.* tyranny, oppression, ill-treatment (ACTION); ill-usage, mistreatment, perversion (MISUSE); attack, mudslinging, invective, opprobrium (MALEDICTION).

abuse, *v.* ill-use, ill-treat, mistreat, oppress (ACTION); misemploy, misapply, prostitute (MISUSE); lash, revile, vilify (MALEDICTION).

abut, *v.* adjoin, meet, border, join, verge on (TOUCH).

abyss, *n.* depths, gulf, pit (DEPTH); chasm, yawn, crater (OPENING).

academic, *adj.* scholarly, classical, educational, collegiate (LEARNING, SCHOOL, TEACHING); suppositional, conjectural, theoretical (SUPPOSITION).

academy, *n.* lyceum, institute, college (SCHOOL).

accelerate, *v.* hasten, hurry, expedite (SPEED).

accent, *n.* accentuation, emphasis, stress (IMPORTANCE, VOICE); brogue, drawl, pronunciation (VOICE); accent mark, diacritical mark, dot (WRITTEN SYMBOL); beat, ictus, meter (POETRY).

ACCEPTANCE *N.* **acceptance,** reception, recipience, admission, adoption; resignation, reconciliation; tolerance, toleration; supposition, assumption, accreditation, honor, approval, recognition; popularity, currency.

V. **accept,** take, buy (*colloq.*),

receive, admit, adopt; resign oneself to, reconcile oneself to, tolerate, abide, bear, stomach, swallow; welcome, lap up; shoulder; suppose, take for granted, grant, assume, accredit, honor, approve, recognize.

Adj. **acceptable,** standard, palatable, tolerable, admissible, receptible.

accepted (*generally*), popular, current, standard, prevalent, prevailing, customary, conventional.

accepting, receptive, recipient, susceptive, open-minded, broad-minded, tolerant.

See also APPROVAL, BELIEF, INTAKE, RECEIVING, TAKING. *Antonyms*—See DENIAL, OPPOSITION, RIDICULE.

access, *n.* avenue, approach, ramp; admission, entry (INGRESS); fit, seizure (ATTACK).

accessible, *adj.* attainable, obtainable, achievable (POSSIBILITY); central, nearby (EASE); amenable, reachable (INFLUENCE); approachable, friendly, affable (APPROACH).

accessory, *adj.* minor, secondary, subordinate, subsidiary (UNIMPORTANCE).

accessory, *n.* collateral, subordinate (UNIMPORTANCE); auxiliary, subsidiary, crutch (AID); *vade mecum* (*L.*), obbligato (ACCOMPANIMENT); adjunct, appanage, appurtenance (ADDITION); accomplice (ILLEGALITY).

accident, *n.* fortune, haphazard, luck (CHANCE); act of God, contingency (OCCURRENCE); unintentionality, inadvertence, unpremeditation (PURPOSELESSNESS).

accidental, *adj.* adventitious, fortuitous, haphazard (CHANCE); unintentional, inadvertent (PURPOSELESSNESS).

acclaim, *n.* acclamation, applause (PRAISE).

acclimate, *v.* habituate, accustom, season (HABIT).

accommodate, *v.* lodge, quarter, board (HABITATION); bed, bed down (SLEEP); have, hold, admit (CONTAINER); adapt, adjust, suit (AGREEMENT).

accommodate with, *v.* lend, loan, advance (DEBT); afford, spare (GIVING).

accommodating, *adj.* hospitable, obliging, kind (KINDNESS); willing, cheerful, alacritous (WILLINGNESS).

accommodation, *n.* adjustment, agreement; benefit, aid; favor, courtesy (KINDNESS); capacity, room, place (SPACE).

accommodations, *pl. n.* quarters,

lodgings, board and room (HABITATION); bunkhouse, dormitory (SLEEP).

ACCOMPANIMENT.—N. accompaniment, attendance, chaperonage, convoy; concomitance, coexistence, collaterality.

accompanier, accompanist (*esp. in music*); companion, associate, colleague, partner, side-kick (*slang*), buddy (*colloq.*), mate, chum, pal, yoke-fellow, *fidus Achates* (*L.*); satellite, hanger-on, shadow; escort, squire, beau, cavalier, gigolo; chaperon, duenna; conductor, convoy, escort, usher.

[*accompanying group*] **retinue**, company, escort, cortege, entourage, suite.

[*accompanying thing*] **accessory**, appanage, obbligato, *vade mecum* (*L.*).

V. **accompany**, attend, be (come, or go) with; chaperon, matronize; conduct, usher, convoy, escort, squire; retinue.

Adj. **accompanying**, attending, attendant, accessory, collateral, concomitant; fellow, twin, joint.

Adv., phrases. **in company with**, together with, along with, therewith, herewith, also, moreover, likewise; hand in hand, side by side, cheek by jowl; collaterally, concomitantly, jointly, together, conjointly, mutually, in a body, in conjunction, collectively.

See also ADDITION, SIMULTANEOUSNESS. *Antonyms*—See DEPARTURE, DESERTION, RELINQUISHMENT, UNITY.

---

accomplice, *n.* confederate, abettor, colluder (AID); accessory, accessory before the fact, accessory after the fact (ILLEGALITY).

accomplish, *v.* achieve, fulfill, attain (COMPLETENESS).

accomplished, *adj.* finished, brilliant, gifted (ABILITY).

accomplishment, *n.* achievement, attainment, acquirement (ABILITY).

accord, *n.* agreement, conformity, keeping (HARMONY); congruity, compliance, correspondence (CONFORMITY); volition, conation (*psychol.*), free will (WILL); zeal, enthusiasm, alacrity (WILLINGNESS).

accordance, *n.* observance, conformity, keeping (OBEDIENCE, AGREEMENT).

accordingly, *adv.* ergo (*L.*), thus, so (REASONING).

accost, *v.* address, buttonhole, harangue (TALK); welcome, hail, salute (GREETING).

account, *n.* bill, check, (ACCOUNTS); yarn, tale, anecdote (STORY); version, report, sketch (DESCRIPTION); *cahier* (*F.*), white paper (INFORMATION); value, worth, benefit (VALUE).

accountable, *adj.* liable, responsible, answerable (DEBT, LIABILITY); attributable, referable, ascribable (ATTRIBUTION); explainable, construable, explicable (EXPLANATION).

accountant, *n.* bookkeeper, auditor, C.P.A. (ACCOUNTS).

ACCOUNTS—N. accounts, money matters, finance, financial affairs, budget.

account, bill, check, chirograph, chit, reckoning, score, statement, tab, tally; debenture, debit, invoice, I.O.U., manifest, memorandum, memo, note, obligation, promissory note.

bookkeeping, accountancy; audit, single entry, double entry; daybook, cashbook, ledger, journal; balance sheet; receipts, assets, accounts receivable; expenditure, liabilities, accounts payable; profit-and-loss account (*or* statement).

accountant, bookkeeper; cashier, teller; auditor, actuary, certified public accountant, C.P.A.

V. **keep accounts**, enter, post, post up, book, credit, debit, balance; cast up accounts, add, add up, tot up; square accounts, settle up, settle an account.

See also DEBT, MONEY, RECORD.

---

accredit, *v.* authorize, charter, commission (POWER).

accrue, *v.* supervene, add up, total (ADDITION); be received, come in (RECEIVING); derive from, come from, issue from (RESULT).

accumulate, *v.* amass, collect, gather (ASSEMBLAGE, STORE); grow, fill out (INCREASE).

accumulation, *n.* store, stock, stock pile (ASSEMBLAGE, QUANTITY, STORE).

accurate, *adj.* actual, factual, correct (TRUTH); exact, precise, nice (RIGHT).

accursed, *adj.* blasted, damnable, foul (HATRED); execrable, anathematized (MALEDICTION); atrocious, heinous, flagitious (WICKEDNESS).

ACCUSATION—N. accusation, accusal, denunciation, arraignment, indictment, impeachment; inculpation, incrimination; charge, complaint, plaint, arraign, true bill,

bill of indictment, bill of particulars, lawsuit; frame-up (*slang*), delation (*esp. by an informer*); witch-hunt, character assassination; counteraccusation, countercharge, recrimination; condemnation, conviction, sentence.

blame, censure, reproach, reprehension, discommendation, upbraiding; odium, obloquy.

libel, slander, slur, smear; aspersion, calumny, defamation, detraction, denigration, vilification, revilement, vituperation, backbiting, traducement; innuendo, insinuation, insinuendo, reflection, obloquy, scandal; witch-hunt.

the accused, defendant, respondent, litigant, prisoner; fall guy (*slang*), scapegoat, whipping boy; libelee.

accuser, accusant, plaintiff, complainant, prosecutor; informant, informer, squealer (*slang*), stool pigeon (*slang*), tattletale, telltale, tattler, talebearer, delator.

V. **accuse,** charge, tax, impute, twit, taunt; denounce, denunciate; arraign, impeach, indict; complain against, lodge a complaint against, prefer charges against; inform on (*or* against), squeal on (*slang*).

incriminate, implicate, criminate, inculpate, frame (*slang*).

blame, censure, reprehend, reproach, upbraid, hold responsible for.

libel, slander; blacken, besmirch, smirch; asperse, backbite, calumniate, defame, denigrate; slur, smear, spatter, bespatter, traduce; blackguard, blaspheme, discredit, revile, vilify, vilipend, vituperate.

Adj. **accusatory,** accusative, complaining, denunciatory; libelous, slanderous, aspersive, calumnious, defamatory, vituperative, insinuative, detractive.

blameworthy, censurable, discommendable, culpable, guilty, reprehensible, reproachable, responsible, blameful.

inexcusable, indefensible, unpardonable, unjustifiable.

See also ATTRIBUTION, DETRACTION, DISAPPROVAL, LAWSUIT, SCOLDING. *Antonyms*—See ACQUITTAL, APPROVAL, JUSTIFICATION.

accustom, *v.* habituate, acclimate, season, inure (HABIT).

accustomed, *adj.* usual, customary, familiar (COMMONNESS); habituated, addicted, wont (HABIT).

ace, *n.* aviator, aeronaut, airman (FLYING); unit, one, integer (UNITY).

acerbity, *n.* acrimony, acridity, sharpness (ANGER).

ache, *n.* pang, lancination, twinge (PAIN); longing, craving, hankering (DESIRE).

ache, *v.* pain, hurt, sting, smart (PAIN).

achievement, *n.* accomplishment, attainment, acquirement; exploit, deed, feat (ABILITY); realization, derivation (ACQUISITION); completion, fulfillment, execution (COMPLETENESS).

acid, *adj.* acrimonious, barbed, vitriolic (SHARPNESS, BAD TEMPER); acerb, acidulous, tart (SOURNESS).

acid test, *n.* crucial test, baptism of fire (TEST).

acknowledge, *v.* admit, concede, grant (STATEMENT); thank, appreciate (GRATITUDE).

acknowledgment, *n.* admission, concession, acceptance (STATEMENT); receipt, voucher, acquittance (RECEIVING).

acne, *n.* blotch, breakout, eruption (SKIN).

acoustic, *adj.* phonic, sonic (SOUND); auditory, auditive, audile (LISTENING).

acquaint, *v.* let know, familiarize, tell (INFORMATION).

acquaintance, *n.* crony, pal, familiar (FRIEND); cognizance, information, familiarity (KNOWLEDGE).

acquainted, *adj.* privy, aware, familiar (KNOWLEDGE).

acquiesce, *v.* assent, concur, agree (AGREEMENT, ASSENT).

acquiescence, *n.* consent, assent, agreement (PERMISSION).

acquire, *v.* win, capture, contract (ACQUISITION).

ACQUISITION—*N.* acquisition, acquirement, procurement, collection, capture, gain; attainment, accomplishment, achievement, realization, derivation; gift, donation, benefaction, grant.

gain, profit, benefit, advantage, harvest, windfall.

beneficiary, heir, heiress, recipient.

V. **acquire,** get, obtain, procure, secure, gain; attain, accomplish, achieve, realize; derive, harvest, reap, win; capture, bag, net, trap, draw, steal, coax, wangle, wheedle, worm; exact, compel, force, wring, pry; fetch, gather, pick up, scrape together, collect; inherit, succeed to, accede to; beg, impetrate; contract (*a disease*), recruit (*members*); receive, accept, share in, profit from, earn.

reacquire, regain, recover, get back, retrieve, redeem, repossess, recapture, retake, recoup, recuperate.

gain, profit, benefit, reap, harvest, realize, clear.

[*try to acquire*] **angle for**, compete for, contest, pursue, seek, snatch at, solicit, strive for, struggle for, sue for, beg; court, woo.

Adj. **acquisitive**, grasping, greedy, avaricious, rapacious, covetous.

profitable, productive, beneficial, fruitful, advantageous; gainful, paying, lucrative, remunerative, well-paying, prosperous.

See also INHERITANCE, RECEIVING, WEALTH. *Antonyms*—See EXPENDITURE, LOSS, PAYMENT, PUNISHMENT.

ACQUITTAL—*N.* **acquittal**, exculpation, clearance, exoneration, discharge, release, absolution, purgation, vindication, disculpation; compurgation.

excusal, pardon, forgiveness, justification; quietus, reprieve, respite.

[*freedom from punishment*] **impunity**, immunity, privilege, exemption.

V. **acquit**, exculpate, disculpate, purge, exonerate, clear, absolve, extenuate, vindicate, whitewash, discharge, release, liberate, free, emancipate; remit, reprieve, respite, pardon, excuse, forgive, justify.

Adj. **acquitted**, exonerated; released, discharged; uncondemned, unpunished.

See also FORGIVENESS, FREEDOM. *Antonyms*—See ACCUSATION, DISAPPROVAL, IMPRISONMENT, RESTRAINT, SCOLDING.

acreage, *n.* acres, lot, parcel (LAND); area, acre, square feet (MEASUREMENT).

acrid, *adj.* bitter, absinthial (SOURNESS); pungent, poignant, acid (SHARPNESS); embittered, sour-tempered, vinegary (ANGER, BAD TEMPER); vexatious, pesky, irritating (ANNOYANCE).

acrimonious, *adj.* bitter, acerb, vitriolic (ANGER); sour-tempered, acid, acrid (BAD TEMPER); caustic, sarcastic (SHARPNESS).

acrobatics, *n.* athletics, calisthenics (GYMNASTICS).

across, *adv.* crosswise, athwart, transversely, aslant (CROSSING, SLOPE).

act, *n.* deed, exploit, step (ACTION); ordinance, edict, mandate (COMMAND); performance, impersonation, impression (DRAMA); measure, statute, bill (LAW).

act, *v.* function, operate, work (ACTION); play, act out, enact (ACTOR); behave, acquit oneself, conduct oneself (BEHAVIOR); pretend to be, impersonate, pose as (PRETENSE); officiate, execute (OFFICIAL).

acting, *adj.* officiating, substituting, delegated (DEPUTY); surrogate, deputy, alternate (SUBSTITUTION); performing, on duty (ACTION).

acting, *n.* theatricals, dramatics, histrionics (DRAMA, ACTOR).

action, *n.* suit, case, litigation (LAWSUIT).

ACTION—*N.* **action**, performance, exercise, pursuit, movement, operation, exertion, execution, commission, perpetration; response, reaction; process, mechanism, working; procedure, conduct, behavior.

act, deed, byplay, ceremonial; *coup* (F.), *coup de grâce* (F.), exploit, achievement, accomplishment, feat, stunt, *tour de force* (F.), undertaking, venture; *beau geste* (F.); measure, step, maneuver, move, *coup de main* (F.), handiwork, stroke, blow.

actions, ceremony, proceedings, *res gestae* (L.).

course of action, campaign, crusade; custom, habit, practice, track; current, drift, trend, tack, tendency, tenor, *démarche* (F.).

treatment, dealings with, management of; ill-treatment, maltreatment, mistreatment, mishandling, abuse, disservice, tyranny, oppression.

principal, star, protagonist, leading participant.

V. **act**, function, operate, work; take action, take steps, put into practice, interact, retroact.

do, carry out, engage in, discharge, execute, pursue, wage, dispose of, fulfill, perform, render, minister, officiate, practice, exercise, prosecute, take care of, transact, undertake, assume, wade into; accomplish, achieve, attain; commit, perpetrate, inflict, wreak; dispatch, expedite; overdo, overwork, supererogate.

treat, act toward, deal with, manage, behave toward, handle.

mistreat, ill-treat, ill-use, maltreat, mishandle, maul, manhandle, abuse, brutalize, disserve, oppress, tyrannize, trample on, violate.

play (*on the stage*), personate, impersonate, represent, perform, enact, take (*or* act) the part of.

Adj. **acting**, performing, officiating, in harness, on duty, at work, in action, operative.

abusive, oppressive, tyrannous, tyrannical, violent.

Adv., phrases. in the act, in the midst of; red-handed, in *flagrante delicto* (*L.*).

See also ACTOR, AGENT, BEHAVIOR, COMPLETENESS, CO-OPERATION, EXERTION, REPETITION, WORK. *Antonyms*—See INACTION, INCOMPLETENESS, REST, SLEEP.

activate, *v.* animate, mobilize, catalyze (MOTIVATION).

ACTIVITY—*N.* activity, bustle, movement, hum, pother, stir, fuss, ado, bother, flurry, buzz, hustle-bustle, turmoil; whirl, whirlwind, bluster, vortex; burst, sally, white heat; niggling, dabbling, tinker; energy, vigor, vibrancy, militancy; agility, legerity.

liveliness, spirit, sparkle, vitality, verve, vivacity, enterprise, vim, snap (*colloq.*), go (*colloq.*), get-up-and-go (*colloq.*), bounce, dash, animal spirits, effervescence, ebullience, ebullition, animation, volatility, alacrity.

[*area of activity*] arena, focus, hub, orbit, province.

V. be active, stir, stir about, bestir oneself; push, go ahead, push forward, make progress; keep moving; have a hand in, take an active part, have a finger in the pie, dabble; hum, buzz, bustle.

become active, resurge, recrudesce, develop, quicken.

effervesce, sparkle, perk up (*colloq.*), sit up, tittup; animate, exhilarate, enliven, pep up (*slang*).

Adj. active, humming, buzzing, bustling, astir, brisk, energetic, vigorous, strenuous, vibrant, aggressive, militant.

agile, spry, nimble, tripping, supple, withy, lissome, light, lightsome, quick.

lively, frisky, spirited, animated, vital, vivacious, alive, chipper, skittish, coltish, bright, vivid, breezy, effervescent, ebullient, peppy (*slang*), perky, sparkling, sprightly, snappy (*colloq.*), dashing.

See also ENERGY, EXERTION, SPEED, WAKEFULNESS. *Antonyms*—See INACTION, LEISURE, REST, SLEEP.

ACTOR—*N.* actor, artist, artiste, entertainer, mummer (*jocose*), performer, player, Thespian (*jocose*), impersonator, personator; vaudevillian, variety artist; tragedian; hero, lead, star, headliner; extra, supernumerary; juvenile; villain, heavy; understudy; traveling actor, barnstormer, trouper.

actress, ingénue, soubrette, show girl; leading lady, star, starlet, heroine, villainess, *première* (*F.*), prima donna, diva; comedienne, tragedienne.

comedian, *farceur* (*F.*), low comedian, comic, comique, mime; straight man, stooge (*colloq.*); top banana (*slang*).

pantomimist, pantomimic, mime, mimer, Harlequin; impersonator.

monologuist, monologist, *diseur* (*F.*), *diseuse* (*F., fem.*); soloist.

acting, dramatics, histrionics; footlights, show business (*colloq.*), the stage, the theater; performance, representation, rendition, impersonation, stage business.

V. act, play, act out, enact, present, take the part of, impersonate, personate; entertain, perform, tread the boards, star, have the lead, solo; understudy; mime, pantomime, mum, tragedize; audition; barnstorm, troupe.

Adj. histrionic, Thespian, theatrical, dramatic; artistic, extra, leading, stellar, starring, straight.

See also AGENT, DRAMA.

actress, *n.* show girl, heroine, soubrette (ACTOR).

actual, *adj.* factual, accurate, correct (TRUTH); concrete, material, objective (REALITY); latest, occurring, instant (PRESENCE).

actuality, *n.* fact, statistic; factuality, verity (REALITY, TRUTH).

actually, *adv.* truly, veritably, in fact (TRUTH).

actuate, *v.* impel, drive, move (MOTIVATION).

acumen, *n.* acuity, discernment, penetration (INTELLIGENCE); perspicacity, perception, judgment (UNDERSTANDING).

acute, *adj.* crucial, climactic, critical (IMPORTANCE); intelligent, agile, alert (INTELLIGENCE); sharp, keen, fine; discerning, penetrating, shrewd; pointy, pointed, pronged (SHARPNESS); quick, perspicacious (UNDERSTANDING).

adage, *n.* proverb, maxim, motto (STATEMENT).

adamant, *adj.* hard, firm (HARDNESS); unyielding, unmovable, inflexible (STUBBORNNESS).

adapt, *v.* accommodate, adjust, reconcile (AGREEMENT).

adaptable, *adj.* flexible, mobile, movable (CHANGEABLENESS); practicable, utilizable, applicable (USE).

addict, *n.* drug fiend, dope fiend (PHARMACY).

addicted, *adj.* habituated, accustomed, used to (HABIT).

adding machine, *n.* calculator, Comptometer (COMPUTATION).

ADDITION—*N.* **addition**, admixture, annexation, apposition, attachment, superaddition.

adjunct, accessory, accretion, additament, additive, additum, appanage, appurtenance, admixture, affix; annex, appendage, appendant, attachment, increment; excrescence, extension, limb, prolongation; prefix; postfix, postscript, subjunction, suffix; subsidiary, supplement, complement; addendum, appendix, codicil, rider; addend, summand.

flap, lug, lappet, cap, leaf, tab, fly, skirt, apron.

[*small amount added*] **dash**, drop, pinch, splash, splatter.

total, aggregate, sum, summation, whole.

V. **add,** admix, annex, append, appose; prefix; affix, attach, superadd, postfix, subjoin, suffix; crown, top, eke out, supplement.

add up, sum, sum up, tot, tot up, total, total up; accrue, supervene.

add up to, aggregate, total, total to.

Adj. **additional,** adscititious, adventitious, auxiliary, subsidiary, supplemental, supplementary, suppletory; added, adjunct, adjunctive, collateral, superadditional; accruing, supervenient.

Adv., phrases. **additionally,** in addition, *au reste* (*F.*), more, and, also, likewise, too, furthermore, further, besides, to boot; over and above, moreover, withal (*archaic*); as well as, together with, along with, in conjunction with, conjointly, *cum multis aliis* (*L.*).

See also ACCOMPANIMENT, INCREASE, NUMBER. *Antonyms*—See DECREASE, DEDUCTION.

---

address, *n.* domicile, residence, home (HABITATION); lecture, speech, discourse (TALK); poise, bearing, demeanor (APPEARANCE, BEHAVIOR); compellation, salutation, appellation (TITLE, NAME); skill, artistry, cleverness (ABILITY).

address, *v.* talk to, hail (TALK); name, call (NAME).

addressee, *n.* occupant, householder, tenant (INHABITANT).

address oneself, *v.* apply oneself, buckle down, devote oneself (ENERGY).

adept, *adj.* skillful, adroit, clever (ABILITY).

adequate, *adj.* enough, ample, plenty (SUFFICIENCY); able, equal, trained (ABILITY).

adhere, *v.* cleave, cohere, cling (STICKINESS).

adherence, *n.* devotion, dedication, faithfulness (LOYALTY); advocacy, backing, championship (SUPPORT); keeping, compliance, obedience (OBSERVANCE).

adherent, *n.* attendant, disciple, proselyte (FOLLOWER); supporter, advocate, ally (SUPPORT).

adhesive, *adj.* sticky, gummy; tenacious, clingy (STICKINESS).

adieu, *n.* leave-taking, farewell, good-by (DEPARTURE).

adjacent, *adj.* bordering, contiguous, neighboring (NEARNESS).

adjoin, *v.* border on, neighbor, lie near (NEARNESS); abut, meet, join (TOUCH).

adjourn, *v.* postpone, put off, defer (DELAY).

adjunct, *n.* accessory, accretion, auxiliary (ADDITION).

adjust, *v.* true, regulate (TRUTH); rectify, correct, remedy (RESTORATION); reconcile, accord, attune (HARMONY); amend, revise, emend (RIGHT).

adjusted, *adj.* neurosis-free, well-balanced (SANITY).

adjustment, *n.* compromise, settlement, arrangement (MID-COURSE).

adjust to, *v.* become accustomed to, get used to (HABIT).

ad lib, *v.* extemporize, improvise, make up (TALK).

administration, *n.* direction, management, government (CONTROL); rule, reign, sway (GOVERNMENT); regime, tenure, incumbency (TIME); officials, brass (*colloq.*); authorities (OFFICIAL); execution, performance, pursuance (RESULT).

admirable, *adj.* estimable, praiseworthy, commendable (APPROVAL); excellent, good, splendid (GOOD).

admiral, *n.* rear admiral, vice-admiral (SAILOR).

admire, *v.* esteem, idolize, venerate (APPROVAL).

admirer, *n.* lover, suitor, swain (LOVE).

admission, *n.* acknowledgment, concession, confession (STATEMENT); access, entrance, entree (INGRESS).

admit, *v.* concede, yield, acknowledge (STATEMENT); suppose, assume, grant (SUPPOSITION); accept, receive (INTAKE).

admonish, *v.* warn, caution, exhort (WARNING); scold, berate, castigate (SCOLDING).

adolescent, *n.* minor, junior, teenager (YOUTH).

Adonis, *n.* Apollo, Greek god (BEAUTY).

adopt, *v.* utilize, employ, apply (USE); take, appropriate, assume (TAKING).

adorable, *adj.* beautiful, angelic, stunning (BEAUTY); lovable, lovely, sweet (LOVE).

adoration, *n.* admiration, worship, idolatry (APPROVAL, LOVE); deification, apotheosis, reverence (WORSHIP).

adorn, *v.* grace, embellish, decorate (BEAUTY, ORNAMENT).

adrift, *adj.* afloat, awaft, natant (FLOAT).

adroit, *adj.* skillful, adept, dexterous (ABILITY).

adult, *adj.* grown, mature, full-blown (MATURITY).

adulterate, *v.* contaminate, debase, pollute (IMPURITY).

adultery, *n.* extramarital relations, infidelity (SEX).

advance, *v.* proceed, go on, go forward (PROGRESS); promote, upgrade (ELEVATION); move, offer, broach (SUGGESTION); lend, loan (DEBT).

advanced, *adj.* beforehand, precocious, ahead of time (EARLINESS); first, *avant-garde* (F.), ahead (FRONT); ultramodern, futurist, futuristic (NEWNESS).

ADVANTAGE—*N.* advantage, avail, behoof, benefit, fringe benefit, vantage; upper hand, whip hand; expedience *or* expediency, opportunism.

V. [be of advantage to] advantage, avail, benefit, boot, favor, serve; accrue; avail oneself of, capitalize on, make capital of, trade on, turn to one's advantage, snatch at; impose upon, presume upon.

Adj. advantageous, beneficial, expedient, favorable, serviceable, useful.

See also GOOD, PRIVILEGE, SUPERIORITY, USE, VALUE. *Antonyms*—See INEXPEDIENCE.

advent, *n.* arrival, appearance, coming (ARRIVAL).

adventure, *n.* experience, escapade, lark (EXPERIENCE).

adventurer, *n.* hero, heroine, daredevil (COURAGE); plotter, racketeer (PLAN).

adventuress, *n.* gold-digger (*slang*), fortune hunter (MONEY).

adventurous, *adj.* venturesome, daring (COURAGE); enterprising, aggressive, resourceful (UNDERTAKING).

adversary, *n.* foe, enemy, opponent (OPPOSITION).

adverse, *adj.* unfortunate, cataclysmic, catastrophic (MISFORTUNE); unfavorable, contrary, disadvantageous (OPPOSITION); repugnant, oppugnant, alien (HOSTILITY).

advertise, *v.* publicize, ballyhoo, puff (PUBLICATION); tell, air, ventilate (DISCLOSURE); show off, parade, display (OSTENTATION); blaze, feature (VISIBILITY).

ADVICE—*N.* advice, counsel, word to the wise, suggestion, recommendation, advisory, aviso, exhortation, persuasion, expostulation, admonition, caution; guidance.

sermon, lecture, preachment, preaching; lesson, moral.

instruction, directions, order, charge, injunction, message, bidding, dictate, mandate.

consultation, conference, parley, palaver, *pourparler* (F.), interview, powwow (*colloq.*), council; deliberation, disquisition, *Kaffeeklatsch* (Ger.), symposium.

adviser, counselor, preacher, councilor, counsel, mentor, Nestor, director, guide; panel, round table.

consultant, conferee, discusser, discussant, deliberator.

V. advise, counsel, suggest, admonish, recommend, urge, move, prescribe, advocate, exhort, persuade, guide; preach, preachify.

instruct, order, charge, enjoin, call upon, direct, dictate.

consult, confer, discuss, palaver; refer to, call in, follow, take (*or* follow) advice; be advised by, have at one's elbow, take one's cue from; advise with, canvas, deliberate, parley, thrash out, ventilate.

Adj. advisable, desirable, commendable, expedient, advantageous, fitting, proper, suitable, meet.

advisory, admonitory, cautionary, exhortative.

See also INFORMATION, PERSUASION, PUBLICATION, SUGGESTION, WARNING. *Antonyms*—See DENIAL, DISSUASION.

advisable, *adj.* rational, sound, well-advised (WISDOM).

advise, *v.* counsel, urge, admonish (ADVICE); suggest, exhort, recommend (SUGGESTION).

adviser, *n.* guide, counselor, mentor (ADVICE, TEACHER).

advocate, *n.* supporter, adherent, ally (SUPPORT); attorney, counsel, counselor (LAWYER).

aeon, *n.* era, epoch, age (TIME).

aerate, *v.* gasify, carbonate, charge (GAS).

aerial, *adj.* aeronautical, volar, volant (FLYING); fanciful, romantic, fantastic (UNREALITY).

aeronautics, *n.* aviation, avigation, airmanship (FLYING).

aesthetic, *adj.* tasteful, refined, cultured (TASTE); beautiful, artistic, well-proportioned (BEAUTY).

afar, *adv.* far, far off, far away (DISTANCE).

affable, *adj.* sociable, amiable, pleasant, agreeable (APPROACH, FRIENDLINESS, KINDNESS, PLEASANTNESS).

affair, *n.* concern, interest, matter (BUSINESS); circumstance, episode, occasion (OCCURRENCE); party, function, gathering (SOCIALITY); business, work, project (UNDERTAKING); affaire, intrigue, liaison (SEX).

affect, *v.* simulate, sham, assume (PRETENSE, UNNATURALNESS); impress, move, touch (INFLUENCE); pertain to, concern (RELATIONSHIP); sicken, upset, afflict (DISEASE).

affected, *adj.* impressed, moved, stirred (FEELING); mannered, chichi, artificial (UNNATURALNESS); ill, sick, afflicted (DISEASE); pretended, make-believe, simulated (PRETENSE).

affecting, *adj.* moving, stirring, impressive (FEELING); touching, heartbreaking, heart-rending (PITY).

affection, *n.* fondness, tenderness, tender feelings (LOVE); malady, ailment, disorder (DISEASE); inclination, passion (LIKING); emotion, sentiment (FEELING).

affinity, *n.* attachment, inclination, partiality (LIKING); intimacy, communion (RELATIONSHIP); resemblance, community, kinship (SIMILARITY).

AFFIRMATION—N. affirmation, confirmation, ratification, corroboration; allegation, profession, acknowledgment, assertion, declaration, statement; predication, avowal, avouchment, averment, asseveration, oath, affidavit, deposition.

V. **affirm,** assert, say, declare, state; put forward, advance, predicate, announce, pose, lay down, allege, propound, enunciate, broach, set forth, maintain, claim, insist, contend.

depose, aver, avow, avouch, asseverate, swear; take one's oath, testify, attest, depone; make an affidavit; vow, vouch, warrant, certify, assure.

Adj. **affirmative,** positive, emphatic, decided, clear, certain, express, declaratory, unmistakable; complying, concurring.

Adv., phrases. **affirmatively,** positively, emphatically, etc. (see *Adjectives*); with emphasis, ex-cathedra, without fear of contradiction.

See also CERTAINTY, STATEMENT.

Antonyms—See DENIAL, UNCERTAINTY.

affix, *n.* adjunct, appendage, supplement (ADDITION); prefix, suffix, particle (WRITTEN SYMBOL).

afflict, *v.* ail, trouble, distress (PAIN); sicken, upset, affect (DISEASE).

affliction, *n.* illness, sickness, ailment, complaint (DISEASE); trouble, hardship, curse (MISFORTUNE).

affluent, *adj.* rich, opulent (WEALTH).

afford, *v.* emit, beam, shed (GIVING); produce, provide, yield (PRODUCTION); result in, beget (RESULT); well afford (WEALTH).

affront, *n.* outrage, indignity, injury (OFFENSE).

afire, *adj.* ablaze, aflame (EXCITEMENT, FIRE).

afoot, *adj.* astir, asimmer, simmering (PREPARATION); current, doing, going on (OCCURRENCE, BUSINESS); itinerant, peripatetic (WALKING).

aforesaid, *adj.* foregoing, aforementioned, aforestated (PRECEDENCE).

aforethought, *adj.* intentional, intended, meant (PURPOSE).

afraid, *adj.* fearful, apprehensive, alarmed (FEAR).

after, *adj.* succeeding, next (FOLLOWING); back, hind, rearmost (REAR).

aftereffect, *n.* afterclap, aftergrowth, aftermath (RESULT).

afterlife, *n.* hereafter, next world, world to come (DESTINY).

aftermath, *n.* outcome, outgrowth, aftereffect (RESULT).

afternoon, *n.* P.M., post meridiem (MORNING).

afterthought, *n.* second thought, reconsideration (THOUGHT).

afterward, *adv.* subsequently, later, behind (FOLLOWING).

again, *adv.* repeatedly, anew, once more (REPETITION).

against, *adj.* opposed, opposing, counter (OPPOSITION).

age, *n.* majority, declining years, old age (OLDNESS); era, epoch, aeon (TIME).

age, *v.* ripen, mature (OLDNESS).

aged, *adj.* elderly, ancient, hoary (OLDNESS).

AGENCY—N. agency, force, function, office, maintenance, exercise, work; action, operation, procedure, method; causation, impelling force, causality; instrumentality, medium, means; influence, pull (*colloq.*), drag (*colloq.*).

mediation, intervention, intercession, interposition.

[*in commerce*] **office**, bureau, business, establishment.

V. **function**, act, operate, work, perform; support, sustain, maintain; take effect, strike; have play, have free play; bring to bear upon.

Adj. **agential**, official, acting, operative; in operation, at work, in force, in action; effective, efficient, practical, effectual, efficacious.

See also ACTION, INFLUENCE, MEANS. *Antonyms*—See DISABLEMENT, INACTION, WEAKNESS.

agenda, *pl. n.* program, procedure (PLAN).

AGENT—N. agent, doer, actor, performer, perpetrator, operator, executor, executrix (*fem.*), practitioner, worker.

representative, deputy, substitute, emissary, proxy, minister, broker, attorney, go-between, mediary; factor, steward.

staff, force, help, helpers, hands, crew; assistants, personnel; faculty.

[*of things*] **cause,** factor, instrument, means.

See also ACTION, DEPUTY, INSTRUMENT, MEANS, REPRESENTATION, SERVICE, SUBSTITUTION, WORK.

aggrandize, *v.* honor, exalt, glorify (ELEVATION); enhance, augment, boost (INCREASE).

aggravate, *v.* acerbate, exasperate, irritate (ANNOYANCE); intensify, exaggerate (SOBRIETY); increase, add to, heighten (INCREASE); make worse, vitiate, corrupt (DETERIORATION).

aggregate, *n.* whole, entirety, sum, total (COMPLETENESS).

aggregate, *v.* add up to, total to (ADDITION).

aggregation, *n.* accumulation, conglomeration (ASSEMBLAGE).

aggression, *n.* inroad, offense, invasion (ATTACK); warlikeness, bellicosity, belligerence (HOSTILITY).

aggressive, *adj.* assaultive, offensive, combative (ATTACK); warlike, belligerent, bellicose (FIGHTING); energetic, dynamic (ENERGY); enterprising, adventurous, venturesome (UNDERTAKING).

aggrieved, *adj.* grief-stricken, grief-laden, grieved (SADNESS); offended, displeased, affronted (UNPLEASANTNESS).

aghast, *adj.* horrified, horror-stricken (HATRED); astonished, taken aback (SURPRISE).

agile, *adj.* spry, nimble (ACTIVITY); lightsome, lithe (LIGHTNESS); intelligent, acute, alert (INTELLIGENCE).

AGITATION—N. agitation, disturbance, stir, tremor, shake, ripple, jog, jolt, jar, jerk, hitch, shock, trepidation, flurry, flutter, fluster; quiver, quaver, dance; twitter, flicker, flutter, pitapat, pulsation.

disquiet, perturbation, discomposure, disconcertion, commotion, hurly-burly.

excitement, turmoil, turbulence; tumult, hubbub, rout, bustle, fuss, racket.

ferment, fermentation, ebullition, effervescence.

V. **agitate,** shake, convulse, toss, tumble, jerk, hitch, jolt, jog, joggle, disturb, stir, shake up, churn.

be agitated, shake, tremble, flutter, fly, flicker, quiver, quaver, quake, shiver, writhe, toss; tumble, stagger, bob, reel, sway, totter, waver.

flurry, fluster, excite, confuse, perturb, trouble, disquiet, rattle (*colloq.*), disconcert, alarm, upset.

ferment, effervesce, work, foam, boil, boil over, bubble, bubble up; simmer.

Adj. **agitated,** tremulous; convulsive, spasmodic, jerky; effervescent, bubbly, bubbling; unquiet, restless.

See also COMMOTION, EXCITEMENT, NERVOUSNESS, OSCILLATION, SHAKE. *Antonyms*—See CALMNESS, INEXCITABILITY, REST, SLEEP, STABILITY.

agitator, *n.* demagogue, rabble-rouser, instigator (DISSATISFACTION).

aglow, *adj.* bright, shiny, ablaze (LIGHT).

agnostic, *n.* non-believer, skeptic, freethinker (IRRELIGION, HETERODOXY, UNBELIEVINGNESS).

ago, *adj.* gone, bygone, long-ago (PAST).

agog, *adj.* excited, twittery, atwitter (EXCITEMENT).

agony, *n.* misery, anguish, torment (PAIN).

agree, *v.* covenant, stipulate, contract (PROMISE); harmonize, correspond (AGREEMENT).

agreeable, *adj.* affable, cheerful, amiable (PLEASANTNESS, SWEETNESS); amenable, inclined, disposed (WILLINGNESS).

AGREEMENT—N. agreement, accord, accordance, coincidence, keeping, unison, consonance, harmony, concord, union, unity, unanimity, reunion, reconcilement; conjunction, coherence; understanding, consort, concert, *entente* (*F.*), compact, contract.

conformity, uniformity, consistency; congruence, congruity; correspondence, parallelism, apposition.

fitness, relevancy, pertinence, aptitude, propriety, applicability, admissiblity, compatibility.

adaptation, adjustment, accommodation: assimilation, reconcilement, reconciliation.

consent, acquiescence, concurrence, consensus.

V. **agree,** accord, harmonize, correspond, fit, tally; consent, acquiesce, assent, accede, accept, fall in with; concur.

adapt, accommodate, graduate, adjust, correct, suit, conform, fit, square, regulate, reconcile.

Adj., phrases. **agreeing,** accordant, correspondent, congenial; harmonious, reconcilable, conformable; consistent, compatible, consonant, congruous; commensurate, proportionate; in accordance with, in harmony with, in keeping with.

suitable, applicable, appropriate, apropos, apt, becoming, befitting, congruous, consentaneous, decent, decorous, expedient, felicitous, happy, fit, fitting, idoneous, likely, meet, pat, proper, right, seemly, suited.

See also ASSENT, CONFORMITY, CO-OPERATION, EQUALITY, HARMONY, SIMILARITY. *Antonyms*—See DISAGREEMENT, INEQUALITY, OPPOSITION.

---

agree to, *v.* concur, acquiesce in, assent to (PERMISSION).

agricultural, *adj.* agrarian, georgic, horticultural (FARMING).

aground, *adj.* grounded, ashore, beached (LAND).

ahead, *adv.* forward, before, vanward (FRONT, PROGRESS).

AID—*N.* aid, assistance, assist, help, succor, support, lift, advance, advancement, furtherance, promotion, co-operation, coadjuvance; accommodation, advantage, avail, benefit, relief, subsidy, subsidization, bounty, subvention, rally; loyal help, yeoman service; secret aid, connivance; recourse, resort, resource, stand-by; auxiliary, accessory, adminicle, subsidiary, crutch.

auxiliary, assistant, help, helper, helpmate, helping hand; colleague, partner, confrere, co-operator, coadjutor, collaborator, right hand, girl Friday, man Friday; adjutant, adjutory, adjuvant, aide (*mil.*), aide-de-camp (*mil.*), ally, second; acolyte (*rel.*); humanitarian, Samaritan.

confederate, accomplice, abettor, accessory, conniver; colluder, conspirator.

ally, associate, coworker; friend, pal, comrade, companion, mate, buddy, chum (*colloq.*).

upholder, seconder, backer, second (*as in a duel*), supporter, advocate, adherent, partisan, champion, patron; friend at court, mediator.

friend in need, special providence, guardian angel, fairy godmother, tutelary genius.

patronage, countenance, favor, interest, advocacy, championship, defense; auspices.

V. **aid,** assist, help, succor, tide over, lend a hand; accommodate, oblige; advantage, avail, benefit, bestead, relieve, serve; abet, connive with, collude with; promote, further, forward, advance, foster, minister to, rally, subserve, subsidize; subvene; contribute, subscribe to; take by the hand, take in tow; set up, set on one's legs, give new life to, be the making of; reinforce.

support, sustain, uphold, prop, hold up, bolster.

serve, tender to, pander to, minister to; tend, attend, wait on; take care of.

second, stand by, back, back up; work for, stick up for (*colloq.*), stick by, take up (*or* espouse) the cause of; advocate, countenance, patronize, smile upon, side with.

turn for help, resort, SOS.

Adj. **aiding,** auxiliary, ancillary, adjuvant, assisting, assistant, apprentice, helping, helpful, subservient, accessory, subsidiary; advantageous, beneficial, useful, constructive; humanitarian; promotive, adjutory, subventionary; accommodating, obliging, accommodative, ministrant.

Phrases. **in aid of,** on (*or* in) behalf of, in favor of, in furtherance of, for the sake of, on the part of.

See also CARE, CO-OPERATION, KINDNESS, SERVICE, WORK. *Antonyms*—See HINDRANCE, NEGLECT, OPPOSITION.

---

ail, *v.* afflict, distress; suffer (PAIN); be ill (DISEASE).

ailment, *n.* illness, malady, complaint (DISEASE).

aim, *n.* goal, target, object (PURPOSE); intention, intent, project (PLAN); set, tack, bent (DIRECTION).

aim, *v.* direct, level, point (DIRECTION); intend, purpose, contemplate (PLAN, PURPOSE); try, strive, endeavor (ATTEMPT).

aimless, *adj.* driftless, random, desultory (PURPOSELESSNESS).

air, *n.* tune, song, aria, strain (MELODY, MUSIC); attitude, bearing, carriage (POSTURE).

air, *v.* publish, make public, report (PUBLICATION); brandish, flaunt, flourish (OSTENTATION).

AIR—*N.* air, ventilation, the open, open air, the outdoors, the out-of-doors; oxygen, ether, ozone (*colloq.*).

    weather, climate, clime; spell.

    airflow, breeze, breath, current, waft, draft, eddy, wind, light wind; blast, flow, puff, whiff.

    atmosphere, troposphere, substratosphere, tropopause, stratosphere, isothermal region, ionosphere; ozone layer, ozone blanket; Heaviside layer; the elements.

    ventilator, ventiduct, funnel, air shaft, flue; transom, louver; fan, electric fan.

    [*air sciences*] **aerodynamics,** aeromechanics, pneumatics, pneumodynamics.

    meteorology, climatology, aerology, barometry, hygrometry.

    barometer, weatherglass, aneroid barometer, barograph, baroscope.

    V. **air,** ventilate, fan; aerate, aerify, purify, oxygenate.

    Adj. **airy,** atmospheric, aerial, aery, pneumatic; windy, breezy, exposed, drafty, roomy.

    open-air, alfresco, outdoor, out-of-door.

    airlike, aeriform, thin, tenuous, unsubstantial, immaterial, ethereal, delicate, graceful.

    Adv., phrases. **in the open air,** in the open, out of doors, outdoors, alfresco; under the stars, *à la belle étoile* (*F.*).

    See also FLYING, GAS, THINNESS, WIND. *Antonyms*—See THICKNESS, WATER.

air-condition, *v.* refrigerate, air-cool, water-cool (COLD).

AIR OPENING—*N.* **air pipe,** air hole, blowhole, breathing hole, vent, spilehole, vent hole, bung, bunghole; shaft, moulin (*in glacier*), air shaft, air trunk; smoke shaft, chimney, flue, funnel, ventilator, louver; air port (*naut.*); air passage, air space.

    nostril, nozzle, throat; trachea, windpipe, weasand (*archaic*).

    blowpipe, blowtube, blowgun.

    See also NOSE, OPENING, THROAT.

airplane, *n.* aircraft, plane, craft (FLYING).

airport, *n.* airdrome, air base, landing field (FLYING).

airs, *n.* haughtiness, hauteur, arrogance (PRIDE).

airship, *n.* dirigible, blimp, balloon (FLYING).

airtight, *adj.* hermetic, airproof (TIGHTNESS).

airy, *adj.* breezy, drafty; atmospheric (AIR); insubstantial, slender (THINNESS); affected, mannered, chichi (UNNATURALNESS); shadowy, gaseous, vaporous (NONEXISTENCE); spiritual, ethereal, rarefied (SPIRITUALITY).

akin, *adj.* kindred, parallel, analogous (SIMILARITY).

alacrity, *n.* accord, zeal, enthusiasm (WILLINGNESS); dispatch, expedition, rapidity (SPEED); animation, spirit, liveliness (ACTIVITY).

alarm, *n.* fright, terror, panic (FEAR); alert, siren, tocsin (WARNING, INDICATION).

alcoholic, *n.* drunkard, souse (*slang*), dipsomaniac (DRUNKENNESS).

ALCOHOLIC LIQUOR—*N.* **alcoholic liquor,** whiskey *or* whisky, liquor, alcohol, spirits, *spiritus frumenti* (*L.*), firewater, drink, schnapps (*Ger.*), booze (*colloq.*), hooch (*slang*), bouse, swill, pot, pottle, the bottle, John Barleycorn.

    intoxicant, inebriant, stimulant, bracer, toxicant; drink, shot, potation, libation (*jocose*), appetizer, *apéritif* (*F.*), nightcap, Mickey Finn, snort (*slang*), pick-me-up (*colloq.*), hooker (*slang*).

    highball, cocktail, pousse-café, toddy, hot toddy, fizz, nog, eggnog, swizzle, sling, rickey.

    brandy, cognac, *eau de vie* (*F.*), applejack, aqua vitae; rye, scotch, rum, grog, gin, bourbon, hard cider, punch, homebrew; liqueur, cordial.

    beer, lager, porter, stout, bock, ale, *sake* (*Jap.*), near-beer.

    wine, vintage, vintage wine, *vin ordinaire* (*F.*), *vin du pays* (*F.*), champagne, sparkling wine.

    God of wine: Bacchus (*Rom.*), Dionysus (*Gr.*).

    viniculture, oenology; zymology, zymurgy.

    alcohol, spirit, spirits, butanol *or* butyl alcohol, ethyl alcohol, grain alcohol *or* grain neutral spirits, isopropyl alcohol, methyl alcohol, wood alcohol; alcoholate.

    distillery, brewery, winery; still, wine press.

    tavern, taphouse, public house *or*

pub (*Brit.*), pothouse (*Brit.*), saloon, dramshop, cantina, gin mill, grogshop, groggery, barrel house, rathskeller; bar, lounge, barroom, taproom; cabaret, café, night club; speak-easy, blind pig, blind tiger; beer parlor, beerhouse, beer garden, alehouse; liquor store, package store, wineshop, *bistro* (*F.*).

bartender, barkeeper, barkeep, barmaid, publican (*Brit.*), tapster, alewife, liquor dealer, wine merchant, vintner; bootlegger, moonshiner (*colloq.*).

[*drinking of liquor*] imbibing, tippling, etc. (see *Verbs*); libation, bibacity, compotation, potation (*jocose*); carousal, debauch, wassail; conviviality.

imbiber, tippler, toper, soak, souse, boozer (*slang*), bouser, guzzler, compotator, winebibber; carouser, wassailer, debauchee, bacchant, bacchanalian, convivialist, barfly.

[*drinking party*] carouse, carousal, wassail, drunk (*colloq.*), spree, jag (*colloq.*).

toast, health, skoal, *prosit* (*L.*), wassail.

V. imbibe, tipple, nip, tope, swizzle, tun, soak, souse, bib, booze (*slang*), bouse, guzzle, fuddle, swill; toast; carouse, wassail, debauch; liquor up (*slang*), raise the elbow, wet one's whistle, hit the bottle, go on a bender (*slang*).

distill, brew, ferment.

Adj. alcoholic, ardent, hard, spirituous, with a kick (*slang*), strong; distilled.

vinous, vinic, vinaceous, winy; dry, *brut* (*F.*).

See also DRINK, DRUNKENNESS. *Antonyms*—See ASCETICISM, MODERATENESS, SOBRIETY.

ale, *n.* beer, porter, lager (ALCOHOLIC LIQUOR).

alert, *adj.* intelligent, acute, sharp (INTELLIGENCE); wide-awake, sleepless, astir (WAKEFULNESS); wary, watchful, vigilant (CARE).

alert, *n.* alarm, siren (WARNING).

alias, *n.* pen name, allonym, nom de plume (NAME).

alibi, *n.* excuse, rationalization, defense (FORGIVENESS).

alien, *adj.* foreign, strange, remote (IRRELATION); repugnant, oppugnant, adverse (HOSTILITY); bizarre, unfamiliar, fantastic (UNUSUALNESS).

alien, *n.* foreigner, stranger, immigrant (IRRELATION).

alienate, *v.* estrange, antagonize, disaffect (HOSTILITY, HATRED).

align, *v.* array, line, line up (ARRANGEMENT); back up, side with (SUPPORT).

alike, *adj.* similar, resembling, identical (SIMILARITY).

alimony, *n.* subsidy, support (PAYMENT).

alive, *adj.* living, live, existing (LIFE); animated, vivacious, brisk (ACTIVITY).

all, *adj.* whole, total, entire (COMPLETENESS).

allay, *v.* alleviate, ease, assuage (CALMNESS, MILDNESS); relieve, qualify, mitigate (RELIEF).

allegiance, *n.* constancy, fidelity, loyalism (LOYALTY).

allegory, *n.* fable, parable, bestiary (STORY); metaphor, simile, metonymy (FIGURE OF SPEECH).

all-embracing, *adj.* all-inclusive, exhaustive, comprehensive (COMPLETENESS, INCLUSION).

allergy, *n.* anaphylaxis (*med.*), idiosyncrasy (*med.*), sensitivity (SENSITIVENESS).

alleviate, *v.* abate, mitigate, ease (MILDNESS, DECREASE); relieve, weaken, temper (RELIEF).

alley, *n.* court, lane, walk (PASSAGE, WALKING).

alliance, *n.* association, union, league (COMBINATION, CO-OPERATION).

allied, *adj.* amalgamated, leagued, federated (COMBINATION); connected, affiliated, associated (RELATIONSHIP).

all-inclusive, *adj.* exhaustive, comprehensive, sweeping, broad (COMPLETENESS, INCLUSION).

all-knowing, *adj.* omniscient, pansophical (WISDOM).

allot, *v.* allocate, assign, distribute (APPORTIONMENT).

allow, *v.* permit, let, suffer, tolerate (PERMISSION); entitle, authorize, qualify (PRIVILEGE); vouchsafe, yield (GIVING); grant, own, profess (STATEMENT).

allowance, *n.* leave, sufferance, tolerance (PERMISSION); bounty, dole, subsidy (PAYMENT); percentage, fee, bonus (COMMISSION); rebate, remission, discount (DEDUCTION).

alloy, *n.* compound, amalgam, blend (COMBINATION, METAL).

alloy, *v.* vitiate, pervert, adulterate (DETERIORATION); intermix, interfuse (COMBINATION).

all-powerful, *adj.* omnipotent, mighty (STRENGTH).

allude to, *v.* refer to, advert to, harp on (TALK).

allure, *v.* lure, entice, tempt (ATTRACTION).

allusion, *n.* reference, advertence, insinuation (TALK).

ally, *n.* supporter, backer, champion (SUPPORT, AID).

ally, *v.* federate, confederate, league (UNITY); relate, connect (RELATIONSHIP).

ally oneself with, *v.* uphold, back, endorse (SUPPORT).

almanac, *n.* yearbook, chronicle, annals (TIME MEASUREMENT, BOOK, RECORD).

almighty, *adj.* omnipotent, potent, all-powerful (POWER).

Almighty, *n.* All Powerful, Supreme Deity (GOD).

almost, *adv.* nearly, approximately, about (NEARNESS, SMALLNESS).

alms, *n.* dole, handout (*colloq.*), relief (CHARITY).

aloft, *adv.* upward, heavenward, skyward (ASCENT); on high, high up, above (HEIGHT).

alone, *adj.* lonely, forlorn, solitary (SECLUSION); sole, lone, single (UNITY).

alongside, *adj.* beside, cheek by jowl (NEARNESS).

alongside, *adv.* abreast, neck and neck, side by side (SIDE).

aloof, *adj.* standoffish, unapproachable, unfriendly (SECLUSION, HOSTILITY); distant, far, remote (DISTANCE).

aloud, *adv. viva voce* (L.), vociferously, clamorously (LOUDNESS).

alphabetic, *adj.* alphabetical, abecedarian (WRITTEN SYMBOL).

alphabetize, *v.* file, index (ARRANGEMENT).

already, *adv.* at this time, now, by now (PRESENT TIME).

also, *adv.* likewise, too, furthermore (ADDITION).

alter, *v.* vary, adjust, modify (CHANGE); castrate, sterilize, geld (CELIBACY).

altercation, *n.* argument, quibble, dispute (DISAGREEMENT).

alternate, *n.* surrogate, proxy, deputy (SUBSTITUTION).

alternate, *v.* change, take turns, interchange (DISCONTINUITY).

alternately, *adv.* by turns, turn and turn about (EXCHANGE).

alternation, *n.* periodicity, rhythm, cycle (UNIFORMITY).

alternative, *n.* horn of a dilemma, option, preference (CHOICE).

although, *conj.* albeit, even though, whereas (OPPOSITION, TIME).

altitude, *n.* stature, elevation, eminence (HEIGHT).

alto, *n.* soprano, treble, tenor (HIGH-PITCHED SOUND).

altogether, *adv.* outright, wholly, totally (COMPLETENESS).

altruist, *n.* philanthropist, good

Samaritan, humanitarian (KINDNESS, UNSELFISHNESS).

alumnus, *n.* alumna (*fem.*), graduate, diplomate (LEARNING).

always, *adv.* ever, forever, perpetually (ENDLESSNESS, UNIFORMITY).

A.M., *n.* forenoon, foreday (MORNING).

amass, *v.* accumulate, collect, gather (ASSEMBLAGE, STORE).

amateur, *n.* layman, laic, nonprofessional (LAITY); hobbyist, dilettante, dabbler (AMUSEMENT, PLAYFULNESS); incompetent, blunderer, fumbler (CLUMSINESS).

amatory, *adj.* amorous, erotic, romantic (LOVE).

amaze, *v.* astonish, astound, dumfound (SURPRISE).

ambassador, *n.* diplomat, minister, consul (DEPUTY); envoy, emissary (MESSENGER).

amber, *adj.* ochery, tawny, carbuncle (YELLOW).

AMBIGUITY—*N.* ambiguity, equivocation, amphibology, doubletalk; riddle, conundrum; sophistry, casuistry.

pun, punning, paronomasia, play upon words, equivoque, *double-entendre* (F.), double meaning.

irony, sarcasm, satire.

equivocator, casuist, sophist; oracle, Delphic oracle, sphinx.

V. equivocate, pun, have a double meaning.

Adj. ambiguous, equivocal, amphibolic, oracular; punning, paronomastic; misleading, fallacious, sophistical, casuistic.

See also CONFUSION, MISINTERPRETATION, UNCERTAINTY, UNCLEARNESS. *Antonyms*—See CERTAINTY, CLARITY.

---

ambition, *n.* aspiration, longing, zeal (DESIRE); aim, goal, target (PURPOSE).

ambitious, *adj.* aspiring, zealous, eager (DESIRE); pretentious, grandiose (OSTENTATION).

amble, *v.* ambulate, perambulate, stroll (WALKING).

ambulance, *n.* litter, stretcher (VEHICLE).

ambush, *n.* ambuscade, lurking place, trap (CONCEALMENT).

amenable, *adj.* open to influence, accessible (INFLUENCE); answerable, accountable, responsible (ANSWER); willing, agreeable (WILLINGNESS).

amend, *v.* revise, emend, adjust (RIGHT); mend, better, ameliorate (IMPROVEMENT).

amends, *n.* redress, reparation,

compensation (RELIEF, ATONE-MENT).

amiable, *adj.* affable, agreeable, sweet-tempered (KINDNESS, PLEAS-ANTNESS, SWEETNESS, FRIENDLI-NESS).

amicable, *adj.* affable, agreeable, friendly (FRIENDLINESS).

amity, *n.* tranquillity, concord, harmony (PEACE); camaraderie, bonhomie (FRIENDLINESS).

ammunition, *n.* explosive, powder (ARMS).

amnesia, *n.* fugue (*med.*), hypomnesia (FORGETFULNESS).

amnesty, *v.* remit, reprieve, respite (FORGIVENESS).

amorous, *adj.* erotic, Paphian, romantic (LOVE); desirous, passionate (SEX).

amorphous, *adj.* shapeless, formless, unshaped (DEFORMITY).

amount, *n.* number, sum, aggregate (QUANTITY, MONEY).

ample, *adj.* enough, sufficient, adequate (SUFFICIENCY); large, tidy (*colloq.*), substantial (SIZE).

amplify, *v.* boost, increase, raise (LOUDNESS); enlarge, pad, bulk (INCREASE); elaborate, embellish, enlarge (DETAIL, WORDINESS).

amputate, *v.* cut away, excise, resect (CUTTING, SURGERY).

amulet, *n.* charm, talisman, periapt (GOOD LUCK, MAGIC).

AMUSEMENT—*N.* amusement, entertainment, diversion, divertissement, distraction, relaxation; pastime, sport, recreation, merriment; avocation, hobby, labor of love; pleasure, mirth.

play, game, gambol, romp, frisk, sport, prank, antic, lark, spree, skylarking, dalliance, escapade, beer and skittles.

fun, frolic, merriment, jollity, joviality, laughter, pleasantry.

merrymaking, festivity, festivities, festival, revel, revelry, carousal, carouse, orgy, racket, bacchanal; celebration, carnival, jollification (*colloq.*), high jinks *or* hijinks (*colloq.*).

radio, wireless, AM, FM, portable, table model, console; reception, static, interference; aerial, antenna, speaker, loud-speaker, tweeter, woofer, amplifier, microphone, transmitter; tube, transistor.

television, TV, audio, video; telecast, broadcast, colorcast, spectacular.

holiday, fiesta, gala, gala day, high holiday, extended holiday, vacation, busman's holiday.

Christmas, Noel, yule, yuletide, Christmas time.

Easter, Eastertide, Easter time.

[*place of amusement*] resort, salon; theater, concert hall, ballroom, dance hall, assembly room, auditorium; movies (*colloq.*), music hall, vaudeville theater; circus, hippodrome.

toy, plaything, kickshaw, gewgaw, bauble; doll, puppet, whirligig, Teddy bear.

sportsman, sport, hobbyist, amateur, dabbler, dilettante.

merrymaker, bacchanalian, bacchant, carouser, celebrant, orgiast, reveler, roisterer, wassailer, frolicker, masquerader; party-goer.

V. amuse, entertain, divert, beguile, charm, occupy, enliven, tickle, please, interest, regale.

amuse oneself, sport, have fun, revel, have one's fling.

play, toy, trifle, twiddle, dally, disport, dabble, frisk, gambol, lark, romp, caper, skylark, sport, roughhouse, dandle (*a child*); kill (while away, *or* beguile) time.

make merry, celebrate, racket, bacchanalize, carouse, revel, roister, wassail, frolic.

Adj. amusing, entertaining, beguiling, regaling, diverting, recreative, pleasant; laughable, droll, funny, priceless, ludicrous, sidesplitting (*colloq.*), comical, witty, jocose; festive, festal, jovial, jolly.

playful, frisky, frolicsome, rompish, rompy, sportive, sportful, arch, roguish, coltish, kittenish, waggish.

Phrases. in play, in the spirit of play, in sport, in jest, in joke.

See also ABSURDITY, CELEBRATION, DANCE, INTERESTINGNESS, MERRIMENT, PLEASURE, SOCIALITY, WITTINESS. *Antonyms*—See BOREDOM, DULLNESS.

---

amusing, *adj.* entertaining, diverting (AMUSEMENT); humorous, funny, comical (WITTINESS, LAUGHTER, ABSURDITY).

anachronous, *adj.* old-fashioned, out-of-date, ahead of time (OLD-NESS, MISTIMING).

analgesic, *adj.* anodyne, lenitive, mitigative (PAINKILLER).

analogy, *n.* similitude, similarity, resemblance (COMPARISON); parallelism, agreement, correspondence (SIMILARITY).

analysis, *n.* ratiocination, generalization, induction (REASONING); examination, quiz, investigation (TEST); therapy, psychiatry, psychoanalysis (PSYCHOTHERAPY).

anarchy, *n.* chaos, pandemonium, turmoil (CONFUSION); lawlessness, disorder, mob rule (ILLEGALITY); terrorism (VIOLENCE).

anathema, n. abomination, *bête noire* (*F.*), hate (HATRED).

anatomy, n. figure, physique; somatology (BODY); dissection, autopsy (SURGERY).

ANCESTRY—N. ancestry, antecedence, bloodline, line, lineage, pedigree, strain, breed, stock, derivation, descent, extraction, origin, family, parentage; branch, stem, offset, offshoot; tree, house, race, family tree, birth.

ancestor, antecedent, sire, forefather, forebear, progenitor, predecessor, primogenitor, parent.

genealogy, heredity, genetics; atavism, atavist, throwback.

father, papa, governor (*slang*), paterfamilias, pater (*colloq.*), patriarch; foster father, godfather, godparent, sponsor, stepfather; author, begetter, originator, procreator; grandfather, grandsire, atavus.

paternity, fatherhood, paternalism.

mother, mamma, mater (*colloq.*), materfamilias, matriarch, progenitress, progenitrix, mulier, matron, dam (*esp. of animals*); foster mother, godmother, godparent, stepmother; proud mother, Niobe (*Gr. myth.*).

grandmother, granny (*colloq.*), grandma, beldam, grandam.

maternity, motherhood; maternology.

Oedipus complex, Electra complex; momism.

V. **father,** create, produce, sire, beget, procreate; godfather, sponsor; paternalize.

mother, maternalize, nurse, godmother.

Adj. **ancestral,** antecedent, familial, genealogical, hereditary, lineal, parental, phyletic.

fatherly, paternal, parental, patriarchal; Oedipal.

motherly, maternal, matronly; affectionate, kind, sympathetic, loving, tender.

See also BIRTH, PAST, RELATIVE. *Antonyms*—See CHILD, FUTURE.

anchorage, n. mooring, harborage, harbor (LOCATION).

ancient, adj. aged, elderly, hoary (OLDNESS).

andiron, n. firedog, fire irons (HEAT).

anecdote, n. narrative, yarn, tale (STORY).

anemic, adj. cadaverous, sallow, bloodless (COLORLESSNESS).

anesthetize, v. chloroform, narcotize, drug (INSENSIBILITY, PAINKILLER).

anew, adv. again, repeatedly, once more (REPETITION).

ANGEL—N. angel, spirit, seraph, cherub, archangel, guardian angel.

Madonna, Our Lady, *Nôtre Dame* (*F.*), The Virgin, The Blessed Virgin, The Virgin Mary, Holy Mary, Queen of Heaven.

Adj. **angelic,** seraphic, cherubic, incorporeal; celestial, heavenly, divine.

See also GOD, SACREDNESS, SUPERNATURAL BEINGS. *Antonyms*—See DEVIL.

ANGER—N. anger, rage, fury, boil, heat, ire, wrath, incensement, dander (*colloq.*), spleen, choler, displeasure; tantrum, conniption or conniption fit (*colloq.*), fume, bluster, flare-up, flounce, bridle; growl, snarl, snort.

resentment, indignation, animosity, animus, offense, dudgeon, high dudgeon, grudge, pique, umbrage, miff (*colloq.*).

bitterness, embitterment, acrimony, acerbity, sardonicism, acridity, exacerbation; gall, wormwood, vitriol.

hothead, tinderbox, wasp, brimstone, spitfire; sulk, grouch (*colloq.*), crank (*colloq.*).

V. **anger,** make one's blood boil, raise one's dander; incense, inflame, arouse, rile (*colloq.*), infuriate, enrage, lash into fury, madden, provoke, offend, miff (*colloq.*), pique, huff, rankle.

be angry, fume, burn, boil, boil with rage, chafe, bridle, storm, rage, madden; become angry, anger, blaze, burst into anger, flare up, lose one's temper, fly into a rage, fly off the handle (*colloq.*), blow one's top (*slang*), shake with anger, flounce off (away, *or* out), stamp one's foot in rage, chew nails (*colloq.*).

growl, snarl, snap, bark, snort, gnarl, gnash.

frown, scowl, glower, look black, look daggers, lower *or* lour; sulk, pout, grouch (*colloq.*); redden, color.

resent, take amiss, take offense, take umbrage, take exception, be miffed (*colloq.*), take in ill part.

embitter, bitter, venom, envenom, exacerbate, acerbate, jaundice.

Adj. **angry,** fuming, boiling, burning, blazing, furious, wild, raging, wrathful, wroth, mad (*colloq.*), irate, ireful, choleric, heated, hot, sulfurous, sultry, hot under the collar (*slang*), worked up, wrought up, spleenful, splenetic;

grouchy, snappish, gowling, snarling; irascent.

angered, aroused, up in arms, incensed, inflamed, enraged, maddened, infuriated, infuriate; irritated, exasperated, provoked, riled, vexed, chafed, galled, acerbated.

irritable, irascible, choleric, cranky, grouchy (*colloq.*), edgy, testy, tetchy, combustible, fiery, hot-blooded, hot-headed, hot-tempered, quick-tempered, short-tempered, inflammable, liverish, peppery, snappish, iracund, spleenish, waspish.

resentful, indignant, hurt, sore (*colloq.*), offended, umbrageous, piqued, miffed (*colloq.*).

sullen, sulky, dour; frowning, scowling, glowering, pouting.

bitter, embittered, acrid, envenomed acerbated, exacerbated, sardonic, jaundiced; acrimonious, acerb, vitriolic.

See also ANNOYANCE, BAD TEMPER, HATRED, OFFENSE, RETALIATION, VIOLENCE. *Antonyms*—See CALMNESS, INEXCITABILITY, LOVE, PLEASURE.

angle, *n.* corner, fork, branch (ANGULARITY); phase, aspect, facet (SIDE).

angle, *v.* color, slant, distort (MISREPRESENTATION, PREJUDICE); fork, branch (ANGULARITY).

anguish, *n.* suffering, misery, agony (PAIN).

ANGULARITY—*N.* angularity, angulation, divarication, bifurcation; rectangularity, squareness, perpendicularity, triangularity.

angle, corner, coin, nook, inglenook, quoin, bight; fork, notch, crotch, branch, V, Y, bend, elbow, zigzag; right angle, straight angle, acute angle, obtuse angle, reflex angle, oblique angle.

V. angle, fork, branch, ramify, bifurcate, bend, elbow, hook, diverge, divaricate.

Adj. angular, bent, crooked, jagged, serrated; forked, bifurcate, bifid, biforked, divaricate, Y-shaped, V-shaped, sharp-cornered, crotched, akimbo; oblique, zigzag, staggered; angled, cornered, sharp-cornered, pointed.

See also BEND, NOTCH, SLOPE, TURNING. *Antonyms*—See CURVATURE, STRAIGHTNESS, VERTICALITY.

ANIMAL—*N.* animal, creature, created being, living thing; dumb animal, brute, beast, quadruped, vertebrate, invertebrate, mammal, animalcule; animal kingdom, fauna, animal life, animality, biota; beasts of the field, flocks and herds, livestock, domestic animals, wild animals, game, wild fowl.

bear, bruin, grizzly bear, polar bear, cub, whelp.

bovine, bovoid, ruminant, cow, ox, bull, bullock, taurine, steer; calf, slink, maverick, yearling, heifer; cattle, stock, kine (*archaic*), neat, oxen.

camel, dromedary, Bactrian camel, llama; giraffe, camelopard.

cat, feline, felid, puss, pussy, grimalkin, tiger cat, tabby, tomcat, tom, mouser, ratter; kitten, kitty, catling.

dog, canine, hound, pointer, hunting dog, ratter, cur, mongrel, mutt (*colloq.*); bitch, slut; pup, puppy.

deer, caribou, chevrotain, elk, moose, musk deer, red deer, reindeer; doe, hind, roe; buck, hart, roebuck, stag; fawn, yearling.

elephant, pachyderm, proboscidian, tusker, mammoth, mastodon.

frog, bullfrog, croaker, toad, amphibian, polliwog, tadpole.

goat, billy goat, she-goat, nanny goat, kid.

hog, sow, pig, porker, swine, boar, tusker, razorback, peccary, wart hog; piggy, piglet, pigling, shoat; litter, farrow.

insect, bug, centipede, earwig, millipede; blight, pest, vermin; louse, flea, cootie (*slang*), bedbug; bee, honeybee, queen bee, drone; wasp, social wasp; ant, termite, formicid, pismire; spider, scorpion, black widow; fly, mosquito, gnat; butterfly, moth, lepidopteran; beetle, weevil, boll weevil, Japanese beetle; locust, grasshopper, cricket, cockroach, roach; pupa, chrysalis, aurelia, nymph, larva, grub, maggot, nit.

kangaroo, marsupial, wallaby, wallaroo.

monkey, primate, anthropoid, simian, Jocko, ape, baboon, chimpanzee, drill, gibbon, gorilla, lemur, macaque, mandrill, marmoset, orangutan, rhesus, tarsier, troglodyte (*loose usage*).

reptile, reptilian, saurian, dragon, dinosaur (*extinct*), ichthyosaur (*extinct*); snake, ophidian, serpent, viper; crocodile, alligator; turtle, tortoise, terrapin; lizard, chameleon, dragon, eft, gecko, Gila monster, horned toad, iguana, newt.

rodent, mouse, rat, squirrel, beaver, chinchilla, chipmunk, nutria, gopher, ground hog, guinea pig, hamster, hedgehog, muskrat, porcupine, prairie dog, woodchuck; rabbit, bunny, cottontail, hare, jack rabbit.

shark, man-eater, tiger of the sea, blue shark, hammerhead, dogfish.

sheep, mouflon, ram, tup, wether, bellwether, ewe, tag, pollard; lamb, lambkin, yearling.

shellfish, oyster, blue point, bivalve, clam, mussel, mollusk, snail, slug, whelk, univalve, scallop, lobster, shrimp, crab, crustacean.

water mammal, beluga, dolphin, dugong, manatee, porpoise, seal, sea lion, sea otter, walrus.

whale, cetacean, bottlehead, bottlenose, blackfish, blue whale, cachalot, finback, grampus, humpback, right whale, sperm whale, sulphur-bottom, whalebone whale.

worm, angleworm, earthworm, tapeworm, leech, roundworm, hookworm (*parasitic*), flatworm.

V. **animalize** (*fig.*), carnalize, sensualize, brutalize, imbrute, brutify, dehumanize.

Adj. **animal,** zoological, faunal, creatural, bestial, beastly, mammalian, brutish; animal-like, zooid, theroid.

animalistic, animalized, brutalized, animalian, carnal, fleshly, bodily, corporeal.

bovine, ruminant, bovoid, cowlike, vaccine, vituline; taurian, taurine.

feline, leonine; canine, lupine, vulpine.

fishy, finny, piscine, piscatory, piscatorial.

hoggish, piggish, swinish, porcine.

insectile, insectival, buggy, verminous, lousy, pedicular.

monkeylike, simian, simious, lemurian, apish.

reptilian, saurian, serpentine, serpentile, ophidian, viperine, snaky, sinuous, viperous.

wormy, vermian, wormlike, vermicular.

See also BIRD, BODY, DOMESTICATION, HORSE, SERVICE, ZOOLOGY. *Antonyms*—See BOTANY, MAN, MANKIND, PLANT LIFE.

ANIMAL SOUND—*N.* animal sound, cry, bark, neigh, etc. (see *Verbs*.)

howl, yowl, wail, ululu, ululation, whine.

V. **cry,** blat, bleat, moo, low; squeak, squeal, grunt; hiss, blow, rattle.

bark, bay, yap, yelp, yip.

neigh, whinny, whicker, snort; bray.

mew, mewl, miaou, miaul, caterwaul; purr *or* pur, curr.

roar, bellow, trumpet; growl, snarl, yarr; troat, bell.

howl, yowl, wail, ululate, whine.

chirp, sing, trill, call, chip, chirrup, chirr, chitter, twitter, tweet, cheep, peep, chuck, churr, chatter, coo, curr, whistle, cuckoo, pipe; crow, cock-a-doodle; cluck, cackle, chuckle, gabble, gaggle, quack, gobble, hiss, clang, honk; scream, screech, squawk, squall, hoot, tuwhit, tu-whoo, whoop, boom, croak, caw, plunk, cronk.

buzz, hum, drone; stridulate, creak, crick, chirr, churr.

Adj. **crying,** etc. (see *Verbs*); howling, ululant, ululatory; bellowing, lowing, mugient; stridulous, stridulent, stridulatory.

See also LOUDNESS. *Antonyms*—See SILENCE.

---

animate, *v.* exhilarate, enliven, vitalize (ACTIVITY, LIFE); activate, mobilize, catalyze (MOTIVATION).

animation, *n.* ebullience, volatility, liveliness (ACTIVITY); vitality, being, existence (LIFE).

animosity, *n.* ill will, bad will (HATRED, HOSTILITY).

ankle, *n.* tarsus, talus (APPENDAGE).

annals, *n.* history, chronicle, archives (PAST, RECORD).

annex, *n.* extension, wing, superstructure (BUILDING); appendage, attachment (ADDITION).

announce, *v.* broadcast, blaze, divulge (DISCLOSURE); promulgate, proclaim (INFORMATION); enunciate, expound, declare (STATEMENT).

ANNOYANCE—*N.* annoyance, irritation, vexation, provocation, exasperation, aggravation (*colloq.*), exacerbation; pet, petulance, fret, displeasure, botheration (*colloq.*); importunity.

nuisance, gadfly, terror, pill (*slang*), pest, plague, nag, nettle, bother, trouble.

V. **annoy,** irritate, grate, rasp, vex, irk, provoke, rile (*colloq.*), exasperate, acerbate, aggravate (*colloq.*), exacerbate; badger, bait, tease, needle; nettle, pique, peeve (*colloq.*), offend, tread on the toes of, roil, displease, gall, fret, get on the nerves of, ruffle; bother, pother, disturb, trouble, prey on (*or* upon), worry; torment, devil, macerate, bedevil, harass, hagride, spite, beset, gall, chafe; persecute, pursue, plague, infest, molest; nag, pester, importune, hector, heckle; fester, rankle.

Adj. **annoying,** etc. (see *Verbs*); vexatious, corrosive, acrid, carking (*archaic* or *poetic*), pesky, irksome, nettlesome, thorny, pesty (*colloq.*), pestiferous, plaguy, pestilent, bothersome, trying, provocative, troublesome, troublous, worrisome, importunate; nerve-racking, maddening, offensive, officious.

See also ANGER, BAD TEMPER, TEASING. *Antonyms*—See HAPPINESS, LIKING, PLEASURE, SWEETNESS.

annual, *adj.* yearly, perennial (TIME).

annul, *v.* nullify, disannul, invalidate (INEFFECTIVENESS).

anodyne, *n.* calmative, sedative, opiate (CALMNESS).

anoint, *v.* sanctify, consecrate, bless (SACREDNESS).

anonymous, *adj.* nameless, innominate, unknown (NAME).

ANSWER—*N.* answer, response, reply, acknowledgment, return, rejoinder, rebuttal; retort, riposte, squelcher (*colloq.*), repartee; password; counterstatement, counterblast, countercharge; echo, return, reverberation; antiphon, antiphony; oracle.

[*in law*] defense, plea, reply, rejoinder, rebutter, surrebutter, surrejoinder, counterclaim, countercharge.

solution, explanation, interpretation, *dénouement* (*F.*), resolution, unravelment, decipherment; cipher, Rosetta stone, *deus ex machina* (*L.*), clue, key.

problem, Gordian knot, puzzle, puzzler, riddle, conundrum, logogriph, rebus; question, quandary, dilemma.

V. answer, respond, reply, say, rebut, retort, return, rejoin, acknowledge; echo.

solve, resolve, unriddle, unravel, ravel, riddle, puzzle out, see through, untangle, unweave, unsnarl, unscramble, disentangle, unfold, explain, cut the Gordian knot; clear up, settle; decipher, decode, interpret.

Adj. answerable, accountable, responsible, liable, amenable.

answering, responsive, respondent, echoing, antiphonal; oracular.

See also EXPLANATION, STATEMENT. *Antonyms*—See DEMAND, INQUIRY.

answerable, *adj.* accountable, amendable, responsible (LIABILITY).

answer for, *v.* be responsible for, sponsor, vouch for (LIABILITY).

ant, *n.* termite, formicid (ANIMAL).

antagonistic, *adj.* averse, inimical, unfriendly (OPPOSITION).

antagonize, *v.* disaffect, offend, displease (HOSTILITY, HATRED).

antarctic, *adj.* southern, southernmost (DIRECTION).

antecedent, *n.* ancestor, forefather, forebear (ANCESTRY); antecessor, precedent (PRECEDENCE).

antedate, *v.* predate, pre-exist, come first (EARLINESS, PRECEDENCE); be older (OLDNESS).

antenna, *n.* tentacle, feeler (APPENDAGE); aerial (AMUSEMENT).

anterior, *adj.* forward, ventral, facial (FRONT).

anteroom, *n.* antechamber, waiting room, sitting room (SPACE).

anthology, *n.* compilation, collectanea, miscellany (TREATISE).

antic, *n.* dido, stunt, caper (MISCHIEF).

anticipate, *v.* expect, hope, foresee (EXPECTATION, FORESIGHT); predict, augur, omen (PREDICTION); be beforehand, forestall (PRECEDENCE).

antidote, *n.* corrective, counteractive, counteragent (CURE, OPPOSITION); counterpoison, mithridate, antitoxin (POISON).

antipathy, *n.* aversion, repugnance, repulsion (HATRED).

antique, *adj.* antiquated, archaic, fossil, dated (OLDNESS).

antiquity, *n.* Bronze Age, Iron Age, ancient times (TIME).

anti-Semite, *n.* bigot, racialist, racist (PREJUDICE).

antiseptic, *n.* disinfectant, germicide, prophylactic (CLEANNESS, CURE).

anti-social, *adj.* unsociable, unsocial, asocial (HOSTILITY); misanthropic, cynical, Diogenic (MISANTHROPY).

antithesis, *n.* contrary, antilogy, antipode (OPPOSITE).

antler, *n.* horn, beam, attire (BONE).

anxious, *adj.* afraid, fearful, apprehensive (FEAR); worried, solicitous, troubled (NERVOUSNESS).

any, *adj.* some (QUANTITY).

apart, *adj.* separate, asunder, loose (DISJUNCTION).

apart, *adv.* independently, separately, one by one (UNITY); a-sunder; wide apart (DISTANCE).

apartment, *n.* flat, suite, rooms (HABITATION); room, chamber, alcove (SPACE).

apathy, *n.* inertia, stupor, torpor (INACTION).

ape, *n.* monkey, primate, gorilla (ANIMAL).

aperture, *n.* cleft, breach, orifice (OPENING).

apex, *n.* tip, vertex, peak (SHARPNESS).

aphrodisiac, *adj.* venereal, stimulating, erogenous (SEXUAL DESIRE).

apocryphal, *adj.* spurious, fictitious, unauthentic (FALSENESS).

apologetic, *adj.* excusatory, deprecatory, sorry (ATONEMENT).

apologize for, *v.* defend, come to the defense of, justify (SUPPORT).

APOSTASY—N. apostasy, recantation, renunciation, abjuration, defection, retraction, withdrawal, disavowal, tergiversation, recreancy, reversal; backsliding, relapse, lapse.

apostate, renegade, turncoat, deserter, recreant, backslider.

timeserver, timepleaser, trimmer, doubledealer, temporizer, opportunist, weathercock.

V. apostatize, secede, lapse, relapse, veer round, change sides, go over, shift one's ground, turn, turn around, change one's mind, abjure, renounce, relinquish, back down, swallow one's words, recant, retract.

hedge, temporize, dodge, shuffle, blow hot and cold, be on the fence, straddle (*colloq.*), wait to see how the cat jumps (*or* how the wind blows), hold with the hare but run with the hounds.

Adj. apostate, recreant, renegade, false, unfaithful.

changeful, irresolute, slippery; trimming, timeserving, opportunistic; reactionary, revulsive, revulsionary; capricious, unreliable.

See also CHANGEABLENESS, DISLOYALTY, IRRELIGION, IRRESOLUTION. *Antonyms*—See CONTINUATION, STABILITY, STUBBORNNESS.

appall, *v.* awe, strike terror, unman (FEAR).

apparatus, *n.* device, contrivance, appliance (INSTRUMENT).

apparel, *n.* garments, garb, trappings (CLOTHING).

apparent, *adj.* unhidden, unconcealed, inescapable (VISIBILITY); seeming, clear, distinct (APPEARANCE); self-evident, manifest, obvious (CLARITY); professed, ostensible, colorable (PRETENSE).

apparition, *n.* specter, spirit, spook (GHOST).

appeal, *n.* solicitation, suit, entreaty (BEGGING); interest, fascination, piquancy (INTERESTINGNESS).

appeal, *v.* request, ask, apply (DEMAND); be interesting, fascinate (INTERESTINGNESS).

appear, *v.* emerge, materialize; seem, look (APPEARANCE, VISIBILITY); be published, come out (PUBLICATION).

APPEARANCE—N. appearance, guise, semblance, superficies, veneer, *vraisemblance* (F.); phenomenon, sight, show, scene, view, *coup d'oeil* (F.); lookout, prospect, vista, perspective, bird's-eye view, scenery, landscape, seascape, picture, tableau, representation, display, exposure; stage setting, *mise en scène* (F.).

spectacle, pageant; peep show, magic lantern, cinematograph, cinema (*Brit.*), moving pictures, movies (*colloq.*), films, photoplay, photodrama; panorama, diorama; exhibition, exposition, review, *revue* (F.), *coup de théâtre* (F.); parade, procession.

aspect, phase, angle, shape, form, guise, likeness, semblance, look, complexion, color, image; mien, air, cast, carriage, port, poise, address, bearing, demeanor; presence, expression, effect, impression, point of view, light.

lineament, feature, trait, lines; outline, outside; contour, *tournure* (F.), silhouette, face, countenance, visage, profile; physiognomy; cut of one's jib (*colloq.*).

sight, apparition, hallucination, illusion, mirage, phantasm, phantasmagoria, phantasmagory, phantom, vision; after-image, photogene; image, concept, eidolon, phantasy, reflection; specter, ghost.

[*misleading appearance*] disguise, gloss, guise, illusion, semblance, varnish.

V. appear, be visible, seem, look, look as if, seem to be, purport to be, show; cut a figure; present to the view; become manifest, come in sight, emerge, issue, arrive, loom, rise, crop up, crop out, dawn, darkle, materialize, occur, visualize, twinkle; reappear, recur.

Adj. apparent, seeming, ostensible, quasi, token; on view, manifest, in sight, clear, distinct; emergent, occurrent, recurrent; *prima facie* (L.).

Adv., phrases. apparently, seemingly, clearly, manifestly, ostensibly, on the face of it, at the first blush, at first sight, to the eye.

See also GHOST, INDICATION, LIGHT, VISIBILITY. *Antonyms*—See DISAPPEARANCE, INVISIBILITY.

appease, *v.* conciliate, propitiate, placate (CALMNESS); assuage, sate, slake (SATISFACTION); pacify, pacificate (PEACE).

append, *v.* add, annex, attach (ADDITION).

APPENDAGE—N. appendage, extremity, limb, appendix, appendicle, process, tentacle, feeler, antenna, flipper, flapper, fin, pinna; finlet, pinnula, pinnule.

arm, limb, member, forearm, elbow, ancon, upper arm, shoulder, shoulder blade, scapular.

hand, extremity, fist, palm, thenar; wrist, carpus.

finger, digit; thumb, pollex, pinkie, index finger, pointer; claw, nail, fingernail, ungula, unguis, talon, pounce, chela.

leg, limb, shank, underpinnings; wooden leg, stump; lower leg, calf, shin; upper leg, thigh; hip, haunch, coxa, loins; kneecap, patella; ankle, tarsus, talus.

foot, extremity, paw, pad, trotter, forefoot, hind foot; hoof, unguis, ungula; sole, heel, toe, digit, pettitoes.

wing, pennon, penna, pinion.

Adj. appendicular, tentacular, brachial, ulnar; manual, chiral; palmar, thenar, volar; carpal.

two-handed, bimanous; four-handed, quadrumanous; many-handed, Briarean.

left-handed, sinistral, sinistro-manual, sinistrous.

right-handed, dexterical, dexterous, dextral, dextromanual.

digital, dactylate, dactyloid, digitate.

clawed, ungual, chelate, cheliferous.

bowlegged, bandy-legged, valgus, varus; knock-kneed; spindle-legged, spindle-shanked.

footed, pedate, pedigerous; two-footed, biped; three-footed, tripedal, tripodal, tripodic; four-footed, quadruped; cloven-footed, bisulcate, cloven-hoofed; flat-footed, splayfooted; lame, crippled, halt, spavined, clubfooted, taliped; pigeon-toed.

winged, alar, alate, alated, pennate; dipterous, tetrapterous, micropterous; alary; winglike, aliform.

See also ADDITION, HANGING, PART, TOUCH.

appendix, *n.* addendum, index (BOOK); codicil, rider (ADDITION).

appetite, *n.* edacity (*jocose*), voracity (HUNGER); palate, penchant, relish (LIKING).

appetizer, *n.* apéritif (*F.*), canapé (*F.*), nightcap (TASTE, ALCOHOLIC LIQUOR).

appetizing, *adj.* piquant, spicy, tangy (TASTE).

applaud, *v.* clap, cheer for, praise (APPROVAL).

appliance, *n.* device, contrivance, apparatus (INSTRUMENT).

applicable, *adj.* usable, utilizable, adaptable (USE); apposite, appurtenant, apropos (PERTINENCE).

application, *n.* request, appeal, bid (DEMAND); usage, employment, adoption (USE); relevance, connection, bearing (PERTINENCE).

apply, *v.* adopt, utilize, employ (USE); pertain, bear upon (PERTINENCE); avail, do, serve (PURPOSE).

apply oneself, *v.* buckle down, devote oneself (ENERGY).

appoint, *v.* assign, name, nominate (PLACE, COMMISSION); engage, billet, berth (SITUATION).

appointment, *n.* nomination, charter, ordination (COMMISSION); employment, engagement, hire; capacity (SITUATION); date, engagement (ARRIVAL).

appointments, *n.* trappings, fittings, accouterments (INSTRUMENT).

APPORTIONMENT—*N.* apportionment, allotment, assignment, allocation, distribution, division, deal; partition, dispensation.

portion, dividend, share, allotment, lot, measure, dose; dole, meed, pittance; ration; ratio, proportion, quota, quantum, modicum, allowance.

V. apportion, prorate, divide, distribute, dispense, allot, allow, allocate, detail, cast, share, mete, spread, portion (parcel, *or* dole) out; dole, award, grant, deal; partition, assign.

Adj. apportionable, divisible, distributable, dispensable.

respective, particular, several, individual, proportionate, proportional, commensurate.

Adv., phrases. respectively, severally, each to each; by lot; in equal shares.

See also GIVING.

appraise, *v.* size up (*colloq.*), estimate, evaluate (VALUE, SIZE); consider, deem (OPINION).

appreciable, *adj.* enough, competent, plenty (SUFFICIENCY).

appreciate, *v.* enjoy (TASTE); think highly of (APPROVAL); value, esteem, prize; rise in value, boom, enhance (VALUE); thank, acknowledge (GRATITUDE); realize, conceive (KNOWLEDGE).

appreciation, *n.* commentary, review, critique (TREATISE).

apprehend, *v.* arrest, pinch (*slang*), seize (TAKING, IMPRISONMENT); understand, grasp, comprehend (UNDERSTANDING); dread, misdoubt, be afraid (FEAR).

apprehension, *n.* phobia, dread, awe (FEAR); misgiving, mistrust, misdoubt (UNBELIEVINGNESS);

seizure, capture, arrest (TAKING).

apprentice, *n.* helper, assistant (WORK); beginner, neophyte (LEARNING, BEGINNING).

apprise, *v.* orient, advise, brief (INFORMATION).

APPROACH—N. approach, access, accession, convergence.

[*means of approach*] **avenue,** adit, path, access, ramp.

overtures, advances, approaches, proposals, offers.

V. **approach,** near, draw near, move toward, drift toward, come near, converge upon; accost, make advances; gain upon, overtake, catch up to, stalk.

Adj. **approaching,** nearing, coming, oncoming, forthcoming, drawing near, convergent, advancing; imminent, impending, threatening.

approachable, accessible, attainable; open, affable, sociable, democratic, friendly.

See also ARRIVAL, FOLLOWING, FRIENDLINESS, FUTURE, NEARNESS, PASSAGE. *Antonyms*—See AVOIDANCE, DISTANCE, REVERSION.

---

approbation, *n.* approval, acceptance, sanction (APPROVAL).

appropriate, *adj.* proper, correct, legitimate (PROPRIETY); particular, peculiar, intrinsic (OWNERSHIP).

appropriate, *v.* assume, confiscate, expropriate (TAKING); abstract, lift (THIEVERY).

APPROVAL—N. approval, approbation, acceptance, endorsement, confirmation, ratification, sanction; esteem, estimation, good opinion, favor; appreciation, regard; account, popularity, credit, repute, renown, kudos (*colloq.*); commendation, congratulation, praise, encomium, homage, hero worship; blessing.

admiration, adoration, worship, veneration, idolatry; tribute, testimonial, recommendation, reference, certificate.

self-admiration, self-love, narcissism, *amour propre* (F.), self-approval, vanity, conceit, pride, self-worship, self-esteem, egotism.

applause, plaudit, clap, handclap, clapping, acclaim, acclamation; cheer, hurrah, huzza; paean, shout (peal, chorus, *or* thunders) of applause, ovation, salvo.

applauder, clapper, rooter, cheerer; cheering squad, claque.

V. **approve,** approbate, commend, boost (*colloq.*), accept, endorse, countenance, smile on, confirm, ratify, sanction; esteem, value, prize, set great store by, honor, like, appreciate, think well of, think highly of; stand up for, stick up for (*colloq.*), uphold, recommend; sympathize with.

admire, esteem, hold in esteem, look up to, adore, worship, venerate, idolize, idolatrize.

excite admiration in, dazzle, impress, strike with wonder, awe.

applaud, clap, acclaim, cheer for, root for (*colloq.*).

Adj. **approbative,** approbatory, applausive, acclamatory, plausive, confirmatory, commendatory, laudatory, complimentary.

approved, popular, standard, acceptable, orthodox, in good odor; in high esteem, in favor, in high favor.

admirable, estimable, venerable, splendid.

praiseworthy, laudable, honorable, commendable, creditable, meritorious, glorious.

See also ACCEPTANCE, FLATTERY, LOVE, PRAISE, PRIDE, RESPECT, WORSHIP. *Antonyms*—See DETRACTION, DISAPPROVAL, DISREPUTE, DISRESPECT, HATRED, UNSAVORINESS.

---

approximate, *adj.* near, close, rough (SIMILARITY).

approximately, *adv.* about, *circa* (L.), nearly (SMALLNESS).

appurtenance, *n.* adjunct, accessory, appanage (ADDITION).

apropos, *adj.* applicable, apposite, appurtenant (PERTINENCE).

apt, *adj.* likely, probable, liable (LIKELIHOOD); inclined, prone (TENDENCY); pat, to the point (PERTINENCE); appropriate, apropos (AGREEMENT).

aptitude, *n.* ability, flair, talent (ABILITY); mental ability (INTELLIGENCE).

aqueduct, *n.* conduit, channel, culvert (PASSAGE).

aquiline, *adj.* eaglelike, hooked, beaked (NOSE).

arable, *adj.* cultivable, cultivatable, tillable (FARMING).

arbitrary, *adj.* peremptory, rigorous, highhanded (CONTROL, OPINION); autocratic, capricious, despotic (WILL).

arbitrator, *n.* arbiter, umpire, referee (JUDGE).

arcade, *n.* cloister, vault, arch (PASSAGE, SUPPORT).

arch, *n.* cove (*arch.*), dome, arcade (SUPPORT).

arch, *v.* bow, crook, loop (CURVE).

archaeology, *n.* paleontology, antiquarianism, paleology (OLDNESS).

archaic, *adj.* antiquated, antique, dated (OLDNESS, DISUSE).

arched, *adj.* arch-shaped, arciform, domed (SUPPORT).

architect, *n.* creator, inventor, originator (PRODUCTION, PLAN).

architecture, *n.* erection, engineering, architectonics (BUILDING); construction, structure, constitution (SHAPE).

archives, *n.* annals, chronicle (RECORD).

arctic, *adj.* polar, hyperborean, northernmost (DIRECTION).

arctics, *n.* overshoes, galoshes, rubber boots (FOOTWEAR).

ardor, *n.* fervor, élan (F.), zeal, passion (FEELING, EAGERNESS, ENTHUSIASM).

arduous, *adj.* hard, tough, toilsome (DIFFICULTY, WORK).

area, *n.* acre, acreage, square feet (MEASUREMENT); tract, space, place (REGION, LAND); field, margin, scope (SPACE).

arena, *n.* scene, theater, stage (ENVIRONMENT); battlefield, battleground, Armageddon (FIGHTING); focus, hub, orbit (ACTIVITY); pit, field (ATTEMPT).

argot, *n.* vernacular, dialect, cant (LANGUAGE).

argue, *v.* altercate, quibble, quarrel (DISAGREEMENT); discuss, deliberate (TALK); debate, agitate, controvert (DEBATE); testify, attest, show (INDICATION).

argue into, *v.* induce, cajole, coax (PERSUASION).

argumentation, *n.* debating, agitation, argument (DEBATE); logic, dialectics, syllogistics (REASONING).

aria, *n.* song, air, arietta (SINGING).

arid, *adj.* dry, droughty, moistless (DRYNESS); sterile, barren, unfertile (UNPRODUCTIVENESS).

arise, *v.* awake, awaken, get up (WAKEFULNESS); ascend, rise, go up (ASCENT); originate, begin (BEGINNING); revolt, riot, rise (DISOBEDIENCE); arrive, crop up, bechance (OCCURRENCE).

aristocracy, *n.* gentry, nobility, peerage (SOCIAL CLASS).

aristocratic, *adj.* patrician, upperclass, well-born (SOCIAL CLASS); superior, condescending, patronizing (PRIDE).

arithmetic, *n.* algorism (COMPUTATION).

arm, *n.* limb, member (APPENDAGE); unit, wing, detachment (PART); bay, gulf, basin (INLET).

arm, *v.* equip, man, fit out (PREPARATION).

armed, *adj.* forearmed, forewarned, forehanded (PREPARATION); armiferous, in (*or* under) arms (FIGHTING).

armistice, *n.* temporary peace, cessation of war, truce (PEACE, CESSATION).

armor, *n.* arms, weapons (ARMS); defense, mail, armature (PROTECTION).

armored, *adj.* armor-plated, ironclad, bullet-proof (COVERING); protected, safe, secure (PROTECTION).

armory, *n.* arsenal, magazine, depot (STORE).

ARMS—N. arms, weapons, deadly weapons, armament, armor.

arrow, missile, dart, shaft, quarrel (*for crossbow*), bolt, vire (*hist.*).

bow, longbow, crossbow, arbalest, arbalester *or* arbalestre, backed bow, carriage bow, selfbow, union bow; sling.

catapult, ballista, ballist, martinet, trebuchet.

firearms, armament, arms, artillery, battery, broadside, cannon, cannonry, gunnery, ordnance, small arms; siege artillery, field artillery, coast artillery, mountain artillery, field battery.

firearm, gun, rifle, weapon, carbine, fowling piece, Garand, musket, muzzle-loader (*obs.*), breechloader, shotgun, sidearm, automatic, blunderbuss (*obs.*), culverin (*hist.*), harquebus (*hist.*), machine gun, Gatling gun, Lewis gun, bazooka.

pistol, revolver, repeater, derringer, automatic, sidearm, shooting iron (*slang*), six-shooter (*slang*), rod (*slang*), zip gun (*slang*), cap pistol.

cannon, mounted gun, gun, fieldpiece, field gun, Big Bertha, Krupp gun, mortar, howitzer, pompom, seventy-five, bombard (*hist.*), culverin (*hist.*), carronade (*hist.*), anti-aircraft cannon, ack-ack; torpedo.

missile, projectile, trajectile, guided missile, ICBM, bolt; bullet, dumdum bullet, ball, slug, shot, pellet; cannon ball, grape, shrapnel; grenade, shell, bomb, blockbuster, robot bomb, rock, napalm bomb, atom bomb, hydrogen bomb, A-bomb, H-bomb, gas bomb, depth bomb.

ammunition, explosive, cartridge, powder, powder and shot, gunpowder, dynamite, explosive, T.N.T.; poison gas, lewisite, chlorine gas, mustard gas, tear gas.

See also ATTACK, CUTTING, FIGHTER, FIGHTING, GAS, PROTECTION.

---

army, *n.* soldiery, troops, armed

forces (FIGHTER); crowd, host, legion (MULTITUDE).

aroma, *n.* fragrance, scent, aura (ODOR).

aromatic, *adj.* flavorful, mellow, savory (TASTE).

around, *adv.* about, on every side, on all sides (ENVIRONMENT).

around, *prep.* via, by way of (PASSAGE).

arouse, *v.* rouse, move, excite (EXCITEMENT); carry away, overpower, transport (FEELING); rise, rouse, wake (WAKEFULNESS).

arraign, *v.* impeach, indict, accuse (ACCUSATION).

arrange, *v.* sort, sift, dispose (ARRANGEMENT); prepare, provide, ready (PLAN, PREPARATION); set to music, harmonize, orchestrate (MUSICIAN).

ARRANGEMENT—*N.* **arrangement,** disposal, disposition, arrayal, array; distribution, allocation, allotment, apportionment; gradation, organization, grouping; analysis, classification, collocation, systematization, orderliness; composition, configuration, ordination, stratification; catalogue, chronology, menology (*of saints*).

method, plan, design, methodology, order, pattern, rank, range, scheme, structure, system, harmony, symmetry, texture, rule, form.

[*science of classification*] **taxonomy,** systematics, nosology (*of diseases*).

V. **arrange,** dispose, fix, place, form; order, set in order, set out, marshal, array, range, align, aline, line, line up, allot, allocate, apportion, distribute, assign the parts, assign places to, dispose of, assort, sort, sift; tidy.

classify, class, assort, bracket, categorize, group, rank, section, sort, type, codify, screen, sift, winnow, pigeonhole, file, catalogue, tabulate, index, alphabetize, grade.

methodize, regulate, systematize, co-ordinate, organize; unravel, disentangle.

Adj. **methodical,** orderly, regular, systematic, routine, businesslike; neat, tidy.

See also CLASS, MAKE-UP, METHOD, NEATNESS, PLAN, RANK, RECORD. *Antonyms*—See CONFUSION, UNTIDINESS.

---

arrant, *adj.* thorough, out-and-out, utter (COMPLETENESS).

arrears, *n.* arrearage, indebtedness, liabilities (DEBT).

arrest, *v.* take into custody, seize,

apprehend (IMPRISONMENT, TAKING); stop, stall, inactivate, suspend (CESSATION, MOTIONLESSNESS, INACTION); retard, retardate, moderate (SLOWNESS).

arresting, *adj.* outstanding, striking, pronounced (VISIBILITY, MAGNIFICENCE).

ARRIVAL—*N.* **arrival,** advent, appearance, home-coming.

visit, call, visitation; date, appointment, engagement, meeting, get-together, gathering; conference, interview.

destination, goal; harbor, haven, port, landing place, anchorage, terminus, terminal; home, journey's end.

[*place frequently visited*] **haunt,** haunts, stamping grounds (*colloq.*), purlieu, resort; ambit, circuit; mecca.

visitor, caller, guest, transient, visitant, *habitué* (*F.*); passenger, arrival, newcomer, late arrival, latecomer, Johnny-come-lately.

visiting card, calling card, card, pasteboard.

V. **arrive,** get to, reach, gain, overtake, join; appear, enter, come in, put in, land, cast anchor, moor, reach port, make port, debark, disembark, come (*or* go) ashore.

come, burst, flare; attain, accede to, hit, make; come from, hail from; come last, bring up the rear; come back, return; come again, rejoin, revisit.

alight, light, dismount, descend, detrain, deplane.

visit, pay a visit, drop in, call, look in on, see, come to see, haunt, frequent; lionize.

throng, crowd, swarm, troop; overcrowd, flood, deluge, swamp, overrun, infest.

Adj. **arriving,** approaching, coming, entering, incoming, homeward, homeward-bound, inward bound, inbound.

See also APPEARANCE, APPROACH, DESCENT, ENCROACHMENT, INGRESS, PUSH, SOCIALITY, VISIBILITY. *Antonyms*—See DEPARTURE, EGRESS.

---

arrogance, *n.* haughtiness, hauteur, assumption (PRIDE).

arrow, *n.* missile, dart, bolt (ARMS).

arsenal, *n.* armory, magazine, depot (STORE).

arsonist, *n.* incendiary, firebug, pyromaniac (FIRE).

art, *n.* skill, artistry, address (ABILITY); painting, design, illustration (FINE ARTS).

artery, *n.* road, highway, thoroughfare (PASSAGE).

artful, *adj.* cunning, crafty, disingenuous (CLEVERNESS); skillful, adept, adroit (ABILITY).

article, *n.* thing, object, commodity (MATERIALITY); script, typescript, manuscript (TREATISE, WRITING).

articles, *n.* stock, produce, goods for sale (SALE).

articulate, *adj.* fluent, vocal, glib, voluble (EXPRESSION).

artifice, *n.* trick, device, subterfuge (DECEPTION).

artificial, *adj.* synthetic, man-made; constrained, contrived, forced (PRODUCTION, UNNATURALNESS).

artillery, *n.* firearms, armament, guns (ARMS).

artisan, *n.* craftsman, technician, artist (WORK).

artist, *n.* painter, drawer, illustrator (ARTIST); actor, entertainer (ACTOR); artiste, performer, virtuoso (MUSICIAN); singer, *cantatrice* (*F., fem.*), songster (SINGING); artisan, craftsman, technician (WORK).

ARTIST—*N.* artist, painter, depicter, drawer, sketcher, designer, engraver, graver, etcher, draftsman *or* draughtsman; copyist; enameler, enamelist; cartoonist, caricaturist; dauber (*derogatory*); watercolorist, pastelist, colorist; portraitist, landscapist, seascapist, miniaturist; Raphael, Titian; aquarellist, chiaroscurist, delineator, drafter, frescoer, illustrator, lithographer, master, old master, mosaicist, muralist, tracer, limner, picturer; primitive.

[*as to school, etc.*] abstractionist, nonobjective painter, cubist, dadaist, expressionist, Fauve, futurist, modernist, pointillist, surrealist, symbolist, vorticist; impressionist, neoimpressionist, post-impressionist; realist, romanticist, romantic, naturalist, classicist, neoclassicist, idealist.

sculptor, sculptress (*fem.*), statuary; molder, modeler, carver, whittler; chaser, embosser, engraver, etcher, mezzotinter, chalcographer, iconographer, wood engraver, xylographer; Phidias, Praxiteles, Michelangelo.

See also FINE ARTS.

---

artistic, *adj.* aesthetic, picturesque, pictorial (BEAUTY); skillful, adept, adroit (ABILITY).

artless, *adj.* unaffected, inartificial, ingenuous (NATURALNESS); guileless, naïve, simple (INNOCENCE); sincere, bona fide, genuine (HONESTY); unskillful, inadept, inapt (CLUMSINESS).

ASCENT—*N.* ascent, rise, ascension, lift; spring, upspring, jump, leap, take-off, zoom; upcropping, emergence, levitation, upheaval.

surge, billow, swell, wallow, resurgence.

climber, scaler, vaulter, steeplejack, cragsman, mountaineer, Alpinist.

climbing irons, crampons; alpenstock.

escalator, elevator, lift (*Brit.*), ladder, stepladder, steppingstone.

step, stile, stair, stairstep; tread, riser, bar, rundle, rung, spoke, stave.

stairs, flight, flight of stairs, staircase, stairway, companionway (*naut.*), stoop; stair well, landing, stairhead.

V. **ascend,** rise, arise, go up, get up, come up, move up, lift, mount, work one's way up; spring up, start up, uprise, jump, leap, rear (*of animals*), take off, go (*or* fly) aloft, uprear, upspring; crop up, surface, emerge; rocket, zoom, skyrocket, shoot up, arrow, spire; levitate.

surge, billow, ripple, swell, well up, wallow, wreathe; resurge.

climb, swarm, swarm over, shin (*colloq.*), shinny up (*colloq.*), clamber, scramble, scrabble; escalade, scale, mount, vault.

tower, soar, dominate, top, overtop, surmount; transcend.

rise and fall, billow, surge, undulate, post (*on a horse*), welter, dip; bob, jog, seesaw, teeter-totter, pump, flap.

Adj. **ascending,** etc. (see *Verbs*); ascendant, emergent, towering, dominant, bluff, lofty, steep.

Adv. **up,** upward, upwards, aloft, heavenward, skyward; uphill, upstairs; upstream.

See also HEIGHT, JUMP, PROGRESS, SLOPE. *Antonyms*—See DESCENT, REVERSION.

---

ascertain, *v.* find out, determine, divine (DISCOVERY).

ascertainable, *adj.* knowable, discoverable, discernible (KNOWLEDGE).

ASCETICISM—*N.* asceticism, austerity, puritanism, total abstinence; mortification, sackcloth and ashes, penance, fasting; scourging, flagellation, self-mortification; hair shirt, martyrdom.

ascetic, anchoret, anchorite, hermit, recluse, monk, solitary, puritan, yogi (*Hindu*), fakir (*Moham.*), dervish (*Moham.*), self-tormentor, martyr.

Adj. ascetic, austere, abstemious, puritanical, flagellant, flagellatory.

See also ATONEMENT, CELIBACY, FASTING, MODERATENESS, SECLUSION, SOBRIETY, UNSELFISHNESS. *Antonyms*—See GLUTTONY, INTEMPERANCE, PLEASURE, SEX, SOCIALITY.

ascribe to, *v.* impute to, accredit with, attribute to (ATTRIBUTION).

asexual, *adj.* sexless, neuter, epicene (CELIBACY).

ash, *n.* cinder, slag, clinker (FIRE).

ashamed, *adj.* compunctious, contrite, sheepish (GUILT).

ashen, *adj.* pale, pallid, ashy (COLORLESSNESS).

ashes, *n.* remains, relics, ruins (DESTRUCTION); bones, *reliquiae* (L.), fossil (REMAINDER).

ashore, *adj.* grounded, aground, beached (LAND).

aside, *adv.* abreast, alongside, side by side (SIDE).

as if, as though, so to speak, as it were (SIMILARITY).

asinine, *adj.* inane, absurd, ridiculous (FOLLY); ass-like, mulish, mule-like (HORSE).

ask, *v.* demand, query, inquire (INQUIRY); request, appeal, apply (DEMAND); levy, impose, charge (EXPENDITURE).

askance, *adv.* with a grain of salt, *cum grano salis* (L.), incredulously (UNBELIEVINGNESS).

askew, *adj.* crooked, wry, awry (WINDING, TURNING, DEFORMITY).

asleep, *adj.* sleeping, dozing, napping (SLEEP).

aspect, *n.* phase, appearance, angle (SIDE, APPEARANCE); view, vista, outlook (VISION).

aspersion, *n.* defamation, calumny, slur (DETRACTION).

asphyxiate, *v.* suffocate, stifle, drown (KILLING).

aspire, *v.* wish, set one's heart upon, desiderate (DESIRE).

ass, *n.* jackass, jack, mule (HORSE); donkey, addlebrain, addlehead, addlepate (STUPIDITY, FOLLY).

assail, *v.* assault, set upon, fall upon (ATTACK).

assassinate, *v.* murder, bump off (*slang*), liquidate (KILLING).

assault, *v.* assail, set upon, fall upon (ATTACK).

assay, *v.* evaluate, appraise, assess (VALUE).

ASSEMBLAGE—*N.* assemblage, collection, levy, conflux, concourse, gathering, mobilization, meet, concentration, convergence, forgathering, muster, congregation.

assembly, meeting, levee, reunion, congress, convocation, caucus, convention, council, committee, association, union, club.

miscellany, medley, miscellanea, collectanea, ana.

crowd, throng; flood, rush, deluge; rabble, mob, host, multitude; press, crush, horde, body, tribe; gang, knot, troop, corps, posse, team, crew, squad, force, band, party; swarm, shoal, covey, flock, herd, roundup, drove, drive, bunch, bevy, array, galaxy.

group, cluster, series, nest (*as of boxes*), set, tissue (*as of lies*), batch, lot, pack; assortment, bunch, parcel, bundle, packet, package, bale, fagot, wisp, truss, tuft, tussock, pompon, shock, clump, thicket; rick, stack, sheaf, swath.

accumulation, amassment, conglomeration, cumulation, store, stock, aggregation, aggregate, congestion, heap, lump, pile, litter, mass, pyramid; drift, snowball, snowdrift; quantity.

V. assemble, come together, collect, muster; meet, unite, join, rejoin; cluster, flock, swarm, rush, surge, stream, herd, mass, crowd, throng, huddle, associate; congregate, concentrate, resort, forgather.

bring together, gather together, collect, muster, gather, round up; hold a meeting, call, convene, convoke; rake up, dredge, heap, mass, pile; pack, bunch, huddle, bundle, cram, lump together; compile, group, concentrate, unite, amass, agglomerate, accumulate, hoard, store.

Adj. dense, compact, solid, close, tight, crowded, thick, thickset, serried, teeming, swarming, populous.

See also COMBINATION, COMPLETENESS, CONVERGENCE, LEGISLATURE, QUANTITY, SOCIALITY, STORE. *Antonyms*—See DISJUNCTION, DISMISSAL, DISPERSION.

ASSENT—*N.* assent, acquiescence, accession, admission; affirmation, nod, acknowledgment.

unanimity, unison, accord, common consent, consensus, acclamation, chorus; concurrence, accordance, consentience.

V. assent, give assent, acquiesce, agree, comply, accept, accede, accord, concur, consent, coincide, echo, go with; recognize; subscribe to, support, conform to, defer to.

confirm, ratify, approve, endorse, visé, seal, countersign; validate, corroborate, sustain, substantiate, clinch (*colloq.*).

Adj. assenting, acquiescing, etc.

(see *Verbs*); assentive, agreed, acquiescent.

unanimous, consentient, concurrent, accordant, consentaneous, like-minded, of one accord (*or* mind), of the same mind, at one.

Adv., phrases. yes, yea, aye, ay, true, granted, even so, just so, to be sure, as you say, surely, assuredly, exactly, precisely, certainly, of course, unquestionably, no doubt, doubtless, indubitably.

unanimously, by common consent, to a man, as one man; with one consent (voice *or* accord), one and all.

See also AGREEMENT, CONFORMITY, PERMISSION, WILLINGNESS. *Antonyms*—See DENIAL, DISAGREEMENT.

---

assert, *v.* say, declare, state (AFFIRMATION).

assertive, *adj.* dogmatic, positive, self-assertive (STATEMENT).

assess, *v.* evaluate, appraise, estimate (VALUE).

asset, *n.* possession, belonging, appurtenance (OWNERSHIP); plum, nugget, treasure (VALUE).

assets, *n.* riches, substance, resources (WEALTH); principal, capital (MONEY); holdings, stocks, bonds (OWNERSHIP).

assiduous, *adj.* hard-working, industrious, laborious (WORK); careful, diligent, punctilious (CARE, ATTENTION); unfailing, unflagging, unrelenting (CONTINUATION).

assign, *v.* appoint, name, nominate (PLACE); apportion, allot (APPORTIONMENT).

assignation, *n.* rendezvous, affair (SEX).

assignment, *n.* practice, drill, homework (TEACHING).

assimilate, *v.* take in, absorb, soak up (INTAKE); make similar, homologize, standardize (SIMILARITY).

assist, *v.* help, lend a hand, be helpful (AID).

assistant, *n.* helper, subordinate, apprentice (WORK); auxiliary, help, aide (AID).

ass-like, *adj.* asinine, mulish, mule-like (HORSE).

associate, *n.* confrere, colleague, cohort (FRIEND); partner, coworker (WORK).

associate, *v.* amalgamate, federate, ally (COMBINATION, UNITY); bracket, group, link (RELATIONSHIP).

association, *n.* alliance, league, society (CO-OPERATION, COMBINATION); relation, connection, affiliation (RELATIONSHIP).

assort, *v.* diversify, vary, variegate (DIFFERENCE); sort, sift (ARRANGEMENT).

assorted, *adj.* hybrid, mixed, varied (CLASS).

assortment, *n.* kind, sort, variety (CLASS).

assuage, *v.* compose, attemper, relieve (CALMNESS); appease, sate, slake (SATISFACTION).

assume, *v.* believe, fall for, accept (BELIEF); suppose, admit, grant (SUPPOSITION); appropriate, confiscate, expropriate (TAKING); simulate, sham, affect (PRETENSE).

assumed, *adj.* tacit, connoted, inferred (MEANING).

assumption, *n.* theory, hypothesis, postulate (BELIEF); supposal, presupposition (SUPPOSITION); arrogance, contumely, insolence (PRIDE); brass, nerve (*colloq.*), presumption (DISCOURTESY).

assurance, *n.* insurance, guarantee, warranty (CERTAINTY); earnest, warrant, guaranty (PROMISE).

astern, *adv.* abaft, rearward, backward (REAR).

astir, *adj.* afoot, asimmer, simmering (PREPARATION); wide-awake, vigilant, alert (WAKEFULNESS).

astonish, *v.* amaze, astound, dumfound (SURPRISE).

astound, *v.* amaze, astonish, dumfound (SURPRISE).

astray, *adj.* lost, gone, strayed (LOSS).

astrologer, *n.* astromancer, Chaldean, soothsayer (WORLD).

astronomer, *n.* stargazer, astrophysicist, uranologist (WORLD).

astute, *adj.* apt, brainy, clever (INTELLIGENCE).

asylum, *n.* insane asylum, mental hospital, state institution (INSANITY); safety, security, shelter (PROTECTION).

at ease, unanxious, carefree, secure (UNANXIETY).

at hand, near, near at hand, close (NEARNESS).

atheist, *n.* irreligionist, heathen, infidel (IRRELIGION).

athletic, *adj.* vigorous, strapping, brawny, muscular (HEALTH, STRENGTH).

athletics, *n.* acrobatics, calisthenics (GYMNASTICS).

at large, escaped, fugitive, loose (FREEDOM, DEPARTURE).

atlas, *n.* globe (MAP); directory, gazetteer (LIST).

atmosphere, *n.* background, aura, surroundings (ENVIRONMENT); troposphere, substratosphere, tropopause (AIR).

atom bomb, *n.* A-bomb, H-bomb (THROW).

atomizer, *n.* sprinkler, sprayer, vaporizer (WATER, GAS).

at once, immediately, directly, instantaneously (EARLINESS).

ATONEMENT—*N.* atonement, reparation, expiation, redemption, propitiation; indemnification, redress, amends, recompense, compensation; peace offering.

apology, explanation, satisfaction, regret, justification, vindication, defense, extenuation, excuse.

penance, fasting, sackcloth and ashes, flagellation, self-mortification, purgation, purgatory.

V. **atone,** expiate, propitiate, appease, make amends; redeem, repair, ransom, absolve, purge, shrive.

apologize, express regret, beg pardon, give satisfaction.

Adj. **atoning,** placular, purgatorial, propitiatory, expiatory, explational, sacrificial.

apologetic, excusatory, deprecatory, sorry, regretful.

atonable, expiable, recoverable, redeemable, retrievable, reparable.

See also JUSTIFICATION, PENITENCE, RECOMPENSE. *Antonyms*—See IMPENITENCE.

---

at present, at this time, at this moment, now (PRESENT TIME).

at random, aimlessly, haphazardly, randomly (PURPOSELESSNESS).

at rest, in repose, settled down, perched (REST); resting, taking it easy, idle (INACTION).

atrocious, *adj.* bad, abominable, dreadful (INFERIORITY); heinous, flagitious, accursed (WICKEDNESS).

atrocity, *n.* brutality, savagery, barbarity (CRUELTY); infamy, iniquity; monster, monstrosity (WICKEDNESS).

attach, *v.* fix, fasten, tie (JUNCTION, FASTENING); add, annex, append (ADDITION); garnishee, usurp, pre-empt (TAKING).

attached to, *adj.* fond of, partial to, affectionate toward (LIKING).

attachment, *n.* affection, fondness, affinity (LIKING); confiscation, expropriation, sequestration (TAKING).

ATTACK—*N.* attack, assault, strike, thrust, aggression, persecution, offense, offensive; onslaught, charge, blitz (*colloq.*), blitzkrieg, incursion, dragonnade, inroad, invasion, irruption, descent, outbreak, sally, sortie, raid, razzia, maraud, air raid, foray; storm, storming, zero hour; boarding, escalade; counterattack, counteroffensive; feint.

siege, investment, blockade, beleaguerment, besiegement, encompassment; bombardment, cannonade, shelling.

fit, seizure, stroke, spell, bout, paroxysm, spasm, convulsion, access, onset.

firing, shooting, discharge, burst, volley, fusillade; sharpshooting, broadside, cross fire, enfilade, barrage.

sharpshooter, dead shot, crack shot, marksman, rifleman, sniper. [*position for attack*] beachhead, bridgehead, offensive.

V. **attack,** assault, assail, descend upon, set upon, pounce upon, fall upon, swoop down on; buck, rush, charge; enter the lists, take the offensive; strike at, thrust at, aim (*or* deal) a blow at; be the aggressor, strike the first blow, fire the first shot; advance (*or* march) against, march upon, ramp, invade, raid, harry, storm, foray, maraud, sally; wade into, aggress, beset, persecute, prey on, devour, tilt at, waylay, ambush, mug (*colloq.*), run amuck; feint, counterattack.

besiege, siege, beset, beleaguer, invest, surround, blockade; sap, mine; storm, board, scale the walls.

fire upon, shoot at, snipe at, open fire, pepper, fusillade, torpedo, bomb, bombard, shell, fire a volley, enfilade, rake; hit, plug (*slang*).

Adj. **aggressive,** assaultive, offensive, combative, pugnacious; invasive, incursive, irruptive; besetting, obsidional.

Phrases. **on the warpath,** on the offensive, over the top, up in arms.

See also FIGHTING, HOSTILITY, PUNISHMENT. *Antonyms*—See FEAR, PROTECTION, SUBMISSION.

---

attain, *v.* accede to, reach, hit (ARRIVAL); achieve, accomplish (ABILITY); gain, get, acquire (ACQUISITION).

attainable, *adj.* obtainable, achievable, accessible (POSSIBILITY).

ATTEMPT—*N.* attempt, try, trial, endeavor, bid, essay, effort; crack, whack, shot (*all colloq.*); exertion, pursuit, contestation.

struggle, contention, tussle, rough-and-tumble, scuffle, brush, skirmish; toil, labor, travail, agony, throes, stress, strain.

competition, contest, bout, match, game, tournament, tug of war, marathon; joust, tourney, duel; rivalry, emulation; easy contest, snap (*colloq.*), setup (*colloq.*), walkaway, walkover, pushover (*slang*).

race, course, marathon; horse race, derby, steeplechase, sweepstake, trotting race, trotters, flats; horse racing, the horses, the turf, the track; rowing race, boat race, regatta.

athletic contest, gymkhana, pentathlon, decathlon; event, heat, course.

place of competition, arena, pit, field; track, race track, racecourse, course, the turf.

draw, dead heat, tie, stalemate, standoff.

competitor, contender, contestant, rival, corrival, entry, protagonist, finalist, dark horse; winner, victor, master, first; runner-up, placer, second; loser, also-ran, underdog.

V. **attempt**, try, aim, essay, assay, endeavor, exert oneself, tackle, attack, strive; angle for, aim for, bid for, dispute, pursue, seek, snatch at, solicit, woo.

struggle, battle, grapple, wrestle, tussle, scuffle, skirmish, scrimmage, buffet, cope with, pit oneself against; toil, labor, travail, agonize, strain, work.

compete, contend, contest, vie, strive; race, duel, joust, tilt, tourney; emulate, rival; place in competition against, pit against, match.

Adj., phrases. **competitive**, rival, corrival, emulous, cutthroat.

tied, even, neck-and-neck, drawn, stalemated.

See also ACTIVITY, ATTACK, ENERGY, FIGHTING, PUSH, TEST. *Antonyms*—See INACTIVITY, RELINQUISHMENT, REST, SLEEP, SUBMISSION.

---

attend, *v.* be present, show (*colloq.*), come to (PRESENCE); tend, do for (*colloq.*), minister to (SERVICE); observe, keep one's eye on, watch (ATTENTION); listen, give ear (LISTENING).

attendant, *n.* nurse, handmaid (CARE); medic, R.N., orderly (MEDICAL SCIENCE); participant, onlooker, spectator (PRESENCE); squire, page, equerry (SERVICE); adherent, disciple, proselyte (FOLLOWER).

ATTENTION—*N.* **attention**, ear, thought, heed, regard, mind, concentration, observance, observation; consideration, reflection; circumspection, vigilance, care; application, devotion, solicitude, study, scrutiny.

preoccupation, attentiveness, absorption, engrossment, immersion, enthrallment, fascination, trance.

considerateness, consideration, gallantry, thoughtfulness, *prévenance* (*F.*), tact, delicacy, diplomacy.

[*center of attention*] **focus**, limelight, spotlight, blazing star, cynosure.

exigency, emergency, urgency, pressingness.

V. **attend**, watch, observe, keep tabs on, keep one's eye on, remark, look, see, notice, regard, take notice, mark, pay attention to, make (*or* take) note of, note, heed, mind, listen, give heed to, address oneself to, apply oneself to, concentrate on, advert to; contemplate, look to, see to; take cognizance of, entertain, recognize.

attract notice, fall under one's notice, be under consideration, catch (*or* strike) the eye.

call attention to, point out, indicate, exhibit, display, reveal, demonstrate, show, direct attention to, bring forward; advertise, show off, parade, make an exhibition of; alert, urge, insist.

Adj. **attentive**, mindful, advertent, assiduous, particular, punctilious, solicitous, heedful, observant, regardful; alive to, awake to, alert, on the *qui vive* (*F.*), vigilant, wakeful, wide-awake; taken up with, occupied with, engrossed in, bemused by, enrapt, enthralled, fascinated, immersed, preoccupied, spellbound, wrapped in; intent, interested, tense, absorbed, rapt, undistracted; single-track, fixated, monomaniacal.

[*demanding attention*] **pressing**, urgent, crying, exigent, insistent, striking.

Interjections. attend! attention! mind! look out! see! look! hark! listen! hear! hear ye! oyez! (*used by court criers*); *nota bene* (*L.*), *N.B.*

See also CARE, LOOKING, THOUGHT, VISIBILITY. *Antonyms*—See INATTENTION, NEGLECT.

---

attest, *v.* affirm, authenticate, aver (TRUTH); countersign, witness (SIGNATURE); testify to, argue, show (INDICATION).

attic, *n.* garret, loft, top floor (SPACE).

attire, *n.* dress, covering, raiment (CLOTHING).

attitude, *n.* disposition, habitude, outlook (CHARACTER); air, bearing, carriage (POSTURE).

attorney, *n.* advocate, counsel, counselor (LAWYER).

ATTRACTION—*N.* attraction, attractiveness; pull, drawing power, affinity, magnetism; allure, seduction, glamour, romance, appeal, enticement, beguilement, bewitchment, witchery, witchcraft, captivation, charm, enchantment, fascination, enthrallment, invitation, temptation, solicitation.

loadstone, lodestone, lodestar, polestar, magnet, attrahent; cynosure, blazing star; lure, bait, charm, decoy, wiles, wisp, will-o'-the-wisp, *ignis fatuus* (*L.*).

V. attract, pull, drag, draw, magnetize; bait, decoy, charm, lure, allure, entice, inveigle, tempt, invite, seduce, solicit, fascinate, appeal, beckon, beguile, bewitch, enthrall, enchant, captivate, intrigue, spellbind, troll, wile, witch; glamorize, romanticize; be attracted to, gravitate toward.

Adj. attractive, drawing, alluring, charming, prepossessing, engaging, winning, fascinating, seductive, appealing, beckoning, beguiling, bewitching, captivating, enchanting, enthralling, inviting, luring, magnetic, intriguing; catchy, catching, fetching, glamorous, romantic, rose-colored, idyllic; orphic, piquant, taking, winsome, adorable.

tempting, enticing, sirenic, siren, suggestive, serpentine, appealing, inviting, seductive, meretricious.

See also DESIRE, INTERESTINGNESS, MOTIVATION, PLEASANTNESS, TRACTION. *Antonyms*—See DISGUST, HATRED, OFFENSE, UNPLEASANTNESS, UNSAVORINESS.

---

attribute, *n.* characteristic, quality, property (CHARACTER).

ATTRIBUTION—*N.* attribution, assignment, reference to, accounting for; ascription, arrogation, imputation, derivation; key, secret, cause, reason why.

V. attribute to, ascribe to, impute to, credit with, accredit with, arrogate to, refer to, lay to, assign to, trace to, blame, saddle, hold responsible for; account for, derive from.

Adj., phrases. attributable, imputable, assignable, traceable, ascribable, referable, referrible, accountable, explicable; due to, owing to.

Adv. hence, therefore, consequently, for that reason, whence. why? wherefore? whence? how so?

Conjunctions. since, seeing that, because, for, on account of, owing to, in as much as, whereas.

See also ACCUSATION, AGENT, CAUSATION, EXPLANATION. *Antonyms*—See CHANCE.

---

auburn, *adj.* red-haired, chestnut, Titian (RED).

auburn, *n.* reddish brown, bay, hazel (BROWN).

audacious, *adj.* brave, bold, aweless (COURAGE); forward, assuming, impudent (DISCOURTESY).

audible, *adj.* distinct, clear, plain (LISTENING).

audience, *n.* hearers, listeners; hearing, interview (LISTENING); playgoers, theatergoers (DRAMA).

audit, *v.* check, inspect, overlook (EXAMINATION).

auditor, *n.* listener, monitor, eavesdropper (LISTENING).

auditorium, *n.* assembly room, theater, playhouse (DRAMA, AMUSEMENT).

augment, *v.* enhance, aggrandize, add to (INCREASE).

augury, *n.* omen, foretoken, harbinger (FUTURE).

august, *adj.* resplendent, glorious, exalted (MAGNIFICENCE, NOBILITY); respectable, estimable (RESPECT).

aura, *n.* atmosphere, surroundings; ring, wreath (ENVIRONMENT).

auspicious, *adj.* promising, favorable, advantageous (FRIENDLINESS, HOPE, SUCCESS); timely, opportune, propitious (TIMELINESS).

austere, *adj.* abstemious, abstinent, abstentious (ASCETICISM, UNSELFISHNESS); primitive, Spartan, rustic (SIMPLICITY).

authentic, *adj.* veritable, valid, bona fide (TRUTH); real, factual, genuine (REALITY); believable, credible, creditable (BELIEF).

author, *n.* *littérateur* (*F.*), essayist, free lance (WRITER); planner, organizer, designer (PLAN); begetter, originator, father (ANCESTRY).

authoritative, *adj.* official, magisterial, officiary (OFFICIAL); commanding, dictatorial, magisterial (COMMAND); weighty, controlling, ruling (POWER).

authorities, *n.* officials, brass (*colloq.*), administration (OFFICIAL).

authority, *n.* weight, control, prestige (POWER); specialist, master (ABILITY); connoisseur, expert (JUDGE).

authorize, *v.* entitle, empower, sanction (POWER, RIGHT, PERMISSION).

autobiography, *n.* memoirs, reminiscences, vita (STORY, TREATISE).

autocracy, *n.* monocracy, despotism, tyranny (CONTROL, GOVERNMENT).

autocrat, *n.* despot, dictator, tyrant (RULER).

autocratic, *adj.* despotic, absolute, absolutistic (POWER); arbitrary, capricious (WILL).

autograph, *v.* sign, inscribe (SIGNATURE, WRITING).

automatic, *adj.* laborsaving, mechanical (INSTRUMENT); self-produced, self-generated, autogenetic (PRODUCTION).

automaton, *n.* mechanical man, robot, android (MANKIND).

automobile, *n.* auto (*colloq.*), motorcar, car, horseless carriage (VEHICLE).

autopsy, *n.* necropsy (*med.*), postmortem (BURIAL); dissection, prosection, anatomy (SURGERY).

autumn, *n.* fall, harvest time, Indian summer (SEASONS).

auxiliary, *adj.* subsidiary, supplementary, accessory (ADDITION).

auxiliary, *n.* accessory, subsidiary, crutch (AID).

avail, *v.* benefit, serve, advantage (GOOD, ADVANTAGE); suffice, do, answer the purpose (SUFFICIENCY, USE).

available, *adj.* handy, convenient, ready (EASE, USE, PREPARATION).

avarice, *n.* cupidity, avidity, rapacity (GREED); illiberality, parsimony (STINGINESS).

avenge, *v.* revenge, requite, repay (PUNISHMENT, RETALIATION).

avenue, *n.* road, boulevard, street (WALKING, PASSAGE); adit, access (APPROACH, INGRESS); outlet, exit, vent (EGRESS).

aver, *v.* avow, avouch, attest (AFFIRMATION, TRUTH).

average, *adj.* usual, everyday, garden-variety, general (COMMONNESS).

average, *n.* mean, medium, middle (MID-COURSE).

averse, *adj.* disinclined, uninclined, indisposed (UNWILLINGNESS); inimical, antagonistic, unfriendly (OPPOSITION).

aversion, *n.* indisposition, disinclination (UNWILLINGNESS); antipathy, repugnance, repulsion (HATRED).

avert, *v.* prevent, forestall, preclude (PREVENTION).

aviation, *n.* aeronautics, avigation, airmanship (FLYING).

avid, *adj.* acquisitive, avaricious, grasping (GREED).

avocation, *n.* hobby (AMUSEMENT).

AVOIDANCE—*N.* avoidance, evasion, dodge, parry, elusion, flight, retreat, recoil, recession, departure, escapism, escape, eschewal, circumvention.

abstinence, abstention, temperance, self-restraint, sobriety, asceticism.

shirker, slacker (*colloq.*), shirk, quitter, malingerer; straddler, fence straddler, whiffler.

V. **avoid,** shun, steer (keep, *or* shy) clear of; fight shy of, keep (*or* stay) away from, give a wide berth to, eschew, blink, evade, shirk, malinger.

ward off, stave off, stall off, avert, fend off, circumvent; bypass, side-step, skirt, parry, dodge, escape.

abstain, refrain, keep from, let alone, not do, not attempt.

avoid the issue, stall, fence, quibble, straddle, straddle the fence, tergiversate.

Adj. **avoidable,** escapable, evadable, eludible, preventable, avertible.

elusive, evasive, tergiversatory; shy, shifty, slippery, tricky.

abstinent, abstentious, sober, moderate, ascetic, abstemious.

See also DEPARTURE, FAILURE, MODERATENESS, PREVENTION, REVERSION, SOBRIETY. *Antonyms*—See APPROACH, ARRIVAL, FOLLOWING.

awake, *v.* rouse, arouse, arise (WAKEFULNESS, EXCITEMENT).

award, *n.* reward, prize (PAYMENT); grant, subsidy, bounty (GIVING).

aware, *adj.* appreciative, conscious, cognizant (KNOWLEDGE).

away, *adv.* absent, not present, elsewhere (ABSENCE); far off, far away, afar (DISTANCE).

awe, *v.* dazzle, stupefy, shock (SURPRISE, APPROVAL); overawe, impress (RESPECT); appall, unman (FEAR).

awful, *adj.* abominable, atrocious, dreadful (INFERIORITY).

awhile, *adv.* transiently, temporarily, for the moment (IMPERMANENCE).

awkward, *adj.* bulky, unwieldy; left-handed, unhandy (CLUMSINESS).

awning, *n.* canopy, marquee, shade (PROTECTION, COVERING, DARKNESS).

awry, *adj.* crooked, wry, askew (WINDING, TURNING).

ax, *n.* adz, tomahawk, hatchet (CUTTING).

axiom, *n.* theorem, postulate, truism (RULE); maxim, aphorism, device (STATEMENT).

axis, *n.* hinge, pivot, axle (ROTATION, CAUSATION); stem, stalk, pedicel (PLANT LIFE).

axle, *n.* pivot, axis, gudgeon (ROTATION).

azure, *n.* cerulean, lapis lazuli, sky color (BLUE).

B

babble, *n.* jargon, jabber, gibberish (ABSURDITY).

babble, *v.* chatter, gibber, gossip (TALK); tattle, squeal (*colloq.*), blab (DISCLOSURE); purl, gurgle, murmur (RIVER); crow, guggle (CHILD).

babel, *n.* bedlam, din, hubbub (CONFUSION).

baby, *adj.* dwarf, miniature, petite (SMALLNESS).

baby, *n.* babe, infant, little one (CHILD).

baby carriage, *n.* bassinet, perambulator, coach (VEHICLE).

bachelor, *n.* celibate (UNMARRIED STATE); graduate, diplomate, collegian (LEARNING).

back, *n.* posterior, hind part, reverse (REAR).

back, *v.* uphold, countenance, endorse (SUPPORT); stand by, abide by (LOYALTY); go back, move back, draw back (REVERSION).

back and forth, to and fro, shuttlewise, in and out (OSCILLATION).

backbiting, *n.* traducement, defamation, denigration (DETRACTION).

backbone, *n.* spine, spinal column, vertebral column (BONE); base, basis (PART).

back down, *v.* back out, back off, backtrack (REVERSION).

backfire, *v.* recoil, rebound, boomerang (REACTION).

backflow, *n.* refluence, reflux, ebb (REVERSION).

background, *n.* training, seasoning, practice (EXPERIENCE); education, literacy, cultivation (LEARNING); atmosphere, aura (ENVIRONMENT).

backhand, *adj.* indirect, oblique, roundabout (INDIRECTNESS).

backhanded, *adj.* sarcastic, mordant, sardonic (RIDICULE); insincere, dishonest, disingenuous (PRETENSE).

backlash, *n.* recoil, reaction, repercussion (REVERSION).

backlog, *n.* supply, reserve, stock (QUANTITY).

back out, *v.* backdown, back off, backtrack (REVERSION).

backside, *n.* rump, rear end, rear (REAR).

backslider, *n.* apostate, turncoat, recidivist (APOSTASY, REVERSION, REPETITION).

back up, *v.* advocate, plead for, champion (SUPPORT); go back, move back, draw back (REVERSION).

backward, *adj.* bashful, shy, diffi-

dent (MODESTY); rearward, tailfirst (REAR).

backwoods, *n.* interior, hinterland, hinterlands (INTERIORITY).

bacterium, *n.* microbe, germ, microorganism (SMALLNESS).

bad, *adj.* abominable, atrocious, dreadful (INFERIORITY); wicked, wrong, naughty (WICKEDNESS).

badge, *n.* hall mark, emblem, scepter (INDICATION, REPRESENTATION).

badger, *v.* needle (*colloq.*), twit, hector (TEASING); nag, pester, importune (DEMAND).

bad luck, *n.* ill-fortune, ill-luck, adversity (MISFORTUNE).

bad-mannered, *adj.* ill-mannered, unrefined, impolite (DISCOURTESY).

BAD TEMPER—*N.* bad temper, temper, dander (*colloq.*), short temper, bad humor, ill-humor (nature, *or* temper), distemper, hot temper, hotheadedness.

sour temper, verjuice, acidity, acrimony, bile, spleen, dyspepsia, asperity; disgruntlement, petulance.

tantrum, temper tantrum, conniption *or* conniption fit (*colloq.*); huff, pet, grouch (*colloq.*); sulk, pout, lower *or* lour.

crab, crabstick, crank (*colloq.*), crosspatch, grouch, grumpy, curmudgeon, splenetic, wasp, sorehead (*colloq.*) pill (*slang*), sulk, churl.

hothead, tinderbox, fire-eater (*colloq.*), hotspur, tartar, pepperpot (*colloq.*), devil.

[*bad- or hot-tempered female*] **spitfire,** brimstone, vixen, virago, termagant, Xanthippe, scold, shrew, harridan, dragon, fury.

V. **have a temper,** fire up, flare up, storm, rage, scold, fly off the handle (*slang*), fly into a temper, lose one's temper; sour; snap, snarl, bark.

sulk, lower *or* lour, pout; crab, fuss, grouch (*colloq.*).

irritate, roil, sour, distemper, peeve (*colloq.*), disgruntle.

Adj. **bad-tempered,** tempery, tempersome, short-tempered, short, sharp-tempered, sharp, ill-humored, ill-natured, ill-tempered.

hot-tempered, fiery, hotheaded, peppery, quick-tempered, excitable.

irascible, irritable, choleric; crabbed, crabby, cranky, cross, cross-tempered, cantankerous, iracund; shrewish (*of women*), snappish, snappy, techy, testy, curmudgeonly, snippy (*colloq.*).

sour-tempered, sour, disagreeable, dour, acid, acrid, acrimonious; bilious, spleenful, splenetic, dyspeptic, ugly, vinegary, waspish, nasty, liverish; mean, mean-tempered.

disgruntled, grumpy, pettish, petulant, peevish; morose, glum, sullen, sulky, sore (*colloq.*); huffish, huffy, moody, temperamental, vapory; grouchy (*colloq.*), querulous, surly, gruff, churlish; out of humor, out of sorts.

See also AGITATION, ANGER, ANNOYANCE, EXCITEMENT, SHARPNESS, UNPLEASANTNESS. *Antonyms*—See CALMNESS, INEXCITABILITY, MILDNESS, MODERATENESS, PLEASANTNESS.

baffle, *v.* puzzle, confound, mystify (CONFUSION, MYSTERY); hinder, thwart, balk (HINDRANCE).

bag, *n.* pouch, sack, sac (CONTAINER).

bag, *v.* capture, net, trap (ACQUISITION, TAKING); lop, flap, hang (LOOSENESS).

baggage, *n.* impedimenta, luggage, grips (CONTAINER); hussy, jade, wench (FEMALE).

baggy, *adj.* flabby, flimsy, loppy (LOOSENESS); pendulous, droopy, saggy (HANGING).

bait, *v.* tease, rag (*colloq.*), badger (TEASING, ANNOYANCE); decoy, lure (ATTRACTION).

bake, *v.* stew, simmer, fricassee (COOKERY).

balance, *n.* symmetry, proportion (SHAPE); counterpoise, equilibrium, equipoise (WEIGHT); surplus, excess (REMAINDER); scale, beam (WEIGHT).

balance, *v.* counterbalance, counterpoise, equilibrate (WEIGHT); countervail, offset, equalize (RECOMPENSE); compare, collate, match (COMPARISON).

bald, *adj.* hairless, bald-headed, glabrous (HAIRLESSNESS); chaste, severe, stark (SIMPLICITY); direct, blunt, forthright (STRAIGHTNESS).

balcony, *n.* gallery, mezzanine (SEAT).

balk, *v.* thwart, baffle, frustrate (HINDRANCE).

balky, *adj.* negative, negativistic, contrary (OPPOSITION).

ball, *n.* masquerade ball, prom (DANCE, SOCIALITY); globe, orb, sphere (ROUNDNESS); bullet (ARMS).

ballad, *n.* ditty, love song, serenade (SINGING).

balloon, *n.* airship, dirigible, blimp (FLYING); belly, billow, bulge (SWELLING).

ballot, *n.* suffrage, franchise (VOTE); ticket, slate (LIST).

balm, *n.* salve, ointment (CURE); analgesic, anodyne (PAINKILLER).

balmy, *adj.* soothing, calmative, bland (CALMNESS); temperate, soft, warm (MILDNESS); analgesic, anodyne, mitigative (PAINKILLER); crackbrained, cracked (*colloq.*), crazy (INSANITY).

ban, *v.* curse, anathematize, damn (MALEDICTION); prohibit, forbid (DENIAL).

banal, *adj.* bromidic, conventional, hackneyed (COMMONNESS, OLDNESS).

band, *n.* binder, fillet, bond (FASTENING, FILAMENT); stripe, streak, line (VARIEGATION); zone, belt (ROUNDNESS); orchestra, ensemble (MUSICIAN, MUSICAL INSTRUMENTS).

bandit, *n.* robber, brigand, bravo (THIEF, ILLEGALITY).

baneful, *adj.* mephitic, pestilent (POISON); evil, wicked (HARM).

bang, *v.* crash, make noise, thunder (LOUDNESS); smash, slam, collide (HITTING).

banish, *v.* exile, deport, cast out (DISMISSAL, PUNISHMENT).

bank, *n.* ledge, reef, cay; riverbank (LAND); terrace, embankment (HEIGHT); treasury, safe, vault (MONEY).

bank, *v.* salt away (*colloq.*), put by (STORE); shelve, rake, bevel (SLOPE).

banker, *n.* moneylender, moneymonger (DEBT).

bank on, *v.* depend on, rely on, trust (DEPENDABILITY, CERTAINTY).

bankrupt, *adj.* insolvent, broke (*colloq.*), ruined (FAILURE, POVERTY).

banner, *n.* flag, ensign, standard (INDICATION); headline, streamer, heading (TITLE).

banquet, *n.* meal, repast, feast (FOOD).

banter, *v.* badinage, chaff, guy (*colloq.*), joke, josh (TEASING, WITTINESS).

baptism, *n.* purgation, purge, sanctification (PURIFICATION).

baptize, *v.* name, christen, godfather (NAME); dip, duck (INSERTION).

bar, *n.* obstruction, barrier, obstacle (RESTRAINT, HINDRANCE); prohibition, injunction, ban (DENIAL); rule, stripe, streak (LENGTH); shallow, shoal, flat (SHALLOWNESS); barroom, lounge, taproom (ALCOHOLIC LIQUOR); legal profession, law, law practice (LAWYER); the bench, bar of justice, judgment seat (COURT OF LAW).

bar, v. obstruct, block, blockade (RESTRAINT, HINDRANCE); prohibit, forbid, enjoin (DENIAL); shut out, keep out, debar (EXCLUSION); bolt, fasten, padlock (CLOSURE).

barb, n. thorn, thistle, prickle (SHARPNESS).

BARBARIANISM—N. barbarianism, barbarism, primitive culture, savagery, savagism, barbarousness, etc. (see Adjectives); savage, barbarian; atavism, primitivism, agriology; primitive desires, id (psychoanal.).

Adj. uncivilized, barbarian, barbaric, barbarous, primitive, rude, savage, unchristian, wild; atavistic, atavic.

See also DISCOURTESY, ROUGHNESS, VIOLENCE, VULGARITY. Antonyms— See COURTESY, MILDNESS.

barbarous, adj. uncivilized, barbaric, primitive (BARBARIANISM); savage, brutal, sadistic (CRUELTY, VIOLENCE).

barbecue, n. clambake, picnic, cookout (COOKERY).

barbed, adj. prickly, echinated, pointed; acid, vitriolic (SHARPNESS).

barber, n. tonsorial artist (HAIRLESSNESS).

bard, n. poet, versifier, rhymer (POETRY).

bare, adj. naked, nude, disrobed (UNDRESS); empty, barren, void (ABSENCE); bald, blunt, severe (SIMPLICITY).

bare, v. show, reveal, unveil (DISCLOSURE, DISPLAY); denude, expose, uncover (UNDRESS).

barefaced, adj. immodest, shameless, brazen (IMMODESTY).

barefoot, adj. barefooted, unshod, discalceate (UNDRESS).

barely, adv. scarcely, hardly, only just (SMALLNESS); solely, simply, purely (UNITY).

bargain, n. pact, understanding, contract (COMPACT); low price, budget price (INEXPENSIVENESS); buy, steal (colloq.), investment (PURCHASE).

bargain, v. negotiate, haggle, dicker (EXCHANGE).

bargain for, v. plan on, count on, reckon on (PLAN).

barge, n. boat, ark, dory (SHIP).

bark, n. peel, rind, husk (COVERING).

bark, v. bay, yap, yip (ANIMAL SOUND); growl, grumble, mutter

(TALK); bawl, bellow, cry (SHOUT); cough, hawk, hack (THROAT); abrade, chafe, gall (RUBBING).

barnyard, n. farmyard, stockyard (INCLOSURE).

barometer, n. weatherglass, barograph (AIR); norm, standard, gauge (JUDGMENT).

baronet, n. knight, sir, esquire (SOCIAL CLASS).

barrage, n. broadside, volley, shower (ATTACK, THROW); boom, thunder, drum fire (ROLL).

barrel, n. drum, keg, tub (CONTAINER); roller, cylinder, drum (ROLL).

barren, adj. unfertile, arid, sterile (UNPRODUCTIVENESS); empty, bare, void (ABSENCE); futile, vain, useless (INEFFECTIVENESS).

barricade, v. obstruct, block, blockade (HINDRANCE).

barrier, n. obstruction, bar (RESTRAINT, HINDRANCE); fence, enclosure (INCLOSURE); limit, bound, confines (BOUNDARY).

bartender, n. barkeeper, barmaid (ALCOHOLIC LIQUOR).

barter, v. trade, traffic, swap (EXCHANGE, SALE).

base, adj. paltry, petty, trifling (WORTHLESSNESS); cowardly, chickenhearted, pigeonhearted (FEAR); coarse, indelicate, offensive (LOWNESS); baseborn, ignoble, scurvy (MEANNESS, LOWNESS).

base, n. bottom, foundation, ground (BASE, LOWNESS); backbone, basis (PART).

base, v. found, ground, prop (SUPPORT).

BASE—N. base, foundation, ground, earth, groundwork, basis, bottom, foot, footing, foothold; bedplate, bed piece, groundsel, groundsill, sill; substructure, substruction, underbuilding, understructure, basement; substratum, bed rock, hardpan.

baseboard, washboard, mopboard; dado, wainscot; plinth, subbase.

floor, flooring, pavement, paving; parquet, deck, surface.

root, radicle, radix, fiber, rhizoid, radicel, rootlet, taproot; fundamental, radical; cause, source, origin.

Adj. basal, basic, fundamental; bottom, undermost, nethermost, lowest, under; founded on, based on, grounded on, built on.

See also LOWNESS, SUPPORT. Antonyms—See HEIGHT.

baseless, adj. flimsy, groundless, ungrounded (NONEXISTENCE).

basement, *n.* cellar, subterrane, vault (SPACE).

bashful, *adj.* reticent, reserved, diffident (MODESTY, SILENCE).

basic, *adj.* indispensable, key, cardinal (IMPORTANCE, NECESSITY); basal, fundamental (BASE).

basin, *n.* vessel, bowl, tub (CONTAINER); watershed, valley (LAND); bay, gulf, pool (INLET, LAKE).

basis, *n.* foundation, ground, support (CAUSATION); backbone, base (PART); keynote, keystone (RULE); root, reason, cause (MOTIVATION).

basket, *n.* hamper, pannier, bassinet (CONTAINER).

bask in, *v.* luxuriate in (PLEASURE).

bass, *adj.* deep, low-toned, low-pitched (LOWNESS).

bassinet, *n.* basket, hamper, pannier (CONTAINER); crib, cradle, bed (SLEEP).

bastard, *n.* by-blow, love-child (CHILD); fraud, fake, sham (FALSENESS).

baste, *v.* sew, stitch, tack (FASTENING); blister, lash, revile (MALEDICTION).

bastion, *n.* fortification, breastwork, earthwork (PROTECTION).

bat, *v.* lob, loft, whack (HITTING).

batch, *n.* amount, volume, assortment (ASSEMBLAGE, QUANTITY).

bath, *n.* shower bath, sponge bath, wash (CLEANNESS).

bathe, *v.* wet, imbue, wash (WATER); steep, soak (INSERTION).

bathing suit, *n.* swim suit, trunks, Bikini (SWIMMING).

bathrobe, *n.* dressing gown, peignoir, robe (CLOTHING).

bathroom, *n.* lavatory, powder room, washroom (CLEANNESS).

baton, *n.* wand, scepter, stick (ROD).

battalion, *n.* regiment, squadron, company (FIGHTER).

batter, *v.* buffet, lash, pommel (HITTING).

battle, *n.* clash, conflict, combat (FIGHTING).

battle, *v.* struggle, wrestle, fight, skirmish, combat (ATTEMPT, FIGHTING).

battlefield, *n.* battleground, arena, Armageddon (FIGHTING).

battleship, *n.* warship, naval vessel, dreadnaught (SHIP).

bauble, *n.* gewgaw, tinsel, trumpery (WORTHLESSNESS).

bawl, *v.* cry, blubber, yowl (WEEPING); shout, bark, roar (SHOUT).

bay, *n.* gulf, basin, arm (INLET).

bayonet, *n.* dagger, dirk, poniard (CUTTING).

bazaar, *n.* marketplace, mart, fair (STORE).

be, *v.* subsist, live, breathe (EXISTENCE).

beach, *n.* waterfront, bank, sea front (LAND).

beach, *v.* ground, strand, land (LAND).

beacon, *v.* guide, pilot, steer (GUIDANCE).

bead, *n.* bubble, globule, blob (FOAM).

beak, *n.* bill, neb, snout (NOSE).

beaked, *adj.* hooked, hook, aquiline (NOSE).

beam, *n.* ray, stream, streak (LIGHT); flicker, gleam, spark (SMALLNESS); plank, stud, post (WOOD); rafter, joist, girder (SUPPORT); balance, scale, scale-beam (WEIGHT).

beam, *v.* emit, radiate, shed (GIVING, THROW); aim, direct, point (DIRECTION); smile, grin (LAUGHTER).

bear, *n.* bruin, grizzly bear (ANIMAL).

bear, *v.* endure, tolerate, suffer (SUPPORT, INEXCITABILITY, OCCURRENCE); bring forth, produce, yield (BIRTH, PRODUCTION); bring, fetch, deliver (TRANSFER).

bearable, *adj.* supportable, endurable, tolerable (SUPPORT).

beard, *n.* whiskers, stubble, goatee (HAIR).

beardless, *adj.* cleanshaven, shaven, unbearded (HAIRLESSNESS).

bear down, *v.* press, depress, clamp (PRESSURE).

bearer, *n.* porter, messenger, transporter (TRANSFER).

bearing, *n.* air, carriage, demeanor (POSTURE, BEHAVIOR); relevance, connection, application (PERTINENCE.)

bearings, *n.* whereabouts, direction, location (SITUATION).

bear out, *v.* verify, substantiate, confirm (SUPPORT).

beast, *n.* brute, quadruped (ANIMAL).

beat, *n.* tick, pulse, throb (RHYTHM); accent, ictus (POETRY); patrol, precinct (REGION).

beat, *v.* throb, flutter, thump (RHYTHM); strike, hit, collide (TOUCH); spank, lash, cane (PUNISHMENT, HITTING); flail, thresh, mash (POWDERINESS, HITTING); best, whip (*colloq.*); triumph over (DEFEAT, SUPERIORITY); gain upon, overhaul, outdo (SPEED, OVERRUNNING).

beau, *n.* squire, cavalier, lover (ACCOMPANIMENT, LOVE).

BEAUTY—*N.* **beauty,** pulchritude, beau ideal, good looks, *beaux yeux* (*F.*), charm; elegance, grace, artistry, symmetry, bloom, delicacy, refinement, style, polish, gloss.

beautiful woman, beauty, reigning beauty, belle, goddess, Venus, Aphrodite, Hebe, Helen of Troy, nymph, vision, knockout (*slang*), bathing beauty, dryad.

handsome man, Adonis, Apollo, Greek god.

cosmetic, cosmetics, make-up, paint, war paint, powder, rouge, lipstick, mascara; beautician, cosmetician; cosmetologist, cosmetology.

aesthetics *or* esthetics, aestheticism, callomania, philocaly; aesthete, aesthetician.

V. **beautify,** prettify, grace; embellish, adorn, deck, bedeck, trim, ornament, decorate, set off; put one's face on (*slang*), make up.

Adj. **beautiful,** beauteous, handsome, pretty, lovely, graceful, elegant, exquisite, delicate, dainty, adorable, angelic, attractive, becoming, cunning, cute, charming, ethereal, gorgeous, personable, pulchritudinous, ravishing, sculpturesque, statuesque, sightly, stunning.

comely, fair, pleasing, good-looking, goodly, bonny, well-favored, presentable.

artistic, aesthetic *or* esthetic, picturesque, pictorial, ornamental; well-composed, well-grouped, well-balanced; well-made, well-formed, well-proportioned, shapely, symmetrical, harmonious; pleasing to the eye, cosmetic.

See also ORNAMENT, SHAPE. *Antonyms*—See DEFORMITY.

because, *conj.* since, for, owing to (ATTRIBUTION).

beckon, *v.* nod, signal, motion (GESTURE); ask, command, summon (SUMMONS).

becoming, *adj.* suitable, befitting, fitting (AGREEMENT); attractive, cute, presentable (BEAUTY).

bed, *n.* bunk, berth, cot (SLEEP); channel, race, river bed (LAND).

bedding, *n.* mattress, feather bed, pallet (SLEEP).

bedlam, *n.* noise, din, pandemonium (CONFUSION, LOUDNESS); insane asylum, asylum, mental hospital (INSANITY).

bedraggled, *adj.* dowdy, sloppy, slovenly (UNTIDINESS).

bedridden, *adj.* confined, shut in, bedfast (DISEASE, INACTION).

bedroom, *n.* bedchamber, cubicle, chamber (SLEEP).

bedspread, *n.* spread, coverlet, counterpane (SLEEP).

bee, *n.* honeybee, queen bee, drone (ANIMAL).

bee keeper, *n.* apiarist, apiculturist (DOMESTICATION).

beer, *n.* lager, porter, ale (ALCOHOLIC LIQUOR).

beetle, *n.* weevil, boll weevil (ANIMAL).

befall, *v.* chance, happen, materialize (OCCURRENCE).

befit, *v.* be proper for, beseem, behoove (PROPRIETY).

before, *adv.* forward, ahead, vanward (FRONT).

beforehand, *adj.* precocious, advanced (EARLINESS).

beget, *v.* breed, engender, sire (BIRTH); generate, give rise to, bring about (PRODUCTION); result in, produce, afford (RESULT).

beggar, *n.* pauper, mendicant, indigent (CHARITY, POVERTY); tramp, vagabond, hobo (REST).

BEGGING—*N.* begging, entreaty, adjuration, plea, supplication, suppliance, prayer; impetration, obsecration, obtestation, petition; appeal, advocacy, solicitation, suit; beggary, mendicance, mendicity; importunity, importunacy, recreance.

supplicant, pleader, suppliant, supplicator, advocate, suitor, wooer.

beggar, mendicant, solicitor, sponge, bum (*slang*), cadger, Lazarus, fakir *or* fakeer (*Moham.*).

V. **beg,** beseech, entreat, adjure, implore, plead, supplicate, pray; impetrate, obsecrate, obtest, petition; whine for, appeal for, plead for, advocate, urge, seek, crave, solicit, sue for, woo; conjure (*someone*) to, importune; panhandle (*slang*), sponge on (*colloq.*), cadge (*colloq.*), bum (*colloq.*).

Adj. **begging,** pleading, whining, supplicatory, supplicant, suppliant, beseeching, entreating, imploring, precatory, adjuratory, appellant, petitionary, importunate; recreant; mendicant, beggarly.

See also CHARITY, DEMAND, POVERTY. *Antonyms*—See DENIAL, GIVING, WEALTH.

BEGINNING—*N.* beginning, commencement, start, dawn, opening, outset, incipience, inception; début (*F.*), coming out (*colloq.*), embarkation; outbreak, onset, outstart; alpha, aurora, first, incunabula, prime, primordium, nucleus; initiative, first move.

origin, fountain, font, fount, source, rise; germ, egg, embryo; genesis, birth, conception, creation, generation, nativity, cradle; ancestry, parentage, authorship, derivation, descent, nascency; ancestor, parent, cunabula, fountainhead, golconda, headspring, well, wellhead, wellspring, matrix, mine, principle, resource, root, spring, springhead, stem, stock, store.

original, antetype, prototype, archetype, model, pattern, type, paradigm.

introduction, prelude, prologue, preamble, preface, foreword, exordium; overture, ritornelle, prelusion, prolegomenon, prolusion, protasis, preliminary; inauguration, induction, initiation, installation, presentation.

rudiments, elements, grammar, alphabet, ABC; first principles, first steps.

starting point, basis, point of departure, threshold.

beginner, novice, tyro, abecedarian, alphabetarian; tenderfoot (*colloq.*), greenhorn, recruit, rookie; initiate, apprentice, probationer, neophyte, catechumen.

introducer, prolegomenist, chairman, toastmaster, master of ceremonies.

V. **begin,** commence, brew; open, start; dawn, set in, take its rise, enter upon; set out, embark on, set about, set forth on, set to work, make a start, break ground, undertake; constitute, establish, organize, set in motion, institute, set up, set afoot, lay the foundations, found, launch; open up, open the door to.

recommence, resume, continue, begin at the beginning, begin again, start afresh, begin *de novo* (*L.*), make a fresh start.

originate, come into existence, take birth; arise, breed, derive, germinate, spring, start, stem, upspring; create, give rise to, father, generate, hatch.

introduce, inaugurate, initiate, induct, install, present, innovate, usher, preface, prelude, prologuize.

Adj. **beginning,** first, opening, maiden; inceptive, incipient, initial, inchoate, nascent, primordial, prime, embryonic; rudimentary, abecedarian, elementary, basic; inaugural, innovational, introductory, organizational; parental, ancestral, lineal.

original, aboriginal, first, genuine, primal, primary, prime, primigenial, pristine, primordial.

introductory, prefatory, preliminary, prelusory, preludial, prolegomenary, prolusory, preparatory, precursory.

Adv., phrases. **from the beginning,** *ab initio* (*L.*), *ab origine* (*L.*), *ab ovo* (*L.*); first, firstly, in

the first place, *imprimis* (*L.*), in the bud, in embryo; to begin with.

See also ANCESTRY, BIRTH, CAUSATION, EARLINESS, FRONT, LEARNING, PRECURSOR, PREGNANCY, PREPARATION. *Antonyms*—See CENTER, DEATH, END, REAR.

begrudge, *v.* pinch, stint, grudge (STINGINESS); covet, envy (DESIRE).

behalf, *n.* interest, cause, part (SIDE).

BEHAVIOR—*N.* **behavior,** conduct, address, bearing, carriage, comportment, demeanor, deportment, mien, manner; decorum, morals, decency, propriety, etiquette, ceremony; reflexive behavior, second nature, ritualism, ritual.

misbehavior, misconduct, naughtiness, impropriety, immorality, indecency; malfeasance, misfeasance, wrongdoing, misdeeds.

science of behavior: sociology, psychology, philosophy, sociometry, anthroponomics, behaviorism.

V. **behave,** acquit onself, act, comport oneself, conduct oneself, demean oneself, deport oneself.

misbehave, misconduct oneself, misdemean (*rare*), be naughty.

See also ACTION, MORALITY, PROPRIETY, WICKEDNESS.

behead, *v.* decapitate, decollate, guillotine (KILLING).

behind, *adj.* behindhand, behind time (DELAY).

behind, *adv.* in the rear (*or* background), in the wake, at the heels of (REAR); subsequently, later, afterward (FOLLOWING).

behind, *n.* buttocks, breech, fundament (REAR).

behold, *v.* see, witness, sight (LOOKING, VISION).

behoove, *v.* be proper for, beseem, befit (PROPRIETY).

beige, *n.* tan, biscuit, ecru (BROWN).

being, *n.* living being, creature, entity; subsistence, vitality, existence (LIFE, EXISTENCE).

belated, *adj.* late, overdue, delayed (DELAY).

belch, *v.* burp (*colloq.*), eruct, eructate (GAS); spew, vomit, disgorge (GIVING); give off, emit, beam (THROW).

belfry, *n.* tower, steeple, campanile (BUILDING, BELL, HEIGHT).

BELIEF—*N.* **belief,** credence, faith, credit, trust, confidence, reliance, acceptance, assumption, orthodoxy.

[a belief] conviction, creed, credo, persuasion; supposition, suspicion, presupposition, notion, impression, opinion, view, conclusion, judgment; theory, hypothesis, postulate, assumption, gospel.

doctrine, teaching, tenet, dogma, propaganda; articles, canons, article (declaration, or profession) of faith, credenda (pl.), ideology, tradition.

misbelief, delusion, illusion, misconception, misimpression; superstition, old wives' tale, shibboleth; heresy, heterodoxy, unorthodoxy.

V. believe, credit, give faith (credit, or credence) to, trust, assume, swallow (colloq.), fall for, accept, take it, take for granted, postulate, posit, presume, presuppose, suppose, premise; suspect, think, hold, opine, account, consider, deem, reckon; have (hold, entertain, adopt, embrace, foster, or cherish) a belief.

believe in, confide in, trust, accredit, have faith in, put one's trust in, place reliance on, rely upon, count on, depend on, swear by, bank on.

Adj. believable, credible, creditable, plausible, authentic; dependable, reliable, trustworthy, trusty, tried; probable, likely, possible; credential, fiduciary; presumptive, a priori (L.).

believed, trusted, accredited, unsuspected, undoubted; accepted, putative, reputed.

orthodox, canonical, authoritative, standard, received, approved, doctrinal.

believing, credulous, gullible, naïve, trusting, unsuspecting, unsuspicious.

See also ACCEPTANCE, CERTAINTY, HOPE, IDEA, JUDGMENT, OPINION, RELIGIOUSNESS, SUPPOSITION. Antonyms —See UNBELIEVINGNESS, UNCERTAINTY.

---

believer, n. religionist, orthodox (RELIGIOUSNESS).

belittle, v. underestimate, run down, depreciate (DETRACTION).

BELL—N. bell, gong, tocsin, vesper, curfew, chime, chimes, carillon, cymbals, peal, Big Ben; clapper, tongue, cannon; bell tower, belfry, campanile; campanology.

ring, ringing, ding, dingdong, ting, ting-a-ling, tinkle, peal, treble, jingle, stroke, tintinnabulation, chime, clang, clangor, clank, carillon, knell, toll.

V. ring, strike, chime, peal, tinkle, ting, tintinnabulate, ding, jingle, clang, clank, clangor, toll, knell.

Adj. ringing, jingly, tinkly; tintinnabulous, bell-like, clear, clangorous.

See also LOUDNESS, RESONANCE, SOUND. Antonyms—See SILENCE.

---

bellboy, n. errand boy, bellhop (slang), page (MESSENGER, SERVICE).

belle, n. beauty, goddess, Venus (BEAUTY).

bellicose, adj. warlike, belligerent, quarrelsome (FIGHTING, DISAGREEMENT, HOSTILITY).

belligerent, adj. military, aggressive, bellicose (FIGHTING, DISAGREEMENT, HOSTILITY).

bellow, v. roar, blare, shout, cry (SHOUT, LOUDNESS).

bell-shaped, adj. campanulate, campaniform (CURVE).

BELLY—N. belly, abdomen, pelvis, solar plexus, paunch, corporation, pot-belly; stomach, venter, maw, bread basket (slang), crop, craw, gizzard; esophagus, gullet.

belly button, navel, omphalos, umbilicus; umbilical cord, silver cord, placenta.

intestines, bowels, entrails, gut, guts, innards, inwards, viscera; small intestine, pylorus, duodenum, jejunum, ileum; large intestine, caecum, colon, sigmoid flexure, appendix, vermiform appendix, rectum, anus; alimentary canal, enteron.

sac, bursa, follicle, saccule; bladder, vesicle, vesica, cyst; pouch, marsupium.

Adj. abdominal, pelvic, ventral, alvine, coeliac; stomachic, gastric, cardiac, esophageal; umbilical, omphalic.

intestinal, visceral, splanchnic, enteric, alvine, duodenal, ileac, caecal, colonic, colic, appendicial, pyloric, sigmoidal, rectal, anal.

See also INTERIORITY, SWELLING. Antonyms—See EXTERIORITY.

---

bellyache (colloq.), n. stomach-ache, colic, cramps (PAIN).

belly button, n. navel, omphalos, umbilicus (BELLY).

belong, v. appertain, pertain, inhere in (OWNERSHIP).

belonging, n. possession, appurtenance, asset (OWNERSHIP).

beloved, adj. loved, adored, cherished (LOVE).

below, adv. under, beneath, underneath (LOWNESS).

belt, *n.* sash, waistband, strap (TROUSERS); cingulum, ring, girdle (VARIEGATION); boundary, cincture, circle (ENVIRONMENT); zone, zonule, band (ROUNDNESS).

belt, *v.* whip, switch, strap (HITTING).

bench, *n.* form, settle, settle bed (SEAT); the bar, bar of justice, judgment seat (COURT OF LAW); the court, his honor (JUDGE).

BEND—*N.* bend, flexure, lean, tilt, twist, crook, curve, curvature, sinus, bight; bow, inclination, crouch, stoop, salaam, nod, nutation; declination, sag; reclination, retroflexion, retroversion; kneel, genuflection.

V. bend, flex, lean, tilt, twist, verge, crook, curve; bow, incline, crouch, nod, stoop, salaam; decline, sag, yield; recline, retroflex, bend back; bend the knee, kneel, genuflect.

Adj. flexible, pliable, pliant, waxen, withy, tough; limber, lissome, lithe, lithesome, supple, svelte.

See also CURVATURE, SLOPE, SOFTNESS, TURNING, WINDING. *Antonyms* —See STRAIGHTNESS, VERTICALITY.

beneath, *adv.* under, underneath, below (LOWNESS).

benefactor, *n.* humanitarian, philanthropist, altruist (KINDNESS).

beneficial, *adj.* profitable, advantageous, favorable (USE, GOOD, ADVANTAGE, AID).

beneficiary, *n.* heir, recipient, inheritor (INHERITANCE, RECEIVING).

benefit, *n.* avail, gain, profit, advantage (VALUE, GOOD).

benefit, *v.* advantage, avail, serve (GOOD, AID).

benevolent, *adj.* kind, beneficent, benignant (KINDNESS); charitable, philanthropic (CHARITY).

benign, *adj.* kind, benignant, benevolent (KINDNESS).

bent, *adj.* intent, bound, determined (PURPOSE, WILL); slouchy, stooped, droopy (POSTURE).

bent, *n.* aptitude, knack, talent (ABILITY); inclination, mind, impulse (TENDENCY); aim, set, tack (DIRECTION).

bequeath, *v.* leave, devise, bequest (GIVING, WILL).

bereft of, *adj.* bereaved of, shorn of, without (LOSS, ABSENCE).

berserk, *adj.* frenzied, frenetic, mad (VIOLENCE).

berth, *n.* bed, bunk, cot (SLEEP); appointment, billet, capacity (SITUATION).

beseech, *v.* beg, entreat, implore (BEGGING).

beside, *adv.* abreast, alongside, neck and neck (SIDE, NEARNESS).

besides, *adv.* furthermore, in addition, moreover (ADDITION).

besiege, *v.* siege, beset, beleaguer (ATTACK); throng, congregate, pack (MULTITUDE).

best, *adj.* capital, choice, prime (SUPERIORITY, PERFECTION).

best, *n.* elite, the select, the cream (SUPERIORITY).

best, *v.* get the better of, gain an advantage over, triumph over (SUPERIORITY, DEFEAT).

bestow, *v.* grant, accord, confer (GIVING).

bet, *n.* gamble, wager (CHANCE).

bête noire (*F.*), *n.* anathema, abhorrence, abomination, hate (HATRED).

betoken, *v.* symbolize, symbol, stand for, mean, denote (REPRESENTATION).

betray, *v.* play false, go back on (DISLOYALTY); report, expose, unmask (INFORMATION).

betrayer, *n.* misleader, decoy, Judas (MISTEACHING).

BETROTHAL—*N.* betrothal, betrothment, engagement, troth, affiance, marriage contract, sponsalia (*Rom. Cath. rel.*); proposal, banns, espousals.

betrothed, fiancé, fiancée, intended.

matchmaker, marriage broker, matrimonial agent.

V. betroth, engage, affiance, troth; propose, ask for the hand of, pop the question (*colloq.*); become engaged, plight one's troth.

Adj. betrothed, engaged, affianced, promised, committed.

marriageable, eligible, nubile.

See also MARRIAGE, PROMISE. *Antonyms*—See DIVORCE.

better, *adj.* improved, preferable, superior (IMPROVEMENT, SUPERIORITY).

better, *v.* mend, amend, ameliorate (IMPROVEMENT); exceed, surpass, top (EXCESS, SUPERIORITY).

between, *prep.* at intervals, in the midst, among (INTERJACENCE).

beverage, *n.* refreshment, refection, potables (DRINK).

bewail, *v.* bemoan, moan, wail (SADNESS); be sorry for, repent, rue (REGRET).

beware, *v.* take care, be careful, take heed (CARE).

bewilder, *v.* perplex, mystify, baffle (CONFUSION, MYSTERY); rattle (*colloq.*), daze, nonplus (UNCERTAINTY).

bewitch, *v.* charm, put under a

magic spell, becharm (MAGIC); beguile, enthrall (ATTRACTION).

beyond, *adv.* more, over, in addition to (SUPERIORITY); past, after (PAST).

bias, *n.* disposition, proclivity, inclination (TENDENCY); slant, preconception, prepossession (PREJUDICE); diagonal, incline (SLOPE).

Bible, *n.* The Scriptures, Holy Scripture, Holy Writ (SACRED WRITINGS).

bicker, *v.* quarrel, wrangle, argue (DISAGREEMENT).

bicycle, *n.* wheel (*colloq.*), cycle (VEHICLE).

bid, *n.* proffer, tender (OFFER); essay, effort (ATTEMPT).

bid, *v.* proffer, present, tender (OFFER); order, instruct, direct (COMMAND).

bier, *n.* litter, hearse, catafalque (BURIAL).

big, *adj.* sizable, large, great, massive (SIZE); generous, bighearted, free (UNSELFISHNESS).

bighearted, *adj.* generous, free, openhanded (UNSELFISHNESS); good-hearted, good-natured (KINDNESS).

bigoted, *adj.* intolerant, unfair, biased (PREJUDICE).

bigwig (*colloq.*), *n.* personage, high-muck-a-muck (*slang*), grandee (IMPORTANCE).

bilk, *v.* cheat, bamboozle, defraud (DECEPTION).

bill, *n.* statement, account, invoice (ACCOUNTS); note, dollar, paper money (MONEY); measure, act (LAW); beak, neb (NOSE); advertisement, placard, handbill (PUBLICATION, INFORMATION).

billfold, *n.* purse, *porte-monnaie* (*F.*), wallet (CONTAINER).

billow, *v.* surge, swell, undulate (RIVER, ROLL, ASCENT); balloon, belly, bulge (SWELLING); roll, rock (ROTATION).

billy, *n.* truncheon, night stick, club (HITTING).

bin, *n.* box, carton, case (CONTAINER).

bind, *v.* tie, attach, fasten (FASTENING); enslave, indenture, yoke (SLAVERY).

binding, *adj.* bounden, incumbent on, obligatory (NECESSITY).

binoculars, *n.* telescope, field glass, spyglass (VISION).

biography, *n.* memoir, vita, profile (TREATISE, STORY).

BIRD—*N.* bird, cageling, songbird, songster, warbler, dickybird (*colloq.*); feathered tribes; bird of prey, eagle, vulture, hawk, falcon, owl.

poultry, fowl, chicken, turkey.

rooster, cock, chanticleer, capon; cob, drake, gander.

hen, biddy, fowl; duck, goose, pen.

birdling, fledgling, nestling; chick, pullet, cockerel; duckling, gosling, squab; brood, clutch, aerie.

birdhouse, aviary, volery, rookery, roost, chicken house, hen house, cote, nest, dovecote, columbary.

Adj. **avian,** avicular, ornithic, ornithological.

See also ANIMAL, FLYING, ZOOLOGY.

BIRTH—*N.* birth, creation, nascency, natality, nativity; abortion, miscarriage, stillbirth; birth rate.

rebirth, palingenesis, recreation, regeneration, renaissance, renascence, revival.

childbirth, accouchement, childbearing, childbed, confinement, delivery, labor, lying-in, parturition, travail; breech delivery, Caesarean operation, Caesarean section; puerperium, parturiency, parity.

V. **give birth,** bear, breed, bring forth, deliver, produce; teem, cub (*derogatory*), spawn (*derogatory*), twin; labor, travail.

[*of animals*] calve, cast, cub, drop, hatch, brood, incubate, slink, sling, throw, whelp, yean, pup, lamb, kid, foal, fawn, farrow, freshen, spawn, fission.

reproduce, breed, multiply, procreate, propagate, pullulate.

beget, breed, engender, father, generate, procreate, produce, sire.

be born, see the light, come into the world; drop, hatch, incubate, pullulate; be reborn, regenerate, revive.

Adj. **born,** née, newborn, just born, yearling (*of animals*), congenital; premature, abortive, stillborn; born alive, viable.

natal, congenital, connate, native, neonatal; prenatal, postnatal.

inborn, connate, indigenous, ingenerate, innate, native, natural, instinctive.

reproductive, generative, genital, procreative, propagative.

giving birth, confined, parturient; oviparous, ovoviviparous, viviparous.

[*pert. to childbirth*] maternity, puerperal, prenatal, postnatal.

See also BEGINNING, CHILD, FERTILITY, LIFE, PREGNANCY, PRODUCTION. *Antonyms*—See DEATH, KILLING.

---

birth control, *n.* contraception, planned parenthood (PREGNANCY).

birthmark, *n.* naevus (*med.*), mole (BLEMISH).

birthright, *n.* heritage, heritance, legacy (INHERITANCE).

biscuit, *n.* roll, cracker, muffin (BREAD, FOOD).

BISECTION—*N.* bisection, dimidiation; bifidity, bipartition; bifurcation, furcation, dichotomy.

half, moiety, hemisphere, fifty per cent.

V. **bisect,** dimidiate, halve, divide, split, cut in two, cleave, dichotomize.

fork, bifurcate, furcate, branch off (*or* out), ramify, divaricate.

Adj. **bisected,** halved, cloven, cleft, bipartible, dimidiate; bipartite, bifid, bilobed, bifurcate, two-pronged, bicuspid, furcate, semi-, demi-, hemi-.

See also CUTTING, PART, TWO.

bishop, *n.* prelate, suffragan, metropolitan (CLERGY).

bit, *n.* crumb, dab, dash (SMALLNESS); piece, lump, cut (PART); morsel, drop, mouthful (TASTE); awl, gimlet, wimble (OPENING).

bite, *n.* mouthful, morsel, snack (FOOD, TASTE).

bite, *v.* browse, graze, crop (FOOD); sting, prickle, smart (CUTTING).

biting, *adj.* cutting, sarcastic, caustic (SHARPNESS); bitter, raw, bleak (COLD).

bitter, *adj.* acrid, absinthal, absinthian (SOURNESS); embittered, sardonic, acrimonious (ANGER).

bizarre, *adj.* strange, alien, fantastic (UNUSUALNESS).

blab, *v.* babble, peach (*slang*), tattle (DISCLOSURE).

black, *adj.* ebony, jet, sable (BLACKNESS); ugly, dire (THREAT).

blacken, *v.* denigrate, nigrify, ebonize (BLACKNESS); defame, besmirch, malign (DETRACTION).

black-haired, *adj.* dark, dark-haired, brunet (HAIR).

blackmail, *n.* bribe, hush money (BRIBERY).

BLACKNESS—*N.* blackness, nigrescence, nigritude, denigration; darkness, lividity, fuliginosity, obscurity.

black, ebony, jet, raven, sable.

V. **black,** blacken, denigrate, nigrify; blot, blotch, smut, smudge, smirch, smutch, sully, begrime, soot, besoot, besmut, besmutch, besmudge; ink, ebonize.

darken, becloud, cloud, obscure.

Adj. **black,** blackish, sable, somber, livid, inky, ink-black, inky-black, atramentous; ebony, nigrescent, coal-black, coaly, jet, jet-black, raven, raven-black, pitch-black, sooty, Cimmerian; melanoid, obsidian, sloe, sloe-black, sloe-colored.

dark, swart, swarthy, dusky, dingy, murky, darkish, darksome, nigricant, nigritudinous.

See also UNCLEARNESS. *Antonyms* —See CLARITY, VISIBILITY, WHITENESS.

blackout, *n.* coma, faint, syncope (INSENSIBILITY); brownout (DARKNESS).

black sheep, *n.* cur, bum (*colloq.*), ne'er-do-well (WORTHLESSNESS).

blacksmith, *n.* ironworker, ironsmith, steelworker (METAL); smith, farrier (*Brit.*), horseshoer (SERVICE).

bladder, *n.* sac, vesicle, cyst (BELLY).

blame, *n.* accountability, responsibility, burden (LIABILITY).

blame, *v.* accuse, censure, hold responsible for (ACCUSATION); ascribe, attribute, lay to (ATTRIBUTION).

blameless, *adj.* guiltless, clear (INNOCENCE).

bland, *adj.* soothing, balmy, calmative (CALMNESS); suave, unctuous, oily (SUAVITY).

blandish, *v.* wheedle, inveigle, seduce (PERSUASION).

blank, *adj.* empty, void, bare (ABSENCE); inexpressive, stupid, vacant (DULLNESS); confounded, dazed (SURPRISE); absolute, utter (COMPLETENESS); hidden, unmarked (BLINDNESS); closed, impassable (CLOSURE).

blank, *n.* nothingness, void (NONEXISTENCE); gap, interstice, hiatus (ABSENCE).

blanket, *n.* cover, quilt, comforter (SLEEP).

blare, *v.* bellow, roar, clangor (LOUDNESS, HARSH SOUND); blast, sound (BLOWING).

blasphemous, *adj.* profane, sacrilegious, impious (DISRESPECT, MALEDICTION, IRRELIGION).

blast, *n.* outburst, eruption, explosion (VIOLENCE); gust, blow, squall (WIND).

blast, *v.* dynamite, bomb, torpedo (BLOWING); lash out at, rail at (MALEDICTION).

blaze, *n.* fire, conflagration, flame (FIRE).

blaze, *v.* burn, flicker, glow (FIRE); flare, glare, shimmer (LIGHT); burst out, jet (EGRESS).

bleach, *v.* whiten, blanch, blench (WHITENESS).

bleak, *adj.* dark, dismal, cheerless (GLOOM, DEJECTION); wind-swept, exposed, raw (WIND).

bleat, *v.* cry, blat, low (ANIMAL SOUND).

bleed, *v.* leech, cup (BLOOD); despoil, strip (TAKING); overcharge, fleece (EXPENDITURE).

BLEMISH—*N.* blemish, disfigurement, defacement, deformity, taint, flaw, injury; imperfection, defect, eyesore, stain, blot, spot, speck, speckle, blur, freckle, patch, blotch, macula, macule, smudge, birthmark, naevus (*med.*), scar, seam, cicatrix, mole.

V. blemish, mar, disfigure, injure, impair, sully, spoil, damage, deform, deface, mutilate, maim, scar, distort, garble, mangle, pervert, wrench, twist, blur, tarnish, taint.

Adj. blemished, etc. (see *Verbs*); defective, imperfect, faulty; discolored, specked, speckled, freckled, pitted, pock-marked, bruised.

See also DEFORMITY, DESTRUCTION, DETERIORATION, IMPERFECTION, SKIN, VARIEGATION. *Antonyms*—See IMPROVEMENT, ORNAMENT, PERFECTION.

blend, *n.* concoction, brew, combination (MIXTURE, PREPARATION).

blend, *v.* merge, fuse, mingle, (COMBINATION, MIXTURE, UNITY).

bless, *v.* hallow, consecrate, sanctify (SACREDNESS).

blessing, *n.* benediction, benison, boon (KINDNESS).

blight, *n.* bane, pest, plague (DESTRUCTION).

blimp, *n.* airship, dirigible, zeppelin (FLYING).

blind, *n.* smoke screen, red herring, disguise; hiding place, hideout (CONCEALMENT).

blind, *v.* darken, seel, purblind (BLINDNESS); dazzle, daze, blur (DIM-SIGHTEDNESS, LIGHT); screen, veil, cloud (INVISIBILITY).

BLINDNESS—*N.* blindness, anopsia (*med.*), amaurosis (*med.*), darkness, typhlosis (*med.*), cataracts; typhlology.

V. be blind, not see; lose one's sight, grope in the dark.

blind, darken, seel, purblind; obscure, eclipse, hide; put one's eyes out, gouge, blindfold; dazzle.

Adj. blind, eyeless, sightless, unsighted, visionless, unseeing, amaurotic (*med.*), typhlotic (*med.*), dark; stone-blind, blindfolded; sand-blind, weak-sighted, blind as a bat.

blind (*fig.*), dark, imperceptive, impercipient, myopic, nearsighted, purblind, shortsighted, undiscern-

ing, unseeing, unperceiving, dim-sighted.

blank, closed at one end, impassable; caecal; hidden, unmarked, concealed.

See also DIM-SIGHTEDNESS, UNCLEARNESS. *Antonyms*—See CLARITY, UNDERSTANDING, VISION.

blink, *v.* wink, bat, nictitate (CLOSURE).

blink at, *v.* wink at, by-pass, ignore (INATTENTION).

blissful, *adj.* ecstatic, enraptured, beatific (HAPPINESS).

blister, *n.* bleb, bulla, vesication (SKIN).

blithe, *adj.* cheerful, gay, joyful (HAPPINESS).

blizzard, *n.* snowstorm, snowfall, precipitation (COLD).

bloat, *v.* balloon, billow, bulge (SWELLING).

block, *n.* snag, blockade, clog (RESTRAINT); mass, lump, cake (THICKNESS).

block, *v.* obstruct, barricade, blockade (HINDRANCE, RESTRAINT).

blockade, *n.* obstruction, embolus (*med.*), bar (CLOSURE); snag, block, clog (RESTRAINT); beleaguerment (SECLUSION).

blockhead, *n.* boob, nincompoop, bonehead (FOLLY, STUPIDITY).

blond, *adj.* flaxen, golden-haired, platinum (YELLOW, HAIR); blondine, light (COLORLESSNESS).

BLOOD—*N.* blood, gore, cruor, clot, plasma.

bleeding, bloodletting, cupping, phlebotomy, venesection, transfusion; bloodsucking, vampirism.

bloodletter, leech, cupper, phlebotomist; bloodsucker, vampire.

heart, auricle, ventricle; pulse, sphygmus; circulation, circulatory system, blood vessels; vein, artery.

V. bleed, let blood, draw blood, leech, cup, phlebotomize; shed blood; transfuse.

Adj. bloody, bleeding, bloodied, gory, ensanguined, imbrued, sanguinary, sanguine, crimson, hemal, hemic; Rh positive, Rh negative; venous, arterial; veiny, varicose, cirsoid, phleboid.

See also KILLING, RELATIVE.

bloodless, *adj.* peaceable, irenic, halcyon (PEACE); pale, cadaverous, sallow (COLORLESSNESS); unemotional, passionless, cold (INSENSITIVITY).

bloodshed, *n.* warfare, war, hostilities (FIGHTING).

bloodsucker, *n.* harpy, vampire, plunderer (PLUNDER).

bloodthirsty, *adj.* sanguinary, gory (KILLING).

bloody, *adj.* hemic, sanguinary, gory (BLOOD, KILLING).

bloom, *n.* prime, heyday, pink (STRENGTH, HEALTH); juvenility, dew (YOUTH); floret, flower, blossom (PLANT LIFE).

bloom, *v.* flourish, thrive (HEALTH); batten, burgeon, prosper (STRENGTH, SUCCESS); flower, blossom (PLANT LIFE).

bloomers, *n.* trouserettes, drawers, shorts (UNDERWEAR).

blossom, *n.* flower, bloom, bud (PLANT LIFE).

blossom, *v.* succeed, bloom, flourish (SUCCESS).

blot, *n.* stain, blemish, blotch (UNCLEANNESS).

blot, *v.* blotch, smut, smudge (BLACKNESS).

blotch, *n.* splotch, stigma, spot (VARIEGATION); breakout, eruption, acne (SKIN).

blotch, *v.* smut, smudge, smirch (BLACKNESS).

blouse, *n.* bodice, middy, shirt (COAT).

blow, *n.* blare, puff, whiff (BLOWING); gust, blast, squall (WIND); impact, shock, stroke (HITTING); casualty, misadventure, mishap (MISFORTUNE); chagrin, frustration, letdown (DISAPPOINTMENT).

blow, *v.* blast, sound, toot (BLOWING); boast, brag, crow (BOASTING).

BLOWING—*N.* blowing, huffing, puffing; blow, blare, blast, honk, puff, whiff, whistle; inflation, insufflation.

ventilator, window, louver, transom, airpipe, funnel.

fan, palm leaf, electric fan, fanner, attic fan, blower, bellows, insufflator; windmill.

bursting, burst, blowout, blowup, detonation, explosion, blast, rupture, shatterment, split, eruption, fulmination; implosion, irruption.

explosive, dynamite, T.N.T., nitroglycerin; bomb, petard (*hist.*), detonator.

V. blow, wind, blast, sound, blare, toot, whistle, honk, tootle; blow out, whiff, puff out; huff, puff, whiffle; fan, ventilate, cool, air-cool, aerate, insufflate.

[*of the wind*] blow, bluster, puff, whiffle, whistle, howl, wail, moan, roar, scream, sing; storm, squall.

inflate, pump, pump up, expand, distend, swell, blow up.

burst, explode, detonate, blow up, pop, rupture, shatter, erupt, fulminate, rend, split, split asunder, rift, rive, blow out; implode,

irrupt; blast, dynamite, bomb, torpedo.

Adj. **blowing** (*of the wind*), blowy, blustering, blusterous, blustery, breezy, gusty, spanking.

explosive, detonative, fulminant, eruptive, irruptive.

See also BREAKAGE, BREATH, DESTRUCTION, VIOLENCE, WIND.

blow out, *v.* extinguish, put out, snuff out (DARKNESS).

blubber, *v.* cry, sob, bawl (WEEPING).

bludgeon, *n.* club, night stick, truncheon (HITTING).

blue, *adj.* cyanic (BLUE); low, depressed (DEJECTION).

BLUE—*N.* blue, light blue, dusty blue, powder blue.

greenish blues: aquamarine, baby blue, beryl, beryl blue, cobalt blue, eggshell blue, glaucous blue, Italian blue, jouvence blue, marine, marine blue, Nile blue, peacock blue, robin's-egg blue, sea blue, turquoise, turquoise blue.

reddish blues: cadet blue, damson, French blue, hyacinth blue, indigo, indigo blue, madder blue, midnight blue, periwinkle, periwinkle blue, mulberry, wisteria blue.

sky blues: azure, azure blue, azury, cerulean, lapis lazuli, sky color.

dark or deep blues: French blue, marine, marine blue, navy, navy blue, royal blue, sapphire, ultramarine.

Adj. **blue,** bluish, slate-blue, steel-blue, cyanic; peacock blue, pavonian, pavonine; greenish-blue, etc. (see *Adjectives*).

blueprint, *n.* diagram, plan, outline (MAP, PLAN).

blues, *n.* the dismals, the mopes (GLOOM, DEJECTION).

bluff, *adj.* brusque, unceremonious, curt (BLUNTNESS); lofty, steep, high (ASCENT).

bluff, *n.* façade, front, false colors (DECEPTION); pretext, stall (*slang*), feint (PRETENSE); faker, bluffer (PRETENSE); precipice, rocky height, cliff (HEIGHT).

bluffer, *n.* deceiver, impostor, fraud (DECEPTION, PRETENSE).

blunder, *v.* nod, slip up, err (MISTAKE); bungle, botch, fumble (CLUMSINESS).

blunt, *adj.* unsharpened; brusque, abrupt, curt (BLUNTNESS); direct, bald, categorical (STRAIGHTNESS); dim-witted, dim, weakminded (STUPIDITY).

BLUNTNESS—*N.* **bluntness**, obtundity, dullness, etc. (see *Adjectives*).

V. **blunt**, dull, take off the edge, obtund, deaden.

Adj. **blunt**, dull, obtuse, deadened, pointless, unpointed, edgeless, unsharpened.

bluff, brusque, unceremonious, abrupt, curt, short, gruff, frank, candid, ungracious, unpolished, rude, rough, uncivil, impolite; downright, outspoken, direct, matter-of-fact, pointed, to the point. See also DISCOURTESY, DULLNESS, SINCERITY. *Antonyms*—See COURTESY, SHARPNESS.

blur, *v.* dazzle, blind, blear (DIMSIGHTEDNESS, DARKNESS).

blush, *v.* color, crimson, flush (MODESTY, RED).

bluster, *n.* braggadocio, braggartism, fanfaronade (BOASTING); fury, rabidity, rage (VIOLENCE).

bluster, *v.* be noisy, roister, ruffle (LOUDNESS).

blustery, *adj.* windy, breezy, blowy (WIND); rampageous, rampant, stormy (VIOLENCE).

board, *n.* slat, stave, slab (WOOD); table, console (SUPPORT); bed and board (SLEEP).

board, *v.* lodge, room, accommodate (HABITATION, INHABITANT).

boarder, *n.* lodger, roomer, tenant (INHABITANT).

boardinghouse, *n.* lodginghouse, *pension* (F.), hotel (HABITATION).

BOASTING—*N.* **boasting**, braggadocio, braggartism, fanfaronade, jactation, rodomontade, vauntage, bluster, gasconade, swagger, swank, swashbucklery; bravado, pretensions, bombast, tall talk, exaggeration, magniloquence, grandiloquence, heroics.

boast, bluff, brag, bounce, vaunt, blow.

boastfulness, egotism, vainglory.

boaster, blow, blowhard, blowoff, bouncer (*colloq.*); brag, braggadocio, braggart, bragger, egotist, fanfaron, gasbag (*slang*), gascon, roisterer, vaporer, vaunter, windbag (*slang*); blatherskite, blusterer, strutter, swaggerer, swashbuckler, swasher; bluffer, fourflusher (*both colloq.*).

V. **boast**, blow, brag, crow, gas (*slang*), rodomontade, roister, spread oneself (*colloq.*), vapor, vaunt; bluster, gasconade, strut, swagger, swank, swash, swashbuckle; puff, show off, flourish, bluff; blow one's own trumpet, talk big (*colloq.*), exaggerate,

draw the long bow; give oneself airs, put on the dog (*slang*).

Adj. **boastful**, boasting, braggart, egotistical; roistering, thrasonical, vainglorious, vaporous, vaunting, windy; blusterous, strutting, swaggering, swashbuckling; pretentious, highfalutin, bombastic, pompous, grandiloquent, magniloquent, tall (*colloq.*), extravagant, toplofty, high-flown, swollen, inflated, turgid, ostentatious, tumid, plethoric, heroic, grandiose, self-praising.

See also EXAGGERATION, PATRIOTISM, PRIDE. *Antonyms*—See MODESTY.

boat, *n.* craft, vessel, skiff (SHIP).

boat, *v.* sail, cruise, voyage (SAILOR).

boat-shaped, *adj.* navicular, naviculoid, naviform (CURVE).

bob, *n.* sled, sleigh, bobsled (VEHICLE); plumb, plumb line (DEPTH).

bob, *v.* leap, bounce, jounce (JUMP); jog, seesaw, pump (ASCENT); shorten, truncate, trim, lop (CUTTING, SHORTNESS).

bodiless, *adj.* immaterial, disembodied, discarnate (SPIRITUALITY).

body, *n.* soul, mortal, person (MANKIND); throng, multitude, corps (ASSEMBLAGE); text, material (READING); density, impermeability (THICKNESS); core, crux, essence (PART).

BODY—*N.* **body**, person, system, tabernacle, protoplasm; torso, trunk; main body, main part, corpus; legal body, legal entity, corporation.

anatomy, figure, physique, constitution.

embodiment, incarnation, personification, avatar, soul.

science of the body: anatomy, physiology, somatology, anthropometry, anthropology.

V. **embody**, incarnate, personify; incorporate, include.

Adj. **bodily**, physical, corporeal, corporal, personal, somatic, systemic, psychosomatic; carnal, fleshly, sensual; embodied, bodied, incarnate, personified, material.

See also APPENDAGE, MATERIALITY, PEOPLE, REALITY, SHAPE, TEXTURE. *Antonyms*—See GHOST, SPIRITUALITY, UNREALITY.

bog, *n.* swamp, morass, quagmire (MARSH).

bogey, *n.* bugbear, bugaboo, bogeyman (FEAR, SUPERNATURAL BEINGS).

bogus, *adj.* false, fake, spurious

(FALSENESS); sham, simulate, counterfeit (PRETENSE).

boil, *n.* sore, excrescence, carbuncle (SKIN).

boil, *v.* coddle, parboil, steam (COOKERY); ferment, effervesce, bubble (AGITATION, FOAM, VIOLENCE).

boiler, *n.* caldron, kettle, urn (CONTAINER); autoclave, pressure cooker (COOKERY).

boisterous, *adj.* noisy, effervescent, rambunctious (LOUDNESS).

bold, *adj.* brave, fearless, intrepid (COURAGE); forward, audacious, assuming (DISCOURTESY); immodest, shameless, barefaced (IMMODESTY); obvious, manifest, evident (VISIBILITY).

bolster up, *v.* shore up, bulwark (SUPPORT).

bolt, *n.* latch, lock, padlock (CLOSURE, FASTENING); lightning, thunderbolt (LIGHT); arrow, missile (ARMS); run, escape, flight (DEPARTURE).

bolt, *v.* devour, gobble, consume (FOOD, RECEIVING); take flight, skip, run (DEPARTURE).

bomb, *n.* blockbuster, atom bomb (ARMS, THROW).

bomb, *v.* bombard, shell, rake (ATTACK).

bombard, *v.* launch, shoot, catapult (THROW).

bombastic, *adj.* grandiloquent, magniloquent, fustian (WORDINESS).

bombshell, *n.* shock, jolt, thunderbolt (SURPRISE).

bona fide, *adj.* genuine, valid, authentic (TRUTH).

bond, *n.* tie, link, joint (FASTENING, JUNCTION); band, binder, binding (FILAMENT); security, surety, collateral (PROMISE).

bondage, *n.* chains, enslavement, helotry (SLAVERY).

bonds, *n.* trammels, chains (RESTRAINT); holdings, securities (OWNERSHIP).

BONE—*N.* bone, os (*L.*), ossicle; collarbone, clavicle; breastbone, chestbone, sternum; leg bone, shinbone, tibia, fibula; radius, ulna; skeleton, bony structure, osteology; wishbone, furculum, merrythought; rib, costa.

backbone, spine, spinal column, vertebral column; vertebra (*pl.* vertebrae), coccyx.

horn, antler, beam; attire.

scale, scurf, dander; scab, eschar.

shell, carapace, crust, test, lorica, chitin, conch.

Adj. bony, osseous, osteal, osteoid; skeletal, osteological; spinal,

vertebral, coccygeal, sacral; vertebrate, invertebrate; costal.

horned, antlered, beamy; bicorn, bicornuate, bicornuous, tricorn.

horny, corneous, chitinous, keratoid, scaly, scabrous, squamate, squamose, squamous, scutellate, scutate, leprose, sclerodermatous; scurfy, scurvy, scabby, scabious.

shell-like, crustaceous, testudinate, testudinal, testudinarious; crustal, testacious.

See also HARDNESS.

boner, *n.* blooper (*slang*), howler, slip (MISTAKE).

bonnet, *n.* hat, capote, sunbonnet (HEADGEAR); hood, cowl (COVERING).

bony, *adj.* skinny, underweight, angular (THINNESS); osseous, osteal (BONE).

boob, *n.* noodle, nincompoop, clod (FOLLY, STUPIDITY).

BOOK—*N.* book, volume, tome, album, edition, writing, work, omnibus, publication, production; codex, treatise, monograph, brochure, pamphlet, booklet, tract, tractate, essay, dissertation; libretto; handbook, manual, guidebook, Baedeker, vade mecum, enchiridion; textbook, text, reader, primer, speller; novel; comic book, pocket book, paperbound book, soft-cover book; bookmobile.

reference book, encyclopedia, dictionary, lexicon, glossary, thesaurus; concordance, anthology, gazetteer, yearbook, almanac.

rare books, first editions, early editions, incunabula.

appendix, addendum, index, contents, frontispiece, colophon.

chapter, division, section, part, article; paragraph, passage, clause.

bookseller, bookman, bibliopole, colporteur, publisher; the trade (*collective*).

book-selling, bibliopoly, colportage, publishing; bookshop, bookstore.

library, public library, lending library, athenaeum, book club, circulating library, bibliotheca; librarian, bibliothecary.

V. book, enter, inscribe, list, register, schedule, engage, reserve, order, hire.

See also DRAMA, POETRY, PRINTING, PUBLICATION, READING, SCHOOL, STORY, TREATISE, WRITER, WRITING.

bookcase, *n.* bookrack, bookstand, bookshelf (CONTAINER).

bookish, *adj.* well-read, literate, learned (READING); studious, scholarly (LEARNING); literary, belletristic, classical (STORY).

bookkeeping, *n.* accountancy, auditing, reckoning (ACCOUNTS).

bookworm, *n.* reader, browser, peruser (READING); bluestocking (*colloq.*), bibliophile, bibliomaniac (LEARNING).

boom, *n.* thunder, cannonade, drumfire (ROLL); prosperity, inflation (BUSINESS).

boom, *v.* roar, thunder, rumble (RESONANCE, ROLL); enhance, appreciate (VALUE).

boomerang, *v.* backfire, recoil, rebound (REACTION).

booming, *adj.* palmy, prosperous, thriving (SUCCESS).

boor, *n.* bounder (*colloq.*), cad, churl (DISCOURTESY); lummox, oaf, lumpkin (CLUMSINESS); yokel (*contemptuous*), rube (*slang*), clodhopper (RURAL REGION).

boorish, *adj.* ill-mannered, unrefined, bad-mannered (DISCOURTESY).

boost, *n.* raise, rise, lift (INCREASE).

boost, *v.* upraise, uprear, heighten (ELEVATION).

boot, *n.* shoe, brogan, oxford (FOOTWEAR).

booth, *n.* stall, cubicle, compartment (SPACE).

bootlegger, *n.* smuggler, contrabandist, rumrunner (ILLEGALITY).

bootlicker, *n.* flunky, truckler, lickspittle (SLAVERY, FOLLOWER).

booty, *n.* loot, spoils, prize (PLUNDER, THIEVERY).

border, *n.* fringe, margin; confines, frontier (BOUNDARY, LAND).

border, *v.* adjoin, abut, join (TOUCH); flank, skirt, lie along (REST, SIDE).

bordering, *adj.* contiguous, adjoining, adjacent (TOUCH, NEARNESS).

bore, *n.* stereotype (BOREDOM); drill, punch, auger (OPENING); caliber, diameter (SIZE, WIDTH).

bore, *v.* tire, weary (BOREDOM); pit, riddle, drill (OPENING).

BOREDOM—*N.* boredom, tedium, ennui, doldrums, weariness, *taedium vitae* (*L.*); apathy, lethargy, languor, lassitude, listlessness; detachment, indifference, incuriosity, unconcern, pococurantism.

tediousness, tedium, monotony, prosaism, vapidity, etc. (see *Adjectives*).

bore, bromide, commonplace, platitude, stereotype; treadmill.

V. **bore,** tire, weary, cloy, pall, stale; tire of, weary of, lose interest in.

Adj. **bored,** uninterested, world-weary, weary, tired, blasé, *ennuyé* (*F.*), jaded; apathetic, lethargic, languid, languorous, lassitudinous, listless; detached, indifferent, incurious, unconcerned, perfunctory, lukewarm, tepid, pococurante.

tedious, uninteresting, monotonous, dull, prosaic, vapid, boring, boresome; commonplace, plebeian, colorless, characterless, drab, arid, dry, flat, humdrum, insipid, lifeless, prosy, stale, threadbare, musty, hackneyed, spiritless, stereotyped, stodgy, stuffy, tame, trite, platitudinous, moth-eaten, unexciting, well-worn, wooden; wearisome, wearying, tiresome, poky, interminable, bromidic, cloying.

See also FATIGUE, INACTIVITY, INATTENTION, UNIFORMITY. *Antonyms*—See ATTENTION, EXCITEMENT, INTERESTINGNESS.

---

born, *adj.* née (*F.*), newborn (BIRTH).

borrowed, *adj.* modeled after, molded on, patterned after (IMITATION).

BORROWING—*N.* borrowing, raising money; pledging, pawning.

renting, rental, charter, hire, lease, sublease, underlease; tenancy.

renter, tenant, lessee, sublessee, underlessee; tenant farmer, sharecropper.

lessor, leaser, sublessor, subletter, underletter.

V. **borrow,** raise money, touch, make a touch, see one's uncle (*slang*), pledge, pawn; run into debt.

hire, engage, charter, rent; lease, take a lease, let, sublease, sublet, underlease, underlet.

See also DEBT, TAKING. *Antonyms*—See GIVING, PAYMENT, RECOMPENSE, RESTORATION.

---

bosom, *n.* bust, chest, breasts (BREAST); interior, inside (INTERIORITY).

boss, *n.* employer, taskmaster, master (WORK, RULER).

bossy, *adj.* domineering, dictatorial, imperious (WILL).

BOTANY—*N.* botany, phytology, biology; floristics; dendrology, pomology, horticulture, flora; botanic garden, arboretum, herbarium.

botanist, dendrologist, pomologist, horticulturist, herborist, herbalist, herbist, herbarian.

Adj. **botanic** or botanical, phytoid, dendroid, dendriform, herby, herbal.

See also FARMING, PLANT LIFE. *Antonyms*—See ANIMAL, ZOOLOGY.

both, *n.* couple, couplet, pair (TWO).
bother, *n.* pother, flurry, to-do (COMMOTION, ACTIVITY); trouble, trial, inconvenience (DIFFICULTY).
bother, *v.* disturb, trouble, perturb (ANNOYANCE, NERVOUSNESS); inconvenience, discommode, disoblige (DIFFICULTY).
bottle, *n.* carafe, decanter, flagon (CONTAINER).
bottom, *n.* lowest point, nadir, base (LOWNESS); substratum, ground, terra firma (SUPPORT); behind, buttocks, fundament (REAR); watercraft, craft, vessel (SHIP).
bottomless, *adj.* fathomless, soundless, unfathomed (DEPTH).
bough, *n.* branch, shoot, limb (PLANT LIFE).
boulder, *n.* slab, dornick, megalith (ROCK).
boulevard, *n.* street, avenue, highway (PASSAGE).
bounce, *v.* ricochet, jounce, bob (JUMP); dismiss, discharge, fire (DISMISSAL).
bound, *adj.* intent, firm, bent (PURPOSE).
bound, *v.* leap, spring, hop (JUMP); limit, confine (BOUNDARY).

BOUNDARY—*N.* boundary, bounds, limits, abuttals, ambit, list, mere, mete, precinct, purlieus, suburbs, terminus; circumference, compass, pale; border, confines, frontier; perimeter; borderline, boundary line.
limit, barrier, borderland, bound, compass, confines, solstice, termination.
edge, border, brim, brink, fringe, margin, rim, verge; burr, selvage.
limitation, restriction, qualification, condition, reservation, restraint; circumscription, confinement, delimitation, demarcation, determination.
V. bound, circumscribe, confine, define, delimit, demarcate, determine, limit, terminate.
edge, border, rim, marginate, list (*cloth*).
be on the edge of (*fig.*), border on, verge on; be on the border (borderline, brim, brink, fringe, *or* verge) of.
Adj. limited, bound, circumscribed, confined, definite, delimited, finite, limitary.
definite, determinate, fixed,

clear-cut, defined, specific, exact, precise, unequivocal.
See also END, PLACE, RESTRAINT. *Antonyms*—See ENDLESSNESS, FREEDOM.

bounder (*colloq.*), *n.* boor, cad, churl (DISCOURTESY).
boundless, *adj.* vast, illimitable, immeasurable (SIZE, ENDLESSNESS).
bounds, *n.* limits, abuttals, border (BOUNDARY).
bountiful, *adj.* abundant, generous (UNSELFISHNESS).
bouquet, *n.* posy, nosegay, corsage (PLANT LIFE); fragrance, aroma, scent (ODOR).
bourgeois, *adj.* conservative, hidebound, old-line (OPPOSITION, PREJUDICE); Philistine, mammonistic, middle-class (WEALTH, MONEY, PEOPLE).
bow, *n.* curtsey, obeisance, salaam (RESPECT, GESTURE); prow, stem, nose (FRONT); long bow, crossbow (ARMS); curve, bend, arch (CURVE, BEND).
bow, *v.* nod, salaam, curtsey (RESPECT, GESTURE); arch, round, incline (CURVE, BEND); cringe, stoop, kneel (SLAVERY); submit, yield, defer (SUBMISSION).
bowels, *n.* insides, recesses, penetralia (INTERIORITY); intestines, entrails, guts (BELLY).
bowl, *n.* plate, platter, dish (CONTAINER).
bow-legged, *adj.* bandy-legged (APPENDAGE).
box, *n.* bin, carton, case (CONTAINER); coffin, casket, pine box (BURIAL).
box, *v.* cuff, punch, slap (HITTING); pen, case, incase (INCLOSURE).
boxer, *n.* pugilist, prize fighter, bruiser (FIGHTER).
boy, *n.* lad, shaver, stripling (YOUTH); buttons (*slang*), bellhop (*slang*), bellboy (SERVICE).
boycott, *n.* blackball, ostracism, black list (DISAPPROVAL).
boycott, *v.* snub, cut, ostracize (INATTENTION).
brace, *n.* vise, grip, clamp (HOLD); bracket, support (STABILITY); couple, pair (TWO).
brace, *v.* strengthen, consolidate, buttress (STRENGTH); stabilize, steady, stiffen (STABILITY).
bracelet, *n.* wristlet, armlet, bangle (JEWELRY).
bracket, *n.* tier, rank, category (CLASS); shelf, ledge, console (SUPPORT); stabilizer, support (STABILITY); parenthesis, brace (WRITTEN SYMBOL).
bracket, *v.* pair, couple, match (TWO); yoke, join (JUNCTION);

group, associate, link (RELATIONSHIP).

brag, v. blow, crow, vaunt (BOASTING).

braid, n. lace, plait, plat (TEXTURE); coil, pigtail, queue (HAIR); cue, wattle (WINDING).

brain, n. encephalon, cerebrum, gray matter (INTELLECT); genius, prodigy, intellect (INTELLIGENCE).

brain, v. fell, blackjack, knock out (HITTING).

brainless, adj. birdbrained, boneheaded, mindless (FOLLY, STUPIDITY).

brainy, adj. brilliant, smart, clever (INTELLIGENCE, CLEVERNESS).

brake, v. slow down, slacken speed, decelerate (SLOWNESS).

branch, n. shoot, limb, bough (PLANT LIFE); division, section, group (PART); extension, wing, arm (STRETCH); divergence, fork, crotch (TURNING); tributary, affluent, confluent (RIVER).

brand, n. variety, description, kind (CLASS); trademark, emblem (INDICATION); blot, scar, stigma (DISGRACE); fagot, cinder, firebrand (WOOD, FIRE).

brandy, n. liquor, brandywine, cognac (ALCOHOLIC LIQUOR).

brash, adj. nervy (colloq.), brazenfaced, brazen (DISCOURTESY).

brass, n. bronze, copper, ormolu (METAL); nerve (colloq.), cheek (colloq.), presumption (DISCOURTESY); officials, authorities, administration (OFFICIAL).

brassière, n. bra (colloq.), bandeau (UNDERWEAR).

brat, n. enfant terrible (F.), devil, urchin (CHILD).

bravado, n. pretensions, bluster, braggadocio (BOASTING).

brave, adj. bold, audacious, intrepid (COURAGE).

brave, v. challenge, dare, throw down the gauntlet (DEFIANCE); bear, go through, support (INEXCITABILITY).

brawl, n. fight, broil, fracas (FIGHTING); quarrel, wrangle, brabble (DISAGREEMENT).

brawny, adj. muscular, athletic, burly (STRENGTH); fleshy, sarcous (SKIN).

brazen, adj. impudent, shameless, bold (IMMODESTY); nervy (colloq.), cheeky (colloq.), brash (DISCOURTESY).

bray, v. bellow, roar, blare (LOUDNESS); grate, rasp, pound (RUBBING, POWDERINESS).

breach, n. fissure, rent, rift (DISJUNCTION); break, crack, chip (BREAKAGE); aperture, cleft, slit (OPENING).

BREAD—N. bread, French toast, hardtack, Melba toast, pizza, pumpernickel, toast; loaf.

[individual] roll, biscuit, brioche, bun, cracker, crouton, crumpet, dumpling, English muffin, fritter, matzo, muffin, pastry shell, patty, timbale, croustade, popover, pretzel, rusk, zwieback, scone, bagel.

pancake, flapjack, griddlecake, hot cake, wheat cake, waffle.

cake, angel cake, cheesecake, coffee cake, coffee ring, Danish pastry, devil's-food cake, French pastry, patisserie, fruit cake, gingerbread, jelly roll, layer cake, marble cake, pastry, pound cake, shortcake, spongecake, Stollen, torte (G.).

[individual cake] bun, cookie, cracker, cream puff, cruller, cupcake, doughnut, sinker, dumpling, éclair, French cruller, gingersnap, ladyfinger, lemon snap, macaroon, napoleon, petits fours (pl.), shortbread, tart, turnover, wafer.

pie, chiffon pie, cream pie, fruit pie, pasty, mince pie, pumpkin pie, shoofly pie.

See also FOOD.

breadth, n. amplitude, extent, expanse (WIDTH).

break, n. crack, chip, breach (BREAKAGE); fracture, discontinuity, cleavage (DISJUNCTION); misunderstanding, rift, clash (DISAGREEMENT); hiatus, lacuna, caesura (INTERVAL); coffee break, recess, respite (REST).

BREAKABLENESS—N. breakableness, brittleness, fragility, frangibility, friability, vitreosity, delicacy.

Adj. breakable, brittle, fragile, frangible, frail, delicate, shivery, splintery, vitreous, shattery; fracturable, rupturable, severable; crumbly, friable, powdery, crisp, crispy, crackly.

See also BREAKAGE, POWDERINESS, WEAKNESS. Antonyms—See STRENGTH.

BREAKAGE—N. breakage, fragmentation, shatterment, smash, fracture, rupture, severance, pulverization, crush.

break, crack, chip, nick, breach, crackle, burst, split, crash, snap.

V. break, crack, snap, split, shiver, splinter, chip, fracture, shatter, sever, crash, crush, burst, give way, stave, rupture; crumble, disintegrate, fall to pieces, pulverize, smash, fragment; breach, nick, crackle.

See also BREAKABLENESS, DESTRUCTION, DISCONTINUITY, DISJUNCTION.
Antonyms — See CONTINUATION, UNCTION.

breakdown, n. crackup, psychasthenia (NEUROSIS).

breaker, n. wave, beachcomber, billow (RIVER).

break in, v. breach, burglarize, raid (INGRESS); tame, gentle, break (DOMESTICATION); master, subdue, vanquish (SLAVERY).

BREAKWATER—N. breakwater, pier, mole, sea wall, dam, dike, embankment, milldam, lock, floodgate, sluice gate, sluice, levee, jetty, revetment.

wharf, pier, dock, quay, landing, dry dock, mole, jetty.

bridge, span; cantilever bridge, covered bridge, drawbridge, lift bridge, bascule bridge; footbridge, gangplank, gangboard, gangway; pontoon bridge, rope bridge, suspension bridge, swing bridge, trestle bridge, truss bridge; viaduct.

V. dam, bank, embank, bay, dike, lock, revet.

dock, wharf, land, put up, dry-dock.

bridge, span, go across, reach, connect, link, cross.

BREAST—N. breast, bosom, bust, chest; breasts, mammary glands, udder, dugs, mammae (*sing.* mamma).

nipple, teat, tit, papilla, mammilla, dug; pacifier, pap.

V. nurse, nurse at the breast, suck, suckle, lactate, give suck to; wet-nurse.

Adj. breast-shaped, mammillary, mastoid; mammary, pectoral; bosomy (*colloq.*), deep-bosomed, bathycolpian, callimastian.

See also FRONT. *Antonyms*—See REAR.

breath, n. puff, flatus, whiff (WIND); trace, whisper, hint (SUGGESTION).

BREATH—N. breath, aspiration, gasp, puff, whiff, huff, pant, gulp; sniffle, sniff, snivel, snuffle, snuff, snore, wheeze; sigh, sough, suspiration; snort, stertor, rhonchus (*med.*), râle (*F., med.*), stridor, murmur, whoop; bad breath, halitosis, ozostomia.

breathing, respiration, aspiration, eupnea (*med.*); expiration, exhalation; inhalation, inspiration, insufflation.

lungs, gills, branchiae; windpipe, throttle, trachea, weasand; bronchi (*pl.*), bronchia (*pl.*); iron lung, aqualung.

consumption, phthisic, phthisis, tuberculosis, pulmonary tuberculosis, white plague; asthma, catarrh, bronchitis.

V. breathe, respire, aspire; breathe in, inspire, insufflate, inhale, sniff, sniffle, snivel, snuff, snuffle; breathe out, expel (*or* emit) the breath, blow, exhale, expire, whiff, pant, puff, snort, huff; gasp, whoop, gulp, sigh, sough, suspire (*poetic*), wheeze, snore.

Adj. breathing, etc. (see *Verbs*); winded, short-winded, pursy, breathless, stertorous, wheezy; respiratory, aspiratory, expiratory, inspiratory.

See also BLOWING, NOSE, WIND.

breathless, *adj.* winded, short-winded, pursy (BREATH); eager, impatient, in suspense (EXPECTATION); agape, open-mouthed, spellbound (SURPRISE).

breath-taking, *adj.* exciting, hair-raising, spine-tingling (EXCITEMENT).

breeches, n. britches (*colloq.*), pants, jeans (TROUSERS).

breed, n. race, genus, kind (CLASS, MANKIND, ANCESTRY).

breed, v. reproduce, procreate, cause (BIRTH, PRODUCTION).

breeding, n. nurture, rearing, upbringing (CHILD); good breeding, good manners, manners (COURTESY); schooling, grounding, culture (LEARNING).

breeze, n. airflow, breath, current (AIR, WIND).

breezy, *adj.* windy, blowy, drafty (WIND, AIR); racy, spicy, salty (INTERESTINGNESS); broad, coarse, ribald (OBSCENITY); effervescent, peppy (*slang*), lively (ACTIVITY).

brevity, n. conciseness, terseness, succinctness (SHORTNESS).

brew, v. compound, concoction, blend (PREPARATION).

brewery, n. distillery, winery (ALCOHOLIC LIQUOR).

BRIBERY—N. bribery, corruption, embracery, subornation, compounding a felony (*all legal*).

bribe, sop, *douceur* (*F.*), graft, payola, boodle, swag (*colloq.*), hush money, blackmail.

V. bribe, buy, corrupt, fix, reach, take care of, smear, tamper with, grease (*or* tickle) the palm of; suborn, embrace (*both legal*).

Adj. bribable, corruptible, rotten, venal, vendible.

See also GIVING, IMMORALITY, PURCHASE. *Antonyms*—See HONESTY.

bric-a-brac, *n.* virtu, *objets d'art* (*F.*), bijouterie (ORNAMENT).

bride, *n.* wife, spouse, helpmate (MARRIAGE).

bridegroom, *n.* groom, husband (MARRIAGE).

bridge, *n.* span, covered bridge (BREAKWATER); extension, wing, branch (STRETCH).

bridge, *v.* span, subtend (STRETCH).

bridle, *v.* curb, govern, control, check (RESTRAINT); become angry (ANGER).

brief, *adj.* concise, terse, succinct (SHORTNESS); short-lived, momentary, meteoric (IMPERMANENCE).

brief, *n.* condensation, abstract, digest (SHORTNESS).

brief, *v.* edify, enlighten, inform (TEACHING); orient, advise, apprise (INFORMATION).

brief case, *n.* brief bag, attaché case, portfolio (CONTAINER).

briefs, *n.* underdrawers, panties, step-ins (UNDERWEAR).

bright, *adj.* clear, shiny, sunny (LIGHT); encouraging, cheering, rosy (CHEERFULNESS, HOPE); brilliant, clever, smart (INTELLIGENCE).

brilliance, *n.* glory, splendor, effulgence (MAGNIFICENCE, LIGHT); genius, brightness, acuteness (ABILITY, INTELLIGENCE).

brim, *n.* edge, brink, rim (BOUNDARY).

brimming, *adj.* full, topfull, brimful (FULLNESS).

brine, *n.* preservative, marinade, pickle (PRESERVING); salt, alkali, sodium chloride (TASTE); sea, deep, briny deep (OCEAN).

bring, *v.* bear, deliver, carry (TRANSFER); fetch, get (SALE).

bring about, *v.* cause, bring, produce (CAUSATION); engender, beget, generate (PRODUCTION); effect, effectuate, make (RESULT).

bring in, *v.* track in, carry in, import (INTAKE); sell for, yield, cost (SALE).

bring together, *v.* collect, gather, amass (ASSEMBLAGE).

bring up, *v.* nurture, raise, rear (CHILD); vomit, retch, throw up (NAUSEA).

brink, *n.* edge, margin, rim (BOUNDARY).

brisk, *adj.* energetic, active, lively (ACTIVITY).

bristle, *n.* quill, vibrissa, whisker (HAIR).

bristly, *adj.* thorny, briery, bristling (SHARPNESS).

brittle, *adj.* frail, fragile, shivery (BREAKABLENESS, WEAKNESS).

broach, *v.* move, propose, offer (SUGGESTION); draw off, tap, decant (ABSENCE).

broad, *adj.* wide, squat, splay (WIDTH); inclusive, all-embracing, all-inclusive (INCLUSION); low-minded, gross, coarse (OBSCENITY, LOWNESS).

broadcast, *v.* promulgate, spread, disseminate (PUBLICATION, DISCLOSURE, SENDING); splatter, splash, strew (THROW).

broaden, *v.* widen, ream, expand (WIDTH).

broad-minded, *adj.* tolerant, liberal, catholic (ACCEPTANCE, IMPARTIALITY).

broke (*colloq.*), *adj.* bankrupt, insolvent, penniless (POVERTY).

brokenhearted, *adj.* heartbroken, sore at heart, heartsore (SADNESS).

brood, *n.* issue, offspring, progeny (CHILD).

brood, *v.* sigh, languish (SADNESS); set, hatch, incubate (SEAT).

brood over, *v.* dwell on, mull over (THOUGHT).

brook, *n.* rivulet, streamlet, brooklet (RIVER).

broom, *n.* brush, besom, whiskbroom (CLEANNESS).

broth, *n.* fluid, liquor, elixir (LIQUID).

brothel, *n.* bordello, disorderly house, house of assignation (PROSTITUTE).

brother, *n.* sibling, twin (RELATIVE).

brow, *n.* forehead, frons, sinciput (HEAD); top, crest, summit (HEIGHT).

browbeat, *v.* domineer, bully, hector (CONTROL).

BROWN—N. brown, amber, café au lait, chocolate, cocoa, coffee, dun, fawn, puce, tawny, Titian, topaz, umber, bister, bistre, ocher, ochre, Vandyke brown.

tan, beige, biscuit, brindle (*of animals*), écru, khaki.

reddish brown, auburn, bay, bronze, burnt almond, burnt umber, chestnut, cinnamon, cocoa, copper, hazel, henna, hyacinth red, mahogany, russet, rust, sorrel.

V. brown, embrown, tan.

sunburn, tan, toast, burn, brown, bronze.

Adj. brown, amber, etc. (see *Nouns*); dun-colored, fulvous, spadiceous; brunet, nut-brown, fawn-colored, fuscous, musteline, brownish, dust-colored.

reddish-brown, etc. (see *Nouns*); rust-colored, rubiginous, ferrugi-

ous; castaneous, roan, foxy, carroty, terra cotta, maroon; bronzy,
coppery, cupreous; hyacinthine.
sunburned, sunburnt, adust,
bronzed, browned, brown, burned,
tanned, tan, toasted.

brown-haired, *adj.* dark-haired,
brunet (HAIR).

brownie, *n.* fairy, elf, sprite (SU-
PERNATURAL BEINGS).

browse, *v.* scan, thumb through,
leaf through (READING); bite,
graze, crop (FOOD).

bruise, *v.* injure, wound, contuse
(HARM); beat, crush, crunch
(POWDERINESS).

brunt, *n.* strain, tension, stress
(PRESSURE).

brush, *n.* broom, whisk, whiskbroom (CLEANNESS); polisher,
buffer, waxer (RUBBING); underbrush, undergrowth, underwood
(PLANT LIFE).

brush, *v.* glance, graze, kiss
(TOUCH).

brusque, *adj.* bluff, unceremonious,
abrupt (BLUNTNESS).

brutal, *adj.* cruel, unkind, inhuman (CRUELTY, VIOLENCE).

brute, *n.* ruffian, savage, cannibal
(CRUELTY, VIOLENCE); beast, quadruped (ANIMAL).

bubble, *n.* globule, bead, blob
(FOAM).

bubble, *v.* effervesce, ferment, boil
(FOAM, EXCITEMENT).

buck, *n.* hart, stag (ANIMAL).

bucket, *n.* pail, brazier, scuttle
(CONTAINER).

buckle, *n.* catch, clasp, hasp (FAS-
TENING).

buckle down, *v.* apply oneself, devote oneself (ENERGY).

bucolic, *adj.* rural, rustic, countrified (RURAL REGION).

bud, *n.* flower, bloom, floret (PLANT
LIFE).

buddy (*colloq.*), *n.* co-worker,
teamworker, fellow worker
(WORK); companion, comrade
(FRIEND).

budge, *v.* move, move around, stir
(MOTION).

buff, *v.* scour, pumice, burnish
(RUBBING, SMOOTHNESS).

buffer, *n.* polisher, brush (RUB-
BING); fender, bumper (PROTEC-
TION).

buffet, *n.* locker, wardrobe, chiffonier (CONTAINER).

buffoon, *n.* clown, jester, merry-
andrew (FOLLY).

bug, *n.* insect, louse, flea (ANI-
MAL); germ, microbe, microorganism (DISEASE, SMALLNESS).

bugbear, *n.* bugaboo, bogey (FEAR,
SUPERNATURAL BEINGS).

buggy, *adj.* insectile, verminous,
lousy (ANIMAL).

buggy, *n.* wagon, cart, van; carriage, clarence (VEHICLE).

build, *n.* constitution, structure,
frame (CONDITION); form, figure,
physique (SHAPE).

BUILDING—*N.* building, structure, edifice, pile, skyscraper, office
building, arcade, rotunda, mausoleum, shed, lean-to; public building, hall, palace, capitol, casino,
castle, chateau, alcazar; annex, extension, wing, superstructure,
dome, cupola; aerie.

tower, steeple, church tower, bell
tower, belfry, beacon, donjon, turret.

porch, patio, piazza, terrace,
lanai, veranda, gallery, loggia,
stoop, portico, porte-cochère.

construction, erection, fabrication, building, engineering, structure, architecture, architectonics,
civil engineering, tectonics.

architect, engineer, civil engineer; builder, erector, fabricator.

V. build, construct, erect, put up,
engineer, fabricate, jerry-build, su-
perstruct; remodel.

See also HABITATION, PRODUCTION.

build up (*colloq.*), *v.* publicize,
ballyhoo, advertise (PUBLICATION).

bulge, *v.* balloon, belly, bloat
(SWELLING); stick out, beetle, extrude (VISIBILITY).

bulk, *n.* majority, greater part,
plurality (SUPERIORITY); extent,
mass, volume (QUANTITY, SIZE).

bulk, *v.* enlarge, pad, amplify (IN-
CREASE).

bulky, *adj.* awkward, cumbersome,
unmanageable (CLUMSINESS, DIF-
FICULTY, SIZE).

bull, *n.* male, buck, tom (MAN);
bullock, taurine, ox (ANIMAL);
slip of the tongue, fluff (MIS-
TAKE); misusage, solecism (MIS-
USE OF WORDS).

bullet, *n.* ball, slug (ARMS).

bulletin, *n.* news, item, dispatch
(PUBLICATION); program, calendar
(LIST).

bullfighter, *n.* tauromachian, *torero*
(*Sp.*), toreador (FIGHTER).

bully, *v.* domineer, browbeat, hector (CONTROL, SEVERITY).

bulwark, *n.* rampart, vallation, defense (PROTECTION).

bum (*slang*), *n.* tramp, vagabond,
hobo (REST); cur, black sheep,
ne'er-do-well (WORTHLESSNESS).

bump, *n.* knob, knurl, lump
(SWELLING).

bump, *v.* jab, bunt, butt (PROPUL-
SION, HITTING).

bumper, *n.* fender, cushion, buffer (PROTECTION).

bumpy, *adj.* uneven, irregular, un-level (ROUGHNESS); knobby, lumpy, nodous (SWELLING).

bun, *n.* Danish pastry, doughnut, cruller (BREAD); topknot, chignon (HAIR).

bunch, *n.* flock, bevy, group (ASSEMBLAGE).

bundle, *n.* packet, package, parcel (ASSEMBLAGE).

bungalow, *n.* cottage, ranch house, cabana (HABITATION).

bungle, *v.* blunder, botch, muff (CLUMSINESS).

bunk (*slang*), *n.* nonsense, poppycock, claptrap (ABSURDITY); bed, berth, cot (SLEEP).

bunk, *v.* slumber, bed down, snooze (SLEEP).

bunting, *n.* streamer, pennant, pennon (INDICATION).

buoyant, *adj.* elastic, resilient, supple (CHEERFULNESS, JUMP); floating, supernatant, afloat (FLOAT).

burden, *n.* load, millstone, cumber (WEIGHT); hardship, uphill work, Herculean task (DIFFICULTY); substance, effect, gist (MEANING, IDEA); accountability, responsibility, blame (LIABILITY); refrain, ritornelle (*mus.*), chorus (REPETITION).

burdensome, *adj.* carking, onerous, oppressive (WEIGHT).

bureau, *n.* chest of drawers, commode, sideboard (CONTAINER); office, department (AGENCY).

bureaucrat, *n.* commissioner, officeholder, incumbent (OFFICIAL).

burglar, *n.* housebreaker, second-story thief, picklock (THIEF).

BURIAL—*N.* burial, entombment, inhumation, interment, sepulture, vivisepulture (*alive*).

cemetery, burial ground (or grounds), campo santo (*It.*), charnel, golgotha, necropolis, catacombs, potter's field, bone yard (*slang*), churchyard.

grave, burial place, tomb, vault, shrine, sepulcher, sepulchre, sepulture, mausoleum, crypt, dolmen (*prehist.*), golgotha, urn (*fig.*); pantheon; charnel house, charnel, ossuary.

tombstone, gravestone, marker, stone, monument, headstone, footstone, shaft, cross, cairn, barrow, tumulus, cromlech; cenotaph; epitaph, inscription.

coffin, box, casket, pine box, pall; shell, sarcophagus; urn, cinerary urn, mortuary urn.

cremation, burning, incineration; pyre, funeral pyre; crematorium,

crematory, cremator, cinerator; furnace; cinerarium, columbarium.

funeral, funeral rites, obsequies, exequies, obit; knell, death bell, tolling; wake, dirge, coronac. (*Scot. and Irish*), requiem, elegy, epicedium, dead march, muffled drum.

bier, litter, hearse, catafalque.

undertaker, funeral director, mortician.

mourner, weeper, lamenter, keener (*Ireland*); pallbearer, bearer.

graveclothes, shroud, winding sheet, cerecloth, cerements.

autopsy, necropsy (*med.*), post mortem.

grave robber, body snatcher, ghoul, resurrectionist.

V. **inter,** bury, entomb, inhume, ensepulcher, sepulcher, inearth, tomb, consign to the grave.

cremate, incinerate, incremate, burn.

disinter, exhume, disinhume, dis entomb.

Adj. **gravelike,** charnel, sepulchral, tomblike; cenotaphic; crematory, cinerary.

funeral, defunctive, feral, funerary, funereal.

Adv., phrases. **in memoriam** (*L.*), *hic jacet* (*L.*), *ci-git* (*F.*), *post obitum* (*L.*), *post mortem* (*L.*), beneath the sod, at rest; R.I.P. (*L.; requiescat in pace*).

See also DEATH, FIRE, KILLING. *Antonyms*—See DIGGING.

burlesque, *n.* parody, caricature, travesty (RIDICULE, IMITATION).

burly, *adj.* brawny, muscular, strapping (SIZE, STRENGTH).

burn, *v.* blaze, flare, glow; sear, singe, scald (FIRE); cremate, incinerate (BURIAL).

burp (*colloq.*), *v.* belch, eruct (GAS).

burrow, *v.* dig, tunnel, sap (DIGGING).

burst, *v.* explode, blow up, pop (BLOWING); breach, broach, fissure (OPENING); teem, pullulate, abound with (FULLNESS).

bury, *v.* inter, entomb (BURIAL).

bus, *n.* omnibus, motorbus (VEHICLE).

bush, *n.* shrub, jungle, forest (PLANT LIFE).

bushy, *adj.* hairy, hirsute, shaggy (HAIR).

BUSINESS—*N.* business, undertaking, pursuit, venture; affair, concern, interest, matter; trade, traffic, truck, merchantry, commerce, industry; dealings, negotiations, intercourse, transactions, deal; technology.

capitalism, commercialism, industrialism, mercantilism.

occupation, calling, line, métier, pursuit, field, employment, business, vocation, work, trade, livelihood; profession, specialty, career; craft.

company, concern, enterprise, establishment, firm, house, institution, organization; corporation, holding company, monopoly, cartel, pool, syndicate, trust; partnership.

[*phases of business cycle*] prosperity, inflation, boom; adjustment, deflation, shakeout, recession, slump, crisis, crash, commercial crisis, depression, hard (*or* bad) times.

businessman, executive, entrepreneur, industrialist, baron, capitalist, tycoon; merchant, tradesman, trader, dealer; Babbitt.

V. **busy oneself,** occupy oneself, employ oneself in; undertake, set about, attempt, turn one's hand to; be engaged in, be occupied with, be at work on, have in hand, ply one's trade, be busy, bustle, hum.

Adj. **business,** commercial, industrial, mercantile.

occupational, professional, vocational, technical.

businesslike, practical, orderly, well-ordered, systematic, methodical, efficient.

busy, employed, occupied, active; going on, on foot, afoot, on hand, in hand; industrious, operose, sedulous, hard-working.

See also ACTIVITY, EXCHANGE, LABOR RELATIONS, UNDERTAKING, WORK. *Antonyms*—See INACTION, INACTIVITY, LEISURE.

bust, *n.* bosom, chest, breasts (BREAST).

bustle, *n.* movement, hum, stir (ACTIVITY).

busy, *adj.* employed, occupied, active (BUSINESS).

busybody, *n.* interferer, meddler, nosybody (INQUIRY, INTERJACENCE).

butchery, *n.* slaughter, bloodshed, carnage; slaughterhouse, abattoir (KILLING).

butler, *n.* valet, manservant, man (SERVICE).

butt, *n.* extremity, tip, edge (END); cigarette, smoke, weed (TOBACCO); grip, lug, grasp (HOLD); laughingstock, jest, byword (LAUGHTER, RIDICULE, CONTEMPT).

butt, *v.* shove, bump, buck (PROPULSION).

butter, *n.* shortening (OIL).

butt in, *v.* interfere, meddle, intervene (INTERJACENCE).

buttocks, *n.* behind, breech, fundament (REAR).

buttress, *v.* shore, bulwark, reinforce (SUPPORT).

buxom, *adj.* plump, chubby, fattish (SIZE).

buy, *v.* shop, market, go shopping (PURCHASE); bribe, corrupt, fix (BRIBERY).

buzz, *v.* hum, drone (ANIMAL SOUND); gossip, tattle, tittletattle (RUMOR).

by, *prep., adv.* by the side of, beside, alongside (SIDE); over, at an end, past, done with (END).

by chance, by accident, by luck (PURPOSELESSNESS).

by degrees, piecemeal, little by little, gradually (PART).

by heart, by (*or* from) memory, *memoriter* (L.), by rote (MEMORY).

bylaw, *n.* regulation, ordinance, rule (LAW).

by-pass, *v.* let go, overlook, omit (INATTENTION, NEGLECT).

by-product, *n.* product, result, output (PRODUCTION); harvest, crop, repercussion (RESULT).

bystander, *n.* spectator, onlooker, witness (LOOKING).

by way of, via, through, by means of (PASSAGE).

byword, *n.* catchword, shibboleth, slogan (WORD); scorn, target, butt (CONTEMPT).

C

cab, *n.* taxi, taxicab, hackney (VEHICLE).

cabaret, *n.* café, night club (ALCOHOLIC LIQUOR).

cabinet, *n.* repository, closet, cupboard (CONTAINER); official family, council (OFFICIAL).

cackle, *v.* chortle, chuckle, giggle (LAUGHTER); gobble, cluck (ANIMAL SOUND).

cacophony, *n.* discord, noise, jangle (HARSH SOUND).

cad, *n.* boor, bounder (*colloq.*), churl (DISCOURTESY).

cadence, *n.* measure, tempo, meter (RHYTHM).

café, *n.* cabaret, night club (ALCOHOLIC LIQUOR).

cafeteria, *n.* diner, restaurant (FOOD).

cage, v. shut in, keep in, confine (IMPRISONMENT).

cajole, v. argue into, coax, wheedle (PERSUASION).

cake, n. pastry, shortcake (BREAD).

cake, v. stiffen, set, fix (THICKNESS).

calamity, n. cataclysm, catastrophe, disaster (MISFORTUNE).

calculate, v. cipher, figure, reckon (COMPUTATION).

calculated, adj. studied, premeditated, conscious (PURPOSE); petty, small, sordid (SELFISHNESS).

calendar, n. time record, almanac, chronology (TIME MEASUREMENT); program, bulletin (LIST).

calf, n. leg, shin, foreleg (APPENDAGE); yearling, heifer, veal (ANIMAL).

caliber, n. worthiness, merit, dignity (VALUE); appetency, habilitation, capacity (ABILITY); diameter, bore, gauge (SIZE, WIDTH).

calisthenics, n. acrobatics, athletics (GYMNASTICS).

call, n. calling, command, invitation (SUMMONS); visit, visitation (ARRIVAL).

call, v. summon, summons, subpoena (SUMMONS); name, address (NAME); visit, drop in (ARRIVAL).

call-girl (slang), n. cocotte, courtesan (PROSTITUTE).

calling, n. occupation, line, métier (BUSINESS).

callous, v. harden, caseharden, brutalize (CRUELTY, INSENSITIVITY).

callow, adj. green, immature, puerile (IMMATURITY, INEXPERIENCE, YOUTH).

call together, v. muster, convene, assemble (SUMMONS, ASSEMBLAGE).

callus, n. callosity, corn, induration (SKIN).

CALMNESS—N. calmness, peace, rest, repose, lull, dispassion, impassivity, stoicism, imperturbation, phlegm, phlegmatism, placidity, quiet, tranquility, serenity; doldrums, windlessness, halcyon days.

composure, self-composure, patience, poise, self-possession, aplomb, sang-froid (F.), nonchalance, insouciance, countenance, presence of mind.

calmative, sedative, anodyne, calmant, nerve tonic, nervine, opiate, paregoric; lullaby; sop, placebo.

soothing agent, soother, balm, demulcent, emollient, lenitive, salve, ointment, unguent, unction, petrolatum, petroleum jelly, Vaseline, mitigative, lotion; pacifier.

V. calm, tranquilize, unruffle, still, quiet, quench, quell, put at rest, ease, compose, becalm, cool, sober; allay, assuage, attemper; drug, narcotize, sedate, relax.

soothe, ease, lull, dulcify, mollify, pacify, pacificate, conciliate, appease, propitiate, placate, smooth, stroke, comfort, console, solace, salve.

calm down, cool down, compose oneself, collect oneself, pull (or get) oneself together, subside, sober down, relax; rest, repose.

Adj. calm, at rest, at peace, in repose, easy, composed, self-composed, collected, self-collected, cool, coolheaded, in countenance, placid, self-possessed, poised, serene, tranquil; passionless, dispassionate, equable, even-tempered, evenminded, levelheaded, even, equanimous, imperturbable, impassive, nonchalant, pococurante, philosophical, stoical, phlegmatic; steady, staid, sober, sedate; quiet, still, reposeful, restful, slumberous, slumbery, smooth, undisturbed, stormless, windless, settled, easeful, halcyon, moderate, peaceful, pacific; patient; unexcited, unagitated, unruffled, unrattled (colloq.), unfluttered, unflurried, unflustered.

soothing, balmy, calmative, bland, soothful, restful, unctuous, dulcet, irenic; paregoric, opiate, nervine, lenitive, emollient, demulcent.

See also INEXCITABILITY, MILDNESS, MODERATENESS, PEACE, RELIEF, REST, SILENCE, UNANXIETY. Antonyms—See AGITATION, EXCITEMENT, SHAKE.

---

calumny, n. defamation, denigration, aspersion (DETRACTION).

camel, n. dromedary, Bactrian camel (ANIMAL).

camouflage, v. disguise, cloak, mask (CONCEALMENT).

camp, n. bivouac, encampment, tents (HABITATION).

campaign, n. crusade, jehad (Moham.), expedition (FIGHTING, ACTION).

campus, n. grounds, terrace, yard (LAND).

can, n. canister, cannikin, tin (CONTAINER).

canal, n. cove, estuary, firth (INLET); aqueduct, channel, watercourse (CHANNEL).

cancel, v. neutralize, counterbalance, repeal (INEFFECTIVENESS).

cancer, n. hydra, curse, plague (WICKEDNESS).

candid, adj. sincere, frank, open (TRUTH, HONESTY, REALITY).

candle, *n.* wax candle, taper, dip (LIGHT).

candy, *n.* confections, confectionery, sweets (SWEETNESS).

cane, *n.* walking stick, pikestaff, staff (WALKING, ROD).

cane, *v.* spank, beat, hit (PUNISHMENT).

cannibal, *n.* brute, ruffian, savage (CRUELTY).

cannon, *n.* mounted gun, mortar, howitzer (ARMS).

canopy, *n.* awning, shade, marquee (COVERING, PROTECTION).

cant, *n.* vernacular, dialect, argot (LANGUAGE); lean, list, tilt (SLOPE).

canter, *v.* skip, trip, buck (JUMP); gallop, run, trot (HORSE).

canvas, *n.* picture, painting, piece (FINE ARTS).

canvass, *v.* peddle, solicit, hawk (SALE).

canyon, *n.* valley, glen, gorge (DEPTH).

cap, *n.* beanie, skullcap, fez (HEADGEAR).

capable, *adj.* competent, able, proficient (ABILITY).

capacity, *n.* room, volume, accommodation (CONTENTS, SPACE); appointment, berth, billet (SITUATION); capability, competence, compass (ABILITY).

cape, *n.* cloak, capote, manteau (COAT); head, headland, promontory (LAND).

caper, *n.* antic, dido, stunt (MISCHIEF).

caper, *v.* frisk, cavort, dance (JUMP).

capital, *adj.* best, champion, crack (GOOD, SUPERIORITY); main, chief, leading (IMPORTANCE).

capital, *n.* property, substance, estate (OWNERSHIP); resources, wherewithal, ways and means (MEANS); principal, assets (MONEY); fortune, treasure, gold (WEALTH); municipality, metropolis, county seat (CITY); majuscule, uncial, upper case (WRITTEN SYMBOL).

capitalism, *n.* commercialism, industrialism (BUSINESS).

capitalist, *n.* bourgeois, plutocrat, moneybags (WEALTH).

capitalize on, *v.* avail oneself of, take advantage of, exploit (USE).

CAPRICE—*N.* caprice, fancy, humor, notion, conceit, whim, whimsy, crotchet, kink, quirk, freak, *capriccio* (*It.*), fad, vagary.

V. be capricious, etc. (see *Adjectives*); take it into one's head, blow hot and cold, play fast and loose.

Adj. capricious, erratic, eccentric, fitful, inconsistent, fanciful, whimsical, crotchety, freakish, wayward, wanton; contrary, captious, unreasonable, variable, changeable, mutable, inconstant, arbitrary; fickle, frivolous, giddy, flighty, volatile, notional, moody, humorsome.

See also CHANGEABLENESS, DESIRE, IRREGULARITY, IRRESOLUTION. *Antonyms*—See STABILITY.

capsize, *v.* turn over, tip, upturn (TURNING).

capsule, *n.* pill, lozenge, tablet (CURE).

captain, *n.* head, chief, chieftain (LEADERSHIP); lord, commander, commandant (RULER); commanding officer, master, skipper (SAILOR).

caption, *n.* heading, head, inscription (TITLE).

captious, *adj.* critical, faultfinding, exceptive (DISAPPROVAL).

captivate, *v.* enchant, fascinate, charm (ATTRACTION).

captive, *n.* prisoner, convict (IMPRISONMENT).

capture, *v.* catch, collar (*colloq.*), seize (TAKING); take prisoner, take captive (IMPRISONMENT); bag, net, trap (ACQUISITION).

car, *n.* conveyance, gondola, train, coach; automobile, machine (*colloq.*), motor (VEHICLE).

carbonated, *adj.* bubbly, effervescent, sparkling (FOAM).

carcass, *n.* corpse, dead body, cadaver (DEATH).

card, *n.* calling card, pasteboard (ARRIVAL); post card, postal card, postal (EPISTLE).

cardinal, *adj.* indispensable, basal, basic; main, central, chief (IMPORTANCE).

cardsharp, *n.* gambler, sharper (CHANCE).

CARE—*N.* care, solicitude, anxiety, responsibility, concern, interest, regard, concernment, apprehension, worry, trouble.

carefulness, assiduity, diligence, solicitude, pains, heed, regard, oversight, precaution, foresight, providence, prudence.

caution, circumspection, Fabian policy, *retenue* (*F.*); admonition, warning.

watchfulness, vigilance, attention, surveillance, watch, vigil, lookout.

charge, supervision, superintendence, ward, custody, tutelage, guardianship, wardship; control, direction, management, safekeeping, protection; auspices, aegis.

tender, attendant, shepherd, nurse, handmaid, handmaiden, wetnurse; caretaker, custodian, curator.

V. be careful, take care, be cautious, take precautions, beware, heed, watch out for, take heed, mind, be on one's guard, think twice, look before one leaps, count the cost, feel one's way, see how the land lies; pussyfoot (*colloq.*), keep out of harm's way, keep at a respectful distance, stand aloof, keep (*or* be) on the safe side.

take care of, pay attention to, look (*or* see) to, look after, keep an eye on, supervise, chaperon, keep watch, mount guard, watch, eye, keep in view (*or* sight), mind, tend, attend to, minister to, watch over; care for, treasure, wet-nurse, shepherd, nurture, nurse, foster, cherish.

care, reck (*poetic*), mind, notice, think, consider; feel inclined, wish, desire.

Adj. careful, assiduous, diligent, studious, calculating, considered, solicitous, heedful, regardful, mindful, precautious, foresighted, provident, prudent, religious.

cautious, chary, circumspect, discreet, Fabian, gingerly, shy, cagey (*colloq.*); overcautious, unenterprising, unadventurous.

scrupulous, meticulous, painstaking, particular, punctilious, strict, thorough, assiduous, conscientious; precise, minute, accurate, exact, elaborate.

watchful, vigilant, attentive, guarded, alert, wary, on one's guard.

See also ATTENTION, CONTROL, NERVOUSNESS, PROTECTION, WARNING. *Antonyms*—See CARELESSNESS, INATTENTION, NEGLECT, UNANXIETY.

---

careen, v. yaw, bicker, lurch, pitch (UNSTEADINESS).

career, n. profession, specialty, field (BUSINESS); orbit, pilgrimage (LIFE).

carefree, adj. unanxious, at ease, secure (UNANXIETY).

care for, v. be enamored of, fancy, be in love with (LOVE); take care of (CARE).

CARELESSNESS—*N.* carelessness, inadvertence, negligence, neglect, laxity, superficiality, pococurantism, sloppiness, etc. (see *Adjectives*).

rashness, incaution, impetuosity, indiscretion, imprudence, improvidence, recklessness, etc. (see *Adjectives*).

V. be careless of, neglect, slur over, plunge into; nap, be caught napping (*or* nodding), not think.

Adj. careless, unthinking, inadvertent, unmindful of, thoughtless, regardless of, napping; negligent, neglectful, remiss, slack; perfunctory, cursory, casual, superficial; pococurante.

rash, reckless, heedless, unwary, incautious, impetuous, harebrained, harum-scarum; precipitate, hasty, madcap; indiscreet, imprudent, improvident.

sloppy, slipshod, slovenly, untidy, lax.

See also INATTENTION, NEGLECT, SURFACE, UNANXIETY. *Antonyms*—See ATTENTION, CARE.

CARESS—*N.* caress, chuck, cuddle, embrace, hug, pat, snuggle, squeeze, stroke, endearment.

kiss, buss, osculation, smack, peck.

V. caress, bill, bill and coo, fondle, cocker, cosset, cuddle, nuzzle, hug, fold in one's arms, embrace, enfold, squeeze, snuggle, pet, pat, stroke, chuck, cosher, dandle; neck (*slang*), spoon (*colloq.*).

kiss, smack, osculate, buss, peck at.

Adj. caressible, cuddly, cuddlesome, embraceable, huggable.

caressive, affectionate, demonstrative; oscular, osculatory.

See also LOVE, TOUCH.

---

caretaker, n. supervisor, curator, custodian (CONTROL, CARE).

cargo, n. freight, load, goods (CONTENTS, TRANSFER).

caricature, n. burlesque, travesty, parody (RIDICULE, IMITATION).

carnage, n. slaughter, butchery, bloodshed (KILLING).

carnal, adj. sensual, voluptuous, fleshly (INTEMPERANCE, SEX, ANIMAL, BODY); worldly, mundane, earthly (IRRELIGION).

carnivorous, adj. omnivorous, flesh-eating, cannibal (FOOD).

carol, v. sing, harmonize (*colloq.*), croon (SINGING).

carousel, n. merry-go-round, whirligig, whirlabout (ROTATION).

carp, v. cavil, grumble, objurgate (DISAPPROVAL, COMPLAINT).

carpenter, n. woodworker, cabinetmaker, joiner (WOODWORKING).

carpet, n. rug, carpeting, runner (COVERING).

carriage, n. chariot, rig, wagonette; baby carriage, perambulator, coach (VEHICLE); air, attitude, bearing (POSTURE).

carry, v. transport, convey, conduct (TRANSFER).

carry in, v. bring in, track in, import (INTAKE).

carry off, v. kidnap, abduct, shanghai (THIEVERY).

carry out, v. execute, perform, discharge (OBSERVANCE).

cart, n. wagon, buggy, van (VEHICLE).

carton, n. box, bin, case (CONTAINER).

cartoonist, n. comic artist, caricaturist (WITTINESS, ARTIST).

carve, v. fashion, sculpture, cut, chisel (CUTTING, SHAPE, FINE ARTS).

Casanova, n. Lothario, Don Juan, rake, roué, gigolo (LOVE, SEX).

cascade, n. waterfall, fall, cataract (RIVER); precipitation, downrush (DESCENT).

case, n. box, bin, carton (CONTAINER); sheath, capsule (COVERING); example, illustration, instance (COPY); suit, action, cause (LAWSUIT).

cash, n. legal tender, funds, wherewithal (MONEY).

cashier, n. purser, paymaster, treasurer (MONEY, RECEIVING).

cask, n. barrel, drum, keg (CONTAINER).

casket, n. coffin, box, pine box (BURIAL); bin, carton, case (CONTAINER).

cast, n. form, embodiment, conformation (SHAPE); dramatis personae (L.), company, actors (DRAMA).

cast, v. fling, heave, hurl (THROW); strew, sprinkle, spatter (DISPERSION); molt, shed, slough (UNDRESS).

caste, n. estate, stratum, station (SOCIAL CLASS).

caster, n. roller, pulley, trolley (ROUNDNESS, ROTATION).

castigate, v. scold, admonish, berate (SCOLDING).

castle, n. palace, château, alcazar (BUILDING).

castoff, n. reject, scrap, discard (ELIMINATION, UNCLEANNESS).

cast off, v. shed, throw off (ELIMINATION).

castrate, v. geld, alter (CELIBACY, DISABLEMENT).

casual, adj. perfunctory, cursory, superficial (CARELESSNESS); nonchalant, pococurante, insouciant (INDIFFERENCE); informal, easygoing, offhand (NONOBSERVANCE); accidental, adventitious (OCCURRENCE).

casualty, n. debacle, misadventure, mishap (MISFORTUNE); victim, basket case (HARM).

cat, n. puss, pussy, tabby (ANIMAL).

catalogue, n. chronology, table, inventory (LIST, ROLL).

cataract, n. cascade, precipitation, downrush (DESCENT).

catarrh, n. nasal catarrh, roup, cold (COLD).

catastrophe, n. calamity, cataclysm, disaster (MISFORTUNE).

catch, n. decoy, trick, deception (TRAP); clasp, hasp, buckle (FASTENING).

catch, v. capture, collar (colloq.), seize (TAKING); lasso, hook, net (TRAP); get, contract (DISEASE).

catching, adj. infectious, communicable, contagious (DISEASE); catchy, fetching (ATTRACTION).

catch on to, v. follow, fathom, figure out (UNDERSTANDING).

catch up to, v. gain on, overtake, overhaul (TRAP).

catchword, n. byword, shibboleth, slogan (WORD).

catchy, adj. tricky, deceptive, treacherous (TRAP); catching, fetching (ATTRACTION).

category, n. classification, department, grouping (CLASS).

cathedral, n. place of worship, house of worship, temple (CHURCH).

catholic, adj. broad-minded, tolerant, liberal (IMPARTIALITY); diffuse, general, universal (PRESENCE); papal, apostolic, Roman (CHURCH).

Catholicism, n. Roman Catholicism, Romanism (derogatory), Catholic Church (RELIGION).

cattle, n. stock, kine (archaic), cows (ANIMAL); mob, canaille, crowd (PEOPLE).

Caucasian, n. white, griffin, paleface (MANKIND).

CAUSATION—N. causation, causality, origination, production, creation, development; contrivance, effectuation, generation, incurrence, inducement, precipitation, provocation, inspiration.

cause, origin, birth; prime mover, author, producer, generator, creator, determinant; parent, ancestor, antecedent, agent, leaven, factor.

pivot, hinge, axis, turning point. reason, purpose, occasion, motive, root, basis, foundation, ground, support, why or wherefore (colloq.), rationale, raison d'être (F.).

rudiment, egg, germ, embryo, root, radix, radical, nucleus, seed, sperm, semen.

V. cause, originate, give rise to, sow the seeds of; bring, bring to pass, bring about, bring on, make, produce, create, develop, set afoot;

beget, brew, contrive, effect, effectuate, engender, foment, generate, incur, induce, precipitate, provoke, prompt, inspire, occasion; maneuver, stage-manage; contribute to, conduce to, trigger, bring down, draw down, evoke, elicit.

Adj. causal, causative, generative, creative, formative, productive, effectual, effective; originative, germinal, embryonic; endogenous, exogenous.

See also ACQUISITION, AGENT, ATTRIBUTION, BEGINNING, JUSTIFICATION, MEANS, MOTIVATION, POWER. *Antonyms*—DISABLEMENT, RESULT.

caustic, *adj.* corrosive, erosive, abrasive (DESTRUCTION); cutting, biting, sarcastic (SHARPNESS).

caution, *n.* notice, caveat, admonition (WARNING); circumspection, Fabian policy, vigilance (CARE); bird (*slang*), character (*colloq.*), customer (UNUSUALNESS).

cautious, *adj.* chary, circumspect, discreet (CARE).

cave, *n.* cavern, grotto, subterrane (OPENING).

cavernous, *adj.* chambered, alveolate, socketed (HOLLOW); spacious, roomy, vast (SPACE).

cavil, *v.* carp, criticize, find fault (DISAPPROVAL).

cavity, *n.* chamber, socket, pocket (HOLLOW); bursa, atrium, sinus (OPENING).

cavort, *v.* romp, prance, caper (PLAYFULNESS, JUMP).

caw, *v.* croak, plunk, cronk (ANIMAL SOUND).

cede, *v.* relinquish, part with, render (GIVING); surrender, concede, capitulate (SUBMISSION).

ceiling, *n.* roof, roofing, housetop (COVERING); top, highest point (HEIGHT); maximum, record (SUPERIORITY).

celebrated, *adj.* storied, immortal, laureate (FAME).

CELEBRATION—*N.* celebration, solemnization, observance, commemoration.

anniversary, biennial, triennial, quadrennial, quinquennial, sextennial, septennial, octennial, decennial; silver wedding, golden wedding, diamond wedding; jubilee, diamond jubilee; centenary, centennial; sesquicentennial; bicentenary, bicentennial; tercentenary, tercentennial.

V. celebrate, keep, observe, signalize, do honor to, lionize, honor, extol, magnify, laud, applaud, glorify, commemorate, solemnize; paint the town red.

See also AMUSEMENT, APPLAUSE, FAME, HAPPINESS, MEMORY, SOCIALITY. *Antonyms*—See DEJECTION, GLOOM.

celebrity, *n.* luminary, personage, notable (FAME).

celerity, *n.* rapidity, acceleration, velocity (SPEED).

celestial, *adj.* heavenly, Olympian, empyreal (HEAVEN, WORLD); godly, godlike (GOD).

CELIBACY—*N.* celibacy, abstinence, abstention, continence, maidenhood, virginity, chastity, purity, virtue; hymen, maidenhead; impotence, frigidity, anaphrodisia.

celibate, maiden, maid, virgin, vestal virgin, vestal; eunuch, androgyne, *castrato* (*It.*); capon, gelding, steer.

V. unsex, unman, emasculate, mutilate, castrate, asexualize, sterilize, caponize, alter, spay, geld.

abstain, virgin it, maid it, refrain, sublimate.

Adj. celibate, abstinent, continent, virginal, virgin, chaste, pure, virtuous; impotent, frigid; anaphrodisiac.

sexless, neuter, asexual, epicene.

See also ASCETICISM, CONTROL, UNMARRIED STATE. *Antonyms*—See SEX.

cellar, *n.* basement, subterrane, vault (LOWNESS, SPACE).

cement, *n.* concrete, sand, mortar (ROCK); plaster, adhesive, mucilage (STICKINESS, FASTENING).

cement, *v.* weld, fuse, solder (JUNCTION, UNITY).

cemetery, *n.* charnel, golgotha, necropolis (BURIAL).

censor, *v.* blue-pencil, bowdlerize, expurgate (ELIMINATION).

censorious, *adj.* critical, captious, carping (DISAPPROVAL).

censure, *v.* chide, exprobrate, lecture, reprehend (DISAPPROVAL, SCOLDING).

CENTER—*N.* center, bull's-eye, middle, navel, omphalos, centroid; intermediacy, equidistance.

middle, midst, deep, thick; median, mean, medium, intermediate, intermediary, compromise; equator; diaphragm, midriff.

core, heart, kernel, hub, pith, focus, nucleus, pivot, axis.

V. center, centralize, concenter, concentrate, focus, focalize, medialize.

Adj. **central**, center, centric, umbilical; pivotal, axial; concentric, homocentric.

middle, halfway, midway, equidistant, medial, mid, midmost, middlemost; mean, median, medium, middling, intermediate.

Adv., phrases. **midway**, halfway, in the middle; amidships (*naut.*), *in medias res* (*L.*).

See also CONVERGENCE, MID-COURSE, *Antonyms*—See BEGINNING, BOUNDARY, END.

central, *adj.* centric, middle, pivotal (CENTER); main, cardinal, chief (IMPORTANCE); accessible, nearby (EASE).

ceremony, *n.* ceremonial, rite, ritual (FORMALITY, OBSERVANCE).

certainly, *adv.* surely, assuredly, exactly (ASSENT).

CERTAINTY—*N.* certainty, certitude, surety, etc. (see *Adjectives*).

self-assurance, self-confidence, confidence, decision, poise, brass, nerve, cheek (*colloq.*), aplomb, presumption.

assurance, insurance, guarantee, security, warranty, certification, corroboration, verification; reassurance, encouragement.

V. **be certain**, be sure, know.

bank on, depend on, rely on, trust.

make certain, make sure, assure, convince, insure, secure.

certify, guarantee, warrant, corroborate, verify, clinch; reassure, encourage; determine, decide.

Adj. **certain**, sure, decided, definite, guaranteed; incontestable, incontrovertible, indisputable, indubitable, irrefutable, undeniable, undoubted, unmistakable, unquestionable, unambiguous.

unavoidable, inevitable, inescapable, ineludible, ineluctable, unfailing.

assured, convinced, absolute, cocksure, confident, secure, positive, overconfident, presumptuous, decisive.

self-assured, self-confident, poised, nervy (*colloq.*), cheeky (*colloq.*), overweening, cocky.

Adv., phrases. **certainly**, surely, undoubtedly, indubitably, definitely, unquestionably, positively, yes, true, just so, precisely, for certain, for sure, no doubt, *sans doute* (*F.*), doubtless, to be sure, of course, without fail.

See also ASSENT, NECESSITY, STABILITY. *Antonyms*—See UNBELIEVINGNESS, UNCERTAINTY.

certificate, *n.* permit, document, paper (COMMISSION, WRITING); sheepskin (*colloq.*), diploma (LEARNING).

certify, *v.* confirm, corroborate, verify (TRUTH, DISCOVERY).

CESSATION—*N.* cessation, stoppage, discontinuance, discontinuation, interruption, hitch, intermission, respite, interval, break, breather, lull, hiatus, halt, recess, rest, truce, armistice; suspense, stop, stay, arrest, pause, block, check, deterrent, impediment, abeyance, suspension, suppression, repression; interregnum; closure, cloture (*in debate*).

deadlock, checkmate, standstill, dead stand, dead stop.

V. **cease**, discontinue, terminate, end, stay, break off, leave off, desist, refrain, quit, hold, stop, check, pull up, stop short, stall, hang fire; halt, pause, rest, come to a stand; go out, die away, wear away, pass away, lapse.

interrupt, break in, interfere, suspend, intermit, remit; obstruct, check, punctuate (*fig.*), break, divide, intersect, separate; stop, cut short, arrest, bring to a stand (*or* standstill), put an end to.

See also DISCONTINUITY, END, HINDRANCE, PREVENTION, RELINQUISHMENT, REST. *Antonyms*—See CONTINUATION.

chafe, *v.* abrade, bark, gall (RUBBING); be impatient, itch (EXPECTATION).

chaff, *n.* banter, badinage, joshing (TEASING, RIDICULE, TALK); rubbish, trash (WORTHLESSNESS).

chagrin, *n.* disgruntlement, frustration, letdown (DISAPPOINTMENT).

chagrin, *v.* humiliate, abash, confuse (HUMILIATION).

chain, *n.* sequence, suite, concatenation (LENGTH, FOLLOWING); lavaliere, locket, pendant (JEWELRY); range, ridge, cordillera (HEIGHT).

chain, *v.* tether, tie, attach (JUNCTION).

chains, *n.* trammels, bonds, fetters (RESTRAINT); bondage, enslavement, helotry (SLAVERY).

chair, *n.* bench, armchair (SEAT); helm, saddle, conn (CONTROL).

chairman, *n.* moderator, leader, symposiarch (OFFICIAL, TALK); toastmaster, master of ceremonies (BEGINNING).

challenge, *v.* brave, dare (DEFIANCE); query, question, impugn (UNBELIEVINGNESS).

chamber, *n.* bedroom, bedchamber (SLEEP); room, alcove (SPACE); cavity, socket, pocket (HOLLOW); legislature, assembly, council (LEGISLATURE).

chameleon, *n.* opportunist, time-server, prima donna (CHANGE-ABLENESS); eft, newt (ANIMAL).

champagne, *n.* sparkling wine (ALCOHOLIC LIQUOR).

champion, *n.* protector, defender, paladin (PROTECTION); partisan, ally, backer (SUPPORT, PITY); non-pareil, paragon, medalist (SU-PERIORITY); victor, master, winner (SUCCESS).

CHANCE—*N.* **chance,** accident, fortune, hap, haphazard, hazard, luck, peradventure; even chance, odds, tossup (*colloq.*), risk.

gamble, lottery, raffle, throw of the dice, fall of the cards; wager, bet, venture, stake.

speculation, plunge, flyer, pig in a poke.

opportunity, occasion, chance, main chance, last chance.

possibility, probability, likeli-hood, contingency.

game of chance, gaming, gam-bling, wagering, betting, drawing lots; gambling scheme, sweep-stakes, Irish sweepstakes, pool; wheel of fortune.

numbers, numbers game, num-bers pool, policy.

gambler, wagerer, bettor, specu-lator, wildcatter, plunger; card player, dice player, crap shooter (*slang*); bookmaker, bookie (*slang*); cardsharp, sharper, rook.

V. **take a chance,** chance it, gamble, gamble on it, risk it, tempt fortune; speculate, wildcat, plunge, take a flyer, draw lots, cast lots, toss up.

chance, happen, arrive, come, befall, turn up, fall to one's lot, be one's fate; chance upon, stum-ble on, light upon, blunder on, hit upon.

gamble, game, wager, bet, stake, venture, risk, hazard, speculate, plunge.

Adj. **chance,** accidental, adventi-tious, at random, casual, contin-gent, fortuitous, haphazard, in-cidental, random; fortunate, happy, lucky.

chancy, hazardous, risky, ven-turesome, venturous, speculative.

unintentional, unpremeditated, unforeseen, contingent, unex-pected, undesigned; incidental, ir-regular, occasional.

Adv., phrases. **by chance,** by ac-cident, at random, accidentally, fortuitously.

See also DANGER, GOOD LUCK, LIKELIHOOD, MISFORTUNE, OCCUR-RENCE, POSSIBILITY. *Antonyms*—See PLANNING, PURPOSE, UNIFORMITY.

chandelier, *n.* candelabra, candle-holder (LIGHT).

CHANGE—*N.* **change,** alteration, amendment, emendation, mutation, permutation, variation, modifica-tion, substitution, transposition; modulation, inflection, qualifica-tion, innovation, deviation, transi-tion, shift; diversion, variety, break, diversification, variegation; conversion, resolution; revolution, revulsion, vicissitude, rotation, turn; inversion, reversal, turn-about, *volte-face* (*F.*), *démarche* (*F.*), transposition, transference; alembic, leaven.

transformation, metamorphosis, transfiguration, transfigurement, transmutation; transition, metas-tasis; transubstantiation; trans-migration, metempsychosis.

[*point or time of change*] crisis, apex, turning point, zero hour, conjuncture, transition.

[*money*] **change,** small change, coins; silver, copper.

deviate, deviator, variant, muta-tion, mutant.

V. **change,** alter, vary, qualify, temper, moderate, modulate, in-flect, diversify, tamper with; turn, shift, switch, shuffle, veer, jib, tack, wear (*naut.*), swerve, deviate, diverge, deflect, take a turn, turn the corner; adapt, adjust; amend, emend.

modify, work a change, trans-form, translate, transfigure, trans-mute, convert, resolve, revolu-tionize; metamorphose, transmog-rify (*jocose*), ring the changes, alternate; innovate, introduce new blood; shuffle the cards, shift the scene, turn over a new leaf, re-form.

recast, revise, remold, recon-struct, remodel; reverse, overturn, upset, invert, transpose, exchange.

Adj. **changed,** etc. (see *Verbs*); changeable, changeful, variable, devious, transitional; newfangled, novel, different.

See also CHANGEABLENESS, DIF-FERENCE, MONEY, ROTATION. *An-tonyms*—See CONTINUATION, STA-BILITY.

CHANGEABLENESS—*N.* change-ableness, modifiability, mutability, versatility, volatility, mobility; in-stability, vacillation, variability, irresolution, indecision, fluctuation, vicissitude; alternation, oscillation; inconstancy, transilience, unreliability, whimsicality, caprice.

adaptability, flexibility, transience, resilience.

[*comparisons*] **moon**, Proteus, chameleon, kaleidoscope, quicksilver, shifting sands, weathercock, vane, weathervane, wheel of fortune.

[*changeable person*] **chameleon**, opportunist, timeserver, prima donna.

V. **be changeable, etc.** (see *Adjectives*); fluctuate, oscillate, vary, waver, shift, vacillate, sway, shift to and fro, alternate.

Adj. **changeable**, alterable, modifiable, mutable, various, variable, versatile, many-sided, kaleidoscopic, abrupt, transilient, protean, chameleon-like, chameleonic, opportunistic, timeserving.

unconstant, changeful, uncertain, unsteady, unstable, unreliable, vacillating, unfixed, fluctuating, wavering, erratic, tangential, fickle, changing, checkered, irresolute, indecisive; capricious, arbitrary, freakish, moody, moonish, streaky, temperamental, whimsical, volatile, skittish, mercurial, irregular, vagrant, wayward; unsettled.

adaptable, flexible, supple, transient, resilient; mobile, movable, plastic.

[*subject to change*] **mutable**, fluid, provisional, tentative, temporary.

[*of colors*] **iridescent**, nacreous, prismatic, rainbowlike, iridian, opalescent, chatoyant.

See also APOSTASY, CAPRICE, CHANGE, IMPERMANENCE, IRREGULARITY, IRRESOLUTION, OSCILLATION. *Antonyms*—See CONTINUATION, DEPENDABILITY, STABILITY, UNIFORMITY.

channel, *n.* ditch, chase, gully (HOLLOW); aqueduct, conduit, culvert (PASSAGE, CHANNEL); bed, race, river bed (LAND); means, agent, medium (INSTRUMENT).

CHANNEL—*N.* **channel**, conduit, duct, watercourse, race, run; raceway, fishway, fish ladder; cañon *or* canyon, coulee, *coulée* (*F.*), gorge, flume, ravine, chasm; aqueduct, canal; gully, arroyo (*Southwest U.S.*), gulch; moat, ditch, dike, gutter, drain, sewer, main, cloaca, culvert; scupper (*naut.*); funnel, trough, siphon, pump, hose; pipe, tube, waterspout, spout, gargoyle; weir, floodgate, water gate, sluice, lock, valve,

sound, strait, neck, fairway; tideway.

See also OPENING, PASSAGE, TRANSFER.

chant, *v.* sing, intonate, cantillate (SINGING); drone, intone (TALK); hymn, doxologize (WORSHIP).

chaos, *n.* anarchy, pandemonium, tumult (CONFUSION).

chapel, *n.* conventicle, oratory (CHURCH); devotions, services, prayer (WORSHIP).

chaperon, *n.* duenna, escort (ACCOMPANIMENT).

chapped, *adj.* rough, cracked (ROUGHNESS).

chapter, *n.* unit, wing, branch (PART); division, section (BOOK).

character, *n.* nature, make-up (CHARACTER); letter, symbol (WRITTEN SYMBOL); numeral, figure (NUMBER); role, impersonation (PART); eccentric (UNUSUALNESS).

CHARACTER—*N.* **character**, nature, temper, temperament, make-up, mettle, emotions, disposition, crasis, personality, constitution; complexion, caliber, ethos.

characteristic, quality, property, attribute, cachet, trait, mannerism; peculiarity, feature, distinction, idiosyncrasy, idiocrasy; savor, streak, vein, tone, token.

eccentricity, foible, idiosyncrasy, idiocrasy, kink, oddity, peculiarity, quirk.

humors (*old physiol.*), blood, phlegm, choler *or* yellow bile, melancholy *or* black bile.

attitude, disposition, habitude, outlook, sentiment, slant, stand, standpoint, turn (*or* bent) of mind, viewpoint, point of view.

V. **characterize**, feature, belong to, symbolize, represent, typify, make up, constitute.

[*have the characteristics of*] **savor of**, smack of, partake of.

Adj. **constitutional**, temperamental, attitudinal, emotional.

[*of the same or similar nature*] **connatural**, connate, cognate.

characteristic, distinctive, distinguishing, peculiar, specific, typical, idiosyncratic, manneristic; [*of a region*] local, regional, vernacular.

See also FEELING, MAKE-UP, TEXTURE, UNUSUALNESS.

characterize, *v.* feature, typify (CHARACTER); differentiate, distinguish (DIFFERENCE); delineate, depict (DESCRIPTION).

charge, *n.* cost, amount, price (EX-PENDITURE); complaint (ACCUSATION); supervision, superintendence, custody (CARE, CONTROL); instructions, directions (COMMAND).

charge, *v.* levy, impose, demand (EXPENDITURE); rush, dash (SPEED, VIOLENCE, ATTACK); cram, crowd (FULLNESS); aerate, carbonate (GAS); accuse, tax (ACCUSATION).

charitable, *adj.* magnanimous, forgiving, generous (FORGIVENESS, UNSELFISHNESS); eleemosynary, philanthropic, benevolent (CHARITY).

charity, *n.* placability, magnanimity (FORGIVENESS); quarter, grace, mercy (PITY); generosity (UNSELFISHNESS); philanthropy, almsgiving (CHARITY).

CHARITY—*N.* charity, largesse, almsgiving, philanthropy, alms, oblation, donation, dole, relief, benefaction, handout (*colloq.*), contribution, widow's mite.

donor, contributor, almsgiver, almoner, philanthropist, benefactor.

almshouse, poorhouse, bedehouse, almonry.

almsman, pauper, mendicant, beggar.

V. donate, contribute, subscribe, hand out, dole out, give.

Adj. charitable, eleemosynary, philanthropic, beneficent, benevolent, generous, openhanded, freehanded, kind.

See also BEGGING, FORGIVENESS, GIVING, KINDNESS, PITY, POVERTY, RECEIVING, UNSELFISHNESS.

charlatan, *n.* empiric, mountebank, quack (PRETENSE, MEDICAL SCIENCE).

charm, *n.* enchantment, fascination, delightfulness (ATTRACTION); spell, hex (MAGIC); amulet, talisman, periapt (GOOD LUCK, JEWELRY).

charm, *v.* please, delight, enchant (PLEASANTNESS); allure, inveigle, entice (ATTRACTION); bewitch, becharm (MAGIC).

charming, *adj.* delightful, lovely (PLEASANTNESS); winsome, engaging (LOVE).

chart, *n.* diagram, sketch (SHAPE); cartogram, plat (MAP).

charter, *n.* patent, franchise, license (PERMISSION); code, constitution (LAW).

charter, *v.* hire, engage, rent (BORROWING).

chase, *n.* hunt, pursuit, quest (SEARCH).

chase, *v.* hunt, pursue (FOLLOWING); course, gun (HUNTING); engrave, enchase (ENGRAVING).

chasm, *n.* gorge, flume (CHANNEL); crater, abyss (OPENING).

chaste, *adj.* virginal, pure, virtuous (CELIBACY, PURIFICATION); maidenly, proper (MODESTY); unpretentious, severe (SIMPLICITY, MODESTY).

chastise, *v.* whip, flog, cowhide (HITTING, PUNISHMENT).

chat, *n.* conversation, tête-à-tête (*F.*), colloquy (TALK).

chatter, *v.* babble, chaffer, gibber (TALK).

chauffeur, *n.* driver, autoist, motorist (VEHICLE).

chauvinism, *n.* nationalism, public spirit, jingoism (PATRIOTISM).

cheap, *adj.* cut-rate, nominal, low-priced (INEXPENSIVENESS); contemptible, abject (CONTEMPT); common, ordinary (COMMONNESS); catchpenny, tinsel (WORTHLESSNESS).

cheapen, *v.* beat down, reduce, lower (INEXPENSIVENESS); decline, depreciate, fall (devaluate, depress (WORTHLESSNESS); vulgarize (COMMONNESS); minimize (DETRACTION); degrade, abase (CONTEMPT).

cheat, *v.* swindle, defraud, fleece (DECEPTION, THIEVERY).

check, *n.* bill, chit, tab (DEBT, ACCOUNTS); plaid, tartan (VARIEGATION); restrainer, curb (RESTRAINT); audit, review (EXAMINATION); trial (TEST).

check, *v.* audit, inspect, overlook (EXAMINATION); examine, quiz, analyze (TEST); tame, curb, restrain (RESTRAINT, MODERATENESS); choke, stunt, retard (SLOWNESS).

checked, *adj.* checkered, mosaic, tessellated (VARIEGATION).

checkmate, *n.* deadlock, standstill, dead stop (CESSATION).

checkmated, *adj.* foiled, thwarted, balked (FAILURE).

cheek, *n.* boldness, audacity, effrontery (DISCOURTESY, CERTAINTY).

cheep, *v.* chirp, twitter, tweet (ANIMAL SOUND, HIGH-PITCHED SOUND).

cheer, *v.* encourage, hearten, inspirit (HOPE, APPROVAL); enliven (CHEERFULNESS).

cheerfully, *adv.* willingly, readily, gladly (WILLINGNESS).

CHEERFULNESS—*N.* cheerfulness, cheer, cheeriness, geniality, gayety, buoyancy, good humor, good spirits, high spirits, light heart, merriment, bonhomie, hilarity, jocundity, jollity, joviality, effervescence, ebullience, ebullition, insouciance; exhilaration, comfort, consolation, encouragement, solace.

V. be cheerful, smile, keep up one's spirits, cheer up, take heart, cast away care, look on the sunny side, perk up, effervesce, brighten, tread (or walk) on air.

cheer, enliven, elate, exhilarate, delight, gladden, blithen, lighten, encourage, hearten, brighten, console, solace, comfort, boost (or raise) the spirits of, buck up (colloq.).

Adj. cheerful, cheery, sunny, beaming, riant, smiling, winsome, blithe, blitheful, blithesome, blithehearted, in good spirits, gay, debonair, light, lightsome, lighthearted, glad, good-natured, good-humored; roseate, rosy, rose-colored, optimistic, hopeful, bright, breezy, airy, jaunty, sprightly, lively, chipper (colloq.); jocund, jovial, jolly, hilarious, ebullient, effervescent, exhilarated, merry.

buoyant, elastic, resilient, supple.

cheering, brightening, cheery, exhilarating, exhilarant, exhilarative, exhilaratory, genial, glad, gladsome, gladdening, winsome, comforting, comfortable, consoling, consolatory, encouraging, enlivening, heartening, solacing.

See also HAPPINESS, HOPE, MERRIMENT, PLEASANTNESS. Antonyms —See DEJECTION, GLOOM, SADNESS, UNPLEASANTNESS.

cheerless, adj. bleak, dismal, dreary (GLOOM, DEJECTION); uncomfortable, jarring (UNPLEASANTNESS).

chemise, n. camisole, slip, shift (UNDERWEAR).

cherish, v. enshrine, prize, treasure (LOVE); cling to, nourish (HOLD); harbor, entertain, imagine (THOUGHT).

cherub, n. angel, seraph, archangel (ANGEL); roly-poly, punchinello (SIZE).

chest, n. box, bin, carton (CONTAINER); bosom, bust (BREAST).

chestbone, n. breastbone, sternum (BONE).

chestnut, adj. red-haired, auburn, sandy, Titian (RED).

chew, v. crunch, masticate, gnaw (FOOD).

chic, adj. fashionable, current, modish (FASHION).

chicanery, n. sharp practices, cozenage, skullduggery (DECEPTION).

chicken, n. poultry, fowl, hen (BIRD).

chide, v. censure, exprobrate, lecture (SCOLDING, DISAPPROVAL).

chief, adj. main, stellar, head (LEADERSHIP); crucial, cardinal, central (IMPORTANCE); preeminent, foremost, principal (SUPERIORITY).

chief, n. head, leader, captain (LEADERSHIP, RANK).

chief executive, n. chief magistrate, governor, mayor (OFFICIAL).

CHILD—N. child, infant, babe, baby, little one, kid (slang), moppet, bairn (Scot.), bambino, bantling, bud, chick, chit, nestling, shaver, sprat, tad, tot, tyke; whelp, youngster, cherub, elf, papoose (N. Amer. Indian), pickaninny, urchin; neonate, suckling, nursling, weanling; orphan; minor (law), ward; foundling, changeling, waif; brat, enfant terrible (F.), oaf, ragamuffin, ugly duckling.

offspring, descendant, scion, heir, sibling; daughter, son, cadet, foster child, fosterling; stepchild.

children, family, issue (law), progeny, seed, spawn (derog.), brood, flock, procreation, generation; small fry (colloq.).

descendant, scion, sprig (jocose), collateral descendant, filiation, offset, offshoot.

descendants, posterity, stock, seed, generations unborn.

mischievous child, devil, devilkin, elf, imp, rascal, rogue, scamp, urchin, villain.

twin, fraternal twin, identical twin, Siamese twin; triplet, quadruplet, quintuplet, sextuplet, septuplet.

unborn child, embryo, foetus, homunculus.

childhood, infancy, babyhood, youth.

nursery, day nursery, crèche; orphanage, orphan asylum.

bastard, bantling, by-blow, illegitimate child, love-child (colloq.).

bastardy, bastardism, illegitimacy; bar sinister, bend sinister.

upbringing, breeding, nurture, rearing, uprearing.

V. bring up (a child), breed, foster, nurture, raise, rear, suckle, uprear, nurse.

gurgle, guggle, babble, crow.

Adj. childish, childlike, babyish, babylike, immature, infantile, infantine, juvenile, panty-waist (colloq.), puerile, pedomorphic.

bastard, baseborn, illegitimate, natural, unfathered.

See also IMMATURITY, YOUTH. *Antonyms*—See ANCESTRY, OLDNESS.

childbirth, *n.* childbearing, confinement, delivery (BIRTH).

chill, *v.* refrigerate, cool, air-condition (COLD); discourage, dishearten, dismay (DEJECTION, HOPELESSNESS).

chilly, *adj.* cool, frigid, unfriendly (HOSTILITY, COLD).

chime, *n.* gong, carillon (BELL).

chimney, *n.* flue, ventilator (AIR OPENING).

chimpanzee, *n.* monkey, baboon, drill (ANIMAL).

china, *n.* crockery, Dresden, Limoges (CONTAINER).

Chinese, *n.* Oriental, Celestial (MANKIND).

chink, *v.* tinkle, jingle, clink (RESONANCE).

chip, *v.* break, crack, splinter (BREAKAGE).

chirp, *v.* warble, trill, cheep (SINGING, ANIMAL SOUND).

chisel, *v.* hew, roughhew, roughcast (SHAPE).

chivalrous, *adj.* courtly, gallant, quixotic (COURTESY).

CHOICE—*N.* choice, option, election, selection, discrimination, predilection, discretion, preference, volition, adoption, decision, cooption; alternative, horn of a dilemma, pick, cull, Hobson's choice; extract, chrestomathy.

V. **choose,** elect, make one's choice, fix upon, settle, decide, determine, make up one's mind; cross the Rubicon.

select, pick, cull, glean, winnow, sift out, single out, prefer, fancy, have rather, had (*or* would) as lief; excerpt, extract, garble.

Adj. **choice,** select, chosen, elect, selected, popular, preferential, preferred.

optional, facultative, alternative, elective, eligible, electoral, discretionary, voluntary, volitional, preferable.

choosy, fastidious, picky, dainty, delicate, discriminating, discriminative, discriminatory, finical, finicky, fussy, particular, pernickety, prissy, queasy, squeamish; eclectic, select, selective.

Phrases. **by choice,** by preference; in preference, first, sooner, rather; at pleasure, at the option of.

See also DESIRE, JUDGMENT, TAKING, VOICE, VOTE, WILL. *Antonyms*—See DENIAL, NECESSITY.

choir, *n.* chorus, glee club, ensemble (SINGING).

choke, *v.* throttle, smother, strangle (PRESSURE, KILLING); stuff, congest, clog (FULLNESS); check, stunt, retard (SLOWNESS).

choose, *v.* pick, select (CHOICE).

chop, *v.* mangle, hack, hackle (CUTTING).

choppy, *adj.* violent, wild, inclement (ROUGHNESS).

chops, *n.* jaws, snout, muzzle (HEAD).

choral, *adj.* cantabile, lyric, vocal (SINGING, MUSIC).

chord, *n.* scale, key, clef (MUSIC).

chore, *n.* stint, task, job (WORK).

chortle, *v.* cackle, chuckle, giggle (LAUGHTER).

chorus, *n.* choir, glee club, ensemble (SINGING); refrain, burden, ritornelle (REPETITION).

CHRIST—*N.* Christ, Jesus, Jesus Christ, the Lord, the Messiah, the Nazarene, the Saviour; the Anointed, the Redeemer, the Mediator, the Intercessor, the Advocate, the Judge; the Son of God, the Son of Man; the Only-Begotten, the Lamb of God, the Word, Logos; the Man of Sorrows; Jesus of Nazareth, King of the Jews, the Son of Mary, the Risen, Immanuel, the Prince of Peace, the Good Shepherd, the Way, the Door, the Truth, the Life, the Bread of Life, the Light of the World.

[*beliefs or doctrines about Christ*] Adventism, chiliasm, millenarianism, millenialism, psilanthropy.

The Virgin Mary, the Holy Virgin, the Madonna, Mater Dolorosa.

See also RELIGION, SACREDNESS. *Antonyms*—See IRRELIGION.

christen, *v.* baptize, godfather, name (NAME).

Christian, *n.* Catholic, Protestant, gentile (RELIGION).

Christmas, *n.* Noel, yuletide (AMUSEMENT).

chronicle, *n.* history, annals, almanac (PAST, RECORD).

chronological, *adj.* temporal, junctural (TIME).

chronology, *n.* chronography, chronometry, calendar (TIME MEASUREMENT).

chubby, *adj.* fat, plump, buxom (SIZE).

chuck, *v.* toss, twirl, cant, flip (THROW); caress, stroke, pat, pet (CARESS, TOUCH).

chuckle, *v.* laugh, cackle, chortle (LAUGHTER).

chum (*colloq.*), *n.* comrade, pal (*slang*), companion (FRIEND).

chunky, *adj.* scrub, stocky, dumpy (SHORTNESS).

CHURCH—*N.* church, house of worship, fane (*archaic*), house of God, house of prayer; cathedral, minster, basilica, kirk (*Scot.*), chapel, conventicle, oratory; abbey, bethel, Catholicity, fold, parish, tabernacle, Zion.

churchgoer, parishioner, worshiper; congregation, flock; novice, novitiate.

temple, synagogue, sanctuary, shrine, holy place, mosque (*Moham.*), pagoda, Chinese temple, joss house (*colloq.*), pantheon.

Adj. **ecclesiastic,** spiritual, parochial, cathedral, abbatial, tabernacular, synagogical; Catholic, papal, apostolic, Roman.

See also CLERGY, RELIGION, RELIGIOUS COMMUNITY, SACREDNESS. *Antonyms*—See IRRELIGION, LAITY.

cigar, *n.* Havana, cheroot, stogie (TOBACCO).

cigarette, *n.* butt (*colloq.*), tailor-made, smoke (TOBACCO).

cinch, *n* push-over, snap, setup (EASE).

cinema, *n.* movie (*colloq.*), film, flicker (MOTION PICTURES).

cipher, *n.* secret writing, code, cryptography (WRITING); nonentity, nobody, insignificancy (UNIMPORTANCE); zero, naught, ought (NONEXISTENCE).

circle, *n.* ring, circlet, band (ROUNDNESS, JEWELRY); clique, coterie, society (FRIEND); orbit, scope, field (POWER).

circle, *v.* gyrate, roll, circulate (ROTATION, ROUNDNESS).

circuit, *n.* cycle, orbit, zone (ROUNDNESS).

circular, *adj.* round, rounded, spheroid (ROUNDNESS).

circular, *n.* handbill, poster, notice (PUBLICATION).

circulate, *v.* circle, gyrate, mill around (ROUNDNESS); issue, bring out, broadcast (PUBLICATION, SENDING); be current, be received (PASSAGE).

circumference, *n.* girth, perimeter, periphery (MEASUREMENT).

circumscribe, *v.* bound, confine, delimit (BOUNDARY).

circumscribed, *adj.* narrow, limited, cramped (NARROWNESS).

circumstance, *n.* episode, occasion, happening (OCCURRENCE).

circumstances, *n.* position, status, situation (CONDITION).

circumstantial, *adj.* concurrent, incidental, fortuitous (OCCURRENCE); detailed, amplified (DETAIL).

circumstantiate, *v.* establish, authenticate, confirm (PROOF).

circumvent, *v.* avoid, prevent, stave off (AVOIDANCE, PREVENTION).

cite, *v.* mention, enumerate, specify (TALK); recite, quote (REPETITION).

CITIZEN—*N.* citizen, civilian, subject; citizens, citizenry, body politic, commonwealth; citizenship, naturalization, enfranchisement, civism, civics; civil liberty, civil rights, Bill of Rights.

immigrant, alien; emigrant, expatriate.

V. **make a citizen of,** naturalize, enfranchise; immigrate, emigrate.

Adj. **civil,** civic, civilian, political.

See also INGRESS, INHABITANT, SERVICE. *Antonyms*—See EXCLUSION.

CITY—*N.* city, municipality, metropolis, megalopolis, town, township, burg (*colloq.*), capital, county seat, borough; suburb, suburbs, village, hamlet.

city dweller, urbanite, town dweller, townsman, oppidan, citizen, metropolitan, megalopolitan; suburbanite, villager, exurbanite; suburbia.

V. **citify,** urbanize, metropolitanize.

Adj. **urban,** civic, municipal, oppidan, citified, metropolitan, megalopolitan; suburban; interurban, intraurban.

See also CITIZEN, HABITATION, INHABITANT. *Antonyms*—See LAND, RURAL REGION.

civil, *adj.* polite, courteous, well-mannered (COURTESY); civic, civilian, political (GOVERNMENT, CITIZEN).

civilian, *n.* private citizen, subject (CITIZEN).

civilization, *n.* cultivation, refinement, culture (IMPROVEMENT).

clad, *adj.* clothed, dressed, appareled (CLOTHING).

claim, *n.* title, interest, privilege (RIGHT, TITLE); counterclaim, lien (DEMAND).

clairvoyant, *adj.* telepathic, extrasensory, psychic (TELEPATHY); farseeing, far-sighted, longsighted (FORESIGHT).

clammy, *adj.* slimy, muculent, mucid (STICKINESS).

clamor, *n.* uproar, hubbub (LOUDNESS); shouting, tumult (SHOUT).

clamp, *n.* vise, brace, grip (PRESSURE, HOLD).

clan, *n.* tribe, race, stock (RELATIVE).

clandestine, *adj.* surreptitious, stealthy, furtive (CONCEALMENT).

clannish, *adj.* select, restrictive, cliquish (EXCLUSION).

clap, *n.* applause, handclap (APPROVAL); thunder, thunderclap, crash (LOUDNESS).

CLARITY—N. clarity, lucidity, limpidity, lucency, luminosity, pellucidity, unambiguity, precision, trenchancy, perspicuity, specificity; transparency, simplicity, tangibility, palpability, intelligibility.

V. clarify, explain, clear, clear up, make clear, become clear; elucidate, illuminate, illumine, illustrate, uncloud, vivify, expound; solve, resolve, ravel, ravel out, unravel, untangle.

Adj. clear, crystalline, limpid, lucent, lucid, pellucid, transparent; cloudless, azure, serene, unclouded, uncloudy, crisp; plain, distinct, articulate, shrill, clarion; inescapable, conspicuous, palpable, tangible, graphic, vivid; clear-cut, definite, decided, pronounced; understandable, intelligible, unambiguous, unequivocal, unmistakable, precise, trenchant, perspicuous, simple, explicit, categorical, specific; evident, obvious, undisguised, manifest, apparent, patent, self-evident, axiomatic.

See also DISCOVERY, EXPLANATION, TRANSPARENCY, UNDERSTANDING. *Antonyms*—See CONCEALMENT, CONFUSION, DARKNESS, MYSTERY, UNCLEARNESS, VISIBILITY.

clash, *n.* discord, discordance, disharmony (DISAGREEMENT); battle, conflict, fight (FIGHTING).

clash, *v.* grate, jar, grind (HARSH SOUND); battle, conflict, contend (FIGHTING).

clasp, *n.* catch, hasp, buckle (FASTENING, HOLD).

clasp, *v.* grasp, grip, clutch (TAKING).

class, *v.* rank, classify, grade (RANK).

CLASS—N. class, classification, category, denomination, department, grade, quality, group, bracket, tier, rank, section, division, subdivision.

kind, sort, description, character, assortment, variety, style, type, brand, cast, color, feather, genre, ilk, manner, kidney, mold, nature, persuasion, stamp, stripe.

family, genus, order, phylum, race, breed, species, stock, strain.

Adj. kindred, consubstantial, homogeneous, congeneric.

assorted, hybrid, mixed, mongrel, multifarious, manifold, omnifarious, varied, variegated, various, varicolored.

See also ARRANGEMENT, ASSEMBLAGE, LEARNING, RANK, SOCIAL CLASS. *Antonyms*—See MIXTURE.

classes, *n.* upper crust, bon ton, society (SOCIAL CLASS).

classical, *adj.* scholastic, academic, liberal (LEARNING); literary, bookish, belletristic (STORY); simple, chaste, Attic (SIMPLICITY).

classics, *n.* literature, letters, belles-lettres (*F.*), humanities (STORY).

classified, *adj.* secret, restricted, top-secret (CONCEALMENT).

classify, *v.* grade, assort, categorize (ARRANGEMENT, RANK).

classmate, *n.* fellow student, condisciple, schoolfellow (LEARNING).

classroom, *n.* schoolroom, recitation room, lecture room (SCHOOL).

clatter, *n.* racket, rattle, clangor (ROLL, COMMOTION).

clatter, *v.* smash, crash, roar (LOUDNESS).

claw, *n.* nail, fingernail (APPENDAGE).

claw, *v.* scratch, scratch about, scrabble (CUTTING).

clay, *n.* earth, argil, potter's clay (LAND).

clean-cut, *adj.* well-defined, sharp-cut, clear (SHARPNESS).

CLEANNESS—N. cleanness, purity, cleanliness, immaculacy; asepsis, sterility; cleansing, abstersion, purgation, purification; disinfection, antisepsis, fumigation, sterilization, sanitation.

bath, shower bath, sponge bath, sitz bath, Turkish bath.

bathroom, lavatory, powder room, rest room, washroom; toilet, latrine, sanitary, urinal, urinary, closet, water closet, cloaca, head (*naut.*), john (*slang*), can (*slang*), outhouse, privy; comfort station.

washing, wash, bath, douche, gargle, rinse, shampoo, ablution, lavage (*med.*), lavation.

cleaner, washerwoman, scrubwoman, laundress, laundryman, washerman; street cleaner, scavenger, street sweeper, whitewing.

brush, broom, besom, clothes brush, wisp, whisk, whisk broom.

cleanser, abstergent, detergent, duster, mop, pumice, scouring powder, sponge, swab, washer, wiper, abluent; dentifrice, toothpaste, tooth powder.

strainer, colander, riddle, sieve, sifter.

antiseptic, disinfectant, fumigant, sterilizer.

V. clean, cleanse, absterge, brush, débride (*med.*), deterge, dry-clean, dust, mop, pumice, purge, scavenge, scour, scrub, sponge, swab, sweep, vacuum, wash, wipe; antisepticize, disinfect, fumigate, sterilize, sanitize; bowdlerize, censor, expurgate.

wash, douche, gargle, launder, lave, rinse, shampoo, swill.

bathe, lave, shower, tub.

comb, rake, scrape, rasp; card, hackle.

strain, riddle, sieve, sift, drain, separate, screen, winnow.

Adj. clean, cleanly, pure, immaculate, spotless, stainless, snowy, neat, spick-and-span.

unstained, spotless, stainless, unblemished, unblotched, unblotted, unblurred, immaculate, unsmeared, unsmudged, unsmutched, unsplotched, unspotted, unsullied, untarnished.

sanitary, hygienic, uncontaminated, uninfected; aseptic, antiseptic, disinfected, sterile.

See also NEATNESS, PURIFICATION, RUBBING, WHITENESS. *Antonyms—* See UNCLEANNESS.

---

clear, *adj.* cloudless, limpid, lucid (CLARITY, TRANSPARENCY); audible, distinct, plain, definite, evident (LISTENING, VISIBILITY); light, bright, sunny (LIGHT); readable, legible, decipherable, intelligible (READING, UNDERSTANDING).

clear, *v.* uncloud, clear up, explain (CLARITY); exonerate, absolve (ACQUITTAL); hurdle, jump over, vault (JUMP).

clear-cut, *adj.* well-defined, sharp-cut, distinct (SHARPNESS).

cleavage, *n.* break, fracture, severance (DISJUNCTION).

cleave, *v.* adhere, cohere, cling (STICKINESS); sever, split; pierce, stab (CUTTING).

cleft, *adj.* pierced, cloven, perforated (CUTTING); cracked, crannied, crenelated (OPENING).

clemency, *n.* leniency, mercy, charity (PITY).

clench, *v.* contract, constrict, constringe (TRACTION).

CLERGY—*N.* clergy, clerical order, clergymen, clericals, ministry, priesthood, the cloth, the pulpit, the desk; the First Estate, the Lords Spiritual, the Spiritualty; canonicate, canonry, cardinalate, deaconry, diaconate, pastorate, prelacy, presbyterate, rabbinate, episcopacy, episcopate; conclave.

clergyman, divine, ecclesiastic, priest, churchman, cleric, pastor, shepherd, minister, preacher, parson, father, padre, abbé (*F.*), curé (*F.*); reverend (*colloq.*), canon, cassock, chaplain, deacon, prelate, presbyter, pulpiteer (*derogatory*), rector, shaveling (*derogatory*), vicar; archbishop, archdeacon bishop, cardinal, dean, metropolitan, monsignor, pontiff, primate; patriarch; rabbi.

Pope, Pontiff, Bishop of Rome, Holy Father, His Holiness, Pontifex.

[*other church officers*] sexton, verger, churchwarden, warden, elder, vestryman, beadle.

[*residence*] parsonage, rectory, manse, pastorage, pastorate, presbytery, deanery, decanate, Vatican.

Adj. ecclesiastical, clerical, ministerial, pastoral, priestly, rabbinical, sacerdotal, churchly, episcopal; papal, pontifical, apostolic.

ordained, in orders, in holy orders.

See also CHURCH, PREACHING, RELIGION, RELIGIOUS COMMUNITY. *Antonyms—*See IRRELIGION, LAITY.

---

clerk, *n.* employee, worker, office worker (WORK); secretary, registrar, transcriber (RECORD, WRITER).

CLEVERNESS—*N.* cleverness, ingenuity, calculation, discernment, sagacity, wisdom.

cunning, craft, subtlety, subtilty, deceit, disingenuity, strategy; chicanery, sharp practice, trickery, knavery, jugglery, guile, duplicity, foul play.

V. be cunning, scheme, plot, intrigue, live by one's wits; maneuver, circumvent, outdo, get the better of, outsmart, outwit.

Adj. clever, brainy, bright, habile, ingenious, resourceful, smart.

shrewd, cagey, calculating, canny, cunning, cute, discerning, hardheaded, politic, sagacious, wise.

cunning, artful, crafty, designing, diabolic, disingenuous, foxy, vulpine, retiary, slick, sly, wily, subtle, subtile, tricky, deep-laid.

See also ABILITY, DECEPTION, IN-

TELLIGENCE, PRETENSE. *Antonyms*—
See SIMPLICITY, STUPIDITY, TRUTH.

cliché, *n.* counterword, bromide, platitude (COMMONNESS).

client, *n.* purchaser, customer, patron (PURCHASE); protégée, ward (PROTECTION).

cliff, *n.* precipice, rocky height, bluff (HEIGHT).

climate, *n.* weather, clime (AIR).

climax, *n.* crisis, turning point, climacteric (IMPORTANCE); tip, tiptop, zenith (HEIGHT); orgasm (SEX).

climb, *v.* mount, scale, clamber (ASCENT).

cling, *v.* adhere, cleave, cohere (STICKINESS); cherish, nourish (HOLD); continue, linger, last (REMAINDER).

clinic, *n.* hospital, infirmary, surgery (CURE); seminar, institute (LEARNING).

clink, *v.* tinkle, jingle, chink (RESONANCE).

clip, *n.* fastener, binder, brace (FASTENING).

clip, *v.* trim, prune, truncate (CUTTING, SHORTNESS); paste (*slang*), sock (*colloq.*), punch (HITTING).

clique, *n.* circle, coterie, set (FRIEND, COMBINATION).

cloak, *n.* cape, manteau, wrap (COAT); disguise, mask, veil (PRETENSE).

clock, *n.* chronometer, watch, timer (TIME MEASUREMENT).

clog, *n.* block, impediment, bar (RESTRAINT, HINDRANCE).

clog up, *v.* stuff, glut, congest (FULLNESS).

cloister, *n.* abbey, priory, priorate, hermitage, monastery (RELIGIOUS COMMUNITY, SECLUSION).

close, *adj.* stuffy, oppressive, stifling (HEAT); intimate, dear, familiar (FRIENDLINESS, NEARNESS); near, near at hand (NEARNESS); approximate (SIMILARITY); faithful, lifelike, accurate (COPY); hairbreadth, bare (NARROWNESS); circumscribed, confined, cramped (NARROWNESS); firm, fast, tight (JUNCTION); dense, compact, impenetrable (THICKNESS).

close, *v.* shut, bolt, seal (CLOSURE); finish, terminate, conclude (COMPLETENESS, END).

closefisted, *adj.* stingy, tight, penurious (STINGINESS).

closemouthed, *adj.* taciturn, uncommunicative, tight-lipped (SILENCE).

closet, *n.* repository, depository, cupboard (CONTAINER).

CLOSURE—*N.* closure, blockade, obstruction, bar, embolism, occlusion, imperforation; contraction.

bolt, fastener, fastening, latch, lock, padlock, seal, closure; bung, cork, occludent, plug, stopper, stopple, tampon, tap.

V. **close,** bolt, fasten, bar, latch, lock, padlock, seal, secure, shut, slam; plug, block up, stop up, fill up, cork up, button up, stuff up, dam up, blockade, barricade; obstruct, occlude, choke, throttle; bung, calk, stopper, stopple.

wink, twink, twinkle, bat, blink, nictitate.

Adj. **closed,** shut, secured, unopened; unpierced, impervious, impermeable, impenetrable; impassable, pathless, wayless, blind.

See also CESSATION, END, HINDRANCE. *Antonyms*—See FREEDOM, OPENING.

clot, *v.* thicken, congeal, coagulate (THICKNESS).

cloth, *n.* fabric, textile, material (TEXTURE).

CLOTHING—*N.* clothing, clothes, things, dress, covering, raiment, attire, array, habiliment, garments, garb, apparel, wearing apparel, duds (*colloq.*), togs (*colloq.*), trappings, toggery, wraps; finery, frippery, gaudery, caparison, panoply; sportswear, sports clothes, casual wear; mufti, plain clothes; baby clothes, smallclothes, swaddling clothes.

outfit, costume, robe, gown, ensemble, suit, wardrobe, trousseau.

canonicals, clericals, pontificals; surplice, cassock, alb, scapular.

uniform, livery, habit, regalia, robe, gown; khaki, olive-drabs, regimentals.

dressing gown, duster, housecoat, house gown, kimono, negligée, peignoir, robe, bathrobe, *robe-de-chambre* (F.), wrapper.

outer clothing, overclothes, outer dress, outer garments, outwear, overgarments, wraps.

formal dress, formal wear, dinner clothes, dress clothes, evening dress, full dress, soup-and-fish (*slang*), tails (*colloq.*); cutaway coat, dress coat, dress suit, fulldress suit, swallow-tailed coat, tail coat; tuxedo, dinner coat, dinner jacket, shell jacket, mess jacket (*mil.* or *naval*).

evening gown, formal gown, cocktail gown, dinner gown.

V. **clothe,** dress, apparel, array, attire, habilitate, garb, raiment, outfit, robe, tog, caparison, livery, costume, habit, panoply, swaddle, bundle up, wrap; endue, invest; bedizen, dizen, dandify, doll up, prank, primp, prink, spruce, titivate, overdress.

get dressed, make one's toilet, preen; wear, don, draw on, get into, get on, pull on, put on, slip into, slip on.

Adj. clothed, clad, dressed, etc. (see *Verbs*).

dapper, groomed, well-groomed, spruce, *soigné* (*F., masc.*), *soignée* (*F., fem.*).

See also CLOTHING WORKER, COAT, COVERING, FOOTWEAR, GLOVE, HEADGEAR, NECKWEAR, ORNAMENT, SKIRT, TROUSERS, UNDERWEAR. *Antonyms*— See UNDRESS.

CLOTHING WORKER—N. clothing worker, clothier, outfitter, costumer, costumier; dressmaker, *couturier* (*F., masc.*), *couturière* (*F., fem.*), tailor, sartor (*jocose*), seamstress, sempstress, needlewoman, *corsetier* (*F., masc.*), *corsetière* (*F., fem.*); milliner, hatter, glovemaker, glover, haberdasher, shirtmaker, hosier, furrier; valet.

clothing trade, dressmaking, tailoring, needlework, needle trade, corsetry; millinery, glovemaking, haberdashery, hosiery, furriery.

See also CLOTHING, FOOTWEAR, WORK.

CLOUD—N. cloud, vapor, fog, smog, smaze, smother, pother, mist, haze, brume, steam, film; scud, rack; rain cloud, thunderhead, thundercloud.

science of clouds: nephology, meteorology.

V. cloud, overcast, overcloud, cloud up; becloud, shadow, overshadow, darken, obscure; fog, befog, mist, envelop.

Adj. cloudy, clouded, overcast, heavy, lowery, nebulous, nubilous, overclouded, skyless; nepheloid, cloudlike; vaporous, steamy, misty, foggy, hazy, brumous, filmy, smoky, dull, murky, dim, dark, shadowy, dusky, indistinct, obscure.

See also DARKNESS, SEMITRANSPARENCY, SMOKE, THICKNESS, UNCLEARNESS, VAPOR. *Antonyms*—See CLARITY, LIGHT.

---

cloudburst, *n.* torrent, shower, pour (RAIN).

cloudless, *adj.* crystal, crystal-like, clear (TRANSPARENCY).

---

cloudy, *adj.* hazy, misty, overcast (CLOUD, SEMITRANSPARENCY); unclear, roily, turbid (UNCLEARNESS).

clown, *n.* buffoon, jester, merry-andrew (FOLLY); quipster, wag, picador (WITTINESS); gawky, lout, rustic (CLUMSINESS).

cloy on, *v.* surfeit, satiate, pall on (SATISFACTION, DISGUST).

club, *n.* association, union, league (ASSEMBLAGE, COMBINATION); bludgeon, cudgel, stick (HITTING).

clue, *n.* inkling, intimation, cue (HINT); solution, key (ANSWER).

clump, *n.* cluster, group, bunch (ASSEMBLAGE).

CLUMSINESS—N. clumsiness, incompetence, improficiency, inefficiency, etc. (see *Adjectives*).

clumsy person, clown, gawk, gawky, lout, rustic, hobbledehoy, booby, lummox, oaf, lubber, lumpkin, boor.

incompetent, amateur, blunderhead, blunderer, fumbler, boggler, botcher, bungler, blunderbuss, cobbler, dabster, duffer, slouch, tinker, ne'er-do-well.

V. bungle, blunder, botch, muff, fumble, boggle, make a mess of (*colloq.*), make a hash of (*colloq.*), muddle, foozle, mar, spoil, flounder, stumble, trip, limp; barge, lumber, shuffle, sprawl, slouch, wobble, waddle.

Adj. clumsy, awkward, backhanded, boorish, footless, heavy-handed, left-handed, ambisinister, unhandy, undexterous, rude, rustic, sternforemost, uncouth; blunderous, botchy, bungling.

ungraceful, ungainly, gawky, gawkish, graceless, ponderous, splay, stiff, untoward, weedy, wooden, inelegant; elephantine, loutish, lubberly, oafish; untactful, tactless, gauche, clownish, inept, maladroit, undiplomatic, uneasy, unresourceful.

unskillful, unskilled, inadept, inapt, inartistic, inept, inexpert, unadept, unadroit, unapt, undexterous, amateurish, artless.

incompetent, improficient, inefficient, unproficient, incapable, inadequate, helpless, shiftless, unable, unqualified, unfit, unworkmanlike; untalented, ungifted, unaccomplished; rusty, inexperienced, green, unpracticed.

bulky, awkward, cumbersome, cumbrous, unwieldy.

See also DIFFICULTY, DISABLEMENT, FOLLY, MISTAKE. *Antonyms*—See ABILITY, CLEVERNESS, EASE, POWER, SUAVITY.

clutch, v. snatch, clasp, grasp (TAKING, HOLD).

clutter, v. litter, jumble, muddle (UNTIDINESS, CONFUSION).

cluttered, adj. crowded, crammed, choked up (FULLNESS).

coach, n. tallyho, stagecoach, diligence; train, car; baby carriage, bassinet, perambulator (VEHICLE); tutor, trainer (TEACHER).

coagulate, v. thicken, congeal, clot (THICKNESS).

coal, n. hard coal, anthracite; soft coal, bituminous coal (FUEL).

coarse, adj. rough, unrefined, unpolished; chapped, harsh (ROUGHNESS); indelicate, offensive, gross (OBSCENITY, LOWNESS); crude, earthy (VULGARITY).

coast, n. shore, littoral, seacoast (LAND).

coat, n. fur, pelage, wool (HAIR); jacket, overcoat (COAT).

coat, v. laminate, plate, foil (LAYER); paint, stain, varnish (COVERING).

COAT—N. coat, overcoat, balmacaan, chesterfield, coonskin, greatcoat, Mackinaw, melton coat, trench coat, pea jacket, peacoat, raglan, redingote, spring coat, topcoat, surcoat, surtout, ulster; frock coat, frock, Prince Albert.

cloak, cape, capote, cardinal, paletot, dolman, manteau, mantelet, mantlet, mantilla, mantle, wrap, pelisse, burnoose.

raincoat, mackintosh, oilskins, slicker, tarpaulin, stormcoat, waterproof, poncho.

jacket, short coat, coatee, Eton jacket, jerkin, sack coat, smoking jacket, sport jacket, sport coat, doublet, lumberjack, jumper, parka, spencer, windbreaker, tunic (mil.), blazer; bolero, sacque, sack, shrug.

sweater, cardigan, pull-over, slipover, slip-on, jersey.

blouse, bodice, halter, middy blouse, middy, shirt, shirtwaist, T-shirt, tunic, waist, basque shirt, sweat shirt, polo shirt, dickey.

See also CLOTHING, COVERING, PROTECTION. Antonyms—See UNDERWEAR, UNDRESS.

coating, n. crust, bloom, encrustation (COVERING).

coax, v. argue into, induce, cajole (PERSUASION); wangle, wheedle, worm (ACQUISITION).

cobweb, n. net, tissue, gossamer (TEXTURE).

cock, n. rooster, capon (BIRD); spout, faucet, tap (EGRESS).

cock, v. erect, stand up, stick up (POSTURE, VISIBILITY, VERTICALITY).

cockeyed, adj. strabismic, crosseyed, esophoric (DIM-SIGHTEDNESS).

cocky, adj. self-assured, self-confident, overweening (CERTAINTY).

coddle, v. indulge, spoil, pamper (MILDNESS); steam, poach, boil (COOKERY).

code, n. rules, discipline (RULE); constitution, charter (LAW); cipher, cryptography (WRITING).

coerce, v. make, compel, drive (FORCE).

coexistent, adj. contemporary, contemporaneous, coeval (SIMULTANEOUSNESS).

coffee, n. café (F.), café au lait (F.), demitasse (DRINK).

coffee pot, n. percolator, dripolator (CONTAINER); coffee shop, diner, restaurant (FOOD).

coffin, n. box, casket, sarcophagus (BURIAL).

cog, n. tooth, fang, prong (TEETH).

cogent, adj. persuasive, convincing, suasive (PERSUASION).

cohabit, v. copulate, conjugate, couple (SEX).

coherence, n. cohesion, adhesion, cleavage (STICKINESS); oneness, identity (UNITY).

coil, n. corkscrew, involution, helix (CURVE, WINDING); braid, plait, pigtail (HAIR).

coin, v. mint, monetize, issue (MONEY); invent, originate, conceive (PRODUCTION).

coincide, v. concur, accompany, synchronize (SIMULTANEOUSNESS, OCCURRENCE); identify, agree, be the same (SIMILARITY).

coincidental, adj. fortuitous, incidental, circumstantial (OCCURRENCE); synchronous, concomitant (SIMULTANEOUSNESS).

COLD—N. cold, chill, gelidity, algidity, frigidity, ague, algor, chills.

ice, sleet, glaze, hail, hailstone; frost, rime, hoarfrost; icicle, iceberg, floe, berg, snow mountain; ice field, ice pack, glacier.

snow, flurry, snowflake, snowball, snowdrift, snowslip, snowslide, snow avalanche; snow ice, névé (F.); snowfall, precipitation, snowstorm, blizzard; slop, slosh, slush.

refrigeration, cooling, infrigidation, gelation, congelation, glaciation.

refrigerator, icebox, ice chest, deepfreeze, freezer; icehouse, cold storage, refrigeratory; frigidarium; ice bag, ice pack, cold pack.

refrigerant, refrigeratory, chiller, coolant, cooler, cryogen; freon, ammonia, dry ice; febrifuge.

[*illness*] **cold,** cold in the head, coryza (*med.*), rhinitis, roup, the sniffles, catarrh, nasal catarrh.

V. **be cold,** shiver, quake, shake, tremble, shudder, chill, freeze; defervesce.

refrigerate, chill, cool; air-condition, air-cool, water-cool; freeze, glaciate, ice; frost, rime; frostbite.

Adj. **cold,** cool, chill, chilly, frigid, ice-cold, algid, bleak, raw, inclement, bitter, biting, cutting, nipping, piercing; shivering, aguish; frostbitten; wintry, hiemal, boreal, hyperborean, arctic, snowbound; marmoreal.

icy, glacial, frosty, freezing, frozen, gelid; icebound, frostbound.

frozen, gelid, glacial, iced, icy; glacé.

See also INDIFFERENCE, INSENSITIVITY, WIND. *Antonyms*—See FIRE, FUEL, HEAT.

---

cold-blooded, *adj.* imperturbable, passionless, dispassionate (INEXCITABILITY); ironhearted, stonyhearted, unfeeling (CRUELTY, INSENSITIVITY).

collaborate, *v.* concur, concert, coact (CO-OPERATION).

collapse, *v.* founder, topple, fall down (DESCENT).

collar, *n.* choker (*colloq.*), dickey, ruff (NECKWEAR).

collar (*colloq.*), *v.* capture, catch, seize (TAKING).

collarbone, *n.* clavicle (BONE).

collateral, *n.* security, surety, bond (PROMISE).

colleague, *n.* confrere, associate, cohort (FRIEND).

collect, *v.* accumulate, amass, gather, assemble (ASSEMBLAGE, STORE, ACQUISITION); compile, anthologize (TREATISE).

collected, *adj.* levelheaded, composed (INEXCITABILITY).

collective, *adj.* shared, common, mutual (CO-OPERATION).

collector, *n.* treasurer, teller, cashier (RECEIVING).

college, *n.* seminary, institute, university (SCHOOL).

collegian, *n.* academic, undergraduate (LEARNING).

collide, *v.* smash, hit, strike (TOUCH, HITTING).

colloquial, *adj.* conversational, chatty, communicative (TALK); vernacular, dialectal, idiomatic (LANGUAGE).

colloquialism, *n.* vernacularism, idiom (WORD).

collusion, *n.* complicity, connivance, guilt (CO-OPERATION).

---

colonist, *n.* immigrant, settler, pioneer (INGRESS).

colonize, *v.* squat, pre-empt, settle (INHABITANT).

color, *v.* dye, tincture, stain (COLOR); blush, crimson, flush (MODESTY); slant, angle, distort (PREJUDICE, MISREPRESENTATION).

COLOR—*N.* **color,** hue, tone; tint, cast, shade, tinge, nuance, tincture; skin color, complexion; chroma, saturation, purity, intensity; coloration, coloring, pigmentation.

pigment, coloring matter, dye, dyestuff; rouge, mascara, lipstick; paint, stain, wash.

[*science*] **chromatics,** chromatology.

[*device*] **chromatometer,** colorimeter, prism.

V. **color,** dye, tincture, tinge, stain, tint, hue (*poetic*), tone, blend; variegate; paint, wash, crayon, distemper, ingrain, grain, illuminate; discolor, tarnish.

Adj. **colored,** colorful, hued, pigmented, prismatic, chromatic.

many-colored, motley, multicolored, parti-colored, piebald, pied, varicolored, varied, variegated, versicolor; blazing, chatoyant, iridescent.

See also BLUE, BROWN, GRAY, GREEN, PURPLE, RED, YELLOW. *Antonyms*—See BLACKNESS, WHITENESS.

---

colorless, *adj.* uncolored, washed out, pale (COLORLESSNESS); characterless, common, nondescript (COMMONNESS); same, drab (UNIFORMITY).

COLORLESSNESS—*N.* **colorlessness,** achromatism; pallor, paleness, pallidity, albinism.

V. **decolor,** decolorize, achromatize, fade, etiolate, washout, tone down.

pale, blanch, bleach, wan (*poetic*), whiten, sallow.

Adj. **colorless,** uncolored, hueless, achromatic, achromatous, etiolated, faded, washed-out.

pale, pallid, ashen, ashy, doughy, pasty, waxen, wan, cadaverous, ghastly, anemic, sallow, bloodless, pale-faced, white, wheyfaced.

light-colored, fair, fair-skinned, light-skinned, blond, blondine, light, white, creamy; leucochroic, leucodermatous, xanthochroid.

See also WHITENESS. *Antonyms*—See BLACKNESS, COLOR, DARKNESS.

colossal, *adj.* mammoth, mountainous, giant (SIZE).

colt, *n.* foal, yearling (HORSE); youngster, youngling, fledgling (YOUTH); greenhorn, babe, virgin (INEXPERIENCE).

column, *n.* pillar, shaft, colonnade (SUPPORT, HEIGHT).

coma, *n.* blackout, faint, syncope (INSENSIBILITY).

comb, *n.* fleshy growth, crest (SKIN).

comb, *v.* scrape, rasp, card (CLEANNESS); ransack, rake, scour (SEARCH).

combat, *v.* fight, battle, clash (FIGHTING).

combed, *adj.* coifed, marcelled (HAIR).

COMBINATION—*N.* combination, union, aggregation, aggregate, composite, mixture, junction, unification, synthesis, incorporation, consolidation, conjuncture, amalgamation, coalescence, fusion, blend, blending, solution, brew.

association, union, alliance, league, order, coalition, federation, confederacy, federacy, guild, club, trade-union, clique, gang, coterie, set, pool, trust, combine, camarilla.

compound, alloy, admixture, amalgam, composition.

V. combine, unite, join, link, incorporate, embody, alloy, intermix, interfuse, interlard, compound, amalgamate, blend, merge, fuse, lump together, consolidate, coalesce.

associate, amalgamate, club, fraternize, unionize, federate, federalize, league, confederate, band together, herd, mass.

Adj. combined, etc. (see *Verbs*); conjoint; coalescent.

allied, amalgamated, leagued, corporate, incorporated, federated, confederate.

See also CO-OPERATION, JUNCTION, MAKE-UP, MIXTURE, TEXTURE, UNITY. *Antonyms*—See DECAY, DISJUNCTION.

combustible, *adj.* burnable, flammable, inflammable (FIRE).

come, *v.* arrive, burst, flare (ARRIVAL); happen, occur, come to pass (OCCURRENCE).

come after, *v.* follow, come next, succeed (FOLLOWING).

come again, *v.* return, rejoin, revisit (ARRIVAL).

come back, *v.* remigrate, return, recur (REVERSION); resume, return to (REPETITION).

come before, *v.* precede, forerun, antecede (PRECEDENCE).

comedian, *n.* comic, humorist, wit (ACTOR, WITTINESS).

come from, *v.* derive from, flow from, accrue (RESULT); hail from (ARRIVAL).

come in, *v.* enter, immigrate (INGRESS).

comely, *adj.* pretty, fair, good-looking (BEAUTY).

come out, *v.* egress, emerge, exit (EGRESS).

comet, *n.* meteor, meteoroid (WORLD).

come together, *v.* assemble, collect, muster (ASSEMBLAGE).

comfort, *v.* calm, soothe, untrouble (CALMNESS, UNANXIETY); condole with, console, solace (RELIEF, PITY).

comfortable, *adj.* restful, peaceful, reposeful (REST).

comic, *n.* comedian, humorist, wag (WITTINESS, ACTOR).

comical, *adj.* funny, humorous, amusing (WITTINESS, AMUSEMENT, ABSURDITY).

coming, *adj.* prospective, impending, overhanging (FUTURE); approaching, nearing (APPROACH).

COMMAND—*N.* command, order, regulation, ordinance, act, fiat, bid, bidding; direction, injunction, behest, precept, commandment, ruling, dictate, dictation, charge, instructions; adjuration, directive, enjoinment, ordainment, prescription, requirement, subpoena, summons; edict, mandate, prescript, rescript, writ.

decree, canon, ukase, bull.

demand, exaction, imposition, requisition, claim, ultimatum; request.

V. command, order, decree, enact, ordain, dictate, enjoin, bid, charge, instruct, prescribe, direct, give orders, issue a command; adjudge, adjure, enjoin, prescribe, require; subpoena, summon.

Adj. commanding, authoritative, imperative, dictatorial, magisterial, imperious; adjuratory, decretive, decretal, decretory, directorial, directive, prescriptive, canonical, injunctive, mandatory.

See also DEMAND, FORCE, NECESSITY, POWER, RULE, SUMMONS. *Antonyms*—See OBEDIENCE, OBSERVANCE.

commander, *n.* head, commandant, captain (RULER, LEADERSHIP).

commanding, *adj.* lofty, striking, arresting (MAGNIFICENCE).

commandment, *n.* command, order, dictate (COMMAND).

commemorate, *v.* celebrate, observe, honor (CELEBRATION); memorialize, perpetuate (MEMORY).

commence, *v.* begin, start, launch (BEGINNING).

commend, *v.* approve, praise, acclaim (APPROVAL); entrust, commit, confide (GIVING).

commendable, *adj.* praiseworthy, laudable, creditable (APPROVAL).

comment, *n.* mention, remark, observation (STATEMENT); commentary, note, gloss (EXPLANATION); hearsay, buzz, report (RUMOR).

commentary, *n.* review, critique, appreciation (TREATISE); note, gloss, comment (EXPLANATION).

commerce, *n.* trade, traffic, merchantry (BUSINESS).

commiseration, *n.* compassion, mercy, humanity (PITY).

COMMISSION—*N.* commission, authorization, warrant, charge, instruction, authority, mandate, trust, brevet; permit, certificate, diploma; delegation; consignment, task, errand, office, assignment; proxy, power of attorney, deputation, legation, mission, embassy; agency.

committing, doing, execution, perpetration, performance.

appointment, nomination, charter; ordination; installation, inauguration, investiture; accession, coronation, enthronement.

percentage, allowance, fee, pay, bonus, rake-off (*slang*), compensation, discount, factorage.

V. commission, delegate, depute; consign, commit, assign, charge, confide to, entrust, authorize, empower, accredit, engage, employ, hire, bespeak, appoint, name, nominate, return; constitute, elect, ordain, install, induct, inaugurate, invest, crown; enroll, enlist; put in commission.

Adv., phrases. instead of, in lieu of, in place of, in one's stead, in one's place; as proxy for, as a substitute for, as an alternative.

See also AGENT, BUSINESS, DEPUTY, PERMISSION, SUBSTITUTION.

commissioner, *n.* officeholder, incumbent, bureaucrat (OFFICIAL).

commit, *v.* entrust, commend, confide (GIVING); perpetrate, do, wreak (ACTION); institutionalize, send to an asylum (INSANITY); imprison, send to prison (IMPRISONMENT).

commitment, *n.* engagement, undertaking (PROMISE).

commodity, *n.* thing, object, article (MATERIALITY).

common, *n.* park, public park, green (LAND).

commoner, *n.* peasant, plebeian, worker (PEOPLE).

COMMONNESS—*N.* commonness, mediocrity, vulgarism, vulgarity.

banality, conventionality, pedestrianism, prosaism, platitude, stereotypy, bathos.

cliché, counterword, banality, bromide, commonplace, platitude.

mediocrity, nondescript, plebeian, vulgarian, bromide, humdrum, stereotype.

V. be common, be usual, prevail; platitudinize, humdrum; make common, cheapen, vulgarize.

Adj. common, ordinary, mediocre, commonplace, characterless, cheap, colorless, middling, nondescript, passable, plain, prosy, tolerable, undistinctive, undistinguished; baseborn, raffish, vulgar, bourgeois, Philistine.

usual, accustomed, average, bread-and-butter, customary, everyday, familiar, frequent, garden variety, general, standard, habitual, normal, ordinary, popular, prevailing, prevalent, regular, stock, typical, unexceptional, wonted, workaday.

banal, bromidic, conventional, drab, hackneyed, humdrum, motheaten, musty, obvious, pedestrian, platitudinous, plebeian, prosaic, slavish, stale, stereotyped, stodgy, threadbare, trite, unexciting, unimaginative, unoriginal, well-worn, bathetic.

See also AGREEMENT, CONFORMITY, DULLNESS, HABIT, VULGARITY. *Antonyms*—See UNUSUALNESS.

commonplace, *adj.* plebeian, colorless, characterless (BOREDOM); mediocre, middling, ordinary (COMMONNESS, MID-COURSE).

common sense, *n.* judgment, acumen, practicality (WISDOM).

commonwealth, *n.* community, citizenry, body politic (PEOPLE, CITIZEN).

COMMOTION—*N.* commotion, excitement, ado, to-do, welter, whirl, whir, fuss, bother, pother, flurry, stir, backwash, combustion; ferment, fermentation, seethe, yeast, simmer; clatter, bluster, ballyhoo (*colloq.*), hurly-burly, pandemonium, uproar, rummage, rumpus.

tumult, turbulence, turmoil, moil, disorder, distemper, fracas, fray, row, ruffle, maelstrom, riot, rabblement, rout, ruction (*colloq.*), ruckus (*colloq.*), squall (*colloq.*), storm, tempest, upheaval, convulsion, disturbance.

V. be in commotion, ferment, seethe, yeast, simmer; riot.

throw into commotion, stir up, disturb, tempest, uncalm, tumult.

Adj. [*in commotion*] **tumultuous,** tumultuary, turbulent, uproarious, hurly-burly, tempestuous, stormy, riotous, disorderly; **simmering,** seething, fermenting, raging.

See also AGITATION, CONFUSION, EXCITEMENT. *Antonyms*—See CALMNESS, PEACE.

communicable, *adj.* contagious, catching, infectious (TRANSFER, DISEASE).

communicate, *v.* tell, disclose, signify (INFORMATION); cede, relinquish, part with (GIVING).

communicate with, *v.* write to, keep in touch with, correspond with (EPISTLE).

communication, *n.* report, statement, communiqué (INFORMATION); missive, letter, note (EPISTLE).

communion, *n.* close relationship, intimacy, affinity (RELATIONSHIP).

communism, *n.* bolshevism, sovietism (GOVERNMENT).

community, *n.* society, commonwealth, commonalty (PEOPLE, INHABITANT); partnership, copartnership (OWNERSHIP); semblance, affinity, kinship (SIMILARITY).

compact, *adj.* dense, close, tight (THICKNESS, ASSEMBLAGE); laconic, pithy, to the point (SHORTNESS).

COMPACT—*N.* compact, contract, deal (*colloq.*), arrangement, understanding, gentlemen's agreement, engagement, stipulation, settlement, agreement, bargain, pact, bond, covenant, indenture (*law*).

treaty, convention, league, alliance, entente (*F.*), concordat.

V. negotiate, treat, stipulate, make terms; bargain, dicker, contract, covenant, engage, agree; conclude, close, close with, complete, strike a bargain; come to terms (*or* an understanding); compromise, settle, adjust.

ratify, confirm, sanction, authorize, approve, establish, fix, clinch; subscribe, underwrite, endorse; sign, seal.

See also AGREEMENT, CONDITION, EXCHANGE, MEDIATION, PROMISE. *Antonyms*—See DISAGREEMENT, FIGHTING, OPPOSITION.

companion, *n.* comrade, chum (*colloq.*), mate (FRIEND); match, fellow, double (SIMILARITY).

companionship, *n.* comradeship, fellowship, company (FRIENDLINESS, SOCIALITY).

company, *n.* association, alliance, league (CO-OPERATION); concern, enterprise, firm (BUSINESS); so-

ciety, companionship, comradeship (FRIENDLINESS, SOCIALITY); retinue, cortege (ACCOMPANIMENT); dramatis personae (*L.*), cast (DRAMA).

comparable, *adj.* commensurable, equivalent, equipollent (COMPARISON, EQUALITY).

comparatively, *adv.* in a certain degree, rather, relatively (SMALLNESS).

COMPARISON—*N.* comparison, collation, parallelism, contrast, balance; likeness, similarity, resemblance, analogy, simile, similitude.

[*basis of comparison*] criterion, norm, standard, yardstick.

V. **compare,** collate, contrast, balance, parallel, liken, match; standardize.

Adj. **comparative,** relative, contrastive; parallel, similar, like, analogous, corresponding.

comparable, commensurable, commensurate.

incomparable, disparate, incommensurable, incommensurate.

See also RELATIONSHIP, SIMILARITY. *Antonyms*—See DIFFERENCE, OPPOSITE.

compartment, *n.* booth, stall, cubicle (SPACE); niche, nook, corner (PLACE).

compassion, *n.* commiseration, mercy, clemency (FORGIVENESS, PITY).

compatible, *adj.* consistent, consonant, congruous (AGREEMENT).

compel, *v.* make, coerce, drive (FORCE); necessitate, make necessary, force (NECESSITY).

compensate, *v.* indemnify, recompense, remunerate (PAYMENT).

compensate for, *v.* indemnify, redress, pay for (RECOMPENSE).

compensation, *n.* payment, indemnification, redress (RECOMPENSE); amends, recompense (ATONEMENT).

compete, *v.* contend, contest, strive (ATTEMPT).

competent, *adj.* able, efficient, proficient (ABILITY); enough, plenty, appreciable (SUFFICIENCY).

competition, *n.* contest, match, game (ATTEMPT).

competitor, *n.* opponent, antagonist, rival (OPPOSITION).

compile, *v.* group, unite, amass (ASSEMBLAGE); anthologize, collect (TREATISE).

complacent, *adj.* smug, self-satisfied, self-complacent (SATISFACTION); compliant, compliable, obsequious (PLEASANTNESS).

C O M P L A I N T—*N.* complaint, plaint, protest, protestation, remonstrance, expostulation, representation, grievance, jeremiad, round robin, bill of particulars, clamor, cavil; gripe (*colloq.*), beef (*slang*), kick (*slang*), squawk (*colloq.*), whine.

complainer, nag, protestant, remonstrant; grumbler, etc. (see *Verbs*).

V. complain, grumble, mutter, whine, pule, snivel, whimper, yammer (*colloq.*), bleat, squawk (*colloq.*), gripe (*colloq.*), carp, cavil; beef, bitch, bellyache, kick (*all slang*); protest, remonstrate, expostulate, nag; clamor, rail, storm.

Adj. complaining, petulant, querulous, grumbly, whiny, clamorous, protestant, remonstrant, remonstrative, expostulatory; grumbling, etc. (see *Verbs*).

See also DISSATISFACTION, SADNESS, WEEPING. *Antonyms*—See BOASTING, HAPPINESS, LAUGHTER, PRIDE, SATISFACTION, SMILE.

complement, *n.* completory, obverse, opposite number (COMPLETENESS).

COMPLETENESS—*N.* completeness, entirety, totality, integrity, perfection, maturity.

completion, accomplishment, attainment, achievement, fulfillment; dispatch, consummation, culmination, realization, perfection, integration, finish, conclusion.

complement, completory, obverse, counterpart, opposite number; copestone, crown, finishing touch.

whole, aggregate, aggregation, entirety, sum, total, totality, unity, body, complex.

all, the whole, everything, everybody; total, aggregate, sum, sum total, gross amount.

V. complete, complement, conclude, consummate, crown, finish, top off, clinch, integrate; accomplish, achieve, fulfill; perfect.

finish, end, terminate, conclude, close, bring to a close, wind up, clinch, seal, put the last (*or* finishing) touch to; crown, cap, round out.

do thoroughly, not do by halves, exhaust; carry through, make good; fill the bill, go the limit, go the whole hog (*all colloq.*).

total, add up to, amount to, come to; constitute a whole, aggregate, assemble, amass, agglomerate, integrate.

Adj. complete, finished, done, through; consummate, full, plenary, full-fledged, entire, aggregate, all-embracing, all-inclusive, exhaustive, comprehensive, sweeping, thorough; perfect.

whole, total, integral, integrated, gross, unitary, entire, all, organic; intact, indiscrete, imperforate; uncut, unbroken, unabridged, undiminished, undivided, unexpurgated, unreduced, unsevered.

indivisible, undividable, inseparable, indiscerptible, indissoluble.

thorough, out-and-out, arrant, utter, outright, circumstantial, intensive, radical, sound, systematic, thoroughgoing.

absolute, blank, blanket, sheer, utter; categorical, unconditional, unqualified, unmitigated.

completive, completing, completory, complemental, complementary, conclusive, integrative, crowning; integral.

Adv., phrases. completely, altogether, outright, wholly, totally, *in toto* (L.), fully, entirely, at all points, utterly, quite; in all respects, in every respect; out and out; throughout, from first to last, from head to foot, cap-a-pie, from top to toe, every whit, every inch; heart and soul, root and branch; lock, stock, and barrel; hook, line, and sinker.

See also ADDITION, ASSEMBLAGE, END, FULLNESS, PERFECTION, SUFFICIENCY, UNITY. *Antonyms*—See ABSENCE, INCOMPLETENESS, INSUFFICIENCY.

complex, *adj.* complicated, entangled, intricate (DIFFICULTY, MYSTERY).

complex, *n.* composite, compound, synthesis (MAKE-UP).

compliance, *n.* keeping, adherence, docility (OBEDIENCE, OBSERVANCE).

complaint, *adj.* submissive, yielding, pliable (SUBMISSION, OBEDIENCE); compliable, complacent, obsequious (PLEASANTNESS).

complicate, *v.* entangle, snag, snarl (DIFFICULTY, MYSTERY); weave, braid, cue (WINDING).

complicity, *n.* collusion, connivance, guilt (CO-OPERATION).

complimentary, *adj.* commendatory, eulogistic, panegyric (PRAISE); flattering, adulatory, courtly (FLATTERY); free, gratuitous, gratis (FREEDOM).

compliments, *n.* respects, regards, devoirs (RESPECT).

component, *n.* constituent, element, factor (PART).

compose, v. make up, form, constitute (MAKE-UP, PART); originate, conceive, coin (PRODUCTION); draft, indite, frame (WRITING); set, set type (PRINTING); calm, still, quiet (PEACE).

composed, adj. level-headed, collected, temperate (INEXCITABILITY).

composer, n. song writer, tunesmith, musician (SINGING, HARMONY); drafter, framer (WRITER).

composite, n. compound, complex, synthesis (MAKE-UP).

composition, n. essay, theme, thesis (WRITING, TREATISE); creation, work, opus (PRODUCTION); concerto, piece (MUSIC); constitution, contents, arrangement (MAKE-UP, TEXTURE); typesetting, presswork (PRINTING).

composure, n. equanimity, equability, poise (CALMNESS, INEXCITABILITY); constraint, reserve, restraint (CONTROL).

compound, n. admixture, amalgam, blend (MIXTURE, COMBINATION, PREPARATION); composite, complex, synthesis (MAKE-UP).

comprehend, v. understand, grasp, apprehend (UNDERSTANDING); include, comprise, subsume (INCLUSION).

comprehensive, adj. sweeping, exhaustive, all-embracing (COMPLETENESS, INCLUSION).

compress, v. contract, condense, constrict (DECREASE); abbreviate, syncopate (SHORTNESS); densen, densify, squeeze (THICKNESS).

comprise, v. subsume, comprehend, consist of (INCLUSION, MAKE-UP).

compromise, v. go halfway, split the difference, meet one halfway (MID-COURSE); settle, adjust (COMPACT); discredit, explode (UNBELIEVINGNESS).

compulsory, adj. requisite, mandatory, obligatory (NECESSITY, FORCE).

compunction, n. contrition, repentance, remorse (GUILT, PENITENCE, REGRET).

COMPUTATION—N. computation, calculation, gauge, estimation, estimate.

[instruments] **calculator,** adding machine, calculating machine, cash register, Comptometer, reckoner, ready reckoner, abacus, slide rule; cybernetics.

mathematics, algebra, arithmetic, algorism, quadratics, trigonometry, calculus, geometry, geodetics, mensuration, topology, statistics.

mathematician, algebraist, arithmetician, geodesist, geometrician, statistician, actuary, abacist.

V. **compute,** calculate, cipher, figure, reckon, sum, tally, estimate, gauge or gage.

See also ADDITION, DEDUCTION, INCREASE, NUMBER.

comrade, n. companion, chum (colloq.), mate (FRIEND).

comradeship, n. companionship, fellowship, good-fellowship (FRIENDLINESS).

concave, adj. incurvate, incurvated, biconcave (CURVE); dented, dimpled, depressed (HOLLOW).

CONCEALMENT—N. concealment, obliteration, obscuration, occultation, secretion, dissimulation, secrecy, privacy.

disguise, camouflage, cloak, masquerade, blind, smoke screen, red herring, defense mechanism (psychoan.); screen, cover, covering, covert, coverture, cover-up (colloq.); curtain, mantle, pall, shade, shroud, veil, wraps; mask, visor, vizard, false face, domino.

masquerader, masquer, domino, mummer, mime, incognito, dissembler, dissimulator.

hider, burrower, coucher, ambuscader, ambusher, lurker, skulker, skulk, stowaway.

ambush, ambuscade, ambushment, lurking place; trap, snare, pitfall.

hiding place, secret place, den, hideaway, hideout, covert, blind, closet, crypt; safe, secret drawer, safe-deposit box, safety-deposit box, cache.

secret, confidence, mystery, arcanum, occult, penetralia (pl.).

secret society, underground, secret service, fraternity, sorority.

secret agent, undercover agent, spy, foreign agent, private investigator.

V. **conceal,** hide, cover, cover up, curtain, veil, cushion, enshroud, mantle, mask, obliterate, blot out, obscure, occult, pall, screen, secrete, cache, harbor, shade, shroud, stow, visor, wrap.

disguise, camouflage, cloak, mask, masquerade, veil.

hide oneself, hide, burrow, couch, keep (or stay) out of sight, hole up (colloq.), lie low (colloq.), secrete oneself; lurk, skulk, sneak, slink, prowl; stow away.

secrete, keep secret, keep quiet, keep from, withhold, keep to oneself; suppress, smother, stifle, hush up, cover up, withhold information, not tell; classify (gov-

ernment documents); dissemble, dissimulate.

ambush, ambuscade, waylay, lie in ambush, lie in wait for; trap, set a trap for, ensnare, entrap.

Adj. concealed, hidden, blind, blotted out, cached, covered, covered up, cushioned, enshrouded, obliterated, obscure, obscured, perdu, recondite, screened, secreted, shrouded, under wraps, unseen.

disguised, camouflaged, cloaked, masked, veiled.

secret, arcane, cryptic, backdoor, backstair, dark, confidential, closet, hush-hush, private, snug, subterranean, underground, classified, restricted, top-secret, incognito.

esoteric, cabalistic, occult, mystical, orphic, recondite.

secretive, backstair, catlike, feline, covert, furtive, hangdog, sly, sneaky, stealthy, surreptitious, clandestine, thievish, undercover, underhand *or* underhanded, *sub rosa* (L.), insidious, subtle; close-lipped, closemouthed, uncommunicative.

unshown, undisclosed, undisplayed, unexposed, unmanifested *or* unmanifest, unrevealed.

untold, hushed-up, occult, smothered, suppressed, unadvertised, unaired, unannounced, unbetrayed, uncommunicated, unconveyed, undeclared, undisclosed, ulterior, undivulged, unheralded, unimparted, unproclaimed, unpromulgated, unpublicized, unpublished, unreported, unrevealed, unvoiced.

Adv., phrases. secretly, clandestinely, covertly, furtively, insidiously, secretively, slyly, stealthily, surreptitiously, thievishly, under cover, underhand, underhandedly.

confidentially, covertly, *in camera* (L.), in privacy, in private, privately, privily, *sotto voce* (It.), *sub rosa* (L.), underground, in secret, between ourselves, *entre nous* (F.), between you and me, off the record, in strict confidence, as a secret, as a confidence.

See also CLEVERNESS, LATENCY, MYSTERY, SECLUSION, TRAP, WRITING. *Antonyms*—See DISCLOSURE, HONESTY, INFORMATION, VISIBILITY.

concede, *v.* admit, allow, grant (PERMISSION, GIVING, STATEMENT); surrender, cede, capitulate (SUBMISSION).

conceit, *n.* vanity, vainglory, egotism (PRIDE); fancy, crotchet, whim (CAPRICE, IDEA).

conceivable, *adj.* possible, thinkable, imaginable (POSSIBILITY).

conceive, *v.* imagine, envisage, envision (IMAGINATION); realize, appreciate (KNOWLEDGE); originate, coin, compose (PRODUCTION); be pregnant, gestate (PREGNANCY).

concentrate, *v.* centralize, focus (CENTER); assemble, congregate, forgather (ASSEMBLAGE); pay attention, give heed (ATTENTION).

concept, *n.* conception, thought, abstraction (IDEA); theory, idea, supposition (THOUGHT); view, consideration, notion (OPINION).

conception, *n.* impression, notion, inkling (UNDERSTANDING).

concern, *n.* distress, disquietude, care (NERVOUSNESS); affair, interest, matter; company, enterprise, firm (BUSINESS).

concern, *v.* touch, affect, pertain to (RELATIONSHIP); trouble, distress, worry (NERVOUSNESS).

concerning, *prep.* as regards, respecting, pertaining to (RELATIONSHIP).

concert, *n.* musicale, musical (*colloq.*), recital (MUSIC).

conciliate, *v.* pacify, appease, propitiate (CALMNESS, PEACE); mollify, placate (FRIENDLINESS).

concise, *adj.* brief, terse, succinct (SHORTNESS).

conclude, *v.* finish, terminate, consummate (END, COMPLETENESS); deduce, ratiocinate, reason (THOUGHT, REASONING); judge, adjudge, reckon (OPINION, UNDERSTANDING); presume, infer, gather (LIKELIHOOD).

conclusion, *n.* finish, termination, completion (END); decision, opinion, determination (JUDGMENT); inference, corollary, illation (REASONING, UNDERSTANDING); development, eventuality, upshot (RESULT).

concoct, *v.* hatch, contrive, project (PLAN).

concoction, *n.* blend, brew, compound (PREPARATION).

concomitant, *adj.* synchronous, concurrent, attendant, accessory, collateral (ACCOMPANIMENT, OCCURRENCE, SIMULTANEOUSNESS).

concrete, *adj.* corporeal, material, physical (REALITY, MATERIALITY).

concrete, *n.* cement, sand, mortar (ROCK).

concubine, *n.* mistress, sultana (SEX).

concur, *v.* agree, acquiesce, assent (PERMISSION, ASSENT); coincide, contemporize, accompany (SIMULTANEOUSNESS); come together, meet (CONVERGENCE); coact, cofunction, collaborate (CO-OPERATION).

concurrent, *adj.* circumstantial, concomitant (OCCURRENCE).

concussion, *n.* jar, jolt, shock (SHAKE, HARM).

condemn, *v.* criticize, chide, castigate (DISAPPROVAL); convict, attaint (GUILT).

condensation, *n.* brief, abstract, digest (SHORTNESS); rainfall, dew, precipitation (RAIN).

condense, *v.* contract, compress, constrict (DECREASE); abridge, compact, telescope (SHORTNESS); densen, consolidate (THICKNESS).

condescend, *v.* deign, stoop, patronize (PRIDE).

condiment, *n.* flavoring, seasoning, spice (TASTE).

CONDITION—*N.* condition, shape, way, form, fettle, tone, trim; state, situation, status, position, circumstances, phase, aspect, appearance; *status quo* (*L.*), *status quo ante* (*L.*); temper, mood.

plight, predicament, scrape, straits, difficult straits, pinch; fix, jam, pickle, hot water (*all colloq.*); stew, mess, muddle, imbroglio; dilemma, quandary; impasse, mire, morass, quagmire, rattrap.

frame, fabric, stamp, mold; structure, framework, texture, constitution, build.

standing, reputation, position, rank, quality, estate, station, sphere.

provision, condition, contingency, proviso, qualification, stipulation, postulate, codicil.

V. provide, condition, postulate, stipulate.

depend on, hinge on, be subject to, be dependent.

Adj. conditional, provisional, tentative, contingent on, dependent on, subject to, provisory, stipulative, codiciliary.

See also COMPACT, MAKE-UP, SHAPE, SUPPOSITION, TEXTURE.

condolence, *n.* consolation, comfort, solace (PITY).

condone, *v.* overlook, pass over, wink at (FORGIVENESS, PERMISSION).

conduct, *n.* address, bearing, comportment (BEHAVIOR).

conduct, *v.* guide, usher, convoy (LEADERSHIP, GUIDANCE, ACCOMPANIMENT); carry, transport, convey (TRANSFER); direct, lead, wield the baton (MUSICIAN).

conductor, *n.* director, *Kapellmeister* (*Ger.*), leader (MUSICIAN).

cone-shaped, *adj.* conical, conic, pyramidal (SHARPNESS).

confederate, *adj.* confederated, leagued, federal (UNITY).

confederate, *n.* accomplice, abettor, accessory (AID).

confederate, *v.* league, federate, associate (COMBINATION).

confer, *v.* bestow, grant, accord (GIVING).

conference, *n.* discussion, argument, consultation (TALK).

confess, *v.* admit, acknowledge, own up (STATEMENT).

confide, *v.* entrust, commend, commit (GIVING); tell, divulge, let know (INFORMATION).

confidence, *n.* self-assurance, poise, assurance (CERTAINTY); inside information, tip, secret (INFORMATION, CONCEALMENT).

confident, *adj.* assured, certain, poised (CERTAINTY); hopeful, secure, expectant (HOPE).

confidential, *adj.* secret, arcane, backstair (CONCEALMENT).

confined, *adj.* cramped, two-by-four, pent (IMPRISONMENT); circumscribed, limited, restricted (NARROWNESS); bedridden, shut in (DISEASE); petty, small-minded, provincial (PREJUDICE).

confinement, *n.* detainment, detention, immurement (IMPRISONMENT); restriction, limitation, delimitation (RESTRAINT); childbirth, delivery, lying-in (BIRTH).

confirm, *v.* establish, authenticate, verify (PROOF, TRUTH, SUPPORT); ratify, sanction, endorse (ASSENT, APPROVAL).

confirmed, *adj.* fixed, rooted, inveterate (HABIT).

confiscate, *v.* appropriate, assume, expropriate (TAKING).

conflagration, *n.* fire, holocaust, flame (FIRE).

conflict, *n.* dissension, strife, friction (DISAGREEMENT).

CONFORMITY—*N.* conformity, correspondence, agreement, accord, harmony, resemblance, likeness, congruity; observance, compliance, acquiescence, assent, submission, consent, obedience.

conventionality, fashion, formalism, ritualism, routinism; orthodoxy, decorum, punctilio, traditionalism, academicism.

conformist, conventionalist, formalist, ritualist; orthodox, traditionalist; purist, precisian, pedant.

V. conform to, adapt oneself to, harmonize, fit, suit, agree with, comply with, fall in with, be guided by, adapt to, adjust to, reconcile.

Adj. conformable, adaptable, tractable, compliant, agreeable, obedient; regular, orderly; similar, like, proper, suitable; harmonious, consistent.

conventional, customary, fashionable, routine, traditional, habitual, usual, ordinary, common; formal, orthodox, punctilious, prim, decorous; academic.

Adv., phrases. **conformably,** by rule; in accordance with, in keeping with; according to; as usual, as a matter of course, invariably.

See also AGREEMENT, COMMONNESS, FORMALITY, HABIT, HARMONY, OBSERVANCE, PROPRIETY, RULE, SUBMISSION. *Antonyms*—See CONFUSION, DISAGREEMENT, DISOBEDIENCE, NONOBSERVANCE, OPPOSITION.

confound, *v.* puzzle, mystify, baffle (CONFUSION, MYSTERY).

confounded, *adj.* blank, dazed, wonder-struck (SURPRISE); damn (*colloq.*), damned, execrated (MALEDICTION).

CONFUSION—*N.* **confusion,** bewilderment, perplexity, mystification, puzzlement, quandary, bafflement, befuddlement, daze, haze, fog, whirl, maze, disorientation, muddle, flurry, fluster, flutter, mix-up, distraction, bedevilment, bemusement.

noisy confusion, bedlam, din, uproar, babel, hubbub, hurly-burly, racket.

disorder, disarrangement, disarray, derangement, clutter, disorganization, mess, mix-up, muddle, snarl, tangle, muss, jumble, litter, entanglement.

chaos, anarchy, pandemonium, tumult, turmoil, turbulence, topsyturvydom, riot, tophet, rummage, pother, maelstrom, welter, whirl, hurry-scurry; wilderness, moil, turbidity.

[*scene or place of confusion*] **bedlam,** maelstrom, shambles, madhouse, babel; labyrinth, maze.

V. **confuse,** bewilder, perplex, mystify, stump, stagger, puzzle, baffle, befuddle, bemuddle, bemuse, confound, fluster, flurry, addle, befog, daze, fog, mix up, muddle, stun, bedevil, disorient, flutter, fuddle; disconcert, discountenance, demoralize, abash, embarrass, nonplus, rattle, distract.

feel confused, whirl, reel; flounce, flounder, tumble, mill around.

disarrange, derange, disorder, disarray, discreate, disorganize, clutter, muddle, jumble, mix up, mess up, litter, rumple, tousle; tangle, snarl, embrangle, entangle, embroil; bedlamize.

becloud (*as an issue, etc.*), befog, obfuscate, fog.

Adj. **confusing,** carking, etc. (see *Verbs*); labyrinthine, mazy.

confused, dizzy, groggy, muzzy, hazy, whirling, addlebrained, addleheaded, addlepated; bewildered, etc. (see *Verbs*).

chaotic, anarchic, turbulent, tumultuous, turbid, macaronic, upside-down, topsy-turvy; rackety, riotous, uproarious.

Adv., phrases. **confusedly,** in confusion, pell-mell, helter-skelter.

See also AGITATION, COMMOTION, EXCITEMENT, INDISCRIMINATION, MYSTERY, SURPRISE, UNCERTAINTY, UNTIDINESS. *Antonyms*—See CONFORMITY, NEATNESS.

congeal, *v.* gelatinize, thicken, jell (THICKNESS, SEMILIQUIDITY).

congenial, *adj.* companionable, convivial, cordial (FRIENDLINESS); complaisant, good-humored, good-natured (PLEASANTNESS).

congested, *adj.* jammed, crowded, massed (MULTITUDE); gorged, chock-full (FULLNESS).

CONGRATULATION—*N.* **congratulation,** felicitation.

V. **congratulate,** felicitate, rejoice with, compliment.

[*congratulate oneself*] **rejoice,** pride oneself, plume oneself, hug oneself, flatter oneself.

Adj. **congratulatory,** gratulatory, complimentary, congratulant.

See also COURTESY, GREETING, HAPPINESS, MERRIMENT. *Antonyms*—See DEJECTION, DISCOURTESY, SADNESS.

congregate, *v.* throng, besiege, pack (MULTITUDE); concentrate, forgather (ASSEMBLAGE).

congregation, *n.* flock, churchgoers, parishioners (CHURCH).

congress, *n.* convocation, caucus, council (ASSEMBLAGE); diet, parliament, senate (LEGISLATURE).

congressman, *n.* senator, representative (LEGISLATURE).

conjecture, *v.* guess, surmise, speculate (SUPPOSITION).

conjugal, *adj.* matrimonial, marital, nuptial (MARRIAGE).

conjure, *v.* perform magic, voodoo, levitate (MAGIC).

connect, *v.* unite, join, combine (JUNCTION, UNITY); bridge, span, link (BREAKWATER); relate, ally, consociate (RELATIONSHIP).

connection, *n.* bond, tie, link (FASTENING); relation, affiliation, association (RELATIONSHIP); relevance, bearing, application (PERTINENCE).

connive, *v.* conspire, collude (CO-OPERATION).

connoisseur, *n.* authority, expert, gourmet (JUDGE).

connote, *v.* imply, intimate, signify (SUGGESTION); denote, designate, evidence (INDICATION).

conquer, *v.* master, overmaster, subjugate (DEFEAT).

conquerable, *adj.* superable, vincible, pregnable (DEFEAT).

conscience, *n.* superego (*psychoanal.*), censor, scruple (PENITENCE).

conscienceless, *adj.* unconscionable, unprincipled, unscrupulous (DISHONESTY, IMPENITENCE).

conscientious, *adj.* moral, scrupulous, principled (HONESTY, RULE); thorough, careful (CARE).

conscious, *adj.* known, supraliminal; aware, appreciative, cognizant (KNOWLEDGE); sensible, aesthetic, passible (SENSITIVENESS); calculated, studied, premeditated (PURPOSE).

conscript, *v.* draft, impress, dragoon (FORCE).

conscript, *n.* drafted man, draftee, inductee (FIGHTER).

consecutive, *adj.* successive, serial, seriate (FOLLOWING).

consecrate, *v.* sanctify, hallow, bless (SACREDNESS).

consent, *n.* acquiescence, assent, concurrence (PERMISSION, AGREEMENT).

consequence, *n.* effect, outcome, aftermath (RESULT); import, moment, weight (IMPORTANCE).

consequently, *adv.* in consequence, therefore, hence (RESULT, REASONING).

conservation, *n.* preservation, salvation, safekeeping (PROTECTION).

conservative, *adj.* moderate, middle-of-the-road (MODERATENESS); bourgeois, hidebound, old-line (OPPOSITION); protective, preservative, defensive (PROTECTION).

conserve, *v.* protect, safeguard, preserve (PROTECTION).

consider, *v.* take into consideration, take account of, view (THOUGHT); deem, estimate, appraise (OPINION).

considerable, *adj.* abundant, ample, large (MULTITUDE, SIZE).

consideration, *n.* considerateness, thoughtfulness, tact (ATTENTION); concept, view, notion (OPINION); thinking, reflection, cogitation (THOUGHT); fee, commission, percentage (PAYMENT).

considered, *adj.* deliberate, voluntary, express (PURPOSE).

consign, *v.* send, dispatch, transmit (SENDING).

consistent, *adj.* uniform, homogeneous, even (UNIFORMITY); compatible, consonant, congruous (AGREEMENT).

consist of, *v.* comprise, contain, include (MAKE-UP).

console, *v.* solace, condole with, comfort (PITY, RELIEF); calm, soothe, untrouble (UNANXIETY).

consolidate, *v.* conjoin, league, band (JUNCTION); densen, compress, condense (THICKNESS).

consonant, *n.* tonic, dental, labial (VOICE, WRITTEN SYMBOL).

conspicuous, *adj.* noticeable, marked, pointed (VISIBILITY).

conspire, *v.* complot, cabal, colleague (PLAN); co-operate, connive, collude (CO-OPERATION).

constable, *n.* police officer, peace officer, sheriff (OFFICIAL).

constant, *adj.* unfailing, unflagging, unremitting (CONTINUATION); uniform, homogeneous, consistent (UNIFORMITY); loyal, faithful, true (LOYALTY).

consternation, *n.* trepidation, dismay, horror (FEAR); awe, shock, wonder (SURPRISE).

constituent, *n.* part, component, factor (PART); voter, elector, balloter (VOTE).

constitute, *v.* compose, compound, construct (MAKE-UP); commission, delegate, deputize (PLACE).

constitution, *n.* composition, content, contents (MAKE-UP); character, structure, organization (TEXTURE, SHAPE); figure, physique, frame (BODY); personality, temperament, make-up (CHARACTER); charter, code; establishment, lawmaking (LAW).

constitutional, *n.* walk, amble, stroll (WALKING).

constrict, *v.* tighten, strain, tauten, tense (TIGHTNESS); contract, constringe, clench (TRACTION).

construct, *v.* build, erect, fabricate (BUILDING); compose, compound, constitute (MAKE-UP).

construction, *n.* structure, constitution, architecture (SHAPE); definition, interpretation, translation (EXPLANATION, UNDERSTANDING).

construe, *v.* interpret, understand, infer (EXPLANATION, UNDERSTANDING).

consult, *v.* confer, ask an opinion, discuss (ADVICE).

consultation, *n.* discussion, argument, conference (TALK).

consume, *v.* use up, exhaust, deplete (USE); swallow, gulp, ingurgitate (RECEIVING); swig, swill, toss off (DRINK).

consummate, *adj.* perfect, absolute, ideal (PERFECTION).

consummate, *v.* perfect, crown,

put the finishing touch to (PER-FECTION).

consumption, *n.* depletion, exhaustion, expenditure (USE); eating, swallowing, deglutition (FOOD, DRINK); waste, atrophy (DECAY); phthisis, tuberculosis, white plague (BREATH).

consumptive, *adj.* wasted, emaciated, cadaverous (THINNESS).

contact, *n.* collision, hit, strike (TOUCH).

contagious, *adj.* catching, infectious, communicable (TRANSFER, DISEASE).

contain, *v.* comprise, consist of, include (MAKE-UP); have, hold, receive (CONTAINER); keep back, check, harness (RESTRAINT).

CONTAINER—*N.* **container,** receptacle, holder, hopper, tabernacle; censer, gallipot, mortar; holster, quiver, scabbard, sheath, horn.

box, bin, carton, case, chest, casket, coffer, crate, firkin, hutch, humidor, caisson.

can, canister, cannikin, tin, growler (*slang*).

vessel, basin, bowl, pot, utensil, tub, churn; tank, cistern, vat.

pail, bucket; brazier, hod, scuttle.

barrel, drum, keg, tub, cask, firkin, tun.

basket, hamper, pannier; bassinet, cradle.

tray, hod, salver, waiter.

bottle, carafe, carboy, censer, canteen, cruet, vinaigrette, vial, phial, decanter, demijohn, stoup, flagon, jeroboam, magnum; flask, ampulla, flacon (*F.*).

jar, amphora, beaker, crock, cruse, jug, pitcher, ewer, Toby; vase, urn.

[*drinking vessel*] **cup,** beaker, bowl, chalice, cruse, demitasse, horn, mug, pannikin, stein; gourd, calabash; cannikin, stoup; glass, goblet, jeroboam, rummer, tankard, tumbler.

plate, platter, dish, porringer, bowl, casserole, tureen.

earthenware, bone china, ceramic ware, china, chinaware, crockery, Dresden, Limoges, porcelain ware, pottery, Sèvres, Spode, stoneware, terra cotta, Lenox, Wedgwood.

ladle, dipper, bail, scoop, spoon. [*for heating or cooking*] **pot,** pan, pannikin, saucepan; frying pan, skillet, spider, griddle; boiler, caldron, kettle, teakettle, teapot, urn, samovar, coffee urn, percolator, dripolator, coffee pot, vacuum coffee maker; retort, crucible.

bag, pouch, sack, poke (*archaic*), caddie bag, saddlebags; purse,

handbag, clutch bag, reticule, pocketbook, French purse, *portemonnaie* (*F.*), wallet, coin purse, money clip, billfold.

traveling bag, traveling case, Boston bag, carpetbag, Gladstone, grip, gripsack, handbag, portmanteau, satchel, suitcase, valise; brief case, brief bag, attaché case, portfolio; duffel bag, haversack, knapsack, wallet, rucksack, kit; trunk, footlocker, wardrobe, wardrobe trunk; baggage, impedimenta, luggage.

repository, depository, closet, cupboard, cabinet, locker, wardrobe, clothespress, chiffonier, buffet, bureau, chest of drawers, commode, sideboard; escritoire, secretary, writing desk, *prie dieu* (*F.*), desk; bookcase, bookrack, bookstand, bookshelf; till, safe, drawer; shelf, whatnot.

V. **contain,** have, hold, receive, admit, include, take in, accommodate, teem with.

See also CONTENTS, GLASSINESS, HOLD, OWNERSHIP, RECEIVING, STORE.

contaminate, *v.* adulterate, debase, pollute (IMPURITY); profane, desecrate, violate (IRRELIGION).

contemplate, *v.* think, reflect, cogitate (THOUGHT); scan, regard, gaze at (LOOKING); plan, meditate, aim (PLAN, PURPOSE).

contemporary, *adj.* contemporaneous, coetaneous, coexistent (SIMULTANEOUSNESS, OLDNESS); present, current, topical (PRESENT TIME).

CONTEMPT—*N.* **contempt,** disdain, disesteem, disregard, ridicule, indignity, contumely, scorn, audacity, impudence, insolence, snobbism, snobbery.

[*object of contempt*] **cur,** bugger, buzzard (*colloq.*), caitiff (*archaic*), scum, sneak, heel (*slang*), swine, wretch; wench, jade; byword, insignificancy, scorn, target, butt.

V. **contemn,** despise, misprize, look down upon, make light of, disdain, disesteem, disregard, vilipend, flout, scout; belittle, huff, pooh-pooh, sneer at, scorn, sneeze at, snub, slight, spurn, upstage (*colloq.*); bridle, sneer, sniff, snort.

ridicule, deride, fleer (*dialectal*), gibe at, hoot at, jeer at, mock, rail at, scoff at, laugh at.

[*cause contempt for*] **cheapen,** degrade, abase, pillory.

Adj. **contemptuous,** disdainful, derisive, scornful, sardonic, snooty, snippy (*colloq.*), supercilious, snobbish, toplofty, haughty, arrogant, upstage (*colloq.*), cavalier, offhand; impudent, insolent, disrespectful, opprobrious, audacious, bold.

contemptible, abject, beggarly, caitiff (*archaic*), cheap, currish, despicable, ignominious, insignificant, low, mean, measly (*slang*), miserable, pitiable, pitiful, scabby (*colloq.*), scummy, scurvy, shabby, sneaky, sorry, swinish, unworthy, wretched, vile.

See also DETRACTION, DISAPPROVAL, DISCOURTESY, DISREPUTE, HATRED, MEANNESS, RIDICULE. *Antonyms*— See APPROVAL, COURTESY, PRIDE, RESPECT.

contend, *v.* compete, contest, vie (ATTEMPT); battle, clash, combat (FIGHTING); dispute, argue, controvert (DISAGREEMENT); assert, maintain, insist (STATEMENT).

content, *adj.* satisfied, complacent, smug (SATISFACTION).

content, *n.* matter, text, subject (MEANING); composition, constitution, contents (MAKE-UP); filling, packing (CONTENTS).

CONTENTS—*N.* contents, content, filling, lading, packing, stuffing, inside, furnishing, furniture; cargo, freight, shipment, load, bale, pack.

capacity, room, burden (*naut.*); cubic capacity, volume; extent, space, size.

content, matter, subject matter, topic, subject, thesis, theme, motif, text; substance, essence, gist.

V. **contain,** have, hold, include, take in, admit, accommodate, receive; teem with, abound with.

See also CONTAINER, FULLNESS, HOLD, OWNERSHIP, RECEIVING, STORE, TOPIC. *Antonyms*—See ABSENCE.

contest, *n.* competition, match, tournament (ATTEMPT).

context, *n.* vocabulary, lexicon, text (WORD).

continent, *n.* mainland, main (LAND).

CONTINUATION—*N.* continuation, continuance, continuity, continuum, durability, stability, survival; duration, term, period; endurance, guts, stamina, vitality.

permanence, perdurability, eternity, immortality, perpetuity, perpetuance, sempiternity.

V. **continue,** go on, keep up, hold on, endure, wear, last, remain, stand; stay, abide, linger; survive, outlast, outlive; proceed, resume; perpetuate, eternalize.

carry on, carry on with, go on with, keep going, keep on with, maintain, prolong, prosecute, pursue, stay with, stick with, sustain, wage.

persevere, persist, hold on, hold out, stick to, cling to, adhere to; keep on, plod, keep to one's course, hold (*or* maintain) one's ground, insist; bear up, keep up, hold up; go to all lengths, go through fire and water.

Adj. **continuous,** endless, perpetual, unbroken, uninterrupted; continual, minutely, steady, stable, constant.

continuing, persisting, abiding, lingering, chronic, persevering, dogged, stubborn, obstinate, persistent, pertinacious, relentless, stick-to-itive (*colloq.*), tenacious; unfailing, unflagging, unrelenting, unremitting, diligent, constant, assiduous.

durable, enduring, lasting, long-continued, long-continuing, long-enduring, long-lasting, long-standing, perennial.

permanent, aeonian, ageless, timeless, agelong, dateless, everlasting, immortal, eternal, perdurable, perpetual, sempiternal.

indelible, ineradicable, inerasable, inexpungeable.

See also ENDLESSNESS, LENGTH, LIFE, REMAINDER, STABILITY, TIME. *Antonyms*—See CESSATION, DISCONTINUITY, DISJUNCTION, ELIMINATION, END.

contour, *n.* outline, lineation, lines (SHAPE).

contraband, *adj.* prohibited, forbidden, taboo (DENIAL).

contraception, *n.* birth control, planned parenthood (PREGNANCY).

contract, *n.* deal (*colloq.*), arrangement, understanding (COMPACT).

contract, *v.* compress, condense, constrict (DECREASE, TRACTION); abbreviate, syncopate (SHORTNESS); shrink, dwindle, wane (SMALLNESS); covenant, agree, stipulate (PROMISE); catch, get (DISEASE).

contraction, *n.* blend, portmanteau word, clipped word (WORD).

contradict, *v.* gainsay, disaffirm, dispute (DENIAL, OPPOSITION, OPPOSITE).

contrary, *adj.* opposed, antithetic, disaffirmatory; unfavorable, adverse, disadvantageous; froward, perverse, wayward (OPPOSITION, OPPOSITE).

contrary, *n.* antilogy, antipode, antithesis (OPPOSITE).

contrast, *n.* antithesis, contradistinction, foil (DIFFERENCE).

contribute, *v.* donate, present, give away (GIVING, CHARITY).

contrite, *adj.* penitent, repentant, remorseful (PENITENCE).

contrivance, *n.* device, apparatus, appliance (INSTRUMENT); design, scheme, stratagem (PLAN).

contrive, *v.* fashion, forge, devise (PRODUCTION); hatch, concoct, project (PLAN).

contrived, *adj.* artificial, constrained, forced (UNNATURALNESS).

CONTROL—*N.* control, determination, manipulation, regulation, regimentation; command, domination, dominion, predomination, sway, ascendancy, upper hand, whip hand, mastery, rule, subjection, subjugation, subordination; check, bridle, rein, curb, restraint, restriction, containment; corner, monopoly, wirepulling, address, strategy.

direction, management, administration, government, regime, charge, supervision, superintendence.

self-control, self-discipline, Spartanism, self-restraint, composure, constraint, reserve, restraint, austerity, temperance, astringency, asceticism, prudence, stoicism, yoga.

position of control: helm, saddle, chair, conn, conning tower.

controlling device: control, controls, regulator, governor, check, determinant, rein, reins, bit; switch, lever, pedal, treadle, robot.

controller, manipulator, governor, commander, master, ruler, wirepuller; navigator, steersman, pilot.

despot, oppressor, tyrant, autocrat, dictator; bully, browbeater, hector, bruiser, bucko.

director, manager, administrator, governor, overseer, supervisor, superintendent; caretaker, curator, custodian, executive, gerent, proctor, steward, comprador; matron.

V. control, determine, manipulate, regulate, regiment; command, dominate, predominate, hold sway over, sway, master, rule, subject, subjugate, subordinate to; check, bridle, rein, curb, contain, restrain, restrict; cow, awe; corner, monopolize; pull strings, pull wires, wirepull; navigate, steer, pilot.

domineer, browbeat, bully, lord over, despotize over, tyrannize over, oppress, hector.

direct, manage, administer, take charge of, govern; oversee, overlook, supervise, superintend.

Adj. despotic, domineering, browbeating, bullying, tyrannous, oppressive, autocratic, dictatorial, imperious, absolutistic, magisterial, peremptory, arbitrary, authoritative, masterful, rigorous.

self-controlled, self-disciplined, Spartan, self-restrained, composed, restrained, reserved.

austere, temperate, abstemious, astringent, ascetic, prudent, stoical.

inhibited, suppressed, repressed, sublimated.

See also CELIBACY, COMMAND, GOVERNMENT, MODERATENESS, OFFICIAL, POWER, RESTRAINT, SOBRIETY. *Antonyms*—See FREEDOM, OBEDIENCE, SUBMISSION.

---

controversial, *adj.* arguable, controvertible, disputable (DISAGREEMENT, UNCERTAINTY, INQUIRY).

controversy, *n.* dispute, conflict, falling-out (DISAGREEMENT).

contusion, *n.* bruise, mouse, wale (HARM).

conundrum, *n.* puzzle, poser, riddle (MYSTERY, INQUIRY, AMBIGUITY).

convalescence, *n.* rally, recovery, recuperation (HEALTH).

convene, *v.* call together, rally, assemble (SUMMONS, ASSEMBLAGE).

convenience, *n.* handiness, availability, accessibility (EASE); leisure, opportunity (TIME).

conveniences, *n.* facilities, utilities, appliances (EASE).

convenient, *adj.* handy, available, commodious (EASE); suitable, suited (USE).

convent, *n.* nunnery, cloister, abbey (RELIGIOUS COMMUNITY).

convention, *n.* custom, customs, proprieties (HABIT); convocation, assembly, meeting (SUMMONS, ASSEMBLAGE).

conventional, *adj.* customary, routine, traditional (CONFORMITY); decorous, demure, proper (PROPRIETY); hackneyed, humdrum (COMMONNESS).

CONVERGENCE—*N.* convergence, conflux, confluence, concourse, concurrence, concentration, focalization, meeting.

V. converge, concur; come together, unite, meet, encounter, close in upon; center, focalize, focus, concentrate, enter in, pour in, assemble, rally.

See also ASSEMBLAGE, CENTER. *Antonyms*—See BISECTION, DISPERSION, SPREAD, TURNING.

conversation, *n.* colloquy, tête-à-tête (*F.*), chat (TALK).

convert, *v.* transform, transmute (CHANGE); persuade, brainwash (PERSUASION); proselytize, proselyte (RELIGION).

convex, *adj.* bulgy, bulged, biconvex (CURVE).

convey, *v.* carry, transport, conduct (TRANSFER); lead, guide (LEADERSHIP).

conveyance, *n.* car, train, omnibus (VEHICLE).

convict, *n.* prisoner, criminal, felon (IMPRISONMENT, ILLEGALITY).

convict, *v.* find guilty, condemn, attaint (GUILT).

conviction, *n.* creed, persuasion (BELIEF).

convince, *v.* prevail on, sway, win over (PERSUASION).

convivial, *adj.* companionable, congenial, conversable (FRIENDLINESS); festive, festal, jovial (SOCIALITY); merry, gay, fun-loving (MERRIMENT).

convulsion, *n.* spasm, paroxysm, algospasm (PAIN); quake, shock, seism (EARTHQUAKE).

COOKERY—*N.* cookery, cuisine, cooking, etc. (see *Verbs*).

cook, chef, *cuisinier* (*F.*, *masc.*), *cuisinière* (*F.*, *fem.*), *cordon bleu* (*F.*; *jocose*), baker.

cookhouse, cuisine, kitchen, galley (*naut.*), cookery, bakehouse, bakery; grillroom, grill, grille, rotisserie, restaurant.

cooker, autoclave, pressure cooker, boiler, broiler, fryer, frying pan, skillet, griddle, gridiron, grill, roasting pan, roaster, rotisserie, pot, pan, double-boiler, waterless cooker, oven, baker, chafing dish, kettle, urn, percolator.

stove, cookstove, range, calefactor.

barbecue, clambake, bake, fry, fishfry, roast, cook-out, picnic.

V. cook, boil, coddle, parboil, steam, precook, poach, scald; heat, warm, prepare, fix (*colloq.*); broil, sizzle, barbecue, grill, fry, frizzle, brown, braise, griddle, roast, rotisserie, sauté, pan-fry, sear, stew, simmer, fricassee, bake, escallop, pressure-cook, autoclave.

Adj. cooked, boiled, etc. (see *Verbs*); well-cooked, well-done; overcooked, overdone; undercooked, underdone, rare; uncooked, raw; underbaked, half-baked, doughy.

[*pert. to cooking*] culinary.

See also CONTAINER, FIRE, FOOD, HEAT. *Antonyms*—See FASTING.

cookie, *n.* bun, cracker (BREAD).

cool, *adj.* chill, chilly, frigid (COLD); calm, unagitated, philosophical (UNANXIETY); self-composed, collected, coolheaded (CALMNESS); hostile, unfriendly (HOSTILITY); insolent, impudent, impertinent (DISCOURTESY); feverless, afebrile, normal (FEVER).

cooler (*colloq.*), *n.* jug (*colloq.*), lockup, jail (IMPRISONMENT).

coolheaded, *adj.* level, cool, self-composed (INEXCITABILITY, CALMNESS); common-sensical, well-balanced, levelheaded (WISDOM).

coop, *n.* cage, fold, pinfold (IMPRISONMENT).

CO-OPERATION—*N.* co-operation, coaction, teamwork, co-ordination, synergism, combination, collaboration, concert, communion, coadjuvancy, union, concurrence; logrolling.

complicity, collusion, connivance, guilt; conspiracy, confederacy.

association, alliance, league, society, company, partnership, pool, gentlemen's agreement; confederation, coalition, fusion, federation, trust, combine; fellowship, comradeship, fraternization, fraternity, freemasonry.

unanimity, agreement, accordance, concord, harmony, consentaneity; morale, *esprit de corps* (*F.*).

V. co-operate, concur, concert, coact, cofunction, collaborate, co-ordinate, synchronize, combine, pool, pull together, stand shoulder to shoulder, work hand in glove, join forces, fraternize; conspire, connive, collude.

side with, go along with, uphold, make common cause with, unite with, join with, take part with, cast in one's lot with; rally round, follow the lead of.

participate, take part, share, be a party to, partake in, lend oneself to; chip in (*colloq.*), contribute.

Adj. co-operative, in league, hand in glove; synergetic.

shared, collective, common, conjoint, mutual, joint; bilateral, trilateral, multilateral.

See also AGREEMENT, AID, COMBINATION, JUNCTION, WORK. *Antonyms*—See OPPOSITION.

coop up, *v.* box up, bottle up, cramp (IMPRISONMENT).

co-ordinate, *adj.* equal, equalized, coequal (EQUALITY).

co-ordinate, *v.* synchronize, conduce, combine (CO-OPERATION).

cope with, *v.* buffet, pit oneself against, struggle with (ATTEMPT).

copious, *adj.* abundant, ample, plentiful (SUFFICIENCY).

copper, *n.* cuprum (*chemistry*), brass, bronze (METAL); change, small change, coins (CHANGE); brownish red, maroon, terra cotta (RED).

copulate, *v.* cohabit, conjugate, couple (SEX).

COPY—*N.* copy, duplicate, manifold, reproduction, tracery, transcription, autotype, carbon copy, ectype, facsimile, likeness, miniature, replica, similitude.

copier, duplicator, engrosser, reproducer, tracer, transcriber, copyist; amanuensis.

model, archetype, original, exemplar, paragon, nonesuch, pattern, prototype, standard, stereotype; ideal, beau ideal.

example, case, illustration, exemplification, instance, specimen, sample, typification, cross section, monotype, precedent, quintessence.

type, antetype, antitype, countertype, paradigm, prototype, prefiguration, exponent; embodiment, incarnation, personification, epitome.

V. copy, duplicate, engross, manifold, reproduce, trace, transcribe, rewrite; mirror, reflect.

exemplify, illustrate, embody, epitomize, typify, personify, incarnate, prefigure; model.

Adj. faithful, lifelike, similar, close, accurate, exact.

Adv., phrases. for example, *exempli gratia* (L.), *e.g.*, *par exemple* (F.), for instance, as an illustration, as a case in point.

literally, verbatim, *literatim* (L.), *sic* (L.), *verbatim et literatim* (L.), *mot à mot* (F.), word for word, precisely, exactly, textually.

See also IMITATION, REPETITION, REPRESENTATION, SIMILARITY. *Antonyms*—See BEGINNING, DIFFERENCE, PRODUCTION.

---

copycat, *n.* imitator, copier, copyist (IMITATION).

coquette, *n.* flirt, vampire, fizgig (LOVE).

coral, *n.* pink, rose, fuchsia (RED).

cord, *n.* string, rope, twine (FILAMENT).

cordial, *adj.* hearty, sincere, glowing (FEELING); heartfelt, heart-to-heart, wholehearted (HONESTY).

core, *n.* heart, kernel, nucleus (CENTER); body, crux, essence (PART); main idea, burden (IDEA).

cork, *n.* plug, stopper, tampon (RESTRAINT, CLOSURE).

corkscrew, *v.* coil, convolute, wrap around (WINDING).

corn, *n.* callus, callosity, induration (SKIN).

corner, *n.* angle, nook, niche (PLACE, ANGULARITY).

cornerstone, *n.* quoin, coin (ROCK); keystone, keynote, core (IMPORTANCE).

corporation, *n.* legal body, legal entity (BODY); paunch, potbelly (BELLY, SIZE).

corpse, *n.* cadaver, remains, the deceased (DEATH).

corpulent, *adj.* fat, stout, fleshy (SIZE).

correct, *adj.* true, actual, factual, accurate (TRUTH); proper, legitimate (PROPRIETY, RIGHT).

correct, *v.* remedy, rectify, adjust (CURE, RIGHT, IMPROVEMENT, RESTORATION); undeceive, set right, set straight (INFORMATION); punish, penalize, discipline (PUNISHMENT).

correlation, *n.* interrelation, interdependence, interconnection (RELATIONSHIP).

correspond, *v.* harmonize, fit, conform (SIMILARITY, AGREEMENT).

correspondence, *n.* agreement, resemblance, likeness (CONFORMITY); regularity, harmony, symmetry (UNIFORMITY, SHAPE); mail, letters, writings (EPISTLE).

corresponding, *adj.* comparative, similar, parallel (SIMILARITY, COMPARISON).

correspond with, *v.* write to, communicate with, keep in touch with (EPISTLE, WRITING).

corridor, *n.* hall, hallway, entranceway (INGRESS, PASSAGE).

corroborate, *v.* substantiate, validate, verify (PROOF, TRUTH).

corrode, *v.* erode, waste, eat away (DESTRUCTION).

corrupt, *adj.* debauched, Augean, base (IMMORALITY); infamous, monstrous, foul (WICKEDNESS); loose, abandoned (SEX).

corrupt, *v.* canker, debauch, degrade (IMMORALITY); seduce, deprave (SEX); bribe, buy, reach (BRIBERY).

corsage, *n.* bouquet, posy, nosegay (PLANT LIFE).

corset, *n.* corselet, foundation, girdle (UNDERWEAR).

cortege, *n.* retinue, procession, company (ACCOMPANIMENT).

cosmetic, *n.* face powder, talcum powder, make-up (BEAUTY, POWDERINESS).

cosmic, *adj.* universal, cosmogonic (WORLD).

cost, *n.* charge, amount, price (EX-

PENDITURE); penalty, forfeiture, forfeit (LOSS).

cost, v. bring in, sell for, yield (SALE).

costly, adj. expensive, high, valuable (EXPENDITURE, VALUE).

costume, n. outfit, ensemble, wardrobe (CLOTHING).

cot, n. bed, bunk, berth (SLEEP).

coterie, n. circle, clique, society (FRIEND).

cottage, n. bungalow, ranch house, cabana (HABITATION).

cottony, adj. villous, lanate, lanuginous (HAIR).

couch, n. davenport, day bed, divan (SEAT).

cough, v. hawk, hack, bark (THROAT).

cough up, v. expectorate, vomit, spit up (THROAT).

council, n. congress, parliament, senate (ASSEMBLAGE, LEGISLATURE); cabinet, official family (OFFICIAL).

counsel, n. attorney, advocate, counselor (LAWYER); suggestion, recommendation (ADVICE).

counselor, n. attorney, advocate, counsel (LAWYER); guide, adviser, mentor (ADVICE, TEACHER).

count, v. enumerate, numerate, reckon (NUMBER); weigh, tell (INFLUENCE).

countenance, n. face, visage, aspect (HEAD, APPEARANCE); composure, self-composure, presence of mind (CALMNESS).

countenance, v. accept, approve, approbate (APPROVAL); invite, encourage (URGING).

counter, adj. opposed, opposing, against (OPPOSITION).

counteract, v. counter, counterwork, contravene (OPPOSITION).

counterattack, n. counteroffensive (ATTACK).

counterbalance, v. neutralize, offset, cancel (OPPOSITION, INEFFECTIVENESS).

counterfeit, v. fake, simulate, feign (FALSENESS, PRETENSE); forge, coin (THIEVERY).

counterpart, n. complement, opposite number, obverse (SIMILARITY, COMPLETENESS).

countersign, n. password, watchword, grip (WORD, INDICATION).

countless, adj. numberless, innumerable, infinite (ENDLESSNESS, MULTITUDE).

count on, v. plan on, aim for, reckon on (PLAN).

countrified, adj. rural, rustic, bucolic (RURAL REGION).

county, n. shire, canton, province (REGION).

coup, n. successful stroke, coup de maitre (F.), master stroke (SUCCESS).

couple, n. couplet, twain (archaic), both (TWO); man and wife, newlyweds, wedded pair (MARRIAGE).

couple, v. link, yoke, pair (TWO, JUNCTION); unite, join, connect (UNITY).

COURAGE—N. courage, bravery, valor, valiancy; heart, spirit, soul; daring, gallantry, intrepidity, heroism, prowess, audacity; foolhardiness, recklessness, temerity, rashness; manhood, manliness, nerve, mettle, grit, guts (colloq.), pluck (colloq.), sand (slang), virtue, hardihood, fortitude, backbone, spunk (colloq.), bulldog courage, resolution; bravado.

exploit, feat, deed, stunt, venture, derring-do, res gestae (L.).

[brave person] hero, heroine, adventurer, daredevil, gallant, lion, Spartan, stalwart, Trojan, yeoman.

desperado, madcap, daredevil, harum-scarum, hotspur, Hector, scapegrace, blade.

V. be courageous, dare, venture, make bold; face, front, confront, face up to; brave, beard, defy.

nerve oneself, summon up (or pluck up) courage, take heart, stand one's ground, brace up, bear up, hold out; present a bold front, show fight, face the music.

hearten, inspire, reassure, encourage, embolden, nerve, rally.

be rash, stick at nothing, play with fire; tempt Providence.

Adj. courageous, brave, bold, audacious, resolute, aweless, dauntless, doughty, fearless, martial, gallant, heroic, impavid, intrepid, lionhearted, redblooded, Spartan, Trojan, stalwart, stout, stouthearted, valiant, valorous; manly, manful, yeomanly, soldierly, two-fisted; game, nervy, spunky, spirited, plucky; daredevil, daring, adventuresome, adventurous, venturesome, venturous, assured, devilish, hardy; unafraid, unalarmed, unapprehensive, undaunted, unfaltering, unflinching, unfrightened, unscared, unshrinking, unterrified; pot-valiant.

reckless, rash, brash, harum-scarum, headlong, impetuous, temerarious, wildcat, wild, madcap, desperate, devil-may-care, death-defying, bold, hotheaded, headstrong, breakneck, foolhardy, harebrained; incautious, indiscreet, injudicious, imprudent, hasty, overhasty, thoughtless, heedless, unwary, careless; overconfident.

See also CARELESSNESS, DEFIANCE.

Antonyms—See FEAR, NERVOUSNESS, SUBMISSION.

courier, *n.* runner, express, intelligencer (MESSENGER).

course, *n.* route, itinerary, run (PASSAGE); current, stream, flow (RIVER, PROGRESS); procedure, *modus operandi* (*L.*), process (METHOD); elapsing, lapse, progress (PASSAGE); subject, study, class (LEARNING); stratum, tier, lap (LAYER).

course, *v.* run, career, dash (SPEED).

court, *n.* yard, compass, close (INCLOSURE); alley, alleyway, lane (PASSAGE); court of justice, tribunal (COURT OF LAW); the bench, his honor (JUDGE); courtship, wooing, suit (LOVE); retinue, train, suite (SERVICE).

court, *v.* make love, woo (LOVE); bootlick, truckle to, pander to (FLATTERY).

courtesan, *n.* cocotte, Cyprian, Delilah (SEX, PROSTITUTE).

COURTESY—*N.* courtesy, affability, breeding, good breeding, good manners, manners, civility, complaisance, comity, bon ton, refinement, ceremony, politesse; suavity, urbanity, gentility.

chivalry, gallantry, knight-errantry, quixotism, attentions, Bushido (*Jap.*).

etiquette, amenities, civilities, suavities, urbanities, niceties, devoirs.

[*courteous person*] gentleman, *caballero* (*Sp.*), lady, gentlewoman, thoroughbred.

[*chivalrous man*] gallant, cavalier, chevalier.

Adj. courteous, polite, attentive, civil, civilized, complaisant, debonair, genteel, gentlemanly, gracious, ladylike, mannerly, refined, well-behaved, well-bred, well-mannered, affable, ceremonious; suave, urbane, well-spoken, soft-spoken.

chivalrous, courtly, chivalric, gallant, knightly, quixotic.

obsequious, servile, subservient.

See also FRIENDLINESS, RESPECT, SOCIALITY. *Antonyms*—See BLUNTNESS, CONTEMPT, DISCOURTESY, DISRESPECT.

courtly, *adj.* flattering, complimentary, adulatory (FLATTERY).

COURT OF LAW—*N.* court of law, court, court of justice, judicatory, judicial tribunal, law court, court of last resort, tribunal; the bar, the bench, bar of justice, judgment seat, courtroom, courthouse; chambers, judge's chambers; Star Chamber (*hist.*); municipal court, police court, criminal court, kangaroo court, court of domestic relations, court of claims, court-martial, superior court, supreme court, court of chancery, court of equity, admiralty, court of admiralty; appellate court, court of appeal, court of review; court system, judiciary; court sessions, juridical days, assizes (*Brit.*).

justice, administration of justice, judicatory, judicature.

decision (*of a court or judge*), decree, ruling, judgment, verdict, adjudication, authority.

court order, summons, process, subpoena, writ, brief, injunction.

V. render judgment, decide on, judge, rule on, hand down a decision, give a verdict; subpoena, summons, issue a writ.

Adj. judicial, forensic, judiciary, juridic *or* juridical, judicatory, justiciary.

See also JUDGE, JUDGMENT, LAW, LAWSUIT, LEGALITY.

courtship, *n.* wooing, suit, court (LOVE).

cousin, *n.* first cousin, full cousin, own cousin (RELATIVE).

cove, *n.* estuary, firth *or* frith (INLET).

covenant, *n.* bargain, pact, agreement (COMPACT).

COVERING—*N.* covering, cover, shelter, screen, coverture, integument, tegument; lid, top, coverlid; rug, carpet, runner, scatter rug, throw rug, carpeting; curtain, drape; blanket, bower, canopy, cap, caparison, cloak, mantle, muffler, pall, panoply, shelter, shroud, shutter, swathe, wraps, antimacassar, cozy.

hood, bonnet, cowl, capote.

crust, coating, coat, bloom, encrustation, incrustation, efflorescence (*chem.*), scale, scab, slough (*med.*), eschar (*med.*).

peel, rind, bark, husk, shell, hull, cortex.

sheath, sheathing, capsule, pod, casing, case, involucrum (*zool.*), wrapping, wrapper, jacket, envelope, vagina.

veneer, facing, leaf, layer; paint, stain, varnish, gloss, enamel, wash, washing, whitewash, plaster, stucco; gilt, gilding, overlay.

horse blanket, horsecloth, body cloth, blanket; caparison, housing, housings, trappings; harness, saddle.

roof, ceiling, roofing, top, housetop; cupola, dome, vault, terrace, spire, thatched roof; canopy, marquee, awning; calash; attic, garret, loft; rafter, coaming, eaves.

V. **cover,** superimpose, overlay, overspread, envelop, clothe, invest, wrap, incase; face, case, veneer, paper; clapboard, weatherboard, shingle; conceal, curtain, hide, cloak, hood, shelter, shield, screen, protect.

coat, paint, stain, varnish, incrust, crust, cement, stucco, plaster; smear, daub, besmear, bedaub; gild, plate, japan, lacquer, enamel; whitewash, calcimine.

Adj. **covered,** protected, screened, shielded, loricated, hooded, cowled, armored, armor-plated, ironclad, bullet-proof.

scaly, squamous, squamate, scalelike, squamosal (*tech.*), ramentaceous *or* ramental (*bot.*); laminate.

overlapping, shingled, imbricate, lapstreak (*said of boats*), clinker-built.

roofed, canopied, ceilinged, domed, spired, vaulted; domal, domical; rooflike, tectiform.

See also CLOTHING, CONCEALMENT, PROTECTION. *Antonyms*—See DISCLOSURE, LINING, UNDRESS, VISIBILITY.

covet, *v.* want, envy, lust after (DESIRE).

cow, *n.* bovine, ruminant (ANIMAL).

cow, *v.* intimidate, daunt, overawe (FEAR).

coward, *n.* poltroon, dastard, sneak (FEAR).

cowboy, *n.* broncobuster, *vaquero* (*Sp.*), buckaroo (SERVICE).

cower, *v.* cringe, crouch, grovel (FEAR, POSTURE).

cowlike, *adj.* bovine, vaccine (ANIMAL).

co-worker, *n.* teamworker, fellow-worker, mate (WORK).

coxcomb, *n.* dandy, dude, exquisite (FASHION).

coy, *adj.* demure, skittish, blushing (MODESTY).

cozy, *adj.* restful, comfortable, snug (REST).

crab, *n.* crabstick, crank (*colloq.*), crosspatch (BAD TEMPER); crustacean (ANIMAL).

crack, *n.* slit, split, cleft (OPENING, DISJUNCTION).

crack, *v.* snap, split, splinter (BREAKAGE).

cracked, *adj.* gruff, roupy, croaky (HARSH SOUND); balmy (*colloq.*), bughouse (SLANG), crackbrained (INSANITY).

cracker, *n.* bun, cookie, biscuit (FOOD, BREAD).

cradle, *n.* crib, bassinet, bed (SLEEP); hamper, pannier (CONTAINER); nativity, ancestry (BEGINNING).

craft, *n.* cunning, subtlety, disingenuity (CLEVERNESS); watercraft, vessel, bottom (SHIP); aircraft, airplane, plane (FLYING).

crafts, *n.* handicraft, manual work (WORK).

crafty, *adj.* cunning, artful, foxy (CLEVERNESS).

cram, *v.* crowd, ram, stuff (FULLNESS).

cramp, *n.* Charley horse, crick, stitch (PAIN).

cramp, *v.* coop up, confine, limit (RESTRAINT, IMPRISONMENT).

cramped, *adj.* confined, two-by-four, close (IMPRISONMENT, NARROWNESS); cacographic, illegible, indecipherable (WRITING).

crane, *v.* elongate, extend, spread (STRETCH).

cranky, *adj.* crabby, cross, irritable (BAD TEMPER).

crash, *n.* smashup, impact, collision (TOUCH); thunder, thunderclap, peal (LOUDNESS).

crash, *v.* smash, clatter, roar (LOUDNESS).

crass, *adj.* lowbrow (*colloq.*), Philistine, illiberal (VULGARITY).

crater, *n.* chasm, yawn, abyss (OPENING).

crave, *v.* long for, hanker, ache for (DESIRE); need, require, want (NECESSITY).

CRAWL—*N.* crawl, creep, grovel, scrabble, scramble, reptation, vermiculation, clamber.

V. **crawl,** creep, grovel, scrabble, scramble, clamber.

Adj. **crawling,** crawly, creepy, reptant, repent, reptatory, reptile, vermicular.

See also ASCENT, SLAVERY, SLOWNESS. *Antonyms*—See SPEED.

craze, *n.* fad, rage, mania (ENTHUSIASM, DESIRE).

crazy, *adj.* insane, daft, touched (INSANITY).

creak, *v.* screak, chirr, crepitate (HARSH SOUND).

cream, *v.* ream, skim, top (REMOVAL).

creamy, *adj.* whitish, cream, cream-color (WHITENESS); fluffy, feathery (SOFTNESS).

crease, *v.* cockle, pucker, ruffle (WRINKLE).

create, *v.* give birth to, bring into being, bring into existence (PRODUCTION).

creation, *n.* coinage, invention, original (PRODUCTION); nascency, nativity (BIRTH); nature, universe (WORLD).

creative, *adj.* productive, prolific, fertile (PRODUCTION); imaginative, original, inventive (IMAGINATION).

creature, *n.* living being, being, organism (LIFE, ANIMAL); product, fruit, offspring (RESULT); cat's-paw, pawn, tool (USE).

credentials, *n.* documents, papers, token (POWER).

credible, *adj.* believable, creditable, plausible (BELIEF).

credit, *n.* installment plan, installment buying (DEBT); trust, confidence (BELIEF); honor, distinction (FAME).

creditable, *adj.* honorable, palmary, estimable (FAME).

creditor, *n.* lender, debtee, mortgagee (DEBT).

credulous, *adj.* believing, gullible, naïve (BELIEF).

creed, *n.* faith, religious persuasion, church (RELIGION); credo, conviction (BELIEF).

creek, *n.* run, burn, rill (RIVER).

creep, *v.* grovel, scrabble, scramble (CRAWL); itch, prickle, tingle (SENSITIVENESS, ITCHING).

creepy, *adj.* itchy, itching, crawly (ITCHING); frightening, shuddersome, dreadful (FEAR); nervous, jittery (*colloq.*), jumpy (NERVOUSNESS).

cremate, *v.* incinerate, cinder, incremate (BURIAL, FIRE).

crescendo, *n.* rise, swell, increase (LOUDNESS).

crescent-shaped, *adj.* crescent, crescentiform, crescentoid (CURVE).

crest, *n.* top, crown, pinnacle (HEIGHT); fleshy growth, comb (SKIN); topknot, panache (FEATHER).

crevice, *n.* crack, cranny, cut (OPENING).

crew, *n.* gang, team (WORK); party, faction, sect (SIDE).

crib, *n.* cradle, bassinet (SLEEP); granary, grain elevator, silo (STORE); pony, horse, trot (EXPLANATION).

crime, *n.* felony, misdemeanor, misdeed (ILLEGALITY).

criminal, *n.* culprit, convict, felon (ILLEGALITY).

crimson, *n.* ruby, ruby red, scarlet (RED).

cringe, *v.* cower, crouch, flinch (FEAR, POSTURE); bow, stoop, kneel (SLAVERY).

crinkle, *v.* rumple, ruffle, cockle (FOLD, WRINKLE, ROUGHNESS).

cripple, *v.* disable, incapacitate, paralyze (WEAKNESS).

crippled, *adj.* disabled, lame, halt (DISABLEMENT, APPENDAGE).

crisis, *n.* turning point, climax, zero hour (IMPORTANCE, CHANGE).

crisp, *adj.* crispy, crusty (HARDNESS); clear, cloudless, azure (CLARITY).

crisscross, *n.* network, reticulation, patchwork (CROSSING).

criterion, *n.* yardstick, touchstone, standard (RULE, JUDGMENT, COMPARISON).

critic, *n.* commentator, annotator, reviewer (TREATISE); hypercritic, censor, Momus (DISAPPROVAL).

critical, *adj.* faultfinding, captious, exceptive (DISAPPROVAL); crucial, acute, strategic (IMPORTANCE, NECESSITY, SOBRIETY).

criticism, *n.* commentary, review, critique (TREATISE, JUDGMENT); stricture, vitriol, opprobrium (DISAPPROVAL).

croak, *v.* hawk, quack, squawk (HARSH SOUND).

crochet, *v.* weave, knit, spin (TEXTURE).

crockery, *n.* china, chinaware, Dresden (CONTAINER).

crony, *n.* acquaintance, intimate, confidant (FRIEND).

crook (*slang*), *n.* pilferer, filcher, purloiner (DISHONESTY, THIEF).

crook, *v.* wind, meander, snake (WINDING).

crooked, *adj.* distorted, contorted, gnarled (DEFORMITY); knurly, tortile, tortuous (WINDING); deceitful, devious, fraudulent (DISHONESTY).

crop, *n.* harvest, yield, output (STORE); byproduct, repercussion (RESULT); handle, shank, haft (HOLD).

crop, *v.* shorten, trim, prune (CUTTING); browse, graze, champ (FOOD).

cross, *adj.* irascible, crabby, irritable (BAD TEMPER).

cross, *n.* rood, crucifix, crux (CROSSING).

cross, *v.* bisect, intersect (CROSSING); sail, voyage, navigate (TRAVELING).

crossbreed, *n.* mixture, mongrel, hybrid (CROSSING).

cross-examine, *v.* cross-question, third-degree (*colloq.*), grill (INQUIRY).

cross-eyed, *adj.* strabismic, squint-eyed (EYE).

CROSSING—*N.* **crossing,** intersection, crosswalk, crossroad, grade crossing; traversal, decussation.

going through, transience; osmosis, dialysis (*chem.*), transudation.

crossbreed, mixture, mongrel, hybrid.

crisscross, network, reticulation, tessellation, patchwork, checkerboard design; net, web, mesh, meshwork, netting, lace, plait; trellis, lattice, latticework, fretwork, filigree, tracery, gridiron, grille, grating; wicker, wickerwork; screen, screening, sieve.

cross, rood, crucifix, crux (*as in heraldry*).

V. **cross**, bisect, cut across, decussate, intersect, traverse, go across, pass over, move across; criss-cross; bridge, ford; nail to the cross, crucify.

go through, pass through, wade through, cross through, cut through; penetrate, percolate, permeate, pierce, transpierce, perforate; disembogue; osmose, transude; cleave, plow, negotiate, scour.

interlace, crisscross, intertwine, intertwist, interweave, interlink, lace; twine, entwine, weave, twist, wattle, wreathe; plait, pleat, plat, braid; tangle, entangle, mat, ravel.

crossbreed, interbreed, intercross, mix, hybridize, cross-fertilize, cross-pollinate (*bot.*).

cross out, cross off, rub out, cancel, strike out, erase, delete, dele (*printing*), remove, obliterate.

Adj. **crossing**, intersecting, bisecting; transverse, transversal, cross, crosswise, diagonal, horizontal.

crossed, matted, intersected, decussate, chiasmal (*anat.*), X-shaped, intertwined, interlaced; cross-shaped, cruciate, cruciform; netlike, retiform, reticular, latticed, grated, barred, streaked.

Adv. **crosswise**, across, athwart, transverse, transversely.

See also CUTTING, ELIMINATION, MANKIND (*hybrid*), MIXTURE, OPPOSITION, PASSAGE.

crossroad, *n.* intersection, crossway, cross-walk (CROSSING, PASSAGE).

crotch, *n.* fork, notch, branch (TURNING, ANGULARITY).

crouch, *v.* stoop, cower, cringe (BEND, LOWNESS, POSTURE).

crow, *v.* exult, gloat, triumph (HAPPINESS); blow, brag, boast (BOASTING); gurgle, guggle, babble (CHILD).

crowd, *n.* mob, mass, throng (MULTITUDE, ASSEMBLAGE).

crowd, *v.* throng, swarm, troop (ARRIVAL); cram, ram, charge (FULLNESS).

crown, *n.* headdress, headband, coronal (HEADGEAR); the throne, crowned head, supreme ruler (RULER); top, crest, pinnacle (HEIGHT); copestone, finishing touch (COMPLETENESS); laurel, garland, bays (FAME, PAYMENT).

crown, *v.* perfect, consummate, top off (END, PERFECTION); enthrone, invest, install (COMMISSION); grace, laureate, adorn (FAME).

crucial, *adj.* acute, climacteric, critical (IMPORTANCE).

crucifix, *n.* cross, rood, crux (CROSSING).

crucify, *v.* excruciate, rack, martyrize (TORTURE); brutalize, illtreat (CRUELTY).

crude, *adj.* raw, unrefined, rustic (NATURALNESS, ROUGHNESS); unbaked, callow, green (IMMATURITY); unpolished, vulgar, indelicate (LOWNESS, VULGARITY).

CRUELTY—*N.* **cruelty**, inclemency, brutality, savagery, savagism, barbarity, atrocity, sadism, cannibalism, ferocity, truculence; unkindness, etc. (see *Adjectives*).

cruel person, brute, ruffian, savage, cannibal, sadist, ogre (ogress, *fem.*), tiger, wolf, vulture; demon, devil, fiend; tyrant, oppressor.

V. **treat cruelly**, be cruel to, brutalize, crucify, ill-treat, maltreat, mistreat, savage, trample on, oppress, tyrannize.

make cruel, barbarize, brutalize, callous, harden, sear.

Adj. **cruel**, unkind, inclement, brutal, ruffianly, inhuman, inhumane, grim, fell, ruthless, savage, barbarous, atrocious, sadistic, unnatural, cannibalistic, ferocious, tigerish; tyrannical, tyrannous, oppressive; vulturous, boarish, ogreish, bloodthirsty, sanguinary.

devilishly cruel, demoniacal, devilish, diabolical, fiendish, satanic.

cruelhearted, heartless, flinthearted, hardhearted, cold-blooded, ironhearted, stonyhearted, unfeeling; unmerciful, unrelenting, relentless, pitiless, merciless.

See also INSENSITIVITY. *Antonyms* —See KINDNESS, PITY.

cruise, *v.* sail, boat, voyage (SAILOR, TRAVELING).

cruiser, *n.* vessel, cabin cruiser, yacht (SHIP); police car, prowl car, squad car (VEHICLE).

crumb, *n.* bit, dab, dash (SMALLNESS); seed, grain, particle (POWDERINESS).

crumble, v. disintegrate, decay, molder (BREAKAGE, DECAY, POWDERINESS).

crumple, v. crinkle, ruffle, rumple (ROUGHNESS).

crunch, v. chew, masticate (FOOD); bruise, beat, crush (PRESSURE, POWDERINESS).

crusade, n. campaign, jehad (Moham.), expedition (FIGHTING).

crush, n. drove, flock, gathering (MULTITUDE); infatuation, flame, passion (LOVE).

crush, v. bruise, beat, crunch (PRESSURE, POWDERINESS); suppress, quell, quash (DEFEAT).

crust, n. coating, bloom, encrustation (COVERING); carapace, lorica (BONE).

crux, n. body, core, essence (PART).

cry, n. scream, screech, shriek (LOUDNESS, SHOUT, HIGH-PITCHED SOUND); exclamation, expletive, ejaculation (VOICE); howl, yowl, bawl (WEEPING).

cry, v. weep, bawl, blubber (WEEPING); screech, scream, shrill (LOUDNESS, SHOUT); blat, bleat, moo (ANIMAL SOUND).

cryptic, adj. secret, arcane, enigmatic (MYSTERY, MEANING, CONCEALMENT).

cub, n. bear, whelp, pup (ANIMAL); newspaperman, reporter (PUBLICATION).

cuddle, v. nestle, nuzzle, snuggle (CARESS, REST, PRESSURE).

cudgel, n. club, bludgeon, stick (HITTING).

cue, n. braid, queue, plait (WINDING); prompt, prod, mnemonic (MEMORY, HINT).

cuff, v. box, punch, slap (HITTING).

culprit, n. criminal, convict, felon (ILLEGALITY).

cultivation, n. delicacy, culture, refinement (IMPROVEMENT, TASTE); education, background, training (LEARNING, TEACHING); agriculture, tillage, agrology (FARMING).

culture, n. cultivation, refinement, civilization (IMPROVEMENT, TASTE); breeding, schooling, grounding (LEARNING); agriculture, agronomics, agrology (FARMING).

cultured, adj. cultivated, educated, erudite (TEACHING, LEARNING); scholarly, well-read, literary (STORY).

cumbersome, adj. bulky, awkward, unwieldy (CLUMSINESS, WEIGHT).

cumulative, adj. increasing, accumulative, increscent (INCREASE).

cunning, n. craft, subtlety, disingenuity (CLEVERNESS).

cup, n. mug, goblet, tumbler (CONTAINER).

cupboard, n. repository, closet, cabinet (CONTAINER).

cup-shaped, adj. calathiform, cyathiform, cupular (HOLLOW).

cur, n. wretch, worm, sneak (WORTHLESSNESS, MEANNESS, CONTEMPT).

curb, v. check, restrain, bridle (RESTRAINT, MODERATENESS).

curdle, v. sour, acidify, turn (SOURNESS).

CURE—N. **cure,** curative, remedy, medication, medicament, medicine, physic, therapeutic, drug, nostrum, placebo, restorative, sanative, proprietary, specific, officinal, vulnerary, glutinative; vaccine, serum; materia medica (L.).

cure-all, panacea, elixir, catholicon.

remedy, help, aid, assistance, relief, reparation, redress; corrective, counteractive, counteractant, antidote.

bactericide, bacteriophage, antibacterial, antibody, antigen, antibiotic (penicillin, etc.), sulfa drugs; disinfectant, germicide, antiseptic, prophylactic.

pill, capsule, lozenge, pellet, troche, tablet.

salve, ointment, lotion, balm, unguent, liniment, lenitive, embrocation, demulcent, slippery elm; poultice, cataplasm, plaster, mustard plaster; compress.

treatment, therapy, therapeutics, medicamentation, doctoring, first-aid; pharmacotherapy, chemotherapy, allopathy, homeopathy; Couéism, cult, naturopathy, Christian Science; physical therapy, physiotherapy, massotherapy, chiropractic; X-ray therapy, roentgenotherapy, radiotherapy, radium therapy.

hospital, infirmary, surgery, clinic, polyclinic, maison de santé (F.), hôtel-Dieu (F.), hôpital (F.); pesthouse, lazaret; sanitarium, sanatorium, nursing home; springs, baths, spa; asylum, home.

therapist, therapeutist, allopath, homeopath, naturopath, physical therapist or physiotherapist, chiropractor, healer, nurse, attendant, doctor, physician, practitioner.

V. **cure,** remedy, heal, glutinate, cicatrize.

medicate, treat, doctor, medicament, physic, drug, dose; attend, nurse, minister to, dress (a wound, etc.).

remedy, relieve, palliate, restore; correct, rectify, right, repair, redress.

Adj. **curing**, curative, remedial, corrective, therapeutic, medicative, medicinal, medical, Aesculapian, sanatory: vulnerary, glutinative; orthogenic.

curable, remediable, medicable, healable; restorable, retrievable, recoverable.

incurable, immedicable, irremediable; inoperable; irretrievable, irrecoverable.

See also IMPROVEMENT, MEDICAL SCIENCE, PHARMACY, RESTORATION, RIGHT. *Antonyms*—See DEATH, DISEASE, KILLING, POISON.

---

curio, *n.* bibelot (*F.*), objet d'art (*F.*), object of art (ORNAMENT).

curiosity, *n.* nosiness (*slang*), inquisitiveness (INQUIRY); oddity, singularity, peculiarity (UNUSUALNESS); phenomenon, *rara avis* (*L.*), rarity (SURPRISE).

curious, *adj.* inquisitive, nosy (*slang*), inquisiturient (INQUIRY, SEARCH); odd, peculiar, singular (UNUSUALNESS); remarkable, salient, prominent (VISIBILITY).

curl, *n.* ringlet, frizzle, friz (HAIR); crispation, crimp, swirl (WINDING); curlicue, flourish, spiral (WRITING).

curl, *v.* crisp, swirl, twist (CURVE, WINDING).

curlicue, *n.* spiral, helix, gyration (WINDING); flourish, quirk, twist (WRITING).

curly-haired, *adj.* curly-headed, woolly, woolly-headed (HAIR).

currency, *n.* coin, specie, cash (MONEY).

current, *adj.* present, contemporary, topical (PRESENT TIME); doing, afoot (OCCURRENCE); common, prevalent, accepted (PRESENCE, ACCEPTANCE, USE).

current, *n.* stream, course, flow (RIVER); run, drift, tide, (DIRECTION); juice, electricity (LIGHT).

curriculum, *n.* syllabus, content (LEARNING).

curry, *v.* groom, tend, brush (DOMESTICATION).

curse, *n.* execration, imprecation, oath (MALEDICTION, DISRESPECT); hydra, cancer, plague (WICKEDNESS); evil eye, whammy (*slang*), hex (HARM).

cursed, *adj.* accursed, blasted, damnable (HATRED); atrocious, heinous, flagitious (WICKEDNESS).

cursory, *adj.* superficial, perfunctory, casual (CARELESSNESS, SPEED).

curt, *adj.* bluff, brusque, abrupt (BLUNTNESS); churlish, crusty, gruff (DISCOURTESY, SHORTNESS).

curtail, *v.* clip, trim, pare down (SHORTNESS).

curtain, *v.* hide, cover, shroud (CONCEALMENT, COVERING).

curtsy, *n.* bow, obeisance, salaam (GESTURE, RESPECT).

CURVE—*N.* **curve**, curvation, curvature, arc, arch, arcade, vault, bow, contour, quirk, bight (*in a coast line*); crook, loop, hook, swerve, curl, swirl; twist, wind, sinuosity; spiral, curlicue, helix, gyration, coil, whorl; outcurve, bulge, convexity; incurve, incurvation, incurvature, concavity; crescent, meniscus, half-moon, horseshoe, festoon; parabola, hyperbola, ellipse, circle.

V. **curve**, bow, arch, round, crook, loop, hook, swerve, curl, swirl, twist, wind, snake, wreathe; spiral, gyrate, coil; outcurve, bulge, convex; concave, incurve.

Adj. **curving**, arching, etc. (see *Verbs*); spiral, gyratory; swirly, aswirl, curly.

curved, curvy, curvate, curvated, compass; round, rounded, circular, elliptical; looped, loopy; curly, swirly, twisty, twisted, snaky, wreathed, wreathy, sinuous, devious, tortuous; S-shaped, sigmate, sigmoid.

outcurved, bandy, bulgy, bulged; convex, biconvex, convexo-concave, convexo-convex.

incurved, incurvate, incurvated, concave, biconcave, concavo-concave, concavo-convex.

bow-shaped, bowed, embowed, arcuate, arclike, arciform; arched, vaulted; sickle-shaped, falcate, falciform; bell-shaped, campanulate, campaniform; boat-shaped, navicular, naviculoid, naviform, scaphoid (*anat.*), cymbiform; helmet-shaped, galeiform, galeate.

spiral, helical, helicoid, whorled, gyrate, gyratory, corkscrew, coiled; tortile, cochleate, volute.

crescent-shaped, crescentic, crescent, crescentiform, crescentlike, crescentoid; meniscal, meniscate, meniscoid, meniscoidal; lunate, lunated, lunar, lunular, moonshaped, moonlike, luniform, semilunar.

heart-shaped, cordiform, cordate.

hook-shaped, hooked, hooklike, uncinate, unciform; aduncous, aduncate, aquiline (*as a nose*).

See also BEND, ROUNDNESS, SLOPE, TURNING, WINDING. *Antonyms*—See STRAIGHTNESS, VERTICALITY.

---

cushion, *n.* pillow, bolster, sham (SLEEP); fender, buffer, bumper (PROTECTION).

cuspidor, *n.* spittoon (SALIVA).

custodian, *n.* supervisor, superintendent, caretaker (CONTROL, CARE).

custody, n. confinement, detention, incarceration (IMPRISONMENT); charge, tutelage, guardianship (CARE); preservation, conservation, safekeeping (PROTECTION).

custom, n. customs, convention, proprieties (HABIT); usage, habit, wont (USE); rite, ceremony, performance (OBSERVANCE); patronage, business, trade (PURCHASE); tax, assessment, dues (PAYMENT).

customary, adj. habitual, wonted, usual (HABIT, COMMONNESS); conventional, routine, traditional (CONFORMITY).

customer, n. purchaser, buyer, patron (PURCHASE); odd person, character (colloq.), eccentric (UNUSUALNESS).

cute, adj. charming, pretty, attractive (BEAUTY).

cut off, v. amputate, mutilate, snip off (CUTTING); disinherit, disherit (WILL).

cut-rate, adj. cheap, nominal, low-priced (INEXPENSIVENESS).

cutting, adj. biting, sarcastic, caustic (SHARPNESS); bitter, raw, piercing (COLD); offensive, insulting, outrageous (OFFENSE).

CUTTING—N. cutting, scission, sculpture, cleavage, shave, section, dissection, incision, scratch, scarification, claw mark; bisection, dichotomy, trisection, intersection, transection, decussation, guillotinade; carving, etc. (see *Verbs*).

amputation, mutilation, truncation, abscission, severance, decollation; excision, exsection; disembowelment, evisceration; retrenchment.

cut, gash, rent, slash, stab, pierce, nip, trim, snip, incision, chip, chop, clip, groove, trench, rabbet, notch, slot, slit, whittle.

shaving, shred, slice, section, cutting, chop, chip, clipping, paring, slip, splinter.

puncture, stab, thrust, prick, pink.

cutting instrument, cutter, carver, slicer, chopper, cleaver, chisel, clippers, nippers, dicer, razor, safety razor, blade, shredder, saw, coping saw, hack saw, jigsaw, skiver, scythe, sickle, mower, lawn mower; scissors, shears, pinking shears; file, rasp, nail file; cutlery.

knife, paring knife, whittling knife, bolo, hunting knife, bowie knife, penknife, pocketknife, machete, snickersnee, switchblade.

sword, blade, broadsword, cutlass, épée, Excalibur, foil, rapier,

scimitar, saber *or* sabre, yataghan.

dagger, bayonet, *couteau* (*F.*), dirk, poniard, stiletto.

ax, axe, adz, adze, battle-ax, poleax, halberd, partisan, tomahawk, hatchet; mattock, pick, pickax.

spear, lance, pike, assagai, javelin, dart, harpoon, shaft, trident.

V. cut, carve, sculpt, whittle, hew, roughhew, chisel; cleave, sever, rive, split, rend, slit, slot, chip, chop, clip, mangle, hack, hackle; dice, cube, mince, shred, shave, slice, section, dissect; slash, dirk, gash, scotch, incise, scarify, rabbet, groove, trench, saw, shear, snip; bisect, decussate, chine, guillotine; cut across, intersect, transect; scratch, claw, scratch about, scrabble.

cut off, cut away, amputate, mutilate, snip off, nip off, pare, poll, pollard, trim, prune, truncate, clip, crop, lop, shave, raze, skive, slip, sever, decollate; cut out, excide, excise, exscind, exsect; disembowel, eviscerate; cut down, retrench.

cut short, bob, shorten, truncate, clip, crop, trim, dock, mow.

pierce, stab, thrust, cleave, plow *or* plough, cut through, go through, push through, come through, puncture; knife, dirk, bayonet, lance, lancinate, prong, spear, stick, transpierce, transfix; impale, spike, spit; prick, pink, sting; penetrate, permeate, perforate, percolate.

sting, prick, prickle, smart, bite, urticate.

Adj. piercing, penetrative, permeative, cutting, pointed, searching (*fig.*), pungent (*fig.*), shrill (*fig.*).

pierced, cleft, cloven, perforated.

stinging, biting, pricking, prickly, prickling, smarting, urticant, aculeate; sharp, pungent, peppery, bitter, acid.

See also BISECTION, DISJUNCTION, REMOVAL, SHARPNESS, SHORTNESS, SURGERY, TEARING. *Antonyms*—See BLUNTNESS, DULLNESS.

---

cycle, n. periodicity, rhythm, alternation (UNIFORMITY); orbit, circuit (ROUNDNESS); bicycle, wheel (colloq.), tricycle (VEHICLE).

cyclone, n. hurricane, tornado, typhoon (WIND).

cylinder, n. roller, barrel, drum (ROLL).

cynical, adj. unbelieving, skeptical, suspicious (UNBELIEVINGNESS).

D

dabble, *v.* toy, twiddle, trifle (PLAYFULNESS); tinker, boondoggle (*slang*), boggle (WORK).

daft, *adj.* crazy, crazed, demented (INSANITY).

dagger, *n.* bayonet, dirk, poniard (CUTTING).

daily, *adj.* quotidian, everyday, per diem (MORNING).

dainty, *adj.* ethereal, exquisite, delicate (WEAKNESS, BEAUTY); palatable, delicious, delectable, toothsome (TASTE).

dainty, *n.* delicacy, tidbit, morsel (TASTE).

dais, *n.* platform, podium, stage (SUPPORT).

dally, *v.* play, be playful, disport (PLAYFULNESS); dawdle, linger, loiter (DELAY, TIME).

dally with, *v.* be insincere with, play with, play fast and loose with (PRETENSE).

dam, *n.* millpond, milldam (LAKE); mare, brood mare (HORSE).

damage, *v.* sabotage, ruin, mutilate (HARM, BLEMISH).

damages, *n.* fine, forfeit, penalty (PUNISHMENT).

dame, *n.* matron, biddy (*colloq.*), dowager (OLDNESS); girl, woman (FEMALE).

damn, *v.* curse, anathematize, ban (MALEDICTION); illegalize, outlaw (ILLEGALITY); cry down, denounce, excoriate (DISAPPROVAL).

damnable, *adj.* accursed, cursed, blasted (HATRED).

damp, *adj.* moist, humid, irriguous, (WATER); drizzly, drippy (RAIN).

dampen, *v.* moisten, damp, humidify (WATER); chill, cloud, dash (DEJECTION).

damsel, *n.* girl, maid, miss (YOUTH).

(THE) DANCE—*N.* dance, step, ballet, buck and wing, cakewalk, cancan, Charleston, clog dance, conga, *contre-danse* (*F.*), cotillion, fandango, fling, folk dance, fox trot, habanera, Highland fling, hornpipe, hula, hula-hula, jig, lindy, mambo, mazurka, *pasodoble* (*Sp.*), peabody, polka, polonaise, promenade, quadrille, reel, rumba, samba, saraband, schottische, shimmy, square dance, tango, tap dance, tarantella, toe dance, two-step, Virginia reel, waltz, zarabanda; rock and roll, jitterbug, hoky poky, cha-cha, Lambeth walk, bunny hug, black bottom, maxixe; gavotte, minuet, one-step, morris dance; frenzied dance, corybantic.

ball, masquerade, masquerade ball, prom, hop (*colloq.*).

dancing, saltation, eurythmics, choregraphy, stage dancing, ballroom dancing; ballet, ballet dancing, choreography; square-dancing, tap-dancing, toe-dancing, waltzing, jitterbugging; tarantism, St. Vitus's dance, chorea.

dancer, artiste, ballerina, choreographer, chorine, clog dancer, coryphee, danseuse, funambulist, geisha girl, nautch girl, tap dancer, taxi dancer, terpsichorean, toe dancer; chorus, *corps de ballet* (*F.*).

writing of ballet dances: choreography, choregraphy.

ballet enthusiast, balletomane.

muse of dancing, Terpsichore.

V. dance, cakewalk, Charleston, etc. (See *Nouns*).

Adj. **terpsichorean,** saltatory, choreographic, gestic, saltant.

See also AMUSEMENT, DRAMA, JUMP, MUSIC, SHAKE.

---

dandruff, *n.* dander, furfur, scurf (HAIR).

dandy, *n.* coxcomb, dude, exquisite (FASHION).

DANGER—*N.* danger, chance, hazard, insecurity, jeopardy, peril, unsafety, risk, pitfall.

[*dangerous person*] **menace,** threat, serpent, viper; dangerous woman, *femme fatale* (*F.*).

V. **endanger,** expose to danger, hazard, jeopardize, peril, imperil, risk, speculate with, venture, compromise.

[*accept danger*] **risk,** hazard, venture, adventure, dare, stake, set at hazard, speculate.

Adj. **dangerous,** chancy, risky, ticklish, touch-and-go, venturous, venturesome, adventurous, adventuresome, speculative; hazardous, perilous, parlous, precarious, insecure, jeopardous, critical, queasy, unsafe, ugly, treacherous, serpentine, viperous.

See also CHANCE, FEAR, THREAT, WARNING. *Antonyms*—See PROTECTION.

---

dangle, *v.* swing, flap (HANGING).

dank, *adj.* clammy, sticky, muggy (WATER).

dapper, *adj.* spruce, natty, jaunty (NEATNESS, FASHION).

dapple, *v.* spot, dot, fleck, stipple (VARIEGATION).

dare, *v.* brave, challenge, throw down the gauntlet (DEFIANCE); venture, make bold (COURAGE); risk, hazard, speculate (DANGER); presume (DISCOURTESY).

daredevil, *n.* hero, heroine, adventurer (COURAGE).

daring, *adj.* adventurous, brave, venturesome (COURAGE).

dark, *adj.* obscure, indistinct, dim (DARKNESS, UNCLEARNESS); confidential, secret, hush-hush (CONCEALMENT); swarthy, dusky, murky (BLACKNESS).

darken, *v.* obscure, dim, fog (DARKNESS, UNCLEARNESS); blind, seel, purblind (BLINDNESS).

dark-haired, *adj.* black-haired, brown-haired, brunet (HAIR).

DARKNESS—*N.* darkness, dark, black, caliginosity, murk, nigritude, obscurity, opacity, shades, shadows, Tophet; gloom, dusk, tenebrosity; blackout, brownout.

shadow, shade, umbra, penumbra (*as in an eclipse*); obscuration, adumbration, eclipse; skiagraph, skiagram, shadowgram, shadowgraph.

night, nightfall, nighttime; midnight, witching hour, dead of night.

[*that which shades*] shade, screen, awning, canopy, sunshade, eyeshade, sunglasses; arbor, bower, shade tree, umbrage; umbrella, parasol, bumbershoot (*jocose*).

V. darken, becloud, bedim, blacken, cloud, dim, dusk, eclipse, gloom, gray, obscure, overshadow, shade, shadow.

extinguish, put out, blow out, snuff out, stifle, smother, douse (*slang*).

dim (*the vision, etc.*), blear, blur, cloud.

shadow, shade, overshadow, adumbrate, eclipse.

Adj. dark, obscure, black, lightless, aphotic, sunless, unilluminated, unlighted, unlit, rayless, inky, atramentous, sooty, caliginous, Cimmerian, murky.

dim, cloudy, overcast, bleak, gray, darkish, darksome, darkling (*poetic*); dusky, adusk, twilight, crepuscular, crepusculous; illlighted, murky, obscure.

[*of the eyes or vision*] dim, blear, bleared, bleary, blurred, blurry, clouded, cloudy.

dismal, dreary, dingy, gloomy, somber, tenebrous, Stygian.

shaded, shady, shadowy, bowery, bosky, adumbral, umbrageous.

See also BLACKNESS, COVERING, GLOOM, SADNESS. *Antonyms*—See FIRE, LIGHT, WHITENESS.

darling, *adj.* beloved, loved, dear (LOVE).

darn, *v.* mend, sew, patch (FASTENING, RESTORATION); curse, anathematize, damn (MALEDICTION).

dart, *n.* arrow, missile, projectile (ARMS, THROW).

dart, *v.* dash, run, course (SPEED).

dash, *n.* drop, pinch, sprinkle (ADDITION, SMALLNESS); line, stroke, score (INDICATION); birr, verve, zip (ENERGY); swank, splash (*colloq.*), flash (OSTENTATION).

dash, *v.* dart, run, career (SPEED); charge, hurtle, lunge (VIOLENCE); chill, cloud, dampen (DEJECTION).

data, *n.* dossier, facts, memoranda (INFORMATION, MATERIALITY).

date, *n.* point, juncture, moment, stage (TIME); appointment, engagement (ARRIVAL).

date, *v.* fix the time, register, record (TIME MEASUREMENT); antiquate, obsolete, outdate (OLDNESS).

daughter, *n.* offspring, descendant (CHILD).

daunt, *v.* intimidate, cow, overawe (FEAR).

dauntless, *adj.* doughty, fearless, brave, gallant (COURAGE).

davenport, *n.* couch, day bed, divan (SEAT).

dawdle, *v.* dally, dillydally, loiter (DELAY, TIME).

dawn, *n.* sunrise, daybreak, daylight (MORNING); commencement, start, origin (BEGINNING).

dawn, *v.* rise, loom, emerge (VISIBILITY).

day, *n.* weekday, Sunday (MORNING).

daydream, *n.* fantasy, reverie, fancy (SLEEP, HOPE).

daydreamer, *n.* dreamer, Don Quixote, romanticist (IMAGINATION).

daze, *v.* benumb, deaden, drug (INSENSIBILITY); addle, muddle, bewilder (CONFUSION, UNCERTAINTY); dazzle, blind, blur (DIM-SIGHTEDNESS, LIGHT).

dazed, *adj.* benumbed, drugged, narcotized (INSENSITIVITY); besotted, besot, bemused (INSENSIBILITY); confounded, blank, wonder-struck (SURPRISE).

dazzle, *v.* daze, blind, glare (LIGHT, DIM-SIGHTEDNESS); excite admiration in (APPROVAL).

dead, adj. deceased, departed, late (DEATH); insensitive, apathic, dull (INSENSIBILITY).

deaden, v. muffle, mute, cushion (NONRESONANCE, WEAKNESS).

dead end, n. blind alley, cul-de-sac (F.), impasse (PASSAGE).

deadlock, n. checkmate, standstill, stalemate (CESSATION, INACTION).

deadly, adj. virulent, lethal, fatal (KILLING); deathlike, deathful, deathly (DEATH).

deafen, v. stun, split the ears, drown out (LISTENING).

deafening, adj. earsplitting, piercing, shrill (LOUDNESS).

deaf-mute, n. mute, laloplegic, aphasiac (SILENCE).

deafness, n. deaf-mutism, defective hearing (LISTENING).

deal, n. arrangement, prearrangement, conception (PLAN); contract, understanding (COMPACT).

deal, v. give out, hand out, distribute (GIVING).

dealer, n. merchant, trader, marketer (SALE).

deal in, v. trade in, traffic in, truck (SALE, PURCHASE).

deal with, v. treat, handle, manage (USE).

dean, n. old stager, doyen (F.), senior (OLDNESS); principal, headmaster, president (SCHOOL).

dear, adj. expensive, high, costly (EXPENDITURE); darling, beloved, loved (LOVE); intimate, familiar, close (NEARNESS).

dearth, n. scarcity, paucity, famine (FEWNESS, ABSENCE).

DEATH—N. death, decease, demise, mortality, extinction, dissolution, departure, release, debt of nature, rest, eternal rest; cessation (loss, or extinction) of life; loss, bereavement; Jordan, Jordan's bank, Stygian shore; the great adventure, last breath, last sleep, night, tomb, quietus; capital punishment, execution, electrocution, hanging, halter.

gangrene, mortification, necrosis, phagedena.

death song, dirge, funeral hymn, coronach, requiem, elegy, threnody.

necrology, obituary, death notice, register of deaths; mortality, death rate.

corpse, dead body, ashes, cadaver, stiff (slang), corpus (humorous), corse (poetic), the deceased, decedent (law), the defunct, the departed; relics (poetic), remains; corpus delicti (law), casualty, victim, zombie, mummy, carcass.

mortuary, undertaking parlor,

morgue; Elysium, Elysian Fields, Hades, other world.

V. die, breathe one's last, croak (slang), decease, depart, expire, fall (drop, sink, etc.) dead, give up the ghost, go to the happy hunting grounds, join one's ancestors, kick the bucket (slang), pass away, pass on, perish, succumb, lose one's life, lay down one's life, go West, make the supreme sacrifice; predecease; drown, smother, stifle, strangle, suffocate, throttle.

Adj. dead, deceased, departed, late, lifeless, stillborn; ad patres (L.), defunct, extinct.

lifeless, brute, exanimate, inanimate, inorganic; arid, inert, languid, languorous, listless, sluggish, spiritless, stodgy, torpid, vapid, washed-out, wooden, zestless; glassy, glazed, glazy, wooden (as a look, stare, etc.).

dying, at death's door, mortal, commorient, moribund.

corpselike, pale, ghastly, cadaverous, cadaveric, defunctive.

[pert. to death] lethal, mortal, mortuary, necrotic, macabre; postmortem, posthumous, post-obit, post obitum (L.); ante-mortem.

deathlike, deadly, deathful, deathly, ghastly, mortal.

See also END, INACTIVITY, INSENSITIVITY, KILLING, SUICIDE, TORTURE. Antonyms—See ACTIVITY, BIRTH, LIFE.

debark, v. disembark, detrain, deplane (DEPARTURE).

debase, v. demean, degrade, humble (HUMILIATION, MEANNESS); devaluate, cheapen, depreciate (WORTHLESSNESS).

debatable, adj. dubious, moot, disputable (UNCERTAINTY, DISAGREEMENT, INQUIRY).

DEBATE—N. debate, agitation, argument, argumentation, controversy, disceptation, contention, disputation, dialectic, dialecticism, polemics.

debater, arguer, disceptator, disputant, disputer, picador, dialectician, polemist, polemician; wrangler.

[art of debate] dialectic, dialectics, polemics.

V. debate, agitate, argue, controvert, discept, dispute, wrangle.

Adj. [relating to debate] forensic, dialectic, polemic.

See also DISAGREEMENT, OPPOSITION, STATEMENT, TALK. Antonyms —See AGREEMENT, ASSENT.

debauchery, *n.* sensuality, dissipation, animalism (PLEASURE, INTEMPERANCE); fornication, fraternization, intimacy (SEX).

debility, *n.* enervation, exhaustion, enfeeblement (WEAKNESS).

debris, *n.* rubbish, trash, rubble (USELESSNESS, UNCLEANNESS).

DEBT—*N.* **debt,** obligation, liability, dues, debit, arrear.

debts, arrears, arrearage, indebtedness, liabilities.

[*record of a debt*] **bill,** statement, account, invoice, manifest; check, tab, reckoning, score, tally; debit, I.O.U., chirograph, chit, memorandum, memo, note, promissory note, obligation, debenture; receipt, voucher, acknowledgment.

debtor, ower, borrower, mortgagor, cosigner.

defaulter, delinquent, repudiator, welsher (*colloq.*), deadbeat; bankrupt, insolvent.

default, repudiation; bankruptcy, insolvency, nonpayment.

credit, trust, installment plan, installment buying, time payments, deferred payments, down payment.

loan, advance, accommodation, mortgage, investment.

creditor, debtee, Shylock, mortgagee.

moneylender, money broker, moneymonger, pawnbroker, uncle (*slang*), banker, usurer.

pawnshop, pawnbroker's, uncle's (*slang*), three balls; loan company.

V. **be in debt,** owe, incur (*or* contract) a debt, run up a bill; borrow, run into debt, be in financial difficulties.

vouch for, answer for, be surety for, guarantee, go bail for; back one's note, cosign.

indebt, obligate, bind, astrict.

default, dishonor, repudiate, welsh (*colloq.*), not pay.

lend, loan, advance, accommodate with; invest.

Adj. **indebted,** obligated, bound, bounden, beholden, astricted; in debt, in embarrassed circumstances, in financial difficulties.

liable, accountable, responsible, chargeable, answerable for.

in default, delinquent; bankrupt, insolvent, broke (*slang*).

unpaid, owing, due, unsettled, unliquidated, unsatisfied, in arrears, outstanding, delinquent, overdue.

on credit, on installment, on account.

Antonyms—See PAYMENT.

debut, *n.* entree, admission, incoming (INGRESS).

decadent, *adj.* degenerate, depraved, corrupt (IMMORALITY, DETERIORATION, DECAY).

DECAY—*N.* **decay,** decomposition, rot, putrefaction, spoilage, breakdown, caries, cariosity; putrescence, putridity, rottenness; pythogenesis, gangrene; decadence, decadency.

wasting away, waste, atrophy, contabescence, marasmus, consumption, blight, blast; decline, disintegration, dissolution, dilapidation.

V. **decay,** decompose, rot, putrefy, putresce, spoil, fester, gangrene, molder, addle (*of eggs*).

waste away, waste, rot away, molder away, shrivel, wither, atrophy, blast, blight, consume, crumble, dilapidate, disintegrate, dissolve, decline, perish; pine, pine away, languish.

Adj. **decayed,** decomposed, moldered, rotten, rotted, putrescent, putrefied, putrid, spoiled, addle (*of eggs*), carious, gangrenous, carrion; decadent.

See also DESTRUCTION, DETERIORATION, DISJUNCTION. *Antonyms*—See COMBINATION, PRODUCTION.

deceive, *v.* delude, dupe, fool (DECEPTION); lie to, be dishonest with (FALSEHOOD).

decent, *adj.* respectable, august, estimable (RESPECT); chaste, maidenly, proper (MODESTY); equitable, ethical, just (PROPRIETY); fair, mediocre, middling (GOOD).

DECEPTION—*N.* **deception,** deceit, fraud, duplicity, fraudulence, misrepresentation, bluff; craft, cunning, dishonesty, obliquity, subtility, subtlety, treachery; sharp practices, chicanery, cozenage, dupery, guile; humbuggery, hocus-pocus, hanky-panky, illusion, imposition, imposture, legerdemain, pettifoggery; knavery, japery, rascality, roguery, shenanigans (*colloq.*), skulduggery, trickery, wiles.

disguise, gloss, varnish; façade, front, false front, bluff, false colors, camouflage, masquerade.

trick, artifice, cheat, chicane, dodge, device, bilk, flam, flimflam (*colloq.*), hoax, humbug, ruse, shift, pretext, stall (*slang*), feint, stratagem, subterfuge, swindle, wile, wrinkle, gimmick; trap, snare, catch, mare's-nest; confidence game.

illusion, mirage, will-o'-the-wisp, wisp, *ignis fatuus* (*L.*); apparition, phantasm, myth, chimera, dream.

deceiver, impostor, bamboozler, beguiler, bluff, bluffer, boggler, chicaner, deluder, duper, fox, fraud, hoaxer, hoodwinker, humbug, humbugger, japer, knave, misleader, pettifogger, picaro, picaroon, rascal, rogue, scamp, schemer, serpent, shammer, slicker (*colloq.*), snake, sneak, snide (*colloq.*), weasel, mountebank.

double-dealer, Janus-face, ambidexter, hypocrite.

cheater, cheat, bilk, blackleg, bunco artist (*colloq.*), cozener, defrauder, fainaiguer, finagler, fleecer, flimflammer (*colloq.*), gouger (*colloq.*), swindler, tricker or trickster, victimizer; shortchanger, shortchange artist; welsher (*colloq.*); con man (*slang*); cardsharp, rook, sharper.

dupe, gull, victim, easy mark, fair game, soft touch, pushover, soft mark, mark (*slang*), sucker (*slang*), greenhorn, fool, April fool.

V. deceive, befool, beguile, blear, bluff, cheat, chicane, delude, dupe, fob, fool, gull, hoax, hocus, hoodwink, hornswoggle (*slang*), humbug, impose on, jape, put something over on, spoof (*slang*), trick, victimize; boggle, pettifog, sham, stall (*slang*).

mislead, lead astray, take in, outwit, steal a march on, throw dust into the eyes; palm off on, take advantage of.

cheat, bamboozle, beguile out of, bilk, bunco (*colloq.*), con (*slang*), cozen, defraud, fainaigue, finagle, flam, fleece, flimflam (*colloq.*), gouge (*colloq.*), mulct, overreach, rook, swindle, trim (*colloq.*), shortchange, welsh (*colloq.*).

Adj. deceptive, deceitful, artful, astucious, astute, beguiling, catchy, crafty, cunning, delusory, designing, dishonest, disingenuous, fallacious, feline, foxy, fraudulent, impostrous, indirect, insidious, knavish, Machiavellian, Mephistophelian, misleading, oblique, obliquitous, rascally, roguish, scheming, serpentine, shifty, slick, slippery, sly, snaky, sneaky, snide (*colloq.*), sophisticated, subtle, subtile, treacherous, tricky, underhanded, vulpine, wily.

[*in appearance*] illusory, illusive, colorable, plausible, specious, varnished.

double-dealing, ambidextrous, Janus-faced, two-faced, hypocritical.

See also CLEVERNESS, DISHONESTY, FALSEHOOD, FALSENESS, SOPHISTRY, THIEVERY, TRAP. *Antonyms*—See HONESTY, REALITY, TRUTH.

decipher, *v.* decode, interpret (ANSWER).

DECISION—*N.* decision, determination, conclusion, settlement; ruling, finding, decree, adjudication, judgment, verdict, oracle; resolution, resolve, resoluteness, firmness, decisiveness, will, will power, volition, iron will, strength of mind (*or* will).

V. decide, determine, conclude, settle; rule, adjudge, judge, pass on, adjudicate, overrule; predetermine, prearrange; will, resolve, make a decision, make up one's mind, take a decisive step, cross the Rubicon, decide upon, fix upon, take upon oneself, take a stand, stand firm.

Adj. decisive, resolute, crisp, conclusive, peremptory, firm, unbending, inflexible, unyielding, strong-willed, strong-minded, deliberate.

decided, resolved, determined, concluded, settled, irrevocable, unalterable, unshaken; predetermined, prearranged, destined, fated.

See also CERTAINTY, CHOICE, JUDGE, JUDGMENT, WILL. *Antonyms*—See IRRESOLUTION, UNCERTAINTY.

decisive, *adj.* eventful, momentous, fateful (RESULT, IMPORTANCE); resolute, crisp, deliberate (DECISION).

deck, *n.* floor, flooring, surface (SUPPORT, BASE).

declare, *v.* proclaim, announce, expound (STATEMENT).

decline, *n.* pitch, dip, descent (SLOPE).

decline, *v.* refuse, say no, not accept (DENIAL); lose value, cheapen, depreciate (WORTHLESSNESS); worsen, corrode, degenerate (DETERIORATION); dwindle, drop, fall (DECREASE, DESCENT).

decompose, *v.* decay, rot, putrefy (DECAY).

decorate, *v.* embellish, enrich, adorn (ORNAMENT); laureate, medal, plume (PAYMENT).

decoration, *n.* ornamentation, adornment, embellishment (ORNAMENT); laurels, medal, ribbon (FAME).

decorous, *adj.* demure, moral, proper (PROPRIETY).

decoy, *n.* catch, trick, deception (TRAP); lure, bait (ATTRACTION); misleader, betrayer, Judas (MISTEACHING).

DECREASE—*N.* **decrease,** decrement, decrescence, decrescendo *or* diminuendo (*of sound*); diminution, reduction, etc. (see *Verbs*).

V. **decrease,** diminish, reduce, lessen, cut, cut down, curtail, lower, dwindle; abridge, impair, pare, pare down, retrench, slash, whittle down; minimize, minify; halve, dimidiate; deflate, deplete, depress; come down, go down, decline, dwindle, drop, fall.

[*in price, value, etc.*] **reduce,** deflate, depress, lower, sag, shade, shave, sink, slash, discount; come down, go down, decline, descend, drop, fall, toboggan.

contract, compress, condense, constrict, constringe, shrink, astringe, shorten.

alleviate, attemper, abate, bate, mitigate, moderate, modify, remit, slacken, slack; subdue, soften, tone down; taper, taper off, wane, decline, subside, peter out.

See also CUTTING, DEDUCTION, LOWNESS, MODERATENESS, REMOVAL, WEAKNESS. *Antonyms*—See ADDITION, INCREASE, SWELLING.

---

decree, *n.* edict, commandment, ukase (LAW, COMMAND).

decrepit, *adj.* infirm, senile, anile (WEAKNESS, OLDNESS).

dedication, *n.* devotion, devotement, adherence (LOYALTY); envoy, *envoi* (F.), inscription (WRITING).

deduce, *v.* reason, analyze, conclude (THOUGHT).

DEDUCTION—*N.* **deduction,** subtraction, removal, excision, abstraction.

inference, a priori reasoning, conclusion, derivation, corollary.

rebate, remission, abatement; discount, offtake, allowance, tare; minuend, subtrahend.

V. **deduct,** subtract, take from, take away, remove, withdraw, abstract, rebate, bate, allow; reduce, diminish.

Adj. **deductive,** deducible, inferable, inferential, *a priori* (L.).

minus, less, negative (*math.*), lacking, deficient, short of, devoid of, diminished, smaller.

Adv. less, to a smaller extent, in a lower degree, not so much.

See also ABSENCE, CUTTING, DECREASE, INSUFFICIENCY, REASONING. *Antonyms*—See ADDITION, INCREASE.

---

deed, *n.* act, feat, stunt (ACTION, ABILITY); document, paper, instrument (WRITING).

deem, *v.* consider, estimate, appraise (OPINION).

deep, *adj.* deep-seated, profound, buried (DEPTH); hard to understand, difficult (MYSTERY); bass, low-pitched, low-toned (LOWNESS).

deep-seated, *adj.* ingrained, implanted, inwrought (INTERIORITY).

deer, *n.* musk deer, red deer, reindeer (ANIMAL).

deface, *v.* disfigure, deform, mar (BLEMISH, DEFORMITY).

defame, *v.* denigrate, blacken, besmirch (DETRACTION).

default, *v.* dishonor, welsh (*colloq.*), repudiate (DEBT).

DEFEAT—*N.* **defeat,** vanquishment, checkmate, discomfiture, rout; overthrow, overturn, setback, upset, debacle, downcome, downthrow, smash, subversion, *coup d'état* (F.); conquest, mastery, subdual, subjugation, triumph, victory.

conqueror, conquistador, winner, master, victor.

V. **defeat,** beat, best, whip (*colloq.*), lick (*colloq.*), trim (*colloq.*), trounce, triumph over, vanquish, worst; checkmate, discomfit, overpower, put to rout, rout, smash, drub, thrash, whitewash, euchre (*colloq.*); overcome, shock, stun, overwhelm; hurdle, negotiate, prevail over, surmount; overthrow, overturn, subvert, upset, topple; put down, crush, quell, quash, squash, squelch, repress, subdue, suppress, tame; conquer, master, overmaster, subjugate, bring to terms.

Adj. **conquerable,** superable, vincible, pregnable, defeatable, etc. (see *Verbs*).

See also CONTROL, OBEDIENCE, SLAVERY, SUBMISSION, SUCCESS. *Antonyms*—See DEFIANCE, DISOBEDIENCE, FAILURE, FIGHTING, OPPOSITION.

---

defeatist, *n.* submitter, yielder, quitter (SUBMISSION).

defect, *n.* flaw, fault, foible (WEAKNESS, IMPERFECTION).

defend, *v.* protect, guard, bulwark (PROTECTION); justify, apologize for (SUPPORT).

defendant, *n.* the accused, prisoner (ACCUSATION); litigant (LAWSUIT).

defender, *n.* protector, paladin, champion (PROTECTION); sympathizer, partisan (PITY).

defense, *n.* armor, bastion, buckler (PROTECTION); excuse, rationalization, alibi (*colloq.*), plea (FORGIVENESS, ANSWER); apology, justification, extenuation (SUPPORT, ATONEMENT).

defensive, *adj.* protective, preservative, conservative (PROTECTION).

defer, *v.* submit, yield, bow to (SUBMISSION); postpone, put off, adjourn (DELAY).

deference, *n.* esteem, homage, honor (RESPECT).

DEFIANCE—*N.* defiance, bravado, defial, defy (*colloq.*), opposition, disobedience, insurgency, insubordination, revolt, rebellion; confrontation, confrontment, affront; recalcitration, recalcitrance; challenge, dare, defi (*colloq.*), the gage, the gauntlet, the glove, cartel.

V. defy, beard, brave, hurl defiance at, mock, flout, laugh at, challenge, dare, throw (or fling) down the gauntlet, square off (*colloq.*); disobey, revolt, mutiny, rebel against, recalcitrate; confront, affront; question, impugn, contest.

Adj. defiant, resistant, resistive, insubmissive, recalcitrant, reckless, mutinous, rebellious, refractory.

Adv., phrases. defiantly, resistively, etc. (see *Adjectives*); in the teeth of, in open rebellion, regardless of consequences.

See also COURAGE, DISAGREEMENT, DISOBEDIENCE, THREAT. *Antonyms*— See ACCEPTANCE, AGREEMENT, ASSENT, OBEDIENCE, SUBMISSION.

deficient, *adj.* wanting, short, inadequate (INCOMPLETENESS, INSUFFICIENCY); imperfect, defective, faulty (IMPERFECTION).

deficit, *n.* deficiency, lack, shortage (INCOMPLETENESS, INSUFFICIENCY).

defile, *v.* taint, pollute, sully (IMPURITY, UNCLEANNESS).

define, *v.* explain, construe, interpret (EXPLANATION); delimit, delimitate, demarcate (BOUNDARY).

definite, *adj.* clear-cut, decided, pronounced; sure, guaranteed (CLARITY, CERTAINTY); fixed, defined, specific (BOUNDARY); distinct, clear, plain (VISIBILITY).

definitely, *adv.* surely, undoubtedly, indubitably (CERTAINTY).

deflation, *n.* recession, slump, depression (BUSINESS).

DEFORMITY—*N.* deformity, deformation, malformation, disfigurement, misshapenness, crookedness; warp, knot, buckle; misproportion, asymmetry, ungracefulness; distortion, contortion, grimace.

[*medical conditions*] humpback, hump, hunchback, kyphosis, curvature of the spine, lordosis, swayback, gibbosity.

eyesore, blemish, disfigurement, blot on the landscape; object, figure, sight (*colloq.*), fright.

hag, harridan, crone, gorgon, witch, ogress.

monster, monstrosity, freak, scarecrow.

humpback, hunchback, Caliban.

V. deform, misshape, skew, distort, contort, twist, gnarl, knot, warp, buckle; grimace, wince.

deface, disfigure, blemish, injure, mar, mangle, mutilate, spoil.

Adj. deformed, ill-made, grotesque, malformed, misshapen, unshaped, unshapen.

shapeless, ungraceful, asymmetrical, unsymmetrical, misproportioned, ill-proportioned, anisometric, baroque, skew, erose, irregular.

distorted, contorted, out of shape, crooked, gnarled, knotted, buckled, twisted, wry, awry, askew.

hunchbacked, humpbacked, gibbous, kyphotic, sway-backed.

ugly, hideous, repulsive, unsightly, ill-favored, ill-formed, illlooking, unfavorable, hard-favored.

unattractive, unaesthetic, plain, homely, unbecoming, unfair, unhandsome, unlovely, unpretty, unbeautiful, unpersonable, uncomely, unseemly.

shapeless, formless, amorphous, unshaped, unshapen, unformed, unhewn, unfashioned.

See also BLEMISH, DISEASE, IRREGULARITY, SWELLING, UNNATURALNESS, WINDING. *Antonyms*—See BEAUTY, SHAPE, STRAIGHTNESS.

defraud, *v.* cheat, bamboozle, swindle (DECEPTION, THIEVERY).

defy, *v.* beard, brave, mock (DEFIANCE); oppose, resist, withstand (OPPOSITION).

degenerate, *adj.* depraved, decadent, degraded (IMMORALITY).

degenerate, *n.* debauchee, pervert (IMMORALITY); sexual deviate, erotopath (SEX).

degenerate, v. worsen, corrode, decline (DETERIORATION).

degrade, v. humble, demean, debase (HUMILIATION, MEANNESS); corrupt, canker, debauch (IMMORALITY); demote, downgrade, abase (RANK).

DEGREE—N. **degree,** grade, step, gradation, extent, measure, amount, point, mark, stage, rate, scale, ratio, standard, height, pitch, plane; reach, range, scope, caliber; tenor, compass; division, interval, space (*music*), line (*music*); shade, intensity, strength.

V. **graduate,** grade, calibrate, measure; classify, range.

Adj. **gradual,** progressive, regular, graduated, gradational.

Adv., phrases. **gradually,** by degrees, regularly, step by step, little by little, inch by inch, drop by drop; to some extent; slowly, gently.

See also GREATNESS, MODERATENESS, QUANTITY, STRENGTH. *Antonyms*—See EXTREMENESS, SUDDENNESS.

deify, v. apotheosize, adore, venerate (GOD, WORSHIP).

deign, v. condescend, stoop, patronize (PRIDE).

deity, n. god, goddess, divinity (GOD).

DEJECTION—N. **dejection,** low spirits, depressed spirits, depression, despondency, melancholy, abjection, disconsolation, gloom, discouragement, dismay.

the blues, the blue devils, the dismals (*colloq.*), the dumps (*colloq.*), the mopes, the doldrums, the megrims, the vapors (*archaic*); damp, slough of despond.

melancholia, hypochondria, hypochondriasis, psycholepsy.

V. **deject,** depress, cast down, discourage, dishearten, dismay, dispirit, gloom; blacken, chill, cloud, dampen, darken, dash.

be dejected, despond, gloom, mope; sag, droop.

Adj. **dejected,** low, low-spirited, heavyhearted, blue, depressed, despondent, dispirited, cast down, chapfallen, crestfallen, downcast, downhearted, gloomy, glum, melancholy, atrabilious, atrabiliar, disconsolate; cheerless, black, bleak, dismal, clouded, dampened, dashed, droopy, drooping, sagging; discouraged, disheartened, dismayed; abject, wretched, spiritless, vaporish, vapory, soul-sick; mopish, mopy, broody, moody.

disheartening, depressing, discouraging, dismaying, dispiriting; somber, chill, chilly, dreary, drearisome, sullen.

See also GLOOM, HOPELESSNESS, REGRET, SADNESS, WEEPING. *Antonyms*—See CHEERFULNESS, HAPPINESS, MERRIMENT, PLEASURE.

DELAY—N. **delay,** wait, dalliance, filibuster, lag, stall, procrastination, cunctation.

postponement, adjournment, deferment, prorogation, reprieve, respite, stay, moratorium.

V. **delay,** dally, dillydally, dawdle, lag, linger, loiter, tarry, stall, temporize, filibuster, demur, procrastinate, take time, mark time.

postpone, put off, adjourn, defer, prorogue, prorogate, stall off, waive, wait; lay aside, lay over, pigeonhole, shelve, table, reserve; hold up, stay, respite, reprieve; detain, retard.

be late, straggle, straggle in, tarry, be tardy.

be kept waiting, dance attendance, cool one's heels (*colloq.*); await, expect, wait for, sit up for.

Adj. **late,** tardy, dilatory; slow, behindhand, behind, behind time, backward, unpunctual; overdue, belated, delayed, long-delayed; posthumous.

recent, not long past, fresh; quondam, former, *ci-devant* (*F.*), sometime, outgoing, retiring, deceased, dead.

delaying, dilatory, Fabian, moratory; dallying, etc. (see *Verbs*).

later (*in time*), subsequent, posterior, ulterior.

Adv., phrases. **late,** backward, behindhand, behind time, too late; ultimately, late in the day, at the eleventh hour, at length, at last, finally.

slowly, leisurely, deliberately, tardily, at one's leisure.

See also PAST, RELIEF, SLOWNESS, TIME. *Antonyms*—See EARLINESS, SPEED.

delectable, *adj.* palatable, delicious, toothsome (TASTE).

delegate, n. ambassador, envoy, emissary (SUBSTITUTION, MESSENGER).

delegate, v. commission, designate, deputize (PLACE, DEPUTY).

deliberate, *adj.* considered, willful, express (PURPOSE).

deliberate, v. think, reflect, contemplate (THOUGHT); discuss, talk over, argue (TALK).

delicacy, n. good taste, cultivation, culture (TASTE); tact, diplomacy (ABILITY); fragility, frailty, subtlety (WEAKNESS); tidbit, dainty (TASTE).

delicate, *adj.* faint, fragile, slight (WEAKNESS, BREAKABLENESS); fine, gauzy, gossamery, filmy (THINNESS, TEXTURE); soft, tender, smooth (SOFTNESS); exquisite, dainty (BEAUTY); thin-skinned, touchy (SENSITIVENESS).

delicious, *adj.* palatable, luscious, savory (TASTE, PLEASANTNESS).

delight, *v.* gratify, enchant, delectate (PLEASURE); please, charm (PLEASURE, PLEASANTNESS); make happy, enrapture (HAPPINESS); satisfy, content (SATISFACTION).

delightful, *adj.* enjoyable, pleasurable, delectable (PLEASURE); cheery, charming, lovely (HAPPINESS, PLEASANTNESS).

delights, *n.* pleasures, joys, enjoyments (SWEETNESS).

delinquent, *adj.* derelict, defaultant, remiss (NEGLECT).

delirious, *adj.* intoxicated, drunk, beside oneself (EXCITEMENT); manic, maniac, maniacal (INSANITY); aberrant, deviant, deviate (WANDERING).

deliver, *v.* transfer, hand, pass (GIVING); bear, bring, fetch (TRANSFER); give tongue to, utter, express (VOICE).

delivery, *n.* liberation, rescue, salvation (FREEDOM); inflection, intonation, modulation (VOICE); childbirth, labor (BIRTH).

deluge, *n.* downpour, drencher, flood (RAIN).

deluge, *v.* flood, engulf, inundate (WATER); crowd, swamp, overcrowd (MULTITUDE); oversupply, glut (EXCESS).

delusion, *n.* fallacy, misbelief, misconception (FALSENESS, BELIEF, UNREALITY).

demagogue, *n.* agitator, political agitator, rabble-rouser (DISSATISFACTION).

DEMAND—*N.* demand, claim, counterclaim, reclaim, lien, ultimatum, clamor, requirement, requisition, imposition, arrogation, stipulation.

request, appeal, application, bid, prayer, entreaty, impetration, supplication; importunity, insistence, invitation, petition, round robin, plea, suit.

V. demand, claim, counterclaim, reclaim, clamor for, urge, press, exact, require, requisition, impose upon, arrogate, stipulate, postulate; abuse, tax.

request, ask, appeal, apply; beg, beseech, pray, entreat, impetrate,

implore, supplicate, plead for, petition, solicit, seek, sue for; nag, pester, importune, insist, badger, besiege, dun, adjure, bid.

Adj. demanding, claiming, etc. (see *Verbs*); clamorous, imperious, dictatorial, ambitious; urgent, insistent, pressing, imperative, exigent.

See also BEGGING, COMMAND, FORCE, URGING. *Antonyms*—See GIVING, SUBMISSION.

demeanor, *n.* poise, bearing, conduct (APPEARANCE, BEHAVIOR).

demented, *adj.* insane, psychotic, psychopathic (INSANITY).

democratic, *adj.* friendly, informal, free and easy (SOCIALITY); self-governing, free, republican (GOVERNMENT).

demolish, *v.* destroy, wreck, smash (DESTRUCTION).

demon, *n.* fiend, imp, evil spirit (DEVIL).

demonstrate, *v.* prove, show, testify to (PROOF).

demonstrative, *adj.* affectionate, warmhearted, tender (LOVE).

demoralize, *v.* disconcert, discountenance, abash (CONFUSION); deprave, pervert, corrupt (IMMORALITY).

demote, *v.* downgrade, degrade, abase (RANK).

demur, *v.* hesitate, stickle, scruple (INACTION); object, take exception, protest (OPPOSITION).

demure, *adj.* conventional, moral, proper (PROPRIETY); earnest, sedate, staid (SOBRIETY); coy, skittish, blushing (MODESTY).

den, *n.* study, studio, atelier (SPACE, WORK); nest, hotbed (WICKEDNESS).

DENIAL—*N.* denial, contradiction, disproof, refutation, denegation, disaffirmation.

refusal, no, declension, nonacceptance, turndown (*colloq.*), flat (*or* point-blank) refusal; negative, negative answer, nay; veto, disapproval, disallowance.

rejection, repulsion, rebuff, discard; thumbs down.

prohibition, forbiddance *or* forbiddal, injunction (*against*), enjoinder, bar, ban, embargo, proscription, interdiction, outlawry, taboo *or* tabu.

V. deny, gainsay, contradict, disprove, refute, controvert, dispute, negate, disaffirm, belie, give the lie to, protest, renege.

refuse, say no, decline, not accept, turn down (*colloq.*), withhold consent (*or* assent); balk.

reject, disdain, spurn, scorn, scout, repel, repulse, rebuff, reprobate; brush aside (*or* away), set aside, cast aside, discard, jilt (*a lover*).

repudiate, disown, disavow, renounce, abnegate, disclaim, divorce oneself from.

veto, negative, discountenance, disapprove, disallow.

prohibit, forbid, enjoin from, forfend (*archaic*), bar, ban, embargo, proscribe, interdict, outlaw, taboo *or* tabu; exclude, debar, keep out, excommunicate (*rel.*); deprive.

Adj. denying, contradictory, contradictive, contrary, disaffirmative *or* disaffirmatory, disputative, protestant; negative, negatory.

rejective, disdainful, reprobatory; disclamatory, abnegative.

prohibitive, prohibitory, injunctive, proscriptive, interdictive.

prohibited, forbidden, contraband, *verboten* (*Ger.*), taboo *or* tabu; barred, banned, etc. (see *Verbs*).

Adv., phrases. no, nay, not, nowise, not at all, not in the least, quite the contrary, *au contraire* (*F.*), on no account, by no means, not for the world, not on your life (*colloq.*), nothing doing (*slang*), out of the question.

See also DISAGREEMENT, DISAPPROVAL, DISPROOF, EXCLUSION, OPPOSITION, UNWILLINGNESS. *Antonyms*—See ACCEPTANCE, APPROVAL, ASSENT, RECEIVING, WILLINGNESS.

---

denomination, *n.* sect, church, religious persuasion (RELIGION); designation, appellation (NAME).

denote, *v.* symbolize, symbol, stand for, mean, betoken (REPRESENTATION); designate, evidence (INDICATION).

denounce, *v.* cry down, damn, denunciate, excoriate (DISAPPROVAL); accuse, charge (ACCUSATION).

dense, *adj.* compact, solid, close, impenetrable (ASSEMBLAGE, THICKNESS); exuberant, luxuriant, rank (PLANT LIFE); stupid, simple, simple-headed, thick, blockheaded (STUPIDITY).

dent, *n.* nick, score, indentation, concavity, dimple, depression (NOTCH, HOLLOW).

dental, *adj.* interdental, periodontal, peridental (TEETH).

dentist, *n.* orthodontist, oral surgeon, dental surgeon (MEDICAL SCIENCE).

deny, *v.* gainsay, contradict, disprove (DENIAL).

department, *n.* classification, category (CLASS); domain, jurisdiction, sphere (POWER); commune, district, parish (REGION).

DEPARTURE—*N.* departure, exit, start, exodus, stampede, migration, emigration, expatriation.

leave-taking, parting, adieu, farewell, good-by, *bon voyage* (*F.*), Godspeed, valediction, valedictory, apopemptic.

escape, wilding, breakout, outbreak, decampment, desertion; flight, hegira, fugue (*psychol.*), bolt, French leave; dispersal, dispersion, diaspora, disbandment; narrow escape, hairbreadth escape, close call (*colloq.*), near (*or* close) shave (*slang*).

[*means of escape*] fire escape, ladder, lifeboat, life raft, parachute; secret passage, tunnel; avenue, egress, exit, outlet, opening, vent, spout, leak; loophole, escape clause.

outlet, egress, port, porthole; sluice, sluice gate, floodgate, hatch; drain, culvert, sewer, cesspool.

departer, migrant, emigrant, expatriate, evacuee, transient; exile, outcast.

escaper, escapee, fugitive, runagate, fugitive from justice, refugee, maroon, deserter, runaway.

V. depart, go away, leave, withdraw, take (*or* make) one's departure, take a powder (*slang*), set out, troop, troop away, start; take leave, part, say good-by, break away; pass away, slip away, lapse, disappear, go by, elapse; migrate, emigrate, expatriate; march out, debouch, sally forth, sally, go forth.

leave, abandon, desert, evacuate, quit, vacate, withdraw from, retire from, retreat from; resign, secede, retire, abdicate, tergiversate.

debark, disembark, detrain, deplane, dismount, get off.

embark, go on board, take ship, go aboard; set sail, put to sea, sail; get under way, weigh anchor.

escape, flee, run away, maroon, decamp, desert, skip; take flight, take wing, fly, flit, steal away, abscond, bolt, skedaddle (*colloq.*), slip away, break out; scatter, disperse, disband, stampede; get away from, elude, evade, avoid, by-pass; wriggle out of, make one's escape, make off, give one the slip; break loose, break away, make a getaway (*slang*), flee (*or* fly) the coop (*slang*).

issue, flow, flow out, emanate, stream, gush, spurt, emerge.

provide escape for, canalize, vent, ventilate.

Adj. departing, etc. (see *Verbs*); outgoing, outbound, outwardbound; migratory, migrant, emigrant.

fleeting, volatile, fugitive, fugacious, transitory, passing, transient; elusive, evasive.

escaped, fugitive, runaway, scot-free, at large.

Interjections. farewell! good-by *or* good-bye! Godspeed! *addio!* (*It.*), *adios!* (*Sp.*), *a mañana!* (*Sp.*), *adeus!* (*Pg.*), *au revoir!* (*F.*), *adieu!* (*F.*), *bonjour!* (*F.*), *auf wiedersehen* (*Ger.*), *a rivederci* (*It.*), *sayonara!* (*Jap.*), *bon voyage!* (*F.*), *gluckliche Reise!* (*Ger.*), *lebewohl!* (*Ger.*), *vale* (*L.*), *vive valeque* (*L.*), *aloha!* (*Hawaiian*), bye-bye! (*colloq.*), so long! (*colloq.*), be seeing you (*colloq.*); good day! good evening! good night!

See also AVOIDANCE, DISAPPEARANCE, EGRESS, FREEDOM, PASSAGE. *Antonyms*—See CONTINUATION.

depend, *v.* bank, hinge, rely (DEPENDABILITY); pend, hang (UNCERTAINTY); hang down, suspend (HANGING).

DEPENDABILITY—*N.* dependability, reliability, responsibility, stability.

dependence, reliance, interdependence.

dependent, client, pensioner, ward, protégée; puppet, figurehead, tool, cat's-paw, Trilby.

recourse, refuge, resort, resource; stand-by, old reliable, old faithful.

V. **depend on,** lean on, bank on, hinge on, reckon on, rely on, interdepend.

Adj. **dependable,** reliable, responsible, stable, steady, trustworthy, trusty, unfailing.

See also BELIEF, CERTAINTY, LIABILITY, STABILITY, UNIFORMITY. *Antonyms*—See CHANGEABLENESS, IRREGULARITY, UNBELIEVINGNESS, UNCERTAINTY.

dependent, *adj.* interdependent, mutual, reciprocal (RELATIONSHIP); subject, subordinate, inferior (SLAVERY); pendent, pending, pensile (HANGING).

dependent, *n.* client, ward, protégée (DEPENDABILITY).

depict, *v.* describe, characterize, delineate (DESCRIPTION, REPRESENTATION).

deplete, *v.* use up, consume, exhaust (USE); empty, drain (ABSENCE).

deplorable, *adj.* lamentable, tragic, regrettable (SADNESS, REGRET).

deport, *v.* banish, cast out, exile (DISMISSAL, PUNISHMENT).

deportment, *n.* conduct, comportment (BEHAVIOR).

depose, *v.* depone, dethrone, unseat (DISMISSAL); aver, avow (AFFIRMATION).

deposit, *n.* alluvion, silt, drift (TRANSFER).

deposit, *v.* lay, rest, set (LOCATION, PLACE).

deprave, *v.* demoralize, pervert, seduce (IMMORALITY, SEX).

depraved, *adj.* debauched, dissolute, abandoned (SEX, WICKEDNESS).

depreciate, *v.* depress, cheapen, decline (WORTHLESSNESS); detract from, deprecate (*loose usage*), derogate from (DETRACTION).

depress, *v.* cast down, dishearten, dispirit (DEJECTION); sink, drop, dip (LOWNESS); clamp, press, bear down (PRESSURE); devaluate, debase, depreciate (WORTHLESSNESS).

depression, *n.* despondency, melancholy, gloom (DEJECTION); deflation, recession, slump (BUSINESS); concavity, dent, dimple (HOLLOW).

deprive, *v.* dispossess, take away (TAKING).

DEPTH—*N.* depth, profundity, intensity, extent.

deep place, deep, depth, depths, abyss, abysm, gulf, valley, pit, shaft, well, crater, depression, hollow, chasm, crevasse; briny deep, benthos.

valley, canyon, cañon, coomb, dale (*poetic*), dell, dingle, gap, glen, gorge, gulch, gully, notch, ravine, strath, vale (*poetic*).

sounding (*naut.*), depth of water; water; plummet, lead, plumb, bob, plumb line, bathometer; sea gauge, fathomer; bathometry.

draft *or* **draught** (*naut.*), submergence, submersion, sinkage, displacement.

V. **deepen,** sink, countersink, dredge, dig, burrow, excavate, mine, sap; intensify, strengthen, increase.

fathom, sound, plumb, take soundings, heave the lead.

Adj. **deep,** deep-seated, profound, buried; sunk, sunken, submerged, subaqueous, submarine, subterranean, underground; inmost, innermost.

bottomless, fathomless, sound-

less, unfathomed, unfathomable,
abysmal, abyssal, depthless, yawning, immeasurable, unplumbed.

[*of sleep*] **profound,** fast, heavy,
undisturbed, sound.

[*of tones*] **sonorous,** resonant,
full-toned, full, rumbling, bass.

See also BURIAL, DIGGING, INCREASE,
INTERIORITY, MYSTERY, STRENGTH,
WISDOM. *Antonyms*—See SHALLOW-
NESS, SURFACE.

---

deputy, *n.* councilman, councilor,
assemblyman (LEGISLATURE); regent, viceroy, minister (DEPUTY).

DEPUTY—*N.* **deputy,** substitute,
surrogate, proxy, *locum tenens*
(L.), delegate, agent, alternate;
vice-president, vice-chairman.

regent, vicegerent, viceroy, minister, vicar, prime minister, premier, chancellor, provost, warden,
lieutenant.

representative, emissary, envoy,
messenger; deputation, committee;
broker, go-between, middleman,
negotiator.

ambassador, diplomat, minister,
legate, envoy, plenipotentiary,
consul, attaché, chargé d'affaires;
nuncio, internuncio; embassy, legation.

V. **depute,** delegate, deputize,
commission, accredit.

represent, stand for, appear for,
answer for, stand in the shoes of,
stand in the stead of.

Adj. **acting,** officiating, substituting, vice, vicegerent, viceregal,
delegated, deputized.

See also AGENT, GOVERNMENT,
MEDIATION, OFFICIAL, REPRESENTA-
TION, SUBSTITUTION. *Antonyms*—See
CONTROL.

---

derange, *v.* discompose, disturb,
upset (UNTIDINESS); disarrange,
disorder, disorganize (CONFU-
SION); dement, distract, frenzy
(INSANITY).

derelict, *adj.* negligent, neglectful,
lax (NEGLECT); ownerless, castoff
(DESERTION).

derisive, *adj.* disdainful, derisory,
scornful (CONTEMPT, RIDICULE).

derogatory, *adj.* depreciatory, detractive, disparaging (DETRAC-
TION).

descendant, *n.* scion, heir, offspring (CHILD).

DESCENT—*N.* **descent,** fall,
header (*colloq.*), drop, coast, slip,
tailspin, slide, settlement; declination, declension, sinkage, dip, subsidence, droop, slump, collapse,

plop, plummet, plunge, sag, cave-
in, crash, toboggan, topple, tumble; duck, nod, nutation; swoop,
pounce; downcome, comedown;
anticlimax, bathos.

cascade, cataract, precipitation,
downrush, chute, avalanche, landslide, snowslide, glissade.

V. **descend,** go (drop *or* come)
down, fall, drop, lower, coast, slip,
slide, settle; decline, sink, swamp,
set, dip, subside, droop, slump,
collapse, plop, plummet, ground,
light, plump, plunge, sag, slough
off, cave in, prolapse (*med.*); cascade, cataract, chute, crash, toboggan, topple, tumble; sink into
mud, poach; duck, nod; swoop,
pounce, swoop down, crouch,
stoop; fall prostrate, precipitate
oneself, throw oneself down.

drip, dribble, drizzle, rain, sleet,
snow, hail, shower, spatter, spray,
sprinkle, trickle, weep.

get down, get off, get down
from, alight, dismount.

fall down, lose one's balance,
fall, stumble, blunder, collapse,
founder, topple, trip, tumble, slip,
slide, come a cropper.

begin to fall, slide, slip, totter,
lurch, trip, pitch.

knock down, bowl down, bowl
over, knock over, overthrow, overturn, topple, tumble, trip.

Adj. **descending,** descendent,
precipitant, precipitous, sheer;
droopy, prolapsed (*med.*); downward, subsident, decursive, decur-
rent; ramshackle, tottery, tumble-
down.

See also ANCESTRY, DEFEAT, LOW-
NESS, SLOPE. *Antonyms*—See ASCENT,
HEIGHT, INCREASE.

DESCRIPTION—*N.* description,
characterization, delineation, depiction, depicture, explication;
portrayal, portrait, portraiture;
topography, chorography, geography, geographics.

account, version, report, sketch,
vignette.

V. **describe,** characterize, delineate, depict, depicture, explicate,
limn, picture, portray; specify, detail, particularize.

Adj. **descriptive,** delineative, depictive, explicatory; specific, detailed, particularized.

[*hard to describe*] **indescribable,**
ineffable, nondescript, subtle.

See also ACCOUNTS, INFORMATION,
MAP, RECORD, REPRESENTATION, STORY,
TALK, WRITING.

---

desecrate, *v.* prostitute, profane,
pervert (MISUSE); violate, com-

mit sacrilege upon, contaminate (DISRESPECT, IRRELIGION).

desert, *n.* wasteland, waste, Sahara (LAND).

deserter, *n.* escaper, maroon, runaway (DEPARTURE).

DESERTION—*N.* **desertion,** abandonment, betrayal, apostasy, tergiversation, defection; derelict, maroon, castoff.

V. **desert,** abandon, forsake, leave, leave in the lurch, go back on (*colloq.*), maroon, strand, beach, betray, bolt; apostatize, tergiversate, run away, go A.W.O.L. (*mil.*).

Adj. **deserted,** abandoned, forsaken, homeless, houseless, left, left in the lurch, marooned, stranded, beached, betrayed, derelict, ownerless, castoff; desolate, forlorn, lorn.

See also ABSENCE, APOSTASY, DEPARTURE, RELINQUISHMENT, SECLUSION. *Antonyms*—See CONTINUATION, FOLLOWING, REMAINDER, REVERSION.

deserve, *v.* be worthy of, merit, rate (VALUE, RIGHT).

design, *n.* painting, depiction, illustration (FINE ARTS); method, plan (ARRANGEMENT); intention, notion, aim (PURPOSE); device, contrivance (PLAN).

design, *v.* plan, devise, contrive (PLAN, PRODUCTION).

designate, *v.* commission, delegate, constitute (PLACE); denote, connote, evidence (INDICATION); denominate, name, nominate (NAME).

DESIRE—*N.* **desire,** wish, desideration, mania, nympholepsy, obsession, oestrus, cacoëthes, passion, yen, zeal, will, accord, ambition, aspiration; want, requirement, preference; envy, lust, avarice, greed, gluttony, appetite.

caprice, fancy, crotchet, whim, notion, vagary.

urge, impulse, itch, conatus, motive, motivation, accord.

incentive, inspiration, motivation, motive, ambition.

[*object of desire*] **desideratum,** desideration, desiderative, plum; rage, craze, fad, passion; temptation, lure, allurement, attraction, magnet.

desirer, aspirant, candidate; nympholept, zealot, enthusiast; glutton, buzzard, cormorant.

V. **desire,** wish, set one's heart upon, desiderate, aspire to, want, require, prefer; covet, lust for (*or* after); envy, grudge, begrudge.

long for, crave, hanker for, ache for, hunger for, thirst for, yearn for, pine for, sigh for, languish for, itch for, gasp for, pant for, starve for.

[*arouse desire*] **inspire,** fire, motivate, suggest, obsess.

Adj. **desirous,** wishful, wistful, wantful, itchy; avid, eager, would-be; nympholeptic, zealous, ambitious, aspiring, aspirant; envious, lustful, greedy, gluttonous, lickerish, liquorish.

desiderative, optative; impulsive, spontaneous, impetuous.

capricious, crotchety, vagarious, flighty; arbitrary.

grasping, acquisitive, greedy, rapacious, ravenous, ravening, cormorant, avaricious, miserly.

desirable, enviable, covetable; agreeable, pleasing, appetizing, savory, tasty; desired, in demand, popular, preferable, advantageous.

[*arousing desire*] **inspiring,** inspirational, motivating, obsessive, suggestive; attractive, alluring, seductive, tempting.

See also ATTRACTION, CAPRICE, EAGERNESS, GLUTTONY, GREED, HUNGER, HOPE, PLEASANTNESS, PLEASURE, SEX. *Antonyms*—See DISAPPROVAL, FULLNESS, HATRED, INDIFFERENCE, UNPLEASANTNESS, UNSAVORINESS.

desist, *v.* not do, abstain, avoid (INACTION).

desk, *n.* reading desk, lectern, pulpit (SCHOOL).

desolate, *adj.* lonely, lonesome, forlorn (SECLUSION); miserable, wretched, tragic (SADNESS).

desolate, *v.* sadden, distress, grieve (SADNESS); lay waste, devastate, ravage (DESTRUCTION).

despair, *n.* dashed hopes, forlorn hope, desperation (HOPELESSNESS).

desperate, *adj.* devil-may-care, death-defying, bold (COURAGE); despondent, despairing, in despair; futile, useless, vain (HOPELESSNESS).

despicable, *adj.* contemptible, ignominious, low (CONTEMPT).

despise, *v.* hate, abhor, abominate (HATRED); misprize, look down upon (CONTEMPT).

despite, *prep.* in spite of, in despite of, in defiance of (OPPOSITION).

despondent, *adj.* depressed, dispirited, cast down (DEJECTION); despairing, desperate, in despair (HOPELESSNESS).

despot, *n.* autocrat, dictator, tyrant (RULER, CONTROL).

despotic, *adj.* autocratic, absolute, arbitrary (POWER, WILL).

dessert, *n.* sweet, sweets, ice cream (SWEETNESS).

destination, *n.* goal, terminus, end (ARRIVAL, PURPOSE).

DESTINY—*N.* destiny, fate, lot, portion, fortune, future, kismet; doom, foredoom; horoscope, constellation; future existence, hereafter, next world, world to come, afterlife, life to come; prospect, expectation.

V. destine, destinate, foreordain, predestine, preordain, predetermine; doom, foredoom; ordain, decree, intend, reserve, set aside.

impend, hang over, overhang, threaten, hover, loom, await, approach.

Adj., phrases. destined, fated, predestined, foreordained, preordained, predetermined; doomed, foredoomed; ordained, decreed, intended, reserved, set aside, planned.

impending, hanging over, overhanging, threatening, looming, awaiting, approaching, brewing, coming, in store, to come; near, at hand, imminent, in the wind, in prospect; in the lap of the gods.

See also DECISION, EXPECTATION, FUTURE, NECESSITY, PLAN, PREDICTION, PURPOSE, THREAT. *Antonyms*—See CHANCE, PURPOSELESSNESS.

destitute, *adj.* poor, beggared, needy (POVERTY).

DESTRUCTION—*N.* destruction, desolation, wreck, wreckage, ruin, ruination, rack and ruin, smash, smashup, demolition, havoc, ravage, dilapidation, blight, breakdown, consumption, dissolution, overthrow, spoilage; sabotage, vandalism.

destroyer, spoiler, wrecker, mutilator, demolitionist, saboteur, vandal, fifth columnist, Trojan horse, nihilist; bane, pest, plague, blast, blight.

remains (*after destruction*), ashes, relics, ruins, wreck, wreckage.

V. destroy, wreck, ruin, ruinate, smash, demolish, raze, ravage, gut, dilapidate, decimate, blast, blight, break down, consume, dissolve, overthrow; mutilate, disintegrate, unmake, pulverize; sabotage, vandalize; annul, blast, blight, damn, dash, extinguish,

invalidate, nullify, quell, quench, scuttle, shatter, shipwreck, torpedo, smash, spoil, undo, void; annihilate, devour, disannul, discreate, exterminate, obliterate, extirpate, subvert.

corrode, erode, sap, undermine, waste, waste away, whittle away; eat away, canker, gnaw; wear away, abrade, batter, excoriate, rust.

lay waste, desolate, devastate, ravage.

Adj. destructive, ruinous, vandalistic, baneful, cutthroat, fell, lethiferous, pernicious, slaughterous, predatory, sinistrous, nihilistic.

corrosive, erosive, cankerous, caustic, abrasive.

See also BLOW, BREAKAGE, DETERIORATION, ELIMINATION, HARM, INEFFECTIVENESS, KILLING, REMOVAL. *Antonyms*—See CURE, PRESERVATION, PRODUCTION, RESTORATION.

detach, *v.* loosen, disjoin, disengage (LOOSENESS); part, separate, sunder (DISJUNCTION).

detached, *adj.* impersonal, candid, disinterested (IMPARTIALITY).

detachment, *n.* indifference, incuriosity, unconcern (BOREDOM); preoccupation, reverie, woolgathering (INATTENTION).

DETAIL—*N.* detail, item, particular, specification, minor point, special point, specific, fact, circumstance, technicality, accessory; schedule, minutiae, trivia, fine points, niceties; counts.

V. detail, amplify, circumstantiate, elaborate, embellish, particularize, itemize, individualize, specify, specialize; recount, recite, rehearse.

Adj. detailed, in detail, elaborate, embellished, amplified, circumstantial, circumstantiated.

See also PART. *Antonyms*—See COMPLETENESS.

detain, *v.* delay, retard, hold up (DELAY); confine, constrain, intern (IMPRISONMENT).

detect, *v.* scent, notice, observe (DISCOVERY, VISION).

detective, *n.* ferret, scout, sleuth (DISCOVERY, SEARCH, OFFICIAL).

detention, *n.* confinement, detainment, immurement (IMPRISONMENT).

deter, *v.* prevent, preclude, stop (PREVENTION); hold back, check, restrain (RESTRAINT).

DETERIORATION—*N.* **deterioration,** worsening, corrosion, decay, decline, declension, degeneration, corruption, impairment, regression, retrogression, retrogradation; degradation, abasement, debasement, decadence, adulteration, disrepair.

V. **deteriorate,** become worse, lose quality (excellence, *or* value), worsen, corrode, decay, decline, degenerate, corrupt, impair, derogate, regress, retrogress, retrograde; make worse, aggravate, vitiate, pervert, adulterate, alloy.

Adj. **deteriorated,** worse, corroded, decayed, decadent, degenerate, corrupt, impaired, regressed, retrogressed, retrograde; degraded, abased, debased, adulterate, alloyed, aggravated, vitiated, perverted.

See also DECAY, DESCENT, DESTRUCTION, HARM, IMMORALITY, REVERSION, WICKEDNESS. *Antonyms*—See CURE, IMPROVEMENT, RESTORATION, RIGHT.

determine, *v.* ascertain, divine, learn (DISCOVERY); intend, resolve, mean (PURPOSE); decide, settle, fix (RULE); mark off, mark out, delimit (LOCATION); control, govern (CONTROL).

determined, *adj.* resolute, resolved, bent (PURPOSE, WILL); stubborn, obstinate, dogged (STUBBORNNESS).

deterrent, *n.* rein, leash, bridle (RESTRAINT); preventive, determent (PREVENTION).

detest, *v.* hate, abhor, despise (HATRED).

detour, *n.* by-pass, side road, byroad (PASSAGE); divergence, deviation, branch (TURNING).

DETRACTION—*N.* **detraction,** depreciation, deprecation (*loose usage*), derogation, disparagement, dispraise, decrial, belittlement, minimization; disesteem, ridicule; pejorative, term of disparagement.

defamation, denigration, calumniation, calumny, scandal, obloquy, slander, libel, aspersion, smear, slur, reflection, traducement, vilification, backbiting; witch hunt, character assassination; revilement, vituperation, abusive language, smear words, accusations; innuendo, insinuation, insinuendo.

V. **detract from,** depreciate, deprecate (*loose usage*), derogate from, disparage, dispraise, decry, cry down, cheapen, minimize, vilipend, disesteem; ridicule, laugh at.

underestimate, undervalue, underrate, underappraise, underassess, misprize, disprize; belittle, run down (*colloq.*), knock (*slang*).

disregard, slight, vilipend, make light of, make little of, set no store by, set at naught.

defame, denigrate, blacken, besmirch, smirch, spatter, bespatter, calumniate, slander, libel, malign, asperse, smear, slur, traduce, vilify, vilipend, backbite; speak evil of, revile, discredit, blaspheme, blackguard, vituperate.

Adj. **derogatory,** depreciatory, derogative, detractive, disparaging, pejorative; defamatory, calumnious, slanderous, libelous, scandalous, aspersive.

See also CONTEMPT, DISAPPROVAL, HATRED, MALEDICTION, RIDICULE, RUMOR, WORTHLESSNESS. *Antonyms*—See APPROVAL, FLATTERY, PRAISE, WORSHIP.

detrimental, *adj.* injurious, prejudicial, deleterious (HARM).

devaluate, *v.* cheapen, debase, depreciate (WORTHLESSNESS).

devastate, *v.* lay waste, desolate, ravage (DESTRUCTION).

develop, *v.* mature, maturate, ripen (MATURITY, UNFOLDMENT); ensue, follow, result (OCCURRENCE); extend, spread, stretch; amplify, dilate on, enlarge on (INCREASE).

deviate, *v.* diverge, deflect, vary (CHANGE, DIFFERENCE); divagate, digress, aberrate (WANDERING).

deviation, *n.* divergence, branch, fork, crotch, detour (TURNING).

device, *n.* contrivance, apparatus, appliance (INSTRUMENT); trick, artifice, design (DECEPTION, PLAN); maxim, aphorism, axiom (STATEMENT).

DEVIL—*N.* **devil,** the Devil, archenemy, archfiend, Beelzebub, Belial, Diabolus, Pluto, Satan, Hades, Lucifer, Mephistopheles, Old Nick, demogorgon; fiend, demon, daemon, imp, evil spirit, devilkin.

demonology, demonism, demonianism, diabolism, diabology, diablery, deviltry, devilry, witchcraft; demonolatry, diabolatry, Satanism.

V. **diabolize,** demonize, diabolify, Satanize.

Adj. **devilish,** demoniac, demonic, demonian, fiendish, impish, diabolical, infernal, serpentine, cloven-footed, cloven-hoofed, chthonian, satanic, Plutonic, Plutonian, Hadean, Mephistophelian, hellborn.

See also HELL, MAGIC, MYTHICAL BEINGS. *Antonyms*—See ANGEL.

devious, *adj.* oblique, obliquitous, roundabout (INDIRECTNESS); ambagious, circuitous, flexuous (WINDING); digressive, digressory, discursive (WANDERING); dishonorable, crooked, deceitful (DISHONESTY).

devise, *v.* contrive, think up, forge (PRODUCTION); plan, design, frame (PLAN); bequeath, bequest, leave (WILL).

devote, *v.* consecrate, consign, dedicate (LOYALTY); give, apportion, assign (GIVING).

devote oneself, *v.* address oneself, apply oneself, buckle down (ENERGY).

devotions, *n.* services, chapel, prayer (WORSHIP).

devour, *v.* take in, swallow, gobble (INTAKE, RECEIVING, FOOD).

devout, *adj.* religious, pious, orthodox (RELIGIOUSNESS); devoted, consecrated, dedicated (LOYALTY).

dew, *n.* vapor, mist, moisture (WATER).

dexterous, *n.* skillful, adept (ABILITY); right-handed, dextral (APPENDAGE).

diagonal, *adj.* bias, oblique, slanting (SLOPE); transverse, cross, crosswise (CROSSING).

diagram, *n.* outline, blueprint, layout (PLAN, MAP); sketch, rough draft, chart (SHAPE).

dialect, *n.* vernacular, cant, argot (LANGUAGE).

dialogue, *n.* colloquy, parlance, repartee (TALK).

diameter, *n.* bore, caliber, module (WIDTH, SIZE).

diamond, *adj.* adamantine, diamantiferous (JEWELRY).

diaphragm, *n.* partition, midriff (INTERJACENCE, CENTER).

diary, *n.* daybook, journal, minutes (RECORD, TIME MEASUREMENT).

dicker, *v.* bargain, negotiate, haggle (EXCHANGE).

dictator, *n.* despot, oppressor, tyrant (CONTROL, RULER).

dictatorial, *adj.* domineering, overbearing, lordly (WILL, PRIDE); clamorous, imperious, ambitious (DEMAND).

dictatorship, *n.* totalitarianism, fascism, nazism (GOVERNMENT, VIOLENCE).

diction, *n.* pronunciation, articulation, enunciation (VOICE).

dictionary, *n.* lexicon, wordbook, glossary (BOOK, WORD).

didactic, *adj.* teacherish, donnish, pedagogical (TEACHER).

die, *v.* breathe one's last, decease, perish (DEATH); run out, lapse, expire (END).

die-hard, *n.* Bourbon, reactionary, standpatter (OPPOSITION).

diet, *n.* dietary, regimen (FOOD); parliament, senate, council (LEGISLATURE).

differ, *v.* diverge, vary, contrast (DIFFERENCE); discept, clash, disagree (DISAGREEMENT).

DIFFERENCE—N. difference, divergence, discrepancy, contrariety, variance; dash, tone, particularity, individuality, individualism; novelty, originality, uniqueness, atypicality; distinction, subtlety, nicety, quiddity; shade of difference, nuance; wide difference, gulf, chasm.

contrast, antithesis, contradistinction, foil.

variation, diversity, heterogeneity, variegation; assortment, miscellany, variety.

differential, distinction, feature, differentia (*logic*), mark, marking, peculiarity, earmark.

[*different thing or person*] deviate, variant, variation, varietist, wilding, novelty, individual, individualist (*sic*).

V. [*be different*] differ, diverge, vary, contrast, deviate.

[*make different*] diversify, vary, assort, variegate; mismate, mismatch; modify, change, alter.

[*set apart as different*] differentiate, distinguish, characterize, demarcate, mark, individuate, individualize; contrast, antithesize.

Adj. different, divergent, motley, discrepant, contrary, variant; distinct, distinctive, special, particular, individual; remote, alien; novel, original, unique, atypical; unwonted, unusual: differential, varietal.

contrasting, antithetic, contradistinct, contradistinctive, colorful, contrastive.

varied, various, divers, sundry, miscellaneous, assorted, diversified, heterogeneous, manifold, multifarious, omnifarious, variegated, varicolored; multiform, diversiform, omniform, variform, biform, triform.

dissimilar, unlike, unrelated, mismatched, mismated, disparate, diverse, incomparable, incommensurable.

special, especial, express, individual, particular, singular, specialized, specific, ad hoc (*L.*).

See also CHANGE, DISAGREEMENT, INEQUALITY, OPPOSITION. *Antonyms* —See SIMILARITY.

DIFFERENTIATION—*N.* differentiation, discrimination, distinction, nicety, discernment, taste, judgment, insight, penetration, perceptivity, subtlety, subtility.

V. differentiate, distinguish, split hairs, subtilize, discriminate, contradistinguish, separate, draw the line, sift, discern.

Adj. discriminating, discriminative, discriminatory, discerning, perceptive; nice, fine, subtle, subtile, schizotrichiatric, hairsplitting, fine-drawn.

See also CHOICE, DIFFERENCE, JUDGE, JUDGMENT, TASTE. *Antonyms*—See INDISCRIMINATION, SIMILARITY.

DIFFICULTY—*N.* difficulty, hardship, uphill work, burden, Herculean (*or* Augean) task.

trouble, trial, bother, inconvenience, pain, severity, snag, vicissitude, pitfall; puzzle, Chinese puzzle, perplexity, problem.

predicament, plight, scrape, straits, difficult straits, pinch; fix, jam, pickle, hot water (*all colloq.*); stew, mess, muddle, imbroglio; dilemma, quandary; impasse, mire, morass, quagmire, rattrap, vicious circle; entanglement, snarl, tangle, knot, Gordian knot, maze, labyrinth, hard nut to crack.

troublemaker, stormy petrel, hellion; nuisance, pest, trial.

V. be difficult, etc. (see *Adjectives*); go against the grain, try one's patience, go hard with one; bother, trouble, inconvenience; perplex, puzzle, baffle, mystify.

meet with difficulty, flounder, struggle, labor, toil, stick fast, be in a predicament, come to a deadlock, be on the horns of a dilemma.

move with difficulty, struggle, toil, work, plow *or* plough, flounder.

render difficult, hamper, encumber, throw obstacles in the way of, impede.

complicate, entangle, snag, snarl, snarl up.

inconvenience, bother, discommode, disoblige, incommode, trouble.

Adj. difficult, hard, tough, uphill; arduous, toilsome, toilful, laborious, onerous, burdensome; Herculean, Sisyphean, Augean; formidable, prohibitive.

complex, complicated, entangled, intricate, elaborate, involved, knotty, ramified, reticular, snarled, tangled, tricky.

troublesome, troublous, painful, queasy, severe, snaggy, spiny, thorny, vicissitudinous, vicissitudi-nary; baffling, puzzling, perplexing, problematic; stubborn, obstinate; delicate, ticklish, trying, awkward.

inconvenient, remote, bothersome, incommodious, untoward; awkward, bulky, unhandy, unmanageable, unwieldy.

in difficulty, in hot water (*colloq.*), in a fix (*colloq.*), in a scrape, between Scylla and Charybdis, between the Devil and the deep blue sea, on the horns of a dilemma.

Adv., phrases. with difficulty, laboriously, arduously, toilsomely, toilfully, onerously, uphill, upstream, against a head wind, against the current.

See also ATTEMPT, CLUMSINESS, CONFUSION, HINDRANCE, IMPOSSIBILITY, MYSTERY, UNCERTAINTY. *Antonyms*—See ABILITY, EASE, POSSIBILITY, UNDERSTANDING.

---

diffident, *adj.* insecure, unconfident, unassured (UNCERTAINTY, UNBELIEVINGNESS); timid, timorous, sheepish (FEAR); bashful, shy, retiring (MODESTY).

diffuse, *adj.* diffusive, broadcast, widespread (DISPERSION); prevalent, general, universal (PRESENCE); verbose, prolix (WORDINESS).

diffuse, *v.* transfuse, overspread, suffuse (SPREAD).

digest, *v.* abridge, abstract, epitomize (SHORTNESS); understand, assimilate (UNDERSTANDING).

DIGGING—*N.* digging, excavation, etc. (see *Verbs*).

digger, burrower, tunneler, sapper, excavator, miner, quarrier, shoveler, delver, dredger, borer, driller.

[*digging instrument*] dredge, dredger, dredging machine, steam shovel, bulldozer; shovel, spade, trowel, scoop, wimble, bore, drill, mattock; bail, bailer, bailing can.

excavation, hole, pit, cutting, trough, furrow, ditch, mine, shaft, quarry.

V. dig, burrow, tunnel, undermine, sap, excavate, mine, quarry, shovel, spade, trowel, delve, dredge; ditch, trench; bore, drill, perforate, pit; dig out, gouge, hollow out, concave, scoop, scoop out, bail out (*water from a boat*); grub, grub up, root, rout.

disentomb, disinter, disinhume, exhume, resurrect.

See also HOLLOW, OPENING. *Antonyms*—See BURIAL.

digit, *n.* cipher, integer, whole number (NUMBER); finger, thumb, toe (APPENDAGE).

dignify, *v.* ennoble, elevate, exalt (FAME, NOBILITY, ELEVATION).

dignitary, *n.* grandee, magnifico (RANK); lion, VIP (*colloq.*), somebody (FAME); officer, functionary (OFFICIAL).

dignity, *n.* solemnity, grandeur, gravity (FAME); worthiness, merit, caliber (VALUE).

digress, *v.* ramble, wander, beat about the bush (WORDINESS); divagate, deviate, aberrate (WANDERING).

dike, *n.* trench, moat, ditch (HOLLOW, PASSAGE); pier, mole, sea wall (BREAKWATER).

dilapidated, *adj.* neglected, unimproved, unkempt (NEGLECT).

dilate, *v.* expand, distend, inflate (INCREASE, SWELLING); expatiate, enlarge, amplify (WORDINESS).

dilatory, *adj.* late, tardy, delaying (DELAY).

dilemma, *n.* quandary, impasse, mire (CONDITION).

dilettante, *n.* dabbler, dallier, amateur (PLAYFULNESS).

diligent, *adj.* hard-working, industrious, assiduous (WORK); unfailing, unflagging, unrelenting (CONTINUATION).

dilute, *adj.* thin, watery, light (WEAKNESS, THINNESS).

dim, *adj.* obscure, indistinct, faint (UNCLEARNESS, INVISIBILITY); cloudy, overcast, gray (DARKNESS); faded, lackluster, lusterless (DULLNESS); stupid, dim-witted, blunt (STUPIDITY).

dimensions, *n.* proportions, measurement, measure (SIZE).

diminish, *v.* reduce, lessen, cut (SMALLNESS, DECREASE).

diminutive, *adj.* little, bantam, Lilliputian (SMALLNESS).

diminutive, *n.* nickname, pet name, byname (NAME).

dimple, *n.* concavity, dent, depression (HOLLOW).

DIM-SIGHTEDNESS—N. [*imperfect vision*] dim-sightedness, amblyopia, myopia, astigmatism, cataract, color blindness, Daltonism, dichromatism; double vision, diplopia, aniseikonia.

farsightedness, hypermetropia, hyperopia, presbyopia.

squint, strabismus, cross-eye, cast in the eye, esophoria, walleye, exophoria.

V. be dim-sighted, see double; blink, squint, screw up the eyes.

dazzle, glare, blind, daze, blur, confuse, dim, bedazzle.

Adj. dim-sighted, weak-sighted, nearsighted, shortsighted, amblyopic, myopic, astigmatic, purblind, sand-blind; color-blind, snow-blind.

squint-eyed, strabismic, cross-eyed, esophoric, cockeyed, walleyed, exophoric.

See also BLINDNESS, DARKNESS, UNCLEARNESS. *Antonyms*—See CLARITY, UNDERSTANDING, VISION.

---

din, *n.* bedlam, uproar, hubbub (CONFUSION, LOUDNESS).

dine, *v.* eat, consume, banquet (FOOD).

dingy, *adj.* murky, dismal, dreary (BLACKNESS, DARKNESS).

dining room, *n.* dining hall, grill, lunchroom (FOOD).

din into, *v.* drum, hammer, harp on (REPETITION).

dip, *n.* pitch, descent, decline (SLOPE).

dip, *v.* sink, set, subside (DESCENT); duck, immerse, baptize (INSERTION).

diploma, *n.* sheepskin (*colloq.*), certificate (LEARNING).

diplomacy, *n.* tact, delicacy, discretion (ABILITY, WISDOM).

diplomat, *n.* ambassador, minister, envoy (DEPUTY); diplomatist, statesman (ABILITY).

dipper, *n.* ladle, scoop, spoon (CONTAINER).

dipsomania, *n.* alcoholism, alcoholomania, bibacity (DRUNKENNESS).

dire, *adj.* ugly, black, threatening (THREAT); extreme, immoderate, drastic (EXTREMENESS); formidable, fierce, redoubtable (FEAR).

direct, *adj.* straight, even, true (STRAIGHTNESS); bald, blunt, categorical (HONESTY, STRAIGHTNESS).

direct, *v.* aim, level, point (DIRECTION); instruct, charge, bid (COMMAND); pilot, shepherd (LEADERSHIP); manage, administer (CONTROL).

DIRECTION—N. direction, course, trend, tenor, tendency, inclination, current, stream, run, drift, tide; aim, set, tack, bent; bearing, aspect, orientation.

line, path, road, track, range, route, beeline, trajectory.

North, northland, northing, ultima Thule, Thule, Scandinavia, North Pole, Arctic.

South, southland, deep South, Auster, Antarctic, South Pole.

East, Eastern Hemisphere, Far East, Orient; Near East, Levant.

West, Western Hemisphere, Occident, Far West, Midwest.

Northerner, northlander, Northman, Scandinavian, Hyperborean, carpetbagger; Southerner, southlander; Easterner, Eastern, Levantine, Oriental; Westerner, Occidental, European, American.

left hand, port *or* larboard (*naut.*), southpaw (*slang*).

right hand, dexter, dextrality, starboard (*naut.*).

V. [*go or point in a direction*] tend, trend, tend toward, aim, drift, incline, verge, dip, bear, bend, course, run, stream, gravitate toward, orient, orientate; make for, steer for, go toward, hold a course toward, be bound for, make a beeline for.

aim, direct, level, beam, train, slant, point, pin-point, address; take aim, sight the target, draw a bead on.

Adj. northern, north, boreal, septentrional, northerly, northward, arctic, polar, hyperborean, northernmost.

southern, south, southerly, meridional, southward, austral, antarctic, southernmost.

eastern, east, easterly, eastward, orient, oriental, Levantine, auroral, easternmost.

western, west, westerly, westward, occidental, Hesperian, westernmost.

left, leftward, left-hand, larboard *or* port (*naut.*), sinister, left-handed, sinistral.

right, dextral, right-handed, dexter.

See also CONVERGENCE, NEARNESS, SIDE, TENDENCY. *Antonyms*—See TURNING.

---

directly, *adv.* immediately, at once, instantaneously (EARLINESS).

director, *n.* controller, leader, master (RULER); manager, administrator, overseer (CONTROL).

directory, *n.* index, gazetteer, atlas (LIST).

dirge, *n.* monody, threnody, requiem (SINGING, DEATH); lament, jeremiad, keen (SADNESS).

dirigible, *n.* airship, zeppelin, blimp (FLYING).

dirt, *n.* impurity, filth, feculence (UNCLEANNESS).

dirty, *adj.* unclean, impure, filthy (UNCLEANNESS); sordid, squalid, nasty (MEANNESS); obscene, immoral (OBSCENITY).

DISABLEMENT—*N.* disablement, disability, incapacity, paralysis, palsy; disqualification, invalidity, impairment.

powerlessness, impotence, incapability, inability, ineffectuality, futility, vanity.

V. disable, incapacitate, disarm; cripple, lame, maim, hamstring, hock, pinion, tie the hands of; paralyze, palsy, prostrate; disqualify, unfit, invalidate, impair; demoralize, weaken, enfeeble, shatter, exhaust, enervate, undermine, deaden, muzzle, strangle, throttle, silence, put *hors de combat* (*F.*), spike the guns of, unhinge, put out of gear.

unman, unnerve, devitalize, eviscerate, attenuate, effeminize, castrate, geld, alter, spay.

Adj. disabled, incapacitated, *hors de combat* (*F.*), disarmed; crippled, lame, halt.

powerless, helpless, impotent, incapable, unable, done for (*colloq.*).

ineffective, ineffectual, fruitless, futile, useless, vain.

See also FAILURE, INEFFECTIVENESS, USELESSNESS, WEAKNESS. *Antonyms*—See ABILITY, FORCE, POWER, RESULT, STRENGTH, USE.

---

disabuse, *v.* set straight, undeceive, disenchant, disillusion (RIGHT, INFORMATION).

disadvantage, *n.* inconvenience, inadvisability, inutility (INEXPEDIENCE).

disadvantageous, *adj.* unfavorable, adverse, contrary (OPPOSITION); unprofitable, objectionable, inopportune (INEXPEDIENCE).

disagreeable, *adj.* unpleasant, unpleasing, unlikable (UNPLEASANTNESS).

DISAGREEMENT—*N.* disagreement, discord, discordance, clash, disharmony, dissonance, incongruity, discongruity, inconsistency, discrepancy, disaccord, divergence, embroilment; conflict, dissension, dissentience, dissidence, strife, faction, factionalism, friction, incompatibility, rift, variance, war, warfare.

dissenter, dissident, factionist, incompatible, irreconcilable.

dispute, disputation, conflict, falling-out, contention, controversy, contest, contestation, disceptation, difference, misunderstanding, rift, rupture, clash, break, breach, split, variance, velitation, war, skirmish.

argument, altercation, affray, bout, polemic, quibble; haggle, higgle; debate.

quarrel, wrangle, bicker, brabble, brawl, embroilment, fracas, fray, words, melee, row, ruckus (*slang*), rumpus, set-to, spat, squabble, scrap (*slang*), tiff, tussle; feud, vendetta; fight, dogfight, cat-and-dog fight, battle, battle royal, Donnybrook Fair, imbroglio, hassle (*slang*), rhubarb (*slang*).

arguer, logomacher, logomachist, logomach; polemist, polemician; quibbler, stickler, haggler, higgler, palterer; debater.

quarreler, wrangler, bickerer, brawler, battler, rower, squabbler, caterwauler; feuder, feudist, vendettist.

troublemaker, mischief-maker, firebrand; shrew, virago, vixen, brimstone, harridan, termagant.

V. disagree, conflict, disaccord, discord, disharmonize, dissent, diverge, war, jar, differ, clash, vary.

dispute, contend, contest, controvert, controversialize, discept, differ, clash, war, skirmish; sue, bring action, engage in litigation.

argue, altercate, logomachize, quibble, spar, stickle; haggle, higgle, palter; debate.

quarrel, pick a quarrel, wrangle, bicker, brawl, battle, have words, row, spat, scrap (*slang*), squabble, fight, caterwaul; feud.

[*cause dissension*] embroil, entangle, disunite, cause factionalism, widen the breach, set (*or* pit) against, set at odds.

Adj. disagreeing, clashing, conflicting, conflictive, disaccordant, discordant, discrepant, disharmonious, unharmonious, inharmonious, dissenting, dissentient, dissident, dissonant, divergent, factious, factional, incompatible, uncongenial, irreconcilable, incongruous, inconsistent, warring; absonant, ajar, alien, jarring.

in disagreement, in strife, in conflict, at odds, at loggerheads, at variance, at issue, at cross-purposes, at sixes and sevens, embroiled, embattled, disunited, torn, up in arms, at daggers drawn.

argumentative, cantankerous, contentious, disputatious, disputative, eristic, polemical.

quarrelsome, bellicose, warlike, belligerent, bickering, combative, scrappy, dissentious, factious, pugnacious, rowdy, rowdyish, ugly; shrewish, vixenish.

[*causing dispute*] disruptive, divisive, factious.

disputable, arguable, contestable, controversial, controvertible, debatable, moot, questionable; actionable.

See also ATTACK, DEBATE, DIFFERENCE, FIGHTER, FIGHTING, HOSTILITY,

IRRELATION, LAWSUIT, OPPOSITION. Antonyms—See AGREEMENT, ASSENT, PEACE.

DISAPPEARANCE—N. disappearance, evanescence, dissolution, departure, dematerialization, evaporation, dissipation, eclipse.

V. disappear, vanish, dissolve, fade, evanesce, melt away, pass, go, depart, be gone, leave no trace, pass away, be lost to view (*or* sight), pass out of sight, perish, dematerialize, evaporate, dissipate.

Adj. evanescent, ephemeral, fugitive, impermanent.

See also DEPARTURE, IMPERMANENCE, NONEXISTENCE. Antonyms—See APPEARANCE, CONTINUATION.

DISAPPOINTMENT—N. disappointment, chagrin, disgruntlement, frustration, letdown, balk, blow, regret, disillusionment, disenchantment.

V. disappoint, balk, belie, bilk, frustrate, let down; chagrin, disgruntle, disillusion, disenchant.

Adj. disappointed, balked, bilked, chagrined, chapfallen, disgruntled, frustrated, let down, disillusioned, disenchanted.

See also DISSATISFACTION, FAILURE, INEFFECTIVENESS. Antonyms—See EXPECTATION, SATISFACTION, SUCCESS.

DISAPPROVAL—N. disapproval, displeasure, disapprobation, etc. (see Verbs); hiss, catcall, boo, brickbat, thumbs down; blackball, ostracism, boycott, black list.

criticism, stricture, vitriol, opprobrium, obloquy, commination; castigation, etc. (see Verbs).

censure, rebuke, odium, blame, etc. (see Verbs).

criticizer, critic, hypercritic, censor, Momus, chider, etc. (see Verbs).

V. disapprove, deprecate, discommend, discountenance, disfavor, dispraise, frown upon, hiss, boo, catcall, object to, take exception to, reflect on.

criticize, find fault with, chide, castigate, condemn, cry down, damn, denounce, denunciate, excoriate, exprobrate, flay, lash, fulminate against, thunder, cavil, carp, objurgate, pan (*slang*), rap (*slang*), reproach, reprobate, scathe, scorch, slam (*colloq.*), slash, slate, taunt with, tax with, twit with, twitter, upbraid for; lacerate, scarify.

censure, call to task, take to task, blame, animadvert on, criminate, decry, rebuke, reprehend, reprimand, reprove, scold, vituperate.

Adj. **disapproving,** disapprobatory, deprecatory, frowning, hissing.

critical, faultfinding, captious, exceptive, censorious, querulous, cynical, pharisaic; comminatory, opprobrious, vitriolic; overcritical, hypercritical, ultracritical; chiding, castigating, condemnatory, damnatory, denunciatory, flaying, lashing, slashing, scathing, scorching, fulminating, fulminant, objurgatory, reproachful, reprobative, taunting, upbraiding; scarifying, lacerative.

censuring, blaming, blameful, criminative, criminatory, rebuking, reprehensive, reproving, scolding, vituperative.

censurable, culpable, condemnable, criticizable, damnable, discommendable, reprehensible, reproachable, reprovable; objectionable, exceptionable; odious, opprobrious.

See also ACCUSATION, DETRACTION, DISGUST, DISREPUTE, HATRED, SCOLDING. *Antonyms*—See APPROVAL, ATTRACTION, FLATTERY, PRAISE, WORSHIP.

---

disarrange, *v.* disorder, disarray, derange (UNTIDINESS, CONFUSION).

disaster, *n.* calamity, cataclysm, catastrophe (MISFORTUNE).

disband, *v.* disperse, scatter, dispel (DISMISSAL).

disbelief, *n.* incredulity, nihilism, agnosticism (UNBELIEVINGNESS).

disbeliever, *n.* scoffer, cynic, skeptic (UNBELIEVINGNESS).

disburden, *v.* disencumber, rid, discharge (FREEDOM).

disburse, *v.* pay, defray, acquit, (PAYMENT); spend, expend, outlay (EXPENDITURE).

disc, *n.* plate, discus, spangle (FLATNESS); phonograph record, platter, release (RECORD).

discard, *v.* eliminate, scrap, reject (ELIMINATION).

discarded, *adj.* exploded, refuted, discredited (MISTAKE).

discern, *v.* distinguish, note, discover (VISION); discriminate, penetrate, see through (INTELLIGENCE).

discernible, *adj.* perceivable, discoverable, observable (VISIBILITY).

discerning, *adj.* perceptive, penetrating, acute (UNDERSTANDING, SHARPNESS); bright, brilliant, clever (INTELLIGENCE).

discernment, *n.* percipience, perception, perspicacity, acumen (UNDERSTANDING, INTELLIGENCE); discrimination, judgment, refinement (TASTE).

discharge, *v.* dismiss, bounce (*colloq.*), fire (DISMISSAL); release, free, liberate (FREEDOM, ACQUITTAL); disburden, rid, unload (FREEDOM); exempt, excuse, relieve (FREEDOM); let off, fire off, shoot (PROPULSION); ejaculate (*physiol.*), vomit, spew (THROW, EXCRETION); erupt, break out (EGRESS); meet, execute, perform (OBSERVANCE); liquidate, settle, square (PAYMENT).

disciple, *n.* learner, student, pupil (LEARNING); attendant, adherent, proselyte (FOLLOWER).

discipline, *n.* training, cultivation, domestication (TEACHING); martinetism, authoritarianism (OBEDIENCE); self-control, self-discipline, Spartanism (CONTROL); rules, rules and regulations, code (RULE).

discipline, *v.* prepare, ground, qualify (TEACHING); punish, penalize, correct (PUNISHMENT); train, tame (OBEDIENCE).

disclaim, *v.* repudiate, disown, renounce (DENIAL, RELINQUISHMENT).

DISCLOSURE—*N.* disclosure, revelation, leak (*colloq.*), exposure, exposal, exposé.

blabber, blabbermouth, blab, blurter.

tattletale, taleteller, tattler, telltale, talebearer, squealer (*colloq.*), informer, snitcher (*slang*), squeaker (*slang*), stool pigeon (*slang*).

V. **disclose,** discover, show, reveal, bare, lay bare, expose, lay open, betray, open to view; uncloak, uncover, uncurtain, unshroud, unthatch, unfold, unfurl, unmask, unveil, bring to light, open up.

tell, air, ventilate, voice, noise it around, advertise, announce, broadcast, blazon, blaze, divulge, impart, reveal; unburden oneself, unbosom oneself, disembosom oneself; betray, report, expose, inform on; blab, babble, tattle, squeal (*colloq.*), peach (*slang*); blurt out, let slip, let fall, tip one's hand; publish, vend, publicize, make known.

be disclosed, come to light, become known, escape the lips, ooze out, leak out, come to one's ears.

See also DISCOVERY, DISPLAY, INFORMATION, RUMOR, PUBLICATION. *Antonyms*—See CONCEALMENT.

---

discomfort, *n.* distress, dysphoria (*med.*), malaise (PAIN); confusion, discomfiture, discomposure (EMBARRASSMENT).

disconcert, *v.* discountenance, embarrass, nonplus (CONFUSION).

disconnect, *v.* disengage, dissever, separate (DISCONTINUITY, DISJUNCTION).

disconnected, *adj.* separate, unconnected (IRRELATION); discontinuous, broken, interrupted (DISCONTINUITY); disjointed, incoherent, irrational (UNREASONABLENESS).

disconsolate, *adj.* inconsolable, unconsolable, distressed (SADNESS).

discontented, *adj.* displeased, disgruntled, disaffected (DISSATISFACTION).

DISCONTINUITY—*N.* **discontinuity,** disconnection, interruption, break, fracture, flaw, fault, crack, cut, gap, opening; broken thread, cessation, intermission, disunion, discontinuance, discontinuation, disruption, disjunction, alternation.

V. **discontinue,** pause, interrupt, break, part, break off, stop, drop, cease, suspend, intervene, interpose, disconnect, dissever, disjoin, separate, disunite.

alternate, change, take turns, interchange, intermit, vary.

Adj. **discontinuous,** disconnected, broken, gaping, interrupted, fitful, irregular, spasmodic, desultory; intermittent, alternate, recurrent, periodic.

Adv., *phrases.* **at intervals,** by snatches, by jerks, by fits and starts.

See also CESSATION, DISJUNCTION, INSERTION, INTERJACENCE, INTERVAL, IRREGULARITY, OPENING. *Antonyms—* See CONTINUATION.

---

discord, *n.* clash, disharmony (DISAGREEMENT); cacophony, noise, jangle (HARSH SOUND).

discount, *n.* rebate, remission, allowance (DEDUCTION).

discount, *v.* undersell, sell at discount, hold a sale (SALE); disbelieve, discredit, reject (UNBELIEVINGNESS).

discourage, *v.* depress, dishearten, dismay (DEJECTION, HOPELESSNESS); disincline, indispose, shake (DISSUASION).

discourse, *n.* disquisition, monologue, descant (TALK).

DISCOURTESY—*N.* **discourtesy,** unchivalry, bad (*or* poor) manners, indelicacy, ill breeding, illiberality, incivility, inurbanity, rusticity, unrefinement, disrespect, contumely.

boldness, audacity, effrontery, cheek, brass (*colloq.*), nerve (*colloq.*), assumption, presumption, procacity.

defiance, insolence, impudence, impertinence, immodesty, flippancy.

[*discourteous person*] **boor,** bounder (*colloq.*), cad, churl, clown.

insolent, malapert, brazenface, flip (*colloq.*), squirt (*colloq.*); chit, hussy (*both fem.*).

V. **be so bold,** dare, presume; brazen out, brazen through, face, have the nerve to (*colloq.*), defy, sass (*slang*).

Adj. **discourteous,** impolite, unpolite, unmannerly, unmannered, ill-mannered, unrefined, bad-mannered, boorish, cavalier, churlish, ill-behaved, ill-bred, illiberal, inurbane, mannerless, offhand, rude, rustic, unbred, uncivil, uncivilized, uncomplaisant, uncourteous, uncouth, ungenteel, ungentlemanly, ungentlemanlike, ungracious, unhandsome, unladylike, disrespectful, contumelious, inaffable; indelicate, uncalled for.

unchivalrous, unchivalric, ungallant, caddish, uncourtly.

bold, forward, audacious, bantam, assuming, assumptive, presumptuous, presuming, cheeky (*colloq.*), brassy (*colloq.*), nervy (*colloq.*), brash, brashy, brazenfaced, brazen, shameless, immodest, barefaced; cool, assured, defiant, insolent, impudent, procacious, impertinent, malapert, pert, saucy, snippy (*colloq.*), fresh, flip (*colloq.*), flippant, sassy (*slang*).

abrupt, unceremonious, blunt, crude, brief, brusque, churlish, crusty, curt, gruff, offhand, outspoken, short, short-spoken, surly.

See also BARBARIANISM, DEFIANCE, DISRESPECT, INSULT, OFFENSE, RIDICULE, VULGARITY. *Antonyms—*See COURTESY, RESPECT, SUAVITY.

DISCOVERY—*N.* **discovery,** location, strike, encounter; detection, discernment, perception.

find, treasure-trove, treasure, chance discovery, accident.

detector, spotter, tracer, tracker, ferret, scout; detective, sleuth, private investigator, private eye (*slang*), snooper (*slang*); radar, sonar.

V. **find,** discover, locate, pinpoint, surprise, turn up, upturn, unearth, dig up, uncover, sight, strike, retrieve, scavenge.

come upon, encounter, chance

upon, alight upon, light upon, stumble upon (or across), meet, overtake.

detect, scent, sniff, snuff, descry, spot, trace, track, ferret out, discern, perceive.

find out, ascertain, determine, divine, learn, tell, get to the bottom of, pinpoint, unravel, fathom, plumb; verify, authenticate, certify; deduce, analyze, diagnose, diagnosticate.

See also DISCLOSURE, LOCATION, VISION. Antonyms—See CONCEALMENT, SEARCH.

---

discredit, v. disgrace, dishonor, reflect on (DISREPUTE); disbelieve, reject, discount; explode, compromise (UNBELIEVINGNESS).

discredited, adj. exploded, refuted, rejected (MISTAKE).

discreet, adj. cautious, chary, circumspect (CARE); prudent, judicious, politic (WISDOM).

discrepancy, n. divergence, variance (DIFFERENCE).

discretion, n. prudence, expedience, politics (WISDOM); caution, chariness (CARE).

discriminate, v. differentiate, distinguish, sift (DIFFERENTIATION); be discerning, judge (TASTE); discern, penetrate, see through (INTELLIGENCE); favor, incline, show prejudice (PREJUDICE).

discrimination, n. discernment, judgment, refinement (TASTE); discretion, preference, decision (CHOICE); favoritism, intolerance, bigotry (UNFAIRNESS, PREJUDICE).

discuss, v. talk over, deliberate, argue (TALK).

disdain, n. ridicule, scorn (CONTEMPT).

disdain, v. reject, spurn, scorn (DENIAL); slight, ignore, disregard (WORTHLESSNESS).

DISEASE—N. disease, epidemic, pest, endemic, idiopathy, infection, contagion, pestilence, plague, bubonic plague, Black Death, autoinfection, pathology, pathosis, morbidity, murrain, complication.

illness, sickness, ailment, malady, affliction, complaint, affection, cachexia, disorder, upset; allergy.

ill-health, unhealthiness, sickliness, delicate health, poor health, indisposition, unsoundness, unwholesomeness, invalidism, infirmity, malaise.

science of disease: pathology, therapeutics, etiology, nosology, symptomatology, semeiology, diagnostics, diagnosis.

invalid, shut-in, valetudinarian, patient, outpatient.

[liability to disease] susceptibility, tendency, predisposition, diathesis.

[cause of disease] germ, microbe, bug, virus, bacterium, pathogen, vector, contagium, carrier.

V. be ill, ail, sicken, suffer from, be affected (or afflicted) with, waste away, pine away; catch, get, contract.

[cause illness or disease] sicken, upset, affect, afflict, invalid, indispose, infect, blight (bot.); shock, traumatize.

Adj. diseased, pathological, morbid, infected, pestiferous; tainted, contaminated, septic.

ill, sick, sickly, poorly, sickish, weakly, delicate, ailing, afflicted, complaining of, affected, cachectic or cachexic, disordered, upset, unwell, not well, peaked, valetudinary, smitten, stricken; in poor (bad, or delicate) health, indisposed, out of sorts, invalid, confined, bedridden, bedfast, shut in, in the hospital, on the sick list, on the critical list, critical; unhealthy, unsound, unwholesome.

[looking ill] sickly, wan, peaked, bilious.

catching, infectious, communicable, contagious, epidemic, endemic, pandemic; zymotic, epizootic.

unhealthful, unhealthy, unwholesome, unsanitary, unhygienic, insanitary, insalubrious, nocuous, noxious; pathogenic, morbific, pestiferous, pestilential, peccant, zymotic.

See also MEDICAL SCIENCE, WEAKNESS. Antonyms—See CURE, HEALTH, STRENGTH.

---

disembark, v. debark, detrain, deplane (DEPARTURE, ARRIVAL).

disembodied, adj. bodiless, immaterial, discarnate (SPIRITUALITY).

disengage, v. detach, disjoin, disunite (DISJUNCTION, LOOSENESS); loose, loosen, extricate (FREEDOM).

disentangle, v. unwind, untwist, disentwine (STRAIGHTNESS); unravel, open, expand (UNFOLDMENT); unfasten, untie, undo (DISJUNCTION); simplify, disinvolve (SIMPLICITY).

disfavor, n. unpopularity, disesteem, disregard (HATRED).

disfigure, v. mar, deform, deface (DEFORMITY, BLEMISH).

disgorge, v. spew, vomit, belch (GIVING).

DISGRACE—N. disgrace, ignominy, infamy, obloquy, odium, opprobrium, reproach, scandal; attaint, attainture, dishonor, shame.

[*mark of disgrace*] **brand**, blot, scar, stigma, mark of Cain.

V. disgrace, bring disgrace upon, attaint, blot, defile, dishonor, shame; expose to disgrace, gibbet.

[*mark with disgrace*] **brand**, blot, scar, stigmatize.

Adj. disgraceful, dishonorable, shameful, ignominious, infamous, opprobrious, scandalous, ignoble, inglorious.

See also BLEMISH, DISAPPROVAL, DISREPUTE, SCOLDING. *Antonyms*—See ACCEPTANCE, APPROVAL, FAME, MAGNIFICENCE, MORALITY, PURIFICATION.

disgruntled, *adj.* discontented, disaffected, peevish (DISSATISFACTION, BAD TEMPER).

disguise, *v.* camouflage, mask, masquerade (CONCEALMENT); cloak, dissemble, dissimulate (PRETENSE); falsify, deacon, doctor (FALSENESS).

DISGUST—N. disgust, repulsion, revulsion, revolt, abomination, loathing; satiety, surfeit, satiation, sickness, nausea.

V. disgust, repel, revolt, nauseate, turn one's stomach, sicken, surfeit, satiate, cloy on; shock, scandalize.

[*feel disgust*] **loathe**, abominate, revolt at, sicken, nauseate.

Adj. disgusting, disgustful, repellent, repulsive, revolting, abominable, loathful, loathsome, vile, hideous, odious, foul, frightful, beastly, offensive, fulsome; shocking, scandalizing, scandalous; nauseating, nauseous, noisome, cloying, sickening, surfeiting, satiating; gruesome, macabre.

disgusted, revolted, repelled, nauseous, nauseated, sick, sickened, satiate, satiated, surfeited; shocked, scandalized; [*easily disgusted*] fastidious, queasy, squeamish.

shocking, frightful, ghastly, hideous, horrible, horrid, horrific, horrifying, monstrous, outrageous, scandalous.

See also HATRED, NAUSEA, UNPLEASANTNESS, UNSAVORINESS. *Antonyms*—See ATTRACTION, LIKING, LOVE.

dish, *n.* plate, platter, bowl (CONTAINER).

disharmony, *n.* discord, discordance, clash (DISAGREEMENT); dissonance, dissonancy (HARSH SOUND).

dishearten, *v.* depress, cast down (DEJECTION); disincline, discourage, indispose (DISSUASION).

disheveled, *adj.* uncombed, rumpled, tousled (UNTIDINESS, UNDRESS).

dishonest, *adj.* untruthful, lying, mendacious (FALSEHOOD); shady, crooked (DISHONESTY).

DISHONESTY—N. dishonesty, improbity, deceit, fraudulence, indirection, knavery, skulduggery, thievery, racket.

[*dishonest person*] **crook**, knave, scoundrel, snollygoster (*colloq.*), thief, racketeer; bezonian, blackguard, rapscallion, rascal, rapscallion, reprobate, rogue, scamp, scapegrace, varlet, villain.

Adj. dishonest, dishonorable, crooked, deceitful, devious, fraudulent, indirect, sinister, thievish, tortuous; conscienceless, unconscionable, unprincipled, unscrupulous; shady, questionable, fishy (*colloq.*).

knavish, scoundrelly, scoundrel, blackguard, blackguardly, rascal, rascally, roguish, villainous.

See also DECEPTION, FALSEHOOD, FALSENESS, ILLEGALITY, IMMORALITY, PRETENSE, SIN, THIEF, THIEVERY, WICKEDNESS. *Antonyms*—See HONESTY, INNOCENCE, MORALITY.

dishonor, *v.* attaint, blot, shame (DISGRACE); discredit, disconsider, reflect on (DISREPUTE).

dishonorable, *adj.* shameful, ignominious, infamous (DISGRACE); disreputable, discreditable, disgraceful (DISREPUTE); crooked, deceitful, fraudulent (DISHONESTY); low, miscreant, putrid (IMMORALITY).

disillusion, *v.* disabuse, open the eyes of, disenchant (INFORMATION, UNBELIEVINGNESS).

disincline, *v.* indispose, shake, discourage (DISSUASION).

disinclined, *adj.* uninclined, indisposed, averse (UNWILLINGNESS).

disinfect, *v.* clean, antisepticize, sterilize (CLEANNESS).

disinfectant, *n.* germicide, antiseptic, prophylactic (CURE).

disinherit, *v.* disherit, cut off (WILL).

disintegrate, *v.* crumble, molder, pulverize (BREAKAGE, POWDERINESS); dilapidate, dissolve, decline (DECAY); unmake, break down (DESTRUCTION).

disinter, *v.* disentomb, disinhume, exhume (DIGGING).

disinterested, *adj.* unconcerned, perfunctory, lackadaisical (INDIFFERENCE); impersonal, candid, detached (IMPARTIALITY).

disjointed, *adj.* disconnected, incoherent, irrational (UNREASONABLENESS).

DISJUNCTION—N. disjunction, disconnection, disunion, separation, partition, disengagement, dissociation, divorce; caesura, division, subdivision; break, breach, hernia, herniation; dissection, dispersion, disruption; detachment, segregation, isolation, insulation, insularity.

fissure, breach, rent, rift, crack, slit, split, cleft, cut, incision.

V. **disjoin,** disconnect, disengage, disunite, dissociate, divorce, part, detach, separate, divide, sunder, subdivide, sever, dissever, cut off, segregate, set apart, keep apart, insulate, isolate; cut adrift, loose, unfasten, disentangle, untie, unravel, undo; rupture, herniate.

disintegrate, dismember, dislocate, disrupt, disband, disperse, break up, crumble.

Adj. **disjoined,** discontinuous, disjunctive, discretive, discrete; detached, unconnected, disjoint, disjunct, isolated, insular; separate, apart, asunder, loose, free, adrift; unattached, unassociated, distinct; reft, cleft, divided, split.

Adv., phrases. **disjointly,** separately, one by one, severally, apart, asunder.

See also BREAKAGE, CUTTING, DISCONTINUITY, DISPERSION, FREEDOM, SECLUSION, TEARING. Antonyms—See COMBINATION, JUNCTION, UNITY.

dislike, *v.* disesteem, disfavor, disrelish (HATRED).

dislodge, *v.* remove, dislocate, oust (REMOVAL, PROPULSION).

DISLOYALTY—N. disloyalty, falsity, perfidy, recreancy, treachery, sedition, treason, disaffection, high treason, lese majesty, infidelity, defection, whoredom; betrayal, Iscariotism, Judas kiss.

traitor, treasonist, quisling, recreant, Judas, betrayer; seditionist, seditionary; renegade, turncoat, apostate; snake, viper, serpent.

V. **betray,** treason, treason against; play false, go back on, sell out to the enemy.

Adj. **disloyal,** faithless, false, perfidious, unfaithful, untrue, traitorous, treacherous, treasonable, treasonous, Punic, recreant, snaky; seditious, seditionary.

See also APOSTASY, DECEPTION, DISHONESTY. Antonyms—See HONESTY, LOYALTY.

dismal, *adj.* dreary, dingy, gloomy (DARKNESS); black, bleak, cheerless (GLOOM, DEJECTION).

dismay, *v.* discourage, dishearten, dispirit (HOPELESSNESS, DEJECTION); frighten, terrify, terrorize (FEAR).

DISMISSAL—N. dismissal, discharge, deposal, deposition, removal, suspension.

ejection, expulsion, ouster, dispossession, eviction; banishment, deportation, exile, expatriation, ostracism, Coventry, relegation, exorcism, dislodgment, displacement.

outcast, deportee, displaced person, D.P., expatriate, exile; pariah, leper.

V. **dismiss,** discharge, give one notice, fire, bounce (*colloq.*), cashier, remove, drum out, depose, depone, dethrone, unseat, disseat; defrock, disfrock, unfrock, unmiter; suspend, shelve.

drive out, force out, smoke out, eject, bounce (*colloq.*), expel, oust, chase, dispossess, put out, turn out, evict; banish, cast out, deport, exile, expatriate, ostracize, relegate, exorcise; dislodge, flush (*birds*), displace.

drive away, chase, disperse, scatter, rout, disband, dispel, rebuff, repulse, repel, send away, laugh away.

Adj. **outcast,** cast out, deported, displaced, exiled, expatriate, homeless.

See also DISPERSION, ELIMINATION, PROPULSION, REMOVAL. Antonyms—See ACCEPTANCE, HOLD, INSERTION, RECEIVING.

dismount, *v.* descend, deplane, disembark (DEPARTURE, ARRIVAL).

DISOBEDIENCE—N. disobedience, insubordination, perversity, noncompliance, nonobservance, recalcitrance; infraction, infringement, violation.

rebelliousness, insurgency, recalcitration, unrest, contumacy, defiance, civil disobedience, sedition; nonconformity, nonconformance, Titanism, revolutionism.

rebellion, insurrection, revolt, revolution, mutiny, outbreak, commotion, *Putsch* (*Ger.*), uprising, rising, riot.

rebel, insurgent, insurrectionist, revolter, revolutionist, revolutionary, mutineer, putschist, upriser, rioter, malcontent, recalcitrant, seditionist; maverick (*politics*), nonconformist.

V. disobey, violate, infringe, transgress, resist; ignore, disregard.

rebel, recalcitrate, insurrect, mutiny, revolutionize, revolution, revolt, arise, riot, rise, rise in arms, defy, set at defiance; not conform.

Adj. disobedient, insubordinate, naughty, perverse, contrary, wayward, fractious, disorderly, uncompliant, noncompliant, froward, resistive.

rebellious, insubordinate, insurgent, insurrectionary, mutinous, malcontent, recalcitrant, restive, revolutionary, contumacious, defiant, seditionary, seditious; nonconformist.

See also DEFIANCE, NONOBSERVANCE, OPPOSITION, ROUGHNESS. *Antonyms*—See MILDNESS, OBEDIENCE, OBSERVANCE, SUBMISSION.

disorder, *n.* riot, tumult, turbulence (UNRULINESS, COMMOTION); lawlessness, anarchy, mob rule (ILLEGALITY); disarrangement, disarray, disorganization (CONFUSION, UNTIDINESS); ailment, affection, upset (DISEASE).

disorderly, *adj.* unruly, unmanageable, uncontrollable (UNRULINESS, COMMOTION, ROUGHNESS); disobedient, wayward, fractious (DISOBEDIENCE); unsystematic, unmethodical, disorganized (UNTIDINESS).

disorganized, *adj.* confused, unsystematic, unmethodical (UNTIDINESS).

disown, *v.* repudiate, disavow, renounce (DENIAL, RELINQUISHMENT).

disparaging, *adj.* derogatory, depreciatory, pejorative (DETRACTION).

disparity, *n.* dissimilarity, dissimilitude, dissemblance (DIFFERENCE).

dispassionate, *adj.* imperturbable, passionless, cold-blooded (INEXCITABILITY, CALMNESS); fairminded, neutral (IMPARTIALITY).

dispatch, *n.* quickness, alacrity, expeditiousness (SPEED); news, bulletin, item (PUBLICATION).

dispatch, *v.* send, issue, transmit (SENDING).

dispel, *v.* disperse, scatter, rout (DISMISSAL).

DISPERSION—*N.* dispersion, dispersal, Diaspora (*of the Jews*); propagation, diffusion, dissipation, dissemination, spread, broadcast, interspersion, radiation.

V. disperse, scatter, sow, disseminate, spatter, spray, propagate, diffuse, radiate, circulate, broadcast, spread, shed, bestrew, besprinkle, intersperse, disband, dispel, dissipate, cast forth, dislodge, eject, banish, rout; strew, cast, sprinkle.

Adj. dispersed, disseminated, sown, strewn, scattered; diffuse, diffusive, broadcast, widespread, epidemic.

See also APPORTIONMENT, DISJUNCTION, DISMISSAL, GIVING, SPREAD, THROW. *Antonyms*—See ASSEMBLAGE, COMBINATION, MIXTURE, SUMMONS, TRACTION.

displace, *v.* replace, supersede, supplant (SUBSTITUTION); disestablish, displant, uproot (REMOVAL); eject, expel, expulse (PROPULSION); shift, relegate, change (TRANSFER).

DISPLAY—*N.* display, show, spread, presentation, emblazonry, blaze, blazonry, exhibit, array, arrayal; exhibition, fair, exposition, pageant, circus, parade, pageantry, panorama, spectacle; bravura, riot, fireworks, pyrotechnics, fanfare; preview.

V. display, show, spread, spread out, unfurl, unfold, unroll, unveil, bare, lay bare, blaze, blazon, emblazon, emblaze, exhibit, expose, feature, open to view, present.

See also CLARITY, DISCLOSURE, INDICATION, ORNAMENT, OSTENTATION, PUBLICATION, VISIBILITY. *Antonyms*—See CONCEALMENT.

displease, *v.* discontent, disgruntle, disappoint (DISSATISFACTION); repel, revolt, antagonize (UNPLEASANTNESS, HATRED); offend, gall, fret (ANNOYANCE).

displeasure, *n.* umbrage, resentment, pique (OFFENSE); incensement, wrath (ANGER); petulance, fret (ANNOYANCE); distaste, repulsion, repugnance (UNPLEASANTNESS); disgruntlement, discontentment (DISSATISFACTION).

dispose, *v.* settle, locate, stand (PLACE); arrange, order (ARRANGEMENT); predispose, sway, govern (INFLUENCE); incline (WILLINGNESS).

disposed, *adj.* minded, inclined, prone (WILLINGNESS); partial, biased, predisposed (TENDENCY).

dispose of, *v.* eliminate, get rid of, dump (ELIMINATION).

disposition, *n.* temperament, make-up, personality (CHARACTER); leaning, proclivity, bias (TENDENCY).

dispossess, *v.* expel, oust, evict (DISMISSAL); take from, deprive, tear from (TAKING).

DISPROOF—N. **disproof**, disproval, confutation, rebuttal, refutation, invalidation; retort, answer, rebutter, clincher (*colloq.*); counterevidence, contradiction, negation.

V. **disprove**, belie, confute, explode, falsify, give the lie to, rebut, refute, negate, negative, demolish, overthrow, invalidate, contradict, oppose, destroy; conflict with.

Adj. **disprovable**, confutable, refutable, defeasible.

contradictory, conflicting, opposing, refutatory, countervailing, contrary, negatory.

unproved, unattested, unauthenticated, unsupported, supposititious, trumped up.

See also ANSWER, DENIAL, OPPOSITION. *Antonyms*—See PROOF.

disputable, *adj.* arguable, contestable, questionable (UNCERTAINTY, DISAGREEMENT, INQUIRY).

dispute, *v.* contend, contest, argue (DISAGREEMENT); contradict, gainsay, deny (DENIAL, OPPOSITION).

disqualify, *v.* unfit, invalidate, impair (DISABLEMENT); disentitle, disfranchise (IMPROPERNESS).

disquieting, *adj.* disturbing, distressing, troublesome (NERVOUSNESS).

disregard, *n.* oversight, omission, (NEGLECT); disdain, scorn (CONTEMPT); unpopularity, disesteem, disfavor (HATRED).

disregard, *v.* miss, overlook, pass by (INATTENTION, NEGLECT); disdain, scorn (WORTHLESSNESS); slight, vilipend (DETRACTION).

DISREPUTE—N. **disrepute**, discredit, dishonor, disesteem, ill repute, ill fame, ill favor, ingloriousness, odium, obloquy, infamy, notoriety, reproach, opprobrium, ignominy, disgrace, shame, scandal.

[*stain on the reputation*] **stigma**, blemish, blot, blur, brand, cloud, maculation, scar, slur, smear, smirch, smutch, spot, stain, taint, attaint, tarnish.

V. **be disreputable**, have a bad name, disgrace oneself, lose caste, fall from one's high estate, cut a sorry figure.

discredit, disconsider, disgrace, dishonor, reflect on, reproach, shame, put to shame; degrade, debase.

stigmatize, befoul, besmear, besmirch, bespatter, blacken, blemish, blot, blur, brand, cloud, darken, defile, denigrate, foul, maculate scar, smear, smirch, smut, smutch, soil, spatter, spot, stain, sully, taint, tarnish, attaint, drag through the mud, make one's name mud (*colloq.*).

Adj. **disreputable**, discreditable, disgraceful, dishonorable, disrespectable, doubtful, infamous, notorious, questionable, raffish, shady, scandalous, shameful.

See also BLEMISH, DETRACTION, DISAPPROVAL, DISGRACE, DISHONESTY, DISRESPECT, UNCLEANNESS. *Antonyms*—See FAME, MAGNIFICENCE, MORALITY.

DISRESPECT—N. **disrespect**, disregard, disesteem; irreverence, flippancy, impertinence, impudence, insolence; sacrilege, impiety.

blasphemy, profanity, swearing, cursing; curse, oath, swear word.

V. **disrespect**, disesteem, disregard, slight, insult, outrage.

profane, desecrate, violate, commit sacrilege upon; blaspheme, curse, swear.

Adj. **disrespectful**, irreverent, aweless, insolent, impudent, impertinent, sassy (*slang*), rude, flip (*colloq.*), flippant, fresh (*colloq.*), snippy (*colloq.*), saucy, insulting; unfilial.

blasphemous, profane, profanatory, sacrilegious, impious.

disrespectable, disreputable, unrespected, in low esteem, of unenviable reputation, of ill repute, notorious, infamous.

See also CONTEMPT, DISCOURTESY, DISREPUTE, INSULT, OFFENSE, RIDICULE. *Antonyms*—See APPROVAL, COURTESY, RESPECT, WORSHIP.

disrobe, *v.* undress, strip, unbusk (UNDRESS).

DISSATISFACTION—N. **dissatisfaction**, discontentment, ennui, discontent, disappointment, displeasure, disgruntlement, malcontentment, disaffection, dysphoria (*med.*), unrest, the grumbles, fret, complaint, lamentation.

envy, jealousy, heartburn.

malcontent, complainer, grumbler, sniveler, discontent, fretter, envier, faultfinder.

[*fomenter of dissatisfaction*] agitator, political agitator, demagogue, rabble-rouser; instigator, *agent provocateur* (*F.*).

agitation, demagoguery, demagogy, demagogism, rabble-rousing.

unsatisfaction, uncontent, unfulfillment, frustration.

V. be dissatisfied, repine, regret, make a wry face, complain, fret, grumble, mutter, mumble, snivel, whine, croak, lament; envy, grudge, begrudge; agitate.

dissatisfy, disaffect, discontent, disgruntle, displease, disappoint, frustrate.

Adj. dissatisfied, discontent, discontented, disappointed, displeased, disgruntled, malcontent, disaffected, dysphoric (*med.*), ennuied, *ennuyé* (*F.*).

envious, jealous, jaundiced, grudging, begrudging.

grumbling, grumbly, grumpy, complaining, plaintive, querulous, fretful, fretted, faultfinding, critical, sniveling, muttering, mumbling; sullen, sulky, glum.

unsatisfied, unappeased, unassuaged, uncomplacent, uncontented, uncontent, unfulfilled, ungratified, unpleased, unsated, unslaked, frustrated.

unsatisfying, unassuaging, unfulfilling, ungratifying, unpleasing, lame, thin, unsatisfactory, unsuitable, frustrating; dissatisfying, displeasing, dissatisfactory.

insatiable, insatiate, unappeasable, unfulfillable, uncontentable, ungratifiable, unsatisfiable.

See also COMPLAINT, REGRET, SADNESS, WEEPING. *Antonyms*—See BOASTING, HAPPINESS, LAUGHTER, PRIDE, SATISFACTION, SMILE.

dissect, *v.* cut, slice, section (CUTTING); prosect, exscind, exsect (SURGERY).

dissemble, *v.* disguise, dissimulate, mask (PRETENSE).

disseminate, *v.* scatter, sow, broadcast (DISPERSION).

dissension, *n.* conflict, strife, faction (DISAGREEMENT).

dissertation, *n.* essay, thesis, composition (TREATISE).

disservice, *n.* hurt, injury, detriment (HARM).

dissimilar, *adj.* unlike, unrelated, mismatched (DIFFERENCE).

dissimulate, *v.* fake, feign, counterfeit (PRETENSE).

dissipate, *v.* fritter away, lavish, squander (WASTEFULNESS); debauch, racket, riot (IMMORALITY, PLEASURE).

dissipated, *adj.* dissolute, debauched, profligate (PLEASURE, INTEMPERANCE).

dissolute, *adj.* dissipated, profligate, depraved, (IMMORALITY, SEX, PLEASURE, INTEMPERANCE); unconstrained, libertine, licentious (FREEDOM).

dissolve, *v.* melt, render, thaw (LIQUID); disintegrate, dilapidate, decline (DECAY); break down, unmake (DESTRUCTION); vanish, fade, evanesce (DISAPPEARANCE).

DISSUASION—*N.* dissuasion, expostulation, remonstrance, deprecation, discouragement, damper, wet blanket.

V. dissuade, remonstrate, expostulate, warn; advise against, deprecate, exhort against, caution against, urge not to.

disincline, indispose, shake; discourage, dishearten, disenchant; deter, hold back, restrain, repel, turn aside, divert from, damp, cool, chill.

Adj. dissuasive, expostulatory, remonstrative, remonstrant; warning, admonitory, monitory, cautionary.

unpersuasive, unconvincing, inconclusive; flimsy, lame, thin, weak.

See also CONTROL, OPPOSITION, RESTRAINT, WARNING. *Antonyms*—See MOTIVATION, PERSUASION, TENDENCY.

DISTANCE—*N.* distance, outskirts, outpost, purlieu, suburbs, hinterland, provinces; extent, length, compass, reach, range, span, stretch; circumference, circuit, perimeter, radius, diameter; light-year; equidistance.

[*instruments*] telemeter, tachymeter, odometer, odograph, pedometer, taximeter, cyclometer, micrometer.

V. be distant, etc. (see *Adjectives*); extend to, stretch to, reach to, lead to, go to, spread to, stretch away to; range, outreach, span.

Adj. distant, far, faraway, faroff, remote, aloof, removed, antipodal, outlying, out-of-the-way, distal (*med.*); farther, more distant, ulterior.

farthest, farthermost, furthermost, furthest, ultimate, endmost, remotest.

Adv., phrases. far off, far away, afar, afar off, away, aloof, beyond range, out of range, out of hearing; wide of, clear of; abroad, yonder, farther, further, beyond; far and wide, from pole to pole, to the ends of the earth.

apart, asunder, separately, wide apart, at arm's length.

See also HOSTILITY, INSENSITIVITY, PROGRESS, ROUNDNESS, SPACE. *Antonyms*—See NEARNESS.

distasteful, *adj.* dislikable, displeasing, unlikable (HATRED); objectionable, unsavory, unappetizing (UNPLEASANTNESS, UNSAVORINESS).

distend, *v.* swell, expand, dilate (SWELLING, INCREASE).

distill, *v.* squeeze out, express, expel (EXTRACTION); clarify, rarefy, refine (PURIFICATION); brew, ferment (ALCOHOLIC LIQUOR).

distillery, *n.* brewery, winery (ALCOHOLIC LIQUOR).

distinct, *adj.* clear, transparent, definite (CLARITY, VISIBILITY); well-defined, sharp-cut, clear-cut (SHARPNESS); audible, clear, plain (LISTENING); distinctive, special, particular (DIFFERENCE); unattached, unassociated (DISJUNCTION).

distinction, *n.* differential, feature, mark, marking, peculiarity, earmark (DIFFERENCE); honor, credit (FAME).

distinctive, *adj.* distinct, special, particular (DIFFERENCE); characteristic, distinguishing, typical (CHARACTER).

distinguish, *v.* note, discern, discover (VISION); discriminate, sift, separate (DIFFERENTIATION, TASTE); differentiate, characterize, demarcate (DIFFERENCE).

distinguished, *adj.* distingué (*F.*), notable, great (IMPORTANCE, FAME).

distort, *v.* deform, gnarl, misshape (DEFORMITY, WINDING); garble, mangle, pervert (BLEMISH); color, slant, angle (MISREPRESENTATION, PREJUDICE).

distract, *v.* abstract (INATTENTION); dement, derange, frenzy (INSANITY).

distress, *v.* afflict, ail, trouble (PAIN, NERVOUSNESS); sadden, desolate (SADNESS).

distribute, *v.* give out, deal out, hand out (GIVING).

district, *n.* department, commune, parish (REGION).

distrust, *v.* doubt, mistrust, disbelieve (UNBELIEVINGNESS).

disturb, *v.* annoy, bother, trouble (ANNOYANCE); disquiet, vex, distress (NERVOUSNESS); stir, churn (AGITATION); derange, discompose, unsettle (UNTIDINESS).

disturbance, *n.* convulsion, upheaval, shock (AGITATION, COMMOTION).

disturbed, *adj.* upset, uneasy, apprehensive (NERVOUSNESS).

DISUSE—*N.* disuse, nonuse, nonemployment, neglect, discontinuance, want of practice; desuetude, obsolescence, obsoletism, archaism.

V. disuse, lay by, lay up, shelve, set aside, lay aside, leave off, have done with; supersede, discard, throw aside, give up, relinquish, abandon; dismantle, idle.

not use, do without, dispense with, let alone, be weaned from; spare, waive, neglect; keep back, reserve.

put out of use, date, antiquate, obsolete, archaize, make unfashionable.

fall into disuse, lapse, obsolesce, become obsolete.

Adj. unused, idle, fallow, vacant, virgin, virginal; unemployed, unapplied, unexercised.

[*no longer in use*] obsolete, out-of-date, passé, old-fashioned, dated, antiquated, obsolescent; archaic, archaistic.

See also ELIMINATION, NEGLECT, OLDNESS, USELESSNESS. *Antonyms*—See USE.

ditch, *n.* moat, dike, gutter (CHANNEL); chase, gully, excavation (OPENING, HOLLOW, PASSAGE).

dither, *n.* twitter, tizzy, whirl (EXCITEMENT).

ditto, *adv.* again, repeatedly, once more (REPETITION).

ditty, *n.* song, vocal (*colloq.*), number (SINGING).

divan, *n.* couch, davenport, day bed (SEAT).

dive, *n.* high-dive, plunge, submergence (DIVING).

diverge, *v.* vary, contrast, deviate (DIFFERENCE); bend, divaricate, fork (TURNING, ANGULARITY).

divergent, *adj.* dissonant, factious, factional (DISAGREEMENT).

diverse, *adj.* different, disparate, incomparable (DIFFERENCE).

diversified, *adj.* variegated, multicolor, many-colored (VARIEGATION).

diversify, *v.* vary, assort, variegate (DIFFERENCE).

diversion, *n.* entertainment, play, sport (AMUSEMENT).

divide, *v.* part, separate, sunder (DISJUNCTION); articulate, factor, partition (PART); share, apportion, distribute (APPORTIONMENT, PART).

divine, *adj.* Olympian, celestial, godly (HEAVEN, GOD).

divine, *n.* clergyman, ecclesiastic, priest (CLERGY).

divine, *v.* forebode, forecast, predict (PREDICTION); find out, ascertain, determine (DISCOVERY); guess, conjecture, suspect (SUPPOSITION).

DIVING—*N.* dive, high-dive, plunge, submergence, submersion, duck; swoop, descent, drop, nose-dive (*aero.*); bathysphere, bentho-scope.

diver, skin-diver, frogman, deep-sea diver, pearl diver, pearler; diving board, high-diving board.

V. dive, plunge, pitch (*of ships*), submerge, submerse, sound, duck; nose-dive (*aero.*), take a header (*colloq.*), swoop, descend, plump, drop, ground, alight, light; sink, founder.

See also DECREASE, DESCENT, LOW-NESS. *Antonyms*—See ASCENT, HEIGHT, INCREASE.

divinity, *n.* godhood, godship; deity, celestial (GOD); theology, hierology (RELIGION).

division, *n.* portion, fraction; section, group (PART); subdivision, department (DISJUNCTION, CLASS).

DIVORCE—*N.* divorce, divorce *a vinculo matrimonii* (L.), decree of nullity; divorce *a mensa et thoro* (L.), legal separation, judicial separation, separate maintenance; annulment.

divorce decrees, decree nisi, interlocutory decree, Enoch Arden decree, final decree.

divorcee, *divorcé* (F., *masc.*), *divorcée* (F., *fem.*); *divorceuse* (F., *fem.*); corespondent.

See also CESSATION, DISJUNCTION, DISMISSAL, ELIMINATION, REMOVAL, UNMARRIED STATE. *Antonyms*—See BETROTHAL, MARRIAGE.

divulge, *v.* disclose, tell, announce (DISCLOSURE).

DIZZINESS—*N.* dizziness, vertigo, giddiness, lightheadedness, whirl, flightiness.

V. dizzy, giddy; reel, whirl, swim.

Adj. dizzy, giddy, lightheaded, swimming, reeling, whirling, vertiginous; harebrained, flighty; dizzying, heady.

See also CONFUSION, DRUNKEN-NESS, ROLL, ROTATION, TURNING, WINDING. *Antonyms*—See SOBRIETY, STABILITY.

dizzy, *adj.* lightheaded, flighty, giddy (DIZZINESS, FRIVOLITY); groggy, muzzy, hazy (CONFUSION).

do, *v.* carry out, engage in, discharge (ACTION); be adequate, avail, suffice (GOOD, SUFFICIENCY, PURPOSE); be of use, be useful, serve (USE).

do again, *v.* redo, reproduce, repeat (REPETITION).

do away with, *v.* eliminate, exterminate, wipe out (ELIMINATION); destroy, slaughter, finish (KILLING).

docile, *adj.* orderly, quiet, manageable (OBEDIENCE); meek, humble, weak-kneed (SUBMISSION).

dock, *n.* wharf, pier, quay (BREAKWATER).

doctor, *n.* medical doctor, medical man, M.D. (MEDICAL SCIENCE).

doctor, *v.* medicate, treat, medicament (CURE); falsify, deacon, disguise (FALSENESS).

doctrine, *n.* indoctrination, inculcation, propaganda (TEACHING); tenet, dogma, gospel (BELIEF, RULE).

document, *n.* paper, deed, instrument (WRITING).

doddering, *adj.* doddery, dotard, senile (WEAKNESS).

dodge, *v.* duck, sidestep, parry (SIDE, AVOIDANCE).

doe, *n.* hind, roe (ANIMAL).

doff, *v.* remove, get out of, slip out of (UNDRESS).

dog, *n.* canine, cur (ANIMAL).

dog, *v.* pursue, dog the footsteps of, track (FOLLOWING).

dogged, *adj.* stubborn, obstinate, determined (STUBBORNNESS, CONTINUATION).

doggerel, *n.* poesy, rhyme, verse (POETRY).

dogma, *n.* doctrine, credenda, gospel (RULE).

dogmatic, *adj.* assertive, positive, self-assertive (STATEMENT); opinionated, opinionative, opinioned (OPINION).

doldrums, *n.* the dismals (*colloq.*), the dumps (*colloq.*), the blues (DEJECTION); inertia, apathy, stupor (INACTION).

dole, *n.* mite, pittance, trifle (INSUFFICIENCY); relief, alms (CHARITY).

doleful, *adj.* mournful, dirgeful, funereal (SADNESS).

doll, *n.* puppet, Teddy bear (AMUSEMENT).

dollar, *n.* paper money, note, bill (MONEY).

doll up (*slang*), *v.* smarten, spruce up (*colloq.*), dress up (ORNAMENT).

domain, *n.* dominion, jurisdiction, province, orbit, realm, sphere (POWER, INFLUENCE).

dome, *n.* arch, arcade, cupola (SUPPORT, COVERING, BUILDING).

domestic, *adj.* internal, intramural, intestine (INTERIORITY); domesticated, tame, gentle (DOMESTICATION).

domestic, *n.* help, servant, maid (SERVICE).

DOMESTICATION—N. domestication, domesticity, taming, reclamation; breeding, raising, rearing.

menagerie, *Tiergarten* (*Ger.*), vivarium, zoological garden, zoo; bear pit; aviary; apiary, beehive, hive; aquarium, fishery, fish hatchery, fish pond; hennery, incubator.

keeper, warden, herder, cowherd, neatherd, ranchero, herdsman, *vaquero* (*Sp. Amer.*), cowboy, cow puncher, cowkeeper, drover; grazier, shepherd, shepherdess; goatherd; trainer, breeder, horse trainer, broncobuster (*slang*); beekeeper, apiarist, apiculturist.

veterinarian, veterinary surgeon, vet (*colloq.*), horse doctor; horseshoer, farrier.

stable, livery, mews, barn, byre; fold, sheepfold; pen, sty; cage, hencoop.

V. domesticate, tame, acclimatize, reclaim, train; corral, round up, herd; raise, breed, bring up.

[*relating to horses*] break in, gentle, break, bust (*slang*), break to harness, yoke, harness, harness up (*colloq.*), hitch, hitch up (*colloq.*), cinch (*U.S.*), drive, ride.

groom, tend, rub down, brush, curry, currycomb; water, feed, fodder; bed down, litter.

Adj. domesticated, tame, habituated, domestic, broken, gentle, docile.

See also ANIMAL, BIRD, HORSE.

domicile, *n.* home, accommodations, residence (HABITATION).

dominance, *n.* domination, ascendancy, paramountcy (POWER); control, upper hand (INFLUENCE).

dominate, *v.* master, rule, subjugate (GOVERNMENT, CONTROL); predominate, preponderate (POWER); prevail, reign, superabound (PRESENCE); lie over, overlie, command (REST).

domineer, *v.* oppress, browbeat, bully over (CONTROL, SEVERITY, POWER).

dominion, *n.* dominance, ascendancy; domain, jurisdiction (POWER); sovereignty, rule (GOVERNMENT, RULE); territory (LAND).

don, *v.* draw on, get into, pull on (CLOTHING).

donation, *n.* gift, present, contribution (CHARITY, GIVING).

Don Juan, *n.* lecher, libertine, Casanova (SEX, LOVE).

donkey, *n.* burro, dickey, mule (HORSE); ass, dolt, booby (FOLLY).

donor, *n.* giver, contributor (CHARITY, GIVING).

doom, *v.* preordain, predetermine, foredoom (DESTINY).

doomed, *adj.* ill-fated, ill-omened, ill-starred (MISFORTUNE).

door, *n.* entrance, gateway, portal (INGRESS, EGRESS).

dope, *n.* narcotic, drug, opiate (PHARMACY); donkey, ass, fool (FOLLY, STUPIDITY).

dormant, *adj.* fallow, quiescent, slack (INACTION); latent, potential, smoldering (PRESENCE).

dormitory, *n.* sleeping quarters, accommodation, bunkhouse (SLEEP).

dot, *n.* spot, fleck, speck (VARIEGATION); diacritical mark, tittle (WRITTEN SYMBOL).

dote on, *v.* like, be fond of, enjoy (LIKING).

double, *adj.* coupled, paired, twin (TWO).

double, *n.* match, mate, twin (SIMILARITY).

double, *v.* duplify, duplicate, redouble (TWO); infold, loop, crease (FOLD).

double-dealing, *adj.* two-faced, Janus-faced, mealymouthed (PRETENSE, DECEPTION).

double talk, *n.* equivocation, mumbo jumbo, rigmarole (AMBIGUITY, ABSURDITY).

doubt, *v.* shilly-shally, back and fill, vacillate (UNCERTAINTY); misdoubt, suspect, wonder at (UNBELIEVINGNESS).

doubtful, *adj.* unconfident, unassured, diffident (UNBELIEVINGNESS); dubious, problematical (UNCERTAINTY).

douse, *v.* drench, saturate, soak (WATER).

dowager, *n.* matron, biddy (*colloq.*), dame (OLDNESS).

dowdy, *adj.* bedraggled, poky, slovenly (UNTIDINESS).

down, *adv.* below, underneath, under (LOWNESS).

down, *n.* fluff, fuzz, lanugo (HAIR); dune, knoll, mesa (HEIGHT).

down-and-out, *adj.* beggared, needy, destitute (POVERTY).

downcast, *adj.* chapfallen, crestfallen, downhearted (DEJECTION).

downfall, *n.* ruin, fall, overthrow (MISFORTUNE).

downgrade, *n.* declivity, pitch, dip (SLOPE).

downhill, *adj.* dipping, descending, downgrade (SLOPE).

downpour, *n.* drencher, deluge, flood (RAIN).

downy, *adj.* fluffy, fuzzy, velutinous (HAIR); feathery, featherlike (FEATHER).

DOZEN—*N.* dozen, twelve; long dozen, baker's dozen, thirteen; duodecimality.

Adj. dozenth, twelfth, duodenary, duodecimal; twelvefold, duodecuple.

dozy, *adj.* sleepy, drowsy, somnolent (SLEEP).

drab, *adj.* arid, dry, flat (BOREDOM); same, unchanging (UNIFORMITY).

draft, *n.* sketch, outline, blueprint (WRITING, PLAN); current, eddy, breeze (AIR); check, order (MONEY); haulage, towage (TRACTION); submersion, displacement (DEPTH); conscription, impressment, induction (FORCE).

draftee, *n.* conscript, drafted man, inductee (FIGHTER).

drag, *v.* tug, tow, trail (TRACTION); pull, draw, magnetize (ATTRACTION).

dragnet, *n.* hook, lasso, net (TRAP).

dragon, *n.* basilisk, cockatrice, dipsas (MYTHICAL BEINGS); wild beast, brute (VIOLENCE); reptile (ANIMAL).

drain, *n.* sewer, cloaca, cesspool (UNCLEANNESS, DEPARTURE).

drake, *n.* rooster, cob, gander (BIRD).

DRAMA—*N.* the drama, the stage, the theater, the play; theatricals, dramaturgy, histrionic art; dramatics, acting, theatrics, showmanship; buskin, sock, cothurnus; Broadway, the Rialto; straw-hat circuit, Borsht Circuit (*slang*).

play, drama, show (*colloq.*), playlet, one-act play, sketch, skit, vehicle; piece, composition; tragedy, opera, curtain raiser, interlude, *entr'acte* (*F.*), *divertissement* (*F.*), afterpiece, farce, extravaganza, harlequinade, pantomime, mime, burlesque, spectacle, pageant, masque, mummery, melodrama; mystery, miracle play, morality play; dialogue, duologue, duodrama; monologue, solo, monodrama, dramalogue; soap opera.

repertory, repertoire, stock, summer stock.

comedy, comedy of manners, drawing-room comedy, light comedy, low comedy, musical comedy, *opéra bouffe* (*F.*), *opéra comique* (*F.*), operetta, revue, slapstick comedy, tragicomedy, comitragedy.

performance, stage show, Broadway show, presentation, act, impersonation, impression, premier, production; aquacade, water ballet; psychodrama; peep show; marionette show, puppet show, Punch-and-Judy show.

vaudeville, variety show, review.

playgoer, theatergoer, firstnighter; audience, house, orchestra, gallery.

dramatist, playwright, dramaturgist.

theater, playhouse, auditorium, bowl, amphitheater.

stage, the boards, wings, footlights, limelight, spotlight; proscenium.

cast, company, *dramatis personae* (*L.*); role, part, character.

V. dramatize, present, show, stage, produce

Adj. dramatic, legitimate, histrionic, theatrical, theatric; stellar, leading, starring; tragic, Thespian, buskined; comic, farcical, slapstick; *Grand Guignol* (*F.*).

See also ACTOR, BOOK, MOTION PICTURES, SEAT, STORY.

dramatize, *v.* romanticize, glamorize (EXCITEMENT, INTERESTINGNESS); stage, show, present (DRAMA).

drastic, *adj.* extreme, immoderate, dire (EXTREMENESS).

draw, *n.* tie, dead heat, stalemate, standoff (EQUALITY, ATTEMPT).

draw, *v.* sketch, design, paint (FINE ARTS); cull, pluck, pick (TAKING); pull, haul, lug (TRACTION); drag, attract (ATTRACTION).

draw back, *v.* retract, sheathe, reel in (TRACTION).

drawback, *n.* weakness, shortcoming, failing (IMPERFECTION).

drawers, *n.* shorts, bloomers, trouserettes (UNDERWEAR).

drawl, *v.* chant, drone, intone, nasalize (TALK).

drawn, *adj.* haggard, pinched, starved (THINNESS); tied, even, neck and neck (EQUALITY).

draw out, *v.* continue, prolong, stretch (LENGTH).

draw together, *v.* contract, constrict, clench (TRACTION).

draw up, *v.* compose, draft, formulate (WRITING).

dread, *v.* apprehend, misdoubt, be afraid (FEAR).

dreadful, *adj.* shuddersome, creepy, dread (FEAR); bad, abominable, awful (INFERIORITY).

dream, *n.* vision, nightmare, incubus (SLEEP).

dreamer, *n.* daydreamer, romanticist, phantast (IMAGINATION, SLEEP).

dreaminess, *n.* musing, reverie, pensiveness (THOUGHT).

dreamy, *adj.* dreamlike, nightmarish, unsubstantial, immaterial (SLEEP, NONEXISTENCE).

dreary, *adj.* dismal, dingy, gloomy (DARKNESS); drearisome, cheerless, wintry (GLOOM).

dredge, *n.* steam shovel, bulldozer, shovel (DIGGING).

dregs, *n.* lees, sediment, silt (REMAINDER); decrement, outscouring, recrement (UNCLEANNESS); trash, scum, riffraff (WORTHLESSNESS, MEANNESS).

drench, *v.* douse, saturate, soak (WATER).

dress, *n.* clothes, things, garments (CLOTHING); frock, gown, robe (SKIRT).

dressmaker, *n.* couturier (F.), couturière (F.), tailor (CLOTHING WORKER).

dress up, *v.* smarten, spruce up (*colloq.*), array (ORNAMENT).

dribble, *v.* drip, drizzle, drop (EGRESS).

drift, *n.* current, stream, tide (DIRECTION); silt, deposit, alluvion (TRANSFER).

drifter, *n.* floater, maunderer, rolling stone (PURPOSELESSNESS).

drill, *n.* practice, assignment, homework (TEACHING); punch, bore, auger (OPENING).

drill, *v.* puncture, punch, perforate (OPENING); exercise, practice (TEACHING).

DRINK—N. drink, gulp, quaff, sip, swig, swill; draught, potation, potion.

drinking, etc. (see *Verbs*); consumption, ingurgitation, libation (*jocose*), compotation.

beverage, refreshment, refection, nightcap, bracer, rickey, chaser; potables.

soda, club soda, Vichy, seltzer, soda water, pop; ginger ale, fruit drink, sherbet, ice-cream soda; punch, ade, soft drink, cola.

coffee, café, café au lait, café noir, demitasse (*all F.*); caffeine; tea, cambric tea.

thirst, dryness, dipsosis (*med.*).

V. drink, imbibe, ingurgitate, partake, quaff, gulp, guzzle, bib, sip, swig, swill, toss off, consume, lap; toast.

Adj. thirsty, dry, athirst, parched; drinkable, potable.

See also ALCOHOLIC LIQUOR, DRUNKENNESS, DRYNESS, FOOD, SOCIALITY.

---

drip, *v.* drizzle, dribble, drop (DESCENT, EGRESS).

dripping, *adj.* wet, doused, saturated (WATER).

drive, *n.* motive, impulse, incentive (MOTIVATION, PROPULSION).

drive, *v.* ride, ride in, motor (VEHICLE); make, compel, oblige (FORCE, NECESSITY); prod, goad, actuate (MOTIVATION, URGING, PROPULSION).

drive at, *v.* signify, intimate, allude to (MEANING).

drive away, *v.* chase, disperse, dispel (DISMISSAL).

drivel, *n.* blather, twaddle, nonsense (ABSURDITY).

drivel, *v.* slaver, slobber, drool (SALIVA).

drive out, *v.* force out, smoke out, eject (DISMISSAL).

drizzle, *v.* mist, sprinkle, rain (RAIN); dribble, drip, drop (EGRESS).

droll, *adj.* comical, whimsical, amusing (WITTINESS, ABSURDITY); queer, quaint, eccentric (UNUSUALNESS).

drone, *n.* idler, sluggard, loafer (REST); leech, lickspittle, parasite (LIFE).

drone, *v.* drawl, chant, intone, nasalize (TALK).

drool, *v.* slaver, slobber, drivel (SALIVA).

droopy, *adj.* languid, languorous, lassitudinous (FATIGUE); pendulous, saggy, flabby (HANGING); slouchy, stooped, bent (POSTURE).

drop, *n.* downward slope, declivity, fall (SLOPE); dash, pinch, splash (ADDITION); morsel, bit, sample (TASTE).

drop, *v.* dribble, drip, drizzle (EGRESS); decline, dwindle, fall (DECREASE, DESCENT); depress, sink, dip (LOWNESS); cheapen, depreciate (WORTHLESSNESS).

drought, *n.* aridity, rainlessness (DRYNESS).

drown, *v.* asphyxiate, suffocate, stifle (KILLING); muffle, deaden, mute (NONRESONANCE).

drowsy, *adj.* sleepy, dozy, somnolent (SLEEP).

drudgery, *n.* toil, travail, labor (WORK).

drug, *v.* dope, knock out, narcotize (PHARMACY); sedate, relax (CALMNESS); benumb, deaden, daze (INSENSIBILITY); anesthetize, analgize, desensitize (PAINKILLER).

druggist, *n.* pharmacist, gallipot (*colloq.*), apothecary (PHARMACY).

drum, *n.* bass drum, kettledrum, snare drum (MUSICAL INSTRUMENTS); roller, cylinder (ROLL); barrel, keg, tub (CONTAINER).

drum, *v.* rap, tap (HITTING); boom, roar, thunder (ROLL).

DRUNKENNESS—N. drunkenness, intoxication, inebriacy, inebriation, inebriety, insobriety.

alcoholism, bibacity, dipsomania, bacchanalianism.

drunkard, drunk, inebriate, bloat (*slang*), lush (*slang*), rummy, soak (*slang*), sot, souse (*slang*), toper, tosspot; barfly; alcoholic, dipsomaniac.

hangover, crapulence, delirium tremens.

V. **intoxicate,** alcoholize, besot, inebriate, stupefy; fuddle, befuddle; mellow, stimulate.

Adj. **drunk,** drunken, alcoholized, besotted, boiled (*slang*), boozy (*colloq.*), bousy, canned (*slang*), half-seas over (*colloq.*), high (*colloq.*), inebriated, inebrious, in one's cups, intoxicated, lit (*slang*), loaded (*slang*), lush (*slang*), pie-eyed (*slang*), potted (*slang*), reeling (*slang*), sodden, sotted, soused (*slang*), three sheets in the wind (*colloq.*), tight (*colloq.*), tipsy, under the influence; bacchic, beery, vinous; mellow, stimulated; groggy, fuddled, befuddled, maudlin; blind-drunk, dead-drunk, stupefied; hung-over, crapulous, crapulent.

See also ALCOHOLIC LIQUOR, INTEMPERANCE. *Antonyms*—See SOBRIETY.

dry, *adj.* arid, sear, stale (DRYNESS); abstinent, ascetic (SOBRIETY); matter-of-fact, naked, plain (SIMPLICITY).

DRYNESS—*N.* **dryness,** aridity, drought; desiccation, dehydration, evaporation, dehumidification, exsiccation, torrefaction.

drier, dryer, towel, wiper, sponge, squeegee.

V. **dry,** soak up, sponge, swab, towel, wipe, drain; parch, scorch, stale, wither, shrivel, wizen, sear; bake, kiln-dry, kiln; desiccate, evaporate, dehumidify, dehydrate, anhydrate, exsiccate, torrefy.

Adj. **dry,** arid, sear, parched, adust, scorched, dried up, stale, withered, wizened, shriveled, desiccated, anhydrous, juiceless, sapless; moistless, moistureless, waterless, thirsty, torrid; waterproof, watertight, staunch.

rainless, fair, pleasant, fine; dry, arid, droughty *or* drouthy.

See also BOREDOM, DULLNESS, SOBRIETY. *Antonyms*—See DRINK, WATER.

dual, *adj.* twofold, bifold, binary (TWO).

dubious, *adj.* suspicious, doubtful; unconfident, unassured (UNBELIEVINGNESS); uncertain, unsure

(UNCERTAINTY); moot, debatable, disputable (INQUIRY).

duck, *n.* plunge, submersion (DIVING); lurch, dodge (SIDE); hen, drake (BIRD).

dude, *n.* coxcomb, dandy, exquisite (FASHION).

due, *adj.* unpaid, owing, payable (DEBT, PAYMENT).

due, *n.* claim, perquisite, prerogative (RIGHT, PRIVILEGE).

duel, *n.* affaire d'honneur (*F.*), monomachy (FIGHTING).

duel, *v.* joust, tilt, tourney (ATTEMPT).

duelist, *n.* swordsman, swashbuckler, fencer (FIGHTER).

dues, *n.* tax, assessment, custom (PAYMENT); obligation, liability, debit (DEBT).

duffer, *n.* incompetent, bungler, cobbler, dabster (CLUMSINESS).

dull, *adj.* blunt, obtuse (BLUNTNESS, DULLNESS); tedious, uninteresting (BOREDOM); murky, dim, dark (CLOUD); dim-witted, stupid (STUPIDITY).

DULLNESS—*N.* **dullness,** stupidity, stagnation, apathy; lackluster, obscurity, opacity, tarnish, mat.

V. **dull,** blunt, obtund; deaden, stupefy, benumb; blur, bedim, obscure, darken, cloud, tarnish, dim, fade, tone down; mat.

Adj. **dull,** dry, uninteresting, heavy-footed, elephantine, ponderous, heavy; jejune, insipid, tasteless, unimaginative; tedious, dreary, dismal, inactive, stagnant, sluggish.

dim, faded, lackluster, lusterless, matted, obscure, opaque, tarnished, unglossy, blurred.

unshined, unbrightened, unbuffed, unburnished, unfurbished, ungilded, unglossed, unplanished, unpolished, unvarnished, unwaxed, unglazed.

expressionless, empty, inexpressive, glassy, stupid, blank, vacant, vacuous, inane.

[*of sounds*] **muffled,** deadened, flat, subdued.

blunt, blunted, dulled, obtuse, unsharpened.

See also BLUNTNESS, BOREDOM, INACTION, INSENSITIVITY, STUPIDITY, UNSAVORINESS. *Antonyms*—See EXPRESSION, INTERESTINGNESS, LIGHT, SHARPNESS, TASTE.

dull-witted, *adj.* dumb, doltish, feeble-witted (STUPIDITY).

dumb, *adj.* silent, inarticulate, tongue-tied (SILENCE); dullwitted, doltish, feeble-witted (STUPIDITY).

dumb-waiter, *n.* elevator, hoist (ELEVATION).

dumfound, *v.* amaze, astonish, astound (SURPRISE).

dummy, *n.* model, mannequin, manikin (FINE ARTS); sphinx, mute, clam (SILENCE); dunce, dumbbell, dullard (STUPIDITY); ringer (*colloq.*), stand-in (SUBSTITUTION).

dump, *v.* unload, dispose of, get rid of (ELIMINATION, SALE); drop, leave, expel (THROW).

dumpy, *adj.* chunky, stocky, squat (SHORTNESS, SIZE).

dunce, *n.* halfwit, nitwit, imbecile (FOLLY, STUPIDITY).

dune, *n.* down, knoll, mesa (HEIGHT).

dungeon, *n.* hole, oubliette, black hole (IMPRISONMENT); vault, crypt, cavern (LOWNESS).

dupe, *n.* victim, gull, easy mark (DECEPTION).

duplicate, *adj.* same, alike, identical (SIMILARITY); twin, duple, duplex (TWO).

duplicate, *n.* copy, reproduction, facsimile (COPY); counterpart, opposite number, obverse (SIMILARITY).

duplicate, *v.* copy, manifold, reproduce (COPY); double, duplify (TWO); redo, repeat (REPETITION).

duplicity, *n.* double-dealing, two-facedness, hypocrisy (DECEPTION); duality, twoness, dualism (TWO).

durable, *adj.* enduring, lasting, long-continued (CONTINUATION).

duration, *n.* term, period, continuance (CONTINUATION, LENGTH, TIME).

duress, *n.* compulsion, constraint, coercion (FORCE).

during, *prep.* until, pending, in the time of (TIME).

dusk, *n.* twilight, gloaming, nightfall (EVENING).

dusky, *adj.* adusk, twilight, crepuscular (DARKNESS); dull, murky, dim (CLOUD); dark, darkish, swarthy (BLACKNESS).

dust, *n.* grime, smut, soot (UNCLEANNESS); soil, earth, ground (LAND); powder, sand, grit (POWDERINESS).

DUTY—*N.* duty, liability, obligation, onus, province, responsibility; service, function, part, task, commission, trust, charge, business, office.

[*science or theory of duty*] ethics, deontology, eudaemonism.

tax, impost, toll, levy, assessment, due, rate, custom, excise.

V. be the duty of, behoove, be incumbent on.

impose a duty, enjoin, require, exact, saddle with, prescribe, assign, call upon, look to, oblige.

Adj. dutiful, duteous, obedient, respectful, filial.

See also DEMAND, LIABILITY, NECESSITY, OBEDIENCE, OBSERVANCE, PAYMENT, RESPECT. *Antonyms*—See DISOBEDIENCE, DISRESPECT, NEGLECT, NONOBSERVANCE.

dwarf, *n.* Tom Thumb, tot, gnome (SMALLNESS).

dwarf, *v.* stunt, micrify, minify (SMALLNESS).

dweller, *n.* denizen, resident (INHABITANT).

dwell in, *v.* inhabit, occupy, reside in (INHABITANT).

dwelling, *n.* abode, haunt, living quarters (HABITATION).

dwindle, *v.* contract, shrink (SMALLNESS); decline, drop, fall (DECREASE); taper, wane, fade (WEAKNESS).

dye, *n.* pigment, coloring matter (COLOR).

dynamic, *adj.* energetic, aggressive, active (ENERGY).

dynamite, *n.* explosive, T.N.T., nitroglycerin (BLOWING, ARMS).

E

each, *adj.* respective, single, exclusive (UNITY).

EAGERNESS—*N.* eagerness, *élan* (*F.*), zeal, ardency, ardor, avidity, vehemence; voracity, thirst.

Adj. eager, zealous, wild (*colloq.*), ablaze, ardent, avid, athirst, ambitious, vehement, whole-souled; warm-blooded; prompt, solicitous; voracious, cormorant, thirsty, liquorish, lickerish.

See also DESIRE, ENTHUSIASM, FEELING, GREED, WILLINGNESS. *Antonyms*—See BOREDOM, DENIAL, DULLNESS, INSENSITIVITY, UNWILLINGNESS.

ear, *n.* auris (*med.*), auricle, pinna (LISTENING).

EARLINESS—*N.* earliness, advancement, pre-existence, precocity, prematurity; promptitude, punctuality; immediacy, instantaneity.

moment, instant, second, split second, twinkling, flash, trice, jiffy (*colloq.*).

V. **be early,** anticipate, foresee, forestall; be beforehand, take time by the forelock, steal a march upon; bespeak, engage, reserve, order, book, hire.

antedate, predate, pre-exist.

Adj. **early,** beforehand, precocious, advanced, ahead of time; matutinal, seasonable, premature, untimely, previous, earlier, pre-existent, former.

earliest, premier, pristine, proleptical; primitive, primeval, primal, primary, primoprimitive, primordial, original, antediluvian, prehistoric.

first, initial, maiden, virgin, premier, prime, primoprime, aboriginal, primigenial, pristine.

on time, prompt, punctual.

immediate, instant, instantaneous, prompt, ready, summary.

Adv., phrases. **early,** soon, anon, betimes, ere long, presently, proximately, shortly, before long; in time, in the fullness of time.

immediately, at once, directly, instantaneously, instanter, instantly, presto, promptly, right away, straightway, thereon, thereupon; summarily, without delay; in no time, in an instant, in a trice, in a jiffy (*colloq.*), in the twinkling of an eye.

See also APPROACH, BEGINNING, PAST, SPEED. *Antonyms*—See DELAY, FUTURE.

---

earmark, *n.* feature, marking, peculiarity (DIFFERENCE).

earn, *v.* make money, be gainfully employed (MONEY); deserve, merit, rate (VALUE).

earnest, *adj.* serious, sedate, staid (SOBRIETY).

earnings, *n.* salary, pay, emolument (PAYMENT); receipts, income, revenue (RECEIVING).

earshot, *n.* hearing, range, reach (SOUND, LISTENING).

earth, *n.* soil, dust, ground (LAND); planet, globe, sphere (WORLD).

earthenware, *n.* crockery, ceramics (CONTAINER).

earthly, *adj.* worldly, mundane, carnal (IRRELIGION); global, planetary (WORLD).

EARTHQUAKE—*N.* **earthquake,** quake, shock, convulsion, seism, temblor, tremor, upheaval, microseism, macroseism, seaquake; seismology, seismography.

seismograph, seismometer, tromometer.

Adj. **seismic,** seismal, seismical.

See also AGITATION, SHAKE. *Antonyms*—See CALMNESS, PEACE.

---

earthy, *adj.* mundane, worldly, earthen (WORLD); coarse, crude, indelicate (VULGARITY).

ease, *n.* security, calm, unapprehension (UNANXIETY); facility, convenience (EASE); repose, quiet, peace (REST).

ease, *v.* facilitate, expedite, simplify (EASE); mitigate, alleviate, allay (MILDNESS); soothe, lull, becalm (CALMNESS); lessen, lighten (PAINKILLER).

EASE—*N.* **ease,** facility, child's play, smooth sailing; cinch, pushover, snap, setup (*all colloq.*); abandon, legerity.

conveniences, facilities, utilities, appliances, aids, helps, advantages, resources, means; comforts, creature comforts; tools, implements, utensils.

V. **ease,** facilitate, expedite, simplify, smooth, pave the way for.

be easy, run smoothly, sail along.

Adj. **easy,** effortless, smooth, simple, simplified, elementary, facile; uncomplicated, uncomplex, uninvolved; feasible, practicable, workable.

manageable, handy, wieldy; flexible, pliant, pliable, ductile; yielding; docile, tractable, easygoing.

convenient, handy, available, commodious; central, accessible, within reach, nearby.

Adv., phrases. **easily,** smoothly, simply, conveniently, handily, swimmingly; without effort, with ease, with the greatest of ease, without a hitch.

See also ABILITY, CALMNESS, POSSIBILITY, SIMPLICITY, SMOOTHNESS. *Antonyms*—See DIFFICULTY, IMPOSSIBILITY.

East, *n.* Eastern Hemisphere, Far East, Orient (DIRECTION).

easy, *adj.* effortless, simple, elementary (EASE); unanxious, carefree, secure (UNANXIETY); calm, at rest, composed (CALMNESS); gentle, moderate, temperate (MILDNESS); leisurely, unhurried, languid (REST).

easygoing, *adj.* complaisant, indulgent, tolerant (MILDNESS); peaceful, placid, calm (INEXCITABILITY); informal, casual, offhand (NONOBSERVANCE).

eat, v. consume, fall to, dine (FOOD).

eatable, adj. edible, esculent, comestible (FOOD).

eatables, n. victuals, viands, edibles (FOOD).

eating, n. consumption, deglutition, mastication (FOOD).

eavesdropper, n. listener, monitor, snoop (LISTENING, INQUIRY).

ebb, v. flow back, recede, retreat (REVERSION).

ebb tide, n. low tide, low water, neap tide (LOWNESS).

eccentric, adj. queer, quizzical, quaint, erratic, outlandish, droll, whimsical (UNUSUALNESS).

eccentricity, n. peculiarity, quirk, foible, idiosyncrasy (UNUSUALNESS, CHARACTER).

ecclesiastical, adj. clerical, pastoral, priestly (CLERGY); spiritual, parochial (CHURCH).

echo, v. vibrate, respond, reverberate (REPETITION, REACTION).

eclipse, v. surmount, tower above, surpass (OVERRUNNING).

economical, adj. low, moderate, reasonable (INEXPENSIVENESS); frugal, thrifty (ECONOMY).

economics, n. plutology, political economy, finance (WEALTH, MONEY).

ECONOMY—N. economy, management, order, careful administration.

frugality, austerity, prudence, thrift, providence, care, husbandry, retrenchment, parsimony.

V. economize, be frugal, husband, save; retrench, cut down expenses, shepherd, skimp, scrimp, scrape, stint, tighten one's belt, spare; make both ends meet, meet one's expenses.

Adj. economical, frugal, Spartan, careful, thrifty, saving, economizing, provident, chary, sparing, parsimonious, canny, penny-wise, penurious, prudent, scrimpy, skimpy, stinting.

See also HOLD, STINGINESS, STORE. Antonyms—See EXPENDITURE, UNSELFISHNESS, WASTEFULNESS.

ecstasy, n. delirium, ebullience (EXCITEMENT); beatitude, bliss, joy (HAPPINESS).

eddy, n. whirlpool, maelstrom, vortex; undercurrent, undertow, underset (RIVER, ROTATION).

edge, n. border, brim, margin (BOUNDARY); extremity, tip, butt (END).

edged, adj. sharp, cutting, keen-edged (SHARPNESS).

edible, adj. eatable, esculent, comestible (FOOD).

edict, n. decree, mandate, writ (LAW, COMMAND).

edifice, n. structure, pile, skyscraper (BUILDING).

edify, v. enlighten, initiate, inform (TEACHING).

edit, v. revise, correct, rectify (IMPROVEMENT).

edition, n. issue, printing, impression (PUBLICATION).

editor, n. compiler, anthologist, journalist (TREATISE, PUBLICATION).

educate, v. instruct, school, tutor (TEACHING).

educated, adj. learned, cultured, erudite, literate, lettered, schooled (LEARNING, TEACHING).

education, n. background, literacy, cultivation (LEARNING), instruction, tuition, edification (TEACHING).

eerie, adj. weird, supernatural, uncanny (UNUSUALNESS, SUPERNATURALISM).

effect, n. consequence, outcome, end (RESULT).

effect, v. cause, make, bring about (RESULT).

effective, adj. potent, telling, trenchant (RESULT).

effects, n. personal possessions, personal effects, paraphernalia (OWNERSHIP).

effeminate, adj. unmanly, unvirile, sissy (WEAKNESS).

effervesce, v. bubble, ferment (EXCITEMENT); be violent, boil (VIOLENCE).

effervescence, n. ebullience, ebullition, animation, volatility (ACTIVITY).

effervescent, adj. exhilarated, merry, ebullient (CHEERFULNESS); bubbly, bubbling (AGITATION).

efficient, adj. competent, proficient, able (ABILITY); businesslike, orderly, systematic (BUSINESS).

effort, n. exertion, toil, labor (ENERGY).

effortless, adj. easy, simple, facile (EASE).

effrontery, n. boldness, audacity, cheek (DISCOURTESY).

egg, n. ovum, ovule, rudiment, embryo (MAKE-UP, CAUSATION).

egghead (slang), n. highbrow (colloq.), double-dome (slang), intellectual (INTELLIGENCE).

egg-shaped, adj. elliptical, oval, elliptoid (ROUNDNESS).

ego, n. self-pride, amour propre (F.), self-admiration (PRIDE); psyche, self (SELFISHNESS).

egoist, n. peacock, egocentric, narcissist (PRIDE, SELFISHNESS).

egotism, n. conceit, vanity, vainglory (PRIDE); egoism, self-praise, self-regard (SELFISHNESS).

egregious, *adj.* flagrant, glaring, gross (INFERIORITY).

EGRESS—*N.* egress, emanation, emergence, exit; issue, escape, leak, leakage, trickle, exudation, seepage, spout, gush, spurt, squirt, outpour, outflow, wallow; outburst, outbreak, explosion, jet, rampage, outrush, sally, debouch, disemboguement; eruption, discharge, efflorescence, appearance, spring, leap; effluvium, efflux, effusion.

outlet, avenue, exit, vent; opening, hole, leak; spout, faucet, escape cock, tap, cock, nozzle; sluice, sluice gate, floodgate; door, doorway, gate, gateway, wicket; port, porthole; skylight, window; loophole.

V. come out, egress, emanate, emerge, exit; issue, escape, leak, trickle, exude, ooze, seep, spout, gush, spurt, squirt, pour out, spill out, flow out, well, well out, wallow; burst out, blaze, explode, jet, jump out, rampage, rush out, sally, debouch, disembogue; come forth, burst forth, effloresce, discharge, erupt, break out, arise, appear, peep through, peer, proceed, rush forth, spring forth, leap forth, break forth.

come out in drops, dribble, drip, drizzle, drop, rain, plash, shower, spatter, splash, splatter, spray, sprinkle, trickle, weep.

See also APPEARANCE, CHANNEL, DEPARTURE, OPENING, PASSAGE, RIVER. *Antonyms*—See IMPRISONMENT, INGRESS.

EIGHT—*N.* eight, octave, octad, octavo, octet, ogdoad, octonary.

V. multiply by eight, octuple, octuplicate.

Adj. eightfold, octuple, octuplicate, octonary; octangular, octagonal, octohedral, octadic.

eject, *v.* evict, oust, dispossess (DISMISSAL); expel, expulse, displace (PROPULSION, THROW).

elaborate, *adj.* complex, complicated, intricate (DIFFICULTY); elegant, ornate, luxurious (ELEGANCE); detailed, embellished (DETAIL).

elaborate, *v.* specify, particularize, embellish (DETAIL).

elapse, *v.* lapse, go by, vanish (PASSAGE).

elastic, *adj.* stretchable, extendible (STRETCH); resilient, supple, buoyant (CHEERFULNESS).

elated, *adj.* exalted, exultant, gleeful (HAPPINESS).

elbow, *n.* ancon (APPENDAGE).

elbow, *v.* push aside, jostle (SIDE); bend, hook (ANGULARITY).

elder, *adj.* older, senior (OLDNESS).

elderly, *adj.* old, aged, ancient (OLDNESS).

eldest, *adj.* oldest, first-born (OLDNESS).

elect, *v.* choose, select, take (CHOICE).

elector, *n.* voter, constituent, balloter (VOTE).

electric, *adj.* electrical, galvanic, voltaic (LIGHT); power-driven, motor-driven (INSTRUMENT); electrifying, galvanizing, galvanic (EXCITEMENT).

ELEGANCE—*N.* elegance, refinement, grace, beauty, polish, finish, distinction; taste, good taste, restraint.

purist, stylist, classicist, Atticist.

Adj. elegant, refined, aesthetic, tasteful, graceful, luxurious, elaborate, ornate; polished, artistic, finished, classical, Attic, Ciceronian.

See also BEAUTY, MAGNIFICENCE, TASTE. *Antonyms*—See CLUMSINESS.

elegy, *n.* lament, requiem, threnody (SADNESS).

element, *n.* component, constituent, factor (PART); material, matter, substance (MATERIALITY); trace, bit, drop (SMALLNESS).

elementary, *adj.* rudimentary, abecedarian (BEGINNING); uncomplex, simplex, elemental (SIMPLICITY); easy, effortless, simplified (EASE).

elementary school, *n.* public school, grade school (SCHOOL).

elephant, *n.* pachyderm, proboscidian (ANIMAL).

ELEVATION—*N.* elevation, uplift, heave, hoist, boost; levitation.

[*elevating device*] lever, crowbar, pry, pulley, crane, derrick, windlass, capstan, winch, hoist, lift, tackle; crank, jack, jackscrew; dredge, dredger, pump; elevator, hoist, dumbwaiter.

V. elevate, raise, lift, erect, hoist, upraise, uprear, rear, ramp, poise, heave, heft, boost, heighten, stilt, perk up, toss up, pry, emboss; levitate; dredge up, drag up, fish up, pump up.

exalt, dignify, ennoble, promote, advance, upgrade, skip, heighten, aggrandize, honor.

uplift, set up, refine, sublimate, glorify, inspire, animate.

See also ASCENT, DIGGING, FAME, HEIGHT, MAGNIFICENCE, NOBILITY, PROGRESS. *Antonyms*—See BURIAL, DESCENT, LOWNESS.

elf, *n.* fairy, brownie, elfin (SUPERNATURAL BEINGS).

elicit, *v.* educe, bring forth, evoke (EXTRACTION).

eligible, *adj.* marriageable, nubile (MARRIAGE); qualified, privileged, authorized (PRIVILEGE).

eliminate, *v.* discharge, egest, ejaculate (EXCRETION); abolish, do away with (ELIMINATION).

ELIMINATION—*N.* **elimination,** abolition, abrogation, extermination.

erasure, deletion, effacement, obliteration, rasure, expunction, cancellation; censorship, bowdlerization, expurgation.

riddance, rejection, discard, disposal; excision, exsection, operation, surgery; eradication, evulsion, extirpation; removal, dismissal, discharge, liquidation; exuviation (*zool.*).

reject, scrap, castoff, discharge; exuviae, slough (*both zool.*).

V. **eliminate,** abolish, do away with, abrogate, scotch, stamp out, exterminate, scuttle, wash out, wipe out.

erase, efface, scratch out, rub out, blot out, obliterate, expunge, cross out, delete, dele (*printing*), strike out, cancel, void; censor, blue-pencil, bowdlerize, expurgate; rub off, scrape off, scrape away.

cut out, cut away, cut off, excise, exscind, exsect, operate on, whittle away, whittle off, hack away at, reduce.

discard, get rid of, scrap, reject, throw out, jilt (*a lover*), burke, cast away, cast out, rid, screen out, unload, dump, dispose of, throw away, jettison.

eradicate, uproot, unroot, weed out, extirpate, pluck out, pull out, deracinate, disroot, outroot, root out.

shed, cast off, throw off, disburden oneself of, relieve oneself of, rid oneself of, get rid of, drop, cast, molt, exuviate (*zool.*), shuffle off, shunt off, slough off.

See also CUTTING, DISMISSAL, DISPERSION, EXCRETION, LOSS, REMOVAL, SURGERY, USELESSNESS. *Antonyms*—See ECONOMY, HOLD, RECEIVING.

ellipse, *n.* oval, ovoid (ROUNDNESS).

elocution, *n.* oratory, eloquence, rhetoric (TALK).

elongated, *adj.* long, elongate, oblong (LENGTH).

elopement, *n.* secret marriage, Gretna Green marriage (MARRIAGE).

eloquent, *adj.* expressive, silvertongued, rhetorical (TALK, EXPRESSION).

elude, *v.* get away from, evade (DEPARTURE, AVOIDANCE).

elusive, *adj.* evasive, shy, slippery (AVOIDANCE); fugitive, fugacious, volatile (IMPERMANENCE).

emaciated, *adj.* wasted, consumptive, cadaverous (THINNESS).

emanate, *v.* issue, flow out, emerge (DEPARTURE, EGRESS).

emancipate, *v.* free, enfranchise, manumit (FREEDOM).

embankment, *n.* terrace, bank, hill (HEIGHT).

embargo, *n.* prohibition, ban, proscription (DENIAL).

embark, *v.* go aboard, ship, go on board, take ship (DEPARTURE, SAILOR); emplane, entrain (INGRESS).

embark on, *v.* begin, set out, set about (BEGINNING).

EMBARRASSMENT—*N.* **embarrassment,** abashment, confusion, discomfiture, discomfort, discomposure, disconcertion, disconcertment, pudency, self-consciousness.

V. **embarrass,** abash, confuse, discomfit, disconcert, discountenance, put out of countenance.

Adj. **embarrassed,** abashed, confused, discomfited, disconcerted, ill-at-ease, uneasy, self-conscious, uncomfortable, sheepish, shamefaced.

embarrassing, discomfiting, disconcerting; awkward, uncomfortable.

See also CONFUSION, MODESTY. *Antonyms*—See CALMNESS, CERTAINTY.

embellish, *v.* enrich, decorate, adorn (BEAUTY, ORNAMENT); amplify, elaborate (DETAIL).

ember, *n.* firebrand, brand, coal (FIRE).

embezzlement, *n.* misappropriation, peculation, defalcation (THIEVERY).

embitter, *v.* bitter, venom (ANGER).

emblem, *n.* badge, mark, scepter (REPRESENTATION); trade-mark, brand (INDICATION).

embodiment, *n.* form, cast, conformation (SHAPE).

embody, *v.* include, embrace, incorporate (INCLUSION); incarnate, personify (BODY).

embrace, *v.* hug, squeeze, press (CARESS, HOLD, PRESSURE); include, comprehend, encompass (INCLUSION).

embroider, v. exaggerate, romanticize, color (EXAGGERATION, FALSENESS).

embroidery, n. needlework, tatting, crochet (ORNAMENT).

embryo, n. rudiment, egg, germ (CAUSATION); fetus, homunculus, unborn child (CHILD).

emerge, v. come out, emanate, exit (EGRESS); stream, gush, spurt (DEPARTURE); rise, loom, dawn (VISIBILITY).

emigrant, n. migrant, expatriate, evacuee (DEPARTURE, TRAVELING, CITIZEN).

eminence, n. highland, upland, rise (HEIGHT).

eminent, adj. famous, noted, renowned (FAME).

emissary, n. ambassador, envoy, representative (DEPUTY, MESSENGER, AGENT).

emit, v. beam, radiate, shed (GIVING, THROW).

emotion, n. sentiment, sensibility, affect (psychol.), feeling (FEELING, SENSITIVENESS).

emotional, adj. demonstrative, sensuous; moving, stirring, touching (FEELING); constitutional, temperamental, attitudinal (CHARACTER).

empathy, n. sympathy, warmth, fellow feeling (PITY).

emperor, n. Caesar, Mikado (Jap.), king (RULER).

emphasize, v. accentuate, accent, stress (IMPORTANCE, VOICE).

empire, n. sway, government, dominion (RULE).

employ, v. adopt, utilize, apply (USE); engage, hire, place (SITUATION).

employee, n. worker, wage earner, clerk (WORK).

employer, n. boss, taskmaster, master (WORK).

empower, v. enable, capacitate (ABILITY); qualify, vest, invest (POWER); authorize, sanction (PERMISSION).

empress, n. czarina, maharani (Hindu), queen (RULER).

empty, adj. bare, barren, vacant (ABSENCE); insincere, dishonest, hollow (PRETENSE); expressionless, stupid, blank (DULLNESS).

emulate, v. follow, pattern after, imitate (IMITATION).

enable, v. provide the means, implement, make possible (MEANS); empower, capacitate, qualify (ABILITY, POWER).

enact, v. decree, ordain (COMMAND); legislate, pass (LAW); act, play (ACTOR).

enamel, n. paint, stain, varnish, gloss (COVERING).

enamored, adj. in love, smitten, infatuated (LOVE).

enchant, v. enthrall, spellbind, bewitch (MAGIC, ATTRACTION); gratify, delight, charm (PLEASURE, PLEASANTNESS); make happy, enrapture (HAPPINESS).

encircle, v. surround, ring, enclose (INCLOSURE, ROUNDNESS); circumscribe, encompass, envelop (ENVIRONMENT, EXTERIORITY).

enclose, v. surround, encircle, encompass (INCLOSURE).

enclosed, adj. walled, fortified, protected (WALL).

encore, adv. de novo (L.), da capo (It.), bis, again (REPETITION).

encore, n. song, aria, number (SINGING); reappearance, return (REPETITION).

encounter, n. meeting, concurrence (CONVERGENCE); battle, conflict, clash (FIGHTING).

encounter, v. come upon, chance upon, meet (DISCOVERY, CONVERGENCE); experience, undergo, sustain (OCCURRENCE, EXPERIENCE).

encourage, v. cheer, hearten, inspirit (HOPE, CHEERFULNESS); inspire, reassure, embolden (COURAGE, CERTAINTY); invite, countenance (URGING).

ENCROACHMENT—N. encroachment, intrusion, infringement, invasion, inroad, overlap, transgression, trespass, violation, transcendence.

V. encroach, extravagate, intrude, overlap, transgress, overstep, trespass; go beyond, impinge, infringe, invade, lap over, run over, overrun, violate, trench on; exceed, surpass, overtop, transcend.

See also ARRIVAL, EXAGGERATION, EXTREMENESS, INGRESS, OVERRUNNING. Antonyms—See MODERATENESS, MODESTY.

encumber, v. burden, load down, lade (WEIGHT).

encyclopedia, n. work of reference, cyclopedia (BOOK).

end, n. limit, extremity, edge (END); effect, consequence, outcome (RESULT); mission, object, objective (PURPOSE).

END—N. end, limit, boundary; antipodes.

extremity, tip, edge, butt, stump; tail, stub, tag; fag end, tail end, tag end, remnant, foot, heel, head, top; ultimate.

[pointed end] tip, cusp, neb, nib, prong, spire, point.

termination, close, closure, completion, conclusion, expiration, finis, finish, last, omega, terminus, terminal, upshot, outcome, windup; dissolution, death, *coup de grâce (F.)*, deathblow.

finale, epilogue, peroration, summation, swan song, conclusion, catastrophe, denouement; last stage; expiration, lapse, wane.

V. **end,** close, crown, complete; top off, finish, terminate, conclude, cease, stop, drop, discontinue, come to a close, perorate, wind up; put an end to, make an end of, abolish, destroy, bring to an end; achieve, accomplish, consummate; run out, lapse, expire, die; wane.

Adj. **final,** terminal, last, supreme, closing, dernier, eventual, conclusive, concluding, terminating, ending, finishing, crowning, definitive, farthest, extreme, ultimate, lattermost.

ended, settled, decided, over, concluded, done, through, finished.

Adv., phrases. **finally,** conclusively, decisively, in fine; at the last; once and for all.

over, at an end, by, past, done with.

See also BOUNDARY, CESSATION, COMPLETENESS, DEATH, DISCONTINUITY, EXTREMENESS, REAR, REMAINDER. *Antonyms*—See BEGINNING, CENTER, CONTINUATION, ENDLESSNESS.

---

endanger, *v.* jeopardize, peril, imperil (DANGER).

endearing, *adj.* affectionate, pet (LOVE).

endeavor, *n.* try, essay, effort (ATTEMPT); enterprise, venture (UNDERTAKING).

ENDLESSNESS—*N.* **endlessness,** incessancy, interminability, perpetuity, continuity; infinity, infinitude.

immortality, athanasia, eternity, imperishability, perdurability; immortal, eternal, phoenix.

V. **perpetuate,** preserve, continue, eternize, eternalize, immortalize.

be infinite, be endless, have no limits (*or* bounds), go on forever, continue without end.

Adj. **perpetual,** endless, ceaseless, eternal, incessant, interminable, interminate, timeless, unceasing, undying, unended, unending, never-ending, unremitting; continuous, continual.

limitless, boundless, illimitable, immeasurable, immense, infinite, measureless, unbounded, unlimitable, unlimited; numberless, countless, innumerable, incalculable.

immortal, undying, deathless, eternal, imperishable, perdurable.

Adv., phrases. **endlessly,** perpetually, etc. (see *Adjectives*); *ad infinitum (L.)*, without end, without limit, without stint; *ad nauseam (L.)*; always, ever, evermore (*archaic*), forever, for aye, to the end of time, till doomsday, to the crack of doom.

See also CONTINUATION, SPACE, STABILITY. *Antonyms*—See BOUNDARY, DISCONTINUITY, IMPERMANENCE, RESTRAINT.

---

endocrine, *n.* hormone, autacoid, secretion (EXCRETION).

endorse, *v.* subscribe, undersign, cosign (SIGNATURE); uphold, countenance, back, second (SUPPORT).

endow, *v.* settle upon, invest, vest in (GIVING).

endowment, *n.* gift, capacity, habilitation, turn (ABILITY).

endurance, *n.* guts, stamina, vitality (CONTINUATION).

endure, *v.* last, remain, stand (CONTINUATION, REMAINDER); outlast, survive (EXISTENCE); tolerate, bear, undergo (SUPPORT, INEXCITABILITY, OCCURRENCE).

enemy, *n.* foe, archenemy, adversary (OPPOSITION, HOSTILITY).

ENERGY—*N.* **energy,** bang, birr, verve, zip, dash, vigor, endurance, fortitude, stamina, vim, vitality; enterprise, initiative; pep, go, getup-and-go, punch (*all colloq.*).

exertion, spurt, struggle, toil, labor, travail, effort, application, devotion.

energetic person: demon, Trojan, dynamo, human dynamo.

V. **energize,** vitalize, invigorate, reinvigorate, innervate, stimulate, pep up (*colloq.*), electrify, excite, animate, enliven.

exert oneself, struggle, toil, labor, work, travail, try, energize, spurt; address oneself, apply oneself, buckle down, devote oneself.

Adj. **energetic,** aggressive, demoniac, dynamic, lively, sappy, strenuous, vibrant, vigorous, vital, zippy (*colloq.*), brisk, enterprising.

tireless, indefatigable, untiring, unwearied, weariless, unfailing, inexhaustible, unflagging; hardy, rugged, stalwart, sturdy, tough.

See also ACTIVITY, ATTEMPT, FORCE, POWER, STRENGTH, UNDERTAKING. *Antonyms*—See FATIGUE, INACTIVITY, WEAKNESS.

enervate, v. exhaust, tire, weary (FATIGUE).

enervated, adj. exhausted, spent, limp (WEAKNESS).

enforce, v. execute, implement, administer (FORCE, RESULT); compel, force (OBEDIENCE).

engage, v. employ, hire, place (SITUATION); charter, rent (BORROWING); promise, bind oneself, guarantee (PROMISE); agree, covenant, contract (COMPACT); attach, fasten, lock (JUNCTION, FASTENING); bespeak, reserve (EARLINESS).

engage in, v. embark on, launch (*or* plunge) into (UNDERTAKING).

engagement, n. troth, marriage contract, betrothment (BETROTHAL); commitment, undertaking (PROMISE); employment, placement, hire (SITUATION); date, appointment (ARRIVAL); combat, contest, encounter (FIGHTING).

engaging, adj. charming, winsome, attractive (LOVE, ATTRACTION).

engender, v. produce, beget, generate, give rise to, bring about (PRODUCTION).

engineering, n. construction, building (BUILDING).

ENGRAVING—N. **engraving,** chiseling, chalcography, xylography, etching, aquatint, dry point, cerography, glyptography; photo-engraving, heliotypography, heliotypy, heliogravure, photogravure, rotogravure, lithography.

impression, print, pull, proof, reprint, engraving, plate; steelplate, copper-plate; etching, acquatint, mezzotint; cut, woodcut; xylograph; cerograph, intaglio, glyphograph, photogravure, rotogravure, rotograph, photoengraving, half tone, heliotype, heliograph; lithograph; illustration, picture; positive, negative.

V. **engrave,** chase, enchase, intaglio, grave, stipple, etch, lithograph, print, imprint.

Adj. **engraved,** graven, cut, incised, sculptured, chalcographic.

See also FINE ARTS, PRINTING.

---

engrossed, adj. lost, rapt, absorbed (INATTENTION).

engrossing, adj. absorbing, enthralling, fascinating (INTERESTINGNESS).

enhance, v. intensify, strengthen,

augment (HEIGHT, INCREASE); boom, appreciate (VALUE).

enigma, n. riddle, puzzle, cryptogram (MYSTERY).

enigmatic, adj. oracular, Delphic, cryptic (MYSTERY).

enjoy, v. like, be fond of, dote on (LIKING); delight in, joy in, relish (PLEASURE, HAPPINESS).

enjoyable, adj. likeable, preferable, relishable (LIKING); delightful, delectable, pleasurable (PLEASURE).

enjoyment, n. fruition, gratification, thrill (PLEASURE).

enlarge, v. pad, amplify, bulk (INCREASE).

enlarge on, v. develop, dilate on, expatiate on (WORDINESS, INCREASE).

enlightening, adj. instructive, informative, edifying (TEACHING).

enliven, v. vitalize, vivify, animate (LIFE).

enmesh, v. snare, ensnare, entrap (TRAP).

enmity, n. antagonism, ill will, animosity (HOSTILITY, OPPOSITION).

ennoble, v. dignify, elevate, exalt (NOBILITY).

enormous, adj. huge, immense, tremendous (SIZE, GREATNESS).

enough, adj. sufficient, adequate, ample (SUFFICIENCY).

enraged, adj. angered, aroused, furious (ANGER).

enroll, v. sign up, register, subscribe (SIGNATURE); serve, enlist (FIGHTING); matriculate, become a student (LEARNING).

ensemble, n. choir, chorus, glee club (SINGING); orchestra, band (MUSICIAN); outfit, costume (CLOTHING).

ensign, n. flag, banner, standard (INDICATION); naval officer, petty officer, lieutenant (SAILOR).

enslave, v. bind, indenture, yoke (SLAVERY).

enslavement, n. bondage, chains, helotry (SLAVERY).

ensnare, v. snare, entrap, enmesh (TRAP).

ensue, v. develop, follow, eventuate (RESULT, OCCURRENCE).

entail, v. require, demand, cause (NECESSITY); involve, tangle, entangle (INDIRECTNESS).

entangle, v. tangle, snarl, embroil (CONFUSION); ensnare, enmesh (TRAP).

enter, v. come in, immigrate, go in (INGRESS); register, record, inscribe (LIST, RECORD).

enterprise, n. endeavor, venture (UNDERTAKING); company, concern, firm (BUSINESS).

enterprising, adj. adventurous, venturesome, resourceful (UN-

DERTAKING); progressive, advancing (PROGRESS).

entertain, v. divert, beguile (AMUSEMENT); enthrall, absorb, pique (INTERESTINGNESS); harbor, cherish, imagine (THOUGHT).

entertainer, n. artist, performer (ACTOR).

entertainment, n. diversion, fun, sport (AMUSEMENT, PLEASURE).

ENTHUSIASM—N. enthusiasm, ardor, fervor, fire, red heat, white heat, zeal, perfervor; zealotry, rabidity, fanaticism; wholeheartedness, heartiness, élan (F.), ebullience, ebullition, esprit de corps (F.), verve; dithyramb, rhapsody, ecstasies; furor scribendi (L.), furor loquendi (L.).

craze, fad, rage, mania, monomania, furor.

enthusiast, zealot, fanatic, monomaniac, faddist, rhapsodist, rooter (colloq.).

V. be enthusiastic, enthuse (colloq.), rhapsodize, rave, cheer, root (colloq.), whoop, fanaticize.

make enthusiastic, enthuse (colloq.), fire, inspire, fanaticize, impassion.

Adj. enthusiastic, enthused (colloq.), ardent, fervent, fervid, redhot, white-hot, zealous, zealotic, perfervid; overenthusiastic, overzealous, rabid, fanatical, monomaniacal; crazy about, wild about (both colloq.); wholehearted, whole-souled, hearty, ebullient; dithyrambic, lyrical, rhapsodic.

See also DESIRE, EAGERNESS, FEELING, HOPE, WILLINGNESS. Antonyms —See BOREDOM, DULLNESS, INSENSITIVITY, UNWILLINGNESS.

---

entirety, n. sum, total, aggregate (COMPLETENESS).

entitle, v. authorize, allow, warrant (POWER, PRIVILEGE, RIGHT); term, subtitle, style (TITLE).

entity, n. individual, single, singleton (UNITY); being, subsistence (EXISTENCE).

entrance, n. ingression, introgression, entry (INGRESS).

entrance hall, n. entranceway, corridor, hallway (INGRESS, PASSAGE).

entreat, v. beg, beseech, implore (BEGGING).

entrust, v. commend, commit, confide (GIVING).

entry, n. ingression, introgression, entrance (INGRESS); hallway, vestibule, lobby (PASSAGE); rival, entrant, contestant (ATTEMPT).

entwine, v. wind, intertwine, interweave (WINDING).

enumerate, v. count, numerate, reckon (NUMBER); name, specify, cite (NAME, TALK).

envelop, v. encompass, encircle, surround (ENVIRONMENT, EXTERIORITY); superimpose, overlay, overspread (COVERING); wrap, wind, muffle (ROLL).

envelope, n. wrapping, wrapper, jacket (COVERING).

envenom, v. poison, taint, venom (POISON); embitter, venom, exacerbate (ANGER).

enviable, adj. desirable, covetable (DESIRE).

envious, adj. jealous, jaundiced, grudging (DISSATISFACTION).

ENVIRONMENT—N. environment, surroundings, scenery, milieu, entourage, circumjacencies, circumambiency, terrain, suburbs, purlieus, precincts, environs, neighborhood, vicinage, vicinity; background, setting, scene, mise en scène (F.), atmosphere, aura.

scenery (on a stage), décor, mise en scène (F.), scene, scenes, setting.

scene (of action, etc.), theater, stage, locale, arena, sphere, panorama, kaleidoscope, phantasmagoria, phantasmagory.

[science of environment] ecology, bionomics, anthroposociology, euthenics.

[that which surrounds] belt, boundary, cincture, circle, bower, envelope, girdle, ring, wreath, cordon, aura.

V. surround, bathe, beleaguer, belt, beset, besiege, bound, box, cincture, circle, circumfuse, circumscribe, circumvallate, compass, corral, embower, encircle, encompass, endue, engulf, enswathe, entrench, envelop, gird, girdle, girth, hedge in, hem in (around or about), invest, ring, siege, swathe, wreathe.

Adj. environmental, environal, environic, suburban, neighboring; ecological, bionomic; atmospheric, aural.

surrounding, beleaguering, besetting, circumfusive, circumscriptive, encircling, encompassing, engulfing, enveloping, circumambient, circumfluent, circumfluous.

Adv., phrases. around, about, on every side, on all sides.

See also BOUNDARY, NEARNESS, RESTRAINT, WALL. Antonyms—See DISTANCE, INTERJACENCE.

---

environs, n. vicinity, neighborhood, surroundings (ENVIRONMENT, NEARNESS).

envisage, v. visualize, envision, image (IDEA, IMAGINATION).

envision, v. reckon on, contemplate, foresee (EXPECTATION); envisage, imagine, conceive (IMAGINATION).

envoy, n. ambassador, minister, emissary (DEPUTY, MESSENGER); representative, vicar, delegate (SUBSTITUTION).

envy, n. jealousy, heartburn, heartburning (DISSATISFACTION).

envy, v. covet, grudge, begrudge (DESIRE).

ephemeral, adj. evanescent, fugitive, fleeting (DISAPPEARANCE, IMPERMANENCE).

epicure, n. gourmet, gastronomer, gourmand (FOOD); hedonist, epicurean (PLEASURE).

epidemic, adj. catching, infectious, communicable (DISEASE); pandemic, rife, widespread (PRESENCE).

epigram, n. saying, quip, quirk, mot (STATEMENT).

epilogue, n. finale, peroration, swan song (END).

episode, n. occasion, affair, circumstance (OCCURRENCE).

EPISTLE—N. epistle, missive, letter, communication, line (colloq.), note, dispatch, message; decretal (eccl.), decretal epistle, rescript, bull (papal), encyclical (papal); post card, card, postal card, postal; love letter, billet-doux; form letter, circular letter, circular.

mail, letters, correspondence, writings, communication, epistolography.

letter writer, correspondent, epistler, epistolarian, epistolographer.

philately, timbrology, deltiology.

V. write to, communicate with, keep in touch with, correspond with; epistolize, correspond.

See also INFORMATION, MESSENGER, PRINTING, WRITING, WRITTEN SYMBOL.

epitaph, n. legend, inscription, epigraph (WRITING).

epithets, n. scurrility, blasphemy, invective (MALEDICTION).

epitomize, v. exemplify, embody, typify (COPY).

epoch, n. era, eon, age (TIME).

EQUALITY—N. equality, equivalence, parallelism, evenness, parity, par, identity, coequality, equipollence, homology, isochronism, isonomy, isopolity; equiponderance, equipoise, equidistance; equalitarianism, egalitarianism.

equal, coequal, peer, compeer, rival, match, equivalent, tit for tat, quid pro quo (L.), parallel, co-ordinate, equipollent, homologue.

tie, draw, dead heat, stalemate, even match, drawn game.

V. equal, match, keep pace with, run abreast; come up to; balance, tie, parallel, commeasure, compare, equiponderate, equipoise; rival, emulate.

equalize, equate, even, even up, level, balance, match, handicap, trim, co-ordinate, poise; strike a balance, equiponderate, equipoise, isochronize.

Adj. equal, equalized, equated, coequal, co-ordinate, matching, parallel, square, even; isonomic, isonomous, isopolitical; equidistant, abreast; same, identical.

equivalent, comparable, equipollent, equipotential, homologous, tantamount, commensurate, commeasurable, equiponderant.

tied, even, drawn, neck and neck, in a dead heat; evenly matched.

Adv., phrases. equally, alike, evenly; pari passu (L.), ceteris paribus (L.).

See also IMPARTIALITY, SIMILARITY, SUBSTITUTION, WEIGHT. Antonyms—See DIFFERENCE, INEQUALITY.

equanimity, n. equability, poise, composure (INEXCITABILITY).

equestrian, n. horse rider, horseman, jockey (HORSE, VEHICLE).

equilibrium, n. balance, counterpoise, equipoise (WEIGHT).

equine, adj. cabaline, horsy (HORSE).

equip, v. furnish, provide, supply (STORE, GIVING, PREPARATION, QUANTITY).

equipment, n. stores, supplies, provisions, furnishings, accouterments, outfit (STORE, QUANTITY).

equitable, adj. fair, just, equal (IMPARTIALITY); decent, ethical (PROPRIETY).

equivalent, adj. equal, comparable, even (EQUALITY).

equivocal, adj. ambiguous, amphibolic (AMBIGUITY).

era, n. epoch, age, generation (TIME).

eradicate, v. uproot, unroot, extirpate (ELIMINATION).

erase, v. efface, scratch out, rub out (ELIMINATION).

erect, adj. upright, cocked, perpendicular (POSTURE, VERTICALITY).

erect, v. build, construct, put up (BUILDING); elevate, raise, lift (ELEVATION, VERTICALITY); stand, cock (POSTURE).

erode, *v.* corrode, waste, eat away (DESTRUCTION).

erotic, *adj.* amorous, Paphian, romantic (LOVE); erogenous, aphrodisiac, carnal (SEX).

err, *v.* be in error, be mistaken, be deceived (MISTAKE); sin, do wrong, transgress (SIN).

errand, *n.* mission, task, assignment (COMMISSION).

errand boy, *n.* bellboy, bellhop (*slang*), page (MESSENGER).

errant, *adj.* erratic, fugitive, planetary (WANDERING); wayward, aberrant, erring (IMMORALITY); sinning, offending (SIN).

erratic, *adj.* fitful, spasmodic, capricious (IRREGULARITY, CAPRICE); errant, fugitive, planetary (WANDERING); queer, outlandish, eccentric (UNUSUALNESS).

erroneous, *adj.* untrue, false, faulty (MISTAKE).

error, *n.* inaccuracy, solecism, blunder (MISTAKE).

erudite, *adj.* learned, cultured, educated (LEARNING).

erupt, *v.* explode, rupture, blow up (BLOWING); discharge, break out (EGRESS).

eruption, *n.* outbreak, outburst, explosion, blast, blow-up (VIOLENCE); blotch, breakout, acne (SKIN).

escapade, *n.* adventure, lark, antic (EXPERIENCE, AMUSEMENT).

escape, *n.* breakout, outbreak, flight (DEPARTURE).

escape, *v.* flee, run away, skip (DEPARTURE).

escaped, *adj.* at large, loose, unloosed (FREEDOM).

escort, *n.* guard, convoyer, warden, company, squire (PROTECTION, ACCOMPANIMENT).

escort, *v.* accompany, convoy, squire (ACCOMPANIMENT).

esoteric, *adj.* cabalistic, occult, mystical, orphic (CONCEALMENT).

esoterica, *n.* erotica, rhyparography, pornography, curiosa (TREATISE, SEX).

especially, *adv.* principally, particularly, notably (SUPERIORITY).

espionage, *n.* spying, espial, counterintelligence (LOOKING).

essay, *n.* endeavor, effort (ATTEMPT); theme, dissertation, thesis (TREATISE, WRITING).

essence, *n.* distillation, pith, quintessence (EXTRACTION, MATERIALITY); substance, gist, burden (MEANING, CONTENTS, IDEA); body, core, crux (PART); perfume, balm, cologne (ODOR).

essential, *adj.* necessary, needed, needful (NECESSITY); fundamental, key, material (IMPORTANCE).

establish, *v.* locate, place, situate (LOCATION, PLACE); constitute organize (BEGINNING); authenti cate, circumstantiate (PROOF).

establishment, *n.* company, con cern, firm (BUSINESS).

estate, *n.* property, substance capital (OWNERSHIP); manor acreage, property (LAND); leg acy, bequest, inheritance (WILL INHERITANCE); caste, stratum, station (SOCIAL CLASS).

esteem, *n.* deference, homage, honor (RESPECT).

esteem, *v.* honor, regard, revere (RESPECT); admire, look up to (APPROVAL); value, appreciate, treasure (VALUE).

estimable, *adj.* respectable, august, decent (RESPECT); honorable, creditable, palmary (FAME).

estimate, *n.* appraisal, appraisement, valuation (JUDGMENT).

estimate, *v.* size up (*colloq.*), rate, appraise (SIZE); consider, deem (OPINION); calculate, figure, tally (COMPUTATION); evaluate, assess, assay (VALUE).

estrange, *v.* antagonize, disaffect, alienate (HOSTILITY, HATRED).

eternal, *adj.* immortal, deathless, imperishable (ENDLESSNESS); perpetual, ceaseless, everlasting (CONTINUATION, ENDLESSNESS, TIME).

eternity, *n.* infinity, endless time, infinite time (TIME); immortality, athanasia, imperishability (ENDLESSNESS).

ethereal, *adj.* airy, rarefied, spiritual (SPIRITUALITY); dainty, exquisite, subtle (WEAKNESS); shadowy, gaseous, vaporous (NONEXISTENCE); ghostly, unearthly, unworldly (SUPERNATURALISM).

ethical, *adj.* virtuous, honorable, moral (RULE, MORALITY); decent, equitable, just (PROPRIETY).

ethics, *n.* morals, moral code, moral principles (MORALITY); convention, conventionalities (PROPRIETY).

etiquette, *n.* amenities, civilities, proprieties (COURTESY, HABIT).

eulogy, *n.* panegyric, encomium, tribute (PRAISE).

eunuch, *n.* androgyne, *castrato* (*It.*), gelding (CELIBACY).

euphonious, *adj.* melodious, melodic, musical (MELODY).

euphony, *n.* consonance, concord, melody, musicality (HARMONY, SWEETNESS).

evacuate, *v.* leave, abandon, desert (DEPARTURE).

evade, *v.* avoid, elude, get away from (AVOIDANCE, DEPARTURE).

evaluate, *v.* appraise, rate, assess (VALUE).

evanescent, *adj.* ephemeral, fugitive, impermanent, fleeting (DISAPPEARANCE, IMPERMANENCE).

evangelist, *n.* preacher, evangelizer, pulpiteer (PREACHING).

evaporate, *v.* vanish, dissolve, disappear (DISAPPEARANCE); desiccate, dehumidify, dehydrate (DRYNESS).

eve, *n.* eventide, sunset, sundown (EVENING).

even, *adj.* level, plane, flat (SMOOTHNESS); flush, horizontal (FLATNESS); straight, direct, true (STRAIGHTNESS); uniform, homogeneous, consistent (UNIFORMITY); balanced, proportional (SHAPE); equal, matching (EQUALITY); tied, drawn (EQUALITY, ATTEMPT); even-tempered, level-headed (CALMNESS).

even, *v.* level, smooth, grade, flatten, roll, plane (UNIFORMITY, SMOOTHNESS, FLATNESS); equalize, even up, balance (EQUALITY).

evenhanded, *adj.* fair, just, equitable, equal (IMPARTIALITY).

EVENING—N. evening, eve, even (*poetic*), decline of day, close of day, eventide, vespers (*eccl.*), sunset, sundown.

twilight, dusk, gloaming, nightfall, gloam (*poetic*), crepuscule, crepuscula.

night, nightfall, nighttime, nighttide; midnight, noontide; night owl (*colloq.*).

Adj. evening, vesper, vespertine, vespertinal.

twilight, crepuscular, crepusculine, crepusculous.

night, nocturnal, midnight, nightly; noctambulant, noctambulous, noctivagant, noctivagous, noctiflorous, noctilucous, noctipotent; overtaken by night, benighted.

See also BLACKNESS, DARKNESS. *Antonyms*—See BEGINNING, LIGHT, MORNING.

event, *n.* milestone, incident, happening (OCCURRENCE).

even-tempered, *adj.* evenminded, level-headed, equanimous (CALMNESS).

eventful, *adj.* momentous, memorable, fateful (OCCURRENCE, IMPORTANCE, RESULT).

eventual, *adj.* ultimate, final, later (FUTURE); indirect, secondary, vicarious (RESULT).

eventuality, *n.* contingency, tossup (*colloq.*), chance (POSSIBILITY).

eventuate, *v.* ensue, eventualize, follow (RESULT).

ever, *adv.* always, evermore, forever (UNIFORMITY, ENDLESSNESS).

everlasting, *adj.* immortal, eternal, perpetual (CONTINUATION).

everybody, *n.* all, the whole, everyone (COMPLETENESS).

everyday, *adj.* common, frequent, familiar (HABIT); daily, quotidian, per diem (MORNING).

everything, *n.* all, the whole (COMPLETENESS).

everywhere, *adv.* far and near, from pole to pole, to the four winds (SPACE)

evict, *v.* expel, oust, dispossess (DISMISSAL).

evidence, *n.* demonstration, testimony, documentation (PROOF).

evidence, *v.* denote, connote, designate (INDICATION).

evident, *adj.* obvious, apparent, patent (CLARITY, VISIBILITY).

evil, *adj.* baneful, wicked, malefic (WICKEDNESS, HARM).

evil, *n.* maleficence, malignancy, sin, vice (WICKEDNESS).

evildoer, *n.* wrongdoer, malefactor, misdoer (WICKEDNESS).

evil eye, *n.* curse, whammy (*slang*), hex, jinx (HARM, MISFORTUNE).

evil spirit, *n.* demon, fiend, devil (SUPERNATURAL BEINGS).

evince, *v.* manifest, signify, suggest (INDICATION).

evoke, *v.* call forth, invoke, elicit (EXTRACTION, SUMMONS).

evolution, *n.* growth, development, maturation (UNFOLDMENT).

exact, *adj.* accurate, precise, nice (RIGHT); specific, definite, unequivocal (BOUNDARY); literal, verbal, verbatim (MEANING).

exact, *v.* extort, squeeze, wrest (FORCE).

EXAGGERATION—N. exaggeration, magnification, overstatement, hyperbole (*rhet.*), amplification, aggrandizement, embroidery; extravagance, stretch, caricature; yarn (*colloq.*), traveler's tale, fish story (*colloq.*), tall story (*colloq.*); puffery, boasting, rant.

V. exaggerate, magnify, amplify, aggrandize, overdo, overestimate, overstate, hyperbolize (*rhet.*), overdraw, caricature, stretch a point, draw a long bow (*colloq.*); overcolor, romance, romanticize, heighten, embroider, color; puff, brag, boast.

Adj. exaggerated, magnified, etc. (see *Verbs*); tall (*colloq.*), bouncing, vaulting, steep (*slang*), overdone, overwrought, hyperbolical (*rhet.*), extravagant.

See also BOASTING, FALSEHOOD, INCREASE, MISREPRESENTATION, OVERESTIMATION. *Antonyms*—See DECREASE, DETRACTION.

exalt, *v.* ennoble. elevate, glorify (NOBILITY, MAGNIFICENCE, ELEVATION); fill with pride, swell, inflate (PRIDE).

exalted, *adj.* august, honorable (NOBILITY); proud, lofty, immodest (PRIDE); self-important, pompous, pretentious (IMPORTANCE).

EXAMINATION—N. examination, check, checkup, canvass, audit, review, inspection, study, scrutiny, survey, *apercu* (F.), *coup d'oeil* (F.), observation, reconnaissance, reconnoiter, assay, analysis.

medical examination, palpation, auscultation; post-mortem, autopsy, necropsy; bacterioscopy, microscopy.

test, quiz, college boards, American boards, orals, practical.

examiner, checker, canvasser, auditor, inspector, student, scrutineer, scrutator, surveyor, observer, assayer, analyst, tester.

V. examine, check, canvass, audit, inspect, overlook, scrutinize, scrutinate, sift, screen, view; assay, analyze, test for, survey, observe, reconnoiter, prospect, search, spy, study, review; test, quiz, question.

See also INQUIRY, LEARNING, LOOKING, SEARCH, TEST. *Antonyms*—See ANSWER, DISCOVERY.

example, *n.* case, illustration, instance (COPY); notice, lesson (WARNING).

exasperate, *v.* provoke, rile (*colloq.*), annoy (ANNOYANCE).

excavate, *v.* mine, quarry, shovel, furrow, gouge, groove (DIGGING, HOLLOW).

excavation, *n.* hole, pit, ditch (DIGGING, OPENING).

exceed, *v.* better, surpass, transcend (EXCESS, ENCROACHMENT, SUPERIORITY).

exceeding, *adj.* excessive, undue, unreasonable (EXTREMENESS).

excel, *v.* be superior, exceed, transcend (SUPERIORITY).

excellence, *n.* merit, virtue, quality (GOOD).

excellent, *adj.* good, ace, admirable (GOOD); superb, peerless, matchless (SUPERIORITY).

except, *prep.* save, saving, but (EXCLUSION).

exception, *n.* anomaly, irregularity (UNUSUALNESS); objection, demurral (OPPOSITION); privileged person, perquisitor, special case (PRIVILEGE).

exceptional, *adj.* unique, unprecedented, unheard-of (UNUSUAL-

NESS); first-class, fine, excellent (GOOD).

excerpt, *n.* extract, portion, quotation, citation, selection (PASSAGE, EXTRACTION, REPETITION).

excerpt, *v.* extract, select, cull (CHOICE).

EXCESS—N. excess, too much, glut, nimiety, overabundance, overflow, overplus, plethora, overstock, oversupply, redundance, superabundance, supererogation, superfluity, surfeit, surplus, surplusage; extra, spare, supernumerary; recrement, embarrassment of riches, *embarras des richesses* (F.), *embarras du choix* (F.), *toujours perdrix* (F.).

V. be in excess, be too much, superabound, overabound.

exceed, better, surpass, transcend, top, improve upon, outnumber; supererogate.

oversupply, deluge, flood, glut, load, overflow, overstock, satiate, saturate, surfeit, swamp.

Adj. excess, excessive, overflowing, superfluous, surplus, superabundant, in excess, *de trop* (F.); excrescent, extra, overabundant, plethoric, recrementitious, redundant, spare, supererogatory, supernumerary.

See also ENCROACHMENT, EXTREMENESS, INTEMPERANCE, UNNECESSITY. *Antonyms*—See ABSENCE, FULLNESS, INSUFFICIENCY, MODERATENESS.

excessively, *adv.* exceedingly, immoderately, inordinately (EXTREMENESS).

EXCHANGE—N. exchange, interchange, commutation, conversion, reciprocation, substitution; *quid pro quo* (L.), give-and-take, intercourse, tit for tat; permutation, transmutation, transposition, shuffle; retaliation, reprisal; retort, repartee.

V. exchange, interchange, commute, convert, substitute; transpose, counterchange, change; give and take, bandy, retaliate, retort, requite, return.

barter, truck, trade, traffic, swap, buy and sell, market, carry on (*or* ply) a trade, deal in.

reciprocate, shuttle, seesaw, give in return.

bargain, drive (make, *or* strike) a bargain, negotiate, bid for; haggle, stickle, higgle, chaffer, dicker; beat down, underbid.

Adj. reciprocal, mutual, give-

and-take, correlative, correspondent, equivalent.

Adv., phrases. **interchangeably,** by turns, turn and turn about, alternately, in succession; in exchange, vice versa, conversely.

See also BUSINESS, CHANGE, CHANGEABLENESS, EQUALITY, PURCHASE, RECOMPENSE, RETALIATION, SALE, SUBSTITUTION, TRANSFER. *Antonyms*—See CONTINUATION, HOLD.

EXCITEMENT—N. excitement, agitation, ferment, fire, flurry, fluster, flutter, frenzy; intoxication, thrill, titillation, tingle, twitter, tizzy, dither, whirl; effervescence, delirium, ebullition, ecstasy; fever, febricity, fury, hysteria, red heat, white heat, oestrus, furor; dramatics, melodramatics, sensationalism, yellow journalism; hoopla, to-do, stir, racket, orgasm; rage, rampage, seethe, simmer.

excitant, stimulant, stimulus, intoxicant, provocation, titillant, thrill, sting, prod, whip, goad.

[*excited person*] **frenetic,** ecstatic, menad (*woman*), berserker (*Scand. myth.*).

V. **excite,** fire, inflame, inspire, intoxicate, provoke, stimulate, rouse, arouse, awake, wake; ferment, electrify, commove, galvanize, frenzy; thrill, titillate, tickle, sting, pique, whet; agitate, flurry, fluster, flustrate, flutter, perturb, ruffle.

be excited, effervesce, bubble, bubble over, rave, ferment, foam, flutter, seethe, simmer, throb, tingle, thrill, twitter; rage, rampage, run amuck, run riot, storm.

dramatize, melodramatize, glamorize, romanticize.

Adj. **excited,** ablaze, afire, aflame, fired, red-hot, white-hot, electrified, galvanized, galvanic, inflamed; intoxicated, drunk, beside oneself, delirious, ecstatic, wild, thrilled, athrill.

frantic, frenetic, furibund, frenzied, hysterical, wrought up, worked up, overwrought, demoniacal; feverish, febrile.

excitable, agitable, combustible, fiery, hot-blooded, hotheaded, inflammable, nervous, passionate, vascular.

seething, simmering, ebullient, bubbling, bubbly, effervescent; throbbing, tingling, tingly, atingle, twittering, twittery, atwitter, agog, charged, emotionally charged, hectic.

raging, rampaging, rampageous, rampant, flaming, furious, storming, stormy.

exciting, breath-taking, hair-raising, spine-tingling, stirring,

wild and woolly, hectic, rip-roaring; sensational, yellow, purple, lurid, melodramatic, dramatic.

stimulating, provocative, heady, intoxicating, electrifying, electric, galvanic, inflaming, inflammatory.

piquant, racy, salty, zestful; thrilling, titillating, tickling, pungent.

See also AGITATION, BAD TEMPER, COMMOTION, FEELING, MOTIVATION, NERVOUSNESS, VIOLENCE. *Antonyms* —See BOREDOM, CALMNESS, INDIFFERENCE, INEXCITABILITY, INSENSIBILITY.

---

exclaim, *v.* state, utter, ejaculate (STATEMENT).

exclamation, *n.* expletive, interjection, cry (VOICE, WORD).

EXCLUSION—N. **exclusion,** debarment, occlusion, lockout, excommunication; prohibition, prevention, preclusion, boycott, embargo; ostracism, coventry.

V. **exclude,** bar, shut out, keep out, debar, lock out, close out, leave out, turn away, **refuse admittance,** occlude; prohibit, prevent, preclude; excommunicate, ostracize, blackball, boycott, embargo.

Adj. **exclusive,** occlusive, preclusive, prohibitive, preventive; select, restrictive, cliquish, clannish.

Prep. **except,** save, saving, but, excepting, exclusive of.

See also DENIAL, PREVENTION, SECLUSION. *Antonyms*—See HOLD, INCLUSION.

---

exclusively, *adv.* only, alone, solely (UNITY).

EXCRETION—N. **excretion,** discharge, elimination, exudation, secernment (*physiol.*), secretion, effusion, egestion, ejaculation, eccrisis, blennorrhea, mucorrhea, flux, leucorrhea; defecation, urination, menstruation, perspiration.

excreta, waste, waste matter, secreta, egesta, exudate, dejecta; afterbirth, secundines (*pl.*), lochia.

secretion, hormone, endocrine, autacoid, chalone; secretin, thyroxin, adrenalin, insulin, bile, gall, gastrin, colostrum.

mucus, phlegm, pituite, rheum, snivel, snot.

science of secretions: endocrinology, eccrinology.

V. **excrete,** eliminate, discharge, egest, ejaculate, exude, exudate, expel, evacuate, pass; defecate, secern (*physiol.*), secrete, produce, elaborate; exhale, emanate.

Adj. excretive, excretory, egestive, eliminative, secretive, menstrual, eccritic.

mucous, pituitary, pituitous, muculent, phlegmy, rheumy.

See also ELIMINATION, PERSPIRATION, REMOVAL, THROW. *Antonyms* —See ACCEPTANCE, RECEIVING.

excruciating, *adj.* grueling, torturous, torturesome (PAIN, TORTURE).

excursion, *n.* outing, picnic, expedition (TRAVELING).

excusable, *adj.* defensible, justifiable, pardonable (FORGIVENESS).

excuse, *n.* apology, justification, extenuation (ATONEMENT); rationalization, alibi (*colloq.*), defense (FORGIVENESS).

excuse, *v.* forgive, pardon, absolve (FORGIVENESS, ACQUITTAL); exempt, release, relieve (FREEDOM).

execute, *v.* put into effect, administer, enforce (RESULT); meet, carry out, perform (ACTION, OBSERVANCE); play, perform, render (MUSICIAN); electrocute, gas, hang (KILLING).

executive, *n.* businessman, entrepreneur, industrialist (BUSINESS).

exemplify, *v.* illustrate, embody, epitomize (COPY).

exempt, *adj.* immune, privileged, excused (FREEDOM, PRIVILEGE).

exempt, *v.* excuse, release, discharge, relieve (FREEDOM).

exercise, *n.* performance, pursuit, discharge (ACTION); lesson, lecture, recitation (TEACHING); daily dozen, workout, calisthenics (GYMNASTICS).

exertion, *n.* toil, labor, effort (ENERGY, ATTEMPT).

exhale, *v.* breathe out, expel (*or* emit) the breath, expire (BREATH).

exhaust, *v.* use, up, consume, deplete (USE, ABSENCE); overfatigue, overtire, sap (FATIGUE, WEAKNESS).

exhaustion, *n.* consumption, depletion, expenditure (USE); enervation, debility (WEAKNESS).

exhaustive, *adj.* comprehensive, embracive, all-inclusive (INCLUSION).

exhibit, *v.* expose, feature, present (DISPLAY); show off, display, advertise (OSTENTATION).

exhibition, *n.* spectacle, exposition, fair (DISPLAY, APPEARANCE).

exhibitionist, *n.* show-off, swaggerer, vulgarian (OSTENTATION).

exhilarate, *v.* inspirit, invigorate, quicken (LIFE).

exhort, *v.* urge, press, spur (URGING); caution, admonish (WARNING).

exhume, *v.* disentomb, disinter, resurrect (DIGGING).

exile, *n.* outcast, deportee, displaced person, D.P., expatriate; deportation, expatriation (DISMISSAL).

exile, *v.* expatriate, banish, deport (DISMISSAL, PUNISHMENT).

EXISTENCE—*N.* existence, being, entity, subsistence, prevalence, survival, life; coexistence, preexistence.

V. exist, be, subsist, live, breathe; stand, lie; occur, prevail, obtain; coexist, pre-exist, antedate, predate; smolder, be latent, be dormant, outlast, survive, continue, endure, remain, stay.

Adj. existent, existing, being, subsistent, extant; current, prevalent, prevailing; coexistent, preexistent; smoldering, latent, dormant.

See also LIFE, MATERIALITY, OCCURRENCE, PRESENCE, REALITY. *Antonyms*—See DEATH, END, NONEXISTENCE, UNREALITY.

exit, *n.* outlet, avenue, vent (EGRESS); exodus, stampede (DEPARTURE).

exonerate, *v.* absolve, clear, exculpate (ACQUITTAL).

exorbitant, *adj.* excessive, extravagant, outrageous (EXTREMENESS, UNREASONABLENESS).

exotic, *adj.* outland, outside, peregrine (IRRELATION); strange, unfamiliar (UNUSUALNESS).

expand, *v.* swell, distend, inflate; expatiate on, extend (INCREASE, SWELLING); unravel, open (UNFOLDMENT).

expanse, *n.* tract, area, extent (LAND, SPACE); breadth, amplitude (WIDTH).

expansion, *n.* distention, dilation, dilatation (INCREASE); growth, development, maturation, evolution (UNFOLDMENT).

expansive, *adj.* expansional, expansile, dilatant (INCREASE); uninhibited, unrepressed, unsuppressed, unreserved (FREEDOM).

expatriate, *n.* emigrant, evacuee, outcast (DEPARTURE, DISMISSAL).

expectant, *adj.* hopeful, eager, impatient (EXPECTATION); pregnant, *enceinte* (F.), big with child (PREGNANCY).

EXPECTATION—*N.* expectation, expectance, prospect, anticipation, calculation, contemplation, view, presumption, hope, trust, confidence, assurance, reliance.

patience, forbearance, longanimity, fortitude, bovinity.

impatience, haste, choler.

V. expect, look for, look out for, look forward to; hope for, anticipate, bargain for; have in prospect, keep in view; contemplate, calculate, reckon on, foresee, prepare for, envision, apprehend, drool.

wait, bide, attend, bide one's time, mark time, be patient, forbear; wait for, watch for, abide, lie in wait for, waylay, ambush, lurk, hover; delay, tarry; line up, wait in line, queue up; wait in suspense, dangle, be left hanging.

be impatient, be unable to wait, itch, chafe; lose patience with, tire of, weary of.

Adj. expectant, hopeful, anticipant, anticipatory; breathless, eager, impatient, in suspense, on tenterhooks, in expectation; anxious, apprehensive.

expected, anticipated, awaited, contemplated, counted on, foreseen, reckoned on, logical, probable, in prospect, prospective, future, coming; in view, on the horizon, impending.

patient, forbearing, longanimous, long-suffering, meek, fortitudinous, bovine.

impatient, itching, chafing, choleric, testy; quick, hasty.

Adv., phrases. expectantly, on the watch, on the alert, on edge (colloq.), with bated breath.

See also CERTAINTY, DEPENDABILITY, EAGERNESS, FUTURE, HOPE, NERVOUSNESS, PREDICTION. Antonyms—See DISAPPOINTMENT, HOPELESSNESS, SUDDENNESS, SURPRISE.

EXPEDIENCE—N. expedience or expediency, fitness, propriety, efficiency, utility, advantage, opportunity; opportunism, policy.

V. be expedient, suit, fit, befit, suit the occasion (or purpose).

Adj. expedient, advisable, wise, acceptable; convenient; worth while, meet, fit, fitting, due, proper, opportune, advantageous, suitable.

practicable, feasible, doable, performable, achievable, attainable, possible; usable.

See also ADVANTAGE, POSSIBILITY, PROPRIETY, TIMELINESS, USE, WISDOM. Antonyms—See IMPOSSIBILITY, INEXPEDIENCE, UNTIMELINESS, USELESSNESS.

expedient, adj. judicious, discreet, politic (EXPEDIENCE, WISDOM); ad hoc (L.), expediential (PURPOSE).

expedient, n. vehicle, way, ways and means (MEANS).

expedite, v. speed up, shoot through, precipitate (SPEED).

expedition, n. outing, excursion, junket (TRAVELING); campaign, jehad (Moham.), crusade (FIGHTING); expeditiousness, alacrity, dispatch (SPEED).

expel, v. oust, dispossess, evict (DISMISSAL, PROPULSION); exude, evacuate, pass (EXCRETION, THROW).

expendable, adj. dispensable, inessential, superfluous (UNNECESSITY).

EXPENDITURE—N. expenditure, expense, disbursement, outlay, outgo; consumption, dissipation, splurge, squander, waste.

cost, charge, amount, price, tariff, toll, bill, fee, dues; overcharge, surcharge; overhead, upkeep, budget.

price, rate, quotation, figure, selling price, list price, market price, markup, market value, valuation.

V. spend, expend, outlay, disburse, consume; lay out, shell out (slang), pay, fork out (slang), ante up (slang), run (or go) through, splurge.

price, set (or fix) a price, appraise, assess, tax, levy, impose, charge, demand, ask, exact.

overcharge, bleed (colloq.) skin (slang), fleece, extort, profiteer, gouge (colloq.); overtax, surcharge.

pay too much, pay dearly, pay through the nose (colloq.).

Adj. expensive, dear, high, high-priced, costly, sky-high, sumptuous, luxurious, extravagant; unreasonable, exorbitant, extortionate, excessive, immoderate, prohibitive.

See also EXCHANGE, GIVING, PAYMENT, PURCHASE, SALE, USE, WASTEFULNESS. Antonyms—See ECONOMY, INEXPENSIVENESS, RECEIVING, STINGINESS.

expense, n. disbursement, outlay, outgo (EXPENDITURE).

expensive, adj. dear, high, costly (EXPENDITURE).

EXPERIENCE—N. experience, training, seasoning, practice, background; worldly wisdom, worldliness, cosomopolitanism, sophistication; practicality, empiricism.

experienced person, veteran; empiric or empiricist; sophisticate, worldling, cosmopolite.

an experience, adventure, escapade, lark; nightmare, ordeal, trial, tribulation.

V. become experienced, practice, train in, train for, become seasoned; train, season.

experience, undergo, sustain, suffer, brave, encounter, go through; bear, endure; feel, apperceive, sense.

Adj. experienced, trained, seasoned, practiced, versed, wellversed, veteran, accustomed; worldly-wise, worldly, practical, sophisticated, cosmopolitan; skilled, capable, qualified.

experiential, empirical or empiric, practical.

See also ABILITY, KNOWLEDGE, LEARNING, OCCURRENCE, TEACHING. Antonyms—See CLUMSINESS, IMMATURITY, INEXPERIENCE.

experiment, n. check, trial, tryout (TEST).

expert, n. ace, specialist, master (ABILITY); connoisseur, authority (JUDGE).

expiate, v. redeem (ATONEMENT).

expire, v. run out, lapse, die (END, DEATH); breathe out, expel the breath (BREATH).

EXPLANATION—N. explanation, elucidation, enucleation, explication, exposition; construction, definition, interpretation; justification, rationalization; solution, resolution; account, accounting; diagram, outline.

commentary, note, gloss, comment, annotation, scholium, exegesis, epexegesis, apostil, postil; glossary, glossography; reflection, animadversion.

translation, rendering, rendition, construction, version, reading; rewording, paraphrase, sense, free translation; metaphrase, verbal (literal, or word-for-word) translation.

crib, pony, horse, trot.

commentator, glossographer, annotator, scholiast.

interpreter, hierophant, mystagogue, exponent; oneirocritic, oracle; translator, paraphraser, dragoman (Far East).

science of explanation: exegetics, hermeneutics.

V. explain, elucidate, enucleate, explicate, expound, account for, spell out; diagram, outline; construe, define, interpret; annotate, gloss; justify, rationalize; solve, resolve, riddle.

translate, construe, render, paraphrase, metaphrase; reword, rephrase, restate, rehash.

Adj. explanatory, explicative, expository, diagrammatic; exegetical, epexegetical, scholiastic.

explainable, accountable, construable, definable, explicable, justifiable, resolvable, solvable, soluble, translatable.

Adv., phrases. in explanation, that is, id est (L.), to wit, namely, videlicet (L.), in other words.

See also ANSWER, CLARITY, MEANING, TREATISE, UNDERSTANDING. Antonyms—See MISINTERPRETATION, UNCLEARNESS.

expletive, n. interjection, exclamation (WORD).

explicable, adj. explainable, accountable, construable (EXPLANATION).

explicit, adj. precise, categorical, specific (CLARITY).

explode, v. go off, detonate, blow up (VIOLENCE, BLOWING); burst out, jet, blaze (EGRESS); disprove, belie, discredit (DISPROOF, UNBELIEVINGNESS).

exploded, adj. refuted, discarded, rejected, discredited (MISTAKE).

exploit, n. deed, feat, stunt (ABILITY, COURAGE).

exploit, v. capitalize on, consume, profit by (USE).

explore, v. investigate, research, inquire (SEARCH).

explosion, n. outbreak, outburst, eruption (VIOLENCE); bang, report, salvo (LOUDNESS).

explosive, n. gunpowder, dynamite, T.N.T. (BLOWING, ARMS).

exponent, n. proponent, second, seconder (SUPPORT); interpreter, hierophant, mystagogue (EXPLANATION); symbol, sign, token (REPRESENTATION).

export, v. ship, smuggle out, freight (SENDING).

expose, v. show, reveal, bare (DISCLOSURE, DISPLAY); denude, uncover, strip (UNDRESS); report, betray, unmask (INFORMATION); subject, make liable (SLAVERY).

exposé, n. betrayal, exposure, exposal (DISCLOSURE).

exposed, adj. vulnerable, unprotected, accessible (WEAKNESS); windswept, bleak, raw (WIND).

exposition, n. exhibition, fair, pageant (DISPLAY); mart, market place, bazaar (STORE); tract, tractate, disquisition (TREATISE); elucidation, enucleation, explication (EXPLANATION).

exposure, n. betrayal, exposal, exposé (DISCLOSURE); nakedness, nudity, denudation (UNDRESS).

expound, v. explain, elucidate, explicate (EXPLANATION).

express, *adj.* considered, deliberate, designful, voluntary, willful, witting (PURPOSE); fast, velocious, accelerated, quick (SPEED).

express, *v.* couch, put, phrase (EXPRESSION, WORD); expel, press out, distill (EXTRACTION).

expressed, *adj.* stated, said, verbal (STATEMENT).

EXPRESSION—*N.* expression, phrase, locution, word, idiom, utterance, statement; verbalization, description, delineation, vocalization, vocalism, verbalism, vent, ventilation; conveyance, conveyal, communication, demonstration, exhibition.

style (*of expression*), phraseology, phrasing, wording, locution, vein, choice of words, language; accents, pronunciation, tone, terms, parlance, delivery, address, tongue.

expressiveness, eloquence, oratory, poetry, sentimentality, soulfulness.

art of expression: composition, rhetoric, oratory, elocution.

orator, elocutionist, rhetorician, rhetor.

V. **express,** couch, phrase, word, put, put in words, say, state, verbalize, describe, delineate, picture; reword, rephrase; voice, vocalize, speak, utter, ventilate, vent; write, indite, frame, draft; show, reveal, exhibit, tell, convey, communicate, demonstrate.

Adj. **expressive,** eloquent, Ciceronian, silver-tongued, soulful, sentimental, poetic, dithyrambic, oratorical; holophrastic, notional.

fluent, articulate, vocal, facile, glib, voluble.

rhetorical, oratorical, elocutionary, linguistic.

See also DESCRIPTION, DISCLOSURE, DISPLAY, LANGUAGE, PUBLICATION, STATEMENT, TALK, VOICE, WORD, WRITING. *Antonyms*—See DULLNESS.

---

expressionless, *adj.* empty, inexpressive, stupid (DULLNESS).

expulsion, *n.* ejection, dispossession, eviction (DISMISSAL).

expurgate, *v.* bowdlerize, censor, blue-pencil (CLEANNESS, ELIMINATION).

exquisite, *adj.* dainty, ethereal, subtle (WEAKNESS); beautiful, lovely (BEAUTY).

extant, *adj.* existent, existing, subsistent (EXISTENCE).

extemporaneous, *adj.* improvised, impromptu, offhand (NONPREPARATION).

extend, *v.* stretch, mantle, elongate (SPREAD, STRETCH); lengthen, prolong (LENGTH); elaborate on,

expatiate on (INCREASE); submit, advance (OFFER); pass, proceed, flow (PASSAGE).

extension, *n.* annex, wing, branch (BUILDING, STRETCH).

extensive, *adj.* wide, far-ranging, far-reaching (STRETCH); spacious, roomy, commodious (SPACE).

extent, *n.* breadth, amplitude, expanse (WIDTH); bulk, mass, magnitude (QUANTITY); range, reach, spread (STRETCH, DISTANCE); duration, continuance (TIME, LENGTH); territory, tract (SPACE).

extenuate, *v.* whitewash, gloss over, varnish (WHITENESS); excuse, justify, condone (FORGIVENESS); palliate, mitigate (SOFTNESS).

EXTERIORITY—*N.* exteriority, externality, superficiality.

exterior, outside, external; outdoors, out-of-doors; surface, superficies, margin; outside layer, superstratum; skin, covering, rind; finish, polish; objectivity, objectivism.

outskirts, limit, limits, bounds, boundary, periphery, perimeter, margin.

V. **exteriorize,** externalize, objectify, objectivate.

be exterior, lie around, environ, envelop, encompass, invest, encircle, cover, shroud, wrap, veil, clothe.

Adj. **exterior,** external, exoteric, outer, outmost, outermost, outlying, outward; outdoor, outdoors, alfresco; extraneous, extrinsic, extrinsical; extramundane, extraterrestrial, extrasolar; extramural, extraterritorial, foreign; peripheral, superficial, surface, marginal; objective.

Adv., phrases. **exteriorly,** externally, outwardly, etc. (see *Adjectives*); out, without, outwards, outdoors, out-of-doors, *extra muros* (L.), in the open air, outside.

See also BOUNDARY, COVERING, ENVIRONMENT, SKIN, SURFACE. *Antonyms*—See DEPTH, INTERIORITY.

---

exterminate, *v.* eliminate, abolish, do away with (ELIMINATION); destroy, obliterate, extirpate (DESTRUCTION).

external, *adj.* exoteric, outer, outermost (EXTERIORITY).

extinct, *adj.* gone, defunct, dead (NONEXISTENCE).

extinguish, *v.* put out, blow out, snuff out (DARKNESS).

extort, *v.* exact, squeeze, wrest (FORCE).

extortion, *n.* shakedown, swindle, blackmail (THIEVERY).

extortionate, adj. inordinate, outrageous, exorbitant (EXTREMENESS).

extra, adj. in reserve, spare, in store (STORE).

EXTRACTION—N. extraction, removal, abstraction, withdrawal, extrication, evulsion, eradication, extirpation; pry, tweeze, wrest, wrench; distillation, evaporation, expression, elicitation, evocation, catheterization (med.), exodontia (of teeth).

descent, lineage, derivation, ancestry, origin, birth, stock, family, parentage.

extract, essence, decoction, abstract, distillation, juice.

quotation, selection, citation, excerpt, abstract, clipping, cutting.

extractor, catheter (med.), siphon, tweezer, tweezers.

V. extract, pull, draw; take out, draw out, draw forth, remove, extricate, abstract, siphon off, catheterize (med.), pluck, crop, pry, tweeze; wring, wrest, extort, wrench; whip out, withdraw, unsheathe, pull out, tear out, pluck out, pick out, get out; root up, eradicate, stub, uproot, pull up, extirpate, stub, weed out.

elicit, educe, evolve, bring forth, evoke, derive, deduce.

squeeze out, express, expel, press out, distill.

See also ANCESTRY, ELIMINATION, REMOVAL, TRACTION. Antonyms—See INSERTION.

extraneous, adj. irrelevant, immaterial, impertinent (IRRELATION); extrinsic, external (EXTERIORITY).

extraordinary, adj. unusual, off the beaten path, out-of-the-way (UNUSUALNESS); inconceivable, incredible, strange (SURPRISE).

extrasensory, adj. telepathic, psychic, clairvoyant (TELEPATHY).

extravagance, n. waste, wastage, improvidence, dissipation (WASTEFULNESS); excess, immoderation, unrestraint (INTEMPERANCE).

extravagant, adj. wasteful, improvident, prodigal (WASTEFULNESS); bountiful, abundant, lavish (UNSELFISHNESS); unreasonable, excessive, exorbitant (UNREASONABLENESS, FOLLY); unrestrained, uncurbed, inordinate (INTEMPERANCE).

EXTREMENESS—N. extremeness, rabidity, radicalism, fanaticism, extremism, ultraism.

extreme, extremes, extremity, excess, nth degree, the ultimate;

maximum, limit, top, utmost, uttermost; last extremity, bitter end, outrance (F.).

extremist, radical, ultraist, fanatic.

Adj. extreme, immoderate, dire, drastic, ultra, utter, rank, extremist, radical, ultraistic, rabid, fanatical.

excessive, undue, exceeding, intemperate, unreasonable, inordinate, outrageous, exorbitant, extortionate, prohibitive, extravagant, unconscionable.

intense, mighty, profound, stupendous, surpassing, towering, transcendent, violent; grievous, severe, mortal; exceptional, extraordinary.

maximum, maximal, supreme, ultimate, top, sovereign, utmost, uttermost, consummate.

Adv., phrases. extremely, drastically, mortally, radically, utterly, violently, with a vengeance; to the nth degree; in extremis (L.).

excessively, exceedingly, exorbitantly, extravagantly, immoderately, inordinately, outrageously, overly, overmuch, prohibitively, terribly (colloq.), unduly, unreasonably.

See also ENCROACHMENT, EXCESS, INTEMPERANCE. Antonyms—See MIDCOURSE, MODERATENESS.

extremity, n. extreme, extremes, excess (EXTREMENESS); tip, edge, butt (END); foot, hand (APPENDAGE).

extricate, v. loose, loosen, disengage (FREEDOM); extract, remove, pull out (EXTRACTION).

exude, v. expel, evacuate, pass (EXCRETION); emit, radiate (GIVING); discharge, eject (THROW).

exult, v. crow, gloat, triumph (HAPPINESS).

exultant, adj. elated, exalted, gleeful (HAPPINESS).

exurbanite, n. villager, suburbanite (RURAL REGION).

eye, n. optic (EYE); hoop, loop, eyelet (ROUNDNESS).

EYE—N. eye, oculus, optic, orb (poetic), peeper (colloq.), glim (slang), lamps (pl., slang); naked eye, eagle (piercing, or penetrating) eye.

[comparisons] eagle, hawk, cat, lynx, Argus.

[parts of the eye] eyeball, pupil, lens, iris, cornea, white, retina, conjunctiva; lid, eyelid, eyebrow, eyelashes, cilia.

V. eye, look at, observe, peer at, gaze at, regard, scan, stare at, view, watch.

Adj. cross-eyed, strabismic, squint-eyed, walleyed; round-eyed, moon-eyed, popeyed, bug-eyed (*slang*), goggle-eyed, exophthalmic; blear-eyed, bleary-eyed, sloe-eyed, starry-eyed, gimlet-eyed; one-eyed, monoptical, monocular.

See also BLINDNESS, DIM-SIGHTED-NESS, LOOKING, VISION.

---

eyeglasses, *n.* spectacles, cheaters (*colloq.*), winkers (VISION).

eyeless, *adj.* blind, sightless, unsighted (BLINDNESS).

eye movements, *n.* saccadic movements, fixations, interfixations (READING).

eyesight, *n.* sight, view, afterimage (VISION).

eyesore, *n.* blot on the landscape, sight (*colloq.*), blemish (DEFORMITY).

eyewitness, *n.* spectator, onlooker, observer (LOOKING, VISION).

F

fable, *n.* allegory, parable, bestiary (STORY); fiction, myth, legend (UNREALITY); lie, fabrication, invention (FALSEHOOD).

fabric, *n.* textile, material, goods (TEXTURE, MATERIALITY); consistency, organization (MAKE-UP); frame, mold, structure (CONDITION).

fabricate, *v.* trump up, lie, prevaricate (FALSEHOOD); counterfeit, fake, sham (FALSENESS); invent, pretend, make up (UNREALITY); build, construct (BUILDING); form, organize, structure (MAKE-UP).

fabulous, *adj.* imaginary, legendary, mythical (UNREALITY); wonderful, wondrous, spectacular (SURPRISE).

façade, *n.* face, frontage, frontal (FRONT); false front, bluff, false colors (DECEPTION); veneer, front (SHALLOWNESS).

face, *n.* countenance, visage, aspect (HEAD, APPEARANCE); frontage, frontispiece (*arch.*), façade (FRONT); obverse, plane, facet (SURFACE); quarter, lee (SIDE).

face, *v.* front, confront, be opposite (HEAD); veneer, overlay (FRONT).

facet, *n.* obverse, plane, level (SURFACE); phase, aspect, angle (SIDE).

facetious, *adj.* frivolous, jocular, humorous (WITTINESS, FRIVOLITY).

facile, *adj.* fluent, glib, voluble (EXPRESSION); easy, effortless, smooth (EASE).

facilitate, *v.* expedite, simplify, smooth (EASE).

facilities, *n.* conveniences, utilities, appliances (EASE).

facility, *n.* smoothness, child's play, smooth sailing (EASE); competence, efficiency, proficiency (ABILITY).

facing, *n.* veneer, leaf, layer (COVERING).

facsimile, *n.* likeness, miniature, replica (COPY, SIMILARITY).

fact, *n.* datum (*pl.* data), statistic, actuality (MATERIALITY, REALITY); particular, specific, circumstance (DETAIL); verity, gospel (TRUTH).

faction, *n.* conflict, dissension, strife, factionalism, friction (DISAGREEMENT); side, party (PART).

factor, *n.* instrument, means, aid (AGENT, MEANS); component, constituent, element (PART); multiple, multiplicand, faciend (NUMBER).

factory, *n.* shop, plant, mill (PRODUCTION, WORK).

factual, *adj.* true, actual, real (TRUTH, REALITY).

faculty, *n.* talent, gift (ABILITY); teachers, staff, professorate (TEACHER).

fad, *n.* rage, craze, passion (DESIRE, FASHION).

fade, *v.* decolor, decolorize, achromatize (COLORLESSNESS); vanish, dissolve, evanesce (DISAPPEARANCE); dwindle, taper, wane (WEAKNESS).

faded, *adj.* dim, lackluster, lusterless (DULLNESS).

fagot, *n.* brand, firebrand, ember (FIRE, WOOD).

failing, *n.* frailty, infirmity, shortcoming (WEAKNESS).

FAILURE—*N.* failure, unsuccess, nonsuccess, unfulfillment, nonfulfillment, forlorn hope; miscarriage, misfire, abortion, stillbirth; fizzle (*colloq.*), flop (*slang*), collapse, debacle, fiasco, dud (*colloq.*), washout (*colloq.*); bankruptcy, insolvency, crash, smash; wreck, ruin, fall, downfall.

unsuccessful person, failure, dud (*colloq.*), washout (*colloq.*), ne'er-do-well; bankrupt, insolvent.

V. fail, miscarry, misfire, abort, fizzle (*colloq.*), flop (*slang*), founder, peter out, collapse, flunk, overreach oneself; go bankrupt, go to the wall, fold, crash; come to naught, go up in smoke, fall through, be futile, be in vain; come (fall, or get) a cropper, come to grief, lay an egg (slang), run aground, break down, meet with disaster, turn out badly; fall short of, miss, miss the mark; lose, be defeated, go down to defeat, meet one's Waterloo, lick the dust, get the worst of it.

Adj. unsuccessful, unprosperous, unthriving, unfruitful, unavailing, fruitless, barren, sterile, successless; stillborn, abortive; futile, bootless, vain, ineffectual, ineffective; bankrupt, insolvent; undone, lost, ruined, wrecked, down, broken down; defeated, vanquished, on the losing side, hard hit; foiled, frustrated, thwarted, balked, checkmated.

inauspicious, ill-starred, starcrossed (poetic), ill-fated, ominous, unlucky, unfortunate, jinxed; disadvantageous.

See also DEFEAT, DISAPPOINTMENT, INCOMPLETENESS, INEFFECTIVENESS, MISFORTUNE, UNPRODUCTIVENESS. Antonyms—See SUCCESS.

faint, adj. inaudible, indistinct, soft (SILENCE, WEAKNESS, LOWNESS); dim, inconspicuous, subtle (INVISIBILITY, UNCLEARNESS); delicate, fragile, frail (WEAKNESS); fainthearted, lily-livered, white-livered (FEAR).

faint, v. swoon, black out, lose consciousness (INSENSIBILITY).

fair, adj. just, equitable, evenhanded (IMPARTIALITY); justifiable, legitimate, logical (REASONABLENESS); decent, mediocre, middling (GOOD); comely, pretty, good-looking (BEAUTY); fairskinned, light-skinned, blond (COLORLESSNESS); rainless, pleasant, fine (DRYNESS).

fair, n. mart, market place, bazaar (STORE); exhibition, exposition, pageant (DISPLAY).

fair-haired, adj. blond, towheaded, flaxen-haired (HAIR, YELLOW).

fairy, n. brownie, elf, elfin (SUPERNATURAL BEINGS).

faith, n. constancy, fidelity, allegiance (LOYALTY); trust, confidence (BELIEF); creed, religious persuasion, church (RELIGION); belief, piety, piousness (RELIGIOUSNESS).

faithful, adj. loyal, constant, true (LOYALTY); close, accurate, exact (COPY).

faithless, adj. false, perfidious, untrue (DISLOYALTY); unconverted, nullifidian, anti-Christian (IRRELIGION).

fake, adj. pretended, make-believe, simulated (PRETENSE); false, bogus, fictitious (FALSENESS).

fake, n. faker, bluffer, bluff, make-believe (PRETENSE); fraud, bastard, phony (colloq.), sham (FALSENESS).

fake, v. dissimulate, feign, counterfeit, fabricate, sham (FALSENESS, PRETENSE).

fall, n. downward slope, declivity, drop (SLOPE); autumn, harvest time, Indian summer (SEASONS); waterfall, cascade, cataract (RIVER); ruin, downfall, overthrow (MISFORTUNE).

fall, v. fall down, stumble (DESCENT); decline, dwindle, drop (DECREASE, DESCENT); cheapen, decline, depreciate (WORTHLESSNESS).

fallacious, adj. sophistic, sophistical, unsound (FALSENESS); illogical, unfounded (MISTAKE).

fallacy, n. delusion, illusion, misbelief (FALSENESS); flaw, fault, pitfall (MISTAKE).

fall guy (slang), n. scapegoat, whipping boy, goat (SUBSTITUTION).

fallout, n. strontium 90 (THROW).

fallow, adj. unused, idle, vacant (DISUSE); unsown, untilled, uncultivated (NONPREPARATION); dormant, quiescent, slack (INACTION).

false, adj. untrue, bogus, fake (FALSENESS); faithless, perfidious, unfaithful (DISLOYALTY).

FALSEHOOD—N. falsehood, lie, half truth, equivocation, fable, fabrication, falsification, fiction, figment, flam, invention, prevarication, romance, story, tale, untruth, fib, white lie, roorback, whopper (colloq.), bouncer (colloq.), tarradiddle (colloq.).

liar, fabler, fabulist, fabricator, falsifier, inventor, prevaricator, romancer, fibber, deceiver, palterer, perjurer, forswearer, pseudologist (jocose), mythomaniac, Ananias, pseudologue; bluffer, bounder, fourflusher, tarrididdler (all colloq.).

untruthfulness, mendacity, dishonesty, aberration; mythomania, pseudologia fantastica (both psych.); deception, pseudology, subreption, perjury.

V. lie, tell a lie, tell an untruth, equivocate, fable, falsify, invent, misrepresent, prevaricate; fib, lie in one's teeth (or throat), palter; perjure oneself, commit perjury, forswear, tarradiddle (colloq.); lie about, belie; lie to, be dishonest with, deceive; fabricate, trump up.

Adj. untruthful, lying, dishonest, mendacious, mythomaniac, perjured, subreptitious.

See also DECEPTION, DISLOYALTY, FALSENESS, DISHONESTY, MISREPRESENTATION, PRETENSE. *Antonyms*—See HONESTY, LOYALTY, REALITY, TRUTH.

FALSENESS—*N.* falseness, falsity, illegitimacy, inaccuracy, unauthenticity, untruth; fraudulence, falsification, misrepresentation, disguise, fakery, fabrication, forgery.

fraud, fake, bastard, phony (*colloq.*), sham, shoddy, simulacrum, *postiche* (*F.*), counterfeit, forgery, pseudograph, fiction, untruth, apocrypha (*pl.*).

delusion, fallacy, idolism, illusion, misbelief, misconception, misimpression.

faker, counterfeiter, pretender, fabricator, forger, pseudographer.

V. falsify, deacon, disguise, doctor, gloss, varnish.

misrepresent, miscolor, trump up, belie, falsify, disguise; misstate, misquote, color, adulterate, dress up, embroider, exaggerate.

counterfeit, fake, fabricate, sham, pretend, forge.

Adj. false, adulterate, bastard, bogus, counterfeit, erroneous, fake, phony (*colloq.*), fictional, fictitious, illegitimate, inaccurate, mistaken, spurious, supposititious, unauthentic, unfathered, untrue, apocryphal, misrepresentative, pseudo.

fallacious, sophistical, unsound, casuistic.

specious, plausible, colorable, delusive, delusory, falsidical, delusional, illusional.

counterfeit, forged, fraudulent, mock, *postiche* (*F.*), sham, shoddy.

See also DECEPTION, EXAGGERATION, FALSEHOOD, MISREPRESENTATION, MISTAKE, MISTEACHING, PRETENSE. *Antonyms*—See HONESTY, REALITY, TRUTH.

false teeth, *n.* denture, plate, partial denture (TEETH).

falter, *v.* shake, reel, totter (UNSTEADINESS); waver, hesitate, scruple (INACTION, UNCERTAINTY); stutter, stammer, stumble (TALK).

FAME—*N.* fame, distinction, notability, eminence, renown, supereminence, pre-eminence, immortality, prominence, prestige, heyday, repute, éclat, kudos; notoriety, rumor; publicity.

reputation, repute, mark, name, good name, popularity, public esteem, high regard, high esteem,

glory, luster, splendor; honor, credit, distinction.

dignity, stateliness, impressiveness, solemnity, grandeur, gravity, nobility, majesty, sublimity.

famous person, celebrity, luminary, personage, notable, notability, immortal, laureate, hero, great man, lion, somebody, VIP (*colloq.*), dignitary.

symbol of honor: crown, garland, bays, palm, laurel, laurels, medal, ribbon, decoration, ornament, distinction, diploma, certificate.

V. make famous, publicize, emblazon, blazon, immortalize, eternize.

honor, give (do, *or* pay) honor to, accredit, dignify, glorify, fête, toast, drink to; lionize, look up to, exalt, aggrandize, elevate, ennoble, enthrone, enshrine, celebrate, grace, crown, laureate, adorn, decorate, cite.

be distinguished, make a splash, shine, glitter, cut a figure, leave one's mark, cut a dash, win laurels, win spurs, be in the limelight, be a household word.

Adj. famous, famed, in the public eye, illustrious, splendent, distinguished, distingué, notable, great, eminent, noted, of note, renowned, redoubted, top-flight, supereminent, pre-eminent, farfamed; celebrated, storied, immortal, laureate, classical; well-known, prominent, outstanding, upmost, foremost, uppermost, familiar, proverbial; notorious, of ill-repute, scandalous, crying.

honorable, creditable, palmary, estimable, respectable, reputable, in good odor; glorious, lustrous, splendid.

dignified, grand, grave, majestic, pontifical, portly, stately, togated, impressive, solemn, noble, sublime, sculpturesque, statuesque.

See also CELEBRATION, ELEVATION, MAGNIFICENCE, PUBLICATION, RESPECT, RUMOR. *Antonyms*—See DISGRACE, DISREPUTE, HUMILITY, IGNORANCE, LOWNESS, MODESTY.

familiar, *adj.* intimate, dear, close (NEARNESS); proverbial, known, well-known (KNOWLEDGE); common, frequent, customary (HABIT, COMMONNESS); informed, apprised, abreast (KNOWLEDGE).

familiarity, *n.* friendship, intimacy, acquaintanceship (FRIENDLINESS).

familiarize, *v.* inform, let know, acquaint (INFORMATION).

family, *n.* children, issue, progeny (CHILD); origin, parentage (ANCESTRY); line, lineage, house

(RELATIVE); genus, order, phylum (CLASS).

famine, *n.* starvation, drought (INSUFFICIENCY); scarcity, dearth, paucity (FEWNESS).

famish, *v.* be hungry, starve, raven (HUNGER).

famous, *adj.* famed, in the public eye, illustrious (FAME).

fan, *n.* palm leaf, electric fan, blower (BLOWING, AIR); follower, devotee (FOLLOWER).

fan, *v.* ventilate, cool, air-cool, aerate (BLOWING).

fanatic, *n.* enthusiast, zealot, monomaniac (ENTHUSIASM); extremist, radical, ultraist (EXTREMENESS).

fanatical, *adj.* overzealous, monomaniacal, radical, ultraistic, rabid (ENTHUSIASM, EXTREMENESS).

fanciful, *adj.* imaginary, romantic, fantastic (UNREALITY).

fancy, *adj.* ornamental, decorative, beautifying (ORNAMENT).

fancy, *n.* fantasy, invention, dream (HOPE, IDEA, UNREALITY); fondness, inclination, penchant (LIKING); notion, conceit, whim (CAPRICE).

fancy, *v.* fantasy, picture (IMAGINATION); favor, prefer (LIKING); care for, be enamored of (LOVE).

fancy-free, *adj.* uncommitted, unattached, foot-loose (FREEDOM).

fang, *n.* tooth, tusk (TEETH).

fantastic, *adj.* strange, bizarre (UNUSUALNESS); fanciful, romantic, aerial (UNREALITY).

fantasy, *n.* fancy, invention, figment (UNREALITY); daydream, reverie, vision (IMAGINATION, SLEEP).

fantasy, *v.* imagine, phantasy, fancy (UNREALITY).

far, *adj.* distant, far-off, remote (DISTANCE).

farce, *n.* burlesque, travesty (ABSURDITY).

fare, *v.* get along, manage, shift (LIFE).

farewell, *n.* leave-taking, parting, adieu (DEPARTURE).

farfetched, *adj.* illogical, incoherent (UNREASONABLENESS); suspicious, fishy (*colloq.*), dubious (UNBELIEVINGNESS).

far-flung, *adj.* wide-flung, outspread, widespread (SPREAD).

FARMING—*N.* farming, agriculture, husbandry, geoponics, agronomy, cultivation, culture, agrology, hydroponics, monoculture, tillage; gardening, horticulture, arboriculture, viniculture, floriculture, landscape gardening, topiary, pedology; green thumb.

garden, nursery, kitchen garden, market (*or* truck) garden, flower garden, botanic garden; greenhouse, hothouse, conservatory; grassplot, lawn, shrubbery, arboretum, orchard; vineyard, vinery, grapery, grape house; orangery.

farmer, agriculturist *or* agriculturalist, agrologist, agronomist, cultivator, husbandman, tiller, harvester, harvestman, reaper, sower, seeder, grower, raiser, planter; plower, plowman, sharecropper, clodhopper, farm laborer, farm hand, hired man, hired hand, plowboy, rancher, ranchman, ranchero (*Southwest U.S.*), granger, farmerette (*colloq.*); peasant, *muzhik* (*Russia*); gardener, landscape gardener, truck farmer, truck gardener, horticulturist, pedologist.

farm, farmstead, grange, plantation, ranch, truck farm, truck garden.

V. **farm,** cultivate the land, till the soil, subdue (*land*), bring under cultivation, grow, raise, garden, landscape; plant, sow, seed, plow, harrow, harvest, reap.

Adj. **agricultural,** geoponic, horticultural, topiary, georgic, agrarian.

arable, cultivable, cultivatable, tillable, plowable.

See also BOTANY, GRASS, PLANT LIFE, RURAL REGION. *Antonyms*—See CITY.

---

farmland, *n.* field, tillage (LAND).

far-reaching, *adj.* extensive, wide, far-ranging (STRETCH).

farsighted, *adj.* sighted, clear-sighted, clear-eyed (VISION); far-seeing, long-sighted, clairvoyant (FORESIGHT); commonsensical, well-balanced, levelheaded (WISDOM).

farsightedness, *n.* hypermetropia, hyperopia, presbyopia (DIMSIGHTEDNESS).

farthest, *adj.* farthermost, furthest, ultimate, (DISTANCE); extreme, lattermost (END).

fascinate, *v.* beguile, bewitch, enthrall (ATTRACTION, INTERESTINGNESS).

fascination, *n.* interest, appeal, piquancy (INTERESTINGNESS); enthrallment, trance (ATTENTION).

fascism, *n.* nazism, dictatorship, totalitarianism (VIOLENCE, GOVERNMENT).

fashion, *n.* manner, form, mode (METHOD, FASHION).

fashion, *v.* form, forge, contrive (PRODUCTION); carve, sculpture, cut (SHAPE).

FASHION—*N.* fashion, style, mode, vogue, *dernier cri* (*F.*), ton (*F.*), *bon ton* (*F.*), the latest thing, the rage, craze, fad, prevailing taste; cult, cultism, faddism.

society, *bon ton* (*F.*), *monde* (*F.*), *beau monde* (*F.*), fashionable society; *haut monde* (*F.*), fashionable world; elite, smart set (*colloq.*), four hundred (*colloq.*); Vanity Fair, Mayfair.

fop, beau, Beau Brummell, buck, coxcomb, dandy, dude, exquisite, jack-a-dandy, jackanapes, popinjay, toff (*British*), swell (*colloq.*), fashion plate.

Adj. fashionable, chic, chichi, current, modish, newfangled (*derogatory*), popular, smart, stylish, in fashion, *à la mode* (*F.*), all the rage (*colloq.*); faddish, faddist.

dapper, dashing, jaunty, natty, nifty (*colloq.*), rakish, saucy, smug, sporty, spruce, swanky (*colloq.*), trim, trig.

See also CLOTHING, HABIT, NEATNESS. *Antonyms*—See OLDNESS, UNTIDINESS.

---

fast, *adj.* rapid, speedy, quick; (*in music*) allegro, prestissimo, presto (SPEED); firm, close, tight (JUNCTION); debauched, depraved, dissolute (SEX); self-indulgent, self-gratifying; wild (INTEMPERANCE).

fast, *v.* starve, famish, go hungry (FASTING).

FASTENING—*N.* fastening, fastener, binder, brace, clip, clinch, clamp, rivet, staple, ring, catch, clasp, hasp, buckle, hook, hook and eye, zipper, slide fastener, button; latch, latchet, bolt, bar, lock, padlock; link, coupler, coupling; tack, brad, thumbtack; nail, screw, pin, dowel, wedge, peg, spike, toggle bolt, cleat; belt, chain, strap; tendril, tentacle.

cement, glue, gum, paste, size, solder, putty; mortar, plaster, stucco.

bond, tie, link, nexus, connection, connective, interconnection, copula (*tech.*); couple, yoke, union; bridge, steppingstone.

band, binder, fillet, snood, braid, bandage; cincture, girdle, girth, cinch (*U.S.*), bellyband, surcingle, belt, sash, cummerbund.

stitch, tack, tuck, baste, seam, hemstitch, suture.

V. tie, attach, fasten, bind, bond, hitch, leash, belt, belay (*naut.*), lash, lace, knot, moor, interlace, interknot, interknit, raddle, rope, tether, string, strap, brace, chain,

colligate; knit, interweave, intertwist, intertwine, interlock, splice, wattle; tie up, truss, trice up (*naut.*), ligate, astrict, astringe, swathe, harness, pinion, girt, girth, gird, enchain, couple, bandage, band.

sew, stitch, tack, baste, seam, hem, hemstitch, tuck; mend, patch, darn, suture.

See also CLOSURE, CLOTHING WORKER, JUNCTION, RESTRAINT, STICKINESS, UNITY. *Antonyms*—See CUTTING, DISJUNCTION, TEARING.

---

fastidious, *adj.* choosy, picky, dainty (CHOICE); queasy, squeamish (DISGUST).

FASTING—*N.* fasting, abstinence, dharma *or* dhurna (*India*).

fast, fast day, fasting day, Lent, Lenten diet, Barmecide feast.

V. fast, starve, famish, go hungry; abstain, diet.

Adj. fasting, Lenten, quadragesimal; unfed, starved, half-starved, hungry.

lack of appetite, inappetency, anorexia (*med.*), anorexia nervosa (*med.*).

See also CONTROL. *Antonyms*—See FOOD, GLUTTONY, GREED, HUNGER.

---

fat, *adj.* corpulent, stout, fleshy (SIZE); fatty, fatlike, adipose (OIL).

fat, *n.* grease, suet, tallow (OIL).

fatal, *adj.* virulent, deadly, lethal (KILLING).

fatalism, *n.* predestinarianism, predestinationism (DESTINY).

fate, *n.* lot, portion, fortune (DESTINY).

fated, *adj.* destined, predestined, foreordained (DESTINY); irreversible, unalterable, unmodifiable (UNIFORMITY).

fateful, *adj.* resultful, momentous, decisive (RESULT, IMPORTANCE).

father, *n.* papa, dad, sire (ANCESTRY); originator, author (BEGINNING); preacher, parson, padre (CLERGY).

father, *v.* beget, generate, procreate, sire (ANCESTRY, BIRTH); originate, create, hatch (BEGINNING).

fathom, *v.* get to the bottom of, unravel (DISCOVERY); get, follow, figure out (UNDERSTANDING); sound, plumb (DEPTH).

FATIGUE—*N.* fatigue, tedium, lassitude, tiredness, etc. (see *Adjectives*).

V. **fatigue,** tire, weary, bush (*colloq.*), enervate, fag, exhaust, overfatigue, overtire, tucker out, wear one out, prostrate, bedraggle; droop, flag, languish, sag, succumb, drop with fatigue, sink.

tax, task, strain; overtask, overwork, overdo, overburden, overtax, overstrain.

Adj. **fatigued,** tired, weary, wearied; bushed, dead-beat, done in, played out, ready to drop, all in, beat (*all colloq.*); enervated, fagged, fagged out, dead-tired, dog-tired, dog-weary, exhausted, spent, outspent, overfatigued, overtired, overwearied, wearyworn, tuckered, tuckered out, washed out, weary-laden, worn out, prostrate, prostrated; bedraggled, drooping, droopy, languid, languorous, lassitudinous, listless; blasé, jaded; footsore, foot-weary, footworn, weary-footed, wayweary, way-worn, weary-winged, wing-weary; tired of living, lifeweary, world-weary; war-weary; fatigable.

tired-looking, weary-looking, wan, haggard, languishing, toilworn.

tiresome, tiring, fatiguing, wearying, weary, wearisome, wearful, wearing; tedious, poky; enervating, exhausting, fagging.

See also BOREDOM, INACTIVITY, REST, WEAKNESS. *Antonyms*—See ENERGY, RESTORATION, POWER, STRENGTH.

fatten, *v.* put flesh on, gain weight (SIZE).

fatty, *adj.* fat, fatlike, adipose (OIL).

fatty (*colloq.*), *n.* roly-poly, punchinello, cherub (SIZE).

faucet, *n.* spout, tap, cock (EGRESS).

fault, *n.* foible, defect, flaw (WEAKNESS, IMPERFECTION); blame, responsibility (ACCUSATION, ATTRIBUTION).

faultfinding, *adj.* critical, captious, carping (DISAPPROVAL, SEVERITY).

faultless, *adj.* flawless, immaculate, impeccable (PERFECTION).

faulty, *adj.* imperfect, deficient, defective (IMPERFECTION); unreliable, unretentive, narrow (SHORTNESS); erroneous, untrue, false (MISTAKE).

favor, *n.* accommodation, benignity, benefaction (KINDNESS).

favor, *v.* fancy, prefer (LIKING); indulge, gratify, humor (MILDNESS); resemble, look like (SIMILARITY).

favorable, *adj.* beneficial, advantageous, good (USE); auspicious, advantageous, benign (FRIENDLI-

NESS); inclined, predisposed (PREJUDICE).

favorite, *n.* fair-haired boy, *persona grata* (*L.*), pet (LIKING).

favoritism, *n.* partiality, partisanship, discrimination (PREJUDICE, UNFAIRNESS).

fawn, *n.* yearling, deer (ANIMAL).

fawn, *v.* crouch, toady, grovel (SLAVERY).

fawning, *adj.* ingratiating, ingratiatory, obsequious (FLATTERY).

fawn on, *v.* ingratiate oneself with, truckle to (LIKING).

FEAR—*N.* **fear,** timidity, diffidence, anxiety, misgiving, misdoubt, qualm, hesitation; apprehension, phobia, dread, awe, consternation, trepidation, dismay, horror.

fright, alarm, terror, panic, scare, startle, shock, start, turn.

cowardice, recreancy, pusillanimity, funk (*colloq.*), white feather, white flag, cold feet (*colloq.*), yellow streak (*colloq.*).

[*object of fear*] **bugbear,** bugaboo, scarecrow, bogy, hobgoblin, nightmare, specter, *bête noire* (*F.*), chimera.

coward, poltroon, dastard, sneak, recreant, craven, caitiff; mollycoddle, milksop, milquetoast, Scaramouch, white feather.

alarmist, scaremonger, fearmonger, panic-monger, Calamity Jane (*colloq.*), terrorist.

bully, hector, browbeater.

V. **fear,** apprehend, dread, misdoubt, be afraid, take fright, take alarm.

cower, cringe, crouch, flinch, shrink, startle, start, shy, wilt.

tremble, quake, quaver, quiver, shiver, shudder.

be cowardly, quail, show the white feather; skulk, sneak, slink, run away, quit.

frighten, terrify, terrorize, dismay, awe, strike terror, appall, unman, petrify, horrify; startle, scare, alarm, stampede, panic, shock; consternate, unstring.

intimidate, daunt, cow, overawe, abash, browbeat, hector, bully, bulldoze (*colloq.*), threaten.

Adj. **afraid,** fearful, apprehensive, anxious, solicitous, creepy, nervous, panicky, jumpy, phobic, qualmish, scary (*colloq.*); timid, timorous, diffident, sheepish, shy, skittish, tremulous.

cowardly, base, chickenhearted, pigeonhearted, craven, dastard, dastardly; faint, fainthearted, lilylivered, white-livered, nerveless, spineless, pusillanimous, pussyfooting (*colloq.*), recreant, sneaky, yellow, unmanly.

frightened, scared, alarmed, aghast, awed, afraid, daunted, dismayed, intimidated, overawed; horrified, petrified, horror-stricken, terrified, terror-stricken, planet-stricken, panic-stricken, awe-stricken; shocked, startled, unmanned, unstrung.

trembling, tremulous, shaky, quivery, shivering, shivery, shuddery.

frightening, alarming, startling, scary, fearful, shocking; awesome, awe-inspiring, awful; terrifying, terrible.

horrifying, horrible, horrific; eerie, unearthly, uncanny, ghastly, ghoulish, gruesome, horrendous, frightful, morbid, shuddersome, creepy, dreadful, dread, bloodcurdling, grisly.

formidable, dire, fierce, redoubtable, redoubted.

See also AGITATION, CARE, GHOST, NERVOUSNESS, SHAKE, THREAT, WARNING. *Antonyms*—See COURAGE, PROTECTION, UNANXIETY.

---

fearless, *adj.* dauntless, doughty, brave (COURAGE).

feasible, *adj.* practicable, performable, workable (POSSIBILITY, EASE).

feast, *n.* repast, spread (*colloq.*), banquet (FOOD).

feat, *n.* deed, exploit, achievement (ABILITY, ACTION, COURAGE).

FEATHER—*N.* feather, plume, plumule, pinna, pinion, pinfeather, penna, quill.

feathers, plumage, tuft, ruff, crest, topknot, panache, hackles, down, fluff.

V. feather, fledge, plume, fletch, preen.

unfeather, pluck, singe, deplume, dress, pinion, molt.

Adj. feathered, fledged, full-fledged, plumed, downy; crested, ruffed, tufted.

feathery, featherlike, downy, fluffy, plumate, pinnate, fledgy.

featherless, plucked, unfeathered, unfledged, squab, callow.

See also HAIR, ORNAMENT, UNDRESS.

---

feature, *n.* distinction, idiosyncrasy, peculiarity (CHARACTER, DIFFERENCE); ingredient, integrant, unit (PART).

feature, *v.* point up, mark, underline (IMPORTANCE).

features, *n.* face, countenance, visage (APPEARANCE, HEAD).

federate, *v.* ally, confederate, league (UNITY, COMBINATION).

---

fed up (*slang*), *adj.* blasé, jaded, sick of (SATISFACTION).

fee, *n.* charge, commission, consideration (PAYMENT).

feeble, *adj.* weak, frail, infirm; faint, gentle, low; lame, flabby, flimsy (WEAKNESS).

feeble-minded, *adj.* defective, retarded, subnormal (STUPIDITY).

feeble-mindedness, *n.* amentia, subnormality, mental defectiveness (*or* deficiency), cretinism (STUPIDITY).

feed, *v.* nourish, sustain, nurture (FOOD).

feel, *n.* sensation, impression, taction (SENSITIVENESS, TOUCH).

feeler, *n.* bristle, quill, vibrissa (HAIR); trial balloon, tentative announcement (TEST).

feel for, *v.* sympathize, empathize, understand (PITY).

FEELING—*N.* feeling, emotion, sentiment, sensibility, sympathy, affect (*psychol.*), affection, pathos; sensation, impression, response.

fervor, fervency, fire, heat, gusto, vehemence, cordiality, ardor, warmth, zeal, passion, verve, ecstasy.

V. feel, touch, handle, thumb, finger, perceive, apperceive, sense, understand, comprehend, know, see, discern.

arouse, carry away, commove, excite, fire, impassion, inflame, overpower, overwhelm, quicken, ravish, rouse, shock, stir up, strike, transport.

Adj. feeling, sentient, sensitive, emotional, demonstrative, susceptible, sensuous.

affecting, exhilarating, impressive, moving, stirring, touching, emotional, pathetic; inflaming, inflammatory, overpowering, overwhelming, ravishing, rousing, striking, poignant.

affected, impressed, moved, stirred, touched.

fervent, fervid, warm, passionate, hearty, cordial, sincere, glowing, ardent; rabid, raving, raging, feverish, fanatical, hysterical, impetuous.

Adv., *phrases.* feelingly, sympathetically, compassionately, emotionally, understandingly; with all one's heart, with heart and soul, from the bottom of one's heart.

See also EAGERNESS, ENTHUSIASM, EXCITEMENT, MOTIVATION, PITY, SENSITIVENESS, SENTIMENTALITY, TOUCH, VIOLENCE. *Antonyms*—See CALMNESS, INACTIVITY, INSENSIBILITY.

---

feign, *v.* dissimulate, fake, counterfeit (PRETENSE).

felicitate, v. congratulate, rejoice with, wish one joy (CONGRATULATION).

fellow, n. match, companion, mate, double (SIMILARITY).

fellowship, n. companionship, comradeship, good-fellowship (FRIENDLINESS).

felony, n. crime, criminality, misdeed (ILLEGALITY).

FEMALE—N. female, she, woman, gentlewoman, girl, lady, mulier, petticoat, weaker vessel, skirt (*slang*), dame (*slang*), matron, dowager, broad (*slang*), frail (*slang*), tomato (*slang*), flapper (*slang*); hussy, jade, shrew, baggage, wench, gold-digger (*slang*), adventuress, grisette; amazon, androgyne; madam, *madame* (*F.*), ma'am (*colloq.*).

women, females, womankind, womanhood, femininity, womenfolk (*colloq.*), distaff side, fair sex, feminality, gentle sex, gentler sex, weaker sex.

womanliness, womanness, womanity, muliebrity; femaleness, femality, feminacy, feminality, femineity, femininity, feminism, feminity.

women's rights, feminism, womanism; female suffrage, woman suffrage, suffragettism.

feminist, womanist, suffragist, woman suffragist (*colloq.*), suffragette.

Adj. **feminine,** female, womanly, gentle, womanlike, womanish, muliebrile, distaff, petticoat, gynecic, gynecomorphous.

maidenly, maidenlike, girlish, girly, modest, virginal, virgin, vestal, chaste, pure.

effeminate, unmanly, womanish, old-womanish, anile, weak, soft, sissyish.

See also SEX, YOUTH. *Antonyms* —See MAN.

---

feminine, *adj.* female, womanly, gentle (FEMALE).

feminism, n. women's rights, female suffrage (FEMALE).

fence, n. barrier, enclosure, pale (INCLOSURE).

fence, v. hedge, hem in, wall in (IMPRISONMENT, INCLOSURE); duel, cross swords (FIGHTING).

fender, n. cushion, buffer, bumper (PROTECTION).

ferment, n. fermentation, seethe, yeast, simmer, ebullition (AGITATION, COMMOTION).

ferment, v. be violent, effervesce, boil (VIOLENCE).

ferocious, *adj.* fierce, grim, savage (VIOLENCE).

FERTILITY—N. fertility, fecundity, prolificacy, uberty; luxuriance, pinguidity, creativity, feracity, productivity; potency, virility, puberty, pubescence.

V. **be fertile,** produce richly, pullulate, teem with, abound in, be rich in.

fertilize, fecundate, fructify, impregnate.

Adj. **fertile,** breedy, fecund, fruitful, prolific, uberous; productive, loamy, luxuriant, mellow, pinguid, rich, vegetative, rank; creative, teeming, plenteous, plentiful, banner, procreant, feracious.

procreative, generative, reproductive, virile, pubescent, hebetic, puberal, pubertal.

See also BIRTH, PREGNANCY, PRODUCTION. *Antonyms*—See UNPRODUCTIVENESS.

---

fertilizer, n. manure, dung, compost (FARMING).

fervent, *adj.* warm, passionate, ardent (FEELING, ENTHUSIASM).

fervor, n. fervency, fire, heat, ardor, ardency (FEELING, ENTHUSIASM).

fester, v. canker, ulcer (UNCLEANNESS); inflame, blister (SWELLING).

festival, n. merrymaking, festivities (AMUSEMENT).

festive, *adj.* convivial, festal, jovial (SOCIALITY).

festivity, n. hilarity, mirth, jocularity, levity, merrymaking (MERRIMENT, AMUSEMENT).

fetch, v. bear, bring, deliver (TRANSFER); be sold for, get (SALE).

fetid, *adj.* malodorous, mephitic, stenchy (ODOR).

fetish, n. talisman, phylactery (JEWELRY); idol, image, golden calf (WORSHIP); stimulant, aphrodisiac (SEXUAL DESIRE).

fetter, v. manacle, handcuff, hobble, shackle (RESTRAINT).

feud, n. blood feud, vendetta, death feud (RETALIATION).

FEUDALISM—N. feudalism, feudal system, fee, feod, feoff, feud, fief, vassalage, manor, lordship; vassal, feudatory, liege, liege man; serf; serfage, serfdom, serfhood, serfism.

feudal ruler, lord, liege, liege lord, overlord, suzerain, lordling, *daimio* (*Jap.*).

Adj. **feudal,** feudalistic, vassal, feudatory, liege, lordly, manorial.

See also GOVERNMENT, SLAVERY, SOCIAL CLASS. *Antonyms*—See FREEDOM.

FEVER—*N.* **fever**, temperature, pyrexia (*med.*), febricity (*med.*), calenture (*med.*), heatstroke, cauma; ague, malarial fever, dengue, breakbone fever, typhoid, enteric fever, typhus, spotted fever, scarlet fever, scarlatina, yellow jack.

feverishness, aguishness, febricity, febrility, pyrexia.

[*producer of fever*] **febrifacient**, pyrogen.

[*remedy for fever*] **antipyretic**, defervescent, febrifuge, refrigerant, aspirin.

V. **fever**, make feverish, raise the temperature of; lose fever, go down in temperature, defervesce.

Adj. **feverish**, fevered, hot, hectic, flushed, aguish, aguey, febrific, febrile, feverous, pyretic, hyperpyretic.

feverless, nonfebrile, afebrile, apyretic, normal, cool.

See also DISEASE, EXCITEMENT, FIRE, HEAT, SKIN. *Antonyms*—See COLD, HEALTH.

---

feverish, *adj.* aguey, febrile, feverous (FEVER); fevered, frantic, frenetic (EXCITEMENT).

FEWNESS—*N.* **fewness**, scantiness, exiguity, sparsity, rarity, infrequency; handful, minority.

scarcity, dearth, paucity, poverty, famine.

V. **render few**, reduce, diminish, lessen, weed out, eliminate, exclude, thin, decimate.

Adj. **few**, scant, scanty; thin, rare, scarce, sparse, few and far between, exiguous, infrequent; inconsequential, inconsiderable, infinitesimal, insignificant, lean, meager, minute, paltry, petty, piddling, short, skimpy, slender, slight, slim, spare, stingy, trifling, trivial, imperceptible.

unabundant, uncopious, unexuberant, unlavish, unluxuriant, unopulent, unplenteous, unplentiful, unprofuse.

infrequent, uncommon, rare, unique, unusual, sporadic, occasional.

Adv., phrases. **infrequently**, seldom, rarely, scarcely, hardly; not often, unoften, uncommonly, scarcely ever, hardly ever; sparsely, occasionally, sporadically; once in a blue moon (*colloq.*).

See also ABSENCE, CUTTING, DECREASE, ELIMINATION, INSUFFICIENCY, POVERTY, SHORTNESS, SMALLNESS, THINNESS, UNUSUALNESS. *Antonyms* —See ADDITION, INCREASE, MULTITUDE, PRESENCE.

fiancé, *n.* betrothed, intended (BETROTHAL).

fiasco, *n.* washout (*colloq.*), debacle, miscarriage (FAILURE).

fib, *v.* lie, invent, prevaricate (FALSEHOOD).

fiber, *n.* fibril (*tech.*), hair, cilia (*pl.*), thread (FILAMENT); grain, nap (TEXTURE).

fickle, *adj.* irresolute, capricious, arbitrary (CHANGEABLENESS); unstable, changeable (CHANGEABLENESS, WEAKNESS).

fiction, *n.* stories, drama, fable, myth, legend (STORY, UNREALITY); figment, invention, prevarication (FALSEHOOD).

fictional, *adj.* narrative, anecdotal, fictive (STORY); fictitious, false, bogus (UNREALITY, FALSENESS).

fiddle, *n.* violin, Cremona, Stradivarius (MUSICAL INSTRUMENTS).

fidelity, *n.* constancy, faith, allegiance (LOYALTY).

fidget, *v.* be nervous, fuss, fret (NERVOUSNESS).

field, *n.* orbit, scope, circle (POWER, SPACE); occupation, calling (BUSINESS); farmland, tillage (LAND).

fiend, *n.* demon, imp, Mephistopheles (DEVIL, WICKEDNESS); devotee, votary, votarist (LOYALTY).

fiendish, *adj.* satanic, demoniac, fiendlike, Mephistophelian (DEVIL, WICKEDNESS).

fierce, *adj.* ferocious, grim, savage (VIOLENCE).

fiery, *adj.* vehement, passionate, inflamed (VIOLENCE); excitable, agitable, combustible (EXCITEMENT); hot-tempered, hotheaded, peppery (BAD TEMPER, ANGER); flaming, flickering, glowing (FIRE); candent, piping-hot (HEAT).

fight, *n.* brawl, broil, fracas (FIGHTING).

FIGHTER—*N.* **fighter**, combatant, contender, battler, wildcat, contestant, brawler, gladiator, jouster, scrapper.

warfarer, warrior, fighting man, military man; belligerent, jingoist, jingo, militarist, warmonger.

soldier, brave, man at arms, serviceman; knight, mercenary, free lance, franc-tireur; private, Tommy Atkins (*Brit.*), doughboy, G.I., Jerry, *poilu* (*F.*), sepoy (*India*); musketeer, rifleman, sharpshooter; guardsman, grenadier, fusilier, infantryman, foot soldier, Zouave, chasseur; artilleryman, gunner, cannoneer, engineer; cavalryman, trooper, dragoon; cuirassier, hussar, lancer; volunteer, recruit, rookie, conscript, drafted man, draftee, inductee, enlisted man; campaigner, veteran.

officer, corporal, sergeant, warrant officer, lieutenant, captain, major, lieutenant colonel, colonel, brigadier general, major general, lieutenant general, general, general of the army; brass hat (*colloq.*), the brass (*colloq.*), commandant, marshal, commander in chief; brevet, cadre.

swordsman, swashbuckler, duelist, dueler, fencer.

boxer, pugilist, prize fighter, bruiser, pug (*slang*), sparring partner.

bullfighter, tauromachian, toreador, *torero* (*Sp.*), picador, matador.

army, soldiery, troops, array; regular army, reserves; corps, division, column, wing, detachment, garrison, flying column, brigade, regiment, battalion, squadron, company, battery, outfit (*colloq.*), section, platoon, squad; detail, patrol, picket, guard, legion, phalanx, cohort.

armed force, military, forces, service, the army, standing army, regulars, the line; militia, national guard, state guard, yeomanry, volunteers, partisans, minutemen (*Am. hist.*), posse; guards, yeomen of the guard (*Eng.*), beefeaters (*Eng.*).

See also FIGHTING, SAILOR.

FIGHTING—*N.* **fighting,** strife, brawling, etc. (see *Verbs*); pugilism, fisticuffs.

battle, conflict, clash, fight, encounter, combat, contest, fray, affray, engagement, action, struggle; brush, dogfight (*aero.*), skirmish, velitation; duel, monomachy, *affaire d'honneur* (*F.*).

fight, brawl, broil, battle royal, fracas, melee, scrap (*slang*), scuffle, scrimmage, set-to, tussle, contention, Donnybrook, free-for-all, scramble; prize fight, bout, match; tournament, tourney, tilt, joust.

scene of battle: battlefield, battleground, arena, Armageddon, aceldama, lists.

warfare, war, rupture, military operations, hostilities, bloodshed; campaign, crusade, jehad (*Moham.*), expedition; warpath, service, campaigning, active service; war to the death, *guerre à mort* (*F.*), *guerre à outrance* (*F.*); *blitzkrieg* (*Ger.*), open war; world war, global war, atomic war, hydrogen war, pushbutton war; chemical (bacteriological, biological, *or* germ) warfare; civil war, internecine strife; war of attrition,

undeclared war, cold war, sabre-rattling, war of nerves.

arms, armor, weapons.

art of war, military art, tactics, strategy, generalship, logistics.

warlikeness, belligerence, bellicosity, militancy, hostility, pugnacity; jingoism, militarism, Prussianism, warmongering; war footing.

V. **fight,** battle, clash, conflict, combat, contend, scramble, contest, scrimmage, skirmish, struggle, buffet, ruffle; come to blows, exchange blows, brawl, tussle, engage in fisticuffs, scuffle, scrap (*slang*), box, spar, fight hand to hand; cross swords, duel, fence, tilt, tourney, joust, tilt at; tilt at windmills, shadow-box.

war, warfare, make war, go to war, declare war, wage war, arm, take up arms.

serve, enroll, enlist; see service, be in service, campaign; be under fire; be on the warpath, keep the field; take by storm; go over the top (*colloq.*); sell one's life dearly.

conscript, draft, induct, enroll, impress.

Adj. **warlike,** military, soldierly, aggressive, belligerent, bellicose, combatant, martial, militant, hostile; jingoistic, jingo, militaristic, warmongering; combative, pugnacious, scrappy (*colloq.*); civil, internecine, guerrilla, irregular, underground; amphibious, triphibious; ante-bellum, post-bellum.

armed, armiferous, armed to the teeth, sword in hand; in battle array, embattled, embroiled.

See also ARMS, ATTACK, CUTTING, DEFEAT, KILLING, OPPOSITION. *Antonyms*—See PEACE, SUBMISSION.

---

figment, *n.* fancy, fantasy, invention (UNREALITY).

figurative, *adj.* symbolic, metaphorical, allegorical (REPRESENTATION, FIGURE OF SPEECH).

figure, *n.* symbol, character, numeral (NUMBER); price, rate, quotation (EXPENDITURE); statue, piece, cast (FINE ARTS); portrait, effigy, model (REPRESENTATION); anatomy, physique, build (BODY, SHAPE).

figure, *v.* calculate, cipher, reckon (COMPUTATION).

figurehead, *n.* puppet, tool, cat's-paw (DEPENDABILITY).

FIGURE OF SPEECH—*N.* **figure of speech,** trope; rhetoric, euphuism, imagery, tropology; metaphor, allegory, simile, metonymy, synecdoche, euphemism, irony, hyperbole; alliteration, anaphora, onomatopoeia, echoism, antithesis, oxymoron, antistrophe, ellipsis, asyndeton, aposiopesis; climax, anticlimax, bathos; personification, pathetic fallacy; understatement, litotes.

Adj. **figurative,** tropal, tropological, pictorial, metaphorical, allegorical, ironic, euphemistic, personified, hyperbolic, echoic.

[*abounding in figures of speech*] florid, flowery, ornate, figured, embellished, rhetorical, high-flown, euphuistic.

See also EXPRESSION, REPRESENTATION, STATEMENT, WORD.

---

figure out, *v.* reason, think out, conclude (REASONING); get, follow, fathom (UNDERSTANDING).

FILAMENT—*N.* **filament,** fiber, fibril (*tech.*), hair, cilia (*pl.*) capillary, vein, strand, tendril, wire, gossamer, cobweb.

thread, yarn, twist, linen, cotton, nap, warp, weft, woof, meshes.

cord, string, rope, twine, tether, thong, torsade, lace, strap, belt, harness, strand, raffia, leash, lashing, lariat, lasso; band, binder, binding, bond, ligament, ligature; chain, cable, wire; bandage; brace, lanyard (*naut.*); braid, tape, ribbon; bight, loop, noose, halter; kink, knot.

Adj. **filamentous,** threadlike, filar, fibrous, thready, stringy, ropy, wiry, hairy, capillary.

See also FASTENING, HAIR, MAKE-UP.

---

filch, *v.* steal, thieve, sneak (THIEVERY).

file, *v.* scrape, abrade, rasp (POWDERINESS, RUBBING); catalogue, index, docket (LIST, ARRANGEMENT); march, debouch, pace (WALKING).

fill, *n.* padding, stuffing, filler (FULLNESS).

fill, *v.* load, lade, pack (FULLNESS).

fill in, *v.* shoal, fill up, silt up (SHALLOWNESS).

filling, *n.* impletion, saturation, replenishment (FULLNESS); content, packing, stuffing (CONTENTS); inlay, crown, bridge (TEETH).

film, *n.* leaf, sheet, membrane (LAYER); cinema, movie (*colloq.*), picture (MOTION PICTURES).

filmy, *adj.* gossamery, diaphanous, sheer (TEXTURE, THINNESS).

filth, *n.* impurity, dirt, feculence, dregs; dirty language, ordure (UNCLEANNESS); immorality, lubricity (OBSCENITY).

filthy, *adj.* unclean, impure, dirty (UNCLEANNESS); vile, nasty, foul-mouthed (OBSCENITY).

fin, *n.* flipper, pinna (APPENDAGE).

final, *adj.* terminal, last, closing (END).

finale, *n.* epilogue, peroration, swan song (END).

finally, *adv.* lastly, in conclusion (END, REASONING).

finance, *n.* accounts, money matters (ACCOUNTS); chrysology, economics, political economy, banking (MONEY).

financial, *adj.* fiscal, monetary, pecuniary (MONEY).

find, *v.* discover, locate, pin-point (DISCOVERY); meet, meet with, fall to the lot of (OCCURRENCE).

finding, *n.* award, verdict, sentence (JUDGMENT).

find out, *v.* ascertain, determine, divine, learn, tell (DISCOVERY).

fine, *adj.* slender, thin, threadlike (NARROWNESS); exceptional, first-class, excellent (GOOD); sharp, keen, acute (SHARPNESS); nice, subtle, hairsplitting (DIFFERENTIATION); rainless, fair, pleasant (DRYNESS); delicate, gauzy, filmy (THINNESS, TEXTURE); dainty, ethereal, exquisite (WEAKNESS).

fine, *n.* forfeit, penalty, damages (PUNISHMENT).

FINE ARTS—*N.* **painting,** depiction, finger painting, drawing, illustration, design, composition, treatment, arrangement, values; *chiaroscuro* (*It.*), black and white; tone, technique, perspective.

style, school, *genre* (*F.*), portraiture, still life; mosaic, fresco, encaustic painting.

picture, painting, piece, collage, mobile, tableau, mural, canvas; fresco, cartoon; drawing, draft, sketch, outline, study, daub; oil, water color.

portrait, likeness, silhouette, profile, miniature.

view, scene, landscape, seascape, interior; panorama, diorama, bird's-eye view.

picture gallery, art gallery, art museum; studio, *atelier* (*F.*).

sculpture, carving, modeling, sculpturing; statuary, marble, bronze.

statue, figure, piece, cast, bust, torso, statuette, figurine, colossus, icon, idol, monument, waxwork, image, effigy, acrolith, abstraction.

dummy, model, mannequin, manikin.

relief, rellevo, low relief, bas-relief, basso-relievo; high relief, alto-relievo; half relief, mezzo-relievo; intaglio, anaglyph, cameo.

architecture, structure, construction, building, architectonics, civil architecture; ecclesiology.

V. paint, design, limn, draw, sketch, color; daub, wash, stencil, depict; miniate (*as a manuscript*), illuminate, rubricate.

sculpture, carve, chisel, cut, cast, mold, model, sculpt.

Adj. pictorial, graphic, picturesque, delineatory.

sculptured, carved, etc. (see *Verbs*); engraved, glyphic, sculptural; Parian, marmorean, marble, marbled.

See also ARTIST, COLOR, ENGRAVING, ORNAMENT, PHOTOGRAPH, REPRESENTATION.

finery, *n.* frippery, gaudery, caparison (CLOTHING, OSTENTATION, ORNAMENT).

finesse, *n.* *savoir faire* (*F.*), skill, competence (ABILITY).

finger, *n.* digit, thumb (APPENDAGE).

finger, *v.* feel, handle, thumb (TOUCH, FEELING).

fingernail, *n.* claw, nail (APPENDAGE).

finish, *n.* finis, last, conclusion (END); refinement, grace, beauty, polish (ELEGANCE).

finish, *v.* close, terminate, conclude (END, COMPLETENESS); slay, slaughter, do in (KILLING).

finished, *adj.* consummate, full, plenary, full-fledged (COMPLETENESS).

finite, *adj.* limited, bound, circumscribed, confined, delimited (BOUNDARY).

fire, *n.* blaze, conflagration (FIRE); red heat, white heat, zeal (ENTHUSIASM).

fire, *v.* ignite, kindle (FIRE); dismiss, discharge (DISMISSAL); inflame, inspire, intoxicate (EXCITEMENT).

FIRE—*N.* fire, blaze, conflagration, wildfire, holocaust, flame, bonfire, balefire, signal fire, beacon, smolder, vortex, hell-fire, phlogiston (*hist.*); tongue of fire, flamelet, flicker; scintilla, spark, sparkle, glow.

combustion, candescence, ignition, spontaneous combustion, thermogenesis.

[*products of combustion*] ash, cinder, coal, embers, scoriae, lava, slag, clinker; coke, carbon, charcoal.

firebrand, brand, charcoal, char, ember, cinder; fagot, firewood, fuel, firing, kindling, peat.

[*setting of fires*] arson, incendiarism, pyromania.

arsonist, incendiary, firebug, pyromaniac.

combustible, inflammable, tin-

derbox, tinder, kindling, ignescent.

incinerator, cinerator, furnace, cremator, ashery.

fireworks, pyrotechnics, pyrotechnic display (*or* exhibition), pyrotechny; firecracker.

V. fire, ignite, kindle, light, set fire to, light a fire, rekindle, inflame (*fig.*).

catch on fire, take fire, catch fire, ignite, fire, kindle, light; blaze, flame, flare, burn, flicker, glow, smolder, spark, sparkle.

burn, sear, singe, scorch, scald, parch, char; incinerate, cremate, cinder, ash, carbonize, cauterize (*med.*).

Adj. **fiery,** igneous, empyreal, ignescent.

afire, on fire, ablaze, aflame, blazing, burning, conflagrant, fiery, flaming, flickering, glowing, candescent, smoldering.

combustible, burnable, flammable, inflammable, fiery, ignitable, piceous, tindery, tinderlike.

ashen, ashy, cindery, cinereous, cineritious.

See also DESTRUCTION, ENTHUSIASM, FIRE FIGHTER, FUEL, HEAT, LIGHT. *Antonyms*—See COLD, DARKNESS.

---

firearms, *n.* armament, arms, artillery (ARMS).

FIRE FIGHTER—*N.* fire fighter, fireman, firewarden, fireward; auxiliary fireman, volunteer fireman, fire buff, buff; fire brigade, fire company, fire department; fire engine, hook and ladder; enginehouse, firehouse, fire station; firebreak, fire drill, fire escape, fire extinguisher, fireplug, fire tower, fire wall.

See also FIRE.

---

firefly, *n.* fire beetle, glowworm (LIGHT).

fire off, *v.* let off, discharge, shoot (PROPULSION).

fireplace, *n.* hearth, fireside, grate (HEAT).

fire upon, *v.* shoot at, snipe at, open fire (ATTACK).

firewood, *n.* fagot, kindlings, brushwood (FUEL).

fireworks, *n.* pyrotechnics, pyrotechny, firecrackers (FIRE).

firm, *adj.* stable, steady, solid (STABILITY); hard, stiff, rigid (HARDNESS, THICKNESS); bulldogged, persistent, tenacious (STUBBORNNESS); intent, bent, bound (PURPOSE); inflexible, staunch (STRENGTH).

firm, *n.* company, concern, house (BUSINESS).

firm, v. stabilize, steady, brace (STABILITY); stiffen, tense (HARDNESS).

first, adj. beginning, opening, maiden (BEGINNING, EARLINESS); ranking, first-string, top-flight (RANK); advanced, avant-garde (F.), ahead (FRONT).

first, adv. firstly, in the first place, to begin with (BEGINNING).

first-rate (colloq.), adj. shipshape, tiptop (colloq.), sound (GOOD).

fish, v. angle, seine, trawl (HUNTING).

fisherman, n. fisher, piscator, angler (HUNTING).

fishy, adj. finny, piscine (ANIMAL); suspicious, farfetched, dubious (UNBELIEVINGNESS); shady, questionable (DISHONESTY).

fissure, n. breach, rent, rift, split (DISJUNCTION).

fit, adj. suitable, fitting, happy (AGREEMENT); trim, trig, hale (HEALTH).

fit, n. seizure, stroke, paroxysm (ATTACK).

fitful, adj. spasmodic, changeable, erratic (IRREGULARITY); restless, restive, uneasy (NERVOUSNESS).

fit out, v. equip, arm, man (PREPARATION).

fitting, adj. proper, suitable, appropriate (AGREEMENT).

fittings, n. trappings, accouterments, appointments (INSTRUMENT).

FIVE—N. five, pentad, cinque (cards and dice); group of five, cinquain, quintet or quintette, quintuplets; quinary, quintuple, quincunx, pentagon (geom.).

V. **quintuple,** quintuplicate, multiply by five; divide into five parts, quinquesect.

Adj. **fivefold,** pentamerous, quinary, quinquefid, quinquepartite, quintuple; fifth, quintan; quinquenary; pentangular, pentagonal (geom.).

fix, n. jam, pickle, hot water (all colloq.), plight (DIFFICULTY, CONDITION).

fix, v. repair, overhaul, mend (RESTORATION); put, set, stick (PLACE, LOCATION); attach, fasten, bind (JUNCTION); bribe, buy, corrupt (BRIBERY); heat, warm, prepare (COOKERY); stop, arrest, stall (MOTIONLESSNESS); decide, determine, settle (RULE); arrange, dispose (ARRANGEMENT).

fixed, adj. situated, located, settled (SITUATION); definite, determinate, specific (BOUNDARY); unchanging, changeless, static (UNIFORMITY); quiet, still, stable (MOTIONLESSNESS); rooted, inveterate, confirmed (HABIT).

fizz, v. seethe, simmer, sparkle (FOAM).

fizzle (colloq.), v. miscarry, misfire, abort (FAILURE).

flabby, adj. flaccid, slack, limp (SOFTNESS, WEAKNESS, INELASTICITY); baggy, loppy, pendulous (LOOSENESS, HANGING); (of abstractions) lame, feeble, flimsy (WEAKNESS).

flaccid, adj. flabby, slack, limp, quaggy, inelastic, irresilient (SOFTNESS, WEAKNESS, INELASTICITY).

flag, n. banner, ensign, standard (INDICATION); stone, cobblestone, flagstone (ROCK).

flag, v. signal, gesture (INDICATION); droop, languish (FATIGUE).

flagrant, adj. egregious, glaring, gross (INFERIORITY).

flair, n. knack, faculty, talent (ABILITY).

flake, n. plate, scale, lamella (LAYER).

flamboyant, adj. ostentatious, showy, flashy (OSTENTATION); luxuriant, orotund, purple (WORDINESS).

flame, n. conflagration, fire, wildfire (FIRE); infatuation, crush (colloq.), passion; swain, spark (LOVE).

flank, n. side, loin, wing (SIDE).

flank, v. skirt, border (SIDE).

flap, n. lug, lappet (ADDITION).

flap, v. wave, flop, flutter (OSCILLATION); hang, swing, dangle (LOOSENESS, HANGING).

flapjack, n. pancake, griddlecake, hot cake, wheat cake (BREAD).

flare, n. signal, beacon, blinker (INDICATION).

flare, v. blaze, burn, flicker (FIRE, LIGHT).

flash, n. gleam, sparkle, glitter (LIGHT); twinkling, trice, instant (TIME, EARLINESS); dash (colloq.), swank, splash (OSTENTATION).

flash, v. glimmer, sparkle, scintillate (LIGHT).

flashlight, n. searchlight, spotlight, torch (LIGHT).

flashy, adj. ostentatious, showy, dashing, dashy, flamboyant, garish, catchpenny, gaudy (OSTENTATION, VULGARITY).

flask, n. ampulla, flacon (F.), flasket (CONTAINER).

flat, adj. level, smooth (FLATNESS); dull, jejune, spiritless (MILDNESS); insipid, vapid, flavorless (UNSAVORINESS, WEAKNESS).

flat, n. shallow, shoal, sandbar (SHALLOWNESS); mud flat, spit, tideland (LAND); apartment, suite, rooms (HABITATION).

flat-footed, n. splayfooted (APPENDAGE).

FLATNESS—N. flatness, levelness, etc. (see *Adjectives*).

plane, level (*or* flat) surface, grade, level; plate, table, tablet, slab; discus, disk *or* disc, spangle.

V. flatten, level, smooth, plane, even, crush, depress, level off, level out, pat, squash; throw down, fell, prostrate, squelch, squash.

Adj. flat, level, smooth, unbroken, plane, even, flush, horizontal; recumbent, supine, prostrate, flattened, complanate, oblate (geom.); discoid, spatulate, splay, squat, squatty, tabular, tabulate; deflated (of tires).

[*without qualification*] positive, unqualified, downright, absolute, peremptory, clear, plain, direct.

See also BOREDOM, DULLNESS, LOWNESS, SMOOTHNESS. Antonyms—See ROUNDNESS, SWELLING, VISIBILITY.

FLATTERY—N. flattery, adulation, cajolery, blandishment, fawning, servility, sycophancy, flunkyism, toadyism, tufthunting, honeyed words, flummery, blarney (colloq.), palaver, soft sawder (slang), soft soap (colloq.), butter (colloq.), compliments, trade-last, salve, puff, puffery, taffy.

toady, truckler, bootlicker, fawner, toadeater, lickspit *or* lickspittle, sycophant, hanger-on, tufthunter, flunky.

V. flatter, beslaver, blandish, blarney, butter, butter up (colloq.), cajole, compliment, salve, sawder (colloq.); soft-soap (colloq.), wheedle, adulate, bedaub, jolly, puff, slaver, slobber.

bootlick, curry favor with, fawn, ingratiate oneself with, toady, insinuate oneself in the good graces of; truckle to, pander to, court.

Adj. flattering, complimentary, adulatory, courtly, sycophantic, blandishing, bootlicking, cajoling, wheedling, assentatory, candied, honeyed, buttery.

fawning, ingratiating, ingratiatory, obsequious, servile, silken.

See also APPROVAL, PRAISE, WORSHIP. Antonyms—See DETRACTION, DISAPPROVAL.

---

flaunt, v. brandish, flourish, air (OSTENTATION).

flavor, n. savor, sapor, smack, tang (TASTE).

flavor, v. season, spice, salt (TASTE, INTERESTINGNESS).

flavorful, adj. mellow, savory, savorous, aromatic, sapid (TASTE).

flavorless, adj. tasteless, flat, insipid (UNSAVORINESS, WEAKNESS).

flaw, n. fault, defect, foible (IMPERFECTION, WEAKNESS); fallacy, fault, pitfall (MISTAKE); windflaw, flurry, gust (WIND).

flawless, adj. faultless, immaculate, impeccable (PERFECTION).

flaxen, adj. blond, leucous, straw-colored, stramineous (YELLOW).

flea, n. cootie (slang), louse (ANIMAL).

fleck, n. spot, dot, mote, speck (VARIEGATION); particle, atom, bit (SMALLNESS).

flee, v. escape, desert, skip (DEPARTURE).

fleece, n. yarn, shag, pelage (WOOL).

fleece, v. cheat, gouge (colloq.), mulct (DECEPTION); despoil, strip, plunder (TAKING).

fleecy, adj. woolly, floccose, flocculent, lanose (WOOL).

fleet, adj. speedy, rapid, swift (SPEED).

fleet, n. navy, armada, flotilla (SHIP).

fleeting, adj. passing, evanescent, impermanent (DEPARTURE, IMPERMANENCE).

flesh, n. brawn, muscular tissue (SKIN); roast, meat (FOOD); man, mortality (MANKIND).

flesh-colored, adj. pink, rosy, incarnadine (SKIN).

fleshly, adj. carnal, sensual, gross (SEX, BODY, ANIMAL, INTEMPERANCE).

fleshy, adj. brawny, sarcous, pulpy (SKIN); fat, corpulent, stout (SIZE).

flex, v. bend, lean, tilt (BEND).

flexible, adj. pliable, pliant, supple (EASE, SOFTNESS, BEND).

flicker, n. beam, gleam, spark (SMALLNESS); cinema, movie (colloq.), film (MOTION PICTURES).

flicker, v. blaze, flare, glow (FIRE, LIGHT).

flight, n. escape, fugue (psychol.), fleeing (DEPARTURE); take-off, volation (FLYING).

flighty, adj. dizzy, lightheaded, giddy (FRIVOLITY).

flimsy, adj. slight, footless, insubstantial, (WEAKNESS, SMALLNESS, THINNESS); unconvincing, lame, thin (DISSUASION, NONEXISTENCE); baggy, flabby, loppy (LOOSENESS).

flinch, v. cower, cringe, wince (FEAR, REVERSION).

fling, v. cast, heave, hurl (THROW).

flip, v. toss, twirl, chuck (THROW).

flippant, adj. frivolous, flip (colloq.), playful (FRIVOLITY); pert, saucy, fresh (DISCOURTESY).

flirt, v. coquette, trifle, philander (LOVE).

flirtation, *n.* love affair, romance, amour (LOVE).

FLOAT—N. float, raft, driftage, driftwood, flotsam, flotsam and jetsam, supernatant; floater, drifter.

V. **float,** drift, waft, ride at anchor, buoy, buoy up.

Adj. **floating,** adrift, afloat, awaft, natant, awash, fluctuant, supernatant, buoyant.

See also FLYING, LIGHTNESS, SWIMMING. *Antonyms*—See DESCENT, WEIGHT.

floater, *n.* drifter, maunderer, rolling stone (PURPOSELESSNESS).

flock, *n.* herd, drove, crush (ASSEMBLAGE, MULTITUDE); churchgoers, parishioners, congregation (CHURCH); procreation, brood, progeny (CHILD).

flock, *v.* gather, herd, huddle (MULTITUDE).

flog, *v.* spank, paddle, whip (HITTING, PUNISHMENT).

flood, *n.* downpour, drencher, deluge (RAIN).

flood, *v.* deluge, engulf, inundate (WATER); oversupply, glut (EXCESS).

floor, *n.* flooring, deck, pavement (BASE, SUPPORT); bottom, lowest point, nadir (LOWNESS).

floor plan, *n.* ground plan, blueprint, diagram, plan, outline (MAP).

floozy (*slang*), *n.* trollop, trull, whore (PROSTITUTE).

flop, *v.* wave, flap, lop, flutter (OSCILLATION).

floral, *adj.* flowery, blossomy, bloomy (PLANT LIFE).

florid, *adj.* ruddy, ruddy-faced, high-colored (RED); embellished, flowery, ornate (WORDINESS, FIGURE OF SPEECH, MUSIC).

flour, *n.* meal, bran, farina (POWDERINESS).

flourish, *n.* curlicue, quirk, curl, twist, spiral (WRITING).

flourish, *v.* batten, burgeon, flower (HEALTH, STRENGTH); succeed, prosper, thrive (SUCCESS); shake, brandish (SHAKE).

flow, *n.* stream, course (RIVER); current, juice, electricity (LIGHT).

flow, *v.* run, stream, gush (RIVER); issue, flow out, emanate (DEPARTURE); pass, proceed, extend (PASSAGE).

flower, *n.* blossom, bloom, floret, bud (PLANT LIFE).

flower, *v.* bloom, batten, burgeon, flourish, prosper, thrive (STRENGTH).

flowery, *adj.* blossomy, bloomy, floral (PLANT LIFE); ornate, ornamented, florid (WORDINESS, FIGURE OF SPEECH).

flowing, *adj.* fluid, fluidic, liquefied (LIQUID); cursive, running, handwritten (WRITING).

fluctuate, *v.* oscillate, shift, swing (CHANGEABLENESS, OSCILLATION); waver, vacillate, be undecided (IRRESOLUTION).

flue, *n.* ventiduct, chimney (AIR, AIR OPENING).

fluent, *adj.* articulate, facile, voluble (EXPRESSION).

fluff, *n.* down, fuzz, lanugo (HAIR); slip of the tongue, *lapsus linguae* (L.), bull (MISTAKE).

fluffy, *adj.* downy, fuzzy, velutinous (HAIR, FEATHER); creamy, feathery (SOFTNESS).

fluid, *adj.* watery, aqueous, serous (WATER, LIQUID).

fluid, *n.* liquor, broth, solution (LIQUID).

fluke, *n.* fortune, good fortune, windfall (GOOD LUCK).

flunky, *n.* help, domestic, domestic servant (SERVICE); hanger-on, ward heeler, truckler, bootlicker (SLAVERY).

flurry, *n.* flutter, fluster (AGITATION); flaw, windflaw, gust (WIND).

flurry, *v.* fluster, fuss up (*colloq.*), disconcert (NERVOUSNESS).

flush, *adj.* even, horizontal (FLATNESS); well-to-do, well-off, mon-eyed (WEALTH).

flush, *n.* glow, bloom, blush (RED).

flush, *v.* blush, color, redden (MODESTY).

fluster, *v.* flurry, fuss up (*colloq.*), flustrate (NERVOUSNESS).

flutter, *v.* wave, flap, flop (OSCILLATION); flitter, drift, hover (FLYING); tremble, throb, vibrate (SHAKE, RHYTHM).

fly, *n.* mosquito, gnat (ANIMAL).

fly, *v.* take off, take wing, aviate (FLYING); escape, take flight, steal away (DEPARTURE); hasten, hurry, hustle (SPEED).

flyer, *n.* aviator, airman (FLYING); advertisement, placard, bill (PUBLICATION).

fly-by-night, *adj.* untrustworthy, shifty, slippery (UNBELIEVINGNESS).

FLYING—N. flying, flight, take-off, volation, aerial maneuvers, aerobatics.

flyer, aviator, ace, aeronaut, airman, airplanist, eagle; aviatrix; pilot, navigator; parachutist, paratrooper, aerialist.

aircraft, airplane, plane, craft, ship (*colloq.*), air liner, air cruiser, clipper, bus (*slang*), crate (*slang*); helicopter, autogyro, monocoupe, glider, sailplane, flying saucer, jet plane, rocket ship, stratocruiser, spaceship, convertiplane, bomber; seaplane, hydroplane, flying boat.

airship, dirigible, zeppelin, blimp, balloon, observation balloon; kite, box kite; parachute.

aviation, aeronautics, avigation, aerodonetics, ballooning.

airport, airdrome, air base, heliport, seadrome.

flying field, airstrip, runway, landing field, landing strip; hangar, shed.

V. fly, take to the air, take flight, take off, take wing, wing, leave the ground; climb, soar, zoom, skirr, whir, sail, glide; flit, flutter, flitter, drift, hover, swarm; pilot, aviate, navigate, volplane; hop, hedgehop, buzz; airplane, plane, take a plane.

Adj. aerial, aeronautical, volar, volant.

See also AIR, FLOAT, HEIGHT.

---

foal, *n.* colt, yearling (HORSE).

FOAM—*N.* foam, froth, spume, scum, head, cream, lather, suds, yeast; surf, spray, sea foam.

bubble, globule, bead, blob.

bubbling, ebullience *or* ebulliency, ebullition, fermentation, effervescence *or* effervescency, boiling, burble *or* burbling, gurgitation, seethe, simmer.

V. foam, spume, froth, scum, cream, despumate; lather, suds; churn, put a head on.

bubble, boil, burble, effervesce, seethe, simmer, sparkle, fizz; hiss, gurgle; aerate.

Adj. foamy, frothy, spumous, spumescent, foaming, spumy, scummy, creamy, yeasty, lathery, sudsy, barmy.

bubbly, bubbling, boiling, burbling, ebullient, effervescent, foaming, foamy, seething, simmering; sparkling, fizzy, carbonated.

See also AGITATION, SHAKE. *Antonyms*—See CALMNESS.

---

focus, *n.* limelight, spotlight, cynosure (ATTENTION).

focus, *v.* centralize, concenter, concentrate (CENTER).

foe, *n.* adversary, enemy, opponent (OPPOSITION, HOSTILITY).

fog, *n.* mist, vapor, smog (GAS, CLOUD); vagueness, haze, confusion (UNCERTAINTY).

fog, *v.* obscure, darken, cloud (UNCLEARNESS).

foggy, *adj.* hazy, murky, fuzzy, misty, filmy, cloudy (UNCLEARNESS, SEMITRANSPARENCY).

foible, *n.* peculiarity, eccentricity, quirk, kink (UNUSUALNESS).

foil, *n.* plate, paillette, leaf (METAL); contrast, antithesis (DIFFERENCE); sword, blade (CUTTING).

foil, *v.* frustrate, thwart, balk (INEFFECTIVENESS).

foiled, *adj.* frustrated, thwarted, balked, checkmated (FAILURE).

FOLD—*N.* fold, dog's ear, ply, plica, plication, plicature, convolution, circumvolution, flection, flexure; loop, crease, crimp; corrugation, groove, furrow, ridge; pucker, rumple, ruffle, cockle, crinkle, crumple, complication.

V. fold, dog-ear, enfold, infold, loop, crease, crimp, double; plait, pleat, plicate, tuck, hem, ruck, seam, gather; corrugate, groove, furrow, ridge; pucker, knit (*as a brow*), purse, rumple, ruffle, cockle, crinkle, crumple, crisp; replicate, complicate.

Adj. folded, dog-eared, double, cockle (*of paper*), corrugate, bullate, convoluted; voluminous, ruffly, rumply, pursy, puckery, loopy, crinkly, crispy, seamy.

See also CLOSURE, TURNING, WINDING, WRINKLE. *Antonyms*—See SMOOTHNESS, UNFOLDMENT.

---

foliage, *n.* leafage, leaves, frondescence (PLANT LIFE).

folks, *n.* the public, the general public, inhabitants (PEOPLE).

folk tale, *n.* legend, myth, folk story (STORY).

follow, *v.* pursue, chase; come next, succeed (FOLLOWING); fathom, figure out (UNDERSTANDING).

FOLLOWER—*N.* follower, attendant, adherent, disciple, proselyte, partisan, sectary, devotee, fan, minion, henchman, myrmidon, vassal, servitor; sycophant, toady, tufthunter, footlicker, bootlicker, lickspittle, satellite, hanger-on, parasite, heeler; client, patron, customer; successor.

following, followers, retinue, rout, train; attendance, devotion, sycophancy, parasitism, sequacity; clientele, clientage, patronage, custom.

V. be a follower of, attend, accompany, serve, dance attendance on, bootlick, toady to.

See also FOLLOWING, LOYALTY, SERVICE.

FOLLOWING—*N.* following, succession, sequence, supervention, catenation.

pursuit, chase, hunt, stalk, persecution.

sequel, sequela, consequence.

series, sequence, succession, run, suite, chain, catena, concatenation, train, continuum, nexus, cycle, litany, consecution, course, ritual; set, suit, *or* run (*in cards*); line, row, range.

pursuer, shadow, tail (*slang*), skip-tracer, chaser, etc. (see *Verbs*).

V. **follow,** come after, go after, come next, go next, succeed; tag after, trail, draggle; catenate, concatenate.

pursue, dog, track, trail, trace, spoor, tag after, chase, hunt, give chase, persecute, hound; shadow, stalk, tail.

Adj. **following,** succeeding, next, after, coming after, coming next, later, posterior, proximate, subsequent, supervenient, trailing; consecutive, successive, serial, seriate, seriatim, quickfire; consequent, consequential, ensuing, attendant, sequential, sequent; in the wake of.

Adv., phrases. **subsequently,** later, behind, afterward, behindhand.

in pursuit, in full cry, in hot pursuit, on the scent, in quest of.

See also BUSINESS, COPY, FOLLOWER, HUNTING, IMITATION, SEARCH, SERVICE. *Antonyms*—See BEGINNING, FRONT, LEADERSHIP, PRECEDENCE.

FOLLY—*N.* folly, fatuity, inanity, unwisdom, absurdity; indiscretion, impracticality, imprudence, insipience; inadvisability, inexpedience, irrationality, obliquity, unintelligence, foolishness, etc. (see *Adjectives*).

fool, idiot, tomfool, witling, dunce, half-wit, nitwit, imbecile, simpleton, Simple Simon; donkey, ass, dolt, booby, boob, noodle, nincompoop, oaf, blockhead, bonehead (*slang*), numskull (*colloq.*), sap *or* saphead (*slang*), owl, goose, chump (*slang*), lunkhead (*slang*); ape, lunatic, ninny, noddy, silly (*colloq.*); pup, puppy, popinjay, fizgig.

clown, buffoon, jester, antic, merry-andrew, harlequin, punchinello, pierrot, Scaramouch; droll, gracioso, mime, mimer, mountebank, zany.

V. **fool,** trifle, play the fool, play, toy, jest, act like a fool; clown, buffoon, mountebank, droll, harlequin.

Adj. **foolish,** silly, senseless, witless, brainless, shallow-brained, shallow; impolitic, unwise, nonsensical, imprudent, misguided, ill-advised, injudicious, inexpedient, indiscreet, unreasonable, irrational, extravagant; fatuous, idiotic, imbecilic, stupid, inane, absurd, ridiculous, laughable, asinine; undiscerning, undiscriminating, shortsighted, imperceptive, impractical, unsagacious, insipient, inadvisable, unsound, obliquitous, unintelligent; trivial, frivolous, useless, vain.

See also ABSURDITY, STUPIDITY, UNREASONABLENESS, WITTINESS. *Antonyms*—See INTELLIGENCE, REASONABLENESS, REASONING, WISDOM.

foment, *v.* incite, instigate, arouse (MOTIVATION).

fond, *adj.* affectionate, tender, doting (LOVE).

fondle, *v.* nuzzle, pet, stroke (CARESS).

fond of, *adj.* partial to, attached to, affectionate toward (LIKING).

FOOD—*N.* food, nourishment, nutriment, foodstuff, sustenance, pabulum, keep, nurture, aliment, sustenance, subsistence; provender, corn, feed, fodder; provision, ration, board; forage, pasture, pasturage; fare, cheer; diet, dietary, regimen.

eatables, victuals, viands, comestibles, edibles, grub (*slang*), eats (*colloq.*), flesh, roast, meat, dainties, delicacies; ambrosia, manna.

biscuit, cracker, pretzel, rusk; hardtack, sea biscuit.

eating, consumption, deglutition, mastication, rumination.

table, cuisine, bill of fare, menu, *table d'hôte* (F.), *à la carte* (F.).

meal, repast, feed (*colloq.*), spread (*colloq.*); mess; course, dish, plate; refreshment, refection, collation, picnic, feast, banquet, junket; potluck.

mouthful, morsel, bite, sop, snack, tidbit.

restaurant, café, chophouse, eating house, cafeteria, Automat, one-arm joint (*slang*); *bistro* (F.), cabaret, coffeepot, coffee shop, diner, grill, inn, lunch wagon, night club, rathskeller, rotisserie, tavern; drive-in (*colloq.*).

dining room, dining hall, grill, lunchroom, mess hall, refectory, commons, canteen.

gourmet, epicure, epicurean, gastronomer, gourmand, *bon vivant* (F.).

V. **feed,** nourish, sustain, foster, nurture, strengthen; graze.

eat, fare, devour, swallow, consume, take, fall to, dine, banquet, feast; gormandize, gluttonize, bolt, dispatch, gulp; crunch, chew, masticate; peck (*colloq.*), nibble, gnaw, live on, batten (*or* feast) upon; bite, browse, graze, crop, champ, munch, ruminate.

Adj. **eatable,** edible, esculent, comestible, dietetic; nourishing, nutrient, nutritive, nutritious, alimentary; succulent.

omnivorous, carnivorous, flesh-eating, cannibal, predaceous; herbivorous, granivorous.

See also ALCOHOLIC LIQUOR, AMUSEMENT, BREAD, COOKERY, DRINK, DRUNKENNESS, GLUTTONY, HUNGER, SOCIALITY. *Antonyms*—See EXCRETION, FASTING.

fool, *n.* idiot, dunce, buffoon (FOLLY).

fool, *v.* deceive, delude, trick (DECEPTION); pretend, make believe, play-act (PRETENSE); jest, jape, spoof (WITTINESS); trifle, play the fool (FOLLY).

foolhardy, *adj.* breakneck, reckless, rash (COURAGE).

foolish, *adj.* silly, senseless, witless (FOLLY); ridiculous, ludicrous (ABSURDITY).

foot, *n.* extremity, paw, hoof (APPENDAGE); bottom, lowest point, nadir (LOWNESS).

foothold, *n.* footing, purchase, hold (SUPPORT); toe hold, bridgehead, open-sesame (INGRESS); foundation, groundwork (BASE).

footing, *n.* status, standing (SITUATION); foundation, underbuilding (BASE).

foot-loose, *adj.* fancy-free, uncommitted, unattached (FREEDOM).

footpath, *n.* foot road, course, walk, path, pathway, sidewalk (WALKING, PASSAGE).

footprint, *n.* trace, vestige, track (INDICATION); fossil footprint, ichnite, ichnolite (REMAINDER).

footsore, *adj.* footweary, footworn, weary-footed, way-weary (FATIGUE).

footstool, *n.* cricket, hassock, ottoman (SEAT).

FOOTWEAR—*N.* **footwear,** footgear, shoes, shoeing; stockings, nylons, socks, bobby socks, hose, hosiery; spats, gaiters.

shoe, boot, brogan, brogue, blucher, clog, gaiter, hobnailed boot, hobnailed shoe, oxford, Oxford tie, Prince Albert, sabot, saddle shoe, Wellington boot; cothurnus, cothurn, buskin (*all hist.*);

slipper, pantofle, step-in, sneaker, scuff, sandal, pump, mule, moccasin, loafer, shuffler; bootee, bed slipper; huaraches, clodhoppers, Hessian boots (*hist.*).

overshoes, arctics, galoshes, rubber boots, rubbers, snowshoes; skis.

stocking, anklet, hose, sock.

leggings, gaiters, gambados, overalls, puttees, spatterdashes; (*armor*) greave, jamb, jambeau, solleret.

shoemaker, bootmaker, cobbler, cordwainer (*archaic*).

bootblack, boots, shoeblack, shoeshine boy.

shoemaking, bootmaking, shoecraft, cobblery, cobbling.

V. **shoe,** boot, slipper; ski, snowshoe.

kick, calcitrate, boot (*colloq.*); paw the ground.

Adj. **shod,** booted, sandaled, slippered, buskined, calced (*rel.*).

See also APPENDAGE, CLOTHING, CLOTHING WORKER. *Antonyms*—See UNDRESS.

fop, *n.* beau, Beau Brummell, buck (FASHION).

foppish, *adj.* foplike, dandyish, dandiacal (FASHION).

forbear, *v.* forgo, refrain, resist (INACTION).

forbearance, *n.* patience, longanimity, fortitude (EXPECTATION).

forbearing, *adj.* humane, humanitarian, clement, merciful, lenient (PITY).

forbid, *v.* prohibit, bar, ban (DENIAL).

forbidden, *adj.* prohibited, contraband, *verboten* (*Ger.*), taboo (DENIAL).

forbidding, *adj.* grim, dour, unapproachable (SEVERITY).

force, *n.* energy, strength, might (FORCE); staff, personnel (WORK).

force, *v.* make, compel, coerce (FORCE); necessitate, make necessary, require (NECESSITY).

FORCE—*N.* **force,** energy, vigor, strength, might, power, punch, fury, dint, pith, birr, brunt, impetus, push, impulse, momentum; strain, stress.

compulsion, constraint, pressure, coercion, duress.

[*science of forces*] **dynamics,** geodynamics, kinetics, mechanics, physics, statics.

V. **force,** make, compel, coerce, drive, impel, constrain, bludgeon; draft, conscript, impress, press, dragoon; require, subject, oblige, insist; exact, extort, squeeze, wrest, wring, pry, twist.

enforce, administer, execute, perform.

Adj. **forceful**, forcible, energetic, mighty, strong, powerful, potent, puissant (*poetic*), vehement, vigorous, violent, stringent, titanic, pithy, punchy, dynamic, elemental.

compulsory, obligatory, enforced, required, binding, peremptory, stringent, compelling, compulsive, coercive.

Adv., phrases. **forcefully**, forcibly, etc. (see *Adj.*); with a vengeance, perforce, by dint of, by main force, by violence, by storm, with might and main; tooth and nail.

compulsorily, compulsively, by force, perforce, against one's will, willy-nilly.

See also ENERGY, NECESSITY, POWER, PROPULSION, RESTRAINT, STRENGTH, VIOLENCE. *Antonyms*— See FATIGUE, INACTION, WEAKNESS.

---

forced, *adj.* grudging, begrudging, involuntary (UNWILLINGNESS); artificial, constrained, contrived (UNNATURALNESS).

forceful, *adj.* forcible, energetic, strong (FORCE, STRENGTH).

forceps, *n.* pliers, pincers, pinchers (TAKING).

forcible, *adj.* strong, forceful, energetic (FORCE, STRENGTH).

forebode, *v.* forecast, foresee, foreshadow (PREDICTION, FUTURE); portend, premonish, forewarn (WARNING).

foreboding, *n.* premonition, misgiving, forewarning (FUTURE, MISFORTUNE, WARNING).

forecast, *n.* prophecy, prognosis, prognostication (PREDICTION).

forecast, *v.* foresee, forebode, divine (PREDICTION).

forefather, *n.* ancestor, antecedent, parent (ANCESTRY).

foregoing, *adj.* aforementioned, aforesaid, aforestated (PRECEDENCE).

foreground, *n.* fore, forepart, forefront (FRONT).

forehead, *n.* brow, frons, sinciput (HEAD, FRONT).

foreign, *adj.* alien, strange, remote (IRRELATION).

foreigner, *n.* stranger, outlander, outsider, alien (IRRELATION).

foreknowledge, *n.* prevision, prescience, prenotion (FORESIGHT).

forelock, *n.* tuft, cowlick, daglock (HAIR).

foreman, *n.* straw boss, superintendent, manager (WORK).

foremost, *adj.* chief, leading, principal (IMPORTANCE, SUPERIORITY).

forenoon, *n.* foreday, ante meridiem, A.M. (MORNING).

---

forerunner, *n.* precursor, harbinger, herald (PRECEDENCE).

foresee, *v.* forecast, expect, anticipate (PREDICTION, EARLINESS, FORESIGHT).

FORESIGHT—*N.* foresight, prevision, foreknowledge, prescience, prenotion, preconception, precognition, prospect, anticipation, premeditation; prudence, sagacity, forethought, providence, second sight, clairvoyance.

V. **foresee**, foreknow, anticipate, expect, contemplate, surmise; look forward to.

Adj. **foresighted**, prudent, discreet, judicious, circumspect, careful, sensible, wise, sagacious, provident.

foreseeing, prescient; farseeing, farsighted, long-sighted, clairvoyant.

See also CARE, EXPECTATION, FUTURE, KNOWLEDGE, PREDICTION, WISDOM. *Antonyms*—See BLINDNESS, SURPRISE.

---

forest, *n.* woodland, woods, wood (PLANT LIFE).

forestall, *v.* prevent, avert, preclude (PREVENTION).

foretaste, *n.* antepast, prelibation (TASTE).

forever, *adv.* always, ever, perpetually (ENDLESSNESS, UNIFORMITY).

forewarn, *v.* portend, forebode, premonish (WARNING).

forewarned, *adj.* armed, forearmed, forehanded (PREPARATION).

forewarning, *n.* foreboding, premonition (WARNING).

foreword, *n.* prelude, preamble, introduction (BEGINNING).

for example, e.g., *par exemple* (*F.*), for instance (COPY).

forfeit, *n.* penalty, fine, damages (LOSS, PUNISHMENT); gambit, pawn, victim (RELINQUISHMENT).

forge, *n.* metalworks, smithy, smithery (METAL); bloomery, kiln, brickkiln (HEAT); factory, manufactory, plant (PRODUCTION).

forge, *v.* fashion, form, contrive, devise (PRODUCTION); counterfeit, coin (THIEVERY).

FORGETFULNESS—*N.* forgetfulness, amnesia, fugue (*med.*), hypomnesia, paramnesia; short (untrustworthy, poor, *or* failing) memory; Lethe, nepenthe, nirvana, amnesty; limbo, oblivion, oblivescence; suppression, repression (*psychoanal.*).

V. **forget**, be forgetful, have a short memory, escape (*or* slip) one's memory, disremember (*archaic or dial.*), efface from the memory, obliterate, lose sight of; consign to oblivion, think no more of, let bygones be bygones; fall (*or* sink) into oblivion.

Adj. **forgetful**, oblivious, unmindful, absent-minded; amnesic *or* amnestic; Lethean, nirvanic; amnemonic.

forgotten, unremembered, past recollection, gone, lost, gone out of one's head, out of mind, buried (*or* sunk) in oblivion; suppressed, repressed; obliviscent.

See also INATTENTION, NEGLECT, SHORTNESS. *Antonyms*—See MEMORY.

FORGIVENESS—*N.* **forgiveness**, pardon, remission, dispensation, absolution, amnesty, immunity, impunity, indemnity; reprieve, respite, purgation.

mercy, clemency, pity, compassion, lenience, lenity, grace, quarter.

excuse, rationalization, alibi (*colloq.*), plea, defense, stall, pretext, subterfuge, allegation, *aeger* (*L.*).

V. **forgive**, pardon, absolve, give absolution, amnesty, remit, reprieve, respite, purge.

excuse, release, exempt, extenuate, mitigate, justify, palliate, overlook, pass over, blink at, wink at, condone, warrant, vindicate; think no more of, let bygones be bygones, bear with, allow for, make allowances for; bury the hatchet, start afresh, wipe the slate clean.

be merciful, show mercy, spare; ask for mercy, throw oneself on the mercy of, ask quarter.

Adj. **forgiving**, placable, unrevengeful, unvindictive; magnanimous, generous, charitable.

merciful, clement, sparing, lenient, compassionate.

forgivable, defensible, excusable, justifiable, pardonable, remissible, venial, vindicable, warrantable; absolvable, exculpable.

See also ACQUITTAL, ATONEMENT, CHARITY. *Antonyms*—See ACCUSATION, RETALIATION.

---

forgo, *v.* forbear, refrain, desist (INACTION).

forgotten, *adj.* unremembered, past recollection, gone (FORGETFULNESS).

for instance, *exempli gratia*, e.g., *par exemple* (*F.*), for example (COPY).

fork, *n.* divergence, branch, crotch, detour, deviation (TURNING, ANGULARITY).

fork, *v.* bifurcate, divaricate, diverge (TURNING, BISECTION, TWO, ANGULARITY).

forked, *adj.* dichotomous, dichotomic, bifid, biforked, bifurcate, divaricate (TWO, ANGULARITY).

forlorn, *adj.* lonely, lonesome, desolate (SECLUSION); miserable, wretched, tragic (SADNESS).

form, *n.* manner, fashion, mode (METHOD); object, thing, phenomenon (VISION); embodiment, cast, conformation (SHAPE); bench, settle (SEAT); class, grade, room (LEARNING).

form, *v.* fabricate, organize, structure (MAKE-UP); compose, make up, constitute (PART); fashion, forge, devise (PRODUCTION); mold, pat, whittle (SHAPE).

formal dress, *n.* formal wear, formals, dinner clothes, dress clothes (CLOTHING).

FORMALITY—*N.* **formality**, ceremony, rite, ritual, tradition, punctilio, convention, etiquette, mummery.

V. **ceremonialize**, conventionalize, formalize; stand on ceremony; solemnize, observe formally (*or* solemnly).

Adj. **formal**, stiff, stilted, angular, bookish, sententious; ritual, ceremonial, ceremonious, academic, conventional, solemn, stereotyped, stereotypical, punctilious; formalistic, ritualistic, ceremonialist.

See also CELEBRATION, CONFORMITY, COURTESY, OBSERVANCE, PROPRIETY, RIGHT, WORSHIP. *Antonyms*—See NONOBSERVANCE.

---

former, *adj.* earlier, prior, previous (PRECEDENCE).

formerly, *adv.* once, erstwhile (*archaic*), of old (TIME, PAST).

formidable, *adj.* overpowering, overwhelming, all-powerful (STRENGTH); dire, fierce, redoubtable (FEAR).

formula, *n.* recipe, receipt, procedure (METHOD); precept, canon, maxim (RULE).

formulate, *v.* compose, draft, draw up (WRITING).

fornicate, *v.* cohabit, copulate, debauch (SEX).

forsake, *v.* desert, abandon, leave (DESERTION).

fort, *n.* citadel, fortress, blockhouse (PROTECTION).

forte, *n.* aptitude, gift, faculty (ABILITY).

forth, *adv.* forward, onward, ahead (PROGRESS).

forthright, *adj.* frank, candid, blunt (HONESTY, STRAIGHTNESS).

fortification, *n.* garrison, presidio, stronghold, bastion, breastwork, earthwork (PROTECTION).

fortified, *adj.* walled, bastioned, battlemented (PROTECTION, WALL).

fortify, *v.* strengthen, brace, buttress (STRENGTH); fortress, bulwark, garrison (PROTECTION).

fortuitous, *adj.* lucky, fortunate, happy (GOOD LUCK); accidental, casual, haphazard (CHANCE).

fortunate, *adj.* happy, lucky, fortuitous (CHANCE, GOOD LUCK).

fortune, *n.* capital, treasure, gold (WEALTH); chance, luck (CHANCE); good fortune, fluke, windfall (GOOD LUCK); fate, lot, portion (DESTINY).

fortune hunter, *n.* adventurer, adventuress, gold-digger (MONEY).

fortuneteller, *n.* predictor, prophet, palmist (PREDICTION).

forward, *adj.* progressive, advancing, onward (PROGRESS); anterior, ventral, facial (FRONT); bold, audacious, assuming (DISCOURTESY).

forward, *adv.* onward, forth, on, ahead, before, vanward (PROGRESS, FRONT).

forward, *v.* promote, cultivate, advance (IMPROVEMENT); send, transmit (SENDING).

fossil, *n.* eolith, paleolith, neolith (OLDNESS).

foster, *v.* advance, help, promote (AID).

foul, *adj.* mucky, nasty, dreggy (UNCLEANNESS); foulmouthed, filthy, obscene (OBSCENITY); monstrous, corrupt (WICKEDNESS).

foul, *v.* dirty, soil, besoil (UNCLEANNESS).

foulmouthed, *adj.* filthy, foul, obscene (UNCLEANNESS).

found, *v.* establish, organize, institute (BEGINNING).

foundation, *n.* bottom, groundwork, basis (BASE); corset, corselet, girdle (UNDERWEAR).

founder, *n.* planner, architect, strategist (PLAN).

foundling, *n.* changeling, waif (CHILD).

fountain, *n.* mine, spring, well (STORE); origin, font, source (BEGINNING).

FOUR—N. four, quaternary, tetrad; square, foursquare, quadrate, quadrilateral, quadrangle, rectangle, tetragon; quarter, quartern.

foursome, quadruplet, quartet, quaternary, quaternion, tetrad.

V. **quadruple,** quadruplicate; quarter, quadrisect.

Adj. **four,** fourfold, quadrigeminal, quadruple, quadruplex, quadruplicate; quadrifid, quadripartite, quaternary, fourth, quartan, quartile.

---

four hundred, *n.* upper class, upper crust, classes, bon ton, society (SOCIAL CLASS).

four-sided, *adj.* quadrilateral, tetrahedral (SIDE).

fowl, *n.* poultry, chicken (BIRD).

foxy, *adj.* cunning, crafty, vulpine (CLEVERNESS).

fracas, *n.* fray, fight, brawl (COMMOTION, FIGHTING); words, melee, row (DISAGREEMENT).

fraction, *n.* portion, fragment, division (PART).

fracture, *n.* break, discontinuity, severance, cleavage (DISJUNCTION).

fracture, *v.* break, snap, split (BREAKAGE).

fragile, *adj.* brittle, frangible, frail (BREAKABLENESS, WEAKNESS).

fragment, *n.* portion, fraction, piece (PART).

fragrance, *n.* aroma, scent, aura (ODOR).

frail, *adj.* weak, feeble, infirm (WEAKNESS); fragile, shattery, brittle (BREAKABLENESS).

frame, *adj.* wooden, wood, timbered (WOOD).

frame, *n.* framework, scaffolding, skeleton (SUPPORT); figure, physique, build (SHAPE, BODY); fabric, mold, structure (CONDITION).

frame, *v.* compose, draft, indite (WRITING); plan, design, devise (PLAN); lath, panel, shingle (WOOD).

framing, *n.* sheathing, lathing, siding, clapboard (WOOD).

franchise, *n.* ballot, suffrage (VOTE); patent, charter (PERMISSION).

frank, *adj.* sincere, candid, aboveboard (HONESTY, TRUTH, REALITY).

frank, *n.* mark, John Hancock (*slang*), cross (SIGNATURE).

frantic, *adj.* frenzied, frenetic, berserk (EXCITEMENT, VIOLENCE).

fraternize, *v.* mingle, hobnob, mix (SOCIALITY).

fraud, *n.* deceit, fraudulence, misrepresentation (DECEPTION); fake, bastard, sham (FALSENESS); humbug, fourflusher (*colloq.*), impostor (PRETENSE, DECEPTION); racket, swindle (THIEVERY).

fraudulent, *adj.* counterfeit, forged, mock, sham (FALSENESS); dishonorable, crooked, deceitful, devious (DISHONESTY).

fray, *n.* combat, contest, affray, engagement (FIGHTING).

fray, *v.* tear, rip, frazzle, shred (TEARING).

frazzle, *v.* tear, rip, fray, shred (TEARING).

freak, *n.* monstrosity, abnormality, aberration (UNNATURALNESS).

freckled, *adj.* spotted, flecked, nevose (VARIEGATION).

free, *adj.* at large, loose (FREEDOM); generous, big, bighearted (UNSELFISHNESS).

free association, *n.* train of thought, association of ideas, flow of ideas, stream of consciousness (THOUGHT, IDEA).

FREEDOM—N. freedom, liberty, *carte blanche* (F.), license, unconstraint, unrestraint, libertinism, profligacy, laxity, rampancy, rein, abandon, abandonment.

liberation, rescue, redemption, release, deliverance, delivery, salvage, salvation, disengagement; disimprisonment, discharge, probation, parole; emancipation, enfranchisement, manumission, abolition; exemption, immunity, impunity, relief.

independence, autonomy, self-government, sovereignty, autocracy, autarchy.

scope, range, latitude, play, free play, swing, full swing, elbow-room, margin, rope.

liberator, rescuer, lifesaver, lifeguard; emancipator, enfranchiser, salvager, salvor, savior, Messiah.

freeman, freedman, parolee, probationer.

independent, free lance, free-thinker, maverick; autocrat, nationalist, autarchist, libertarian, libertine, wanton.

V. free, liberate, set free, rescue, save, salve, salvage, deliver, let loose, let go, release, set loose, unloose, unloosen, let escape, unhand; emancipate, enfranchise, affranchise, manumit; ransom, redeem; unimprison, disimprison, discharge, unmew, uncoop, uncage, parole, spring (*slang*), go bail for, bail, bail out; loose, loosen, extricate, disengage, unbind, unchain, unfetter, unhobble, unleash, unpinion, untie, unfasten, unstick, unshackle; unhandcuff, unmanacle, untrammel; unmuzzle, unbridle, ungag.

be free, have scope, do what one likes, have one's fling; paddle one's own canoe (*colloq.*); go at large, feel at home, stand on one's rights; relax, thaw, unbend.

exempt, excuse, release, discharge, relieve.

disburden, disencumber, rid, discharge, unload, unpack, unlade, disengage.

unblock, deobstruct, unclog, uncork, unplug, unstop, unstopple.

Adj. free, at large, loose, unloosed, escaped; fancy-free, uncommitted, unattached, foot-loose, uninhibited, expansive, unrepressed, unsuppressed, unreserved.

exempt, immune, privileged, special, excused, released.

unrestrained, unrestricted, unlimited, unqualified; unconstrained, dissolute, libertine, licentious, licentiate, profligate, loose, lax, unprincipled, unconscionable, unscrupulous, wanton, wild, rampant, riotous, abandoned; uncontrolled, ungoverned, madcap, wildcat, reinless, unreined, unchecked, uncurbed, unbridled; uncircumscribed, unconfined, unbound, uncontained, unconstricted.

independent, autonomous, self-governing, sovereign; absolute, substantive; undominated, unregulated, ungoverned.

unencumbered, unburdened, unhampered, unhindered, unimpeded, unobstructed, unstemmed, unsuppressed, unstifled, untrammeled; disburdened, disencumbered, rid; unblocked, unclogged, unplugged, unstopped.

[*without cost*] free, complimentary, gratuitous, gratis, costless, chargeless; for nothing, for love; without obligation.

free and easy, unconventional, unceremonious, careless, casual, slack, unmindful, regardless, informal, Bohemian; at ease, *dégagé* (F.), at one's ease, quite at home.

Adv., *phrases*, freely, at will, *ad libitum* (L.), with no restraint.

See also ACQUITTAL, DEPARTURE, DISJUNCTION, RELIEF. Antonyms— See HINDRANCE, IMPRISONMENT, RESTRAINT.

---

free lance, *n.* author, *littérateur* (F.), essayist (WRITER); franctireur, mercenary (FIGHTER).

freely, *adv.* willingly, gladly, cheerfully (WILLINGNESS); *ad libitum* (L.), at will (FREEDOM).

freethinker, *n.* skeptic, unbeliever, agnostic (IRRELIGION).

freeze, *v.* glaciate, ice, frost (COLD).

freezer, *n.* refrigerator, icebox, ice chest, deep-freeze (COLD).

freight, *n.* cargo, load, shipment (TRANSFER, CONTENTS).

freighter, *n.* merchant ship, lighter, tanker (SHIP).

frenetic, *adj.* frantic, phrenetic, furibund, frenzied (EXCITEMENT).

frenzied, *adj.* frenetic, insane, frantic (EXCITEMENT, VIOLENCE).

frenzy, *n.* distemper, distraction, madness (INSANITY); ferment, phrensy, fever (EXCITEMENT).

frenzy, *v.* dement, derange, distract (INSANITY); excite, ferment (EXCITEMENT).

FREQUENCY—N. frequency, repetition, iteration, persistence, reiteration, recurrence; density, abundance.

V. **frequent,** resort to, visit, revisit, attend, haunt; infest, overrun, swarm over.

Adj. **frequent,** repeated, incessant, perpetual, continual, constant; habitual, persistent, common, customary, general; numerous, abundant, thick.

Adv., phrases. **frequently,** repeatedly, recurrently, in quick succession, at short intervals; often, oft *(archaic or poetic)*; oftentimes, ofttimes *(archaic)*; habitually, commonly.

See also ARRIVAL, COMMONNESS, CONTINUATION, HABIT, MULTITUDE, OCCURRENCE, PRESENCE, REPETITION. *Antonyms*—See FEWNESS, INSUFFICIENCY.

---

fresh, *adj.* novel, original, Promethean (NEWNESS, UNUSUALNESS); untried, untouched, unbeaten (NEWNESS); saucy, snippy *(colloq.)*, flippant (DISCOURTESY).

fret, *v.* worry, stew *(colloq.)*, fuss (NERVOUSNESS); displease, gall (ANNOYANCE).

friction, *n.* conflict, dissension, strife (DISAGREEMENT); traction, attrition, trituration (RUBBING).

FRIEND—N. friend, acquaintance, crony, well-wisher, intimate, confidant; *alter ego* (L.), other self; best (bosom, trusty, or fast) friend, *fidus Achates* (L.).

comrade, mate, companion, chum *(colloq.)*, pal *(slang)*, buddy *(colloq.)*, confrere, associate, colleague, cohort, consort, side-kick *(slang)*, playmate, schoolmate, classmate; roommate, shipmate, messmate, comate, compeer; compatriot, countryman.

friends (collectively), circle *or* social circle, clique, company, coterie, society.

See also FRIENDLINESS.

FRIENDLINESS—N. friendliness, camaraderie, comradery, bonhomie, amity, affability.

friendship, familiarity, intimacy, acquaintanceship, companionship, comradeship, camaraderie or comradery, fellowship, company, society, sodality, solidarity; harmony, concord, peace; partiality, favoritism.

V. **be friendly,** be friends, be acquainted with, know; have dealings with, sympathize with, favor, have a leaning to, bear good will; befriend, cultivate, curry favor with, ingratiate oneself with; companion.

become friendly, make friends with, break the ice, be introduced to, scrape up an acquaintance with; thaw, unbend.

[*make friendly*] conciliate, appease, mollify, placate, propitiate, soothe, reconcile, disarm, win over.

Adj. **friendly,** affable, amiable, boon, chummy, clubby, companionable, congenial, conversable, convivial, jovial, cordial, debonair, familiar, genial, gregarious, hearty, homey, intimate, bosom, close, matey, neighborly, pally *(slang)*, sociable, social, thick *(colloq.)*.

favorable, auspicious, advantageous, benign, favonian, fortunate, opportune, propitious; in favor of, well disposed toward, favorably disposed (*or* inclined), inclinable.

See also AID, KINDNESS, LOVE, PEACE, PLEASANTNESS, SOCIALITY. *Antonyms*—See FIGHTING, HOSTILITY, OPPOSITION, SECLUSION, UNPLEASANTNESS.

---

fright, *n.* alarm, terror, panic (FEAR).

frighten, *v.* terrify, alarm, intimidate (FEAR).

frightening, *adj.* fearful, shocking, terrifying, terrible (FEAR).

frightful, *adj.* gruesome, morbid, grisly (FEAR); shocking, hideous, horrible (DISGUST).

frigid, *adj.* cool, chill, frigid (COLD); impotent, unresponsive (CELIBACY).

fringe, *n.* tassel, knot, frog (ORNAMENT); mane, ruff (HAIR).

frisk, *v.* caper, cavort, dance (JUMP); gambol, lark, frolic (AMUSEMENT, PLAYFULNESS).

fritter, *v.* dissipate, lavish, squander (WASTEFULNESS).

FRIVOLITY—N. frivolity, levity, volatility, flippancy, fribble, trifling, whimsicality, whimsey.

frivoler, fribbler, trifler; lighthead, flip *(colloq.)*, rattlebrain, rattlehead, rattlepate, whiffler; soubrette, flibbertigibbet (*both fem.*).

V. act frivolously, frivol, fribble, trifle, flibbertigibbet; play with, toy with, trifle with.

Adj. frivolous, idle, fribble, trivial, frothy, facetious, tongue-in-cheek, sportive; dizzy, light-headed, flighty, giddy, hare-brained, barmy, barmybrained, rattlebrained, rattleheaded, rattlepated; flippant, flip (*colloq.*), playful, trifling, skittish, whimsical, yeasty, volatile.

See also ABSURDITY, DIZZINESS, FOLLY, PLAYFULNESS, UNIMPORTANCE, WITTINESS. *Antonyms*—See IMPORTANCE, SOBRIETY.

frock, *n.* gown, robe, dress (SKIRT).

frog, *n.* bullfrog, croaker, toad (ANIMAL); fringe, tassel, knot (ORNAMENT).

frolic, *n.* fun, sport, gaiety (MERRIMENT); trick, gambol, lark (MISCHIEF).

frolic, *v.* sport, frisk, gambol (PLAYFULNESS); prance, romp (JUMP).

frolicsome, *adj.* gleeful, hilarious, jocular (MERRIMENT).

FRONT—*N.* front, foreground, fore, forepart, beginning, forefront; face, frontage, frontispiece (*arch.*), frontal, façade, obverse, proscenium; anterior; brow, forehead.

van, head, vanguard, *avant-garde* (*F.*).

[*of a ship*] prow, stem, nose, bow; rostrum, beak, jib, bowsprit.

V. front, face, confront, meet; veneer, overlay, cover.

Adj. front, frontal, foremost, fore, headmost; forward, anterior, ventral, facial, foreground, obverse; vanward, first, advanced, *avant-garde* (*F.*), ahead.

Adv., phrases. frontward, forward, before, ahead, vanward, onward; in front, in the van, in advance, in the foreground; anteriad (*anat.*).

See also BEGINNING, EXTERIORITY, HEAD, LEADERSHIP, PRECEDENCE. *Antonyms*—See REAR.

frontier, *n.* border, confines, march (BOUNDARY, LAND).

frost, *n.* rime, hoarfrost (COLD).

frosted, *adj.* milky, opalescent, pearly (WHITENESS, SEMITRANSPARENCY).

froth, *n.* foam, spume, head (FOAM).

frown, *v.* scowl, glower, lour (ANGER).

frowzy, *adj.* slovenly, sloppy, messy, blowzy, grubby (UNTIDINESS, UNCLEANNESS).

frugal, *adj.* economical, Spartan, thrifty (ECONOMY).

fruit, *n.* crop, harvest (RESULT).

fruitful, *adj.* fertile, fecund, prolific (FERTILITY); successful, blooming, flourishing (SUCCESS).

fruitless, *adj.* unprofitable, unproductive, profitless (USELESSNESS, INEFFECTIVENESS); sterile, barren, unfruitful (UNPRODUCTIVENESS).

frump, *n.* draggletail, drab, trollop (UNTIDINESS).

frustrate, *v.* thwart, baffle, foil (HINDRANCE, INEFFECTIVENESS).

frustrated, *adj.* foiled, thwarted, balked, checkmated (FAILURE); ungratified, unsated, unslaked (DISSATISFACTION).

frustration, *n.* unsatisfaction, uncontent, unfulfillment (DISSATISFACTION); chagrin, disgruntlement, letdown (DISAPPOINTMENT).

frying pan, *n.* fryer, fry pan, skillet (COOKERY).

FUEL—*N.* fuel, firing, combustible, coal, hard coal, anthracite, soft coal, bituminous coal, cannel coal, lignite, carbon, gasoline, petrol; gas, natural gas; electricity.

firewood, fagot, kindling wood, kindlings, brushwood; log, stump, block, backlog, yule log.

match, light, lucifer, safety match, vesuvian; flint and steel; pocket lighter, cigarette lighter.

V. fuel, supply with fuel, coal, stoke.

See also FIRE, HEAT, OIL.

fugitive, *adj.* fugacious, volatile, elusive, evanescent, ephemeral, impermanent (DISAPPEARANCE, IMPERMANENCE); errant, erratic, planetary (WANDERING).

fugitive, *n.* escaper, escapee, runagate (DEPARTURE).

fulfill, *v.* perform, render, do (ACTION); please, suit, suffice (SATISFACTION).

fulfilled, *adj.* delighted, gratified, pleased (SATISFACTION).

fulfillment, *n.* contentment, contentedness, gratification (SATISFACTION).

FULLNESS—*N.* fullness, congestion, repletion, plenitude, plenum.

filling, padding, stuffing, fill, filler, pad, load.

overfullness, satiety, satiation, surfeit, repletion, glut.

V. fill, load, lade, pack, pad, bulk out, saturate, impregnate, imbue, suffuse, swamp; stuff, choke up, clog up, glut, congest, cram, crowd, ram, charge, overcrowd, overstuff, overfill, overflow; clutter, lumber; refill, replenish; be full, burst, teem, pullulate, abound with; sate, satiate, surfeit, stodge.

fill oneself (*as with food*), cram oneself, gorge oneself, stuff, stuff oneself.

Adj. full, voluminous, loaded, laden, packed, padded, teeming, replete; saturated, suffused, impregnated, impregnate, imbued, charged.

cluttered, crowded, crammed, choked up, clogged up, gorged, chock-full, chuck-full, congested, overcrowded.

topfull, full to the top, brimming, brimful, cram-full, overfull, full to overflowing, overflowing, overfilled, bursting, plethoric, swollen.

absolute, plenary, complete, thorough.

sated, satiated, satiate, surfeited, gorged, stuffed, glutted.

See also COMPLETENESS, FOOD, SATISFACTION, SUFFICIENCY. *Antonyms*—See ABSENCE, FASTING, HUNGER, INSUFFICIENCY.

---

fully, *adv.* outright, wholly, totally (COMPLETENESS).

fume, *v.* smoke, reek, smolder (GAS); burn, boil with rage (ANGER).

fumigate, *v.* smoke, steam (GAS).

fun, *n.* sport, frolic, gaiety (MERRIMENT, AMUSEMENT, PLEASURE).

function, *n.* utility, service, purpose (USE); party, affair, gathering (SOCIALITY).

function, *v.* act, operate, work (ACTION, AGENCY); officiate, officialize (OFFICIAL).

functional, *adj.* practical, useful, utile, utilitarian (USE).

fund, *n.* stock, supply, reservoir (STORE).

fundamental, *adj.* essential, key, primary (IMPORTANCE); basal, basic (BASE).

funds, *n.* wealth, means, resources (MONEY).

funeral, *n.* obsequies, exequies, obit (BURIAL).

funeral song, *n.* dirge, monody, threnody (SINGING).

funereal, *adj.* mournful, dirgeful, doleful, elegiac (SADNESS); serious, solemn, grim, somber (SOBRIETY); funeral, defunctive, feral, funerary (BURIAL).

fun-loving, *adj.* merry, convivial, gay (MERRIMENT).

funnel, *n.* ventilator, ventiduct, air shaft (AIR).

funny, *adj.* witty, humorous, jocular (WITTINESS); odd, peculiar, curious (UNUSUALNESS).

fur, *n.* coat, pelage, wool (HAIR).

furbish, *v.* refurbish, rehabilitate, recondition (RESTORATION).

furious, *adj.* angry, enraged, raging (ANGER); rampageous, flaming, rabid (EXCITEMENT, VIOLENCE).

furl, *v.* swathe, fold, lap (ROLL).

furlough, *n.* leave, leave of absence, liberty (ABSENCE).

furnace, *n.* incinerator, calefactor (FIRE, HEAT).

furnish, *v.* supply, provide, equip (GIVING, STORE, QUANTITY).

furor, *n.* craze, fad, rage (ENTHUSIASM); agitation, ferment, hysteria (EXCITEMENT).

furrow, *n.* corrugation, groove, ridge (FOLD, WRINKLE); rabbet, rut (HOLLOW).

furry, *adj.* hairy, woolly, bushy (HAIR).

further, *v.* promote, forward, advance (AID).

furthermore, *adv.* further, besides, also (ADDITION).

furthest, *adj.* farthest, furthermost, ultimate (DISTANCE).

furtive, *adj.* secretive, sly, sneaky (CONCEALMENT).

fury, *n.* rage, ire, wrath (ANGER); rabidity, rampancy, storm (VIOLENCE); energy, might, power (FORCE); spitfire, virago, shrew (BAD TEMPER, VIOLENCE).

fuse, *v.* blend, cement, weld (UNITY, JUNCTION).

fusillade, *n.* barrage, volley, discharge, shower (THROW).

fusion, *n.* amalgamation, coalescence, blend, blending (COMBINATION); union, junction, coadunation (UNITY).

fuss, *n.* pother, ado, to-do (ACTIVITY, COMMOTION); fret, solicitude, perturbation (NERVOUSNESS).

fuss, *v.* worry, stew (*colloq.*), fret, fidget (NERVOUSNESS).

fuss-budget (*colloq.*), *n.* worrier, fusser, fretter (NERVOUSNESS).

fussy, *adj.* overfastidious, overparticular, dainty (CHOICE); garish, gew-gaw, gimcrack (OSTENTATION).

futile, *adj.* sterile, barren, unavailing (USELESSNESS, INEFFECTIVENESS, HOPELESSNESS, FAILURE).

FUTURE—*N.* future, futurity, aftertime, offing, posterity, time to come; morrow, tomorrow, by and by; millennium, doomsday, day of judgment, crack of doom; hereafter, future state, afterlife, life to come; destiny.

prospect, outlook, forecast, foresight, prescience; hope, anticipation, expectation.

[*sign of the future*] omen, augury; auspice, forerunner, foreshadower, foretoken, harbinger, herald, precursor, preindication, prodigy, prognostic, prognostication, apocalypse.

foreboding, portent, premonition, presage.

V. augur, adumbrate, bespeak, betoken, bode, forebode, forecast, foreshadow, foreshow, foretell, foretoken, harbinger, herald, omen, portend, prefigure, preindicate, presage, preshow, presignify, prognosticate, prophesy.

Adj. future, coming; prospective; impending, overhanging, imminent; next, near, close at hand;

eventual, ulterior, final, later.
Adv., phrases. in future, hereafter, prospectively, in the course of time, eventually, ultimately, sooner or later, one of these days.

soon, presently, shortly, anon (*archaic*), on the eve (*or* point) of, about to.

See also APPROACH, CHILD, DESTINY, EARLINESS, EXPECTATION, FORESIGHT, PRECEDENCE, PREDICTION. *Antonyms*—See PAST, PRESENT TIME.

futuristic, *adj.* ultramodern, ultramodernistic, futurist, advanced (NEWNESS).

fuzz, *n.* down, fluff, lanugo (HAIR).

fuzzy, *adj.* downy, fluffy, velutinous (HAIR); hazy, murky, foggy (UNCLEARNESS).

G

gab, *v.* gabble, jaw (*slang*), jabber (TALK).

gabble, *v.* cackle, chuckle, gaggle (ANIMAL SOUND); gab, jabber (TALK).

gadabout, *n.* gallivanter, rover, roamer (WANDERING).

gag (*colloq.*), *n.* joke, jest, jape (WITTINESS).

gag, *v.* muzzle, suppress, muffle (SILENCE, RESTRAINT); be nauseous, nauseate (NAUSEA).

gaiety, *n.* fun, sport, frolic (MERRIMENT).

gain, *v.* win, acquire, profit (TAKING, ACQUISITION).

gainful, *adj.* well-paying, profitable, lucrative (PAYMENT).

gain on, *v.* overtake, overhaul, beat (TRAP, SPEED).

gainsay, *v.* contradict, disaffirm, dispute, disprove, deny (OPPOSITION, DENIAL).

gait, *n.* walk, tread, stride (WALKING).

gale, *n.* windstorm, big blow, cyclone (WIND).

gallant, *adj.* chivalrous, courtly, knightly (COURTESY); dauntless, doughty, fearless (COURAGE).

gallant, *n.* squire, cavalier, chevalier (LOVE, COURTESY); paramour, lover (SEX).

gallery, *n.* balcony, mezzanine (SEAT); porch, patio, veranda (BUILDING).

galley, *n.* kitchen, scullery, pantry (SPACE); bireme, trireme, quadrireme (SHIP).

gallivant, *v.* cruise, gad, jaunt (WANDERING).

gallop, *v.* run, career, course (SPEED).

gallows, *n.* gibbet, scaffold (KILLING, HANGING).

galoshes, *n.* overshoes, arctics, rubber boots (FOOTWEAR).

galvanize, *v.* electrify, commove, arouse (EXCITEMENT).

gamble, *n.* lottery, raffle, throw of the dice (CHANCE).

gamble, *v.* game, wager, hazard (CHANCE).

gambol, *v.* prance, romp (JUMP); sport, frisk, frolic (PLAYFULNESS).

game, *adj.* nervy, spunky, plucky (COURAGE); willing, ready (WILLINGNESS).

game, *n.* object of ridicule, butt, derision (RIDICULE); wild animals, wild fowl (ANIMAL).

game, *v.* gamble, bet, wager (CHANCE).

gamin, *n.* urchin, street Arab, guttersnipe (YOUTH).

gang, *n.* workers, crew, team (WORK); knot, troop, cluster (ASSEMBLAGE).

gangling, *adj.* lanky, lank, slabsided, stringy (THINNESS).

gangrene, *n.* mortification, necrosis, phagedena (DEATH).

gangster, *n.* mobster, gunman, hoodlum (ILLEGALITY, VIOLENCE).

gap, *n.* space, interstice, blank (INTERVAL, ABSENCE); pass, defile, cut (NOTCH).

gape, *v.* stare, yawp, gawk (LOOKING); dehisce, frondesce, gap (OPENING).

garb, *n.* dress, raiment, garments (CLOTHING).

garbage, *n.* refuse, waste, swill (UNCLEANNESS).

gardening, *n.* horticulture, floriculture (FARMING).

garish, *adj.* showy, ostentatious, flashy (OSTENTATION, VULGARITY).

garland, *n.* crown, bays, palm, laurel (FAME, PAYMENT).

garment, *n.* dress, raiment, attire (CLOTHING).

garret, *n.* attic, loft (SPACE).

garrison, *n.* fortification, presidio, stronghold (PROTECTION).

GAS—*N.* gas, fluid, oxygen, nitrogen, hydrogen, carbon monoxide, coal gas, carbon dioxide.

vapor, steam, reek, effluvium, miasma; fog, mist, brume, pea-soup fog.

vaporizer, atomizer, spray, evaporator, still, retort.

smoke, fume, fumes, smolder, smudge, soot, smother; puff, whiff, wisp, drag; flue, smokestack, chimney.

belch, burp (*colloq.*), eructation, flatus, flatulence.

V. gasify, aerate, aerify, carbonate, charge.

vaporize, atomize, spray; distill, finestill, evaporate, volatilize.

smoke, drag, puff, suck, whiff, inhale; fume, seek, smoulder, fumigate, steam, smudge.

belch, burp (*colloq.*), eruct, eructate, bubble (*an infant*).

Adj. gaseous, ethereal, fluid, gassy, effervescent, charged.

vaporous, vapory, vaporish, steamy, miasmal; volatile, vaporable, effluvial.

smoky, fumy, reeky, smouldering; fuliginous, fumatory, sooty.

belching, flatulent, eructative, carminative.

See also AIR, FOAM, THINNESS, TOBACCO. *Antonyms*—See THICKNESS.

---

gasp, *v.* whoop, gulp, sigh (BREATH).

gate, *n.* door, portal, gateway (INGRESS, EGRESS); returns, proceeds (RECEIVING).

gather, *v.* accumulate, amass, collect (STORE, ACQUISITION); pluck, pick, draw (TAKING); convene, flock, huddle (ASSEMBLAGE, MULTITUDE); infer, conclude, judge (LIKELIHOOD, UNDERSTANDING).

gathering, *n.* drove, crush, flock (MULTITUDE); assembly, meeting (ASSEMBLAGE); party, affair (SOCIALITY).

gaudy, *adj.* flashy, meretricious, loud (OSTENTATION, VULGARITY).

gauge, *n.* measure, meter, rule (MEASUREMENT); norm, standard, criterion (JUDGMENT).

gauge, *v.* measure, meter (MEASUREMENT); calculate, estimate (COMPUTATION).

gauzy, *adj.* transparent, diaphanous, sheer (TRANSPARENCY).

gawk, *v.* stare, gape, yawp (LOOKING).

gay, *adj.* blithe, glad, joyful (HAPPINESS); debonair, cheerful, cheery (CHEERFULNESS); merry, convivial, fun-loving (MERRIMENT); primrose, saturnalian, sensual (PLEASURE).

gaze, *v.* moon, glare, stare (LOOKING).

gear, *n.* equipment, tackle (INSTRUMENT).

gem, *n.* jewel, bijou, stone (JEWELRY).

general, *adj.* normal, usual, accustomed (COMMONNESS, HABIT); diffuse, universal, catholic (PRESENCE); public, vernacular, national (VULGARITY).

generalization, *n.* analysis, ratiocination, induction (REASONING).

generally, *adv.* thereabouts, roughly, roundly (NEARNESS).

generate, *v.* engender, beget (PRODUCTION).

generation, *n.* era, epoch, age (TIME).

generous, *adj.* big, bighearted, free, charitable (UNSELFISHNESS).

genesis, *n.* birth, creation (BEGINNING).

genial, *adj.* sunny, cheerful, cheery (CHEERFULNESS).

genital, *adj.* reproductive, generative (BIRTH).

genius, *n.* brilliance, prowess, superability (ABILITY); prodigy, brain (*slang*), intellect (INTELLIGENCE).

genteel, *adj.* refined, cultivated, urbane (IMPROVEMENT).

gentile, *n.* Christian, Catholic, Protestant (RELIGION).

gentle, *adj.* mild, moderate, temperate (MILDNESS); kind, kindly, genial (SOFTNESS); low-pitched, low-toned, faint (LOWNESS, WEAKNESS).

gentleman, *n.* sir, esquire (MAN, COURTESY).

gentry, *n.* gentlefolk, aristocracy (SOCIAL CLASS).

genuine, *adj.* real, authentic, factual (REALITY); valid, bona fide, veritable (TRUTH); sincere, candid, frank (HONESTY, REALITY).

germ, *n.* microbe, microorganism, bug (SMALLNESS, DISEASE); egg, embryo (BEGINNING).

germane, *adj.* pertinent, relevant, material (PERTINENCE).

germinate, *v.* vegetate, sprout, grow (PLANT LIFE).

GESTURE—*N.* gesture, gesticulation, pantomime, mime, dumb show; sign, high sign, signal, wave.

V. **gesture,** gesticulate, pantomime, mime; signal, wave, wigwag, give the high sign, bow, scrape, curtsy, genuflect, bend the knee, salaam, salute, toast; nod, beckon, beck, shrug, wink.

Adj. **gestural,** gesticular, gesticulative, gesticulatory, gestic, nodding, cernuous.

See also INDICATION, MOTION, RESPECT. *Antonyms*—See MOTIONLESSNESS.

get, *v.* obtain, gain, win (ACQUISITION); receive, inherit (RECEIVING); follow, figure out (UNDERSTANDING); bring, fetch (SALE); catch, contract (DISEASE).

get along, *v.* fare, manage, shift (LIFE).

get down, *v.* get off, descend, dismount (DESCENT).

get rid of, *v.* discard, scrap, reject (ELIMINATION).

get up, *v.* awake, arise, awaken (WAKEFULNESS).

get well, *v.* convalesce, heal, mend (HEALTH).

ghastly, *adj.* shocking, frightful, horrible (DISGUST); horrid, grim, grisly (HATRED); ghostly, ghostlike, spectral (GHOST); anemic, sallow, cadaverous (COLORLESSNESS).

GHOST—*N.* **ghost,** apparition, specter, spirit, spook, wraith, shade, revenant, sprite; phantom, phantasm, fantasm; eidolon, bogle, banshee, poltergeist, vampire; eidolism, vampirism.

Adj. **ghostly,** ghostlike, apparitional, eidolic, phantasmal, phantom, spectral, spooky, vampiric, wraithy, wraithlike, ghastly, shadowy; eerie *or* eery, uncanny, haunted.

See also FEAR, MYTHICAL BEINGS, SUPERNATURALISM, SUPERNATURAL BEINGS, UNREALITY. *Antonyms*—See BODY, REALITY.

ghoul, *n.* grave robber, body snatcher, resurrectionist (BURIAL); lamia, harpy, vampire (SUPERNATURAL BEINGS).

G.I., *n.* soldier, infantryman, private, doughboy (FIGHTER).

giant, *adj.* mammoth, mountainous, colossal (SIZE).

giant, *n.* Brobdingnagian, goliath, Cyclops (SIZE, MYTHICAL BEINGS).

gibbet, *n.* gallows, scaffold (KILLING, HANGING).

gibbet, *v.* hang, lynch (KILLING).

giddy, *adj.* dizzy, reeling, whirling (DIZZINESS); lightheaded, flighty (FRIVOLITY).

gift, *n.* present, presentation, donation (GIVING); bent, turn, talent (ABILITY).

gigantic, *adj.* titanic, stupendous, monster (SIZE).

giggle, *v.* cackle, chortle, chuckle (LAUGHTER).

gigolo, *n.* Lothario, Casanova, Don Juan (SEX).

gild, *v.* aureate, aurify, begild (METAL, YELLOW).

gills, *n.* lungs, branchiae (BREATH).

gimmick (*slang*), *n.* shift, ruse, trick (PLAN); aid, factor, instrument (MEANS).

girder, *n.* beam, rafter, joist (SUPPORT).

girdle, *n.* corset, corselet, foundation (UNDERWEAR); belt, sash, waistband (TROUSERS); cingulum, ring, cincture (VARIEGATION).

girl, *n.* maid, miss, damsel (YOUTH); she, woman (FEMALE); maidservant, maid, hired girl (SERVICE).

girlish, *adj.* maidenly, maidenlike, girly (FEMALE).

girth, *n.* perimeter, circumference (MEASUREMENT); fatness, corpulence, avoirdupois (SIZE).

gist, *n.* substance, effect, essence (MEANING, CONTENTS); kernel, keynote, nub (IDEA).

give, *v.* grant, donate, distribute (GIVING); bend, yield, relax (SOFTNESS).

give-and-take, *n. quid pro quo* (*L.*), tit for tat (EXCHANGE).

give back, *v.* restore, return, rebate (RESTORATION, GIVING).

give forth, *v.* emit, beam, radiate (GIVING).

give in, *v.* surrender, yield, capitulate (RELINQUISHMENT, SUBMISSION).

given to, addicted to, accustomed to (HABIT).

give off, *v.* throw off, give forth, emit, beam, belch, exude, radiate (THROW, GIVING).

give up, *v.* surrender, quit, yield (RELINQUISHMENT, SUBMISSION); deliver, hand over, transfer (GIVING).

GIVING—*N.* **giving,** bestowal, presentation, conferral, concession, cession; delivery, consignment, disposition, dispensation, endowment.

gift, present, presentation, donation, donative, boon; lagniappe, handsel, sop, sportula; keepsake, token, tribute, *amatorio* (*It.*); gratuity, *douceur* (*F.*), tip; offering, oblation (*both, to the church*), benefice.

grant, subsidy, bounty, award, reward, subvention.

giver, donor, bestower, etc. (see *Verbs*).

restitution, rebate, reciprocation, rendition, restoration, return.

V. give, bestow, grant, accord, award, donate, confer; apportion, allot, devote, assign, present, give away, dispense, dispose of, deal, give (or deal) out, hand out, distribute; allow, contribute, subscribe.

deliver, transfer, hand, hand over, pass, assign, turn over, make over, consign, surrender, give up, cede, relinquish, part with, render, impart, communicate.

concede, vouchsafe, yield, admit, allow, grant, permit; award.

endow, settle upon, invest, inform, vest in, enrich, bequeath, dower, leave, devise.

furnish, supply, provide, equip, administer to, afford, accommodate with, indulge with, favor with; lavish, shower, pour on, thrust upon.

[give for safekeeping] entrust, commend, commit, confide, consign, deliver.

[give back] restore, return, render, rebate.

[give in return] reciprocate, render, requite, return.

[give forth] give off, emit, beam, radiate, shed, yield, afford, exude, secrete; spew, vomit, disgorge, belch.

Adj. restitutive, restitutory, restorative, reciprocal.

See also APPORTIONMENT, CHARITY, DISPERSION, INHERITANCE, PAYMENT, PERMISSION, RELINQUISHMENT, RESTORATION, THROW, TRANSFER, UNSELFISHNESS. Antonyms—See ACCEPTANCE, RECEIVING, TAKING, THIEVERY.

glad, adj. happy, joyful, delighted (HAPPINESS).

gladly, adv. willingly, freely, cheerfully (WILLINGNESS).

glamorize, v. dramatize, melodramatize, romanticize (EXCITEMENT, INTERESTINGNESS).

glamour, n. romance, interest, color (INTERESTINGNESS, ATTRACTION).

glance, v. peep, peek, peer (LOOKING); brush, graze, sideswipe (TOUCH, HITTING).

glare, v. flare, blaze, glow (LIGHT); stare, gaze, moon (LOOKING); dazzle, blind, daze (DIM-SIGHTEDNESS).

glaring, adj. crying, blatant, protrusive (VISIBILITY); egregious, flagrant, gross (INFERIORITY).

glass, n. cup, goblet, tumbler (CONTAINER, GLASSINESS); mirror, looking-glass, reflector (VISION).

glasses, n. eyeglasses, spectacles, goggles (VISION).

GLASSINESS—N. glassiness, hyalescence, vitreosity, vitrescence.

glassware, glasswork, vitrics, stemware.

glassmaking, glasswork, vitrifacture, vitrics, glass blowing; glaziery.

glassworker, glass blower, glazier.

pane (of glass), light, panel, window, windowpane, quarry; windshield.

V. glaze, vitrify.

Adj. glassy, glasslike, glazy, hyalescent, hyaline, vitreal, vitreous, vitric, vitrescent.

See also CONTAINER, SMOOTHNESS, VISION.

glassy, adj. glazy, hyaline, vitreous (TRANSPARENCY, GLASSINESS); glossy, burnished, shiny (LIGHT); expressionless, stupid, blank (DULLNESS).

glaze, n. polish, gloss, shine (SMOOTHNESS).

gleam, n. flash, sparkle, glitter (LIGHT); beam, flicker, spark (SMALLNESS).

gleam, v. shine, glow, glisten (LIGHT, VISIBILITY).

glee, n. elation, exultation, triumph (HAPPINESS); round, roundelay, madrigal (SINGING, MUSIC).

glee club, n. choir, chorus, ensemble (SINGING).

gleeful, adj. elated, exalted, exultant (HAPPINESS); frolicsome, hilarious, jocular (MERRIMENT).

glen, n. valley, canyon, gorge (DEPTH).

glib, adj. fluent, articulate, facile (EXPRESSION); slick, smooth, urbane (SUAVITY).

glide, v. soar, skirr, sail (FLYING); slide, slip, slither (SMOOTHNESS).

glimmer, v. flicker, sparkle, scintillate (LIGHT, VISIBILITY).

glimpse, v. descry, espy, spy (VISION).

glint, n. flash, gleam, sparkle (LIGHT).

glisten, v. shine, glow, gleam (LIGHT).

glitter, v. glimmer, glow, twinkle (LIGHT, VISIBILITY).

gloat, v. crow, exult, whoop (HAPPINESS).

globe, n. ball, orb, sphere (ROUNDNESS); earth, planet, terrene (WORLD).

globe-trotter, n. excursionist, expeditionist, migrator, migrant (TRAVELING).

gloom, n. melancholy, bleakness (GLOOM); shadows, Tophet, dusk (DARKNESS).

GLOOM—N. gloom, disconsolation, melancholy, desolation, saturninity; the blues, the blue devils, the dismals, the mopes.

V. gloom, blacken, darken, cloud, overcast, overcloud, overshadow, shadow, darkle; mope.

Adj. gloomy, cheerless, uncheerful, black, dark, bleak, blue; cloudy, clouded, overcast, overclouded, overshadowed; disconsolate, dismal, dour; dyspeptic, glum, melancholy, melancholic, mirthless, moody, broody, mopish, mopy, morose, saturnine.

dreary, drearisome, cheerless, wintry, desolate, forlorn; black, bleak, dark, dismal, Stygian, tenebrous; sepulchral, funereal, somber.

See also BLACKNESS, DARKNESS, DEJECTION, SADNESS. Antonyms—See CHEERFULNESS, HAPPINESS, LIGHT, MERRIMENT.

---

glorify, v. honor, dignify, exalt (FAME, MAGNIFICENCE, NOBILITY).

glorious, adj. lustrous, splendid, resplendent (FAME, MAGNIFICENCE).

glory, n. splendor, resplendence, brilliance (MAGNIFICENCE); halo, nimbus, aureole (LIGHT).

gloss, n. luster, sheen, polish (LIGHT, SMOOTHNESS); commentary, note, annotation (EXPLANATION).

gloss, v. falsify, deacon, disguise, doctor (FALSENESS).

glossary, n. dictionary, lexicon, wordbook, thesaurus (WORD).

gloss over, v. whitewash, extenuate, varnish (WHITENESS).

GLOVE—N. glove, gauntlet, mousquetaire, kid glove, mitt, mitten, muff.

sleeve, armlet, cap sleeve, balloon sleeve, bouffant sleeve, dolman sleeve, puffed sleeve, raglan sleeve, set-in sleeve; wristband, wristlet.

handkerchief, kerchief, bandanna, foulard.

See also APPENDAGE, CLOTHING, CLOTHING WORKER.

---

glow, n. bloom, blush, flush (RED).

glow, v. shine, glitter, twinkle (LIGHT, VISIBILITY).

glue, n. paste, adhesive, mucilage (STICKINESS).

glum, adj. gloomy, melancholy, mirthless (DEJECTION, GLOOM);

sullen, sulky, saturnine (SILENCE, BAD TEMPER).

glut, n. surfeit, saturation, plenitude (SATISFACTION); too much, nimiety, overabundance, superabundance (EXCESS, MULTITUDE).

glut, v. oversupply, deluge, flood (EXCESS, MULTITUDE); surfeit, jade, pall (SATISFACTION); stuff, clog up, congest (FULLNESS).

GLUTTONY—N. gluttony, voracity, edacity, greed.

glutton, gormandizer, cormorant, hog, pig (colloq.).

V. gluttonize, gormandize, gorge, stuff, cram, overeat, devour, gobble up, gulp, raven.

Adj. gluttonous, greedy, edacious, ravenous, cormorant, ravening, voracious, hoggish, piggish; overfed, gorged.

See also DESIRE, FOOD, FULLNESS, GREED, HUNGER. Antonyms—See ASCETICISM, FASTING, MODERATENESS, SOBRIETY.

---

gnarled, adj. distorted, contorted, crooked (DEFORMITY); gnarly, knotted, knotty (ROUGHNESS).

gnaw, v. chew, masticate, nibble (FOOD).

go, v. advance, proceed (PROGRESS).

goad, n. urge, pressure, impetus (PROPULSION); prod, lash, whip (MOTIVATION).

goad, v. drive, prod, incite (URGING, PROPULSION).

go after, v. come after, come next, succeed; pursue, chase (FOLLOWING).

go ahead, v. shoot ahead, edge forward, dash ahead (PROGRESS).

goal, n. aim, ambition, target (PURPOSE).

goat, n. billy goat, she-goat (ANIMAL); scapegoat, fall guy (slang); whipping boy (SUBSTITUTION).

go away, v. depart, leave, withdraw (DEPARTURE).

gob (colloq.), n. salt (colloq.), windjammer, tar (colloq.), seaman (SAILOR).

go back, v. move back, back, draw back (REVERSION); resume, return to (REPETITION).

gobble, v. bolt, devour, gorge (RECEIVING); gabble, cackle (ANIMAL SOUND).

go-between, n. intermediary, interagent, middleman (INTERJACENCE, DEPUTY).

go beyond, v. outrace, pass, go by (OVERRUNNING); encroach, trespass (ENCROACHMENT).

goblin, n. ouphe, barghest, bogle (SUPERNATURAL BEINGS).

go by, v. pass, skirt, elapse, lapse, vanish (PASSAGE).

GOD—N. God, the Supreme Deity, the Deity, the Absolute Being, the All Holy, the All Knowing, the All Merciful, the Almighty, the All Powerful, the All Wise, Ancient of Days, the Creator, the Divinity, the Eternal, the Eternal Being, Father, the Godhead, the Holy Spirit, the Infinite, the Infinite Being, Jehovah, the King of Kings, the Lord, the Lord of Lords, the Maker, the Master Workman, the Omnipotent, the Omniscient, Providence, the Spirit, the Supreme Being.

deity, god, goddess, celestial, divinity, satyr, numen (*Rom. myth.*), Titan (*Gr. myth.*); daimon (*Gr. myth.*); demigod, demigoddess, godling, siren, tutelary deity, Demiurge; false god, Baal.

gods, pantheon, *lares* (L.), *penates* (L.).

nymph, dryad, hamadryad, naiad, Nereid, oceanid, oread; Hyades.

Muses: Calliope, Clio, Erato, Euterpe, Melpomene, Polyhymnia, Terpsichore, Thalia, Urania.

divinity, godhead, godhood, theomorphism, avatar, theophany, theurgy; theology; deification, apotheosis.

[*beliefs about God or gods*] monotheism, theism, deism, pantheism, anthropolatry, anthropomorphism; ditheism, bitheism, henotheism, polytheism; agnosticism, freethinking; atheism, godlessness, heathenism.

theologian, divinity student, theologizer, seminarian, Doctor of Divinity.

V. **deify**, apotheosize, god, theologize.

Adj. **divine**, godly, ambrosial, celestial, Olympian, providential; godlike, deiform, theomorphic.

See also CHURCH, HEAVEN, RELIGION, SUPERNATURAL BEINGS, WORSHIP. Antonyms—See IRRELIGION.

---

godless, adj. irreligious, undevout, graceless (IRRELIGION); ungodly, unholy, unclean (WICKEDNESS).

godly, adj. divine, celestial (GOD); holy, saintly (RELIGIOUSNESS).

goggles, n. glasses, eyeglasses, spectacles (VISION).

go in, v. enter, come in, immigrate (INGRESS).

going on, adj. in progress, in hand, proceeding (INCOMPLETENESS).

gold, adj. auric, auriferous, aurous (METAL); golden, aureate, aurulent (YELLOW).

gold, n. bullion, gold dust, gilding, gilt (METAL); capital, fortune, treasure (WEALTH).

gold-digger (*fem.*), n. fortune hunter, adventuress (MONEY).

golden-haired, adj. flaxen-haired, auricomous, blonde, blond (YELLOW).

golden mean, n. middle course, mean, moderation, temperance (MID-COURSE, MODERATENESS).

gone, adj. missing, lost (ABSENCE); astray, strayed, vanished (LOSS); ago, bygone, long-ago (PAST).

go next, v. come after, go after, succeed (FOLLOWING).

gong, n. tocsin, chime (BELL).

good, adj. ethical, virtuous, honorable (MORALITY); excellent, admirable, fine (GOOD); beneficial, advantageous, favorable (USE).

GOOD—N. good, benefit, advantage, avail, gain, profit, boon, nugget, plum, treasure, favor, blessing, prize, windfall, godsend, good fortune, happiness, well-being, welfare, commonweal; *summum bonum* (L.).

excellence, goodness, dignity, merit, supereminence, superexcellence, value, virtue, worth, quality, class (*colloq.*).

[*excellent condition*] prime, pink, soundness, trim.

[*belief about what is good*] meliorism, utilitarianism, Benthamism.

V. **be good for**, advantage, avail, benefit, serve.

be good enough for, avail, do, serve, suffice, suit, satisfy.

Adj. **excellent**, good, ace, admirable, bully (*colloq.*), capital, choice, crack, de luxe, exceptional, fine, first-class, first-rate (*colloq.*), marvelous, prime, recherché (F.), select, spanking, splendid, sterling, stupendous, superb, supereminent, superexcellent, wonderful, worthy; *par excellence* (F.; *follows the noun*).

[*in good condition*] first-rate (*colloq.*), shipshape, sound, tip-top (*colloq.*); trim, well-kept.

advantageous, beneficent, beneficial, benignant, fruitful, salutary, serviceable, useful, wholesome.

good enough, satisfactory, sufficient, suitable; decent, fair, mediocre, middling, moderate, passable, respectable, tolerable.

well-behaved, obedient, well-mannered, orderly, decorous, well-conducted, seemly, proper.

See also ADVANTAGE, APPROVAL, BEHAVIOR, HAPPINESS, MORALITY, OBEDIENCE, SUPERIORITY, USE, VALUE. Antonyms—See DETERIORATION, INFERIORITY, WICKEDNESS.

---

good-by, n. leave-taking, parting, farewell (DEPARTURE).

good-fellowship, *n.* companionship, comradeship, fellowship (FRIEND-LINESS).

good-for-nothing, *n.* scalawag, scapegrace, scamp (WORTHLESS-NESS).

goodhearted, *adj.* bighearted, good-natured, gracious (KINDNESS).

good-humored, *adj.* good-natured, complaisant, congenial (PLEAS-ANTNESS).

GOOD LUCK—*N.* good luck, fortune, good fortune; fluke, windfall, stroke.

lucky charm, charm, rabbit's foot, amulet, talisman, periapt, grigri, mascot.

Adj. lucky, fortunate, happy, fortuitous, providential, auspicious, propitious, aleatory.

See also CHANCE. *Antonyms*—See MISFORTUNE.

---

good-natured, *adj.* complaisant, congenial, amiable (PLEASANT-NESS, SWEETNESS).

goodness, *n.* excellence, merit, worth (GOOD); virtue, ethicality, honesty (MORALITY).

goods, *n.* fabric, textile, material (TEXTURE, MATERIALITY); merchandise, wares, commodities (SALE); freight, cargo, load (TRANSFER).

good Samaritan, *n.* altruist, philanthropist, humanitarian (UNSELF-ISHNESS).

go off, *v.* explode, blow up (VIO-LENCE).

go on, *v.* continue, keep up, hold on (CONTINUATION); advance, proceed, go ahead (PROGRESS).

go on board, *v.* embark, emplane, entrain (INGRESS).

gorge, *n.* flume, ravine, chasm (CHANNEL); valley, canyon, glen (DEPTH); craw, gullet, maw (THROAT).

gorged, *adj.* packed, jammed, congested (FULLNESS); replete, overfed, satiated (SATISFACTION).

gorgeous, *adj.* beautiful, stunning, ravishing (BEAUTY).

gorilla, *n.* monkey, ape (ANIMAL).

gory, *adj.* bloody, bleeding, ensanguined (BLOOD); bloodthirsty, bloody-minded (KILLING).

Gospel, *n.* The Scriptures, The Bible, the Good Book (SACRED WRITING).

gossip, *n.* talk, idle rumor, scandal; rumormonger, newsmonger, quidnunc (RUMOR).

gossip, *v.* chatter, babble, chaffer (TALK); tattle, tittle-tattle, buzz (RUMOR).

go through, *v.* pass through, wade through, cross through (CROSS-ING); pierce, cleave, stab (CUT-TING); endure, suffer, brave (OC-CURRENCE, INEXCITABILITY).

gouge, *v.* excavate, furrow, groove (HOLLOW).

go up, *v.* ascend, climb, rise (AS-CENT).

gourmet, *n.* epicure, epicurean, gastronomer (FOOD).

govern, *v.* rule, reign, manage (GOVERNMENT, CONTROL, RULE); dispose, incline, sway (IN-FLUENCE).

government, *n.* direction, management, administration, sway, dominion, empire (GOVERNMENT, RULE, CONTROL).

GOVERNMENT—*N.* government, rule, administration, domination, dominion, empire, governance, regency (*delegated*), reign, sway, polity, regime, politics.

national government, federal government, the Administration (*U.S.*), the White House (*U.S.*), the executive branch (*U.S.*); Whitehall (*Gr. Brit.*), the Wilhelmstrasse (*Germany*), the Quirinal (*Italy*), the Vatican, the Reich (*Germany*), the Kremlin (*U.S.S.R.*).

[*types or systems*] absolutism, Caesarism, kaiserism, autarchy, autocracy, monocracy, despotism, benevolent despotism, paternalism; monarchy, aristocracy, oligarchy; dictatorship, totalitarianism, fascism, nazism, communism, bolshevism, sovietism, czarism, tzarism; terrorism, coercion; collectivism, socialism; feudalism, feudal system; matriarchy, metrocracy, patriarchy, thearchy, theocracy, divine rule, papacy (*Rom. Cath. Ch.*), hierarchy, hierocracy (*church*); imperialism; federalism, statism.

self-government, self-rule, freedom, independence, political liberty, autonomy, autarchy, home rule, pantisocracy, democracy, republicanism; republic, commonwealth, Dominion (*Brit. Emp.*).

[*harsh government*] tyranny, absolutism, autocracy, Caesarism, despotism, oppression.

[*power or authority to govern*] dominion, sovereignty, jurisdiction, scepter, empire, crown.

communist, red, pink, card-carrying member, fellow traveler, commie (*slang*), leftist; anti-communist, red baiter.

V. govern, rule, control, direct, administer, command, manage, hold sway, reign; dominate, head, hold sway over, reign over, sway, wield power over; subject, subjugate; misgovern, misrule; tyrannize, despotize.

Adj. ruling, regnant, reigning, sovereign, dominant, predominant, governing, regnal, regent.

governmental, civil, political; municipal, domestic, internal.

self-governing, self-ruling, independent, free, autonomous, municipal; democratic, republican.

autocratic, absolutist, autarchic, monocratic, despotic, tyrannical, tyrannous.

totalitarian, fascist, nazi, communist, bolshevist, czarist; terroristic, coercionary.

See also CONTROL, FEUDALISM, FREEDOM, LAW, LEGISLATURE, OFFICIAL, POWER, RULE, RULER, SEVERITY. *Antonyms*—See ILLEGALITY.

governor, *n.* director, manager, leader (CONTROL, RULER); check, determinant, rein (CONTROL).

gown, *n.* frock, robe, dress (SKIRT).

grace, *n.* elegance, symmetry, shapeliness (BEAUTY); refinement, polish, finish (ELEGANCE); charity, quarter, lenience (FORGIVENESS, PITY); praise, benediction, thanksgiving (WORSHIP).

grace, *v.* beautify, embellish, adorn (BEAUTY); crown, laureate (FAME).

graceful, *adj.* beautiful, lovely, elegant (BEAUTY); shapely, curvaceous (SHAPE); refined, aesthetic, tasteful (ELEGANCE).

gracious, *adj.* kind, amiable, good-natured (KINDNESS, SOFTNESS); suave, urbane, bland (PLEASANTNESS).

graciously, *adv.* with good grace, without demur, cheerfully (WILLINGNESS).

grade, *n.* quality, group, class (RANK, CLASS); form, room (LEARNING); step, gradation (DEGREE); plane, level (FLATNESS); slant, gradient, incline (SLOPE).

grade, *v.* rank, class, classify (RANK); level, even (UNIFORMITY); smooth, flatten, roll (SMOOTHNESS).

gradual, *adj.* piecemeal, step-by-step, bit-by-bit (SLOWNESS); by degrees, progressive, graduated (DEGREE).

graduate, *n.* diplomate, collegian, bachelor (LEARNING).

graduate, *v.* grade, calibrate, measure (DEGREE).

graduation, *n.* commencement, commencement exercises (LEARNING).

graft, *n.* bribe, boodle, hush money (BRIBERY).

graft, *v.* insert, ingraft, bud (INSERTION).

grain, *n.* fiber, nap, warp and woof (TEXTURE); crumb, seed, particle (POWDERINESS); atom, bit, drop (SMALLNESS).

gram, *n.* iota, jot, grain (SMALLNESS).

grammar, *n.* syntax, accidence, linguistics (LANGUAGE).

grand, *adj.* grandiose, splendid, magnificent (MAGNIFICENCE, NOBILITY); dignified, grave, majestic (FAME).

grandeur, *n.* magnificence, majesty, sublimity, grandiosity (MAGNIFICENCE, NOBILITY); dignity, solemnity, gravity (FAME).

grandfather, *n.* grandsire, atavus (ANCESTRY); ancient, graybeard, Nestor (OLDNESS).

grandiose, *adj.* pretentious, ambitious, splashy (OSTENTATION); grand, splendid, splendrous (MAGNIFICENCE); grandiloquent, magniloquent, bombastic (WORDINESS).

grandmother, *n.* granny (*colloq.*), beldame, grandam (ANCESTRY, OLDNESS).

grant, *v.* bestow, accord, award (GIVING); own, profess, concede (GIVING, STATEMENT, PERMISSION); suppose, assume, admit (SUPPOSITION).

granted, *adv.* yes, indeed, just so (ASSENT).

granulate, *v.* pulverize, comminute, triturate (POWDERINESS).

grapple, *v.* struggle, tussle, wrestle (ATTEMPT); seize, grasp (TAKING).

grasp, *v.* seize, grip, clutch (HOLD, TAKING); understand, comprehend, apprehend (UNDERSTANDING).

grasping, *adj.* acquisitive, greedy, rapacious (DESIRE, GREED).

GRASS—*N.* grass, pasturage, hay, soilage, sedge, cereal, grain; bamboo, reed.

grassland, meadow, prairie, lea, green, lawn, terrace; sod, turf, sward, greensward, greenyard; pasture, hayfield; pampas (*esp. Argentina*), veld *or* veldt (*S. Africa*), the Steppes (*Russia*).

haycock, hayrick, haystack; haymow, hayloft.

V. grass, turf, sward, sod.

graze, grass, pasture, soil.

Adj. grassy, gramineous, poaceous, grass-green, turfy, verdant, verdurous.

See also LAND, PLANT LIFE.

grate, *v.* rasp, pound, bray (RUBBING, POWDERINESS); jar, clash, grind (HARSH SOUND); annoy, irritate, vex (ANNOYANCE).

grateful, *adj.* appreciative, thankful (GRATITUDE); pleasing, desirable, welcome (PLEASANTNESS).

gratify, *v.* satisfy, content, delight (SATISFACTION); enchant, delectate (PLEASURE); indulge, favor, humor (MILDNESS).

grating, *adj.* harsh, jarring (HARSH SOUND).

gratis, *adj.* free, complimentary, gratuitous (FREEDOM).

GRATITUDE—N. gratitude, thankfulness, thanks, appreciation, acknowledgment; thanksgiving.

V. **be grateful,** thank, appreciate, acknowledge.

Adj. **grateful,** appreciative, thankful, much obliged; thankworthy.

Interj. thanks! many thanks! *merci!* (*F.*), *danke!* (*Ger.*), *danke schön!* (*Ger.*), *grazie!* (*It.*), gramercy! (*archaic*), much obliged! thank you!

See also KINDNESS. *Antonyms—* See INGRATITUDE.

grave, *adj.* sober, solemn, momentous (SOBRIETY); dignified, grand, majestic (FAME).

grave, *n.* tomb, vault, mausoleum (BURIAL).

gravel, *n.* stones, pebbles, riprap (ROCK).

grave robber, *n.* body snatcher, ghoul, resurrectionist (BURIAL).

gravestone, *n.* tombstone, marker, headstone (BURIAL).

gravity, *n.* seriousness, severity, solemnity (SOBRIETY); grandeur, dignity (FAME); consequence, significance (IMPORTANCE); avoirdupois (*colloq.*), heaviness (WEIGHT); fetation, gestation (PREGNANCY).

gravy, *n.* juice, fluid (LIQUID).

GRAY—N. gray *or* **grey,** silver, dove color, pepper and salt, *chiaroscuro* (*It.*); dun, drab, etc. (see *Adjectives*).

V. **gray** *or* **grey,** grizzle, silver, dapple.

Adj. **gray** *or* **grey,** grizzled, grizzly, griseous, ash-gray, ashen, ashy, cinereous; dingy, leaden, pearly, pearl-gray, clouded, cloudy, misty, foggy, hoary, hoar, canescent, silver, silvery, silver-gray; iron-gray, dun, drab, dappled, dapple-gray, brindle, brindled, mouse-colored, stone-colored, slate-gray; dove-gray, columbine, fulvous, taupe, oyster-white; sad, dull, somber.

gray-haired, silver-haired, gray-headed, hoary, grizzly.

See also CLOUD, DARKNESS, DULLNESS, OLDNESS, SADNESS, WHITENESS. *Antonyms* — See CHEERFULNESS, LIGHT.

graze, *v.* brush, glance, shave (TOUCH); bite, browse, crop (FOOD); grass, pasture, soil (GRASS).

grease, *n.* fat, suet, tallow (OIL).

grease, *v.* lubricate, tallow, lard (OIL).

greasy, *adj.* unctuous, oleaginous, slick (OIL).

greater, *adj.* superior, higher, major (SUPERIORITY).

greatest, *adj.* supreme, highest, maximum (SUPERIORITY).

GREATNESS—N. greatness, largeness, etc. (see *Adjectives*); magnitude, size, bulk, mass, amplitude, abundance, immensity, infinity, enormity, might, strength, intensity.

eminence, distinction, grandeur, dignity; nobility, fame, importance.

V. **be great,** soar, tower, loom, rise above, transcend; bulk, bulk large, know no bounds.

Adj. **great,** large, considerable, big, bulky, huge, titanic; voluminous, ample, abundant.

vast, immense, enormous, extreme; towering, stupendous, prodigious; terrible (*colloq.*), terrific (*colloq.*), dreadful (*colloq.*), fearful (*colloq.*).

eminent, distinguished, remarkable, extraordinary, important, elevated, lofty, noble, mighty, supreme; notable, noteworthy, noticeable, esteemed, noted, signal, conspicuous, prominent, renowned, illustrious, famous, glorious, grand, majestic, august, dignified, sublime.

Adv., phrases. [*in a great or high degree*] greatly, largely, etc. (see *Adjectives*); much, indeed, very, very much, most; in a great measure, passing, richly; on a large scale; mightily, powerfully; extremely, exceedingly, intensely, indefinitely, immeasurably, incalculably, infinitely.

[*in a supreme degree*] pre-eminently, superlatively, eminently, supremely, inimitably, incomparably.

[*in a marked degree*] remarkably, particularly, singularly, curiously, uncommonly, unusually, peculiarly, notably, signally, strikingly; famously, prominently, conspicuously, glaringly, emphatically, incredibly, amazingly, surprisingly, stupendously.

See also ELEVATION, ENDLESSNESS, FAME, FULLNESS, HEIGHT, IMPORTANCE, MAGNIFICENCE, POWER, QUANTITY, SIZE, STRENGTH, SUPERIORITY. *Antonyms*—See SMALLNESS, UNIMPORTANCE.

GREED—*N.* greed, cupidity, avarice, avidity, gluttony, rapacity, voracity, esurience; greediness, etc. (see *Adjectives*).

[*greedy person*] hog, pig, swine, wolf, vulture; buzzard, harpy, Shylock, miser, curmudgeon; cormorant, esurient, glutton.

Adj. greedy, acquisitive, avaricious, avid, grasping, covetous, gluttonous, lickerish, liquorish, miserly, openmouthed, sordid; hoggish, piggish, swinish, vulturous, wolfish; voracious, ravening, ravenous, rapacious, cormorant, esurient.

See also DESIRE, EAGERNESS, FOOD, GLUTTONY, HUNGER. *Antonyms*—See FASTING, INDIFFERENCE.

green, *adj.* emerald, chartreuse (GREEN); callow, raw, untrained (INEXPERIENCE); immature, ungrown, puerile (YOUTH).
green, *n.* lawn, terrace, common (GRASS, LAND).

GREEN—*N.* [*yellowish greens*] apple green, bladder green, boa, chartreuse, emerald, fir green, glaucous green, jade, mignonette, moss green, mousse, Nile green, olive, olive drab, Paris green, pea green, peacock green, reseda, sea green, shamrock, verdet, verdigris, viridian.

[*bluish greens*] aquamarine, bird's-egg green, glaucous green, jade, myrtle, Nile green, sea green, turquoise.

greenness, viridity, verdancy, patina; greenery, verdure, virescence.

Adj. greenish, viridescent, virescent, verdant.

See also GRASS, PLANT LIFE.

greenery, *n.* botany, herbage, verdure (PLANT LIFE).
greenhorn, *n.* babe, colt, virgin (INEXPERIENCE).
greenhouse, *n.* garden, nursery, hothouse (FARMING).
GREETING—*N.* greeting, greet-

ings, hail, salaam, salute, salutation, nod; welcome, ovation, compellation; aloha (*Hawaiian*), banzai (*Jap.*).
V. greet, accost, welcome, hail, talk to, nod to, salute, salaam.

See also ACCEPTANCE, FRIENDLINESS, SOCIALITY, TALK, TITLE.

gregarious, *adj.* sociable, social, companionable (SOCIALITY, FRIENDLINESS).
gremlin, *n.* hobgoblin, puck, spirit (SUPERNATURAL BEINGS).
grief, *n.* sorrow, grieving, woe (SADNESS).
grievance, *n.* round robin, beef (*slang*), jeremiad (COMPLAINT); violence, outrage, wrong (HARM).
grieve, *v.* lament, deplore, sorrow (SADNESS).
grieved, *adj.* grief-stricken, grief-laden, aggrieved (SADNESS).
grieve with, *v.* lament with, express sympathy for, send one's condolences (PITY).
grievous, *adj.* lamentable, deplorable, tragic (SADNESS); grave, critical, momentous (SOBRIETY); severe, mortal (EXTREMENESS).
grill, *v.* question, catechize, inquisition (INQUIRY); fry, broil, griddle (COOKERY).
grim, *adj.* serious, solemn, somber (SOBRIETY); forbidding, dour (SEVERITY); horrible, horrid, grisly (HATRED); fell, ruthless, savage (CRUELTY, VIOLENCE).
grime, *n.* smut, soil, soot (UNCLEANNESS).
grimy, *adj.* grubby, messy, Augean, collied (UNCLEANNESS).
grin, *v.* smile, smirk, simper (LAUGHTER).
grind, *n.* toiler, drudge, plodder (WORK).
grind, *v.* bray, levigate, comminute (RUBBING); scrape, file, abrade (POWDERINESS).
grip, *n.* grasp, purchase; lug, butt (HOLD); brace, vise, clamp (HOLD, TAKING); gripsack, handbag, portmanteau (CONTAINER); ken, comprehension, mastery (UNDERSTANDING).
grip, *v.* grasp, seize, clutch, snatch, clasp (HOLD, TAKING).
grisly, *adj.* horrible, horrid, ghastly, grim (HATRED).
grit, *n.* powder, dust, sand (POWDERINESS); nerve, mettle, pluck (COURAGE).
grizzly, *adj.* gray, gray-haired, gray-headed, hoary, grizzled, griseous (GRAY).
groggy, *adj.* dizzy, muzzy, hazy,

whirling (CONFUSION); reeling, swaying, staggering (UNSTEADINESS).

groom, *n.* bridegroom, husband (MARRIAGE); hostler, stable boy (SERVICE).

groom, *v.* sleek, prim, spruce (NEATNESS); prime, train, ground (PREPARATION, TEACHING); brush, curry (DOMESTICATION).

groove, *n.* corrugation, furrow, ridge (FOLD); rabbet, rut (HOLLOW).

grope, *v.* feel, handle, finger (TOUCH).

gross, *adj.* large, unwieldy, massive (SIZE); broad, coarse, improper (OBSCENITY, LOWNESS); egregious, flagrant, glaring (INFERIORITY); voluptuous, carnal, venereal (INTEMPERANCE, SEX); lustful, sensual, Cyprian (SEX).

grotesque, *adj.* deformed, malformed, misshapen (DEFORMITY); monstrous, freakish, abnormal (UNNATURALNESS); strange, bizarre, baroque (UNUSUALNESS).

grouchy, *adj.* irritable, snappish, growling (ANGER, BAD TEMPER).

ground, *n.* soil, earth, dust (LAND); substratum, bottom, foundation (SUPPORT, BASE); sphere, realm, zone (REGION); basis, root, reason (MOTIVATION).

ground, *v.* train, prepare (TEACHING); beach, strand, land (LAND).

grounding, *n.* breeding, schooling, culture (LEARNING).

groundless, *adj.* flimsy, baseless, ungrounded (NONEXISTENCE).

ground plan, *n.* floor plan, blueprint, diagram, plan, outline (MAP).

grounds, *n.* premises (*law*), campus, terrace (LAND); foundation, reason, basis (MOTIVATION).

group, *n.* division, section, branch (PART); cluster, gang (ASSEMBLAGE).

group, *v.* arrange, classify, rank (ARRANGEMENT); bracket, associate, link (RELATIONSHIP).

grove, *n.* orchard, copse, coppice (PLANT LIFE).

grovel, fawn, crawl, toady (SLAVERY); cower, cringe (POSTURE); creep, scrabble, scramble (CRAWL).

grow, *v.* raise, plant, sow (FARMING); vegetate, germinate, sprout (PLANT LIFE); fill out, wax, accumulate (INCREASE).

growl, *v.* snarl, snap, gnarl (ANGER); utter threats, thunder (THREAT); grumble, mutter, bark (TALK).

growth, *n.* expansion, development, maturation (UNFOLDMENT); surge, swell, rise (INCREASE).

grow up, *v.* mature, develop, ripen (MATURITY).

grubby, *adj.* frowzy, messy, blowzy (UNTIDINESS).

grudge, *n.* ill will, bad will, bad blood (HOSTILITY).

grudge, *v.* covet, envy, begrudge (DESIRE); be stingy, pinch, stint (STINGINESS).

grudging, *adj.* begrudging, forced, compelled (UNWILLINGNESS).

grueling, *adj.* racking, punishing, torturous (PAIN, PUNISHMENT).

gruesome, *adj.* hideous, macabre, monstrous (FEAR, HATRED).

gruff, *adj.* throaty, guttural, husky (THROAT); roupy, croaky, cracked (HARSH SOUND); churlish, crusty, curt (DISCOURTESY); grouchy (*colloq.*), surly (BAD TEMPER); rough, boisterous, bearish (VIOLENCE).

grumble, *v.* whine, mutter, complain (COMPLAINT).

grumpy, *adj.* disgruntled, pettish, dissatisfied (BAD TEMPER, DISSATISFACTION).

G string, *n.* loincloth, breechclout, dhoti, diaper (TROUSERS).

guarantee, *n.* assurance, insurance, security, warranty (CERTAINTY); earnest, warrant (PROMISE).

guarantee, *v.* assure, insure, warrant (CERTAINTY); promise, bind oneself, commit oneself (PROMISE); vouch for, answer for, be surety for (DEBT).

guard, *n.* protector, escort, warden; safeguard, shield, screen (PROTECTION); sentinel, sentry, watchman (WARNING); screw (*slang*), turnkey (IMPRISONMENT).

guard, *v.* protect, defend, bulwark, panoply (PROTECTION).

guarded, *adj.* watchful, vigilant, wary (CARE).

guardian, *n.* shepherd, Argus (PROTECTION).

guess, *n.* guesswork, surmise, conjecture, speculation, suspicion (SUPPOSITION).

guess, *v.* surmise, conjecture, speculate (SUPPOSITION).

guest, *n.* visitor, caller, transient (ARRIVAL).

guffaw, *v.* horselaugh, howl, scream (LAUGHTER).

GUIDANCE—*N.* guidance, navigation, direction; counsel, advice.

guide, pilot, steersman, navigator, helmsman, coxswain; conductor, usher, marshal, director, shepherd, fugleman; counselor, advisor; cicerone (*ciceroni or cicerones, pl.*), guiding spirit, genius, genie; rudder, tiller; guiding star, lodestar, North Star, Polaris, polestar, cynosure; beacon, lighthouse, lightship, guideboard, guidepost, signpost; guidebook, Baedeker, handbook.

[*guiding position*] **conning tower,** conn, helm, saddle, reins.

V. **guide,** beacon, pilot, steer, navigate, helm, coxswain, conn; conduct, usher, marshal, direct, convey, shepherd, fugle; counsel, advise.

Adj. **guiding,** polar, directive, navigational.

guidable, steerable, dirigible, navigable.

See also ADVICE, CONTROL, EXPLANATION, INDICATION, LEADERSHIP, TEACHER, TEACHING. *Antonyms*—See MISTEACHING.

guidebook, *n.* manual, Baedeker, vade mecum (BOOK, GUIDANCE).

guild, *n.* trade-union, federation, association (COMBINATION).

guile, *n.* chicanery, knavery, duplicity (CLEVERNESS, DECEPTION).

guileless, *adj.* unguileful, undeceitful, ingenuous (HONESTY); naïve, artless, simple (INNOCENCE).

GUILT—*N.* **guilt,** culpability, criminality, reprehensibility, censurability.

shame, compunction, contrition, penitence, remorse, repentance.

repenter, penitent, confesser; convict, culprit.

conviction, attainder, attainture, condemnation; suspicion, accusation, indictment.

V. [*prove guilty*] **convict,** condemn, attaint.

suspect, accuse, indict.

Adj. **guilty,** blamable, culpable, censurable, condemnable, reprehensible, blameworthy, delinquent; redhanded, *flagrante delicto* (L.), caught in the act; suspect, open to suspicion.

ashamed, compunctious, contrite, penitent, remorseful, repentant; shamefaced, sheepish.

See also ACCUSATION, DISAPPROVAL, ILLEGALITY, IMMORALITY, PENITENCE, SIN, WICKEDNESS. *Antonyms*—See IMPENITENCE, INNOCENCE, LEGALITY, MORALITY.

guiltless, *adj.* innocent, unguilty (INNOCENCE).

guise, *n.* pose, posture, role (PRETENSE); likeness, semblance,

similitude (SIMILARITY); aspect, mien (APPEARANCE).

gulch, *n.* valley, gully, notch, ravine (DEPTH).

gulf, *n.* bay, basin, arm (INLET); abyss, depths (DEPTH).

gullet, *n.* craw, gorge, esophagus (THROAT, BELLY).

gullible, *adj.* credulous, naïve, trusting (BELIEF).

gully, *n.* ditch, dike, trench (PASSAGE, HOLLOW); notch, ravine (DEPTH).

gulp, *v.* swallow, ingurgitate, consume (RECEIVING); guzzle, imbibe (DRINK); eat, devour, bolt (FOOD); gasp, sigh (BREATH).

gum, *n.* glue, cement, mucilage (STICKINESS).

gun, *n.* rifle, cannon, revolver (ARMS).

gunman, *n.* gangster, murderer, assassin (ILLEGALITY, KILLING).

gurgle, *v.* purl, murmur (RIVER); guggle, babble, crow (CHILD).

gush, *v.* stream, spurt, emerge (DEPARTURE); flow, run (RIVER); spout, slobber, vapor (TALK).

gushy, *adj.* sentimental, bathetic, maudlin (SENTIMENTALITY).

gust, *n.* blast, blow, squall (WIND).

gusto, *n.* relish, zest (PLEASURE).

gut, *v.* ravage, dilapidate, decimate (DESTRUCTION); loot, pillage, ransack (PLUNDER).

guts, *n.* intestines, innards, viscera (BELLY); pluck (*colloq.*), nerve, grit (COURAGE).

gutter, *n.* ditch, drain, gully (CHANNEL, HOLLOW).

guttural, *adj.* throaty, husky, gruff (THROAT, HARSH SOUND).

guzzle, *v.* gulp, imbibe (DRINK); fuddle, swill (ALCOHOLIC LIQUOR).

GYMNASTICS—*N.* **gymnastics,** acrobatics, athletics, calisthenics, hydrogymnastics, agonistics, palaestra; exercise, daily dozen, work-out.

gymnast, acrobat, athlete, hydrogymnast, aerialist, contortionist, tumbler, turner (*Ger.*).

gymnasium, gym; athletic club, *Turnverein* (*Ger.*).

See also ACTIVITY, MOTION.

gypsy, *adj.* vagabond, nomadic, migratory (WANDERING).

gypsy, *n.* *tzigane* (*Hungarian*), *zingaro* (*It.*), Romany (WANDERING).

gyrate, *v.* circle, gyre, roll, circulate, mill around (ROTATION, ROUNDNESS).

H

HABIT—*N.* habit, wont, habitude, rule, practice, addiction, way, usage, routine, second nature.

custom, convention, proprieties, stereotype, *mores* (*L.*), etiquette, fashion, vogue, amenities, consuetude, orthodoxy, observance, tradition.

V. **habituate,** accustom, acclimate, acclimatize, naturalize, season, inure, addict.

become habituated, get used to, adjust to; ossify.

be in the habit, be addicted, practice, follow, be confirmed; be customary, prevail, obtain.

Adj. **habitual,** customary, wonted, usual, routine, general, common, frequent, everyday, familiar, well-trodden, regular, set, stock, established, stereotyped; fixed, rooted, inveterate, confirmed, ingrained; consuetudinary, conventional, practiced, second nature; prevalent, prevailing.

habituated, addicted, accustomed, wont, used to, given to, in the habit of; adjusted to, acclimated to, acclimatized, inured, seasoned.

conventional, academic, formal, formalistic, orthodox, traditional, punctilious, prim, decorous; fashionable.

See also COMMONNESS, CONFORMITY, FORMALITY, FREQUENCY, OBSERVANCE, PROPRIETY, UNIFORMITY. *Antonyms*—See DISUSE, IRREGULARITY, NONOBSERVANCE, UNUSUALNESS.

HABITATION—*N.* habitation, abode, haunt, living quarters, dwelling, quarters, lodgings, digs (*slang*), accommodations, roost, domicile, residence, seat, place, address, berth, billet, hermitage, tabernacle, *pied-à-terre* (*F.*); habitat, biosphere, cunabula, cradle.

home, homestead, hearth, hearthstone, fireside, roof, household, housing, shelter.

house, mansion, villa, palace, castle, château, country house, country seat, hacienda, lodge, split-level house, building; premises.

cottage, cot, bower, chalet, bungalow, ranch house, cabana.

hut, hutch, hovel, shack, shanty, wickiup, igloo (*Eskimo*), cabin, log cabin.

multiple dwelling, apartment house, tenement, barracks, development, tract houses, row houses; duplex, two-family house.

apartment, flat, suite, rooms, penthouse.

hotel, inn, tavern, lodge, lodginghouse, boardinghouse, pension, rooming house, resort, hostel, hospice, caravansary, motel, roadhouse, tourist house.

hotelkeeper, boniface, hosteler, hotelier, innkeeper, host,

tent, canvas, pavilion, tabernacle, tepee, wigwam; camp, bivouac, encampment.

homesickness, nostalgia, *Heimweh* (*Ger.*), *mal du pays* (*F.*).

home management, domestic arts, home economics, homemaking, household arts, housekeeping.

householder, homeowner, homemaker, housekeeper; household, ménage.

V. **house,** barrack, berth, billet, domicile, lodge, quarter, canton, board, accommodate.

Adj. **habitable,** inhabitable, livable, lodgeable, tenantable, occupiable, abidable.

residential, domal, domiciliary, domestic; at home, *en famille* (*F.*).

See also BUILDING, CITY, INHABITANT, LAND, LOCATION, REGION, RURAL REGION, SPACE.

---

hack, *v.* chop, clip, hackle (CUTTING); cough, hawk, whoop (THROAT).

hackney, *n.* taxi, cab, hansom (VEHICLE).

hackneyed, *adj.* well-worn, stale, trite (USE, OLDNESS).

Hades, *n.* Gehenna, the inferno, the lower regions (HELL).

hag, *n.* crone, harridan, gorgon (OLDNESS, DEFORMITY).

haggard, *adj.* drawn, pinched, starved (THINNESS); wan, tired-looking (FATIGUE).

hail, *n.* ice, hailstone (COLD).

hail, *v.* salute, greet, welcome (GREETING, TALK).

HAIR—*N.* hair, bristle, quill, vibrissa, feeler, whisker, filament; tuft, cowlick, forelock, daglock, hackles, mane, fringe, ruff; lock, strand, tress; pubic hair, pubescence, pubes; topknot, bun, chignon.

locks, mop, thatch, shag, tousle, crop, bangs, tresses, mane, patch, shock; pile, nap, widow's peak.

fur, coat, pelage, wool, hirsuties.

down, fluff, fuzz, lanugo, pubescence, moss.

curl, ringlet, frizzle, friz; braid, plait, coil, pigtail, queue.

beard, whiskers, stubble, goatee, Vandyke, imperial, mutton chops, sideburns, burnsides, sideboards (*slang*).

mustache, mustachio, handlebar mustache, walrus mustache, Kaiser Wilhelm mustache.

wig, periwig, peruke, toupee, transformation, switch.

hairiness, hispidity, hirsutism, hypertrichosis, villosity, pubescence.

hair style, coiffure, hair-do; pompadour, updo, upsweep, permanent wave, croquignole, cold wave, marcel, bob, poodle cut, crew cut, pony tail.

hairdresser, barber, *coiffeur* (F.), *coiffeuse* (F., *fem.*).

hairdressing, brilliantine, pomade, pomatum.

dandruff, dander, furfur, scurf.

Adj. hairy, hirsute, hispid, bristly, bristled, barbigerous, comate, shaggy, pileous, bushy, woolly, furry, tufted; hairlike, capillary, trichoid.

downy, fluffy, fuzzy, velutinous, villous, cottony, lanate, lanuginous, pubescent, velvety.

curly-headed, woolly, woolly-headed, ulotrichous, fuzzy-haired, wire-haired, wavy-haired.

blond-haired, blond, golden-haired, auricomous, fair-haired, sandy, sandy-haired, xanthochroid, auburn; towheaded, albino; gray-haired, grizzled.

dark-haired, black-haired, brown-haired, brunet, melanous.

combed, coifed, marcelled, permanented (*colloq.*), curled, curly, waved, wavy; bobbed; upswept; braided, plaited, tressed; straight, lank.

bearded, whiskered, bewhiskered, barbate, barbigerous, goateed, unshaved or unshaven, stubbled; mustached, mustachioed.

See also FEATHER, GRAY, OLDNESS. *Antonyms*—See HAIRLESSNESS.

---

haircut, n. trim, shave, tonsure (HAIRLESSNESS).

hairdresser, n. *coiffeur* (F.), barber (HAIR).

hairdressing, n. brilliantine, pomade, pomatum (HAIR).

HAIRLESSNESS—N. hairlessness, baldness, bald-headedness, baldpatedness.

loss of hair, alopecia, defluvium, trichorrhea, the mange.

hair removal, depilation, coupage, electrolysis; haircut, trim, shave, tonsure; depilatory.

bald person, baldhead, baldpate.

barber, haircutter, tonsorial artist; barbershop, tonsorial parlor, hairdresser's, beauty salon, beauty parlor.

V. barber, cut, trim, shave, tonsure, depilate.

Adj. bald, hairless, baldheaded, glabrous (*zool.*), smooth.

beardless, clean-shaven, shaven, unbearded, unwhiskered, smoothfaced.

See also CUTTING, SMOOTHNESS, UNDRESS. *Antonyms*—See HAIR.

---

hair-raising, adj. exciting, breathtaking, spine-tingling (EXCITEMENT).

hairsplitting, adj. nice, fine, subtle (DIFFERENTIATION).

hale, adj. healthy, trim, fit (HEALTH).

half, n. moiety, 50 per cent (BISECTION).

half-baked, adj. underbaked, doughy (COOKERY); underdeveloped, undergrown, sophomoric (IMMATURITY).

half-breed, n. hybrid, half-blood, half-caste (MANKIND).

halfway, adv. midway, in the midst (CENTER, INTERJACENCE).

half-wit, n. nitwit (*colloq.*), dunce, imbecile (STUPIDITY, FOLLY).

hall, n. corridor, entrance hall, entranceway (PASSAGE, INGRESS); rotunda, saloon, casino (SPACE).

hallmark, n. badge, countermark, emblem (INDICATION).

hallowed, adj. inviolable, sacrosanct, holy (SACREDNESS).

hallucination, n. delusion, illusion, mirage (UNREALITY, APPEARANCE).

hallway, n. vestibule, lobby, entry (PASSAGE).

halo, n. glory, nimbus, aureole (LIGHT).

halt, v. stop, pause, rest (END, CESSATION).

halting, adj. hesitant, faltering, wavering (INACTION).

halve, v. divide, split, cut in two, dichotomize (BISECTION).

hammer, n. mallet, maul, gavel (HITTING).

hammer, v. drum, din into, harp on (REPETITION).

hamper, n. basket, pannier, bassinet (CONTAINER).

hamper, v. hinder, interfere with, impede (HINDRANCE).

hand, n. extremity, fist, palm (APPENDAGE); penmanship, handwriting, longhand (WRITING); hired man, handy man, employee (WORK).

hand, v. deliver, transfer, pass (GIVING, PASSAGE).

handbag, n. purse, pocketbook; grip, portmanteau (CONTAINER).

handbill, n. poster, placard, notice (INFORMATION, PUBLICATION).

handbook, n. manual, guidebook, Baedeker (BOOK).

handcuffs, n. bracelets (slang), manacles (RESTRAINT).

handicraft, n. handiness, dexterity, skill (ABILITY); crafts, manual work (WORK).

handkerchief, n. kerchief, bandanna (GLOVE).

handle, n. hilt, hold, shaft (HOLD).

handle, v. feel, touch, finger (FEELING, TOUCH); work, wield, manipulate (USE); treat, manage (USE, ACTION).

handsome, adj. comely, beautiful, graceful (BEAUTY); generous, princely, unsparing (UNSELFISHNESS).

handwriting, n. longhand, chirography, manuscription (WRITING).

handy, adj. convenient, central; wieldy, manageable (USE, EASE, PREPARATION); adroit, deft, dexterous (ABILITY).

hang, v. suspend, loll, hover (HANGING); gibbet, lynch (KILLING); depend, pend, hang in suspense (UNCERTAINTY).

hangdog, adj. secretive, furtive, sneaky (CONCEALMENT).

hanger-on, n. satellite, parasite, heeler (FOLLOWER); flunky, truckler, bootlicker (SLAVERY).

HANGING—N. hanging, suspension, loll, poise, hover, sag, droop; swing, dangle; overhang, projection, jut.

gallows, gibbet, scaffold, halter; pendant, rack, suspenders.

V. **hang,** hang down, depend, suspend, loll, lop, poise, hover, brood over, sag, droop; swing, dangle, flap; overhang, project, beetle, jut, topple; gibbet, lynch, hang in effigy.

Adj. **hanging,** pendent, pending, pensile, dependent, suspended, suspensory, loppy, lop, poised.

pendulous, cernuous, nutant, droopy, saggy, flabby, baggy, loppy.

overhanging, beetling, beetle, jutting, projecting; overlapping, overlying, imbricate.

See also DESCENT, OSCILLATION, VISIBILITY. Antonyms—See SUPPORT.

---

hangover, n. crapulence, delirium tremens (DRUNKENNESS).

hang over, v. overhang, project, beetle, jut (HANGING).

hanker, v. long for, crave, ache for (DESIRE).

haphazard, adj. accidental, random, incidental (CHANCE); aimless, driftless (PURPOSELESSNESS).

happen, v. occur, take place, transpire (OCCURRENCE).

happening, n. event, milestone, incident (OCCURRENCE).

HAPPINESS—N. happiness, beatitude, beatification, bliss, cheer, contentment, content, delight, ecstasy, enchantment, gaiety, joy, jubilation, jubilation, rapture, ravishment, enjoyment, eudaemonia, felicity, rejoicing, well-being, welfare.

elation, exaltation, exultation, exultance, glee, triumph.

[state or place of perfect happiness] Eden, Elysium, Elysian fields, paradise, seventh heaven, Shangri-La, utopia.

[time of happiness] red-letter day, jubilee, millennium, golden age, Saturnian period.

science of happiness: eudaemonics.

V. **feel happy,** be content, jubilate, purr, joy, delight in, enjoy, enjoy oneself, revel in, rhapsodize about, rejoice, tread (or walk) on air, soar, cheer up; crow, exult, gloat, triumph, whoop; congratulate, felicitate.

make happy, blithen, cheer, content, delight, rejoice, enchant, enrapture, exalt, gladden, joy, ravish, thrill, elate.

Adj. **happy,** beatific, blissful, blithe, blitheful, blithesome, cheerful, content, contented, delighted, ecstatic, enchanted, enraptured, exalted, gay, glad, joyful, joyous, overjoyed, rapturous, ravished, rhapsodic, thrilled.

elated, exalted, exultant, gleeful, gleesome, jubilant, triumphant.

cheery, delightful, delightsome, delighting, enchanting, enrapturing, exalting, glad, gladsome, joyful, joyous, jubilant, ravishing, thrilling, Elysian, enjoyable, eudaemonical, felicific, happy, winsome.

See also CHEERFULNESS, MERRIMENT, PLEASANTNESS, PLEASURE, SATISFACTION. Antonyms—See DEJECTION, DISAPPOINTMENT, DISSATISFACTION, GLOOM, SADNESS.

---

harangue, n. tirade, screed, diatribe (MALEDICTION).

harangue, v. address, apostrophize, accost; spout, orate (TALK).

harass, v. torment, devil, beset (ANNOYANCE).

harbinger, *n.* precursor, forerunner, herald (PRECEDENCE); omen, augury, foretoken (FUTURE).

harbor, *n.* port, anchorage, mooring (LOCATION, ARRIVAL); refuge, asylum, haven (PROTECTION).

hard, *adj.* difficult, tough, uphill (DIFFICULTY); firm, stony, rocky (HARDNESS).

hard-boiled (*colloq.*), *adj.* casehardened, hard-bitten, callous (INSENSITIVITY).

harden, *v.* temper, anneal, planish, toughen (HARDNESS); caseharden, callous, indurate (INSENSITIVITY).

hardened, *adj.* case-hardened, hard-bitten, hard-boiled (*colloq.*), callous (INSENSITIVITY); indurated, sclerosed (HARDNESS).

hardhearted, *adj.* cruel-hearted, heartless, flinthearted (CRUELTY); cold-blooded, cold, heartless (INSENSITIVITY).

hardly, *adv.* infrequently, seldom, rarely (FEWNESS, SMALLNESS).

HARDNESS—*N.* **hardness,** solidity, impermeability, ossification, petrifaction.

[*comparisons*] adamant, diamond, flint, stone, brick, cobblestone, rock, granite, iron, steel.

stiffness, tension, tensity, rigidity, inflexibility, consistency, firmness, etc. (see *Adjectives*).

V. **harden,** temper, anneal, planish, toughen, steel, braze; callous, crust, solidify, congeal, crisp, indurate, petrify, ossify.

stiffen, tense, firm, brace, petrify.

Adj. **hard,** firm, solid, adamantine, adamant, stony, rocky, petrous, petrified, flinty, steely, brassy, brazen; horny, callous, bony, ossified, cartilaginous; hardened, indurate, sclerotic, sclerous; crisp, crispy, crusty, impermeable, leathern, leathery, coriaceous, tough, planished, weather-beaten; stale (*of bread, etc.*), congealed, frozen.

stiff, firm, rigid, tense, inflexible, unbending, unyielding.

See also BONE, DIFFICULTY, ROCK, SEVERITY, SKIN. *Antonyms*—See EASE, SOFTNESS.

---

hardship, *n.* uphill work, burden, Herculean task (DIFFICULTY); affliction, trouble, curse (MISFORTUNE).

hardware, *n.* ironware, metalware, enamelware (METAL).

hard-working, *adj.* industrious, diligent, assiduous (WORK).

hardy, *adj.* rugged, indefatigable, unflagging (ENERGY, STRENGTH).

hare, *n.* rabbit, jack rabbit (ANIMAL).

harebrained, *adj.* scatterbrained, flighty, giddy (FRIVOLITY, INATTENTION).

harem, *n.* seraglio (SEX).

harken, *v.* listen, give ear, lend an ear (LISTENING).

harlot, *n.* cocotte, *fille de joie* (*F.*), Jezebel (PROSTITUTE, SEX).

HARM—*N.* **harm,** damage, mischief, malicious mischief, sabotage, vandalism, hurt, ruination; disservice, hurt, injury, prejudice, detriment, violence, outrage, wrong, grievance, ravage, ravages, wear and tear.

injury, lesion, mar, spoilage, scuff; shock, trauma; sprain, wrench; wound, concussion, stab; mutilation, mayhem, battery, casualty.

bruise, contusion, mouse, wale, weal, welt, wheal; blemish, scar, abrasion.

[*cause of harm*] **curse,** evil eye, whammy (*slang*), hex, evil, cancer.

[*injured person*] **victim,** casualty, basket case, litter case.

V. **harm,** damage, sabotage, vandalize, ruin; disserve, hurt, injure, prejudice, outrage, do violence to, wrong, trample on, ravage.

injure, hurt, mar, spoil, blemish, shatter, scotch, scuff, scathe; shock, traumatize; sprain, wrench; wound, bruise, contuse, raze, stab, wing; maim, mutilate, mangle, crush.

Adj. **harmful,** damaging, hurtful, ruinous, injurious, prejudicial, deleterious, detrimental; vandalistic, mischievous; baneful, evil, wicked, maleficent, mephitic, nasty, outrageous, pernicious, scatheful; nocuous, noisome, noxious, vicious, virulent, unhealthy, unwholesome, demoralizing, pestiferous, pestilential, anti-social, dysgenic, predatory; contraindicated, traumatic.

malevolent, malicious, malign, malignant, evil-minded.

See also BLEMISH, CUTTING, DESTRUCTION, DETERIORATION, DISEASE, HATRED, HOSTILITY, IMPROPERNESS, MALEDICTION, THREAT, VIOLENCE, WICKEDNESS. *Antonyms*—See CURE, HEALTH, INNOCENCE, RESTORATION.

---

harmless, *adj.* inoffensive, innocuous, safe (INNOCENCE).

harmonious, *adj.* congruous, undiscordant (HARMONY); canorous, cantabile, Lydian (SWEETNESS, HARMONY); concordant, unanimous (UNITY).

HARMONY—*N.* **harmony,** agreement, adaptation, conformity, accord, accordance, concord, concurrence, unity, unanimity, congruity, consistency, correspondence, unison; order, symmetry, proportion.

[*in music*] **consonance,** accordance, accord, concord, tunefulness, euphony, chord, diapason, music, symphony.

V. [*to be harmonious*] **harmonize,** agree, accord, combine, co-operate, blend, unite, correspond, tally, suit.

[*to make harmonious*] **adjust,** reconcile, accord, attune, string, tune, modulate, adapt, set, orchestrate, symphonize, transpose, arrange.

Adj. **harmonious,** symmetrical, congruous, congruent, accordant, undiscordant, correspondent, conformable, proportionate.

agreeable, pleasing, sweet-sounding, pleasant-sounding, musical.

See also AGREEMENT, CONFORMITY, CO-OPERATION, MELODY, MUSIC, SINGING, SOUND, SWEETNESS, UNITY. *Antonyms*—See DISAGREEMENT, HARSH SOUND, HIGH-PITCHED SOUND, LOUDNESS, OPPOSITION.

---

harness, *n.* strap, belt (FILAMENT).
harp, *n.* lyre, lute, zither (MUSICAL INSTRUMENTS).
harp on, *v.* drum, hammer, din (REPETITION); refer to, advert to, allude to (TALK).
harsh, *adj.* coarse, chapped (ROUGHNESS); strict, hard, rigid (SEVERITY); grating, jarring (HARSH SOUND).

HARSH SOUND—*N.* **harsh sound,** dissonance, disharmony, discord, cacophony, noise, jangle, stridor, clangor, clash, crepitation, stridulation; stridence, stridency.

V. **grate,** jar, clash, grind, burr, rasp, set the teeth on edge, jangle, clangor, blare, bray, bark, croak, hawk, quack, squawk, yawp, caterwaul; creak, screak, chirr, crepitate, stridulate, saw, buzz.

Adj. **harsh-sounding,** harsh, grating, etc. (see *Verbs*); unmusical, unmelodious, unharmonious, uneuphonious, inharmonious, barbarous, raucous, rugged, rude, scrannel, brazen, cacophonous, discordant, dissonant, disharmonious, strident, raspy, noisy, clangorous; creaky, screaky, crepitant, stridulous, squawky.

hoarse, guttural, husky, throaty, gruff, roupy, croaky, cracked.

See also HIGH-PITCHED SOUND, ROUGHNESS, SOUND, THROAT. *Anto-*

nyms—See MELODY, MUSIC, SILENCE, SINGING, SWEETNESS.

---

harvest, *n.* crop, yield, output (STORE); by-product, repercussion (RESULT).
harvest, *v.* plow, harrow, reap (FARMING); get as a result, get (RESULT).
hash, *n.* mess, olla-podrida (*Sp.*), salmagundi (MIXTURE).
haste, *n.* hurry, rush, precipitance (SPEED).
hasten, *v.* fly, hurry, hustle, speed up, quicken, accelerate (SPEED).
hasty, *adj.* hurried, rushed, precipitate, precipitant, abrupt (SPEED).
hat, *n.* chapeau, fedora, Homburg (HEADGEAR).
hatch, *v.* set, brood, incubate (SEAT); improvise, make up, invent (PRODUCTION); contrive, concoct, project (PLAN).
hatchet, *n.* tomahawk, ax (CUTTING).

HATRED—*N.* **hatred,** hate, abhorrence, abomination, detestation, loathing, shudders, enmity, rancor, horror, animosity, animus, odium.

dislike, mislike, objection, disesteem, disfavor, disrelish, distaste, grudge, aversion, antipathy, repugnance, repulsion, disgust.

unpopularity, disesteem, disfavor, disregard.

[*object of hatred*] **anathema,** abhorrence, abomination, detestation, execration, bête noire (*F.*), hate; monster, monstrosity, horror.

[*object of dislike*] **aversion,** antipathy, dislike, objection, *persona non grata* (*L.*), rotter.

V. **hate,** abhor, abominate, detest, loathe, despise; shudder, recoil, shrink.

dislike, disesteem, disfavor, disrelish, mislike, object to, begrudge, grudge, have no stomach for, have no taste for, revolt against.

[*arouse dislike or hatred in*] **offend,** antagonize, displease, horrify, shock, disgust, repel, scandalize, envenom, venom; alienate, estrange, set against, turn against.

Adj. **hateful,** abhorrent, abominable, despicable, detestable, execrable, loathsome, shuddersome, shuddery; accursed, cursed, blasted, damnable, confounded, damned, foul, odious, heinous, invidious, infamous.

horrible, horrid, horrendous, horrifying, horrific, ghastly, grim, grisly, gruesome, hideous, macabre, monstrous, morbid.

dislikable, distasteful, displeasing, unlikable, objectionable, exceptionable, antipathetic, disgusting, disgustful, repugnant, repulsive, repellent, obnoxious, revolting, offensive, villainous.

unpopular, disesteemed, disfavored, disliked, disrelished, distasteful, in the bad graces of, misliked, out of favor, unesteemed, unfavored, unliked, unrelished, in bad odor, in the doghouse (*slang*).

horrified, horror-stricken, aghast, abhorrent of; rancorous, despiteful, malicious, malevolent, grudgeful; averse, antipathetic; repelled, repulsed, disgusted, revolted.

See also ANGER, DISAPPROVAL, DISGUST, HOSTILITY, MALEDICTION, OFFENSE, OPPOSITION, UNPLEASANTNESS. *Antonyms*—See APPROVAL, FRIENDLINESS, LOVE, PLEASANTNESS.

haughty, *adj.* arrogant, cavalier, toplofty (PRIDE).

haul (*colloq.*), *n.* loot, swag (*colloq.*), booty (THIEVERY).

haul, *v.* pull, draw, lug (TRACTION).

haunt, *n.* abode, living quarters, dwelling (HABITATION); haunts, stamping grounds (ARRIVAL).

haunt, *v.* frequent, visit, infest (PRESENCE).

have, *v.* include, accommodate, teem with (CONTAINER); possess, occupy, own (HOLD).

haven, *n.* refuge, asylum, harbor (PROTECTION).

havoc, *n.* wreckage, ruin, dilapidation (DESTRUCTION).

hay, *n.* pasture, pasturage, soilage (GRASS).

hay fever, *n.* allergic rhinitis, pollinosis (NOSE).

hazard, *v.* risk, dare, speculate, venture (DANGER, CHANCE).

hazardous, *adj.* perilous, precarious, insecure (DANGER); chancy, risky, venturesome (CHANCE).

haze, *n.* vapor, fog, smaze (CLOUD); vagueness, obscurity, confusion (UNCERTAINTY).

hazy, *adj.* misty, cloudy, foggy (SEMITRANSPARENCY, UNCLEARNESS); dizzy, groggy, muzzy (CONFUSION).

H-bomb, *n.* hydrogen bomb, hell bomb (THROW).

he, *n.* male, buck, tom (MAN).

head, *adj.* leading, chief, main (LEADERSHIP); pioneer, *avantgarde* (*F.*), advanced (PRECEDENCE); cephalic, frontal (HEAD).

head, *n.* pate, skull (HEAD); chief, leader, commander (RANK, LEADERSHIP); fountainhead, headspring, riverhead (RIVER); heading, caption, inscription (TITLE).

head, *v.* dominate, hold sway over (GOVERNMENT); lead, pioneer (PRECEDENCE); go, proceed, hie (HEAD).

HEAD—*N.* head, *caput* (*L.*), pate, noddle (*colloq.*), noggin (*colloq.*), noodle (*slang*), poll (*dial. or jocose*), costard (*jocose*), nob *or* knob (*slang*), bean (*slang*), dome (*slang*); skull, cranium.

forehead, brow, frons, sinciput; temple.

face, countenance, visage, aspect, physiognomy, features, lineament, profile, silhouette; poker face, dead pan (*both colloq.*).

jaw, jowl, maxilla, underjaw, submaxilla, mandible; jaws, chops, snout, muzzle.

mouth, maw, stoma (*zool.*), neb; palate, soft palate, velum; river mouth, embouchure; tongue, lips, cupid's bow.

neck, cervix; nape, nucha, nuque, poll, scruff.

science of the head or skull: cephalology, craniology, phrenology.

V. head, go, proceed, hie; lead, guide, supervise, manage, be in charge of.

Adj. cephalic, frontal, metopic, sinciptial; headless, acephalous; [*pert to the neck*] cervical, jugular; thick-necked, bull-necked.

facial, physiognomical; twofaced, Janus-faced, bifacial; pokerfaced (*colloq.*), dead-pan (*colloq.*), stony-faced, stony, expressionless.

lantern-jawed, underhung, underjawed, undershot, prognathous; gnathic, maxillary.

pert. to the mouth, etc.: oral, oscular, stomatic, stomatous; buccal, malar (*cheeks*); labial (*lips*); lingual, glossal (*tongue*).

See also APPEARANCE, BODY, CONTROL, FRONT, LEADERSHIP.

---

headache, *n.* sick headache, nervous headache, migraine (PAIN).

HEADGEAR—*N.* headgear, millinery, headcloth, headpiece, babushka, cowl, fascinator, hood, kerchief, mantilla, scarf, shawl, wrap, snood, turban, tiara, veil, veiling, wimple.

headdress, headband, crown, coronal, coronet, tiara, garland, bandeau, fillet, circlet, frontlet, frontal, aigrette, egret, snood (*Scot.*); hair ribbon, barrette, hairpin, bobble pin.

hat, chapeau, fedora, Homburg, kelly (*slang*), Stetson (*slang*), panama, pork pie, straw hat, skimmer (*slang*), derby, bowler (*Brit.*); castor, busby, cocked hat, coonskin hat, pith helmet, shako, sombrero, southwester *or* sou'-wester, tricorn; bonnet, capote, sunbonnet, calash, breton, cloche, picture hat, pillbox, sailor, toque.

cap, beanie, beret, biretta *or* barret (*R. C. Ch.*), coif, fez, tarboosh, garrison cap, overseas cap, kepi, mobcap, mob (*hist.*), mortarboard, nightcap, bedcap, skullcap, tam-o'-shanter, tam, tuque; cap and bells, fool's cap, dunce cap.

high hat, beaver, crush hat, opera hat, plug hat (*slang*), silk hat, stovepipe hat (*colloq.*), top hat, topper (*colloq.*).

helmet, headpiece, crest, casque (*poetic*); visor, beaver.

See also CLOTHING, CLOTHING WORKER, COVERING, HEAD, ORNAMENT. *Antonyms*—See FOOTWEAR.

---

heading, *n.* caption, rubric, inscription (TITLE).

headland, *n.* promontory, cape, head (LAND).

headline, *n.* banner, streamer, heading (TITLE).

headlong, *adv.* full-tilt, posthaste, pell-mell (SPEED); violently, headfirst, precipitately (VIOLENCE).

headstrong, *adj.* self-willed, obstinate, willful (STUBBORNNESS, WILL, UNRULINESS); ungovernable, uncontrollable, unruly (VIOLENCE).

headway, *n.* headroom, elbowroom, leeway, seaway (SPACE).

heady, *adj.* provocative, intoxicating, stimulating (EXCITEMENT).

heal, *v.* convalesce, mend, cure (HEALTH, CURE).

healer, *n.* medicine man, witch doctor, shaman (MEDICAL SCIENCE).

HEALTH—N. health, vigor, euphoria, eudaemonia, well-being; trim, bloom, pink, verdure, prime.

hygiene, sanitation, prophylaxis.

health resort, sanatorium, sanitarium, spa, watering place, rest home, convalescent home, hospital.

V. be in health, enjoy good health, bloom, flourish, thrive.

get well, convalesce, heal, mend, rally, recover, recuperate, revalesce, get better; cure, heal, restore to health, make well.

Adj. healthy, sound, well, robust, hearty, robustious (*jocose*), trim, trig, hale, fit, blooming, bouncing, strapping, vigorous, whole, wholesome, able-bodied, athletic, eudaemonic, euphoric, tonic.

convalescent, recovering, on the mend, recuperating, revalescent.

healthful, nutritious, salutary, salubrious, wholesome, beneficial; hygienic, sanatory, sanitary, prophylactic.

[*concerned about one's health*] hypochondriac, valetudinary, atrabilious.

unharmed, intact, untouched, scatheless, scot-free, sound, spared, unblemished, unbruised, undamaged, unhurt, uninjured, unmarred, unscarred, unscathed, unspoiled, unwounded, whole.

See also CURE, MEDICAL SCIENCE, RESTORATION, STRENGTH. *Antonyms*—See DISEASE.

---

heap, *n.* lump, pile, mass (ASSEMBLAGE).

heap up, *v.* pile up, stack, load (STORE).

hear, *v.* give a hearing to, overhear (LISTENING); try, sit in judgment (LAWSUIT).

hearing, *n.* audience, interview, conference (LISTENING); earshot, range (SOUND).

hearing aid, *n.* ear trumpet, auriphone, audiphone (LISTENING).

hearsay, *n.* comment, buzz, report (RUMOR).

heart, *n.* core, pith, kernel (CENTER, INTERIORITY); auricle, ventricle (BLOOD).

heartache, *n.* heavy heart, broken heart, heartbreak (SADNESS).

heartbreaking, *adj.* affecting, heart-rending, moving (PITY).

hearten, *v.* inspire, reassure, encourage (COURAGE).

heartfelt, *adj.* cordial, wholehearted (HONESTY).

hearth, *n.* fireplace, fireside, grate (HEAT); home, homestead, hearthstone (HABITATION).

heartless, *adj.* cruelhearted, flinthearted, hardhearted (CRUELTY); coldhearted, cold-blooded, cold (INSENSITIVITY).

heart-shaped, *adj.* cordiform, cordate (CURVE).

heartsick, *adj.* heartsore, heartstricken, heavyhearted (SADNESS).

hearty, *adj.* healthy, well, robust (HEALTH); cordial, sincere, glowing (FEELING).

HEAT—N. heat, warmth, temperature, calefaction, calescence, incalescence, candescence, incandescence.

[*instruments*] thermometer, calorimeter, pyrometer, centigrade *or* Celsius thermometer, Fahrenheit thermometer; thermostat, pyrostat, cryometer.

heater, radiator, calefactor, furnace, boiler; electric heater, heating pad, brazier, foot warmer; stove, cookstove, range, oven; bloomery, forge, kiln, brickkiln, limekiln.

fireplace, hearth, fireside, grate, firebox; andiron, firedog, fire irons; poker, tongs, shovel, hob, trivet; damper, crane, pothooks, chains, turnspit, spit, gridiron.

V. **heat,** calorify, fire, chafe, cook, bake, bask, toast, warm, tepefy, broil, roast, scald, scorch, parch, torrefy (*drugs, etc.*), pasteurize (*milk*), irradiate; thaw, melt.

be hot, glow, flush, bask, bake, toast, sweat, perspire, swelter, stew, simmer, seethe, boil, burn, sizzle, broil, roast, incandesce.

Adj. **hot,** broiling, burning, roasting, scorching, sizzling, steaming, steamy, sweltering, torrid, tropical; close, heavy, stuffy, oppressive, stifling, suffocating, sultry, muggy; candent, fiery, piping-hot, red-hot, white-hot.

warm, lukewarm, tepid, hypothermal, thermal.

[*pert. to heat*] **thermal,** caloric; thermonuclear.

See also COOKERY, FEVER, FIRE, FUEL. Antonyms—See COLD.

heath, *n.* moor, moors, moorland (LAND).

heathen, *n.* pagan, paganist (RELIGION); irreligionist, atheist, infidel (IRRELIGION).

heave, *v.* cast, fling, hurl (THROW); lift, hoist, raise (ELEVATION); keck, retch, vomit (NAUSEA).

HEAVEN—N. heaven, seventh heaven, abode of God.

[*mythological heaven or paradise*] Olympus, Elysium (*Greek*), Elysian fields, Island (*or* Isles) of the Blessed, Happy Isles, Fortunate Isles, garden of the Hesperides; Valhalla (*Scandinavian*), Asgard (*Scandinavian*); happy hunting grounds (*N. Amer. Indian*).

the heavens, sky, welkin (*archaic*), firmament, canopy, sphere (*poetic*), empyrean, azure, hyaline (*poetic*), ether, starry cope, the wide blue yonder.

paradise, Canaan, Elysium, empyrean (*poetic*).

[*inhabitant of heaven*] **celestial,** Olympian, angel, god, God.

Adj. **heavenly,** uranic, firmamental, empyreal, Olympian, celestial, divine, ethereal, superlunary, supernal; paradisaical, paradisiac, Elysian.

See also GOD, LIGHT, WORLD. Antonyms—See HELL.

heavy, *adj.* weighty, hefty (*colloq.*), ponderous (WEIGHT); fat, fleshy, stout (SIZE); close, stuffy, oppressive (HEAT); dull, lethargic, listless (INACTION); pregnant, *enceinte* (*F.*), expectant (PREGNANCY).

heavyhearted, *adj.* heartsick, heartsore, heart-stricken (SADNESS).

hectic, *adj.* exciting, rip-roaring, rip-roarious (EXCITEMENT).

hedge, *v.* girdle, fence, ring (ENVIRONMENT, INCLOSURE); temporize, blow hot and cold (APOSTASY).

heed, *v.* listen, give ear, attend (LISTENING); mind, do one's bidding, follow orders (OBEDIENCE).

heedless, *adj.* disregardful, thoughtless, careless (INATTENTION); reckless, unwary, impetuous (CARELESSNESS).

heel, *v.* tag, shadow, follow (REAR); lean, list, tilt (SLOPE).

hefty (*colloq.*), *adj.* strapping, husky (*colloq.*), burly (SIZE).

HEIGHT—N. height, altitude, stature, elevation, sublimity, heyday, high point; eminence, highland, upland, promontory, rise, terrace, bank, embankment.

precipice, rocky height, cliff, bluff, escarpment, scarp, crag, scar; cliffside, palisades.

top, highest point, ceiling, acme, apex, cusp, climax, tip, tiptop, zenith, apogee, solstice, vertex, cope, summit, peak, crown, crest, brow, pinnacle, *ne plus ultra* (*L.*), culmination, noontide, noon, meridian; lid, cover.

hill, hillock, hummock, hurst, dune, down, knoll, mesa, mound, mount, tumulus; mountain, alp, volcano; mountain range, ridge, cordillera, chain.

tower, pillar, column, obelisk, monument, belfry, steeple, spire, minaret, campanile, turret, pagoda, pyramid.

mountain dweller, mountaineer, hillbilly (*colloq.*).

V. **heighten,** elevate, exalt, upraise, uphoist, uplift, uprear, raise, rear, hoist, erect, set up.

intensify, strengthen, enhance, augment, increase, aggravate, advance, sharpen.

top, command, dominate, transcend, overtop, overlook, surmount, soar above, rise above, tower above, jut above, overhang; mount; crown, culminate.

Adj. **high,** tall, towering,

alpine; elevated, lofty, exalted, upborne; winged, sublime, supernal; steep, abrupt, precipitous, declivitous.

higher, superior, upper, upward, transcendent.

highest, top, tiptop, topmost, uppermost, upmost, utmost, maximal; supreme, top-drawer, topflight; crowning, apical, climactic, coronal, meridian, solstitial, zenithal.

tall (of persons), lanky, lank, rangy, gangling, slab-sided, spindly, spindling, stringy; slender, statuesque, sculpturesque, Junoesque, willowy, Amazonian.

hilly, highland, hillocked, hummocky, knolly, precipitous, tumulose; mountainous, alpine, alpestrine, volcanic, vulcanian.

Adv., phrases. **on high,** high up, aloft, up, upward, above, overhead, in the clouds.

See also ASCENT, BUILDING, COVERING, ELEVATION, EXPENDITURE, HIGH-PITCHED SOUND, INHABITANT, SLOPE, SUPERIORITY, SURFACE, THINNESS. Antonyms—See DEPTH, DESCENT, LOWNESS.

heinous, adj. atrocious, flagitious, accursed (WICKEDNESS).

heir, n. inheritor, heiress (fem.), beneficiary (INHERITANCE).

HELL—N. hell, the abyss, Acheron, Avernus, Gehenna, Hades, the inferno, the lower regions, the lower world, pandemonium, the pit, Tartarus (Greek myth.), Tophet, the underworld.

Adj. hellish, Avernal, Hadean, infernal, Plutonian or Plutonic, hellborn, Stygian, sulphurous.

See also DEPTH, DEVIL. Antonyms—See HEAVEN, HEIGHT.

helm, n. conning tower, conn, saddle, position of control, chair (CONTROL, GUIDANCE).

helmet, n. headpiece, casque (poetic), crest (HEADGEAR).

helmet-shaped, adj. galeiform, galeate (CURVE).

help, n. aid, assistance, hand (AID); domestic, domestic servant, employees (SERVICE, WORK).

help, v. assist, lend a hand, succor (AID).

helper, n. aide, assistant, apprentice (AID, WORK).

helpless, adj. powerless, impotent, incapable (DISABLEMENT, WEAKNESS); incompetent, inefficient, shiftless (CLUMSINESS).

helter-skelter, adv. pell-mell, in confusion (CONFUSION).

hem, v. sew, seam, hemstitch (FASTENING).

hem in, v. hedge, girdle, fence (INCLOSURE).

hen, n. biddy, fowl (BIRD).

hence, adv. therefore, consequently, ergo (L.), wherefore (REASONING, RESULT, ATTRIBUTION).

henchman, n. minion, myrmidon, vassal (FOLLOWER).

henpecked, adj. downtrodden, under one's thumb, tied to one's apron strings (SLAVERY).

herald, n. precursor, forerunner, harbinger (PRECEDENCE).

herald, v. usher in, preface, prelude (PRECEDENCE).

herb, n. plant, vegetable (PLANT LIFE).

herd, n. flock, drove, gathering (ASSEMBLAGE).

herd, v. flock, gather, huddle (MULTITUDE).

herder, n. keeper, warden, cowherd (DOMESTICATION).

here, present, attending, on-the-spot (PRESENCE, SITUATION).

hereafter, n. next world, afterlife, future state (DESTINY, FUTURE, LIFE).

hereafter, adv. in future, eventually, ultimately (FUTURE).

hereditary, adj. legitimate, heritable, inheritable (INHERITANCE); genealogical, lineal (ANCESTRY).

heredity, n. genetics, geneslology, eugenics (INHERITANCE).

heresy, n. heterodoxy, unorthodoxy, disbelief (HETERODOXY, BELIEF, UNBELIEVINGNESS).

heretic, n. infidel, misbeliever, unbeliever, nonbeliever, unorthodox, skeptic, freethinker, agnostic (IRRELIGION, HETERODOXY, UNBELIEVINGNESS).

heritage, n. heritance, legacy, estate (INHERITANCE).

hermaphrodite, n. gynandroid, androgyne (SEX).

hermit, n. recluse, solitaire, monk (ASCETICISM, SECLUSION).

hernia, n. rupture, breach, herniation (DISJUNCTION).

hero, n. adventurer, daredevil (COURAGE); lead, star (ACTOR).

heroic, adj. fearless, brave, impavid, intrepid, lionhearted (COURAGE).

hero worship, n. idolatry, idolism (WORSHIP).

hesitant, adj. halting, wavering, indecisive (INACTION).

hesitate, v. demur, scruple, falter (INACTION, UNCERTAINTY); be unwilling, stickle (UNWILLINGNESS).

hesitation, n. hesitance, demurral,

scruple, doubt, misgiving, qualm (INACTION, UNCERTAINTY); reluctance, reluctancy, scruples (UNWILLINGNESS).

HETERODOXY—N. heterodoxy, unorthodoxy, error, false doctrine, heresy, schism, recusancy, backsliding, apostasy.

sectarianism, nonconformity, dissent, disagreement, dissidence, secularism, denominationalism, separation, division.

heretic, infidel, misbeliever, unbeliever, apostate, backslider; antichrist, irreligionist, atheist, agnostic, skeptic, freethinker, iconoclast.

sectarian, sectary; seceder, separatist, recusant, dissenter, dissentient, dissident, nonconformist.

Adj. heterodox, heretical, unorthodox, unscriptural, uncanonical, unchristian, apocryphal; antichristian, antiscriptural, schismatic, recusant, iconoclastic; sectarian, dissenting, secular; agnostic, atheistic, unbelieving, freethinking, skeptical.

See also APOSTASY, IRRELIGION, UNBELIEVINGNESS. Antonyms—See BELIEF, CONFORMITY, RELIGION.

hew, v. carve, sculpt, whittle (CUTTING, SHAPE).

hex, n. curse, evil eye, jinx (HARM, MISFORTUNE); magic spell, charm (MAGIC).

heyday, n. prime, bloom, vitality (STRENGTH); popularity, prevalence, currency (USE).

hidden, adj. concealed, blind, blotted out, cached, covered (CONCEALMENT).

hide, n. pelt, peltry, slough (SKIN).

hide, v. conceal, cover, curtain (CONCEALMENT).

hideaway, n. hiding place, den, hideout (CONCEALMENT).

hidebound, adj. old-line, illiberal, Mid-Victorian (PREJUDICE, OPPOSITION).

hideous, adj. ugly, repulsive, unsightly (DEFORMITY); gruesome, macabre, morbid (HATRED); shocking, frightful, ghastly (DISGUST).

high, adj. tall, towering, alpine (HEIGHT); shrill, treble, sharp (HIGH-PITCHED SOUND); expensive, dear, costly (EXPENDITURE); inebriated, intoxicated, tipsy (DRUNKENNESS).

highball, n. cocktail, apéritif (F.), pousse-café (F.) (ALCOHOLIC LIQUOR).

highbrow (colloq.), adj. double-dome (slang), egghead (slang), intellectual (INTELLIGENCE).

higher, adj. upper, upward (HEIGHT); superior, greater, major (SUPERIORITY).

highest, adj. top, tiptop, topmost (HEIGHT); supreme, greatest, maximum (SUPERIORITY).

highfalutin (colloq.), adj. grandiloquent, high-flown, high-sounding (WORDINESS).

highhanded, adj. peremptory, arbitrary, dogmatic (OPINION).

highland, n. upland, promontory, rise (HEIGHT, LAND).

HIGH-PITCHED SOUND—N. high-pitched sound, high note, shrill note; soprano, treble, tenor, alto, falsetto, shrill; head voice, head tone; cheep, peep, squeak, squeal, skirl, clarion, zing, ting, chirr, stridulation, stridor, whistle, whine.

V. be high-pitched, cheep, peep, squeak, squeal, skirl, pipe, whistle, whine, zing, ting, stridulate, chirr.

shrill, scream, screech, cry, shriek, squawk, squall, yelp, yip, yap, yawp.

Adj. high-pitched, shrill, high, treble, sharp, thin, reedy, penetrating, piercing, clarion; strident, stridulous, squeaky; screechy, squally, squawky.

See also LOUDNESS, MELODY, MUSIC, SINGING. Antonyms—See HARMONY, LOWNESS, SILENCE.

high school, n. secondary school, lycée (F.), preparatory school (SCHOOL).

high-sounding, adj. highfalutin (colloq.), high-flown, grandiloquent (WORDINESS).

high-strung, adj. tense, taut, wire-drawn (NERVOUSNESS).

highway, n. road, artery, thoroughfare (PASSAGE).

highwayman, n. footpad, highway robber, hijacker (THIEF).

hiker, n. walker, hitchhiker, marcher (WALKING).

hilarious, adj. laughable, amusing, jocular (ABSURDITY, MERRIMENT).

hill, n. hillock, hummock, hurst (HEIGHT).

hillbilly (colloq.), n. mountain dweller, mountaineer (HEIGHT).

hilly, adj. steep, abrupt, precipitous (SLOPE, HEIGHT).

hilt, n. handle, hold, shaft (HOLD).

hind, n. hindquarters, dorsum (anat.), behind (REAR); deer, doe, roe (ANIMAL).

HINDRANCE—N. hindrance, astriction, constriction, bafflement, frustration, interference, circumscription, obstruction, blockage, restriction, retardation, obscurantism, obstructionism; impediment, bar, barricade, block, blockade, encumbrance, clog, fetter, hobble, shackle, bridle, muzzle, trammel, retardant, snag, strait jacket; obstacle, obstruent (med.), barrier, rampart, stumbling block, hitch, hurdle, hopple, strangle hold, bottleneck, baffle.

V. hinder, interfere with, hamper, impede, hobble, hopple, hamstring, pinion, shackle, fetter, strait-jacket, trammel, spike, snag, obstruct, retard, bar, barricade, block, blockade, clog, cumber, encumber.

thwart, baffle, balk, frustrate, stymie.

restrict, astrict, bridle, circumscribe, constrict, cramp.

See also CESSATION, DIFFICULTY, DISAPPOINTMENT, EMBARRASSMENT, IMPRISONMENT, OPPOSITION, PREVENTION, RESTRAINT, WEIGHT. Antonyms—See AID, FREEDOM.

hinge, n. swivel, pivot, axis (CAUSATION, ROTATION); joint, juncture, articulation (JUNCTION).
hinge, v. rest, be subject, depend (UNCERTAINTY, CONDITION).

HINT—N. hint, inkling, clue, suspicion, whisper, innuendo, insinuation, insinuendo, intimation, implication, suggestion, tip, pointer, wrinkle, word to the wise, verbum sat sapienti (L.); cue, prompt, tag.

V. hint, hint at, give a hint to, imply, intimate, suggest, tip or tip off, insinuate, prompt, cue.

See also INFORMATION, MEANING, MEMORY, SUGGESTION. Antonyms—See IGNORANCE.

hinterland, n. interior, backwoods, hinterlands (INTERIORITY); outskirts, outpost, purlieu, suburb, suburbs (DISTANCE).
hire, v. employ, engage, place (SITUATION); charter, rent, lease (BORROWING).
hireling, n. pensionary, mercenary (MONEY).
hiss, v. sibilate, sizz, spit (SIBILATION, ANIMAL SOUND).
historian, n. annalist, chronicler, archivist (PAST, RECORD).
history, n. chronicle, annals (PAST).
hitch, n. stoppage, discontinuance,

interruption (CESSATION); obstacle, stumbling block (HINDRANCE); shift, tour, trick (WORK).
hitherto, adv. ere now, before now, hereto (PAST).

HITTING—N. hitting, percussion, impact, concussion, collision, smashup (colloq.); beating, fustigation, lapidation, bastinado or bastinade, whipping, spanking, chastisement, flagellation.

blow, impact, shock, stroke, strike, hit, slap, smack, box, cuff, punch, uppercut, clip (slang), paste (slang), sock (slang), wallop (colloq.), swat, clout, smite, knock, bust (slang), bash, swipe; slam, slash, stamp, thump, thud, crash, bang, smash, clap; bat, lob, whack, thwack; bump, butt, bunt; pat, tap, rap, spat, tamp; sideswipe, glance, glancing blow, carom; buffet, lash, drum, drub, whack; spank, switch, belt (slang); poke, jab, push.

final blow, deathblow, coup de grâce (F.), quietus.

club, bludgeon, cudgel, stick, quarterstaff; bastinado or bastinade, bat, blackjack, pike, shillelagh, stave; truncheon, billy, night stick; ferule, flail, pestle.

whip, switch, strap, belt, scourge, quirt, birch, cat-o'-nine-tails, cat, crop, horsewhip, lash, knout, rawhide; thong, whiplash.

hammer, mallet, maul, mall, sledge, sledge hammer, gravel, cock (of a gun).

V. hit, strike, percuss, slap, smack box, cuff, punch, uppercut, clip (slang), paste (slang), sock (slang), wallop (colloq.), swat, clout, clobber (slang), smite, fell, blackjack, brain, knock out, knock down, knock, slug (slang), bust (slang), bash, swipe; slam, dash, slash, stamp, slog, stub, thump; bat, lob, loft, whack, thwack; buck, bunt, butt, bump, bunk (slang); bang, smash, collide, clang, clap; pellet, stone, lapidate; poke, jab, push.

hit lightly, pat, tap, tip, rap, bob, tamp, tag, drum, thrum; bounce, sideswipe, glance, carom.

beat, flail, thresh, mash, pound, pestle, hammer; knock about, buffet, lash, batter, pummel, belabor, pelt, drum, drub; club, cudgel, fustigate, bludgeon, truncheon, bastinade, lambaste (slang), maul, whack, ferule; whip, stir, whisk.

whip, switch, knout, swinge, slate, chastise, horsewhip, cowhide, quirt, scourge, strap, belt, birch, flagellate, pistol-whip, baste, larrup; spank, paddle, paddywhack (*colloq.*), lick (*colloq.*), flog, cane, tan (*colloq.*), thrash, whale, trounce; urticate (*med.*).

See also PUNISHMENT, TOUCH.

---

hoard, *n.* store, stockpile, accumulation (STORE, QUANTITY).

hoard, *v.* lay away, save, stow away, stock, stock-pile (STORE).

hoarse, *adj.* raucous, croaky, guttural (THROAT, HARSH SOUND).

hoax, *n.* trick, ruse, shift (DECEPTION).

hobble, *v.* limp, clump, scuff (WALKING); fetter, shackle, trammel (RESTRAINT).

hobnob, *v.* mingle, mix, fraternize (SOCIALITY).

hobo, *n.* tramp, bum (*slang*), vagabond (REST).

hocus-pocus, *n.* abracadabra, mumbo-jumbo, open-sesame (MAGIC).

hodgepodge, *n.* jumble, mélange (*F.*), hash (MIXTURE).

hog, *n.* sow, pig (ANIMAL); glutton, gormandizer, cormorant (GLUTTONY); self-seeker, timeserver (SELFISHNESS).

hoist, *v.* elevate, raise, lift (ELEVATION).

HOLD—*N.* hold, control, possession, retention, occupancy, occupation, tenure, ownership, reception, maintenance; tenacity, pertinacity.

grip, grasp, purchase, clutch, clasp, clench; seizure, suspension, wring.

gripping or holding device: brace, vise, grip, clamp, grippers, clutch, cradle, net, suspensory; clasp, pin, safety pin, diaper pin, snap, hook; pincers *or* pinchers, nippers, pliers, tweezers, forceps; Stillson wrench, monkey wrench, lug wrench.

handle, hilt, hold, shaft, grip, lug, grasp, butt, stock, shank, crop, haft, helve, stele, withe, brace, snath, snead, bail, crank, ear, knob, knocker.

V. **hold,** have, possess, occupy, own, retain, hold back, withhold, contain, receive, keep, maintain, keep hold of; hold fast, hold on, cling to, cherish, nourish.

grasp, seize, grip, clutch, clasp, clench; brace, vise; wring.

hug, embrace, cuddle, cradle, clinch, grapple, wrap one's arms around, enfold.

Adj. **holding,** etc. (see *Verbs*) possessive, retentive, tenacious, pertinacious, viselike; tenable, retainable.

See also CONTAINER, CONTENTS, CONTROL, OWNERSHIP, RECEIVING, STINGINESS, STORE, SUPPORT, TAKING. *Antonyms*—See DESERTION, EXCRETION, GIVING, RELINQUISHMENT.

---

hold back, *v.* restrain, stop, prevent (RESTRAINT); withhold, keep (HOLD).

holder, *n.* possessor, occupant, tenant (OWNERSHIP); receptacle, holster, box (CONTAINER).

hold forth, *v.* discourse, descant, dissertate (TALK).

hold in, *v.* suppress, repress, inhibit (RESTRAINT).

holdings, *n.* stocks, bonds, securities (OWNERSHIP).

hold on, *v.* continue, go on, keep up (CONTINUATION); hold fast, cling (HOLD).

hold out, *v.* continue, persevere, persist (CONTINUATION, STUBBORNNESS).

holdup, *n.* highway robbery, stickup (*slang*), robbery (THIEVERY).

hold up, *v.* uphold, upbear, sustain (SUPPORT).

hole, *n.* perforation, slot, puncture (OPENING); dungeon, oubliette, black hole (IMPRISONMENT).

holiday, *n.* fiesta, day of rest, vacation (REST, AMUSEMENT).

hollow, *adj.* concave, gullied (HOLLOW); insincere, dishonest, empty (PRETENSE); Pyrrhic, trifling (WORTHLESSNESS).

HOLLOW—*N.* hollow, concavity, dent, dimple, depression, dip, wallow, recess, sinus, umbilication, trough, cleft, bight, bowl, gouge, excavation, gulf, notch, pit; cavity, chamber, pocket.

furrow, groove, rabbet, rut, track, corrugation, gutter, sulcation, gully.

recess, niche, indentation, socket. ditch, channel, chase, gully, trench, dike, moat, trough.

V. **hollow,** hollow out, channel, chase, corrugate, dent, excavate, furrow, gouge, groove, indent, notch, pit, rabbet, rut, socket, trench, ditch, concave, scoop out.

Adj. **hollow,** concave; dented, dimpled, depressed, umbilicate, cleft, notched, pitted; cavernous, chambered, alveolate, socketed; flatulent, fistulous; troughlike, channeled, chased, gullied, sunken.

furrowed, grooved, rabbeted, rutted, corrugated, sulcate, gullied; recessed, indented, canaliferous; striated, fluted, ribbed, corduroy.

cup-shaped, calathiform, cyathiform, cupped, cupular.

pitted, foveate, punctate, pockmarked, variolar.

See also CONTAINER, DIGGING, FOLD, OPENING. *Antonyms*—See ROUNDNESS, SMOOTHNESS.

---

holster, *n.* quiver, scabbard, sheath (CONTAINER).

holy, *adj.* righteous, sainted, godly (MORALITY, RELIGIOUSNESS); inviolable, sacrosanct, hallowed (SACREDNESS).

homage, *n.* deference, esteem, honor (RESPECT); obeisance, genuflection (SUBMISSION).

home, *n.* homestead, hearth, house (HABITATION).

home-coming, *n.* arrival, advent, return (ARRIVAL).

home-grown, *adj.* native, indigenous, native-grown, homebred (INHABITANT).

homeland, *n.* native land, mother country, motherland (LAND).

homeless, *adj.* deserted, abandoned (DESERTION); outcast, displaced, exiled (DISMISSAL).

homely, *adj.* unattractive, unaesthetic, plain (DEFORMITY); humble, lowly, mean (MODESTY); homespun, rustic, provincial (VULGARITY); unpretentious, unelaborate (SIMPLICITY).

homemaking, *n.* home management, domestic arts, home economics (HABITATION).

homeowner, *n.* householder, homemaker, housekeeper (HABITATION).

homesickness, *n.* *Heimweh* (*Ger.*), *mal du pays* (*F.*), nostalgia (HABITATION).

homeward, *adj.* incoming, homeward-bound, inbound (ARRIVAL).

homework, *n.* practice, drill, assignment (TEACHING).

homicide, *n.* murder, assassination, manslaughter (KILLING).

homogeneous, *adj.* homologous, homological, homotaxic (SIMILARITY).

homosexual, *n.* homosexualist, sexual invert (SEX).

hone, *n.* sharpener, strop, grindstone (SHARPNESS).

HONESTY—*N.* **honesty,** integrity, probity, rectitude, veracity, veridicality, honor, clean hands, morality, scruples.

V. **be honest,** be honorable, play the game (*colloq.*), keep one's promise (*or* word), keep faith with, not fail, be on the up-and-up (*slang*), be on the level (*slang*), level with (*slang*).

Adj. **honest,** aboveboard, straightforward, truthful, upright, veracious, veridical, honorable, upstanding.

conscientious, moral, conscionable, scrupulous; principled, high-principled, high-minded, right-minded.

frank, bluff, aboveboard, candid, direct, forthright, heart-to-heart, open, openhearted, outspoken, square, straightforward, unreserved; blunt, point-blank, plump; guileless, unguileful, undeceitful, ingenuous, childlike, transparent.

sincere, artless, bona fide, cordial, devout, earnest, genuine, heartfelt, heart-to-heart, wholehearted, whole-souled, hearty, simple, simplehearted, singlehearted, single-minded; unaffected, unartful, undesigning, unequivocal.

Adv., phrases. **honestly,** etc. (see *Adjectives*); on the square (*colloq.*), in good faith, on the up-and-up (*slang*), with clean hands.

See also LEGALITY, MORALITY, PENITENCE, TRUTH. *Antonyms*—See DECEPTION, DISHONESTY, FALSEHOOD, FALSENESS, ILLEGALITY, PRETENSE, THIEVERY.

---

honey, *n.* mel (*pharm.*), hydromel, mead (SWEETNESS).

honeyed, *adj.* sugary, saccharine, candied (SWEETNESS).

honor, *n.* rectitude, integrity, probity (HONESTY, MORALITY); deference, esteem, homage (RESPECT); credit, distinction (FAME).

honor, *v.* esteem, regard, revere (RESPECT); dignify, glorify, exalt (FAME); celebrate, keep, lionize (CELEBRATION).

honorable, *adj.* ethical, virtuous, moral (HONESTY, MORALITY, RULE); august, exalted (NOBILITY); creditable, palmary, estimable (FAME).

honorary, *adj.* titular, nominal (NAME).

honored, *adj.* esteemed, redoubted, reputable (RESPECT).

hood, *n.* bonnet, cowl, capote (COVERING); gangster, mobster (*slang*), gunman (ILLEGALITY).

hoodlum, *n.* thug, tough, gangster (VIOLENCE).

hoof, *n.* unguis, ungula (APPENDAGE).

hook, *n.* grapple, grapnel, grip, tongs (TAKING); lasso, net, dragnet (TRAP).

hook, v. catch, net, bag (TAKING, TRAP).

hooked, adj. uncinate, hook-shaped (CURVE); beaked, aquiline (NOSE).

hooligan, n. ruffian, roughneck (colloq.), rowdy (VIOLENCE); outlaw, bandit, highwayman (ILLEGALITY).

hoop, n. loop, eyelet, eye (ROUNDNESS).

hoot, v. jeer, laugh, mock (INSULT).

hop, v. leap, spring, bound (JUMP).

HOPE—N. hope, desire, expectation, expectancy, trust, confidence, reliance, faith, belief, assurance, security; reassurance, encouragement; prospect.

[hopeful person] optimist, Pollyanna, daydreamer.

daydream, pipe dream (colloq.), fancy, reverie, golden dream, mirage, castles in the air, utopia, millennium, fool's paradise.

V. hope, trust, rely, lean upon.

hope for, desire, wish for; expect, anticipate, aspire.

be hopeful, look on the bright side, hope for the best, hope against hope, take heart, be of good cheer; flatter oneself.

encourage, cheer, hearten, inspirit, hold out hope to, comfort, fortify, assure, reassure, buoy up, boost, brace up, buck up, embolden; promise, bid fair, augur well.

Adj. hopeful, confident, in hopes, secure, expectant, anticipatory, optimistic, Pollyanna-like, roseate, rose-colored, rosy, sanguine.

auspicious, promising, favorable, propitious, reassuring, encouraging, heartening, cheering, inspiriting, bright, rosy.

See also BELIEF, CHEERFULNESS, DESIRE, EXPECTATION, PROMISE, SUPPORT. Antonyms—See HOPELESSNESS.

HOPELESSNESS—N. hopelessness, despair, forlorn hope, desperation; despondency, Slough of Despond, melancholy, depression, dejection, psycholepsy (psych.).

pessimism, dyspepsia, futilitarianism, Weltschmerz (G.), miserabilism, malism.

discourager, wet blanket (colloq.), spoilsport.

pessimist, futilitarian, miserabilist, malist, Job's comforter.

V. be hopeless, despair, despond, lose (give up, or abandon) all hope.

discourage, dishearten, dismay, chill, dampen, daunt.

Adj. hopeless, despondent, despairing, desperate, in despair, inconsolable, abject, chilled, dampened, disconsolate, discouraged, disheartened, downhearted, dismayed, pessimistic, futilitarian.

futile, useless, vain, desperate, forlorn.

discouraging, disheartening, dampening, chilly.

unpropitious, unpromising, unfavorable, inauspicious, ill-omened, ominous, ill-boding.

incurable, cureless, irremediable, remediless, irreparable, irrecoverable, irretrievable, irreclaimable, irredeemable, irrevocable, ruined.

See also DEJECTION, DISAPPOINTMENT, INEFFECTIVENESS, USELESSNESS. Antonyms—See CURE, HOPE.

hopper, n. container, receptacle, bin (CONTAINER).

horde, n. throng, crush, mob (ASSEMBLAGE, MULTITUDE).

horizontal, adj. even, flush, plane (FLATNESS); lying, recumbent, accumbent (REST).

hormone, n. endocrine, autacoid, secretion (EXCRETION).

horn, n. antler, beam, attire (BONE); foghorn, hooter, siren (INDICATION).

horn-shaped, adj. cornute, corniform (SHARPNESS).

horrible, adj. horrid, ghastly, grisly (HATRED); execrable, outrageous (INFERIORITY); frightful, horrifying (FEAR); shocking, hideous (DISGUST).

horrid, adj. horrible, ghastly, grim (HATRED); nasty, ungodly, unholy (INFERIORITY); monstrous, scandalous (DISGUST).

horrified, adj. horror-stricken, horror-struck, aghast (HATRED).

horrifying, adj. horrible, eerie (FEAR); horrid, monstrous, outrageous (DISGUST).

horror, n. dread, consternation, trepidation (FEAR); monster, monstrosity (HATRED).

HORSE—N. horse, equine, steed, Dobbin, mount; war horse, courser, charger, hunter; race horse, racer, steeplechaser, pacer, trotter, ambler, maiden; roadster, gigster, pad, padnag, sumpter, stepper, clipper, cob, palfrey; hack, hackney, saddle horse; carriage horse, shaft horse, thill horse, thiller, wheeler, wheel horse, leader; pack horse, cart horse, dray horse, draft horse, shire horse.

sire, stallion, stud, studhorse, gelding.

mare, brood mare, dam, filly.

foal, colt, yearling.

nag, jade, hack, Rosinante, tit.

pony, Shetland, bronco, cayuse, cow pony, Indian pony, polo pony.

thoroughbred, blood horse, Arab, Belgian, jennet, Morgan, mustang, palomino, Percheron, Percheron Norman, Shire, Waler; unicorn, eohippus.

horses, team, stable, tandem, bloodstock, stud, rig, pair, span.

horse rider, horseman, equestrian, jockey; horsemanship, equitation, manège.

ass, jackass, jack; she-ass, jenny ass, jenny, jennet; donkey, burro, dickey; mule, hybrid, sumpter, sumpter mule, pack mule.

V. horse, unhorse, mount, dismount, remount.

canter, gallop, run, trot, walk, amble, single-foot; prance, capriole.

Adj. equine, cabaline, horsy; equestrian, mounted, on horseback, horsed, à cheval (F.), bareback.

asslike, asinine, mulish, mulelike.

See also ANIMAL, DOMESTICATION, VEHICLE.

---

horse doctor, n. veterinarian, farrier (MEDICAL SCIENCE).

horseman, n. horse rider, equestrian, jockey (HORSE, VEHICLE).

horse race, n. derby, steeplechase, sweepstake (ATTEMPT).

horse sense (colloq.), n. judgment, acumen, common sense (WISDOM).

horse thief, n. rustler (THIEF).

horsewhip, n. cat-o'-nine-tails, cat, crop (HITTING).

horsewhip, v. whip, chastise, cowhide (HITTING).

horticulture, n. gardening, floriculture, landscape gardening (FARMING).

hosiery, n. stockings, nylons, hose (FOOTWEAR).

hospitable, adj. obliging, accommodating (KINDNESS, SOCIALITY, UNSELFISHNESS).

hospital, n. infirmary, surgery, clinic (CURE).

hospitality, n. conviviality, hospitableness, welcome (SOCIALITY).

host, n. army, crowd, legion (MULTITUDE); hotelkeeper, boniface, innkeeper (HABITATION).

hostess, n. waitress, stewardess (SERVICE).

HOSTILITY—N. hostility, ill will, bad will, bad blood, grudge, animosity, enmity; disaffection, estrangement, heartburn; war, warfare, warpath; antagonism, inimicality, malevolence, malice, malignance, malignity, spite, despite; rancor, spleen, venom, virulence.

[hostile person] enemy, foe, archenemy; viper, snake, splenetic, dastard.

V. be hostile, show ill will, aggress, bristle, growl, begrudge, grudge, spite, canker; keep (or hold) at arm's length, stand off (colloq.), bear malice, fall out.

antagonize, disaffect, estrange, alienate.

Adj. hostile, antagonistic, deadly, inimical, malevolent, malicious, malign, malignant, nasty (colloq.), poisonous, rancorous, repugnant, oppugnant, adverse, alien, spiteful, spleenful, squint-eyed, vicious (colloq.); viperous, snaky, venomous, virulent; catty, cattish; wanton.

unfriendly, chill, chilly, cool, cold; ill-affected, ill-disposed, unamiable, uncongenial, unamicable, uncompanionable, uncordial, unneighborly; unsociable, unsocial, asocial, dissociable, dissocial, antisocial; aloof, standoff, standoffish, gruff, surly; alienated, disaffected, estranged, antagonized; on bad terms, not on speaking terms.

warlike, bellicose, belligerent, hostile, aggressive.

unapproachable, inaccessible, remote; formidable, forbidding, undemocratic, inaffable.

See also ATTACK, CRUELTY, DISAGREEMENT, FIGHTING, HATRED. Antonyms—See AGREEMENT, FRIEND, FRIENDLINESS, LOVE.

---

hot, adj. broiling, burning, roasting (HEAT); pungent, peppery (TASTE); vehement, passionate, fiery (VIOLENCE).

hotbed, n. den, nest, place of vice (WICKEDNESS).

hot-blooded, adj. excitable, combustible, fiery (EXCITEMENT).

hotel, n. inn, tavern, lodge (HABITATION).

hotelkeeper, n. boniface, hosteler, hotelier, host (HABITATION).

hothead, n. tinderbox, spitfire, fire-eater (ANGER, BAD TEMPER).

hotheaded, adj. hot-tempered, fiery, combustible, peppery, quick-tempered (BAD TEMPER).

hothouse, n. garden, nursery, greenhouse (FARMING).

hot-tempered, adj. fiery, hotheaded, quick-tempered (BAD TEMPER).

house, n. mansion, building, home

(HABITATION); family, line, lineage (RELATIVE).

house, v. barrack, berth, billet (HABITATION).

housecoat, n. dressing gown, duster, house gown, kimono (CLOTHING).

householder, n. occupant, indweller, addressee, tenant (INHABITANT); homeowner, homemaker, housekeeper (HABITATION).

housekeeper, n. dayworker, charwoman, houseworker (SERVICE); homeowner, householder (HABITATION).

housekeeping, n. home management, domestic arts, homemaking (HABITATION).

house of prostitution, n. brothel, house, bagnio, bawdyhouse, bordel (PROSTITUTE).

hovel, n. hut, shack, shanty (HABITATION).

hover, v. poise, brood over (HANGING); flutter, flitter, drift (FLYING).

however, adv. notwithstanding, nevertheless, nonetheless (OPPOSITION).

howl, v. weep, bawl, blubber (WEEPING); yowl, wail, whine (ANIMAL SOUND).

hubbub, n. bedlam, din, uproar (CONFUSION, LOUDNESS).

huckster, n. moneygrubber, miser, mammonist (MONEY); publicist, press agent (PUBLICATION).

huddle, v. flock, gather, herd (MULTITUDE).

hue, n. tone, tint, shade (COLOR); bellow, cry, outcry (SHOUT).

huff, v. expire, pant, puff (BREATH, BLOWING).

hug, v. embrace, cuddle, squeeze (HOLD, CARESS, PRESSURE).

huge, adj. immense, tremendous, enormous (SIZE).

hulking, adj. oversized, lubberly, lumpish (SIZE).

hum, v. buzz, drone (ANIMAL SOUND); warble, trill (SINGING); whir, rustle (ROLL); be busy, bustle (BUSINESS).

human, adj. mortal, bipedal, creatural (MANKIND).

human being, n. human, biped, man (MANKIND).

human beings, n. humanity, Homo sapiens (L.), man, people (MANKIND).

humane, adj. clement, merciful, lenient (PITY); philanthropic, humanitarian, charitable (KINDNESS).

humanitarian, n. altruist, philanthropist, good Samaritan (KINDNESS).

humanity, n. Homo sapiens (L.),

human beings, man (MANKIND); commiseration, compassion, mercy (PITY); humaneness, humanitarianism, charity (KINDNESS).

humanize, v. make human, hominify, personify, personalize (MANKIND).

humble, adj. lowly, modest, unpretentious (HUMILITY, MODESTY, LOWNESS); docile, meek, weak-kneed (SUBMISSION).

humble, v. abase, debase, degrade (HUMILIATION).

humbug, n. fraud, fourflusher (colloq.), faker (PRETENSE).

humdrum, adj. monotonous, tiresome, unrelieved (UNIFORMITY); drab, insipid, prosy (BOREDOM).

humidity, n. moisture, damp, wet (WATER).

HUMILIATION—N. humiliation, abashment, chagrin, confusion, degradation, discomfiture, disgrace, embarrassment, ignominy, mortification, pudency, shame.

V. **humiliate,** abash, chagrin, confuse, dash, degrade, discountenance, put out of countenance, disgrace, embarrass, mortify, shame, put to shame, wither.

feel humiliated, blush at, blush for; eat humble pie, eat crow.

humble, abase, bemean, debase, degrade, demean, vilify.

humble oneself, abase oneself, bemean oneself, debase oneself, degrade oneself, demean oneself, descend, stoop.

Adj. **humiliated,** abashed, ashamed, chagrined, chapfallen, confused, degraded, disgraced, embarrassed, hangdog, mortified, put out of countenance, shamed, shamefaced.

humiliating, abject, degrading, disgraceful, embarrassing, ignominious, mortifying, shameful, withering.

See also CONFUSION, DISGRACE, EMBARRASSMENT, HUMILITY, LOWNESS, MEANNESS. Antonyms—See ASCENT, ELEVATION, FAME, MAGNIFICENCE.

HUMILITY—N. humility, modesty, abasement, self-abasement, submission.

V. **be humble,** humble oneself, grovel, submit, be meek, etc. (see Adjectives).

humble, humiliate, abash, abase, lower, cast into the shade, degrade, debase.

Adj. **humble,** lowly, meek, modest, unassuming, unpretending, unpretentious, unambitious, humble-minded; poor, lowborn, baseborn, plain, simple, mean, inglorious, undistinguished, obscure; submissive, servile.

humbled, bowed down, abashed, ashamed, dashed, crestfallen, chapfallen.

Adv., phrases. humbly, lowly, etc. (see *Adjectives*); with downcast eyes, on bended knee.

See also EMBARRASSMENT, HUMILIATION, INFERIORITY, LOWNESS, MEANNESS, SLAVERY, SUBMISSION. *Antonyms*—See ELEVATION, FAME, MAGNIFICENCE, PRIDE, SUPERIORITY.

humor, *n.* wit, whimsey, facetiousness (WITTINESS); fancy, notion, whim (CAPRICE).

humor, *v.* indulge, favor, gratify (MILDNESS, PERMISSION).

humorous, *adj.* funny, jocose, waggish, amusing, droll, comical, whimsical, facetious (WITTINESS).

hunchbacked, *adj.* humpbacked, gibbous, kyphotic (DEFORMITY).

HUNDRED—N. hundred, fivescore, century; centennial, centenary.

V. multiply by a hundred, centuple, centuplicate.

Adj. hundredth, centuple, centesimal, cental; centennial, centenary; secular.

See also CELEBRATION.

HUNGER—N. hunger, esurience, starvation, famine; appetite, edacity (*jocose*), appetency, voracity, gluttony.

V. hunger, be hungry, famish, starve, raven.

Adj. hungry, esurient, empty (*colloq.*), hollow, starving, starveling, famished; ravening, ravenous, voracious, gluttonous.

See also DESIRE, DRINK, DRYNESS, FOOD, GLUTTONY, GREED. *Antonyms*—See FASTING, FULLNESS, SATISFACTION.

hunt, *n.* chase, pursuit, quest (SEARCH, HUNTING).

HUNTING—N. hunting, venery, the chase, the hunt, sport; man hunt, dragnet.

fishing, angling, etc. (see *Verbs*) piscatology, piscary; tackle, fishing gear, line, hook, bait, lure, rod, troll.

hunter, huntsman, chasseur, gunner, Nimrod, woodman, woodsman; Diana, huntress; big-game hunter, sealer, wolver; sportsman,

stalker, deerstalker, deerslayer; poacher, trapper, ferreter, falconer.

fisherman, fisher, piscator, angler, trawler, troller; poacher.

V. hunt, chase, course, gun, scent, poach, wolf.

fish, angle, seine, trawl, chum; poach.

Adj. venatic (*pert. to hunting*); piscatory *or* piscatorial (*pert. to fishing*).

See also ANIMAL, KILLING, LOOKING, SEARCH. *Antonyms*—See DISCOVERY.

hurdle, *n.* obstacle, barrier, stumbling block (HINDRANCE).

hurdle, *v.* clear, jump over, vault (JUMP).

hurl, *v.* cast, fling, heave (THROW).

hurricane, *n.* cyclone, tornado, typhoon (WIND).

hurry, *n.* haste, rush, precipitance (SPEED).

hurry, *v.* fly, hasten, hustle (SPEED).

hurt, *adj.* aching, sore (PAIN); resentful, indignant, offended, piqued (ANGER, OFFENSE).

hurt, *n.* ill, injury, mischief, disservice, prejudice, detriment (HARM, WICKEDNESS).

hurt, *v.* pain, ache, smart (PAIN); injure, prejudice, mar (HARM).

hurtle, *v.* charge, dash, lunge (VIOLENCE); smash, clatter, roar (LOUDNESS).

husband, *n.* spouse, mate (MARRIAGE).

hush, *v.* quiet, quieten, still (SILENCE).

hushed, *adj.* silent, noiseless, soundless, quiet, still (SILENCE).

hush-hush, *adj.* secret, confidential, dark (CONCEALMENT).

husk, *v.* hull, pod, shell (UNDRESS).

husky, *adj.* throaty, guttural, gruff (THROAT, HARSH SOUND); brawny, muscular, stocky (STRENGTH); thickset, burly (SIZE).

hussy, *n.* jade, shrew, wench (FEMALE, WORTHLESSNESS).

hustle, *v.* fly, hasten, hurry (SPEED).

hut, *n.* hovel, shack, shanty (HABITATION).

hybrid, *adj.* mixed, assorted, mongrel, varied (CLASS).

hybrid, *n.* half-breed, half-blood, half-caste (MANKIND, CROSSING).

hygienic, *adj.* sanitary, uncontaminated, aseptic (CLEANNESS, HEALTH).

hymn, *n.* chorale, psalm, chant (SINGING, WORSHIP); paean, laud (PRAISE).

hypnotism, *n.* animal magnetism, magnetism, mesmerism (SLEEP).

hypocrisy, *n.* double-dealing, duplicity, Pecksniffery (DECEPTION, PRETENSE).

hypocrite, *n.* pharisee, tartufe, whited sepulcher (PRETENSE).

hypocritical, *adj.* Pecksniffian, canting, sanctimonious (PRETENSE).

hypothesis, *n.* premise, proposition, postulate (SUPPOSITION).

hypothetical, *adj.* suppositional, conjectural, presumptive, academic, theoretical (SUPPOSITION).

hysterical, *adj.* wrought up, worked up, overwrought (EXCITEMENT).

hysterics, *n.* mirth, convulsions, hysteria (LAUGHTER).

I

ice, *n.* sleet, glaze, hail (COLD).

icebox, *n.* refrigerator, ice chest, freezer (COLD).

icy, *adj.* glacial, freezing, gelid (COLD); cold, frigid, frosty (INSENSITIVITY).

id (*psychoanal.*), *n.* self, ego, psyche (SELFISHNESS).

IDEA—*N.* idea, impression, notion, view, brain storm, inspiration, concept, conception, thought, abstraction, obsession, *idée fixe* (*F.*), theory, surmise, prenotion, preconception, stereotype.

image, vision, phantasm, construct, eidolon, phantasy; anticipation, foresight, prevision.

[*foolish, unrealistic, etc., idea*] fancy, fantasy, phantasy, dream, reverie, bubble, whim, whimsey, wrinkle, crank, crinkum-crankum, conceit, crotchet, fallacy, vagary, vagrancy, vapor, maggot, chimera, castle in the air, castle in Spain, caprice, capriccio, vacuity, megrim, old wives' tale.

main idea, burden, core, essence, gist, kernel, keynote, nub, purport, substance, sum, sum and substance.

ideas, train of thought, stream of consciousness, ideation, free association (*psychoanal.*), complex, imagery.

V. ideate, conceive, preconceive; free-associate (*psychoanal.*).

visualize, envisage, envision, image, imagine, picture, vision; anticipate, foresee.

Adj. ideational, conceptual, notional, theoretical, impressional, prenotional, holophrastic.

See also FORESIGHT, IMAGINATION, MEANING, OPINION, THOUGHT, VISION.

ideal, *adj.* perfect, absolute, consummate (PERFECTION).

ideal, *n.* nonesuch, nonpareil (PERFECTION); pattern, standard (COPY).

idealism, *n.* perfectionism, romanticism, utopianism (PERFECTION, IMAGINATION).

identical, *adj.* same, self-same, duplicate (SIMILARITY).

identify, *v.* coincide, agree; homologize (SIMILARITY).

identify with, *v.* feel for, empathize, understand (PITY).

identity, *n.* coincidence, congruence, congruity (SIMILARITY); oneness, coherence, singleness (UNITY).

ideology, *n.* philosophy, theory, system (RULE).

idiom, *n.* provincialism, localism, colloquialism (WORD); phrase, locution, word (EXPRESSION); jargon, lingo, patois (LANGUAGE).

idiosyncrasy, *n.* distinction, feature, peculiarity (CHARACTER).

idiot, *n.* mental defective, imbecile, moron (STUPIDITY); fool, tomfool, witling (FOLLY).

idle, *adj.* leisured, unoccupied, unemployed (REST); at rest, resting (INACTION); unused, fallow, vacant (DISUSE); frivolous, fribble (FRIVOLITY).

idle, *v.* loaf, dally, gold-brick (*slang*), waste time, dawdle (REST, TIME).

idol, *n.* image, golden calf, fetish (WORSHIP); beloved, darling, dear (LOVE).

idolize, *v.* idolatrize, admire (WORSHIP, APPROVAL).

if, *conj.* provided, in the event (SUPPOSITION).

ignite, *v.* kindle, light, set fire to (LIGHT, FIRE).

ignoble, *adj.* baseborn, menial, lowly (MEANNESS).

ignominious, *adj.* dishonorable, shameful, infamous (DISGRACE); despicable, insignificant, low (CONTEMPT).

ignoramus, *n.* troglodyte, illiterate, dunce (IGNORANCE).

IGNORANCE—*N.* ignorance, nescience, unacquaintance, dark, insensibility, incognizance, unfamiliarity; sealed book, virgin soil, unexplored ground, terra incognita (L.), Dark Ages; illiteracy, inerudition, unenlightenment.

[*imperfect knowledge*] **smattering**, smatter, superficiality, sciolism, half-learning, glimmering.

[*affectation of knowledge*] **charlatanry**, charlatanism, quackery, bluff, empiricism; pedantry, pedantism.

ignoramus, troglodyte, illiterate, dunce, bonehead (*slang*), dolt, blockhead, dumbbell (*slang*), thickhead (*colloq.*), numskull (*colloq.*), low-brow (*colloq.*), Philistine; empiric.

smatterer, dabbler, sciolist, charlatan, quack.

V. **be ignorant** (*or* uninformed), be uneducated, know nothing of; **ignore**, be blind to, disregard.

Adj. **ignorant**, unknowing, unaware, unacquainted, uninformed, unwitting, unconscious, insensible, unconversant, nescient, incognizant, unfamiliar with, unversed in, troglodytic, benighted, in the dark; sophomoric.

uneducated, inerudite, unlearned, illiterate, unread, uncultivated, uninstructed, untaught, untutored, unschooled, unlettered, uncoached, unedified, unenlightened, unilluminated, unindoctrinated, uninitiated; low-brow (*colloq.*), Philistine, raw, unbred, ill-bred.

shallow, superficial, sciolistic, green, rude, empty, half-learned, half-baked (*colloq.*), unscholarly.

unknown, unapprehended, unexplained, unascertained, unperceived, unfamiliar, uninvestigated, unexplored, unheard of, strange, undetermined, undiagnosed, undiscovered, unfathomed, unlearned, unplumbed, imponderable; concealed, hidden.

See also FOLLY, INEXPERIENCE, INNOCENCE, STUPIDITY, UNCERTAINTY. *Antonyms*—See INFORMATION, KNOWLEDGE, LEARNING, TEACHING.

---

ignore, *v.* scorn, slight, disregard (INATTENTION, UNIMPORTANCE, WORTHLESSNESS).

ill, *adj.* sick, sickly, ailing (DISEASE).

ill, *n.* harm, hurt, injury, mischief (WICKEDNESS).

ill-advised, *adj.* inadvisable, impolitic, imprudent (INEXPEDIENCE).

ill-at-ease, *adj.* discomfited, self-conscious, uncomfortable (EMBARRASSMENT).

ill-bred, *adj.* ill-mannered, underbred, uncivil (VULGARITY); vulgar, unrefined, crude (LOWNESS).

ILLEGALITY—*N.* illegality, illegitimacy, unconstitutionality, invalidity.

smuggling, contrabandism, bootlegging.

malfeasance, malversation, misfeasance, misprision, malpractice, misconduct, wrongdoing, malefaction.

breach of law, infringement, infraction, transgression, violation, lawbreaking, offense, misdeed, outlawry, sin.

lawlessness, anarchy, disorder, violence, misrule, mob rule, lynch law.

crime, criminality, felony, misdemeanor, villainy.

lawbreaker, offender, sinner, transgressor, violator; scofflaw, outlaw; smuggler, bootlegger, contrabandist, rumrunner; poacher.

malfeasant, misfeasor, wrongdoer, malefactor, malpractitioner.

criminal, culprit, convict, felon, misdemeanant, villain, desperado, bravo, resolute, gangster, mobster (*slang*), gunman, hood (*slang*), hoodlum, goon (*slang*), hooligan, outlaw, bandit, highwayman, brigand, racketeer, thief; juvenile delinquent; accessory, accessory before the fact, accessory after the fact, accomplice; suspect.

criminal class, felonry, the underworld.

science of crime, criminals, etc.: criminology, penology.

V. **break the law**, violate the law, commit a violation, commit a crime, transgress, offend, trespass, sin.

[*involve in, or connect with, a crime*] **incriminate**, criminate, inculpate.

Adj. **illegal**, contrary to law, in violation of law, illicit, lawbreaking, illegitimate, unauthorized, unlawful, lawless, wrongful, unconstitutional, extrajudicial; contraband, bootleg; outlawed, proscribed, prohibited, invalid.

criminal, felonious, malfeasant, villainous, wide-open; red-handed, *flagrante delicto* (L.).

See also ACCUSATION, SIN, THIEF, THIEVERY. *Antonyms*—See HONESTY, LAW, LEGALITY.

---

illegible, *adj.* indecipherable, unintelligible, unreadable (MYSTERY, READING, WRITING).

illegitimate, *adj.* lawbreaking, unlawful, lawless (ILLEGALITY);

bastard, natural, unfathered (CHILD); unauthorized, illicit, wrong (IMPROPERNESS).

ill-fated, adj. doomed, ill-omened, ill-starred (MISFORTUNE).

ill-health, n. indisposition, invalidism, infirmity (DISEASE).

illicit, adj. illegal, contrary to law (ILLEGALITY).

illiterate, adj. uneducated, unlearned, unschooled (IGNORANCE, READING); solecistic, ungrammatical (MISUSE OF WORDS).

ill-mannered, adj. unrefined, bad-mannered, boorish (DISCOURTESY).

illness, n. sickness, ailment, malady (DISEASE).

illogical, adj. farfetched, fallacious, ungrounded (UNREASONABLENESS, MISTAKE).

ill-starred, adj. ill-fated, doomed, ill-omened (MISFORTUNE).

ill-timed, adj. unseasonable, mistimed (UNTIMELINESS).

ill-treat, v. abuse, maltreat, mistreat (MISUSE).

illuminating, adj. instructive, informative, edifying (TEACHING).

illuminate, v. brighten, illumine, lighten (LIGHT); clarify, elucidate, illustrate (CLARITY).

illusion, n. fallacy, idolism, mis-impression (FALSENESS, BELIEF); hallucination, optical illusion, mirage (UNREALITY, DECEPTION); humbuggery, hocus-pocus, hanky-panky (DECEPTION).

illustrate, v. represent, picture, portray (REPRESENTATION); exemplify, embody, epitomize (COPY); illuminate, elucidate (CLARITY).

illustration, n. painting, depiction, drawing, design, picture (FINE ARTS, REPRESENTATION); example, case, instance (COPY).

illustrious, adj. renowned, famous, famed (FAME).

ill will, n. bad will, bad blood, grudge (HOSTILITY).

image, n. portrait, figure, picture (REPRESENTATION); reflection, simulacrum (SIMILARITY); vision, phantasm, construct (IDEA); idol, golden calf, fetish (WORSHIP).

imaginary, adj. unreal, legendary, mythical (UNREALITY).

IMAGINATION—N. imagination, enterprise, fancy, sally, verve; flight of fancy, creation, inspiration, originality, invention, imagery, romanticism, utopianism, castle-building, dreaming, reverie, daydream.

fantasy, phantasy, vision, dream, conceit, concept, fancy, notion, whim, vagary, figment, myth; romance, extravaganza; shadow, chimera, phantasm, will-o'-the-wisp,

illusion, phantom, bugbear, nightmare.

visionary, idealist, seer, romancer, dreamer, daydreamer, Don Quixote, romanticist.

V. imagine, conceive, depicture, envisage, envision, fancy, fantasy, phantasy, picture, surmise, vision, visualize; invent, make up, create, create out of whole cloth, fabricate.

Adj. imaginative, original, inventive, creative, enterprising, fictive, fertile, productive, forgetive; romantic, visionary, utopian, quixotic, extravagant, high-flown.

fanciful, fantastical, fabulous, legendary, mythical, mythological, chimerical; whimsical, notional, fictitious, figmental, dreamy, imaginary.

impractical, quixotic, theoretical, abstract, utopian, visionary, impracticable; ideal, idealistic.

See also FORESIGHT, IDEA, PRODUCTION, SLEEP, UNREALITY, VISION. Antonyms—See IMITATION, REALITY.

---

imagined, adj. unreal, delusive, illusory (UNREALITY).

imbecile, n. dunce, moron, idiot (FOLLY, STUPIDITY).

imbibe, v. consume, ingurgitate, partake (DRINK); tipple, souse (ALCOHOLIC LIQUOR); absorb, assimilate (INTAKE).

imbue, v. saturate, impregnate, infuse (FULLNESS, MIXTURE); instill, infix, inoculate (INSERTION).

IMITATION—N. imitation, emulation, mimicry, mimesis (rhet.), apery, mockery, parrotism, echo, simulation, impersonation, masquerade, plagiarism; forgery, sham, counterfeit, mock, postiche (F.), fake, fraud; copy, reproduction, facsimile.

parody, burlesque, caricature, pastiche, travesty.

imitator, copier, copyist, copycat, mimicker, mime, mimic, aper, emulator, echo; cuckoo, parrot, mocking bird, ape, monkey.

V. imitate, simulate, copy, mirror, reflect, reproduce, repeat; feign, follow, pattern after, emulate, follow suit (colloq.), take after, model after, borrow, echo, re-echo; match, parallel; forge, counterfeit, sham.

mimic, mime, parrot, ape, mock, take off on, personate, impersonate, parody, travesty, caricature, burlesque.

Adj. imitative, mock, mimic,

apish, mimetic, echoic, reflective; counterfeit, sham; parrotlike; emulous, rivalrous.

imitated, secondhand, pretended, feigned, modeled after, molded on, borrowed, counterfeit, forged, imitation, simulated, sham, pseudo.

See also COPY, DECEPTION, FALSENESS, PRETENSE. Antonyms—See IMAGINATION, PRODUCTION.

immaculate, adj. clean, spotless, snowy (CLEANNESS); pure, taintless (PURIFICATION); faultless, stainless (INNOCENCE).

immaterial, adj. unimportant, inconsequential, insignificant (UNIMPORTANCE); irrelevant, extraneous, impertinent (IRRELATION); bodiless, disembodied, discarnate (SPIRITUALITY); incorporeal, spectral, wraithlike (SUPERNATURAL BEINGS); unsubstantial, dreamy, dreamlike (NONEXISTENCE).

IMMATURITY—N. immaturity, crudity, infantilism, infantility, youth, juvenility, puerility, nonage, verdancy (colloq.), salad days, chrysalis.

bud, larva, embryo, vestige.

Adj. immature, bread-and-butter, unbaked, callow, raw, crude, green, young, tender, childish, infantile, infantine, juvenile, puerile, unfledged, ungrown, unlicked, unripe, unfinished, unseasoned, verdant (colloq.), sophomoric, halfbaked, underdeveloped, undergrown, half-grown.

undeveloped, abortive, embryonic, latent, rudimentary, vestigial, larval, primitive, protomorphic.

See also CHILD, CLUMSINESS, INEXPERIENCE, NEWNESS, YOUTH. Antonyms—See EXPERIENCE, MATURITY.

immediate, adj. instant, instantaneous (EARLINESS); nearest, contiguous, nearby (NEARNESS).

immediately, adv. at once, directly, instantaneously (EARLINESS); hereupon, thereupon, whereupon (TIME).

immense, adj. tremendous, enormous, vast (SIZE, GREATNESS); infinite, boundless, immeasurable (ENDLESSNESS, SIZE).

immerse, v. merge, immerge, plunge (INSERTION).

immigrant, n. foreigner, outsider, alien (IRRELATION); colonist, settler, pioneer (INGRESS).

imminent, adj. impending, threatening, looming (APPROACH).

immobile, adj. motionless, immovable, quiescent (MOTIONLESSNESS).

immoderate, adj. intemperate, excessive, unbridled (INTEMPERANCE).

immodest, adj. shameless, barefaced (IMMODESTY); proud, exalted, lofty (PRIDE).

IMMODESTY—N. immodesty, brass (colloq.) impudence, impudicity, indecency, obscenity, indelicacy.

Adj. immodest, shameless, barefaced, bold, brassy (colloq.), brazen, brazenfaced, impudent, indecent, indelicate, obscene, shameful, unblushing, unseemly.

See also DISPLAY, OBSCENITY, PRIDE, SEX. Antonyms—See HUMILITY, MODESTY.

IMMORALITY—N. immorality, vice, dissipation, evil, profligacy, villainy; corruption, miscreancy, degeneracy, depravity, decadence, degradation, debauchery, perversion, moral turpitude.

profligate, rakehell, rake, roué, reprobate, rotter (slang), miscreant.

degenerate, debauchee, pervert, yahoo, wretch.

[corrupting influence] canker, smutch, ulcer, virus.

V. corrupt, canker, debauch, degrade, demoralize, deprave, pervert, seduce, soil, stain, subvert, taint, vilify.

debauch, dissipate, go astray, wander, fall (of women); canker, corrupt, taint, decay.

Adj. immoral, dissipated, dissolute, evil, loose, graceless, profligate, rakish, reprobate, saturnalian; unethical, unprincipled, unscrupulous, unwholesome; vicious, vile, wicked, villainous, fallen (of women); supine.

corrupt, abandoned, Augean, base, dishonorable, low, miscreant, putrid, rotten.

degenerate, depraved, decadent, degraded, demoralized, debauched, perverted.

wayward, aberrant, errant, obliquitous, sinuous, wandering.

[injurious to morals] unwholesome, noxious, pestiferous, pestilent, pestilential, unhealthy.

See also DISHONESTY, IMPROPERNESS, OBSCENITY, SEX, SIN, UNCLEANNESS, WICKEDNESS. Antonyms—See ELEVATION, HONESTY, MORALITY, PURIFICATION.

immortal, *adj.* deathless, eternal, imperishable (ENDLESSNESS); everlasting, perpetual (CONTINUATION).

immortality, *n.* athanasia, eternity, imperishability (ENDLESSNESS).

immovable, *adj.* motionless, immobile, quiescent (MOTIONLESSNESS); inflexible, uncompromising, intransigent (STUBBORNNESS).

immunity, *n.* exemption, impunity (FREEDOM); mithridatism, prophylaxis (PROTECTION).

immunize, *v.* inoculate, vaccinate, variolate (PROTECTION).

imp, *n.* rogue, villain, scamp (MISCHIEF, CHILD); fiend, demon (DEVIL).

impact, *n.* blow, shock, crash (TOUCH, HITTING).

impair, *v.* destroy, spoil (USELESSNESS); unfit, invalidate (DISABLEMENT); cheapen, debase (WORTHLESSNESS).

impart, *v.* cede, relinquish, communicate (GIVING).

IMPARTIALITY—N. impartiality, unprejudice, objectivity, impersonality, candor, detachment, disinterest, dispassion, neutrality, nonpartisanship.

broad-mindedness, tolerance, liberality, catholicity, breadth of mind, cosmopolitanism.

fairness, fair play, justice, fair treatment, equity, square deal (*colloq.*), reasonability, sportsmanship.

neutral, neutralist, nonpartisan; cosmopolitan, cosmopolite; sportsman, square shooter.

V. unprejudice, unbias, liberalize.

Adj. impartial, unprejudiced, unbiased, unbigoted, objective, impersonal, candid, detached, disinterested, dispassionate, fairminded, neutral, nonpartisan; uncolored, unslanted.

broad-minded, tolerant, liberal, catholic, broad, cosmopolitan.

fair, just, equitable, equal, evenhanded, reasonable, right, sporting, sportsmanlike, square.

See also ACCEPTANCE, EQUALITY. *Antonyms*—See INEQUALITY, PREJUDICE, UNFAIRNESS.

---

impasse, *n.* dead end, *cul-de-sac* (*F.*), closed passage (PASSAGE); dilemma, quandary (CONDITION).

impassive, *adj.* imperturbable, nonchalant, stoical (CALMNESS).

impatience, *n.* expectancy, suspense (EXPECTATION).

impatient, *adj.* itching, chafing, choleric, testy (EXPECTATION).

impeach, *v.* challenge, question, impugn (UNBELIEVINGNESS); accuse, indict (ACCUSATION).

impede, *v.* hinder, interfere with, hamper (HINDRANCE).

impediment, *n.* bar, barricade, obstacle (HINDRANCE).

impel, *v.* prod, goad, actuate (URGING, MOTIVATION); drive, push, propel (PROPULSION).

impend, *v.* threaten, portend, loom (DESTINY, THREAT).

impenetrable, *adj.* dense, compact, close (THICKNESS).

IMPENITENCE—N. impenitence, obduracy, incorrigibility, irreclaimability, irrepentance.

Adj. impenitent, unashamed, uncontrite, unpenitent, unremorseful, remorseless, unrepentant, unrepented; obdurate, incorrigible, irreclaimable, lost, unreformable.

conscienceless, unconscionable, unscrupulous; unregretful, regretless, unsorry, unrueful, uncontrite.

See also SIN. *Antonyms*—See ATONEMENT, PENITENCE, REGRET.

---

imperative, *adj.* urgent, pressing, exigent (IMPORTANCE, NECESSITY, DEMAND).

imperceptible, *adj.* inappreciable, inconsiderable, insignificant (SMALLNESS).

IMPERFECTION—N. imperfection, frailty, deficiency, inadequacy, defection.

fault, defect, flaw, foible, failing, weak point; mar, demerit, delinquency, taint, blemish, spot, stain; weakness, shortcoming, drawback; peccadillo, vice.

V. be imperfect, have a defect, not pass muster, fall short, miss the mark, be amiss.

Adj. imperfect, deficient, defective, faulty, unsound, blemished, flawed, marred, tainted, out of order; warped, injured, impaired, disfigured; crude, incomplete, unfinished, undeveloped, below par.

See also BLEMISH, DEFORMITY, INCOMPLETENESS, INFERIORITY, NONPREPARATION, WEAKNESS. *Antonyms* —See PERFECTION.

---

imperil, *v.* endanger, jeopardize, peril (DANGER).

imperious, *adj.* overbearing, magisterial, lordly (PRIDE); clamorous, dictatorial (DEMAND).

IMPERMANENCE—*N.* **imperma-nence,** transience, fugitivity, eva-nescence, fugacity, ephemerality, temporality, volatility, caducity, mortality, brevity.

transient, ephemeron, vapor; makeshift, stopgap.

V. **be impermanent,** flit, pass away, fly, vanish, evanesce, melt, fade, blow over, evaporate.

Adj. **transient,** transitory, pass-ing, evanescent, fleeting, fleet, fugitive, fugacious, volatile, elu-sive, caducous, impermanent, pâ-pier-maché (*F.*), temporal, tem-porary, ad interim (*L.*), pro tem-pore (*L.*), sometime, provisional, tentative, provisionary, short-lived, ephemeral, deciduous, perishable, mortal.

brief, short; instantaneous, mo-mentary, spasmodic, meteoric; hasty, hurried, cursory, quick.

Adv., phrases. **transiently,** tran-sitorily, in passing, *en passant* (*F.*), temporarily, for the moment, pro tempore (*L.*), for a time, awhile, briefly.

See also CESSATION, CHANGE, CHANGEABLENESS, DISAPPEARANCE, NONEXISTENCE, SHORTNESS. *Anto-nyms*—See CONTINUATION, ENDLESS-NESS.

impersonal, *adj.* candid, detached, disinterested (IMPARTIALITY).

impersonate, *v.* act, play, represent (ACTOR, ACTION); masquerade as, pass oneself off as (PRETENSE).

impertinent, *adj.* insolent, impu-dent, procacious (DISCOURTESY); irrelevant, extraneous, immate-rial (IRRELATION).

impetuous, *adj.* unexpected, abrupt, impulsive (SUDDENNESS, NONPREPARATION).

impetus, *n.* urge, pressure, goad (PROPULSION); momentum, push (FORCE).

impious, *adj.* blasphemous, pro-fane, sacrilegious (DISRESPECT, IRRELIGION, MALEDICTION).

implausible, *adj.* improbable, un-likely, doubtful (IMPROBABILITY).

implement, *n.* utensil, machine, tool (INSTRUMENT).

implement, *v.* put into effect, ex-ecute, enforce (RESULT); provide the means, enable, make possi-ble (MEANS).

implication, *n.* overtone, intima-tion, innuendo (SUGGESTION, MEANING).

implicit, *adj.* inferential, implied, understood (MEANING, INDIRECT-NESS, SUGGESTION); tacit, unut-tered, unexpressed (SILENCE).

implied, *adj.* inferential, implicit,

understood (INDIRECTNESS, SUG-GESTION); unspoken, tacit, word-less (SILENCE, MEANING).

implore, *v.* beg, beseech, entreat (BEGGING).

imply, *v.* hint at, intimate, insinu-ate (HINT, SUGGESTION); signify, mean, denote (MEANING).

impolite, *adj.* discourteous, un-mannerly, rude (DISCOURTESY, VULGARITY).

impolitic, *adj.* inadvisable, ill-advised, unwise, imprudent (IN-EXPEDIENCE, FOLLY).

import, *n.* purport, sense, signifi-cance, signification (MEANING).

import, *v.* bring in, track in, carry in (INTAKE).

IMPORTANCE—*N.* **importance,** import, moment, consequence, weight, significance, gravity, ma-teriality, notability, prominence, substantiality, concern; para-mountcy, preponderance; preced-ence, priority.

[*important person*] personage, bigwig (*colloq.*), grandee, high-muck-a-muck (*slang*), magnifico, mogul, notable, notability, worthy (*jocose*), big wheel (*colloq.*), VIP, kingpin, magnate, tycoon, figure, somebody, panjandrum, lion; key man, indispensable, pivot, princi-pal, protagonist.

crisis, turning point, climax, cli-macteric, apex; pinch, clutch, crux; milestone.

[*important thing or part*] cor-nerstone, keystone, keynote, core, pivot, heart, fundamental, essen-tial, indispensable, *sine qua non* (*L.*).

V. **be important,** bulk, bulk large, import, signify, matter, carry weight; preponderate, pre-cede, outweigh, overshadow.

treat as important, lionize, exalt, inflate, publicize, puff up.

emphasize, stress, accent, accen-tuate, feature, point up, punctuate, lay (*or* place) stress on; mark, un-derline, underscore.

Adj. **important,** eventful, grave, key, material, momentous, notable, outstanding, prominent, serious, significant, substantial, weighty; major, overshadowing; distingué (*F.*), distinguished, important-looking.

main, arch, banner, capital, cardinal, central, chief, foremost, leading, master, palmary, para-mount, premier, preponderant, primal, primary, prime, principal, sovereign, stellar, top, top-drawer, staple (*as a commodity*).

crucial, acute, climacteric, critical, decisive, fateful, key, momentous, pivotal, climactic.

urgent, pressing, instant, imperative, exigent.

indispensable, basal, basic, cardinal, essential, fundamental, key, material, pivotal, primary, radical, substantial, vital, strategic.

self-important, consequential, pompous, pretentious, toplofty, exalted.

Adv., phrases. importantly, substantially, etc. (see *Adjectives*); in the main, above all, in the first place.

See also GREATNESS, ELEVATION, INFLUENCE, NECESSITY, PRECEDENCE, PRETENSE, SOBRIETY, VALUE, WEIGHT. *Antonyms*—See HUMILITY, MEANNESS, UNIMPORTANCE.

importune, *v.* nag, pester, badger (DEMAND, ANNOYANCE).

imposing, *adj.* impressive, stately, towering (SIZE, MAGNIFICENCE).

IMPOSSIBILITY—*N.* impossibility, impracticability, infeasibility.

Adj. impossible, absurd, unreasonable, visionary, impractical, hopeless, unimaginable, unthinkable, inconceivable.

impracticable, unachievable, infeasible *or* unfeasible, insurmountable, insuperable, inaccessible, unattainable, unobtainable; out of the question.

See also HOPELESSNESS, IMAGINATION, IMPROBABILITY, UNREALITY. *Antonyms*—See LIKELIHOOD, POSSIBILITY.

impostor, *n.* impersonator, actor, masquerader (PRETENSE); deceiver, bluffer, fraud (DECEPTION).

impotent, *adj.* powerless, helpless, prostrate (DISABLEMENT, WEAKNESS); frigid (CELIBACY).

impoverished, *adj.* poor, indigent, poverty-stricken (POVERTY).

impracticable, *adj.* unusable, impractical, inapplicable (USELESSNESS); unachievable, infeasible (IMPOSSIBILITY).

impractical, *adj.* quixotic, theoretical, abstract (IMAGINATION); unusable, inapplicable (USELESSNESS).

impregnate, *v.* inseminate, fecundate (PREGNANCY); saturate, imbue, suffuse (FULLNESS); infuse, instill, inoculate (INSERTION).

impress, *v.* affect, move, touch (INFLUENCE); awe, overawe (RESPECT); draft, conscript, dragoon (FORCE).

impression, *n.* sensation, feel, sense (SENSITIVENESS); notion, conception, view (UNDERSTANDING, IDEA); mold, *moulage* (F.), pattern (SHAPE); imprint, mark (INDICATION).

impressionable, *adj.* susceptible, suggestible, waxy (SUGGESTION, INFLUENCE, SENSITIVENESS).

impressive, *adj.* affecting, inspiring, moving (FEELING, INFLUENCE); grand, magnificent (NOBILITY, SIZE, MAGNIFICENCE).

imprint, *n.* mark, impression, trace (INDICATION).

imprint, *v.* offset, impress, stamp (PRINTING).

IMPRISONMENT—*N.* imprisonment, confinement, detention, immurement, incarceration, internment, custody, duress, durance (*poetic*), captivity, bonds.

prison, jail, gaol (*Brit.*), bridewell, penitentiary, penal institution, penal colony, pen, reformatory, reform school, house of correction, workhouse, stir (*slang*), jug (*colloq.*), lockup, coop (*colloq.*), cooler (*colloq.*), clink (*slang*), bastille, calaboose (*colloq.*), hoosegow (*slang*), big house (*slang*), brig, guardhouse (*mil.*); cell, cell block; ward.

dungeon, hole, oubliette, black hole.

cage, coop, fold, pinfold, pound; stockade, bullpen, barracoon.

prisoner, captive, convict, con (*slang*), felon, inmate, *détenu* (F.), intern *or* internee, jailbird (*slang*); trusty; convicts, felonry; shut-in.

jailer, keeper, gaoler (*Brit.*), warden, guard, screw (*slang*), turnkey.

V. imprison, incarcerate, immure, mure, jail, lock up, jug (*colloq.*); put in irons; send to prison, commit; remand, recommit; take prisoner, take captive, capture.

confine, constrain, detain, intern, hold in custody, restrain, trammel, keep confined; impound, pen, pound, pinfold (*animals*), fold (*sheep*), fence in, wall in, rail in, stockade; shut in, shut up, keep in, cage, encage, occlude, box up, bottle up, coop up, cramp, closet.

arrest, apprehend, pinch (*slang*), nab (*colloq.*), take into custody, take prisoner.

Adj. imprisoned, in prison, doing time (*slang*), behind bars, in custody, under lock and key, captive, incommunicado; incarcerated, etc. (see *Verbs*).

confined, cramped, two-by-four; pent, pent up; snowbound, icebound, stormbound, weatherbound; constrained, detained, etc. (see *Verbs*).

See also ACCUSATION, CLOSURE, FASTENING, HINDRANCE, PUNISHMENT, RESTRAINT. *Antonyms*—See ACQUITTAL, FREEDOM.

IMPROBABILITY—N. improbability, unlikelihood, bare possibility, long odds.

Adj. **improbable,** unlikely, rare, unheard of, inconceivable, unimaginable, implausible, doubtful, questionable.

See also IMPOSSIBILITY. *Antonyms* —See CHANCE, LIKELIHOOD, OCCURRENCE.

impromptu, *adj.* improvised, offhand, extemporaneous (NONPREPARATION).

IMPROPERNESS—N. improperness, impropriety, illegitimacy, aberration, perversity; immorality, indecency, indecorum, injustice, inequity.

V. **be improper,** be amiss; be unsuitable to, misbecome, unbecome, unbefit, unbeseem; unfit, unsuit.

wrong, injure, harm, damage, hurt, serve ill, misserve, disserve, do injury to, maltreat, abuse, cheat, defraud; dishonor, disgrace.

infringe, encroach, trench on, trespass, intrude; exact, arrogate, usurp, violate; get under false pretenses, sail under false colors.

disentitle, dispossess, disfranchise, disqualify, invalidate; illegitimatize, bastardize.

Adj. **improper,** inappropriate, wrong, unseemly, incorrect, illegitimate, illicit, solecistic; uncalled-for, gratuitous; perverse, perverted, aberrant; immoderate, exorbitant.

[*morally improper*] **immoral,** indecent, inequitable, unethical, unjust, unrighteous, wrong, wrongful; indecorous, unconventional.

unsuitable, ill-befitting, ill-beseeming, ill-suiting, impertinent, inapplicable, inappropriate, inapropos, inapt, incongruous, inexpedient, infelicitous, unhappy, malapropos, misbecoming, unapt, unbecoming, unbefitting, unbeseeming, uncomely, unfitting, unhandsome, unmeet, unseemly, unsuited, unworthy, wrong; undue, unseasonable, untimely.

unjustifiable, unreasonable, unwarrantable, objectionable, inexcusable, indefensible, unpardonable, unforgivable; unjustified, unwarranted, unsanctioned, unauthorized.

See also HARM, IMMODESTY, IMMORALITY, INEXPEDIENCE, IRRELATION, MISTAKE, PREJUDICE, SEX, UNFAIRNESS, UNTIMELINESS. *Antonyms* —See IMPARTIALITY, PROPRIETY, TIMELINESS.

IMPROVEMENT—N. improvement, amelioration, betterment, enrichment, advancement, promotion, preferment, elevation, recovery.

cultivation, refinement, culture, civilization, *Kultur* (*Ger.*), polish; euthenics, eugenics.

reform, reformation; revision, correction, repair, reclamation.

reformer, reformist, progressive, radical; do-gooder (*colloq.*), crusader.

V. **improve,** mend, amend, better, ameliorate, help, relieve, rectify, correct, repair, restore; improve upon; enrich, mellow, refine, develop, rarefy, polish, civilize, culture, cultivate.

promote, advance, forward, further, speed, push, enhance, foster, aid, profit, benefit.

revise, edit, review, doctor, emend, correct, rectify, touch up, polish, amend.

reform, remodel, re-establish, reconstruct, refashion, reorganize, reclaim, civilize, lift, uplift, raise, regenerate.

Adj. **improved,** etc. (see *Verbs*); better, preferable, superior.

refined (*fig.*), civilized, cultivated, cultured, genteel, polished, rarefied, suave, urbane; Attic.

See also CHANGE, ELEVATION, HEALTH, PROGRESS, PURIFICATION, RESTORATION. *Antonyms*—See BARBARIANISM, DETERIORATION, DISEASE.

improvident, *adj.* extravagant, lavish, prodigal, profligate (WASTEFULNESS).

improvise, *v.* extemporize, ad-lib, (NONPREPARATION, TALK); make up, invent (PRODUCTION).

imprudent, *adj.* incautious, indiscreet, injudicious, hasty (CARELESSNESS, COURAGE); inadvisable, impolitic, unwise (INEXPEDIENCE, FOLLY).

impudent, *adj.* cool, insolent, impertinent (DISCOURTESY).

impulse, *n.* motive, incentive, urge (MOTIVATION, DESIRE); inclination, bent, mind (TENDENCY).

impulsive, *adj.* sudden, unexpected, spontaneous (SUDDENNESS, NONPREPARATION).

impunity, *n.* immunity, privilege, exemption (FREEDOM, ACQUITTAL).

IMPURITY—*N.* impurity, uncleanness, foulness, filth, corruption, pollution.

contamination, defilement, debasement, taint, adulteration, vitiation, sullage, infection.

V. contaminate, adulterate, alloy, debase, pollute; corrupt, defile, maculate, taint, infect, vitiate, tarnish.

Adj. impure, adulterated, alloyed, contaminated, debased, polluted; corrupt, corrupted, defiled, maculate, tainted, unclean, vitiated, feculent, foul, filthy, infected.

[*ceremonially impure*] unpurified, uncleansed, defiled, unholy, unhallowed, unsanctified, unblessed.

See also SEX, UNCLEANNESS. *Antonyms*—See CLEANNESS, PURIFICATION.

impute to, *v.* ascribe to, refer to (ATTRIBUTION).

inability, *n.* powerlessness, impotence, incapability (DISABLEMENT).

inaccessible, *adj.* unapproachable, unaccessible, remote (HOSTILITY).

inaccuracy, *n.* error, solecism, blunder (MISTAKE).

inaccurate, *adj.* erroneous, incorrect, imprecise (MISTAKE).

INACTION—*N.* inaction, inactivity, rest, peace, *laissez faire* (F.), noninterference, fainéance, *dolce far niente* (*It.*); standstill, arrest, deadlock, stalemate, entropy, suspension, abeyance, subsidence.

sluggishness, languor, lassitude, lethargy, doldrums, inertia, apathy, stupor, torpor, oscitancy, sloth, inanimation.

stagnation, stagnancy, vegetation; slumber, sleep, hibernation, estivation (*zool.*).

unemployment, ease, leisure, retirement, superannuation.

hesitation, hesitance, demurral, indecision, waver, scruple, doubt.

V. inactivate, arrest, suspend, deadlock, stalemate, quiet, still, slake.

be inactive, slumber, sleep, stagnate, vegetate, hibernate, estivate (*zool.*), do nothing, take it easy, idle, rest, stop, cease; quiet, still, slack, slacken, slack off, lull, languish, subside, abate, decline, droop, sink, relax.

not do, not act, do nothing; abstain, avoid, desist, forbear, forgo, refrain, resist; shirk, default; leave alone, let be, let pass, pass, let things take their course; rest upon one's oars, rest upon one's laurels, relax one's efforts.

hesitate, boggle, demur, stickle, scruple, falter, shilly-shally, stagger, waver.

Adj. inactive, passive, inert, stagnant, still, quiet, peaceful, static, deedless; sedentary, recumbent; bedridden, bedfast, shut-in.

sluggish, languid, languorous, leaden, dull, heavy, lethargic, listless, phlegmatic, apathetic, stuporous, supine, torpid, vegetative, slothful, spiritless, lifeless, inanimate, droopy (*colloq.*), logy (*colloq.*), in the doldrums; unresisting, nonresistant, unresistant.

unoccupied, unemployed, unengaged, laid off, at ease, at leisure, at rest, resting, taking it easy, idle; retired, superannuated, emeritus.

dormant, fallow, quiescent, slack, abeyant, subsident, slumberous, asleep, sleeping, latescent, latent, potential.

hesitant, faltering, halting, hesitative, hesitatory, wavering, indecisive.

See also AVOIDANCE, FAILURE, INSENSIBILITY, NEGLECT, MOTIONLESSNESS, PEACE, REST, SEAT, SLEEP. *Antonyms*—See ACTION, ACTIVITY, MOTION, WORK.

inactive, *adj.* passive, inert, static (INACTION).

inactivity, *n.* rest, peace, *dolce far niente* (*It.*), standstill (INACTION).

inadequate, *adj.* helpless, unqualified, unfit (CLUMSINESS); not enough, deficient, unequal (INSUFFICIENCY, INCOMPLETENESS).

inadvertent, *adj.* unintentional, accidental (PURPOSELESSNESS); unthinking, unmindful, thoughtless (CARELESSNESS).

inadvisable, *adj.* ill-advised, impolitic, imprudent (INEXPEDIENCE).

inane, *adj.* absurd, ridiculous, asinine (FOLLY); meaningless, senseless, pointless (ABSURDITY); vapid, vacuous, vacant (STUPIDITY).

inanimate, *adj.* lifeless, brute, inorganic (DEATH); sluggish, slothful, spiritless (INACTION).

inapplicable, *adj.* inapposite, inappurtenant, inapropos (IRRELATION).

inappropriate, *adj.* inapropos, incongruous, unseemly (IMPROPERNESS).

inarticulate, *adj.* dumb, tongue-tied, mum (SILENCE).

INATTENTION—N. inattention, oblivion, disregard, unconcern, inadvertence, negligence, oversight, neglect, inattentiveness, etc. (see *Adjectives*); distraction, red herring.

absent-mindedness, abstraction, absorption, engrossment, bemusement, detachment, preoccupation, distraction, reverie, brown study (*colloq.*), woolgathering, daydream.

V. **disregard,** pay no attention to, overlook, pass by, neglect, miss, skip, slur over; override, ride roughshod over, ignore, turn a deaf ear to, shrug off, slight, wink at, blink at, by-pass, cushion; snub, cut, brush off (*slang*), ostracize, boycott.

distract, abstract, confuse, befuddle, muddle, giddy.

Adj. **inattentive,** unobservant, undiscerning, unmindful, oblivious, unaware, unconscious, unheeding, regardless; indifferent, blind, deaf; scatterbrained, harebrained, flighty, giddy; heedless, disregardful, thoughtless, careless, neglectful, negligent.

absent-minded, absent, lost, rapt, engrossed, preoccupied, abstracted, bemused, distrait, distracted, removed, woolgathering, dreamy, faraway, dazed; lost in thought, musing, in the clouds, off one's guard, caught napping.

inconsiderate, unconsiderate, tactless, thoughtless, unthinking, untactful, indelicate, wanton, outrageous.

See also CARELESSNESS, DIZZINESS, FORGETFULNESS, INDIFFERENCE, NEGLECT. *Antonyms*—See ATTENTION, CARE.

---

inaudible, *adj.* indistinct, unclear, unheard (SILENCE).

inaugurate, *v.* initiate, introduce, launch (BEGINNING); install, induct, invest (COMMISSION).

inauspicious, *adj.* untimely, inopportune, unpropitious (UNTIMELINESS); ill-omened, ominous, ill-

boding (HOPELESSNESS, OPPOSITION).

inborn, *adj.* inbred, intrinsic, innate (BIRTH, NATURALNESS, INTERIORITY).

incalculable, *adj.* countless, infinite, innumerable (MULTITUDE, ENDLESSNESS).

incapable, *adj.* powerless, helpless, impotent (DISABLEMENT); incompetent, improficient, inefficient (CLUMSINESS).

incapacitate, *v.* disable, paralyze, cripple (DISABLEMENT, WEAKNESS).

incendiary, *n.* arsonist, firebug, pyromaniac (FIRE).

incentive, *n.* motive, impulse, inspiration (MOTIVATION, DESIRE).

incessant, *adj.* interminable, timeless, unending (ENDLESSNESS).

incident, *n.* event, milestone, happening (OCCURRENCE).

incidental, *adj.* fortuitous, concurrent, concomitant (OCCURRENCE); casual, chance, accidental (CHANCE, IRRELATION); irregular, occasional (CHANCE).

incinerator, *n.* cinerator, furnace, cremator (FIRE).

incision, *n.* surgical operation, operation, the knife, section (SURGERY).

incisive, *adj.* keen, penetrating, acute, trenchant (INTELLIGENCE, SHARPNESS).

incite, *v.* prod, goad, impel (URGING); instigate, foment (MOTIVATION).

inclement, *adj.* violent, extreme, rough (SEVERITY).

inclination, *n.* mind, impulse, bent, predilection, predisposition, propensity (TENDENCY, PREJUDICE); appetite, partiality (LIKING); slant, grade, gradient, cant, incline (SLOPE, TURNING).

incline, *n.* slant, grade, inclination (SLOPE, TURNING).

incline, *v.* tend, trend, verge (TENDENCY); be willing, lean to, not mind (WILLINGNESS); discriminate, be partial, favor (PREJUDICE); make willing, dispose (WILLINGNESS); prejudice, bias, predispose (PREJUDICE, INFLUENCE); turn, bend, yaw (TURNING); lean, slant, cant (SLOPE).

inclined, *adj.* apt, liable, minded, disposed, prone (WILLINGNESS, TENDENCY); predisposed, favorable, partial (PREJUDICE); sloping, slanting, banked (SLOPE).

INCLOSURE—N. inclosure *or* enclosure, receptacle, case, wrapper, envelope; cincture, girdle.

[*inclosed place*] pen, fold, corral, pound, pinfold, compound, coop, cote, cubbyhole, cubby, pale, stockade; sty, shed, hutch, stall; paddock, pasture, croft.

yard, compass, court, courtyard, close, garth, quadrangle; barnyard, farmyard, stockyard, cattlefold.

fence, barrier, enclosure, pale, paling, palisade, railing, barricade, wall; panel, picket, post, rail, stake, upright; hedge, hedgerow.

V. **inclose** or **enclose,** surround, encircle, encompass, ring, circumscribe, hedge, girdle, fence, hem in, gird, impound, corral, pen, box, case, incase, envelop, shut in; insert.

See also BOUNDARY, CLOSURE, CONTAINER, ENVIRONMENT, IMPRISONMENT, INSERTION, PROTECTION, RESTRAINT, SECLUSION, WALL. *Antonyms*—See FREEDOM, SPACE.

INCLUSION—*N.* inclusion, admission, subsumption, comprisal; embodiment, incorporation, involvement.

V. **include,** comprise, subsume, comprehend, contain, encompass, hold, admit, embrace, involve, incorporate, cover, embody, reckon among, number among, count among.

Adj. **inclusive,** all-embracing, all-inclusive, broad, comprehensive, embracive, exhaustive, expansive, extensive, full, sweeping, vast, wide, indiscriminate.

See also CONTAINER, CONTENTS, BODY, COVERING, FULLNESS, MAKE-UP. *Antonyms*—See ABSENCE, EXCLUSION, INCOMPLETENESS.

---

incoherent, *adj.* irrational, disconnected, disjointed (UNREASONABLENESS).

income, *n.* receipts, revenue, earnings (RECEIVING, PAYMENT).

incoming, *adj.* entering, inbound, approaching (INGRESS, ARRIVAL).

incommunicado, *adj.* quarantined, sequestered, isolated (SECLUSION); imprisoned, in custody (IMPRISONMENT).

incomparable, *adj.* disparate, diverse, incommensurable (DIFFERENCE, COMPARISON); second to none, sovereign, transcendent (SUPERIORITY).

incompatible, *adj.* irreconcilable, incongruous, inconsistent (DISAGREEMENT).

incompetent, *adj.* improficient, inefficient, inept, (CLUMSINESS, USELESSNESS).

INCOMPLETENESS—*N.* incompleteness, crudity, deficiency, deficit, shortcoming, lack, want, insufficiency, shortage, inadequacy, omission.

noncompletion, nonfulfillment, nonperformance, inexecution, neglect, incompletion.

V. **be incomplete,** fall short of, lack, want, need, require.

leave unfinished, leave undone, neglect, fail to obtain (attain or reach), do things by halves.

Adj. **incomplete,** uncompleted, imperfect, unfinished, fragmentary, inchoate, partial, rude, crude, rudimentary, sketchy, unconsummated, unpolished, incondite; deficient, wanting, short; immature, undeveloped; abridged, expurgated.

in progress, in hand, going on, proceeding, in preparation, under construction.

See also ABSENCE, CUTTING, IMMATURITY, IMPERFECTION, INSUFFICIENCY, NECESSITY, NEGLECT, NONPREPARATION, PART, SHORTNESS. *Antonyms*—See COMPLETENESS, INCLUSION.

---

incomprehensible, *adj.* unintelligible, unfathomable, fathomless (MYSTERY).

inconceivable, *adj.* incredible, strange, unheard of (IMPROBABILITY, SURPRISE).

in conclusion, finally, lastly, in fine (REASONING).

inconclusive, *adj.* uneventful, indecisive, unfateful (UNIMPORTANCE); unpersuasive, unconvincing, lame (DISSUASION).

incongruous, *adj.* inappropriate, inapropos, inapt (IMPROPERNESS); incompatible, irreconcilable, inconsistent (DISAGREEMENT); strange, alien (UNUSUALNESS).

inconsiderate, *adj.* unconsiderate, tactless, thoughtless (INATTENTION).

inconsistent, *adj.* incompatible, incongruous, warring (DISAGREEMENT).

inconsolable, *adj.* disconsolate, unconsolable, distressed (SADNESS).

inconspicuous, *adj.* indistinct, dim, faint (INVISIBILITY, UNCLEARNESS).

inconvenient, *adj.* remote, bothersome, unhandy (DIFFICULTY).

incorporate, *v.* include, involve, cover (INCLUSION, BODY); embody, link (COMBINATION).

incorrect, *adj.* erroneous, inaccurate, imprecise (MISTAKE); improper, inappropriate, wrong (IMPROPERNESS).

incorrigible, *adj.* irreclaimable,

recidivous, irreformable (WICKED-NESS, LOSS).

INCREASE—N. increase, raise, rise, boost, step-up; addition, increment, accrual, access.

growth, surge, swell, rise, accretion; accumulation, overgrowth, spread.

[abnormal bodily enlargement] giantism, gigantism, elephantiasis, acromegaly.

V. increase, enhance, aggrandize, augment, add to, heighten, aggravate, intensify, step up, raise, lift, boost, up; multiply, propagate, redouble, magnify, exaggerate, maximize, lengthen.

grow, surge, swell, fill out, inflate; wax, accumulate, rise, skyrocket; overgrow, overrun, spread.

expand, distend, dilate, inflate, swell, develop, extend, spread, stretch, widen; enlarge, pad, amplify, bulk.

enlarge on (a subject, etc.), amplify, develop, dilate on, elaborate on, expand, expatiate on, extend.

Adj. increasing, etc. (see Verbs); accretive, crescent, crescive, incremental, increscent, addititious, cumulative, accumulative.

See also ADDITION, EXAGGERATION, SPREAD, SWELLING. Antonyms—See DECREASE, DEDUCTION.

---

incredible, adj. unbelievable, questionable, suspect (UNBELIEVINGNESS).

incredulous, adj. unbelieving, skeptical, suspicious (UNBELIEVINGNESS).

incriminate, v. implicate, inculpate (ACCUSATION).

incubate, v. set, brood, hatch (SEAT).

inculcate, v. instill, implant, indoctrinate (TEACHING).

incumbent, n. commissioner, officeholder, bureaucrat (OFFICIAL).

incur, v. lay onself open to, be subjected to, run the chance (LIABILITY).

incurable, adj. irremediable, remediless, immedicable (HOPELESSNESS, CURE).

incursion, n. invasion, raid, irruption (INGRESS).

indebtedness, n. arrears, arrearage, liabilities (DEBT).

indecision, n. fluctuation, vacillation, incertitude (UNCERTAINTY, IRRESOLUTION, CHANGEABLENESS); hesitancy, waver, doubt (INACTION).

indecisive, adj. irresolute, vacillating (WEAKNESS); hesitant, waver-ing (INACTION); inconclusive, unfateful (UNIMPORTANCE).

indeed, adv. actually, veritably, truly (TRUTH); much, very, very much (GREATNESS).

indefatigable, adj. tireless, untiring, unwearied (ENERGY).

indefensible, adj. inexcusable, unpardonable, unforgivable (IMPROPERNESS); vulnerable, untenable, unprotected (WEAKNESS).

indefinable, adj. obscure, undefinable, ambiguous (UNCERTAINTY).

indefinite, adj. uncertain, unsure, undependable (UNCERTAINTY); obscure, shadowy, vague (INVISIBILITY, UNCERTAINTY); undecided, intangible, indeterminate (UNCLEARNESS).

indelible, adj. ineradicable, inerasable, inexpungeable (CONTINUATION); memorable, rememberable, unforgettable (MEMORY).

indelicate, adj. indecent, obscene, shameful (IMMODESTY, OBSCENITY); coarse, crude, earthy (VULGARITY, LOWNESS); unthinking, untactful (INATTENTION).

indemnify, v. pay, compensate for, redress (RECOMPENSE).

indent, v. notch, pit, rabbet (HOLLOW).

indentation, n. dent, nick, score (NOTCH).

independence, n. autonomy, self-government, sovereignty (FREEDOM, GOVERNMENT).

independent, adj. free, autonomous, sovereign (FREEDOM); unrelated, unallied (IRRELATION); well-fixed, wealthy, rich (WEALTH).

independently, adv. apart, separately, one by one (UNITY).

indescribable, adj. inexpressible, unutterable, ineffable (SILENCE); nondescript, subtle (DESCRIPTION).

index, v. file, alphabetize, catalogue (ARRANGEMENT, LIST).

INDICATION—N. indication, indicator, show, token, evidence, symptom, testimony, augury, auspice, omen.

sign, mark, symbol, emblem, brassard, chevron, ensign, index, indicium.

[of locality] signpost, sign, signboard, guidepost, waypost, milestone, landmark, beacon, hand, pointer; vane, cock, weathercock, weather vane; North Star, polestar, Polaris.

signal, beacon, flare, blinker, rocket, watchtower, signal tower, signal smoke.

call, reveille, taps, bugle call, tattoo, whistle, hooter, siren, horn, bell, alarm, alert, tocsin, curfew, foghorn, toll; battle cry, rallying cry.

mark, impression, imprint, line, stroke, dash, score, lineation, streak, scratch, dot, notch, nick, blaze; brand, stigma, sear, earmark, birthmark, scar, ring, scuff; trace, vestige, track, footprint, wake.

[for identification] badge, countermark, hallmark, trade-mark, brand, emblem, insignia (pl.), decoration, regalia; voucher, docket, countercheck, counterfoil, stub, duplicate, tally, tag, slip, label, ticket, counter, check, stamp; credentials; monogram, seal, signet; fingerprint, dactylogram; shibboleth, watchword, catchword, password, sign, countersign, pass, grip; open-sesame.

flag, banner, colors, streamer, bunting, pennant, pennon, ensign, standard; eagle, oriflamme, blue peter, burgee, jack, union jack; banderole, bannerette, gonfalon, guidon; tricolor; flag of truce, white flag; flagpole, flagstaff.

U. S. Flag, Old Glory, the Red, White, and Blue, the Star-Spangled Banner, the Stars and Stripes; the Stars and Bars.

symptom, prodrome, syndrome; symptomatology, semeiology.

V. indicate, show, token, betoken, bespeak, denote, connote, designate, evidence, evince, manifest, signify, suggest, symbolize, mark, symptomatize; testify, argue, adumbrate, attest, augur.

signal, signalize, flag, semaphore, wave, wigwag, heliograph; flash, beacon.

Adj. indicative, expressive, denotative, connotative, designative, evidential, evincive, significant, suggestive, representative, symbolic, symptomatic; diagnostic, prognostic, augural, auspicious, apocalyptic; emblematic.

See also DISCLOSURE, DISPLAY, GESTURE, INFORMATION, MEANING, PREDICTION, REPRESENTATION, SUMMONS, WARNING. Antonyms—See CONCEALMENT, ELIMINATION.

indict, v. charge, accuse, arraign (ACCUSATION).

INDIFFERENCE—N. indifference, tepidity, cold shoulder (colloq.), disinterest, unconcern, insouciance, nonchalance, pococurantism; languor, lethargy, apathy, stoicism.

[person who is indifferent] apathist, Laodicean, pococurante.

V. be indifferent, take no interest in, have no desire for, have no taste for, not care for, care nothing for (or about), not mind; spurn, disdain, cold-shoulder (colloq.).

Adj. indifferent, lukewarm, tepid, superior to, casual, nonchalant, pococurante, disinterested, unconcerned, insouciant, perfunctory, lackadaisical, languid, languorous, Laodicean, lethargic, apathetic, listless.

See also INATTENTION, INSENSITIVITY, NEGLECT. Antonyms—See EAGERNESS, ENTHUSIASM, FEELING, SENSITIVENESS.

indigenous, adj. native, original, home-grown (INHABITANT).
indigent, adj. poverty-stricken, poor, impoverished (POVERTY).
indignation, n. resentment, animus, displeasure (ANGER).
indignity, n. slur, slap, taunt (INSULT); affront, outrage, injury (OFFENSE).
indirect, adj. devious, oblique (INDIRECTNESS, WORDINESS); secondary, vicarious (RESULT).

INDIRECTNESS—N. indirectness, indirection, circuity, sinuosity, tortuosity, circularity, obliquity, ambagiosity; ambages (pl.), circumbendibus (jocose), circumlocution, circumvolution, periphrasis.
V. involve, entail, tangle, entangle, mire.
Adj. indirect, devious, oblique, obliquitous, roundabout, ambagious, ambagitory, backhand, backhanded, circuitous, circular, collateral, sinuous, tortuous, circumlocutory, periphrastic.
inferential, implied, implicit, understood, unexpressed, tacit, allusive, covert.
See also MEANING, WANDERING, WINDING, WORDINESS. Antonyms—See HONESTY, STRAIGHTNESS.

indiscreet, adj. imprudent, hasty, thoughtless (COURAGE, CARELESSNESS); misguided, ill-advised, inexpedient (FOLLY).
indiscriminate, adj. promiscuous, imperceptive (INDISCRIMINATION); motley, variegated, miscellaneous (MIXTURE); sweeping, vast, wide (INCLUSION).

INDISCRIMINATION—N. indiscrimination, promiscuity; confusion, mix-up, jumble.

V. **confuse,** not tell apart, mix up, confound.

Adj. **undiscriminating,** indiscriminate, promiscuous, imperceptive, undiscerning; confused, confounded, mixed-up, baffled, bewildered, lost.

See also CONFUSION, MIXTURE, UNCERTAINTY. *Antonyms*—See DIFFERENTIATION, JUDGMENT.

indispensable, *adj.* essential, basic, vital (NECESSITY, IMPORTANCE).

indisposed, *adj.* disinclined, uninclined, averse (UNWILLINGNESS).

indisposition, *n.* ill-health, invalidism, infirmity (DISEASE).

indisputable, *adj.* incontestable, incontrovertible, indubitable (CERTAINTY).

indistinct, *adj.* dim, faint, inconspicuous (INVISIBILITY); inaudible, unclear, unheard (SILENCE); obscure, dark, shadowy (UNCLEARNESS, CLOUD).

individual, *adj.* exclusive, particular; single, odd, unitary (UNITY); special, especial, express (DIFFERENCE).

individual, *n.* entity, single, singleton (UNITY); person, soul, cog (PEOPLE).

indivisible, *adj.* undividable, inseparable, indiscerptible (COMPLETENESS).

indoctrinate, *v.* instill, implant, inculcate (TEACHING).

indolent, *adj.* lazy, slothful, shiftless (REST).

indorse, *v.* sign, undersign (SIGNATURE); countenance, back, sanction (SUPPORT, ASSENT).

induce, *v.* inspire, prompt, provoke (MOTIVATION); persuade, cajole, coax (PERSUASION).

induct, *v.* install, inaugurate, invest (COMMISSION).

indulge, *v.* favor, humor, pamper (MILDNESS, PERMISSION).

indulgence, *n.* allowance, toleration (PERMISSION); license, sensuality, debauchery (INTEMPERANCE).

indulgent, *adj.* complaisant, easygoing, lenient (MILDNESS); permissive, tolerant, overpermissive (PERMISSION).

industrialist, *n.* businessman, executive, entrepreneur (BUSINESS).

industrious, *adj.* busy, diligent, assiduous (BUSINESS, WORK).

inebriated, *adj.* high (*colloq.*), intoxicated, tipsy (DRUNKENNESS).

ineffable, *adj.* indescribable, inexpressible, unutterable, unspeakable (SILENCE).

INEFFECTIVENESS—*N.* ineffectiveness, ineffectuality, futility, vanity, impotence, sterility, inefficacy, anticlimax, bathos; futilitarianism.

V. **annul,** nullify, disannul, vitiate, discharge (*legal*), invalidate, quash (*legal*), repeal, rescind, revoke, recall, vacate, void, abolish, abrogate; neutralize, counterbalance, cancel, countermand, countermine, negate, override; scotch, spike, destroy, ruin, stultify, supersede, suspend; weaken, wither.

frustrate, thwart, foil, stymie, balk, bilk, blight, dash, countervail, defeat, circumvent, discomfit.

Adj. **ineffective,** ineffectual, inefficacious, fruitless, unfruitful, sterile, barren, futile, vain, feckless, bootless, null, null and void, void, unavailing, defeasible, innocuous, inoperative, invalid, nugatory; weak, impotent, powerless, withered, indecisive, inexpedient, stillborn; anticlimactic, bathetic.

See also DEFEAT, DENIAL, DESTRUCTION, DISABLEMENT, DISAPPOINTMENT, INEXPEDIENCE, OPPOSITION, PREVENTION, UNPRODUCTIVENESS, USELESSNESS, WEAKNESS. *Antonyms*—See POWER, RESULT, STRENGTH.

inefficient, *adj.* incompetent, improficient, inadequate (CLUMSINESS); inept, ineffectual (USELESSNESS).

INELASTICITY—*N.* inelasticity, flaccidity, laxity.

Adj. **inelastic,** flaccid, flabby, irresilient, inductile, unyielding, inflexible, inextensible.

See also LOOSENESS, SOFTNESS. *Antonyms*—See HARDNESS, JUMP, STRENGTH, STRETCH, TIGHTNESS.

inelegant, *adj.* graceless, stiff, wooden (CLUMSINESS); unrefined, unpolished, uncultured (VULGARITY).

inept, *adj.* unskillful, inadept, inartistic (CLUMSINESS); inefficient, ineffectual, incompetent (USELESSNESS).

INEQUALITY—*N.* inequality, imparity, unequality, unequivalence, disparity; dissimilarity, dissimilitude, disproportion, diversity.

[*person or thing without equal*] nonesuch, nonpareil; *rara avis* (L.), freak, sport.

Adj. **unequal,** disparate, incommensurate, unequivalent, uneven; inadequate, deficient, insufficient; overbalanced, unbalanced, top-heavy, lopsided, irregular; disquiparant (*logic*).

unequaled, unmatched, peerless, unique, nonpareil, unexampled, incomparable, unapproached, unparalleled, unrivaled, matchless.

See also DIFFERENCE, INSUFFICIENCY, IRREGULARITY, OPPOSITE. *Antonyms*—See EQUALITY.

inequity, *n.* discrimination, favoritism, injustice (UNFAIRNESS).

ineradicable, *adj.* indelible, inerasable, inexpungeable (CONTINUATION).

inert, *adj.* inactive, passive, static (INACTION); sluggish, languid, listless (SLOWNESS, DEATH); torpid, numb, paralyzed (MOTIONLESSNESS).

inertia, *n.* apathy, stupor, torpor, oscitancy (INACTION); immobilization, paralysis (MOTIONLESSNESS).

inescapable, *adj.* apparent, unhidden, unconcealed (VISIBILITY); unavoidable, inevitable, ineluctable (CERTAINTY).

inevitable, *adj.* certain, sure, ineluctable (CERTAINTY).

INEXCITABILITY—*N.* inexcitability, imperturbability, even temper, dispassion, tolerance, patience, inertia, impassibility, stupefaction.

equanimity, equability, poise, sobriety, composure, placidity, *sang-froid* (*F.*), tranquillity, serenity; quiet, quietude, peace of mind; philosophy, stoicism, self-possession, self-control, self-command, self-restraint; presence of mind.

V. bear, endure, undergo, suffer, bear with, put up with, tolerate, brook, abide, stand, submit to, resign oneself to, acquiesce in, go through, support, brave, swallow, pocket, stomach; carry on, carry through; make light of, make the best of.

Adj. inexcitable, imperturbable, passionless, dispassionate, cold-blooded, enduring, stoical, philosophical, staid, sober, sedate, cool-headed, level, well-balanced, steady, levelheaded, composed, collected, temperate; unstirred, unruffled, unperturbed; easygoing, peaceful, placid, calm; quiet, tranquil, serene, cool.

See also ACCEPTANCE, CALMNESS, PEACE, SOBRIETY, SUBMISSION. *Anto-*

nyms—See ANGER, BAD TEMPER, EXCITEMENT.

---

inexcusable, *adj.* indefensible, unpardonable, unforgivable (IMPROPERNESS).

inexorable, *adj.* unyielding, adamant, unmovable (STUBBORNNESS).

INEXPEDIENCE—*N.* inexpedience, undesirability, inadvisability, impropriety, inutility, disadvantage, inconvenience, discommodity.

V. be inexpedient, come amiss, embarrass, put to inconvenience.

Adj. inexpedient, undesirable, inadvisable, ill-advised, impolitic, unwise, imprudent, inopportune, disadvantageous, unprofitable, unfit, inappropriate, unsuitable, objectionable, inconvenient.

See also DIFFICULTY, IMPROPERNESS, UNTIMELINESS, USELESSNESS. *Antonyms*—See ADVANTAGE, PROPRIETY, TIMELINESS, USE.

INEXPENSIVENESS—*N.* inexpensiveness, low price, budget price, bargain, sale; drug on the market; seconds, rejects, samples, cancellations.

V. be inexpensive, cost little, come down (*or* fall) in price, be marked down, buy at a bargain, buy dirt-cheap, get one's money's worth.

cheapen, beat down, reduce, lower, depreciate, undervalue.

Adj. inexpensive, cheap, cut-rate, nominal, low-priced, popular-priced, budget-priced, low, moderate, reasonable, economical, dirt-cheap; catchpenny, tin-horn; reduced, marked down, half-price; shopworn, shelf-worn.

Adv., phrases. cheaply, inexpensively, at a bargain, at a discount, for a song; at a reduction, at cost, at wholesale.

See also ECONOMY, LOWNESS, SALE. *Antonyms*—See EXPENDITURE.

INEXPERIENCE—*N.* inexperience, innocence, naïveté, unsophistication, verdancy, salad days.

[*inexperienced person*] greenhorn, babe, colt, virgin.

Adj. inexperienced, young, callow, green, raw, untrained, unskilled, inexpert, unseasoned, unpracticed, undisciplined, strange at, unfamiliar with, unacquainted, unaccustomed to, unversed, virgin to; unsophisticated, innocent, naïve, unworldly, verdant, sophomoric.

See also CLUMSINESS, IMMATURITY, INNOCENCE, NEWNESS, YOUTH. *Antonyms*—See EXPERIENCE, MATURITY, TEACHING, WISDOM.

inexpressible, *adj.* unutterable, indescribable, ineffable (SILENCE).

infallible, *adj.* perfect, unerring, inerrable (PERFECTION, RIGHT).

infamous, *adj.* notorious, ignoble, inglorious (DISREPUTE, DISGRACE); monstrous, corrupt, foul (WICKEDNESS).

infancy, *n.* youth, childhood, nursery (CHILD, YOUTH).

infantry, *n.* foot, rifles, foot soldiers (FIGHTER).

infatuated, *adj.* in love, enamored, smitten (LOVE).

infected, *adj.* insanitary, unhygienic, contaminated (UNCLEANNESS); diseased, pathological (DISEASE).

infectious, *adj.* catching, communicable, contagious (DISEASE, TRANSFER).

infer, *v.* deduce, conclude, judge (REASON, UNDERSTANDING); presume, gather (LIKELIHOOD).

inference, *n.* conclusion, corollary, illation (DEDUCTION, REASONING, UNDERSTANDING).

inferior, *adj.* poor, bad, (INFERIORITY); subordinate, junior (RANK); lesser, smaller (SMALLNESS); lower, under (LOWNESS).

inferior, *n.* junior, subordinate, subaltern (RANK).

INFERIORITY—*N.* inferiority, poor quality, mediocrity; inferiority complex, inadequacy feelings, diffidence.

V. be inferior, fall short of, not come up to, not measure up to.

Adj. inferior, poor, mediocre, indifferent, bad, base, bum (*colloq.*), coarse, common, low, meager, scrub, second-rate, third-rate, crummy (*slang*), shoddy, substandard, wretched, sleazy, dubious.

very bad, abominable, atrocious, awful, dreadful, execrable, horrible, outrageous, putrid, rotten (*slang*), terrible, worthless; beastly, frightful, horrid, nasty, ungodly, unholy, vicious, vile, villainous, wicked.

[*conspicuously bad*] egregious, flagrant, glaring, gross, monstrous, outrageous, rank.

See also DETERIORATION, LOWNESS, MEANNESS, UNPLEASANTNESS, WORTHLESSNESS. *Antonyms*—GOOD, PLEASANTNESS, SUPERIORITY, VALUE.

infernal, *adj.* demonic, fiendish, diabolical (DEVIL); hellish, Avernal, Hadean (HELL); wicked, monstrous (WICKEDNESS).

inferred, *adj.* tacit, assumed, implicit (MEANING).

infest, *v.* overrun, swarm over (FREQUENCY, MULTITUDE).

infidel, *n.* irreligionist, atheist, heathen (IRRELIGION); heretic, misbeliever, unbeliever (HETERODOXY, UNBELIEVINGNESS); pagan, paganist (RELIGION).

infidelity, *n.* perfidy, unfaithfulness, faithlessness (DISLOYALTY).

infinite, *adj.* eternal, unending, endless (TIME); countless, incalculable, innumerable (MULTITUDE); immense, measureless, limitless (SIZE, ENDLESSNESS).

infinitesimal, *adj.* inappreciable, inconsiderable, imperceptible (SMALLNESS).

infinity, *n.* endless time, eternity (TIME); immensity, vastitude (SPACE); infinitude, myriad (MULTITUDE); illimitability, immeasurability, immensity (ENDLESSNESS).

infirm, *adj.* weak, feeble, frail (WEAKNESS); senile, decrepit, anile (OLDNESS).

infirmary, *n.* hospital, surgery, clinic (CURE).

inflame, *v.* fire, inspire, intoxicate (EXCITEMENT); stimulate (SEXUAL DESIRE); arouse, rile (*colloq.*), incense (ANGER); fester, blister (SWELLING).

inflamed, *adj.* vehement, passionate, fiery (VIOLENCE).

inflammable, *adj.* combustible, burnable, flammable (FIRE).

inflate, *v.* distend, swell, blow up (BLOWING, SWELLING); expand, dilate (INCREASE); fill with pride, exalt (PRIDE).

inflation, *n.* prosperity, boom (BUSINESS).

inflection, *n.* modulation, pitch, intonation (SOUND, VOICE).

inflexible, *adj.* unbending, unyielding, firm (HARDNESS, STRENGTH); immovable, uncompromising, obdurate (STUBBORNNESS, SEVERITY); unchangeable, immutable, invariable (UNIFORMITY).

INFLUENCE—*N.* influence, power, force, authority, effect, pressure, stress, weight; prestige, ascendancy, pull (*colloq.*), drag (*slang*); sway, hold, control, dominance, upper hand, whip hand; bias, prejudice; inspiration, obsession, impression, leaven, miasma; lobby, embracery.

region of influence: circle, demesne, domain, orbit, province, realm, sphere.

V. **influence,** affect, impress, move, touch; bias, prejudice, dispose, incline, predispose, sway, govern, inspire; possess, obsess; outweigh, predominate, preponderate, weigh against, militate against, counterbalance; pull strings, pull wires, wirepull; weigh, tell, count.

pervade, impregnate, permeate, penetrate, infiltrate, fill, run through, be rife, rage, prevail.

Adj. **influential,** powerful, potent, effective, weighty, strong, governing, dominant, controlling; affecting, impressive, inspiring, moving, touching.

[*easily influenced*] **impressionable,** impressible, plastic, pliable, pliant, sensitive, suggestible, susceptible, waxen, waxy; accessible, amenable; subject, subordinate.

See also CONTROL, EXCITEMENT, IMPORTANCE, MOTIVATION, PERSUASION, POWER, PREJUDICE, RESULT. *Antonyms*—See DISABLEMENT, INACTIVITY, INEFFECTIVENESS.

influx, *n.* inflow, inpour, inrush (INGRESS).

inform, *v.* let know, acquaint, familiarize (INFORMATION); edify, enlighten, initiate (TEACHING); endow, invest (GIVING).

informal, *adj.* casual, easygoing, offhand (FREEDOM, NONOBSERVANCE, SOCIALITY).

INFORMATION—*N.* information, knowledge, intelligence, news, propaganda, advice, advisory, aviso, data, dossier, side light; inside information, confidence, tip, tip-off.

communication, report, statement, communiqué, message, missive, letter.

announcement, proclamation, manifesto, bull (*by the pope*), pronouncement, pronunciamento, notice; poster, placard, bill, handbill; trial balloon.

report, account, white paper; tale, story, version, recital, recitation, narrative, narration, revelation, confidence.

informant, adviser, notifier, propagandist, source; messenger, herald, announcer, crier; tout, tipster.

informer, betrayer, blab, blabber, snitcher (*slang*), squealer (*colloq.*), stool pigeon (*slang*), talebearer, taleteller, tattletale, telltale.

V. **inform,** let know, acquaint, familiarize, orient, brief, advise, apprize, enlighten, notify, warn, confide in; communicate with, write, call, telephone, wire, telegraph, cable; circularize, advertise of, give the low-down (*slang*), tip off, tout.

inform on, bear (*or* carry) tales, peach (*slang*), snitch (*slang*), squeal (*colloq.*), tattle; report, betray, expose, unmask.

announce, annunciate, promulgate, proclaim, blazon, herald, publish, trumpet.

tell, disclose, signify, communicate, confide, report, reveal, relate, rehearse, recount, recite; tell about, describe, outline, detail, narrate, testify to.

undeceive, set right, set straight, correct, disabuse, open the eyes of, disenchant, disillusion.

Adj. **informative,** advisory, newsy, instructive, informational, educational; communicative, revelatory, significant, descriptive.

See also ADVICE, AFFIRMATION, DISCLOSURE, EPISTLE, INDICATION, KNOWLEDGE, PUBLICATION, TEACHING. *Antonyms*—See CONCEALMENT.

informed, *adj.* familiar, apprized, abreast (KNOWLEDGE).

infraction, *n.* infringement, transgression, violation (ILLEGALITY).

infrequent, *adj.* rare, sporadic, occasional (FEWNESS); unusual, uncommon, scarce (UNUSUALNESS).

infringe, *v.* disobey, violate, transgress (DISOBEDIENCE, NONOBSERVANCE); encroach, trench on, trespass (IMPROPERNESS).

infringement, *n.* infraction, transgression, violation (ILLEGALITY).

infuriate, *v.* enrage, lash into fury, incense (ANGER).

infuse, *v.* instill, inoculate, impregnate (INSERTION).

ingenious, *adj.* inventive, adroit, forgetive (PRODUCTION); clever, resourceful, shrewd (CLEVERNESS).

ingenuous, *adj.* guileless, naïve, artless (INNOCENCE); natural, unaffected, inartificial (NATURALNESS).

ingrained, *adj.* deep-seated, implanted, inwrought (INTERIORITY); rooted, inveterate, confirmed (HABIT).

ingratiating, *adj.* ingratiatory, silken, soft (LIKING).

INGRATITUDE—*N.* ingratitude, inappreciation, unappreciation; ungrateful person, ingrate.

V. be ungrateful, feel no obligation, bite the hand that feeds one.

Adj. ungrateful, thankless, unappreciative, inappreciative, unthankful.

unappreciated, unacknowledged, unavowed, unthanked, unrequited, unreturned, unrewarded, thankless, unthankful; misunderstood, ill-requited, ill-rewarded, forgotten, unremembered.

Antonyms—See GRATITUDE.

ingredient, *n.* component, element, constituent (PART).

INGRESS—*N.* ingress, ingression, introgression, entrance, entry, entree, admission, debut (*into society, etc.*), incoming; influx, inflow, inpour, inrush, immigration.

invasion, raid, incursion, irruption, inroad, violation, breach, burglary, escalade.

entrant, entry (*in a contest*), newcomer, incomer, straggler; immigrant, colonist, settler, pioneer; debutante.

access, entrance, adit, avenue; opening, orifice, inlet, mouth; entering wedge, opening wedge, wedge, toe hold, foothold, bridgehead, open-sesame; admission, admittance.

entrance hall, corridor, hall, hallway, lobby, vestibule; entranceway, doorway, gateway; door, gate, portal, portcullis (*hist.*), wicket; threshold, sill, doorsill.

doorkeeper, gatekeeper, concierge, porter, janitor.

V. enter, come in, immigrate, go in, pass into, flow in, burst in, barge in; break in, breach, burglarize, invade, raid, violate, escalade; straggle in, drop in, plunge, dive.

penetrate, permeate, interpenetrate, filter, infiltrate, percolate, pierce, stab.

embark, go on board, emplane, entrain.

Adj. entering, ingressive, immigrant, incoming, inbound.

enterable, accessible, penetrable, permeable, pervious, porous.

See also APPROACH, ARRIVAL, CUTTING, ENCROACHMENT, INLET, INSERTION, OPENING, PASSAGE. *Antonyms* —See DEPARTURE, EGRESS.

inhabit, *v.* live in, dwell in, occupy, reside in (INHABITANT).

inhabitable, *adj.* habitable, livable, lodgeable (HABITATION).

INHABITANT—*N.* inhabitant, habitant, commorant, denizen, resident, dweller, residentiary; inmate, occupant, householder, indweller, addressee, tenant; settler, squatter, pre-emptor, colonist; islander, villager, cottager; boarder, lodger, roomer; cohabitant, neighbor; urbanite, suburbanite, exurbanite.

earth dweller, earthling, terrestrial, tellurian.

transient, sojourner, visitor, visitant, migrant.

native, aborigine, aboriginal, autochthon, indigene.

population, inhabitants, people, folk, nation, state, community; colony, settlement.

inhabitation, inhabitancy, habitation, residence, residency, occupancy, occupation, tenancy, tenantry; stay, sojourn, visit; cohabitation, coexistence.

V. inhabit, live in, dwell in, occupy, indwell, reside in, tenant; settle, squat, pre-empt, colonize; sojourn, stay, visit, abide, live, take up one's abode; lodge, room, board, roost (*colloq.*), bunk (*colloq.*); populate, people; cohabit, coexist.

Adj. inhabited, lived in, settled, populated, occupied, tenanted, peopled, populous.

resident, commorant, inhabiting, etc. (see *Verbs*); urban, suburban, exurban; residential.

native, indigenous, original, natal, natural, aboriginal, autochthonous, endemic, domestic, homegrown, native-grown, homebred; naturalized; vernacular.

See also HABITATION, LIFE, PEOPLE. *Antonyms*—See TRAVELING.

inhale, *v.* breathe in, inspire, sniff (BREATH).

inherent, *adj.* innate, inborn, intrinsic (INTERIORITY, NATURALNESS); component, appertaining, resident (PART).

INHERITANCE—*N.* inheritance, coinheritance, coparcenary, coparceny, parceny, joint inheritance; primogeniture, ultimogeniture, matriheritage.

heritage, heritance, legacy, estate, birthright, heirloom, patrimony.

inheritor, heir, heiress (*fem.*), beneficiary, legatee, coheir, coparcener, parcener; heir apparent, crown prince, heir presumptive.

heredity, genetics, genesiology, eugenics, dysgenics; Mendelian theory, chromosome, gene, Mendelian characteristic, allelomorph, dominant character, recessive character, strain.

V. inherit, get, receive, fall heir to, acquire; succeed to, accede to.

Adj. hereditary, legitimate; heritable, inheritable.

See also ACQUISITION, CHILD, FOLLOWER, PAST, RECEIVING, WILL. *Antonyms*—See ANCESTRY, FUTURE, GIVING.

---

inhibition, *n.* constraint, reserve, restraint (INSENSITIVITY); suppression, repression, sublimation (CONTROL, RESTRAINT).

inhuman, *adj.* unkind, brutal, inhumane (CRUELTY).

inimical, *adj.* antagonistic, unfriendly (OPPOSITION).

inimitable, *adj.* unparalleled, unparagoned, unequaled (PERFECTION).

iniquity, *n.* wrong, miscreancy, sin (WICKEDNESS).

initial, *adj.* first, opening, maiden (BEGINNING, EARLINESS).

initial, *v.* stamp, mark, sign (WRITTEN SYMBOL).

initiate, *v.* start, begin, launch (BEGINNING); edify, enlighten, inform (TEACHING).

inject, *v.* interpolate, interjaculate, insert (INTERJACENCE, INSERTION).

injudicious, *adj.* misguided, ill-advised, inexpedient (FOLLY, INEXPEDIENCE).

injunction, *n.* prohibition, enjoinder, ban (DENIAL).

injure, *v.* deface, disfigure, blemish (BLEMISH, DEFORMITY); hurt, mar, spoil (HARM); pique, sting, wound (OFFENSE).

injury, *n.* disservice, prejudice, mischief (HARM, WICKEDNESS); lesion, wound (HARM); affront, outrage, indignity (OFFENSE).

injustice, *n.* wrong, favoritism, inequity (UNFAIRNESS).

inkling, *n.* suspicion, suggestion, tip (HINT); impression, notion, conception (UNDERSTANDING).

inland, *n.* inlands, midlands, upcountry (INTERIORITY).

inlay, *n.* insert, inset, panel (INSERTION).

INLET—*N.* inlet, bay, gulf, basin, arm, bight, fiord *or* fjord (*esp. Norway*), slough, slew *or* slue, bayou (*Southern U.S.*), cove, estuary, firth *or* frith (*esp. Scotland*), canal; sound, strait, narrows; harbor.

See also INGRESS, OCEAN, RIVER, WATER. *Antonyms*—See EGRESS.

---

inmate, *n.* felon, detenu, intern (IMPRISONMENT); inhabiter, occupant (INHABITANT).

inn, *n.* hotel, tavern, lodge (HABITATION).

innate, *adj.* inbred, intrinsic, inherent (INTERIORITY); natural, inborn, native (NATURALNESS, BIRTH).

inner, *adj.* internal, inside, inward (INTERIORITY).

INNOCENCE—*N.* innocence, naiveté, simplicity, purity, chastity, incorruption, impeccability, clean hands, clear conscience.

innocent, newborn babe, lamb, dove; Caesar's wife.

Adj. innocent, guiltless, blameless, cleanhanded, guilt-free, impeccable, impeccant, incorrupt, inculpable, irreprehensible, irreproachable, reproachless, sinless, uncensurable, uncorrupt, unexceptionable, unimpeachable, unreproachable; faultless, stainless, spotless, immaculate, unsullied, untainted, pure, unoffending, above suspicion; virtuous, chaste; guileless, naïve, unsophisticated, ingenuous, artless, simple.

harmless, inoffensive, offenseless, innocuous, safe; undamaging, undetrimental, unhurtful, uninjurious, unpernicious, unprejudicial.

See also CLEANNESS, HONESTY, INEXPERIENCE, MORALITY, NATURALNESS, PURIFICATION. *Antonyms*—See ACCUSATION, GUILT, HARM, ILLEGALITY, IMPURITY, SIN, UNCLEANNESS.

---

innuendo, *n.* implication, overtone, insinuation (HINT, SUGGESTION, ACCUSATION); reference, allusion (TALK).

innumerable, *adj.* countless, incalculable, infinite (MULTITUDE, ENDLESSNESS).

inoculate, *v.* immunize, vaccinate, variolate (PROTECTION); infuse, instill, infix (INSERTION).

INODOROUSNESS—*N.* inodorousness, deodorization, purification, fumigation; deodorizer, deodorant.

V. deodorize, remove the odor of.

Adj. inodorous, scentless, odorless, unscented, unaromatic, unperfumed; deodorized.

See also GAS, PURIFICATION. *Antonyms*—See ODOR.

---

inoffensive, *adj.* harmless, innocuous, safe (INNOCENCE).

inoperative, *adj.* ineffective, ineffectual, innocuous (INEFFECTIVENESS).

inopportune, *adj.* untimely, inauspicious, unpropitious (UNTIMELINESS); unfavorable, contrary, disadvantageous (MISFORTUNE).

inordinate, *adj.* unrestrained, uncurbed, extravagant (INTEMPERANCE); outrageous, exorbitant, extortionate (EXTREMENESS).

inorganic, *adj.* lifeless, exanimate, inanimate (DEATH); mineral (METAL).

INQUIRY—*N.* inquiry, investigation, research, study, examination; scrutiny, search, quest, pursuit, exploration.

interrogation, examination, quiz, test, third degree (*colloq.*), grilling, catechism, cross-examination, inquisition, interview, inquest, questionnaire.

question, interrogatory, query, rhetorical question; conundrum, riddle, poser, problem; issue, crux, moot point.

[*inquisitive person*] nosybody (*colloq.*), bluenose, busybody, inquisitive, pry, quidnunc, Paul Pry, eavesdropper, snoop, snooper.

V. inquire, inquisite, pry into, investigate, research, study, examine; scrutinize, search, explore.

question, interrogate, pump, query, catechize, grill, inquisition, interview, ply with questions, pry; examine, test, quiz, sound out, cross-examine, cross-question, third-degree (*colloq.*); challenge, badger, heckle.

ask, demand, query, inquire.

Adj. inquiring, curious, inquisiturient; interrogative, catechistic, quizzical.

inquisitive, nosy (*slang*), prying, personal.

questionable, doubtful, uncertain, undecided, problematical, dubious, moot, debatable, disputable, controversial, arguable, controvertible, suspicious.

See also EXAMINATION, FOLLOWING, SEARCH, UNBELIEVINGNESS, UNCERTAINTY. *Antonyms*—See ANSWER.

inquisition, *n.* interrogation, cross-examination, grilling (INQUIRY).

inquisitive, *adj.* nosy (*slang*), prying, personal (INQUIRY, SEARCH).

inroad, *n.* intrusion, infringement, trespass (ENCROACHMENT); invasion, irruption, incursion (ATTACK, INGRESS).

insane, *adj.* frenzied, frenetic, mad (VIOLENCE); psychotic, demented (INSANITY).

insanitary, *adj.* unhygienic, insalubrious, contaminated (DISEASE, UNCLEANNESS).

INSANITY—*N.* insanity, lunacy, mental imbalance, psychosis, psychopathy, mental disorder, mental ailment, aberration, alienation, cachexia, madness, mania, deliration, delirium, phrenitis, delirium tremens, D.T.'s, dementia, derangement, distemper, distraction, frenzy, phrensy; schizophrenia, schizothymia, schizomania, catatonia, hebephrenia, dementia praecox, manic-depressive psychosis, cyclothymia, involutional melancholia, paranoia; megalomania, monomania.

lunatic, madman, madwoman, maniac, bedlamite, frenetic, psychotic, psychopath, crackpot, crackbrain, loon *or* loony (*colloq.*), nut (*slang*), mental patient.

insane asylum, asylum, bedlam, booby hatch (*slang*), bughouse (*slang*), lunatic asylum, madhouse, nuthouse (*slang*), psychiatric ward, state hospital, crazy house (*slang*), mental institution (*or* hospital).

V. be (*or* become) insane, craze, madden, lose one's senses (mind, *or* reason), go mad, rave, become delirious, wander.

dement, derange, disorder, distemper, distract, frenzy, madden, craze, unbalance, unhinge, unsettle.

Adj. insane, psychotic, psychopathic, demented, disordered, deranged, lunatic, mad, manic, maniac, maniacal, delirious, mentally unbalanced (unhinged, *or* disordered), cachectic, distracted, distempered, frenzied, frenetic, pixilated; balmy (*colloq.*), bughouse (*slang*), crackbrained, cracked (*colloq.*), crackpot, crazy, crazed, daffy (*colloq.*), daft, distraught, irrational, loco (*colloq.*), loony (*colloq.*), moonstruck, *non compos mentis* (*L.*), nutty (*slang*), out of one's mind (*or* head), potty (*colloq.*), touched, touched in the head, unbalanced, unhinged, unsettled, unsound of mind, wild, zany.

See also DISEASE, NEUROSIS, PSYCHOTHERAPY.   *Antonyms*—See HEALTH, SANITY.

insatiable, *adj.* unappeasable, unquenchable (DISSATISFACTION).

inscribe, *v.* enter, list, register (LIST, BOOK); letter, stamp, mark (WRITTEN SYMBOL).

inscription, n. heading, caption, legend (TITLE).

insect, n. bug, mite, fly (ANIMAL).

insecure, adj. hazardous, perilous, precarious (DANGER); unconfident, unassured, diffident (UNCERTAINTY).

INSENSIBILITY—N. insensibility, blackout, coma, faint, syncope, swoon, trance, catalepsy, anesthesia, impassivity, insentience, analgesia (to pain), twilight sleep, suspended animation.

[lack or dullness of sensations] insensitivity, apathism, torpor, torpidity, stupor, stupefaction, petrification, daze, bemusement, hebetude, hypesthesia.

anesthetic, stupefacient, analgesic, narcotic; opium, ether, chloroform, chloral hydrate, morphine, morphia; nitrous oxide, scopolamine, laughing gas, cocaine, novocaine, knockout drops (slang).

V. render insensible, knock out, stun, knock unconscious, chloroform, etherize, anesthetize, narcotize (fig.).

numb, dull, blunt, obtund, benumb, deaden, daze, drug, besot, bemuse, hebetate, stupefy, torpify, petrify.

faint, swoon, black out, lose consciousness.

Adj. insensible, senseless, unconscious, comatose, knocked out, stunned, anesthetized, chloroformed, etherized, drugged, in a trance, cataleptic, impassive, insensate, insentient.

insensitive, apathic, dead, deadened, dull, dulled, numb, numbed, benumbed, torpid, stuporous, stupid, stupefied, narcous, petrified, dazed, besotted, bemused, hebetate, bloodless, hypesthesic.

See also DULLNESS, INACTION, INSENSITIVITY, PAINKILLER, PHARMACY, SLEEP. Antonyms—See FEELING, PAIN, SENSITIVENESS.

INSENSITIVITY—N. insensitivity, impassivity, impassibility, indifference, insentience, unimpressionability.

daze, narcosis, shock, stupefaction, stupor, torpor.

unemotionalism, phlegmatism, phlegm, apathy, bovinity, dispassion, lethargy, oscitancy, stoicism, stolidity.

undemonstrativeness, constraint, inhibition, reserve, restraint, selfrestraint, reticence, self-control.

detachment, disinterest, impartiality, objectivity.

V. be insensitive, not mind, not care, not be affected by; brutalize, callous, indurate.

daze, benumb, drug, narcotize, numb, shock, stupefy.

harden, caseharden, callous, indurate, sear, steel, toughen, inure, brutalize.

Adj. insensitive, unsensitive, impassive, impassible, indifferent, insensate, insensible, anesthetic (to), insentient, obtuse, blunt, blunted, dull; unresponsive, insusceptible, unimpressionable, unimpressible; thick-skinned, pachydermatous, imperceptive.

unaffected, unruffled, unimpressed, unexcited, unmoved, unstirred, untouched.

dazed, benumbed, drugged, narcotized, numb, numbed, shocked, stunned, stupefied, stuporous, stupid, torpid.

unemotional, phlegmatic, passionless, marble, apathetic, bovine, dispassionate, cool, lethargic, lowstrung, matter-of-fact, pragmatical, oscitant, stolid, stoical, bloodless, torpid.

cold, cool, frigid, frosty, icy, wintry, chill, chilly; lukewarm, tepid, nonchalant; offish, standoffish, standoff, aloof, remote, distant; uncordial, unaffectionate, unresponsive, unhearty, unfervent, spiritless, bloodless; mechanical, perfunctory.

undemonstrative, constrained, inhibited, reserved, restrained, selfrestrained, reticent, self-controlled, shy, unaffectionate, undemonstrative, uneffusive, unresponsive, unspontaneous.

unfeeling, feelingless, callous, calloused, hardened, casehardened, hard-bitten, hard-boiled (colloq.); coldhearted, cold-blooded, cold, hardhearted, heartless, unkind, soulless; rockhearted, rocky, stonehearted, stony, flinthearted, ironhearted.

detached, disinterested, dispassionate, impartial, indifferent, objective, unprejudiced.

merciless, pitiless, unmerciful, unpitying, bowelless; cutthroat (as competition, etc.), dispiteous, grim, inclement, implacable, inexorable, obdurate, relentless, remorseless, ruthless; unsparing, unrelenting, slashing, sanguinary, cruel, inhuman, inhumane, brutal, brutish.

unsympathetic, uncompassionate, aloof, alien.

See also CALMNESS, CONTROL, CRUELTY, DULLNESS, IMPARTIALITY, INACTION, INDIFFERENCE, INEXCITABILITY, INSENSIBILITY. Antonyms—

See EAGERNESS, ENTHUSIASM, FEELING, KINDNESS, PITY, PREJUDICE, SENSITIVENESS.

inseparable, adj. indivisible, indissoluble, secure (COMPLETENESS, JUNCTION).

INSERTION—N. insertion, implantation, introduction, interpolation, intercalation, embolism, interlineation, insinuation, injection, inoculation, infusion; immersion, submersion, submergence, dip, plunge.

insert, inset, inlay, panel, addition.

V. insert, introduce, put in (or into), inject, imbed, inlay, inweave, interject, interpolate, inset, intercalate, interline, interlineate, infuse, instill, infix, inoculate, impregnate, imbue.

graft, ingraft, bud, plant, implant.

obtrude, thrust in, stick in, ram in, stuff in, tuck in, press in, drive in, pierce; intrude, intervene.

immerse, merge, immerge, plunge, dip, duck, baptize; bathe, steep, soak; sink, bury.

See also ADDITION, INGRESS, INTERJACENCE. Antonyms—See EGRESS, ELIMINATION, EXTRACTION, REMOVAL.

inside, adj. internal, inner, inward (INTERIORITY).

insight, n. intuitiveness, penetration, perceptivity (INTUITION, UNDERSTANDING).

insignia, n. regalia, badges, decorations (ROD, INDICATION).

insignificant, adj. minute, minuscule, imperceptible (SMALLNESS); unimportant, immaterial, inconsequential (UNIMPORTANCE); contemptible, pitiful, despicable (CONTEMPT, PITY).

insincere, adj. backhanded, dishonest, disingenuous (PRETENSE).

insincerity, n. hypocrisy, pharisaism, Pecksniffery (PRETENSE).

insinuation, n. implication, overtone, innuendo (SUGGESTION); reference, allusion, advertence (TALK).

insipid, adj. tasteless, flat, flavorless (UNSAVORINESS); strengthless, characterless, namby-pamby (WEAKNESS).

insist, v. maintain, assert, contend (STATEMENT); require, request, importune (DEMAND).

insistent, adj. pressing, urgent, exigent (ATTENTION, DEMAND).

insolent, adj. cool, impudent, impertinent (DISCOURTESY); insulting, contumelious, outrageous (INSULT).

insolvent, adj. bankrupt, broke (colloq.), ruined (FAILURE, POVERTY).

insomnia, n. vigilance, vigil (WAKEFULNESS).

inspect, v. eye, watch, oversee (LOOKING); examine, check, audit (EXAMINATION).

inspiration, n. incentive, motivation, motive (DESIRE).

inspire, v. hearten, reassure, encourage (COURAGE); move, induce, prompt (MOTIVATION, CAUSATION); fire, inflame (EXCITEMENT).

inspiring, adj. affecting, impressive, moving (INFLUENCE).

install, v. establish, plant, set (PLACE, LOCATION); induct, inaugurate, invest (COMMISSION, BEGINNING).

installment, n. earnest, token payment, part payment (PAYMENT).

instance, n. example, case, illustration (COPY).

instant, n. flash, jiffy (colloq.), moment (EARLINESS, TIME).

instantaneous, adj. immediate, instant (EARLINESS).

instead of, in lieu of, in place of (COMMISSION).

instigate, v. incite, foment (MOTIVATION).

instill, v. implant, inculcate, indoctrinate (TEACHING); infuse, inoculate, impregnate (INSERTION).

instinctive, adj. reflexive, second-nature (WILL, HABIT); natural, inborn, innate (NATURALNESS, BIRTH).

institute, n. seminar, clinic (LEARNING); college, university, institution (SCHOOL).

institute, v. begin, start, found (BEGINNING).

institution, n. college, institute, university (SCHOOL); company, establishment, organization (BUSINESS); lunatic asylum, madhouse, mental hospital (INSANITY).

instruct, v. direct, order, charge (COMMAND, ADVICE); educate, school, coach (TEACHING).

instructive, adj. informative, newsy (INFORMATION); edifying, enlightening, illuminating (TEACHING).

instructor, n. educator, master, tutor (TEACHER).

INSTRUMENT—N. instrument, instrumentality, agency, vehicle, means, agent, medium, channel, machinery, wherewithal, material.

device, contrivance, apparatus, appliance, convenience, mechanism; tool, implement, utensil, machine, motor, engine; lathe, gin; automation, mechanical man, robot.

gear, equipment, plant, matériel (*F.*), outfit, appliances, contrivances, tools, tackle, rigging, harness, trappings, fittings, accouterments, appointments, furniture, upholstery, chattels, paraphernalia, belongings.

lever, crow, crowbar, jimmy, jack, tumbler, trigger; treadle, pedal, knob; arm, limb, wing, oar, sweep, paddle, helm, tiller, swingle, cant hook, handspike, marlinespike (*naut.*); pulley, tackle, purchase, crane, derrick.

wedge, chock, shim, quoin, keystone, cleat, block.

Adj. labor-saving, useful, mechanical, automatic; power-driven, motor-driven, electric.

See also AGENCY, AGENT, MEANS, MUSICAL INSTRUMENTS, USE.

insubordinate, *adj.* rebellious, perverse, contrary (DISOBEDIENCE).

insubstantial, *adj.* airy, slight, flimsy (WEAKNESS, SMALLNESS, THINNESS); imponderable, tenuous (NONEXISTENCE).

INSUFFICIENCY—*N.* insufficiency, deficiency, deficit, shortage, inadequacy, poverty, paucity, scantity, scarcity, dearth, lack; incompetence, imperfection, shortcoming.

dole, mite, pittance; trifle, modicum.

V. be insufficient, want, lack, need, require.

have insufficient, be lacking, be short, be shy; be in want, live from hand to mouth, eke out.

render insufficient, impoverish, beggar, stint, drain, ruin, pauperize, exhaust.

Adj. insufficient, deficient, inadequate, unequal, incommensurate, incompetent, lacking, scant, scanty, scarce, short, shy, skimpy, unample, infrequent, rare, wanting, lacking, incomplete, imperfect; ill-provided; short of, out of, destitute of, devoid of, bereft of, denuded of, dry, drained.

meager, thin, spare, slim, poor, slight, slender, bare, barren, stingy, stinted; starved, emaciated, undernourished, underfed, half-starved, famine-stricken, famished; without resources, in want.

See also ABSENCE, FEWNESS, HUNGER, IMPERFECTION, INCOMPLETENESS,

POVERTY. *Antonyms*—See MULTITUDE, SUFFICIENCY.

insulate, *v.* protect, cushion, seclude (PROTECTION); set apart, keep apart, isolate (DISJUNCTION, ISLAND).

INSULT—*N.* insult, affront, flout, slight, snub, slur, indignity, slap, taunt, Bronx cheer (*slang*), bird (*slang*), raspberry (*slang*), brickbat, despite, contumely, insolence, epithet, innuendo; dishonor, offense, outrage.

V. insult, affront, disoblige, flout, dishonor, outrage, offend, slight, snub, slur, pan (*slang*).

jeer at, hoot, laugh at, mock, razz (*slang*).

Adj. insulting, insolent, contumelious, despiteful, offensive, disobliging, outrageous; *infra dignitatem* (*L.*), infra dig.

See also CONTEMPT, DISCOURTESY, DISRESPECT, LAUGHTER, OFFENSE, RIDICULE. *Antonyms*—See COURTESY, RESPECT.

insuperable, *adj.* insurmountable, inaccessible, unattainable (IMPOSSIBILITY); undefeatable, unbeatable, unconquerable (SUCCESS).

insurance, *n.* assurance, guarantee, warranty (CERTAINTY).

insurgent, *adj.* rebellious, insubordinate, insurrectionary (DISOBEDIENCE).

insurmountable, *adj.* insuperable, inaccessible, unattainable (IMPOSSIBILITY); unmasterable, impregnable, ineluctable (SUCCESS).

insurrection, *n.* rebellion, revolt, mutiny (DISOBEDIENCE).

intact, *adj.* whole, indiscrete, uncut (COMPLETENESS); unharmed, uninjured, scatheless (HEALTH).

INTAKE—*N.* intake, absorption, assimilation, suction, resorption; acceptance, admission, reception, capillarity.

V. take in, absorb, assimilate, soak up, sponge, sop up, suck, swallow, devour, imbibe, resorb; accept, admit, receive.

bring in, track in, carry in, adhibit, import, superinduce.

Adj. absorbent, absorptive, spongy, suctorial, bibulous, porous, hygroscopic; resorbent, resorptive, siccative.

See also ACCEPTANCE, INGRESS, RECEIVING, TAKING, TRACTION. *Anto-*

nyms—See EGRESS, ELIMINATION, EXCRETION, GIVING, REMOVAL.

---

intangible, *adj.* impalpable, abstract, unsubstantial (MYSTERY, SPIRITUALITY).

integer, *n.* cipher, digit, unit (NUMBER, UNITY).

integrity, *n.* probity, rectitude, honor (HONESTY, RIGHT); entirety, totality, wholeness (COMPLETENESS).

INTELLECT—*N.* intellect, mind, mental faculties, intellectuality, brains, intelligence, cerebration, mentality, wits, mother wit, psyche.

brain, encephalon, cerebellum, cerebrum, gray matter, ganglion, cortex, cerebral cortex, white matter, alba; convolutions, gyri, fissures, sulci, pons; medulla oblongata.

Adj. **intellectual,** mental, phrenic, psychic, psychological; conscious, subconscious, subliminal, unconscious, subjective.

See also IDEA, IMAGINATION, INTELLIGENCE, LEARNING, PSYCHOTHERAPY, THOUGHT, WISDOM. *Antonyms* —See STUPIDITY.

INTELLIGENCE—*N.* intelligence, sense, wit, mental ability, aptitude, mental agility, acuity, acumen, discernment, penetration, perception, percipience, perspicacity, subtlety, trenchancy; precocity, coruscation, brilliance, luminosity; intelligence quotient, I.Q.

genius, prodigy, brain (*slang*), intellect, child prodigy.

intellectual, highbrow (*colloq.*), doubledome (*slang*), egghead (*slang*), longhair (*slang*), Brahman, literatus.

intellectual class, intelligentsia, clerisy, literati (*pl.*).

intelligence test, alpha test, beta test, Binet test, Binet-Simon test, Stanford-Binet test.

V. **be intelligent,** understand, comprehend, see at a glance, discern, discriminate, penetrate, see through, seize, apprehend, follow; have one's wits about one, scintillate, be brilliant, coruscate.

Adj. **intelligent,** acute, agile, alert, apt, astucious, astute, brainy, bright, brilliant, clever, discerning, incisive, intellectual, keen, keen-minded, knowledgeable, luminous, nimble, penetrating, penetrative, perceptive, percipient, perspicacious, quick-witted, rational, sagacious, sensible, sharp, sharp-witted, shrewd, smart, subtle, trenchant, wide-awake.

See also CLEVERNESS, INTELLECT, LEARNING, UNDERSTANDING, WISDOM. *Antonyms*—See STUPIDITY.

---

intelligible, *adj.* understandable, clear, unambiguous (UNDERSTANDING, CLARITY).

INTEMPERANCE—*N.* intemperance, excess, immoderation, excessiveness, extravagance, unrestraint.

self-indulgence, self-gratification, free living, dissipation, high living, indulgence, prodigalism, dissoluteness, license, sensuality, animalism, debauchery.

V. **be intemperate,** indulge, exceed; run riot, sow one's wild oats, paint the town red (*colloq.*).

Adj. **intemperate,** excessive, immoderate, unbridled, unrestrained, uncurbed, inordinate, extravagant, ungovernable.

self-indulgent, self-gratifying, wild, fast, dissolute, dissipated, profligate.

sensual, voluptuous, carnal, fleshly, gross, animal.

See also DRUNKENNESS, EXTREMENESS, FREEDOM, PLEASURE. *Antonyms* —See MODERATENESS, SOBRIETY.

---

intend, *v.* determine, resolve, purpose (PLAN, PURPOSE); reserve, set aside (DESTINY).

intended, *n.* betrothed, fiancé (BETROTHAL).

intense, *adj.* strong, concentrated, profound (STRENGTH, EXTREMENESS); steady, steadfast, unwavering (PURPOSE).

intensify, *v.* strengthen, enhance, augment (HEIGHT, STRENGTH); aggravate, exaggerate (SOBRIETY).

intensity, *n.* force, might, energy, vigor (STRENGTH); power, volume, sonority (LOUDNESS).

intensive, *adj.* complete, radical, thorough (COMPLETENESS).

intent, *adj.* firm, bent, bound (PURPOSE); absorbed, rapt, engrossed (THOUGHT).

intention, *n.* aim, intent, design (PLAN, PURPOSE).

intentional, *adj.* deliberate, purposeful, aforethought (PURPOSE).

inter, *v.* bury, entomb, inhume, ensepulcher (BURIAL).

intercede, *v.* mediate, step in, negotiate (MEDIATION).

interchange, *v.* swap, switch, change (EXCHANGE, SUBSTITUTION).

intercourse, *n.* dealings, transactions, negotiations (BUSINESS); give-and-take, exchange, interchange (EXCHANGE); relations, sexual act (SEX).

INTERESTINGNESS—*N.* interestingness, interest, appeal, fascination, piquancy, color, glamour, succulence, zest, salt, spice, savor.

V. **interest,** be interesting to, appeal to, fascinate, enthrall, absorb, pique, entertain; concern; become interested, perk up, sit up.

make interesting, season, flavor, spice, salt, savor; romanticize, glamorize, dramatize.

Adj. **interesting,** racy, spicy, breezy, salty; succulent, piquant, appealing, zestful, glamorous, colorful, picturesque; absorbing, enthralling, engrossing, fascinating, entertaining, ageless, dateless.

See also AMUSEMENT, ATTENTION, ATTRACTION, RIGHT. *Antonyms*—See BOREDOM, DULLNESS, INATTENTION.

---

interfere, *v.* meddle, butt in, intervene (INTERJACENCE); interrupt, suspend, intermit (CESSATION).

interfere with, *v.* hinder, hamper, impede (HINDRANCE).

interim, *n.* pause, interlude, intermission (INTERVAL).

INTERIORITY—*N.* interiority, internality, intrinsicality; interior, bosom, inside, inward, innermost; midst, center, core, pulp, heart, pith, marrow, substance, soul.

insides, innermost recesses, bowels, penetralia (*pl.*).

inland, inlands, midlands, upcountry, interior, backwoods, hinterland, hinterlands.

Adj. **interior,** internal, inner, inside, inward, inmost, innermost, intimate, intrinsic, within; endogenous, autogenous.

innate, inborn, inbred, intrinsic, inherent, deep-seated, ingrained, implanted, inwrought, inwoven, infixed, indwelling, immanent.

inland, midland, upcountry, interior; hinterland, backwoods; internal, domestic, intramural, intestine, home, intraterritorial.

See also CENTER, BELLY, DEPTH, INSERTION, INTERJACENCE. *Antonyms* —See EXTERIORITY.

INTERJACENCE—*N.* interjacence, interposition, interlocation, intercurrence, intermediation, interpenetration.

interference, intrusion, obtrusion, intervention, opposition.

interferer, busybody, meddler, tamperer, buttinsky (*slang*), marplot, interventionist; interloper, intruder, obtruder, trespasser.

intermediary, go-between, interagent, middleman, medium.

partition, septum (*tech.*), diaphragm, midriff; panel, bulkhead, wall, party wall.

V. **permeate,** penetrate, interpenetrate, pervade, interfuse.

interject, interpose, introduce, insert, intercalate, implant, insinuate, inject, interpolate, interjaculate, throw in, force in, lug in, parenthesize, interlard, intersperse, infiltrate, ingrain, infuse; dovetail, mortise, splice.

interfere, meddle, intermeddle, interrupt, break in, butt in, intervene, horn in (*slang*), tamper with; intrude, obtrude; clash, conflict, get (*or* stand) in the way.

Adj. **interjacent,** intervening, interjectional, parenthetical, episodic; medial, mesial (*zool.*), intermediate, mean, middle, intermediary, intrusive.

interfering, officious, meddlesome, pragmatic, interventional.

Adv., phrases, prep. **between,** at intervals, in the midst, betwixt and between (*colloq.*), in the thick of, midway, halfway.

See also CUTTING, ENCROACHMENT, HINDRANCE, INSERTION. *Antonyms*— See ENVIRONMENT, EXTERIORITY, SURFACE.

---

interject, *v.* interpose, introduce, insert, interpolate (INTERJACENCE, INSERTION).

interjection, *n.* exclamation, expletive (WORD).

interloper, *n.* intruder, obtruder, trespasser (INTERJACENCE).

interlude, *n.* recess, intermission, interim (TIME, INTERVAL, REST).

intermarriage, *n.* miscegenation, mixed marriage (MARRIAGE).

intermediary, *n.* negotiator, go-between, middleman (INTERJACENCE, MEDIATION).

intermediate, *adj.* mean, medium, middle (MID-COURSE).

interminable, *adj.* endless, incessant (ENDLESSNESS).

intermission, *n.* interlude, interim, recess (INTERVAL, REST, TIME).

internal, *adj.* inner, inside, domestic (INTERIORITY).

interpose, *v.* interject, introduce, insert, inject (INTERJACENCE, INSERTION).

interpret, *v.* explain, define, construe (EXPLANATION).

interrogate, *v.* question, pump, grill (INQUIRY).

interrupt, *v.* break in, butt in (INTERJACENCE); punctuate, break, divide (CESSATION).

interruption, *n.* pause, hitch, cessation, break (CESSATION); interlude, recess, intermission (TIME).

intersect, *v.* cross, bisect, cut across, decussate, traverse (CROSSING).

intersection, *n.* crossroad, crossway, crosswalk (PASSAGE, CROSSING).

interval, *v.* space, period, term (INTERVAL); breathing spell, intermission, interlude (REST); interim, meantime, while (TIME).

INTERVAL—N. [*intervening time*] interval, space, period, spell, term, season, pause, interlude, interim, intermission, parenthesis, meantime, interregnum, recess, interruption.

[*intervening space*] interspace, space, interstice, gap, break, hiatus, lacuna, caesura, separation, division; void, vacancy, vacuum.

V. interval, space, dispart, separate, set at intervals.

See also ABSENCE, DEGREE, DISCONTINUITY, DISJUNCTION, INTERJACENCE, OPENING, SPACE, TIME. *Antonyms*—See TOUCH.

---

intervene, *v.* interrupt, break in, interfere, meddle (INTERJACENCE); intrude, obtrude (ARRIVAL).

intervention, *n.* mediation, intercession (AGENCY); interference, intrusion, obtrusion (INTERJACENCE).

interview, *n.* conference, parley, audience (ADVICE, LISTENING).

interview, *v.* question, interrogate, examine (INQUIRY).

intestines, *n.* bowels, gut, entrails (BELLY).

intimacy, *n.* communion, affinity (RELATIONSHIP); friendship, familiarity (FRIENDLINESS); sexual relations, fornication (SEX).

intimate, *adj.* familiar, close, bosom (NEARNESS, FRIENDLINESS); inmost, innermost, intrinsic (INTERIORITY).

intimate, *v.* hint at, imply, insinuate (HINT, SUGGESTION).

intimidate, *v.* daunt, cow, overawe (FEAR).

intolerant, *adj.* unfair, jaundiced, bigoted (PREJUDICE).

intonation, *n.* inflection, delivery, modulation (VOICE).

intoxicated, *adj.* drunk, beside oneself, delirious (EXCITEMENT);

high (*colloq.*), inebriated, tipsy (DRUNKENNESS).

intrepid, *adj.* fearless, heroic, lion-hearted (COURAGE).

intricate, *adj.* complex, complicated, entangled (MYSTERY, DIFFICULTY); mazy, labyrinthine, involved (WINDING).

intrigue, *n.* plot, scheme, machination (PLAN); love affair, romance, flirtation (LOVE); liaison, affair (SEX).

intrigue, *v.* attract, enchant, captivate (ATTRACTION); plot, scheme, maneuver (PLAN).

intrinsic, *adj.* innate, inborn, inbred (INTERIORITY); constitutive, essential, material (PART); appropriate, particular, peculiar (OWNERSHIP).

introduce, *v.* inject, interpose, insert (INTERJACENCE, INSERTION); inaugurate, initiate, present (BEGINNING).

introduction, *n.* prelude, preface, foreword (BEGINNING).

introspective, *adj.* self-absorbed, introverted, autistic (SELFISHNESS).

introverted, *adj.* self-absorbed, autistic, introspective (SELFISHNESS).

intrude, *v.* obtrude, interlope, intervene (ARRIVAL); transgress, overstep, go beyond (ENCROACHMENT).

intruder, *n.* interloper, obtruder, trespasser (INTERJACENCE).

INTUITION—N. intuition, second sight, clairvoyance, spiritual insight, perception, insight, penetration, perceptivity, divination, presentiment, inspiration.

Adj. intuitive, instinctive, intuitional, inspirational, perceptive, innate.

See also KNOWLEDGE, UNDERSTANDING. *Antonyms*—See REASONING.

---

inundate, *v.* flood, deluge, engulf (WATER).

inure, *v.* toughen, brutalize, brutify (INSENSITIVITY); habituate, accustom (HABIT).

invade, *v.* break in, breach, raid (INGRESS); storm, foray, maraud (ATTACK).

invalid, *adj.* inoperative, nugatory, void (INEFFECTIVENESS).

invalid, *n.* shut-in, valetudinarian, patient (DISEASE).

invaluable, *adj.* valuable, priceless, worth-while (VALUE); useful, serviceable, helpful (USE).

invariable, *adj.* unchangeable, immutable, unvarying (UNIFORMITY).

invasion, *n.* raid, incursion, irruption (INGRESS).

invective, *n.* scurrility, vituperation, epithets (MALEDICTION).

inveigle, *v.* wheedle, blandish, seduce (PERSUASION); lead on, decoy (MISTEACHING).

invent, *v.* coin, hatch, improvise (PRODUCTION); fabricate, pretend, make up (UNREALITY); lie, tell a lie (FALSEHOOD).

inventive, *adj.* imaginative, original, creative (IMAGINATION); ingenious, adroit, forgetive (PRODUCTION).

invert, *v.* reverse, upend, overturn (TURNING).

invest, *v.* empower, qualify, vest (POWER); endow, inform, vest in (GIVING).

investigate, *v.* inquire, inquisite, pry into (INQUIRY); explore, research (SEARCH).

investigation, *n.* inquiry, exploration, research (SEARCH); examination, quiz, analysis (TEST).

invigorate, *v.* exhilarate, inspirit, quicken (LIFE); strengthen, vivify, vitalize (STRENGTH).

invincible, *adj.* irresistible, unconquerable, indomitable (STRENGTH, SUCCESS).

INVISIBILITY—*N.* invisibility, imperceptibility, concealment, obliteration.

V. be invisible, hide, lurk, escape notice.

screen, veil, cloud, blind, mask, conceal.

Adj. invisible, imperceptible, undiscernible, unperceivable, indistinguishable, unevident, unapparent, unnoticeable; microscopic, submicroscopic; hidden, concealed, masked, ulterior, screened, veiled; out of sight, not in sight, unseen, lost to view, perdu, obliterated.

indistinct, dim, faint, inconspicuous, tenuous, unobvious, unpronounced; obscure, shadowy, indefinite, undefined, ill-defined, blurred, misty, hazy, feeble, nebulous.

See also BLINDNESS, CONCEALMENT, DARKNESS. *Antonyms*—See VISIBILITY.

invite, *v.* ask, beckon (SUMMONS); attract, appeal to, tempt (ATTRACTION); urge, encourage, countenance (URGING).

invoice, *n.* bill, statement, manifest (DEBT).

invoke, *v.* call forth, evoke, conjure up (SUMMONS); pray, supplicate (WORSHIP).

involuntary, *adj.* unwilled, reflex, reflexive (WILL); uncalculated, unconscious, unintentional (PURPOSELESSNESS); grudging, begrudging, forced (UNWILLINGNESS).

involve, *v.* entail, comprise, consist of (INCLUSION, MAKE-UP); complicate, tangle, entangle (MYSTERY, INDIRECTNESS).

involved, *adj.* complex, intricate, ramified (MYSTERY, DIFFICULTY); winding, mazy (WINDING).

invulnerable, *adj.* impregnable, inviolable, unassailable (PROTECTION).

iota, *n.* gram, infinitesimal, jot (SMALLNESS).

irascible, *adj.* irritable, choleric, liverish (BAD TEMPER, ANGER).

irate, *adj.* ireful, choleric, incensed (ANGER).

iridescent, *adj.* opalescent, prismatic, nacreous (VARIEGATION, CHANGEABLENESS); many-colored, chatoyant (COLOR).

irk, *v.* annoy, provoke, vex (ANNOYANCE).

iron, *adj.* ironlike, steel, steely (STRENGTH); ferric, ferrous (METAL).

iron, *n.* wrought iron, cast iron, pig (METAL); mangle, flatiron, sadiron (SMOOTHNESS, PRESSURE).

irony, *n.* sarcasm, satire, sardonicism (AMBIGUITY, RIDICULE).

irrational, *adj.* nonsensical, senseless, incoherent (UNREASONABLENESS); distraught, delirious (INSANITY).

irrefutable, *adj.* unimpeachable, unquestionable, undeniable (TRUTH).

IRREGULARITY—*N.* irregularity, aberration, abnormality, abnormity, singularity, anomaly.

Adj. irregular, uncertain, unpunctual, capricious, fitful, flickering, spasmodic, variable, unsettled, mutable, changeable, erratic, uneven, unmethodical, unsystematic, confused, disordered, disarranged, unsymmetrical, asymmetrical; unnatural, abnormal, anomalous, unconformable, exceptional, illegitimate, unusual, singular, odd.

[*of surfaces*] uneven, rough, bumpy, unlevel, humpy, jagged, hummocky, hilly, rugged, lumpy, broken; holey, pitted.

See also CHANGEABLENESS, DEFORMITY, DISCONTINUITY, INEQUALITY, ROUGHNESS, UNUSUALNESS, VARIEGATION. *Antonyms*—See RHYTHM, RULE, UNIFORMITY.

IRRELATION—*N.* irrelation, dissociation, disconnection, disjunction, irrelevance, immateriality.

foreigner, stranger, outlander, outsider, alien, immigrant, exotic, newcomer.

Adj. **irrelative**, unrelated, unallied, independent, separate, disconnected, unconnected.

irrelevant, extraneous, immaterial, impertinent, inapplicable, inapposite, inappurtenant, inapropos, inconsequential, non-germane, pointless, remote, unapt, unconnected.

foreign, alien, strange, remote, exotic, outland, outside, peregrine; outlandish, barbaric, barbarian.

incidental, casual, chance, accidental, coincidental, fortuitous, parenthetical.

See also CHANCE, DIFFERENCE, DISAGREEMENT, DISJUNCTION, IMPROPERNESS. *Antonyms*—See PERTINENCE, RELATIONSHIP.

---

irrelevant, *adj.* extraneous, immaterial, impertinent (IRRELATION).

IRRELIGION—*N.* irreligion, impiety, irreligionism, irreverence, athleism, heathenism, infidelity, paganism, unchristianity.

[*hypocritical or affected religiousness*] religionism, pharisaism, phariseeism, pietism, piety, religiosity, sanctimony, lip service; religionist, pharisee.

skepticism, doubt, unbelief, disbelief, agnosticism, freethinking.

irreligionist, atheist, heathen, infidel, pagan, paganist, paynim, unchristian.

skeptic, unbeliever, heretic, freethinker, rationalist, materialist, positivist, Comtist, agnostic, Pyrrhonist, nullifidian.

V. **be irreligious**, doubt, disbelieve, skepticize, scoff, question, lack faith.

profane, desecrate, violate, contaminate, defile, pollute, blaspheme; commit sacrilege.

Adj. **irreligious**, undevout, godless, graceless, ungodly, unholy, irreverent, profane, impious, blasphemous; atheistic, heathen, infidel, pagan, unchristian, uncircumcized.

religionistic, pharisaical, pietistic, pious, religionist, sanctimonious, self-righteous.

skeptical, freethinking, agnostic, Pyrrhonian, positivistic, materialistic, unbelieving, unconverted, faithless, nullifidian, antichristian.

worldly, mundane, earthly, carnal, worldly-minded, unspiritual; secular, temporal.

See also HETERODOXY, LAITY, UNBELIEVINGNESS. *Antonyms*—See BELIEF, RELIGIOUSNESS, SACREDNESS, SPIRITUALITY.

---

irreparable, *adj.* irrecoverable, irretrievable, irreclaimable (HOPELESSNESS).

irreproachable, *adj.* inculpable, irreprehensible, reproachless (INNOCENCE).

irresistible, *adj.* invincible, unconquerable, indomitable (STRENGTH).

IRRESOLUTION—*N.* irresolution, indecision, indetermination, instability, uncertainty, caprice, vacillation, fluctuation.

waverer, trimmer, timeserver, opportunist, turncoat, shilly-shallier; shuttlecock; butterfly.

V. **be irresolute**, dillydally, hover, shilly-shally, hem and haw, debate, balance.

waver, vacillate, fluctuate, change, alternate, shuffle, straddle, palter, shirk, trim; blow hot and cold, back and fill.

Adj. **irresolute**, wavering, undecided, undetermined, uncertain, fickle, unreliable, halfhearted, capricious, inconstant, vacillating, variable, changeful, changeable, mutable, unstable, unsteady.

See also CAPRICE, CHANGE, CHANGEABLENESS, UNCERTAINTY, UNSTEADINESS. *Antonyms*—See CERTAINTY, DECISION, STABILITY.

---

irreverent, *adj.* disrespectful, insolent, impudent (DISRESPECT); ungodly, unholy (IRRELIGION).

irrevocable, *adj.* irreparable, irreclaimable, irredeemable (HOPELESSNESS).

irritable, *adj.* irascible, cranky, choleric (ANGER, BAD TEMPER).

irritate, *v.* annoy, vex, irk (ANNOYANCE); peeve (*colloq.*), exasperate, provoke (BAD TEMPER, ANGER); sensitize, sharpen (SENSITIVENESS).

ISLAND—*N.* island, cay, isle, islet, key, atoll; archipelago.

V. **island**, insulate, isolate; isle, enisle.

Adj. **insular**, island, seagirt (*chiefly poetic*), isolated.

See also LAND.

---

isolate, *v.* segregate, quarantine, sequester (SECLUSION, DISJUNCTION, ISLAND).

issue, *n.* edition, printing, impression (PUBLICATION); problem, question (TOPIC); children, progeny, offspring (CHILD); consequence, product, fruit (RESULT).

issue, *v.* flow, emanate, spurt (DEPARTURE, RIVER); send, dispatch, transmit (SENDING); bring out, circulate (PUBLICATION).

isthmus, *n.* neck, spit, tongue (LAND).

itch, *n.* pruritus, prurigo, scabies (SKIN); urge, impulse, motive (DESIRE).

itch, *v.* crawl, prickle, tingle (SENSITIVENESS, ITCHING); be impatient, chafe (EXPECTATION).

ITCHING—*N.* itching, formication (*med.*), paresthesia (*med.*).

  V. **itch,** tingle, creep, thrill, sting; prick, prickle; tickle, titillate.

  Adj. **itchy,** itching, crawly, creepy, tingling; formicative, pruriginous, pruritic (*med.*); ticklish, tickly.

  See also EXCITEMENT, SENSITIVENESS, SKIN. *Antonyms*—See INSENSIBILITY.

item, *n.* particular, minor point, specific (DETAIL); news, bulletin, dispatch (PUBLICATION); thing, object, article (MATERIALITY).

itemize, *v.* particularize, individualize, specify (DETAIL); recite, recount, relate (TALK).

itinerant, *adj.* afoot, on foot, peripatetic (WALKING).

itinerary, *n.* route, way, run (PASSAGE).

J

jab, *v.* poke, push, bump (PROPULSION).

jabber, *v.* jargon, gab, gabble (TALK).

jacket, *n.* coatee, jerkin, sack coat (COAT); wrapping, wrapper, envelope (COVERING).

jade, *n.* hussy, shrew, wench (FEMALE); drab, harlot, Jezebel (SEX); nag, hack, Rosinante (HORSE).

jaded, *adj.* blasé (*F.*), sick of, surfeited (SATISFACTION).

jag, *n.* point, spike, pike (SHARPNESS); orgy, saturnalia (PLEASURE).

jail, *n.* prison, penitentiary, reformatory (IMPRISONMENT).

jail, *v.* imprison, incarcerate, lock up (IMPRISONMENT).

jalopy (*slang*), *n.* hot rod (*slang*), flivver (*slang*), auto (VEHICLE).

jam, *n.* conserves, preserves, jelly (SEMILIQUIDITY); crowd, mob, crush (MULTITUDE); fix, pickle, hot water (*colloq.*) (DIFFICULTY).

janitor, *n.* doorkeeper, gatekeeper, porter (INGRESS).

Japanese, *n.* Nipponese, Issei, Nisei (MANKIND).

jar, *n.* amphora, beaker, urn (CONTAINER); jolt, jounce, concussion (SHAKE).

jar, *v.* jog, jounce, rock (SHAKE); offend, outrage, shock (UNPLEASANTNESS); grate, clash, grind (HARSH SOUND).

jargon, *n.* lingo, idiom, patois (LANGUAGE).

jaunt, *n.* travel, trip, journey (TRAVELING); stroll, tramp, ramble (WANDERING).

javelin, *n.* shaft, spear, lance (CUTTING).

jaw, *n.* jowl, maxilla (HEAD).

jaw (*colloq.*), *v* chatter, clack, jabber (TALK).

jazz, *n.* syncopation, ragtime, jive (MUSIC).

jealous, *adj.* envious, jaundiced, grudging (DISSATISFACTION).

jeer, *v.* deride, mock, hoot (RIDICULE, INSULT).

jell, *v.* congeal, gelatinate, thicken, jelly (SEMILIQUIDITY, THICKNESS).

jeopardy, *n.* hazard, insecurity, peril (DANGER).

jerk, *v.* jiggle, wiggle, bob (SUDDENNESS, NERVOUSNESS); yank (*colloq.*), pull (TRACTION).

jerky, *adj.* joggly, jolty, jouncy (SHAKE).

jest, *n.* joke, gag (*colloq.*), jape (WITTINESS); laughingstock, butt, derision (LAUGHTER).

jest, *v.* fool, jape, kid (*slang*), spoof (WITTINESS).

jester, *n.* clown, buffoon, merryandrew (FOLLY); japer, larker, prankster (WITTINESS).

Jesus, *n.* Jesus Christ, the Saviour, the Nazarene (CHRIST).

jet, *adj.* raven, pitch-black (BLACKNESS).

jet, *v.* pour, spout, spurt (RIVER).

jetty, *n.* wharf, dock, quay (BREAKWATER).

Jew, *n.* Judaist, Israelite, Hebrew (RELIGION).

JEWELRY—*N.* jewelry, bijouterie; jewel, bijou, gem, stone, precious stone, birthstone, brilliant, baguette, semiprecious stone; bead, rhinestone, trinket, bauble; stickpin, tiepin, pin, brooch, chatelaine; cameo, intaglio.

necklace, necklet, choker, beads, rosary, pearls, crystals, torque, lavaliere, locket, pendant, chain.

bracelet, wristlet, armlet, bangle, anklet, circlet.

ring, circlet, circle, band, wedding ring, wedding band, engagement ring, solitaire, diamond ring; earring, pendant.

V. jewel, bejewel, enchase, encrust, gem, set, diamond, pearl.

Adj. diamond, adamantine, diamantiferous.

pearl, pearly, nacreous, mother-of-pearl.

See also METAL, ORNAMENT, ROCK.

Jezebel, *n.* drab, harlot, jade (SEX).

jiffy, (*colloq.*), *n.* twinkling, flash, trice (EARLINESS, TIME).

jiggle, *v.* shimmer, wiggle, jog (SHAKE); jerk, twitch (SUDDENNESS, NERVOUSNESS).

Jim Crow, *n.* apartheid (*South Africa*), negrophobia, segregation (SECLUSION, PREJUDICE).

jingle, *v.* tinkle, clink, ring (BELL, RESONANCE).

jingoist, *n.* jingo, militarist, warmonger (FIGHTER); flag waver, ultranationalist, spread-eagleist (PATRIOTISM).

jinx, *n.* hex, evil eye, whammy (MISFORTUNE).

jittery, (*colloq.*), *adj.* nervous, jumpy, creepy (NERVOUSNESS).

job, *n.* task, chore, stint (WORK); position, place, post (SITUATION).

jobber, *n.* middleman, wholesaler (SALE).

jocular, *adj.* frolicsome, gleeful, hilarious (MERRIMENT); witty, humorous, joking (WITTINESS).

jog, *v.* jounce, rock, jar (SHAKE); push, press, prod (PROPULSION).

join, *v.* unite, associate, connect (JUNCTION, UNITY, COMBINATION, MIXTURE); adjoin, abut, meet (TOUCH); couple, mate, wed (MARRIAGE).

joint, *adj.* joined, united, hand in hand (JUNCTION); shared, collective, mutual (CO-OPERATION).

jointly, *adv.* unitedly, together, conjointly (UNITY, JUNCTION).

joke, *n.* jest, gag (*colloq.*), jape (WITTINESS); jestingstock, laughingstock (LAUGHTER); trick, frolic, lark (MISCHIEF).

joke, *v.* banter, chaff, josh (WITTINESS).

jolly, *adj.* hilarious, jocund, jovial (CHEERFULNESS, MERRIMENT).

jolly, *v.* chaff, rally, make fun of (RIDICULE).

jolt, *n.* jar, jounce, concussion (SHAKE); bombshell, shock, thunderbolt (SURPRISE).

josh, *v.* joke, banter, chaff (WITTINESS); guy (*colloq.*), banter, rally (RIDICULE, TEASING).

jostle, *v.* push, shove, jab (PROPULSION).

jot, *n.* gram, infinitesimal, iota (SMALLNESS).

jot down, *v.* note, put down, set down (WRITING).

jounce, *v.* jog, rock, jar (SHAKE).

journal, *n.* daybook, ledger (ACCOUNTS); diary, annals, minutes (TIME MEASUREMENT, RECORD); periodical, magazine (PUBLICATION).

journalist, *n.* editor, newsman (PUBLICATION).

journey, *n.* travel, trip, tour (TRAVELING).

journey, *v.* tour, jaunt, peregrinate, circuit (TRAVELING).

joust, *n.* tournament, tourney, tilt (FIGHTING).

jovial, *adj.* merry, jocund, jolly (MERRIMENT); convivial, festive, festal (SOCIALITY); companionable, congenial, cordial (FRIENDLINESS).

jowl, *n.* jaw, maxilla (HEAD); dewlap, wattle (SKIN).

joy, *n.* rapture, ravishment, jubilance (HAPPINESS); enchantment, delight (PLEASURE).

joyful, *adj.* joyous, overjoyed, rapturous (HAPPINESS); pleasurable, enjoyable (PLEASURE).

jubilant, *adj.* exultant, gleeful, gleesome (HAPPINESS).

JUDGE—*N.* judge, jurist, justice, justice of the peace, justiciary, magistrate, police justice, police magistrate, surrogate, chancellor, chief justice; the bench, the court, his honor, his lordship (*Brit.*); [*collectively*] judiciary, judicature, magistracy, magistrature.

arbitrator, arbiter, adjudicator, judicator, umpire, referee, czar, moderator.

connoisseur, *arbiter elegantiae* or *arbiter elegantiarum* (*L.*), authority, expert; critic, reviewer; gourmet, epicure.

jury, panel, blue-ribbon jury, coroner's jury, grand jury, petty jury, trial jury.

juror, juryman, venireman, talesman; grand juror, petty juror; panel, tales (*pl.*).

V. **judge**, adjudicate, decide, settle, adjudge, try, arbitrate, referee, umpire; decree, pronounce. rule, rule on; sentence, award, find; try a case, sit in judgment, pronounce judgment.

appraise, estimate, rate, assess, rank, value, size up (*colloq.*).

[*to exercise the judgment*] **distinguish**, discern, discriminate, determine, ascertain, decide, resolve, form an opinion; come to (*or* arrive at) a conclusion.

impanel, empanel, call for jury duty.

Adj. **juridical**, justiciary, magisterial, magistratic, judicial, arbitrative, adjudicative; critical, judicative, judgmental.

See also COURT OF LAW, DECISION, DIFFERENTIATION, JUDGMENT, LAWSUIT, VALUE, WISDOM.

JUDGMENT—N. judgment, conclusion, decision, opinion, determination; finding, award, verdict, sentence, decree; arbitration, adjudication, arbitrament; prejudgment, misjudgment.

[*standard of judgment*] **criterion**, yardstick, canon, touchstone, measure, norm, standard; barometer, gauge.

critique, criticism, review, notice, report.

estimate, appraisal, appraisement, valuation, assessment.

discernment, discrimination, perspicacity, astuteness, taste, acumen.

See also CHOICE, DECISION, DIFFERENTIATION, JUDGE, OPINION, VALUE, WISDOM. *Antonyms*—See MISINTERPRETATION.

---

judicial, *adj.* forensic, judiciary, juridic (COURT OF LAW).

judicious, *adj.* prudent, discreet, politic (WISDOM).

jug, *n.* jar, vase, urn (CONTAINER); lockup, cooler (*colloq.*), jail (IMPRISONMENT).

juggler, *n.* sleight-of-hand artist, prestidigitator (MAGIC).

juice, *n.* essence, abstract, distillation (EXTRACTION); sap, latex, lymph (LIQUID); current, flow, electricity (LIGHT).

juicy, *adj.* succulent, luscious, mellow (LIQUID).

jumble, *n.* medley, hodgepodge, mélange (MIXTURE); muddle, snarl, tangle (CONFUSION); derangement, litter, clutter (UNTIDINESS).

JUMP—N. jump, leap, spring, bound, hop, skip, buck, canter, bob, gambade, somersault, upspring, capriole, saltation, vault, hurdle.

V. **jump**, leap, spring, bound, hop, lollop, skip, trip, buck, canter, curvet, somersault; hurdle, clear, jump over, vault; parachute, hit the silk (*slang*), bail out.

caper, frisk, cavort, dance, gambol, prance, frolic, romp.

rebound, recoil, carom, ricochet, bounce, jounce, bob.

Adj. **jumping**, saltant, salient, transilient (*fig.*), saltatory.

jumpy, frisky, skittish; resilient, buoyant, elastic, springy, rubbery, spongy.

See also ASCENT, NERVOUSNESS. *Antonyms*—CALMNESS, INELASTICITY.

---

jumpy, *adj.* frisky, skittish (JUMP); jittery (*colloq.*), creepy (NERVOUSNESS).

JUNCTION—N. junction, union, connection, combination, conjugation, concatenation, confluence, meeting, conjunction, coherence, attachment, annexation, assemblage, reunion; concourse, consolidation, alliance, coalition.

joint, juncture, articulation, pivot, hinge, mortise, miter, dovetail, splice, weld, knee, elbow, knot, node (*bot.*), suture (*anat.*), closure, seam, gore, gusset; link, bond.

V. **join**, unite, connect, associate, piece, coalesce, blend, merge, mix, mingle, combine, embody, incorporate, compound, conjoin, consolidate, league, band.

attach, fix, fasten, bind, secure, tighten, clinch, tie, pinion, strap, sew, lace, stitch, knit, button, buckle, hitch, lash, truss, splice, gird, tether, moor, chain; fetter, hook, link, yoke, couple, bracket; marry, bridge, span; pin, nail, screw, bolt, hasp, lock, clasp, clamp, rivet; solder, cement, weld, fuse; rabbet, mortise, miter, dovetail; graft, ingraft; append, add, annex, adjoin.

Adj. **joining**, etc. (see *Verbs*); conjunctive, connective, copulative (*gram.*).

joint, joined, united, etc. (see *Verbs*); corporate, conjunct, compact, concurrent, coincident; hand in hand.

firm, fast, close, tight, taut, secure, inseparable, indissoluble.

See also ADDITION, ASSEMBLAGE, COMBINATION, FASTENING, MIXTURE, STICKINESS, TEXTURE, TIGHTNESS,

UNITY. *Antonyms*—See DISJUNCTION.

jungle, *n.* bush, chaparral, forest (PLANT LIFE).

junior, *adj.* minor, subordinate, second-string (LOWNESS, RANK); puisne (*law*), younger (YOUTH).

junk (*colloq.*), *n.* rubbish, trash, debris (USELESSNESS, UNCLEANNESS).

jurisdiction, *n.* province, domain, dominion (POWER, GOVERNMENT).

jurist, *n.* judge, justice, magistrate (JUDGE); jurisconsult, jurisprudent (LAW).

jury, *n.* panel, grand jury, petty jury (JUDGE).

just, *adj.* fair, equitable, evenhanded (IMPARTIALITY); decent, ethical (PROPRIETY).

justice, *n.* fairness, fair play, equity (IMPARTIALITY); judicatory (COURT OF LAW).

justifiable, *adj.* defensible, excusable, pardonable (FORGIVENESS); rightful, legitimate, lawful (RIGHT); fair, logical, reasonable (REASONABLE).

justification, *n.* apology, vindication, defense (ATONEMENT).

justify, *v.* defend, apologize for (SUPPORT); excuse, mitigate, palliate (FORGIVENESS).

jut, *n.* overhang, projection (HANGING).

jut, *v.* project, protrude, protuberate (VISIBILITY).

juvenile, *adj.* childish, immature, infantile (CHILD); young, youthful, vernal (YOUTH).

K

kangaroo, *n.* marsupial, wallaby (ANIMAL).

keen, *adj.* sharp, acute, fine (SHARPNESS); incisive, penetrating (INTELLIGENCE).

keep, *n.* sustenance, provisions, food (SUPPORT).

keep, *v.* hold, retain (HOLD); maintain, sustain, provide for (SUPPORT); preserve, retard decay, corn (PRESERVING).

keep away from, *v.* eschew, avoid, shun (AVOIDANCE).

keep back, *v.* check, contain, harness (RESTRAINT).

keeper, *n.* jailer, warden (IMPRISONMENT); herder, cowherd (DOMESTICATION).

keep in, *v.* suppress, repress, inhibit (RESTRAINT); shut in, shut up, cage (IMPRISONMENT).

keeping, *n.* adherence, compliance, accordance (OBSERVANCE, AGREEMENT).

keep on, *v.* continue, go on (CONTINUATION).

keep out, *v.* exclude, bar, debar (EXCLUSION).

keepsake, *n.* memento, token, souvenir (MEMORY).

keep up, *v.* continue, go on, keep on (CONTINUATION).

keg, *n.* barrel, drum, tub (CONTAINER).

kerchief, *n.* neckcloth, neckerchief, neckpiece (NECKWEAR).

kernel, *n.* core, heart, hub (CENTER); gist, keynote, nub (IDEA).

kettle, *n.* boiler, cauldron, teapot (CONTAINER).

key, *adj.* essential, fundamental, material (IMPORTANCE); indispensable, basic, vital (NECESSITY).

key, *n.* opener, passkey, master key (OPENING); solution, clue (ANSWER); cay, isle, atoll (ISLAND); scale, clef, chord (MUSIC).

keynote, *n.* cornerstone, keystone, basis (IMPORTANCE, RULE); gist, kernel, nub (IDEA).

khaki, *n.* tan, biscuit (BROWN); uniform, olive-drabs, regimentals (CLOTHING).

kick, *n.* rebound, recoil, backlash (REACTION).

kick, *v.* boot (*colloq.*), calcitrate (FOOTWEAR); gripe (*colloq.*), complain, grumble (COMPLAINT).

kid (*slang*), *n.* sprig, juvenile, teen-ager (YOUTH); infant, baby, little one (CHILD).

kid (*slang*), *v.* fool, jest, spoof (WITTINESS); make fun of, make game of, make sport of (RIDICULE).

kidnap, *v.* abduct, shanghai, spirit away (TAKING, THIEVERY).

KILLING—*N.* killing, slaying, destruction, decimation, extermination, dispatch, holocaust (*by fire*), mercy killing, euthanasia.

slaughter, butchery, bloodshed, battue, carnage, hecatomb, trucidation, massacre, pogrom, genocide.

murder, assassination, lapidation, thuggery, homicide, manslaughter.

execution, capital punishment, electrocution, hanging, lynching, auto-da-fé (*of a heretic*), crucifixion; immolation, sacrifice.

slaughterhouse, abattoir, butchery, shamble, shambles, Aceldama.

gallows, gibbet, scaffold.

[*killing of a specific person*] patricide, parricide, matricide, filicide, infanticide, fratricide, sororicide, uxoricide, mariticide, deicide, regicide, tyrannicide, vaticide; lupicide (*of a wolf*), vulpicide (*of a fox*).

murderer, assassin, bravo, Cain, cutthroat, highbinder, hatchet man, gunman, Bluebeard, thug; slaughterer, killer, slayer, butcher, poisoner; manslayer, homicide, homicidal maniac.

executioner, electrocutioner, hangman.

insecticide, pesticide, raticide, rodenticide, disinfector, disinfectant.

deathblow, finishing stroke, *coup de grâce* (F.), quietus.

[*devices, etc.*] iron collar, garotte, guillotine, electric chair, gas chamber, gun, knife, sword, rope, poison, bane.

V. **kill,** slay, slaughter, shed blood; finish, do in, put to the sword, butcher, destroy, dispatch, do away with, liquidate (*slang*), put an end to, put an end to the suffering of, put to death, smite, strike dead, strike down, cut down, take the life of; decimate, exterminate, massacre, pith, devitalize (*fig.*); murder, assassinate, burke, liquidate, poison, stone, lapidate, take for a ride (*slang*), bump off (*slang*).

execute, electrocute, gas, hang, gibbet, lynch, immolate, sacrifice to the gods.

strangle, strangulate, bowstring, garotte, burke, choke, throttle, smother, suffocate, stifle, asphyxiate; drown.

behead, decapitate, decollate, guillotine.

Adj. **murderous,** homicidal, bloodguilty, slaughterous, destructive, poisonous, cutthroat, internecine; sanguinary, bloody, bloodstained, gory, red-handed, bloodthirsty, bloody-minded.

lethal, killing, lethiferous, virulent, deadly, deathly, deathful, fatal, vital, mortal, baneful, fell, feral, malign, malignant, pestilent, baleful.

See also ARMS, CUTTING, DEATH, FIGHTER, FIGHTING, POISON, SUICIDE, TORTURE. *Antonyms*—See AID, FREEDOM, LIFE, PROTECTION.

---

kill-joy, *n.* spoilsport, wet blanket, dampener (SADNESS).

kilt, *n.* filibeg, philibeg (SKIRT).

kimono, *n.* dressing gown, duster, housecoat (CLOTHING).

kin, *n.* kith, kindred, kinfolk (RELATIVE); analogue, homologue, parallel (SIMILARITY).

kind, *n.* sort, variety, type (CLASS).

kind, *adj.* gentle, kindly, genial, goodhearted, amiable (KINDNESS, SOFTNESS).

kindle, *v.* light, ignite, enkindle (LIGHT, FIRE).

kindling, *n.* inflammable, tinderbox, tinder (FIRE).

KINDNESS—*N.* kindness, kindliness, affability, amiability, beneficence, benevolence, benignity, benignancy, good nature, grace, graciosity, humanity, humanitarianism, bonhomie, charity, philanthropy, clemency, indulgence, lenience, lenity, mercy, hospitality.

favor, accommodation, benignity, benefaction, courtesy.

blessing, benediction, benison, boon.

[*kind person*] philanthropist, good Samaritan, altruist, humanitarian; benefactor.

V. **bear good will,** wish well, take (or feel) an interest in; sympathize with, feel for; treat well, give comfort, do good, do a good turn, benefit.

Adj. **kind,** kindly, affable, amiable; beneficent, benevolent, benign, benignant; bighearted, goodhearted, good-natured, gracious, clement, indulgent, tender, lenient, merciful, hospitable, obliging, accommodating; humane, philanthropic, humanitarian, charitable.

See also AID, CHARITY, FRIEND, FRIENDLINESS, PITY. *Antonyms*—See CRUELTY, HATRED, HOSTILITY, MALEDICTION, MISANTHROPY, OPPOSITION, WICKEDNESS.

---

kindred, *adj.* parallel, analogous, corresponding (SIMILARITY); consubstantial, homogeneous, congeneric (CLASS).

king, *n.* monarch, sovereign, majesty (RULER).

king-size (*colloq.*), *adj.* big, large (SIZE).

kink, *n.* knot, loop, mat (WINDING); peculiarity, eccentricity, quirk (UNUSUALNESS); cramp, Charley horse, crick (PAIN).

kinky, *adj.* matted, matty, knotted (WINDING).

kiss, *v.* smack, buss, osculate (CARESS); brush, graze, shave (TOUCH).

kitchen, *n.* cookhouse, galley (*naut.*), scullery (COOKERY, SPACE).

kitten, *n.* kitty, catling, pussy (ANIMAL).

knack, *n.* flair, talent, forte (ABILITY).

knave, *n.* rascal, rogue, scamp (DECEPTION).

knavish, *adj.* scoundrelly, black-guardly (DISHONESTY).

kneel, *v.* genuflect, kowtow (RE-SPECT, BEND); bow down and worship (WORSHIP).

knickers, *n.* knickerbockers, knee breeches (TROUSERS).

knife, *n.* bolo, scalpel, lancet (CUT-TING, SURGERY).

knight, *n.* sir, cavalier, esquire (SOCIAL CLASS).

knightly, *adj.* chivalrous, courtly, gallant (COURTESY).

knit, *v.* weave, crochet, twill (TEX-TURE); pucker, purse (FOLD).

knob, *n.* bump, knurl, lump (SWELLING); lever, opener, handle (INSTRUMENT, OPENING).

knock, *v.* hit, bash, slap, punch (HITTING).

knock down, *v.* bowl down, overthrow (DESCENT).

knock out, *v.* knock unconscious, drug, narcotize (INSENSIBILITY, PHARMACY).

knoll, *n.* dune, down, mesa (HEIGHT).

knot, *n.* loop, mat, kink (WIND-ING); gathering, swarm, group (MULTITUDE).

knotty, *adj.* involved, ramified, mazy (DIFFICULTY, MYSTERY); gnarled, knotted (ROUGHNESS).

know, *v.* perceive, cognize, discern (KNOWLEDGE); be friends with, be acquainted with (FRIENDLI-NESS).

knowingly, *adv.* willfully, wittingly, purposely (PURPOSE).

KNOWLEDGE—*N.* knowledge, cognizance, acquaintance, information, know-how, ken, daylight; lore, learning, erudition, wisdom, worldly wisdom, experience, sophistication; omniscience, pansophism, cabalism, afflatus; intuition, insight, privity; foreknowledge, prescience, prevision; smatter, smattering, sciolism.

knowing, realization, appreciation, cognition, perception, recognition.

epistemology, pantology, science, cyclopedia, encyclopedia, empiricism, organon.

knower, one in the know, *cognoscente* (*It.*), worldling, sophisticate.

V. **know,** perceive, cognize, discern, ken, recognize, see, comprehend, understand, realize, conceive, appreciate, fathom, make out, experience; wot (*archaic*), be aware of, ween (*archaic*), trow (*archaic*), savvy (*slang*); foreknow.

Adj. **aware,** appreciative, conscious, cognizant, conversant, familiar, informed, alert, wide-awake, apprised, abreast, acquainted, privy, sensible, alive to, alert to, versed in, learned, erudite; omniscient, pansophical, prescient; wise, knowing, worldly, worldly-wise, sophisticated, experienced, knowledgeable, sciential, well-informed, *au fait* (*F.*), well-rounded.

knowing, cognitive, percipient, perceptive, apperceptive (*psychol.*), apperceptive (*psychol.*), understanding, intelligent.

knowable, ascertainable, discoverable, discernible, distinguishable, understandable, cognizable, cognoscible, perceptible, comprehensible.

known, conscious, supraliminal; well-known, common, exoteric, familiar, proverbial, famous, notorious.

little-known, obscure, orphic, recondite, secret, unfamiliar.

See also DISCOVERY, EXPERIENCE, FAME, INFORMATION, INTELLIGENCE, INTUITION, LEARNING, TEACHING, UNDERSTANDING, WISDOM. *Antonyms*—See IGNORANCE, INEXPERIENCE.

L

label, *n.* tag, slip, ticket (NAME, INDICATION).

labor, *n.* toil, travail, drudgery (WORK); childbirth, delivery (BIRTH).

labor, *v.* toil, sweat, struggle (WORK, ENERGY, ATTEMPT).

laborer, *n.* proletarian, manual worker (WORK).

laborious, *adj.* industrious, diligent, assiduous (WORK); arduous, toilsome, strenuous (DIFFI-CULTY, WORK).

LABOR RELATIONS—*N.* labor relations, labor union, union, trade union, guild; unionism, syndicalism; union shop; nonunion shop, nonunionism, antilabor policy; shape-up, hiring, firing.

strike, sit-down strike, walkout, wildcat strike; lockout.

unionist, union organizer, labor leader; striker, picket *or* picketer; grievance committee, union delegate.

strikebreaker, scab, fink, goon.

V. unionize, organize; strike, picket, scab; hire, fire.

See also BUSINESS, WORK.

---

laborsaving, *adj.* mechanical, automatic (INSTRUMENT).

labor union, *n.* union, trade union, guild (LABOR RELATIONS).

labyrinth, *n.* maze, intricacy, perplexity (CONFUSION).

lace, *v.* interlace, raddle, pleach (TEXTURE).

lacerate, *v.* tear, rip (TEARING); lance, puncture (OPENING).

lack, *n.* want, need, deficiency (ABSENCE).

lackadaisical, *adj.* languid, languorous, listless (WEAKNESS); disinterested, unconcerned, perfunctory (INDIFFERENCE).

laconic, *adj.* terse, concise, compact, pithy (SHORTNESS).

lad, *n.* boy, shaver, stripling (YOUTH).

laden, *adj.* burdened, encumbered, loaded (WEIGHT).

ladle, *n.* dipper, bail, scoop (CONTAINER).

lady, *n.* woman, petticoat, weaker vessel (FEMALE).

lady-killer (*slang*), *n.* rake, Don Juan, Lothario (LOVE).

lag, *v.* dally, dawdle, linger (DELAY, SLOWNESS).

laggard, *n.* slowpoke, loiterer, snail (SLOWNESS).

lagoon, *n.* basin, pool, pond (LAKE).

laid off, *adj.* unoccupied, unemployed, unengaged (INACTION).

LAITY—*N.* laity, laymen; laymanship, amateurism, dilettantism.

layman, laic, nonprofessional, amateur, dilettante, dabbler.

V. laicize, secularize, democratize, popularize.

Adj. lay, laic *or* laical, layman, secular; civil, temporal; nonclerical, nonprofessional, nonexpert, unprofessional; amateur, dilettante.

See also IRRELIGION. *Antonyms*—See ABILITY, CLERGY.

LAKE—*N.* lake, lagoon, lagune, loch (*Scot.*), lough (*Irish*); pond, basin, pool, lakelet, mere, tarn, spring, reservoir; salt pond, salina; dam, millpond, milldam, sluice; limnology; lake dweller, lacustrian, pile dweller.

Adj. lake, lacustrine, laky; riparian; fluvial, fluviatile.

See also OCEAN, RIVER, WATER. *Antonyms*—See LAND.

---

lamb, *n.* lambkin, yeanling (ANIMAL).

lame, *adj.* crippled, halt, spavined (DISABLEMENT, APPENDAGE); unpersuasive, unconvincing, flimsy (DISSUASION, WEAKNESS).

lament, *v.* deplore, mourn, sorrow (REGRET, SADNESS).

lamentable, *adj.* regrettable, deplorable, unfortunate (REGRET); tragic, grievous (SADNESS).

laminate, *v.* plate, coat, foil (LAYER).

lamp, *n.* lantern, bull's-eye (LIGHT).

lampoon, *v.* satirize, parody, travesty (RIDICULE).

lance, *n.* spear, pike, javelin (CUTTING).

lance, *v.* lancinate, puncture, pierce (CUTTING, OPENING).

LAND—*N.* land, earth, ground, dry land, landscape, terra firma; continent, mainland, main; farmland, field, tillage; highland, downs, ridge, upland, wold; lowland, polder (*esp.* Holland), valley; lot, patch, plot, plat, cantle.

native land, mother country, motherland, fatherland, home, homeland.

tract, area, expanse, extent, stretch, sweep, purlieu, region, terrain, territory, terrene.

neck, isthmus, spit, tongue, cape, head, headland, promontory, peninsula, chersonese.

plain, level, plains, pampas (*esp. Argentina*), plateau, tableland, table, platform, prairie, cove, steppe, tundra (*Arctic*), bay; heath, moor, moors, moorland; savanna, campo (*S. Amer.*), playa, mesilla, veld (*S. Africa*).

wasteland, waste, desert, Sahara, barrens, Barren Lands (*Northern Canada*); wilderness, wilds, heath or moor (*Gr. Brit.*); oasis.

territory, dominion, enclave, exclave.

grounds, premises (*law*), campus, terrace, yard, lawn.

park, common, green, plaza, square, village green (*New England*); preserve, sanctuary.

borderland, border, frontier, march.

real estate, real property, realty, property, freehold, holding, acreage, acres, lot, parcel, plot, estate, manor (*Gr. Brit.*).

soil, earth, ground, dust, divot (*golf*), loam, muck, mold, mud, peat; sod, sward, turf; alluvium, silt, sullage; topsoil; subsoil, substratum, underearth.

clay, argil, potter's clay, slip.

coast, littoral, seaboard, seacoast, seashore, seaside, shore, strand, tidewater, waterfront, beach, bank, terrace, sea front.

coastline, shore line, seaboard, strand line.

shoal, shallow, sandbank, sand bar, mud flat, flat, spit, tideland, bank, ledge, reef, cay, key, shelf, swash.

bed, channel, race; river bed, river bottom, watercourse.

watershed, river basin, basin, valley, divide, continental divide, delta.

riverside, riverbank, bank, shore.

landsman, landlubber (slang), landman.

landowner, freeholder, landholder, landlord, landlady, squire; landed gentry.

real estate agent, real estate broker, realtor.

geography, topography, topology; scenery.

V. land, disembark, debark, come (or go) ashore, cast anchor, arrive; alight, descend.

beach, ground, strand, land, dock, wharf.

Adj. terrestrial, agrarian, continental, outland, highland, upland; regional, areal, territorial, peninsular; landowning, landed.

grounded, aground, ashore, beached, stranded.

coastal, seaboard, seaside, littoral; riparian, riverside, alluvial.

See also DEPTH, GRASS, HABITATION, INHABITANT, ISLAND, REGION, RURAL REGION, WORLD. Antonyms—See LAKE, OCEAN, RIVER, WATER.

---

landing, n. level, storey (SUPPORT); wharf, dock, quay (BREAKWATER).

landlord, n. landowner, freeholder, squire (LAND, OWNERSHIP).

landmark, n. waypoint, milestone, milepost (INDICATION).

landslide, n. avalanche, snowslide, glissade (DESCENT).

lane, n. alley, alleyway, court (PASSAGE).

LANGUAGE—N. language, speech, parlance, tongue, mother tongue, native tongue, prose, parent language, Ursprache (Ger.); king's English; secret language, cryptology; flowery language, sillabub, rhetoric, poetry; babel, polyglot.

vernacular, dialect, cant, argot, idiom, jargon, lingo, patois, patter, slang, jive (slang), vulgate; commercialism, lingua franca, basic English, journalese, legalese, telegraphese, gobbledygook (colloq.).

universal language, pasigraphy, international language; Volapük, Esperanto, Ido, Mondolingue, Kosmos, Myrana, Spelin, Universala, Idiom Neutral, Ro.

linguistics, glossology, glottology, philology, lexicology, morphology, etymology; grammar, rhetoric, syntax, accidence; Anglistics.

Adj. linguistic, glottic, glossological, philological, etymological, grammatical, syntactical, rhetorical.

vernacular, colloquial, dialectal, idiomatic, slangy, vulgar.

multilingual, polylingual, polyglot, bilingual, diglot, trilingual, quadrilingual.

See also EXPRESSION, STATEMENT, TALK, WORD. Antonyms—See SILENCE.

---

languid, adj. languorous, lackadaisical, listless (INACTION, WEAKNESS); leisurely, unhurried, easy (REST).

languish, v. sigh, snivel, brood (SADNESS).

languor, n. lassitude, inanition, lethargy (INACTION, WEAKNESS).

lanky, adj. tall, gangling, slabsided (HEIGHT, THINNESS).

lantern, n. flashlight, lamp, bull's-eye (LIGHT).

lap, v. lick, lap at (TOUCH).

lapse, v. run out, expire, die (END); pass, elapse, go by (PASSAGE).

larceny, n. stealing, robbery (THIEVERY).

larder, n. storeroom, buttery, pantry (STORE).

large, adj. big, ample, substantial (SIZE).

lark, n. adventure, escapade, spree (AMUSEMENT, EXPERIENCE); practical joke, prank, trick (WITTINESS, MISCHIEF).

larva, n. grub, maggot (ANIMAL).

lascivious, adj. lewd, licentious, libidinous (OBSCENITY, SEX).

lash, v. buffet, batter, pommel (HITTING); spank, beat, cane (PUNISHMENT); abuse, baste, blister (MALEDICTION, DISAPPROVAL); drive, urge, impel (PROPULSION).

lass, n. lassie, petticoat, girl (YOUTH).

lassitude, n. sluggishness, languor, lethargy (INACTION).

lasso, n. lariat, net, dragnet (FILAMENT, TRAP).

last, adj. concluding, final, terminal (END).

last, v. endure, continue, abide (REMAINDER, CONTINUATION).

lastly, *adv.* finally, in conclusion, in fine (REASONING).

latch, *n.* bolt, bar, lock (FASTENING, CLOSURE).

late, *adj.* tardy, dilatory, behindhand (DELAY); dead, deceased, departed (DEATH).

lately, *adv.* recently, latterly, of late (PAST).

latent, *adj.* undeveloped, rudimentary, vestigial (IMMATURITY); potential, dormant (INACTION).

later, *adj.* subsequent, posterior, ulterior (DELAY, FOLLOWING).

later, *adv.* subsequently, behind, afterward (FOLLOWING, TIME).

lateral, *adj.* side, flanking, skirting (SIDE).

lather, *n.* head, cream, suds (FOAM).

latitude, *n.* sweep, play, swing (SPACE, FREEDOM).

lattice, *n.* trellis, fretwork, tracery (CROSSING).

laud, *v.* compliment, praise, applaud (PRAISE).

laudable, *adj.* praiseworthy, commendable (APPROVAL).

laudatory, *adj.* approbative, applausive, acclamatory (PRAISE, APPROVAL).

laugh, *v.* snicker, giggle (LAUGHTER).

laughable, *adj.* inane, absurd, ridiculous, asinine (FOLLY, ABSURDITY).

laugh at, *v.* jeer at, hoot, mock, deride (INSULT, RIDICULE).

LAUGHTER—*N.* laughter, mirth, Homeric laughter, gelasmus, hysterics, convulsions, hysteria; cachinnation, chuckles, giggles, guffaws, horselaughter, howls, roars, gales, screams (*or* shrieks) of laughter, titters, snickers, sniggers.

laugh, cackle, chortle, chuckle, giggle, snicker, snigger, twitter, titter, guffaw, haw-haw, horselaugh, belly laugh (*colloq.*).

laughingstock, butt, derision, jest, jestingstock, joke, laugh.

V. laugh, snicker, snigger, titter, cachinnate, giggle, twitter, cackle, chortle, chuckle, guffaw, horselaugh, howl, scream, roar, shriek.

smile, beam, grin, smirk, simper.

laugh at, deride, fleer, ridicule, howl down, laugh down.

tickle, titillate, tickle the funny bone of, tickle the risibilities of, amuse, convulse, convulse with laughter.

Adj. laughing, riant, hysterical, convulsive, in stitches, mirthful, giggly; cachinnatory, gelastic, risible; derisive, derisory.

smiling, riant, beaming, beamish, grinning, simpering, smirking, grinny.

laughable, amusing, convulsing, tickling, titillative, funny, side-splitting, rib-tickling; ridiculous, derisible.

See also ABSURDITY, AMUSEMENT, CONTEMPT, FOLLY, MERRIMENT, RIDICULE. *Antonyms*—See DEJECTION, GLOOM, SADNESS, WEEPING.

launch, *v.* start, begin, institute (BEGINNING); shoot, catapult (THROW).

launder, *v.* wash, lave, rinse (CLEANNESS).

lava, *n.* molten rock, scoria, cinders (ROCK).

lavatory, *n.* bathroom, powder room, washroom (CLEANNESS).

lavender, *adj.* orchid, perse, amethyst (PURPLE).

lavish, *adj.* munificent, prodigal, profuse (UNSELFISHNESS); extravagant, improvident, profligate (WASTEFULNESS).

lavish, *v.* dissipate, fritter away, squander (WASTEFULNESS); pour on, thrust upon, be generous with (GIVING).

LAW—*N.* law, rule, ordinance, regulation, decree, edict, canon (*rel.*), commandment, bylaw.

legislation, act, enactment, measure, statute, bill.

laws, body of law, civil law, common law, criminal law, penal code, international law, statute law, unwritten law, blue laws, admiralty law, maritime law; corpus juris, jurisprudence, equity, chancery, pandect, constitution, charter, code.

lawmaking, legislation, constitution, establishment, passage.

science of laws: jurisprudence, nomology.

[*expert in the law*] jurist, jurisconsult, jurisprudent, legalist, legist, nomologist.

V. make laws, legislate, enact, pass, establish, constitute, set up; codify.

Adj. legislative, statutory, constitutional, common-law, canonical (*church law*); juridical, legal.

See also COMMAND, COURT OF LAW, GOVERNMENT, JUDGE, JUDGMENT, LAWSUIT, LAWYER, LEGALITY, LEGISLATURE, OFFICIAL, RULE. *Antonyms*—See ILLEGALITY.

lawbreaker, *n.* offender, transgressor, violator (ILLEGALITY).

lawful, *adj.* legal, legitimate, licit (LEGALITY, PERMISSION); rightful, justifiable (RIGHT).

lawless, *adj.* lawbreaking, illegitimate, unlawful (ILLEGALITY).

lawn, *n.* green, terrace, grassplot (GRASS, LAND).

LAWSUIT—*N.* lawsuit, suit, action, case, cause, litigation; legal proceedings (*or* action); prosecution, arraignment, accusation, impeachment; presentment, true bill, indictment.

summons, subpoena, citation; writ, habeas corpus (*L.*).

pleadings, allegations, procès-verbal (*F.*), declaration, bill, claim; affidavit; answer, counter-allegations, counterclaim, plea, demurrer, rebutter, rejoinder; surre-butter, surrejoinder; interpleader.

hearing, trial; judgment, sentence, finding, verdict; appeal, writ of error; decision, precedent.

litigant, suitor, appellant, plaintiff, defendant.

V. litigate, go to law, appeal to the law, contest; bring to justice (trial, *or* the bar), put on trial, accuse, prefer (*or* file) a claim; cite, summon, summons, subpoena, serve with a writ, arraign; sue, prosecute, indict, impeach; attach, distrain.

try, hear a cause, hear, sit in judgment; adjudicate, judge, adjudge, decide.

Adj. litigious, contentious, litigatory.

See also ACCUSATION, ANSWER, COURT OF LAW, DECISION, IMPRISONMENT, JUDGE, JUDGMENT, LAW, LAWYER, OPPOSITION.

LAWYER—*N.* lawyer, attorney, member of the bar, attorney at law, advocate, counsel, counselor, counselor at law, legal advisor, corporation lawyer, criminal lawyer (*or* attorney), defense lawyer (*or* attorney), lawyer (*or* attorney) for the defense, mouthpiece (*slang*), plaintiff's lawyer (*or* attorney), lawyer (*or* attorney) for the plaintiff; legal light, jurist, legist, jurisconsult, jurisprudent; shyster (*colloq.*), Philadelphia lawyer (*colloq.*), pettifogger, judge advocate (*mil.*).

British lawyer, solicitor, barrister, barrister-at-law, king's counsel *or* K.C., bencher, sergeant-at-law.

government lawyer, attorney general, corporation counsel, district attorney, prosecutor *or* public prosecutor, public defender, solicitor, solicitor general.

legal profession, the bar, law, law practice, the practice of law.

V. practice law, practice at the bar, plead; be called to (*or* within) the bar, be admitted to the bar; take silk (*become a K.C.*).

See also COURT OF LAW, JUDGE, LAW, LAWSUIT, OFFICIAL.

lax, *adj.* negligent, neglectful, derelict (NEGLECT); loose, slack, relaxed (LOOSENESS).

lay, *adj.* laic, laical, secular (LAITY).

lay, *n.* ditty, chantey, ballad (SINGING).

lay, *v.* put, set, rest (LOCATION, PLACE).

lay aside, *v.* pigeonhole, shelve, table (DELAY).

lay away, *v.* store away, save (STORE).

LAYER—*N.* layer, stratum, course, bed, seam, coping, substratum, floor, stage, story, tier; fold, lap, ply; slab, tablet, flag.

plate, scale, flake, lamella, lamina, leaf, sheet, film, membrane, skin, coat, peel, slice, shaving, paring, wafer.

V. laminate, plate, coat, foil, veneer, overlay, cover, stratify.

scale, flake, delaminate, exfoliate, peel, pare, shave, slice, skive.

Adj. lamellar, scaly, scalelike, lamelliform, laminate, platelike, laminated, flaky, filmy, foliated, squamous, stratified, leafy, micaceous, schistose.

See also COVERING, CUTTING, FOLD, SKIN, SURFACE.

layman, *n.* laic, nonprofessional, amateur (LAITY).

layout, *n.* map, diagram, chart (PLAN).

lay waste, *v.* desolate, devastate, ravage (DESTRUCTION).

lazy, *adj.* slothful, shiftless, indolent (REST).

lea, *n.* grassland, meadow, prairie (GRASS).

lead, *adj.* pioneer, *avant-garde* (*F.*), front (PRECEDENCE).

lead, *v.* convey, conduct, guide (LEADERSHIP).

leaden, *adj.* plumbeous, plumbic, saturnine (METAL); heavy, cumbersome, unwieldy (WEIGHT); sluggish, languid, languorous (INACTION).

leader, *n.* guide, pilot, captain (LEADERSHIP); master, controller, manager (RULER); conductor,

Kapellmeister (*Ger.*), director (MUSICIAN); chief, head, officer (RANK).

leaderless, *adj.* pilotless, acephalous (MISTEACHING).

LEADERSHIP—*N.* leadership, conveyance, conduction, direction, guidance, pilotage, hegemony.

leader, conductor, conveyor, guide, pilot, shepherd, director, marshal, pioneer; captain, skipper, chief, chieftain, president, commander, commander in chief, head, head man, standard-bearer, *Führer* (*Ger.*), *gauleiter* (*Ger.*), *caudillo* (*Sp.*), ringleader, bellwether; pioneers, vanguard, *avant-garde* (*F.*).

V. lead, convey, conduct, guide, direct, pilot, shepherd, marshal; take the lead, pioneer.

Adj. leading, chief, main, principal, stellar, head, important.

See also CONTROL, FRONT, GUIDANCE, IMPORTANCE, PRECEDENCE. *Antonyms*—See FOLLOWER, FOLLOWING, IMITATION, MISTEACHING, REAR, UNIMPORTANCE.

lead on, *v.* decoy, inveigle (MISTEACHING).

leaf, *n.* frond, petal, needle (PLANT LIFE); film, membrane (LAYER); plate, paillette, foil (METAL); page, sheet (PAPER).

league, *n.* association, alliance, society (CO-OPERATION).

league, *v.* consolidate, ally, confederate (UNITY, JUNCTION, COMBINATION).

leak, *n.* puncture, pit, perforation (OPENING).

leak, *v.* trickle, exude, seep (EGRESS).

lean, *adj.* spare, willowy, svelte (THINNESS).

lean, *v.* list, careen, tilt (SLOPE, BEND, ROLL).

leaning, *n.* disposition, proclivity, bias (TENDENCY).

lean on, *v.* depend on, bank on, hinge on (DEPENDABILITY).

leap, *v.* spring, bound, hop (JUMP).

learn, *v.* acquire knowledge, master (LEARNING); find out, ascertain, determine (DISCOVERY).

LEARNING—*N.* learning, lore, erudition, scholarship, education, knowledge, wisdom.

education, background, literacy, cultivation, culture, breeding, schooling, grounding, opsimathy (*late in life*).

learned person, scholar, savant, bookman, intellectual, highbrow (*colloq.*), doubledome (*slang*), egghead (*slang*), longhair (*slang*),

Brahman, literatus, polyhistor, pundit; Minerva (*fem.*), *savante* (*F.*, *fem.*); man of letters, man of learning, walking encyclopedia; philosopher, philomath, scientist; pedant.

bookworm, bibliophile, bibliomaniac, *bas bleu* (*F.*, *fem.*), bluestocking (*colloq.*).

learned class, intelligentsia, literati, clerisy.

learner, beginner, alphabetarian, abecedarian, apprentice, probationer, neophyte, catechumen, novice, tyro, disciple, initiate; self-learner, autodidact.

student, pupil, scholar, schoolboy, schoolgirl, coed (*fem.*), cadet (*in military school*); specialist, major, trainee, grind (*slang*); freshman, plebe (*West Point*), sophomore, lowerclassman, junior, senior, upperclassman.

collegian, academic, undergraduate, postgraduate, seminarian, divinity student; matriculant, matriculator.

classmate, fellow student (*or* pupil), condisciple, schoolfellow, schoolmate.

class, form, grade, room, division; seminar, clinic, institute.

graduate, diplomate, collegian, bachelor, master, doctor, alumnus (*masc.*), alumna (*fem.*).

subject, course, study, class, lesson; major, specialty, minor; course of study, syllabus, curriculum, content, seminar.

graduation, commencement, commencement exercises; sheepskin (*colloq.*), certificate, diploma; degree, bachelor's degree, baccalaureate; master's degree, master, master's, masterate; doctor's degree, doctorate.

V. learn, acquire (gain, imbibe, pick up, *or* obtain) knowledge *or* learning; master, learn by heart.

study, coach in, tutor in, train in, major in, specialize in, minor in, brush up on, review, lucubrate, burn the midnight oil, grind (*slang*), cram (*colloq.*), prepare, read, peruse, con, pore over, wade through; enroll, take courses, matriculate.

Adj. learned, cultured, educated, erudite, scholarly, schooled, literate, abstruse, cultural, Palladian, Chaldean; well-informed, well-read, widely-read, well-rounded, well-educated, accomplished, grounded, well-grounded; pedantic.

studious, bookish, scholarly; apt.

scholastic, academic, classical, liberal, curricular; extension, Chautauquan.

See also BEGINNING, EXPERIENCE, INTELLECT, INTELLIGENCE, KNOWLEDGE, MATURITY, READING, SCHOOL, TEACHING, WISDOM. *Antonyms*—See IGNORANCE, IMMATURITY, INEXPERIENCE, STUPIDITY.

lease, *v.* let, sublet (BORROWING).

leash, *n.* rein, bridle, deterrent (RESTRAINT).

leash, *v.* curb, rein in, bridle (RESTRAINT).

least, *adj.* smallest, slightest, minimum (SMALLNESS).

leather, *n.* alligator, buckskin, buff (SKIN).

leave, *n.* furlough, liberty, sabbatical (ABSENCE); allowance, sufferance, tolerance (PERMISSION).

leave, *v.* abandon, forsake, evacuate (DEPARTURE, DESERTION); bequeath, devise (WILL, GIVING); quit, drop out, give notice (RELINQUISHMENT).

leaves, *n.* leafage, foliage, frondescence (PLANT LIFE).

leave-taking, *n.* parting, adieu, farewell (DEPARTURE).

leavings, *n.* remnants, odds and ends, rest (REMAINDER).

lecherous, *adj.* lewd, libidinous, lascivious (SEX).

lecture, *n.* speech, address (TALK); sermon, preachment (MORALITY, ADVICE).

lecture, *v.* speak, prelect, recite (TALK); moralize, preach, sermonize (MORALITY); censure, chide (SCOLDING).

ledge, *n.* shelf, bracket, console (SUPPORT); bank, reef, cay (LAND).

leech, *n.* worm, hookworm (ANIMAL); bloodletter, cupper, phlebotomist (BLOOD); parasite, drone, lickspittle (LIFE).

leer, *v.* stare, goggle, ogle (LOOKING).

leeway, *n.* elbowroom, headroom, headway (SPACE).

left, *adj.* remaining, left over, residual (REMAINDER); abandoned, forsaken, marooned (DESERTION); leftward, left-hand, sinister (DIRECTION).

left-handed, *adj.* sinistral, sinistromanual (APPENDAGE); awkward, backhanded, heavy-handed (CLUMSINESS).

leg, *n.* limb, shank (APPENDAGE); pile, post, stilt (SUPPORT).

legacy, *n.* bequest, inheritance, estate (WILL, INHERITANCE).

LEGALITY—*N.* legality, validity, conformity to law, legitimacy; legalism, nomism.

V. legalize, legitimatize, authorize, validate, constitute, sanction.

Adj. legal, legitimate, licit, lawful, legalized, authorized, juristic, valid, sound, according to law; law-abiding.

Adv., phrases. legally, legitimately, etc. (see *Adjectives*); in the eye of the law; by right, by law, *de jure* (L.).

See also HONESTY, LAW, PERMISSION. *Antonyms*—See ILLEGALITY, THIEVERY.

legend, *n.* fiction, fable, myth (UNREALITY); folk tale, folk story (STORY); inscription, epigraph, epitaph (WRITING); heading, head, caption (TITLE).

legendary, *adj.* imaginary, mythical, fabulous (UNREALITY).

legerdemain, *n.* sleight of hand, conjuration, jugglery (MAGIC).

leggings, *n.* gaiters, gambados, puttees (FOOTWEAR).

legible, *adj.* readable, clear, decipherable (READING).

legislate, *v.* make laws, enact, pass (LAW).

LEGISLATURE—*N.* legislature, legislative assembly, chamber, congress, council, diet, parliament, senate.

legislator, legislatress (*fem.*), lawgiver, lawmaker, Solon; senator, representative, congressman, congresswoman; Member of Parliament, M.P., parliamentarian, lord, peer, peer of the realm (*all Gt. Brit.*); councilman, councilor, assemblyman, deputy, alderman; whip, party whip, floor leader.

Adj. legislative, congressional, parliamentary; bicameral, unicameral.

See also GOVERNMENT, LAW, OFFICIAL.

legitimate, *adj.* logical, reasonable, fair (REASONABLENESS); proper, appropriate, correct (PROPRIETY); legal, licit, lawful (LEGALITY); orthodox, canonical, official (TRUTH); rightful, justifiable (RIGHT); dramatic, Broadway, theatrical (DRAMA).

leisure, *n.* spare time, spare moments, freedom (REST); convenience, opportunity, chance (TIME); unemployment, ease, retirement (INACTION).

leisurely, *adj.* unhurried, slow, easy (REST, SLOWNESS).

leisurely, *adv.* slowly, deliberately, tardily (DELAY).

lend, *v.* loan, advance, accommodate with (DEBT).

LENGTH—*N.* length, extent, span, measure, distance, mileage; range, reach, compass, magnitude, size.

line, row, series, sequence, succession, chain, concatenation, train, string, queue, stream, course; bar, rule, stripe, streak, stroke; chord, radius.

[*of time*] **duration**, extent, stretch, continuance, term, space, period.

[*single piece*] **piece**, portion, part, fragment, coil, roll.

V. **lengthen**, let out, extend, elongate, stretch, draw out, continue, prolong, prolongate, produce (*geom.*), protract, pad; fine-draw, wiredraw, spin out.

be long, stretch out, sprawl; extend to, reach to, stretch to.

Adj. **lengthy** (*used of speech, writing, etc.*), long, longish, protracted, drawn out, long-drawn-out, padded, long-spun, interminable, diffuse, prolix, sesquipedalian, windy, long-winded, wordy, tedious, wearisome, tiresome.

long, elongate, elongated, oblong; stringy, reedy, spindly, spindling.

See also CONTINUATION, MEASUREMENT, NARROWNESS, SIZE, SLOWNESS, STRETCH, TIME, VARIEGATION, WORDINESS. *Antonyms*—See DECREASE, SHORTNESS, SMALLNESS.

---

lenient, *adj.* easygoing, indulgent, tolerant (MILDNESS); merciful, sparing, forbearing (FORGIVENESS, PITY).

leper, *n.* outcast, pariah (DISMISSAL).

Lesbianism, *n.* Sapphism, tribadism (SEX).

lesion, *n.* injury, wound (HARM).

less, *adj.* lesser, smaller, minor (SMALLNESS); minus, lacking (DEDUCTION).

lessen, *v.* reduce, cut (DECREASE); ease, lighten, mitigate (PAINKILLER, RELIEF); diminish, decrease (SMALLNESS).

lesson, *n.* lecture, recitation, exercise (TEACHING); notice, example (WARNING).

let, *v.* allow, permit, tolerate (PERMISSION); lease, sublease (BORROWING).

let down, *v.* lower, pull down, take down, (LOWNESS).

letdown, *n.* chagrin, disgruntlement, blow (DISAPPOINTMENT).

lethal, *adj.* virulent, deadly, fatal (KILLING).

lethargic, *adj.* dull, heavy, listless (INACTION).

lethargy, *n.* sluggishness, languor, lassitude (INACTION).

let out, *v.* lengthen, extend, elongate (LENGTH).

letter, *n.* missive, communication, note (EPISTLE); character, symbol, type (WRITTEN SYMBOL).

letter, *v.* inscribe, stamp, sign, initial (WRITTEN SYMBOL).

letter carrier, *n.* postman, mailman (MESSENGER).

letup (*colloq.*), *n.* lull, pause, stop (REST).

level, *adj.* even, plane, flat, unwrinkled (SMOOTHNESS); coolheaded, well-balanced (INEXCITABILITY).

level, *n.* plane, grade (FLATNESS); plain, plateau, tableland (LAND); landing, storey (SUPPORT); obverse, face, facet (SURFACE); position, sphere, station (RANK).

level, *v.* smooth, grade, press (SMOOTHNESS, FLATNESS, UNIFORMITY, ROLL); equalize, equate (EQUALITY); aim, direct, point (DIRECTION).

levelheaded, *adj.* commonsensical, well-balanced, coolheaded (WISDOM).

lever, *n.* crowbar, jimmy (ELEVATION, INSTRUMENT); switch, pedal, treadle (CONTROL).

levity, *n.* flippancy, trifling, whimsey (FRIVOLITY); pleasantry, wit, repartee (WITTINESS); hilarity, mirth, jocularity (MERRIMENT).

levy, *n.* collection, gathering, muster (ASSEMBLAGE); tax, impost, toll, assessment, duty, excise (DUTY, PAYMENT).

levy, *v.* impose, tax, assess (EXPENDITURE).

lewd, *adj.* lascivious, licentious, lecherous (SEX, OBSCENITY).

liabilities, *n.* obligations, dues, arrears (DEBT).

LIABILITY—*N.* liability, accountability, responsibility, blame, burden, onus.

V. **be liable**, incur, lay oneself open to, be subjected to, run the chance, expose oneself to.

be responsible for, answer for, sponsor, vouch for.

Adj. **liable**, subject, susceptible, in danger, open to, exposed to, apt to; answerable, accountable, amenable, responsible.

See also DANGER, DEBT, DEPENDABILITY, DUTY, LIKELIHOOD, TEND-

ENCY, WEIGHT. *Antonyms*—See
FREEDOM, UNCERTAINTY.

---

liable, *adj.* inclined, apt, prone
(TENDENCY); subject, in danger,
open (LIABILITY).

liar, *n.* fabler, fabulist, fabricator
(FALSEHOOD).

libel, *v.* slander, malign, asperse
(DETRACTION, ACCUSATION).

liberal, *adj.* generous, openhanded,
unstinting (UNSELFISHNESS);
broad-minded, tolerant, catholic
(IMPARTIALITY); scholastic, academic, classical (LEARNING).

liberate, *v.* emancipate, set free,
rescue (FREEDOM).

liberation, *n.* rescue, delivery,
salvation (FREEDOM).

libertine, *n.* erotic, sensualist,
lecher (SEX); libertarian, wanton
(FREEDOM).

liberty, *n.* license, unconstraint;
independence (FREEDOM); chance,
leisure, opportunity (TIME);
leave, furlough (ABSENCE).

libidinous, *adj.* lascivious, lecherous, lewd, libertine (SEX).

libido (*psychoanal.*), *n.* sex drive,
sexuality, heterosexuality (SEX).

library, *n.* public library, lending
library, athenaeum (BOOK);
studio, workroom, study (WORK,
SPACE).

license, *n.* permit, warrant, authorization (PERMISSION); indulgence,
sensuality, debauchery (INTEM-
PERANCE); liberty, carte blanche
(*F.*), unconstraint (FREEDOM).

licentious, *adj.* unconstrained, dissolute, libertine (FREEDOM); lascivious, lewd, lubricous (OBSCEN-
ITY); loose, profligate, promiscuous (SEX).

lick, *v.* lap, suck (TOUCH); hit,
beat, spank (HITTING).

lid, *n.* top, coverlid (COVERING).

lie, *n.* fabrication, invention, untruth (FALSEHOOD).

lie, *v.* recline, loll, lounge (REST);
be situated, be located (SITUA-
TION); fabricate, invent (FALSE-
HOOD).

lie along, *v.* border, skirt (REST).

lie down, *v.* recline, prostrate oneself (REST).

lien, *n.* claim, counterclaim (DE-
MAND).

lie over, *v.* overlie, dominate,
tower above (REST).

LIFE—*N.* life, vitality, animation,
being, existence, entity, essence;
course of life, career, orbit, pilgrimage; survival, longevity.

afterlife, hereafter, future life;
everlasting life, eternity, immortality.

life force, vital spark, vital flame,
lifeblood, *élan vital* (*F.*), soul,
spirit, vital force (energy, impulse,
or principle).

science of life, physiology, biology, biochemistry, embryology;
biometry, biometrics, ecology,
bionomics; sociology, demotics.

living being, being, creature,
organism, animal, person, human
being.

[*one who lives off another*] parasite, sponge, sponger, free loader
(*slang*), sycophant, leech, drone,
lickspittle, lickspit, trencherman;
symbiont (*biol.*).

V. live, be alive, breathe, subsist,
exist, be, walk the earth; survive,
continue, remain, endure, last,
outlast, outlive, outride; coexist,
pre-exist, postexist.

get along, make out, fare,
manage, shift, scrape along, fend
for oneself.

vitalize, vivify, animate, enliven,
exhilarate, inspirit, invigorate,
quicken.

revivify, reanimate, re-create, regenerate, reinvigorate, rejuvenate,
renew, revitalize.

revive, resuscitate, resurrect,
rally, quicken; come alive, come
to life.

live off, leech on, sponge on,
drone.

Adj. living, alive, live, existing,
extant, subsistent, breathing,
quick (*archaic*), animate, alive and
kicking (*colloq.*); longevous, long-
lived, long-living; short-lived;
viable, facultative (*biol.*); organic,
biotic, zoetic (*all biol.*).

lifelike, true to life, photographic.

See also ACTIVITY, ANIMAL, CON-
TINUATION, EXISTENCE, PEOPLE, PRES-
ENCE, REMAINDER. *Antonyms*—See
DEATH, DESTRUCTION, KILLING.

---

lifeless, *adj.* exanimate, inanimate,
inorganic (DEATH); slothful,
spiritless (INACTION); dull, insipid, prosy (BOREDOM).

lifelike, *adj.* faithful, exact, photographic (SIMILARITY, LIFE).

lifesaver, *n.* liberator, rescuer, lifeguard (FREEDOM).

lift, *v.* elevate, raise, hoist (ELEVA-
TION); step up, raise, boost up
(INCREASE); come up, move up
(ASCENT); steal, abstract, ap-
propriate (THIEVERY).

light, *adj.* bright, clear, sunny
(LIGHT); featherweight, bantam,
lightweight (LIGHTNESS).

LIGHT—*N.* light, ray, beam,
stream, streak, pencil, sunbeam,
moonbeam, sunshine, sunlight,

sun, starlight, moonlight; illumination, radiation, phosphorescence, lucency, glare, glow, afterglow.

[*phenomena*] **reflection**, reflex, refraction, dispersion, interference, polarization.

halo, glory, nimbus, aureole, aura, corona.

luster, sheen, shimmer, gloss, resplendence, brilliancy, splendor, effulgence, radiance, iridescence, refulgence, luminosity.

flash, gleam, sparkle, glint, glitter, coruscation, scintillation, flame, blaze, glare, shimmer, spark, scintilla, glance, glisten.

lightning, fulmination, thunderbolt, bolt.

sciences of light: optics, photology, photics, photometry, catoptrics.

illuminant, light giver; gas, gaslight, electric light, headlight, searchlight, flashlight, spotlight, limelight; lamplight, lamp, lantern, bull's-eye; candle, taper, rushlight, night light, night lamp, torch, flambeau, gaselier, chandelier, electrolier.

polar lights, northern lights, merry dancers, aurora borealis (L.), aurora australis (L.); aurora, zodiacal light.

will-o'-the-wisp, *ignis fatuus* (L.), jack-o'-lantern, friar's lantern; St. Elmo's fire (*or* light), corposant.

electricity, galvanism, hydroelectricity; current, juice, flow; ampere, coulomb, farad, henry, ohm, volt, watt; electron; cathode, electrode; electrochemistry, electrodynamics, electrokinetics, electronics, electrostatics, voltaism; ammeter, electrometer, galvanometer, voltameter, wattmeter, voltmeter.

candle, wax candle, taper, dip, tallow candle, tallow; chandler, chandlery.

candleholder, candelabrum, candelabra, candlestick, flambeau, hurricane lamp, pricket, chandelier, Menorah.

V. **light**, ignite, kindle, enkindle, set fire to; rekindle, relume, relight.

illuminate, brighten, illumine, light up, lighten, irradiate.

shine, glow, glitter, glisten, gleam; flare, blaze, glare, shimmer, glimmer, flicker, sparkle, scintillate, coruscate, flash, beam.

dazzle, bedazzle, daze, blind.

electrify, electrize, galvanize.

Adj. **light** (*not dark*), bright, clear, shiny, sunny, lucent, ablaze,

aglow, cloudless, unobscured, unclouded, sunshiny.

luminous, shining, radiant, brilliant, illuminated, lustrous, vivid, lucid, resplendent, refulgent, lambent; fulgurant, flashing, scintillant, phosphorescent.

glossy, burnished, glassy, sheeny, shiny, polished.

self-luminous, phosphorescent, phosphoric, luminescent, fluorescent, radiant.

electric, electrical, galvanic, voltaic.

See also FIRE, HEAT, MORNING, PHOTOGRAPH, SMOOTHNESS, WAX, WORLD. *Antonyms*—See BLACKNESS, DARKNESS, EVENING.

---

light-colored, *adj.* fair, blond (COLORLESSNESS).

lightheaded, *adj.* giddy, reeling, whirling (DIZZINESS).

LIGHTNESS—*N.* lightness, buoyancy, levity, ethereality; legerity, agility, lambency.

lightweight, featherweight, underweight, bantamweight (*boxing*).

[*comparisons*] feather, fluff, down, thistledown, cobweb, gossamer, straw, cork, bubble, air.

V. **lighten**, ease, disburden, disencumber, disload, unload; relieve, alleviate, mitigate.

levitate, float, swim, rise, soar, hang, waft.

Adj. **light** (*not heavy*), featherweight, bantam, lightweight, underweight, buoyant, floating, portable; airy, aerial, lightsome, feathery, frothy, yeasty, gossamer.

[*light in movement, etc.*] **nimble**, agile, lightsome, lithe, airy, nimble-stepping, tripping, light-footed, nimble-footed, lively, lambent; light-fingered, light-handed, nimble-fingered.

See also ASCENT, EASE, FLOAT, FREEDOM, RELIEF, SWIMMING. *Antonyms* —See WEIGHT.

---

lightning, *n.* fulmination, thunderbolt, bolt (LIGHT).

likable, *adj.* enjoyable, preferable, relishable (LIKING); sweet-natured, winsome, pleasant (PLEASANTNESS).

like, *adj.* similar, resembling, alike (SIMILARITY).

like, *v.* be fond of, dote on, enjoy (LIKING).

LIKELIHOOD—*N.* likelihood, probability, chance, prospect; presumption, tendency, trend, direction.

V. be likely, be probable; tend to, incline toward, trend toward; lend color to, point to; promise, bid fair, suggest, imply, stand a good chance; seem to, appear to.

presume, infer, gather, conclude, deduce, suppose, take for granted, expect, count upon, rely upon, depend upon.

Adj. likely, probable, presumable, presumptive, moral, apt, liable; eventual, contingent, imminent; impendent, impending, looming, threatening.

credible, believable, trustworthy; reasonable, well-founded, plausible, ostensible.

Adv., phrases. probably, presumably, etc. (see *Adjectives*); seemingly, in all probability, in all likelihood, most likely, to all appearance; prima facie (*L.*).

See also BELIEF, CHANCE, DEPENDABILITY, DIRECTION, EXPECTATION, POSSIBILITY, TENDENCY. *Antonyms*—See IMPROBABILITY, UNCERTAINTY.

liken, *v.* compare, collate (SIMILARITY).

likeness, *n.* resemblance, similitude, semblance (SIMILARITY); photograph, picture, portrait (PHOTOGRAPH, FINE ARTS).

likewise, *adv.* too, furthermore, also (ADDITION).

LIKING—*N.* liking, affection, attachment, affinity, appetite, fancy, fondness, inclination, palate, partiality, passion, penchant, predilection, propensity, preference, stomach, taste, relish, tooth; sympathy, mutual attraction; favoritism, popularity, fashion, vogue.

favorite, fair-haired boy, *persona grata* (*L.*), pet, white-headed boy (*Irish*).

V. like, be fond of, dote on, enjoy, fancy, have a fancy for, favor, prefer, relish, cotton to (*colloq.*).

ingratiate oneself with, fawn on, become popular with, truckle to.

Adj. fond of, partial to, attached to, affectionate toward, sympathetic to; catholic, omnivorous.

likable, enjoyable, preferable, relishable.

popular, newfangled, new-fashioned, in vogue, in demand, in favor; liked, enjoyed, doted on, preferred, in the good graces of; favorite, fair-haired, favored, pet.

ingratiating, ingratiatory, silken, soft, saccharine, suave, urbane, unctuous.

See also FASHION, LOVE, PLEASANTNESS, PLEASURE. *Antonyms*—See DISGUST, HATRED, UNPLEASANTNESS.

lilt, *n.* cadence, swing, meter (RHYTHM); tune, melody (SINGING).

limb, *n.* branch, shoot, bough (PLANT LIFE); extremity, leg, arm (APPENDAGE); extension, wing, unit (ADDITION, PART).

limber, *adj.* lissome, lithe, flexible (BEND).

limelight, *n.* focus, cynosure (ATTENTION); spotlight (LIGHT); publicity, fame (PUBLICATION).

limit, *n.* borderland, bound, confines (BOUNDARY).

limit, *v.* narrow, restrict, confine, cramp (NARROWNESS, RESTRAINT).

limited, *adj.* bound, delimited, finite (BOUNDARY); circumscribed, confined, cramped (NARROWNESS); local, sectional, regional (SITUATION).

limitless, *adj.* boundless, infinite, measureless (ENDLESSNESS, SIZE).

limp, *adj.* flabby, flaccid, slack (WEAKNESS, SOFTNESS); spent, enervated, exhausted (WEAKNESS).

limp, *v.* hobble, clump, scuff (WALKING).

line, *n.* stripe, streak, band (VARIEGATION); stroke, dash, score (INDICATION); row, string, queue (LENGTH); track, range, route (DIRECTION); occupation, calling, pursuit (BUSINESS); family, lineage, ancestry (RELATIVE, ANCESTRY).

line, *v.* pad, quilt, face (LINING).

lineage, *n.* family, line, house (RELATIVE).

lines, *n.* outline, contour, figuration (SHAPE).

linger, *v.* loiter, lag, trail (SLOWNESS); dally, dillydally, dawdle (DELAY); last, cling, stay (REMAINDER, CONTINUATION).

lingerie, *n.* underclothes, undergarments, underthings (UNDERWEAR).

lingo, *n.* idiom, jargon, patois (LANGUAGE).

linguistics, *n.* philology, lexicology, etymology (LANGUAGE).

LINING—*N.* lining, coating, inner surface; filling, stuffing, wadding, padding; facing, bushing; sheathing, wainscoting, panelwork.

V. line, stuff, incrust, wad, pad, quilt, fur, fill, face, overlay, bush, sheathe, wainscot.

See also INTERIORITY. *Antonyms* —See COVERING, EXTERIORITY, SURFACE.

link, *n.* bond, tie, joint (FASTENING, JUNCTION).

link, *v.* unite, join, couple (COMBINATION, JUNCTION); bracket, group, associate (RELATIONSHIP).

lipstick, *n.* rouge, lip rouge (COLOR).

liqueur, *n.* cordial, pousse-café (ALCOHOLIC LIQUOR).

LIQUID—*N.* liquid, fluid, liquor, aqua (*pharmacy*), elixir, nectar, broth, solution, soakage, slop, swill; blob, bubble; juice, sap, latex, lymph, chyle, rheum, verjuice, gravy.

dissolvent, dissolver, liquefacient, menstruum, solvent.

V. liquefy, liquidize, fluidify, fluidize; dissolve, fuse, melt, render (*fat*), smelt (*ore*), thaw; solubilize, deliquesce; leach, leach out.

Adj. liquid, fluid, fluidic, flowing, liquefied, uncongealed; watery, sappy; juicy, succulent, pulpy, luscious, mellow, *au jus* (*F.*), melted, molten, thawed; liquescent.

dissoluble, dissolvable, fusible, hydrosoluble, meltable, soluble, solvable, solvent, liquefiable.

See also GAS, RIVER, WATER. *Antonyms*—See POWDERINESS, STABILITY, THICKNESS.

liquor, *n.* whiskey, alcohol, grog (ALCOHOLIC LIQUOR); fluid, elixir, broth (LIQUID).

list, *v.* enter, record (LIST); lean, careen, tilt (SLOPE).

LIST—*N.* list, catalogue, screed, table, canon, inventory, scroll, register, roll, rota, roster, poll, ballot, ticket (*politics*), slate (*politics*), docket; prospectus, program, syllabus, contents, index, bulletin, schedule, timetable, calendar; census, statistics, returns; directory, gazetteer, atlas; book, ledger; score, tally; file, row.

cataloguer, cataloguist, indexer, registrar, tabulator; statistician, actuary.

V. list, register, enter, record, inscribe, tally, enroll, inventory, schedule, catalogue, file, index, docket, calendar, tabulate, tabularize, post (*bookkeeping*), slate, book, census, enroll, draft, poll.

See also ARRANGEMENT, LENGTH, NAME, RECORD. *Antonyms*—See CONFUSION, UNTIDINESS.

LISTENING—*N.* listening, attention, audition, auscultation, stethoscopy (*med.*); wiretapping, bugging (*slang*).

hearing, audience, interview, conference; trial, judicial examination; earshot, range, reach, carrying distance, sound; science of hearing, audiology; earful.

ear, auris (*med.*); auricle, pinna; eardrum, tympanic membrane, middle ear, tympanum.

listener, auditor, monitor, eavesdropper, hearer; audience, captive audience.

hearing aid, ear trumpet, auriphone, audiphone, dentiphone, osteophone.

[*other devices*] audiometer, sonometer, telephone, detectaphone, hydrophone, Dictograph; stethoscope, auscultator.

[*hearing defect*] deafness, stone deafness, deaf-mutism, defective hearing, otosis, pseudacusis, tinnitus.

V. listen, give ear, lend an ear, harken, hearken, hark (*chiefly in the imperative*), eavesdrop, attend, heed, audit, monitor, audition; stethoscope, auscultate, ausculte; strain one's ears, prick up one's ears, give ear, give a hearing to, give an audience to, hear, overhear, mishear.

deafen, stun, split the ears; drown out.

Adj. auditory, auditive, acoustic, audile, audiovisual; listening, audient, attentive.

aural, auricular, otic; binaural, binotic, dichotic.

eared, aurated, auriculate, lopeared, dog-eared.

audible, distinct, clear, plain.

See also ATTENTION, LAWSUIT, SOUND. *Antonyms*—See BOREDOM, INATTENTION.

listless, *adj.* energyless, languid, languorous (WEAKNESS); dull, heavy, lethargic (INACTION).

literacy, *n.* education, background, cultivation (LEARNING).

literal, *adj.* verbal, verbatim, exact (MEANING).

literally, *adv.* verbatim, *literatim* (*L.*), textually (COPY).

literary, *adj.* bookish, belletristic, classical (STORY).

literate, *adj.* lettered, educated, schooled (TEACHING, LEARNING); well-read, bookish, learned (READING).

literature, *n.* letters, humanities, classics (STORY).

lithe, *adj.* nimble, agile, lightsome (LIGHTNESS).

litigation, *n.* cause, action, case (LAWSUIT).

litter, *n.* mess, jumble, clutter (UNTIDINESS); stretcher, ambulance (VEHICLE).

little, *adj.* small, tiny, diminutive (SMALLNESS); short, brief (SHORTNESS).

little by little, piecemeal, by degrees, gradually (DEGREE, SLOWNESS).

little-known, *adj.* obscure, orphic, recondite (KNOWLEDGE).

livable, *adj.* habitable, inhabitable, lodgeable (HABITATION).

live, *v.* be, subsist, exist (LIFE, EXISTENCE).

live in, *v.* inhabit, dwell in, occupy (INHABITANT).

livelihood, *n.* vocation, work, trade (BUSINESS).

lively, *adj.* active, brisk, vivacious (ACTIVITY).

live off, *v.* leech on, sponge on, drone (LIFE).

livery, *n.* uniform, habit (CLOTHING).

livestock, *n.* flocks and herds, domestic animals (ANIMAL).

living, *adj.* alive, live, existing (LIFE).

living room, *n.* drawing room, front room, parlor (SPACE).

lizard, *n.* chameleon, Gila monster (ANIMAL).

load, *n.* freight, cargo, goods, shipment, bale, pack (TRANSFER, CONTENTS); burden, millstone, cumber (WEIGHT).

load, *v.* fill, lade, pack (FULLNESS); load down, burden, oppress (WEIGHT); pile up, heap up, stack (STORE).

loadstone, *n.* lodestar, magnet (ATTRACTION).

loaf, *v.* idle, dally, dawdle (TIME, REST).

loafer, *n.* lazybones, slouch, idler, indolent (REST).

loan, *v.* lend, advance, accommodate with (DEBT).

loath, *adj.* reluctant, disinclined, averse (UNWILLINGNESS).

loathe, *v.* abhor, detest, despise (HATRED); abominate, revolt at (DISGUST).

loathsome, *adj.* abhorrent, hateful, detestable (HATRED); disgusting, repulsive, revolting (DISGUST).

lobby, *n.* vestibule, entranceway, hallway (INGRESS, PASSAGE).

local, *adj.* sectional, topical, regional (REGION, SITUATION, TOPIC, CHARACTER).

locale, *n.* locality, spot, place (REGION, LOCATION); scene, theater, stage (ENVIRONMENT).

locality, *n.* spot, site, locale (LOCATION, REGION, PLACE).

locate, *v.* find, discover, pin-point (DISCOVERY); place, situate, establish (PLACE, LOCATION).

located, *adj.* situated, fixed, established, settled (SITUATION).

LOCATION—*N.* **location,** establishment, settlement, installation, fixation, emplacement, placement.

place, situation, position, spot, locality, locale, region, tract, part, neighborhood, district; site, station, post, locus, whereabouts.

anchorage, mooring, harborage, harbor, shelter.

V. **locate,** place, situate, establish, settle, repose, set, seat, put, lay, deposit, plant, store, station, park, stand, pitch, camp, post, quarter, lodge, stop, remain, stow, house, cradle, install; fix, root, graft; moor, tether, picket, tie, stake; embed, insert.

settle, take root, anchor, cast anchor; bivouac, encamp, pitch one's tent.

determine (*the location of*), mark off, mark out, delimit, limit, localize, bound, define.

Adj. **located,** placed, etc. (see *Verbs*); situate, ensconced, imbedded, rooted; moored, at anchor.

See also BOUNDARY, FASTENING, HABITATION, INSERTION, JUNCTION, PLACE, REGION, SEAT, SITUATION. *Antonyms*—See DISMISSAL, ELIMINATION, REMOVAL.

---

lock, *n.* bolt, latch, padlock (CLOSURE, FASTENING); floodgate, sluice gate (BREAKWATER); strand, tress (HAIR).

locker, *n.* wardrobe, clothespress, chiffonier (CONTAINER).

locket, *n.* lavaliere, pendant, chain (JEWELRY).

lock out, *v.* close out, leave out, occlude (EXCLUSION).

lock up, *v.* imprison, incarcerate, jail (IMPRISONMENT).

lodge, *n.* hotel, inn, tavern; country house (HABITATION).

lodge, *v.* station, establish, install (PLACE); quarter, canton, accommodate (HABITATION); room, board (INHABITANT); stop, remain (LOCATION).

lodger, *n.* boarder, roomer (INHABITANT).

lodgings, *n.* dwellings, quarters, rooms (HABITATION).

loft, *n.* attic, garret (SPACE).

lofty, *adj.* high, tall, elevated (HEIGHT); commanding, striking, arresting (MAGNIFICENCE); noble, great, dignified (NOBILITY); proud, exalted, immodest (PRIDE).

log, *n.* stump, block, backlog (FUEL).

logger, *n.* woodcutter, lumberjack (WOODWORKING).

logic, *n.* sense, rationality, sanity (REASONABLENESS); dialectics, argumentation, syllogistics (REASONING).

logical, *adj.* reasonable, fair, legitimate (REASONABLENESS); syllogistic, dialectical (REASONING).

loincloth, *n.* breechclout, dhoti, diaper (TROUSERS).

loins, *n.* dorsal region, withers (REAR).

loiter, *v.* lag, trail, linger (SLOWNESS); dally, dillydally, dawdle (DELAY).

loll, *v.* lie, recline, sprawl (REST).

lone, *adj.* one, sole, single (UNITY); alone, lonely (SECLUSION).

lonely, *adj.* lonesome, desolate, forlorn (SECLUSION).

lonesome, *adj.* lonely, desolate, forlorn (SECLUSION).

long, *adj.* elongated, lengthy, protracted (LENGTH).

long, *v.* crave, hanker, hunger (DESIRE).

long-drawn-out, *adj.* padded, longspun, interminable (LENGTH).

longevity, *n.* survival, survivance (LIFE).

longhand, *n.* handwriting, chirography, manuscription (WRITING).

long-winded, *adj.* tedious, lengthy, windy (LENGTH, WORDINESS).

look, *n.* peek, peep, glance (LOOKING).

look, *v.* appear, seem (APPEARANCE); peer, glance (LOOKING).

look for, *v.* search for, seek, quest (SEARCH).

look forward to, *v.* expect, look for, look out for (EXPECTATION).

LOOKING—*N.* **looking,** inspection, observation, examination, scrutiny, supervision, surveillance, scansion; beholding, etc. (see *Verbs*).

look, peek, peep, glance, blink, squint, scowl, regard, scan; appearance.

stare, gape, yawp, gaze, glare, gloat, glower, goggle, leer, ogle.

spying, espionage, espial, counterintelligence, cloak and dagger.

spy, snoop, snooper, scout; secret agent, intelligence agent; fifth columnist.

spectator, onlooker, looker-on, bystander, witness, eyewitness, beholder, sightseer, rubberneck (*slang*), observer, watcher, peeper, peeker, pry, viewer; Peeping Tom, voyeur.

V. **look,** spy, snoop, pry, peep, peek, peer, blink, squint, glance, strain one's eyes; scowl, lower; appear.

look at, view, feast one's eyes, look one's fill, behold, eye, inspect, watch, keep one's eye on, oversee, supervise, survey, spy upon, sight, scan, regard, pore over, overlook, contemplate, examine, scrutinize, admire, muse on; review.

stare, gape, yawp, gawk (*colloq.*), gaze, moon, glare, gloat over, glower, goggle, leer, ogle; rivet (*or* fix) the eyes upon.

observe, remark, note, notice, witness, see, scout, trace.

Adj. **observant,** watchful, vigilant, regardful, attentive.

staring, gaping, etc. (see *Verbs*); moony, openmouthed, walleyed.

See also APPEARANCE, ATTENTION, CARE, EXAMINATION, VISION. *Antonyms*—See CARELESSNESS, INATTENTION.

---

looking-glass, *n.* mirror, glass, reflector (VISION).

look like, *v.* favor (*colloq.*), resemble (SIMILARITY).

lookout, *n.* spotter, sentinel, sentry (WARNING, PROTECTION); observation tower, watchtower (VISION); watch, vigil (CARE).

loom, *v.* hover, await, approach (DESTINY); overhang, portend, impend (THREAT); rise, emerge, dawn (VISIBILITY).

loop, *n.* bight, noose (FILAMENT); hoop, eyelet, eye (ROUNDNESS); knot, mat, kink (WINDING).

loop, *v.* bow, arch, crook (CURVE).

loose, *adj.* baggy, flabby, slack (LOOSENESS); separate, apart, asunder (DISJUNCTION); at large, unloosed, escaped (FREEDOM); immoral, promiscuous, abandoned, corrupt (SEX).

LOOSENESS—*N.* **looseness,** laxity, relaxation, slack.

V. **loosen,** slack, slacken, relax, unstring; bag, lop, flap, hang.

loose, detach, disjoin, disengage, undo, free, release, unfasten.

Adj. **loose,** baggy, flabby, filmsy, loppy, ramshackle, slack, slackened, relaxed, lax, ungirt.

See also DISJUNCTION, FREEDOM, HANGING, INELASTICITY, SEX. *Antonyms*—See HARDNESS, STRENGTH, TIGHTNESS.

---

loot, *n.* booty, haul (*colloq.*), swag (*colloq.*), spoils, prize (THIEVERY, PLUNDER).

loot, *v.* rifle, burglarize, rob (THIEVERY); ravage, pillage, ransack (PLUNDER).

lope, *v.* pad, trot, race, scamper, scoot (SPEED).

loppy, *adj.* loose, baggy, flabby (LOOSENESS).

lopsided, *adj.* unbalanced, topheavy (INEQUALITY); leaning, inclinatory (SLOPE).

loquacious, *adj.* talkative, gabby, chatty (TALK).

lord, *n.* commander, commandant, captain (RULER); liege, liege lord (FEUDALISM); parliamentarian, peer, nobleman (LEGISLATURE, SOCIAL CLASS).

Lord, *n.* the Supreme Deity, the Deity, the Almighty (GOD).

lordly, *adj.* overbearing, imperious, magisterial (PRIDE).

lore, *n.* knowledge, learning, information (LEARNING, KNOWLEDGE).

lose, *v.* mislay, misplace, miss (LOSS); be defeated, go down to defeat, meet one's Waterloo (FAILURE).

loser, *n.* also-ran, underdog (ATTEMPT).

LOSS—*N.* loss, deprivation, privation, decrement, bereavement, penalty, cost, forfeiture, forfeit, lapse, dispossession; damage, harm, misfortune, injury, waste, leakage, death, casualties (*mil.*), toll; perdition, ruin, destruction, failure, defeat, undoing, downfall.

lost person, thing, or animal: stray, waif.

V. lose, mislay, misplace, miss; incur a loss, be deprived of, fail to win, drop (*slang*), be without, forfeit.

be (*or* become) **lost,** go astray, stray, wander away, disappear, vanish, vanish into thin air, get lost, slip away.

Adj. lost, mislaid, misplaced, missing, gone, astray, strayed, vanished; forfeited, forfeit, unredeemed; destroyed, wrecked, ruined.

bereft of, bereaved of, shorn of, cut off.

incorrigible, irredeemable, irreclaimable, unreformable, abandoned.

See also ABSENCE, ATTENTION, CONCEALMENT, DEFEAT, DESTRUCTION, DISAPPEARANCE, FAILURE, HARM, IMPENITENCE, PUNISHMENT. *Antonyms*—See ACQUISITION, INCREASE, PRESENCE.

---

lost, *adj.* mislaid, misplaced, missing (LOSS); obdurate, incorrigi-

ble, irreclaimable (IMPENITENCE); rapt, engrossed (INATTENTION).

lot, *n.* group, batch, assortment (ASSEMBLAGE); fate, portion, fortune (DESTINY); patch, plot, parcel (LAND).

Lothario, *n.* Casanova, Don Juan, roué (LOVE, SEX).

lotion, *n.* balm, salve, ointment (CALMNESS, CURE).

lots, *n.* numbers, scores, heap (MULTITUDE).

lottery, *n.* gamble, raffle (CHANCE).

loud, *adj.* clangorous, noisy, powerful (LOUDNESS); grandiose, pretentious, gaudy (OSTENTATION, VULGARITY).

loudmouthed, *adj.* blatant, vulgar, scurrilous (UNPLEASANTNESS).

LOUDNESS—*N.* loudness, vociferance, sonority, intensity, power, volume.

noise, din, disquiet, bedlam, pandemonium; bluster, brawl, clamor, uproar, hubbub, hullabaloo, hurlyburly, racket, riot, rumpus, tumult; bang, explosion, report, salvo, thunder, thunderclap, slam, crash, clash, clap, chirm, peal.

crescendo, rise, swell, uprise, increase, amplification, boost, resonance.

noisy person, terror, rowdy, stentor; virago, scold, termagant.

V. be loud, bellow, roar, blare, bray, clangor, clang, crackle, crepitate; cry, screech, scream, yell, shrill, squall, shriek, skirl, screak, shout, squawk, yawp, bark; zing, zoom, roll.

deafen, drown out, stun, rend the air, awake the echoes, resound.

be noisy, bluster, roister, ruffle, brawl, clamor, noise, racket; din, bang, thunder, slam, crash, clap, clash, peal.

[*make louder*] amplify, boost, increase, raise.

[*become louder*] increase, rise, swell, uprise.

[*move loudly*] smash, crash, clatter, roar, hurtle, bicker; whir, whiz, whish, swish, skirr, birr, chug, rumble.

Adj. loud, clangorous, clarion, crepitant, screechy, squally, squawky, thunderous, blatant, brazen; canorous, resonant, forte (*music*), fortissimo (*music*), sonorous, deep, full, powerful; deafening, earsplitting, piercing, shrill; loud-voiced, stentorian, vociferous.

noisy, blusterous, blustery, brawly, clamorous, hurly-burly, rackety, riotous, tumultuous, uproarious, bedlam; boisterous, effervescent, obstreperous, rambunctious, rip-roaring, rowdy, disorderly; strepitant.

Adv., phrases. **loudly,** noisily, etc. (see *Adjectives*); lustily, aloud, viva voce (*L.*), at the top of one's lungs, in full cry; crescendo.

See also HIGH-PITCHED SOUND, RESONANCE, ROLL, SHOUT, SOUND. *Antonyms*—See LOWNESS, SILENCE.

lounge, *n.* resting place, roost, perch (REST); cocktail lounge, bar (ALCOHOLIC LIQUOR).

lounge, *v.* lie, recline, loll (REST).

lousy (*slang*), *adj.* execrable, horrible, outrageous (INFERIORITY).

lout, *n.* lummox, gawk, blunderbuss (STUPIDITY).

LOVE—*N.* love, ardor, infatuation, crush (*colloq.*), flame, passion, desire, attraction, venery; puppy love, calf love, platonic love.

affection, tender passion, tender feelings, yearning, devotion, liking, fancy, attachment, endearment.

self-love, amour propre (*F.*), autophilia (*psych.*), narcissism (*psychoanal.*).

[god of love] **Cupid** or **Amor** (*Rom.*), Eros (*Gr.*), Kama (*Hindu*), Freya or Freyja (*Norse*); Astarte (*Phoenician*), Aphrodite (*Gr.*), Venus (*Rom.*).

courtship, wooing, suit, court, attention, addresses, serenading.

beloved, darling, dear, idol, passion, pet, precious, sweetheart, treasure, love, truelove, sweetie (*colloq.*).

love affair, romance, amour, flirtation, intrigue, affaire de coeur (*F.*), affaire d'amour (*F.*); tryst.

lover, suitor, admirer, adorer, idolizer, wooer, courter, spooner, beau, boy friend (*colloq.*), inamorato, paramour, swain, young man (*colloq.*), flame (*colloq.*), spark, valentine; amorist, gallant, squire, cavalier, cicisbeo (*It.*); Lothario, lady-killer (*slang*), Casanova, Don Juan, Corydon, Romeo, Strephon.

ladylove, Dulcinea, mistress, inamorata.

flirt, coquette, vampire, vamp (*slang*), gold-digger, soubrette, fizgig, Sheba (*slang*), wanton.

love potion, philter or philtre, aphrodisiac.

V. **love,** care for, be enamored of, fancy, be in love with, fall for, lose one's heart to, be taken with; adore, idolize, worship, dote on, yearn; revere, reverence.

cherish, enshrine, prize, treasure.

make love, spoon, gallant, court, woo, spark, tryst.

flirt, coquette, vampirize, wanton, gallivant, dally, trifle, philander.

enamor, infatuate, excite with love; captivate, charm, attract, bewitch; win the favor of, win the affections of, capture the fancy of.

Adj. **in love,** enamored, smitten, infatuated.

loving, adoring, idolatrous, worshipful, reverent, reverential; amorous, amative, romantic (*colloq.*), ardent.

lovesick, lovelorn, languishing, pining.

affectionate, warmhearted, demonstrative, tender, yearning, devoted, fond, doting, attached; uxorious.

[expressive of love] **endearing,** pet, amatory, amatorial.

loved, adored, beloved, cherished, darling, dear, doted on, idolized, pet, precious, prized, revered, treasured, worshiped.

lovable, adorable, lovely, sweet, winning, winsome, charming, engaging, alluring, seductive, attractive, enchanting, captivating, fascinating, bewitching, angelic.

amatorial, amatorian, amatorious, amatory, amorous, erotic, Paphian, romantic, venereal.

flirtatious, coquettish, coquet, philandering, dallying.

See also APPROVAL, ATTRACTION, LIKING, SEX, WORSHIP. *Antonyms*—See DISGUST, HATRED.

---

lovely, *adj.* charming, delightful (PLEASANTNESS); beautiful, graceful (BEAUTY); lovable, sweet (LOVE).

love potion, *n.* aphrodisiac, philter (SEX).

lover, *n.* admirer, sweetheart (LOVE); gallant, gigolo (SEX).

lovesick, *adj.* lovelorn, languishing, pining (LOVE).

love song, *n.* serenade, strephonade, ballad (SINGING).

love story, *n.* romance, fiction, novel (STORY).

lowbrow (*colloq.*), *adj.* Philistine, raw, unbred (IGNORANCE).

lowbrow (*colloq.*), *n.* vulgarian, barbarian, savage (VULGARITY).

low-cut, *adj.* low-necked, décolleté (*F.*), plunging (LOWNESS).

lower, *adj.* nether, under (LOWNESS); less, lesser, inferior (SMALLNESS).

lower-class, *adj.* baseborn, lowborn, proletarian (PEOPLE).

lowest, *adj.* bottom, rock-bottom, undermost (LOWNESS, BASE); least, smallest, minimum (SMALLNESS).

lowland, *n.* polder, valley, glen (LAND, DEPTH).

lowly, *adj.* humble, unpretentious (LOWNESS); meek, modest (HUMILITY); baseborn, ignoble, menial (MEANNESS).

low-necked, *adj.* low-cut, décolleté (*F.*), plunging (LOWNESS).

LOWNESS—*N.* lowness, depression, depth; bottom, lowest point, base, basement, bedrock, bed, depths, floor, foundation, fundament, nadir; abyss, benthos.

vault, crypt, dungeon, cavern, cellar, underground room, basement, subbasement, hold.

low tide, low water, ebb tide, neap tide, neap.

low person, bugger, cur, sneak, whoreson (*archaic*), worm, wretch; dregs, raff, scum; junior, subordinate.

V. be low, lie low, underlie; crouch, cower, squat, grovel, wallow, welter.

lower, let down, pull down, haul down, take down, depress, sink, drop, dip, duck, strike (*as sail*), douse (*naut.*); droop, plunge, tumble, knock down.

reduce, diminish, decrease, curtail, shorten, lessen, flatten, slacken, abate.

Adj. low, flat, level, squat, low-lying, low-slung; depressed, deep; decumbent, prostrate.

lower, inferior, nether, under, subjacent; minor, junior, subordinate, second-string.

lowest, bottom, rock-bottom, bottommost, nethermost, lowermost, undermost.

low-pitched, low-toned, subdued, gentle, soft, faint, inaudible, piano, pianissimo, velvety, throaty, muffled, murmurous, whisperous, whispery; deep, bass.

humble, unpretentious, modest, lowly, obscure, lowborn, inferior, submissive, unimportant, commonplace, common, undignified, ordinary, mean, plebeian, menial.

coarse, indelicate, base, offensive, broad, low-minded, gross, improper, unbecoming, vulgar, unrefined, ill-bred, unpolished, crude; depraved, abandoned, degraded, abject, disreputable, dishonorable, mean, scurvy, rascally, low-down.

low-necked, low-cut, décolleté (*F.*), plunging.

Adv., phrases. under, beneath, underneath, below, down, downward; underfoot, underground, downstairs, belowstairs; at a low ebb; below par.

See also BASE, DECREASE, DEPTH, FLATNESS, HUMILIATION, HUMILITY, INEXPENSIVENESS, MEANNESS, SILENCE, SOFTNESS, VULGARITY. *Antonyms*—See ASCENT, BELL, ELEVATION, HEIGHT, HIGH-PITCHED SOUND, LOUDNESS, RESONANCE.

low-priced, *adj.* cheap, cut-rate, nominal (INEXPENSIVENESS).

low-spirited, *adj.* low, heavy-hearted, blue (DEJECTION).

LOYALTY—*N.* loyalty, constancy, fidelity, faith, troth, attachment, allegiance, fealty, loyalism, *esprit de corps* (*F.*).

devotion, adherence, dedication, idolatry, idolism, worship, fetishism, cult, consecration, consignment.

devotee, votary, votarist, friend, adherent, cultist, fetishist, idolater, idolist, religionist, sectarian; *fidus Achates* (*L.*), loyalist.

V. be loyal to, stand by, abide by, stick up for (*slang*), back, support, adhere to; fetish, idolatrize, idolize, worship.

devote, consecrate, consign, dedicate.

Adj. loyal, constant, faithful, staunch, true, unfailing, tried, tried-and-true, true-blue, steadfast, unwavering, unswerving, steady, attached, liege, loyalist.

devoted, adherent, consecrated, dedicated, devout, idolatrous, idolistic, sectarian, worshipful, religious, wrapped up in; votive, votary.

See also APPROVAL, PRAISE, WORSHIP. *Antonyms*—See DETRACTION, DISLOYALTY.

lubricate, *v.* grease, oil, wax (OIL, SMOOTHNESS).

lucid, *adj.* pellucid, limpid, lucent (CLARITY); clear, obvious, intelligible (UNDERSTANDING); sane, rational, normal (SANITY).

luck, *n.* chance, accident, fortune (CHANCE).

lucky, *adj.* fortunate, fortuitous (GOOD LUCK); promising, auspicious, happy (SUCCESS).

ludicrous, *adj.* absurd, ridiculous, foolish (ABSURDITY).

lug, *v.* pull, draw, haul, rake, trawl (TRACTION).

luggage, *n.* baggage, impedimenta (CONTAINER).

lukewarm, *adj.* warm, tepid (HEAT); indifferent, uninterested (INDIFFERENCE).

lull, *n.* break, breather, pause (CESSATION, REST).

lullaby, *n.* berceuse (*F.*), cradlesong (MUSIC).

lumber, n. timber, hardwood, plank (WOOD).

luminary, n. sun, orb, fireball (WORLD); celebrity, personage, notable (FAME).

luminous, adj. shining, radiant (LIGHT); bright, brilliant (INTELLIGENCE).

lummox, n. lout, gawk, blunderbuss (STUPIDITY).

lump, n. piece, bit, cut (PART); solid, mass, block (THICKNESS); bump, knob, knurl (SWELLING).

lumpy, adj. bumpy, knobby, nodous (SWELLING).

lunacy, n. mental imbalance, psychosis, psychopathy (INSANITY).

lunatic, adj. insane, mad, psychotic (INSANITY); nonsensical, zany, absurd (ABSURDITY).

lunatic, n. madman, madwoman, maniac (INSANITY); ape, ninny, noddy (FOLLY).

lunatic asylum, n. institution, madhouse, nuthouse (slang), mental hospital (INSANITY).

lunchroom, n. dining room, dining hall, grill (FOOD).

lunge, v. push, thrust, plunge (PROPULSION).

lungs, n. gills, branchiae (BREATH).

lurch, v. reel, pitch, toss (ROLL, ROTATION, UNSTEADINESS, OSCILLATION).

lurid, adj. sensational, yellow, purple (EXCITEMENT); racy, risqué (OBSCENITY); rust-colored, rufous (YELLOW).

lurk, v. skulk, slink (CONCEALMENT).

luscious, adj. juicy, succulent (LIQUID); palatable, savory, delicious (PLEASANTNESS).

lush, adj. wild, luxuriant, rich (PLANT LIFE).

lust, n. concupiscence, sensuality, animalism (SEX).

luster, n. sheen, shimmer, gloss (LIGHT).

lustful, adj. sensual, Cyprian, gross, lecherous (SEX).

lustrous, adj. shining, resplendent, refulgent (LIGHT); polished, glacé (F.), waxy (SMOOTHNESS); glorious, splendid (FAME).

lusty, adj. vigorous, energetic, tough (STRENGTH).

lute, n. harp, lyre, zither (MUSICAL INSTRUMENTS).

luxuriant, adj. rank, dense, exuberant (PLANT LIFE); productive, loamy, mellow (FERTILITY); orotund, purple, flamboyant (WORDINESS).

luxurious, adj. silken, nectareous, pleasurable (PLEASURE); Corinthian, plush, palatial (WEALTH).

luxury, n. opulence, affluence, richness (WEALTH).

lying, adj. recumbent, accumbent, decumbent (REST); untruthful, mendacious (FALSEHOOD).

lynch, v. hang, gibbet (KILLING, HANGING).

lyre, n. harp, lute, zither (MUSICAL INSTRUMENTS).

lyric, adj. cantabile, vocal, choral (SINGING, MUSIC).

M

machine, n. tool, implement, utensil (INSTRUMENT); automobile, motor, car (VEHICLE).

machine gun, n. Gatling gun, Lewis gun (ARMS).

mad, adj. deranged, lunatic, insane (INSANITY); frenzied, frenetic, berserk (VIOLENCE); absurd, nonsensical (ABSURDITY).

madam, n. lady, woman (FEMALE); procuress, bawd (PROSTITUTE).

madden, v. craze, unbalance, unhinge (INSANITY).

madhouse, n. institution, lunatic asylum, mental hospital (INSANITY); bedlam, maelstrom, babel (CONFUSION).

madman, n. lunatic, maniac, psychotic (INSANITY).

Madonna, n. Our Lady, Notre Dame (F.), The Blessed Virgin, The Virgin Mary, Holy Mary (ANGEL).

magazine, n. periodical, publication, journal (PUBLICATION).

MAGIC—N. magic, thaumaturgy, rune, conjury, necromancy, black magic, the black art, theurgy; sorcery, sortilege, enchantment, deviltry, deviltry, diablerie, diabolism, demonology, witchcraft, witchery, wizardry, fetishism, hoodoo, voodoo, voodooism; obsession, possession; levitation.

magic spell, spell, charm, hex, incantation; evil eye; invocation, rune, conjuration, hocus-pocus, abracadabra, mumbo jumbo, open-sesame.

magic charm, charm, amulet, periapt, talisman, phylactery, fetich; mascot, rabbit's foot, scarab.

wand, caduceus, rod, divining rod, witch hazel, Aaron's rod.

[*magic wishgivers*] Aladdin's lamp, Aladdin's casket, magic casket, magic ring, magic belt, magic spectacles, wishing cap, Fortunatus's cap, seven-league boots, magic carpet.

sleight of hand, conjurement, jugglery, legerdemain, prestidigitation.

sleight-of-hand artist, prestidigitator, *prestidigitateur* (*F.*), juggler.

magician, thaumaturgist, conjuror, necromancer, magus, archimage, theurgist; sorcerer, sorceress (*fem.*), enchanter, enchantress (*fem.*), Circe, siren, diabolist, wizard, witch, voodoo; jinni, genie (*myth.*); medicine man, shaman, witch doctor; Cagliostro, Merlin, Comus.

V. **perform magic**, voodoo, conjure, levitate, juggle, prestidigitate.

bewitch, becharm, charm, enchant, enthrall, spellbind, ensorcell, bedevil, witch, hex, jinx, hoodoo, wile; cast a spell, call up (*or* invoke) spirits, raise ghosts, wave a wand.

Adj. **magic**, magical, weird, occult, hermetic, necromantic, runic, thaumaturgical, voodoo, incantatory.

See also DEVIL, MYSTERY, ROD, SUPERNATURALISM. *Antonyms*—See REALITY.

magistrate, *n.* judge, jurist, justice (JUDGE); chief of state, president, chief magistrate (RULER).

magnanimous, *adj.* forgiving, generous, charitable (FORGIVENESS).

magnet, *n.* loadstone, attrahent, lodestar (ATTRACTION).

MAGNIFICENCE—*N.* **magnificence**, grandeur, grandiosity, sublimity, brilliance, glory, splendor, resplendence, luster, majesty, nobility, pomp, royalty; halo, nimbus, aureole.

V. **glorify**, exalt, transfigure, halo, aggrandize.

Adj. **magnificent**, majestic, noble, sublime, grand, grandiose, splendid, splendorous, resplendent, glorious, august, brilliant, lustrous, Olympian, palatial, pompous, regal, royal, sculpturesque, sumptuous, superb; arresting, striking, commanding, lofty, towering, imperial, imposing, impressive, stately.

See also ASCENT, ELEVATION, FAME, GOOD, NOBILITY, SOCIAL CLASS. *Antonyms*—See COMMONNESS, HUMILITY, LOWNESS, MEANNESS.

magnify, *v.* amplify, enlarge, aggrandize (EXAGGERATION, INCREASE).

magnifying glass, *n.* magnifier, jeweler's loupe, reading glass (VISION).

magnitude, *n.* extent, bulk, mass (QUANTITY, GREATNESS, SIZE); range, reach, compass (LENGTH).

maharajah, *n.* rajah, gaekwar, nizam (RULER).

maid, *n.* maiden, virgin, miss (CELIBACY, UNMARRIED STATE); girl, teen-ager, damsel (YOUTH); maidservant, domestic, hired girl (SERVICE).

maiden, *adj.* first, initial, virgin (EARLINESS).

maidenly, *adj.* maidenlike, girlish (FEMALE).

mail, *n.* defense, armor, shield (PROTECTION); letters, correspondence, writings (EPISTLE); post, air mail (MESSENGER).

mail, *v.* send, transmit, post (SENDING).

mailman, *n.* postman, letter carrier (MESSENGER).

maim, *v.* mutilate, mangle, crush (HARM).

main, *adj.* leading, principal, head (LEADERSHIP); cardinal, central, chief (IMPORTANCE).

mainstay, *n.* support, staff, prop (HOPE).

maintain, *v.* carry on, go on with (CONTINUATION); claim, insist, assert (AFFIRMATION, STATEMENT); sustain, keep, provide for (SUPPORT).

maintenance, *n.* sustenance, subsistence, sustentation, upkeep (SUPPORT).

majestic, *adj.* grand, magnificent, sublime (FAME, NOBILITY, MAGNIFICENCE).

majesty, *n.* grandeur, magnificence, sublimity (NOBILITY); king, monarch, sovereign (RULER).

major, *adj.* senior, chief, leading (RANK); superior, higher, greater (SUPERIORITY); more important, overshadowing (IMPORTANCE).

major, *n.* grandee, magnifico, prince (RANK); officer, military man (FIGHTER); specialty (LEARNING).

majority, *n.* bulk, plurality (SUPERIORITY).

make, *v.* build, construct, synthesize (PRODUCTION); effect, effectuate, cause (RESULT); compel, coerce, drive (FORCE); constrain, oblige (NECESSITY); realize, receive, get (RECEIVING).

MAKE BELIEVE   255   MAMMOTH

make believe, *v.* pretend, fool, play-act (PRETENSE).

make love, *v.* spoon, gallant, court, woo (LOVE).

make merry, *v.* be merry, frolic (MERRIMENT).

make out, *v.* get along, manage, fare (LIFE); remark, observe, notice (VISION).

makeshift, *n.* stopgap, temporary expedient, shift (SUBSTITUTION, IMPERMANENCE, USE).

make up, *v.* pretend, fabricate, invent (UNREALITY); hatch, improvise (PRODUCTION); compose, constitute (MAKE-UP).

MAKE-UP—N. make-up, composition, constitution, content, contents, formation; structure, texture, consistency, fabric, nature, construction, organization; combination, mixture.

composite, compound, complex, fabrication, organism, network, system; synthesis.

protoplasm, plasm, bioplasm, cytoplasm, metaplasm, nucleoplasm.

ovum, egg cell, egg, germ cell, germ plasm; oöspore, zygote, oösperm, oösphere, ovule; oöcyte, gamete; spawn, roe.

sperm, sperm cell, spermatozoon (*pl.* spermatozoa), seed, semen, milt.

V. **comprise**, consist of, contain, include, involve; be composed of, be made of, be formed of.

make up, compose, compound, constitute, construct, fabricate, form, mix, organize, structure, synthesize, texture, weave; compile, put together.

Adj. **composite**, compound, mixed, synthesized, synthetic; complex, complicated; articulate, segmented.

[*made up of*] **composed of**, comprised of, consisting of, constituted of, constructed of, containing, fabricated of, formed of, organized from, structured of, textured of, combined of, compact of.

See also BUILDING, COMBINATION, COMPLETENESS, CONTENTS, MIXTURE, PART, SHADE, TEXTURE. *Antonyms*—See DESTRUCTION.

---

make up for, *v.* atone, make amends for, expiate (RECOMPENSE).

maladjusted, *adj.* neurotic, psychoneurotic, neurasthenic (NEUROSIS).

malady, *n* illness, sickness, ailment (DISEASE).

malcontent, *n.* complainer, grumbler, sniveler (DISSATISFACTION).

male, *adj.* manly, masculine (MAN).

MALEDICTION—N. malediction, curse, execration, imprecation, damnation, anathema, ban (*eccl.*), malison; curseword, swearword, oath, expletive, damn, darn.

cursing, blasphemy, profanity, impiety.

abuse (*in words*), attack, assailment, assault, denunciation, excoriation, revilement, mudslinging, tongue-lashing; barrage, bombardment, broadside; diatribe, tirade, harangue, screed, philippic, snipe, smear, character assassination; billingsgate, blasphemy, invective, obloquy, scurrility, vituperation, epithets.

V. **curse**, anathematize, ban, damn, darn (*colloq.*), execrate, imprecate, swear at; swear, blaspheme.

abuse (*in words*), attack, assail, assault, belabor, baste, blister, lash, lash out at, whip, blast, rail at, snipe at, vituperate, blaspheme, blackguard, revile, smear, inveigh against, excoriate, denounce; bombard, barrage; pillory.

Adj. **maledictory**, execrative, imprecatory; blasphemous, impious, profane.

cursed, accursed, anathematized, banned, blasted, confounded, damn (*colloq.*), damned, darn or darned (*colloq.*), execrated; damnable, execrable.

See also DETRACTION, DISAPPROVAL, DISRESPECT, HARM, HATRED, OBSCENITY, RIDICULE, SHARPNESS. *Antonyms* —See APPROVAL, SACREDNESS.

---

malefactor, *n.* evildoer, wrongdoer, misdoer (WICKEDNESS).

malevolent, *adj.* malicious, malign, malignant (HOSTILITY, HATRED, HARM).

malicious, *adj.* malevolent, malign, malignant (HOSTILITY, HATRED, HARM).

malign, *adj.* malevolent, malicious, malignant (HARM).

malign, *v.* slander, libel, asperse (DETRACTION).

malignant, *adj.* malign, vicious, malevolent (WICKEDNESS, HARM).

malinger, *v.* gold-brick (*slang*), soldier, laze (REST).

malingerer, *n.* gold-brick (*slang*), slacker (*colloq.*), shirker (AVOIDANCE).

malleable, *adj.* ductile, tractable, plastic, yielding (SOFTNESS).

malodorous, *adj.* smelly, fetid, mephitic (ODOR).

mammoth, *adj.* mountainous, giant, colossal (SIZE).

man, *n.* gentleman, male (MAN); mankind, human race (MANKIND); person, soul (PEOPLE).

MAN—*N.* man, gentleman, sir, esquire; male, he, buck, bull, tom; masculinity, virility, manhood.

sissy, milksop, cotquean, mollycoddle, betty, pantywaist, effeminate, androgyne.

V. man, people, garrison.

effeminate, womanize, sissify.

Adj. manly, male, masculine, manful, brave, undaunted, virile, two-fisted, courageous.

See also COURAGE, MANKIND, SEX. *Antonyms*—See FEMALE, WEAKNESS.

---

manage, *v.* direct, administer (CONTROL); get along, fare, shift (LIFE); treat, deal with (USE).

manageable, *adj.* docile, orderly, quiet (OBEDIENCE); handy, wieldy, convenient (EASE).

management, *n.* direction, administration, government (CONTROL).

manager, *n.* director, administrator, overseer (CONTROL); foreman, superintendent (WORK).

mandatory, *adj.* required, requisite, compulsory (NECESSITY).

mane, *n.* locks, mop, ruff (HAIR).

maneuver, *v.* plot, scheme (PLAN).

mangle, *v.* maim, mutilate, crush (HARM).

mania, *n.* delirium, phrenitis, dementia (INSANITY); craze, fad, rage (ENTHUSIASM).

maniac, *n.* lunatic, madman, psychotic (INSANITY).

maniacal, *adj.* insane, mad, psychotic (INSANITY).

manifest, *adj.* apparent, patent, evident (CLARITY, VISIBILITY).

manifest, *v.* evince, signify, suggest (INDICATION).

manikin, *n.* dummy, model, mannequin (FINE ARTS).

manipulate, *v.* work, wield, handle (USE); feel, finger, thumb (TOUCH).

MANKIND—*N.* mankind, man, mortality, flesh; Hominidae, homo, Primates (*all biol.*); *Homo sapiens* (L.), humanity, humankind, human race.

human being, human, biped, man, person, mortal, soul, living soul, worldling, earthling, creature, body, anthropos; mechanical man, automaton, robot, android; humanoid, hominoid.

[*science of mankind*] anthropology, anthroponomy, ethnology, eugenics, genetics; philosophy, psychology, sociology.

race, strain, stock, breed, lineage.

Negro, Afro-American, colored person, blackamoor, Ethiopian; Negroid, Negrillo.

Caucasian, white, xanthochroid, griffin, paleface.

American Indian, Amerind, red man, redskin, squaw.

Oriental, Mongoloid; Japanese, Nipponese, Issei, Nisei, Sansei; Chinese, Chinaman (*slang*), Celestial.

hybrid, half-breed, half-blood, half-caste, miscegenate, Eurasian; mulatto, quadroon, quintroon, octoroon; albino, creole.

V. humanize, hominify, anthropomorphose, virify, personify, personalize, personate.

Adj. human, mortal, bipedal, creatural; manlike, anthropomorphous, hominiform, anthropoid.

racial, ethnic, phyletic, phylogenetic; Caucasian, Mongoloid, Negroid.

See also HEREDITY, LIFE, MAN, PEOPLE. *Antonyms*—See ANIMAL.

---

manly, *adj.* male, masculine, manful (MAN).

man-made, *adj.* synthetic, artificial (PRODUCTION).

manner, *n.* fashion, form, mode (METHOD); demeanor, address, bearing (APPEARANCE, BEHAVIOR); kind, sort, type (CLASS).

manners, *n.* breeding, good breeding (COURTESY).

manor, *n.* estate, acreage, property (LAND).

manservant, *n.* butler, valet, man (SERVICE).

mansion, *n.* house, palace, building (HABITATION).

manual, *adj.* chiral (APPENDAGE).

manual, *n.* textbook, text, workbook (SCHOOL); handbook, guidebook, Baedeker (BOOK).

manufacture, *v.* make, build, construct (PRODUCTION).

manuscript, *n.* script, composition, essay (TREATISE, WRITING).

many, *adj.* numerous, multitudinous, rife (MULTITUDE).

many-sided, *adj.* multilateral, multifaceted (*fig.*), versatile (SIDE).

MAP—*N.* map, chart, cartogram, plat; atlas, globe; ground plan, floor plan, blueprint, diagram, plan, outline; projection, elevation. map-making, cartography, topography, chorography.

V. map, plan, outline, lay out, plot, chart, project.

See also DESCRIPTION, EXPLANA-TION, PLAN, REPRESENTATION.

mar, n. blemish, demerit, delin-quency, vice (WEAKNESS).

mar, v. deface, disfigure, blemish (DEFORMITY, HARM, BLEMISH).

marbled, adj. marmoraceous, mar-moreal (VARIEGATION).

march, v. defile, file, pace (WALK-ING).

mare, n. brood mare, dam, filly (HORSE).

margin, n. edge, border, rim (BOUNDARY); field, area, scope (SPACE).

marine, adj. nautical, maritime, naval (SAILOR, OCEAN).

marine, n. leatherneck, devil dog (SAILOR).

mariner, n. seaman, seafarer (SAILOR).

marionette show, n. puppet show, Punch-and-Judy show (DRAMA).

marital, adj. matrimonial, nuptial, conjugal (MARRIAGE).

maritime, adj. marine, pelagic, nautical (OCEAN, SAILOR).

mark, n. distinction, feature, peculiarity (DIFFERENCE); badge, emblem, scepter (REPRESENTA-TION); impression, imprint (IN-DICATION); cross, frank (SIGNA-TURE); criterion, gauge, measure (MEASUREMENT).

mark, v. inscribe, stamp (WRITTEN SYMBOL); eye, watch (OBSERV-ANCE); point up, signalize, fea-ture (VISIBILITY, IMPORTANCE).

marked, adj. conspicuous, notice-able, pointed (VISIBILITY).

market, n. shop, department store chain store (STORE).

market, v. sell, vend, merchandise (SALE); shop, go shopping (PUR-CHASE).

marksman, n. sharpshooter, dead shot, crack shot (ATTACK).

maroon, n. terra cotta, copper (RED).

maroon, v. desert, strand, beach (DESERTION).

marquee, n. canopy, awning (COV-ERING).

MARRIAGE—N. marriage, matri-mony, wedlock, alliance, con-sortium (law), union; intermar-riage, miscegenation, mixed mar-riage; nuptial tie, nuptial knot, vinculum matrimonii (L.), match.

[kinds of marriage] monogamy, monogyny, monandry; bigamy, deuterogamy, second marriage, re-marriage, digamy; trigamy; poly-gamy, polygyny, polyandry; endog-amy, exogamy; morganatic mar-riage, mésalliance (F.), misal-liance, mismarriage, mismatch; marriage de convenance (F.), mar-riage of convenience; companionate marriage, trial marriage, common-law marriage.

wedding, nuptials, espousals, bridal; civil marriage, elopement, Gretna Green marriage; honey-moon; bridesmaid, maid of honor, matron of honor; best man, groomsman, bridesman, attendant, usher.

marriage song, nuptial ode, hy-meneal, epithalamium.

married man, benedict, partner, spouse, mate, yokemate, husband, lord and master (jocose), consort; groom, bridegroom.

married woman, wife, wedded wife, spouse, helpmeet, helpmate, better half (jocose), ball and chain (slang), squaw, matron, feme covert (law), mulier; bride.

married couple, man and wife, newlyweds, wedded pair, wedded couple, Darby and Joan, Philemon and Baucis.

V. marry, get married, lead to the altar, espouse, wed, wive (archaic), be made one, mate; re-marry, rewed; mismate, inter-marry, miscegenate.

unite in marriage, marry, unite in holy wedlock, unite, join, couple, mate, wed, splice (colloq.); ally.

Adj. married, conjugate, coupled, joined, matched, mated, united, wed.

marriageable, eligible, nubile.

matrimonial, marital, nuptial, spousal, conjugal, connubial, hy-meneal (poetic), wedded, bridal; premarital, postmarital, extra-marital.

See also BETROTHAL. Antonyms—See CELIBACY, DIVORCE, UNMARRIED STATE.

MARSH—N. marsh, marshland, swamp, swampland, slough, slew, slue, bog, fen, mire, moor or moor-land (esp. Gr. Brit.), morass, ooze, peat bog, quagmire, quag, swale, everglade, salt marsh, salina.

Adj. marshy, swampy, boggy, fenny, miry, moory, oozy, quaggy, sloughy, paludal, plashy, water-logged, spongy, poachy, muddy.

See also SEMILIQUIDITY, WATER. Antonyms—See DRYNESS, LAND.

martial, adj. military, militant, hostile (FIGHTING).

martyrdom, n. mortification, sack-cloth and ashes, self-mortification (ASCETICISM); self-sacrifice, self-immolation (UNSELFISHNESS, SUI-CIDE).

marvel, *n.* phenomenon, portent, *rara avis* (*L.*), prodigy, miracle, wonder (UNUSUALNESS, SURPRISE).

marvel, *v.* feel surprise, be amazed, wonder (SURPRISE).

marvelous, *adj.* wonderful, fabulous, spectacular (SURPRISE); remarkable, outstanding, prodigious (UNUSUALNESS); prime, splendid, superb (GOOD).

masculine, *adj.* manly, male, manful (MAN).

mash, *v.* crush, squash, triturate (PRESSURE); beat, flail, thresh (HITTING).

mask, *n.* visor, false face, domino (CONCEALMENT); disguise, cloak, veil (PRETENSE).

mask, *v.* hide, camouflage, cover up (CONCEALMENT); disguise, cloak, dissimulate (PRETENSE).

mason, *n.* stoneworker, stonecutter, lapicide (ROCK).

masquerade, *n.* imposture, impersonation, personation (PRETENSE).

masquerader, *n.* masker, domino, mummer (CONCEALMENT).

mass, *n.* crowd, mob, jam (MULTITUDE); solid, block, lump (THICKNESS); magnitude, size, bulk (QUANTITY, GREATNESS).

mass, *v.* jam, mob, swarm (MULTITUDE).

massacre, *n.* slaughter, pogrom, genocide (KILLING).

massage, *v.* rub down, stroke, pat (RUBBING).

masses, *n.* common people, vulgus, lower class (PEOPLE).

massive, *adj.* big, large, gross (SIZE); bulky, unwieldy, cumbersome (WEIGHT, SIZE); impressive, imposing, stately (SIZE).

master, *n.* controller, director, leader (RULER); employer, boss, taskmaster (WORK); commanding officer, captain, skipper (SAILOR); expert, authority, whiz (ABILITY); conqueror, subjugator (DEFEAT); victor, winner, champion (SUCCESS); educator, instructor, tutor (TEACHER).

master, *v.* tame, subdue, vanquish, conquer (SLAVERY, DEFEAT); excel in (ABILITY).

masterpiece, *n.* magnum opus (*L.*), chef-d'oeuvre (*F.*), monument (PRODUCTION).

match, *n.* light, lucifer (FUEL); companion, mate, double (SIMILARITY); contest, game (ATTEMPT).

match, *v.* pair, couple, bracket (TWO); parallel, imitate, copy (SIMILARITY); keep pace with, come up to, balance (EQUALITY); place in competition against, pit against (ATTEMPT).

matchless, *adj.* unparalleled, unrivaled (INEQUALITY).

matchmaker, *n.* marriage broker, matrimonial agent (BETROTHAL).

mate, *n.* spouse, husband, wife (MARRIAGE); buddy (*colloq.*), comrade (FRIEND); co-worker, fellow worker (WORK); match, fellow, twin (SIMILARITY).

material, *adj.* actual, real, concrete (REALITY, MATERIALITY, TOUCH, BODY); pertinent, relevant, germane (PERTINENCE); important, essential, fundamental (IMPORTANCE, PART).

material, *n.* fabric, textile, goods (TEXTURE); matter, substance, element (MATERIALITY); text, body (READING).

MATERIALITY—*N.* materiality, substantiality, corporeity, physical nature, corporality.

material, matter, substance, constituent, component, element; stuff, goods, fabric, grist, staple; pith, essence, distillation, quiddity, quintessence.

data, facts, memoranda, notes, documents, information.

materials, substances, elements, raw materials; supplies, essentials, stores, matériel (*F.*), munitions, provisions, means.

thing, object, article, something, commodity, substance, item, novelty, conversation piece; novelties, notions.

materialism, hylotheism, hylism, hylozoism, somatism.

V. materialize, incorporate, substantialize, exteriorize, externalize, substantiate; objectify, reify; solidify, concrete.

Adj. material, physical, substantial, solid, concrete; chemical, chemurgic, somatological; tangible, palpable, ponderable, sensible; unspiritual, temporal, materialistic.

See also BODY, EXISTENCE, LIFE, MEANS, REALITY, THICKNESS, TOUCH, USE. *Antonyms*—See NONEXISTENCE, SPIRITUALITY, THINNESS, UNREALITY.

materialize, *v.* visualize, appear (VISIBILITY); actualize, corporealize, realize, exteriorize (REALITY, MATERIALITY).

maternal, *adj.* motherly, parental, affectionate (ANCESTRY, KINDNESS, LOVE).

maternity, *adj.* puerperal, prenatal (BIRTH).

maternity, *n.* motherhood, maternology (ANCESTRY).

mathematics, *n.* algebra, arithmetic, trigonometry (COMPUTATION).

matrimonial, *adj.* marital, nuptial, conjugal (MARRIAGE).

matrimony, *n.* wedlock, alliance, union (MARRIAGE).

matron, *n.* dowager, lady, woman (OLDNESS, FEMALE).

matted, *adj.* kinky, matty, knotted (WINDING).

matter, *n.* material, substance, element (MATERIALITY); object, thing, phenomenon (REALITY); affair, concern, interest (BUSINESS); subject, subject matter, theme (CONTENTS, TOPIC); content, text (MEANING); pus, purulence, suppuration (UNCLEANNESS).

matter, *v.* import, signify, carry weight (IMPORTANCE).

matter-of-fact, *adj.* dry, naked, plain (SIMPLICITY).

mattress, *n.* bedding, feather bed, pallet (SLEEP).

MATURITY—N. maturity, adulthood, full growth, development, maturation.

V. **mature**, maturate, grow up, develop, mellow, ripen, season.

Adj. **mature**, matured, adult, full-blown, full-fledged, full-grown, fully grown, full-ripe, grown, grown-up, mellow, mellowed, ripe, seasoned, well-developed; maturing, maturescent; overgrown, overdeveloped.

See also EXPERIENCE, INCREASE, OLDNESS. *Antonyms—*See IMMATURITY, INEXPERIENCE, YOUTH.

maudlin, *adj.* sentimental, bathetic, gushy (SENTIMENTALITY).

mauve, *adj.* violaceous, plumcolored, plum (PURPLE).

maw, *n.* craw, gorge, gullet (THROAT).

maxim, *n.* saying, aphorism, axiom (STATEMENT).

maximum, *adj.* highest, most, greatest, maximal, top (SUPERIORITY, EXTREMENESS).

maximum, *n.* limit, top, utmost (EXTREMENESS); ceiling, record (SUPERIORITY).

maybe, *adv.* possibly, perhaps, perchance (POSSIBILITY).

maze, *n.* labyrinth, perplexity, bewilderment (CONFUSION).

meadow, *n.* grassland, prairie, lea (GRASS).

meager, *adj.* thin, spare, slim (INSUFFICIENCY); insubstantial, slight, flimsy (THINNESS).

meal, *n.* repast, spread (*colloq.*), dinner (FOOD); bran, flour, farina (POWDERINESS).

mean, *adj.* nasty, liverish, mean-tempered (BAD TEMPER); low, miserable, vile (MEANNESS); poor, miserable, sordid (POVERTY); intermediate, medium, middle (MID-COURSE).

mean, *n.* medium, average, middle (MID-COURSE).

mean, *v.* signify, denote, symbolize, stand for, betoken (MEANING, REPRESENTATION); intend, determine, resolve (MEANING, PURPOSE).

meander, *v.* ramble, peregrinate, extravagate (WANDERING).

MEANING—N. [*that which is meant*] meaning, intent, purpose, intention, aim, object, design.

[*that which is signified*] **sense**, significance, signification, import, point, tenor, purport, drift, bearing, pith, meat, essence, spirit; implication, denotation, suggestion, nuance, allusion, acceptation, interpretation, connotation, hidden meaning, *arrière-pensée* (F.), substance, effect, burden, gist, sum and substance, argument, content, matter, text, subject matter, subject.

[*science of meaning*] **semantics**, semantology, sematology, significs, semasiology, hermeneutics.

V. **mean**, have in mind, intend, purpose, resolve, destine, aim, direct.

signify, denote, import, imply, argue, connote, suggest, intimate, allude to, point to, indicate, convey, symbolize, express, purport, drive at, spell.

Adj. **meaningful**, meaty, pithy, sappy, pointed, pregnant, sententious, succinct, concise; expressive, significant, suggestive, allusive, indicative, eloquent, explicit, clear, intelligible.

oracular, mystical, cryptic, cabalistic; connotative, denotative, semantic.

literal, verbal, verbatim, exact, word-for-word, textual; figurative, metaphorical.

implied, implicit, understood, unexpressed, tacit, assumed, connoted, inferred.

synonymous, tantamount, equivalent, equal, equipollent.

See also EQUALITY, EXPLANATION, HINT, IDEA, INDICATION, PLAN, PURPOSE, REPRESENTATION, SUGGESTION, TOPIC, UNDERSTANDING. *Antonyms—*See ABSURDITY.

meaningless, *adj.* senseless, pointless, inane (ABSURDITY).

MEANNESS—N. meanness, pusillanimity, ignobility, lowness, etc. (see *Adjectives*).

[*mean person*] **wretch,** worm, cur, sneak, bugger, huckster, whoreson (*archaic*); scum, dregs, raff, riffraff (*all collective*).

V. **demean,** degrade, debase, abase, humiliate, humble, disgrace, shame.

Adj. **mean,** low, miserable, wretched, vile, unhandsome, ungenerous, small-minded, pusillanimous, mean-minded, petty, picayune, picayunish ornery (*colloq.*), currish, hangdog, sneaky, soulless, scummy, scurvy, scabby (*colloq.*); sordid, squalid, dirty, nasty, shabby; rascally, scoundrelly, raffish.

baseborn, ignoble, menial, lowly, base, beggarly, humble, slavish, abject.

valueless, worthless, unimportant, measly (*slang*), piddling, poky, scummy, unworthy, sorry, pitiful, pitiable.

See also BAD TEMPER, DISREPUTE, LOWNESS, MODESTY, POVERTY, UNCLEANNESS, WORTHLESSNESS. *Antonyms*—See BOASTING, FAME, MAGNIFICENCE, NOBILITY, OSTENTATION, PRIDE.

MEANS—*N.* **means,** instrumentality, agency, medium, measure, instrument, factor, aid, gimmick (*slang*), agent, avenue, method, mode, path, road, route, step, steppingstone, tactics, technique, technic, tool, vehicle, way, ways and means, expedient, means to an end; *modus operandi, modus vivendi* (*both L.*).

resources, wherewithal, capital, wealth, money, revenue, income; property, estate, stock, reserves; stocks, stocks and bonds, securities.

V. **provide the means,** enable, implement, make possible; permit, allow; help, aid, assist; arm.

See also AGENCY, AGENT, AID, EXPEDIENCE, MATERIALITY, METHOD, MONEY, PASSAGE, POSSIBILITY, POWER, STORE, WEALTH. *Antonyms*—See IMPOSSIBILITY, INEXPEDIENCE, POVERTY.

---

meantime, *n.* interval, interim (TIME, INTERVAL).

meanwhile, *adv.* meantime, in the interim (TIME).

measly (*slang*), *adj.* valueless, worthless, insignificant (MEANNESS, PITY).

measure, *n.* mensuration, admeasurement (MEASUREMENT); instrumentality, agency, medium (MEANS); extent, span (LENGTH); step, maneuver (ACTION); cadence, tempo, beat (RHYTHM);

foot, mora (POETRY); legislation, act, bill (LAW).

measure, *v.* gauge, quantify (MEASUREMENT); time, regulate, adjust (TIME).

measureless, *adj.* immense, infinite, limitless (ENDLESSNESS, SIZE).

MEASUREMENT—*N.* measurement, mensuration, admeasurement, admensuration, meterage, quantification, survey; size, dimensions, capacity, limit.

[*device for measuring*] **measure,** meter, gauge, rule, scale, yardstick; level, spirit level; plumb line, plumb rule, plummet, plumb bob; calipers, dividers, compass; square, try square, T square.

[*standard of measurement*] **criterion,** gauge, mark, measure, norm, standard, touchstone, yardstick.

surveyor, geodesist, topographer, cartographer.

linear or distance measure: inch, foot, yard, rod, mile, statute mile, nautical (geographical *or* sea) mile, furlong, league, light-year (*astron.*), parsec (*astron.*); fathom, hand, pace, span, rood, cubit (*ancient unit*); bolt, ell; link, chain (*both surveying*); agate, pica, point (*all printing*); cable, mil; circumference, girth, perimeter; diameter, radius; module.

metric measure: meter, millimeter, centimeter, decimeter, decameter, hectometer, kilometer; micron, millimicron, angstrom (*light waves*).

square measure: area, acre, acreage, square feet, etc., rood; hectare, centare *or* centiare, are.

circular measure: second, minute, degree; pi.

fluid measure: ounce, gill, pint, quart, gallon; minim, drop, dram, jigger; flagon, firkin, barrel, hogshead, pipe, tun.

dry measure: pint, quart, peck, bushel.

metric capacity: liter, milliliter, centiliter, deciliter, dekaliter, hectoliter, kiloliter.

cubic measure, volume, volumetry; volumeter.

V. **measure,** gauge *or* gage, meter, quantify, quantitate, admeasure, span, survey, pace off; plumb, plumb-line, fathom, sound; graduate, calibrate, caliper, commeasure, commensurate.

Adj. **measurable,** mensurable, gaugeable, plumbable, fathomable, quantifiable, surveyable; commensurable, commeasurable, commensurate.

mensurational, mensural, mensurative, quantitative, quantitive; metrological, modular.

See also APPORTIONMENT, DEGREE, LENGTH, QUANTITY, SIZE, WEIGHT.

---

meat, n. flesh, roast (FOOD); brawn, muscular tissue (SKIN); point, pith, essence (MEANING); nucleus, principle (PART).

mechanic, n. toolman, tooler, operator (WORK).

mechanical, adj. laborsaving, useful, automatic (INSTRUMENT).

mechanical man, n. automaton, robot (INSTRUMENT).

mechanics, n. physics, statics, dynamics (FORCE).

medal, n. decoration, medallion (FAME, PAYMENT).

meddle, v. interfere, butt in, intervene (INTERJACENCE).

median, n. middle, mean, intermediate (CENTER).

MEDIATION—N. mediation, instrumentality, intermediation, intervention, interposition, interference, intercession; parley, negotiation, arbitration, good offices; compromise.

mediator, intercessor, reconciler, propitiator, peacemaker, pacificator, negotiator, interagent, intermediary, diplomatist, arbitrator, umpire, moderator.

V. mediate, intercede, interpose, interfere, intervene, step in, negotiate; meet halfway, arbitrate, propitiate, reconcile.

See also AGENCY, JUDGE, JUDGMENT, MID-COURSE, MODERATENESS, PEACE.

MEDICAL SCIENCE—N. medical science, medicine, physic (archaic), practice of medicine, general practice, healing art, surgery; medical jurisprudence, legal medicine, forensic medicine; diagnostics, internal medicine, materia medica, dosology, posology, etiology, pathology, nosology, therapeutics, physiology, symptomatology, semeiology, serology, toxicology, somatology or somatics, histology, anatomy; anesthetics, anesthesiology; epidemiology, endemiology, immunology, virology; veterinary medicine; specialty, specialism.

obstetrics, maieutics, tocology, midwifery; gynecology, gyniatrics.

doctor, medical doctor, medical man, medico, M.D., medic, physician, Aesculapian, general practitioner, G.P., interne or intern, resident, leech (contemptuous), surgeon; diagnostician, clinician,

internist, therapeutist, specialist; pediatrician, geriatrician, allergist, anesthetist, aurist; oculist, ophthalmologist, optometrist; chiropodist, podiatrist, osteopath, chiropractor.

healer, medicine man, witch doctor, shaman; quack, quacksalver, charlatan.

obstetrician, accoucheur, accoucheuse (fem.), midwife; gynecologist.

dentist, orthodontist, pedodontist, periodontist, evodontist, oral surgeon, dental surgeon, prosthetist, prosthodontist.

veterinarian, veterinary, farrier, horse doctor.

nurse, attendant, medic, trained nurse, registered nurse, R.N., visiting nurse, practical nurse, sister, nursing sister; orderly.

See also CURE, DISEASE, HEALTH, PSYCHOTHERAPY, SURGERY.

---

medicate, v. treat, doctor (CURE).

medicine, n. remedy, medication, medicament (CURE); physic (archaic), practice of medicine, general practice (MEDICAL SCIENCE).

medicine man, n. healer, witch doctor, shaman (MEDICAL SCIENCE, MAGIC).

mediocre, adj. common, ordinary, commonplace (MID-COURSE, COMMONNESS); decent, fair, middling (GOOD); poor, indifferent (INFERIORITY).

meditate, v. ponder, puzzle over, muse (THOUGHT).

meditation, n. contemplation, rumination, study (THOUGHT).

medium, n. instrumentality, instrument, agent (MEANS, AGENCY); spiritualist, seer, clairvoyant (SUPERNATURALISM, TELEPATHY).

medley, n. hodgepodge, mélange (F.), jumble (MIXTURE).

meek, adj. docile, humble, weak-kneed (SUBMISSION); orderly, quiet, manageable (OBEDIENCE); patient, forbearing, longanimous (EXPECTATION).

meet, v. join, rejoin, flock (ASSEMBLAGE); concur, come together, converge (CONVERGENCE); adjoin, abut, border (TOUCH); execute, perform, discharge (OBSERVANCE); find, meet with, encounter (OCCURRENCE).

meeting, n. assembly, convention, convocation (ASSEMBLAGE); get-together, gathering (ARRIVAL).

melancholy, adj. mirthless, gloomy, atrabilious (GLOOM, SADNESS, DEJECTION).

melancholy, n. unhappiness, dejection, gloom (SADNESS).

melee, *n*. fracas, fray, words, row (DISAGREEMENT).

mellow, *adj*. dulcet, smooth, soothing (SWEETNESS); mellifluous, mellifluent, sweet-sounding (MELODY); flavorful, savory, delicious (TASTE, PLEASANTNESS); juicy, succulent (LIQUID); seasoned, ripe, mature (MATURITY).

mellow, *v*. soften, mollify, milden (SOFTNESS); mature, ripen, season (MATURITY).

melodious, *adj*. melodic, musical, tuneful, euphonious (MELODY, SWEETNESS).

melodrama, *n*. dramatics, drama, sensationalism (EXCITEMENT, DRAMA); sentimentalism, bathos, melodramatics (SENTIMENTALITY).

MELODY—*N*. melody, euphony, mellifluence, musical quality.

air, tune, chime, carillon, measure, lay, song, aria, run, chant; theme.

timbre, clang, tone color, quality.

Adj. melodious, melodic, musical, tuneful, euphonious; sweet, mellow, mellifluous, mellifluent, sweet-sounding, dulcet, soft; lyric, melic, songful; clear, silvery, silver-toned, fine-toned, full-toned, deep-toned, rich, Orphean, canorous, resonant, ringing.

See also HARMONY, MUSIC, RESONANCE, SINGING, SOUND, SWEETNESS. *Antonyms*—See HARSH SOUND.

melt, *v*. dissolve, thaw (LIQUID); unsteel, sweeten, soften (RELIEF).

member, *n*. arm, limb (APPENDAGE); unit, component (PART).

membrane, *n*. pellicle, mucosa (SKIN); leaf, sheet, film (LAYER).

memento, *n*. token, souvenir, keepsake (MEMORY).

memoirs, *n*. autobiography, vita, reminiscences (TREATISE, STORY).

memorable, *adj*. rememberable, unforgettable, indelible, (MEMORY).

memorandum, *n*. memo, *aide-mémoire* (F.), note (MEMORY).

memorial, *n*. monument, cairn, testimonial (MEMORY).

memorize, *v*. commit to memory, learn by heart (MEMORY).

MEMORY—*N*. memory, remembrance, recall, recognition, recollection, reminiscence, mneme, reproduction, retention, memorization; memoirs, memorials, reminiscences, memoirism; Mnemosyne.

reminder, phylactery, suggestion, hint, cue, twit, jog, prompt, prod, mnemonic, mnemonicon; memorandum, memo, memoir, *aide-mémoire* (F.), note, admonition.

memento, token, souvenir, remembrance, keepsake, relic, memorabilia (*pl.*).

memorial, monument, cairn, testimonial, trophy; commemoration, jubilee.

V. remember, retain, keep in mind, bear in mind; brood over, dwell upon.

recall, recollect, recognize, bethink oneself, call up, summon up, retrace, call (*or* bring) to mind, review, reminisce, retrospect, look back upon, reproduce; rake up the past, revive, renew.

memorize, commit to memory; fix in the mind, engrave (stamp, *or* impress) upon the memory; learn by heart, learn by rote, keep at one's fingertips.

remind, suggest, hint, cue, prompt, prod, jog the memory, admonish, put in mind, refresh the memory, recall to, din into; twit.

commemorate, memorialize, perpetuate, perpetuate the memory of.

Adj. mnemonic, eidetic, memorial.

memorable, rememberable, unforgettable, fresh, vivid, red-letter, indelible, catchy.

remindful, suggestive, mnemonic, redolent of, reminiscent, admonitory; commemorative, memorial.

Adv., phrases. by heart, by rote, by (*or* from) memory, *memoriter* (L.), word for word.

in memory of, in memoriam (L.), to the memory of.

See also CELEBRATION, HINT, RECORD. *Antonyms*—See FORGETFULNESS.

menace, *n*. threats, intimidation, thunder (THREAT).

menace, *v*. threaten, overhang, impend (THREAT).

menagerie, *n*. zoological garden, zoo (DOMESTICATION).

mend, *v*. repair, fix, overhaul (RESTORATION); sew, darn, suture (FASTENING); amend, better, ameliorate (IMPROVEMENT); get well, convalesce, heal (HEALTH).

mendacious, *adj*. untruthful, dishonest (FALSEHOOD).

mendicant, *n*. beggar, pauper, solicitor (BEGGING, CHARITY).

menial, *adj*. baseborn, ignoble, lowly (MEANNESS).

menial, *n*. domestic, servant, retainer (SERVICE).

mental, *adj*. intellectual, intellective, phrenic (INTELLECT).

mental health, *n.* sound mind, mental balance (SANITY).

mention, *v.* name, cite, enumerate (TALK, NAME); remark, observe (STATEMENT).

menu, *n.* table, cuisine, bill of fare (FOOD).

mercenary, *adj.* sordid, venal, hireling (MONEY).

merchandise, *n.* wares, commodities, goods (SALE).

merchant, *n.* dealer, trader, marketer (SALE).

merciful, *adj.* humane, lenient, compassionate (FORGIVENESS, PITY).

merciless, *adj.* pitiless, unmerciful, unrelenting (INSENSITIVITY, CRUELTY).

mercury, *n.* quicksilver (METAL).

mercy, *n.* clemency, commiseration, compassion (FORGIVENESS, PITY).

mercy-killing, *n.* euthanasia (KILLING).

mere, *adj.* simple, bald, blunt (SIMPLICITY, SMALLNESS).

merely, *adv.* only, solely, simply (UNITY, SMALLNESS).

merge, *v.* mix, mingle, combine (JUNCTION); fuse, blend, weld (UNITY).

merit, *n.* excellence, virtue, quality (GOOD); worthiness, dignity, caliber (VALUE).

merit, *v.* deserve, be worthy of, rate (RIGHT, VALUE).

meritorious, *adj.* laudable, praiseworthy, creditable (APPROVAL); worthy, deserving (VALUE).

mermaid, *n.* siren, Lorelei, Lurlei (MYTHICAL BEINGS); swimmer, naiad, natator (SWIMMING).

MERRIMENT—*N.* merriment, fun, sport, frolic, gaiety, hilarity, mirth, festivity, jocularity, levity.

V. be merry, make merry, frolic, riot, lark, skylark, rollick; celebrate, jubilate, revel.

Adj. merry, convivial, gay, fun-loving, sportive, festive, frolicsome, gleeful, hilarious, jocular, jocund, jolly, jovial, larking, skylarking, mirthful, riant, rip-roaring, rollicking, saturnalian, sunny, winsome, Falstaffian; boisterous, riotous, uproarious.

See also AMUSEMENT, CHEERFULNESS, HAPPINESS, LAUGHTER, PLAYFULNESS, SOCIALITY. *Antonyms*—See DEJECTION, NERVOUSNESS, SADNESS, WEEPING.

merry-go-round, *n.* carousel, whirligig, whirlabout (ROTATION).

merrymaking, *n.* sport, festivity, revel (AMUSEMENT).

mesh, *n.* web, net, lace, (CROSSING, TEXTURE).

meshes, *n.* snare, pitfall, quicksand (TRAP).

mess, *n.* confusion, mix-up, muddle (UNTIDINESS); imbroglio, stew (CONDITION); hash, olla-podrida, salmagundi (MIXTURE).

mess, *v.* dirty, soil, smear (UNCLEANNESS); clutter, litter, jumble (UNTIDINESS).

message, *n.* letter, missive, communication (EPISTLE).

MESSENGER—*N.* messenger, ambassador, envoy, emissary, angel (*Biblical*), delegate, intermediary, go-between, herald, harbinger, forerunner, precursor; trumpeter, crier, bellman; Gabriel, Hermes, Mercury, Iris, Ariel.

courier, runner, express, intelligencer; postboy, errand boy, bellboy, bellhop (*slang*), page.

mail, post, post office, air mail; postman, mailman, letter carrier.

telegraph, cable, wire (*colloq.*), radiotelegraph, radio, wireless.

telephone, phone (*colloq.*), radiotelephone.

See also INFORMATION, MEDIATION, PRECEDENCE, SENDING.

Messiah, *n.* Jesus, Jesus Christ, the Saviour (CHRIST).

messy, *adj.* dirty, Augean, grimy (UNCLEANNESS); frowzy, blowzy, grubby (UNTIDINESS).

METAL—*N.* metal, plate, *paillon* (*F.*), paillette, leaf, foil, casting, ingot, sheet metal, mail; mineral, ore, vein, load; alloy, solder; hardware, ironware, metalware, enamelware; metalloid.

metallurgy, metallography, mineralogy; metalworking, metalwork, hydrometallurgy, pyrometallurgy, smithery, smelting, soldering, brazing, forging, casting, liquation, plating, puddling, acieration.

metalworker, metalist, smith, armorer, smelter, plater, brazer, solderer, forger; goldsmith, aurifex; silversmith; coppersmith, brazier; ironworker, blacksmith, ironsmith, steelworker, puddler; tinsmith, whitesmith; tinman, tinner, tinsman, pewterer.

metalworks, smithy, smithery, forge, smeltery; anvil; ironworks, steelworks, bloomery; tinworks.

precious metals: gold, iridium,

osmium, palladium, platinum, rhodium, ruthenium, silver.

gold, bullion, gold dust; gilding, gilt, ormolu, vermeil, gold plate, solid gold, aurum (chemistry), nugget; fool's gold, iron pyrites, pyrite.

silver, argent (poetic or archaic), argentine; argentum (chemistry), sterling; silver plate, flatware, hollow ware, silverware, tableware; gadroon.

copper, cuprum (chemistry), German silver, albata, ormolu, brass, bronze, cupronickel; verdigris, patina.

iron, bloom, wrought iron, cast iron, pig, pig iron, steel, cast steel; ironware, steelware.

lead, plumbum; zinc; tin, stannum, pewter, tinwork, tinware, tin plate; mercury, quicksilver.

V. metal, metalize, mineralize; mail, armor; cast, ingot, foil, liquate, braze, solder, plate, forge, smelt, alloy; platinize, silver, cupel, bronze; puddle, acierate; lead, tin, tin-plate, mercurialize; zincify, galvanize.

gild, aureate, transmute, alchemize, aurify.

Adj. metallic, metalline, metal, metalliferous, metal-bearing, metalloid; monometallic, bimetallic; inorganic, mineral; vulcanian.

gold, auriferous, aurous, golden, gilt, gilded, vermeil, aurate, aurulent, chryselephantine, gold-plated, gold-filled.

silver, argental, argentic (chemistry), argentine, lunar, silvery, silverlike, argent.

coppery, copperlike, cupreous, cupric (chemistry); brassy, brass, brazen, bronzy.

iron, irony, ferric, ferrous, ferruginous, steel, steely, rubiginous; ironbound, ironclad, iron-plated.

leaden, lead, plumbeous, plumbic, saturnine.

zincky, zincic, zincous, galvanized.

tin, tinny, stannic, stannous, pewter.

mercuric, mercurous, mercurial. See also JEWELRY, ROCK.

---

metamorphosis, n. transfiguration, transmutation, transformation (CHANGE).

metaphor, n. allegory, simile, metonymy (FIGURE OF SPEECH).

metaphysical, adj. oversubtle, abstruse, jesuitic (SOPHISTRY).

meteor, n. comet, falling star, meteoroid (WORLD).

meteorology, n. climatology, aerology (AIR).

meter, n. measure, gauge, rule (MEASUREMENT); cadence, lilt, swing (RHYTHM); foot, mora (POETRY).

METHOD—N. method, formula, form, routine, route, rubric, tack, technique, technic, theory, usage, way, ways and means, means, short cut.

procedure, course, modus operandi (L.), modus vivendi (L.), process, proceeding, proceedings, ritual, routine, rote, tactics, system, scheme, strategy, receipt, recipe.

manner, fashion, form, style, mode.

methodology, methods, methodics, tactics, technics, strategy.

V. methodize, organize, systematize, systemize, routinize.

See also ACTION, ARRANGEMENT, FORMALITY, MEANS.

---

methodical, adj. systematic, businesslike, orderly (BUSINESS).

meticulous, adj. scrupulous, painstaking, punctilious (CARE).

metrical, adj. measured, metered, lilting (RHYTHM); anapaestic, dactylic, iambic (POETRY).

metropolis, n. municipality, megalopolis, town (CITY).

mew, v. mewl, miaou, caterwaul (ANIMAL SOUND).

mezzanine, n. balcony, gallery (SEAT).

miasma, n. vapor, steam, effluvium (GAS).

microbe, n. bug, microorganism, bacterium (SMALLNESS); germ, virus, pathogen (DISEASE).

microscopic, adj. tiny, teeny, wee (SMALLNESS).

MID-COURSE—N. mid-course, middle way, middle course, mean, golden mean, moderation; half measure.

compromise, adjustment, settlement, arrangement, give-and-take.

mean, medium, average, norm, golden mean, middle.

V. steer a middle course, keep the golden mean, avoid extremes; sit on the fence, straddle the issue.

compromise, go halfway, give a little, split the difference, meet one halfway, give and take, come to terms, settle; make the best of, make a virtue of necessity, settle for half a loaf.

Adj. mean, intermediate, medium, middle, medial, median, average, normal.

mediocre, middling, ordinary, commonplace.

See also CENTER, COMMONNESS, EQUALITY, MODERATENESS. *Antonyms* —See EXTREMENESS, INEQUALITY, INTEMPERANCE.

midday, *n.* noon, noonday, noontime (MORNING).

middle, *n.* midst, thick, median (CENTER).

middle age, *n.* middle years, summer, autumn (OLDNESS).

middle class, *n.* bourgeoisie, whitecollar class (PEOPLE).

middleman, *n.* jobber, wholesaler (SALE); broker, go-between, intermediary (DEPUTY, INTERJACENCE).

middling, *adj.* decent, fair, mediocre (GOOD).

midget, *n.* peewee, pygmy, shrimp (SMALLNESS).

midriff, *n.* partition, septum, diaphragm (INTERJACENCE).

midst, *n.* middle, deep, thick (CENTER).

mid-Victorian, *adj.* illiberal, hidebound, bourgeois (PREJUDICE).

midway, *adv.* in the midst, halfway, in the middle (INTERJACENCE, CENTER).

midwife, *n.* obstetrician, accoucheur, accoucheuse (MEDICAL SCIENCE).

mighty, *adj.* strong, powerful, potent (POWER, STRENGTH); prodigious, monumental (SIZE); intense, profound, stupendous (EXTREMENESS).

migrant, *n.* emigrant, expatriate, evacuee (DEPARTURE, TRAVELING).

migration, *n.* pilgrimage, hadj (*Arabic*), travel, tour (TRAVELING).

migratory, *adj.* wandering, vagabond, vagrant, gypsy, nomadic (WANDERING).

MILDNESS—*N.* mildness, moderation, lenity, clemency, humanity, compassion, mercy, quarter, indulgence, tolerance, toleration, favor, forbearance.

V. indulge, favor, gratify, humor, spoil, coddle, pamper, pet, cosset.

milden, soften, tame, mollify, calm, mellow, sweeten; mitigate, alleviate, allay, ease, relieve, ameliorate.

Adj. mild, gentle, easy, moderate, temperate, tranquil, calm, placid, bland, soft, suave; kind, considerate, conciliatory, gracious, amiable, benign, complaisant, easygoing, indulgent, tolerant; lenient, merciful, clement, compassionate,

tender, humane; forbearing, meek, submissive, pacific, unassuming, mild-spoken.

tame, feeble, insipid, vapid, dull, flat, jejune, spiritless, halfhearted. [*of weather*] temperate, balmy, soft, warm, pleasant, calm, summery, moderate.

See also CALMNESS, INEXCITABILITY, KINDNESS, MODERATENESS, PITY, RELIEF, SOFTNESS. *Antonyms*—See FORCE, ROUGHNESS, SEVERITY, STRENGTH, VIOLENCE.

milestone, *n.* waypost, milepost, landmark (INDICATION); occasion, event (OCCURRENCE).

militant, *adj.* aggressive, combative, active (FIGHTING, ACTIVITY).

militarism, *n.* jingoism, Prussianism, warmongering (FIGHTING).

military, *adj.* martial, soldierly, armed (FIGHTING).

military, *n.* armed force, army, soldiery (FIGHTER).

milksop, *n.* sissy, mollycoddle, milquetoast (MAN, FEAR).

milky, *adj.* lacteal, lacteous (SEMILIQUIDITY); milk-white, lactescent (WHITENESS); frosted, opalescent, pearly (SEMITRANSPARENCY).

mill, *n.* shop, plant, factory (WORK); grater, pestle, grindstone (POWDERINESS).

million, *n.* thousand thousand, billion, trillion (THOUSAND).

millionaire, *n.* Croesus, Midas, nabob (WEALTH).

millstone, *n.* burden, load, cumber (WEIGHT).

mimic, *v.* mime, parrot, ape (IMITATION).

mince, *v.* dice, cube, shred (CUTTING); simper, attitudinize (UNNATURALNESS); walk, tiptoe (WALKING).

mind, *n.* mental faculties, intellectuality, brain (INTELLECT); inclination, impulse, bent (TENDENCY).

mind, *v.* listen, give heed to (ATTENTION); obey, follow orders (OBEDIENCE); take care of, tend (CARE).

mindful, *adj.* attentive, heedful, observant (ATTENTION, CARE).

mine, *n.* excavation, ditch, trench (OPENING); lode, spring, fount (STORE).

mine, *v.* excavate, quarry, shovel (DIGGING).

miner, *n.* digger, burrower, sapper, excavator (DIGGING).

mineral, *n.* ore, vein, load (METAL).

mineral, *adj.* inorganic (METAL).

mingle, *v.* hobnob, mix, fraternize (SOCIALITY); blend, combine, mix (MIXTURE, JUNCTION).

miniature, *n.* midget, insignificancy, toy (SMALLNESS).

minimize, *v.* depreciate, derogate from, cheapen (DETRACTION).

minimum, *adj.* least, smallest, lowest (SMALLNESS).

minister, *n.* clergyman, priest, cleric (CLERGY); ambassador, diplomat (DEPUTY); prime minister, premier (OFFICIAL); fosterer, succorer (AID).

minister to, *v.* take care of, attend, tend (CARE); help, succor, foster (SERVICE, AID).

minor, *adj.* less, lesser, smaller (SMALLNESS); lower, junior, subordinate (LOWNESS, RANK); accessory, subsidiary (UNIMPORTANCE).

minor, *n.* adolescent, junior, teenager (YOUTH).

minority, *n.* juniority, nonage (YOUTH); the smaller number, the less (FEWNESS).

minstrel, *n.* bard, singer, songster (SINGING).

mint, *v.* coin, monetize, issue (MONEY).

minus, *adj.* less, negative, lacking (DEDUCTION, ABSENCE).

minute, *adj.* minuscule, infinitesimal, insignificant (SMALLNESS).

minutes, *n.* diary, journal (RECORD).

miracle, *n.* rarity, prodigy, wonderwork (UNUSUALNESS, SURPRISE, SUPERNATURALISM).

miraculous, *adj.* phenomenal, preternatural, prodigious, supernatural (SUPERNATURALISM, UNUSUALNESS).

mirage, *n.* delusion, hallucination, optical illusion (UNREALITY, DECEPTION).

mire, *n.* slime, ooze, muck (SEMILIQUIDITY).

mirror, *n.* glass, looking-glass, reflector (VISION).

mirror, *v.* imitate, simulate, reflect, copy (IMITATION).

mirth, *n.* hysterics, hysteria, convulsions (LAUGHTER); hilarity, festivity, levity (MERRIMENT).

MISANTHROPY—*N.* misanthropy, cynicism; hatred of women, misogyny.

misanthrope, man-hater, misanthropist, cynic, Timonist; Timon, Diogenes; misogynist.

Adj. misanthropic, antisocial, cynical, Diogenic; misogynous, misogynistic.

See also HATRED. *Antonyms*—See CHARITY, COURTESY, KINDNESS, LOVE.

---

misappropriation, *n.* embezzlement, peculation, defalcation (THIEVERY).

misbehave, *v.* do wrong, do evil, sin (WICKEDNESS).

misbehavior, *n.* misconduct, impropriety, immorality (WICKEDNESS, BEHAVIOR).

misbelief, *n.* delusion, misconception, fallacy (BELIEF, FALSENESS).

miscalculate, *v.* misreckon, miscount, misjudge (MISTAKE).

miscarriage, *n.* misfire, abortion, stillbirth (FAILURE); aborticide, feticide, curettage (PREGNANCY, BIRTH).

miscarry, *v.* misfire, fizzle (*colloq.*), go amiss, go wrong (FAILURE, MISTAKE); abort (PREGNANCY).

miscellaneous, *adj.* varied, divers, sundry (DIFFERENCE, MIXTURE).

miscellany, *n.* olio, omnium-gatherum (*colloq.*), farrago, medley (MIXTURE, ASSEMBLAGE); anthology, compilation (TREATISE).

mischance, *n.* misadventure, mishap, reverse (MISFORTUNE).

mischief, *n.* pranks, deviltry (MISCHIEF); damage, sabotage, vandalism (HARM); ill, harm, hurt, injury (WICKEDNESS).

MISCHIEF—*N.* mischief, pranks, villainy, knaveries, rascality, roguery, shenanigans (*colloq.*); devilry, deviltry, devilment; waggery.

trick, frolic, gambol, joke, lark, practical joke, prank; antic, dido, stunt, caper, capriccio; trickery.

mischief-maker, rascal, rogue, villain, devil, puck, gremlin, harlequin, hellion; scamp, imp, tyke, devilkin, vagabond, urchin; hoyden, minx; wag.

trickster, prankster, practical joker, larker, frolicker.

V. play tricks, prank, lark, frolic.

Adj. mischievous, roguish, rascal, rascally, villainous, devilish, naughty, parlous; waggish, puckish, arch, sly; impish, elfin, hoydenish.

trickish, pranky, pranksome, prankish, larksome, frolicsome.

See also CHILD, DECEPTION, HARM, PLAYFULNESS, WICKEDNESS, WITTINESS.

---

mischief-maker, *n.* rascal, rogue, villain (MISCHIEF); troublemaker, firebrand (DISAGREEMENT); evil worker, misdemeanant, monster (WICKEDNESS).

misconception, *n.* misapprehension, misunderstanding, misconstruction (MISINTERPRETATION).

misconduct, *n.* misbehavior, immorality, wrongdoing (BEHAVIOR, WICKEDNESS).

misconstrue, *v.* misinterpret, misapprehend, miscomprehend, misunderstand (MISINTERPRETATION).

misdeed, *n.* wrong, malefaction, transgression (SIN, WICKEDNESS); breach of law (ILLEGALITY).

miser, *n.* moneygrubber, huckster, mammonist (MONEY, GREED); niggard, penny pincher, Scrooge (STINGINESS).

miserable, *adj.* wretched, tragic, forlorn (SADNESS); sad, pathetic, contemptible (PITY); suffering, in pain (PAIN); poor, mean, vile (POVERTY, MEANNESS).

miserly, *adj.* penny-pinching, niggardly (STINGINESS).

misery, *n.* sorrow, grief, woe (SADNESS); suffering, anguish, agony (PAIN).

MISFORTUNE—*N.* misfortune, calamity, cataclysm, catastrophe, disaster, reverse, tragedy; casualty, debacle, misadventure, mishap, blow, contretemps.

adversity, bad (ill, evil, adverse, *or* hard) fortune (*or* luck), frowns of fortune; broken fortunes; evil day, hard times, rainy day, cloud, gathering clouds, ill wind; affliction, trouble, hardship, curse, blight, load, pressure, humiliation; evil, harm.

bad luck, ambsace, ill fortune, ill luck, misadventure, mischance, mishap, reverse.

foreboding, misgiving, premonition, presage, presentiment, presurmise; portent.

ruin, downfall, fall, overthrow, failure, crash, wreck; losing game; undoing, extremity.

jinx, hex, evil eye; whammy, double whammy (*both slang*).

V. come to grief, go downhill, be up against it (*colloq.*), go to rack and ruin, go to the dogs (*colloq.*); decay, sink, decline, fall, go down in the world; have seen better days; be all up with (*colloq.*).

Adj. unfortunate, adverse, cataclysmic, catastrophic, tragic; direful, foreboding, premonitory, sinister.

adverse, untoward, opposed, opposite, contrary, conflicting, opposing, disastrous, calamitous, ruinous, dire.

unlucky, unhappy, black, hapless, luckless, misadventurous, unpropitious, untoward; unblessed, unprosperous, unsuccessful, out of luck; badly off, in adverse circumstances, poor, wretched.

ill-fated, doomed, ill-omened, ill-starred, jinxed, star-crossed (*poetic*).

unfavorable, contrary, disadvantageous, inauspicious, inopportune, ominous, prejudicial, ill-disposed.

See also DESTRUCTION, FAILURE, OPPOSITION. *Antonyms*—See FRIENDLINESS, GOOD LUCK, SUCCESS.

misgiving, *n.* distrust, mistrust, apprehension (UNBELIEVINGNESS); doubt, scruple, hesitation (UNCERTAINTY); anxiety, qualm (FEAR); foreboding, premonition, presage (MISFORTUNE).

misguided, *adj.* ill-advised, injudicious, indiscreet (FOLLY).

mishap, *n.* casualty, debacle, blow (MISFORTUNE).

misinform, *v.* mislead, misguide, lead astray (MISTAKE, MISTEACHING).

MISINTERPRETATION—*N.* misinterpretation, misapprehension, miscomprehension, misconstruction, misunderstanding, misintelligence, misconception; cross-purposes; mistake.

misjudgment, miscalculation, hasty conclusion.

V. misinterpret, mistranslate, misread, misconstrue, misapprehend, miscomprehend, misunderstand, misconceive, misrender, mistake, confuse.

misjudge, miscalculate, misconjecture, overestimate, underestimate.

See also AMBIGUITY, CONFUSION, MISTAKE, MYSTERY, OVERESTIMATION, UNCLEARNESS. *Antonyms*—See CLARITY, EXPLANATION, JUDGMENT, MISREPRESENTATION, MISTEACHING, RIGHT, UNDERSTANDING.

misjudge, *n.* miscalculate, overestimate, underestimate (MISINTERPRETATION).

mislay, *v.* misplace, miss, lose (LOSS).

mislead, *v.* misguide, pervert, misinform (MISTAKE, MISTEACHING); deceive, lead astray, take in (DECEPTION).

misleading, *adj.* deceptive, delusive, sophistical (DECEPTION, MISTEACHING).

misname, *v.* miscall, misnomer, misterm (NAME).

misplace, *v.* lose, mislay, miss (LOSS).

misprint, *n.* typographical error, typo, corrigendum (MISTAKE).

mispronunciation, *n.* misenunciation, incorrect pronunciation (VOICE).

misquote, v. misstate, color, adulterate (FALSENESS).

MISREPRESENTATION—N. misrepresentation, perversion, distortion, contortion, twist, twisting; misstatement, exaggeration, falsification.

burlesque, travesty, take-off, parody, caricature, extravaganza, burletta, mockery, ridicule.

V. misrepresent, distort, contort, pervert, wrench, twist, skew; color, miscolor, trump up, slant, angle; overdraw, exaggerate, falsify, misstate, understate, overstate, stretch.

See also DISHONESTY, EXAGGERATION, FALSEHOOD, FALSENESS, RIDICULE, SOPHISTRY. Antonyms—See HONESTY, REPRESENTATION, RIGHT, TRUTH.

miss, n. unmarried woman, maiden, virgin (UNMARRIED STATE); maid, damsel (YOUTH).
Miss, n. Mademoiselle (F.), Señorita (Sp.), Mistress (TITLE).
miss, v. fail, fall short of, miss the mark (FAILURE); neglect, skip, disregard (NEGLECT); lose, mislay, misplace (LOSS).
misshapen, adj. deformed, ill-made, grotesque (DEFORMITY).
missile, n. projectile, trajectile, bolt (ARMS, THROW).
missing, adj. lost, mislaid, misplaced (LOSS); absent, gone, away (ABSENCE).
mission, n. errand, task, assignment (COMMISSION); object, objective, end (PURPOSE).
misspelling, n. incorrect spelling, pseudography (WRITTEN SYMBOL).
misstate, v. misquote, falsify, misrepresent (FALSENESS, MISREPRESENTATION).
mist, n. fog, smog, smaze (WATER, CLOUD).

MISTAKE—N. mistake, error, inaccuracy, solecism, blunder, boner, blooper (slang), howler, slip, slip-up; misprint, typographical error, typo, corrigendum, erratum; slip of the tongue, lapsus linguae (L.), fluff, bull, spoonerism, malapropism, lapse; faux pas (F.), gaffe (F.), misstep, oversight; fallacy, flaw, fault.

V. err, be in error, be mistaken, be deceived; mistake, deceive oneself, blunder, nod, slip, slip up, fluff (one's lines), stumble, trip; mistake or confuse (one for the other).

misunderstand, misapprehend, misconceive, misconstrue, misinterpret, misreckon, miscount, miscalculate, misjudge.
miscarry, misfire, go amiss, go wrong, go astray, stray; be wrong, be amiss.

Adj. erroneous, untrue, false, faulty, erring, fallacious, illogical, unreal, unfounded, ungrounded, groundless, unsubstantial, unsound, inexact, inaccurate, incorrect, imprecise, improper, wrong, unexact, unprecise; mistaken, in error, deceived; wide of the mark, at fault; solecistic; wrongful, wrongheaded.

exploded, refuted, discarded, rejected, discredited, obsolete, outworn, passé (F.).

See also DECEPTION, FALSENESS, MISINTERPRETATION, MISTEACHING, MISTIMING. Antonyms—See RIGHT, TRUTH.

MISTEACHING—N. misteaching, misinstruction, misinformation, misguidance, misdirection, demagoguery, perversion, sophistry, the blind leading the blind.

misleader, betrayer, seducer, perverter, decoy, Judas goat, demagogue.

V. misteach, misinstruct, misinform, miseducate, misdirect, misguide; lead astray, seduce, pervert, mislead, deceive, betray, lead on, decoy, inveigle.

Adj. misleading, deceptive, sophistical, demagogic, seductive, perversive.

leaderless, pilotless, acephalous; unlead, uncaptained, unchaired, unguided, unpiloted.

See also DECEPTION, FALSEHOOD, FALSENESS, MISREPRESENTATION, PRETENSE, SOPHISTRY. Antonyms—See GUIDANCE, HONESTY, LEADERSHIP, TEACHING.

mistimed, adj. unseasonable, ill-timed (UNTIMELINESS).

MISTIMING—N. mistiming, anachronism, prolepsis, anticipation, prochronism, metachronism, parachronism.

V. mistime, misdate; antedate, postdate, overdate, anticipate.

Adj. anachronistic, anachronous, misdated; antedated, postdated, overdated; overdue; out of date, behind time, outdated; ahead of time.

See also MISTAKE, UNTIMELINESS.
Antonyms—See MEASUREMENT, TIME.

---

mistreat, *n.* abuse, ill-use, ill-treat (MISUSE, ACTION).

mistress, *n.* paramour, kept woman (SEX).

mistrust, *n.* distrust, misgiving, misdoubt (UNBELIEVINGNESS).

mistrust, *v.* distrust, doubt, disbelieve (UNBELIEVINGNESS).

misty, *adj.* dewy, vaporous, vapory (WATER); hazy, murky, foggy (UNCLEARNESS, SEMITRANSPARENCY).

misunderstand, *v.* misconstrue, misapprehend, miscomprehend (MISINTERPRETATION); take amiss, take wrongly (OFFENSE).

misunderstanding, *n.* misapprehension, misconstruction, misconception (MISINTERPRETATION); rift, rupture, break (DISAGREEMENT).

misunderstood, *adj.* unappreciated (INGRATITUDE).

MISUSE—*N.* misuse, misusage, misemployment, misapplication, perversion; abuse, ill-usage, maltreatment, mistreatment, profanation, prostitution, desecration; waste.

V. misuse, misemploy, misapply, exploit; desecrate, abuse, ill-use, ill-treat, maltreat, mistreat, prostitute, profane, pervert; squander, waste.

overwork, overtax, overtask, overlabor, overburden, overstrain.

See also ACTION, DISRESPECT, MISUSE OF WORDS, WASTEFULNESS, WEIGHT, WORK. *Antonyms*—See RESPECT, USE.

MISUSE OF WORDS—*N.* misuse of words, misusage, bull, grammatical error, error in grammar, solecism, syllepsis, slip of the tongue, *lapsus linguae* (L.), barbarism, catachresis, malapropism, impropriety.

Adj. misused, solecistic, catachrestic, sylleptic, ungrammatical, unidiomatic, improper, incorrect, illiterate.

See also IMPROPERNESS, MISTAKE. *Antonyms*—See LANGUAGE, PROPRIETY, RIGHT.

---

mite, *n.* small thing, peewee, tot; minim, modicum, particle (SMALLNESS).

mitigate, *v.* alleviate, allay, ease (MILDNESS); abate, moderate, attemper (DECREASE, WEAKNESS); justify, palliate (FORGIVENESS).

mitten, *n.* gauntlet, mousquetaire, mitt (GLOVE).

mix, *v.* blend, combine, compound (MIXTURE, COMBINATION); mingle, hobnob, fraternize (SOCIALITY).

mixed, *adj.* composite, motley, assorted, mongrel, hybrid, varied, various (MIXTURE, CLASS).

MIXTURE—*N.* mixture, admixture, minglement, blend, compound, combination, union, association, amalgamation, mix, intermixture, immixture, composite, junction; alloy, amalgam; instillation, infusion, transfusion; impregnation, infiltration.

medley, jumble, hodgepodge, mélange (F.), hash, mess, ollapodrida, salmagundi, olio, miscellany, omnium-gatherum (*colloq.*), farrago, *pasticcio* (It.), potpourri, patchwork, pastiche (F.), gallimaufry; mosaic, motley.

V. mix, blend, stir, whip, combine, mingle, commingle, intermingle, scramble, interlard, join, compound, amalgamate, alloy, cross; adulterate.

imbue, infuse, diffuse, suffuse, transfuse, instill, infiltrate, saturate, impregnate, lace (*a beverage*), tinge, tincture.

unite, associate, join, conjoin; fraternize.

Adj. mixed, etc. (see *Verbs*): composite, half-and-half, heterogeneous; motley, variegated, miscellaneous, promiscuous, indiscriminate; hybrid, mongrel.

See also COMBINATION, JUNCTION, LIQUID, MAKE-UP, TEXTURE, UNITY, VARIEGATION. *Antonyms*—See DISJUNCTION, UNIFORMITY, SIMPLICITY.

---

mix-up, *n.* confusion, muddle, mess (CONFUSION, UNTIDINESS).

mix up, *v.* confuse, confound (INDISCRIMINATION); derange, muddle, jumble (CONFUSION).

moan, *v.* bemoan, bewail, keen (SADNESS).

moat, *n.* ditch, dike, trough (CHANNEL, HOLLOW).

mob, *n.* crowd, mass, jam (ASSEMBLAGE, MULTITUDE); rabble, canaille, cattle (PEOPLE).

mob, *v.* jam, mass, swarm (MULTITUDE).

mobile, *adj.* motile, ambulatory (MOTION).

mobilize, *v.* catalyze, activate, animate (MOTIVATION).

mob rule, *n.* lawlessness, anarchy, disorder (ILLEGALITY).

mock, *adj.* imitative, mimic, apish (IMITATION); pretended, make-believe, fake (PRETENSE); counterfeit, forged, fraudulent (FALSE-NESS).

mock, *v.* mimic, ape, imitate (IMI-TATION); jeer at, hoot, deride (IN-SULT, RIDICULE).

mockery, *n.* derision, scorn, sport; jestingstock, laughingstock (RIDI-CULE).

mode, *n.* fashion, style, vogue (FASHION); manner, way, form (METHOD).

model, *n.* archetype, original, exemplar (BEGINNING, COPY); portrait, figure, image (REPRESENTATION); paragon, pattern, ideal (PERFECTION); dummy, mannequin, poser (FINE ARTS, POSTURE).

MODERATENESS—*N.* moderateness, moderation, conservatism, golden mean, moderatism, temperance.

moderate, moderatist, conservative, middle-of-the-roader.

V. **moderate,** temper, soften, mitigate, palliate; lessen, abate, decrease; check, tame, curb, restrain, subdue.

Adj. **moderate,** temperate, reasonable, medium, conservative, middle-of-the-road; abstemious; gentle, mild, calm, quiet.

unexcessive, unexorbitant, unextravagant, unprohibitive; unextreme, unradical, unfanatical.

Adv., phrases. **moderately,** temperately, etc. (see *Adjectives*); in moderation, in reason, within bounds.

See also CALMNESS, CONTROL, DECREASE, JUDGE, MEDIATION, MIDCOURSE, REASONABLENESS, SOBRIETY, WEAKNESS. *Antonyms*—See EXTREMENESS, FORCE, INTEMPERANCE, STRENGTH, VIOLENCE.

modern, *adj.* new, up-to-date, neoteric (NEWNESS).

modernize, *v.* renew, renovate, refurbish (NEWNESS).

MODESTY—*N.* modesty, humility, diffidence, reserve, retiring disposition; simplicity, unostentation; decency, propriety, pudicity, overmodesty, prudery, Victorianism, pudency, pudibundity, Grundyism.

prude, Victorian, Grundyist.

V. be modest, retire, keep one's distance, keep in the background; hide one's light under a bushel.

blush, color, crimson, flush, mantle, redden; prim.

Adj. **modest,** humble, meek, sheepish, unassuming; diffident, retiring, reserved.

unpretentious, unpretending, unpresumptuous, chaste, homely, humble, lowly, mean, plain, quiet, simple, unassuming, unobtrusive, unostentatious.

decent, chaste, maidenly, proper, pudent, pudibund.

demure, coy, skittish, blushing, overmodest, prim, prudish, straitlaced, Victorian, squeamish, queasy.

bashful, shy, chary, backward, diffident, mousy, timid, timorous; recessive, self-effacing, shrinking; self-conscious, sheepish, shamefaced, verecund.

See also HUMILITY, LOWNESS, MEANNESS, UNCERTAINTY. *Antonyms*—See BOASTING, CERTAINTY, OSTENTATION, PRIDE.

modify, *v.* transform, transmute, convert (CHANGE); relax, remit, slacken (WEAKNESS).

modulation, *n.* pitch, intonation, inflection (SOUND, VOICE).

mogul, *n.* baron, potentate, sachem (POWER).

Mohammedanism, *n.* Moslemism, Mussulmanism, Islamism (RELIGION).

moist, *adj.* damp, humid, irriguous (WATER); rainy, drizzly, drippy (RAIN).

moisten, *v.* wet, damp, dampen, humidify (WATER).

moisture, *n.* humidity, damp, wet (WATER).

molasses, *n.* syrup, treacle (*Brit.*), sorghum (SWEETNESS).

mold, *n.* moulage (*F.*), impression, pattern (SHAPE).

mold, *v.* form, pat, whittle (SHAPE); mildew, rust, stale (OLDNESS).

moldy, *adj.* putrid, gamy, high (ODOR); stale, timeworn (OLDNESS).

molest, *v.* annoy, bother, plague (ANNOYANCE).

mollify, *v.* soothe, ease, pacify (CALMNESS); soften, mellow, milden (SOFTNESS).

mollycoddle, *n.* weakling, sissy, pantywaist (WEAKNESS, FEAR, MAN).

molt, *v.* shed, cast, exuviate (UNDRESS, ELIMINATION).

molten, *adj.* melted, liquefied, thawed (LIQUID).

moment, *n.* second, twinkling, instant (TIME, EARLINESS); point, date, stage (TIME); import, consequence, weight (IMPORTANCE).

momentary, *adj.* brief, short, instantaneous (IMPERMANENCE).

momentous, *adj.* eventful, important, outstanding (OCCUR-

RENCE, IMPORTANCE, RESULT); grave, critical, fateful (IMPORTANCE, SOBRIETY).

momentum, n. impetus, push, impulse (FORCE).

monarch, n. king, sovereign, majesty (RULER).

monastery, n. lamasery, abbey, priory (RELIGIOUS COMMUNITY).

monastic, adj. monkish (derogatory), cenobitic, hermitlike, anchoritic (RELIGIOUS COMMUNITY, SECLUSION).

monetary, adj. financial, fiscal, pecuniary (MONEY).

MONEY—N. money, legal tender, pelf (derogatory), lucre or filthy lucre (derogatory), medium of exchange, funds, treasure, wealth, means, ways and means, wherewithal, cash, currency.

coin, specie, change, token.

[slang terms] jack, spondulics, simoleons, mazuma, shekels, the needful, the ready, grand ($1000), century ($100), C-note; tenner ($10), ten-spot; fiver ($5), five-spot; deuce; cart wheel (silver dollar), bob (shilling), two bits (quarter).

petty cash, pocket money, pin money, spending money, change, small coin, chicken feed (slang).

paper money, note, bill, dollar, dollar bill, money order, bank note, bond, bill of exchange, check, promissory note, IOU, draft, order, warrant, coupon, debenture, greenback, roll, bank roll, wad (colloq.); lettuce, folding money, long green, the green stuff (all slang).

money-maker, earner, wage earner, provider, breadwinner; livelihood.

treasurer, bursar, controller, comptroller, chamberlain, steward, purser, paymaster, cashier, teller, financier, banker; cambist, money-changer, money broker; economist, political economist; accountant, bookkeeper.

treasury, bursary, exchequer, fisc, purse, bank, vault, safe, coffer, till, cash register, cash drawer.

[science of money, coins, etc.] finance, numismatics, numismatology, chrysology, economics, political economy.

coinage, mintage, monometallism, bimetallism; mint.

[one interested in money] moneygrubber, miser, huckster, mammonist, bourgeois, Philistine, fortune hunter, adventuress, gold-digger (fem.); hireling, pensionary, mercenary (mil.).

V. coin, mint, monetize, remonetize, issue, circulate; counterfeit; demonetize, devaluate, repudiate.

make money, earn, earn money, be gainfully employed, be paid, eke out an existence.

Adj. financial, fiscal, monetary, pecuniary, nummary, nummular, economic, budgetary.

mercenary, sordid, venal, hireling, pensionary, Philistine, mammonish, mammonistic, bourgeois.

See also ACCOUNTS, MEANS, WEALTH. Antonyms—See POVERTY.

moneyed, adj. well-to-do, well-off, flush (WEALTH).

moneylender, n. money broker, moneymonger, pawnbroker (DEBT).

mongrel, adj. hybrid, mixed (CLASS).

mongrel, n. dog, mutt (colloq.), cur (ANIMAL); crossbreed, mixture, hybrid (CROSSING).

monitor, n. listener, auditor, eavesdropper (LISTENING); watchdog, Cerberus, Cassandra (WARNING).

monk, n. monastic, cenobite, anchorite (RELIGIOUS COMMUNITY, SECLUSION).

monkey, n. simian, ape, baboon (ANIMAL).

monologue, n. soliloquy, discourse, disquisition (TALK).

monopoly, n. corner, oligopoly (CONTROL); holding company, cartel, trust (BUSINESS).

monotonous, adj. tedious, uninteresting, dull (BOREDOM); toneless, unrelieved (UNIFORMITY).

monster, n. devil, evil worker, mischief-maker (WICKEDNESS); colossus, titan, mammoth (SIZE); monstrosity, horror (HATRED); freak, scarecrow, grotesque (DEFORMITY, UNNATURALNESS, UNUSUALNESS); griffin, Chimera (MYTHICAL BEINGS).

monstrous, adj. infamous, evil, corrupt (WICKEDNESS); gruesome, hideous, macabre (HATRED); horrid, outrageous, scandalous (DISGUST); grotesque, freakish, abnormal (UNNATURALNESS, UNUSUALNESS).

monthly, adj. mensal (TIME).

monument, n. pillar, column, obelisk (HEIGHT); memorial, cairn, testimonial (MEMORY); tombstone, gravestone, stone (BURIAL); magnum opus (L.), chef-d'oeuvre (F.), masterpiece (PRODUCTION).

moody, adj. mopish, broody, temperamental (GLOOM, DEJECTION, BAD TEMPER).

moon, *n.* satellite, Sputnik, crescent (WORLD).

moon-shaped, *adj.* moonlike, luniform, semilunar (CURVE).

moor, *n.* heath, moors, moorland (LAND).

moor, *v.* tether, picket, tie (LOCATION, JUNCTION).

moot, *adj.* dubious, debatable, disputable, questionable, controversial, contestable (INQUIRY, UNCERTAINTY, DISAGREEMENT).

mop, *n.* sponge, swab, wiper (RUBBING); locks, tresses, mane (HAIR).

mope, *v.* despond, gloom (DEJECTION).

moral, *n.* gnome, moralism, precept (STATEMENT).

morale, *n. esprit de corps* (*F.*), party spirit (CO-OPERATION).

MORALITY—*N.* morality, morals, moral code, moral principles, ethics.

goodness, virtue, ethicality, honesty, honor, incorruptibility, rectitude.

sermon, lecture, preachment, moralism, moral, lesson.

V. moralize, preach, sermonize, lecture.

Adj. moral, ethical, virtuous, good, honest, honorable, incorrupt, incorruptible, righteous, sainted, holy, saintly, upright, scrupulous, conscientious.

strait-laced, strict, puritanical, prudish; preachy, self-righteous, sanctimonious, pharisaical.

See also GOOD, HONESTY, MODESTY, PREACHING. *Antonyms*—See DISHONESTY, IMMORALITY.

---

morbid, *adj.* gruesome, hideous, macabre (HATRED, FEAR); pathological, infected, diseased (DISEASE).

more, *adv.* in addition, also, beyond (ADDITION, SUPERIORITY).

moreover, *adv.* additionally, also, furthermore (ADDITION).

morgue, *n.* mortuary, undertaking parlor (DEATH).

MORNING—*N.* morning, morn, morningtide (*poetic*), matins (*eccl.*), forenoon, foreday, ante meridiem, A.M., midmorning.

sunrise, dawn, daybreak, daylight, dayspring, sunup, aurora, peep of day, break of day, crack of dawn, cockcrow.

noon, midday, noonday, noontime, noontide, midnoon.

afternoon, P.M., post meridiem, midafternoon.

day, weekday; Sunday, Sabbath, weekend.

Adj. **morning,** matin, matinal, matutinal, antemeridian; noon, noonday, noontide, midday, meridian; afternoon, postmeridian, midafternoon.

daily, diurnal (*astron.*), quotidian, everyday, per diem, semidiurnal (*twice a day*); noctidiurnal (*day and night*), bissextile (*extra day in leap year*); quintan (*every fifth day*), hebdomadal (*every seven days*).

See also EARLINESS, LIGHT. *Antonyms*—See DARKNESS, EVENING.

---

moron, *n.* cretin, idiot, imbecile (STUPIDITY).

morose, *adj.* glum, sullen, sulky (BAD TEMPER); moody, broody, mopish (GLOOM).

morsel, *n.* bit, sample, drop (TASTE); snack, tidbit (FOOD, SMALLNESS).

mortal, *adj.* human, bipedal, creatural (MANKIND); fatal, lethal, deadly (KILLING); grievous, severe (EXTREMENESS).

mortician, *n.* undertaker, funeral director (BURIAL).

mortification, *n.* penance, hair shirt, martyrdom (ASCETICISM).

mortuary, *n.* undertaking parlor, morgue (DEATH).

mosaic, *n.* parquet, parquetry, checkerwork (VARIEGATION).

mosquito, *n.* fly, gnat (ANIMAL).

mossy, *adj.* turfy, grassy, verdant (PLANT LIFE).

mote, *n.* spot, dot, fleck (VARIEGATION).

moth-eaten, *adj.* hackneyed, stale, trite (USE).

mother, *n.* parent, mamma, matriarch (ANCESTRY).

MOTION—*N.* motion, movement, locomotion, ambulation, sweep, move, action, gesture; direction, inclination, tendency, drift, driftage, set, course, circuit, current, stream, flow, flux, progress, advance.

mobility, motility, locomobility, locomotion, movability.

science of motion: dynamics, physics, kinetics, kinematics.

V. move, move about, move around, locomote, stir, budge, drift, maunder; ambulate, circulate, sweep; toss, twist, wind; mill around, swarm, stream, throng, troop, stampede; progress, advance, act, take action.

motion, gesture, sign, gesticulate, beckon, nod, wave, direct, guide, invite.

set in motion, move, stir, budge, circulate, manipulate.

make a motion, propose, suggest, offer, recommend.

wheel, roll, truckle, trundle.

Adj. mobile, motile, locomotive, locomobile, ambulatory; automotive, automobile; movable.

Phrases. on the move, on the march, under way.

See also ACTION, GESTURE, OFFER, OSCILLATION, PROGRESS, RHYTHM, ROLL, SUGGESTION, TENDENCY, TRANSFER, VEHICLE WINDING. *Antonyms*— See INACTIVITY, MOTIONLESSNESS, REST.

MOTIONLESSNESS—*N.* motionlessness, immobility, immovability, quiescence; quiet, quietude, stability, stagnation, entropy, stagnancy, stall, stand, standstill; immobilization, inertia, torpor, paralysis, palsy, apoplexy, petrifaction, transfixture, transfixion, trance.

V. be motionless, not move, stand still, stand, stall, stagnate.

stop, arrest, fix, stall, still, quiet, immobilize; numb, paralyze, palsy, transfix, spellbind, petrify.

Adj. motionless, immobile, immovable, quiescent, fixed, quiet, still, stable, stagnant, stalled, standing, static, stationary, steadfast; immobilized; inert, torpid, numb, paralyzed, palsied, apoplectic, petrified, transfixed, spellbound, sessile (*zool.*).

See also CESSATION, END, INACTIVITY, REST, STABILITY. *Antonyms*—See CONTINUATION, ENDLESSNESS, MOTION, PROGRESS.

MOTION PICTURES—*N.* motion picture, cinema, film, flicker (*colloq.*), movie (*colloq.*), feature, moving picture, photodrama, photoplay, picture, picture show (*colloq.*), screen play, show (*colloq.*); travelogue, cartoon, newsreel, documentary; Western, horse opera (*colloq.*); trailer, preview, sneak preview.

[*motion-picture industry, etc.*] films, filmland (*colloq.*), motion pictures, moviedom, movieland (*colloq.*), the movies (*colloq.*), moving pictures, pictures (*colloq.*), the screen, the silver screen, Hollywood; cinematography.

screen writer, photodramatist, photoplaywright, scenarist.

motion-picture theater, cinema (*Brit.*), movie theater *or* house (*colloq.*), nickelodeon (*hist.*), picture theater (*colloq.*), drive-in.

V. film, shoot, cinematograph.

See also AMUSEMENT, DRAMA, PHOTOGRAPH, STORY, WRITER.

MOTIVATION—*N.* motivation, actuation, impulsion, inducement, etc. (see *Verbs*).

motive, impulse, drive, inducement, incentive, influence, bias; reason, cause, springs, root, basis, ground, foundation, underlying motive, ulterior motive.

stimulus, stimulant, spur, urge, prod, goad, lash, whip, push; excitant, shock, activator, catalytic agent, catalyst; sting, prick, needle; temptation, lure, enticement, blandishment, consideration.

V. motivate, actuate, impel, drive, move, induce, inspire, prompt, provoke, suggest; influence, sway, lead, prevail on, persuade, encourage, egg on; incline, dispose, predispose, bias; predetermine.

stimulate, spur, urge, prod, goad, lash, whip, innervate, jog, push.

excite, arouse, rouse, waken, stir, stir up, bestir, galvanize, shock, whip, quicken; activate, animate, mobilize, develop, catalyze, sting, prick, pique, needle; incite, instigate, foment.

tempt, lure, entice, allure; coax, wheedle, inveigle.

bestir oneself, bestir, quicken, rouse, stir, waken, mobilize.

Adj. motivating, etc. (see *Verbs*); motivational, inspirational, provocative, suggestive, influential, persuasive; excitative, stimulative, urgent.

See also ATTRACTION, CAUSATION, EXCITEMENT, INFLUENCE, PERSUASION, PROPULSION. *Antonyms*—See DISSUASION, PREVENTION.

---

motive, *n.* reason, purpose, root, basis (CAUSATION); impulse, drive, incentive (MOTIVATION).

motley, *adj.* variegated, mottled (VARIEGATION); varied, mixed, miscellaneous (MIXTURE).

motorist, *n.* driver, chauffeur, autoist (VEHICLE).

mottle, *v.* speckle, speck, bespot (VARIEGATION).

motto, *n.* saying, slogan, watchword (STATEMENT).

mound, *n.* mount, tumulus, rise (HEIGHT).

mount, *v.* ascend, rise, climb (ASCENT).

mountain, *n.* alp, volcano, hill (HEIGHT).

mountainous, *adj.* hilly, alpine, alpestrine (HEIGHT); mammoth, giant, colossal (SIZE).

mourn, *v.* lament, grieve, sorrow (SADNESS, REGRET).

mournful, *adj.* dirgeful, doleful, eleglac, funereal, somber (SADNESS).

mouse, *n.* rodent, rat (ANIMAL); bruise, contusion, wale (HARM).

mousy, *adj.* timid, bashful, diffident (MODESTY).

mouth, *n.* maw, stoma (*zool.*), neb (HEAD); entrance, opening, orifice (INGRESS).

mouthful, *n.* morsel, bite, snack (TASTE, FOOD).

move, *v.* locomote, stir, budge; propose, recommend (MOTION); shift, change residence, transfer; carry, convey (TRANSFER); induce, inspire, prompt (MOTIVATION); affect, touch, impress (PITY, INFLUENCE).

moved, *adj.* affected, impressed, stirred (FEELING).

movement, *n.* locomotion, action, gesture (MOTION).

moving, *adj.* affecting, impressive, inspiring (INFLUENCE); stirring, touching, emotional (FEELING); heartbreaking, heart-rending, poignant (PITY).

moving picture, *n.* photodrama, photoplay, picture (MOTION PICTURES).

Mr., *n.* Mister, *Monsieur* (*F.*), Master (TITLE).

Mrs., *n. Madame* or *Mme.* (*F.*), *Doña* (*Sp.*), Mistress (TITLE).

much, *n.* lot, loads, lots (MULTITUDE).

mucilage, *n.* glue, cement, gum (STICKINESS).

muck, *n.* slime, ooze, mire (SEMILIQUIDITY).

mucus, *n.* phlegm, pituite, rheum (EXCRETION).

mud, *n.* slush, slop, slosh (SEMILIQUIDITY).

muddle, *n.* confusion, mix-up, mess (UNTIDINESS); haze, daze, fog (CONFUSION).

muddle, *v.* bewilder, rattle (*colloq.*), nonplus (UNCERTAINTY); bungle, blunder (CLUMSINESS); confuse, mix up, bemuddle (CONFUSION).

muddy, *adj.* slushy, sloughy, squashy (SEMILIQUIDITY); unclear, cloudy, turbid (UNCLEARNESS).

mudslinging, *n.* abuse, attack, assailment (MALEDICTION).

muffin, *n.* crumpet, English muffin (BREAD).

muffle, *v.* wrap, envelop, wind (ROLL); gag, muzzle, squelch

(SILENCE); dreaden, drown, cushion (NONRESONANCE, WEAKNESS).

muffled, *adj.* silenced, mute (NONRESONANCE); deadened, flat, subdued (DULLNESS).

muffler, *n.* bandanna, comforter, scarf (NECKWEAR).

muggy, *adj.* sultry, stuffy, oppressive (HEAT).

mulatto, *n.* Negro, quadroon, octoroon (MANKIND).

mule, *n.* ass, hybrid, sumpter (HORSE); bullhead, intransigent (STUBBORNNESS); scuff, sandal, pump (FOOTWEAR).

mull over, *v.* brood over, pore over, study (THOUGHT).

multiple, *n.* factor, multiplicand, faciend (NUMBER).

multiply, *v.* reproduce, procreate, propagate (BIRTH).

MULTITUDE—*N.* multitude, army, crowd, host, legion, loads, lots, multiplicity, raft (*colloq.*), sea, ocean, slew *or* slue (*colloq.*); infinity, infinitude, myriad; majority, plurality; numbers, scores, heap (*colloq.*), power (*colloq.*), sight (*colloq.*), lot, much.

crowd, mob, mass, jam, throng, press, swarm, horde, pack, herd (*derogatory*), drove, crush, flock, gathering, conglomeration, huddle, knot, posse, push (*colloq.*).

crowded place, packed house; slums, slum, warren.

[*large amount or quantity*] **abundance,** affluence, dollop, flood, deluge, shower, torrent, immensity, mass, mint, oodles (*colloq.*), peck (*colloq.*), pile, plenitude, plenty, profusion, raft (*colloq.*), superabundance, wealth, opulence, luxuriance.

overabundance, excess, glut, superabundance.

V. **be numerous,** abound, exuberate, pullulate, superabound, swarm, teem; infest, swarm over, overrun; outnumber.

abound in, swarm with, teem with, superabound in; be crowded (packed, jammed, swarming, teeming, alive, rife, abounding *or* superabounding) with; be crawling (infested, *or* overrun) with.

crowd, deluge, swamp, overcrowd, flood; conglomerate, flock, gather, herd, huddle, jam, mass, mob, swarm, throng, besiege, congregate, pack, serry.

Adj. **many,** numerous, multitudinous, rife, thick, considerable, great, several, endless, unending, galore (*colloq.*).

various, divers, manifold, multiple, sundry.

[*large in amount or quantity*] considerable, abundant, ample, astronomical, copious, exuberant, great, legion (*in the predicate*), overwhelming, plenteous, plentiful, profuse, rife, substantial, superabundant, tidy (*colloq.*), vast, torrential.

countless, incalculable, infinite, innumerable, innumerous, myriad, numberless, uncountable, uncounted, unnumberable, unnumbered, untold.

crowded, jammed, crammed, massed, mobbed, swarming, thronged, packed, jam-packed, serried, tumid, teeming, bristling, chockablock, congested, conglomerate, crammed, overcrowded; slum, slummy.

See also ASSEMBLAGE, EXCESS, GREATNESS, PRESENCE, QUANTITY, SUFFICIENCY, WEALTH. *Antonyms*—See FEWNESS, LACK, INSUFFICIENCY, SMALLNESS.

mum, *adj.* dumb, silent, quiet (SILENCE).

mumble, *v.* whisper, murmur, mutter (TALK).

mummy, *n.* corpse, remains, carcass (DEATH).

munch, *v.* crunch, chew, masticate (FOOD).

mundane, *adj.* worldly, carnal, temporal, unspiritual (WORLD, IRRELIGION); earthly, global, planetary (WORLD).

municipality, *n.* metropolis, town, township (CITY).

murder, *n.* slaying, assassination, homicide (KILLING).

murder, *v.* assassinate, slay (KILLING).

murderer, *n.* assassin, cutthroat (KILLING).

murderous, *adj.* homicidal, slaughterous (KILLING).

murky, *adj.* hazy, fuzzy, foggy (UNCLEARNESS); dull, dim, dark (CLOUD).

murmur, *v.* whisper, susurrate, mumble (TALK); purl, gurgle, babble (RIVER).

muscular, *adj.* brawny, athletic, burly (STRENGTH).

muse, *n.* Calliope, Clio (GOD).

muse, *v.* meditate, ponder, puzzle over (THOUGHT).

MUSIC—*N.* music, melody, harmony; polyphony; strain, tune, air, measure; medley, potpourri; composition, opus (*L.*), piece; concerto; symphony, sonata, symphonic poem, tone poem; chamber music; movement; overture, prelude.

jazz, syncopation, ragtime; jive, swing, bop, bebop, rock-'n-roll, boogie-woogie (*all slang or colloq.*); calypso.

[*vocal music*] opera, grand opera, music drama, operetta.

solo, duet, duo (*It.*), trio, quartet, quintet, sestet *or* sextet, septet, double quartet, chorus; part song, descant, glee, madrigal, catch, round, chorale; antiphon.

concert, musicale, musical (*colloq.*), recital, pop (*colloq.*), sing (*colloq.*).

note, symbol, character, musical note; sharp, flat, natural; grace, grace note, appoggiatura (*It.*).

Adj. musical, melodious, melodic, tuneful, canorous, euphonious, harmonious, symphonic, contrapuntal; orchestral, instrumental; classical, popular, modern; vocal, choral, lyric, operatic, dramatic; philharmonic.

florid, embellished, brilliant, flowery, elaborate, ornate, figured.

See also HARMONY, MELODY, MUSICAL INSTRUMENTS, MUSICIAN, SINGING, SWEETNESS, VOICE.

MUSICAL INSTRUMENTS—*N.* musical instruments: orchestra (*including* strings, wood winds, brass winds, *and* percussives), concert orchestra, *Kappelle* (*Ger.*); band, military band, brass band, jazz band.

[*stringed instruments*] violin, Cremona, Stradivarius, fiddle (*colloq.*), rebec, viol, viola, viola d'amore, viola da braccio, tenor viol, viola da gamba, bass viol, violoncello *or* cello, double bass, contrabass, contrabasso, violone.

harp, lyre, lute, archlute, cithara, cither, zither, psaltery, balalaika, guitar, banjo, mandolin, ukulele, uke (*colloq.*).

piano *or* pianoforte, harpsichord, clavichord, clavier, spinet, virginal.

[*wind instruments*] organ, pipe organ, reed organ; harmonium, melodion, accordion, concertina; bagpipes, doodlesack; Panpipe, Pandean pipes; mouth organ, harmonica; whistle.

wood winds, flute, fife, piccolo, pipe, flageolet, clarinet, oboe, bassoon, saxophone, reed instrument.

brass winds, trumpet, cornet, horn, bugle, French horn, saxhorn, trombone, tuba.

[*percussion instruments*] drum, bass drum, kettledrum, timbal, timpano (*pl.* timpani), side drum, snare drum, tambour, taboret, tom-tom, tambourine, timbrel; cymbals, bells, glockenspiel, carillon, xylophone, marimba, vibraphone, triangle, etc.

[*mechanical*] player piano, hurdy-gurdy, hand organ, barrel organ; phonograph, Victrola, record player, turntable, gramophone, music box; calliope.

See also MUSIC, MUSICIAN.

MUSICIAN—*N.* musician, artist, artiste, performer, virtuoso, player, instrumentalist, organist, pianist, accompanist; violinist, fiddler (*colloq. or derogatory*), flutist or flautist, harpist or harper, lutist or lutanist, fifer, trumpeter, cornettist, bugler, piper, drummer; disc-jockey.

orchestra, band, ensemble, strings, wood wind, brass; brass band, military band, German band, jazz band.

conductor, director, leader, *Kapellmeister* (*Ger.*), bandmaster, choirmaster, concertmaster, drum major.

V. play, perform, execute, render, read, tune, tune up, pipe, flute, whistle, pipe up, strike up; fiddle, bow, scrape (*derogatory*); twang, pluck, pick; pound, thump, tickle the ivories (*slang*), strum, thrum, drum; accompany.

conduct, direct, lead, wield the baton, beat time.

compose, set to music, arrange, harmonize, orchestrate.

See also MUSIC, SINGING, WRITER.

---

muss up (*colloq.*), *v.* rumple, dishevel, tousle; mess up, clutter (UNTIDINESS, CONFUSION).

mustache, *n.* mustachio, handlebar mustache (HAIR).

mute, *adj.* silent, speechless, wordless; unpronounced, unsounded (SILENCE); muffled, silenced (NONRESONANCE).

mutilate, *v.* maim, mangle, crush (HARM).

mutiny, *n.* rebellion, insurrection, revolt (DISOBEDIENCE).

mutter, *v.* growl, mumble (TALK); grumble, complain (COMPLAINT).

mutual, *adj.* shared, collective joint (CO-OPERATION); reciprocal, give-and-take, correlative (EXCHANGE); dependent, interdependent (RELATIONSHIP).

muzzle, *n.* jaws, chops, snout (HEAD).

muzzle, *v.* gag, suppress, squelch (SILENCE, RESTRAINT).

myriad, *adj.* numberless, uncountable, uncounted (MULTITUDE).

MYSTERY—*N.* mystery, secret, oracle, occult, arcana (*pl.*), rune,

subtlety, riddle, cryptogram, enigma, sphinx.

mysticism, cabalism, occultism; cabalist, mystic, occultist, hierophant, mystagogue.

puzzle, perplexity, puzzlement, puzzler, poser, riddle, conundrum, Chinese puzzle, crux, charade, rebus, logogriph.

complexity, complication, complicacy, snarl, intricacy, involvement, labyrinth, maze, reticularity.

V. make difficult (*to understand*), obscure, confuse, darken; complicate, snarl, involve.

puzzle, mystify, baffle, bewilder, perplex, confound.

Adj. mysterious, secret, weird, uncanny, preternatural, transcendental, subtle, enigmatic, oracular, Delphic, cryptic, runic, inscrutable, sphinxian, occult, arcane, cabalistic; unexplainable, unaccountable, inexplicable; mystical, esoteric.

unintelligible, unfathomable, fathomless, incomprehensible, inconceivable, impenetrable; indecipherable, illegible.

hard to understand, difficult, deep, profound, elusive, dark, obscure, recondite, intangible, impalpable, opaque, abstract, abstruse, metaphysical, unclear, turbid.

puzzling, mystifying, baffling, bewildering, confusing, perplexing, confounding, carking, problematical.

complex, complicated, tricky, intricate, knotty, involved, labyrinthine, mazy, reticular, scabrous.

See also AMBIGUITY, CONCEALMENT, CONFUSION, DIFFICULTY, MISINTERPRETATION, UNCLEARNESS. *Antonyms*—See CLARITY, DISCOVERY, EXPLANATION, UNDERSTANDING.

---

mystical, *adj.* esoteric, cabalistic, occult (CONCEALMENT, MYSTERY); oracular, cryptic (MEANING).

mysticism, *n.* cabalism, occultism (MYSTERY).

mystify, *v.* puzzle, baffle, bewilder (CONFUSION, MYSTERY).

myth, *n.* fiction, fable, legend (UNREALITY, STORY).

mythical, *adj.* imaginary, legendary, fabulous (UNREALITY).

MYTHICAL BEINGS—*N.* monster, monstrosity, griffin, hippogriff, Chimera, thunderbird.

dragon, basilisk, cockatrice, dipsas, Python, salamander.

[*part human, part animal*] centaur, bucentaur, Minotaur, satyr, Pan, Harpy, lamia, sphinx; siren, Lorelei or Lurlei, mermaid, merman, Triton.

sphinx (*Egypt. archeol.*), androsphinx, criosphinx, hieracosphinx.

[*others*] **giant**, Cyclops, ogre, ogress, Gorgon; werewolf, lycanthrope; Charon.

Adj. **monstrous**, chimeric, draconic, salamandrine; giant, gigantic, gigantean, ogreish, Cyclopean, Cyclopic.

[*both human and animal*] **biform**, biformed, therianthropic, androcephalous, androtauric.

See also GHOST, SUPERNATURAL BEINGS.

N

nab (*colloq.*), *v.* arrest, apprehend (IMPRISONMENT); seize, snatch, grab (TAKING).

nag, *n.* nuisance, pest (ANNOYANCE); jade, hack, Rosinante (HORSE).

nag, *v.* pester, importune, badger (ANNOYANCE, DEMAND).

nail, *n.* screw, pin, dowel (FASTENING); claw, fingernail (APPENDAGE).

naïve, *adj.* unsophisticated, innocent, unworldly (INEXPERIENCE); ingenuous, simple, guileless (NATURALNESS, INNOCENCE); gullible, believing, credulous (BELIEF).

naked, *adj.* nude, bare, stripped (UNDRESS); dry, matter-of-fact, plain (SIMPLICITY).

NAME—*N.* **name**, appellation, appellative, compellation, address, denomination, designation, epithet, handle (*slang*), moniker (*slang*), signature, autonym, autonym, tag, term, title, trade name; style; place name, toponym; heading, head; monogram.

given name, first name, Christian name; middle name.

family name, cognomen, cognomination, last name, surname, second name; metronymic, patronymic.

false name, alias, pen name, allonym, nom de plume (F.), nom de théâtre (F.), stage name, nom de guerre (F.), pseudonym, anonym; misnomer.

nickname, diminutive, pet name, moniker (*slang*), agnomen, byname, byword, sobriquet.

label, docket, tag, ticket.

[*person named*] **nominee**, designate; namesake, cognominal.

nomenclature, glossology, terminology, orismology, technology, toponymy, synonymy; roll, roster, register, rota, onomasticon.

V. **name**, denominate, cognominate, designate, nominate, nomenclature, dub (*poetic or archaic*),

term, tag, title, style, entitle, christen, baptize, godfather, nickname, dignify; enumerate, specify, mention; call, address; acclaim, declare.

label, tag, tally, docket, ticket.

misname, miscall, misnomer, misterm.

Adj. **named**, nominated, designate, called, etc. (see *Verbs*); hight (*archaic*), y-clept (*archaic or jocose*), known as; titular, nominal, honorary.

self-named, self-called, self-christened, self-styled, soi-disant (F.); so-called.

nameless, anonymous, innominate, unnamed, unknown, unacknowledged; pseudonymous, allonymous, incognito.

Adv. **namely**, to wit, viz. (abbr. of L. videlicet).

See also ROLL, SIGNATURE, TITLE.

nameless, *adj.* anonymous, innominate, unknown (NAME); inexpressible, unutterable, ineffable (SILENCE).

namely, *adv.* that is, id est (L.), to wit (EXPLANATION, NAME).

nap, *n.* cat nap, forty winks, doze (SLEEP); grain, fiber, pile (TEXTURE).

narcotic, *n.* dope, drug, opiate (INSENSIBILITY, PHARMACY); lenitive, sedative (PAINKILLER); hypnotic, somnifacient, soporific (SLEEP).

narrate, *v.* tell, yarn, spin (STORY).

narrative, *n.* account, yarn, tale (STORY).

NARROWNESS—*N.* **narrowness**, exiguity, hairsbreadth; constriction, compression, contraction, stricture.

V. **narrow**, taper, reduce, constrict, contract, limit, restrict.

Adj. **narrow**, slender, thin, fine, threadlike, linear, finespun, taper, slim; contracted, circumscribed, limited, close, confined, confining, pent, cramped, exiguous, incapacious, straitened, meager, small, restricted; necessitous.

[*with little margin*] **near,** close, hairbreadth, bare.

See also DECREASE, LENGTH, SMALLNESS. *Antonyms*—See WIDTH.

narrow-minded, *adj.* narrow, insular, provincial (PREJUDICE).

narrows, *n.* sound, strait (INLET).

nasty, *adj.* dirty, mucky, foul (UNCLEANNESS); offensive, unpleasant (UNPLEASANTNESS); ugly, vinegary, waspish (BAD TEMPER); mean, sordid, squalid (MEANNESS); horrid, ungodly, unholy (INFERIORITY); obscene, filthy, smutty (OBSCENITY).

natal, *adj.* congenital, connate (BIRTH).

nation, *n.* state, community (INHABITANT).

national, *adj.* general, public, vernacular (VULGARITY).

nationalism, *n.* public spirit, chauvinism, jingoism (PATRIOTISM).

native, *adj.* indigenous, original, aboriginal (INHABITANT); natural, inborn, innate (NATURALNESS, BIRTH).

native, *n.* aborigine, aboriginal, autochthon (INHABITANT).

native land, *n.* mother country, motherland, homeland (LAND).

natty, *adj.* spruce, dapper, jaunty (NEATNESS, FASHION).

naturalist, *n.* botanist, zoologist (BOTANY, ZOOLOGY).

naturalize, *v.* habituate, accustom, acclimatize (HABIT); enfranchise (CITIZEN).

NATURALNESS—*N.* naturalness, naturalism, inherency; unsophistication, naïveté, unconstraint, unartificiality, spontaneity, innocence.

Adj. **natural,** inborn, inbred, ingenerate, instinctive, inherent, innate, native; crude, raw, unrefined, unperverted.

unaffected, artless, inartificial, ingenuous, innocent, naïve, rustic, simple, simplehearted, spontaneous, unartful, unartificial, unconstrained, uncontrived, unforced, unlabored, unsophisticated, unstudied.

See also COMMONNESS, HABIT, INHABITANT, INNOCENCE, SIMPLICITY. *Antonyms*—See PRETENSE, SUPERNATURALISM, UNNATURALNESS, UNUSUALNESS.

nature, *n.* temper, temperament, personality (CHARACTER); crea-

tion, universe (WORLD); ilk, brand, kind (CLASS).

naughty, *adj.* mischievous, roguish, rascally (MISCHIEF); wicked, bad, ill-behaved (WICKEDNESS); disobedient, insubordinate, contrary (DISOBEDIENCE).

NAUSEA—*N.* nausea, disgust, qualm, seasickness, *mal de mer* (*F.*); vomit, puke, spew, bloody vomit, black vomit; regurgitation, rejection.

emetic, vomitive, vomitory, ipecac, nauseant (*med.*).

V. **be nauseous,** gag, sicken, nauseate; heave, keck; retch, vomit, puke, throw up, spit up, upchuck (*slang*), regurgitate, reject.

nauseate, sicken, disgust, turn the stomach.

Adj. **nauseated,** nauseous, queasy, squeamish, sick, seasick.

nauseating, nauseous, nauseant (*med.*), disgustful, disgusting, brackish (*of fluids*).

Phrases. to the point of nausea, ad nauseam (*L.*).

See also DISGUST.

nautical, *adj.* maritime, sailorly (SAILOR).

naval, *adj.* nautical, maritime (SAILOR).

navel, *n.* belly button, umbilicus (BELLY).

navigate, *v.* voyage, cruise, sail (TRAVELING); helm, coxswain, conn (GUIDANCE).

navigation, *n.* nautics, seamanship, boatmanship (SAILOR).

navigator, *n.* seafarer, seafaring man, mariner (SAILOR).

navy, *n.* naval ships, fleet, armada (SHIP).

nay, *n.* negative vote, blackball (VOTE); no (DENIAL).

nazism, *n.* totalitarianism, fascism (GOVERNMENT, VIOLENCE).

nearly, *adv.* almost, well-nigh, nigh (SMALLNESS); approximately, circa (*L.*), about (NEARNESS).

NEARNESS—*N.* nearness, proximity, propinquity, contiguity, adjacency; short distance, close quarters, stone's throw.

nearby regions, vicinity, neighborhood, environs, precincts, purlieus, vicinage.

V. **be near,** border on, neighbor; adjoin, lie near, lie next to, border, abut, verge on.

near, come (*or* draw) near *or* close, close in upon, approach, converge, approximate, border on, shave, verge on, trench on.

Adj. near, at hand, near at hand, close, close by, contiguous, immediate, nearby, nigh, proximate, vicinal; adjacent, approximate, bordering, contiguous, neighboring; available, convenient, handy, ready; narrow, hairbreadth.

next, touching, abutting, adjacent, adjoining, approximal (*anat.*), bordering, conterminous, contiguous, immediate, neighboring, vicinal; side by side, abreast, juxtaposed.

nearest, immediate, proximal, proximate.

intimate, dear, familiar, close.

Adv., phrases. near, nigh, hard by, close to, close upon, hard upon; next door to; within reach (call, hearing, earshot, *or* range), in sight of; at close quarters; beside, alongside, cheek by jowl, side by side, in juxtaposition; at the heels of, on the verge of, at the point of; closely.

nearly, approximately, almost, about, all but, thereabouts, roughly, in round numbers, roundly, generally, well-nigh, barely.

See also APPROACH, EASE, ENVIRONMENT, NARROWNESS, RELATIONSHIP, SIMILARITY, TOUCH. *Antonyms*—See DISTANCE.

---

nearsighted, *adj.* weak-sighted, short-sighted, amblyopic (DIMSIGHTEDNESS).

neat, *adj.* tidy, spruce (NEATNESS); undiluted, unmixed, plain (STRAIGHTNESS).

NEATNESS—*N.* neatness, order, orderliness, etc. (see *Adjectives*).

V. neaten, tidy, tidy up, tauten, groom, sleek, prim, spruce, slick up (*colloq.*), titivate, smarten, trim; unscramble (*colloq.*).

Adj. neat, tidy, spick-and-span, taut, well-kept, spruce, prim, dapper, natty, smug, sleek, groomed, well-groomed, trig.

orderly, shipshape, trim, uncluttered, unlittered; methodical, systematic.

See also ARRANGEMENT, CLEANNESS, METHOD. *Antonyms*—See UNCLEANNESS, UNTIDINESS.

NECESSITY—*N.* necessity, requirement, demand, requisite, *sine qua non* (L.), prerequisite, qualification, postulate; necessary, essential, indispensable; desideratum, godsend, vitals, essence, competence.

need, craving, want, demand, exigency, urgency, extremity; compulsion, compulsiveness, blind impulse, instinct.

V. necessitate, compel, force, drive, constrain, oblige, make, require, demand, cause, entail, postulate; behoove.

need, crave, require, want, demand, postulate, desiderate.

Adj. necessary, needed, needful, essential, indispensable, basic, key, vital, substantive, organic, strategic, critical, integral; imperative, urgent, pressing; inevitable, unavoidable.

required, requisite, compulsory, mandatory, demanded, *de rigueur* (F.), entailed, obligatory, postulated, prerequisite; binding, bounden, incumbent on; necessitated, necessitous.

Adv., phrases. necessarily, perforce, of necessity, of course; willy-nilly, *nolens volens* (L.).

See also ABSENCE, CAUSATION, IMPORTANCE, POVERTY. *Antonyms*—See UNIMPORTANCE, UNNECESSITY.

---

neck, *n.* cervix, nape, nucha (HEAD); isthmus, spit, tongue (LAND).

neck (*slang*), *v.* pet (*slang*), cuddle, caress (CARESS, HEAD).

necklace, *n.* necklet, choker (JEWELRY).

necktie, *n.* cravat, tie, scarf (NECKWEAR).

NECKWEAR—*N.* neckwear, kerchief, neckcloth, neckerchief, neckpiece, bandanna, muffler, comforter, ruff, scarf; choker, boa, fichu, guimpe, chemisette, jabot, tucker, neckband, tippet.

necktie, cravat, tie, scarf, foulard, ascot, Windsor tie, four-in-hand, bow tie, white tie.

collar, choker (*colloq.*), dickey, Eton collar, Peter Pan collar, ruff, stock; lapel, revers *or* revere.

shawl, stole, wrap, fichu.

See also CLOTHING, HEAD, HEADGEAR, ORNAMENT.

---

need, *n.* extremity, exigency, requirement (NECESSITY); distress, indigence, want (POVERTY).

need, *v.* crave, require, want (NECESSITY).

needed, *adj.* necessary, needful, essential (NECESSITY).

needle, *n.* quill, spine, spur (SHARPNESS); leaf, frond (PLANT LIFE).

needle, *v.* sting, prick, pique (MOTIVATION); badger, annoy, bait (ANNOYANCE, TEASING).

needless, *adj.* unnecessary, gratuitous, uncalled for (UNNECESSITY).

needy, *adj.* poor, beggared, destitute (POVERTY).

ne'er-do-well, *n.* black sheep, bum (*colloq.*), cur (WORTHLESSNESS); incompetent, duffer, slouch (CLUMSINESS).

nefarious, *adj.* iniquitous, miscreant, pernicious (WICKEDNESS).

negate, *v.* rebut, refute, negative, disprove (DISPROOF); controvert, dispute, disaffirm (DENIAL).

negative, *adj.* balky, contrary, resistive (OPPOSITION, OPPOSITE).

NEGLECT—N. neglect, disregard, oversight, omission, pretermission, default; negligence, laxity, delinquency, laches (*law*); dilapidation, limbo.

[*of duty, etc.*] **dereliction,** nonfeasance, nonobservance, nonperformance, defection, misprision, violation, breach, delinquency.

V. **neglect,** disregard, pass over, miss, skip, let pass, let slip, let go, overlook, by-pass, omit, pretermit, slight; default, violate.

Adj. **negligent,** neglectful, lax, derelict, remiss, delinquent, defaultant; disregardful, disregardant, omissive.

neglected, uncared for, unheeded, disregarded, unattended to, shelved; dilapidated, unimproved, unkempt; abandoned.

See also CARELESSNESS, DETERIORATION, FORGETFULNESS, INACTIVITY, INATTENTION, NONOBSERVANCE, NONPREPARATION. *Antonyms*—See ATTENTION, CARE.

negligee, *n.* undress, dishabille, divestment (UNDRESS); dressing gown, peignoir, bathrobe (CLOTHING).

negligence, *n.* neglectfulness, remissness, laxity, laxness, delinquency (NEGLECT).

negligent, *adj.* neglectful, lax, derelict (NEGLECT).

negotiable, *adj.* transferable, assignable, transmissible (TRANSFER); salable, marketable, vendible (SALE).

negotiate, *v.* treat, stipulate, make terms (COMPACT); bargain, haggle, dicker (EXCHANGE); mediate, intercede, step in (MEDIATION).

Negro, *n.* Afro-American, colored person (MANKIND).

neigh, *v.* whinny, whicker, snort (ANIMAL SOUND).

neighborhood, *n.* vicinity, environs, surroundings (NEARNESS, ENVIRONMENT).

neighboring, *adj.* adjacent, bordering, contiguous (NEARNESS).

neighborly, *adj.* hospitable, friendly (SOCIALITY).

nerve, *n.* mettle, guts (*colloq.*), grit (COURAGE); brass, cheek (*colloq.*), presumption (DISCOURTESY, CERTAINTY).

NERVOUSNESS—N. nervousness, nervosity, fluster, flustration, the jitters (*colloq.*), the fidgets, the willies (*slang*), the heebie-jeebies (*slang*); stage fright.

tension, nervous tension, strain, stress.

restlessness, unrest, dysphoria (*med.*), inquietude.

anxiety, worry, worriment, apprehension, fear; distress, disquietude, concern, care, fuss, fret, solicitude, perturbation, unease, upset, trouble.

worrier, fuss-budget (*colloq.*), fusser, fretter.

V. **be nervous,** fidget, fuss, fret, jitter (*colloq.*), tittup; fear, apprehend.

twitch, jerk, vellicate, jiggle, stir, toss, thrash, shy, start, buck, startle.

tense, tense up, string, unstring, flurry, fluster, flustrate, fuss up (*colloq.*).

worry, stew (*colloq.*), fret, fuss, trouble, trouble oneself; disquiet, vex, distress, disturb, faze (*colloq.*), upset, perturb, bother, pother; unnerve, unhinge, uncalm, unsettle.

Adj. **nervous,** tense, highstrung, taut, wiredrawn, uneasy, unstrung, overwrought, overstrung, jumpy, creepy, jittery (*colloq.*); fussed-up (*colloq.*), flustered, flurried; skittish, twitchy, jerky, jiggly.

restless, fitful, restive, uneasy, unquiet, dysphoric (*med.*), fidgeting, fidgety, tittupy.

anxious, worried, solicitous, troubled, upset, uneasy, apprehensive, disturbed, concerned, bothered, distressed, perturbed, exercised, fussed up (*colloq.*), fretted, carking (*archaic or poetic*), fazed (*colloq.*); fussy, worrisome, fearful; careworn.

See also AGITATION, COMMOTION, EXCITEMENT, FEAR, JUMP, NEUROSIS, PRESSURE. *Antonyms*—See CALMNESS, INEXCITABILITY, UNANXIETY.

nervy, *adj.* game, spunky, plucky (COURAGE).

nest, *n.* birdhouse, aviary (BIRD); den, hotbed (WICKEDNESS).

nestle, *v.* cuddle, nuzzle, snuggle (REST, PRESSURE, WINDING).

net, *n.* snare, lasso, dragnet (TRAP); mesh, web, lace (CROSSING, TEXTURE).

netlike, *adj.* retiform, reticular, latticed (CROSSING).

network, *n.* crisscross, reticulation, tessellation, patchwork, checkerboard design (CROSSING).

NEUROSIS—N. neurosis, psychoneurosis, emotional disorder, personality disorder, nervous ailment, maladjustment, neurasthenia, breakdown, nervous breakdown, crack-up, psychasthenia; psychopathy, psychopathic personality, sociopathic personality; hysteria.

neurotic, psychoneurotic, neuropath, neurasthenic, psychasthenic; psychopath, psychopathic personality, sociopath, sociopathic personality; hysteric *or* hysteriac.

Adj. **neurotic,** psychoneurotic, maladjusted, neurasthenic, sick, psychasthenic; psychopathic, sociopathic; hysteric *or* hysterical.

See also INSANITY, NERVOUSNESS, PSYCHOTHERAPY. *Antonyms*—See HEALTH, SANITY.

---

neuter, *adj.* sexless, asexual, epicene (CELIBACY).

neutral, *adj.* impartial, unbiased, fair-minded (IMPARTIALITY); pacifistic, nonbelligerent (PEACE).

neutral, *n.* neutralist, nonpartisan (IMPARTIALITY).

neutralize, *v.* offset, counterbalance, cancel (OPPOSITION, INEFFECTIVENESS).

nevertheless, *adv.* notwithstanding, nonetheless, however (OPPOSITION).

new, *adj.* newfangled (*derogatory*), recent, just out (*colloq.*), fresh, novel (NEWNESS).

newcomer, *n.* late arrival, latecomer, Johnny-come-lately (ARRIVAL); outsider, immigrant (IRRELATION).

NEWNESS—N. newness, recency, novelty, originality.

[*something new*] **novelty,** wrinkle, original, rehash, neoterism, neoteric, modernism, modernity, *dernier cri* (*F.*), latest thing, latest fashion.

freshness, viridity, crispness, succulence, dew, revirescence.

modern, modernist, neoteric, ultramodern, ultramodernist, futurist; vanguard, *avant-garde* (*F.*); innovator.

V. **renew,** renovate, refurbish, modernize, streamline, bring up to date, revamp, recast, revise, rehash; refresh, reinvigorate, rejuvenate, restore, resurrect; innovate.

Adj. **new,** brand-new, span-new, spick-and-span; new-made, new-fledged, new-fashioned, newfangled (*derogatory*), newborn, recent, just out (*colloq.*), just made, just published; fresh, novel, original, Promethean, unprecedented.

fresh, untried, untouched, unbeaten, untrod, untrodden, virgin, virginal; vernal, youthful, succulent, crisp, crispy; dewy, revirescent.

modern, up-to-date, up-to-the-minute, neoteric, new-fashioned, streamlined, modernistic, modernist, moderne (*commercial cant*), ultramodern, ultramodernistic, futurist, futuristic, advanced, twentieth-century.

See also BEGINNING, IMMATURITY, INEXPERIENCE, RESTORATION, YOUTH. *Antonyms*—See DETERIORATION, DISUSE, OLDNESS.

---

news, *n.* information, intelligence, tidings (PUBLICATION).

newspaper, *n.* paper, daily, gazette (PUBLICATION).

newsy, *adj.* informative, advisory, instructive (INFORMATION).

New Testament, *n.* Gospels, Evangelists, Acts (SACRED WRITINGS).

next, *adj.* following, succeeding, after (FOLLOWING); abutting, adjacent, adjoining (NEARNESS).

nibble, *v.* bite, crop, graze (FOOD).

nice, *adj.* pleasant, agreeable, amiable (PLEASANTNESS); precise, accurate (RIGHT).

nicety, *n.* discernment, taste, judgment (DIFFERENTIATION); correctness, precision, accuracy (RIGHT).

niceties, *n.* minutiae, trivia, fine points (DETAIL); etiquette, amenities, civilities (COURTESY).

niche, *n.* compartment, nook, corner (PLACE); recess, recession, indentation (HOLLOW).

nick, *n.* dent, score, indentation (NOTCH).

nick, *v.* mill, score, cut (NOTCH).

nickname, *n.* diminutive, pet name, byname (NAME).

nicotine, *n.* Lady Nicotine, the weed (*colloq.*), smokes (TOBACCO).

niggardly, *adj.* miserly, churlish, penny-pinching (STINGINESS).

night, *n.* nighttime, nighttide, nightfall (EVENING, DARKNESS).

night club, *n.* cabaret, café (ALCOHOLIC LIQUOR).

nightgown, *n.* nightdress, bedgown, night robe (SLEEP).

nightmare, *n.* dream, incubus, succubus (SLEEP, SUPERNATURAL BEINGS); ordeal, trial, tribulation (EXPERIENCE).

nimble, *adj.* active, agile, spry (ACTIVITY, LIGHTNESS); skillful, deft, dexterous (ABILITY).

NINE—*N.* nine, ennead, novenary, nonagon (*geom.*), enneastyle (*arch.*), novena (*R. C. Ch.*), nonuplet (*music*).

Adj. ninefold, nonuple, nonary, novenary.

---

nip, *v.* cut, cut off, snip off (CUTTING); twinge, pinch (PRESSURE).

nippers, *n.* pliers, tweezers, forceps (HOLD).

nipple, *n.* teat, tit, papilla (BREAST).

nitwit (*colloq.*), *n.* half-wit, jackass, muddlehead (STUPIDITY).

no, *n.* refusal, declination, declension (DENIAL).

nobility, *n.* dignity, grandeur, magnificence (NOBILITY); peerage, aristocracy, elite (SOCIAL CLASS).

NOBILITY—*N.* nobility, dignity, generosity, magnanimity; grandeur, magnificence, majesty, sublimity.

noble person, greatheart, prince, sublimity.

V. ennoble, dignify, elevate, exalt, glorify, sublimate, sublime.

Adj. noble, great, dignified, lofty, generous, magnanimous; impressive, grand, stately, magnificent; august, exalted, greathearted, great-minded, highminded, honorable, princely, sublime, superb, whole-souled; elevated, empyreal, empyrean, majestic, winged.

See also ELEVATION, FAME, MAGNIFICENCE, SOCIAL CLASS, UNSELFISHNESS. *Antonyms*—See COMMONNESS, HUMILITY, LOWNESS, MEANNESS, SELFISHNESS, STINGINESS.

---

noble, *adj.* great, dignified, lofty (NOBILITY); magnificent, majestic, sublime (MAGNIFICENCE); nobiliary, titled, lordly, princely (SOCIAL CLASS).

nobleman, *n.* noble, lord, peer (SOCIAL CLASS).

nobody, *n.* nonentity, cipher, insignificancy (UNIMPORTANCE).

nod, *v.* beckon, beck, signal (GESTURE); blunder, slip, slip up (MISTAKE).

noise, *n.* din, disquiet, pandemonium (LOUDNESS); discord, cacophony, jangle (HARSH SOUND).

noiseless, *adj.* soundless, quiet, still (SILENCE).

nomad, *n.* Bedouin, wanderer, vagabond (WANDERING).

nom de plume, *n.* false name, alias, pen name (NAME).

nominal, *adj.* titular, honorary (NAME); cheap, inexpensive, low-priced (INEXPENSIVENESS).

nominate, *v.* name, designate (NAME); appoint, assign (PLACE).

nonchalant, *adj.* casual, pococurante, insouciant (INDIFFERENCE); unalarmed, unperturbed, unconcerned (UNANXIETY).

nondescript, *adj.* colorless, characterless, commonplace (COMMONNESS).

nonentity, *n.* nonessential, nullity, picayune; nobody, cipher (UNIMPORTANCE); nonbeing, nonsubsistence (NONEXISTENCE).

nonesuch, *n.* paragon, *rara avis* (*L.*), nonpareil (PERFECTION, INEQUALITY).

NONEXISTENCE—*N.* nonexistence, nonbeing, nonsubsistence, nonentity.

nothingness, nullity, nihility, blank, void, vacuum.

nothing, nil, naught *or* nought (*archaic or literary*).

zero, cipher, naught *or* nought, ought *or* aught.

V. not exist, pass away, perish, be extinct, die out, disappear, vanish, fade, dissolve, melt away, be no more, die.

annihilate, render null, nullify, abrogate, extinguish, blot out, destroy, remove, vacate; obliterate.

Adj. nonexistent, negative, blank, null, missing, absent, vacant, empty, void.

unsubstantial, immaterial, dreamy, dreamlike, illusory, unreal, gossamery, shadowy, ethereal, airy, gaseous, vaporous, insubstantial, imponderable, tenuous, vague; flimsy, groundless, baseless, ungrounded, without foundation.

unborn, uncreated, unconceived, unproduced, unmade, unbegotten.

extinct, gone, lost, departed, defunct, dead, passed away, passed on, perished; extinguished, quenched.

See also ABSENCE, DEATH, DESTRUCTION, DISAPPEARANCE, REMOVAL, UN-

REALITY. *Antonyms*—See EXISTENCE, FULLNESS, LIFE, MATERIALITY, REALITY.

NONOBSERVANCE—*N.* **nonobservance**, nonperformance, noncompliance, evasion, failure, omission, neglect, laches (*law*).

V. **omit**, leave undone, evade, neglect, skip, slip, elude, cut (*colloq.*), set aside, ignore; shut one's eyes to.

Adj. **nonobservant**, inattentive, neglectful, elusive, evasive, slippery, casual, lax; transgressive, lawless.

informal, casual, easygoing, offhand, unacademic, unceremonial, unceremonious, unconventional, unstereotyped, summary.

See also AVOIDANCE, DISOBEDIENCE, FAILURE, ILLEGALITY, INACTIVITY, INATTENTION, NEGLECT. *Antonyms*—See ACTION, ATTENTION, CARE, FORMALITY, OBSERVANCE.

---

nonpartisan, *n.* impartial, neutral, neutralist (IMPARTIALITY).

nonplus, *v.* bewilder, rattle (*colloq.*), daze (UNCERTAINTY).

NONPREPARATION—*N.* **nonpreparation**, negligence, inadvertence, improvidence.

V. **be unprepared**, live from day to day, live from hand to mouth.

improvise, improvisate, extemporize, do offhand, do impromptu; cook up, fix up.

Adj. **unprepared**, unequipped, unprovided, unorganized, unready, unfit, unadapted, unfitted, unqualified, unsuited.

improvised, impromptu, offhand, improviso, extemporaneous, extemporary, extemporal, extempore; extemporized, unplanned, unprepared, unpremeditated; impulsive, impetuous, spontaneous.

fallow, unsown, untilled, uncultivated, unplowed, idle.

Phrases. **without preparation**, on the spur of the moment.

See also PURPOSELESSNESS, SUDDENNESS, SURPRISE. *Antonyms*—See PLAN, PURPOSE, PREPARATION.

---

nonprofessional, *adj.* nonexpert, unprofessional, amateur (LAITY).

NONRESONANCE—*N.* **nonresonance**, dead sound, pounding, pound, thud, thump; muffler, silencer.

V. **muffle**, deaden, dampen, drown, overwhelm, overpower, mute.

Adj. **nonresonant**, nonvibrant, deadened, dead, hollow, heavy, muffled, silenced, mute.

Antonyms—See RESONANCE.

---

nonsense, *n.* poppycock, claptrap, trash (ABSURDITY).

nook, *n.* compartment, niche, corner (PLACE); inglenook, quoin (ANGULARITY).

noon, *n.* midday, noonday, noontime (MORNING).

noose, *n.* bight, loop (FILAMENT); snare, pitfall, toils (TRAP).

norm, *n.* standard, touchstone, yardstick (MEASUREMENT, JUDGMENT); average, mean, medium (MID-COURSE).

normal, *adj.* usual, general, habitual (COMMONNESS); average, mean, median (MID-COURSE); sane, lucid, rational (SANITY); feverless, afebrile, cool (FEVER).

north, *n.* northland, northing, ultima Thule (DIRECTION).

NOSE—*N.* [*human*] **nose**, beak, bill (*both contemptuous*), proboscis (*jocose*); snoot (*slang*); bridge, nostrils, nares, adenoids.

[*animal*] **beak**, bill, neb, snout, proboscis, trunk.

sneeze, sneezing, sternutation.

ailments: catarrh, rhinitis, coryza; hay fever, allergic rhinitis, pollinosis; a cold, rheum, roup; the sniffles.

Adj. **nasal**, rhinal; aquiline, beaked, hooked, hook, Roman, pug, retroussé (*F.*), snub, uptilted, upturned.

See also BREATH, FRONT, ODOR.

---

nostalgia, *n. Heimweh* (*Ger.*), *mal du pays* (*F.*), homesickness (HABITATION).

nosy (*slang*), *adj.* inquisitive, prying, personal (INQUIRY, SEARCH).

nosybody, *n.* bluenose, busybody, inquisitive (INQUIRY).

notable, *adj.* eventful, momentous, outstanding (IMPORTANCE); famous, great, distinguished (FAME).

notable, *n.* notability, VIP (IMPORTANCE); celebrity, luminary (FAME).

notably, *adv.* principally, especially, particularly (SUPERIORITY).

NOTCH—*N.* **notch**, dent, nick, score, cut, indentation, serration, denticulation, serrulation; saw, tooth, crenel, scallop, jag; machicolation, crenelation, castellation.

pass, defile, cut, gap, neck, gully, passage, gorge.

V. notch, nick, mill, score, cut, dent, indent, jag, scarify, scallop, gash, crimp; crenelate.

Adj. notched, crenate, scalloped, dentate, toothed, palmate, serrate, serrated, serriform, sawlike; machicolated, castellated.

See also HOLLOW, INTERVAL, PASSAGE. Antonyms—See SMOOTHNESS.

---

note, n. letter, communication, message (EPISTLE); memorandum (MEMORY); bill, paper money (MONEY); jotting, record (WRITING); commentary, annotation (EXPLANATION).

note, v. write, jot down (WRITING); observe, remark, notice (LOOKING); distinguish, discover (VISION).

notebook, n. diary, daybook (RECORD).

noted, adj. eminent, renowned (FAME).

nothing, n. nil, zero, cipher (NONEXISTENCE).

nothingness, n. nullity, nihility, void (NONEXISTENCE).

notice, n. announcement, proclamation, manifesto (INFORMATION); handbill, poster, circular (PUBLICATION); caution, caveat, admonition (WARNING).

notice, v. remark, observe, perceive (VISION, LOOKING).

noticeable, adj. conspicuous, marked, pointed (VISIBILITY).

notify, v. inform, let know, acquaint (INFORMATION).

notion, n. impression, conception, inkling (UNDERSTANDING, IDEA); concept, view (OPINION); fancy, humor, whim (CAPRICE).

notorious, adj. infamous, shady, scandalous (DISREPUTE, FAME).

notwithstanding, adv. nevertheless, nonetheless, however (OPPOSITION).

nourish, v. feed, sustain, foster, nurture (FOOD).

nourishing, adj. nutrient, nutritive, nutritious (FOOD).

nourishment, n. nutriment, foodstuff, sustenance (FOOD).

nouveau riche (F.), n. parvenu, arriviste (F.), upstart (SOCIAL CLASS, WEALTH).

novel, adj. fresh, off-beat (colloq.), unusual (UNUSUALNESS); original, Promethean (NEWNESS); unique, atypical (DIFFERENCE).

novel, n. fiction, novelette, novella (STORY).

novelist, n. fictionist, anecdotist (WRITER).

novelty, n. freshness, recency, originality; original, dernier cri (F.), wrinkle (NEWNESS); item, conversation piece (MATERIALITY).

novice, n. beginner, tyro, neophyte (BEGINNING, LEARNING); novitiate, postulant (RELIGIOUS COMMUNITY).

now, adv. at this time, at this moment, at present (PRESENT TIME).

noxious, adj. virulent, unhealthy (HARM); unwholesome, pestiferous, pestilent (IMMORALITY).

nozzle, n. spout, faucet (EGRESS, OPENING).

nuance, n. shade of difference (DIFFERENCE); implication, suggestion (MEANING).

nucleus, n. heart, hub, focus (CENTER); meat, pith, principle (PART).

nude, adj. stripped, naked, bare (UNDRESS).

nudge, v. push, poke, prod (PROPULSION).

nudity, n. nakedness, denudation, exposure (UNDRESS).

nuisance, n. gadfly, terror, pest (ANNOYANCE).

nullify, v. annul, disannul, invalidate (INEFFECTIVENESS).

numb, adj. dazed, torpid, stuporous (INSENSIBILITY).

numb, v. dull, blunt, obtund (INSENSIBILITY).

number, n. amount (QUANTITY); numeral (NUMBER); song (SINGING).

NUMBER—N. number, symbol, character, numeral, figure, statistic, Arabic number, cipher, digit, integer, whole number, folio, round number; cardinal number, ordinal number, Roman number; decimal, fraction, infinity, googol; numerator, denominator; prime number.

sum, difference, product, quotient; addend, summand, augend; dividend, divisor; factor, multiple, multiplicand, faciend, multiplier; minuend, subtrahend, remainder; total, summation, aggregate, tally; quantity, amount.

ratio, proportion, quota, percentage; progression, arithmetical progression, geometric progression.

power, root, exponent, index, logarithm.

numeration, notation, algorism, cipher, algebra; enumeration, count, tally, census, poll; statistics; numerology.

V. count, enumerate, numerate, reckon, tally; count down, tell, tell out (off, or down).

page, number, foliate, paginate, mark.

Adj. **numeral,** numerary, numeric, numerical; numbered, numerate.

proportional, commeasurable, commensurate, proportionate.

See also ADDITION, COMPUTATION, LIST, MULTITUDE, QUANTITY, TWO, THREE, ETC.

---

numbers, *n.* scores, heaps, lots (MULTITUDE).

numberless, *adj.* countless, innumerable, myriad (MULTITUDE, ENDLESSNESS).

numeral, *n.* symbol, character, figure (NUMBER).

numerical, *adj.* numeral, numerary (NUMBER).

numerous, *adj.* many, multitudinous, abundant (MULTITUDE, FREQUENCE)

nun, *n.* sister, *religieuse* (F.), vestal, vestal virgin (RELIGIOUS COMMUNITY, UNMARRIED STATE).

nunnery, *n.* convent, abbey, cloister (RELIGIOUS COMMUNITY).

nuptial, *adj.* matrimonial, marital, conjugal (MARRIAGE).

nurse, *n.* attendant, medic, R.N. (MEDICAL SCIENCE).

nurse, *v.* attend, tend, care for (CARE); suck, suckle, lactate (BREAST).

nursery, *n.* day nursery, crèche (CHILD); garden, greenhouse, hothouse (FARMING); cradle, childhood, infancy (YOUTH).

nurture, *v.* feed, nourish, sustain (FOOD); care for, cherish, foster (CARE).

nuthouse (*slang*), *n.* lunatic asylum, madhouse (INSANITY).

nutritious, *adj.* nourishing, wholesome (FOOD, HEALTH).

nutty (*slang*), *adj.* potty (*colloq.*), touched, crazy (INSANITY).

nuzzle, *v.* nestle, snuggle, cuddle (PRESSURE, REST).

nymph, *n.* dryad, hamadryad, hyad (GOD).

nymphomania, *n.* erotomania, andromania (SEX).

O

oaf, *n.* lummox, lout, gawky (CLUMSINESS); boob, nincompoop, blockhead (FOLLY).

oar, *n.* paddle, scull (SAILOR).

oath, *n.* curse, curseword, swearword (MALEDICTION, DISRESPECT); affidavit, deposition (AFFIRMATION); word of honor, vow (PROMISE).

OBEDIENCE—*N.* **obedience,** observance, conformance, conformity, accordance, compliance, docility, servility, subservience, tameness.

[*one who demands obedience*] **disciplinarian,** martinet, authoritarian, precisian.

[*obedient person*] **servant,** minion, myrmidon, slave.

discipline, training; military discipline, blind obedience.

V. **obey,** observe, comply, conform, submit; mind, heed, do one's bidding, follow orders, do what one is told; behave.

discipline, train, tame; enforce, compel, force; put teeth in.

Adj. **obedient,** compliant, compliable, observant, law-abiding; dutiful, duteous; orderly, quiet, docile, meek, manageable, tractable, biddable, well-behaved; submissive, servile, subservient, tame.

disciplinary, strict, stern, authoritative, authoritarian.

See also DUTY, FORCE, OBSERVANCE, SLAVERY, SUBMISSION, TEACHING. *Antonyms*—See DISOBEDIENCE, NONOBSERVANCE.

---

obese, *adj.* paunchy, pursy, fat (SIZE).

obey, *v.* observe, comply, submit (OBEDIENCE).

object, *n.* thing, article, commodity (MATERIALITY); matter, phenomenon, substance (REALITY); mission, objective, end (PURPOSE).

object, *v.* demur, protest, remonstrate (OPPOSITION, UNPLEASANTNESS).

objection, *n.* exception, demurral (OPPOSITION); dislike, disesteem (HATRED).

objectionable, *adj.* displeasing, distasteful, unpalatable (UNPLEASANTNESS, HATRED); exceptionable, opprobrious (DISAPPROVAL).

objective, *adj.* impartial, unprejudiced, unbiased (IMPARTIALITY); actual, concrete, material (REALITY).

objective, *n.* mission, object, end (PURPOSE).

object of art, *n.* bibelot (F.), objet d'art (F.), curio (ORNAMENT).

object to, *v.* dislike, have no stomach for, be displeased by, protest (HATRED, UNPLEASANTNESS).

obligate, *v.* indebt, bind, astrict (DEBT).

obligation, n. liability, responsibility, dues, debit (DUTY, DEBT).

obligatory, adj. compulsory, enforced, required (FORCE).

oblige, v. require, compel, constrain (NECESSITY).

obliging, adj. hospitable, accommodating, cheerful (KINDNESS, (WILLINGNESS).

oblique, adj. diagonal, bias (SLOPE); bent, crooked (ANGULARITY); devious, roundabout (INDIRECTNESS).

obliterate, v. exterminate, extirpate, expunge (DESTRUCTION); blot out, obscure, cover (CONCEALMENT).

oblivion, n. disregard, unconcern, inadvertence (INATTENTION).

oblivious, adj. unobservant, undiscerning, (INATTENTION); unmindful, absent-minded, amnesic (FORGETFULNESS).

oblong, adj. long, elongate, elongated (LENGTH).

obnoxious, adj. repugnant, repulsive, offensive (UNPLEASANTNESS, HATRED).

OBSCENITY—N. obscenity, immorality, dirt, filth, lubricity, salacity, smut, pornography, scatology, coprophemia.

indelicacy, immodesty, indecency, impropriety, indecorum; ribaldry, scurrility, vulgarity, bawdry.

Adj. obscene, immoral, dirty, unclean, vile, filthy, foulmouthed, foul, nasty; lascivious, lewd, licentious, lubricous, salacious, sexy (slang), smutty, pornographic, scatological, coprophemic, ithyphallic, raw, shameless, shameful.

indelicate, immodest, indecent, improper, indecorous; breezy, broad, coarse, gross, lurid, purple, racy, risqué, scabrous, Rabelaisian, ribald, scurrilous, off-color, spicy, suggestive, vulgar, low, bawdy, Fescennine.

See also IMMODESTY, IMMORALITY, IMPROPERNESS, MALEDICTION, SEX, UNCLEANNESS, VULGARITY. Antonyms. —See CLEANNESS, MORALITY, PROPRIETY.

obscure, adj. little-known, orphic, recondite (KNOWLEDGE); indefinable, ambiguous (UNCERTAINTY); shadowy, indefinite (INVISIBILITY); dark, indistinct, dim (UNCLEARNESS); hidden (CONCEALMENT).

obscure, v. conceal, screen, hide (CONCEALMENT); darken, dim, fog, cloud (UNCLEARNESS); gray, overshadow, shade (DARKNESS).

obsequious, adj. servile, subservient, deferential (SUBMISSION, COURTESY, RESPECT); fawning, ingratiatory (FLATTERY); compliant, compliable (PLEASANTNESS).

observable, adj. perceivable, discernible, discoverable (VISIBILITY).

OBSERVANCE—N. observance, attention, keeping, acknowledgment, adherence, compliance, obedience, fulfillment, satisfaction, discharge; acquittance, acquittal; fidelity.

rite, ceremony, custom, performance, practice, form, rule.

V. observe, comply with, respect, acknowledge, abide by, keep, hold, heed, obey, follow, cling to, adhere to, be faithful to; meet, carry out, execute, perform, discharge, keep one's word (or pledge), redeem, fulfill (as a promise), keep faith with; celebrate, honor, solemnize, regard.

notice, perceive, see, discover, detect.

Adj. observant, attentive, mindful, heedful, watchful, regardful.

obedient, submissive, faithful, true, loyal, honorable; punctual, punctilious, scrupulous.

See also ACTION, ATTENTION, CELEBRATION, CONFORMITY, DUTY, EXAMINATION, FORMALITY, LOOKING, OBEDIENCE, RULE, STATEMENT, VISION. Antonyms—See DISOBEDIENCE, NONOBSERVANCE.

observation, n. examination, supervision, surveillance (LOOKING); mention, comment, remark (STATEMENT).

observe, v. obey, comply with (OBEDIENCE); honor, respect (OBSERVANCE); watch, keep one's eye on (ATTENTION); note, notice (LOOKING, VISION); say, remark, mention (STATEMENT).

obsolete, adj. outdated, outmoded, passé (OLDNESS, DISUSE).

obstacle, n. obstruction, barrier, hurdle (RESTRAINT, HINDRANCE).

obstetrician, n. accoucheur, midwife (MEDICAL SCIENCE).

obstinate, adj. stubborn, dogged (STUBBORNNESS); persistent, tenacious (CONTINUATION).

obstreperous, adj. noisy, boisterous, rambunctious (LOUDNESS).

obstruct, v. hinder, impede, block (HINDRANCE, RESTRAINT); occlude, choke, throttle (CLOSURE).

obtain, v. get, procure, secure (ACQUISITION); be prevalent, prevail, abound (PRESENCE).

obtrude, v. thrust in, stick in, ram in (INSERTION).

obtuse, *adj.* thick, imperceptive, opaque (STUPIDITY).

obvious, *adj.* evident, manifest, apparent (CLARITY); conspicuous, striking (VISIBILITY); intelligible, understandable (UNDERSTANDING); banal, hackneyed (COMMONNESS).

occasion, *n.* affair, circumstance, episode (OCCURRENCE); chance, opportunity (CHANCE).

occasion, *v.* provoke, prompt, inspire (CAUSATION).

occasional, *adj.* infrequent, uncommon, sporadic (FEWNESS, CHANCE).

occult, *adj.* arcane, mystic (MYSTERY, CONCEALMENT); preternatural, psychic (SUPERNATURALISM); magical, weird (MAGIC).

occupancy, *n.* control, possession, retention, occupation, tenancy (HOLD, OWNERSHIP).

occupant, *n.* householder, addressee, tenant (INHABITANT); possessor, occupier (OWNERSHIP).

occupation, *n.* calling, line (BUSINESS); possession, occupancy, tenancy (OWNERSHIP).

occupied, *adj.* busy, employed, active (BUSINESS).

occupy, *v.* inhabit, live in (INHABITANT); own, hold, possess (OWNERSHIP, HOLD).

OCCURRENCE—*N.* **occurrence,** transpiration, materialization, development, eventuation, incidence.

recurrence, repetition, persistence, perseverance, recrudescence, relapse.

concurrence, accompaniment, coincidence, conjunction, synchronization.

event, milestone, incident, happening, affair, circumstance, episode, occasion; adventure, experience; accident, act of God, happenstance, contingency, eventuality.

V. **occur,** happen, take place, transpire, turn out, come, come to pass, turn up, present itself, arise, arrive, crop up, bechance, chance, befall, betide, materialize; ensue, develop, follow, result, eventualize, eventuate.

recur, repeat, persist, persevere (*in the mind*), recrudesce.

concur, accompany, coincide, synchronize.

experience, encounter, undergo, bear, endure, go through; pass through, suffer, find, meet, taste, receive, have, meet with, fall to the lot of, be one's lot.

Adj. **occurrent,** current, doing, afoot, passing, topical.

eventful, momentous, memorable, important.

concurrent, circumstantial, incidental, concomitant, accompanying, conjunctional, conjunctural, synchronous.

accidental, by chance, adventitious, casual, circumstantial, incidental, coincidental, contingent, fortuitous, haphazard, random.

recurrent, regular, periodic, repeated, recrudescent, intermittent, isochronous, minutely, continual, persistent.

See also ACCOMPANIMENT, ARRIVAL, CHANCE, DESTINY, EXPERIENCE, PRESENCE, REPETITION, RESULT, SIMULTANEOUSNESS. *Antonyms*—See ABSENCE, NONEXISTENCE.

---

occur to, *v.* come to mind, cross the mind (THOUGHT, SUGGESTION).

OCEAN—*N.* **ocean,** sea, main (*poetic*), high seas, seaway, deep, briny deep, brine, watery waste, the hyaline (*poetic*), the Seven Seas; waters, waves, billows, tide.

[*mythological*] Neptune, Poseidon, Oceanus, Thetis, Triton, naiad, Nereid; sea nymph, Siren, mermaid, merman; trident.

oceanography, hydrography, bathymetry.

Adj. **oceanic,** marine, maritime, pelagic, Neptunian, briny, thalassic, sea-born, oceanlike; seagirt.

deep-sea, abyssal, bathic, bathyal; benthonic, benthic.

seagoing, ocean-going, seafaring, seaworthy, sea-borne; aeromarine.

overseas, transoceanic, transatlantic, transpacific.

See also DEPTH, LAKE, RIVER, WATER. *Antonyms*—See LAND.

---

ocular, *adj.* visual, optical (VISION).

oculist, *n.* ophthalmologist (VISION, MEDICAL SCIENCE).

odd, *adj.* peculiar, singular, curious (UNUSUALNESS); single, individual, unitary (UNITY); surplus, left over (REMAINDER).

oddity, *n.* singularity, incongruity (UNUSUALNESS); quirk, eccentricity, kink (CHARACTER).

odds, *n.* chance, tossup (CHANCE).

odds and ends, *n.* leavings (REMAINDER).

odium, *n.* censure, rebuke, blame (DISAPPROVAL); obloquy, opprobrium, dishonor (DISGRACE).

ODOR—*N.* **odor,** smell, pungency, tang; effluvium, efflux, emanation, exhalation; sniff, snuff, whiff, tinge, tincture; scent, trail; musk.

malodor, fetor, mephitis, stench, stink, fumet, must, reek.

fragrance, aroma, scent, aura, bouquet (*of wine*), spice, perfume, essence, incense, savor.

perfume, balm, cologne, eau de cologne, essence, patchouli, scent, toilet water; sachet; attar, frankincense, myrrh, musk, civet, ambergris.

olfaction, osmesis, scent; osmology; olfactory organs, olfactories.

V. smell, scent, sniff, snuff, inhale; smell of, reek, savor of, stink.

odorize, aromatize, perfume, savor, scent, tincture, tinge, cense, fumigate.

Adj. odorous, odoriferous, pungent, musky, tangy, effluvious, scentful, redolent.

malodorous, fetid, mephitic, stenchy, stenching, smelly, stinky, stinking, musty, dank, reeking; evil-smelling, rank, rancid, rotten, putrid, gamy, high, moldy, foul, noisome, ill-smelling, stagnant, fusty, unsavory; acrid.

fragrant, aromatic, balmy, scented, spicy, perfumed, sweetsmelling; savory, flavorous, flavorsome, delicious, redolent.

olfactory, osmotic.

See also NOSE, TASTE. *Antonyms* —See INODOROUSNESS.

odorless, *adj.* scentless, unscented, unaromatic (INODOROUSNESS).

Oedipus complex, *n.* Electra complex, momism (ANCESTRY).

of course, *adv.* unquestionably, no doubt, indubitably (ASSENT, CERTAINTY).

off-beat (*colloq.*), *adj.* novel, fresh, unusual (UNUSUALNESS).

off-color, *adj.* spicy, suggestive, vulgar (OBSCENITY).

offend, *v.* affront, insult, outrage (OFFENSE); slight, snub, slur (INSULT); shock, jar (UNPLEASANTNESS); antagonize, displease, horrify (HATRED); sin, transgress, trespass (SIN).

offense, *n.* insult, outrage (OFFENSE); breach of law, infraction, violation (ILLEGALITY); transgression, trespass, wrong (SIN).

OFFENSE—*N.* offense, insult, affront, outrage, indignity, injury, wound, sting.

displeasure, umbrage, resentment, pique, dudgeon, high dudgeon, huff.

V. offend, affront, insult, outrage, pique, sting, injure, wound, cut, huff, disoblige, hurt (injure, bruise, wound, lacerate, *or* scarify) the feelings, tread on the toes.

be (*or* feel) offended, resent, take exception to, take amiss, take wrongly, misunderstand.

Adj. offensive, insulting, outrageous, cutting, sarcastic, wounding, stinging, biting, disobliging.

offended, resentful, umbrageous, hurt, etc. (see *Verbs*).

[*easily offended*] thin-skinned, huffy, sensitive, testy, techy, ticklish, touchy.

See also ANGER, DISRESPECT, INSULT, SENSITIVENESS, UNPLEASANTNESS. *Antonyms*—See PLEASANTNESS.

OFFER—*N.* offer, proffer, tender, bid, advance, submission, suggestion, presentation, overture, proposal, proposition, motion.

V. offer, proffer, present, tender, render, bid, propose, suggest, propound, adduce, lay before, submit, put forward, bring forward, advance, extend, press, ply, urge upon, hold out; move, make a motion; offer up, sacrifice.

volunteer, proffer, tender, come forward, be a candidate, present oneself, stand for, bid for; be at one's service.

See also GIVING, MOTION, SUGGESTION, URGING, WILLINGNESS. *Antonyms*—See DEMAND, DENIAL.

offhand, *adj.* informal, casual, easygoing (NONOBSERVANCE); improvised, impromptu, extemporaneous (NONPREPARATION).

office, *n.* bureau, department (AGENCY); position, post (SITUATION).

office girl, *n.* secretary, typist, stenographer (WORK).

officeholder, *n.* commissioner, incumbent, bureaucrat (OFFICIAL).

officer, *n.* chief, head, leader (RANK); policeman, cop (*colloq.*); dignitary, functionary (OFFICIAL); captain, major (FIGHTER).

official, *adj.* ex-cathedra, authoritative (POWER, OFFICIAL); orthodox, canonical (TRUTH).

OFFICIAL—*N.* official, officer, dignitary, civil servant, functionary, panjandrum, syndic, chamberlain, executive, commissioner, officeholder, incumbent, bureaucrat; chief executive, chief magistrate, governor, mayor, burgomaster, president, prexy (*colloq.*), chancellor, archon, doge, magistrate, minister, prime minister, premier, secretary; vice-president, vice-chancellor, vice-gerent, deputy, councilman, selectman, alderman; coroner, medical examiner; marshal.

officials, authorities, bureaucracy, officialdom, officialism, brass (*colloq.*), administration, cabinet, official family, council, civil service, board of governors, magistracy, ministry.

officialism, beadledom, bureaucracy, officialdom, red tape, Bumbledom.

chairman, the chair, moderator, president, presider, presiding officer.

police officer, arm of the law, minion of the law, officer of the law, officer, peace officer; policeman, cop (*colloq.*), bluecoat (*colloq.*), patrolman, copper (*slang*), detective, bull (*slang*), harness bull (*slang*), bobby (*Brit.*), peeler (*Brit.*), tipstaff (*Brit.*); constable, bailiff, sheriff, trooper, state trooper, gendarme (*F.*), marshal; policewoman, matron; sergeant, lieutenant, captain, inspector, chief, police commissioner; sergeant at arms, proctor, vigilante; brown shirt, storm trooper, black shirt.

police, constabulary, police force, *Polizei* (*Ger.*), *gendarmerie* (*F.*); vigilance committee; secret police, Gestapo (*Ger.*), Gay-Pay-Oo or Ogpu (*Russ.*), MVD (*Russ.*), NKVD (*Russ.*); platoon, squad, posse; precinct, shrievalty, bailiwick; police station, station house, headquarters, police headquarters.

V. **officiate,** officialize, act, function; moderate, preside, take the chair; police, patrol, policize; seek (*or* run for) office, stump.

Adj. **official,** authoritative, magisterial, officiary; bureaucratic, red-tape, officious.

See also GOVERNMENT, POWER, RULER.

officiate, *v.* act, function, preside (OFFICIAL).

officious, *adj.* interfering, meddlesome, pragmatic (INTERJACENCE); bureaucratic, red-tape (OFFICIAL).

offing, *n.* futurity, aftertime (FUTURE).

offset, *v.* balance, equalize, neutralize (RECOMPENSE, OPPOSITION, WEIGHT).

offspring, *n.* descendant, scion, heir (CHILD).

off the record, *entre nous* (*F.*), confidentially (CONCEALMENT).

often, *adv.* frequently, recurrently (FREQUENCY).

ogle, *v.* stare, goggle, leer (LOOKING).

OIL—N. oil, petroleum, lubricant, lubricator, mineral oil, petrolatum, *oleum* (*L.*); olein; petroleum jelly, Vaseline; ointment, pomade, pomatum, brilliantine, unguent, unction, glycerin.

fat, grease, suet, tallow, blubber, lard, drippings, lanolin, margarine, oleomargarine; butter, butterfat, cream, shortening; sebum.

V. **oil,** pomade, lubricate, grease, tallow, lard, smear, begrease, pinguefy; anoint.

Adj. **oily,** unctuous, oleaginous, greasy, slick, oleic, unguinous, slippery, lubricous, lubricative.

fatty, fat, fatlike, adipose, sebaceous, lipoid, pinguid, blubbery; buttery, butyraceous, creamy, lardy, lardaceous.

smooth, glib, unctuous, plausible, suave, bland, fawning, ingratiating.

See also SMOOTHNESS, THICKNESS. *Antonyms*—See ROUGHNESS, THINNESS, VULGARITY.

ointment, *n.* lenitive, salve, unguent (CALMNESS).

O.K. (*colloq.*), *n.* acceptance, agreement, assent (PERMISSION).

old-fashioned, *adj.* out-of-date, anachronous, dated (OLDNESS, DISUSE).

old maid, *n.* bachelor girl, spinster (UNMARRIED STATE).

OLDNESS—N. oldness, old age, declining years, winter, senectitude, ancientry, antiquity, superannuation; anecdotage, longevity.

age, chronological age, majority, minority.

middle age, middle years, summer, autumn, fall, maturity.

senility, dotage, caducity, second childhood; senile decay, anility, decrepitude, debility, infirmity.

[*sciences of old age*] gerontology, nostology, geriatrics.

[*sciences of old things*] archaeology, paleontology, Assyriology, Egyptology, antiquarianism, paleology.

old man, patriarch, ancient, graybeard, Nestor, grandfather, gaffer (*contemptuous*), geezer (*colloq.*), codger, dotard; Methuselah, antediluvian, preadamite, veteran, old-timer (*colloq.*), oldster, old soldier, old stager, dean, doyen; senior, elder; oldest, firstborn; seniority, primogeniture.

old woman, old lady, grandmother, grandam, granny, grimal-kin (contemptuous), matriarch; matron, biddy (colloq.), dame, dowager; crone, hag, witch, bel-dame.

[as to years] quinquagenarian (50–60), sexagenarian (60–70), sep-tuagenarian (70–80), octogenarian (80–90), nonagenarian (90–100), centenarian (100 or over).

[one of the same age] contem-porary, coeval.

antique, antiquity, archaism, relic, fossil, eolith, paleolith, neo-lith; antiquities, remains, relics, reliquiae.

[old-fashioned thing, word, etc.] anachronism, antique, archaism, obsoletism.

[old-fashioned person] old fogy, fogy, square-toes, fossil, antedilu-vian, anachronism.

V. be old, have had its day, have seen its day.

become old, age, ripen, mature; fade, deteriorate, decay; mildew, mold, rust, stale, wither.

antiquate, archaize, date, obsolete, outdate, outmode, stale; obso-lesce.

be older, antedate, predate, have seniority, have priority; pre-exist.

Adj. old, aged, elderly, olden (poetic), senectuous, wintry or wintery; ancient, hoary, anti-quated, age-old, archaic, antique, fossil, superannuated; dateless, timeless, antediluvian, preadamitic, Noachian; time-honored, venera-ble; overage; geratic, gerontal (biol.); patriarchal, matriarchal; senile, decrepit, infirm, aging, senescent; old-womanish, anile.

older, elder, senior.

oldest, eldest, first-born; primo-genital.

[of the same age] contemporary, coeval, coetaneous.

[not, or no longer, new or fresh] stale, musty, rancid, threadbare, timeworn, worm-eaten, moss-grown, moth-eaten, outworn, moldy, mildewed, fusty, seedy, rusty, withered; trite, hackneyed, banal, stock.

old-fashioned, out-of-date, corny (slang), anachronistic, anachron-ous, antediluvian, antiquated, an-tique, archaic, dated, moss-grown, moth-eaten, obsolete, old-fangled, outdated, outmoded, passé, stale, superannuated, timeworn, worm-eaten, unfashionable; obsolescent.

veteran, old, experienced, prac-ticed, seasoned, disciplined.

See also DECAY, DETERIORATION, EX-PERIENCE, GRAY, MATURITY, TIME.

Antonyms—See CHILD, NEWNESS, YOUTH.

Old Testament, n. Septuagint, Genesis, Pentateuch (SACRED WRITINGS).

olive, adj. olive-colored, olive-drab (YELLOW).

olive branch, n. peace offering (PEACE).

omen, n. augury, foretoken, har-binger (FUTURE); sign, presage, token (PRECEDENCE); auspice, prophecy (PREDICTION).

ominous, adj. inauspicious, ill-omened (HOPELESSNESS).

omission, n. disregard, disregard-ance, oversight (NEGLECT).

omit, v. neglect, overlook, by-pass (NEGLECT, NONOBSERVANCE).

omnipotent, adj. powerful, al-mighty, mighty (POWER).

omnipresent, adj. pervasive, preva-lent, ubiquitous (PRESENCE).

omniscient, adj. all-wise, all-know-ing, pansophical (WISDOM, KNOWLEDGE).

omnivorous, adj. devouring, all-devouring (FOOD).

on, adv. forward, onward, forth (PROGRESS).

once, adv. formerly, at one time (TIME, PAST).

once more, again, over (REPETI-TION).

one, n. unit, ace, integer (UNITY).

one by one, independently, sepa-rately, severally (UNITY, DISJUNC-TION).

one-eyed, adj. monoptical, monocu-lar (EYE).

onerous, adj. burdensome, carking, oppressive (WEIGHT).

one-sided, adj. unilateral, partial, biased (SIDE, PREJUDICE).

on hand, in hand, in store, in stock (OWNERSHIP).

onlooker, n. spectator, witness, eyewitness (LOOKING, PRESENCE).

only, adj. exclusive, single, sole, unique (UNITY).

only, adv. exclusively, alone, solely (UNITY); merely, purely, simply (SMALLNESS).

on purpose, advisedly, calculatedly, deliberately (PURPOSE).

onset, n. start, outbreak, outstart (BEGINNING); access, seizure (AT-TACK).

onslaught, n. charge, blitz (col-loq.), incursion (ATTACK).

on the contrary, per contra (L.), au contraire (F.), in opposition (OPPOSITE).

on time, prompt, punctual (EARLI-NESS).

ooze, n. slime, mire, muck (SEMI-LIQUIDITY).

ooze, v. leak, trickle, seep (EGRESS); well, issue, spurt (RIVER); perspire, sweat, swelter (PERSPIRATION).

oozy, adj. quaggy, spongy, miry (MARSH).

opaque, adj. nontranslucent, nontransparent, intransparent (THICKNESS); obtuse, imperceptive, purblind (STUPIDITY).

open, adj. unlocked, unfastened (OPENING); outspoken, candid, frank (TRUTH); revealed, in view (VISIBILITY).

open, v. breach, lance, pop (OPENING); unravel, disentangle, expand (UNFOLDMENT).

open-air, adj. alfresco, outdoor (AIR).

OPENING—N. opening, aperture, mouth, orifice, cleft, breach, slit, crack, cranny, crevice, cut, rent, tear, rift, chink, break, split, fissure, vein, gap, cavity, loculus; vent, outlet, spout, vomitory, nozzle, hiatus, interstice, space; recess, slot, socket; scupper, scuttle, hatch, hatchway; wicket, window, door.

[opening in the earth] chasm, yawn, crater, abyss, cañon, gulf; excavation, ditch, trench, mine, quarry, tunnel.

cave, cavern, grotto, subterrane, hole, loophole, peephole, keyhole, pinhole, venthole, blowhole, airhole, bung, bunghole, pothole, eye, eyelet; puncture, pit, perforation, leak; burrow, wallow; well.

window, casement, french window, lattice, light, skylight, fanlight, bay window, bow window, oriel, dormer, port, porthole, embrasure; clerestory window, picture window, transom, wicket; fenestella; windshield; mullion, jamb; fenestration (arch.).

opener, key, passkey, master key, skeleton key, knob, handle, passe-partout (F.), open-sesame; can opener, bottle opener.

[instrument for making holes] drill, punch, bore, auger, awl, bit, gimlet, wimble, reamer; broach.

cave dweller, cave man, troglodyte.

[cave science] speleology, spelunking.

V. open, breach, broach, tap, burst, fissure, lacerate, lance, pop, puncture, scuttle, sever, slit, slot, socket, split, spread, stave, tap, unbolt, uncork, unfasten, unlatch, unlock, unplug, unseal, unstop, unstopper, unwrap, vent, ventilate; dehisce, frondesce, gap, gape, unfold, yawn, yawp.

puncture, punch, perforate, drill, bore, pit, riddle, scuttle (naut.).

Adj. open, opened, breached, broached, burst, fissured, lacerated, lanced, popped, punctured, scuttled, severed, slit, slotted, socketed, split, staved in, tapped; unbolted, uncorked, unfastened, unlatched, unlocked, unplugged, unsealed, unstopped, unstoppered, unwrapped, vented, ventilated; dihiscent, frondescent, gaping, gapy, unfolded, yawning; cleft, cracked, crannied, crenelated, cut, excavated, dug-out, holey, leaky, louvered, perforated, rent, torn, veined, vented, windowed; leachy, spongy, porous, cavernous, rimose; spread, spread open, patulous; unclosed, ajar.

See also AIR OPENING, BREAKAGE, CUTTING, HOLLOW, TEARING. Antonyms—See CLOSURE.

open-minded, adj. recipient, receptive, interested (RECEIVING).

openmouthed, adj. breathless, agape, spellbound (SURPRISE).

open to, liable to, subject to, in danger of (LIABILITY).

opera, n. grand opera, music drama, operetta (MUSIC).

operate, v. function, work (RESULT, ACTION); run, manage, drive (WORK); cut out, remove (SURGERY).

opiate, n. calmative, sedative, anodyne (CALMNESS); hypnotic, narcotic, soporific (SLEEP).

OPINION—N. opinion, concept, view, consideration, notion, judgment, persuasion, sentiment, slant, estimate, estimation, conclusion, apprehension; preconceived opinion, parti pris (F.), preconception, prejudgment, prejudice; dogma, pronouncement, address, resolution, deliverance; sense, pulse, tidal wave; thesis, symposium, rostrum, soapbox.

V. opine, suppose, think; judge, adjudge, conclude, reckon, account, consider, deem, estimate, appraise, hold; prejudge, preconceive.

Adj. opinionated, opinionative, opinioned, dogmatic, assertive, positive, pragmatic, peremptory, arbitrary, highhanded, oracular; uncompromising, intransigent.

See also BELIEF, CERTAINTY, IDEA, JUDGMENT, PREJUDICE, SUPPOSITION, THOUGHT. Antonyms—See UNCERTAINTY.

opium, n. morphine, morphia, paregoric (PHARMACY).

opponent, *n.* antagonist, competitor, rival (OPPOSITION).

opportune, *adj.* timely, auspicious, propitious (TIMELINESS).

opportunist, *n.* timeserver, trimmer, chameleon (CHANGEABLENESS, APOSTASY, IRRESOLUTION).

opportunity, *n.* occasion, chance, scope (CHANCE); leisure, freedom, convenience (TIME).

oppose, *v.* violate, defy, resist (OPPOSITION).

opposed, *adj.* opposing, against, counter (OPPOSITION); contrary, antithetic, contradictory (OPPOSITE).

OPPOSITE—*N.* opposite, contrary, antilogy, antipode, antithesis, antonym, contradiction, converse, inverse, paradox, reverse.

V. **be contrary,** contrast with, differ from, contradict, gainsay, contravene, thwart, oppose, violate.

Adj. **opposite,** opposed, contrary, absonant, antilogical, antipodal, antipodean, antithetic, contradictory, contradictive, contrariant, converse, counter, crosswise, diametric, inverse, reverse, polar, vis-à-vis (*F.*), repugnant, violative of; paradoxical, self-contradictory; antonymous.

contrary, froward, perverse, wayward, negative, negativistic, resistive.

Phrases. **on the contrary,** per contra (*L.*), au contraire (*F.*), in opposition; vis-à-vis (*F.*).

See also DIFFERENCE, OPPOSITION. *Antonyms*—See SIMILARITY.

OPPOSITION—*N.* opposition, defiance, violation, oppugnancy; repulsion, repugnance, aversion, resistance, negativism, renitence, contrariety, civil disobedience; antithesis, antinomy; competition, rivalry.

counteraction, contravention, neutralization, counterbalance, counterpoise, counterweight, counterwork, counteragent, antidote.

objection, exception, demurral, demur, demurrer, protestation, protest, remonstrance, remonstrance, challenge, recalcitration, recalcitrance.

enmity, hostility, antagonism, inimicality.

opponent, antagonist, competitor, rival, adversary, foe, enemy; rebel, Guelph, iconoclast, die-hard, bitter-ender.

conservative, Bourbon, Bourbonist, reactionary, Philistine, standpatter, die-hard.

V. **oppose,** violate, defy, oppugn, oppugnate, repel, repulse, resist, withstand; buck, bar, balk, antagonize; compete.

counter, counteract, counterwork, contravene, neutralize, offset, counterbalance, counterpoise, counterweigh, countermine.

object, demur, take exception, protest, remonstrate, stickle, challenge, recalcitrate.

contradict, gainsay, disaffirm, dispute, disagree with, rebut, controvert.

Adj. **opposed,** opposing, against, counter, versus, alien, contrarient; violative, oppugnant, repugnant, repellent, repulsive, defiant, resistant, resistive, unbowed, underground, balky, negative, negativistic, renitent, contrary; antithetic, antinomous, adverse, averse, inimical, antagonistic, unfriendly; competitive, rival; counteractive, counteractant.

objecting, demurring, exceptive, captious, protestive, protestant, recalcitrant.

contradictory, contradictive, disaffirmatory, contrary, in contradiction.

[*opposed to change or progress*] **conservative,** bourgeois, hidebound, old-line, square-toed, standpat, die-hard, Philistine, reactionary.

unfavorable, adverse, contrary, disadvantageous, inauspicious, inopportune, ominous, prejudicial, unfortunate, untoward, ill-disposed, unpropitious.

Adv., conjunctions, phrases. **although,** though, albeit, even though, supposing that, despite, in spite of; notwithstanding, nevertheless, nonetheless, however.

Prep., phrases. **against,** facing, opposite to, versus (*L.*), adverse to, in opposition to, counter to.

despite, in spite of, in despite of, in defiance of, notwithstanding, against, in the teeth of, in the face of.

See also ATTEMPT, DEFIANCE, DENIAL, DISAGREEMENT, HINDRANCE, HOSTILITY, OPPOSITE, UNWILLINGNESS. *Antonyms*—See ACCEPTANCE, CO-OPERATION, FRIEND, FRIENDLINESS, WILLINGNESS.

---

oppress, *v.* load, prey on, tax (WEIGHT); despotize, tyrannize (POWER, CONTROL).

oppression, *n.* despotism, tyranny, autocracy (CONTROL).

oppressive, *adj.* burdensome, carking, onerous (WEIGHT); hardhanded, ironhanded, grinding (POWER).

opprobrium, *n.* criticism, stricture, vitriol (DISAPPROVAL); obloquy, reproach, dishonor (DISGRACE).

optical, *adj.* visual, ocular (VISION).

optimism, *n.* hopefulness, buoyancy, Pollyannaism (HOPE).

optimistic, *adj.* hopeful, roseate, rose-colored (CHEERFULNESS, HOPE).

optimum, *adj.* best, capital, superlative (SUPERIORITY).

option, *n.* election, selection, preference (CHOICE).

optional, *adj.* discretionary, elective, voluntary (CHOICE, WILL).

optometrist, *n.* oculist, ophthalmologist (VISION).

opulent, *adj.* wealthy, rich, affluent, prosperous (WEALTH).

oracle, *n.* soothsayer, prophet, seer (PREDICTION).

oracular, *adj.* mystical, cryptic, cabalistic (MEANING).

oral, *adj.* spoken, phonic, unwritten (STATEMENT, TALK); oscular, stomatic (HEAD).

orange, *adj.* peach, apricot, tangerine (YELLOW, RED).

orate, *v.* speechify (*jocose*), spout, harangue, spellbind (TALK).

orator, *n.* discourser, public speaker, elocutionist, rhetorician (TALK, EXPRESSION).

oratorical, *adj.* rhetorical, elocutionary; soulful, sentimental, poetic, dithyrambic (EXPRESSION).

oratory, *n.* elocution, eloquence, rhetoric (TALK, EXPRESSION).

orbit, *n.* trajectory, locus, path (PASSAGE); cycle, circuit (ROUNDNESS); scope, circle, realm (POWER, INFLUENCE).

orchard, *n.* grove, copse, coppice (PLANT LIFE).

orchestra, *n.* band, ensemble, strings (MUSICIAN); parquet circle (SEAT).

orchid, *adj.* lavender, perse, amethyst (PURPLE).

ordain, *v.* decree, order, dictate (COMMAND); commission, constitute, appoint (COMMISSION).

ordained, *adj.* in orders, in holy orders (CLERGY).

ordeal, *n.* nightmare, trial, tribulation (EXPERIENCE).

order, *n.* disposition, distribution, pattern (ARRANGEMENT); orderliness, tidiness, system (NEATNESS); regulation, direction (COMMAND).

order, *v.* decree, ordain, dictate (COMMAND); book, engage, reserve (EARLINESS, BOOK).

orderly, *adj.* methodical, regular, systematic (ARRANGEMENT); shipshape, trim, uncluttered (NEATNESS); well-behaved, docile, manageable (GOOD, OBEDIENCE).

ordinance, *n.* rule, regulation (LAW).

ordinary, *adj.* common, usual, habitual; mediocre, commonplace, characterless (COMMONNESS).

ore, *n.* mineral, vein, lode (METAL).

organ, *n.* pipe organ, reed organ, harmonium (MUSICAL INSTRUMENTS).

organism, *n.* living being, being, creature (LIFE).

organization, *n.* disposition, grouping, orderliness (ARRANGEMENT); constitution, character, structure (MAKE-UP, TEXTURE); company, establishment (BUSINESS).

organize, *v.* methodize, systematize (ARRANGEMENT, METHOD); constitute, establish (BEGINNING).

organizer, *n.* planner, designer, author (PLAN).

orgy, *n.* merrymaking, revel, carousal (AMUSEMENT, PLEASURE).

oriental, *adj.* Far Eastern, Chinese, Japanese (DIRECTION, MANKIND).

origin, *n.* source, derivation (BEGINNING).

original, *adj.* aboriginal, first (BEGINNING); fresh, novel, Promethean (NEWNESS); imaginative, inventive, creative (IMAGINATION, PRODUCTION); different, unique, atypical (DIFFERENCE).

original, *n.* model, archetype (COPY, BEGINNING); creation, invention (PRODUCTION); wrinkle, novelty (NEWNESS); manuscript, holograph (WRITING).

originate, *v.* come into existence, arise, derive (BEGINNING); create, conceive, compose (PRODUCTION).

ORNAMENT—*N.* ornament, ornamentation, adornment, decoration, embellishment, flamboyance, enrichment; illustration, illumination.

decorative design: fretwork, tracery, filigree, arabesque, foliation, imbrication; scroll, spiral, wave, flourish, zigzag, interlacing, strapwork, checkering, striping, paneling, panelwork, spotting; frostwork, tooling, inlaid work, parquetry, figurework, appliqué (*F.*), enamel, cloisonné (*F.*).

[*fancywork*] embroidery, needlework; lace, tatting, crochet, edging; brocade, brocatel, tapestry.

[*trimmings*] fringe, tassel, knot, frog; shoulder knot, aiglet, aiguillette, epaulet; rosette, bow; feather, plume, panache, aigrette; fillet, snood; sash, scarf, baldric, girdle, belt.

finery, frippery, tinsel, clinquant, spangle,

object of art, *bibelot* (*F.*), curio, *objet d'art* (*F.*), knicknack *or* nicknack; bric-a-brac, virtu, bijouterie.

V. **ornament,** embellish, enrich, decorate, adorn, beautify, ornamentalize, deck, bedeck; trick up (*or* out), prink, bedizen, trim, dress out, dress up, dress, array, smarten, spruce up (*colloq.*), doll up (*slang*); garnish, furbish, polish, gild, varnish, enamel, paint; spangle, bespangle, bead, embroider; chase, tool; emblazon, blazon, illuminate, miniate (*as a manuscript*), rubricate.

Adj. **ornamental,** decorative, fancy; inwrought, inlaid, filigreed, fretted, festooned.

ornate, ornamented, decorated, adorned, beautified, flowery, rich; gilt, begilt, gilded, glittering, refulgent, resplendent; showy, flashy, gorgeous, garish, flamboyant, gaudy, tawdry, meretricious.

See also BEAUTY, JEWELRY, OSTENTATION, WORDINESS. *Antonyms*— See BLEMISH, SIMPLICITY.

ornate, *adj.* rich, ornamented, decorated, adorned (ORNAMENT); embellished, florid, flowery, figured (WORDINESS, FIGURE OF SPEECH).

orphanage, *n.* orphan asylum (CHILD).

orthodox, *adj.* religious, pious, devout (RELIGIOUSNESS); rightful, legitimate, official (TRUTH); standard, canonical, authoritative (APPROVAL, BELIEF); traditional, punctilious, prim (HABIT).

OSCILLATION—*N.* **oscillation,** undulation, pendulation, vibration, fluctuation, swing, switch, whirl, waltz; pendulum, pivot, swivel.

V. **oscillate,** undulate, ripple, pendulate, vibrate, librate, fluctuate, swing, switch; swivel, pivot; whirl, waltz.

wave, flap, flop, lop, flutter, dangle, flicker; wag, waggle, wiggle.

sway, careen, rock, roll, pitch, toss, thrash, seesaw, teeter, teetertotter, lurch, reel, stagger, totter, waver, wobble, waddle.

Adj. **oscillatory,** undulatory, undulant, pendulant, pendulous, vibratory, vibratile, vibrant, libratory, fluctuant, billowy, aswing, zigzag; whirly, awhirl, whirligig.

wavy, wavery, floppy, fluttery, aflutter, dangly, adangle, flickery, aflicker; waggy, awag, waggly, wiggly, awiggle.

swaying, asway, seesaw, tottery, totterish, wavery, wobbly, waddly.

Adv., phrases. to and fro, back and forth, shuttlewise, in and out, up and down, zigzag, wibble-wobble (*colloq.*), from side to side.

See also AGITATION, CHANGEABLENESS, HANGING, MOTION, ROLL, SHAKE, TURNING, UNSTEADINESS. *Antonyms*—See MOTIONLESSNESS, REST, STABILITY.

ostensible, *adj.* apparent, seeming, quasi (APPEARANCE); professed, colorable (PRETENSE).

OSTENTATION—*N.* **ostentation,** display, show, parade, pretension, pretense, flourish, pomp, magnificence, splendor, pageant, pageantry; dash (*colloq.*), splurge (*colloq.*), swank, flash, splash (*colloq.*), swagger, swash, front (*slang*), veneer, gloss, glitter, clinquant, tinsel, frippery, gaudery, foppery; show-off, flaunt, fanfare, mummery, puppetry, vainglory; exhibitionism.

show-off, flaunter, splurger, swaggerer, exhibitionist, parader, tinhorn (*slang*), vulgarian.

[*showy thing or things*] tinsel, brummagem, gewgaw, gimcrack, catchpenny; trumpery, peddlery, finery, frippery, gaudery, regalia.

V. **show off,** display, advertise, exhibit, brandish, flaunt, flourish, air, parade, prank, wave, dangle, sport; cut a dash (*colloq.*), put up a front (*slang*), swagger, swank, swash, make a splurge (*colloq.*), spread oneself (*colloq.*); gloss, tinsel, varnish.

Adj. **ostentatious,** showy, dashing, dashy, flamboyant, flashy, flatulent, flaunty, gay, glittery, grandiose, jaunty, loud (*colloq.*), pretentious, splashy (*colloq.*), sporty, theatrical, stagy, spectacular; tinsel, fussy, garish, gewgaw, gimcrack, brummagem, trumpery; exhibitionistic.

pretentious, grandiose, ambitious, highfalutin (*colloq.*), pompous, stilted, toplofty (*colloq.*), vainglorious.

flashy, catchpenny, gaudy, meretricious, raffish, sporty (*colloq.*), tawdry, tinhorn (*slang*), tinsel, swank *or* swanky (*colloq.*).

See also BOASTING, DISPLAY, IMMODESTY, ORNAMENT, PRETENSE, PRIDE, VULGARITY. *Antonyms*—See MODESTY, SIMPLICITY.

ostracism, *n.* exclusion, coventry, boycott, black list (EXCLUSION, DISAPPROVAL).

ostracize, *v.* snub, cut, boycott (INATTENTION, EXCLUSION).

oust, *v.* expel, eject, evict (DISMISSAL, PROPULSION).

ouster, *n.* ejection, expulsion, dispossession, eviction (DISMISSAL).

out, *adv.* without, outward (EXTERIORITY).

outbreak, *n.* rebellion, insurrection, uprising (DISOBEDIENCE); outburst, eruption, explosion (VIOLENCE); sally, sortie, invasion (ATTACK).

outburst, *n.* outbreak, eruption, explosion (VIOLENCE).

outcast, *n.* deportee, displaced person, D.P., exile (DISMISSAL).

outcome, *n.* aftermath, effect, consequence (RESULT).

outcry, *n.* cry, screech, scream (LOUDNESS, SHOUT).

outdated, *adj.* obsolete, outmoded, passé, unfashionable, anachronous, out-of-date, behind time (OLDNESS, MISTIMING).

outdistance, *v.* outrun, outstrip, outpace, outstride (OVERRUNNING).

outdo, *v.* surpass, top, excel (SUPERIORITY, OVERRUNNING).

outdoor, *adj.* open-air, alfresco (AIR).

outer, *adj.* exterior, external (EXTERIORITY).

outfit, *n.* supplies, equipment, provisions, (QUANTITY); appliances, tackle, rigging (INSTRUMENT); costume, ensemble, wardrobe (CLOTHING).

outfit, *v.* equip, accouter (PREPARATION, QUANTITY).

outing, *n.* excursion, picnic (TRAVELING).

outlandish, *adj.* queer, quaint, eccentric (UNUSUALNESS); barbaric, barbarian (IRRELATION).

outlast, *v.* survive, outlive (CONTINUATION, LIFE).

outlaw, *n.* hooligan, bandit, highwayman (ILLEGALITY).

outlaw, *v.* ban, proscribe, interdict (DENIAL).

outlet, *n.* avenue, exit, vent (EGRESS, DEPARTURE, OPENING).

outline, *n.* contour, lineation, lines (SHAPE); diagram, plan (MAP, PLAN); draft, rough draft, sketch (WRITING).

outline, *v.* describe (INFORMATION);

summarize, recapitulate (SHORTNESS).

outlive, *v.* survive, outlast (CONTINUATION, LIFE).

outlook, *n.* view, perspective (VISION); viewpoint, attitude (CHARACTER); prospect, forecast (FUTURE).

outmoded, *adj.* obsolete, outdated, passé (OLDNESS).

out-of-date, *adj.* old-fashioned, anachronous (OLDNESS, MISTIMING); obsolete, passé, dated (DISUSE).

out-of-the-way, *adj.* secluded, unfrequented, lonely (SECLUSION).

outpost, *n.* outskirts, purlieu, suburb (DISTANCE).

output, *n.* harvest, yield, product (STORE).

outrage, *n.* affront, indignity, injury (OFFENSE); evildoing, malefaction, misdoing, wrongdoing (WICKEDNESS), violation, ravishment, rapine (VIOLENCE).

outrage, *v.* offend, affront, insult (OFFENSE); scandalize, shock, jar (UNPLEASANTNESS); do violence to, wrong (HARM).

outrageous, *adj.* offensive, insolent, contumelious (INSULT, OFFENSE); inordinate, exorbitant, extortionate (EXTREMENESS); horrifying, monstrous, scandalous (DISGUST, UNPLEASANTNESS).

outright, *adj.* complete, thorough, out-and-out (COMPLETENESS).

outrun, *v.* outstrip, outdistance (OVERRUNNING).

outset, *n.* first, start, opening (BEGINNING).

outside, *n.* external, outdoors, out-of-doors (EXTERIORITY).

outsider, *n.* foreigner, stranger, outlander (IRRELATION).

outskirts, *n.* limits, bounds, boundary (EXTERIORITY); outpost, purlieu, suburbs (DISTANCE).

outspoken, *adj.* straightforward, unreserved, frank (HONESTY, TRUTH).

outstanding, *adj.* conspicuous, striking, arresting (VISIBILITY); extrusive, jutting (VISIBILITY); remarkable, phenomenal, marvelous (UNUSUALNESS); famous, well-known, prominent (FAME); eventful, momentous (IMPORTANCE); unpaid, owing, unsettled (DEBT).

outstrip, *v.* outrun, outdistance (OVERRUNNING); gain upon, overhaul, overtake (SPEED).

outweigh, *v.* overweigh, overbalance (SUPERIORITY, WEIGHT); preponderate, overshadow (IMPORTANCE).

outwit, *v.* outgeneral, outmaneuver, overreach (SUPERIORITY);

mislead, lead astray, take in (DECEPTION).

outworn, *adj.* moldy, mildewed, fusty (OLDNESS).

oval, *n.* ellipse, ovoid, ellipsoid (ROUNDNESS).

ovation, *n.* applause, salvo (APPROVAL); tribute, testimonial (RESPECT).

oven, *n.* stove, cookstove, range (HEAT).

over, *adj.* finished, settled, concluded (END); remaining, left, surplus (REMAINDER).

over, *adv.* at an end, done with (END); again, anew, once more (REPETITION); beyond, in addition to (SUPERIORITY).

over, *prep.* through, throughout (TIME).

overabundance, *n.* too much, glut, nimiety, superabundance (EXCESS, MULTITUDE).

overbearing, *adj.* imperious, dictatorial, lordly (PRIDE).

overburden, *v.* overlade, overload (WEIGHT); overtax, overwork (FATIGUE).

overcast, *adj.* cloudy, heavy, lowery (CLOUD).

overcharge, *v.* bleed (*colloq.*), skin (*slang*), fleece (EXPENDITURE).

overcoat, *n.* balmacaan, chesterfield, ulster (COAT).

overcome, *v.* surmount, prevail over; stun, overwhelm (DEFEAT).

overcrowd, *v.* crowd, deluge, swamp, flood, overrun (MULTITUDE, ARRIVAL).

overdo, *v.* overburden, overtax (FATIGUE); overwork, supererogate (ACTION).

overdue, *adj.* belated, delayed, long-delayed (DELAY); unpaid, delinquent, outstanding (DEBT).

overeat, *v.* gorge, stuff, cram (GLUTTONY).

OVERESTIMATION—*N.* overestimation, overvaluation, overrating, megalomania, eulogy, overpraise; exaggeration, hyperbole; tempest in a teacup.

V. **overestimate**, overvalue, overstate, overprize; overpraise, overesteem, overrate, magnify, glorify, extol, panegyrize, eulogize, puff (*colloq.*), boost (*colloq.*).

See also EXAGGERATION, PRAISE, VALUE. *Antonyms*—See DETRACTION.

---

overfed, *adj.* overweight, overstuffed, rotund (SIZE).

overflow, *v.* overwhelm, deluge, inundate (OVERRUNNING, WATER).

overflowing, *adj.* brimful, overfilled, bursting (FULLNESS).

overhang, *n.* projection, jut (HANGING).

overhang, *v.* stick out, jut, project, beetle (VISIBILITY); rise above, tower above, jut above (HEIGHT); menace, portend, impend, loom (THREAT).

overhaul, *v.* repair, fix, mend (RESTORATION); gain upon, catch up to, overtake (TRAP, SPEED).

overhead, *adv.* upward, above (HEIGHT).

overhead, *n.* cost, upkeep, budget (EXPENDITURE).

overjoyed, *adj.* joyous, rapturous, ravished (HAPPINESS).

overlap, *v.* run over, overrun (ENCROACHMENT, OVERRUNNING).

overlapping, *adj.* overlying, imbricated, shingled, lapstreak (HANGING, COVERING).

overlook, *v.* overtop, surmount, soar above (HEIGHT); inspect, scrutinize, scan (EXAMINATION, LOOKING); oversee, supervise, superintend (CONTROL); disregard, omit (INATTENTION, NEGLECT); blink at, condone (FORGIVENESS).

overly, *adv.* excessively, exceedingly, inordinately (EXTREMENESS).

overpower, *v.* put to rout, smash, overwhelm (DEFEAT).

overpowering, *adj.* overwhelming, formidable (STRENGTH).

overrate, *v.* overestimate, overvalue, overassess (OVERESTIMATION, VALUE).

override, *v.* trample, ride roughshod over (SEVERITY).

OVERRUNNING—*N.* overrunning, overflowing, overspreading, overstepping, transgression, encroachment, infraction, inroad, infringement, transcendence, advance, overrun.

V. **overrun**, run over, overlap, spread over, overspread, overgrow, infest, swarm over, grow over; overflow, overwhelm, deluge, inundate.

outrun, outstrip, outpace, outstride, outdistance, outrace, pass, go beyond, go by, shoot ahead of, override, outride, outrival, outdo, beat, distance, throw into the shade, eclipse; surmount, tower above, surpass; overshoot the mark.

overstep, transgress, trespass, encroach, infringe, intrude, invade.

See also ENCROACHMENT, EXCESS,

SPREAD, STRETCH, SUPERIORITY. *Antonyms*—See REVERSION.

---

overseas, *adj.* transoceanic, transatlantic, transpacific (OCEAN).

oversee, *v.* overlook, supervise, superintend (CONTROL); inspect, watch (LOOKING).

overshadow, *v.* outweigh, preponderate, overweigh (IMPORTANCE).

overshoes, *n.* arctics, galoshes, rubber boots (FOOTWEAR).

oversight, *n.* disregard, omission (NEGLECT).

oversized, *adj.* large, lubberly, hulking (SIZE).

overspread, *v.* suffuse, transfuse, diffuse (SPREAD); overrun, overgrow, run over (OVERRUNNING); superimpose, overlay, envelop (COVERING).

overstate, *v.* exaggerate, hyperbolize (*rhet.*), overdraw (EXAGGERATION).

overstep, *v.* transgress, trespass, encroach (OVERRUNNING, ENCROACHMENT).

overstuffed, *adj.* fat, overweight, overfed (SIZE).

oversupply, *v.* deluge, flood, glut (EXCESS).

overtake, *v.* catch up to, gain on, reach (APPROACH, TRAP); overhaul, outstrip, beat (SPEED).

overtax, *v.* overwork, overburden, overstrain (MISUSE).

overthrow, *v.* knock down, overturn, topple (DESCENT, DEFEAT).

overtone, *n.* implication, intimation, innuendo (SUGGESTION).

overture, *n.* presentation, proposal, advance (OFFER); prelude, ritornel, prelusion (MUSIC, BEGINNING).

overtures, *n.* advances, proposals (APPROACH).

overturn, *v.* upend, reverse, invert (TURNING); overthrow, upset, topple (DEFEAT, DESCENT).

overused, *adj.* overworked, worn, shabby (USE).

overweight, *adj.* fat, overfed, overstuffed (SIZE).

overwhelm, *v.* overcome, overpower, rout (DEFEAT); overflow, deluge, inundate (OVERRUNNING).

overwhelming, *adj.* formidable, overpowering (STRENGTH).

overwrought, *adj.* uneasy, unstrung, overstrung (NERVOUSNESS).

ovum, *n.* egg cell, egg (MAKE-UP).

owe, *v.* be in debt, run up a bill (DEBT).

owing, *adj.* payable, due, matured, unpaid, unsettled, outstanding (PAYMENT, DEBT).

own, *v.* possess, occupy, hold (OWNERSHIP); admit, confess, grant (STATEMENT).

OWNERSHIP—*N.* ownership, proprietorship, possession, occupation, occupancy, tenancy, tenure; partnership, copartnership, community, coparcency (*law*); monopoly.

possession, belonging, appurtenance, asset, chattel; white elephant (*colloq*).

personal possessions, effects, paraphernalia, traps, baggage; goods, movables, stock.

property, substance, capital, estate, holdings, stocks, bonds, securities, assets; real estate, real property, realty, land, lands, acreage; capitalism.

owner, proprietor, co-owner, partner, copartner; landowner, landlord, landholder, squire.

possessor, holder, occupant, occupier, tenant, freeholder, lessee, leaseholder, renter, lodger.

owners (*collectively*), proprietariat, landed gentry, squirearchy, bourgeoisie.

V. **own,** possess, be possessed of, occupy, hold, have, contain.

belong, appertain, pertain, belong to, reside in, inhere in.

Adj. **possessing,** worth, possessed of, master of, in possession of; endowed with; on hand, in store, in stock; at one's command, at one's disposal.

belonging, appurtenant, inherent, pertinent, resident; appropriate, particular, peculiar, endemic, intrinsic.

See also CONTENTS, HOLD, INHABITANT, WEALTH. *Antonyms*—See LOSS, POVERTY, RELINQUISHMENT, TRANSFER.

---

ox, *n.* bull, bullock (ANIMAL).
oxygen, *n.* ozone (*colloq.*), ether (AIR).

P

pace, *n.* rate, velocity, tempo (SPEED); step, footstep, tread (WALKING).

pace, *v.* step, walk, tread, march (WALKING).

pacify, *v.* tranquilize, appease (PEACE).

pack, *n.* group, bundle, bunch; horde, swarm, crowd, mass (ASSEMBLAGE, MULTITUDE).

pack, *v.* cram, fill, load (FULL-NESS); bunch, bundle, group (ASSEMBLAGE); throng, besiege, congregate (MULTITUDE).

package, *n.* bundle, parcel, packet (ASSEMBLAGE).

packed, *adj.* jam-packed, serried, tumid (MULTITUDE).

packing, *n.* content, filling, stuffing (CONTENTS).

pact, *n.* agreement, contract, deal (*colloq.*), arrangement (COMPACT).

pad, *n.* tablet, quire, ream (PAPER); foot, paw (APPENDAGE).

pad, *v.* pat, patter, pitter-patter (WALKING); enlarge, amplify, bulk (INCREASE).

padded, *adj.* long-drawn-out, long-spun, interminable (LENGTH).

padding, *n.* stuffing, fill, filler (FULLNESS).

paddle, *n.* oar, scull, sweep (SAILOR).

paddle, *v.* row, pull, scull (SAILOR); swim (SWIMMING).

padlock, *n.* latch, bolt, lock (FASTENING).

pagan, *n.* heathen, infidel (RELIGION, IRRELIGION).

page, *n.* equerry, squire (SERVICE); leaf, sheet, signature (PAPER); errand boy, bellboy, attendant (MESSENGER).

pageant, *n.* exhibition, fair, exposition (DISPLAY); parade, procession, motorcade (WALKING).

pail, *n.* bucket, hod, scuttle (CONTAINER).

PAIN—*N.* **pain,** ache, pang, throe, lancination, twinge, twitch, tingle, prickle, prick, sting, smart; spasm, paroxysm, convulsion; earache, otalgia, otodynia; toothache, odontalgia; heartburn, cardialgia, pyrosis; sciatica, neuralgia, myalgia, arthritis, rheumatism, lumbago, gout, podagra, backache.

cramp, Charley horse, crick, kink, stitch, algospasm; writer's cramp, graphospasm.

stomach-ache, bellyache (*colloq.*), colic, cramps, gripe, gripes, gastralgia, tormina.

headache, migraine, cephalalgia.

childbirth pains, labor pains, throes.

suffering, misery, anguish, agony, torment, torture, rack, affliction, throes, travail.

distress, discomfort, malaise, dysphoria (*med.*).

sufferer, victim, prey, martyr, wretch.

V. **pain,** hurt, sting, smart, ache, twinge, burn, bite, tingle, prick, prickle; agonize, convulse, torture,

---

torment, rack, scourge, punish, chasten, excruciate, anguish; afflict, ail, trouble, distress; chafe, gall; cramp, crick, gripe.

be in pain, suffer, ail, pain, writhe, travail (*in childbirth*), agonize, anguish, hurt, ache; tingle, prickle, prick, sting, smart, burn, twinge; cringe, wince, flinch.

Adj. **painful,** hurtful, algetic, stinging, smarting, aching, throbbing, splitting (*esp. of a headache*), burning, biting, prickly, sore, tender; agonizing, torturous, torturesome, torturing, tormenting, lancinating, racking, punishing, grueling, chastening, excruciating, anguishing; distressing, cruel, dire, grievous.

unbearable, intolerable, insufferable, insupportable, unendurable.

suffering, in pain, miserable, afflicted, ailing, writhing, agonized, anguished, hurt, aching, achy, tingling, tingly, smarting, twinged, sore, tender; tormented, tortured, excruciated, on the rack, racked, convulsed; distressed, uncomfortable, dysphoric.

See also CRUELTY, PUNISHMENT, TORTURE, UNPLEASANTNESS. *Antonyms*—See INSENSIBILITY, INSENSITIVITY, PAINKILLER, PLEASANTNESS, PLEASURE.

PAINKILLER—*N.* **painkiller,** analgesic, anodyne, aspirin, balm, lenitive, mitigative, narcotic, sedative, opiate; analgetic, anesthetic, desensitizer.

relief (*of pain*), anesthesia, analgesia.

V. **relieve** (*pain*), soothe, reduce, allay, alleviate, assuage, deaden, decrease, diminish, dull, ease, lessen, lighten, mitigate, quiet, salve, soften, still, palliate.

anesthetize, analgize, desensitize, narcotize, drug.

Adj. **insensitive** (*to pain*), anesthetic, anesthetized, desensitized, impassible.

painless, unpainful; unpaining, indolent (*med.*).

See also INSENSIBILITY, INSENSITIVITY, RELIEF. *Antonyms*—See PAIN.

---

painless, *adj.* unpainful, unpaining (PAINKILLER).

painstaking, *adj.* scrupulous, meticulous, punctilious (CARE).

paint, *n.* stain, varnish, enamel (COVERING).

paint, *v.* color, draw, daub (FINE ARTS).

painter, *n.* colorist, drawer, sketcher (ARTIST).

painting, *n.* drawing, illustration,

design; picture, piece, canvas (FINE ARTS).

pair, *n.* couple, brace, mates (TWO).

pajamas, *n.* nightshirt, nightdress, nightwear (SLEEP).

pal (*slang*), *n.* companion, chum (*colloq.*), comrade (FRIEND).

palace, *n.* castle, château, alcazar (BUILDING).

palatable, *adj.* luscious, delicious, toothsome (PLEASANTNESS, TASTE).

palate, *n.* appetite, relish, tooth (LIKING); sense of taste, gustation (TASTE).

palatial, *adj.* luxurious, silken, plush (WEALTH).

pale, *adj.* pallid, ashen, pasty (COLORLESSNESS).

pall, *v.* cloy, jade, surfeit (SATISFACTION).

palliate, *v.* soften, mitigate, extenuate (SOFTNESS); excuse, justify (FORGIVENESS).

pallor, *n.* sallowness, pastiness (COLORLESSNESS).

palmist, *n.* fortuneteller, chiromancer (PREDICTION).

palpable, *adj.* perceptible, perceivable, tangible (SENSITIVENESS, TOUCH).

palpitate, *v.* throb, pulsate, flutter (RHYTHM).

paltry, *adj.* petty, picayune, piddling (UNIMPORTANCE, WORTHLESSNESS); pitiful, contemptible, miserable (PITY).

pamper, *v.* humor, indulge, spoil (MILDNESS).

pamphlet, *n.* brochure, booklet, tract (BOOK).

pan, *n.* pot, pannikin, saucepan (CONTAINER).

panacea, *n.* cure-all, elixir, catholicon (CURE).

pancake, *n.* flapjack, griddlecake, hot cake (BREAD).

pandemonium, *n.* uproar, rumpus, clatter (COMMOTION, LOUDNESS); chaos, tumult (CONFUSION).

panderer, *n.* procurer, pimp, whiteslaver (PROSTITUTE).

pane (*of glass*), *n.* light, panel (GLASSINESS).

panel, *n.* insert, inset, inlay (INSERTION); pane, light, window (GLASSINESS); jury (JUDGE); round table, discussion group (ADVICE).

pang, *n.* ache, throe, twinge (PAIN).

panic, *n.* fright, alarm, terror (FEAR).

panic, *v.* startle, scare, alarm, stampede (FEAR).

panorama, *n.* spectacle, diorama, bird's-eye view (APPEARANCE, FINE ARTS).

pant, *v.* whiff, puff, huff (BREATH).

panties, *n.* briefs, step-ins (UNDERWEAR).

pantomime, *n.* gesticulation, pantomimicry (GESTURE).

pantry, *n.* larder, buttery, storeroom (STORE).

pants, *n.* breeches, britches (*colloq.*), jeans (TROUSERS).

papal, *adj.* pontifical, apostolic (CLERGY).

PAPER—N. paper, stationery, parchment, vellum, note paper, papyrus, onionskin, tissue, tissue paper, foolscap; pad, tablet, quire, ream; scroll; newspaper, newsprint; wrapping paper, gift wrap; confetti, streamers, crepe paper; papier-mâché, cardboard, paperboard; page, leaf, sheet, signature, folio.

Adj. papery, paperlike, chartaceous; paper-thin, wafer-thin, papier-mâché.

See also RECORD, ROLL, WRITING.

---

papers, *n.* credentials, documents (PROOF, POWER).

par, *n.* equivalence, parity, coequality (EQUALITY).

parable, *n.* bestiary, fable, allegory (STORY).

parachute, *v.* hit the silk (*slang*), bail out (JUMP).

parachutist, *n.* paratrooper, aerialist (FLYING).

parade, *n.* procession, march, motorcade (WALKING); display, show (OSTENTATION).

paradise, *n.* Eden, Elysium (HAPPINESS, HEAVEN); Utopia, Erewhon (PERFECTION).

paradox, *n.* contradiction, inconsistency (OPPOSITE, ABSURDITY).

paragon, *n.* model, pattern, ideal (PERFECTION, COPY).

parallel, *adj.* comparative, analogous, corresponding (COMPARISON, SIMILARITY).

parallelism, *n.* agreement, analogy, correspondence (SIMILARITY); uniformity, regularity, evenness (SHAPE).

paralysis, *n.* palsy, inertia, torpor (MOTIONLESSNESS).

paralyze, *v.* disable, cripple (WEAKNESS).

paramount, *adj.* leading, supreme, chief (IMPORTANCE).

paramour, *n.* lover, gallant (LOVE).

paraphernalia, *n.* effects, personal effects (OWNERSHIP); regalia, insignia (ROD).

paraphrase, *v.* restate, recapitulate, reword (REPETITION).

parasite, *n.* sponge, free loader (*slang*), sponger (LIFE).

parasol, n. shade, sunshade, umbrella (PROTECTION).

parcel, n. package, bundle (ASSEMBLAGE); lot, property, plot (LAND).

parch, v. scorch, stale, shrivel (DRYNESS).

pardon, v. excuse, forgive, absolve (FORGIVENESS, ACQUITTAL).

pardonable, adj. defensible, excusable, justifiable (FORGIVENESS).

pare, v. skin, peel, decorticate (SKIN, UNDRESS); thin, prune, scrape (DEDUCTION).

parent, n. origin, source (BEGINNING); ancestor, sire, father (ANCESTRY).

parentheses, n. braces, brackets (WRITTEN SYMBOL).

pariah, n. outcast, leper (DISMISSAL).

parish, n. fold, congregation (CHURCH).

parity, n. equivalence, coequality (EQUALITY).

park, n. common, green (LAND).

park, v. station, stand (LOCATION).

parkway, n. state road, roadway, way (PASSAGE).

parley, n. discussion, negotiation, palaver (TALK).

parliament, n. council, diet, senate (LEGISLATURE).

parlor, n. living room, drawing room, front room (SPACE).

parochial, adj. cathedral, ecclesiastic, synagogical (CHURCH); narrow-minded, narrow, insular (PREJUDICE).

parody, n. burlesque, caricature, satire (IMITATION, RIDICULE).

parole, n. discharge, probation (FREEDOM).

paroxysm, n. convulsion, fit, seizure (ATTACK, PAIN).

parry, v. by-pass, side-step (AVOIDANCE).

parsimonious, adj. stingy, avaricious, illiberal (STINGINESS); penurious, prudent (ECONOMY).

parson, n. shepherd, minister, preacher (CLERGY).

part, v. take leave, break away (DEPARTURE); detach, separate (DISJUNCTION, PART).

PART—N. part, portion, helping, fragment, fraction, sector, articulation; item, detail, factor, particular; aught, any; installment.

piece, lump, bit, cut, cutting; chip, chunk, slice, scrap, sample, crumb, morsel, moiety, particle; cantlet, shred, stitch; slab, slat, strip, patch.

important part, backbone, base, basis, bedrock, body, core, crux, essence, kernel, keynote, marrow,

mass, meat, nucleus, pith, principle, substance, trunk.

division, section, branch, group, member, partition, subdivision, segment; unit, arm, limb, chapter, wing, detachment, detail.

component, constituent, element, factor, ingredient, feature, integrant, unit, staple; base, basis; contents.

share, allotment, portion, partition, section, quota, proportion, quantum, lot, dividend.

role, character, personification, impersonation.

side, party, faction, interest, cause, behalf.

V. divide, articulate, factor, itemize, particularize, partition, portion, section, segment, slice, strip, subdivide; fraction, fractionize; shred, slab, strip.

[be a part of] compose, make up, form, constitute, appertain to, inhere in, reside in.

share, apportion, portion, allot, divide, distribute, parcel out.

Adj. partial, fragmentary, fractional, sectional, incomplete; bipartite, tripartite, multipartite.

component, appertaining, appurtenant, constituent, inherent, resident; constitutive, essential, intrinsic, material.

Adv., phrases. partly, in part, partially, incompletely, in some measure (or degree).

piecemeal, by degrees, little by little, piece by piece, bit by bit, by installments.

See also APPORTIONMENT, DETAIL, DISJUNCTION, INCOMPLETENESS, MAKE-UP. Antonyms—See COMPLETENESS.

---

partake, v. savor, sip, sample (TASTE); take part, share (CO-OPERATION).

partial, adj. fragmentary, sectional, fractional (PART); incomplete, unfinished (INCOMPLETENESS); partisan, biased (PREJUDICE); disposed, minded (TENDENCY).

partiality, n. (partisanship, favoritism, onesidedness (PREJUDICE); fondness, inclination (LIKING).

partial to, adj. fond of, attached to (LIKING).

participate, v. take part, share (CO-OPERATION).

participator, n. attendant, onlooker, spectator (PRESENCE).

particle, n. cantlet, shred, stitch (PART); crumb, seed, grain (POWDERINESS); bit, modicum (SMALLNESS).

particular, adj. choosy, pernickety,

fastidious (CHOICE); scrupulous, meticulous, painstaking (CARE); individual, exclusive, personal (UNITY); appropriate, intrinsic (OWNERSHIP); distinct, special (DIFFERENCE).

particular, *n.* item, specific, fact (DETAIL).

particularly, *adv.* principally, especially, notably (SUPERIORITY).

partisan, *n.* sympathizer, champion, zealot (PREJUDICE, PITY).

partition, *n.* separation, parting (DISJUNCTION); separating wall (WALL).

partly, *adv.* in part, partially, incompletely (PART).

partner, *n.* co-owner (OWNERSHIP); colleague, confrere (AID); associate, co-worker (WORK).

parts of speech, *n.* adjective, adverb, conjunction (WORD).

part with, *v.* cede, relinquish, give up (GIVING).

party, *n.* affair, gathering (SOCIALITY); force, band, group (ASSEMBLAGE); faction, sect (SIDE).

pass, *n.* defile, cut, gap (NOTCH); passage, path (PASSAGE); safe-conduct, passport (PERMISSION).

pass, *v.* proceed, extend, flow (PASSAGE); deliver, transfer, hand (GIVING); outrace, go beyond, go by (OVERRUNNING); legislate, enact (LAW).

passable, *adj.* moderate, respectable, tolerable (GOOD).

PASSAGE—*N.* passage, movement, motion; transition, transit, transmigration.

voyage, journey, crossing, cruise, sail, route.

[*literary passage*] excerpt, extract, portion, quotation, citation, text, selection; paragraph, section, clause, sentence, verse, chapter.

passageway, passage, pass, path, pathway, way, lane, road, thoroughfare; access, approach, avenue; alley, alleyway, defile, notch, cut, mountain pass, gap, gorge; arcade, cloister, vault; corridor, entrance hall, entranceway, hall, hallway, vestibule, lobby, entry, gallery; overpass, viaduct; underpass, underground passage, underground, subway, shaft, tunnel; labyrinth, maze; elevator shaft, hoistway; course, run, driveway.

dead end, closed passage, blind alley, cul-de-sac (*F.*), impasse.

watercourse, waterway, water gap, canal, channel, aqueduct, conduit, arroyo (*Southwest U.S.*), culvert; ditch, dike, trench, gully; millrace, mill run; sluice, sluiceway, spillway, runnel, race.

road, artery, highway, thoroughfare, course, highroad, parkway, state road, roadway, way; speedway, freeway, thruway, expressway, superhighway, turnpike, toll road; access road, access, approach, ramp, cloverleaf, gradient; bypass, side road, byroad, shunpike, detour, short cut, beeline; causeway, overpass, viaduct; underpass, subway, tunnel; mountain road, gap, switchback; boardwalk (*mil.*); crossroad, crossway, crossroads, intersection, four corners; roadside, wayside; driveway.

street, avenue, boulevard, alley, alleyway, court, lane, place, row, terrace, road, gutter.

foot road, footpath, course, walk, path, pass, passage, pathway, track, trail, towpath; bypath, byroad, bystreet, byway; sidewalk, pavement.

route, itinerary, way, run, circuit, course.

orbit, trajectory, locus, path.

V. **pass,** pass along (down, on, over, etc.), go, move, proceed, extend, flow, stream, run, continue, move past, flow past; transit, transmigrate; pass along the edge of, skirt.

circulate, be current, be received, be popular.

elapse, lapse, go by, glide by, be spent, be lost, vanish, flit, disappear, expire, slip by (*or* away).

pass (*time*), pass away, spend, expend, while away, beguile, idle away, moon away; use, employ, consume, take.

hand over, deliver, give, transfer; surrender, yield control of, consign, relinquish.

pass (*a bill, law, etc.*), enact, ratify, approve, vote for, sanction, establish; ordain, decree.

Adj. **passing,** going by, transient, transmigratory, transitional, transitory; fleeting, ephemeral, evanescent, fugacious.

arterial, viatic, vestibular; quadrivial.

Prep., phrases. via, through, by way of, by means of, around, over, under.

See also CHANNEL, CROSSING, DEPARTURE, DISAPPEARANCE, EGRESS, MEANS, MOTION, NOTCH, OCCURRENCE, OPENING, TRANSFER, TRAVELING, WALKING. *Antonyms*—See MOTIONLESSNESS.

---

passenger, *n.* traveler, wayfarer, rider (TRAVELING, VEHICLE).

passer-by, *n.* walker, pedestrian, ambler (WALKING).

passing, *adj.* fleeting, transient,

evanescent (DEPARTURE, IMPERMA-
NENCE, PASSAGE).

passion, *n.* vehemence, fire, heat
(VIOLENCE); desire, infatuation,
flame (LOVE); sexual desire, pas-
sions (SEXUAL DESIRE); rage,
craze, fad (DESIRE); appetite,
fancy (LIKING).

passionate, *adj.* vehement, inflamed, fiery (VIOLENCE); fervent,
warm (FEELING); amorous, desirous (SEXUAL DESIRE).

passive, *adj.* inactive, inert, static
(INACTION); unresistant, resistless (SUBMISSION).

pass over, *v.* cross, intersect
(CROSSING); disregard, miss, skip
(NEGLECT).

passport, *n.* pass, safe-conduct,
visa (PERMISSION).

pass through, *v.* cross, penetrate,
pierce (CROSSING); suffer, endure
(OCCURRENCE).

password, *n.* watchword, countersign (WORD).

PAST—*N.* past, time gone by, past
time, yore, days of yore, former
days (*or* times), days of old, times
past, langsyne, long ago, bygone
days, yesterday, yesteryear (*poetic*); time immemorial, remote
time, remote past.

history, prehistory, chronicle,
annals, topology, historiography.

V. be past, have expired, have
run its course, have had its day.

Adj. past, gone, ago, bygone,
long-ago, gone by, over; latter,
latter-day, recent.

former, earlier, prior, previous,
antecedent, whilom, erstwhile,
sometime, quondam, late.

historical, prehistorical, ancient,
medieval, early.

Adv., phrases. formerly, of old,
of yore, time was, ago, since, an-
ciently, aforetime, once, one day,
long ago; lately, latterly, of late;
ere now, before now, hitherto,
hereto, hereunto, up to this time,
heretofore; theretofore, thitherto,
up to that time; already, yet, from
time immemorial.

past, by, beyond, gone.

Prep. past, beyond (*in time*),
after; beyond (*in place*), farther
than.

See also EARLINESS, OLDNESS, PRE-
CEDENCE, RECORD. *Antonyms*—See
FUTURE, PRESENT TIME.

paste, *n.* glue, cement, mucilage
(STICKINESS).

pastime, *n.* fun, sport, recreation
(AMUSEMENT).

pastor, *n.* priest, shepherd, minister (CLERGY).

pasture, *v.* graze, grass, soil
(GRASS).

pat, *adj.* timely, auspicious, opportune (TIMELINESS); put-up,
primed, rehearsed (PREPARATION);
pertinent, apropos (PERTINENCE).

pat, *v.* tap, rap (HITTING); massage, stroke (RUBBING); pet, caress, chuck (TOUCH); form, mold,
whittle (SHAPE).

patch, *n.* piece, strip, slat (PART);
lot, plot, plat (LAND).

patch, *v.* mend, cobble (RESTORA-
TION); sew, darn (FASTENING).

paternity, *n.* fathership, fatherhood (ANCESTRY).

path, *n.* pathway, passageway,
pass (WALKING, PASSAGE); orbit,
trajectory, locus (PASSAGE); line,
track, route (DIRECTION).

pathetic, *adj.* miserable, pitiable,
wretched (SADNESS, PITY).

pathological, *adj.* morbid, infected,
diseased (DISEASE).

patient, *adj.* forbearing, longanimous, long-suffering (EXPECTA-
TION).

patient, *n.* invalid, shut-in (DIS-
EASE).

patio, *n.* porch, piazza, terrace
(BUILDING).

patrician, *adj.* aristocratic, upper-
class, well-born (SOCIAL CLASS).

PATRIOTISM—*N.* patriotism, nationalism, public spirit; chauvinism, jingoism, flag waving, ultra-
nationalism, spread-eagleism.

patriot, nationalist, public-spir-
ited citizen; chauvinist, jingoist
or jingo, flag waver, ultranationalist, spread-eagleist; loyalist.

Adj. patriotic, nationalistic, pub-
lic-spirited, civic-minded, commu-
nity-minded; chauvinistic, jingoistic, flag-waving, ultranational-
istic, spread-eagle.

patrol, *n.* spotter, lookout (WARN-
ING).

patrol, *v.* watch, police (PROTEC-
TION, OFFICIAL); march, pace
(WALKING).

patrolman, *n.* bluecoat (*colloq.*),
policeman (OFFICIAL).

patron, *n.* customer, client (PUR-
CHASE); supporter, backer, champion (SUPPORT).

patronize, *v.* buy from, do business
with (PURCHASE); condescend,
deign, stoop (PRIDE).

patronizing, *adj.* superior, condescending, snobbish (PRIDE).

patter, *n.* jive (*slang*), slang (LAN-
GUAGE).

patter, *v.* pad, pat, pitter-patter
(WALKING).

pattern, *n.* model, standard, stereotype (COPY, BEGINNING, PERFECTION); method, design (ARRANGEMENT); mold, impression (SHAPE).

paunch, *n.* potbelly, corporation (*colloq.*), abdomen (SIZE, BELLY).

pauper, *n.* indigent, beggar, mendicant (POVERTY, CHARITY).

pause, *n.* lull, cessation, stop (REST); interlude, interim, intermission (INTERVAL, TIME).

pause, *v.* stop, halt, cease (REST, CESSATION).

pavement, *n.* cobblestones, concrete, flagstones (ROCK, BASE, SUPPORT).

paw, *n.* foot, pad (APPENDAGE).

pawn, *n.* cat's-paw, tool, puppet (USE); forfeit, gambit, victim (RELINQUISHMENT); gage, pledge, earnest (PROMISE).

pawnbroker, *n.* moneylender, uncle (*slang*), usurer (DEBT).

PAYMENT—*N.* payment, acquittance, acquittal, award, compensation, defrayal, defrayment, discharge, ransom, recompense, redemption, remittance, remuneration, return, satisfaction, settlement, clearance, quittance, reckoning; subsidy, support, pension, alimony, allowance, annuity, bounty, dole, relief, grant, perquisite, subvention, installment, earnest, token payment, part payment, budget payment, time payment, deposit; reparation, solatium, award, arbitrament, compensation, recompense.

reward, prize, award, accolade, booty, desert, meed (*poetic*), purse, stake, guerdon (*poetic*), palm, plume, trophy, wreath, medal, medallion, laurel, garland, crown, bays; Oscar, Emmy; decoration, laureation; medalist, laureate.

salary, pay, earnings, emolument, pittance, stipend, stipendium, wage, wages, portal-to-portal pay, take-home pay.

income, receipts, revenue, royalty, tontine, interest, dividends, earnings.

fee, commission, percentage, consideration, honorarium.

tip, bonus, *douceur* (F.), premium, primage, gratuity, *pourboire* (F.), perquisite, cumshaw, baksheesh.

repayment, rebate, refund, reimbursement, kickback (*slang*), replacement, requital, restitution, retribution.

tax, assessment, custom, dues, duty, excise, excise tax, levy, rate, tariff, tithe, toll, capitation, poll, poll tax, impost; gabelle.

V. **pay,** defray, disburse, acquit, amortize, discharge, liquidate, redeem, remit, render, return, satisfy, settle, square, deposit; compensate, indemnify, recompense, remunerate, reward, tip, award; pension, subsidize, support; prepay; ransom.

repay, pay back, rebate, refund, reimburse, replace, requite.

reward, award, crown, garland, laurel, laureate, medal, decorate, plume.

Adj. **well-paying,** profitable, lucrative, remunerative; gainful, paying, paid.

payable, due, owing, matured, maturing.

See also ACCOUNTS, ATONEMENT, EXPENDITURE, GIVING, MONEY, RECOMPENSE, RETALIATION, SUPPORT. *Antonyms*—See ACCEPTANCE, DEBT, RECEIVING.

PEACE—*N.* peace, tranquillity, serenity, calm, quiet, amity, concord, harmony; pacifism, neutrality; armistice, truce.

peace offering, olive branch, irenicon, dove, pipe of peace, calumet.

inner peace, peace of mind, peace of soul, repose, rest, serenity, tranquillity, composure, nirvana (*Buddhist*).

peacemaker, peacemonger (*contemptuous*), pacifier, pacificator, appeaser; pacifist, peaceman.

V. **pacify,** pacificate, tranquilize, compose, calm, still, quiet, appease, assuage, soothe; reconcile, propitiate, placate, conciliate; heal the breach, make peace, make one's peace with, restore harmony, bring to terms, win over; bury the hatchet, lay down one's arms, turn swords into plowshares.

Adj. **peaceful,** placid, quiet, restful, easeful, at peace, tranquil, serene, peaceable, bloodless, irenic, halcyon, pacific, amicable, friendly, harmonious, calm, undisturbed, untroubled; pacifistic, peacemongering (*contemptuous*), neutral, neutralist, nonbelligerent.

unwarlike, unbelligerent, unbellicose, unmilitant, unmilitaristic, unpugnacious, peace-loving.

See also CALMNESS, FRIENDLINESS, HARMONY, REST, SILENCE. *Antonyms*—See ARMS, ATTACK, FIGHTING, OPPOSITION.

---

peace of mind, *n.* serenity, composure, nirvana (*Buddhist*), tranquillity (PEACE).

peak, *n.* tip, vertex, apex (HEIGHT, SHARPNESS).

peaked, *adj.* sickly, wan, bilious (DISEASE).

peal, *n.* thunderclap, crash, clap (LOUDNESS).

peal, *v.* ring, strike (BELL).

pearl, *adj.* pearly, nacreous (JEWELRY).

pearly, *adj.* opalescent, opaline (SEMITRANSPARENCY); off-white, ivory (WHITENESS).

peasant, *n.* commoner, plebeian, worker (PEOPLE); rustic, bucolic, farmer (RURAL REGION).

pebble, *n.* stone, gravel, riprap (ROCK).

peculiar, *adj.* odd, singular, curious (UNUSUALNESS); individual, personal (UNITY); appropriate, intrinsic (OWNERSHIP); typical, characteristic (CHARACTER).

peculiarity, *n.* eccentricity, idiosyncrasy, foible; feature, distinction (UNUSUALNESS, CHARACTER).

pecuniary, *adj.* financial, fiscal, monetary (MONEY).

pedagogue, *n.* schoolmaster, schoolteacher, schoolman (TEACHER).

pedant, *n.* precisianist, purist, prig (RIGHT).

peddle, *v.* canvass, solicit, hawk (SALE).

pedestrian, *n.* walker, passer-by, ambler (WALKING).

pedigree, *n.* lineage, strain (ANCESTRY).

peek, *v.* look, peer (LOOKING).

peel, *n.* rind, pellicle, bark, husk (SKIN, COVERING).

peel, *v.* pare, uncover, strip (SKIN, UNDRESS); scale, flake (LAYER).

peep, *v.* chirp, chuck, churr (ANIMAL SOUND); cheep, squeak, squeal (HIGH-PITCHED SOUND); look, peek, snoop (LOOKING); peer out, emerge (VISIBILITY).

peer, *n.* equal, compeer (EQUALITY); parliamentarian, lord (LEGISLATURE); nobleman, noble (SOCIAL CLASS).

peer, *v.* peep, stare, peek (LOOKING).

peerless, *adj.* unequaled, unmatched, unique (INEQUALITY).

peevish, *adj.* cross, cranky, petulant (BAD TEMPER).

pell-mell, *adv.* full-tilt, headlong, helter-skelter (SPEED, CONFUSION).

pelt, *n.* hide, skin, epidermis (SKIN).

pelt, *v.* pellet, pepper, stone (THROW).

pelvis, *n.* abdomen, paunch (BELLY).

pen, *n.* fountain pen, stylograph (WRITING).

pen, *v.* write, autograph (WRITING); confine, box (INCLOSURE).

penalize, *v.* punish, discipline, correct (PUNISHMENT).

penalty, *n.* fine, forfeit, damages (PUNISHMENT); cost, forfeiture (LOSS).

penance, *n.* shrift, purgation (ATONEMENT).

pencil, *n.* stylus, crayon (WRITING).

penchant, *n.* partiality, predilection, propensity (LIKING).

pend, *v.* depend, hang in suspense, hang (UNCERTAINTY).

pending, *adj.* doubtful, dubious (UNCERTAINTY); pendent, pensile, dependent (HANGING).

pendulous, *adj.* droopy, saggy, flabby (HANGING).

penetrate, *v.* pierce, stab (CUTTING); pervade, permeate (SPREAD); filter, infiltrate (INGRESS); discern, see through (INTELLIGENCE).

penetrating, *adj.* perceptive, percipient (UNDERSTANDING); perspicacious, sharp, trenchant (INTELLIGENCE).

penetration, *n.* acumen, discernment (UNDERSTANDING, INTELLIGENCE); insight, perceptiveness (INTUITION).

peninsula, *n.* isthmus, tongue (LAND).

PENITENCE—*N.* penitence, contrition, compunction, repentance, remorse, regret; self-reproach, self-reproof, self-accusation, self-condemnation.

conscience, superego (*psychoanal.*), censor; scruple, compunction, prick (pang, qualm, twitch, twinge, misgiving, *or* remorse) of conscience.

penitent, penitential, repenter, ruer.

V. **repent,** be sorry for, rue, regret, think better of, recant; humble oneself, turn over a new leaf, reform.

Adj. **penitent,** repentant, remorseful, contrite, compunctious, sorry, regretful, penitential; conscience-smitten, conscience-stricken.

See also ATONEMENT, GUILT, RECOMPENSE, REGRET. *Antonyms*—See IMPENITENCE.

---

penitentiary, *n.* prison, jail (IMPRISONMENT).

penmanship, *n.* handwriting, longhand (WRITING).

pen name, *n.* alias, nom de plume (*F.*), allonym (NAME).

pennant, *n.* flag, streamer, bunting (INDICATION).

penniless, *adj.* strapped (*colloq.*), unmoneyed, moneyless (POVERTY).

pension, *n.* subsidy, support, alimony (PAYMENT).

pensive, *adj.* thoughtful, attentive, reflective (THOUGHT); melancholy, melancholic, wistful (SADNESS).

penurious, *adj.* parsimonious, prudent (ECONOMY).

penury, *n.* impecuniosity, indigence (POVERTY).

PEOPLE—*N.* **people,** the public, populace, inhabitants, population, folk, folks, the world, rank and file; Tom, Dick, and Harry; society, community, commonwealth, commonalty, body politic.

the common people, commonalty, commonality, commonage, commons, crowd, demos, hoi polloi, masses, multitude, plebs, populace, Third Estate; lower class, peasantry, proletariat, working classes; middle class, bourgeoisie, white-collar class.

commoner, peasant, plebeian, proletarian, worker, underdog, untouchable (*India*); bourgeois, white-collar worker.

mob, canaille, cattle, crowd, dregs, herd, horde, peasantry, rabble, raff, ragtag; rag, tag, and bobtail; ribble-rabble, riffraff, rout, ruck, scum, varletry; the great unwashed.

person, man, personage, soul, individual, specimen (*colloq.*), cog, cog in the wheel, average man, man in the street, John Q. Public (*slang*), John Doe, Richard Roe, Joe Blow (*slang*); workingman, proletarian.

sociology, demotics, demography, larithmics, vital statistics.

V. **people,** populate, inhabit, settle.

Adj. **public,** popular, social, societal, communal, community, folk, demotic, pandemic, democratic.

common, plebeian, peasant, vulgar, mass; baseborn, lowborn, lower-class; proletarian, workingclass; middle-class, bourgeois.

peopled, populous, occupied, settled, populated.

See also COMMONNESS, HUMILITY, INHABITANT, LOWNESS, MANKIND, MEANNESS, WORK. *Antonyms*—See ANIMAL, SOCIAL CLASS.

pep, *n.* go, get-up-and-go, punch (ENERGY).

peppery, *adj.* angry, sharp-tempered, irritable (SHARPNESS); pungent, racy, hot (TASTE).

peppy (*slang*), *adj.* perky, sparkling (ACTIVITY).

perambulate, *v.* walk, amble, ambulate (WALKING).

perceivable, *adj.* discernible, discoverable, observable (VISIBILITY).

perceive, *v.* sense, feel, apperceive (SENSITIVENESS); remark, observe, notice (VISION); understand, grasp, comprehend (UNDERSTANDING).

percentage, *n.* ratio, proportion, quota (NUMBER); fee, allowance, bonus (PAYMENT, COMMISSION).

perceptible, *adj.* perceivable, palpable, tangible (SENSITIVENESS).

perceptive, *adj.* percipient, discerning, perspicacious (UNDERSTANDING, INTELLIGENCE).

perch, *n.* resting place, lounge, roost (REST).

perch, *v.* light, roost, sit (REST, SEAT).

percolator, *n.* coffeepot (CONTAINER).

perdition, *n.* annihilation, discreation, extermination (DESTRUCTION).

peremptory, *adj.* magisterial, arbitrary, authoritative (CONTROL).

perennial, *adj.* yearly, annual (TIME); long-enduring, long-lasting (CONTINUATION); seasonal, seasonable (SEASONS).

PERFECTION—*N.* **perfection,** consummation, indefectibility, excellence, finish, superexcellence, transcendence, sublimity, purity, impeccability, immaculacy; perfectionism, idealism, idealization, utopianism.

paragon, quintessence, impeccable, model, pattern, beau ideal (*F.*), ideal, *ne plus ultra* (*L.*), standard; nonesuch, nonpareil, phoenix, flower, queen (*fig.*), masterpiece.

Utopia, Elysian fields, Elysium, Erewhon, paradise, Shangri-La.

V. **perfect,** crown, consummate, put the finishing touch to, complete; idealize; be perfect, transcend.

Adj. **perfect,** absolute, consummate, ideal, sublime, utopian, Elysian, Erewhonian, paradisiacal.

faultless, flawless, immaculate, impeccable, indefectible, pure, sound, unblemished, unflawed, unmarred.

infallible, unerring, inerrable.

best, model, standard; inimitable, unparalleled, unparagoned, unequaled, choice, prime, beyond all praise.

See also COMPLETENESS, GOOD, HEAVEN, HEIGHT, SUPERIORITY. *An-*

tonyms—See BLEMISH, IMPERFECTION, IMPURITY.

perfidy, *n.* treachery, disaffection, infidelity (DISLOYALTY).

perforate, *v.* puncture, punch, drill (OPENING); pierce, penetrate, permeate (CUTTING).

perform, *v.* do, fulfill, accomplish (ACTION); meet, carry out, discharge (OBSERVANCE); play, execute, render (MUSICIAN).

performance, *n.* exercise, pursuit (ACTION); administration, execution, pursuance (RESULT); presentation (DRAMA).

performer, *n.* entertainer, player (ACTOR, ACTIVITY); artist, instrumentalist (MUSICIAN).

perfume, *n.* balm, cologne, essence (ODOR).

perfume, *v.* odorize, aromatize, savor, scent (ODOR).

perfunctory, *adj.* cursory, casual, superficial (CARELESSNESS); indifferent, unconcerned (INDIFFERENCE).

perhaps, *adv.* possibly, conceivably, perchance (POSSIBILITY).

peril, *n.* hazard, insecurity, jeopardy (DANGER).

perilous, *adj.* hazardous, precarious, insecure (DANGER).

perimeter, *n.* circumference, periphery, margin, (EXTERIORITY, MEASUREMENT).

period, *n.* term, space, duration (TIME, INTERVAL, CONTINUATION).

periodic, *adj.* regular, routine, repeated (UNIFORMITY, OCCURRENCE); cyclic, seasonal (TIME).

periodical, *n.* magazine, journal (PUBLICATION).

perish, *v.* die, pass away, pass on (DEATH).

perjure oneself, *v.* commit perjury, forswear (FALSEHOOD).

permanent, *adj.* continuous, endless, timeless (CONTINUATION).

permeable, *adj.* enterable, accessible, penetrable (INGRESS).

permeate, *v.* penetrate, pervade (SPREAD); pierce, stab (CUTTING); filter, infiltrate (INGRESS).

PERMISSION—*N.* permission, leave, allowance, sufferance, tolerance, toleration, indulgence; warrant, privilege, license, concession, imprimatur, dispensation; carte blanche (*F.*).

permit, license, warrant, patent, charter, franchise, authorization; green light (*colloq.*), go-ahead signal (*colloq.*); pass, safe-conduct, passport, visa; admittance.

consent, yes, acceptance, accession, agreement, concurrence, acquiescence, assent, subscription to, okay *or* O.K. (*colloq.*), approval.

licensee, licentiate, diplomate, permittee, privileged character.

V. permit, allow, let, suffer, tolerate, indulge, humor; empower, authorize, sanction, sanctify, warrant, license, canonize, charter, franchise, privilege.

condone, blink at, wink at, let pass, shut one's eyes to, ignore; abet.

consent, say yes, accept, accede to, agree to, concur, acquiesce in, assent to, subscribe to, okay *or* O.K. (*colloq.*).

Adj. permissible, allowable, admissible, unprohibited, unforbidden, licit, lawful, legitimate, legal, legalized.

permissive, indulgent, tolerant, overpermissive; permitting, susceptible of.

consenting, assentive, assentient, acquiescent, willing, agreeable (*colloq.*), consentant, consentive.

See also ABSENCE, AGREEMENT, APPROVAL, INGRESS, PRIVILEGE, WILLINGNESS. *Antonyms*—See DENIAL, UNWILLINGNESS.

pernicious, *adj.* injurious, deleterious, detrimental (HARM); iniquitous, nefarious, vile (WICKEDNESS).

perpendicular, *adj.* upright, erect, sheer (VERTICALITY).

perpetual, *adj.* everlasting, immortal, sempiternal (CONTINUATION); endless, ceaseless, eternal (ENDLESSNESS).

perplex, *v.* puzzle, mystify, baffle (MYSTERY, CONFUSION, UNCERTAINTY).

persecute, *v.* harass, plague, molest (ANNOYANCE).

perseverance, *n.* resolution, determination, immovability (STUBBORNNESS).

persevere, *v.* persist, die hard (STUBBORNNESS); continue, hold on (CONTINUATION).

persist, *v.* continue, persevere, hold out (CONTINUATION); recur, repeat (OCCURRENCE); die hard (STUBBORNNESS).

persistent, *adj.* bulldogged, tenacious, pertinacious (STUBBORNNESS, CONTINUATION).

person, *n.* mortal, soul (PEOPLE, MANKIND).

personage, *n.* bigwig (*colloq.*), grandee, VIP (IMPORTANCE); celebrity, luminary, notable (FAME); person, man, soul (PEOPLE).

personal, *adj.* individual, exclusive, particular (UNITY); bodily, physical, corporal (BODY); inquisitive, prying (INQUIRY).

personality, *n.* make-up, emotions, disposition (CHARACTER); individuality, individualism, particularity (UNITY).

personify, *v.* humanize, personalize (MANKIND); embody, incarnate (BODY).

personnel, *n.* staff, force (WORK).

PERSPIRATION—*N.* perspiration, sweat, exudation, ooze, sudor, transpiration, transudation.

V. perspire, sweat, swelter, ooze, exude, exudate, transpire; transude.

Adj. perspiratory, sudoral, sudoric; sudoriferous; sudorific, sudatory, diaphoretic.

See also EXCRETION, HEAT.

PERSUASION—*N.* persuasion, alignment, conversion, brainwashing, convincement, conviction, enlistment, proselytism, seduction, subornation, suasion; propagandism.

[*that which persuades*] argument, blandishment, blarney, cajolery, taffy, inducement, propaganda.

V. persuade, convert, brainwash, proselytize, proselyte, convince, prevail on, sway, win over, argue into, induce; align, enlist; cajole, coax, wheedle, blandish, blarney (*colloq.*), inveigle, seduce, suborn; propagandize, urge, woo.

Adj. persuasive, convincing, convictive, suasive, cogent, conclusive, stringent, unctuous, seductive, subornative; propagandistic, missionary.

See also INFLUENCE, MOTIVATION, TEACHING, URGING. *Antonyms*—See BELIEF, DISSUASION.

---

pert, *adj.* malapert, saucy, flippant (DISCOURTESY).

pertain, *v.* appertain, apply (PERTINENCE); belong, inhere in (OWNERSHIP); affect, concern, touch (RELATIONSHIP).

PERTINENCE—*N.* pertinence, relevance, connection, bearing, applicability, application, materiality, appurtenance.

V. pertain, appertain, apply, bear upon, connect.

Adj. pertinent, relevant, germane, material, applicable, apposite, appurtenant, apropos, apt, connected, pat, to the point, opportune.

See also RELATIONSHIP. *Antonyms* —See IRRELATION.

---

perturb, *v.* upset, bother, disturb (NERVOUSNESS, AGITATION, EXCITEMENT).

peruse, *v.* read, pore over, study (READING).

pervade, *v.* penetrate, permeate, impregnate (SPREAD, PRESENCE, INFLUENCE).

perverse, *adj.* contrary, froward, wayward (OPPOSITE); disobedient, insubordinate, naughty (DISOBEDIENCE); obstinate, dogged (STUBBORNNESS); self-willed, headstrong (WILL).

perversion, *n.* misusage, misemployment, misapplication (MISUSE); depravity, immorality (WICKEDNESS); abnormality, aberration (UNNATURALNESS); sexual perversion (SEX).

pervert, *n.* degenerate, debauchee, yahoo (IMMORALITY, SEX).

pervert, *v.* misuse, desecrate, prostitute (MISUSE); vitiate, adulterate, alloy (DETERIORATION); demoralize, deprave, seduce (IMMORALITY).

perverted, *adj.* depraved, abandoned, unnatural (WICKEDNESS); grotesque, monstrous, abnormal (UNNATURALNESS).

pesky, *adj.* annoying, vexing, irksome (ANNOYANCE).

pessimism, *n.* futilitarianism, *Weltschmerz* (*Ger.*), dyspepsia (HOPELESSNESS).

pest, *n.* nuisance, plague, nag (ANNOYANCE); bane, blast, blight (DESTRUCTION).

pester, *v.* nag, importune, badger (ANNOYANCE, DEMAND).

pestilence, *n.* contagion, plague (DISEASE); hydra, curse, cancer (WICKEDNESS).

pet, *adj.* endearing, affectionate, amatory (LOVE).

pet, *n.* petulance, fret, displeasure (ANNOYANCE); *persona grata* (*L.*), favorite, fair-haired boy (LIKING); beloved, darling, dear (LOVE).

pet, *v.* pat, stroke, fondle (CARESS, TOUCH).

petite, *adj.* dwarf, miniature, minikin (SMALLNESS).

petition, *n.* round robin, plea, suit (DEMAND).

petition, *v.* beg, plead, impetrate (BEGGING).

pet name, *n.* nickname, diminutive (NAME).

petrified, *adj.* transfixed, spellbound (MOTIONLESSNESS); frightened, terrified (FEAR); stony, petrous, calcified (ROCK).

petroleum, *n.* lubricant, petrolatum (OIL).

petticoat, *n.* underskirt, crinoline, bustle (UNDERWEAR); girl, lass, lassie (YOUTH); lady, woman, weaker vessel (FEMALE).

petty, *adj.* paltry, peddling, piddling (UNIMPORTANCE, WORTHLESSNESS); mean, picayune (MEANNESS); small-minded, provincial, narrow-minded (PREJUDICE).

petulant, *adj.* grumpy, peevish, fretful (BAD TEMPER, ANNOYANCE); querulous, grumbly, whiny (COMPLAINT).

phantom, *n.* apparition, specter, spook (GHOST); shadow, dream, vision (UNREALITY).

PHARMACY—*N.* **pharmacy,** pharmaceutics, pharmacology, drugstore, apothecary's, dispensary, dispensatory, pharmacopoeia.

pharmacist, druggist, apothecary, gallipot (*colloq.*), pharmaceutist, pharmacologist.

narcotic, dope, drug, opiate, sedative, hypnotic, soporific, sleeping pill, barbiturate, phenobarbital; opium, morphine, morphia, paregoric, codeine, laudanum, heroin, hashish, cocaine, marijuana.

narcotics addict, drug fiend, dope fiend, cokey (*slang*), junkey (*slang*), narcotic, morphinist, cocainist, cocainomaniac, opium eater, snowbird (*slang*), hophead (*slang*).

[*narcotic state*] **narcosis,** narcotism, sedation, narcoma, jag (*colloq.*).

V. **drug,** dope, knock out, narcotize, sedate.

See also CURE, DULLNESS, INSENSIBILITY, MEDICAL SCIENCE, PAINKILLER, SLEEP.

phase, *n.* aspect, angle, facet (CONDITION, SIDE).

phenomenal, *adj.* remarkable, outstanding, marvelous (UNUSUALNESS); miraculous, preternatural, prodigious (UNUSUALNESS); physical, sensible, substantial (REALITY); factual, true, valid (REALITY).

phenomenon, *n.* marvel, *rara avis* (*L.*), rarity (UNUSUALNESS, SURPRISE); matter, object, thing (VISION, REALITY).

philander, *v.* flirt, coquette, trifle (LOVE).

philanthropic, *adj.* charitable, magnanimous, humane (UNSELFISHNESS, KINDNESS).

philanthropist, *n.* altruist, humanitarian, almsgiver (KINDNESS, CHARITY, UNSELFISHNESS).

Philistine, *adj.* mammonish, bourgeois (MONEY); standpat, diehard, reactionary (OPPOSITION).

philosopher, *n.* pundit, thinker, solon (WISDOM).

philosophical, *adj.* stoical, imperturbable, impassive (CALMNESS, INEXCITABILITY, UNANXIETY).

philosophy, *n.* ontology, metaphysics, transcendentalism (REALITY); ideology, theory, system (RULE).

philter, *n.* aphrodisiac, love potion (SEX).

phlegm, *n.* mucus, pituite, rheum (EXCRETION).

phlegmatic, *adj.* unemotional, passionless, cold (INSENSITIVITY); imperturbable, impassive, stoical (CALMNESS, UNANXIETY).

phobia, *n.* apprehension, dread, awe (FEAR).

phonetic, *adj.* phonic, lingual, vocal (TALK, VOICE).

phonetics, *n.* phonology, phonography, phonemics (SOUND, VOICE).

phonograph, *n.* Victrola, record player, turntable (MUSICAL INSTRUMENTS).

phonograph record, *n.* disc, platter, release (RECORD).

phony (*colloq.*), *n.* fraud, fake, sham (FALSENESS).

PHOTOGRAPH—*N.* **photograph,** photo (*colloq.*), daguerreotype, photochrome, picture, portrait, likeness, tintype, snapshot, snap, shot, candid shot; print, positive, negative; photostat, photomural, photomontage, cheesecake (*slang*).

X-ray photograph, roentgenogram, tomogram, radiogram, skiagram.

radioactive rays, alpha rays, Becquerel rays, beta rays, gamma rays; X-ray, Roentgen ray; radiation, radiant energy, radioactivity, uranium, radium; fallout, strontium 90; Geiger counter.

X-ray therapy, roentgenotherapy, radiotherapy, radium therapy, irradiation, radiothermy; radiology, radiologist.

camera, television camera, flash camera, Kodak; fluoroscope, roentgenoscope.

photographer, cameraman, daguerreotypist, photoengraver, photogravurist, portraitist.

V. **photograph,** shoot, snap, snap a picture of, take a picture of; photostat, print, photoengrave; X-ray, fluoroscope, radiograph, skiagraph.

See also FINE ARTS, MOTION PICTURES, REPRESENTATION.

photographic, *adj.* lifelike, faithful, exact (SIMILARITY, LIFE).

photoplay, *n.* moving picture, photodrama, picture (MOTION PICTURES).

phrase, *n.* locution, word, idiom (EXPRESSION); wordage, phraseology, terminology (WORD); measure, bar (PASSAGE).

phrase, *v.* couch, put, express (EXPRESSION, WORD).

phraseology, *n.* terminology, style, phrasing (EXPRESSION, WORD).

physical, *adj.* bodily, corporeal, corporal (BODY); material, substantial, concrete (MATERIALITY); real, phenomenal, sensible (REALITY).

physician, *n.* general practitioner, doctor (MEDICAL SCIENCE).

physique, *n.* anatomy, figure, constitution (BODY).

piano, *n.* pianoforte, harpsichord, clavichord (MUSICAL INSTRUMENTS).

picayune, *adj.* piddling, paltry, peddling (UNIMPORTANCE); small-minded, pusillanimous, petty (MEANNESS).

pick, *v.* select, cull, winnow (CHOICE); gather, draw (TAKING).

picket, *n.* patrol, sentinel, guard (WARNING, PROTECTION); panel, post, rail (INCLOSURE).

pickle, *n.* fix, jam, hot water (*all colloq.*) (DIFFICULTY).

pickle, *v.* cure, salt, souse (PRESERVING).

pickpocket, *n.* dip (*slang*), cutpurse (THIEF).

picky, *adj.* choosy, fastidious, finical (CHOICE).

picnic, *n.* outing, barbecue, cookout (TRAVELING, COOKERY).

picture, *n.* painting, piece, canvas (FINE ARTS); portrait, tintype, snapshot (PHOTOGRAPH); illustration, image (REPRESENTATION); moving picture, photoplay (MOTION PICTURES).

picture, *v.* represent, illustrate, portray (REPRESENTATION); describe, delineate, depict (DESCRIPTION); imagine, fancy, fantasy (IDEA, IMAGINATION).

picturesque, *adj.* artistic, pictorial (BEAUTY).

piddling, *adj.* paltry, petty, picayune (UNIMPORTANCE).

pie, *n.* chiffon pie, cream pie (BREAD).

piece, *n.* portion, fragment, bit (PART, LENGTH); paper, article (TREATISE, WRITING).

piecemeal, *adv.* step by step, by degrees, little by little (SLOWNESS, PART).

pied, *adj.* mottled, piebald, skewbald (VARIEGATION).

pier, *n.* wharf, dock, quay (BREAKWATER).

pierce, *v.* stab, thrust, cleave (CUTTING).

piercing, *adj.* keen, sharp, searching (SEARCH); nipping, cutting, biting (COLD); loud, deafening, earsplitting (LOUDNESS); shrill, thin, penetrating (HIGH-PITCHED SOUND).

piety, *n.* faith, belief, piousness (RELIGIOUSNESS); religionism, pietism, religiosity (IRRELIGION).

pig, *n.* porker, swine, hog (ANIMAL); glutton, gormandizer, cormorant (GLUTTONY).

pigeonhole, *v.* put aside, shelve, table (SIDE).

pigment, *n.* coloring matter, dye, dyestuff (COLOR).

pigsty, *n.* sty, Augean stable (UNCLEANNESS).

pigtail, *n.* braid, plait, coil (HAIR).

pike, *n.* point, spike, pricket (SHARPNESS).

pile, *n.* heap, mass, accumulation (ASSEMBLAGE); post, stilt, pole (SUPPORT).

pile, *v.* mass, heap, stack (ASSEMBLAGE, STORE).

pilfer, *v.* steal, purloin, crib (THIEVERY).

pilgrim, *n.* migrator, wanderer (TRAVELING, WANDERING).

pill, *n.* capsule, lozenge, tablet (CURE).

pillage, *v.* ravage, gut, loot (PLUNDER).

pillar, *n.* column, shaft, colonnade (SUPPORT); tower, obelisk (HEIGHT).

pillow, *n.* cushion, bolster, sham (SLEEP).

pilot, *n.* guide, steersman (GUIDANCE); helmsman, coxswain (SAILOR); flyer, aviator (FLYING).

pimp, *n.* procurer, panderer, white slaver (PROSTITUTE).

pimple, *n.* fester, papule, pustule (SKIN).

pin, *n.* clasp, safety pin, diaper pin (HOLD, FASTENING).

pinch, *n.* dash, drop, splash (ADDITION); nip, squeeze (PRESSURE); predicament, plight, straits (DIFFICULTY, CONDITION); crisis, clutch (IMPORTANCE).

pinch, *v.* nip, twinge, squeeze (PRESSURE); be stingy, stint (STINGINESS); arrest, apprehend (IMPRISONMENT); pilfer, crib, cabbage (THIEVERY).

pinched, *adj.* drawn, haggard (THINNESS).

pinch hitter (*colloq.*), understudy, replacement, supplanter (SUBSTITUTION).

pine for, *v.* long for, sigh for, languish for (DESIRE).

pink, *adj.* flesh-colored, rosy, incarnadine (SKIN); rose, coral (RED).

pink, *n.* rose, coral, fuchsia (RED); prime, trim, bloom (HEALTH, GOOD).

pinnacle, *n.* top, summit, peak (HEIGHT).

pipe, *n.* briar, brierroot, meerschaum (TOBACCO); air pipe, vent (AIR OPENING); tube, spout (CHANNEL).

pioneer, *adj.* lead, *avant-garde* (*F.*), head (PRECEDENCE).

pioneer, *n.* immigrant, colonist, settler (INGRESS).

pious, *adj.* religious, devout, orthodox (RELIGIOUSNESS); religionistic, pharisaical, sanctimonious (IRRELIGION).

piquant, *adj.* racy, salty, pungent (EXCITEMENT); appetizing, spicy, tangy (TASTE); appealing, attractive, winsome (ATTRACTION).

pique, *v.* enthrall, absorb, entertain (INTERESTINGNESS); nettle, peeve (*colloq.*), offend (ANNOYANCE).

pirate, *n.* corsair, buccaneer, privateer (THIEF).

pirate ship, *n.* corsair, rover, brigantine (SHIP).

pistol, *n.* gun, revolver, automatic (ARMS).

pit, *n.* dent, depression, notch (HOLLOW); pock, pockmark (VARIEGATION); hole, puncture, perforation (OPENING); shaft, well (DEPTH).

pitch, *n.* dip, descent, decline (SLOPE); modulation, intonation, inflection (SOUND); bitumen, tar, asphalt (RESIN).

pitch, *v.* lob, shy, fling (THROW); yaw, bicker, lurch (UNSTEADINESS, ROLL, OSCILLATION); drop, dip, descend (SLOPE).

pitcher, *n.* ewer, vase, urn (CONTAINER).

pitfall, *n.* snare, booby trap, quicksand (TRAP).

pith, *n.* point, meat, essence (MEANING); distillation, quiddity, quintessence (MATERIALITY); nucleus, principle (PART).

pithy, *adj.* meaty, pointed, pregnant (MEANING); compact, laconic (SHORTNESS).

pitiful, *adj.* sad, sorry, wretched (SADNESS); paltry, contemptible; compassionate (PITY).

pitiless, *adj.* merciless, cruel, unrelenting (INSENSITIVITY, CRUELTY).

pittance, *n.* dole, mite, trifle (INSUFFICIENCY, APPORTIONMENT).

PITY—N. pity, commiseration, compassion, yearning, mercy, humanity, clemency, leniency, lenity, charity, quarter, grace.

sympathy, warmth, fellow-feeling, empathy, identification.

condolence, consolation, comfort, solace.

sympathizer, friend, well-wisher, advocate, patron, partisan, champion, defender; softy (*colloq.*), tenderheart.

V. **pity,** commiserate, compassion, compassionate, have mercy on, have (*or* take) pity on, be sorry for; relent, give quarter to, spare.

sympathize, feel for, empathize, identify with, understand.

condole with, console, solace, comfort, soothe, afford consolation; lament with, express sympathy for, grieve with.

[*excite pity*] **affect,** move, touch, tug at the heart (*or* heartstrings), wring the heart; soften, melt, melt the heart.

Adj. **pitying,** pitiful, commiserative, compassionate, rueful, soft, softhearted, sorry, tender, tenderhearted, touched; humane, humanitarian, clement, merciful, forbearing, lenient.

sympathetic, warm, warmhearted, empathetic, vicarious; condolatory, condolent.

pitiable, piteous, pitiful, poignant, touching, affecting, heartbreaking, heart-rending, moving; pathetic, miserable, rueful, sad, wretched, distressing, woeful.

pitiful (*in degree, quantity, etc.*), paltry, contemptible, miserable, despicable, insignificant, abject, base, mean, measly.

See also CHARITY, FRIEND, KINDNESS, MEANNESS, PROTECTION, SUPPORT. *Antonyms*—See CRUELTY, INSENSITIVITY, SEVERITY.

pivot, *n.* axle, axis, gudgeon (ROTATION); hinge, turning point (CAUSATION).

pixie, *n.* fairy, fay, sprite (SUPERNATURAL BEINGS).

placard, *n.* advertisement, bill, flyer (PUBLICATION, INFORMATION).

placate, *v.* propitiate, conciliate, appease (PEACE, FRIENDLINESS, CALMNESS).

PLACE—*N.* **place,** spot, locality, situation, site, location, locus (*esp. tech.*), situs, position, region, neighborhood, locale, scene, tract; latitude, longitude, whereabouts; point, part; compartment, niche, nook, hole, corner.

V. **place,** put, fix, set, stick, lay, deposit, rest, repose, settle, locate, dispose, stand, station, lodge, establish, plant, install; order, arrange, array, marshal, organize.

appoint, assign, name, nominate, commission, delegate, ordain, designate, constitute, deputize, depute.

Adv., phrases. **somewhere,** in some place, here and there.

See also ARRANGEMENT, HABITATION, LOCATION, NEARNESS, REGION, SITUATION. *Antonyms*—See ELIMINATION, REMOVAL.

placid, *adj.* peaceful, quiet, serene (PEACE, CALMNESS).

plagiarism, *n.* piracy, plagiary, stealing (THIEVERY).

plague, *n.* epidemic, contagion, pestilence (DISEASE); bane, pest, blight (DESTRUCTION); hydra, curse, cancer (WICKEDNESS).

plague, *v.* persecute, infest, molest (ANNOYANCE).

plaid, *n.* check, tartan, patchwork (VARIEGATION).

plain, *adj.* unornamented, unadorned (SIMPLICITY, SEVERITY); visible, clear, transparent (CLARITY, VISIBILITY); audible, distinct (LISTENING); unattractive, unaesthetic, homely (DEFORMITY); understandable, simple, unmistakable (UNDERSTANDING); modest, quiet, unassuming (MODESTY); undiluted, neat, unmixed (STRAIGHTNESS); dry, matter-of-fact, naked (SIMPLICITY).

plain, *n.* level, plateau, tableland (LAND).

plaintiff, *n.* litigant, complainant (LAWSUIT, ACCUSATION).

plaintive, *adj.* lugubrious, moanful, lamentatory (SADNESS).

plait, *n.* braid, cue, wattle (WINDING); coil, pigtail, queue (HAIR).

plait, *v.* pleat, braid, wattle (CROSSING).

PLAN—*N.* **plan,** design, device, contrivance, aim, intention, intent, project, arrangement, prearrangement, conception, deal, proposal, proposition; strategy, strategics.

outline, blueprint, sketch, draft, map, layout, diagram, chart; program, agendum, agenda (*pl.*), procedure, prospectus.

plot, scheme, intrigue, machination, schemery, maneuver; subterfuge, stratagem, gimmick (*slang*), trick, shift; racket; conspiracy, complot, countermine, counterplot.

planner, organizer, designer, author, architect, founder, strategist.

plotter, schemer, intriguer, intrigant, machinator, agitator, maneuverer; conspirator, complotter, counterplotter; adventurer, racketeer; cabal, junto, junta.

V. **plan,** cogitate, contemplate, meditate; design, devise, frame, contrive, hatch, concoct, project; prearrange, premeditate, forecast; arrange, prepare, block out, map out, outline, sketch out, shape up; aim, intend, purpose, propose.

plan on, aim for, bargain for, count on, reckon on.

plot, scheme, intrigue, maneuver, machinate, agitate, brew, conspire, complot, cabal, colleague, countermine, counterplot.

See also ARRANGEMENT, MAP, METHOD, PREPARATION, PURPOSE. *Antonyms*—See NONPREPARATION, PURPOSELESSNESS.

plane, *adj.* even, level, flat (SMOOTHNESS).

plane, *n.* aircraft, airplane (FLYING); level, face, facet (SURFACE); grade (FLATNESS).

plane, *v.* level, smooth, even (FLATNESS).

planet, *n.* earth, globe, sphere (WORLD).

plank, *n.* pole, stud, post (WOOD).

plant, *n.* vegetable, shrub, bush (PLANT LIFE); shop, factory, mill, forge (WORK, PRODUCTION).

plant, *v.* sow, grow, raise (FARMING); set, deposit, station (LOCATION, PLACE).

plantation, *n.* farm, grange, ranch (FARMING).

PLANT LIFE—*N.* **plant life,** plants, vegetation, flora, vegetable kingdom, vegetable life, biota, botany, herbage, verdure, greenery; pasture, pasturage, grass; plankton, benthos.

plant, vegetable, herb; shrub, bush, creeper, vine; perennial, annual; cereal, grain; moss, bryophyte, lichen, liverwort; bulb, bud, tuber.

tree, stand, pollard, espalier (*hort.*), arbor, arbuscle; sapling, seedling; fruit tree, timber tree, oak, elm, beech, birch, pine, maple, etc.

forest, woodland, woods, wood, forest land, timber, timberland, greenwood, wildwood; grove, orchard, copse, coppice, thicket, canebrake, covert, bosk, shrubbery, hurst, clump, wood lot; bush, jungle, chaparral, park.

underbrush, undergrowth, underwood, brush, brushwood, scrub, brake, boscage, heath, heather, fern, bracken, furze, gorse, broom, sedge, rush, bulrush.

seaweed, wrack, kelp, rockweed, tangle, alga (*pl.* algae).

leafage, foliage, leaves, wreath, frondescence, foliation, foliature, frondage, greenery, umbrage, herbage.

leaf, frond, petal, needle, leaflet, blade.

stem, stalk, axis, pedicel, petiole, sprout, shoot.

branch, shoot, limb, bough, offshoot, twig, switch, sprig, spray, branchlet, branchling, vimen, ramulus (*bot.*), ramule, runner, tendril; osier, wicker, withe, ramage (*collective*).

flower, blossom, bloom, floret, bud; inflorescence, flowering, flowerage, florescence, blossoming, florification; full bloom, anthesis (*bot.*).

bouquet, posy, nosegay, corsage; wreath.

V. **vegetate,** germinate, sprout, grow, shoot up, live, develop, increase, luxuriate, grow rank, flourish; flower, blossom, bloom, bud.

Adj. **vegetable,** vegetative, vegetal, vegetational, vegetarian; leguminous, herbaceous, herblike, herbal, botanical; arboreal, sylvan; ligneous, xyloid, woody, wooden; bosky, copsy; mossy, turfy, grassy, verdant, verdurous.

flowery, blossomy, bloomy, floral, florescent, floriated (*decorative art*); blooming, blossoming, flowering, floriferous, efflorescent, inflorescent.

luxuriant, rank, dense, exuberant, prolific, lush, wild.

See also BOTANY, GRASS, WOOD. *Antonyms*—See ANIMAL, ZOOLOGY.

---

plaster, *n.* cement, gum, paste (STICKINESS).

plaster, *v.* spread, smear, daub (SPREAD).

plastic, *adj.* ductile, tractable, yielding (SOFTNESS); shapable, formable, malleable (SHAPE); impressionable, pliable, pliant (INFLUENCE).

plate, *n.* platter, dish, bowl (CONTAINER); discus, disc, spangle (FLATNESS); paillette, leaf, foil (METAL); coat, lamella (LAYER); denture (TEETH).

plateau, *n.* plain, level, tableland (LAND).

platform, *n.* scaffold, scaffolding, stage, dais (SUPPORT).

platitude, *n.* cliché, bromide, commonplace (COMMONNESS).

platonic love, *n.* spiritual relationship, platonism (SPIRITUALITY).

platter, *n.* plate, dish, bowl (CONTAINER); phonograph record, disc, release (RECORD).

plausible, *adj.* believable, credible (BELIEF); sound, valid, reasonable (REASONABLENESS); specious, colorable (FALSENESS).

play, *n.* drama, legitimate drama (DRAMA); swing, latitude, sweep (SPACE).

play, *v.* dally, disport (PLAYFULNESS); toy, trifle (AMUSEMENT); personate, impersonate, act (ACTION); perform, execute, render (MUSICIAN).

play-act, *v.* pretend, make believe (PRETENSE).

PLAYFULNESS—*N.* **playfulness,** play, dalliance, frisk, frolic, gambol, romp, sport; beer and skittles, recreation.

dabbler, dallier, dilettante, amateur, hobbyist.

V. **play,** dally, disport, sport, frisk, frolic, gambol, lark, skylark, cut capers; cavort, romp, prance, caper; toy, twiddle, trifle, dabble.

Adj. **playful,** frisky, frolicsome, rompish, rompy, sportive, sportful, waggish.

See also AMUSEMENT, DRAMA, FRIVOLITY, MISCHIEF, MUSICIAN, PRETENSE. *Antonyms*—See SOBRIETY, WORK.

---

playgoer, *n.* theatergoer, firstnighter (DRAMA).

play with, v. be insincere with, dally with, trifle with (PRE-TENSE).

plaza, n. park, square, village green (LAND).

plea, n. petition, round robin, suit (DEMAND); appeal, prayer, entreaty (BEGGING); excuse, defense (FORGIVENESS).

plead, v. supplicate, pray, implore (BEGGING).

plead for, v. advocate, champion, back up (SUPPORT).

pleadings, n. allegations, procès-verbal (F.), declaration (LAW-SUIT).

PLEASANTNESS—N. pleasant-ness, affability, agreeability, amenity, amiability, charm, con-geniality, companionability, good humor, good nature, bonhomie; compliancy, complaisance, compla-cency.

suavity, urbanity, unction, unc-tuosity.

V. please, charm, delight, en-chant, gratify, tickle; suit, sat-isfy.

Adj. pleasant, affable, compan-ionable, conversable, agreeable, nice, cheerful, cheery, amiable; charming, delightful, delightsome, lovely, enchanting; complaisant, congenial, good-humored, good-natured, sweet-natured, winsome, likable, sweet.

suave, urbane, bland, unctuous, gracious.

pleasing, desirable, gratifying, welcome, grateful; luscious, mel-low, palatable, savory, delicious; dulcet, musical, sweet.

compliant, compliable, compla-cent, complaisant, courtly, obse-quious.

See also ATTRACTION, CHEERFUL-NESS, PLEASURE, SATISFACTION, SUAV-ITY, SWEETNESS. Antonyms—See DISGUST, PAIN, UNPLEASANTNESS.

---

pleasantry, n. witticism, levity, wit (WITTINESS).

please, v. satisfy, suit (SATISFAC-TION); charm, delight, enchant (PLEASANTNESS).

pleased, adj. delighted, gratified, fulfilled (SATISFACTION).

PLEASURE—N. pleasure, joy, en-chantment, delight, delectation, enjoyment, fruition, gratification, thrill, titillation; fun, amusement, entertainment; relish, gusto, zest,

spice, seasoning, nectar, ambrosia, luxury; zest for life (or living), joie de vivre (F.); primrose path, gay life, life of pleasure, joy ride (colloq.), honeymoon, beer and skittles.

pleasurableness, charm, savor, delectability, gaiety, sensuality.

pleasure seeking, epicureanism, epicurism, hedonism, sensualism, sensuality, sybaritism, dissipation, debauchery, debauch, luxuriation; jag, orgy, saturnalia.

pleasure seeker, pleasurer, pleas-urist, epicurean, epicure, hedonist, sensualist, sybarite, voluptuary, debauchee, dissipator, rioter, sport.

V. pleasure, gratify, delight, en-chant, delectate, hit the spot (col-loq.), titillate, tickle; amuse, en-tertain; season, spice, zest.

enjoy, pleasure in, delight in, joy in, relish, revel in, riot in, savor, luxuriate in, bask in; enjoy oneself, have a good time, have a ball (slang), have a picnic (slang), live high off the hog (colloq.), de-bauch, dissipate, racket, riot.

Adj. pleasurable, pleasure-giving, amusing, entertaining, delectable, delightful, delightsome, enchant-ing, enjoyable, gratifying, joyful, joyous, relishable, titillating, zest-ful, zesty, ambrosial, luxurious, silken, nectareous, spicy, spiceful, charming, gay, delicious, savory, sweet, pleasant, pleasing, pleasure-ful, voluptuous, sensual, primrose, sensuous, welcome, winsome; bit-tersweet.

pleasure-seeking, hedonistic, syb-aritic, voluptuous, voluptuary, epicurean, gay, primrose, satur-nalian, sensual, sensualistic, sen-suous, sporty, fast; debauched, dis-sipated, dissolute, rackety, riotous.

See also AMUSEMENT, ATTRACTION, PLEASANTNESS, SATISFACTION, SWEET-NESS. Antonyms—See PAIN, UN-PLEASANTNESS.

---

pleat, v. tuck, hem, seam (FOLD).

plebeian, adj. banal, pedestrian, platitudinous (COMMONNESS); ·vulgar, common, popular (VUL-GARITY).

plebiscite, n. ballot, suffrage, ref-erendum (VOTE).

pledge, n. gage, earnest; word, sa-cred word (PROMISE); toast, health (RESPECT).

plentiful, adj. plenteous, profuse, rife (MULTITUDE).

plenty, adj. enough, appreciable (SUFFICIENCY).

pliable, *adj.* supple, flexible, pliant (SHAPE, BEND, EASE, SOFTNESS); submissive, yielding, obedient (SUBMISSION); impressionable, plastic (INFLUENCE).

pliant, *adj.* supple, pliable, flexible (SHAPE, SOFTNESS); submissive, yielding, compliant (SUBMISSION); impressionable, plastic (INFLUENCE).

pliers, *n.* nippers, pincers, pinchers (HOLD, TAKING).

plight, *n.* predicament, scrape, straits (DIFFICULTY, CONDITION).

plodder, *n.* drudge, grind, grub (WORK).

plot, *n.* scheme, intrigue, machination (PLAN); lot, patch, plat (LAND).

plot, *v.* scheme, intrigue, maneuver (PLAN); outline, lay out, chart (MAP).

pluck, *v.* cull, gather, pick (TAKING); unfeather, deplume (FEATHER).

plucky, *adj.* game, nervy, spunky (COURAGE).

plug, *n.* stopper, cork, tampon (RESTRAINT, CLOSURE).

plum, *n.* asset, nugget, treasure (VALUE).

plumage, *n.* tuft, ruff, feathers (FEATHER).

plumb, *adj.* straight, vertical, sheer (VERTICALITY, STRAIGHTNESS).

plumb, *v.* unravel, fathom (DISCOVERY); sound, take soundings (DEPTH).

plume, *n.* feather, plumule, pinna (FEATHER); reward, palm, trophy (PAYMENT).

plump, *adj.* stout, buxom, chubby (SIZE).

PLUNDER—*N.* **plunder,** plunderage, ravage, pillage, robbery, depredation, spoliation, despoliation, despoilment.

booty, loot, spoils, swag (*colloq.*); prize; prey, quarry, raven.

preying, predacity, ravin, brigandage, brigandism, vampirism.

plunderer, depredationist, spoiler, filibuster, freebooter; preyer, predator, robber, brigand, vampire, bloodsucker, harpy.

V. **plunder,** depredate, spoil, spoliate, despoil, fleece, rob, sack, strip, ravage, gut, loot, pillage, ransack, ravin, prey on, prey; filibuster, maraud, prowl, foray, forage.

Adj. **plunderous,** spoliatory, spoliative, predatory, predative, predacious, depredatory, rapacious, raptorial, ravenous.

See also TAKING, THIEVERY. *Antonyms—*See GIVING.

---

plunge, *n.* dive, submersion, duck (DIVING).

plunge, *v.* dive, submerge, duck (DIVING); immerse, immerge (INSERTION).

plurality, *n.* majority, bulk, greater part (SUPERIORITY).

plush, *adj.* luxurious, silken, palatial (WEALTH).

ply, *n.* plica, plication, plicature (FOLD); twist, quirk (WINDING).

ply, *v.* travel regularly over, range (TRAVELING).

pock, *n.* notch, gouge, pockmark (VARIEGATION, HOLLOW).

pocket, *n.* cavity, chamber, socket (HOLLOW).

pocketbook, *n.* purse, handbag, reticule (CONTAINER).

pock-marked, *adj.* variolar, variolous (*med.*), pitted (HOLLOW).

pod, *n.* sheath, capsule, case (COVERING).

podium, *n.* rostrum, soapbox, stump, pulpit (SUPPORT).

poetic, *adj.* epic, lyrical, dithyrambic (POETRY); soulful, sentimental (EXPRESSION).

POETRY—*N.* **poetry,** poesy, rhyme, rhymes, rime, verse, blank verse, free verse, vers libre (*F.*), doggerel, narrative poetry, balladry, epic poetry; Pegasus, Muse, Apollo.

poem, poesy, rhyme, rime, verse, ballad, ballade, epic, ditty, lay, lyric, madrigal, ode, epode; palinode; psalm, hymn; elegy, bucolic, dithyramb, jingle, limerick, epithalamion, erotic, amphigory, telestich; sonnet, monostich, couplet, distich, tristich, quatrain, tetrastich, pentastich, rondelet, sestet, hexastich, heptastich, rhyme royal, octastich, roundel, decastich, rondeau, rondel.

canto, stanza, verse, stave, strophe, antistrophe, envoy, *envoi* (*F.*), sestiad; tercet, sestet, octet.

accent, beat, ictus; meter, measure, foot, mora, caesura; monometer, dimeter, trimeter, tetrameter, pentameter, hexameter, heptameter, octameter, decameter; amphibrach, anapest, dactyl, iamb, spondee, trochee; Alexandrine; dipody, tripody, tetrapody, pentapody, hexapody, heptapody, octapody.

poetics, metrics, prosody, versification.

poet, bard, versifier, poetizer, rhymer *or* rimer, metrifier, metrist, minstrel, lutanist, troubadour, vers librist; coupleteer, sonneteer; ballader, dithyrambic, elegist, epithalamiast, lyrist, madrigalist *or* madrigaler, palinodist, psalmodist, hymnist.

[*inferior poet*] poetaster, rhymer *or* rimer, rhymester *or* rimester, versiflaster, versifier.

V. poetize, rhyme *or* rime, versify, sonnetize; berhyme *or* berime, metrify; scan.

Adj. poetic *or* poetical, epic, lyrical *or* lyric, elegiac, dithyrambic, odic, sonnetary; Heliconian, Parnassian, Pierian; Ionic, Sapphic, Alcaic, Pindaric.

metrical, anapestic, dactylic, iambic, spondaic, trochaic.

See also RHYTHM, SINGING, WRITER.

poignant, *adj.* moving, touching, pathetic (FEELING); pitiable, piteous, pitiful (PITY); sharp, pungent, acrid (SHARPNESS).

point, *n.* spike, pike, pricket (SHARPNESS); cusp, nib, prong (END); juncture, moment (TIME); pith, meat, essence (MEANING).

point, *v.* aim, direct, slant (DIRECTION).

pointed, *adj.* acute, pronged (SHARPNESS); barbed, acid, vitriolic (SHARPNESS); conspicuous, noticeable (VISIBILITY); meaty, pregnant (MEANING).

pointedly, *adv.* willfully, wittingly, knowingly (PURPOSE).

pointless, *adj.* absurd, meaningless, senseless (ABSURDITY); inconsequential, nongermane, remote (IRRELATION).

pointy, *adj.* pointed, acute, pronged (SHARPNESS).

poise, *n.* self-assurance, self-confidence, confidence (CERTAINTY); self-possession, aplomb, presence of mind (CALMNESS); equanimity, equability, composure (INEXCITABILITY); address, bearing (APPEARANCE); balance, equilibrium, equipoise (WEIGHT).

poise, *v.* stand, stand poised, stand up (POSTURE); hover, brood over (HANGING).

POISON—*N.* poison, bane, toxin, toxicant, venom, virus, venin, ratsbane, endotoxin, exotoxin, toxoid; miasma.

[*common poisons*] arsenic, atropine, belladonna, bichloride of mercury, carbolic acid, phenol, corrosive sublimate, cyanide, hemlock, prussic acid, strychnine.

counterpoison, antidote, mithridate, antitoxin, toxicide, antivenin.

science of poisons: toxicology.

V. poison, taint, venom, envenom; fester.

Adj. poisonous, baneful, mephitic, pestilent, toxic, venomous, viperous, virulent; septic.

See also DISEASE. *Antonyms*—See CURE, GOOD.

poke, *v.* jab, push, nudge (HITTING); jostle, shoulder, ram (PROPULSION).

poky, *adj.* slow, bovine, lentitudinous (SLOWNESS); shabby, mangy, seedy (UNTIDINESS).

pole, *n.* stick, stave, stake (ROD); plank, stud, beam (WOOD); pile, stilt, leg (SUPPORT).

police, *n.* constabulary, police force (OFFICIAL).

police car, *n.* prowl car, squad car, cruiser (VEHICLE).

policeman, *n.* officer, peace officer, patrolman (OFFICIAL).

polish, *n.* refinement, grace, finish (ELEGANCE, IMPROVEMENT, BEAUTY).

polish, *v.* burnish, sleek, buff (SMOOTHNESS, RUBBING); touch up, make improvements, amend (IMPROVEMENT).

polished, *adj.* glossy, burnished, lustrous (LIGHT, SMOOTHNESS); refined, cultivated, cultured (IMPROVEMENT).

polite, *adj.* courteous, civil, well-bred (COURTESY).

politic, *adj.* prudent, judicious, expedient (WISDOM, CLEVERNESS).

political, *adj.* civil, civic, governmental (CITIZEN, GOVERNMENT).

politics, *n.* statesmanship, statecraft, government (RULER).

poll, *v.* vote, ballot, plump for (VOTE).

pollute, *v.* contaminate, adulterate, sully (IMPURITY, UNCLEANNESS).

pomp, *n.* magnificence, splendor, pageant (OSTENTATION).

pompous, *adj.* self-important, pretentious, toplofty (IMPORTANCE).

pond, *n.* lagoon, pool, basin (LAKE).

ponder, *v.* meditate, puzzle over, muse (THOUGHT).

ponderous, *adj.* weighty, heavy (WEIGHT).

pony, *n.* Shetland, bronco, cayuse (HORSE); crib, horse, trot (EXPLANATION).

pool, *n.* lagoon, basin, pond (LAKE); swimming pool, natatorium (SWIMMING).

poor, *adj.* impoverished, indigent (POVERTY); mean, miserable, sordid (POVERTY); mediocre, indifferent (INFERIORITY).

poorhouse, *n.* almshouse (CHARITY).

Pope, *n.* Pontiff, Bishop of Rome, His Holiness (CLERGY).

popeyed, *adj.* round-eyed, bug-eyed (*slang*), moon-eyed (EYE).

popular, *adj.* current, prevailing, prevalent (USE, COMMONNESS); accepted, standard, approved (ACCEPTANCE, APPROVAL); staple, in demand (SALE); in vogue, liked (LIKING); public, social, societal (PEOPLE); vulgar, plebeian, common (VULGARITY).

popularity, *n.* fashion, vogue (LIKING); prevalence, currency, heyday (USE).

popularize, *v.* restore, resurrect, revive (USE).

populate, *v.* people, inhabit, settle (PEOPLE).

populated, *adj.* inhabited, settled, occupied (INHABITANT, PEOPLE).

population, *n.* inhabitants, people, populace (INHABITANT, PEOPLE).

porch, *n.* patio, piazza, veranda (BUILDING).

pore over, *v.* scan, regard, contemplate (LOOKING).

pornography, *n.* smut, scatology, coprophemia (OBSCENITY); erotica, curiosa, rhyparography (TREATISE, SEX).

porous, *adj.* absorbent, absorptive, spongy (INTAKE); penetrable, permeable, pervious (INGRESS).

port, *n.* harbor, anchorage (ARRIVAL); pose, position, carriage (POSTURE).

portable, *adj.* cartable, movable, haulable (TRANSFER).

portal, *n.* door, gate, entry (INGRESS).

portend, *v.* forebode, premonish, forewarn (WARNING).

portent, *n.* foreboding, premonition, presage (FUTURE); marvel, phenomenon (UNUSUALNESS).

porter, *n.* doorkeeper, gatekeeper, janitor (INGRESS); transporter, bearer (TRANSFER).

portfolio, *n.* valise, brief case, attaché case (CONTAINER).

portion, *n.* piece, fragment, fraction (PART, LENGTH); dividend, share, allotment (APPORTIONMENT, PART).

portly, *adj.* fat, corpulent, stout (SIZE); stately, togated, impressive (FAME).

portrait, *n.* likeness, silhouette, profile (FINE ARTS); picture, tintype, snapshot (PHOTOGRAPH); figure, model, image (REPRESENTATION).

portray, *v.* describe, characterize, depict (DESCRIPTION); represent, picture, illustrate (REPRESENTATION).

pose, *n.* position, stance, carriage (POSTURE); role, guise (PRETENSE).

pose, *v.* stand, model, poise (POSTURE); simper, mince, attitudinize (UNNATURALNESS); pretend, posture, peacock (PRETENSE).

position, *n.* spot, situation, site (PLACE, LOCATION); job (*colloq.*), place, post (SITUATION); sphere, station, status (RANK, CONDITION); stand, pose (POSTURE).

positive, *adj.* unqualified, downright, absolute (FLATNESS); assured, cocksure, confident (CERTAINTY); assertive, dogmatic (OPINION, STATEMENT).

possess, *v.* have, occupy, own (HOLD, OWNERSHIP).

possession, *n.* control, occupancy, tenancy (HOLD, OWNERSHIP); belonging, appurtenance, asset (OWNERSHIP).

possessive, *adj.* retentive, tenacious, pertinacious (HOLD).

POSSIBILITY—*N.* possibility, contingency, likelihood, eventuality, chance, tossup (*colloq.*), potentiality.

V. be **possible,** stand a chance, be contingent on, depend on, admit of.

Adj. possible, thinkable, contingent; eventual, potential; conceivable, imaginable, likely.

practicable, feasible, performable, doable, actable, workable; within reach, accessible, surmountable; attainable, obtainable, achievable.

Adv., phrases. possibly, conceivably, perhaps, perchance, peradventure, haply, mayhap (*archaic*), maybe; if possible, God willing, *Deo volente* (L.), *D.V.*; not impossibly, within the realm of possibility, could be (*colloq.*).

See also CHANCE, EXPEDIENCE, LIKELIHOOD. *Antonyms*—See IMPOSSIBILITY, IMPROBABILITY.

---

post, *n.* panel, picket, rail (INCLOSURE); plank, pole, beam (WOOD); pile, stilt, leg (SUPPORT); site, station (LOCATION, SITUATION); position, place, office (SITUATION).

post card, *n.* postal (EPISTLE).

poster, *n.* placard, bill, handbill (INFORMATION).

posterior, *adj.* hinder, caudal (*anat.*), dorsal (REAR).

posterior, *n.* back, hind part, hindmost part (REAR).

posterity, *n.* descendants, generations unborn (CHILD).

postman, *n.* mailman, letter carrier (MESSENGER).

postpone, v. delay, adjourn, defer (DELAY).

POSTURE—N. **posture,** air, attitude, bearing, carriage, demeanor, port, pose, position.

stance, stand, poise.

stander, standee, straphanger; bystander, onlooker, spectator, passer-by; poser, model.

V. **stand,** poise, **stand poised;** bestraddle, bestride, straddle, stride; slouch, lounge, droop, stoop, totter; stand up, erect, stand erect, cock; pose, model, posture, posturize.

crouch, grovel, cower, cringe, squat.

Adj. **postural,** attitudinal, positional; standing, poised, posed, astraddle, astride, straddle-legged; droopy, slouchy, stopped, bent, tottery; upright, cocked, erect, upstanding.

See also APPEARANCE, MOTIONLESSNESS, PLACE, PRETENSE, REST, SITUATION, STRAIGHTNESS, VERTICALITY. Antonyms—See REST, SEAT.

posy, n. flower, bouquet, nosegay (PLANT LIFE).

pot, n. pan, saucepan (CONTAINER).

potbelly, n. paunch, corporation (colloq.), ventricosity (SIZE, BELLY).

potency, n. force, strength, vigor (RESULT, POWER); virility, puberty (SEX, FERTILITY).

potent, adj. powerful, mighty, almighty (POWER); effective, telling, trenchant (RESULT); virile, vigorous (SEX).

potential, adj. latent, dormant (INACTION).

pottery, n. porcelain, porcelainware (CONTAINER).

pouch, n. bag, sack (CONTAINER); sac, marsupium (BELLY).

poultry, n. fowl, chickens, turkeys (BIRD).

pound, v. pestle, hammer, beat (HITTING).

pour, v. spout, roll, jet (RIVER); teem, shower, rain (RAIN).

pout, v. sulk (ANGER).

poverty, n. want, destitution (POVERTY); scarcity, dearth (FEWNESS, INSUFFICIENCY).

POVERTY—N. **poverty,** impoverishment, indigence, want, destitution, need, distress; beggary, pauperism, pauperage; bankruptcy, insolvency; impecuniosity, penury, adversity.

poor person, pauper, poorling, indigent, beggar, mendicant, starveling; insolvent, bankrupt.

V. **be poor,** want, starve, live from hand to mouth, eke out a bare living, have seen better days.

impoverish, destitute, pauperize, beggar; straiten, strap, distress, break (colloq.), bankrupt, strip.

Adj. **poverty-stricken,** poor, impoverished, indigent, destitute, down-and-out, beggared, beggarly, necessitous, in want, needy, needful, pauperized; bankrupt, broke (colloq.), insolvent; in embarrassed (distressed, pinched, reduced, or straitened) circumstances; penniless, strapped (colloq.), unmoneyed, moneyless, impecunious, badly off, hard up, short, stranded.

[of surroundings, etc.] **poor,** mean, miserable, sordid, squalid, seedy, shabby.

See also DEBT, MEANNESS, NECESSITY. Antonyms—See MONEY, OWNERSHIP, WEALTH.

POWDERINESS—N. **powderiness,** friability, pulverulence, arenosity, granulation.

powder, dust, sand, grit; sawdust; meal, bran, flour, farina, rice; crumb, seed, grain, particle; cosmetic, face powder, talc, talcum powder; explosive, gunpowder.

[pulverizing instruments] **mill,** grater, rasp, file, pestle and mortar, grindstone, quern, millstone.

V. **powder,** pulverize, comminute, granulate, triturate, levigate; scrape, file, abrade, grind, grate, rasp, pound, bray, bruise, beat, crush, smash, craunch, crunch, crumble, disintegrate, molder.

sprinkle, besprinkle, scatter, strew, powder, flour, dust.

Adj. **powderable,** pulverizable, friable, crumbly, shivery.

powdery, pulverulent, granular, mealy, floury, farinaceous, branny, dusty, sandy, arenaceous, arenose, sabulous, gritty, scurfy.

See also DECAY, PRESSURE, RUBBING. Antonyms—See LIQUID, THICKNESS.

POWER—N. **power,** potency, prepotency, omnipotence, puissance (poetic), vigor, vim, force, energy.

dominance, domination, ascendancy, dominion, imperium, paramountcy, predominance, preponderance, regency, scepter, sovereignty, diadem, supremacy; autocracy, absolutism.

authority, weight, control, prestige, command, sway; authorization, warrant, right, accreditation, jurisdiction, license, charter, commission.

domain, dominion, jurisdiction, province, realm, sphere, precinct, bourn, demesne, department; bailiwick, orbit, scope, circle, field, purview.

[*proof of authority*] **credentials**, documents, paper, token.

powerful person, Hercules, titan, leviathan, behemoth; official, influence, plenipotentiary; commander, emperor, autocrat, plutocrat; baron, mogul, potentate, sachem.

V. **empower**, qualify, vest, invest, enthrone, enable; arm, endow, strengthen, soup up (*slang*), implement; aggrandize.

authorize, accredit, charter, commission, license, warrant, permit, sanction, entitle; delegate, deputize, depute.

dominate, control, predominate, preponderate, reign, reign supreme, rule; have the upper (*or* whip) hand, prevail, boss (*colloq.*).

despotize, tyrannize, oppress, bend to one's will, lay down the law, lord it over, domineer, override, overrule.

Adj. **powerful**, high-powered, potent, prepotent, plenipotentiary, omnipotent, puissant (*poetic*), mighty, almighty, vigorous, forceful, able; strong, Herculean, titanic.

effective, effectual, efficacious, influential.

dominant, ascendant, predominant, preponderant, paramount, sovereign, supreme.

authoritative, weighty, controlling, ruling, influential, prestigious, commanding; official, cathedral, ex cathedra (*L.*), thetic; top, top-drawer, upmost, uppermost.

despotic, autocratic, absolute, absolutistic, arbitrary, tyrannous, hard, hardhanded, ironhanded, oppressive, grinding, Draconian, dictatorial, domineering.

See also ABILITY, AGENT, COMMAND, ENERGY, FORCE, GOVERNMENT, INFLUENCE, OFFICIAL, PERMISSION, RESULT, RULE, SEVERITY, STRENGTH. *Antonyms*—See DISABLEMENT, WEAKNESS.

powerless, *adj.* helpless, impotent, prostrate (WEAKNESS, DISABLEMENT).

pox, *n.* chicken pox, varicella, cowpox (SKIN).

practicable, *adj.* feasible, performable, workable (POSSIBILITY, EASE); usable, utilizable, applicable (USE).

practical, *adj.* workaday, useful, applied (USE); businesslike, orderly, systematic (BUSINESS); realistic, unromantic, down-to-earth (REALITY); worldly, sophisticated, cosmopolitan (EXPERIENCE, WISDOM).

practical joke, *n.* lark, prank, trick (MISCHIEF, WITTINESS).

practice, *n.* training, seasoning, background (EXPERIENCE); drill, assignment, homework (TEACHING); usage, custom, way (USE); wont, rule, routine (HABIT).

practice, *v.* train in, drill exercise (EXPERIENCE, TEACHING); repeat, rehearse (REPETITION); be in the habit, follow (HABIT).

praise, *n.* grassland, meadow, lea (GRASS); plateau, plain (LAND).

PRAISE—*N.* **praise**, acclaim, acclamation, applause, boost (*colloq.*), celebration, commendation, laudation; citation, flattery, hymn, paean, puff, puffery; eulogy, panegyric, encomium, tribute, accolade, éclat (*F.*), kudos (*colloq.*), plaudit; compliment, trade-last (*colloq.*); blurb (*colloq.*).

V. **praise**, acclaim, applaud, boost (*colloq.*), celebrate, commend, glorify, laud, eulogize, panegyrize, exalt, extol, cite, paean, hymn; compliment, flatter, overpraise, puff, tout (*colloq.*).

Adj. **laudatory**, acclamatory, applausive, commendatory, complimentary, eulogistic, panegyric, flattering, encomiastic, plausive.

See also APPROVAL, EXAGGERATION, FLATTERY, OVERESTIMATION, WORSHIP. *Antonyms*—See CONTEMPT, DETRACTION.

praiseworthy, *adj.* laudable, commendable, meritorious (APPROVAL).

prance, *v.* gambol, frolic, romp (JUMP); cavort, caper (PLAYFULNESS); strut, swagger, stalk (WALKING, PRIDE).

prank, *n.* trick, joke, practical joke (MISCHIEF, WITTINESS).

pray, *v.* invoke, supplicate, commune with God (WORSHIP); beg, adjure, plead (BEGGING).

prayer, *n.* devotions, services, chapel (WORSHIP); entreaty, supplication, petition (BEGGING).

preacher, *n.* pastor, shepherd, parson (CLERGY); evangelist (PREACHING).

PREACHING—*N.* **preaching**, evangelism, homiletics, pulpitism.

sermon, preachment, homily, lecture, pastoral, exhortation.

preacher, evangelist, evangelizer, evangel, preachifier, pulpiter, pulpiteer (*often contemptuous*), sermonizer, homilist, predicant, predicator, pulpitarian.

V. preach, sermonize, pulpiteer, pulpit, evangelize, preachify, preacherize.

Adj. preaching, predicant, predicatory, evangelistic, pulpitarian, homilectic.

See also CLERGY, MORALITY.

preamble, *n.* introduction, prelude, preface (BEGINNING).

precarious, *adj.* hazardous, perilous, insecure (DANGER); chancy (*colloq.*), rocky, contingent (UNCERTAINTY).

PRECEDENCE—*N.* precedence, antecedence, priority, prevenience.

antecedent, antecessor, precess, precedent, ancestor, forebear, progenitor, predecessor.

precursor, forerunner, harbinger, herald, avant-courier (*F.*), vauntcourier (*F.*), outrider, pioneer; prognostic, omen, sign, presage, token.

V. precede, forerun, come before, antecede, come first, antedate, pre-exist; head, lead, lead the way, pioneer, guide; rank, take precedence over, outrank; be beforehand, anticipate, forestall, steal a march upon, have a head start, be ahead of.

introduce, pave the way, prepare the ground, harbinger, announce, usher in, herald, preface, prelude, precurse.

Adj. preceding, antecedent, precursory, preliminary, prevenient, prodromal (*esp. med.*), pre-existent; foregoing, aforementioned, aforesaid, aforestated, said, above, above-mentioned, above-stated, before-mentioned; prior, anterior, previous, former, earlier; leading, lead, head, pioneer, pioneering, avant-garde (*F.*).

See also ANCESTRY, BEGINNING, EARLINESS, FRONT, GUIDANCE, LEADERSHIP, MESSENGER, PAST, PREDICTION. *Antonyms*—See DELAY, END, FOLLOWING, REAR.

precept, *n.* canon, maxim, formula (RULE).

precious, *adj.* valuable, costly, priceless (VALUE); affected, sophisticated, stagy (UNNATURALNESS).

precipice, *n.* cliff, bluff (HEIGHT).

precise, *adj.* accurate, exact, nice (RIGHT, BOUNDARY); explicit, categorical, specific (CLARITY).

preclude, *v.* prevent, avert, forestall (PREVENTION).

precocious, *adj.* beforehand, advanced (EARLINESS).

preconception, *n.* prejudgment, prepossession, bias (OPINION, PREJUDICE).

precursor, *n.* forerunner, harbinger, herald (PRECEDENCE).

predatory, *adj.* predacious, depredatory, rapacious (PLUNDER).

predestine, *v.* destine, foreordain (DESTINY).

predicament, *n.* plight, scrape, straits (DIFFICULTY, CONDITION).

PREDICTION—*N.* prediction, anticipation, divination, fortunetelling, palmistry, crystal gazing, hariolation, mantic, manticism, prognostication, pythonism, soothsaying, vaticination; omen, augury, auspice, foreboding, forecast, presage, prognosis, prognostic, prophecy; horoscope, zodiac.

predictor, augur, Chaldean, diviner, foreboder, forecaster, foreseer, foreteller, fortuneteller, presager, prognosticator, prophesier, prophet, pythoness (*fem.*), pythonist, seer, sibyl (*fem.*), soothsayer, sortileger, Cassandra; oracle, astrologer, astromancer, crystal gazer, hydromancer, oneiromancer, palmist, chiromancer, sorcerer, necromancer, clairvoyant, horoscoper.

V. predict, anticipate, augur, omen, croak, divine, envision, forebode, forecast, foresee, forespeak, foretell, presage, prognosticate, prophesy, vaticinate; hariolate, pythonize, soothsay.

Adj. predictive, divinatory, fatidic, mantic, prognostic.

prophetic, pythonic, sibyllic.

See also EXPECTATION, FUTURE, PRECEDENCE, SUPPOSITION, WARNING.

predilection, *n.* preference, partiality, penchant (LIKING); inclination, predisposition, propensity (PREJUDICE).

predispose, *v.* dispose, sway, govern (INFLUENCE); prejudice, bias, incline (PREJUDICE).

predisposed, *adj.* disposed, minded, partial (TENDENCY).

predisposition, *n.* propensity, predilection, inclination (PREJUDICE).

predominant, *adj.* powerful, ascendant, preponderant (POWER); dominant, reigning, obtaining (PRESENCE).

pre-exist, *v.* antedate, predate (EXISTENCE, EARLINESS).

preface, *n.* introduction, foreword, prelude (BEGINNING).

prefer, *v.* fancy, have rather, favor (CHOICE, LIKING).

preferable, *adj.* better, superior (IMPROVEMENT); likable, enjoyable, relishable (LIKING).

preference, *n.* partiality, predilection, propensity (LIKING); choice, say (*colloq.*), option (VOICE).

PREGNANCY—N. pregnancy, fetation, gestation, gravity; conception, quickening, lightening, labor, term.

impregnation, fecundation, fertilization, insemination, artificial insemination.

birth control, contraception, planned parenthood.

abortion, feticide, aborticide, curettage, miscarriage, spontaneous abortion.

V. **be pregnant,** gestate, conceive, quicken; miscarry, abort.

impregnate, inseminate, fecundate (*biol.*), fertilize (*biol.*).

Adj. **pregnant,** big, big with child, childing, *enceinte* (*F.*), expectant, expecting, full, gravid, great, great with child, heavy, heavy with child, laden, anticipating (*slang*).

See also BIRTH, CHILD, FERTILITY. *Antonyms*—See UNPRODUCTIVENESS.

---

pregnant, *adj.* expectant (PREGNANCY); meaty, pithy, pointed (MEANING); suggestive, redolent, remindful (SUGGESTION).

prejudge, *v.* forejudge (PREJUDICE).

prejudgment, *n.* preconception, prejudice (OPINION).

PREJUDICE—N. prejudice, preconception, prepossession, prejudgment, bias, slant, bigotry, illiberality, intolerance, discrimination, subjectivity, jaundice.

race prejudice, racism, racialism, sectarianism, sectionalism; anti-Semitism; negrophobia, Jim Crowism, Jim Crow, segregation, apartheid; nativism, xenophobia.

partiality, partisanship, favoritism, *parti pris* (*F.*), predilection, inclination, predisposition, propensity, zealotry.

narrow-mindedness, illiberality, provincialism, parochialism, insularity, Victorianism, mid-Victorianism, sectarianism, sectionalism, localism.

bigot, racialist, racist, sectarian, sectionalist, nativist, xenophobe, anti-Semite, negrophobe, segregationist.

partisan, zealot, zealotist.

provincial, provincialist, paro-

chialist, Victorian, mid-Victorian, sectarian, sectionalist, localist.

V. **prejudice,** bias, predispose, prepossess, predetermine, incline, influence, indoctrinate; jaundice, warp, twist.

be prejudiced, prejudge, forejudge, favor, incline, discriminate; color, slant, angle, distort.

Adj. **prejudiced,** prepossessed, biased, squint-eyed, bigoted, intolerant, unfair, jaundiced, discriminatory, subjective; slanted, colored.

partial, partisan, one-sided, favorable, inclined, predisposed.

narrow-minded, narrow, insular, parochial, provincial, petty, small-minded, confined, hidebound, bourgeois, illiberal, Victorian, mid-Victorian; sectarian, sectional, local, localistic.

See also INFLUENCE, JUDGMENT, OPINION, TENDENCY, UNFAIRNESS. *Antonyms*—See IMPARTIALITY.

---

prejudicial, *adj.* injurious, deleterious, detrimental (HARM).

preliminary, *adj.* introductory, preceding, preparatory (PRECEDENCE, PREPARATION).

prelude, *n.* introduction, preamble, preface (BEGINNING); overture (MUSIC).

premature, *adj.* untimely, previous (*colloq.*), inopportune (EARLINESS, UNTIMELINESS).

premeditate, *v.* prearrange, plan, plot (PLAN).

premeditated, *adj.* calculated, studied, conscious (PURPOSE, WILL).

premise, *n.* proposition, hypothesis (REASONING).

premises, *n.* grounds, campus, terrace (LAND); house, building, home (HABITATION).

premonition, *n.* forewarning, foreboding, presage (FUTURE, WARNING, MISFORTUNE).

preoccupation, *n.* attentiveness, absorption, abstraction (ATTENTION, THOUGHT); reverie, brown study (*colloq.*), woolgathering (INATTENTION).

preoccupied, *adj.* immersed, absorbed, rapt, engrossed, lost in thought (ATTENTION, THOUGHT).

PREPARATION—N. preparation, arrangement, provision, rehearsal; anticipation, expectation, precaution; groundwork, substructure, base, basis, foundation.

concoction, blend, brew, compound, decoction, confection.

V. **prepare,** arrange, provide, ready, unlimber, brew; block out, roughhew; prepare the ground for, lay the foundation of; prime, groom, rehearse; arm, forearm.

prepare for, guard against, provide against.

equip, arm, man; fit out, rig, dress, accouter, array, outfit, appoint, gird, furnish, provide.

concoct, blend, brew, compound, decoct, confect, cook, fix.

prepare oneself, get ready, compose oneself, rehearse, unlimber, arm, forearm; hold oneself in readiness, be on guard.

Adj. **prepared,** ready, readied, arranged, unlimbered; available, handy; primed, groomed, rehearsed, pat, put-up; armed, forearmed, forewarned, on guard, forehanded, foresighted.

preparatory, preparative, preliminary, introductory, precautionary.

See also ARRANGEMENT, BASE, COMPLETENESS, COOKERY, EXPECTATION, EXPERIENCE, FORESIGHT, MATURITY, PLAN. *Antonyms*—See IMMATURITY, INEXPERIENCE, NONPREPARATION, SUDDENNESS, SURPRISE.

---

prepare, *v.* arrange, provide, ready (PREPARATION); train, ground, prime (TEACHING).

preposterous, *adj.* absurd, unreasonable, ridiculous (ABSURDITY).

prerequisite, *n.* qualification, postulate (NECESSITY).

prerogative, *n.* right, due, perquisite (PRIVILEGE).

presage, *n.* foreboding, portent, premonition (FUTURE).

presage, *v.* foretell, prognosticate, prophesy (PREDICTION).

PRESENCE—*N.* **presence,** attendance; whereabouts, ubiety, ubiquity, omnipresence; existence, subsistence.

attender, attendant, participator; onlooker, spectator, bystander.

V. **be present,** attend, make it (*colloq.*), show (*colloq.*), arrive, look on; present oneself, show up (*colloq.*), find oneself; be situated, be located, be found, lie, stand; stay, remain, outlast, continue; exist, subsist, be extant.

be prevalent, prevail, obtain, abound, superabound, dominate, reign, predominate.

frequent, haunt, visit; infest, overrun.

pervade, permeate, penetrate, diffuse; overspread, fill, run through, saturate.

Adj. **present,** here, on-the-spot, attendant, participating, taking part; omnipresent, ubiquitous, ubiquitary; situated, situate, located, found; existent, existing, extant, subsistent; latent, dormant, potential, smoldering.

actual, latest, occurring; instant, immediate.

prevalent, prevailing, current, common, abundant, extensive, diffuse, general, universal, catholic; ecumenical, widespread, epidemic, pandemic, rife, dominant, predominant, reigning, obtaining.

Adv., phrases. **here,** here, there, and everywhere; on the spot, in person; at home; aboard, on board.

See also ARRIVAL, EXISTENCE, LOCATION, VISIT. *Antonyms*—See ABSENCE, INSUFFICIENCY.

---

presence of mind, *n.* composure, self-possession, aplomb (CALMNESS).

present, *adj.* here, on-the-spot, attendant, existent (PRESENCE); current, contemporary, topical (PRESENT TIME).

present, *n.* gift, donation (GIVING); now, nowadays (PRESENT TIME).

present, *v.* offer, proffer, tender (OFFER); give, bestow, award (GIVING); exhibit, expose (DISPLAY); act, play (ACTOR).

presentation, *n.* overture, proposal, proposition (OFFER); act, performance, stage show (DRAMA).

presently, *adv.* soon, shortly, before long (FUTURE, EARLINESS).

PRESENT TIME—*N.* **present time,** the present, now, nowadays, the nonce, the present juncture (or occasion); the times, time being; twentieth century.

Adj. **present,** current, contemporary, topical, modern, up-to-date, latter-day.

Adv., phrases. **at this time,** at this moment, now, at present; today, nowadays; by now, already; even now, but now, just now; for the time being, for the nonce.

See also NEWNESS. *Antonyms*—See DELAY, FUTURE, PAST.

---

preservation, *n.* conservation, salvation, safekeeping (PROTECTION); corning, refrigeration (PRESERVING).

preserve, *n.* retreat, sanctuary, shelter (PROTECTION, LAND); jam, conserve, jelly (SEMILIQUIDITY).

preserve, *v.* protect, safeguard (PROTECTION); perpetuate, continue (ENDLESSNESS); corn (PRE-SERVING).

PRESERVING—N. preserving, preservation.

preservative, brine, marinade, pickle, salt, spices.

V. preserve, keep, retard decay, corn, cure, salt, pickle, souse, marinate, marinade, brine, kipper, smoke, confect, conserve; dehydrate, dry, tan, refrigerate, freeze, quick-freeze, can; embalm, mummify.

See also HOLD, STORE, TASTE. Antonyms—See DECAY.

president, n. chief of state, chief magistrate (RULER); principal, headmaster (SCHOOL); commander, head (LEADERSHIP); chairman, moderator (OFFICIAL).

press, v. depress, clamp, push (PRESSURE, PROPULSION); weigh, cumber (WEIGHT); iron, smooth, flatten (SMOOTHNESS, ROLL); urge, exhort, prod (URGING).

press agent, n. publicity agent, huckster (derogatory), publicist (PUBLICATION).

pressing, adj. urgent, imperative, exigent (DEMAND, IMPORTANCE, ATTENTION, NECESSITY, PRESSURE).

pressure, n. strain, tension (PRESSURE); compulsion, constraint, coercion (FORCE).

PRESSURE—N. pressure, brunt, strain, tension, stress, urgency.

clamp, vise, nipper, nippers, masher, wringer, crusher.

V. press, bear down, depress, clamp, cram, jam, mash, ram, wedge, stuff, wad, knead; compress, astringe; iron, smooth.

cuddle, hug, embrace, squeeze, nestle, nuzzle, snuggle, strain.

crush, crunch, trample, tread, mash, squash, squelch, triturate.

squeeze, choke, throttle, strangle, wring; pinch, sandwich, nip, twinge, vellicate, tweak.

Adj. pressing, urgent, insistent, persistent, important.

See also IMPORTANCE, NERVOUSNESS, POWDERINESS, PROPULSION, RUBBING, SMOOTHNESS, URGING. Antonyms—See ROUGHNESS, UNANXIETY.

prestige, n. pre-eminence, repute, prominence (FAME); authority, weight, control (POWER).

presumably, adv. supposedly, theoretically, hypothetically (SUPPOSITION).

presume, v. infer, gather, conclude (LIKELIHOOD); suppose, grant

(SUPPOSITION); be so bold, dare (DISCOURTESY).

presumption, n. premise, assumption, presupposition (SUPPOSITION); arrogance, insolence (PRIDE); brass (colloq.), nerve (colloq.), cheek (DISCOURTESY).

presumptuous, adj. cheeky (colloq.), brassy (colloq.), presuming (DISCOURTESY); arrogant, contumelious (PRIDE).

PRETENSE—N. pretense, make-believe, fakery, dissimulation, play-acting, simulation, affectation, pretension, shoddy, outward show, histrionics, humbuggery, postiche (F.); bravado.

pretext, stall (slang), bluff, feint.

imposture, masquerade, impersonation, personation; charlatanism, quackery.

pose, posture, role, guise, false show, sham, simulacrum.

disguise, mask, cloak, veil.

hypocrisy, phariseeism, insincerity, Pecksniffery, dishonesty, unctuosity.

pretender, counterfeiter, dissembler, dissimulator, feigner, shammer, simulator; fake, faker, bluffer, bluff, boggler, make-believe, humbug, play-actor, fraud, fourflusher (colloq.), mountebank, shoddy, tinhorn.

impostor, impersonator, personator, actor, masquerader.

poser, poseur, posturer, posturist, attitudinizer, attitudinarian.

charlatan, empiric, mountebank, quack, quacksalver.

hypocrite, pharisee, tartuffe, whited sepulcher, snuffler, palterer.

V. pretend, make believe, fool, play-act, dissimulate, fake, feign, counterfeit, simulate, sham, profess, purport, assume, affect, put on, masquerade, boggle, bluff, malinger.

pretend to be, act, assume the character, part, role, etc., of; impersonate, masquerade as, pass oneself off as, personate, pose as, purport to be, represent oneself as.

pose, posture, posturize, peacock, attitudinize, strike an attitude (or pose).

be insincere with, dally with, play with, play fast and loose with, toy with, trifle with; snuffle, palter, act insincerely.

disguise, cloak, dissemble, dissimulate, mask, veil.

Adj. pretending, dissimulative.

pretended, make-believe, simulated, fake, affected, artificial, dissimulated, sham, bogus, simulate, counterfeit, feigned, false, factitious, mock, pseudo; imposturous, quack, charlatanic, shoddy.

pretentious, histrionic, theatrical, stagy, *postiche* (F.), ostentatious, showy.

professed, ostensible, colorable, apparent, purported, *soi-disant* (F.), self-styled, so-called, token.

hypocritical, Pecksniffian, pharisaical, canting, tartuffish, sanctimonious.

insincere, backhanded, dishonest, disingenuous, empty, hollow, two-faced, double-dealing, Janus-faced, mealy-mouthed, fulsome, unctuous.

See also FALSENESS, IMITATION, OSTENTATION, UNNATURALNESS, UNREALITY. *Antonyms*—See HONESTY, NATURALNESS, REALITY, SIMPLICITY.

---

pretentious, *adj.* ostentatious, showy, grandiose (PRETENSE, OSTENTATION); self-important, pompous, toplofty (IMPORTANCE); swollen, inflated (WORDINESS).

pretext, *n.* stall (*slang*), bluff, feint (PRETENSE, DECEPTION); excuse, subterfuge (FORGIVENESS).

pretty, *adj.* attractive, comely, lovely (BEAUTY).

prevail, *v.* obtain, abound (PRESENCE, COMMONNESS).

prevail against, *v.* resist, withstand, weather (SUCCESS).

prevailing, *adj.* prevalent, current, common (PRESENCE).

prevail on, *v.* convince, sway, win over (PERSUASION).

prevalent, *adj.* prevailing, current, common (PRESENCE); in use, popular (USE).

prevaricate, *v.* lie, invent, fabricate (FALSEHOOD).

preventable, *adj.* avoidable, avertible (AVOIDANCE).

PREVENTION—*N.* prevention, forestallment, preclusion, avoidance; deterrence, determent.

preventive, preventative, deterrent, determent, prohibition.

V. prevent, avert, forestall, preclude, stay, stave off, stop, ward off, avoid, rule out; deter, discourage; forbid, prohibit; frustrate, thwart.

See also AVOIDANCE, CESSATION, DENIAL, HINDRANCE, INEFFECTIVENESS, RESTRAINT. *Antonyms*—See AID.

---

previous, *adj.* prior, former, earlier (PRECEDENCE, EARLINESS); untimely, inopportune, premature (UNTIMELINESS).

prey, *n.* quest, quarry, chase (SEARCH, PLUNDER); sufferer, victim (PAIN).

prey on, *v.* plunder, depredate, fleece (PLUNDER); weigh on, oppress (WEIGHT).

price, *n.* rate, figure, cost (EXPENDITURE).

priceless, *adj.* valuable, invaluable, precious (VALUE); funny, amusing, humorous (WITTINESS).

prick, *v.* prickle, sting, smart (CUTTING); goad, pique, needle (MOTIVATION).

prickle, *n.* thorn, thistle, barb (SHARPNESS).

PRIDE—*N.* pride, exaltation, immodesty, swagger; superiority, condescension, patronage, snobbery, snobbism; self-esteem, self-respect.

haughtiness, hauteur, airs; arrogance, assumption, presumption, contumely, insolence, huff.

conceit, vanity, vainglory, self-conceit, self-praise, egotism, egoism, self-importance, pragmatism, tympany, swelled head (*slang*).

self-pride, *amour propre* (F.), ego, self-admiration, self-love, self-laudation, self-glorification.

egotist, egoist, peacock, swellhead (*slang*), snob; popinjay, prima donna (*fem.*), puppy, pup, coxcomb.

V. be proud, hold one's head high, pride oneself, plume oneself, pique oneself, preen oneself, give oneself airs; crow; puff up, swell, swagger, strut, prance, bridle; cavalier, presume, overween, overbear, huff.

condescend, deign, stoop, patronize, lower oneself, talk down to.

be conceited, peacock, peacock oneself, vaunt, boast, have a high opinion of oneself.

fill with pride, exalt, swell, inflate, bloat, puff up, turn one's head.

Adj. proud, exalted, lofty, highminded, immodest, prideful, overproud; superior, condescending, patronizing, snobbish, snooty (*colloq.*), aristocratic; puffed up, swollen, inflated, purse-proud, pursy.

haughty, cavalier, toplofty, uppity, uppish, overweening, vaulting.

arrogant, supercilious, assumptive, assuming, presumptuous, contumelious, insolent, snippy (*colloq.*), peremptory.

overbearing, imperious, dictatorial, magisterial, lordly.

conceited, vain, vainglorious, self-conceited, cocky (*colloq.*), chesty (*slang*), egotistical, egoistical, bloated, bumptious, peacocky, coxcombical, self-important, stuck-up (*colloq.*), pragmatic, perky.

See also BOASTING, ELEVATION, IMMODESTY, IMPORTANCE. *Antonyms—* See HUMILITY, MODESTY.

priest, *n.* divine, ecclesiastic; cleric (CLERGY).

prig, *n.* precisianist, pedant, purist (RIGHT); prude, bluenose, puritan (PROPRIETY).

prim, *adj.* spruce, dapper, natty (NEATNESS); prudish, overmodest, strait-laced (PROPRIETY, MODESTY).

primary, *adj.* beginning, first, original (BEGINNING); essential, fundamental, key (IMPORTANCE).

prime, *adj.* principal, chief, fundamental (IMPORTANCE); original, beginning, first (BEGINNING); best, unparalleled, choice (PERFECTION); marvelous, splendid, superb (GOOD).

prime, *n.* bloom, pink, heyday (HEALTH, STRENGTH).

prime minister, *n.* minister, premier, secretary (OFFICIAL).

primitive, *adj.* rudimentary, vestigial, larval (IMMATURITY); primeval, primal, primary (EARLINESS); uncivilized, savage (BARBARIANISM); simple, austere, Spartan (SIMPLICITY).

primp, *v.* prink, spruce, titivate (CLOTHING).

prince, *n.* king, monarch, grand duke (RULER, SOCIAL CLASS); greatheart, sublimity (NOBILITY); dignitary, grandee, magnifico (RANK).

princess, *n.* noblewoman, peeress (SOCIAL CLASS, RULER).

principal, *adj.* leading, chief, main (LEADERSHIP, IMPORTANCE, SUPERIORITY).

principal, *n.* dean, preceptor, headmaster (SCHOOL); star, protagonist (ACTION); capital, assets (MONEY).

principle, *n.* regulation, law prescript (RULE).

PRINTING—*N.* printing, typography, lithography, photogravure, rotogravure, thermography, gravure, offset, letterpress; composition, typesetting, presswork; type, Linotype, Monotype.

print, impression, impress, imprint.

proof, pull, slip, trial impression, galley, galley proof, page proof, foundry proof, plate proof; revise.

printer, compositor, typesetter, pressman, typographer, lithographer, linotypist, photogravurist; printer's devil.

printing press, press, cylinder press, rotary press, web press.

V. **print**, offset, impress, imprint, stamp, strike off; compose, set, set type; reprint, reissue.

Adj. **typographical**, printed, in print, in type, in black and white.

See also BOOK, ENGRAVING, PUBLICATION, WRITING.

prior, *adj.* previous, former, earlier (PRECEDENCE).

prison, *n.* jail, penitentiary, reformatory (IMPRISONMENT).

prissy (*colloq.*), *adj.* puritanical, prim, prudish (PROPRIETY).

privacy, *n.* quiet, isolation, retirement (SECLUSION).

private, *adj.* remote, quiet, isolated (SECLUSION); hush-hush, secret, confidential (CONCEALMENT).

private, *n.* doughboy, G.I. (FIGHTER).

privately, *adv.* in private, *in camera* (L.), tête-à-tête (F.), covertly, *sub rosa* (L.), confidentially (SECLUSION, CONCEALMENT).

PRIVILEGE—*N.* privilege, right, due, authority, appurtenance, perquisite, prerogative; franchise, charter; grant, license, exemption, concession, immunity.

privileged person, perquisitor, special case, exception.

V. **privilege**, entitle, authorize, allow, sanction, qualify; charter, franchise; give, confer, grant, concede, vouchsafe, *or* delegate (*a right or privilege to*).

Adj. **privileged**, exempt, excused, immune, allowed, authorized, special, licensed, eligible, qualified; entitled; chartered, franchised; palatine.

See also ADVANTAGE, FREEDOM, PERMISSION, POWER. *Antonyms—See* RESTRAINT.

prize, *n.* reward, award, accolade (PAYMENT).

prize, *v.* value, appreciate, esteem (VALUE); cherish, enshrine, treasure (LOVE).

prize fight, *n.* bout, match (FIGHTING).

prize fighter, *n.* boxer, pugilist (FIGHTER).

probability, *n.* likelihood, chance, prospect (LIKELIHOOD).

probable, *adj.* likely, presumable (LIKELIHOOD).

probably, *adv.* presumably, in all probability, in all likelihood (LIKELIHOOD).

probation, n. disimprisonment, discharge, parole (FREEDOM); trial, tryout, approval (TEST).

problem, n. puzzle, puzzler, riddle (ANSWER); question, issue (TOPIC).

procedure, n. course, *modus operandi* (L.), process (METHOD, USE); program, agendum (PLAN).

proceed, v. advance, go, go on (PROGRESS); pass, extend, flow (PASSAGE).

proceeding, adj. in progress, in hand, going on (INCOMPLETENESS).

proceeds, n. returns, take (slang), income (RECEIVING).

process, n. procedure, *modus operandi* (L.), course (METHOD); mechanism, working (ACTION).

procession, n. course, movement, passage (PROGRESS); parade, march, cavalcade (WALKING).

proclaim, v. declare, announce, expound (STATEMENT, INFORMATION).

procrastinate, v. postpone, put off, stall (DELAY).

procreate, v. multiply, breed, reproduce (BIRTH).

procure, v. gain, secure, acquire (ACQUISITION, TAKING).

procurer, n. pimp, panderer (PROSTITUTE).

prod, n. goad, lash, whip, push (MOTIVATION).

prod, v. drive, goad, impel (URGING); motivate, stimulate, spur (MOTIVATION); push, press, nudge (PROPULSION); remind, prompt (MEMORY).

prodigal, adj. extravagant, improvident, profligate (WASTEFULNESS, UNSELFISHNESS).

prodigal, n. wastrel, profligate, spendthrift (WASTEFULNESS).

prodigious, adj. miraculous, phenomenal, preternatural (UNUSUALNESS); monumental, herculean, mighty (SIZE).

prodigy, n. marvel, wonder, rarity (SURPRISE, UNUSUALNESS); genius, brain (slang), intellect (INTELLIGENCE).

produce, v. turn out, provide, yield (PRODUCTION); result in, afford, beget (RESULT).

product, n. yield, output, crop (PRODUCTION, STORE); result, fruit, offspring (RESULT).

PRODUCTION—N. production, origination, generation.

product, result, by-product, production; yield, fruit, output, outturn, provision, produce; work, artifact, synthetic, synthesis, concoction, confection, compound, decoction, blend, brew, fabrication, device, contrivance.

creation, coinage, invention, original, improvisation, conception, execution; creature, artistic creation, composition, work, opus, magnum opus (L.), masterpiece, chef-d'oeuvre (F.), monument; petty creation, opuscule.

creator, inventor, artificer, originator, architect, composer, designer.

factory, manufactory, mill, plant, forge; factories, industry.

V. **produce,** turn out, provide, yield, bear, afford, breed, pullulate (fig.), cause, effect, engender, beget, generate, give rise to, bring about, result in.

create, give birth to, bring into being, bring into existence, originate, conceive, coin, compose, execute, design, contrive, devise, think up, hatch, improvise, make up, invent, fabricate, manufacture, concoct.

make, build, construct, synthesize, manufacture, fabricate; fashion, form, forge, contrive, devise; prepare, concoct, confect, mix, compound, blend, brew, decoct.

Adj. **produced,** etc. (see *Verbs*); synthetic, man-made, artificial; wrought of, compact of.

creative, productive, prolific, fertile; original, Promethean, demiurgic; creational, creationary.

inventive, ingenious, adroit, forgetive, clever.

See also BIRTH, CAUSATION, FERTILITY, IMAGINATION, MIXTURE, RESULT. *Antonyms*—See DESTRUCTION, IMITATION, UNPRODUCTIVENESS.

---

productive, adj. loamy, luxuriant, mellow (FERTILITY); creative, prolific, inventive (PRODUCTION).

profane, adj. blasphemous, sacrilegious, impious (IRRELIGION, DISRESPECT, MALEDICTION).

profane, v. desecrate, violate, contaminate (IRRELIGION, DISRESPECT); misuse, pervert, prostitute (MISUSE).

profanity, n. cursing, swearing, blasphemy, impiety (MALEDICTION, DISRESPECT).

professed, adj. purported, ostensible, colorable (PRETENSE).

profession, n. occupation, specialty, career (BUSINESS).

professor, n. educator, instructor (TEACHER).

proffer, v. volunteer, tender, present (OFFER).

proficient, adj. able, competent, skillful (ABILITY).

profile, *n.* silhouette, shadow (FINE ARTS, SHAPE).

profit, *n.* gain, benefit, advantage, harvest (ACQUISITION).

profit, *v.* gain, benefit, clear (ACQUISITION).

profitable, *adj.* beneficial, productive, fruitful (USE, ACQUISITION); lucrative, remunerative (PAYMENT).

profit by, *v.* capitalize on, exploit (USE).

profiteer, *v.* bleed (*colloq.*), gouge (*colloq.*), overcharge (EXPENDITURE).

profligate, *adj.* dissolute, dissipated, loose (INTEMPERANCE, FREEDOM); immoral, licentious, promiscuous (SEX); extravagant, improvident, prodigal (WASTEFULNESS).

profound, *adj.* deep, deep-seated, buried (DEPTH); wise, shrewd (WISDOM); difficult (MYSTERY).

profuse, *adj.* lavish, munificent, prodigal (UNSELFISHNESS).

program, *n.* agendum, procedure (PLAN); schedule, bulletin, calendar (LIST).

PROGRESS—*N.* progress, progression, advance, advancement, ongoing, march, onward motion, speed, headway; rise, improvement, development, growth.

V. progress, advance, proceed, go, go on, get on, gain ground, forge ahead, press onward, step forward, speed, make headway; go ahead, shoot ahead, edge forward, dash ahead, lunge forward, move ahead, move on, keep going.

Adj. progressive, advancing, increasing; advanced, enterprising, forward, onward, forward-looking, up-to-date, modern.

See also ASCENT, CONTINUATION, ELEVATION, IMPROVEMENT, MOTION, NEWNESS, RANK, SPEED. *Antonyms*—See DESCENT, DETERIORATION, MOTIONLESSNESS, REVERSION, SLOWNESS.

---

progressive, *adj.* advancing, enterprising (PROGRESS); gradual, by degrees (DEGREE).

progressive, *n.* improver, reformer (IMPROVEMENT).

prohibit, *v.* forbid, enjoin, bar (DENIAL).

prohibited, *adj.* forbidden, contraband, *verboten* (*Ger.*), taboo (DENIAL).

prohibition, *n.* ban, bar, embargo (DENIAL).

Prohibition, *n.* temperance act, Volstead Act (SOBRIETY).

project, *n.* business, work, affair (UNDERTAKING); aim, intention, proposition (PLAN).

project, *v.* jut, protrude, protuberate (VISIBILITY); plan, contemplate, intend (PLAN).

projectile, *n.* missile, shot (THROW).

projection, *n.* overhang, jut (HANGING); prominence, protrusion (RELIEF).

prolific, *adj.* breedy, fecund, fruitful (FERTILITY); creative, productive (PRODUCTION).

prolong, *v.* stretch, draw out, continue (LENGTH).

promenade, *v.* saunter, stroll, march (WALKING).

prominent, *adj.* famous, well-known, outstanding (FAME); conspicuous, remarkable, protrusive (VISIBILITY).

promiscuous, *adj.* undiscriminating (INDISCRIMINATION); loose, immoral, licentious (SEXUAL IMMORALITY).

PROMISE—*N.* promise, engagement, commitment, undertaking, word, sacred word, pledge, parole, word of honor, vow, oath, profession, assurance, earnest, warrant, warranty, guarantee, bond (*law*), promissory note, mortgage, obligation, stipulation, contract, covenant.

security, surety, bond, collateral, gage, pawn, pledge, earnest, token payment, bail, hostage.

V. promise, bind oneself, commit oneself, engage, guarantee; give one's word; obligate oneself, swear, undertake, vow, warrant, assure; covenant, contract, agree, stipulate; pledge, plight, mortgage, subscribe to; plight one's troth; hypothecate; pawn, hock (*slang*).

Adj. promissory, contractual, covenantal, votive, votary.

See also AFFIRMATION, AGREEMENT, BETROTHAL, COMPACT, LOYALTY. *Antonyms*—See DISLOYALTY.

---

promising, *adj.* auspicious, favorable, propitious (SUCCESS, HOPE).

promote, *v.* cultivate, forward, further (IMPROVEMENT, AID); advance, elevate, upgrade (RANK, ELEVATION).

prompt, *adj.* on time, punctual (EARLINESS).

prompt, *n.* hint, cue, mnemonic (MEMORY, HINT).

prompt, *v.* cause, provoke, occasion (CAUSATION); move, induce, inspire (MOTIVATION); prod, jog the memory (MEMORY).

promptly, *adv.* sharp, precisely, punctually, on time (SHARPNESS); right away, straightway (EARLINESS).

prone, *adj.* inclined, apt, liable (TENDENCY); minded, disposed (WILLINGNESS); procumbent, prostrate (REST).

prong, *n.* tooth, tine, cog (TEETH, SHARPNESS); tip, cusp (END).

pronounce, *v.* speak, say, utter (TALK); articulate, enunciate (VOICE).

pronounced, *adj.* outstanding, striking, arresting (VISIBILITY).

pronunciation, *n.* diction, articulation, enunciation (VOICE).

PROOF—*N.* proof, demonstration, evidence, testimony, documentation; credentials, documents, papers, token.

V. prove, demonstrate, show, testify to, establish, authenticate, circumstantiate, confirm, vindicate, corroborate, substantiate, validate, verify, vouch for, attest, argue; document.

Adj. [*serving as proof*] **probative,** probatory, confirmatory, corroborative, demonstrative, evincive, substantiative, verificative, documentary, conclusive, decisive.

[*capable of proof*] **demonstrable,** attestable, confirmable, establishable, verifiable; irrefutable, undeniable, unanswerable.

See also BELIEF, PAPER, PERSUASION. *Antonyms*—See DISPROOF.

---

proofread, *v.* copy-edit, correct, revise (WRITTEN SYMBOL).

prop, *n.* stay, mainstay, strut (SUPPORT).

prop, *v.* brace, truss, shore (SUPPORT, STRENGTH).

propaganda, *n.* doctrine, indoctrination (TEACHING, BELIEF).

propel, *v.* push, start, set in motion (PROPULSION).

propensity, *n.* partiality, penchant, predilection (LIKING).

proper, *adj.* correct, free of error, unmistaken (RIGHT); appropriate, suitable (PROPRIETY).

property, *n.* real estate (LAND); substance, capital, estate (OWNERSHIP); attribute, quality, trait (CHARACTER).

prophecy, *n.* augury, presage, forecast (PREDICTION).

prophesy, *v.* predict, foretell, forecast (PREDICTION).

prophet, *n.* predictor, diviner, seer (PREDICTION).

propinquity, *n.* proximity, contiguity, adjacency (NEARNESS).

propitiate, *v.* placate, conciliate,

appease (PEACE, CALMNESS, ATONEMENT).

propitious, *adj.* timely, auspicious, opportune (TIMELINESS).

proponent, *n.* supporter, exponent, champion (SUPPORT).

proportion, *n.* ratio, percentage, quota (RELATIONSHIP, NUMBER); symmetry, balance (SHAPE); division, portion (PART).

proportional, *adj.* commeasurable, commensurate, proportionate (NUMBER); balanced, well-balanced, uniform, even (SHAPE).

proportions, *n.* dimensions, measurement (SIZE).

proposal, *n.* presentation, overture, proposition (OFFER).

propose, *v.* advance, broach, put forward (SUGGESTION, SUBMISSION, OFFER); aim, contemplate, intend (PURPOSE); pop the question (*colloq.*), ask for the hand of (BETROTHAL).

proposition, *n.* presentation, overture, proposal (OFFER); premise, hypothesis (REASONING).

proprietor, *n.* owner, possessor (OWNERSHIP).

PROPRIETY—*N.* propriety, legitimacy, decency, ethicality, rectitude, correctitude, justice, morality; respectability, conventionality, decorum, etiquette, politesse.

ethics, convention, conventionalities; morals, proprieties.

puritanism, prudery, rigidity, Grundyism.

puritan, prude, prig, bluenose, Grundyist, Grundyite, Mrs. Grundy.

V. be proper for, beseem, befit, behoove, suit, fit.

Adj. **proper,** appropriate, suitable, correct, legitimate, right, seemly.

[*morally proper*] **decent,** equitable, ethical, just, moral, respectable, right, righteous, rightful.

conventional, decorous, demure, moral, proper, staid.

puritanical, prim, prissy (*colloq.*), prudish, priggish, squeamish, rigid, square-toed, strait-laced.

See also CONFORMITY, COURTESY, FORMALITY, MORALITY, RIGHT, SOBRIETY. *Antonyms*—See IMPROPERNESS.

PROPULSION—*N.* propulsion, projection, push, propelment, jet propulsion.

drive, impellent, impulse, lash, urge, pressure, goad, propellant, driving force, impetus, drift.

V. propel, start, set in motion, set going, force, dash, project, throw, send, let off, fire off, discharge, shoot; launch, send forth, let fly; drive, lash, urge, goad, impel.

push, press, prod, jog, nudge, shove, slam, lunge, plunge, thrust; jab, bump, buck, bunt, butt, jostle, shoulder, nuzzle, plump, poke, ram, pack, wedge.

eject, expel, expulse, displace, dislodge, flush (*birds*), extrude, obtrude, oust, thrust out, outthrust, protrude.

repel, repulse, rebuff, retrude.

Adj. propulsive, driving, urging, impellent; projectile, ballistic; protrusible, protrusile, protractile.

See also ARMS, MOTIVATION, PRESSURE, SENDING, THROW, URGING. *Antonyms*—See RECEIVING, TRACTION.

prosaic, *adj.* plebeian, platitudinous, pedestrian (COMMONNESS); tedious, monotonous, dull (BOREDOM).

proscribe, *v.* ban, embargo, outlaw (DENIAL).

prose, *n.* speech, parlance, tongue (LANGUAGE); composition, essay, text (WRITING).

prosecute, *v.* sue, indict, put on trial (LAWSUIT); carry on, pursue, wage (CONTINUATION).

prospect, *n.* outlook, forecast (FUTURE); likelihood, probability, chance (LIKELIHOOD); vista, perspective, view (APPEARANCE, VISION).

prospective, *adj.* coming, impending (FUTURE, EXPECTATION).

prosper, *v.* thrive, flourish, bloom (SUCCESS, STRENGTH).

prosperity, *n.* opulence, affluence, luxury (WEALTH); inflation, boom, good times (BUSINESS).

prosperous, *adj.* wealthy, rich, affluent (WEALTH); palmy, thriving, booming (SUCCESS).

prostitute, *v.* desecrate, profane, pervert (MISUSE).

PROSTITUTE—*N.* prostitute, cocotte, courtesan, Cyprian, Delilah, doxy (*slang*), drab, fallen woman, fancy woman, *fille de joie* (F.), *fille de nuit* (F.), call girl, harlot, meretrix, painted woman, Paphian, quean, scarlet woman, slut, stew, strumpet, tart (*slang*), trollop, trull, whore, floozy (*slang*), woman of the town, woman of easy virtue, chippie (*slang*), harridan, streetwalker, white slave.

prostitution, harlotry, white slavery, whoredom.

house of prostitution, house, bagnio, bawdyhouse, bordel, bordello, brothel, disorderly house, house of assignation, house of ill-fame, house of ill-repute, panel den (*or* house), seraglio, stews, whorehouse.

red-light district, Yashiwara (*Jap.*), tenderloin.

procurer, pimp, pander, panderer, white slaver; procuress, bawd, madam.

V. pimp, pander, procure; solicit, whore.

Adj. whorish, sluttish, meretricious; wide-open; pornographic.

See also SEX.

prostrate, *adj.* overtired, spent (FATIGUE); powerless, helpless, impotent (WEAKNESS); flat, prone, procumbent (REST).

PROTECTION—*N.* protection, defense, preservation, conservation, salvation, safekeeping, custody; tutelage, guardianship, wardship; self-defense, self-preservation, judo, jujitsu.

safety, security, shelter, asylum, seclusion, assurance, panoply.

refuge, asylum, harbor, haven, retreat, preserve, sanctuary, shelter, coverture, covert, citadel, burrow, ark, fastness, lee, oasis.

[*fortified place*] fort, citadel, fortress, blockhouse, alcazar, redoubt; garrison, presidio, stronghold, tower, castle, château.

fortification, bastion, breastwork, earthwork, outwork, ravelin, redoubt, work, parapet, machicolation, battlement; bulwark, rampart, vallation; barricade, stockade, barrier, moat, trench, ditch.

[*protective device*] safeguard, guard, shield, screen, shutter, protector, fender, cushion, buffer, bumper.

[*against light, sun, rain, etc.*] awning, canopy, parasol, screen, shade, sunshade, umbrella, bumbershoot (*jocose*).

defense, armor, bastion, ammunition, weapon, tower, mail, armature; shield, buckler, breastplate; helmet.

protector, defender, paladin, champion, conserver, savior, messiah, shepherd, guardian, Argus, guardian angel.

guard, convoyer, escort, warden; lifeguard, bodyguard; convoy, cordon, garrison, patrol; chaperon, duenna; watchdog, Cerberus.

sentinel, lookout, sentry, picket, vedette, watch (*pl.*); watchman, warder, warden.

protégé, protégée (*fem.*), ward, client.

vaccine, inoculant, toxin-antitoxin; injection, shot; immunity, prophylaxis.

V. protect, safeguard, preserve, conserve, defend, guard, bulwark, panoply, save, secure, assure, champion, shepherd, shield, treasure, watch over, mount guard, patrol, sentinel; shelter, sheathe, shade, screen, shutter, veil, cushion, insulate, seclude; convoy, escort; harbor.

immunize, inoculate, vaccinate, variolate.

fortify, fortress, bulwark, garrison, rampart, barricade, stockade; crenelate, machicolate.

Adj. protective, preservative, conservative, conservational, defensive, guardian, custodial, tutelary, Cerberean.

protected, safe, secure, armored, bastioned, snug; impregnable, inviolable, invulnerable, unassailable; under the wing of.

fortified, walled, bastioned, battlemented, garrisoned, barricaded.

See also ARMS, CARE, COVERING, HEADGEAR, SUPPORT, WALL. *Antonyms*—See DANGER, DESERTION, RELINQUISHMENT, THREAT.

protégé, *n.* ward, dependent, pensioner (DEPENDABILITY, PROTECTION).

protest, *v.* complain, remonstrate, expostulate (COMPLAINT); object, demur (OPPOSITION).

protracted, *adj.* lengthy, long, drawn out (LENGTH).

protrude, *v.* jut, project, protuberate (VISIBILITY); extrude, obtrude, thrust out (PROPULSION).

proud, *adj.* exalted, lofty (PRIDE).

prove, *v.* demonstrate, show, testify to (PROOF); put to a test, verify, try (TEST).

proverb, *n.* saying, adage, byword (STATEMENT).

provide, *v.* furnish, supply, stock (GIVING, STORE); prepare, arrange, ready (PREPARATION); produce, turn out, yield (PRODUCTION); postulate, stipulate (CONDITION).

provide for, *v.* maintain, sustain, keep (SUPPORT).

province, *n.* orbit, realm, sphere (INFLUENCE, ACTIVITY); domain, dominion, jurisdiction (POWER); county, shire, canton (REGION).

provincial, *adj.* local, sectional, regional (SITUATION); rustic, countrified, bucolic (RURAL REGION); homely, homespun (VULGARITY); petty, small-minded, parochial (PREJUDICE).

provision, *n.* arrangement, groundwork, foundation (PREPARATION); condition, proviso, qualification (CONDITION).

provisional, *adj.* conditional, tentative, temporary (CONDITION, TEST, IMPERMANENCE).

provisions, *n.* supplies, equipment, accouterments (QUANTITY).

provocative, *adj.* exciting, intoxicating (EXCITEMENT); inspirational, suggestive, influential (MOTIVATION).

provoke, *v.* prompt, move, induce (MOTIVATION); fire, inflame (EXCITEMENT); vex, irk (ANNOYANCE, ANGER).

prow, *n.* stem, nose, bow (FRONT).

prowl, *v.* stroll, rove, roam (WANDERING).

proximity, *n.* propinquity, contiguity, adjacency (NEARNESS).

proxy, *n.* representative, surrogate, alternate (SUBSTITUTION, DEPUTY, AGENT).

prude, *n.* prig, puritan, bluenose (MODESTY, PROPRIETY).

prudence, *n.* caution, foresight (CARE); discretion, expedience (WISDOM).

prudent, *adj.* careful, cautious, discreet (CARE); judicious, expedient, politic (WISDOM); economical, frugal (ECONOMY).

prudish, *adj.* strait-laced, overmodest, prim (MODESTY); puritanical, prissy (*colloq.*), priggish, (PROPRIETY).

prune, *v.* trim, cut, shorten (SHORTNESS, CUTTING).

pry, *v.* spy, snoop, peep (LOOKING); tear, wrest, wring (TAKING, EXTRACTION); elevate, raise, lift (ELEVATION).

prying, *adj.* inquisitive, nosy (*slang*), personal (INQUIRY).

psalm, *n.* hymn, canticle, chant (SINGING, WORSHIP).

pseudo, *adj.* imitation, simulated, sham (IMITATION, SIMILARITY, PRETENSE).

pseudonym, *n.* false name, non de plume (*F.*), pen name (NAME).

psyche, *n.* soul, spirit, pneuma (SPIRITUALITY); self, ego (SELFISHNESS).

psychiatry, *n.* psychoanalysis, analysis (PSYCHOTHERAPY).

psychic, *adj.* supernatural, preternatural, occult (SUPERNATURALISM); metaphysical, supersensible, supersensual (SPIRITUALITY); telepathic, extrasensory, clairvoyant (TELEPATHY).

psychoanalysis, *n.* therapy, psychiatry, analysis (PSYCHOTHERAPY).

psychologist, *n.* social worker, case worker (PSYCHOTHERAPY).

psychopath, *n.* psychopathic personality, sociopath (NEUROSIS).

psychosis, *n.* lunacy, mental imbalance, psychopathy (INSANITY).

PSYCHOTHERAPY—*N.* psychotherapy, therapy, treatment, psychiatry, orthopsychiatry, neuropsychiatry, psychopathology, psychoanalysis, analysis, lay analysis, Freudian analysis, group therapy, hypnoanalysis, hypnotherapy, narcosynthesis; metrazol shock therapy, electrotherapy, electroshock therapy, insulin therapy; occupational therapy, bibliotherapy, play therapy; psychosomatic medicine, psychosomatics; psychodrama; mental hygiene, mental health.

psychotherapist, therapist, psychoanalyst, analyst, lay analyst, head shrinker (*slang*), psychologist, social worker, case worker, clinical psychologist; Freudian; psychiatrist, orthopsychiatrist, alienist; mental healer, mind healer.

the unconscious, the subconscious; transference, countertransference; patient, analysand.

V. psychoanalyze, analyze, treat; be psychoanalyzed, undergo analysis, be in therapy (or analysis).

Adj. psychotherapeutic, psychiatric, psychoanalytic, analytic; psychosomatic, psychogenic; Freudian.

See also INSANITY, NEUROSIS.

psychotic, *adj.* insane, psychopathic, demented (INSANITY).

psychotic, *n.* psychopath, crackpot, crackbrain, lunatic, madman (INSANITY).

puberty, *n.* adolescence, preadolescence, pubescence (FERTILITY, YOUTH).

public, *adj.* societal, general, national (PEOPLE, VULGARITY).

public, *n.* people, populace, society (PEOPLE).

PUBLICATION—*N.* publication, announcement, promulgation, propagation, proclamation, pronouncement, ventilation, divulgation; issuance, appearance.

publicity, ballyhoo, build-up (*colloq.*), puffery, *réclame* (*F.*), notoriety, limelight (*colloq.*), spotlight (*colloq.*), fame; public relations, press-agentry.

publicity agent, press agent, publicist, huckster (*derogatory*), public-relations counselor.

periodical, magazine, journal, review, digest; newspaper, paper, daily, gazette, sheet, tabloid; annual, quarterly, monthly, bimonthly; slick, pulp.

edition, issue, printing, impression; revision, new edition.

advertisement, placard, bill, flyer, throwaway, leaflet, broadside, handbill, poster, circular, notice, commercial.

the press, Fourth Estate, journalism.

news, information, intelligence, tidings; story, bulletin, item, dispatch, copy, beat, scoop, report; newscast, news report, news broadcast.

journalist, member of the press, editor, newsman, newspaperman, reporter, cub, columnist, publisher; newscaster, commentator; copy editor, proofreader.

V. publish, make public, make known, report, air, broadcast, put on the air, promulgate, spread, disseminate, propagandize; issue, print, bring out, circulate, circularize; syndicate.

be published, appear, come out, be brought out.

publicize, ballyhoo, puff, advertise, build up (*colloq.*).

See also BOOK, DISCLOSURE, INFORMATION, STORY, TREATISE, WRITER. *Antonyms*—See CONCEALMENT.

publicity, *n.* ballyhoo, build-up (*colloq.*), puffery (PUBLICATION).

publicize, *v.* ballyhoo, advertise, build up (*colloq.*), puff (PUBLICATION); emblazon, immortalize (FAME).

publish, *v.* report, air; issue, print (PUBLICATION).

pucker, *v.* purse, crease, cockle (FOLD, WRINKLE).

pudgy, *adj.* roly-poly, chunky (SIZE).

puerile, *adj.* callow, green, juvenile (IMMATURITY, YOUTH, CHILD).

puff, *n.* breath, whiff, wisp (WIND, AIR, GAS).

puff, *v.* blow, exhale, huff (BREATH, BLOWING); smoke, suck, inhale (TOBACCO); publicize, ballyhoo, advertise (PUBLICATION).

puff up, *v.* inflate, swell, distend (SWELLING); exalt, bloat (PRIDE).

puffy, *adj.* swollen, billowy, bulgy, distent (SWELLING).

pug, *adj.* snub, uptilted, upturned (NOSE, SHORTNESS).

pugnacious, *adj.* quarrelsome, combative, bellicose (FIGHTING, DISAGREEMENT).

puke, *v.* vomit, throw up, bring up (NAUSEA).

pull, *v.* haul, tow, lug (TRACTION); draw, magnetize (ATTRACTION).

pull back, *v.* draw back, retract (TRACTION).

pull down, *v.* lower, haul down (LOWNESS).

pulley, *n.* roller, caster, wheel (ROTATION).

pull in, *v.* draw in, suck, absorb (TRACTION).

pull up, *v.* pluck, uproot, extirpate (EXTRACTION).

PULP—*N.* pulp, flesh (*as of fruit*), pap, sponge, paste, pomace, mash, dough, batter, curd, grume, jam, poultice.

V. pulp, mash, squash (*colloq.*), macerate; inspissate, incrassate, gelatinate, coagulate.

Adj. pulpy, grumous, fleshy (*as fruit*), pulpous, spongy, pappy, crass, thick, gelatinous.

See also SEMILIQUIDITY, SKIN, THICKNESS. *Antonyms*—See LIQUID.

pulpit, *n.* rostrum, soapbox, podium (SUPPORT); desk, lectern (SCHOOL).

pulse, *v.* beat, pulsate, throb (RHYTHM).

pump, *v.* inflate, expand, swell (BLOWING); question, interrogate, query (INQUIRY).

pun, *n.* play upon words, *double-entendre* (*F.*), equivoque (AMBIGUITY).

punch, *v.* puncture, perforate, drill (OPENING); hit, box, cuff (HITTING).

punctual, *adj.* on time, prompt (EARLINESS).

punctually, *adv.* sharp, precisely, promptly (SHARPNESS).

punctuate, *v.* emphasize, stress, accent (IMPORTANCE); break, divide, intersect (CESSATION).

punctuation mark, *n.* period, comma, colon, etc. (WRITTEN SYMBOL).

puncture, *n.* hole, perforation, leak (OPENING).

puncture, *v.* perforate, lacerate, lance (OPENING); pierce, knife (CUTTING).

pungent, *adj.* sharp, acrid, poignant (SHARPNESS); odoriferous, tangy (ODOR); spicy, peppery, hot (TASTE); racy, salty, zestful (EXCITEMENT).

PUNISHMENT—*N.* punishment, penalty, penalization, discipline, correction, castigation; deserts, nemesis, penance; damnation, purgatory.

fine, forfeit, penalty, amende (*F.*), damages, assessment.

device for punishing: scourge, whip, ferule, rod, ruler, cane, strappado, tar and feathers, pillory, stocks, cutty stool; rack; ducking stool, cucking stool.

vengeance, revenge, requital,

payment, repayment, just deserts, retribution, wrath.

avenging spirits: Erinyes, Eumenides, Furies, Semnae (*all pl.*); Nemesis.

V. punish, penalize, discipline, correct, castigate, scourge, slate, smite, trounce; teach a lesson to, make an example of; fine, mulct, amerce.

[*punish physically*] chastise, whip, flog, ferule, chasten, bastinade, scourge, spank, beat, lash, cane; keelhaul, masthead, tar and feather, draw and quarter, strappado, impale; torture, crucify, martyrize.

avenge, revenge, requite, pay back, repay, pay off, get even with, give just deserts to.

banish, exile, transport, deport, expel, ostracize, rusticate; drum out (*esp. mil.*), dismiss, disbar, unfrock.

impose punishment, inflict, visit, impose (assess, *or* levy) a fine; sentence, condemn.

Adj. punitive, penal, punitory, corrective, disciplinary; punishing, grueling, torturous.

avenging, vengeful, wrathful, vindicatory, nemesic, retributive, revengeful, vindictive.

See also HITTING, IMPRISONMENT, RETALIATION, TORTURE. *Antonyms*—See ACQUITTAL, FREEDOM, PAYMENT (REWARD).

puny, *adj.* tiny, sawed-off, pint-size (SMALLNESS).

pupil, *n.* student, scholar, schoolboy (LEARNING); eyeball (EYE).

puppet, *n.* figurehead, cat's-paw, pawn (USE, DEPENDABILITY); doll, Teddy bear, marionette (AMUSEMENT).

puppet show, *n.* marionette show, Punch-and-Judy show (DRAMA).

purchase, *n.* footing, foothold, grasp (SUPPORT, HOLD).

PURCHASE—*N.* purchase, patronage, custom, business; buying on time, deferred payments, installment buying.

buy, bargain, steal (*colloq.*), investment.

purchaser, buyer, customer, client, patron, shopper, marketer; dealer, trader, trafficker.

customers (*collectively*), trade, patronage, custom, clientele.

V. purchase, buy, shop, market, go shopping (*or* marketing); buy from, patronize, do business with; buy back, repurchase, redeem, ransom; deal in, traffic in, trade in, truck; coempt, engross, pre-empt; invest in.

See also BRIBERY, BUSINESS, EXPENDITURE, PAYMENT, STORE. *Antonyms*—See SALE.

pure, *adj.* immaculate, taintless, spotless (CLEANNESS, PURIFICATION); virginal, chaste, virtuous (CELIBACY).

purely, *adv.* solely, simply, merely (UNITY, SMALLNESS).

purge, *v.* purify, cleanse, depurate (PURIFICATION).

PURIFICATION—*N.* purification, clarification, depuration, distillation, rarefaction, refinement; lustration, purgation, purge, sanctification, baptism.

purifier, cleanser, depurator *or* depurative, refiner, alembic.

purity, immaculacy, chastity, innocence, virginity, virtue.

V. **purify,** cleanse, clean, depurate, clarify, distill, rarefy, refine, render; ventilate, decontaminate; chasten, immaculate, lustrate, purge, sanctify, baptize; expurgate.

Adj. **pure,** clean, immaculate, intemerate, pristine, snowy, taintless, untainted; unadulterated, unalloyed, uncontaminated, undebased, unpolluted, unvitiated, unmixed, single, sheer; undefiled, inviolate, unviolated, unprofaned; spotless, unspotted, unstained, stainless, impeccable, unsmirched, unsmeared, unblackened, unblemished, unblotted, unblurred, unclouded, undarkened, unfouled, unscarred, unsoiled, unspattered, unsullied, untarnished.

chaste, innocent, intemerate, virtuous, white, virginal, angelic.

See also CLEANNESS, IMPROVEMENT, INNOCENCE, MORALITY. *Antonyms*—See IMPURITY, WICKEDNESS.

purist, *n.* precisianist, pedant, prig (RIGHT, CONFORMITY).

puritanical, *adj.* prim, prudish, strict (PROPRIETY, MORALITY).

purple, *adj.* racy, lurid, risqué (OBSCENITY); orotund, flamboyant (WORDINESS).

PURPLE—*N.* purple, etc. (see *Adjectives*); gridelin, amethyst, damson.

Adj. **purple,** violet, lilac, lilaceous, mulberry, heliotrope, mauve, violaceous, plum-colored, plum, orchid, lavender, perse, amethyst, magenta, solferino.

purplish, livid, purplescent, violescent.

purported, *adj.* soi-disant (F.), self-styled, so-called (PRETENSE).

PURPOSE—*N.* purpose, design, intention, intent, notion; fixed purpose, resolve, resolution, will, aim, ambition, goal, target, mission, object, objective, end; ulterior purpose, *arrière-pensée* (F.).

V. **purpose,** propose, aim, contemplate, determine, intend, resolve; mean, have in view, bid for, work for, aspire to, aim at, pursue.

Adj. **purposeful,** calculated, purposive, teleological, telic; intent, firm, bent, bound, decided, determined, resolute, staunch, resolved, stalwart, intense, single-minded, steady, steadfast, unwavering, undeviating.

intentional, intended, meant, aforethought, calculated, studied, premeditated, conscious, considered, deliberate, designful, voluntary, willful, witting, express.

well-intentioned, well-meaning; well-intended, well-meant.

Adv., phrases. **on purpose,** advisedly, calculatedly, consciously, deliberately, designedly, intentionally, purposely, voluntarily, willfully, wittingly, knowingly, pointedly, premeditatedly, with premeditation, in cold blood, by design.

See also DECISION, DESTINY, EXPEDIENCE, MEANING, PLAN, STUBBORNNESS, WILL. *Antonyms*—See PURPOSELESSNESS.

PURPOSELESSNESS—*N.* purposelessness, *flânerie* (F.), accident, inadvertence, chance, luck.

drifter, floater, maunderer, rolling stone, *flâneur* (F.).

Adj. **purposeless,** aimless, designless, driftless, haphazard, random, undirected, drifting, desultory, maundering, floundering.

unintentional, accidental, inadvertent, involuntary, uncalculated, unconscious, undeliberate, unintended, unmeant, unpremeditated, unthinking, unwilled, unwitting, unknowing.

Adv., phrases. **aimlessly,** haphazard, haphazardly, randomly, at random, desultorily, driftingly, maunderingly.

unintentionally, accidentally, inadvertently, involuntarily, reflexively, spontaneously, unconsciously, uncalculatedly, unpremeditatedly, unthinkingly, unwittingly, unknowingly, without premeditation, by accident, by chance, by luck.

See also NONPREPARATION, SURPRISE. *Antonyms*—See PLAN, PURPOSE.

purposely, *adv.* deliberately, designedly, intentionally (PURPOSE).

purr, *v.* feel happy, be content (HAPPINESS); curr, mew (ANIMAL SOUND).

purse, *n.* handbag, reticule, pocketbook (CONTAINER); prize, award, stake (PAYMENT).

purse, *v.* pucker, knit, crease (FOLD, WRINKLE).

purser, *n.* paymaster, cashier, teller (MONEY).

pursue, *v.* chase, dog (FOLLOWING); trail, track, trace (SEARCH); aspire to, aim at (PURPOSE).

pursuit, *n.* performance, exercise, execution (ACTION); undertaking, venture, work (UNDERTAKING); occupation, calling, career (BUSINESS); chase, hunt, quest (FOLLOWING, SEARCH).

pus, *n.* matter, purulence, suppuration (UNCLEANNESS).

push, *v.* press, nudge, shove (PROPULSION); inspire, prod, goad (MOTIVATION).

push back, *v.* repel, repulse, rebuff (PROPULSION).

push-over, *n.* child's play, smooth sailing, cinch (EASE).

pussy, *adj.* purulent, pylc, abscessed (UNCLEANNESS).

pussy, *n.* cat, feline, tabby (ANIMAL).

put, *v.* repose, set, lay (LOCATION, PLACE).

put aside, *v.* shelve, table, pigeonhole (SIDE).

put back, *v.* reinsert, return, give back (RESTORATION).

put by, *v.* salt away (*colloq.*), bank, save (STORE).

put down, *v.* write, jot down, note (WRITING); crush, quell, subdue (DEFEAT).

put in, *v.* insert, introduce, inject (INSERTION).

put off, *v.* postpone, adjourn, defer (DELAY).

put on, *v.* don, get into (CLOTHING); pretend, assume, affect (PRETENSE).

put out, *v.* extinguish, blow out, snuff out (DARKNESS); evict, oust, dispossess (DISMISSAL).

putrefy, *v.* decompose, rot, spoil (DECAY).

putrid, *adj.* decomposed, moldered, rotten (DECAY).

putter, *v.* niggle, potter, tinker (TIME).

put together, *v.* piece together, coalesce, blend (JUNCTION).

put-up, *adj.* pat, rehearsed, primed (PREPARATION).

put up with, *v.* bear with, tolerate, brook (INEXCITABILITY, SUPPORT).

puzzle, *n.* conundrum, charade, rebus (MYSTERY).

puzzle, *v.* baffle, mystify, perplex (CONFUSION, MYSTERY, UNCERTAINTY).

pygmy, *n.* midget, peewee, shrimp (SMALLNESS).

pyromaniac, *n.* arsonist, incendiary, firebug (FIRE).

Q

quack, *n.* impostor, empiric, charlatan (PRETENSE, MEDICAL SCIENCE).

quack, *v.* gabble, gobble, honk (ANIMAL SOUND).

quadruple, *adj.* fourfold, quadrigeminal, quadruplex (FOUR).

quaff, *v.* imbibe, ingurgitate, partake of (DRINK).

quagmire, *n.* morass, ooze (MARSH); predicament, mire, impasse (DIFFICULTY).

quaint, *adj.* queer, outlandish, eccentric (UNUSUALNESS).

quake, *n.* shock, convulsion, seism (EARTHQUAKE).

quake, *v.* tremble, quaver, shudder (SHAKE, FEAR).

qualification, *n.* provision, condition, stipulation (CONDITION); limitation, restriction, reservation (BOUNDARY); prerequisite, postulate (NECESSITY).

qualified, *adj.* capable, skilled (EXPERIENCE); licensed, eligible, authorized (PRIVILEGE).

qualify, *v.* enable, empower, capacitate (ABILITY, POWER); train, prepare, ground (TEACHING); temper, moderate (CHANGE, RELIEF).

quality, *n.* characteristic, property, trait (CHARACTER); rank, grade (CLASS); goodness, excellence, worth (GOOD); upper class, society (SOCIAL CLASS).

qualm, *n.* doubt, misgiving, scruple (UNCERTAINTY, FEAR); nausea, seasickness (NAUSEA).

quandary, *n.* impasse, mire, dilemma (CONDITION, DIFFICULTY).

QUANTITY—*N.* quantity, amount, number, figure, volume, sum, measure, deal, variety, batch; extent, bulk, mass, magnitude.

supply, backlog, reserve, stock, store, stockpile, hoard, accumulation, abundance, resources; adequacy, sufficiency.

supplies, equipment, accouterments, outfit, provisions, victuals, sustenance, subsistence, accommodations; munitions, ordnance (*both mil.*).

supplier, provider, furnisher, provisioner, purveyor, purveyancer, victualer, caterer, quartermaster, steward, sutler, vivandière (*F., hist.*), chandler, grocer.

science of military supply: logistics.

V. **supply,** provide, furnish, purvey, serve, administer, provision, victual, cater; equip, outfit, accouter; afford, maintain, sustain, endow, render, accommodate, dower (*with a dowry*), endue (*with a quality*); provender, forage; replenish, refill, fill up.

Adj. **quantitative,** of quantity; some, any, more or less.

See also COMPLETENESS, DEGREE, MEASUREMENT, MULTITUDE, SIZE, STORE, SUFFICIENCY. *Antonyms*—See INSUFFICIENCY.

---

quarantine, *n.* segregation, isolation, sequestration (SECLUSION).

quarrel, *n.* dispute, wrangle, brawl (DISAGREEMENT).

quarrel, *v.* argue, wrangle, bicker (DISAGREEMENT).

quarrelsome, *adj.* argumentative, contentious, belligerent (DISAGREEMENT).

quarry, *n.* quest, chase, prey (SEARCH, PLUNDER); excavation, mine (OPENING).

quarry, *v.* dig, excavate, mine (DIGGING).

quarter, *n.* lenience, clemency, mercy (FORGIVENESS, PITY); place, domain, territory (REGION); lee, face (SIDE); fourth (FOUR).

quarter, *v.* lodge, canton, board, accommodate (HABITATION).

quarterly, *adj.* trimonthly, trimestral, trimestral (TIME).

quartermaster, *n.* victualer, caterer, steward (QUANTITY).

quarters, *n.* dwellings, lodgings, rooms (HABITATION).

quartet, *n.* foursome (FOUR).

quaver, *v.* tremble, quiver, twitter (SHAKE); quake, shiver, shudder (FEAR).

quay, *n.* wharf, pier, dock, landing (BREAKWATER).

queen, *n.* czarina (*Russia*), maharani (*Moham.*), empress (RULER).

queer, *adj.* strange, quaint, peculiar (UNUSUALNESS).

quell, *v.* put down, crush, quash (DEFEAT); still, quiet, ease (CALMNESS).

querulous, *adj.* petulant, grumbly, whiny (COMPLAINT).

query, *v.* ask, question, interrogate (INQUIRY); challenge, impugn, impeach (UNBELIEVINGNESS).

quest, *n.* hunt, pursuit; quarry, prey (SEARCH).

question, *n.* interrogatory, query (INQUIRY); doubt, dubiety (UNBELIEVINGNESS); problem, issue (TOPIC).

question, *v.* ask, interrogate (INQUIRY); challenge, impugn (UNBELIEVINGNESS).

questionable, *adj.* moot, disputable, controversial (DISAGREEMENT, UNCERTAINTY); doubtful, uncertain, undecided (INQUIRY); incredible, suspect (UNBELIEVINGNESS).

quibble, *v.* argue, altercate, spar (DISAGREEMENT); sophisticate, paralogize (SOPHISTRY); fence, straddle the fence (AVOIDANCE).

quick, *adj.* rapid, speedy, accelerated (SPEED); acute, perspicacious (UNDERSTANDING).

quicken, *v.* hasten, hurry (SPEED).

quick-tempered, *adj.* inflammable, hot-tempered, excitable (ANGER, BAD TEMPER).

quick-witted, *adj.* sharp, keenminded, agile (INTELLIGENCE).

quiescent, *adj.* motionless, immobile, immovable (MOTIONLESSNESS).

quiet, *adj.* noiseless, soundless, hushed (SILENCE); inactive, stagnant, still (INACTION, MOTIONLESSNESS); peaceful, placid, restful (PEACE); private, remote, isolated (SECLUSION); orderly, docile, meek (OBEDIENCE); plain, simple, unassuming (MODESTY).

quiet, *n.* hush, still (SILENCE); ease, peace (REST).

quiet, *v.* still, hush (SILENCE); compose, calm, tranquilize (CALMNESS, PEACE); inactivate, slack, lull (INACTION).

quill, *n.* spine, spur, needle (SHARPNESS); bristle, vibrissa, feeler (HAIR).

quilt, *n.* blanket, cover, comforter (SLEEP).

quintessence, *n.* pith, essence, distillation (MATERIALITY).

quintet, *n.* cinquain, pentad (FIVE).

quip, *n.* spoof, bon mot, sally (WITTINESS); saying, epigram (STATEMENT); whimsey, crank (UNUSUALNESS).

quirk, *n.* peculiarity, eccentricity, foible (UNUSUALNESS); twist, ply (WINDING); curlicue, flourish (WRITING); quip, epigram (STATEMENT).

quit, *v.* stop, cease, desist (CESSATION); leave, drop out (RELINQUISHMENT); abandon, desert, evacuate (DEPARTURE); give up, surrender, yield (RELINQUISHMENT).

quite, *adv.* altogether, wholly, totally (COMPLETENESS).

quitter, *n.* submitter, yielder, defeatist (SUBMISSION).

quiver, *n.* holster, scabbard, sheath (CONTAINER).

quiver, *v.* quaver, twitter, thrill (SHAKE); tremble, quake, shiver (FEAR).

quiz, *v.* question, cross-examine, cross-question (INQUIRY); check, test, examine (TEST).

quizzical, *adj.* incredulous, skeptical, suspicious (UNBELIEVINGNESS); inquisitive, searching, curious (SEARCH); chaffing, joshing (TEASING); queer, quaint, erratic (UNUSUALNESS).

quota, *n.* ratio, proportion, percentage (APPORTIONMENT, NUMBER, PART).

quotation, *n.* extract, selection, citation (REPETITION, PASSAGE, EXTRACTION).

R

rabbit, *n.* bunny, cottontail, hare (ANIMAL).

rabble, *n.* mob, crowd, canaille (PEOPLE).

rabble-rouser, *n.* agitator, demagogue, instigator (DISSATISFACTION).

rabid, *adj.* radical, fanatical (EXTREMENESS); overzealous, fervent (ENTHUSIASM); furious, raging (VIOLENCE).

race, *n.* competition, contest (ATTEMPT); strain, stock (MANKIND, RELATIVE); tide, sluice (RIVER); duct, run (CHANNEL).

race, *v.* run, hurry, scamper (SPEED).

race prejudice, *n.* racism, racialism, sectarianism (PREJUDICE).

racial, *adj.* ethnic, phyletic, phylogenetic (MANKIND).

racial segregation, *n.* Jim Crow, apartheid (*South Africa*), ghettoism (SECLUSION).

racist, *n.* bigot, sectarian, anti-Semite (PREJUDICE).

rack, *n.* spreader, stretcher, extender (SPREAD, STRETCH).

racket, *n.* din, uproar, hubbub (CONFUSION, LOUDNESS); rattle, clatter (ROLL); extortion, shakedown (THIEVERY).

racking, *adj.* punishing, grueling, excruciating (PAIN).

racy, *adj.* piquant, zestful, pungent (EXCITEMENT); spicy, breezy, salty (INTERESTINGNESS); lurid, purple, risqué (OBSCENITY).

radial, *adj.* rayed, actiniform, actinoid (ROUNDNESS).

radiant, *adj.* glowing, bright, luminous (LIGHT).

radiate, *v.* proliferate, ramify (SPREAD); emit, beam, shed (GIVING).

radical, *adj.* ultraistic, rabid, fanatical (EXTREMENESS).

radical, *n.* extremist, ultraist, fanatic (EXTREMENESS).

radio, *n.* wireless, AM, FM (AMUSEMENT).

radioactivity, *n.* radiation, radiant energy (PHOTOGRAPH).

rafter, *n.* beam, joist, girder (SUPPORT).

ragamuffin, *n.* tatterdemalion, scarecrow (UNTIDINESS).

rage, *n.* fury, wrath, spleen (ANGER); storm, bluster (VIOLENCE); craze, fad, passion (DESIRE).

rage, *v.* storm, fume, boil (BAD TEMPER, ANGER); rampage, run amuck (EXCITEMENT).

ragged, *adj.* torn, shabby, seedy (TEARING); ruffled, shaggy, jagged (ROUGHNESS).

raging, *adj.* violent, furious, rabid (VIOLENCE).

ragtime, *n.* jazz, syncopation, jive (MUSIC).

raid, *n.* invasion, incursion, irruption (INGRESS); descent, foray (ATTACK).

raid, *v.* break in, breach, invade (INGRESS); storm, foray, sally (ATTACK).

rail, *n.* panel, picket, post (INCLOSURE).

rail at, *v.* scold, objurgate, rant at (SCOLDING); whip, blast (MALEDICTION).

RAIN—*N.* rain, rainfall, rainstorm, precipitation, condensation; downpour, drencher, deluge, flood, cloudburst, torrent, shower, pour, sun shower, thundershower, flurry; drizzle, sprinkle; sleet, hail; rainy season, rains, monsoon; raindrop, drop, drops; rain water; rain check; rain making, cloud seeding.

rain gauge, pluviometer, pluviograph, pluvioscope, ombrometer, ombrograph, udomograph, udometer, hyetometrograph, hyetometer, hyetograph.

science of rainfall: hyetography, hyetology; udometry, pluviometry.

rainbow, iris, sunbow, sundog.

rain god, Jupiter Pluvius; rain maker, rain doctor; Iris.

V. rain, drizzle, mist, sprinkle; teem, pour, shower; sleet, hail.

Adj. raining, drizzling, sprinkling, teeming, showering, pouring, sleeting, hailing.

rainy, wet, soppy, moisty, moist, damp, drizzly, drippy, showery, pluvial, pluvious, sleety.

See also WATER. *Antonyms*—See DRYNESS.

rainbow, *n.* iris, sunbow, sundog (RAIN).

rainbowlike, *adj.* iridescent, prismatic, opalescent (CHANGEABLENESS).

raincoat, *n.* mackintosh, oilskins, slicker (COAT).

rainless, *adj.* fair, pleasant, fine (DRYNESS).

raise, *v.* step up, lift, boost (INCREASE); elevate, erect, hoist (ELEVATION, HEIGHT, VERTICALITY); grow, plant, sow (FARMING); rear, bring up, nurture (CHILD).

rajah, *n.* maharajah, gaekwar, nizam (RULER).

rake, *n.* profligate, roué, lecher (IMMORALITY, SEX).

rake, *v.* ransack, scour, fine-comb (SEARCH); comb, card, rasp (CLEANNESS); bombard, shell (ATTACK); shelve, bank, bevel (SLOPE).

rakish, *adj.* tipsy, slanting (SLOPE); saucy, sporty (FASHION).

rally, *n.* convocation, convention, assembly (SUMMONS).

rally, *v.* muster, convene (SUMMONS); revive, resuscitate, resurrect (LIFE); refresh, rejuvenate (STRENGTH).

ram, *v.* push, poke, wedge (PROPULSION); cram, crowd, pack (FULLNESS).

ramble, *v.* stroll, meander, peregrinate (WANDERING); proliferate, ramify, radiate (SPREAD); digress (WORDINESS).

rambler, *n.* rover, roamer (WANDERING).

ramp, *n.* adit, access (APPROACH).

ramp, *v.* rear, erect, uprear (ELEVATION).

rampage, *v.* storm, rage (EXCITEMENT).

rampant, *adj.* rampageous, stormy, blustery (VIOLENCE).

rampart, *n.* fortification, bulwark, vallation (PROTECTION).

ramshackle, *adj.* unsteady, unstable, shaky (UNSTEADINESS).

ranch, *n.* farm, grange, plantation (FARMING).

rancid, *adj.* soured, turned, curdled (SOURNESS); rank, evil-smelling, rotten (ODOR).

rancor, *n.* spleen, venom, virulence (HOSTILITY).

random, *adj.* aimless, driftless, haphazard (PURPOSELESSNESS); casual, incidental (CHANCE).

range, *n.* extent, compass, magnitude (DISTANCE, LENGTH, STRETCH); latitude, sweep, play (SPACE); earshot, hearing, reach (LISTENING, SOUND); ridge, chain (HEIGHT); stove, calefactor (COOKERY, HEAT).

range, *v.* ply, make a circuit of (TRAVELING); stroll, tramp, roam (WANDERING).

rangy, *adj.* thin, reedy, spindly (THINNESS).

rank, *adj.* luxuriant, dense, exuberant (PLANT LIFE); evil-smelling, rancid, rotten (ODOR).

RANK—*N.* rank, position, sphere, station, level, grade, class, classification, estate, echelon; higher rank, majority, seniority; highest rank, paramountcy, primacy, sovereignty, supremacy; higher ranks, hierarchy.

advancement (*in rank*), promotion, upgrading, preferment, advance, skipping, skip, ascent.

[*person of high rank*] **chief,** head, leader, officer; dignitary, grandee, magnifico, major, prince; senior, superior.

[*person of lower rank*] **junior,** subordinate, inferior.

V. rank, class, classify, grade; outrank.

advance, push up, promote, upgrade, skip; rise, go up, ascend.

demote, downgrade, degrade, abase, disrate (*naval*); go down, drop, descend, fall.

Adj. [*high in rank*] senior, major, chief, leading, first, ranking, first-string, top-flight, top-drawer, paramount, premier, prime, sovereign, supreme.

[*low or lower in rank*] **junior,** minor, second-string, subordinate, inferior, rude.

See also ARRANGEMENT, ASCENT, CLASS, DESCENT, INFERIORITY, PROGRESS, SOCIAL CLASS, SUPERIORITY.

ransack, *v.* rake, scour, comb (SEARCH); loot, pillage (PLUNDER).

ransom, *v.* repurchase, redeem (PURCHASE).

rant at, *v.* objurgate, rag, rail at (SCOLDING).

rap, *v.* pat, tap (HITTING); criticize, pan (*slang*), lash (DISAPPROVAL).

rape, *n.* assault, ravishment (SEX); plunder, pillage, rapine (THIEVERY).

rape, *v.* abuse, assault, ruin, violate (SEX).

rapid, adj. quick, fast, speedy, swift, fleet (SPEED).

rapt, adj. absorbed, engrossed, intent (THOUGHT).

rapture, n. bliss, ecstasy, ravishment (HAPPINESS).

rare, adj. uncommon, scarce, infrequent (UNUSUALNESS, FEWNESS); unlikely, unheard of, inconceivable (IMPROBABILITY); thin, rarefied, tenuous (THINNESS); undercooked, underdone (COOKERY).

rarefied, adj. airy, ethereal, spiritual (SPIRITUALITY); thin, attenuated, rare (THINNESS).

rarely, adv. infrequently, seldom, scarcely, hardly (FEWNESS).

rarity, n. phenomenon, rara avis (L.), curiosity (SURPRISE); prodigy, miracle, wonderwork (UNUSUALNESS).

rascal, n. villain, imp, scamp (MISCHIEF, CHILD); knave, rogue, reprobate (DISHONESTY, DECEPTION).

rash, adj. heedless, incautious, impetuous (CARELESSNESS); reckless, brash, headlong (COURAGE).

rash, n. breakout, eruption (SKIN).

rasp, v. grate, file, raze (RUBBING); pound, bray (POWDERINESS); irritate, vex, irk (ANNOYANCE).

raspy, adj. strident, noisy, clangorous (HARSH SOUND).

rat, n. rodent, mouse (ANIMAL).

rate, n. velocity, pace, tempo (SPEED); price, quotation, figure (EXPENDITURE); tariff, toll (PAYMENT).

rate, v. evaluate, appraise, estimate (VALUE); deserve, merit (VALUE).

rather, adv. comparatively, somewhat (SMALLNESS); first, sooner, preferably (CHOICE).

ratify, v. confirm, approve, endorse (COMPACT, APPROVAL, ASSENT).

ratio, n. proportion, quota, percentage (NUMBER, APPORTIONMENT); proportionality, equation (RELATIONSHIP).

ration, n. portion, share, allotment (APPORTIONMENT).

rational, adj. sensible, sound (REASONABLENESS); thinking, thoughtful (REASONING); sane, lucid, normal (SANITY); advisable, well-advised (WISDOM).

rationalization, n. excuse, alibi (colloq.), defense (FORGIVENESS).

rattle, n. racket, clatter, clangor (ROLL).

rattle, v. hiss, blow (ANIMAL SOUND); bewilder, muddle, nonplus (UNCERTAINTY).

rattrap, n. morass, quagmire, pitfall (TRAP).

raucous, adj. inharmonious, scrannel, cacophonous (HARSH SOUND).

ravage, v. dilapidate, desolate, devastate (DESTRUCTION); gut, loot, pillage (PLUNDER).

rave, v. go mad, become delirious, wander (INSANITY); rant, prate, prattle (ABSURDITY); effervesce, bubble (EXCITEMENT); enthuse (colloq.), rhapsodize (ENTHUSIASM).

ravel, v. plait, raddle, wattle (WINDING); unwind, untwist, disentangle (STRAIGHTNESS).

ravenous, adj. hungry, starving, famished (HUNGER); greedy, voracious, rapacious (GREED).

ravine, n. chasm, gorge, flume (CHANNEL, DEPTH).

ravings, n. wanderings, raving, deliration (INSANITY).

ravish, v. rape, abuse, violate (SEX); kidnap, abduct, shanghai (THIEVERY).

raw, adj. immature, unbaked, callow (IMMATURITY); inexperienced, green, untrained (INEXPERIENCE); crude, unrefined (NATURALNESS); bleak, bitter, biting (COLD); wind-swept, exposed (WIND); vulgar, pornographic (OBSCENITY); undercooked, underdone, uncooked (COOKERY).

ray, n. beam, stream, streak (LIGHT); flicker, gleam, spark (SMALLNESS).

rayed, adj. actiniform, actinoid, radial (ROUNDNESS).

reach, n. range, span, magnitude (DISTANCE, LENGTH, STRETCH); latitude, sweep, play (SPACE).

reach, v. get to, gain (ARRIVAL); catch up to, overtake (TRAP).

REACTION—N. reaction, response, reagency, reverberation, echo, re-echo, repercussion, revulsion, chain reaction, delayed reaction, double-take; boomerang, backfire; backlash, recoil, rebound, kick; reactivity; reactology, psychology; reactor, reagent, reagency.

V. react, respond, reverberate, echo, re-echo; boomerang, backfire, recoil, rebound, fly back.

Adj. reacting, reactive, reactional, responsive, sensitive, susceptible.

See also JUMP, REVERSION, SENSITIVENESS. Antonyms—See INSENSIBILITY, INSENSITIVITY.

reactionary, adj. standpat, diehard, Philistine (OPPOSITION).

readily, adv. freely, gladly, cheerfully (WILLINGNESS).

READING—N. reading, perusal, skimming, etc. (see Verbs); interpretation, rendition, translation; text, body, material; recital; [*teaching of reading*] phonics.

eye movements, saccadic movements, fixation, interfixation; recognition span, eye span, macular image, peripheral image; tachistoscope, Flashmeter.

reading difficulties: word blindness, alexia, paralexia, strephosymbolia.

reader, bookworm, browser, peruser, skimmer; censor; editor, proofreader, copy editor; lip reader.

V. **read,** peruse, pore over, study, con, spell out; browse, scan, thumb through, leaf through, thumb, skim, turn the pages; censor, edit, revise; interpret, render, translate; misread, misinterpret, misunderstand; lip-read; read aloud, say, pronounce, speak.

Adj. **readable,** clear, legible, decipherable, understandable, smooth, flowing, simple.

well-read, literate, bookish, learned, studious, scholarly; thumbed, dog-eared.

unread, unlettered, illiterate, unschooled.

unreadable, illegible, undecipherable.

See also CLARITY, IGNORANCE, KNOWLEDGE, LEARNING, MISINTERPRETATION, UNDERSTANDING. *Antonyms* —See WRITING.

---

ready, *adj.* available, unlimbered, prepared (PREPARATION); willing, game (*colloq.*), prompt (WILLINGNESS).

ready, *v.* prepare, arrange, provide (PREPARATION).

real, *adj.* authentic, factual, genuine (REALITY); material, substantial, concrete (TOUCH).

real estate, *n.* realty, property (LAND).

realism, *n.* fidelity, naturalism, verism (REALITY).

realistic, *adj.* practical, unromantic, down-to-earth (REALITY).

REALITY—*N.* reality, actuality, fact, verity; entity, matter, object, phenomenal, phenomenon, substance, substantial, substantive, concrete.

realness, authenticity, factuality, actuality, truth; corporeality, corporeity, materiality, objectivity, palpability, phenomenality, physicality, substantiality, tangibility.

science of reality: ontology; philosophy, metaphysics; transcendentalism.

[*in literature and art*] realism,

fidelity, graphicalness, naturalism, Zolaism, verism.

fact, datum (*pl. data*), statistic, actuality; accomplished fact, *fait accompli* (*F.*); statistics, vital statistics; statistician.

V. **make real,** actualize, corporealize, materialize; realize; assume as real, hypostatize *or* hypostasize.

Adj. **real,** authentic, factual, genuine, simon-pure, veritable; the McCoy, the real McCoy (*both slang*).

actual, concrete, corporeal, material, objective, palpable, phenomenal, physical, sensible, substantial, substantive, tangible.

factual, phenomenal, true, valid, veritable, *de facto* (*L.*).

unpretended, candid, frank, genuine, simplehearted, sincere, single, true, unaffected, unashamed, undissembled, undissimulated, unfaked, unfeigned.

realistic, practical, unromantic, feet-on-the-ground, down-to-earth; naturalistic.

See also BODY, MATERIALITY, NATURALNESS, TRUTH. *Antonyms*—See FALSENESS, IMITATION, MAGIC, PRETENSE, SUPERNATURALISM, UNREALITY.

---

realize, *v.* know, conceive, appreciate (KNOWLEDGE); gain, acquire, accomplish (ACQUISITION, RECEIVING); actualize, corporealize, materialize (REALITY).

realm, *n.* domain, orbit, province (INFLUENCE, POWER); place, zone, ground (REGION).

ream, *v.* widen, broaden, expand (WIDTH); skim, top, cream (REMOVAL).

reanimate, *v.* revivify, re-create, regenerate (LIFE).

reap, *v.* plow, harrow, harvest (FARMING); acquire, gather, get (ACQUISITION, RESULT).

reappear, *v.* recur, return (REPETITION).

rear, *v.* raise, bring up, breed (CHILD); set up, raise up, erect (VERTICALITY); jump, leap, rise (ASCENT).

REAR—*N.* rear, back, posterior, hind part, hindmost part, hind, hindquarters, dorsum (*anat.*), tergum (*anat.*), dorsal region, withers, loins; small of the back; behind, reverse, tail; rearward, rear rank, rear guard; background, setting; afterpart, stern, poop; tailpiece, heel, heelpiece; back door, postern, postern door; rumble, rumble seat; occiput (*tech.*); nape, scruff.

rump, backside, rear end, rear, tail (*slang*), can (*slang*), bum (*vulgar*), behind, buttocks, breech, prat (*slang*), fundament, seat, bottom; croup, crupper; buttock, cheek; haunch.

tail, brush (*of a fox*), scut (*as of a hare*), flag (*as of a setter*), dock, caudal appendage, cauda (*tech.*), empennage (*of an airplane*, F.).

wake, train, trail, track, path, trace.

V. be behind, bring up the rear, fall astern; heel, tag, shadow, follow, pursue; turn the back, tergiversate.

Adj. rear, back, hindermost, hindmost, hindhand, hind, after, mizzen (*naut.*), rearmost, postern, tail, stern, behind, reverse, astern; backward, rearward, tailfirst; tandem; posterior, hinder, caudal (*anat.*), dorsal, tergal (*anat.*); tergiversatory, tergiversant.

Adv., phrases. behind, in the rear (or background), tandem, in the wake, at the heels of; aft, abaft, astern, rearward, backward; caudad, caudalward (*anat.*).

See also END, FOLLOWING. *Antonyms*—See BEGINNING, FRONT.

---

reason, n. purpose, root, basis (CAUSATION, MOTIVATION).

reason, v. think out, figure out (REASONING); analyze, conclude, deduce (THOUGHT).

REASONABLENESS—N. reasonableness, justifiability, legitimacy, logic, logicality, moderateness, rationality, sanity, sensibleness, soundness, temperateness, validity, plausibility.

V. make reasonable, keep within reason, temper, moderate; justify, explain.

Adj. reasonable, justifiable, fair, legitimate, logical, moderate, philosophical, rational, sane, sensible, sound, temperate, valid, plausible.

See also EXPLANATION, IMPARTIALITY, MODERATENESS. *Antonyms*—See EXTREMENESS, PREJUDICE.

REASONING—N. reasoning, analysis, ratiocination, generalization, induction, deduction, syllogization, apriority; conclusion, inference, corollary, illation, analogism, dianoetic, rationalization, rationalism, rationale, consecution; logic, dialectics or dialectic, argumentation, syllogistics, syllogism; premise, proposition, hypothesis.

reasoner, logician, dialectician, syllogist, ratiocinator, analogist, rationalist, rationalizer.

V. reason, reason out, think out, figure out, conclude, decide, infer, deduce or deduct, induce; ratiocinate, analyze, syllogize, analogize, philosophize.

Adj. reasoning, thinking, thoughtful, rational, rationalistic, ratiocinative, analytical or analytic, dianoetic; inductive, a posteriori (*L.*), deductive, inferential, illative, a priori (*L.*), corollary; logical, syllogistic, dialectic or dialectical.

valid, sound, legitimate, relevant, germane.

Adv., phrases. therefore, hence, as a deduction, consequently, accordingly, ergo (*L.*); thus, so, wherefore, then, thence, whence.

finally, lastly, in conclusion, in fine, after all, on the whole.

See also DECISION, JUDGMENT, THOUGHT. *Antonyms*—See INTUITION, SOPHISTRY.

---

reassure, v. hearten, inspire, encourage (COURAGE); assure, convince (CERTAINTY).

rebate, n. repayment, refund, reimbursement (PAYMENT); discount, allowance (DEDUCTION).

rebate, v. repay, refund, reimburse (PAYMENT); restore, return, render (GIVING).

rebel, n. insurgent, insurrectionist, revolter (DISOBEDIENCE); Guelph, iconoclast (OPPOSITION).

rebel, v. insurrect, mutiny, revolt (DISOBEDIENCE).

rebellion, n. insurrection, revolt, revolution, mutiny (DISOBEDIENCE).

rebellious, adj. insubordinate, insurgent, insurrectionary (DISOBEDIENCE).

rebirth, n. recreation, renaissance (BIRTH).

rebound, v. jump back, recoil, carom (JUMP); backfire, boomerang (REACTION); reverberate, redound, resound (REPETITION).

rebuff, v. repel, repulse (PROPULSION, DENIAL).

rebuild, v. reconstruct, reconstitute, reproduce (RESTORATION).

rebuke, v. censure, reprimand, reproach (DISAPPROVAL, SCOLDING).

rebut, v. refute, negate, negative (DISPROOF).

recalcitrant, adj. resistant, resistive (DEFIANCE).

recall, v. remember; recollect, bethink oneself (MEMORY); revoke, repeal (SUMMONS, INEFFECTIVENESS).

recant, v. retract, backtrack (APOSTASY, REVERSION).

recapitulate, v. restate, reword, rephrase (REPETITION).

recast, *v.* remodel, reform, reshape (CHANGE, SHAPE).

recede, *v.* ebb, retreat (REVERSION).

receipt, *n.* reception, recipience, acceptance; acknowledgment, voucher (RECEIVING).

RECEIVING—*N.* receiving, reception, receipt, recipience, receptivity, acceptance, inheritance; inhalation, suction, immission.

swallowing, deglutition, ingurgitation, resorption; swallow, gulp.

receiver, recipient, inheritor, heir (heiress, *fem.*), beneficiary, donee, grantee, fence (*of stolen goods*); treasurer, teller, cashier, collector; receptionist, greeter.

receipt, acknowledgment, voucher, acquittance; recipe.

receipts, income, revenue, earnings, returns, proceeds, take (*slang*), gate (*colloq.*).

V. **receive,** get, take in, inherit, make, realize, relay, accept, come by, take, catch, pocket; greet, welcome, admit, entertain; show in, usher in, let in; initiate; receipt, acknowledge.

be received, come in, come to hand, go into one's pocket; accrue.

give entrance to, give the entrée, introduce; import, bring in; absorb, ingest, drink in, assimilate, imbibe; instill, implant, induct, inhale.

swallow, gulp, gulp down, ingurgitate, consume, englut, bolt, devour, gorge, gobble, gobble up, glut, wolf, suck in (*or* up), drink, swig, swill, pouch, resorb, engulf (*fig*).

Adj. **receivable,** receptible, inheritable, realizable, acceptable, welcome.

receiving, recipient, receptive, open-minded, interested; absorbent, absorptive.

See also ACCEPTANCE, ACQUISITION, DRINK, INCLUSION, INHERITANCE, INTAKE, PAYMENT, SOCIALITY, TAKING. *Antonyms*—See EXPENDITURE, GIVING, PROPULSION.

recent, *adj.* new, fresh (NEWNESS); latter, latter-day (PAST).

receptacle, *n.* holder, hopper, vessel (CONTAINER).

reception, *n.* receipt, recipience, acceptance (RECEIVING); party, gathering (SOCIALITY).

receptive, *adj.* recipient, open-minded, interested (RECEIVING).

recess, *n.* interlude, intermission, pause (TIME, CESSATION); break, respite (REST); slot, socket, niche (OPENING, HOLLOW).

recesses, *n.* insides, penetralia (*pl.*), bowels (INTERIORITY).

recession, *n.* deflation, shakeout, slump (BUSINESS).

recessive, *adj.* reserved, shy, shrinking (SECLUSION, MODESTY).

recipe, *n.* receipt, formula, procedure (METHOD).

recipient, *n.* receiver, inheritor, beneficiary (RECEIVING).

reciprocal, *adj.* give-and-take, correlative, interchangeable (EXCHANGE, SUBSTITUTION); mutual, interdependent (RELATIONSHIP).

reciprocate, *v.* render, requite, return (GIVING).

reciprocity, *n.* repayment, requital (RECOMPENSE).

recital, *n.* concert, musicale (MUSIC).

recitation, *n.* lesson, lecture, exercise (TEACHING).

recite, *v.* parrot, chant, quote (REPETITION); speak, declaim (TALK); itemize, recount (TALK).

reckless, *adj.* heedless, unwary, incautious (CARELESSNESS); rash, daring, brash (COURAGE).

reckon, *v.* calculate, cipher, figure (COMPUTATION); count, enumerate, tally (NUMBER); judge, conclude (OPINION).

reckon on, *v.* aim for, bargain for, count on (PLAN).

reclaim, *v.* reform, regenerate (IMPROVEMENT); recover, redeem, retrieve (RESTORATION).

recline, *v.* lie, loll, sprawl (REST).

recluse, *n.* solitaire, hermit, monk (SECLUSION, ASCETICISM).

recognize, *v.* see, comprehend, understand (KNOWLEDGE); recall, recollect (MEMORY).

recoil, *n.* backlash, reaction, repercussion (REVERSION).

recoil, *v.* jump back, rebound, carom (JUMP); backfire, boomerang (REACTION); demur, stick at, refuse (UNWILLINGNESS); shrink, flinch, quail (REVERSION, HATRED).

recollect, *v.* remember, recall (MEMORY).

recommend, *v.* suggest, advise, exhort (SUGGESTION).

recommendation, *n.* reference, certificate, testimonial (APPROVAL).

RECOMPENSE—*N.* recompense, payment, compensation, indemnification, redress, restitution, solatium; reparation, amende (*F.*), amende honorable (*F.*), amende profitable (*F.*), amends, atonement, expiation, propitiation (*rel.*), redemption, satisfaction, retrieval, retrievement; recovery, recoupment; overcompensation.

repayment, payment in kind, reciprocation, reciprocity, requital, requitement, retribution, *quid pro quo* (*L.*), retort.

V. recompense, pay, compensate for, indemnify, redress, requite; countervail, offset, equalize, balance, counterpoise, counterbalance, square; overcompensate; make amends, make amends for, make up for, atone, atone for, expiate, propitiate (*rel.*). satisfy, give satisfaction for, retrieve, redeem; recover, recoup.

See also ATONEMENT, GIVING, PAYMENT, WEIGHT.

---

reconcile, v. adjust, accord, attune (HARMONY); propitiate, placate, conciliate (PEACE).

reconciled, adj. resigned, submissive, defeatist (SUBMISSION).

reconcile oneself, v. accede, resign oneself, abide (SUBMISSION).

recondite, adj. esoteric, cabalistic, mystical (CONCEALMENT); littleknown, obscure (KNOWLEDGE).

recondition, v. refurbish, rehabilitate (RESTORATION).

reconnaissance, n. survey, observation, reconnoiter (EXAMINATION).

reconsideration, n. mature thought, afterthought, reflection (THOUGHT).

reconstruct, v. reconstitute, rebuild, reproduce (RESTORATION); remodel, recast, remold (CHANGE); re-establish, refashion, reorganize (IMPROVEMENT).

record, n. note, memo (RECORD); maximum, ceiling (SUPERIORITY).

record, v. register, enter, inscribe (LIST, RECORD).

RECORD—N. record, note, memorandum, memo, script, transcript; diary, journal, minutes, ship's log; annals, archives, chronicle, almanac, registry, report, scroll.

phonograph record, disc, platter, release, pressing, recording, transcription; album; tape, wire; disc jockey, discographer, discophile.

recorder, annalist, archivist, diarist, scribe, historian, chronicler; clerk, secretary, recording secretary, registrar; tape recorder, wire recorder, phonograph.

record book, notebook, memorandum book, diary, daybook, journal; bulletin, bulletin board, scoreboard, score sheet; card index, file.

V. record, put on record, chronicle, report, enter, post, jot down, note, write; transcribe.

See also ACCOUNTS, DESCRIPTION, LIST, MEMORY, PAPER, PAST, SIGNA-

TURE, TIME MEASUREMENT, WRITER, WRITING.

---

recount, v. itemize, recite, relate (TALK).

recourse, n. resort, resource, refuge (AID, DEPENDABILITY).

recover, v. regain, get back, reacquire (ACQUISITION); reclaim, redeem, retrieve (RESTORATION); rally, recuperate, convalesce (HEALTH).

recreation, n. pastime, sport (AMUSEMENT); rebirth, regeneration (BIRTH).

recrimination, n. counteraccusation, countercharge (ACCUSATION).

rectify, v. remedy, correct, redress (CURE, RESTORATION, RIGHT).

rectitude, n. integrity, probity, honor (RIGHT, HONESTY).

recumbent, adj. lying, accumbent, decumbent (REST).

recuperate, v. rally, recover, convalesce (HEALTH).

recur, v. reappear, return (OCCURRENCE, REPETITION, REVERSION).

recurrent, adj. regular, periodic, repeated (OCCURRENCE).

red, n. communist, pink (GOVERNMENT).

RED—N. red, crimson, ruby, scarlet, vermilion, minium, cardinal, carmine, cherry, cerise, wine, murrey; blood red, incarnadine; brownish red, maroon, terra cotta, copper; puce.

pink, rose, coral, fuchsia, apricot, peach, tea rose, salmon; flesh, flesh color, carnelian, incarnadine.

redness, erubescence, rubedity, rubescence, rubricity.

blue or purple reds: burgundy, carmine, carnation, claret, crimson, dahlia, fuchsia, gridelin, heliotrope, hellebore red, hyacinth, lilac, magenta, mallow, mauve, solferino.

yellow reds: blossom, orange, tangerine, tea rose, titian, Venetian pink.

redness of complexion: high color, ruddiness, rosiness, floridness or floridity, rubicundity; glow, bloom, blush, flush, rubescence, erubescence; inflammation, erythema.

V. redden, ruby, vermilion, crimson, carmine, incarnadine, ruddle, rubric; rouge; rubricate or rubricize (*a manuscript, etc.*).

blush, redden, crimson, mantle, flush, color; glow, bloom.

Adj. red, carmine, incarmined, cerise, cherry, crimson, incarnadine, pink, puce, ruby, scarlet, vermilion, wine-colored, rubescent, erubescent, rubineous; blood-red, hematic, sanguine; beet-red, brick-red, flame-colored.

pink, rose, rose-colored, rosy, roseate, coral, coralline, fuchsia, apricot, peach, tea-rose, salmon, salmon-colored; flesh-color, flesh-colored, incarnadine.

brownish-red, maroon, terra-cotta, rufous; rust-colored, ferruginous, rubiginous, rubiginose.

bluish-red, carmine, claret, crimson, fuchsia, hyacinthine, lilac or lilaceous, magenta, mauve, purple.

yellowish-red, orange, carroty, rufous, sandy, tea-rose.

reddish, carnelian, carroty, copper, coppery, erubescent, puce, rubedinous, rubescent, rubicund, rubricose, ruddy, rufescent, rufous.

red-complexioned, red-faced, high-colored, rosy, blooming, glowing, ruddy, ruddy-faced, ruddy-complexioned, florid, flush, flushed, rubicund, sanguine, blowzy, blowzed; inflamed, erythematous.

blushing, ablush, blushful, crimson, flush, aflush, red, red-faced, rosy, rubescent, erubescent.

red-haired, auburn, auburn-haired, chestnut, carroty, red-headed, sandy, sandy-haired, titian.

See also HAIR, SKIN.

redeem, v. repurchase, ransom (PURCHASE); reclaim, recover, retrieve (RESTORATION); balance, counterweight, offset (WEIGHT, RECOMPENSE).

red-haired, adj. auburn, chestnut, sandy (RED).

red-handed, adj. or adv. in flagrante delicto (L.), caught in the act (GUILT, ACTION).

red-letter, adj. memorable, unforgettable, indelible (MEMORY).

red-light district, n. Yashiwara (Jap.), tenderloin (PROSTITUTE).

redolent, adj. remindful, suggestive, reminiscent (MEMORY, SUGGESTION).

redress, n. payment, compensation, indemnification (RECOMPENSE); reparation, rectification, correction (RELIEF).

redress, v. remedy, correct, rectify (RIGHT, RELIEF, CURE).

redskin, n. American Indian, Amerind, red man (MANKIND).

red-tape, n. officialism, beadledom, Bumbledom (OFFICIAL).

reduce, v. diminish, lessen, cut (DECREASE); subjugate, defeat, overcome (SLAVERY).

redundant, adj. tautological, pleonastic (WORDINESS).

reedy, adj. stringy, spindly, spindling (LENGTH); soft, small, thin (WEAKNESS).

reef, n. bank, ledge, cay (LAND).

reek, v. smell, stink (ODOR).

reel, n. spool, bobbin (ROTATION).

reel, v. totter, falter, lurch (UNSTEADINESS, ROLL, OSCILLATION).

reel in, v. retract, pull back, draw back (TRACTION).

reeling, adj. giddy, lightheaded, whirling (DIZZINESS).

re-establish, v. restore, replace, reinstate (RESTORATION).

referee, n. arbitrator, arbiter, umpire (JUDGE).

reference, n. allusion, advertence, innuendo (TALK); recommendation, certificate, tribute (APPROVAL).

referendum, n. ballot, suffrage, plebiscite (VOTE).

refer to, v. advert to, allude to, harp on (TALK); relate to, bear upon, regard (RELATIONSHIP).

refine, v. purify, clarify, rarefy (PURIFICATION); sensitize, irritate, sharpen (SENSITIVENESS).

refined, adj. civilized, cultivated, cultured (IMPROVEMENT); tasteful, aesthetic, graceful (TASTE, ELEGANCE).

refinement, n. depuration, distillation, rarefaction (PURIFICATION); discrimination, discernment, judgment (TASTE); grace, polish, finish (ELEGANCE, BEAUTY); cultivation, culture, civilization (IMPROVEMENT).

reflect, v. cogitate, deliberate, contemplate (THOUGHT); simulate, copy, mirror (IMITATION); revert, reverse, turn back (TURNING).

reflection, n. thinking, cogitation, consideration (THOUGHT); image, likeness, simulacrum (SIMILARITY).

reflective, adj. thoughtful, pensive, meditative (THOUGHT).

reflect on, v. discredit, disgrace, dishonor (DISREPUTE).

reflector, n. mirror, glass, looking-glass (VISION).

reflexive, adj. unwilled, involuntary, reflex (WILL).

reform, v. remodel, reclaim, regenerate (IMPROVEMENT); recast, reshape (SHAPE).

reformatory, n. prison, reform school (IMPRISONMENT).

reformer, n. reformist, progressive (IMPROVEMENT).

refrain, n. burden (of a song), ritornel (mus.), chorus (REPETITION).

refrain, v. avoid, forbear, forgo (AVOIDANCE, INACTION); be temperate, abstain (SOBRIETY); desist, quit, stop (CESSATION).

refresh, v. reinvigorate, rejuvenate, restore (NEWNESS, STRENGTH); renew, renovate, remodel (RESTORATION).

refrigerate, v. chill, cool (COLD).

refuge, n. haven, asylum, sanctuary (PROTECTION); recourse, resort, resource (DEPENDABILITY).

refugee, n. maroon, deserter, runaway (DEPARTURE).

refund, v. repay, rebate, reimburse (PAYMENT).

refurbish, v. renew, renovate, modernize (NEWNESS); rehabilitate, furbish, recondition (RESTORATION).

refusal, n. no, declination, declension (DENIAL).

refuse, n. waste, garbage, slops (UNCLEANNESS, REMAINDER).

refuse, v. decline (DENIAL); demur, stick at, recoil (UNWILLINGNESS).

refute, v. disprove, controvert, rebut (DENIAL, DISPROOF).

refuted, adj. exploded, discarded, rejected (MISTAKE).

regain, v. recover, get back, retrieve (ACQUISITION).

regal, adj. royal, sovereign, princely (RULER).

regalia, n. insignia (pl.), paraphernalia, decorations (ROD, INDICATION).

regard, n. reverence, veneration, worship (RESPECT).

regard, v. esteem, honor, revere (RESPECT); scan, contemplate (LOOKING); relate to, refer to, bear upon (RELATIONSHIP).

regards, n. respects, devoirs, compliments (RESPECT).

regenerate, v. revivify, reanimate, re-create (LIFE); rejuvenate, reinvigorate, refresh (STRENGTH).

regent, n. vicegerent, viceroy, vicar (DEPUTY, RULER).

regime, n. tenure, incumbency, rule, (TIME, GOVERNMENT).

regiment, n. battalion, squadron, company (FIGHTER).

REGION—N. region, sphere, realm, zone, ground, area, tract, space, place, arena, clearing, domain, territory, quarter, scene, terrain (mil.), locality, locale, spot, location, situation, part.

county, shire, canton, province, department, commune, district, parish, diocese, township, ward, precinct, bailiwick; walk, march, beat; principality, duchy, palatinate, archduchy, dukedom, dominion, colony, commonwealth, country; kingdom, empire.

Adj. regional, sectional, local,

parochial; regionalistic, regionary, insular, provincial.

See also HABITATION, LAND, LOCATION, PLACE, PREJUDICE, SPACE.

register, n. roll, roster, scroll (NAME, ROLL, LIST).

register, v. enter, record, inscribe (LIST, BOOK); sign up, enroll, subscribe (SIGNATURE).

registrar, n. recorder, clerk (RECORD, WRITER).

regress, v. revert, relapse, backslide (REVERSION).

REGRET—N. regret, regrets, compunction, contrition, penitence, remorse, repentance, sorrow; apology, apologies.

V. regret, be sorry for, bewail, repent, rue, deplore, lament, mourn; apologize.

Adj. regretful, full of regret, sad, sorry, rueful, compunctious, contrite, penitent, repentant, remorseful; apologetic.

regrettable, deplorable, lamentable, unfortunate.

See also ATONEMENT, PENITENCE, SADNESS. Antonyms—See IMPENITENCE, SATISFACTION.

regular, adj. well-regulated, orderly (CONFORMITY); common, ordinary, typical (COMMONNESS); set, stock, established (HABIT); uniform, periodic, routine (UNIFORMITY, OCCURRENCE); symmetrical, well-balanced, even (UNIFORMITY, SHAPE).

regulate, v. govern, manage, determine (CONTROL); adjust, time (TIME); true, true up (TRUTH).

regulation, n. principle, law, ordinance (RULE, LAW, COMMAND).

rehabilitate, v. refurbish, furbish, recondition (RESTORATION).

rehash, v. revamp, recast, revise (NEWNESS); rephrase, restate (EXPLANATION).

rehearse, v. repeat, practice (REPETITION); itemize, recite, recount (TALK).

reign, n. regime, incumbency, tenure (GOVERNMENT, TIME).

reign, v. govern, hold sway (GOVERNMENT, RULE); prevail, dominate (PRESENCE).

reigning, adj. ruling, regnant, sovereign (GOVERNMENT); obtaining, dominant, predominant (PRESENCE).

reimburse, v. repay, rebate, refund (PAYMENT).

rein, n. leash, bridle, deterrent (RESTRAINT, CONTROL).

reincarnation, n. transmigration, palingenesis (SPIRITUALITY).

reinvigorate, v. regenerate, rejuvenate, refresh (STRENGTH).

reiterate, v. repeat, iterate, ingeminate (REPETITION).

reject, n. scrap, discard, cast-off (UNCLEANNESS, ELIMINATION).

reject, v. discard, get rid of, scrap (ELIMINATION); refuse, disdain, spurn (DENIAL); disbelieve, discredit (UNBELIEVINGNESS).

rejoice, v. revel, exult; delight, enchant (HAPPINESS); pride oneself (CONGRATULATION).

rejuvenate, v. refresh, revitalize, restore (STRENGTH, NEWNESS, LIFE).

relapse, n. recurrence, repetition, recrudescence (OCCURRENCE).

relapse, v. backslide, regress (REVERSION).

RELATIONSHIP—N. relationship, relation, connection, affiliation, alliance, association, consociation, interrelation, interrelationship, interdependence, interconnection, correlation, contingency, dependence or dependency, mutuality, reciprocity; concern, bearing, pertinence or pertinency, reference, linkage, link; close relationship, intimacy, communion, affinity, liaison, sympathy, bonds of sympathy, contact, terms, friendly terms; union, unity, integration.

ratio, proportion, commensurateness, proportionality, proportionateness, equation.

[*related thing or person*] **correlate,** consociate, associate, cognate, congener, cousin, dependent, reciprocal.

V. **relate,** connect, ally, consociate; interrelate, interdepend, interconnect, correlate, depend; unite, integrate, link; bracket, group, associate; adjust, orient or orientate.

relate to, refer to, bear upon, regard, concern, touch, affect, pertain to, belong to, appertain to.

recount, narrate, tell, recite, rehearse, report, state, describe, detail.

Adj. **related,** connected, affiliated, allied, associated, consociate, connatural; interrelated, interdependent, interconnected, correlative, contingent, dependent, mutual, reciprocal, equiparent (*logic*); proportional, proportionate, commensurate.

relative, pertaining, referring, referential, connective, relating to, belonging to, referable to, in respect to, with reference to; germane, relevant, pertinent, applicable, in the same category; comparative, comparable.

Prep., phrases. **concerning,** as regards, respecting, pertaining to, with regard to, as to, as for, with relation to, anent, about, in respect to, in (or with) reference to, in connection with, in the matter of.

See also AGREEMENT, COMPARISON, DEPENDABILITY, DESCRIPTION, JUNCTION, PERTINENCE, RELATIVE, SIMILARITY, UNITY. *Antonyms*—See DISJUNCTION, IRRELATION.

RELATIVE—N. relative, relation, cognate, agnate, collateral, consanguinean, kinsman, kinswoman, sib, clansman; cousin, first cousin, full cousin, own cousin, cousingerman, cater-cousin; second cousin, etc.; nephew, nepote; uncle, aunt, etc.

relationship (*by blood or family*), consanguinity, collaterality, kindred, kindredship, kinship; filiation, affiliation, agnation, cognation, lineality, direct descent; avunculate.

family, line, lineage, house; kin, kith, kindred, kinfolk, kinfolks, kinsfolk, sib, sept (*anthropol.*), blood group; clan, tribe, gens (*ancient Rome*), phratry (*ancient Greece*); race, stock, strain, breed.

brother, blood brother, brother-german, sib (*genetics*), sibling, twin brother, twin; younger brother, cadet; half brother, step-brother, brother-in-law; brothers, brethren; brotherhood, fraternity.

sister, sibling, sib (*genetics*), sister-german, twin sister, twin; half sister, stepsister, sister-in-law; sisterhood.

Adj. **related** (*by blood or family*), cognate, collateral, consanguineous, consanguine, agnate, agnatic, kindred, lineal; unilateral, bilateral; affinal (*by marriage*).

familial, gentilitial, gentilitious, kindred.

tribal, racial, gentile, gentilic, gentilitian, phyletic.

[*pert. to a family member*] **brotherly,** fraternal; sisterly, sororal; filial; fatherly, paternal, motherly, maternal, parental, ancestral; nepotal (*nephew*), avuncular (*uncle*), noverical (*stepmother*).

See also ANCESTRY, BIRTH, CHILD, RELATIONSHIP. *Antonyms*—See IRRELATION.

relax, v. slack, slacken (LOOSENESS); modify, modulate, remit (WEAKNESS, RELIEF); lose speed, (SLOWNESS); bend, give, yield (SOFTNESS); thaw, unbend (FREEDOM); take it easy, take time out (REST).

release, *v.* unloose, undo, unfasten (FREEDOM, LOOSENESS); exempt, excuse, relieve (FREEDOM).

relent, *v.* yield, relax, give in (SOFTNESS); have mercy, give quarter (PITY).

relentless, *adj.* unmerciful, pitiless, merciless (CRUELTY); obdurate, inexorable, implacable (INSENSITIVITY); stubborn, unbending, unrelenting (STUBBORNNESS); persistent, tenacious (CONTINUATION).

relevant, *adj.* germane, material, applicable (PERTINENCE, RELATIONSHIP).

reliable, *adj.* dependable, responsible, stable (DEPENDABILITY); believable, trustworthy (BELIEF); truthful, veracious (TRUTH).

reliance, *n.* dependence, interdependency (DEPENDABILITY).

relic, *n.* trace, vestige, survival (REMAINDER); antique, antiquity, archaism (OLDNESS).

RELIEF—*N.* relief, alleviation, qualification, moderation, palliation, assuagement, mitigation; relaxation, remission *or* remittal; help, aid, assistance; respite, rest, reprieve, truce, solace; lenitive, palliative, alleviative, mitigative, moderant, relaxative.

lessening, decrease, reduction, diminution, diminishment, abatement, easement.

redress, reparation, amends, rectification, correction, indemnification, repair, remedy.

prominence, projection, protrusion, excrescency, embossment.

[*in sculpture*] **relievo,** *rilievo* (*It.*); high relief, *alto-rilievo* (*It.*); half relief, *mezzo-rilievo* (*It.*); low relief, bas-relief, *basso-rilievo* (*It.*); hollow relief, *cavo-rilievo* (*It.*), cameo.

[*distinctness of outline*] **vividness,** sharpness, distinctness, definition, prominence.

V. **relieve,** alleviate, weaken, temper, attemper, qualify, moderate, palliate, allay, quell, assuage, mitigate; relax, remit, slacken, slack; reprieve, respite, solace, console, comfort; help, aid, assist.

lessen, decrease, reduce, diminish, abate, ease, lighten.

soften, tame, tame down, tone down, season; dull, deaden; melt (*as the heart*), unsteel, sweeten, mollify, cool, soothe.

redress, repair, remedy, readjust, right, indemnify, make amends to (*or* for).

[*to take one's turn*] **free,** release, spell, take the place of, substitute for, alternate with, replace.

Adj. **relieving,** alleviative, alleviatory, lenitive, palliative, palliatory, assuasive, mitigative, mitigant, mitigatory; relaxative; solaceful, consolatory.

See also AID, CALMNESS, DECREASE, PAINKILLER, REST, RESTORATION, RIGHT, SOFTNESS, SUBSTITUTE, UNANXIETY, VISIBILITY, WEAKNESS. *Antonyms*—See INCREASE, STRENGTH.

RELIGION—*N.* religion, creed, faith, religious persuasion, church, religious preference, orthodoxy; cult, cultism; denomination, sect; theology, divinity, hierology.

Christianity, Catholicism, Protestantism, Christian faith, gospel; Roman Catholicism, papistry, popishness, popery, Romanism, Romishness (*the last five derogatory*).

Jewish religion, Jewish faith, Judaism, Hebrew religion.

[*Asian religions*] **Mohammedanism,** Moslemism, Mussulmanism, Islamism, Islam; Hinduism, Brahmanism; Jainism, Sikhism; Buddhism, Taoism, Confucianism; Shinto *or* Shintoism; Zoroastrianism *or* Zoroastrism.

paganism, heathenism, therianthropism.

Christian, Catholic, Protestant, gentile, Nazarene, *giaour* (*Turk.*); Roman Catholic, Roman (*derogatory*), papist (*derogatory*), Romanist (*derogatory*); Christians, Christendom.

Jew, Judaist, Judean *or* Judaean, Israelite, Hebrew; Jews, Jewry, Zion; Zionism.

Mohammedan, Moslem, Moslemite, Mussulman, Islamist, Islamite, paynim.

[*others*] **Hindu,** Jain, Jaina, Jainist, Sikh, Buddhist, Taoist, Confucian, Confucianist, Shintoist, Zoroastrian; pagan, paganist, heathen, infidel; coreligionist; heathendom, pagandom.

convert (*to a religion*), proselyte, novice, novitiate, neophyte.

V. **convert** (*to a religion*), proselytize, proselyte; Christianize, evangelize, Protestantize, Catholicize, Romanize; Judaize; Mohammedanize, Islamize; paganize, heathenize.

Adj. **Christian,** Catholic, Protestant, gentile; Roman Catholic, Roman, Romanist, Romanistic, Romish, popish, papist, papistic, papistical (*the last seven derogatory*).

Jewish, Judaic, Judaistic, Judean, Hebrew, Israelite, Israelitish; orthodox, conservative, reformed, liberal.

Mohammedan, Moslem, Moslemic, Moslemite, Mussulmanic, Islam, Islamic, Islamistic, Islamitic.

pagan, paganist, paganistic, heathen, therianthropic.

theological, hierological; denominational, sectarial, sectarian; evangelical, evangelistic, proselytical.

See also CHURCH, GOD, RELIGIOUSNESS, SACREDNESS, SACRED WRITINGS. Antonyms—See HETERODOXY, IRRELIGION.

RELIGIOUS COMMUNITY—N. abbey, cloister, priory, priorate; monastery, lamasery; convent, nunnery.

monk, monastic, cenobite, religieux (F.), conventual; stylite, pillarist, pillar saint; friar, fra (It.), dervish.

abbot, prior, archimandrite, hegumen.

nun, sister, religieuse (F.), cenobite, cloistress, vestal virgin, conventual; canoness.

abbess, prioress, mother superior, the reverend mother.

novitiate, noviciate, novice; postulant.

votary, votarist, devotee; votaress, votress (both fem.).

monasticism, cenobitism; abbacy, priorate; sisterhood.

Adj. monastic, monachal, monkish (derogatory), cenobitic; abbatial, cloistral, conventual; votary.

See also CHURCH, RELIGION. Antonyms—See IRRELIGION, LAITY.

RELIGIOUSNESS—N. religiousness, religiosity, orthodoxy, religionism, faith, belief, piety, piousness, pietism, devotion, devoutness, godliness, holiness; theopathy, Sabbatarianism, sabbatism.

religious person, religionist, orthodox, believer, saint, devotee, religious fanatic, convulsionary; Sabbatarian, Sabbatist.

V. be religious, etc. (see Adjectives); have faith, believe, receive Christ, stand up for Jesus, keep the faith.

Adj. religious, pious, pietistic, pietistical, religionistic, devout, orthodox, devoted, God-fearing, godly, holy, saintly, saintlike, faithful, believing.

See also BELIEF, RELIGION, SACREDNESS. Antonyms—See HETERODOXY, IRRELIGION, UNBELIEVINGNESS.

RELINQUISHMENT—N. relinquishment, renunciation, renouncement, abjuration, abjurement, abnegation, disownment, renege,

waiver, disclaimer, disclamation; release, cession, abandonment; surrender, submission; delivery, betrayal, betrayment, extradition (law).

sacrifice, forfeiture, immolation, hecatomb, self-sacrifice, martyrdom; forfeit, gambit, pawn, victim.

resignation, retirement, abdication, demission, divorce, withdrawal, secession, vacation.

relinquisher, renouncer or renunciator, etc. (see Verbs); self-sacrificer, martyr, protomartyr.

that to which one is sacrificed: juggernaut, moloch.

V. relinquish, renounce, forswear, abjure, abnegate, disown, renege, waive, disclaim; let go, release, drop, cede, abandon.

give up, surrender, give in, quit, yield, submit; forfeit, abandon, sacrifice, immolate; deliver, extradite (a prisoner), disgorge, betray; abandon oneself to, resign oneself to.

resign, retire (from), abdicate, divorce oneself from, quit, leave, give notice, drop out, withdraw, secede, vacate.

See also DESERTION, DISLOYALTY, FREEDOM, GIVING. Antonyms—See HOLD, OWNERSHIP, PROTECTION, STINGINESS.

---

relish, n. appetite, stomach, taste (LIKING); savor, flavor, tang (TASTE); gusto, zest (PLEASURE).

relish, v. enjoy, delight in (PLEASURE).

reluctant, adj. loath, disinclined, averse (UNWILLINGNESS).

rely on, v. depend on, lean on, reckon on (DEPENDABILITY); believe in, count on, bank on (BELIEF).

REMAINDER—N. remainder, residue, residuum, remains, remnant, rest, carry-over, leavings, odds and ends, oddment; refuse, waste, ruins, wreckage, wreck, detritus, stump, butt.

dregs, lees, sediment, silt.

surplus, excess, overplus, surplusage, balance.

trace, vestige, vestigium, rack, ashes, bones, fossil, reliquiae, survival, relic; footprint, fossil footprint, ichnite, ichnolite.

trail, track, trace, spoor, wake. [science of fossils] paleontology, ichnology, ichnolithology, paleontography.

V. remain, be left, survive, subsist, exist, stay, continue, cling, linger, last, endure; rest, tarry, loiter, hover, wait, halt; sojourn, abide, dwell, stop, live, reside, roost, visit, bivouac, lodge.

Adj. remaining, left, leftover, residual, residuary, surplus, remanent, remainder, over, odd, surviving; net, superfluous, over and above; outstanding; vestigial, vestigiary, fossil.

See also CONTINUATION, DESTRUCTION, EXCESS, EXISTENCE, LIFE, SLOWNESS, UNCLEANNESS. *Antonyms*— See ADDITION.

---

remains, *n.* residue, remnant (REMAINDER); ashes, relics, ruins (DESTRUCTION); corpse, cadaver (DEATH).

remark, *n.* mention, comment, observation (STATEMENT).

remark, *v.* say, mention, observe (STATEMENT, OBSERVANCE); see, notice, perceive (VISION, LOOKING).

remarkable, *adj.* curious, salient, prominent (VISIBILITY); unprecedented, singular, signal (SURPRISE); outstanding, phenomenal (UNUSUALNESS).

remedy, *n.* corrective, counteractant; medication, medicine (CURE).

remedy, *v.* correct, rectify, right, repair, redress (CURE, RELIEF, RIGHT, RESTORATION).

remember, *v.* recall, recollect (MEMORY).

remembrance, *n.* recall, recollection, reminiscence (MEMORY).

remind, *v.* prod, suggest, hint, cue (MEMORY).

reminder, *n.* phylactery, suggestion, hint (MEMORY).

remindful, *adj.* mnemonic, redolent, reminiscent (MEMORY).

reminisce, *v.* review, retrospect, look back upon (MEMORY).

reminiscent, *adj.* remindful, suggestive, redolent (MEMORY).

remiss, *adj.* negligent, derelict, delinquent (NEGLECT).

remit, *v.* slacken, slack, relax (RELIEF, WEAKNESS); settle, square, pay (PAYMENT); amnesty, reprieve, respite (FORGIVENESS).

remnant, *n.* residue, remains (REMAINDER).

remodel, *v.* refresh, renew, renovate (RESTORATION); recast, remold, reconstruct (CHANGE); reform, reclaim, regenerate (IMPROVEMENT).

remonstrate, *v.* object, demur, expostulate (OPPOSITION, COMPLAINT).

remorse, *n.* repentance, sorrow, contrition (PENITENCE, REGRET).

remorseful, *adj.* penitent, repentant, contrite, sorry (PENITENCE, REGRET).

remorseless, *adj.* unrepentant, unrepented (IMPENITENCE); ruthless, merciless, pitiless (INSENSITIVITY).

remote, *adj.* distant, far (DISTANCE); irrelevant, pointless; foreign, strange (IRRELATION); private, quiet, isolated (SECLUSION); standoff, aloof, unapproachable (INSENSITIVITY, HOSTILITY).

REMOVAL—*N.* removal, detachment; relegation, cartage, carriage, transplantation; withdrawal, departure, abstraction.

displacement, transference, shift, transshipment, transposition, transfer, replacement, dislocation.

V. remove, dislodge, dislocate, delocalize, disroot, decenter, detach, take away, brush away, sweep away, relegate, cart off, carry off, transplant.

strip, take off, withdraw, tear, rend, abstract, cream, ream, skim, top; pit, stone.

displace, disestablish, displant, uproot; set aside, transfer, transpose.

See also DEPARTURE, DISMISSAL, DISPERSION, ELIMINATION, TRANSFER. *Antonyms*—See HOLD, LOCATION, REMAINDER, STABILITY.

---

remove, *v.* dislodge, take away (REMOVAL); doff, get out of (UNDRESS); operate, cut out, excise (SURGERY).

remunerate, *v.* pay, compensate, indemnify (PAYMENT).

rend, *v.* sunder, rive (TEARING).

render, *v.* cede, relinquish (GIVING); play, perform, execute (MUSICIAN); translate, construe (EXPLANATION).

renegade, *n.* apostate, turncoat (APOSTASY).

renew, *v.* renovate, refurbish, modernize (NEWNESS, RESTORATION); rejuvenate, revitalize (LIFE, STRENGTH).

renounce, *v.* repudiate, disown, disavow (DENIAL); give up, forswear, abjure (RELINQUISHMENT).

renovate, *v.* modernize, refresh, remodel (NEWNESS, RESTORATION).

renowned, *adj.* redoubted, eminent, noted (FAME).

rent, *n.* rip, tear, tatter (TEARING); fissure, breach, rift (DISJUNCTION).

rent, *v.* lease, let, hire (BORROWING).

renunciation, *n.* abjuration, abnegation, disavowal (DENIAL, RELINQUISHMENT).

reorganize, *v.* reconstruct, remodel, recast (IMPROVEMENT, CHANGE).

repair, *v.* remedy, correct, rectify (CURE, RELIEF, RIGHT); fix, overhaul, mend (RESTORATION).

reparation, *n.* rectification, correction (RELIEF); explation, redress (ATONEMENT, RECOMPENSE).

repartee, *n.* retort, riposte (ANSWER); pleasantry, levity, wit (WITTINESS).

repast, *n.* meal, spread (*colloq.*), banquet (FOOD).

repay, *v.* rebate, refund, reimburse (PAYMENT); return, avenge, revenge (RETALIATION, PUNISHMENT).

repeal, *v.* rescind, revoke (INEFFECTIVENESS).

repeat, *v.* duplicate, reproduce; retell (REPETITION); recur, persist (OCCURRENCE).

repeated, *adj.* recurrent, regular, periodic (OCCURRENCE).

repeatedly, *adv.* again, again and again (REPETITION).

repeater, *n.* parrot, recidivist, backslider (REPETITION).

repel, *v.* repulse, rebuff (PROPULSION); revolt, nauseate, sicken (DISGUST).

repent, *v.* be sorry for, rue, regret (PENITENCE, REGRET).

repentance, *n.* contrition, compunction, remorse (PENITENCE).

repentant, *adj.* penitent, remorseful, contrite (PENITENCE).

repercussion, *n.* re-echo, echo, reverberation (REACTION, REPETITION).

repertory, *n.* repertoire, stock (DRAMA).

REPETITION—*N.* repetition, reiteration, iteration, iterance, broken record, ingemination; restatement, recapitulation, paraphrase; chant, recitation, rote, report, rehearsal, practice; repetitiveness, repetitiousness, nimiety; recurrence, reappearance, encore, return, perseveration, periodicity, rhythm; duplication, reproduction; alliteration, pallilogy; litany.

redundance, tautology, pleonasm, wordiness, verbosity.

echo, reverberation, repercussion, rebound, replication, re-echo, reflection, reply; echolalia.

quotation, quote (*colloq.*), passage, excerpt, extract, snippet; *disjecta membra* (*L., pl.*); misquotation.

refrain, burden (*of a song*), ritornel (*mus.*), ritornello (*It.*), chorus, reprise (*mus.*), repetend.

repeater, echo, parrot; tautologist, recidivist, backslider.

V. **repeat,** say again, tell again, retell, reiterate, iterate, ingeminate; drum, hammer, din into, harp on (*or* upon); restate, recapitulate, reword, rephrase, paraphrase; parrot, chant, recite, rehearse, report, quote, cite; misquote; alliterate, tautologize.

echo, re-echo, vibrate, redouble, reverb, reverberate, rebound, redound, resound, echo back.

do again, redo, duplicate, reproduce, repeat, reiterate, practice, rehearse; resume, return to, go back, come back, turn back, revert.

be repeated, recur, reappear, return, come back, come again, perseverate.

Adj. **repetitive,** repetitious, reiterative, iterative, iterant, recapitulatory; echoic, echolalic, plangent, reboant, resonant, alliterative, pallilogetic; tautological, redundant, pleonastic.

Adv., phrases. again, repeatedly, again and again, anew, afresh, once more, over; ditto, encore, *de novo* (*L.*), *da capo* (*It.*), bis; over and over, frequently, often.

See also COPY, FREQUENCY, OCCURRENCE, RHYTHM, WORDINESS. *Antonyms*—See FEWNESS.

rephrase, *v.* restate, rehash, recapitulate, reword (EXPLANATION, REPETITION).

replace, *v.* supersede, supplant, displace (SUBSTITUTION); reinstate, re-establish (RESTORATION).

replacement, *n.* pinch hitter (*colloq.*), understudy (SUBSTITUTION); reinstatement, re-establishment (RESTORATION); transposition, transfer (REMOVAL).

replete, *adj.* gorged, satiated, full (SATISFACTION, FULLNESS).

replica, *n.* facsimile, likeness, miniature (COPY).

reply, *n.* response, rejoinder, retort (ANSWER).

report, *n.* statement, account, story (INFORMATION, DESCRIPTION); hearsay, comment, buzz (RUMOR); bang, explosion (LOUDNESS).

report, *v.* tell, disclose, reveal (INFORMATION); publish, air (PUBLICATION); betray, expose, unmask (INFORMATION).

reporter, *n.* journalist, newspaperman (PUBLICATION).

repose, *n.* ease, quiet, peace (REST).

repose, *v.* put, place, lay (PLACE, LOCATION); rest, settle (REST).

repository, *n.* depository, closet, cupboard (CONTAINER); magazine, depot (STORE).

REPRESENTATION—*N.* representation, portrayal, portraiture, depiction, depicture, delineation, presentation (*theatrical*), symbolization, typification, denotation, prefiguration, prefigurement, adumbration; picture, illustration, image, tableau, *tableau vivant* (*F.*), spectacle.

symbol, denotation, exponent, sign, token; badge, emblem, mark, scepter, totem, totem pole, totem post, zoomorph, swastika, cryptogram, cryptograph; portrait, figure, effigy, model, image; rebus.

symbolism, symbology, iconology, totemism.

V. represent, depict, depicture, delineate, picture, illustrate, portray, limn, feature; stage, present; prefigure, pretypify, adumbrate.

symbolize, symbol, stand for, mean, denote, betoken, token, image, typify, emblematize.

Adj. representative, delineative, depictive, illustrative, representational, presentational; prefigurative, adumbrative.

symbolic, symbolical, symbolistic, figurative, denotative, emblematic, typical.

See also DESCRIPTION, DRAMA, FINE ARTS, INDICATION, MAP, MEANING.

representative, *n.* emissary, vicar, envoy (AGENT, DEPUTY, SUBSTITUTION); senator, congressman (LEGISLATURE).

repress, *v.* restrain, suppress, keep in, inhibit (RESTRAINT).

repression, *n.* suppression, inhibition, sublimation (RESTRAINT, CONTROL).

reprieve, *n.* respite, truce (REST).

reprieve, *v.* amnesty, remit, respite (FORGIVENESS).

reprimand, *v.* reproach, reprove, rebuke (DISAPPROVAL, SCOLDING).

reprisal, *n.* retribution, revenge, vengeance (RETALIATION).

reproach, *n.* rebuke, reprehension, reprimand (SCOLDING); obloquy, opprobrium, dishonor (DISGRACE).

reproach, *v.* censure, reprove, rebuke (DISAPPROVAL, SCOLDING).

reproduce, *v.* breed, multiply, procreate (BIRTH); reconstruct, reconstitute, rebuild (RESTORATION); duplicate, manifold, trace (COPY); repeat, redo (REPETITION).

reptile, *n.* saurian, serpent, viper (ANIMAL).

repudiate, *v.* disown, disavow, renounce (DENIAL); default, dishonor (DEBT).

repugnance, *n.* aversion, antipathy,

repulsion, displeasure, distaste (UNPLEASANTNESS, HATRED).

repugnant, *adj.* obnoxious, repulsive, revolting (UNPLEASANTNESS, HATRED).

repulse, *v.* repel, rebuff (PROPULSION).

repulsion, *n.* repugnance, aversion, antipathy (UNPLEASANTNESS, HATRED); revulsion, revolt, loathing (DISGUST).

repulsive, *adj.* revolting, offensive, loathsome (UNPLEASANTNESS, HATRED, DISGUST); unsightly, ugly, hideous (DEFORMITY).

reputable, *adj.* esteemed, honored, redoubted (RESPECT).

reputation, *n.* repute, mark, name (FAME); standing, position, rank (CONDITION).

repute, *n.* renown, prominence, prestige (FAME, APPROVAL).

reputed, *adj.* assumed, supposed, putative (SUPPOSITION); gossiped, noised around, reported (RUMOR).

request, *v.* ask, appeal, apply (DEMAND).

require, *v.* need, want; demand, cause, entail (NECESSITY).

required, *adj.* compulsory, obligatory, requisite (FORCE, NECESSITY).

requirement, *n.* demand, requisite, *sine qua non* (*L.*), prescription (NECESSITY, COMMAND).

requisite, *adj.* required, compulsory, mandatory (NECESSITY).

requisite, *n.* need, requirement, *sine qua non* (*L.*), demand (NECESSITY).

rescue, *n.* liberation, delivery, salvation (FREEDOM).

rescue, *v.* liberate, set free, save (FREEDOM).

research, *n.* exploration, investigation, inquiry (SEARCH).

research, *v.* investigate, explore, inquire (INQUIRY, SEARCH).

resemble, *v.* look like, favor (*colloq.*), be like (SIMILARITY).

resent, *v.* take amiss, take offense, take umbrage (OFFENSE, ANGER).

resentful, *adj.* offended, umbrageous, piqued, hurt, indignant (OFFENSE, ANGER).

resentment, *n.* umbrage, pique, indignation (OFFENSE, ANGER).

reserve, *n.* supply, backlog, stock (QUANTITY); savings, nest egg (STORE); self-restraint, composure, constraint (RESTRAINT, CONTROL); aloofness, coldness (INSENSITIVITY); shyness, diffidence (MODESTY); quietness, taciturnity, reticence (SILENCE).

reserve, *v.* keep, hoard, stock-pile (STORE); engage, book, schedule (EARLINESS, BOOK).

reserved, *adj.* unaffectionate, undemonstrative, inhibited (INSENSITIVITY); recessive, retiring, bashful (SECLUSION, MODESTY, SILENCE).

reservoir, *n.* stock, fund, supply (STORE); tarn, spring (LAKE).

reshape, *v.* recast, reform, remodel (SHAPE).

reside in, *v.* inhabit, dwell in, occupy (INHABITANT).

residence, *n.* home, domicile (HABITATION); inhabitation, habitation (INHABITANT).

resident, *n.* denizen, occupant, tenant (INHABITANT).

residue, *n.* remains, remnant (REMAINDER).

resign, *v.* secede, retire, abdicate (DEPARTURE, RELINQUISHMENT).

resigned, *adj.* submissive, reconciled, unassertive (SUBMISSION).

resign oneself to, *v.* accept, submit to, reconcile oneself to (SUBMISSION, ACCEPTANCE).

resilient, *adj.* buoyant, elastic, springy (JUMP).

RESIN—*N.* resin, rosin, gum, lac, shellac, varnish, mastic, oleoresin, meglip, copal, japan, lacquer, sealing wax; amber, ambergris; bitumen, pitch, tar, asphalt.

Adj. resinous, resiny, rosiny, gummous, gummy, gummed, waxed, lacquered, tarry, pitched, pitchy, bituminous, asphaltic.

resist, *v.* prevail against, withstand, weather (SUCCESS); oppose, violate, defy (OPPOSITION); forbear, forgo, refrain (INACTION).

resistant, *adj.* unbowed, insubmissive, negative (OPPOSITION, OPPOSITE, DEFIANCE).

resolute, *adj.* determined, set, bent (PURPOSE, WILL); stubborn, obstinate, dogged (STUBBORNNESS).

resolution, *n.* fixed purpose, resolve, will power (WILL); perseverance, determination, immovability (STUBBORNNESS); motion, proposition, proposal (SUGGESTION).

resolve, *n.* fixed purpose, resolution, will (PURPOSE).

resolve, *v.* determine, intend, mean (PURPOSE); decide, will, make up one's mind (DECISION); solve, unravel, untangle (ANSWER).

resolved, *adj.* determined, set, bent (WILL, PURPOSE).

RESONANCE—*N.* resonance, vibration, reverberation, reflection; ringing, tintinnabulation, bell

note, ring, chime, boom, roar, clang, clangor, rumble, thunder, roll.

V. resound, reverberate, re-echo, sound, echo, peal, vibrate, tintinnabulate, ring, chime, tinkle, jingle, chink, clink; gurgle, mutter, murmur, plash; boom, roar, thunder, roll, rumble.

Adj. resonant, resounding, reverberant, reverberating, sonorous, vibrant, ringing, plangent, roaring, booming, thunderous, thundering; deep-toned, hollow-sounding.

See also BELL, MELODY, LOUDNESS, REPETITION, ROLL, SOUND. *Antonyms* —See LOWNESS, SILENCE.

resort, *n.* recourse, refuge, resource (DEPENDABILITY); hotel, inn (HABITATION).

resound, *v.* reverberate, re-echo, rebound (RESONANCE, REPETITION).

resourceful, *adj.* enterprising, venturesome (UNDERTAKING); clever, ingenious (CLEVERNESS).

resources, *n.* riches, substance, assets (WEALTH, MEANS).

RESPECT—*N.* respect, adoration, deference, esteem, homage, honor, obeisance, regard, reverence, veneration, worship; consideration, courtesy, repute, dignity; ovation, tribute, testimonial.

respects, regards, devoirs, compliments, greetings.

gesture of respect: bow, curtsey, obeisance, salaam, kowtow, genuflection, scrape; toast, health, pledge.

V. respect, adore, esteem, honor, regard, revere, reverence, venerate, worship; look up to, defer to, pay homage to; awe, overawe, impress.

pay respects, bow, curtsey, salaam, scrape, bend the knee, kneel, genuflect, kowtow, prostrate oneself, pay tribute; toast, pledge.

Adj. respected, esteemed, honored, redoubted, reputable, revered, reverenced, reverend, venerated, well-thought-of, time-honored.

respectable, august, decent, estimable, redoubtable, venerable, sublime.

respectful, deferent, deferential, obeisant, regardful, reverent, reverential, obsequious.

Adv., phrases. respectfully, etc. (see *Adjectives*); with all respect, with due respect, with the highest respect; in deference to.

See also APPROVAL, COURTESY, GESTURE, GREETING, OBSERVANCE, PROPRIETY, WORSHIP. Antonyms—See DISCOURTESY, DISRESPECT, INSULT.

respecting, prep. concerning, as regards, pertaining to (RELATIONSHIP).

respective, adj. particular, several (APPORTIONMENT).

respectively, adv. individually, severally (UNITY).

respiration, n. breathing, aspiration (BREATH).

respite, n. reprieve, letup (colloq.), lull (REST).

respond, v. answer, reply, retort (ANSWER); react (REACTION).

response, n. retort, reply, rejoinder (ANSWER); reverberation, echo (REACTION).

responsibility, n. accountability, blame, burden (LIABILITY); encumbrance, incubus, onus (WEIGHT).

responsible, adj. liable, answerable, accountable (LIABILITY); dependable, reliable, stable (DEPENDABILITY).

responsive, adj. sensitive, sentient, passible (SENSITIVENESS); answering, respondent (ANSWER); reactive, reactional (REACTION).

rest, n. remains, leavings (REMAINDER).

rest, v. roost, settle, pause (REST); put, lay, deposit (PLACE).

REST—N. rest, repose, ease, quiet, quietude, peace, relaxation, recumbency; statics.

period of rest, midday rest, siesta, noonday rest, nooning; break, coffee break; recess, respite, reprieve, truce, spell, breathing spell, interval, intermission, interlude; lull, pause, cessation, stop, letup (colloq.).

resting place, lounge, roost, perch, shelter, refuge, retreat, haven.

holiday, fiesta, day of rest, vacation, busman's holiday.

leisure, spare time, spare moments; freedom, otiosity, time to spare, time.

laziness, do-nothingness, do-nothingism, indolence, sloth, acedia, lymphatism, fainéance (F.), ergophobia.

idler, sluggard, slugabed, do-nothing, fainéant (F.), sloth, sloven, acediast, indolent; tramp, bum (slang), vagabond, vagrant, hobo, beggar, lazzarone; lazybones, loafer, slouch, hooligan, lounger, poke, slowpoke; drone, gold-bricker (slang), malingerer.

recumbency, dormience, accumbency, decumbency, procumbency, prostration, subjacency.

V. rest, repose, bed, settle, settle down, let up (colloq.); alight, light, roost, perch; be still, be quiet, keep quiet, lie still; pause, stop, halt, cease, relax, take it easy, take time out, pause for breath, take a breather.

idle, loaf, dally, gold-brick (slang), soldier, malinger, laze, lounge.

lie, recline, loll, sprawl, lounge, squat, wallow, welter, puddle; lie down, couch, prostrate oneself, grovel, lay oneself down; lie along, border, skirt; cuddle, nestle, nuzzle, snuggle, bundle, bask in; lie over, overlie, dominate, command, tower above.

Adj. resting, at rest, in repose, settled, still, quiet, relaxed.

restful, peaceful, reposeful, comfortable, cozy, snug, quiet, still, calm, tranquil.

leisured, unoccupied, unemployed, disengaged, inactive, idle, otiose.

leisurely, unhurried, slow, easy, languid, hasteless.

lazy, slothful, shiftless, indolent, sluggard, fainéant (F.), do-nothing; sluggish, supine, lymphatic.

lying, recumbent, accumbent, decumbent, horizontal, flat, cubatory, couchant, dormient, couché (F.), incumbent, prone, procumbent, prostrate; supine, resupine; underlying, subjacent; overlying, superincumbent, superjacent.

See also CALMNESS, CESSATION, INACTION, INTERVAL, MOTIONLESSNESS, PEACE, RELIEF, REMAINDER, SEAT, SLEEP, SLOWNESS, TIME. Antonyms —See ACTION, ACTIVITY, ATTEMPT, ENERGY, MOTION, WORK.

---

restate, v. reword, rephrase, paraphrase (REPETITION, EXPLANATION).

restaurant, n. café, chophouse, cafeteria (FOOD).

restful, adj. peaceful, placid, quiet (REST, PEACE).

restitution, n. restoration, return, requital (GIVING, PAYMENT).

restless, adj. fitful, restive, uneasy (NERVOUSNESS, AGITATION).

RESTORATION—N. restoration, replacement, reinstatement, reestablishment, reinstallation, reinstallment, reinsertion; rehabilitation, remodeling, reconstruction, instauration, reconstitution, reproduction, renovation, redintegration, repair, reparation, renewal, revival, resuscitation, resurrection, revivification, reanimation, reorganization; redemption, restitution, return, rectification, correction, relief, redress, retrieval, reclamation, recovery, regainment.

restorer, furbisher, mender, repairer, tinker, patcher, tinkerer, cobbler, shoemaker.

V. **restore,** replace, reinstate, reestablish, reinstall, reinsert, return, put back, give back.

refurbish, rehabilitate, furbish, recondition, refresh, renew, renovate, remodel, reconstruct, reconstitute, rebuild, reproduce, redintegrate, reorganize, rearrange.

reclaim, recover, redeem, retrieve, rescue.

repair, fix, overhaul, mend, put in repair, retouch, tinker, cobble, patch, patch up, darn; staunch, calk, splice.

rectify, adjust, redress, correct, remedy, right.

revive, resuscitate, resurrect, revivify, reanimate.

Adj. **restorable,** repairable, renewable, reparable, mendable, remediable, curable, redressable; reclaimable, recoverable, retrievable; replaceable.

restorative, reparative, reparatory, recuperative, recuperatory, curative, remedial, corrective; resuscitative, resurrectionary.

See also CURE, GIVING, HARM, IMPROVEMENT, RELIEF, RIGHT. *Antonyms*—See BREAKAGE, DESTRUCTION, DETERIORATION.

---

restrain, *v.* stop, prevent (RESTRAINT); subdue, temper (SOFTNESS); chasten (SIMPLICITY).

restrained, *adj.* self-restrained, reticent, self-controlled (INSENSITIVITY); unadorned, unornamented, plain (SEVERITY).

RESTRAINT—N. restraint, containment, control, deterrence, determent, reservation, stop, stoppage, prevention; suppression, repression, inhibition, reserve, constraint, reticence.

restrainer, check, harness, curb, rein, leash, bridle, deterrent, stay, muzzle, gag, strangle hold.

shackles, fetter, fetters, bilboes, gyves, shackle, manacles, handcuffs, bracelets (*slang*), hobble, hopple, strait jacket, trammel, trammels, chain, chains, bonds, hindrance.

obstruction, bar, barrier, pale, obstacle, snag, block, blockade, clog, dam, plug, occlusion, stopper, stopple, cork, obstruent (*med.*); iron curtain, bamboo curtain.

restriction, confinement, limitation, determination, delimitation, bounds, boundary, circumscription, demarcation, localization, qualification, astriction, constriction, taboo or tabu.

restricted place, ghetto, pale, precinct.

V. **restrain,** hold back, stop, prevent, keep back, check, contain, harness, control, curb, rein in, leash, bridle, govern, constrain, deter, overawe, stay, checkmate, stymie; strangle; withhold, reserve; muzzle, gag.

fetter, manacle, handcuff, hobble, shackle, strait-jacket, trammel, chain, hinder, pinion.

restrict, confine, limit, determine, bound, circumscribe, cramp, delimit, delimitate, demarcate, localize, qualify, astrict, constrict, taboo or tabu, stop short.

suppress, keep in, hold in, repress, inhibit, burke, stifle, choke back, smother, quench, throttle, cork.

obstruct, bar, block, blockade, clog, dam, daggle, plug, plug up, occlude, thwart, stop up, stem, choke, snag.

See also BOUNDARY, CESSATION, CONTROL, DENIAL, DISSUASION, HINDRANCE, IMPRISONMENT, PREVENTION, SLAVERY, UNNATURALNESS. *Antonyms*

—See FREEDOM, PERMISSION.

restrict, *v.* narrow, constrict, confine (RESTRAINT, NARROWNESS).

restriction, *n.* confinement, limitation (RESTRAINT); qualification, condition, reservation (BOUNDARY).

restrictive, *adj.* select, exclusive, cliquish (EXCLUSION); astrictive, circumscriptive (HINDRANCE).

RESULT—N. result, effect, consequence, resultant, aftermath, outcome, end, outgrowth, corollary, development, eventuality, upshot, conclusion, denouement; sequel, sequence, sequela, sequelant, sequent; product, creature, fruit, offspring, issue, spawn (*derogatory*), offshoot; aftereffect, afterclap, aftergrowth, harvest, crop, by-product, repercussion; derivative, derivation; engram (*psychol.*).

results, fruit, crop, harvest, spawn (*derogatory*), sequelae (*pl.*).

concern with practical results: pragmatism.

effectiveness, efficacy, efficaciousness, effectuality, weight, force, forcefulness, power, validity, potency, strength, vigor, virtue, fruitfulness, productiveness, trenchancy.

V. result, ensue, eventuate, eventualize, follow, happen, pan out, turn out, issue from, spring from, derive from, flow from, come from, accrue, attend, redound upon.

result in, produce, afford, beget, determine, effect, effectuate, spawn (*derogatory*), cause, make, bring about; fulfill, realize; contribute to; produce a result, operate, work; backfire.

put into effect, administer, administrate, perform, execute; enforce, implement.

get as a result, get, obtain, secure, harvest, reap.

Adj. resultful, eventful, momentous, decisive, fateful, efficient, expedient; indirect, eventual, secondary, contingent, vicarious; potential.

resultant, consequent, consequential, ensuing, sequent, sequential, resultative, accruing, attendant, attending, corollary; attributable to, ascribable to, due to, caused by.

effective, effectual, efficacious, forceful, fruitful, operative, potent, telling, trenchant, valid, strong, vigorous, productive.

Adv., conjunctions, phrases. as a result, as a natural result, as a consequence, in consequence, consequently, therefore, and so, *ergo* (*L.*), hence, wherefore, it follows that; inevitably, necessarily; eventually.

See also ACQUISITION, EXPEDIENCE, FOLLOWING, FORCE, OCCURRENCE, POWER, PRODUCTION, REACTION, STRENGTH. *Antonyms*—See CAUSATION, INEFFECTIVENESS, UNPRODUCTIVENESS.

---

resume, *v.* continue, go on, proceed (CONTINUATION); return to, go back, come back (REPETITION).

resurrect, *v.* revive, resuscitate, revivify (LIFE, RESTORATION); restore (USE).

resuscitate, *v.* revive, resurrect, rally (LIFE).

retain, *v.* keep, keep hold of, hold fast (HOLD); remember, keep in mind (MEMORY).

RETALIATION—*N.* retaliation, repayment, reprisal, requital, retribution, desert, just deserts, punishment, talion, *lex talionis* (*L.*), retort, recrimination; tit for tat, give-and-take, blow for blow.

revenge, vengeance, revengefulness, reprisal, feud, blood feud,

vendetta, death feud; eye for an eye, tooth for a tooth.

avenger, Nemesis, Erinys (*pl.* Erinyes), Eumenides (*pl.*), Furies; retaliator, retaliationist, feudist, feuder.

V. retaliate, return, repay, requite, retort, turn upon; pay, pay off, pay back; turn the tables upon, return the compliment, return like for like, exchange blows; give and take, be quits, be even with, pay off old scores.

revenge, avenge, take revenge.

Adj. retaliatory, retaliative, retributive, talionic; vindictive, grudgeful, vengeful, avenging, unforgiving.

See also ACCUSATION, EXCHANGE, PAYMENT, PUNISHMENT, RECOMPENSE. *Antonyms*—See FORGIVENESS, SUBMISSION.

---

retard, *v.* decelerate, arrest, check, (SLOWNESS); delay, detain, hold up (DELAY).

retarded, *adj.* feeble-minded, defective, subnormal (STUPIDITY).

retch, *v.* heave, keck, vomit (NAUSEA).

retention, *n.* holding, keeping, possession (HOLD); remembrance, recall, recollection (MEMORY).

reticent, *adj.* reserved, shy, uncommunicative (SILENCE); restrained, self-restrained (INSENSITIVITY).

retinue, *n.* train, suite, cortege (FOLLOWER, ACCOMPANIMENT, SERVICE).

retire, *v.* withdraw, retreat, go back (DEPARTURE, REVERSION); rusticate (SECLUSION); go to bed (SLEEP); resign, secede, abdicate (DEPARTURE, RELINQUISHMENT).

retired, *adj.* superannuated, emeritus (INACTION).

retirement, *n.* retreat, withdrawal (REVERSION); resignation, abdication (DEPARTURE, RELINQUISHMENT); privacy, isolation (SECLUSION); unemployment, leisure, superannuation (INACTION).

retiring, *adj.* recessive, unsociable, nongregarious (SECLUSION); unassuming, diffident, shy (MODESTY).

retort, *n.* riposte, repartee, rejoinder, reply (ANSWER).

retort, *v.* return, rebut, reply (ANSWER); repay (RETALIATION).

retract, *v.* back down, recant, back water (APOSTASY, REVERSION); pull back, draw back, reel in (TRACTION).

retreat, *n.* seclusion, sanctum, adytum (SECLUSION); preserve, sanctuary, shelter (PROTECTION); retirement, withdrawal (REVERSION, DEPARTURE).

retreat, *v.* withdraw, retire (AB-SENCE, DEPARTURE); retire from the world, rusticate (SECLUSION); flow back, ebb, recede (REVERSION).

retribution, *n.* repayment, reprisal, vengeance (RETALIATION, PAYMENT).

retrieve, *v.* reclaim, recover, redeem (ACQUISITION, RESTORATION).

retrospect, *v.* review, reminisce, look back (MEMORY).

return, *v.* go back, recur, reappear (REPETITION, REVERSION); give back, put back, restore (GIVING, RESTORATION); retaliate, repay, requite (RETALIATION); reply, retort, respond (ANSWER).

returns, *n.* proceeds, take (*slang*), income (RECEIVING).

reunion, *n.* meeting, assembly, convention (ASSEMBLAGE).

reveal, *v.* show, bare, expose (DISCLOSURE).

revealed, *adj.* open, in view (VISIBILITY).

revel, *n.* gala, celebration, wassail (SOCIALITY).

revelry, *n.* merrymaking, carousal, carouse (AMUSEMENT).

revenge, *n.* vengeance, retribution, reprisal (RETALIATION, PUNISHMENT).

revenue, *n.* receipts, income, earnings (RECEIVING, PAYMENT).

reverberate, *v.* echo, rebound, resound (REPETITION); react, have repercussions (REACTION).

reverberating, *adj.* resounding, sonorous, vibrant (RESONANCE).

revere, *v.* esteem, honor, regard (RESPECT); adore, deify, venerate (WORSHIP).

reverence, *n.* regard, veneration (RESPECT); adoration, deification, apotheosis (WORSHIP).

reverend, *adj.* reverenced, venerated, venerable (RESPECT, WORSHIP).

reverent, *adj.* respectful, deferential (RESPECT).

reverie, *n.* daydream, fantasy, fancy (HOPE, SLEEP); preoccupation, woolgathering, dreaminess (INATTENTION, THOUGHT).

reversal, *n.* retroflexion, regression (TURNING, REVERSION); turnabout, *volte-face* (F.), change of mind (CHANGE).

reverse, *n.* tail, behind (REAR); bad luck, mischance, adversity (MISFORTUNE); contradiction, paradox (OPPOSITE).

reverse, *v.* invert, upend, turn back (TURNING, REVERSION).

REVERSION—*N.* reversion, reversal, relapse, backslide, regres-sion, retrogradation, retrogression, recidivism, atavism, throwback.

retreat, retirement, withdrawal; backflow, refluence, reflux, retro-flux, ebb, recession, retrocession, retrocedence; return, remigration, repatriation.

backout, backdown, retraction, change of mind, change of heart, about-face, *volte-face* (F.).

recoil, backlash, reaction, repercussion, echo.

reverter, backslider, regressor, recidivist, atavist, throwback; backtracker, remigrant, repatriate, revenant.

V. **revert,** reverse, relapse, backslide, turn back, regress, retrograde, retrogress, retrocede.

go back, move back, back, draw back, drop back, slip back, fall back, pull back, flow back, ebb, recede, retreat, retire, withdraw, retrace one's steps; remigrate, repatriate, come back, return, recur.

shrink, wince, flinch, cringe, blench, quail, recoil.

back out, back down, back off, backtrack, crawfish (*slang*), backwater, retract, recant, take back, change one's mind, have a change of heart, do an about-face.

Adj. **reverting,** regressive, retrograde, retrogressive, recidivous, atavistic; refluent, reflux, recessive, retrocessive.

See also LOWNESS, OCCURRENCE, RE-ACTION, REPETITION, TRACTION, TURN-ING. *Antonyms*—See CONTINUATION, OVERRUNNING, PROGRESS.

---

revert, *v.* relapse, backslide (REVERSION).

review, *n.* criticism, notice, commentary (JUDGMENT, TREATISE); résumé, recapitulation (SHORT-NESS); study, scrutiny, survey (EXAMINATION).

revile, *v.* smear, defame, denigrate (MALEDICTION, DETRACTION).

revise, *v.* amend, edit, correct (IM-PROVEMENT, RIGHT); change, recast, revamp (NEWNESS, CHANGE).

revival, *n.* rebirth, renaissance (BIRTH).

revive, *v.* resuscitate, resurrect, re-vivify (LIFE, RESTORATION); refresh, rejuvenate, renew (STRENGTH); restore, popularize (USE).

revoke, *v.* repeal, rescind, void (IN-EFFECTIVENESS).

revolt, *n.* rebellion, insurrection, mutiny (DISOBEDIENCE); distaste, repulsion, repugnance (UNPLEAS-ANTNESS, DISGUST).

revolt, *v.* rebel, arise (DISOBEDI-ENCE); repel, nauseate (DISGUST).

revolting, *adj.* obnoxious, repugnant, repulsive (HATRED, UNPLEAS-ANTNESS).

revolution, *n.* turning, gyration (ROTATION); rebellion, insurrection, mutiny (DISOBEDIENCE); change, reversal, revulsion (CHANGE).

revolve, *v.* rotate, spin, whirl (ROTATION).

revolver, *n.* gun, pistol, sidearm (ARMS).

revulsion, *n.* repulsion, revolt, loathing (DISGUST); revolution, transformation (CHANGE).

reward, *n.* prize, award, crown (PAYMENT).

reword, *v.* restate, rephrase, paraphrase (REPETITION).

rhetoric, *n.* tropology, imagery (FIGURE OF SPEECH, LANGUAGE); grammar, syntax (LANGUAGE); oratory, elocution (TALK).

rhetorical, *adj.* eloquent, grandiloquent, magniloquent (TALK); figured, ornate, embellished, florid (FIGURE OF SPEECH); linguistic, grammatical (LANGUAGE).

rhyme, *n.* poem, verse, doggerel (POETRY).

RHYTHM—*N.* rhythm, cadence, measure, tempo, meter, lilt, eurythmy, swing; regularity, periodicity, uniformity.

beat, tick, pulse, pulsation, throb, stroke, tattoo, flutter, vibration, palpitation, pitter-patter, thump, pant.

V. beat, tick, pulse, pulsate, throb, flutter, vibrate, palpitate, pitter-patter, thump, pant.

Adj. rhythmical, cadent, measured, metrical, metered, lilting, eurythmical; pulsatile, pulsative, fluttery, vibrant, vibratory, palpitant, pitapat.

See also MOTION, OSCILLATION, POETRY, REPETITION, RULE, SEASONS, UNIFORMITY. *Antonyms*—See IRREGULARITY.

---

rib (*colloq.*), *v.* tease, rag (*colloq.*), bait (TEASING); chaff, jolly (RIDICULE).

ribald, *adj.* scabrous, Rabelaisian, scurrilous (OBSCENITY, WITTINESS).

ribbon, *n.* braid, tape (FILAMENT); laurels, medal, decoration (FAME).

rich, *adj.* wealthy, affluent, opulent (WEALTH); loamy, luxuriant (FERTILITY); sonorous, rotund, resonant (SWEETNESS, MELODY).

riches, *n.* substance, assets, means, resources (WEALTH).

rickety, *adj.* wobbly, tottery, shaky (UNSTEADINESS, WEAKNESS).

rid, *v.* disburden, disencumber, discharge (FREEDOM); eliminate, dispose of (ELIMINATION).

riddle, *n.* cryptogram, enigma, conundrum (MYSTERY, INQUIRY, AMBIGUITY).

riddle, *v.* perforate, puncture, bore (OPENING).

ride, *v.* drive, ride in, motor (VEHICLE).

rider, *n.* traveler, journeyer, passenger (TRAVELING, VEHICLE).

ridge, *n.* corrugation, groove, furrow (FOLD); highland, downs, upland (LAND); range, cordillera, chain (HEIGHT).

RIDICULE—*N.* ridicule, derision, scorn, sport, mockery; satire, parody, pasquinade, caricature, burlesque, lampoonery, travesty; lampoon, squib, pasquil, pastiche; iconoclasm, sarcasm, mordancy, backhandedness, sardonicism, irony, asteism (*rhet.*); razz, raspberry (*both slang*).

banter, raillery, chaff, badinage, persiflage.

jeer, jibe *or* gibe, hoot, scoff, taunt, twit.

satirist, lampoonist, parodist, caricaturist.

Greek god of ridicule: Momus.

object of ridicule, butt, derision, game, jestingstock, laughingstock, mockery, scoff, scorn, sport, target, victim.

V. ridicule, laugh at, deride, mock, jeer, jibe *or* gibe, fleer (*dial.*), josh (*colloq.*), guy (*colloq.*), poke fun at, banter, chaff, jolly, rally, rib (*colloq.*), kid (*slang*), make fun of, make game of, make sport of; hoot at, scoff at; taunt, twit, twitter; pillory.

satirize, lampoon, parody, travesty, burlesque, caricature, pasquinade, squib.

Adj. derisive, derisory, quizzical, iconoclastic.

sarcastic, backhanded, mordant, sardonic, ironic, ironical, satiric, satirical, Hudibrastic, burlesque.

See also CONTEMPT, DETRACTION, DISCOURTESY, DISRESPECT, INSULT, LAUGHTER, MALEDICTION, OFFENSE, TEASING. *Antonyms*—See ACCEPTANCE, APPROVAL.

---

ridiculous, *adj.* preposterous, ludicrous, laughable (ABSURDITY).

rife, *adj.* prevalent, widespread, epidemic (PRESENCE); many, numerous, multitudinous (MULTITUDE).

riffraff, *n.* scum, dregs, raff (MEANNESS).

rifle, v. loot, burglarize, rob (THIEVERY).

rift, n. fissure, breach, rent (DISJUNCTION); misunderstanding, rupture, break (DISAGREEMENT).

right, adj. correct, proper (RIGHT); right-handed, dexter (DIRECTION).

right, n. authorization, warrant, accreditation (POWER); due, perquisite, prerogative (PRIVILEGE).

RIGHT—N. right, rectitude, integrity, probity, propriety, morality, virtue, honor, straight course.

claim, title, interest, due, privilege, droit (law).

correctness, correctitude, accuracy, exactitude, precision, nicety.

precisianist, precisian, precisioner, formalist, pedant, purist, prig.

purism, pedantry, pedantism, precisianism, formalism, priggery, priggism.

V. right, regulate, rule, make straight; do right, recompense, vindicate, do justice to, see justice done, see fair play, give everyone his due.

correct, rectify, remedy, redress, repair, fix, cure, mend; amend, revise, emend or emendate, adjust; set straight, disabuse, undeceive.

have right to, have claim (or title) to, be entitled to, belong to; deserve, merit, be worthy of.

entitle, give (or confer) a right, authorize, sanction, legalize, ordain, prescribe, allot; qualify, capacitate, name.

Adj. right, correct, proper, free of error, perfect, inerrant, unmistaken, watertight, immaculate, Augustan; unerring, infallible, inerrable; rigorous, scrupulous, strict, punctilious, solemn; accurate, exact, precise, nice.

pedantic, priggish, puristic, formalistic, pernickety (colloq.).

rightful, justifiable, legitimate, lawful, legal, fitting.

See also CURE, FORMALITY, LEGALITY, MORALITY, PERFECTION, PRIVILEGE, PROPRIETY, REASONABLENESS, RESTORATION. Antonyms—See DISHONESTY, IMMORALITY, IMPROPERNESS, WICKEDNESS.

right-angled, adj. rectangular, orthogonal (VERTICALITY).

right away, adv. promptly, straightway, immediately (EARLINESS).

righteous, adj. ethical, honorable, virtuous (RULE); holy, saintly (MORALITY).

rightful, adj. legitimate, orthodox, canonical (TRUTH).

right-handed, adj. right, dextral (DIRECTION, APPENDAGE).

rigid, adj. stiff, firm, tense (HARDNESS); stiff, hard, harsh (SEVERITY); square-toed, strait-laced (PROPRIETY); fixed, static (UNIFORMITY); relentless, unbending (STUBBORNNESS).

rigorous, adj. strict, stern, harsh (SEVERITY); scrupulous, punctilious (RIGHT).

rile (colloq.), v. irk, provoke, exasperate (ANNOYANCE).

rim, n. edge, border, margin (BOUNDARY).

rind, n. peel, pellicle, bark (SKIN, COVERING).

ring, n. circle, band, ringlet (JEWELRY, ROUNDNESS); chime, tinkle (BELL); belt, cincture, girdle (VARIEGATION).

ring, v. jingle, tinkle, strike (BELL); encircle, surround, inclose (ROUNDNESS).

ringer (colloq.), n. substitute, dummy, stand-in (SUBSTITUTION).

ringlet, n. curl, frizzle, friz (HAIR); circle, circlet, ring (ROUNDNESS).

riot, n. disorder, tumult, uproar (UNRULINESS, LOUDNESS, COMMOTION).

riot, v. revolt, arise, rise (DISOBEDIENCE); debauch, dissipate, racket (PLEASURE); lark, skylark, rollick (MERRIMENT).

rip, v. fray, frazzle, shred (TEARING).

ripe, adj. mature, mellow, seasoned (MATURITY).

ripen, v. mature, mellow (MATURITY); evolve, develop (UNFOLDMENT); age (OLDNESS).

ripple, v. billow, surge, swell (RIVER); oscillate, undulate, vibrate (OSCILLATION).

ripply, adj. wavy, undulating, undulant (WINDING).

rise, n. upgrade, uprise (SLOPE); eminence, highland, promontory (HEIGHT); boost, step-up, growth (INCREASE).

rise, v. ascend, climb (ASCENT); awake, rouse (WAKEFULNESS); crop up, appear (SURFACE); emerge, dawn (VISIBILITY); rebel, revolt (DISOBEDIENCE).

rise above, v. tower above, jut above, overhang (HEIGHT).

rise and fall, v. billow, surge, undulate (ASCENT).

risk, v. gamble, hazard, speculate (CHANCE, DANGER).

risqué, adj. lurid, purple, racy, off-color (OBSCENITY).

rite, n. ceremony, custom, ritual (FORMALITY, OBSERVANCE).

rites, n. liturgy, ritual, ritualism (WORSHIP).

ritual, *n.* liturgy, rites, ritualism (WORSHIP); ceremonial, ceremony, rite (FORMALITY).

rival, *adj.* opposing, competitive, emulous (OPPOSITION, ATTEMPT).

rival, *n.* opponent, antagonist, competitor (OPPOSITION, ATTEMPT).

RIVER—N. river, stream, watercourse, water system, waterway, canal, bourn, millstream; branch, tributary, affluent, confluent; headwaters.

rivulet, streamlet, brook, brooklet, runlet, runnel, creek, run, burn, rill, bayou, spring.

current, stream, course, flow, tide, race, sluice, tiderace, millrace, torrent; undercurrent, undertow, underset, crosscurrent, eddy, rip tide; seiche; billow, surge, tidal wave.

whirlpool, maelstrom, vortex, eddy, Charybdis.

tide, spring tide, high tide, flood tide, full tide, neap tide, ebb tide, low tide.

waterfall, fall, cascade, torrent, cataract, Niagara, chute, chutes, rapids.

wave, beachcomber, billow, breaker, comber, decuman, surge, tidal wave, whitecap; wavelet, ripple, ripplet; surf, sea, swell; trough.

source (*of a river*), origin, spring, fount, fountain, fountainhead, head, headspring, riverhead.

spring, hot spring, thermal spring, geyser, mineral spring, spa.

V. billow, ripple, surge, swell, roll, rise, flow, eddy; break against (on, *or* upon), dash against (on, *or* upon); fall, cascade, cataract.

flow, run, stream, gush, pour, spout, roll, jet, well, issue, ooze, spill, spurt, geyser; purl, gurgle, babble, murmur, meander, swirl, splash, plash, swash.

flow into, fall into, open into, empty into, drain into; discharge itself, disembogue.

Adj. **riverine,** fluvial, fluviatile, fluviomarine, riverlike; riverside, riparian; Nilotic, Rhenish, transpadane.

billowy, billowing, surgy, surging; eddying, flowing, streaming, tidal, torrent, torrentful, torrential, torrentuous; vortical, vorticose, vortiginous; rippling, ripply, rolling, swelling; choppy, chopping.

See also EGRESS, LAKE, OCEAN, WATER. *Antonyms*—See LAND.

riverside, *n.* riverbank, bank, shore (LAND).

road, *n.* artery, highway, thoroughfare (WALKING, PASSAGE).

roam, *v.* stroll, tramp, rove (WANDERING).

roar, *v.* bellow, blare, trumpet (LOUDNESS, ANIMAL SOUND); bawl, clamor (SHOUT); boom, thunder (ROLL, RESONANCE); crash, clatter (LOUDNESS); howl, guffaw (LAUGHTER).

roast, *v.* cook, bake, rotisserie (COOKERY); be hot, swelter, broil (HEAT).

rob, *v.* loot, rifle, burglarize (THIEVERY).

robber, *n.* burglar, bandit, brigand (THIEF).

robbery, *n.* brigandage, plunderage, pillage (THIEVERY, PLUNDER).

robe, *n.* outfit, costume (CLOTHING); frock, gown, dress (SKIRT).

robust, *adj.* stout, sturdy, strapping (STRENGTH, HEALTH).

rock, *v.* roll, sway, careen (ROTATION, OSCILLATION); jog, jounce, jiggle (SHAKE); stagger, reel, totter (UNSTEADINESS).

ROCK—N. rock, boulder, slab, dornick; megalith, monolith, menhir (*all prehist.*); bedrock, shelf, ledge; molten rock, lava, scoria, cinders, slag; marble, Carrara marble, Carrara; gneiss, granite, schist, mica schist, limestone, travertine, chalk, chalkstone, shale, slate.

stone, cobblestone, cobble, flagstone, flag, flint, pebble, gravel, riprap, rubble; cornerstone, quoin, coin; tile, quarry; obelisk, shaft; concrete, cement, sand, mortar; stonework, masonry, rubblework; stoneworks, quarry; cairn, cromlech, dolmen.

pavement, cobblestones, concrete, flagstones, flagging, gravel, pebbles, asphalt, macadam.

[*sciences*] **lithology,** petrography, petrology, stratigraphy.

stoneworker, mason, stonecutter, lapicide, tiler.

V. **stone,** concrete, cement, gravel, mortar, pebble, slate, tile, mason, riprap, quoin; quarry.

pave, cobble, cobblestone, concrete, flag, flagstone, gravel, pebble, macadamize, asphalt.

[*turn into stone*] **petrify,** lapidify, mineralize, calcify.

Adj. **rocky,** stony, lithic, rupestral, rupestrian, lapidarian; stonelike, rocklike, petrous, lithoid; petrified, calcified.

See also HARDNESS, HEIGHT, JEW-

ELRY, METAL. *Antonyms*—See SOFT-NESS.

rocky, *adj.* stony, petrous, calcified (ROCK); wavery, wobbly, tottery (UNSTEADINESS); uncertain, chancy (*colloq.*), precarious (UNCERTAINTY).

ROD—*N.* rod, wand, baton, scepter *or* sceptre, verge, crosier *or* crozier, mace, caduceus, Hermes' staff, crook.

stick, stave, stake, pole, pikestaff, walking stick, Malacca cane, cane; skewer, broach, brochette, spit.

regalia, insignia, paraphernalia, badges, emblems, ensigns, decorations.

See also HITTING, MAGIC, ORNAMENT, SEARCH.

rodent, *n.* mouse, rat (ANIMAL).

rogue, *n.* rascal, knave, scamp (DISHONESTY, DECEPTION); mischief-maker, villain (MISCHIEF); monstrosity, sport (UNUSUALNESS).

role, *n.* character, personification, impersonation (PART); pose, posture, guise (PRETENSE).

roll, *n.* scroll, roster (LIST, ROLL, NAME); biscuit, bun (BREAD).

ROLL—*N.* roll, scroll, document; register, record, list, rota, catalogue, inventory, schedule.

roller, cylinder, barrel, drum, trundle, rundle, truck, trolley, wheel.

reverberation, echoing, rumbling, rumble, drumming, resonance, bombilation, bombination, booming, boom, thunder, cannonade, drumfire, barrage; rat-a-tat, rub-a-dub, pitapat, quaver, pitter-patter, tattoo, racket, rattle, clatter, clangor, whir, drone.

V. roll, revolve, rotate, wheel, trundle, turn, turn over, whirl, gyrate; bowl.

wrap, envelop, wind, muffle, swathe, fold, furl, lap, bind; infold, inwrap, involve, inclose.

smooth, level, press, flatten.

sway, incline, lean, lurch, reel, pitch, swing, jibe, yaw (*as a ship*), wallow, welter.

reverberate, re-echo, resound; drum, boom, roar, thunder, bombinate, rumble; clack, clatter, rattle; patter, pitapat, pitpat, pitter-patter; whir, rustle, hum; trill, quaver; tootle, chime, peal.

undulate, wave, swell, billow.

See also FLATNESS, INCLOSURE, LOUDNESS, MOTION, PAPER, RECORD, REPETITION, RESONANCE, ROTATION,

ROUNDNESS, SMOOTHNESS, TURNING. *Antonyms*—See UNFOLDMENT.

roller, *n.* cylinder, barrel, drum (ROLL); caster, pulley (ROTATION); smoother, steam roller (SMOOTHNESS).

rollicking, *adj.* merry, rip-roaring, rip-roarious (MERRIMENT).

roly-poly, *adj.* fat, pudgy, chunky (SIZE).

romance, *n.* love story, fiction, novel (STORY); love affair, amour, flirtation (LOVE).

romantic, *adj.* amorous, erotic, Paphian (LOVE); fanciful, aerial, fantastic (UNREALITY); visionary, utopian, quixotic (IMAGINATION).

romanticist, *n.* dreamer, daydreamer, Don Quixote (IMAGINATION).

romanticize, *v.* dramatize, melodramatize, glamorize (EXCITEMENT, INTERESTINGNESS); heighten, embroider, color (EXAGGERATION).

Romeo, *n.* Casanova, Don Juan, Lothario (LOVE).

romp, *n.* frolic, gambol, antic (AMUSEMENT); tomboy, hoyden, chit (YOUTH).

romp, *v.* lark, caper, skylark (AMUSEMENT, PLAYFULNESS, JUMP).

roof, *n.* ceiling, top (COVERING).

room, *n.* apartment, chamber, alcove (SPACE); capacity, accommodation, volume (SPACE, CONTENTS).

room, *v.* lodge, board, live (INHABITANT).

rooming house, *n.* lodginghouse, boardinghouse, pension (HABITATION).

rooms, *n.* apartment, flat, suite (HABITATION).

roomy, *adj.* spacious, commodious, capacious (SPACE, WIDTH).

roost, *n.* resting place, lounge, perch (REST).

roost, *v.* alight, perch, sit (REST, SEAT).

rooster, *n.* cock, capon, cockerel (BIRD).

root, *n.* radicle, radix (BASE); reason, cause, basis (MOTIVATION, CAUSATION); etymon, stem (WORD).

root, *v.* place, fix, graft (LOCATION); dig, grub, rout (DIGGING).

rope, *n.* cord, string, twine (FILAMENT).

rose-colored, *adj.* pink, rosy, coral (RED); optimistic, Pollyanna, roseate (HOPE).

roster, *n.* roll, register (NAME).

rostrum, *n.* soapbox, stump, podium (SUPPORT).

rosy, *adj.* pink, coral, peach (RED); flesh-colored, incarnadine (SKIN); glowing, blooming; blushing (RED); cheerful, optimistic, bright (CHEERFULNESS, HOPE).

rot, *v.* decompose, putrefy, spoil (DECAY).

ROTATION—*N.* rotation, revolution, turning, gyration, circumvolution; pronation, supination; revolvency.

spin, turn, roll, trundle, twirl, whirl, birl, swirl, troll, tumble, pirouette; vortex, eddy, whirlpool, maelstrom, Charybdis; vertigo.

merry-go-round, carousel, whirligig, whirlabout, Ixion's wheel, top, teetotum; rotator, rotor, rundle; gyroscope, gyrostat; wheel, screw, turbine, propeller; windmill, treadmill; turnspit, jack, smokejack; flywheel, gear wheel, cogwheel, roller, caster, sheave, pulley.

pivot, axle, axis, gudgeon, swivel, hinge, pin, gimbals; arbor, mandrel, reel, spool, bobbin, cop, quill, whorl, wharve.

science of rotary motions: trochilics, gyrostatics.

V. rotate, revolve, turn round, turn, circle, gyrate, gyre, roll, trundle, twirl, whirl, whirligig, whirr, spin, birl, swirl, circumvolve, pivot, swivel, wheel, troll, tumble, pirouette, waltz; pronate, supinate; bowl, twiddle (*as the thumbs, etc.*).

roll, rock, billow, toss, pitch, lurch; wallow, welter; trundle, tumble, convolve, devolve.

Adj. rotatory, rotary, rotative; gyratory, gyral, whirligig, vertiginous, voluble; vortical, vorticular, vorticose, vortiginous.

See also DIZZINESS, ROLL, ROUNDNESS, TURNING. *Antonyms*—See FLATNESS, UNFOLDMENT.

---

rotten, *adj.* putrid, decomposed (DECAY); corruptible, venal (BRIBERY).

rotund, *adj.* fat, corpulent, overweight (SIZE); rounded, spheroid (ROUNDNESS).

roué, *n.* lecher, rake, Casanova (IMMORALITY, SEX).

rouge, *n.* paint, lipstick, pigment (BEAUTY, COLOR).

roughly, *adv.* thereabouts, in round numbers, roundly (NEARNESS).

ROUGHNESS—*N.* roughness, irregularity, asperity, nodosity, nodulation, stubble, burr.

V. roughen, rough, rough up,

crinkle, ruffle, crumple, rumple; corrugate; stroke the wrong way, rub the fur the wrong way; chap, coarsen, crisp, shag, splinter, wrinkle.

Adj. rough, uneven, bumpy, irregular, unlevel, rocky, broken, craggy, cragged, rugged, ragged, ruffled, shaggy, brambly, jagged; cross-grained, gnarled, gnarly, knotted, knotty, nodose (*tech.*), nodular, nodulated, nodulose, scraggly, scraggy; wrinkled, wrinkly, crisp, crispy, corrugated, scaly, scabrous; coarse, chapped, harsh, splintery.

crude, unwrought, roughhewn, rustic, rude, unfashioned, uncut, formless, shapeless; incomplete, unfinished, imperfect, rudimentary, vague.

[*of the sea or the weather*] stormy, tempestuous, boisterous, turbulent, violent, wild, choppy, inclement.

unrefined, coarse, rugged, unpolished, unkempt, uncultivated, uncultured, rude, blunt, gruff, brusque, churlish, uncivil, discourteous.

disorderly, riotous, noisy, unrestrained, vehement, rowdy, rowdyish, uproarious.

Adv. roughly, etc. (see *Adjectives*); harshly, cruelly, severely; incompletely, approximately, generally.

See also DEFORMITY, DISCOURTESY, FOLD, HARDNESS, INCOMPLETENESS, NATURALNESS, SEVERITY, UNRULINESS, VIOLENCE, VULGARITY, WIND, WRINKLE. *Antonyms*—See GLASSINESS, MILDNESS, OIL, RUBBING, SMOOTHNESS, THINNESS.

---

roundabout, *adj.* devious, oblique, obliquitous (INDIRECTNESS); circumlocutory, ambagious (WORDINESS).

roundelay, *n.* round, glee, madrigal (SINGING).

ROUNDNESS—*N.* roundness, circularity, annularity, rotundity, sphericity, cylindricality, orbicularity, globosity, globularity, spheroidicity.

circle, ring, circlet, ringlet, gyre (*poetic*), wreath, equator, annulation, annulet, annulus; hoop, loop, eyelet, eye, grommet; roller, drum, caster, trolley, wheel, cycle, orb, orbit, disc, circuit, zone, belt, zonule, band; noose, lasso, bight, coil.

[*parts of a circle*] semicircle, hemicycle; quadrant, sextant, octant, sector; arc, circumference, diameter, radius.

ellipse, oval, ovoid, ellipsoid, cycloid, epicycle, epicycloid.

ball, globe, orb, sphere; globule, cylinder, spheroid, lobe, lobation.

V. circle, circulate, gyrate, mill around, purl, revolve, ring, roll, rotate, wheel, pivot, turn.

encircle, surround, ring, inclose, environ, encompass, girdle, wreathe.

Adj. round, rounded, spheroid, circular, orbiculate, rotund, lobate, cylindrical, beady; compass, cycloid, orbicular; discoid.

ringlike, annular, annulate, annulose, armillary.

spherical, ampullaceous, global, globate, globoid, globular, orbicular, spheriform.

elliptical, oval, ovoid, elliptoid, egg-shaped.

See also CENTER, CURVE, ENVIRONMENT, INCLOSURE, JEWELRY, ROLL, ROTATION, SWELLING. Antonyms—See STRAIGHTNESS, VERTICALITY.

rouse, v. excite, arouse, waken (MOTIVATION, EXCITEMENT); rise, wake, wake up (WAKEFULNESS).

route, n. line, path, road, track (DIRECTION); itinerary, way, run (PASSAGE).

routine, adj. habitual, customary, usual (HABIT); periodic, regular (UNIFORMITY).

routine, n. usage, practice (HABIT); formula, technique (METHOD).

rove, v. stroll, roam, range (WANDERING).

rover, n. gadabout, gallivanter, roamer, rambler (WANDERING).

row, n. line, string, queue (LENGTH); fracas, fray, words (DISAGREEMENT).

row, v. paddle, pull, scull (SAILOR); quarrel, fight, squabble (DISAGREEMENT).

rowdy, adj. noisy, uproarious, disorderly (ROUGHNESS, VIOLENCE).

rowdy, n. ruffian, roughneck (colloq.), hooligan (VIOLENCE).

rower, n. oar, oarsman, paddler (SAILOR).

rowing race, n. boat race, regatta (ATTEMPT).

royal, adj. regal, sovereign, princely (RULER).

royalty, n. crowned heads, the crown, the throne (RULER); income, receipts, revenue (PAYMENT).

rub, v. abrade, bark, chafe; massage, stroke, pat (RUBBING).

rubberneck (slang), n. onlooker, beholder, sightseer (LOOKING).

rubbers, n. overshoes, galoshes (FOOTWEAR).

rubbery, adj. spongy, resilient, elastic (JUMP).

RUBBING—N. rubbing, friction, wear, traction, attrition, trituration; massage, rubdown, chirapsia; pat, stroke, sponge, swab, wipe, polish, shine, smear; scrape, scrub, scour, scuff; abrasion, excoriation, chafe, chafing; anointment, unction.

abrasive, pumice, file, rasp, razor, triturator, grate, grater; sponge, swab, towel, wiper, mop; polisher, buffer, brush, waxer.

rubber, burnisher, furbisher; masseur, masseuse (fem.).

V. rub, abrade, bark, chafe, gall, excoriate, grate, file, rasp, raze, scrape, scuff, wear, triturate, bray; wipe, towel, swab, sponge, scrub, scour, mop, brush; anoint, massage, rub down, stroke, pat, plaster, smear.

polish, buff, burnish, furbish, pumice, shine, sleek, wax.

grind, bray, levigate, comminute, pulverize, bruise, crunch.

See also CLEANNESS, LIGHT, OIL, POWDERINESS, PRESSURE, SMOOTHNESS, SPREAD, WAX. Antonyms—See ROUGHNESS, WRINKLE.

rubbish, n. trash, junk (colloq.), debris (USELESSNESS, WORTHLESSNESS, UNCLEANNESS).

rubble, n. scrap, waste, trash (USELESSNESS, UNCLEANNESS).

rubdown, n. massage, chirapsia (RUBBING).

rube (slang), n. clodhopper, boor, yokel (RURAL REGION).

ruby, adj. crimson, scarlet (RED).

ruddy, adj. flushed, florid, rubicund (RED).

rude, adj. ill-bred, mannerless, uncivil (DISCOURTESY); unkempt, uncultivated, uncultured, (ROUGHNESS); rough, rowdy (VIOLENCE); unfashioned, formless, shapeless (ROUGHNESS).

rudimentary, adj. immature, vestigial, primitive (IMMATURITY); elementary, basic (BEGINNING).

rueful, adj. doleful, mournful, sorry (SADNESS); penitent, remorseful, contrite (REGRET).

ruff, n. mane, fringe (HAIR); feathers, plumage, tuft (FEATHER); collar, choker (colloq.), dickey (NECKWEAR).

ruffian, n. roughneck (colloq.), rowdy, hooligan (VIOLENCE).

ruffle, v. agitate, flurry, fluster (EXCITEMENT); crinkle, crumple, rumple (ROUGHNESS); crease, cockle, pucker (WRINKLE).

rug, *n.* carpet, carpeting, runner (COVERING).

rugged, *adj.* tough, lusty, hardy (STRENGTH, ENERGY); stormy, tempestuous (WIND); unrefined, coarse (ROUGHNESS).

ruin, *n.* wreck, wreckage, demolition (DESTRUCTION); downfall, fall, overthrow (MISFORTUNE).

ruin, *v.* wreck, smash, demolish (DESTRUCTION); damage, sabotage, vandalize (HARM).

ruinous, *adj.* harmful, damaging, hurtful (HARM).

ruins, *n.* remains, ashes, relics (DESTRUCTION).

RULE—N. rule, principle, regulation, law, prescript, dictum, prescription, regimen, precept, canon, maxim, formula, convention, punctilio; axiom, theorem, postulate, fundamental, basis, keynote, keystone; guide, polestar, lodestar, evangel, tenet, logos (*philos.*); standard, test, criterion, model, precedent; habit, routine, custom, order, method; normality, normalcy; hard-and-fast rule, Procrustean law, law of the Medes and Persians.

rules, discipline, rules and regulations, code, ideology, philosophy, theory, system, protocol, platform; doctrine, dogma, credenda, gospel.

conventionality, formalism, legalism, rigidity, ceremony; nomism, rationalism.

sway, government, dominion, empire, authority, control, direction, jurisdiction, sovereignty, regnancy, reign.

ruler, straightedge, slide rule.

V. **rule,** control, govern, reign, guide, conduct, direct, command, manage; curb, bridle, restrain.

decide, determine, settle, fix, establish, conclude, decree, adjudicate, judge, hold, pass upon; postulate, prescribe, theorize.

Adj. **punctilious,** conventional, formal, formalistic, ceremonious, legalistic, rigid, scrupulous; conscientious, principled, highly principled, ethical, honorable, moral, righteous, upright, virtuous.

See also CONTROL, DECISION, FORMALITY, GOVERNMENT, GUIDANCE, HABIT, JUDGMENT, METHOD, OBSERVANCE, POWER, RESTRAINT, RULER, TEST, UNIFORMITY. *Antonyms*—See DISOBEDIENCE, IRREGULARITY, NONOBSERVANCE, UNNATURALNESS.

ruler, *n.* straightedge, slide rule (RULE).

RULER—N. ruler, master, controller, director, leader, boss (*slang*),

big shot (*slang*), kingpin (*colloq.*), mastermind; lord, commander, commandant, captain, chief, chieftain; paterfamilias, patriarch, head, senior, governor, margrave (*hist.*); sirdar, sachem, sagamore, *burra sahib* (*India*), emir, aga *or* agha (*Turkish*), *Führer* (*Ger.*); statesman, politician.

chief of state, president, gerent, governor-general, magistrate, chief magistrate, first magistrate, archon, overlord, potentate, tetrarch; bey, khan, dey, kaiser, shogun, tycoon; maharajah, rajah, rao, gaekwar, thakur, nizam, amir *or* ameer, mirza, nawab (*Indian ruling chiefs*).

autocrat, despot, benevolent despot, dictator, tyrant, czar, Caesar, kaiser, oppressor; oligarch.

king, monarch, sovereign, majesty, dynast, prince, overking, suzerain, the crown, the throne, crowned head, supreme ruler, imperator; kinglet; rana, shah, padishah, sultan, pharaoh (*anc. Egypt*), mogul; crowned heads, royalty.

emperor, Caesar, mikado (*Jap.*), Tenno (*Jap.*); czar, tsar, *or* tzar (*Russia*); kaiser, imperator (*anc. Rome*).

queen, empress, czarina, maharani (*Moham.*), rani (*India*), begum (*Moslem*); queen consort, queen dowager, queen mother, sultana, sultaness, vicereine.

princess, princess royal, crown princess, czarevna.

prince, crown prince, prince royal, Prince of Wales (*Gr. Brit.*), prince consort, czarevitch, grand duke, archduke.

regent, viceroy, khedive, mandarin, tetrarch, satrap, bey, pasha, vicegerent, vice-regent, prince regent; *gauleiter* (*Ger.*), deputy.

group of rulers: triarchy *or* triumvirate (*three*), tetrarchy (*four*), pentarchy (*five*), decemvirate (*ten*).

one of a group of rulers: duarch (*two*), triumvir (*three*), tetrarch (*four*), pentarch (*five*), decemvir (*ten*).

statesmanship, statecraft, politics, kingcraft.

Adj. **kingly,** monarchal, monarchic, monarchial, royal, regal, sovereign, princely, suzerain, imperatorial; queenly.

See also CONTROL, DEPUTY, GOVERNMENT, LEADERSHIP, RULE, SOCIAL CLASS. *Antonyms*—See SERVICE, SLAVERY.

ruling, *adj.* regnant, reigning, sovereign (GOVERNMENT).

rumble, v. boom, thunder, roll (RESONANCE, LOUDNESS).

RUMOR—N. **rumor,** hearsay, comment, buzz, report, repute, talk, *ouidire* (*F.*); idle rumor, gossip, scandal, tales, tattle, tittle-tattle, canard, tale.

rumormonger, gossip, newsmonger, quidnunc, rumorer, talebearer, taleteller, tattler, telltale, tittle-tattle.

V. [*spread rumor*] **gossip,** tattle, tittle-tattle, buzz, noise it about (abroad, *or* around), rumor.

Adj. **rumored,** bruited, bruited about, buzzed, gossiped, noised around, reported, reputed; rumorous, gossipy.

See also DISCLOSURE, INFORMATION, PUBLICATION. *Antonyms*—See REALITY, TRUTH.

rump, n. backside, tail (*slang*), buttocks (REAR).

rumple, v. tousle, dishevel, bedraggle (CONFUSION, UNTIDINESS); ruffle, crumple, cockle (FOLD, ROUGHNESS); seam, wreathe (WRINKLE).

rumpled, *adj.* disheveled, tousled, unkempt, untidy (UNTIDINESS).

rumpus, n. pandemonium, uproar, tumult (COMMOTION, LOUDNESS).

run, n. series, sequence, succession (FOLLOWING); trip, journey, tour (TRAVELING).

run, v. race, dart, dash, gallop (SPEED); flow, stream, gush (RIVER); continue, move past (PASSAGE).

run amuck, v. run wild, rage, riot (VIOLENCE).

runaway, n. refugee, maroon, deserter (DEPARTURE).

run away, v. escape, flee, desert (DEPARTURE).

run away with, v. abduct, kidnap (TAKING).

runner, n. courier, intelligencer (MESSENGER); scatter rug, throw rug (COVERING).

running, *adj.* speeding, procursive, cursorial (SPEED); cursive, flowing (WRITING).

run over, v. spread over, overspread, overgrow (OVERRUNNING).

runt, n. midget, peewee, shrimp (SMALLNESS).

rupture, n. breach, hernia (DISJUNCTION); misunderstanding, clash, rift (DISAGREEMENT).

rupture, v. burst, shatter, erupt (BLOWING).

RURAL REGION—N. **rural region,** country, countryside, suburbs.

rurality, rusticity, ruralism, pastoralism, pastorality, peasantry, provincialism, provinciality.

country dweller, countryman, rural, ruralist, ruralite, rustic, bucolic (*jocose*); farmer, peasant, churl, chuff, clodhopper, rube (*slang*), boor, yokel (*contemptuous*), bumpkin, swain; villager, exurbanite, suburbanite, native.

pastorale (*music*), pastoral, idyl, bucolic, eclogue.

V. **ruralize,** rusticate.

Adj. **rural,** rustic, countrified, countrylike, bucolic, Arcadian, provincial, geoponic, georgic, pastoral, villatic, sylvan.

See also FARMING, LAND. *Antonyms*—See CITY.

ruse, n. hoax, shift, subterfuge (DECEPTION).

rush, n. haste, hurry, precipitance (SPEED); trifle, trinket, picayune (WORTHLESSNESS).

rush, v. hurry, hasten, tear off (SPEED); surge, thrash, whip (VIOLENCE).

rust, v. mildew, mold, stale, wither (OLDNESS).

rust-colored, *adj.* reddish-brown, ferruginous (BROWN).

rustic, *adj.* rural, countrified (RURAL REGION); crude, unwrought, roughhewn (ROUGHNESS); austere, primitive, Spartan (SIMPLICITY); homely, homespun, provincial (VULGARITY).

rustle, v. whir, hum (ROLL).

rusty, *adj.* inexperienced, green, unpracticed (CLUMSINESS).

rut, n. furrow, groove, rabbet (HOLLOW); heat, oestrus (SEX).

ruthless, *adj.* sadistic, merciless, pitiless (CRUELTY); obdurate, relentless, remorseless (INSENSITIVITY).

S

saber, n. foil, rapier, scimitar (CUTTING).

sabotage, n. damage, malicious mischief, vandalism (HARM, DESTRUCTION).

sac, n. bursa, bladder, cyst (BELLY).

saccharine, *adj.* sugary, candied, honeyed (SWEETNESS).

sack, n. pouch, bag (CONTAINER).

sack, v. strip, rob, gut (PLUNDER).

SACREDNESS—N. **sacredness,** inviolability, sanctity, solemnity, spirituality, spiritualism, venerability; sacred cow.

[*sacred place*] **shrine, sanctuary,** bethel, sanctum, sanctum sanctorum.

saint, sainthood, beatification (*R.C.Ch.*), canonization (*R.C.Ch.*); hierology, hagiology, sanctilogy, canon (*R.C.Ch.*); menology, hagiography.

V. **sanctify,** consecrate, hallow, enshrine, anoint, bless; saint, canonize, beatify.

Adj. **sacred,** inviolable, sacrosanct, holy, blessed, hallowed, enshrined, consecrated, anointed, hieratic, sanctified, venerable, spiritual, solemn, pious, taboo.

sainted, saintly, angelic *or* angelical; venerable, beatified, canonized (*all R.C.Ch.*).

See also RELIGION, SACRED WRITINGS, SPIRITUALITY. *Antonyms*—See DISRESPECT, IRRELIGION, MALEDICTION.

SACRED WRITINGS—*N.* **sacred writings,** Scripture, the Scriptures, Holy Scripture, Holy Writ, the Bible, the Book, the Book of Books, the Good Book, the Word, the Word of God, Gospel; Vulgate, King James Bible, Douay Bible; Talmud, Torah, Haggadah; oracles; Ten Commandments, Decalogue; codex, concordance; pseudepigrapha.

Old Testament, Septuagint, Genesis, Pentateuch, Heptateuch, Hexateuch, Octateuch, Apocrypha.

New Testament, Gospels, Evangelists, Acts, Epistles, Apocalypse, Revelation, Revelations.

[*non-Biblical*] the Vedas, Upanishads, puranas, sutras, sasta *or* shastra, tantra, Bhagavad-Gita (*all Brahmanic*); the Koran *or* Alcoran (*Moham.*); Zend-Avesta, Avesta (*Zoroastrian*); Tripitaka, Dhammapada (*Buddhist*); agamas (*Jain*); Granth, Adigranth (*Sikh*); the Kings (*Chinese*); the Eddas (*Scandinavian*).

Bible scholar, Biblist, Biblicist, Talmudist; textualist; Biblicism, textualism.

Adj. **Biblical,** Scriptural, sacred, Vulgate, apocalyptic, revealed; apocryphal, Genesiac *or* Genesitic, Talmudic, Vedaic; pseudepigraphic, pseudepigraphous; ecclesiastical, canonical, textual, textuary, Biblicistic.

See also GOD, RELIGION, SACREDNESS. *Antonyms*—See IRRELIGION.

sacrifice, *n.* forfeiture, immolation; victim, gambit, pawn (RELINQUISHMENT).

sacrifice, *v.* forfeit, give up, immolate (RELINQUISHMENT).

sacrilegious, *adj.* blasphemous, profane, impious (DISRESPECT).

sad, *adj.* melancholy, sorry, sorrowful (SADNESS).

sadden, *v.* distress, desolate (SADNESS).

sadistic, *adj.* brutal, ruthless, barbarous (CRUELTY).

SADNESS—*N.* **sadness,** melancholy, unhappiness, dolor (*poetic*), tristesse (*F.*); disconsolation, inconsolability, distress, wrench.

sorrow, grief, woe; heavy heart, broken heart, heartbreak, heartache, tribulation; world sorrow, *Weltschmerz* (*Ger.*); misery, desolation, languishment; lamentation.

lament, jeremiad, keen, dirge, elegy, requiem, threnody; the blues.

kill-joy, spoilsport, wet blanket, dampener.

V. **sadden,** distress, desolate; lament, deplore, mourn, grieve, sorrow; bemoan, bewail, keen, moan, wail, sigh, snivel, brood, languish; elegize.

Adj. **sad,** melancholy, melancholic, pensive, wistful, broody; adust, atrabilious, dolorous, doleful, tristful, *triste* (*F.*), mournful, rueful, somber, sorry; disconsolate, inconsolable, unconsolable, distressed, distressful.

sorrowful, sorrowing, sorrowburdened, sorrow-laden, sorrowworn, sorrow-stricken; griefstricken, grief-laden, aggrieved, grieved; sick at heart, heartsick, heartsore, heart-stricken, heavyhearted, sore at heart; woe-laden, woeful, woe-stricken, woe-dejected; brokenhearted, heartbroken.

miserable, wretched, tragic, desolate, desolated, forlorn.

unhappy, mirthless, blissless, cheerless, joyless, unblissful, uncheerful, unecstatic, unglad, ungleeful, unjoyful, unjoyous.

mournful, dirgeful, doleful, elegiac, funereal; lugubrious, moanful, plaintive, lamentatory, wailful, wailsome, rueful, woebegone, woeful.

lamentable, deplorable, tragic, rueful, grievous, miserable, pathetic, pitiable, pitiful, sorry, wretched.

See also DEJECTION, GLOOM, HOPELESSNESS, REGRET, WEEPING. *Antonyms*—See CHEERFULNESS, HAPPINESS, IMPENITENCE, MERRIMENT, PLEASURE.

safe, *adj.* protected, secure, armored (PROTECTION).

safe, *n.* coffer, bank, vault (MONEY); cache, hiding place (CONCEALMENT).

safebreaker, *n.* yegg, Raffles (THIEF).

safeguard, *n.* guard, shield, screen (PROTECTION).

safeguard, *v.* protect, preserve, conserve (PROTECTION).

safekeeping, *n.* preservation, conservation, custody (PROTECTION).

safety, *n.* security, shelter, asylum (PROTECTION).

sag, *v.* lean, curve, bow (BEND); drop, fall (DECREASE); droop, flag, languish (FATIGUE, WEAKNESS, HANGING).

sagacious, *adj.* sage, wise, shrewd (WISDOM).

sage, *n.* wise man, Solomon, Nestor (WISDOM).

saggy, *adj.* pendulous, flabby, droopy (HANGING).

said, *adj.* stated, expressed, verbal (STATEMENT); above, above-mentioned, above-stated (PRECEDENCE).

sail, *v.* cruise, cross, navigate (SAILOR, TRAVELING).

sailboat, *n.* clipper, schooner (SHIP).

SAILOR—N. sailor, sailorman, seaman, seafarer, seafaring man, sea dog (*colloq.*), cruiser, voyager, mariner; navigator, circumnavigator; deck hand, gob (*colloq.*), salt (*colloq.*), windjammer, tar (*colloq.*), limey (*Brit.*); able seaman, A.B., midshipman, mate, boatswain; crew, ship.

marine, leatherneck, devil dog.

boatman, boater, yachtsman, gondolier; ferryman, charon (*jocose*); rower, oar, oarsman, paddler, sculler, stroke.

steersman, helmsman, pilot, coxswain.

commanding officer, captain, master, skipper, old man (*colloq.*).

naval officer (*U.S.*), petty officer, ensign, lieutenant j.g., lieutenant, lieutenant commander, commander, captain, commodore, rear admiral, vice-admiral, admiral, admiral of the fleet.

rowing, paddling, canoeing; oarsmanship, watermanship.

oar, paddle, scull, sweep, pole.

navigation, nautics, seamanship, pilotship, boatmanship; circumnavigation, cabotage.

V. sail, cruise, boat, voyage, steam; navigate, pilot, circumnavigate; put to sea, set sail, gather way; go aboard, embark, ship.

row, paddle, pull, scull, punt, oar (*poetic*), propel, ply the oar.

Adj. nautical, maritime, sailorly, navigational, marine, naval; seafaring, seagoing, ocean-going; coasting, coastwise, coastal; navigable.

See also FIGHTING, SHIP, TRAVELING. *Antonyms*—See LAND.

saintly, *adj.* sainted, angelic, godly (SACREDNESS, RELIGIOUSNESS); righteous, holy (MORALITY).

salacious, *adj.* lascivious, licentious, libidinous, pornographic (SEX, OBSCENITY).

salary, *n.* pay, earnings, emolument (PAYMENT).

SALE—N. sale, disposal, negotiation, vendition, auction, vendue; resale, clearance sale, mongering *or* mongery (*derogatory*), simony; salesmanship.

seller, vender *or* vendor, auctioneer, regrater, trafficker, bootlegger, monger, chandler; salesman, salesperson, saleswoman, salesclerk, salesgirl.

merchant, dealer, trader, tradesman, shopkeeper, marketer, commission merchant, mercantile agent, factor; retailer, middleman, jobber, wholesaler.

peddler, canvasser, solicitor, costermonger (*Brit.*), pedlar, hawker, higgler, packman, butcher, chapman (*Brit.*), colporteur *or* colporter, huckster.

traveling salesman, commercial traveler, drummer, traveler.

merchandise, wares, commodities, goods, effects, articles, stock, produce, vendibles, stock in trade, cargo.

V. sell, vend, market, merchandise, merchant, regrate, negotiate, retail, wholesale, trade in, traffic in, truck, deal in, dispense, furnish; barter, exchange, trade; auction, sell at auction, put up at auction; bootleg; resell.

undersell, discount, sell at discount, hold a sale, clear out, dump, unload, get rid of, give away.

peddle, canvass, solicit, hawk, higgle, costermonger (*Brit.*).

be sold for, bring, fetch, get, bring in, sell for, yield, cost.

Adj. salable, marketable, vendible, negotiable, trafficable, merchantable; staple, in demand, popular.

See also EXCHANGE, STORE. *Antonyms*—See EXPENDITURE, PAYMENT, PURCHASE.

salient, *adj.* conspicuous, prominent; protruding, jutting (VISIBILITY); saltant (JUMP).

SALIVA—*N.* saliva, spittle, sputum, spit, slaver, slobber, drool, drivel.

salivation, spitting, expectoration, splutter, sputter, ptyalism (*med.*), hemoptysis (*med.*).

[*vessel*] cuspidor, spittoon.

expectorant, salivant, salivator, sialogogue.

V. spit, expectorate, salivate, slaver, slobber, drool, drivel, disgorge, splutter, sputter.

Adj. salivary, salivous, sialoid; salivant, salivatory, sialagogic.

See also EXCRETION, THROAT.

sallow, *adj.* bloodless, pale-faced, anemic (COLORLESSNESS, YELLOW).

sally, *n.* witticism, squib, pleasantry (WITTINESS); outrush, debouch (EGRESS).

saloon, *n.* dramshop, gin mill (*colloq.*), bar (ALCOHOLIC LIQUOR); rotunda, casino, hall (SPACE).

salt, *n.* zest, spice, savor (INTERESTINGNESS); sodium chloride, brine; flavoring, seasoning (TASTE).

salt, *v.* flavor, season, spice (TASTE, INTERESTINGNESS); cure, pickle, souse (PRESERVING).

salty, *adj.* salt, saline, briny (TASTE); racy, breezy, pungent (INTERESTINGNESS, EXCITEMENT); ribald, spicy (WITTINESS).

salutation, *n.* greetings, hail, salute (GREETING); address, compellation (TITLE).

salute, *v.* greet, welcome (GREETING, TALK).

salvation, *n.* liberation, delivery, salvage (FREEDOM); preservation, safekeeping, custody (PROTECTION).

salve, *n.* ointment, lotion, balm (CURE, CALMNESS).

same, *adj.* alike, identical, duplicate (SIMILARITY); colorless, drab (UNIFORMITY).

sample, *n.* example, specimen (COPY); morsel, bit, drop (TASTE).

sample, *v.* partake of, savor, sip (TASTE).

sanatorium, *n.* rest home, convalescent home (HEALTH).

sanctify, *v.* consecrate, hallow, bless (SACREDNESS).

sanctimonious, *adj.* self-righteous, pharisaical (MORALITY); religionistic, pietistical (IRRELIGION); hypocritical, canting (PRETENSE).

sanction, *v.* empower, authorize, allow (PERMISSION); confirm, ratify (APPROVAL).

sanctity, *n.* inviolability, solemnity, spirituality (SACREDNESS).

sanctuary, *n.* retreat, preserve, shelter (PROTECTION); temple, shrine, sanctum (SACREDNESS, CHURCH).

sand, *n.* powder, dust, grit (POWDERINESS).

sandal, *n.* scuff, pump, mule (FOOTWEAR).

sand bar, *n.* shallow, shoal, flat (SHALLOWNESS, LAND).

sandy, *adj.* dusty, arenaceous (POWDERINESS); fair-haired, xanthochroid (HAIR).

sane, *adj.* rational, sensible, normal (SANITY, REASONABLENESS).

sang-froid (*F.*), *n.* nonchalance, insouciance, coolness (CALMNESS).

sanguinary, *adj.* bloody, gory (BLOOD, KILLING).

sanitarium, *n.* sanatorium, rest home (HEALTH).

sanitary, *adj.* hygienic, uncontaminated, uninfected (HEALTH, CLEANNESS).

sanitation, *n.* hygiene, prophylaxis (HEALTH); disinfection, antisepsis (CLEANNESS).

SANITY—*N.* sanity, sound mind, mental health, mental balance, soundness of mind, rationality, lucidity, senses, *mens sana* (*L.*).

V. become sane, come to one's senses, sober down, cool down.

render sane, bring to one's senses, sober.

Adj. sane, lucid, rational, normal, wholesome, healthy, in possession of one's faculties, compos mentis (*L.*), mentally sound, sound of (*or* in) mind, sound-minded, of sound mind, well-balanced, in one's right mind; uncrazed, underanged, undistempered, undistraught, unfrenzied, uninsane.

neurosis-free, adjusted, balanced, unneurotic, well-adjusted, well-balanced; fully (*or* successfully) analyzed.

See also HEALTH, PSYCHOTHERAPY, WISDOM. *Antonyms*—See INSANITY, NERVOUSNESS, NEUROSIS.

sap, *n.* juice, latex, lymph (LIQUID).

sap, *v.* exhaust, impair, prostrate (WEAKNESS); burrow, tunnel, undermine (DIGGING).

sarcasm, *n.* sardonicism, irony, satire (RIDICULE, AMBIGUITY).

sarcastic, *adj.* cutting, biting, caustic (SHARPNESS, RIDICULE).

sardonic, *adj.* sarcastic, backhanded, mordant (RIDICULE); bitter, jaundiced (ANGER).

sash, *n.* belt, cummerbund, waistband (FASTENING, TROUSERS).

sassy, (*slang*), *adj.* saucy, snippy (*colloq.*), fresh (DISCOURTESY).

Satan, *n.* the devil, Pluto, Lucifer (DEVIL).

satanic, *adj.* demoniac, fiendish, Mephistophelian (DEVIL, WICKEDNESS).

satchel, *n.* suitcase, valise, grip (CONTAINER).

sate, *v.* appease, assuage, slake (SATISFACTION).

sated, *adj.* satiated, satiate, surfeited (FULLNESS).

satellite, *n.* moon, Sputnik, Vanguard (WORLD); hanger-on, parasite, heeler (ACCOMPANIMENT, FOLLOWER).

satiate, *v.* sate, saturate, surfeit (SATISFACTION, FULLNESS, DISGUST).

satire, *n.* parody, pasquinade, irony (RIDICULE, AMBIGUITY).

satirical, *adj.* ironic, Hudibrastic, burlesque (RIDICULE).

satirize, *v.* lampoon, parody, travesty (RIDICULE).

SATISFACTION—*N.* satisfaction, contentment, delight, fulfillment, gratification; ease, peace of mind, serenity; appeasement, assuagement; self-satisfaction, self-complacence, complacence.

satiety, satiation, repletion, saturation, plenitude, glut, surfeit.

V. **be satisfied,** be content, let well enough alone; be reconciled to, put up with.

satisfy, content, delight, gratify, fulfill, please, suit, suffice, appease, assuage, sate, slake; indulge, overindulge.

satiate, sate, saturate, cloy, jade, pall, glut, surfeit; bore, tire, weary, spoil.

[*satisfy hunger or thirst*] appease, assuage, gratify, pacify, sate, slake, quench; allay, alleviate, quiet, relieve, still.

Adj. **satisfied,** content, contented, well-content, well-satisfied, delighted, gratified, fulfilled, pleased, suited, sated, slaked, appeased, assuaged; self-satisfied, self-complacent, complacent, smug.

satiated, satiate, cloyed, glutted, palled, sated, surfeited; full, replete, gorged, overgorged, overfed; blasé (*F.*), jaded, sick of, fed up (*slang*).

satisfactory, satisfying, appeasing, assuaging, assuasive, contenting, delighting, delightful, delightsome, fulfilling, gratifying, indulgent, overindulgent, pleasing, sating; suitable, adequate, sufficient, ample, enough.

satisfiable, appeasable, gratifiable, satiable.

See also BOREDOM, FULLNESS, MILDNESS, PEACE, PLEASANTNESS, PLEASURE, SUFFICIENCY. *Antonyms*—See ABSENCE, INSUFFICIENCY, REGRET, UNPLEASANTNESS.

---

satisfy, *v.* answer, serve, tide over (SUFFICIENCY); content, delight, gratify (SATISFACTION).

saturate, *v.* impregnate, imbue, suffuse (FULLNESS); douse, drench, soak (WATER); satiate, surfeit, sate (EXCESS, SATISFACTION).

satyr, *n.* centaur, bucentaur, Minotaur (MYTHICAL BEINGS).

saucy, *adj.* malapert, pert, fresh (DISCOURTESY); rakish, sporty (FASHION).

saunter, *v.* promenade, stroll, amble (WALKING).

savage, *adj.* uncivilized, barbarian, barbaric (BARBARIANISM); barbarous, brutal, ferocious (VIOLENCE).

savagery, *n.* brutality, savagism, barbarity, atrocity, sadism, fierceness, ferocity (CRUELTY, VIOLENCE); barbarism, primitive culture (BARBARIANISM).

savant, *n.* learned person, scholar, bookman (LEARNING).

save, *v.* liberate, set free, rescue (FREEDOM); safeguard, protect, preserve (PROTECTION); lay away, be frugal, husband (STORE, ECONOMY).

savings, *n.* reserve, stockpile, nest egg (STORE).

savior, *n.* conservator, messiah (PROTECTION, FREEDOM).

Saviour, *n.* Jesus, the Messiah (CHRIST).

savor, *n.* flavor, smack, tang (TASTE); zest, salt, spice (INTERESTINGNESS).

savor, *v.* partake of, sip, sample (TASTE).

savor of, *v.* smack of, partake of (CHARACTER).

savory, *adj.* flavorful, luscious, delicious (TASTE, PLEASANTNESS).

say, *v.* speak, utter, pronounce (TALK, STATEMENT, VOICE).

saying, *n.* adage, proverb, byword (STATEMENT).

scabbard, *n.* holster, quiver, sheath (CONTAINER).

scaffold, *n.* platform, stage, dais (SUPPORT); gallows, gibbet (HANGING, KILLING).

scald, *v.* burn, sear, scorch (FIRE).

scale, *n.* balance, steelyard (WEIGHT); flake, lamella (LAYER); scurf, dander (BONE); gamut, key, clef (MUSIC).

scale, *v.* flake, delaminate, exfoliate, peel (LAYER).

scalpel, *n.* knife, lancet (SURGERY).

scaly, *adj.* lamellar, scalelike, lamelliform (LAYER); horny, scabrous, squamous (BONE).

scamp, *n.* rogue, imp, tyke (MISCHIEF); offscouring, scalawag (WORTHLESSNESS); scapegrace, varlet, villain (DISHONESTY).

scamper, *v.* run, hurry, scoot (SPEED).

scan, *v.* regard, pore over, contemplate (LOOKING); browse, thumb through, leaf through (READING).

scandal, *n.* ignominy, infamy, dishonor (DISGRACE); talk, gossip (RUMOR).

scandalous, *adj.* opprobrious, infamous, notorious (DISGRACE, DISREPUTE); shocking, ugly (UNPLEASANTNESS).

scant, *adj.* thin, scarce, inadequate (FEWNESS, INSUFFICIENCY, SHORTNESS).

scapegoat, *n.* fall guy (*slang*), whipping boy, goat (SUBSTITUTION, ACCUSATION).

scar, *n.* cicatrice, cicatrix, seam (BLEMISH).

scarce, *adj.* sparse, exiguous (FEWNESS); scant, short (INSUFFICIENCY); uncommon, rare (UNUSUALNESS).

scarcely, *adv.* hardly, barely, imperceptibly (SMALLNESS); infrequently, seldom, rarely (FEWNESS).

scarcity, *n.* dearth, paucity, poverty, famine, scantity (FEWNESS, INSUFFICIENCY).

scare, *v.* frighten, alarm, startle (FEAR).

scarf, *n.* bandanna, muffler; necktie, cravat (NECKWEAR); mantilla, shawl (HEADGEAR).

scarlet, *adj.* crimson, ruby, ruby-red (RED).

scatter, *v.* shower, spray, sprinkle (THROW); sow, disseminate, broadcast (DISPERSION).

scatterbrained, *adj.* harebrained, flighty, giddy (INATTENTION).

scattering, *n.* sprinkling, dash (SMALLNESS).

scene, *n.* sight, spectacle, view (VISION); locale, spot, setting (ENVIRONMENT, REGION); theater, stage, arena (ENVIRONMENT); picture, landscape, seascape (FINE ARTS).

scenery, *n.* surroundings, setting (ENVIRONMENT, DRAMA).

scent, *n.* smell, tang, fragrance, aroma, aura (ODOR).

scent, *v.* smell, sniff; perfume (ODOR); detect (DISCOVERY).

scepter, *n.* mace, verge, wand (ROD); badge, emblem, mark (REPRESENTATION).

schedule, *n.* timetable, calendar, program (LIST, ROLL).

scheme, *n.* plot, intrigue, machination (PLAN); tactics, system, strategy (METHOD).

scholar, *n.* student, pupil, schoolboy; learned person, savant, bookman (LEARNING).

scholarly, *adj.* schooled, literate, educated; studious, bookish (LEARNING); cultured, literary (STORY).

scholarship, *n.* lore, erudition, education (LEARNING).

scholastic, *adj.* academic, educational, collegiate (LEARNING, SCHOOL, TEACHING).

school, *v.* instruct, educate, tutor (TEACHING).

SCHOOL—*N.* school, academy, lyceum, palaestra (*wrestling*), manège (*riding*); seminary, college, institution, educational institution, institute, university, varsity (*colloq.*), alma mater; day school, boarding school, private school, finishing school, junior college, pension.

elementary school, public school, common school, grade (district, primary, nursery, kindergarten, *or* grammar) school.

secondary school, preparatory school, high school; *lycée* (*F.*), Gymnasium (*Ger.*), Realschule (*Ger.*); normal school, teachers' college; military academy, naval academy; summer school, university extension, adult classes, adult school.

vocational school, trade school, school of art, commercial (*or* business) school, conservatory, conservatoire.

Sunday school, Sabbath school, Bible school, Bible class.

schoolroom, classroom, recitation room, lecture room, lecture hall, theater, amphitheater, clinic.

desk, reading desk, lectern, pulpit, rostrum, platform, dais.

schoolbook, textbook, text, workbook, manual; grammar, primer, hornbook (*hist.*), reader, speller.

dean, principal, preceptor, headmaster, president.

Adj. **scholastic,** academic, vocational, professional, elementary, secondary, collegiate; educational, intramural, extramural, extracurricular.

See also BOOK, LEARNING, TEACHER, TEACHING.

schoolbook, *n.* textbook, workbook, manual (SCHOOL).

schooled, *adj.* literate, lettered, educated (TEACHING, LEARNING).

schooling, *n.* education, grounding, culture (LEARNING).

schoolroom, *n.* classroom, recitation room, lecture room (SCHOOL).

schoolteacher, *n.* schoolmaster, schoolmistress, pedagogue (TEACHER).

scimitar, *n.* foil, rapier, saber (CUTTING).

scintillate, *v.* glimmer, flicker, sparkle (LIGHT); be brilliant, coruscate (INTELLIGENCE); flash, be the life of the party (WITTINESS).

scoff at, *v.* disbelieve, discredit, reject (UNBELIEVINGNESS); jeer at, taunt, twit (RIDICULE).

SCOLDING—*N.* **scolding,** admonishment, admonition, castigation, censure, chiding, exprobration, lecture, objurgation, ragging, rag, rebuke, reprehension, reprimand, reproach, reproval, reproof, revilement, tongue-lashing, twit, whipping, upbraiding; comeuppance (*colloq.*), curtain lecture (*colloq.*), dressing-down, jobation (*colloq.*), lashing, speaking-to, talking-to.

scold, harridan, shrew, termagant, virago, Xanthippe.

V. **scold,** admonish, berate, bring to book, call to account, castigate, censure, chide, exprobrate, flay, lecture, objurgate, rag, rail at, rant at, rebuke, reprehend, reprimand, reproach, reprove, revile, slate, tax, tongue-lash, twit, whip, upbraid.

See also BAD TEMPER, DISAPPROVAL, MALEDICTION, SHARPNESS. *Antonyms* —See ACCEPTANCE, APPROVAL, PRAISE.

---

scoop, *n.* ladle, dipper, spoon (CONTAINER); shovel, spade, trowel (DIGGING); beat, story (PUBLICATION).

scope, *n.* margin, latitude, play (SPACE, FREEDOM); orbit, circle, field (POWER).

scorch, *v.* burn, singe, scald (FIRE); parch, stale, shrivel (DRYNESS).

score, *v.* nick, mill, cut (NOTCH).

scorn, *n.* derision, sport, mockery; target, butt (RIDICULE, CONTEMPT).

scorn, *v.* sneer at, despise (CONTEMPT); reject, disdain, spurn (DENIAL); slight, ignore, disregard (WORTHLESSNESS).

scoundrel, *n.* knave, rascal, rogue (DISHONESTY); scamp, imp, tyke (MISCHIEF).

scour, *v.* sandpaper, pumice, buff (SMOOTHNESS); scrub, mop, brush (RUBBING); ransack, rake, comb (SEARCH).

scout, *n.* patrol, picket, spotter (WARNING, LOOKING); ferret, detective, sleuth (DISCOVERY).

scowl, *v.* frown, glower, lour (ANGER).

scrap, *n.* rubble, wastements, re-

ject (USELESSNESS, ELIMINATION, UNCLEANNESS); quarrel, row, squabble (DISAGREEMENT).

scrap, *v.* discard, reject (ELIMINATION); quarrel, spat, have words (DISAGREEMENT).

scrape, *n.* predicament, plight, trouble (DIFFICULTY); kowtow, genuflection (RESPECT).

scrape, *v.* file, abrade, bray (POWDERINESS, RUBBING); pare, thin (DEDUCTION); peel, shave (SKIN); scrimp, skimp, stint (ECONOMY).

scratch, *v.* claw, scrabble (CUTTING); scrawl, scribble (WRITING).

scrawl, *v.* scribble, scrabble, scratch (WRITING).

scrawny, *adj.* skinny, bony, rawboned (THINNESS).

scream, *n.* screech, cry, shriek, outcry (HIGH-PITCHED SOUND, LOUDNESS).

scream, *v.* screech, shrill, shriek (LOUDNESS, SHOUT); laugh, guffaw, howl (LAUGHTER).

screech, *n.* cry, outcry, scream, shriek (HIGH-PITCHED SOUND, LOUDNESS).

screech, *v.* scream, shrill, shriek (LOUDNESS, SHOUT).

screen, *n.* shade, awning, canopy (DARKNESS); cover, curtain, shroud (CONCEALMENT); safeguard, guard, shield (PROTECTION); pictures (*colloq.*), Hollywood (MOTION PICTURES).

screen, *v.* protect, shade, shutter (PROTECTION); conceal, hide, obscure (CONCEALMENT); veil, cloud, blind (INVISIBILITY).

scribble, *v.* scrawl, scrabble, scratch (WRITING).

scribe, *n.* penman, chirographer, clerk (WRITER); annalist, archivist, diarist (RECORD).

scrimp, *v.* skimp, scrape, stint (ECONOMY).

script, *n.* printing, longhand, handwriting (WRITING); typescript, manuscript, article (TREATISE, WRITING).

Scriptural, *adj.* Biblical, sacred, Vulgate (SACRED WRITINGS).

Scriptures, *n.* Holy Scripture, Holy Writ, the Bible (SACRED WRITINGS).

scrub, *n.* brake, boscage, brushwood (PLANT LIFE).

scrub, *v.* scour, mop, brush (RUBBING).

scruple, *n.* doubt, misgiving, qualm (UNCERTAINTY); reluctance, hesitation (UNWILLINGNESS); conscience (PENITENCE).

scruple, *v.* have misgivings, falter (UNCERTAINTY); be unwilling, hesitate, stickle (UNWILLINGNESS).

scrupulous, *adj.* meticulous, painstaking, particular (CARE); rigorous, strict, punctilious (RIGHT); conscientious, moral, principled (HONESTY, RULE).

scrutinize, *v.* examine, inspect, contemplate (EXAMINATION, LOOKING).

scrutiny, *n.* survey, observation, inspection, study (EXAMINATION, LOOKING).

scuff, *n.* sandal, pump, mule (FOOTWEAR).

scuff, *v.* scrape, triturate, bray (RUBBING).

scuffle, *v.* struggle, tussle, skirmish (ATTEMPT, FIGHTING).

sculptor, *n.* carver, statuary, molder (ARTIST).

sculpture, *n.* carving, modeling, sculpturing (FINE ARTS).

sculpture, *v.* fashion, carve, hew (CUTTING, FINE ARTS, SHAPE).

scum, *n.* foam, froth, spume (FOAM); dregs, riffraff, vermin; cur, bugger (WORTHLESSNESS, MEANNESS, CONTEMPT).

scurrilous, *adj.* ribald, Rabelaisian, scabrous, (WITTINESS, OBSCENITY); blasphemous, vituperative (MALEDICTION).

scurry, *v.* hurry, hasten, sprint (SPEED).

scurvy, *adj.* mean, shabby, scummy (MEANNESS).

sea, *n.* deep, briny deep, brine (OCEAN); surf, swell (RIVER).

seacoast, *n.* coast, littoral, seaboard (LAND).

seagoing, *adj.* ocean-going, seafaring, seaworthy (OCEAN, SAILOR).

seal, *n.* sigil, signet, cachet (SIGNATURE); sea lion (ANIMAL).

seal, *v.* gum, paste, plaster (STICKINESS); close, secure, shut (CLOSURE).

seam, *n.* gore, gusset, joint (JUNCTION); ruffle, rumple, crinkle (WRINKLE); pleat, tuck, hem (FOLD).

seam, *v.* sew, hem, hemstitch (FASTENING); plait, pleat, tuck (FOLD).

seaman, *n.* seafarer, mariner (SAILOR).

seamstress, *n.* sempstress, needlewoman (CLOTHING WORKER).

seaplane, *n.* hydroplane, flying boat (FLYING).

SEARCH—*N.* search, hunt, chase, pursuit, quest, rummage, perquisition, wild-goose chase, witch hunt; investigation, inquiry, inquest, exploration, research.

searcher, seeker, ferret, sleuth, detective, snoop, perquisitor, quidnunc; dowser, hydroscopist.

quest, quarry, chase, prey, big game.

dowsing rod, dowser, dipping rod, divining rod, divining stick.

V. **search,** seek, look for, quest, go in quest of, hunt, hunt for, chase after, gun for, cast about, pursue, trail, track, trace, mouse, prospect, root, rout, scout, scrimmage, ferret, court; ransack, rake, scour, rummage, comb, fine-comb, rifle; forage, maraud; dowse; shop around.

investigate, explore, research, inquire, delve, burrow; pry, snoop, sleuth.

Adj. **searching,** curious, inquisitive, nosy, snoopy, prying, rogatory, exploratory, investigative, investigatory; piercing, keen, sharp, penetrating, quizzical.

See also EXAMINATION, FOLLOWING, INQUIRY, LOOKING, ROD. *Antonyms*—See DISCOVERY.

searchlight, *n.* torch, flashlight, spotlight (LIGHT).

seashore, *n.* seaside, shore, strand (LAND).

seasick, *adj.* nauseated, nauseous, queasy (NAUSEA).

season, *v.* flavor, spice, salt (TASTE, INTERESTINGNESS, PLEASURE); habituate, accustom, inure (HABIT, EXPERIENCE).

seasonable, *adj.* timely, well-timed, providential (TIMELINESS).

seasonal, *adj.* periodic, regular, uniform (UNIFORMITY); epochal, cyclic (TIME); seasonable, annual (SEASONS).

seasoned, *adj.* trained, practiced, well-versed (EXPERIENCE); veteran, old (OLDNESS); mellowed, ripe, well-developed (MATURITY).

seasoning, *n.* flavoring, zest, spice (TASTE).

SEASONS—*N.* spring, springtime, springtide, prime, germinal, seedtime, vernal season, blossomtime; vernal equinox.

summer, summertime, summertide, midsummer; estivation.

autumn, fall, harvesttime, midautumn, autumnal equinox; Indian summer.

winter, wintertime, wintertide, midwinter; hibernation.

V. **spend the season,** winter, hibernate; summer, estivate (*zool.*).

Adj. **spring,** springtime, vernal; springlike.

summer, aestival *or* estival, midsummer; summerlike, summery, midsummery.

autumn, autumnal, fall, autumnlike.

winter, midwinter, brumal, hiemal; winterlike, hibernal, midwinterly, midwintry, wintery, wintry.

seasonal, seasonable; annual, perennial (*of plants*).

See also RHYTHM, TIME.

seat, *n.* chair, stool, couch (SEAT); station, post, spot (SITUATION); fundament, bottom, breech (REAR).

seat, *v.* plant, set, put (LOCATION).

SEAT—*N.* seat, chair, folding chair, camp chair, bridge chair; armchair, easy chair, wing chair, slipper chair, club chair, *fauteuil* (*F.*), Morris chair; armless chair, pouf; bench, form, settle, settle bed, stall, still, taboret; throne, cathedra; musnud (*Oriental*), ottoman, squab, perch, roost, rocker, rocking chair; howdah, saddle.

stool, camp stool, folding stool; footstool, cricket, hassock, ottoman, squab.

couch, *causeuse* (*F.*), chaise longue, chesterfield, davenport, day bed, divan, lounge, love seat, settee, sofa, squab, tête-à-tête (*F*).

structure of seats, amphitheater, bleachers, grandstand, pew; balcony, box, dress circle, gallery, mezzanine, orchestra, parquet, orchestra circle, parquet circle, parterre, pit.

sitting, séance (*F.*), session, wake.

V. sit, be seated, seat oneself, take (*or* have) a seat (*or* chair); squat, roost, perch, lounge, slouch, nestle; straddle, stride, bestraddle, bestride; sit with, baby-sit; set, brood, hatch, incubate.

Adj. sitting, seated, astraddle, perched, squatting, squat, sedentary, insessorial (*of birds*).

See also INACTIVITY, LOCATION, PLACE, POSTURE, REST. *Antonyms*—See MOTION, WALKING.

seaweed, *n.* wrack, kelp, rockweed (PLANT LIFE).

secede, *v.* withdraw, resign, retire (DEPARTURE, RELINQUISHMENT).

SECLUSION—*N.* seclusion, beleaguerment, blockade.

segregation, isolation, quarantine, insularity, sequestration; racial segregation, Jim Crow, Jim Crowism, apartheid (*South Africa*), ghettoism.

privacy, isolation, penetralia (*pl.*); retirement, withdrawal, retreat, voluntary exile; solitude, desolation.

[*state of living in seclusion*] reclusion, asceticism, eremitism, anchoritism, monasticism, monkhood, monkery (*derogatory*).

[*private place*] **retreat,** seclusion, sanctum, adytum, sanctum sanctorum.

hermitage, monastery, ribat (*Algeria*), cloister, cell.

recluse, solitaire, solitary, solitudinarian, ascetic; hermit, eremite, santon, troglodyte, anchorite, anchoret, anchoress (*fem.*), Hieronymite, Hieronymian, Marabout (*Mohammedan*), stylite, pillarist, monk.

V. seclude, shut off, beleaguer, blockade; ostracize, boycott, embargo.

segregate, isolate, quarantine, sequester, cloister.

seclude oneself, keep aloof, withdraw, keep apart, separate oneself, shut oneself up; rusticate, retire, retreat, retire from the world; take the veil.

Adj. secluded, shut off, beleaguered, blockaded; segregated, isolated, isolate, insular, sequestered, cloistered, quarantined, incommunicado; retired, withdrawn.

private, remote, quiet, isolated, out-of-the-way, cloistered, singular, secluded, unfrequented, lonely; secret, covert, personal, confidential, closet.

uninhabited, unoccupied, untenanted, tenantless, abandoned, deserted.

alone, lone, sole, single, stray; unaccompanied, unattended; unassisted, unaided, singlehanded.

lonely, lonesome, desolate, forlorn, lorn, solitary, solitudinous; companionless, friendless.

unsociable, withdrawn, nongregarious, retiring, shy, recessive, reserved, unsocial, self-sufficient, standoffish, aloof, unapproachable, unclubbable (*colloq.*), insociable, dissocial, asocial.

Adv., phrases. privately, in private, *in camera* (*L.*), tête-à-tête (*F.*), sotto voce (*It.*).

See also ASCETICISM, CONCEALMENT, DESERTION, EXCLUSION, PREJUDICE, RELIGIOUS COMMUNITY. *Antonyms*—See FRIENDLINESS, SOCIALITY.

second, *n.* moment, trice, instant (TIME, EARLINESS); exponent, proponent, seconder (SUPPORT); runner-up, placer (ATTEMPT).

second, *v.* uphold, endorse, back (SUPPORT, AID).

secondary, *adj.* accessory, minor, subordinate (UNIMPORTANCE); indirect, eventual, vicarious (RESULT).

second-rate, *adj.* inferior, shoddy, substandard (INFERIORITY).

secret, *adj.* arcane, cryptic, dark (CONCEALMENT); mysterious, weird, uncanny (MYSTERY).

secret, *n.* confidence, mystery, oracle, occult (CONCEALMENT, MYSTERY).

secret agent, *n.* undercover agent, spy, foreign agent (CONCEALMENT).

secretary, *n.* clerk, registrar, amanuensis (RECORD, WRITER); typist, stenographer (WORK, WRITER); minister, prime minister, premier (OFFICIAL); escritoire, writing desk (CONTAINER).

secrete, *v.* hide, shroud; keep secret, keep to oneself (CONCEALMENT); produce, secern (EXCRETION).

secretive, *adj.* backstairs, covert, furtive (CONCEALMENT); eccritic, secretional (EXCRETION).

secretly, *adv.* clandestinely, covertly, furtively (CONCEALMENT).

secret writing, *n.* code, cipher, cryptography (WRITING).

sect, *n.* party, faction (SIDE); religious persuasion, church (RELIGION).

sectarianism, *n.* nonconformity, dissent, disagreement (HETERODOXY).

section, *n.* division, category, branch (CLASS, PART); surgical operation (SURGERY).

secular, *adj.* lay, laic, layman (LAITY); subcelestial, temporal, worldly (WORLD, IRRELIGION).

secure, *adj.* unanxious, carefree, easy (UNANXIETY); hopeful, confident (HOPE); certain, positive, assured (CERTAINTY); protected, safe (PROTECTION).

secure, *v.* acquire, procure, gain (ACQUISITION); close, lock, padlock (CLOSURE); tighten, clinch, tie (JUNCTION).

securities, *n.* holdings, stocks, bonds (OWNERSHIP, MEANS).

security, *n.* ease, calm, unapprehension (UNANXIETY); assurance, guarantee, warranty (CERTAINTY); safety, shelter, asylum (PROTECTION); surety, bond, collateral (PROMISE).

sedate, *adj.* staid, sober, demure (CALMNESS, SOBRIETY).

sedative, *n.* anodyne, opiate (CALMNESS); analgesic, lenitive (PAINKILLER); hypnotic, soporofic (PHARMACY, SLEEP).

sedition, *n.* unrest, defiance (DISOBEDIENCE).

seduce, *v.* wheedle, blandish, in-

veigle (PERSUASION); entice, invite (ATTRACTION); deprave, pervert, corrupt (IMMORALITY, SEX).

see, *v.* behold, witness, view (VISION); recognize, comprehend, understand (KNOWLEDGE).

seed, *n.* semen, milt, sperm (MAKEUP); spawn, progeny, issue (CHILD); crumb, grain, particle (POWDERINESS).

seedy, *adj.* squalid, shabby, poor (POVERTY); torn, ragged (TEARING); mangy, ratty (*colloq.*); tacky (*colloq.*), poky (UNTIDINESS).

seek, *v.* look for, quest (SEARCH).

seem, *v.* appear, look (APPEARANCE).

seeming, *adj.* apparent, ostensible, quasi (APPEARANCE).

seep, *v.* leak, trickle, ooze (EGRESS).

seer, *n.* soothsayer, prophet (PREDICTION); psychic, medium, clairvoyant (TELEPATHY).

seesaw, *v.* pitch, toss, thrash (OSCILLATION).

seethe, *v.* simmer, bubble (FOAM, EXCITEMENT).

seething, *adj.* simmering, ebullient, bubbling (EXCITEMENT).

see through, *v.* discern, discriminate, penetrate (INTELLIGENCE).

segment, *n.* subdivision, sector, articulation (PART).

segregate, *v.* isolate, quarantine, sequester (SECLUSION).

segregation, *n.* isolation, quarantine, sequestration (SECLUSION); apartheid, negrophobia, Jim Crowism (PREJUDICE).

seize, *v.* take, grasp, clutch (TAKING, HOLD); capture, catch, arrest (TAKING).

seizure, *n.* fit, stroke, convulsion (ATTACK); capture, apprehension, arrest (TAKING, LAWSUIT).

seldom, *adv.* infrequently, rarely, scarcely (FEWNESS).

select, *adj.* chosen, popular, preferred (CHOICE); best, top-notch, unexcelled (SUPERIORITY); restrictive, cliquish, clannish (EXCLUSION); choosy, selective, discriminating (CHOICE).

select, *n.* best, élite, cream (SUPERIORITY).

select, *v.* pick, cull, winnow (CHOICE).

self, *n.* ego, psyche, id (SELFISHNESS).

self-abasement, *n.* self-humiliation, masochism, self-debasement (HUMILIATION).

self-absorbed, *adj.* introverted, autistic, introspective (SELFISHNESS).

self-admiration, *n.* *amour-propre* (*F.*), self-love (APPROVAL).

self-approval, *n.* vanity, conceit, self-esteem (APPROVAL).

self-assurance, *n.* self-confidence, poise (CERTAINTY).

self-centered, *adj.* egocentric, ego-centered (SELFISHNESS).

self-concern, *n.* self-devotion, self-seeking, self-interest (SELFISHNESS).

self-confidence, *n.* confidence, poise, self-assurance (CERTAINTY).

self-conscious, *adj.* discomfited, ill-at-ease, uncomfortable (EMBARRASSMENT); sheepish, shamefaced, verecund (MODESTY).

self-control, *n.* stoicism, self-restraint, discipline (INEXCITABILITY, CONTROL).

self-defense, *n.* self-preservation, judo, jujitsu (PROTECTION).

self-denial, *n.* self-begrudgment, self-renunciation, self-abnegation (UNSELFISHNESS).

self-discipline, *n.* self-control, Spartanism (CONTROL).

self-effacing, *adj.* recessive, shrinking, shy (MODESTY).

self-esteem, *n.* self-approval, conceit, egotism (APPROVAL).

self-government, *n.* independence, autonomy, self-rule (FREEDOM, GOVERNMENT).

self-important, *adj.* pompous, pretentious, toplofty (IMPORTANCE); conceited, egoistical (PRIDE).

self-indulgence, *n.* self-gratification, free-living, dissipation (INTEMPERANCE).

self-interest, *n.* self-concern, self-devotion, self-seeking (SELFISHNESS).

SELFISHNESS—*N.* selfishness, calculation, illiberality; self-interest, self-concern, self-devotion, self-seeking, expedience; egocentricity, self-centerment, self-indulgence, self-worship, egoism, egotism, self-praise, self-regard, egomania, self-love, narcissism (*psychoanal.*).

self-absorption, introversion, autism, introspection, self-contemplation, self-reflection.

egoist, egocentric, egotist, narcissist (*psychoanal.*), egomaniac; introvert, autist.

self-seeker, timeserver, dog in the manger, hog, roadhog (*colloq.*); toady, sycophant, tufthunter; fortune hunter, golddigger (*slang*).

self, ego, psyche, id (*psychoanal.*), superego (*psychoanal.*).

other self, alter ego, alter idem.
V. be selfish, indulge (or pamper) oneself, feather one's nest; have an eye to the main chance.
Adj. selfish, calculated, small,

small-minded, sordid, base; illiberal, hoggish, piggish.

self-interested, self-concerned, self-intent, self-devoted, self-seeking, egocentric, egocentered, self-centered, self-indulgent, self-worshiping, egoistic, egotistic, egomaniacal, narcissistic (*psychoanal.*); expedient.

self-absorbed, introverted, autistic, introspective, self-contemplative, self-reflective, subjective, personal.

Adv., phrases. by and of itself, per se (*L.*), intrinsically.

See also EXPEDIENCE, MEANNESS, PRAISE, PRIDE, STINGINESS, TAKING. *Antonyms*—See GIVING, UNSELFISHNESS.

selfless, *adj.* uncalculating, ungrudging, altruistic (UNSELFISHNESS).

self-love, *n.* *amour-propre* (*F.*), narcissism (*psychoanal.*), conceit (LOVE, APPROVAL).

self-praise, *n.* egoism, egotism, self-regard (SELFISHNESS).

self-pride, *n.* *amour-propre* (*F.*), ego, self-admiration (PRIDE).

self-regard, *n.* egoism, egotism, self-praise (SELFISHNESS).

self-righteous, *adj.* sanctimonious, pharisaical, pietistical (MORALITY, IRRELIGION).

self-sacrifice, *n.* self-immolation, martyrdom (UNSELFISHNESS, SUICIDE).

self-satisfaction, *n.* self-complacence, complacency, smugness (SATISFACTION).

self-seeking, *n.* self-concern, self-devotion, self-interest (SELFISHNESS).

self-styled, *adj.* purported, *soi-disant* (*F.*), so-called (PRETENSE, TITLE).

self-sufficient, *adj.* reserved, unsocial (SECLUSION).

self-suggestion, *n.* autosuggestion, Couéism (SUGGESTION).

self-willed, *adj.* obstinate, unyielding, headstrong (WILL).

sell, *v.* vend, market, merchandise (SALE).

sell for, *v.* bring in, yield, cost (SALE).

seltzer, *n.* soda, club soda, vichy (DRINK).

semantics, *n.* semantology, significs (MEANING).

semaphore, *n.* wigwag, wave, heliogram (INDICATION).

semen, *n.* seed, sperm (MAKE-UP).

semicircle, *n.* half circle, hemicycle (ROUNDNESS).

SEMILIQUIDITY—*N.* semiliquidity, semifluidity, colloidality; jellification, gelatination, gelatinization.

mud, slush, slop, slosh, sludge, slime, ooze, mire, muck, clay, sullage; mudhole, slough.

jelly, colloid, suspension, emulsion, gelatin; fruit jelly, jam, conserve, conserves, preserves, marmalade; pectin.

V. jell or gel, congeal, gelatinate, gelatinize, jelly, jellify; mash, squash.

muddy, muddle, puddle, roil, rile (colloq.); mire, poach.

Adj. semiliquid, semifluid, semifluidic, half-melted, half-frozen; milky, lacteal, lacteous, emulsive.

muddy, slushy, sludgy, sloppy, oozy, miry, clayey, slimy, sloughy, squashy, uliginose; turbid, muddled, roily, roiled, riley (colloq.).

gelatinous, gelatinoid, colloidal, jellied.

See also MARSH, OIL, STICKINESS, THICKNESS. Antonyms—See FOAM, LIQUID, THINNESS.

seminar, n. clinic, institute (LEARNING).

seminary, n. college, institute, university (SCHOOL).

SEMITRANSPARENCY—N. semitransparency, opalescence, translucence.

V. cloud, frost, cloud over, frost over, opalize.

Adj. semitransparent, translucent, semidiaphanous, semiopaque, semipellucid, opalescent, opaline, pearly, nacreous, milky, frosted; hazy, misty, cloudy, clouded, filmy, foggy.

See also CLOUD, JEWELRY. Antonyms—See THICKNESS, TRANSPARENCY.

senate, n. council, diet, parliament, congress (LEGISLATURE).

senator, n. congressman (LEGISLATURE).

SENDING—N. sending, consignment, dispatch, issuance, issue, transmission, transmittal, accompaniment; circulation, broadcast, exportation, export, smuggling, contraband; mission, errand.

V. send, consign, dispatch, issue, forward, transmit; broadcast, circulate, troll; export, ship, smuggle out, freight, route, mail, post, express; direct, detail

See also GIVING, MESSENGER, PROPULSION, THROW, TRANSFER. Antonyms—See RECEIVING.

senile, adj. decrepit, infirm, anile (OLDNESS, WEAKNESS).

senility, n. dotage, caducity, second childhood, decrepitude (OLDNESS, WEAKNESS).

senior, adj. older, elder (OLDNESS); major, chief, leading (RANK).

senior, n. old stager, dean, doyen (OLDNESS); paterfamilias, patriarch, head (RULER).

sensation, n. impression, feel, sense (SENSITIVENESS).

sensational, adj. yellow, purple, lurid (EXCITEMENT).

sense, n. sensation, impression, feel (SENSITIVENESS); wit, mental ability (INTELLIGENCE); significance, signification, import (MEANING).

sense, v. feel, perceive, apperceive (SENSITIVENESS).

senseless, adj. stupid, silly, witless (STUPIDITY, FOLLY); nonsensical, pointless, inane (ABSURDITY); irrational, unsound (UNREASONABLENESS); insensible, unconscious (INSENSIBILITY).

sensible, adj. sagacious, shrewd, astute (INTELLIGENCE, WISDOM); rational, sane, sound (REASONABLENESS); conscious, passible (SENSITIVENESS); perceptible, palpable, tangible (REALITY, MATERIALITY, SENSITIVENESS).

sensitive, adj. thin-skinned, huffy, touchy (OFFENSE); reactive, reactional, responsive (REACTION); passible, impressionable (SENSITIVENESS).

SENSITIVENESS—N. sensitiveness, sensitivity, sensibility, esthesia, passibility, sentience; impressibility, susceptibility, susceptivity, affectibility, suggestibility, delicacy; hypersensitivity, hyperesthesia; allergy, anaphylaxis (med.), idiosyncrasy (med.); algesia, hyperalgesia, irritation.

sensation, impression, feel, sense, apperception, percipience.

feeling, emotion, sentiment, affect (psychol.), affection, attitude, passion.

V. sense, feel, perceive, apperceive; be sensitive to, appreciate.

sensitize, irritate, sharpen, refine, cultivate; impress, excite.

feel a sensation, crawl, creep, itch, prickle, tickle, tingle, thrill, sting.

Adj. sensitive, sentient, passible, responsive; impressible, susceptible, susceptive, impressionable, waxen, suggestible; thin-skinned, touchy, tender, delicate, temperamental; hypersensitive, hyperesthetic; allergic, anaphylactic (med.), sore, irritated.

[capable of having sensations] sensible, conscious, aesthetic, passible, sensitive, sentient; apperceptive, perceptive, percipient.

sensory, sensational, perceptive, apperceptive, perceptional, perceptual, sensorial, sensual.

[*pert. to feelings*] **affective**, affectional, attitudinal, passional, passionary.

perceptible, perceivable, palpable, sensible, tangible.

See also EXCITEMENT, FEELING, INFLUENCE, ITCHING, OFFENSE, REACTION, SENTIMENTALITY, TOUCH. *Antonyms*—See INSENSIBILITY, INSENSITIVITY.

---

sensitize, v. irritate, sharpen, refine (SENSITIVENESS).

sensory, adj. sensational, perceptual, sensorial (SENSITIVENESS).

sensual, adj. sexual, carnal, fleshy (SEX, BODY); gross, voluptuous (INTEMPERANCE); gay, primrose, saturnalian (PLEASURE); sensory, sensorial (SENSITIVENESS).

sensualism, n. epicureanism, epicurism (PLEASURE); lust, sensuality, animalism, sexuality, eroticism, erotism (SEX).

sensuality, n. indulgence, license, animalism, debauchery (INTEMPERANCE).

sensuous, adj. gay, primrose (PLEASURE).

sentiment, n. feeling, affect (*psychol.*), emotion (SENSITIVENESS); view, judgment, slant (OPINION); sentimentalism, gush (SENTIMENTALITY).

SENTIMENTALITY—N. sentimentality, sentimentalism, sentiment, bathos, melodrama, melodramatics, namby-pambyism, namby-pambics, unctuosity, unction; gush, mush, slush.

Adj. **sentimental,** bathetic, gushy, lackadaisical, maudlin, melodramatic, namby-pamby, namby-pambical, slushy, unctuous.

See also FEELING, SENSITIVENESS. *Antonyms*—See INSENSITIVITY.

---

sentinel, n. lookout, sentry, picket (PROTECTION, WARNING).

sentry, n. sentinel, watch, guard (PROTECTION, WARNING).

separate, adj. apart, asunder, loose (DISJUNCTION); disconnected, unconnected (IRRELATION).

separate, v. part, detach, divide (DISJUNCTION); break, intersect (CESSATION); disconnect, dissever, disjoin (DISCONTINUITY); interval, space (INTERVAL); riddle, sift, screen (CLEANNESS).

separately, adv. apart, independ-

ently (UNITY); disjointly, severally (DISJUNCTION).

sequel, n. result, sequent (FOLLOWING, RESULT).

sequence, n. series, succession, chain (LENGTH, FOLLOWING).

serenade, n. love song, strephonade, ballad (SINGING).

serene, adj. tranquil, calm (PEACE); phlegmatic, unruffled (UNANXIETY).

serenity, n. peace of mind, tranquillity, composure (PEACE).

serf, n. slave, chattel, vassal (SLAVERY).

series, n. sequence, succession, run (LENGTH, FOLLOWING).

serious, adj. solemn, grim, somber (SOBRIETY).

sermon, n. preachment, homily, lecture (PREACHING, MORALITY, ADVICE).

serpent, n. snake, viper, reptile (ANIMAL).

serpentine, adj. meandrous, snaky, sinuous (WINDING).

servant, n. minion, menial, retainer, domestic (OBEDIENCE, SERVICE).

serve, v. minister to, help, aid (SERVICE); administer, provision, victual (QUANTITY); avail, apply, do (PURPOSE); be useful (USE); answer, satisfy (SUFFICIENCY); enroll, enlist (FIGHTING).

SERVICE—N. service, help, aid, assistance, ministration, attendance; domestic service (*or* employment); use, usefulness, employment, value.

servant, menial, minion, retainer, servitor, slavey, vassal, help, domestic, domestic servant, flunkey *or* flunky (*contemptuous*), lackey, footman, steward, majordomo, maître d'hôtel (*F.*), butler, valet, valet de chambre (*F.*), manservant, man, boy, bellboy, buttons (*slang*), bellhop (*slang*).

attendant, squire, page, usher, cupbearer, trainbearer, equerry; caddie.

retinue, train, suite, cortege, following, bodyguard, court.

groom, hostler; blacksmith, smith, horseshoer, farrier (*Brit.*); saddler.

cowboy, broncobuster, buckaroo, buckayro; cowpuncher, vaquero (*Sp.*); cowherd, neatherd, shepherd, sheepherder.

maidservant, maid, girl, hired girl, housemaid, house worker, bonne (*F.*), housekeeper, dayworker, charwoman, cleaning woman, chambermaid, femme de chambre (*F.*), maid of all work, domestic, laundress, washerwoman, scrubwoman, cook, scullion, Cinderella, scullery maid; handmaid, handmaiden, amah (*Orient*), ayah (*India*), lady's maid, lady in waiting, nurse, governess.

waiter, server, carhop, *garçon* (*F.*), steward; bus boy, dishwasher; headwaiter, captain, maître d'hôtel (*F.*), maître de (*colloq.*); waitress, hostess, stewardess.

subject, liege, liegeman, liege subject, citizen.

V. **serve**, minister to, help, aid, assist, wait (attend, *or* dance attendance) upon; squire, valet, lackey, tend, do for (*colloq.*), attend; work for, be useful to, cooperate with, oblige; officiate, act.

Adj. **serving**, tending, ministering, helping out, filling in, menial, vassal, domestic; working for, in the employ of, on the payroll.

See also ACTION, AID, CARE, CITIZEN, FOLLOWER, FOLLOWING, SLAVERY, USE, WORK. *Antonyms*—See RULER, UNWILLINGNESS.

---

serviceable, *adj.* useful, helpful, valuable (USE).

services, *n.* devotions, chapel, prayer (WORSHIP).

servile, *adj.* slavish, submissive, subservient (SLAVERY).

servitude, *n.* subjection, subjugation, vassalage (SLAVERY).

session, *n.* sitting, séance (*F.*), wake (SEAT).

set, *adj.* determined, resolved, bent (WILL); jelled, stiff, fixed (THICKNESS).

set, *n.* group, series, pack (ASSEMBLAGE).

set, *v.* put, settle, stick (LOCATION, PLACE); stiffen, fix, cake (THICKNESS); decline, sink, dip (DESCENT); jewel, bejewel, incrust (JEWELRY); brood, hatch, incubate (SEAT).

set apart, *v.* insulate, isolate (DISJUNCTION).

set down, *v.* put down, jot down, note (WRITING).

set out, *v.* troop away, start (DEPARTURE); begin, embark on, set about (BEGINNING).

settle, *v.* put, lay, dispose, stand (LOCATION, PLACE); repose, settle down (REST); take up one's abode (LOCATION); squat, preempt, colonize (INHABITANT); populate, inhabit (PEOPLE); judge, decide, determine (JUDGE, RULE); discharge, liquidate (PAYMENT).

settled, *adj.* inhabited, populated, occupied (INHABITANT, PEOPLE);

located, fixed, established (SITUATION); serious, sedate, staid (SOBRIETY); stormless, windless, smooth (CALMNESS).

settler, *n.* immigrant, colonist, pioneer (INGRESS).

settle up, *v.* square accounts (ACCOUNTS).

set up, *v.* erect, rear, raise (VERTICALITY).

setup (*colloq.*), *n.* easy victory, snap, walkaway (SUCCESS).

SEVEN—*N.* **seven**, heptad, hebdomad; heptagon (*geom.*), heptahedron (*geom.*), heptameter (*pros.*), heptastich (*pros.*); septet, septette, septuor, heptarchy.

V. **multiply by seven**, septuple, septuplicate.

Adj. **sevenfold**, septuplicate, septuple; heptad (*chem.*), heptavalent (*chem.*); heptangular, heptagonal, heptahedral, heptamerous (*bot.*), heptasyllabic; septennial, septenary, weekly, hebdomadal, hebdomadary, septenary.

SEVENTY—*N.* **seventy**, threescore and ten; septuagenarian, septuagenary.

Adj. **seventieth**, septuagenary, septuagenarian, septuagesimal.

---

sever, *v.* rive, split, rend (CUTTING); disunite, sunder, dissever (DISJUNCTION).

several, *adj.* many, various, sundry (MULTITUDE); respective, proportionate (APPORTIONMENT).

severally, *adv.* singly, individually, respectively (UNITY).

SEVERITY—*N.* **severity**, rigor, stringency, inclemency; austerity, gravity.

[*arbitrary power*] **tyranny**, despotism, absolutism, autocracy, domination, oppression, dictatorship; inquisition, reign of terror, iron rule, coercion, martial law.

tyrant, despot, autocrat, Draco, oppressor, inquisitor; disciplinarian, martinet, stickler.

V. **domineer**, bully, tyrannize, be hard upon, ill-treat, rule with an iron hand, oppress, override, trample, trample underfoot, ride roughshod over, coerce.

Adj. **severe**, strict, hard, harsh, rigid, stern, rigorous, unkind, uncompromising, unyielding, hardshell (*colloq.*), exacting, searching, inexorable, inflexible, obdurate, austere, relentless, stringent, peremptory, absolute, arbitrary, imperative, coercive, tyrannical, extortionate, oppressive, Draconian, barbarous, grinding, inquisitorial, ironhanded, cruel, arrogant; forbidding, grim, dour.

unadorned, unornamented, unrelieved, plain, restrained, strict, chaste.

[*strict in judgment*] **censorious,** carping, faultfinding, caviling, hypercritical, sharp, biting, cutting, condemnatory, acrimonious, tart, sarcastic, bitter, keen, satirical.

[*of weather*] **inclement,** violent, extreme, rough, stormy, stark, cold, bitter, rigorous.

[*of conditions, pain, punishment, etc.*] **acute,** austere, crucial, drastic, grievous, hard, harsh, inclement, mortal, rigid, rigorous, rugged, sharp, smart, sore, tough, vicious, wicked, nasty.

See also ACTION, CRUELTY, DISAPPROVAL, FORCE, GOVERNMENT, INSENSITIVITY, ROUGHNESS, SIMPLICITY, SOBRIETY, WIND. *Antonyms—See* MILDNESS, PITY.

sew, v. stitch, tack, baste (FASTENING).

sewer, n. drain, cesspool, cloaca (UNCLEANNESS, CHANNEL).

SEX—N. sex, sexuality, venery; sexology; gender.

sexual power, virility, potency, vigor; puberty, pubescence.

sexual desire, passion, libido (*psychoanal.*), aphrodisiomania, eroticism, erotomania, nymphomania, andromania; satyriasis, priapism (*psychol.*), gynecomania.

[*of animals*] heat, oestrus, rut.

lust, sensualism, sensuality, animalism, animality, bestiality, carnality, concupiscence, prurience.

sexual intercourse, cohabitation, coition, coitus, congress, conjugation, connection, copulation, carnal knowledge (*archaic*), sexual relations, sexual union; defloration; climax, orgasm.

fornication, debauchery, fraternization, intimacy, intrigue, liaison, affair *or* affaire, premarital relations, prostitution, concubinage; assignation, rendezvous; incest.

adultery, extramarital relations, infidelity, unfaithfulness; scarlet letter; cuckoldry.

rape, abuse, assault, ravishment, stupration, violation.

sexual immorality, sexual looseness, corruption, debauchery, depravity, lechery, libertinism, lubricity, profligacy, promiscuity, salacity, vice.

sexual deviation, sexual perversion; homosexuality, sexual inversion, sodomy, buggery, pederasty; Lesbianism, Lesbian love, Sapphism, tribadism; bisexualism; fetishism, masochism, flagellation, sadism; exhibitionism, voyeurism, transvestism; hermaphroditism, gynandry.

erotic, sensualist, ram, boar, goat, satyr, satyromaniac, masher (*colloq.*), nymphomaniac.

paramour, lover, gallant, gigolo.

mistress, kept woman, fancy woman, hetaera (*ancient Greece*), concubine, doxy (*archaic or dial.*), sultana, bona roba (*It.*); odalisque.

[*sexually immoral man*] **lecher,** debauchee, Don Juan, Lothario, Casanova, libertine, profligate, rake, roué, swine, wanton, whoremaster.

[*sexually immoral woman*] **slut,** debauchee, cocotte, courtesan, Cyprian, Delilah, demimondaine, bitch (*slang*), drab, harlot, jade, Jezebel, libertine, Messalina, profligate, strumpet, tart (*slang*), trollop, trull, wanton, wench (*somewhat archaic*), frail (*slang*), broad (*slang*), pickup (*slang*), chippy (*slang*), woman of easy virtue, demirep.

sexual deviate, sexual pervert, degenerate, erotopath.

homosexual, homosexualist, sexual invert, fairy (*slang*), queer (*slang*), nance (*slang*), fag (*slang*), sodomist *or* sodomite, bugger, pederast; Lesbian, Sapphist, tribade; bisexual; third sex.

[*others*] fetishist, masochist, flagellator, sadist, exhibitionist, voyeur, Peeping Tom, transvestite.

hermaphrodite, gynandroid, androgyne.

harem, seraglio, zenana.

aphrodisiac, love potion, philter, stimulant, Spanish fly, blister beetle, cantharis, fetish.

erotica, curiosa, pornography, scatology.

V. **sexualize,** eroticize, libidinize.

desire sexually, desire, want, make advances to, lust for (*or* after); [*of animals*] rut, oestruate, be in heat.

excite sexually, excite, stimulate, inflame.

copulate, cohabit, conjugate, couple, have intercourse, sleep together, be intimate, make love, consummate a marriage; go to bed with, go to sleep with, sleep with, bed, know (*archaic*), deflower, possess, have; [*of animals*] mate, cover, serve.

fornicate, fraternize, debauch,

intrigue, prostitute, wench, whore.

seduce, betray, initiate, debauch; corrupt, deprave.

rape, abuse, assault, defile (*archaic*), outrage, ravish, ruin, violate.

Adj. **sexual,** sensual, animal, animalistic, bestial, brutish, carnal, erotic, fleshly, gross, venereal, voluptuous.

heterosexual, bisexual, intersexual; unisexual, homosexual, Lesbian; sexological, libidinal, libidinous.

[*of gender*] masculine, feminine, common, neuter.

pubescent, hebetic, puberal, pubertal, pubertic; virile, vigorous, potent.

amorous, desirous, passionate, stimulated, sultry, erotic; nymphomaniacal, priapistic (*psychol.*), narcissistic (*psychoanal.*).

lustful, sensual, Cyprian, gross, swinish, animal, boarish, bestial, brutish, goatish, rammish, hircine, carnal, concupiscent, prurient; lecherous, lewd, libidinous, libertine, licentious, lickerish, liquorish, lubricous, salacious, ruttish, rutty, lascivious, incontinent.

loose, immoral, abandoned, corrupt, Cyprian, debauched, depraved, dissolute, fast (*colloq.*), Jezebelian (*of the female*), pornerastic, profligate, promiscuous, rakehell, rakish, shameful, shameless, sluttish (*of the female*), unchaste, vicious, wanton, whorish.

[*causing sexual desire*] aphrodisiac, venereal, stimulating, estrogenic, erotic, erogenous.

copulatory, coital, venereal; Paphian, Sapphic; adulterous, adulterine, unfaithful; intimate; concubinal, concubinary; incestuous.

See also FERTILITY, FREEDOM, IMMODESTY, IMMORALITY, LOVE, PROSTITUTE. *Antonyms*—See ASCETICISM, CELIBACY, CONTROL, MODERATENESS, MODESTY, MORALITY, PROPRIETY, UNMARRIED STATE.

sexless, *adj.* neuter, asexual, epicene (CELIBACY).

sexy (*slang*), *adj.* smutty, pornographic, salacious (OBSCENITY).

shabby, *adj.* torn, ragged, seedy (TEARING); squalid, mean (POVERTY); mangy, ratty (*colloq.*), poky (UNTIDINESS); scurvy, sneaky (CONTEMPT); underhand, unjust (UNFAIRNESS); overused, overworked, worn (USE).

shack, *n.* hut, hovel, shanty (HABITATION).

shackle, *v.* fetter, manacle, hobble (RESTRAINT).

shackles, *n.* manacles, fetters, bilboes (RESTRAINT).

shade, *n.* screen, awning, blind; shadow, dark, gloom (DARKNESS); hue, tone, cast (COLOR); wraith, revenant, sprite (GHOST).

shade, *v.* screen, shutter, veil, (PROTECTION); darken, gray, shadow (DARKNESS).

shadow, *n.* dark, shade, umbra (DARKNESS); pursuer, tail (*slang*), skip-tracer (FOLLOWING); profile, silhouette (SHAPE).

shadow, *v.* shade, obscure, gray (DARKNESS); follow, stalk, tail (FOLLOWING).

shadowy, *adj.* shaded, bowery, bosky (DARKNESS); obscure, indefinite, undefined (INVISIBILITY); ethereal, airy, vaporous (NON-EXISTENCE).

shady, *adj.* shaded, shadowy, umbrageous (DARKNESS); disreputable, infamous, notorious (DISREPUTE); dishonest, fishy (*colloq.*), questionable (DISHONESTY).

shaft, *n.* column, pillar, colonnade (SUPPORT); handle, hilt, helve (HOLD); underpass, subway, tunnel (PASSAGE); pit, well (DEPTH).

shaggy, *adj.* hairy, hirsute (HAIR); rugged, ragged, ruffled (ROUGHNESS).

SHAKE—*N.* shake, shaking, ague, jactation, churn, convulsion; jiggle, jog, joggle, rock, shimmy, totter, dodder, jar, succussion, jolt, jounce, concussion, agitation; flourish, brandish.

V. shake, churn, convulse, joggle, jolt, jiggle, shimmy, shimmer, wiggle, jog, jounce, rock, jar, succuss, agitate; flourish, brandish; totter, dodder.

tremble, flutter, palpitate, throb, thrill, quaver, quiver, twitter, twiddle, flicker, bicker, vibrate; shiver, shudder, quake.

Adj. **shaky,** jiggly, joggly, jolty, jerky, jouncy, rocky, tottery, doddery, loose-jointed.

trembly, atremble, fluttery, quavery, quivery, twittery, twiddly, flickery, lambent; tremulous, tremulant, aspen, blubbery; shivery, shuddery, quaky.

See also AGITATION, FEAR, OSCILLATION, RHYTHM, ROLL, UNSTEADINESS. *Antonyms*—See MOTIONLESSNESS, REST, STABILITY.

shaky, *adj.* rocky, tottery, unstable (UNSTEADINESS, SHAKE); rickety, tumble-down (WEAKNESS).

SHALLOWNESS—*N.* shallowness,

superficiality, triviality; veneer, front, façade.

shallow, shoal, flat; bar, sandbank, sand bar.

V. shallow, shoal, fill in, fill up, silt up.

Adj. shallow, depthless, shoal, shoaly, skin-deep, trifling.

superficial, trivial, empty, silly, inane, frivolous, shallow-brained, shallowpated; half-learned, half-baked (*colloq.*), ignorant, empty-headed, unthinking.

See also FOLLY, FRIVOLITY, IGNORANCE, LAND, SURFACE. *Antonyms*—See DEPTH, SOBRIETY.

sham, *adj.* simulated, bogus (IMITATION, PRETENSE); counterfeit, forged, fraudulent (FALSENESS).

sham, *n.* forgery, counterfeit, mock (IMITATION); fraud, fake (FALSENESS).

sham, *v.* simulate, assume, affect, counterfeit, fake (PRETENSE, FALSENESS).

shamble, *v.* shuffle, slog (WALKING).

shambles, *n.* bedlam, maelstrom, madhouse, babel (CONFUSION).

shame, *n.* mortification, pudency, shamefacedness (HUMILIATION); compunction, contrition, remorse (GUILT); infamy, scandal, dishonor (DISGRACE).

shame, *v.* humiliate, embarrass, mortify (HUMILIATION); attaint, defile, dishonor (DISGRACE).

shamefaced, *adj.* self-conscious, sheepish (MODESTY); abashed, discomfited (EMBARRASSMENT); guilty, ashamed (GUILT).

shameful, *adj.* disgraceful, infamous, notorious (DISREPUTE, DISGRACE); indelicate, obscene, unseemly (IMMODESTY); immoral, unchaste (SEXUAL IMMORALITY).

shameless, *adj.* immodest, barefaced, bold (IMMODESTY); immoral, sluttish, unchaste (SEXUAL IMMORALITY).

shank, *n.* handle, crop, stock (HOLD).

shanty, *n.* hut, hovel, shack (HABITATION).

SHAPE—*N.* shape, figuration, configuration, mold, moulage (*F.*), impression, pattern, embouchure (*music*), figure, build, cut of one's jib, frame.

form, embodiment, cast, conformation, species, formation, format, getup (*colloq.*), construction, structure, constitution, architecture; metamorphosis, recast, rough cast; simulacrum.

symmetry, proportion, proportionality, balance, correspondence, harmony, congruity, conformity, uniformity, regularity, evenness, parallelism.

outline, contour, lineation, figuration, lines, circumscription, conformation; shadow, profile, silhouette; diagram, sketch, rough draft, chart.

condition, trim (*colloq.*), fettle, state, kilter (*colloq.*).

V. shape, form, mold, pat, whittle, fashion, carve, sculpture, cut, chisel, hew, roughcast, sketch, block out; trim, model, knead, pattern, cast, stamp, mint; crystallize, canalize, embody, streamline; recast, reform, reshape.

symmetrize, proportion, regularize, balance.

outline, contour, profile, silhouette, circumscribe, roughhew; diagram, chart, sketch.

Adj. shapely, graceful, curvaceous, sculpturesque, statuesque, sylphlike, petite, chiseled.

symmetrical, regular, balanced, well-balanced, uniform, even, proportional, proportionate, corresponding.

shapable, formable, plastic; malleable, viscous, moldable, pliant, pliable.

multiform, polymorphic, polymorphous; biform, biformed, dimorphic, dimorphous; triform.

See also ARRANGEMENT, BODY, CONDITION, CUTTING, MAKE-UP, TEXTURE, UNIFORMITY. *Antonyms*—See DEFORMITY.

shapeless, *adj.* formless, amorphous; ungraceful, unsymmetrical (DEFORMITY).

shapely, *adj.* well-proportioned, graceful, curvaceous (BEAUTY, SHAPE).

share, *n.* portion, allotment, quota (APPORTIONMENT, PART).

share, *v.* apportion, allot, divide (PART); participate, take part, partake in (CO-OPERATION).

shared, *adj.* collective, mutual, joint (CO-OPERATION).

shark, *n.* man-eater, tiger of the sea (ANIMAL).

SHARPNESS—*N.* sharpness, acuity, trenchancy; keenness, etc. (see *Adjectives*).

point, spike, pike, pricket, jag, nib, neb, pen point, prong, tine, tip, vertex, peak, apex, spire, taper, wedge, cusp, fang; thorn, thistle, barb, prickle, quill, spine, spur; needle, pin.

sharpener, hone, strop, grindstone, whetstone, oilstone, rubstone, steel, emery, carborundum.

V. sharpen, whet, hone, strop, grind, acuminate; come to a point, taper.

Adj. sharp, keen, acute, fine, incisive, trenchant; acuate, corrosive, cutting, edged, sharp-edged, keen-edged, knife-edged, razorsharp, splintery, pointed, pointy.

well-defined, sharp-cut, clear, distinct, clean-cut, clear-cut.

[*of taste or smell*] pungent, acrid, poignant, acid, tart, sour, biting, piquant.

[*of sound*] shrill, piercing, penetrating, penetrative, high-pitched.

[*trying to the feelings*] severe, intense, painful, excruciating, shooting, lancinating, keen.

[*of perception*] discerning, penetrating, acute, shrewd, quick, clever, sharp-sighted, sharp-eyed, sharp-witted, keen-witted, discriminating, critical, sensitive.

vigilant, alert, attentive, observant, wary, circumspect, searching.

steep, abrupt, precipitous, sheer, vertical, sudden.

[*of language*] cutting, biting, sarcastic, caustic, acrimonious, bitter, tart, harsh, pointed, barbed, acid, vitriolic, angry, sharp-tempered, peppery, pungent.

[*quick to take advantage*] unscrupulous, artful, dishonest, unprincipled.

pointy, pointed, acute, pronged, tapering, tapered, spired, peaked, apical, cuspate, cuspidate, jagged, jaggy, tined, tipped, acuate, acuminate (*biol.*), mucronate, muricate; bicuspid, tricuspidate, trident, tridentate, trifid, multifid; needle-shaped, acerate, acerose.

prickly, barbed, echinated, spiny, thorny, briery, bristly, bristling, aculeate, hispid, acanthoid.

cone-shaped, conical, conic; pyramidal.

horn-shaped, cornuted, corniform, hornlike, corniculate, horned.

spear-shaped, hastate, lance-shaped.

star-shaped, stellate, stelliform, stellular, starlike, radiated, starry.

sword-shaped, ensate (*bot.*), ensiform (*as a leaf*), gladiate (*bot.*), xiphoid (*anat.*).

Adv., phrases. sharp, precisely, promptly, punctually, exactly, on the dot, on the button.

See also ANGER, ATTENTION, CLARITY, CUTTING, HEIGHT, HIGH-PITCHED SOUND, MALEDICTION, SCOLDING, SEVERITY, SOURNESS, VERTICAL-ITY. *Antonyms*—See BLUNTNESS, DULLNESS, UNSAVORINESS.

sharpshooter, *n.* dead shot, crack shot, marksman (ATTACK).

sharp-sighted, *adj.* sharp-eyed, keen-eyed, eagle-eyed (VISION).

sharp-tempered, *adj.* short, sharp, irritable (BAD TEMPER).

sharp-witted, *adj.* acute, alert, quick-witted (INTELLIGENCE).

shatter, *v.* break, smash, fracture (BREAKAGE); wreck, ruin, blast (DESTRUCTION).

shave, *v.* slice, shred, mince (CUTTING); peel, decorticate, pare (SKIN); prune, shear, crop (SHORTNESS); brush, glance, graze (TOUCH); barber, cut, trim (HAIRLESSNESS).

shawl, *n.* stole, wrap (NECKWEAR); mantilla, scarf (HEADGEAR).

she, *n.* woman, gentlewoman, girl (FEMALE).

sheaf, *n.* stack, bundle, swath (ASSEMBLAGE).

sheath, *n.* holster, quiver, scabbard (CONTAINER); capsule, pod, case (COVERING).

shed, *n.* storehouse, warehouse, depository (STORE); lean-to, extension, wing (BUILDING).

shed, *v.* cast off, throw off (ELIMINATION); molt, cast, slough (UNDRESS); radiate, yield, afford (GIVING).

sheen, *n.* luster, shimmer, gloss (LIGHT).

sheep, *n.* mouflon, ram (ANIMAL).

sheepish, *adj.* shamefaced, verecund, self-conscious (MODESTY); timid, timorous, diffident (FEAR); guilty, ashamed (GUILT).

sheer, *adj.* diaphanous, gauzy (TRANSPARENCY); filmy, gossamer (THINNESS); pure, unalloyed (PURIFICATION); steep, abrupt, precipitous (VERTICALITY, SHARPNESS).

sheet, *n.* film, membrane (LAYER); page, leaf, folio (PAPER).

shelf, *n.* ledge, bracket, console (SUPPORT).

shell, *n.* carapace, test, chitin (BONE).

shell, *v.* husk, hull, pod (UNDRESS); pepper, bombard, bomb (ATTACK).

shellfish, *n.* oyster, bivalve (ANIMAL).

shelter, *n.* home, roof, housing (HABITATION); safety, security, asylum (PROTECTION); cover, screen, coverture (COVERING).

shelve, *v.* pigeonhole, table (DELAY, SIDE); rake, bank, bevel (SLOPE).

shepherd, *n.* cowherd, neatherd,

sheepherder (SERVICE); guardian, Argus (PROTECTION); attendant, nurse (CARE); pastor, minister, parson (CLERGY).

shepherd, v. lead, direct, pilot (LEADERSHIP).

sheriff, n. police officer, peace officer, constable (OFFICIAL).

shibboleth, n. slogan, catchword, byword (WORD).

shield, n. safeguard, guard, buckler (PROTECTION).

shift, n. transference, change, translocation (TRANSFER); subterfuge, stratagem, trick (DECEPTION, PLAN); makeshift, stopgap (SUBSTITUTION, USE); tour, hitch, turn (WORK); camisole, slip, chemise (UNDERWEAR).

shift, v. turn, veer, swerve (CHANGE); change, transpose, displace (TRANSFER); get along, fare, manage (LIFE).

shiftless, adj. lazy, slothful, indolent (REST).

shifty, adj. untrustworthy, slippery, treacherous (UNBELIEVINGNESS).

shimmer, n. luster, sheen, gloss (LIGHT).

shimmer, v. shine, flare, blaze (LIGHT); jiggle, shimmy, wiggle (SHAKE).

shimmy, v. jiggle, shimmer, wiggle (SHAKE).

shine, n. polish, gloss, glaze (SMOOTHNESS).

shine, v. glitter, glisten, gleam (LIGHT); polish, sleek, wax (RUBBING).

shingle, v. lath, panel, frame (WOOD).

shingled, adj. overlapping, imbricated, lapstreak (COVERING).

shining, adj. luminous, radiant, brilliant (LIGHT).

shiny, adj. glossy, sheeny, polished (LIGHT, SMOOTHNESS); bright, clear, sunny (LIGHT).

ship, v. send, export (SENDING); go aboard, embark (SAILOR).

SHIP—N. ship, watercraft, craft, vessel, bottom.

boat, ark, barge, canoe, craft, cutter, dinghy, dory, gig, kayak, punt, rowboat, sampan, scull, skiff, tender, trawler, umiak, wherry, yawl, shallop, pinnace, launch; lifeboat, pilot boat, longboat, jolly boat, pair-oar, cockboat, cockleshell; iceboat, ice yacht, icebreaker; dugout, outrigger; pontoon, catamaran; gondola, calque (Levant).

motorboat, power boat, cabin cruiser, speedboat.

vessel, cruiser, cabin cruiser, yacht, barge; mail boat, packet;

ferry, ferryboat, steamship, steamboat, steamer, liner, ocean liner; tug, tugboat, scow, garbage scow; whaler, pearler, sealer; lightship, bathysphere.

merchant ship, merchantman, argosy, lighter, freighter, tanker, flatboat, ark, collier.

warship, naval vessel, battleship, dreadnaught, man-of-war, cruiser, destroyer, sloop of war, frigate, galleon, aircraft carrier, flattop, gunboat, corvette, flagship, submarine, U-boat, privateer, corsair.

pirate ship, corsair, rover, brigantine (hist.).

galley, bireme, trireme, quadrireme, quinquereme.

sailing vessel, sailboat, sailing boat, sailer, sailship, shipentine, full-rigged ship, windjammer (colloq.), galleon, clipper, schooner; two-master, three-master, fourmaster; bark, barque, barkentine, brig, brigantine, cutter, ketch, lugger, sloop, dinghy, smack, yawl, junk (Chinese), dhow (Arab), felucca, caravel.

ships collectively, craft, watercraft, shipping, tonnage, fleet, flotilla, argosy, marine, merchant marine.

naval ships, navy, fleet, armada, squadron, flotilla, division, task force; convoy, escort.

shipbuilder, boatman, waterman.

See also FLOAT, SAILOR, TRAVELING, VEHICLE, WATER.

shipment, n. cargo, freight, load (CONTENTS).

shipshape, adj. orderly, trim, uncluttered (NEATNESS); first-rate (colloq.), tiptop (colloq.), sound (GOOD).

shirker, n. slacker (colloq.), quitter, malingerer (AVOIDANCE, ABSENCE).

shirt, n. blouse, waist (COAT); undershirt, undervest (UNDERWEAR).

shiver, v. tremble, quake, shudder (FEAR, SHAKE); shake, freeze (COLD).

shoal, n. shallow, flat, bar (SHALLOWNESS, LAND).

shock, n. blow, impact (HITTING, TOUCH); trauma, concussion (HARM); brunt, strain (VIOLENCE); bombshell, jolt (SURPRISE); scare, start, turn (FEAR); daze, narcosis, stupefaction (INSENSITIVITY); awe, consternation, wonder (SURPRISE); quake, convulsion, seism (EARTHQUAKE).

shock, v. daze, stupefy (INSENSITIVITY); awe, flabbergast (SURPRISE); stun, overwhelm (DE-

FEAT); offend, outrage (UNPLEAS-ANTNESS, HATRED).

shocking, *adj.* frightful, ghastly, horrible (DISGUST); ugly, scandalous (UNPLEASANTNESS).

shoe, *n.* boot, brogan, oxford (FOOTWEAR).

shoemaker, *n.* bootmaker, cobbler (FOOTWEAR).

shoot, *n.* branch, limb, bough (PLANT LIFE).

shoot, *v.* let off, fire off, discharge (PROPULSION); bombard, barrage (THROW); photograph, snap (PHOTOGRAPH); film (MOTION PICTURES); hurry, run (SPEED).

shoot at, *v.* fire upon, snipe at, shell (ATTACK).

shop, *n.* emporium, market (STORE); plant, factory (WORK); carpentry (WOODWORKING).

shop, *v.* buy, market, go shopping (PURCHASE).

shopkeeper, *n.* merchant, tradesman, retailer (SALE).

shore, *n.* strand, seashore, seaside; riverbank, bank (LAND).

shore, *v.* bolster up, shore up, bulwark (SUPPORT).

short, *adj.* brief, concise, undersized (SHORTNESS); deficient, wanting (INCOMPLETENESS); bad-tempered, sharp-tempered (BAD TEMPER).

shortage, *n.* want, deficit (INCOMPLETENESS, INSUFFICIENCY).

shortcoming, *n.* drawback, frailty, failing (IMPERFECTION, WEAKNESS); deficiency, deficit, lack (INCOMPLETENESS).

shorten, *v.* cut, bob, lop (SHORTNESS).

shortening, *n.* butter, butterfat, cream (OIL).

shorthand, *n.* stenography, stenotypy (WRITING).

shortly, *adv.* soon, presently (FUTURE, EARLINESS).

SHORTNESS—*N.* **shortness,** brevity, conciseness, concision.

abridgment, abbreviation, curtailment, detruncation, truncation, epitomization, summarization, contraction, reduction; elision, ellipsis, syncopation, syncope; brief, condensation, abstract, digest.

summary, synopsis, sum, compendium, compend, conspectus, *aperçu* (*F.*), epitome, précis, résumé, recapitulation, review, outline, summation.

V. **shorten,** cut, bob, lop, prune, shear, shave, crop, bobtail, clip, trim, pare down, curtail, detruncate, truncate, dock; abbreviate, syncopate, contract, compress, take in; be concise, come to the point.

abridge, condense, compact, telescope, abstract, digest, epitomize; summarize, outline, précis, recapitulate, review, sum, sum up, synopsize.

Adj. **short,** brief, little; pug, retroussé (*F.*), turned-up; stubby, pudgy, squatty, stumpy.

[*not tall*] **undersized,** undergrown, stunted, thickset, chunky, scrub, stocky, squat, dumpy, runty (*colloq.*), dwarfish, diminutive.

abridged, condensed, capsule, tabloid, summarized, synoptic, abstractive, recapitulative.

concise, brief, terse, succinct, summary, compendious, compact, laconic, pithy, to the point, trenchant.

curt, abrupt, uncivil, snappish, harsh, cross.

scant, scanty, inadequate, deficient, insufficient, niggardly, scrimpy, poor, small, limited.

[*of memory*] **faulty,** unreliable, unretentive, narrow.

Adv., phrases. **in short,** in brief, briefly, in fine, in substance, in few words, in a nutshell, in a word.

See also CUTTING, DECREASE, DEDUCTION, DISCOURTESY, FORGETFULNESS, INCOMPLETENESS, INSUFFICIENCY, PRESSURE, SHARPNESS, SMALLNESS. *Antonyms*—See HEIGHT, LENGTH, OVERRUNNING, PERFECTION, SIZE, WORDINESS.

shorts, *n.* knickers, Bermudas (TROUSERS); bloomers, drawers (UNDERWEAR).

shortsighted, *adj.* impractical, myopic (FOLLY, BLINDNESS); weak-sighted, nearsighted, amblyopic (DIM-SIGHTEDNESS).

shot, *n.* dart, missile, projectile (THROW); bullet, slug, ball (ARMS); drink, snort (*slang*), bracer (ALCOHOLIC LIQUOR).

shoulder, *v.* nudge, thrust, jostle (PROPULSION).

SHOUT—*N.* **shout,** bellow, whoop, cry, hue, outcry, roar, bark, bawl; scream, scream, screech, shriek, squall, squawk; yell, yammer, yap, yawp; cheer, salvo, tallyho!, view halloa, yoicks; oyez, oyes; shouting, tumult, vociferation, clamor.

V. **shout,** bark, bawl, bellow, cheer, clamor, cry, roar, screak, scream, screech, shriek, squall, squawk, vociferate, whoop, yammer, yap, yawp, yell.

Adj. **shouting,** clamorous, screechy, squally, squawky, tumultuous, tumultuary, vociferant, vociferous.

See also ANIMAL SOUND, LOUDNESS. *Antonyms*—See LOWNESS, SILENCE, SOFTNESS.

shove, *v.* push, press, nudge (PROPULSION).

shovel, *n.* dredge, spade, trowel (DIGGING).

show, *n.* display, *étalage* (F.), parade (OSTENTATION); play, drama (DRAMA); picture show (*colloq.*), motion-picture show (MOTION PICTURES).

show, *v.* spread out, unfurl, unfold (DISPLAY); reveal, bare, expose (DISCLOSURE); indicate, token, betoken (INDICATION); prove, demonstrate (PROOF); come in sight, come into view (VISIBILITY).

shower, *n.* barrage, volley, fusillade (THROW); pour, cloudburst, torrent (RAIN); bath, shower bath (CLEANNESS).

shower, *v.* scatter, spray, sprinkle (THROW); furnish, lavish (GIVING); teem, pour, rain (RAIN).

show off, *v.* display, advertise, exhibit (OSTENTATION).

show-off, *n.* swaggerer, exhibitionist, vulgarian (OSTENTATION).

showy, *adj.* flamboyant, flashy, garish (OSTENTATION, VULGARITY); pretentious, histrionic (PRETENSE).

shred, *n.* particle, cantlet, stitch (PART); scintilla, shadow, speck (SMALLNESS).

shred, *v.* rip, fray, frazzle (TEARING).

shrew, *n.* scold, termagant, virago (SCOLDING, BAD TEMPER, VIOLENCE, DISAGREEMENT); hussy, jade, baggage (FEMALE).

shrewd, *adj.* cagey (*colloq.*), calculating, canny (CLEVERNESS); discerning, penetrating, acute (SHARPNESS); wise, deep, profound (WISDOM).

shriek, *n.* scream, screech, cry (HIGH-PITCHED SOUND, SHOUT).

shrill, *adj.* high, treble, sharp (HIGH-PITCHED SOUND).

shrill, *v.* screech, scream, shriek (LOUDNESS, HIGH-PITCHED SOUND).

shrimp, *n.* midget, peewee, runt (SMALLNESS).

shrine, *n.* temple, sanctuary, sanctum (CHURCH, SACREDNESS); grave, sepulcher, mausoleum (BURIAL).

shrink, *v.* contract, dwindle, wane (SMALLNESS); compress, constrict, reduce (DECREASE); shudder, recoil (HATRED); wince, flinch, cringe (REVERSION); demur, stick at, refuse (UNWILLINGNESS).

shrinking, *adj.* recessive, self-effacing, shy (MODESTY).

shrivel, *v.* parch, scorch, wither (DRYNESS).

shriveled, *adj.* wizened, withered, macerated (THINNESS).

shroud, *n.* cerecloth, cerements (BURIAL).

shrub, *n.* bush, creeper, vine (PLANT LIFE).

shrug off, *v.* ignore, turn a deaf ear to, slight (INACTION).

shudder, *v.* tremble, quake, shiver (FEAR, SHAKE).

shun, *v.* avoid, eschew (AVOIDANCE).

shunt, *v.* veer, swing, swerve (TURNING).

shut, *v.* fasten, secure, slam (CLOSURE).

shut in, *adj.* confined, bedridden, bedfast (DISEASE, INACTION).

shut in, *v.* keep in, cage (IMPRISONMENT).

shut off, *v.* beleaguer, blockade (SECLUSION).

shutter, *v.* shade, screen, veil (PROTECTION).

shut up, *v.* shut in, keep in, cage (IMPRISONMENT); be silent, hold one's tongue, dummy up (SILENCE).

shy, *adj.* reserved, unsocial, reticent (MODESTY, SILENCE, SECLUSION); unaffectionate, uneffusive, unresponsive (INSENSITIVITY); scant, scanty, short (INSUFFICIENCY); careful, cagey (*colloq.*), gingerly (CARE).

shy, *v.* start, buck, startle (NERVOUSNESS, FEAR).

shyster (*colloq.*), *n.* Philadelphia lawyer (*colloq.*), pettifogger (LAWYER).

SIBILATION—N. sibilation, sibilance, sibilant, "S" sound, hissing; hiss, whisper, buzz; zip, siss (*colloq.*), fizz, fizzle, sizzle, spit (*as of a cat*), swish, whiz, wheeze, sniffle (*med.*), whistle, râle (F., *med.*); sneeze, sneezing, sternutation; lisp.

V. sibilate, hiss, sizz, siss (*colloq.*), spit, fizz, fizzle, sizzle, whiz, buzz, whisper, rustle, swish, wheeze, whistle, lisp; sneeze, sternutate.

Adj. sibilant, hissing, rustling, wheezy, lisping, whisperous, whispery.

See also VOICE.

---

sick, *adj.* ill, ailing, afflicted (DISEASE); neurotic, maladjusted (NEUROSIS); nauseated, queasy (NAUSEA).

sicken, *v.* upset, afflict; become ill, get sick (DISEASE); repel, revolt

(DISGUST, NAUSEA, UNSAVORINESS).

sickle-shaped, *adj.* falcate, falciform (CURVE).

sickly, *adj.* wan, peaked, bilious, valetudinarian, adynamic (DISEASE, WEAKNESS).

sickness, *n.* illness, ailment, malady (DISEASE).

sick of, *adj.* blasé (*F.*), fed up (*slang*), jaded (SATISFACTION).

SIDE—*N.* side, flank, flitch (*of bacon*), loin, wing, hand, haunch, hip, leg (*of a triangle*), jamb, quarter, lee, face.

phase, aspect, appearance, angle, point of view, facet.

party, faction, sect; team, crew; interest, cause, part, behalf.

V. flank, skirt, border, juxtapose; outflank, outmaneuver (*mil.*), enfilade.

put aside, shelve, table, pigeonhole; push aside, jostle, elbow.

move to the side, dodge, duck, lurch, side-skip, sideslip, side-step, sidle, skew, skid, swerve, veer.

side with, take the part of, befriend, aid, uphold, back up, second, advocate, unite with, rally round.

Adj. side, lateral, flanking, skirting; sidelong, sidewise, sideward, sideway, postern.

side-by-side, abreast, collateral, juxtaposed.

one-sided, unilateral; partial, biased, unfair, unjust, prejudiced, influenced.

two-sided, bilateral, dihedral (*tech.*); bifacial.

three-sided, trilateral (*geom.*), triquetrous (*tech.*).

four-sided, quadrilateral (*esp. geom.*), tetrahedral (*tech.*).

many-sided, multilateral, polyhedral (*geom.*); multifaceted (*fig.*), versatile.

Adv., phrases. sidelong, laterally, obliquely, indirectly; askew, askance *or* askant.

sidewise, sideways, laterally, broadside on; abreast, alongside, neck and neck, side by side, beside, aside; by, by the side of, right and left; to windward, to leeward (*naut.*).

See also AID, BOUNDARY, CO-OPERATION, DIRECTION, PREJUDICE, SUPPORT. *Antonyms*—See FRONT, IMPARTIALITY, REAR.

sideboard, *n.* bureau, commode (CONTAINER).

sideburns, *n.* mutton chops, burrsides (HAIR).

side by side, abreast, juxtaposed, cheek by jowl (NEARNESS, SIDE).

sidelong, *adj.* sidewise, sideward, sideway (SIDE).

sidelong, *adv.* indirectly, askew, askance (SIDE).

side-step, *v.* by-pass, parry (AVOIDANCE); slip, sidle (SIDE).

sideswipe, *v.* glance, carom (HITTING).

sidewalk, *n.* boardwalk, street, footpath (WALKING).

sidewise, *adj.* sideward, sideway, sidelong (SIDE).

sidewise, *adv.* slantwise, aslant, athwart (SLOPE, SIDE).

side with, *v.* rally to, subscribe to, go along with (SUPPORT, CO-OPERATION).

siding, *n.* framing, sheathing, clapboard (WOOD).

siege, *v.* besiege, beset, beleaguer (ATTACK).

siesta, *n.* midday rest (REST); nap, snooze (SLEEP).

sieve, *n.* strainer, colander, sifter (CLEANNESS).

sift, *v.* strain, drain; separate, screen (CLEANNESS).

sigh, *v.* sough, wheeze (BREATH); snivel, brood, languish (SADNESS).

sigh for, *v.* ache for, pine for, languish for (DESIRE).

sight, *n.* spectacle, view, scene (VISION); apparition, mirage, phantasm (APPEARANCE); eyesight, afterimage (VISION).

sight, *v.* see, witness, view (VISION).

sightless, *adj.* eyeless, unsighted, visionless (BLINDNESS).

sightly, *adj.* beautiful, ravishing, stunning (BEAUTY).

sightseer, *n.* beholder, rubberneck (*slang*), spectator (LOOKING).

sign, *n.* mark, symbol, emblem (INDICATION, REPRESENTATION); omen, presage, token (PRECEDENCE); signpost, signboard, guidepost (INDICATION); signal, wave (GESTURE); countersign, grip (INDICATION).

sign, *v.* autograph, inscribe, initial (SIGNATURE, WRITTEN SYMBOL); motion, gesture, gesticulate (MOTION).

signal, *adj.* outstanding, striking, arresting (VISIBILITY).

signal, *n.* beacon, flare, blinker (INDICATION).

signal, *v.* wave, wigwag (GESTURE); indicate, signalize (INDICATION).

SIGNATURE—*N.* signature, autograph, endorsement, undersignature, subscription, sign manual, official signature, visa *or* vise, cosignature, countersignature, frank, mark, cross, John Hancock (*slang*); forgery; enrollment, registration.

signer, signatory, attestor *or* attestant, witness, autographer, cosigner *or* cosignatory, countersigner, endorser, undersigner, subscriber; forger.

enroller, registrant, registerer, subscriber; recorder, registrar.

seal, sigil, signet, cachet, bulla, bull; science of seals, sphragistics.

V. **sign,** autograph, inscribe, subscribe, endorse, undersign, cosign, countersign, attest, witness; forge; seal, signet.

sign up, enroll, register, subscribe; enter, inscribe, record.

See also NAME, RECORD, WRITING, WRITTEN SYMBOL.

significance, *n.* sense, signification, import (MEANING); consequence, gravity (IMPORTANCE).

significant, *adj.* meaningful, suggestive, eloquent (MEANING); indicative, representative, symbolic (INDICATION); serious, weighty, momentous (IMPORTANCE).

signify, *v.* mean, denote, import (MEANING); evince, manifest (INDICATION); imply, intimate, connote (SUGGESTION); tell, disclose, communicate (INFORMATION); import, matter (IMPORTANCE).

signpost, *n.* signboard, guidepost (INDICATION, GUIDANCE).

sign up, *v.* enroll, register, subscribe (SIGNATURE).

SILENCE—*N.* **silence,** quiet, quietude, hush, still; sullenness, sulk, saturninity, taciturnity, laconism, reticence, reserve.

muteness, mutism, deaf-mutism, laloplegia, anarthria, aphasia, aphonia, dysphasia.

speech impediment, stammering, stuttering, baryphony, dysphonia, paralalia.

dummy, sphinx, sulk, sulker, calm; mute, deaf-mute, laloplegic, aphasiac, aphonic, dysphasiac.

V. **silence,** quiet, quieten, still, hush; gag, muzzle, squelch, tongue-tie; muffle, stifle, strike dumb.

be silent, quiet down, quiet, hush, dummy up, hold one's tongue, sulk, say nothing, keep silent, shut up (*slang*).

Adj. **silent,** noiseless, soundless, quiet, hushed, still.

speechless, wordless, voiceless, mute, dumb, inarticulate, tongue-tied, mousy, mum, sphinxian.

sullen, sulky, glum, saturnine.

taciturn, uncommunicative, close-mouthed, tight-lipped, unvocal, nonvocal, laconic; reticent, reserved, shy, bashful.

unspoken, tacit, wordless, implied, implicit, understood, unsaid, unuttered, unexpressed, unvoiced, unbreathed, unmentioned, untold.

unpronounced, mute, silent, unsounded, surd, voiceless.

inaudible, indistinct, unclear, faint, unheard.

inexpressible, unutterable, indescribable, ineffable, unspeakable, nameless, unnamable; fabulous.

See also MODESTY, PEACE. *Antonyms*—See LOUDNESS, SHOUT.

---

silent, *adj.* noiseless, soundless, quiet, hushed, still; unpronounced, mute, unsounded (SILENCE).

silken, *adj.* silk, silky (WOOL); luxurious, Corinthian, plush (WEALTH); flocculent, fleecy, cottony (SOFTNESS); satiny, velvety (SMOOTHNESS).

sill, *n.* limen (*psychol.*), threshold, doorsill (INGRESS); bedplate, groundsill (BASE).

silly, *adj.* asinine, nonsensical (ABSURDITY); foolish, senseless, fatuous (FOLLY, STUPIDITY).

silt, *n.* deposit, alluvion, drift (TRANSFER).

silver, *adj.* lunar, argent (METAL, WHITENESS).

silver, *n.* argentine, sterling (METAL); small change, coins (CHANGE).

silverware, *n.* silverplate, flatware, tableware (METAL).

SIMILARITY—*N.* **similarity,** resemblance, likeness, similitude, semblance, affinity, approximation, parallelism, agreement, analogy, correspondence, conformity, conformance, community, kinship, consubstantiality, reciprocity; homogeneity, homology, solidarity (*of interests*); protective coloration, mimicry, mimesis.

identity, coincidence, congruence, congruity, unity.

lifelikeness, verisimilitude, *vraisemblance* (*F.*) fidelity to life.

counterpart, opposite number, obverse, duplicate, facsimile, copy, equal, likeness, kin, analogue, homologue, parallel, congener, match, fellow, companion, mate, twin, double, mirror image, *Doppelgänger* (*Ger.*), doubleganger, image, reflection, simulacre, simulacrum, correspondent, reciprocal, semblance, similitude, alter ego, chip off the old block, birds of a feather, tweedledum and tweedledee.

V. **resemble,** look alike, look like, favor (*colloq.*), follow, echo, reproduce, duplicate, take after, bear resemblance; savor of, smack of; approximate, parallel, match, imitate, copy.

correspond, reciprocate, conform, assimilate, compare, border on, approximate; be the same, coincide, identify, agree.

make similar, homologize, identify, reciprocalize, symmetrize, conform, assimilate, reconcile, standardize.

liken, compare, collate.

Adj. **similar,** resembling, like, alike, akin, kindred, kin, parallel, analogous, corresponding, correspondent, collateral, companion, matching, allied, consubstantial, reciprocal; homogeneous, homologous, homological, homotactic (*esp. geol.*), congenerous (*esp. biol.*).

same, self-same, very same, alike, identical, twin, duplicate, coincident, coincidental, coinciding, congruent, one.

approximate, near, close, something like, fairly close; pseudo, mock, simulating, representing.

lifelike (*as a portrait*), faithful, photographic, exact, true, accurate, true to life, the very image of, cast in the same mold.

Adv., phrases. as if, as though, so to speak; as it were; quasi (*L.*).

See also AGREEMENT, COMPARISON, CONFORMITY, COPY, EQUALITY, IMITATION, NEARNESS, UNIFORMITY. *Antonyms*—See DIFFERENCE, DIFFERENTIATION, INEQUALITY, OPPOSITE.

---

simmer, *v.* cook, stew, fricassee (COOKERY); foam, bubble, effervesce (EXCITEMENT).

simper, *v.* smile, grin, smirk (LAUGHTER); mince, attitudinize, pose (UNNATURALNESS).

simple, *adj.* easy, elementary, effortless (EASE); self-explanatory, unmistakable, transparent (UNDERSTANDING); plain, quiet, unassuming (MODESTY); guileless, naïve, unaffected (INNOCENCE, NATURALNESS); austere, primitive, rustic (SIMPLICITY); thick, dense (STUPIDITY).

simpleton, *n.* moron, thickwit (STUPIDITY).

SIMPLICITY—*N.* simplicity, austerity, plainness, unadornment, chastity, severity, Spartanism, classicality, rusticity.

V. **simplify,** simplicize, disin-

volve, disentangle; chasten, restrain; facilitate.

Adj. **simple,** austere, primitive, Spartan, rustic, unpretentious, unelaborate, homely, homespun; idyllic; Attic, Augustan, classic, classical; artless, unsophisticated, ingenuous.

uncomplex, uncomplicated, uninvolved, uncompounded, simplex, elementary, elemental; single, unmixed, unblended, unadulterated, pure, uniform, homogeneous; easy.

plain, unornamented, unrelieved, unadorned, unornate, chaste, severe, stark, bare, bald.

unfancy, unflamboyant, ungaudy, unfrilled, unbedecked, undecked, undecorated, unembellished, unemblazoned, ungarnished, unpranked, untrimmed, unvarnished, unbedaubed, unbedizened, unelaborated, unembossed, unengraved, unfestooned, unflounced, unflourished, unfoliated, unfringed, unfurbelowed, ungarlanded, ungarnished, unscalloped, unstudded, untessellated, untinseled, unruffled.

[*of facts, truths, statements, etc.*] **unadorned,** mere, bald, bare, blunt, crude, dry, matter-of-fact, naked, plain, simple, stark, unembellished, unvarnished.

See also EASE, NATURALNESS, PURIFICATION. *Antonyms*—See DIFFICULTY, MIXTURE, ORNAMENT, PRETENSE, UNNATURALNESS.

---

simply, *adv.* merely, purely, only (UNITY, SMALLNESS).

simulate, *v.* sham, assume, affect (PRETENSE); imitate, copy, counterfeit (IMITATION).

simulated, *adj.* pretended, make-believe, fake (PRETENSE); mock, sham, pseudo (IMITATION).

SIMULTANEOUSNESS—*N.* simultaneousness, coinstantaneity, simultaneity, synchronism, synchronization, accompaniment, coexistence, coincidence, concurrence, coevality, isochronism.

V. **coincide,** concur, contemporize, accompany, keep pace with, synchronize, coexist.

Adj. **simultaneous,** coinstantaneous, coincident, coincidental, synchronous, synchronal, concomitant, accompanying, concurrent; contemporary, contemporaneous, coeval, coetaneous, coexistent, coexisting.

Adv., phrases. **simultaneously,** etc. (see *Adj.*); at the same time, together, in unison, all together, in concert; in the same breath.

See also ACCOMPANIMENT, OCCURRENCE.

SIN—*N.* sin, offense, transgression, trespass, misdeed, wrong, vice, peccadillo, damnation.

seven deadly sins: anger, covetousness, envy, gluttony, lust, pride, sloth.

sinner, offender, transgressor, trespasser, wrongdoer.

V. sin, do wrong, err, fall from grace, offend, transgress, trespass, fall (*esp. of women, sexually*), stray.

Adj. sinning, erring, errant, offending, peccant, transgressive, transgressing, trespassing; peccable.

sinful, piacular, unregenerate, unrighteous, vile, wrong.

See also GUILT, ILLEGALITY, IMMORALITY, WICKEDNESS. *Antonyms* —See ACQUITTAL, INNOCENCE.

since, *conj.* because, for, in as much as (ATTRIBUTION).
sincere, *adj.* bona fide, true, unaffected (HONESTY, REALITY); candid, frank, outspoken (TRUTH).
sing, *v.* warble, yodel, croon (SINGING).
singe, *v.* burn, sear, scorch (FIRE).

SINGING—*N.* singing, accompaniment, cantillation, chant, croon, hum, intonation, serenade, trill, vocalization *or* vocalism, warble, yodel; minstrelsy, antiphony, psalmody, calypso.

singer, songster, *cantatrice* (*F., fem.*), artist, artiste, *chanteuse* (*F., fem.*), cantor; chorister, choralist, chorine (*colloq.*), chorus girl; opera singer, buffo, prima donna, diva (*fem.*); caroler, chanter, crooner, hummer, intoner, serenader, soloist, vocalizer, vocalist, warbler, yodeler, calypso singer, minstrel, melodist, accompanist; songbird, thrush, nightingale; minnesinger, troubadour.

singing voice: bass, basso profundo, contrabass, baritone, tenor, countertenor; alto, contralto, mezzo-soprano, soprano, coloratura soprano, coloratura, falsetto.

singing group: choir, chorus, glee club, ensemble; duo, duet, trio, quartet, quintet, sextet, sestet, septet, septuor, octet.

song, aria, air, arietta, vocal (*colloq.*), number, encore, tune, melody, lilt, chant, croon, trill, warble, yodel, *Lied* (*Ger.*), chanson, canzonet, ditty, folk song,

minstrelsy, chantey, lay, ballad; solo, duo, duet; carol, cantata, oratorio; lullaby, *berceuse* (*F.*).

round, roundelay, antiphony, canon, troll, glee, madrigal; Christmas carol, noel.

hymn, canticle, chorale, choral, psalm, requiem, spiritual, vesper, anthem.

love song, serenade, strephonade, ballad, ballade.

marriage song, epithalamion, charivari, callithump, hymeneal, hymen, prothalamion.

song of grief, dirge, monody, threnody.

song writer, tunesmith, composer, ballader, bard, lyricist, melodist.

V. sing, vocalize, warble, yodel, chant, intonate, intone, cantillate, carol, harmonize (*colloq.*), croon, serenade, hum, trill, troll, solo, accompany, chirp, chirrup.

Adj. singing, cantabile, lyric, melic, vocal, choral.

See also HARMONY, MELODY, MUSIC, SWEETNESS, VOICE.

single, *adj.* unmarried, unwed (UNMARRIED STATE); only, exclusive, sole (UNITY); alone, lone (SECLUSION); odd, individual (UNITY); unadulterated, unalloyed (PURIFICATION, SIMPLICITY); unaffected, sincere (REALITY).
singlehanded, *adj.* unassisted, unaided (SECLUSION).
single-minded, *adj.* intense, steadfast, unwavering (PURPOSE).
singly, *adv.* individually, severally, respectively (UNITY).
singular, *adj.* odd, peculiar, curious (UNUSUALNESS); surprising, remarkable, unprecedented (SURPRISE).
sinister, *adj.* threatening, menacing, minacious (THREAT); evil, blackhearted, malefic (WICKEDNESS); left, leftward (DIRECTION).
sink, *v.* fall, drop, dip (LOWNESS, DESCENT).
sip, *v.* partake, imbibe (DRINK); savor, sample (TASTE).
sir, *n.* esquire, don (*Sp.*), gentleman (MAN); baronet, knight, cavalier (SOCIAL CLASS).
sire, *n.* ancestor, antecedent, forefather (ANCESTRY); stallion, stud (HORSE).
siren, *n.* alarm, alert (WARNING); Lorelei *or* Lurlei (MYTHICAL BEINGS); sorceress, enchantress, witch (MAGIC).
sissy, *adj.* effeminate, unmanly, unvirile (WEAKNESS).
sissy, *n.* milksop, mollycoddle, pantywaist (MAN, WEAKNESS).

sister, *n.* sibling, sib (*genetics*), sister-german (RELATIVE); nun, *religieuse* (*F.*), vestal virgin (RELIGIOUS COMMUNITY).

sit, *v.* squat, roost, perch (SEAT).

site, *n.* post, spot, locality (LOCATION, PLACE).

sitting, *adj.* seated, astraddle, sedentary (SEAT).

sitting, *n.* séance (*F.*), session, wake (SEAT).

situate, *v.* locate, place, establish (LOCATION).

SITUATION—*N.* situation, position, locality, location, place, site, station, seat, post, spot, whereabouts, bearings, direction, latitude and longitude; footing, status, standing, standpoint, stage.

position (*as a worker*), job, place, post, office; appointment, berth, billet, capacity.

V. be situated, be located, lie.

employ, engage, hire, place, billet, berth, appoint.

Adj. situated, located, fixed, established, settled; conditioned, circumstanced.

local, sectional, topical (*esp. med. in this sense*), limited, regional, provincial, territorial.

Adv., phrases. in position, *in situ* (*L.*), *in loco* (*L.*), in place; here and there; here, hereabouts; there, thereabouts.

See also BUSINESS, CONDITION, LOCATION, PLACE, REGION, WORK. *Antonyms*—See REST.

SIX—*N.* six, half a dozen, hexad (*esp. chem.*), sextuplet, sextet, sestet (*of a sonnet*), hexagram, hexagon (*geom.*), hexahedron (*geom.*), hexameter (*pros.*), hexarchy, hexastich (*pros.*), hexapody (*pros.*), hexastyle (*arch.*), Hexateuch (*Bible*).

V. multiply by six, sextuple, sextiply, sectuplicate.

Adj. sixfold, sextuple, sexpartite, sextipartite, hexamerous, hexadic; hexangular, hexagonal, hexahedral, hexastyle (*arch.*), hexatomic (*chem.*), sexennial.

SIXTY—*N.* sixty, threescore; sexagenarian, sexagenary.

Adj. sixtieth, sexagesimal, sexagenary.

SIZE—*N.* size, dimensions, proportions, measurement, admeasurement, measure; magnitude, bulk, volume; expanse, extent, area, amplitude, mass; capacity, content, tonnage; caliber, diameter, bore.

fatness, corpulence, avoirdupois (*colloq.*), girth, *embonpoint* (*F.*), obesity, polysarcia (*med.*), adiposity (*med.*), overweight, rotundity; potbelly, paunch, corporation (*colloq.*), ventricosity.

giant, Brobdingnagian, Goliath, Antaeus, Polyphemus, colossus, titan, Briareus, Cyclops, Gog and Magog, Gargantua, Pantagruel; monster, mammoth, whale, behemoth, leviathan, elephant, jumbo, lubber, oversize, whopper (*colloq.*).

fat person, tub (*colloq.*), fatty (*colloq.*), roly-poly, punchinello, cherub.

V. size, adjust, arrange, grade, gauge, classify, range, graduate, group, sort, match.

Adj. sizable, big, great, large, ample, substantial, tidy (*colloq.*), voluminous, capacious, spacious, comprehensive; beamy, bouncing, bull, decuman, gross, king-size (*colloq.*), magnitudinous, thumping (*colloq.*), thundering, whacking, whopping (*colloq.*), massive, ponderous; strapping, burly, hefty (*colloq.*), husky (*colloq.*).

impressive, imposing, massive, monumental, stately, mighty, towering, magnificent, sculpturesque, statuesque.

bulky, unwieldy, gross, massive, ponderous, unmanageable, cumbersome, cumbrous.

oversized, oversize, outsized, outsize, overgrown, lubberly, lumpish, hulking, hulky, hippopotamic, elephantine, lumbering.

huge, immense, tremendous, enormous, gigantic, gigantean, titanic, titan, stupendous, monster, monstrous, elephantine, jumbo (*colloq.*), megatherian, mammoth, mountainous, giant, colossal, Cyclopean, Cyclopic, Brobdingnagian, Gargantuan, goliath; prodigious, monumental, herculean, mighty, thumping (*colloq.*), whopping (*colloq.*), cosmic, astronomical.

vast, boundless, illimitable, immeasurable, immense, infinite, limitless, measureless, unbounded, unlimitable, unlimited.

fat, corpulent, stout, fleshy, fleshly, beefy, blubbery, heavy, overweight, overfed, overstuffed, broad in the beam (*slang*), rotund, well-fed, plump, buxom, chubby, fattish, Falstaffian, paunchy, pursy, obese, adipose (*med.*), blowzy, blowzed, bouncing, burly, portly; pudgy, podgy, roly-poly, chunky, dumpy, tubby, stubby, stocky, husky (*colloq.*), squat, squatty, thickset, big as a house.

See also ARRANGEMENT, ENDLESSNESS, GREATNESS, INCREASE, MAGNIFICENCE. MEASUREMENT, OIL, RANK, WEIGHT. *Antonyms*—See SHORTNESS, SMALLNESS, THINNESS.

sizzle, *v.* hiss, sizz, spit (SIBILATION); roast, broil (HEAT).

skeleton, *n.* bony structure, osteology (BONE); frame, framework, scaffolding (SUPPORT); cadaver, scrag (THINNESS).

skeptic, *n.* disbeliever, scoffer, doubting Thomas (UNBELIEVINGNESS); freethinker, agnostic (IRRELIGION, HETERODOXY).

skeptical, *adj.* unbelieving, incredulous, suspicious, quizzical (UNBELIEVINGNESS); freethinking, agnostic (IRRELIGION).

skepticism, *n.* doubt, incredulity, suspicion, cynicism (UNBELIEVINGNESS); unbelief, agnosticism, freethinking (IRRELIGION).

sketch, *n.* picture, drawing, cartoon (FINE ARTS); draft, chart, blueprint (PLAN, SHAPE, WRITING); piece, vignette, monograph (TREATISE); account, version, report (DESCRIPTION).

skewer, *n.* broach, brochette, spit (ROD).

skid, *v.* skew, swerve, veer (SIDE).

skill, *n.* dexterity, deftness, artistry (ABILITY).

skillet, *n.* frying pan, griddle (COOKERY).

skillful, *adj.* dexterous, practiced, adroit, adept (ABILITY).

skim, *v.* remove, ream, cream (REMOVAL); thumb, turn the pages (READING); skip, trip, skitter (SPEED).

skimp, *v.* scrape, stint, scrimp (ECONOMY).

SKIN—*N.* skin, epidermis, dermis, integument, corium, cuticle, cutis, derma; hide, pelt, peltry, slough, exuviae; peel, rind, pellicle; callus, hangnail, agnail; parchment, vellum; scalp; taxidermy, taxidermist.

flesh, brawn, muscular tissue, meat, pulp; quick; crest, comb, caruncle, jowl, dewlap, wattle; incarnation.

leather, alligator, buckskin, buff, calfskin, capeskin, chamois, cowhide, crocodile, deerskin, doeskin, goatskin, horsehide, kid *or* kidskin, lizard, morocco, pigskin, pin seal, seal, sheepskin, snakeskin, cordovan, suede, skiver, rawhide; belt, strap, thong, sandal; leatherette, plastic; tannery.

membrane, pellicle, mucous membrane, mucosa, peritoneum, caul; meninges (*pl.*), arachnoid, dura, dura mater, pia mater; pleura, endometrium, endocardium, pericardium; frenum.

pimple, fester, papule, phlyctena, pustule, pustulation, whelk; blackhead, comedo; blotch, breakout, rash, eruption, acne.

boil, sore, excrescence, carbuncle, furuncle, anthrax.

blister, bleb, bulla, vesication, vesicle.

rash, roseola, hives, uredo, urticaria; frambesia, yaws; measles, morbilli, German measles, rubella, rubeola; scarlet fever, scarlatina; pityriasis, impetigo; ringworm, tinea.

pox, chicken pox, varicella; cowpox, vaccinia, smallpox, variola, varioloid; leprosy, lepra; lupus.

the itch, pruritis, prurigo, scabies, the mange.

callus, callosity, corn, induration; elephantiasis, pachydermia, ichthyosis, myxedema, scleroderma, xeroderma.

leper, lazar; leprosarium, lazaret, leprosery.

V. skin, peel, decorticate, pare, scrape, uncover, strip, shave; tan, curry.

put flesh on, gain weight, fatten; incarnate, carnify.

blister, vesicate, vesiculate; pimple, pustulate.

Adj. dermal, epidermal, cuticular, cutaneous; subcutaneous, hypodermic, intradermal; skinlike, dermatoid; membranous, membranaceous, membranate.

fleshy, brawny, fleshly, sarcous, pulpy, pulpous; flesh-colored, pink, rosy, incarnadine, incarnate.

leathery, coriaceous, leather, leatherlike, leathern.

See also BLEMISH, COVERING, HARDNESS, ITCHING, PULP, RED, SURFACE.

---

skinny, *adj.* bony, rawboned, scrawny (THINNESS).

skip, *v.* disregard, pass over, miss (NEGLECT, INATTENTION); step, trip (WALKING); buck, canter (JUMP); escape, flee, desert (DEPARTURE); promote, advance, upgrade (ELEVATION, RANK).

skipper, *n.* captain, master, chief (SAILOR, LEADERSHIP).

skirmish, *v.* scuffle, scrimmage, buffet (FIGHTING, ATTEMPT).

skirt, *v.* lie along, border, flank (REST, SIDE).

SKIRT—*N.* skirt, overskirt, underskirt, peg-top skirt, peg tops, dirndl, culottes, hobble skirt, hoop skirt, crinoline, pannier, peplum, lava-lava (*Samoa*), pareu (*Polynesia*); kilt, filibeg, philibeg.

frock, gown, robe, dress, dirndl, jumper, pinafore, princess dress, sheath, housedress, mantua (*hist.*), Mother Hubbard, *décolletage* (*F.*); hostess gown, housecoat, house gown; riding dress, habit.

See also CLOTHING, TROUSERS.

---

skullcap, *n.* cap, beanie, fez (HEADGEAR).

sky, *n.* the heavens, firmament (HEAVEN).

skylark, *v.* lark, gambol, rollick (PLAYFULNESS, MERRIMENT).

skyrocket, *v.* rocket, shoot up, arrow (ASCENT).

slab, *n.* stone, boulder, dornick (ROCK); board, slat, stave (WOOD); piece, strip, cut (PART).

slack, *adj.* flabby, flaccid, limp (WEAKNESS, SOFTNESS); lax, baggy (LOOSENESS); quiet, inactive (INACTION).

slacken, *v.* loosen, relax (LOOSENESS); slow down (SLOWNESS); weaken, modify (WEAKNESS, RELIEF).

slack off, *v.* dwindle, taper, wane (WEAKNESS).

slacks, *n.* breeches, pants (TROUSERS).

slake, *v.* appease, assuage, sate (SATISFACTION).

slander, *v.* libel, blacken, besmirch (ACCUSATION, DETRACTION).

slang, *n.* patter, patois, jargon (LANGUAGE).

slant, *n.* grade, gradient, cant, incline (SLOPE); bias, preconception, prepossession (PREJUDICE); view, judgment, sentiment (OPINION).

slant, *v.* cant, incline, skew, (SLOPE); aim, level, point (DIRECTION); color, angle, distort (PREJUDICE, MISREPRESENTATION).

slap, *v.* hit, strike, smack (HITTING).

slat, *n.* board, stave, slab (WOOD).

slate, *n.* stone, shale, chalkstone (ROCK); ballot, ticket (LIST).

slattern, *n.* dowd, slut (UNTIDINESS).

slaughter, *n.* butchery, bloodshed, carnage (KILLING).

slaughter, *v.* kill, slay, finish, do in (KILLING).

slaughterhouse, *n.* abattoir, butchery, shamble (KILLING).

SLAVERY—*N.* **slavery**, bondage, chains, enslavement, helotry, serfdom, bondservice, servitude, subjection, subjugation, vassalage, yoke, indenture; enthrallment, thrall, thralldom.

slave, bondsman, bondman, bond servant; bondswoman, bondmaid, odalisque; chattel, helot, mameluke (*Moham.*), serf, thrall, vassal.

servility, submissiveness, abjectness, slavishness, subservience, supineness; obsequiousness, humility, abasement, prostration, toadeating, fawning, flunkyism, sycophancy.

sycophant, fawner, toady, toadeater, flunky, hanger-on, ward heeler, truckler, bootlicker.

V. **enslave**, bind, indenture, yoke; enthrall, thrall, bethrall.

subject, control, tame, break in, master, subdue, vanquish, subjugate, reduce, defeat, overcome; tread down, weigh down, keep under rule.

be servile, cringe, bow, stoop, kneel; fawn, crouch, crawl, toady, grovel.

be subject, be at the mercy of, depend upon; fall a prey to, fall under the spell of; serve, obey, submit to.

Adj. **slavish**, servile, submissive, abject, subservient, supine, enslaved; obsequious, pliant, cringing, fawning, truckling, groveling, sycophantic, prostrate, base, mean.

subject, dependent, subordinate; feudal, feudatory; downtrodden, henpecked; under one's thumb, tied to one's apron strings, at one's beck and call, at the mercy of.

See also CONTROL, CRAWL, DEFEAT, FEUDALISM, FOLLOWER, HUMILITY, LIABILITY, OBEDIENCE, RESTRAINT, RULE, SERVICE, SUBMISSION. *Antonyms*—See OPPOSITION, RULER.

---

slavish, *adj.* servile, submissive, abject, subservient (SLAVERY).

slay, *v.* kill, slaughter, do in (KILLING).

sleazy, *adj.* flimsy, papery, gimcrack (WEAKNESS).

sled, *n.* sleigh, bob, bobsled (VEHICLE).

sleek, *adj.* glossy, slick, shiny (SMOOTHNESS); groomed, well-groomed, trig (NEATNESS).

SLEEP—*N.* sleep, slumber, slumbers, shut-eye (*colloq.*), nap, cat nap, forty winks, doze, drowse, snooze, siesta, land of nod; dormience, repose, deep sleep, sopor; cataplexy, trance, narcolepsy; dormition.

sleepiness, doziness, drowsiness, narcosis, narcotism, oscitancy, slumberousness; lethargy, somnolence.

science of sleep: hypnology.

god of sleep: Morpheus.

sleeping quarters, accommodation, bunkhouse, cubicle, dormitory; board, bed and board, board and keep.

bedroom, bedchamber, cubicle, chamber, sleeping porch, stateroom, cabin, nursery; dressing room, boudoir.

nightgown, nightdress, bedgown, night robe, *robe-de-nuit* (F.), nightshirt, pajamas, night clothes, nightwear.

sleepwalking, somnambulism, noctambulism.

bed, bunk, berth, pallet, truckle bed, trundle bed, cot, army cot, folding cot, folding bed, day bed, settle bed, couch, four-poster, hammock; crib, cradle, bassinet.

bedding, mattress, feather bed, pallet, paillasse, palliasse, litter.

bedspread, spread, bedcover, coverlet, counterpane, blanket, comfort, comforter, comfortable, quilt; bedclothes, bedding.

blanket, cover, quilt, crazy quilt, patchwork quilt; comforter, comfort, comfortable, puff; feather bed, eider down.

pillow, cushion, bolster, sham; pillowcase, pillow slip, slip.

dream, vision, nightmare.

daydream, fantasy, phantasy, reverie, castle in the air, castle in Spain, fancy.

hypnotism, animal magnetism, mesmerism; hypnosis, trance; autohypnosis, self-hypnosis.

sleepwalker, somnambulist, noctambulist.

dreamer, visionary, phantast.

hypnotist, magnetizer, mesmerist, Svengali.

sleeping pill, sedative, barbiturate, dormitive, hypnotic, narcotic, opiate, somnifacient, soporific.

V. sleep, slumber, bunk, bed down, snooze, nap, catch forty winks, take a cat nap, get some shut-eye (*colloq.*), drowze, drop off, doze, fall asleep; go to sleep, go to bed, hit the hay (*colloq.*), retire; oversleep.

bed, bed down, put to bed, accommodate, lodge, camp, board.

hypnotize, magnetize, mesmerize.

Adj. asleep, sleeping, dozing, napping, slumbering, snoozing, dormient, retired.

sleepy, dozy, drowsy, somnolent, poppied, slumberous, slumbery, soporific.

sleeplike, hypnoid, trancelike.

sleep-producing, sleep-inducing, dormitive, hypnagogic, hypnogenetic, hypnotic, narcotic, opiate, somnifacient, somniferous, somnific, soporiferous, soporific.

hypnotic, hypnogenetic, magnetic, mesmeric.

dreamlike, dreamy, nightmarish, phantasmagoric, phantasmagorial, moony, visionary.

See also CALMNESS, COVERING, IMAGINATION, INACTION, INSENSIBILITY, PHARMACY, REST. *Antonyms*—See ACTION, ACTIVITY, WAKEFULNESS.

---

sleeping pill, *n.* sedative, barbiturate, hypnotic (SLEEP, PHARMACY).

sleepless, *adj.* wide-awake, alert, insomniac (WAKEFULNESS).

sleep together, *v.* be intimate, make love (SEX).

sleepwalking, *n.* somnambulism, noctambulism (SLEEP).

sleet, *n.* ice, glaze, hail (COLD).

sleeve, *n.* armlet, cap sleeve (GLOVE).

sleight of hand, *n.* jugglery, legerdemain (MAGIC).

slender, *adj.* slim, slight, skinny (THINNESS); thin, fine, threadlike (NARROWNESS); insubstantial, airy (THINNESS); bare, little, scant (SMALLNESS).

sleuth, *n.* ferret, detective, snoop (SEARCH, DISCOVERY).

slice, *v.* shred, shave, section (CUTTING, PART).

slick, *adj.* glossy, shiny; slippery, lubricous (SMOOTHNESS); urbane, glib, unctuous (SUAVITY, OIL).

slide, *v.* glide, slip, slither (SMOOTHNESS).

slight, *adj.* delicate, faint (WEAKNESS); meager, insubstantial (SMALLNESS); trifling, unessential (UNIMPORTANCE); slender, slim (THINNESS).

slight, *v.* snub, disdain, scorn (INSULT, CONTEMPT, WORTHLESSNESS); disregard, ignore (DETRACTION, UNIMPORTANCE, INACTION).

slightest, *adj.* least, lowest, minimum (SMALLNESS).

slightly, *adv.* imperceptibly, hardly, scarcely (SMALLNESS).

slim, *adj.* slender, fine (NARROWNESS); thin, lean (THINNESS); insubstantial, remote (SMALLNESS, WEAKNESS).

slime, *n.* ooze, mire, muck (SEMILIQUIDITY).

slimy, *adj.* mucous, mucid, clammy (STICKINESS).

slink, *v.* steal, pass quietly, sneak (THIEVERY).

slip, *n.* error, boner (MISTAKE); tag, label, ticket (INDICATION); camisole, chemise (UNDERWEAR).

slip, *v.* glide, slide, slither (SMOOTHNESS); err, blunder

(MISTAKE); drop, fall, totter (DE-SCENT).

slipper, *n.* pantofle, step-in, sneaker (FOOTWEAR).

slippery, *adj.* slick, lubricous (SMOOTHNESS, OIL); untrust-worthy, fly-by-night, shifty (UN-BELIEVINGNESS); elusive, tricky (AVOIDANCE).

slipshod, *adj.* careless, sloppy, slovenly (CARELESSNESS, UNTIDI-NESS).

slit, *n.* aperture, cleft, breach (OPENING, DISJUNCTION).

slither, *v.* crook, meander, snake, zigzag (WINDING); glide, slide, slip (SMOOTHNESS).

sliver, *n.* snip, snippet, splinter (SMALLNESS).

slob, *n.* sloven, slattern (UNTIDI-NESS).

slobber, *v.* slaver, drool, drivel (SALIVA).

slogan, *n.* saying, motto, catchword (STATEMENT, WORD).

slop, *v.* smear, spatter, smudge (UNCLEANNESS); spill, splash, spray (WATER).

SLOPE—*N.* slope, slant, grade, gradient, cant, incline, inclination, shelf, rake, bank, bevel, hill, pre-cipice, cliff, talus, versant; dia-gonal, bias.

upward slope, acclivity, ascent, helicline, upgrade, uprise, upris-ing, rise.

downward slope, declivity, fall, drop, pitch, dip, descent, decline, chute, downgrade.

lean, leaning, list, careen, cant, tilt.

V. slope, slant, cant, incline, skew, splay, shelve, rake, bank, bevel; rise, ascend; fall, drop, pitch, dip, descend, decline.

lean, list, heel, careen, cant, tilt, tip.

Adj. **sloping,** slanting, aslope, aslant, sloped, slanted, inclined, tilted, atilt, skew, rakish, tipsy, banked, beveled; diagonal, bias, oblique; hilly, steep, abrupt, pre-cipitous; synclinal.

sloping upward, ascending, ris-ing, acclivous, uprising, uphill; steep, abrupt, precipitous.

sloping downward, declivitous, declivous, declivate, pendent, pre-cipitant; falling, dropping, pitched, dipping, descending, de-clining, downgrade, downhill.

leaning, inclinatory, incumbent, recumbent, reclining; lopsided.

Adv., phrases. **slopingly,** slant-ingly, rakishly, tipsily, on the bias, on a slant, diagonally, obliquely; steeply, abruptly, precipitously;

downhill, uphill; slantly, across, slantwise, aslant, aslantwise, aslope, athwart, sidewise, at an angle.

See also ASCENT, BEND, CURVATURE, DESCENT, HEIGHT, TURNING. *Anto-nyms*—See FLATNESS, STRAIGHTNESS, VERTICALITY.

sloppy, *adj.* dirty, dingy (UNCLEAN-NESS); bedraggled, dowdy, tacky (UNTIDINESS); slipshod, slovenly (CARELESSNESS).

slops, *n.* refuse, garbage, swill (UN-CLEANNESS).

slot, *n.* recess, socket, slit (OPEN-ING).

slothful, *adj.* lazy, shiftless, indo-lent (REST); spiritless, lifeless, inanimate (INACTION).

slouchy, *adj.* stooped, bent, droopy (POSTURE).

slovenly, *adj.* slipshod, sloppy (CARELESSNESS); bedraggled, dowdy, tacky (UNTIDINESS); dirty, dingy, frowzy (UNCLEAN-NESS).

SLOWNESS—*N.* slowness, inertia, snail's pace, bovinity, lentitude.

retardation, retardment, retard-ance, delay, deceleration, arrested development, arrest, abortion, hy-poplasia (*med.*), infantilism.

slowpoke, poke, laggard, loiterer, tarrier, snail, turtle, tortoise, slug (*ship, vehicle, etc.*), gradualist.

gradualness, graduality, grada-tion, gradualism.

V. slow, lose speed, slow down, slow up, relax, slack, slacken, de-celerate, brake, backwater; retard, retardate, moderate, arrest (*med.*), check, choke, stunt.

move slowly, crawl, creep, slug; toil, labor, work, forge, struggle; walk, saunter, trudge, barge, plow, plod, lumber, drag, worm one's way, inch, inch along, limp; delay, stall, tarry, take one's time, drag one's feet, loiter, lag, lag behind, trail, linger, jog, prowl; taxi.

Adj. **slow,** leisurely, slack, slow-footed, slow-moving, slow-paced, slow-gaited, laggard, sluggard, sluggish, sullen, inert, snail-like, snail-paced, tardy, late, behind-hand, tardigrade, poky, bovine, lentitudinous; turtle-like, tortoise-like, testudineous; slow-witted, slow on the uptake.

slowed, slowed down, slowed up, retarded, delayed, decelerated, slackened, arrested (*med.*), pau-peritic (*med.*), dwarfed, stunted, checked, choked.

slow (*in music*), allegretto, an-dante, adagio, andantino, larghetto, largo, lentando, lentissimo, lento.

gradual, piecemeal, step-by-step, bit-by-bit, drop-by-drop, inch-by-inch, gradational, gradative, imperceptible; gradualistic.

Adv., phrases. **slowly**, slow, leisurely, sluggishly, tardily, pokily.

gradually, bit by bit, by degrees, by slow degrees, drop by drop, *gradatim* (*L.*), gradationally, gradatively, imperceptibly, inch by inch, little by little, piece by piece, piecemeal, step by step, by regular steps, by gradations; *pas à pas, peu à peu* (*both F.*).

See also CRAWL, DELAY, INACTION, STUPIDITY, UNWILLINGNESS. *Antonyms*—See ACTIVITY, SPEED.

sluggard, *n.* idler, slugabed, do-nothing (REST).

sluggish, *adj.* languid, languorous, leaden, lethargic (INACTION); sluggard, sullen (SLOWNESS).

sluice, *n.* sluice gate, floodgate, hatch (DEPARTURE).

slumber, *n.* doze, drowse, snooze (SLEEP).

slummy, *adj.* dirty, squalid, sordid (UNCLEANNESS).

slump, *n.* shakeout, recession, depression (BUSINESS).

slums, *n.* warren (MULTITUDE).

slur, *v.* offend, slight, snub (INSULT); smear, traduce, vilify (ACCUSATION, DETRACTION).

slur over, *v.* neglect, miss, skip (INATTENTION).

slush, *n.* snow, slosh, slop (COLD, SEMILIQUIDITY).

slut, *n.* strumpet, cocotte, courtesan (PROSTITUTE, SEX); slattern, dowd (UNTIDINESS).

sly, *n.* cunning, subtle, tricky (CLEVERNESS); sneaky, stealthy, furtive (CONCEALMENT).

smack, *n.* slap, blow (HITTING); flavor, savor, tang (TASTE).

smack, *v.* hit, strike, slap (HITTING).

small, *adj.* little, tiny, petite (SMALLNESS); soft, thin, reedy (WEAKNESS); sordid, small-minded (SELFISHNESS).

smaller, *adj.* less, lesser (SMALLNESS).

smallest, *adj.* least, minimum (SMALLNESS).

small-minded, *adj.* calculated, small, sordid (SELFISHNESS).

SMALLNESS—*N.* smallness, littleness, etc. (see *Adjectives*); dwarfism, nanism.

small person, bantam, diminutive being, Lilliputian, midge, midget, peewee, pygmy, runt, shrimp, snip (*colloq.*), Tom Thumb, hop-o'-my-thumb, tot, dwarf, gnome, homunculus, manikin; Negrillo (*African*), Negrito (*Asiatic*); Pygmy *or* Pigmy; insignificancy.

small creature, runt, shrimp, stunt, toy (*dog*), pygmy, midget, dwarf, mite.

microbe, germ, bug, microorganism, bacterium (*pl.* bacteria), bacillus (*pl.* bacilli), micrococcus.

small thing, mite, peewee, pygmy, scrub, shrimp, snippet, tot, minim, miniature, midget, insignificancy, toy, ambsace.

[*small amount*] **bit,** crumb, dab, dash, dribble, driblet, gram, infinitesimal, iota, jot, little, minim, mite (*colloq.*), modicum, particle, patch, pittance, scantling, scintilla, shade, snuff, soupçon, speck, tittle, tot, trace, trickle, trifle, vestige, whit, atom; morsel, tidbit *or* titbit; scattering, sprinkle, sprinkling; dash, drop, pinch, splash, splatter; scrap, shred; snip, snippet, sliver, splinter, chip, shaving, hair; thimbleful; drop in the bucket, a drop in the ocean.

particle, ambsace, atom, bit, corpuscle, fleck, grain, granule, molecule, mote (*esp. of dust*), scintilla, speck.

trace, bit, drop, element, iota, jot, mite, modicum, patch, rack, shade, show, smack, soupçon, spice, strain, streak, suggestion, suspicion, tang, tincture, tinge, vein, vestige, whisper, wisp; atom, beam, flicker, gleam, ray, spark, breath, grain, inkling, molecule, particle, scintilla, shadow, shred, speck.

V. **make small,** dwarf, stunt, micrify, minify; make smaller, decrease, contract, diminish.

become smaller, diminish, lessen, decrease, contract, shrink, dwindle, wane.

Adj. **small,** little, bantam, diminutive, Lilliputian, microscopic, tiny, teeny, wee, vest-pocket, pocket-size, undersized, undergrown, stunted, scrub, scrubby, runty, puny, sawed-off, pygmy, pint-size *or* pint-sized, dwarf, dwarfish, baby, miniature, minikin, petite, minute, minuscule, minimal, minim, infinitesimal, insignificant, submicroscopic, slight, smallish, toy (*of dogs*), fine; cramped, limited, poky.

slight, flimsy, footless, insubstantial, tenuous, unsubstantial; bare, frail, insignificant, lean, little, meager, rare, remote, scant, slender, slim, small, tiny, weak.

inappreciable, inconsiderable, imperceptible, homeopathic, infinitesimal, insignificant.

mere, simple, sheer, stark, bare, naked, plain, nothing but.

less, lesser, smaller, inferior, minor, lower.

least, smallest, slightest, lowest, minimum, minimal, minim.

Adv., phrases. little, a little, not much, somewhat, rather, to some degree (*or* extent); in a nutshell; on a small scale.

slightly, imperceptibly, faintly, feebly, barely, hardly, scarcely.

merely, only, purely, simply.

partially, in part, incompletely, somewhat, to a certain extent, in a certain degree, comparatively, rather, in some degree (*or* measure); at least, at most, ever so little, after a fashion.

almost, nearly, well-nigh, nigh, not quite, all but, close to; within an ace (*or* inch) of, on the brink of.

scarcely, hardly, barely, only just, no more than.

about, nearly, approximately, *circa* (*L.*), say, thereabouts, somewhere about, somewhere near.

nowise, noway *or* noways, in no manner, not at all, not in the least, not a bit, not a jot, in no wise, in no respect, by no means, on no account.

See also DECREASE, FEWNESS, SHORTNESS, THINNESS. *Antonyms* —See ADDITION, GREATNESS, INCREASE, MULTITUDE, SIZE.

smart, *adj.* bright, brilliant, intelligent (INTELLIGENCE); clever, ingenious, resourceful (CLEVERNESS); stylish, in fashion (FASHION).

smart, *v.* hurt, sting, ache (PAIN); prick, prickle, bite (CUTTING).

smash, *v.* bang, hit, collide (HITTING); pound, crush (POWDERINESS); wreck, ruin, demolish (DESTRUCTION); crash, clatter (LOUDNESS); charge, stampede (SPEED).

smashup, *n.* collision, impact, crash (TOUCH).

smattering, *n.* smatter, superficiality, sciolism (IGNORANCE).

smear, *n.* macule, smudge, smutch (UNCLEANNESS); character assassination (MALEDICTION).

smear, *v.* dirty, spatter, smudge (UNCLEANNESS); bespread, besmear, spray (SPREAD); slur, traduce, revile (DETRACTION, MALEDICTION, ACCUSATION); bribe, corrupt, reach (BRIBERY).

smell, *n.* tang, scent, trail (ODOR).

smell, *v.* scent, sniff, snuff; stink, reek (ODOR).

smelt, *v.* dissolve, fuse, melt, render (LIQUID).

smile, *v.* beam, grin, smirk (LAUGHTER).

smirk, *v.* grin, simper (LAUGHTER).

smith, *n.* metalworker, metalist, armorer (METAL); blacksmith, farrier (*Brit.*), horseshoer (SERVICE).

smithy, *n.* metalworks, smithery, forge (METAL).

smitten, *adj.* in love, enamored, infatuated (LOVE); attracted, drawn (ATTRACTION).

smoke, *n.* fume, fumes, smolder (GAS); cigar, Havana, cheroot, stogie; cigarette, fag (*slang*), tailor-made (TOBACCO).

smoke, *v.* whiff, fume, reek, smolder (GAS); puff, inhale (TOBACCO).

smoky, *adj.* fumy, reeky, smoldering (GAS).

smoldering, *adj.* latent, dormant, potential (PRESENCE).

smooth, *adj.* even, level; creamy (SMOOTHNESS); calm, windless (CALMNESS); urbane, glib (SUAVITY).

smooth, *v.* press, iron (SMOOTHNESS, ROLL); level, even (UNIFORMITY); stroke, pat (CALMNESS).

SMOOTHNESS—N. smoothness, evenness, etc. (see *Adjectives*); polish, gloss, glaze, shine.

smoother, roller, steam roller; mangle, iron, flatiron, emery paper; plane; polisher, waxer, burnisher.

V. smooth, even, level, flatten, roll, grade; unwrinkle, press, mangle, iron; scour, sandpaper, pumice, buff, file; plane, shave; lubricate, oil, grease, wax; pat, planish, levigate.

polish, burnish, sleek, slick, luster, varnish, glaze, gloss.

[*move smoothly*] glide, slide, slip, slither, skitter, flow.

Adj. smooth, even, level, plane, flat, unwrinkled; satiny, silken, silky, velvety, velutinous, glassy, glabrous, creamy, bland, levigate.

glossy, sleek, slick, shiny, polished, lustrous, *glacé* (*F.*), waxen, waxy.

slippery, slick, saponaceous, lubricous.

See also CALMNESS, FLATNESS, GLASSINESS, LIGHT, OIL, PRESSURE, RUBBING, SUAVITY, WAX. *Antonyms* —See FOLD, NOTCH, ROUGHNESS, WRINKLE.

smooth-spoken, *adj.* slick, urbane, glib (SUAVITY).

smother, v. burke, choke, throttle (KILLING); restrain, stifle, choke back (RESTRAINT).

smudge, n. macule, smear, smutch (UNCLEANNESS).

smudge, v. slop, smear, spatter (UNCLEANNESS).

smug, adj. complacent, self-satisfied (SATISFACTION); spruce, trim, natty (NEATNESS).

smuggler, n. bootlegger, contrabandist, rumrunner (ILLEGALITY).

smut, n. pornography, scatology, coprophemia (OBSCENITY).

smutty, adj. pornographic, salacious (OBSCENITY).

snack, n. mouthful, morsel, bite (FOOD).

snag, n. block, blockade, clog (RESTRAINT).

snake, n. reptile, serpent, viper (ANIMAL).

snake, v. wind, crook, meander, slither (WINDING).

snaky, adj. meandrous, serpentine, sinuous (WINDING); vipery, venomous, virulent (HOSTILITY).

snap, n. crack, break, fracture (BREAKAGE); easy contest, setup (colloq.), walkaway (ATTEMPT, SUCCESS); child's play, smooth sailing, cinch (EASE).

snap, v. break, crack, fracture (BREAKAGE); photograph, shoot (PHOTOGRAPH); snarl, bark, growl (ANGER, BAD TEMPER).

snapshot, n. picture, portrait, tintype (PHOTOGRAPH).

snare, n. pitfall, booby trap, meshes, noose, toils, quicksand (TRAP).

snare, v. trap, ensnare, enmesh (TRAP).

snarl, n. muss, tangle, rummage (UNTIDINESS).

snarl, v. tangle, complicate, involve (CONFUSION, MYSTERY); thunder, growl, snap (THREAT, ANGER, BAD TEMPER).

snatch, v. grab, seize, grip, clutch (TAKING).

snatch at, v. be willing, jump at (WILLINGNESS).

sneak, n. wretch, worm, cur (MEANNESS, CONTEMPT); coward, poltroon, dastard (FEAR).

sneak, v. slink, prowl, skulk (THIEVERY, CONCEALMENT); steal, filch, thieve (THIEVERY).

sneaker, n. slipper, pantofle, step-in (FOOTWEAR).

sneaky, adj. stealthy, surreptitious, furtive (CONCEALMENT); cowardly, recreant, yellow (FEAR).

sneer, v. jeer, scoff, snort (CONTEMPT).

sneeze, n. sneezing, sternutation (NOSE).

sneeze at, v. snub, upstage (colloq.), spurn (CONTEMPT); ignore, pooh-pooh, slight (UNIMPORTANCE).

snicker, v. laugh, snigger, titter (LAUGHTER).

sniff, v. inspire, insufflate, inhale (BREATH); smell, snuff (ODOR); detect, scent (DISCOVERY).

sniffle, v. snivel, snuff, snuffle (BREATH).

sniffles, n. a cold, rheum, rhinitis (NOSE).

snippy, (colloq.), adj. sassy (slang), saucy, fresh (DISCOURTESY).

snitch (slang), v. peach (slang), squeal (colloq.), inform on (INFORMATION); steal, filch, lift (THIEVERY).

snivel, v. sniffle, snuff, snuffle (BREATH); mewl, pule, cry (WEEPING).

snobbish, adj. superior, condescending, patronizing (PRIDE).

snoop, n. pry, quidnunc, spy (INQUIRY, LOOKING); detective, ferret, sleuth (SEARCH).

snoop, v. spy, pry, peep (LOOKING).

snore, v. breathe, wheeze (BREATH).

snort, v. exhale, whiff (BREATH); sneer, jeer, scoff (CONTEMPT).

snout, n. jaws, chops, muzzle (HEAD).

snow, n. flurry, snowflake, snowdrift, snowslip (COLD).

snowfall, n. precipitation, snowstorm, blizzard (COLD).

snowslide, n. avalanche, landslide, glissade (DESCENT).

snub, adj. pug, retroussé (F.), upturned (NOSE).

snub, v. slight, slur, upstage (INSULT, CONTEMPT); cut, brush off (slang), boycott (INATTENTION).

snug, adj. restful, cozy, comfortable (REST); tight, compact, close (TIGHTNESS); protected, secure, safe (PROTECTION).

snuggle, v. cuddle, nestle, nuzzle (REST, PRESSURE, WINDING).

so, adv. thus, accordingly, therefore (REASONING).

soak, v. douse, drench, saturate (WATER); bathe, steep (INSERTION).

soak up, v. absorb, assimilate (INTAKE).

soapbox, n. rostrum, stump, pulpit (SUPPORT).

soar, v. fly, climb, glide (FLYING); ascend, rise (ASCENT).

sob, v. wail, whimper, cry (WEEPING).

sober, adj. uninebriated, unintoxicated (SOBRIETY); steady, staid, serious, serious-minded, settled (CALMNESS, SOBRIETY).

SOBRIETY—*N.* sobriety, soberness, uninebriation, unintoxication, temperance, temperateness, moderation, abstemiousness.

teetotalism, abstinence, total abstinence, asceticism, nephalism, Rechabitism, Encratism, temperance; temperance act, Volstead Act, Prohibition; Alcoholics Anonymous.

teetotaler, teetotalist, abstainer, total abstainer, ascetic, nephalist, Rechabite, Encratite; dry, prohibitionist, Women's Christian Temperance Union (W.C.T.U.), Carry Nation.

seriousness, austerity, astringency, gravity, severity, solemnity; soberness, etc. (See *Adjectives*).

V. be temperate, abstain, refrain, go on the water wagon (*slang*), teetotal, take (*or* sign) the pledge; sober, sober up.

make serious, treat seriously, solemnize, solemnify; aggravate, intensify, exaggerate.

Adj. sober, uninebriated, uninebrious, unintoxicated; temperate, moderate, abstemious; on the water wagon (*slang*), abstinent, ascetic, teetotal; dry, antisaloon.

serious, solemn, grim, funereal, pontifical, saturnine, somber, demure, earnest, sedate, settled, staid, sober-minded; severe, sore, weighty, important, grave, critical, momentous, grievous, astringent, austere.

See also ASCETICISM, CONTROL, EXAGGERATION, IMPORTANCE, MODERATENESS, SEVERITY. *Antonyms*—See DRUNKENNESS, FRIVOLITY, PLAYFULNESS, UNIMPORTANCE.

so-called, *adj.* soi-disant (*F.*), purported, self-styled (NAME, PRETENSE).

sociable, *adj.* gregarious, companionable, friendly (SOCIABILITY, FRIENDLINESS, APPROACH).

social, *adj.* public, popular, societal (PEOPLE); sociable, gregarious, companionable (SOCIABILITY, FRIENDLINESS).

social, *n.* sociable, soirée, tea party (SOCIALITY).

SOCIAL CLASS—*N.* social class, caste, estate, stratum, station, sphere, class.

gentry, gentlefolk, gentlefolks, aristocracy, beau monde (*F.*), elite, nobility, peerage, patricians (*anc. Rome*), equites (*anc. Rome*); upper class, upper crust, classes, bon ton (*F.*), society, quality, café society, the four hundred.

aristocrat, patrician, noble, blue blood, socialite; parvenu (*F.*), arriviste (*F.*), nouveau riche (*F.*), upstart (*all derogatory*).

nobleman, noble, lord (*Gr. Brit.*), peer, prince, archduke (*Austria*), grandee (*Spain or Portugal*), grand duke, duke, marchese (*Italy*), marquis, margrave, earl (*Gr. Brit.*), count, landgrave (*Germany*), viscount, baron, chevalier (*F.*).

noblewoman, peeress, princess, archduchess (*Austria*), grand duchess, duchess, marchesa (*Italy*), marquise *or* marchioness, margravine, countess (*Gr. Brit.*), landgravine *or* landgravess (*Germany*), viscountess, baroness.

[*collectively*] nobility, peerage, Second Estate, baronage, aristocracy.

[*titles below nobility*] baronet (*abbr.* Bart.), knight, sir, cavalier, esquire.

Adj. aristocratic, patrician, upper-class, well-born, highborn, blue-blooded, equestrian (*anc. Rome*).

noble, nobiliary, titled, lordly, princely.

See also ARRANGEMENT, CLASS, RANK, RULER. *Antonyms*—See HUMILITY, LOWNESS, MEANNESS, PEOPLE.

SOCIALITY—*N.* sociality, sociability, companionability, social intercourse; association, company, society, companionship, comradeship, fellowship, consociation, clubbism; social circle, circle of acquaintances.

conviviality, good fellowship, joviality, jollity, festivity, merrymaking; hospitality, heartiness, cheer.

welcome, greeting, salutation, hearty (*or* warm) reception, glad hand (*slang*).

good fellow, boon companion, good scout (*colloq.*), good mixer (*colloq.*), joiner (*colloq.*), bon vivant (*F.*).

party, affair, function, social function, gathering, house party, Kaffeeklatsch (*Ger.*), reception, at home, social, sociable, soirée, tea, tea party; feast, festival, festivity, frolic, spree; gala, celebration, revel, wassail, Bacchanalia, bacchanals (*Rom.*); housewarming, shower, masquerade, masquerade party, surprise party, birthday party, garden party, coming-out party (*colloq.*); hen party (*colloq.*), stag or stag party, smoker; Dutch treat (*colloq.*); ball, dance, thé dansant (*F.*), dinner dance;

bee, corn husking, husking bee; social whirl.

V. **be sociable,** know, be acquainted, associate with, consort with, club together, keep one company, join, make advances, mingle, hobnob, mix, fraternize.

entertain, receive, welcome; keep open house, have the latchstring out.

Adj. **sociable,** social, gregarious, companionable, clubbable (*colloq.*), cozy, chatty, conversable, communicative, conversational, convivial, festive, festal, jovial, jolly, hospitable, neighborly, familiar, intimate, friendly, genial, affable; accessible, informal, democratic, free and easy, hail-fellow-well-met.

See also AMUSEMENT, FOOD, FRIEND, FRIENDLINESS, MERRIMENT. *Antonyms*—See EXCLUSION, HATRED, HOSTILITY, SECLUSION.

---

society, *n.* association, alliance, company (CO-OPERATION); circle, clique, coterie (FRIEND); companionship, comradeship (SOCIALITY, FRIENDLINESS); community, commonwealth, commonalty (PEOPLE); *beau monde* (*F.*), *haut monde* (*F.*), the four hundred (FASHION, SOCIAL CLASS); wealthy class, plutocracy (WEALTH).

sociology, *n.* demotics, demography, larithmics (PEOPLE).

sock, *n.* stocking, anklet, hose (FOOTWEAR); punch, smack, slap (HITTING).

socket, *n.* cavity, chamber, pocket (HOLLOW); recess, slot, slit (OPENING).

sod, *n.* turf, sward, greensward (GRASS, LAND).

soda, *n.* vichy, seltzer (DRINK).

sodden, *adj.* soaked, soggy, sopping (WATER); pasty, spongy (SOFTNESS).

sofa, *n.* settee, davenport, couch (SEAT).

softhearted, *adj.* soft, tender, tenderhearted (PITY).

SOFTNESS—*N.* **softness,** flexibility, pliancy, pliability, malleability, ductility, plasticity, flaccidity, laxity, flocculence, mollescence.

V. **soften,** mollify, mellow, milden, dulcify; melt, thaw, dissolve, moisten, macerate, intenerate, sodden; squash (*colloq.*), mash, knead.

bend, give, yield, relax, relent. **palliate,** mitigate, assuage, extenuate, alleviate, allay, appease, lessen, abate.

subdue (*as tone or color*), temper, tone down, restrain, chasten, modify, moderate, lower, reduce, cushion, modulate, depress, muffle, mute, deaden.

Adj. **soft,** supple, pliant, pliable, flexible, flexile; ductile, malleable, tractable, tractile, plastic, yielding; relaxed, softened, flabby, flaccid, slack, flexuous, limp, flimsy; mellow, pulpy, doughy, pithy, pasty, spongy, sodden, soggy, quaggy, squashy; tender, delicate, smooth, velvety, velutinous (*bot.*), sleek, silken, silky, flocculent, fleecy, cottony, creamy, fluffy, feathery.

gentle, kind, kindly, genial, amiable, benign, gracious, mild, tender, softhearted, tenderhearted, sympathetic, compassionate.

soft-spoken, conciliatory, complimentary, affable.

[*of sounds*] low, low-toned, low-pitched, subdued, faint, murmurous, whisperous.

[*of muscles*] flaccid, flabby, lax, unstrung, untrained, undertrained, unhardened.

softening, emollient, mollescent, demulcent, assuasive, lenitive.

See also BEND, FEATHER, LOWNESS, MILDNESS, MODERATENESS, PITY, PULP, SILENCE, SMOOTHNESS, SWEETNESS, WEAKNESS. *Antonyms*—See HARDNESS, LOUDNESS, SHOUT.

---

soft-spoken, *adj.* conciliatory, affable (SOFTNESS).

soggy, *adj.* sodden, sopping; clammy, sticky (WATER); soft, pasty, spongy (SOFTNESS).

soil, *n.* earth, ground, dust (LAND); grime, smut, soot (UNCLEANNESS).

soil, *v.* dirty, foul (UNCLEANNESS).

sojourn, *v.* stay, visit, abide (INHABITANT).

solace, *n.* condolence, consolation, comfort (PITY).

solace, *v.* console, comfort (PITY, RELIEF).

solder, *v.* cement, weld, fuse (JUNCTION).

soldier, *n.* warrior, private, serviceman (FIGHTER).

soldier, *v.* gold-brick (*slang*), malinger, laze (REST).

sole, *adj.* only, single, unique (UNITY); one, alone, lone (SECLUSION, UNITY).

solely, *adv.* simply, merely, purely (UNITY).

solemn, *adj.* serious, grim, somber (SOBRIETY).

solicit, *v.* peddle, canvass, hawk

(SALE); beg, sue for, seek (BEGGING); pimp, procure, whore (PROSTITUTE).

solicitor, n. peddler, canvasser, hawker (SALE); beggar, mendicant (BEGGING); barrister (LAWYER).

solicitous, adj. heedful, regardful, mindful (CARE); anxious, concerned, troubled (NERVOUSNESS).

solid, adj. stable, steady, firm (STABILITY); stalwart, sturdy (STRENGTH); material, physical, concrete (MATERIALITY); hard, consolidated (THICKNESS); dense, compact, tight (ASSEMBLAGE).

solid, n. mass, block, lump (THICKNESS).

solitary, adj. alone, lonely, friendless (SECLUSION).

soluble, adj. dissoluble, dissolvable, meltable (LIQUID); solvable, resolvable, explainable (CLARITY).

solution, n. blend, brew, mixture (COMBINATION); fluid, elixir (LIQUID); unravelment, clarification, resolution (CLARITY, ANSWER).

solve, v. resolve, unravel, untangle (CLARITY, ANSWER).

solvent, n. dissolvent, dissolver, menstruum (LIQUID).

somber, adj. sober, serious, solemn (SOBRIETY); mournful, rueful, doleful (SADNESS); sepulchral, funereal (GLOOM); dismal, dreary, dingy (DARKNESS).

some, adj. any, more or less (QUANTITY).

something, n. commodity, thing, article (MATERIALITY).

somewhat, adv. partially, in part, incompletely (SMALLNESS).

somewhere, adv. here and there (PLACE).

somnambulism, n. sleepwalking, noctambulism (SLEEP).

somnolent, adj. sleepy, dozy, drowsy (SLEEP).

son, n. offspring, descendant, scion (CHILD).

song, n. aria, air, number (SINGING).

sonorous, adj. deep, full, powerful (LOUDNESS); sounding, resonant, resounding (SOUND, RESONANCE); rich, orotund, silvery (SWEETNESS).

soon, adv. ere long, presently, shortly (EARLINESS, FUTURE).

soot, n. grime, smut, soil (UNCLEANNESS).

soothe, v. lull, dulcify, mollify (CALMNESS); untrouble, comfort, console (UNANXIETY).

soothing, adj. balmy, calmative, bland (CALMNESS).

soothsayer, n. seer, prophet, pre-

dictor (PREDICTION); astrologer, astromancer, Chaldean (WORLD).

sophisticate, n. worldling, cosmopolite (WISDOM).

sophisticated, adj. practical, worldly-wise, worldly (WISDOM); precious, stagy, artificial (UNNATURALNESS).

SOPHISTRY—N. sophistry, specious reasoning, casuistry, Jesuitry, paralogy, equivocation, philosophism, evasion, fallaciousness, speciousness, deception, sophistication, mental reservation, hairsplitting, quibbling, begging of the question, *post hoc ergo propter hoc* (L.), *non sequitur* (L.), nonsense, absurdity, error.

sophism, paralogism (*logic*), amphibology *or* amphiboly, ambiguity, fallacy, quibble, subterfuge, shift, subtlety, *quodlibet* (L.), antilogy, inconsistency.

sophist, casuist, quibbler, paralogist, prevaricator, shuffler, philosophist.

V. **sophisticate,** paralogize, quibble, subtilize, split hairs, equivocate, prevaricate, shuffle, cavil, palter, shift, dodge, evade, mislead, varnish, gloss over, falsify, misrepresent, pervert, misteach, beg the question, reason in a circle, beat about the bush.

Adj. **sophistical** *or* **sophistic,** specious, captious, casuistic, pilpulistic, hairsplitting, paralogistic, vermiculate, Jesuitic, oversubtle, metaphysical, abstruse, fallacious, misleading, paralogical, unsound, invalid, illogical, deceptive, illusory, illusive, plausible, evasive, false, groundless, hollow, unscientific, untenable, inconclusive, incorrect, fallible, unproved; inconsequent, irrational, incongruous, unreasonable, inconsequential, self-contradictory, inconsistent, unconnected, irrelevant, inapplicable, unwarranted, gratuitous.

See also ABSURDITY, AMBIGUITY, DECEPTION, FALSEHOOD, FALSENESS, MISREPRESENTATION, MISTAKE, MISTEACHING, UNREASONABLENESS. *Antonyms*—See REALITY, REASONING, TRUTH.

---

soprano, n. mezzo-soprano, coloratura (SINGING).

sop up, take in, soak up, absorb (INTAKE).

sorcerer, n. magician, enchanter, wizard (MAGIC).

sorceress, n. enchantress, Circe, siren (MAGIC).

sorcery, *n.* sortilege, enchantment, witchcraft (MAGIC, SUPERNATURAL-ISM).

sordid, *adj.* poor, mean, miserable (POVERTY); squalid, dirty, slum-my (UNCLEANNESS, MEANNESS); mercenary, venal, hireling (MONEY); calculated, small, small-minded (SELFISHNESS).

sore, *adj.* painful, aching, tender (PAIN); severe, weighty, impor-tant (SOBRIETY); resentful, in-dignant, hurt (ANGER).

sore, *n.* boil, excrescence, carbun-cle (SKIN).

sorrow, *n.* grief, grieving, woe (SADNESS); remorse, repentance (REGRET).

sorrow, *v.* lament, deplore, mourn, grieve (SADNESS).

sorrowful, *adj.* sad, sorrowing, sor-row-burdened, sorrow-laden (SAD-NESS).

sorry, *adj.* doleful, mournful, rue-ful (SADNESS); remorseful, re-pentant, contrite (REGRET, PENI-TENCE); pitiful, wretched, mis-erable (SADNESS); scummy, scurvy, shabby (CONTEMPT).

sort, *n.* kind, variety, type (CLASS).

sort, *v.* arrange, assort, sift (AR-RANGEMENT).

soul, *n.* spirit, psyche, pneuma (SPIRITUALITY); *élan vital* (*F.*), vital force (LIFE); marrow, sub-stance (INTERIORITY); person, mortal, man (MANKIND, PEOPLE).

soulful, *adj.* sentimental, poetic, dithyrambic (EXPRESSION).

sound, *adj.* well, robust, hearty (HEALTH, STRENGTH); rational, sane, sensible (WISDOM, REASON-ABLENESS); first-rate (*colloq.*), tiptop (*colloq.*), ship-shape (GOOD).

sound, *n.* noise, static (SOUND); strait, narrows (INLET).

sound, *v.* toot, blare, blast (BLOW-ING, SOUND); dive, plunge, sub-merge (DIVING); fathom, plumb (DEPTH).

SOUND—*N.* sound, noise, peep, sonance, static, report, sonifica-tion; decibel; audibility, vibra-tion, undulation, reverberation, polyphony; strain, key, tune, note, accent, twang; utterance, phona-tion, sonancy, articulation, voice; binaural sound, stereophonic sound, high fidelity *or* hi-fi.

quality, resonance, sonority, tone, inflection, modulation, pitch, intonation, cadence, rhythm, mel-ody, monotony, volume, intensity; assonance, consonance, homoph-ony, unison, harmony, accord.

earshot, hearing, range, hearing distance.

science of sound: acoustics, dia-coustics, phonics, supersonics, cat-acoustics; phonetics, phonology, phonography; telephony, radioph-ony; harmonics.

V. sound, ring, resound, rever-berate; blow, blare.

Adj. sounding, sonorous, sonif-erous, soniferous, sonant, multi-sonous, multisonant, resonant, sonoric, melodious, ringing; ear-splitting; audible, distinct, clear.

acoustic, phonic, sonic, stereo-phonic, supersonic, ultrasonic, polyphonic, isacoustic, auditory, audiogenic, phonetic.

See also ANIMAL SOUND, HAR-MONY, HARSH SOUND, HIGH-PITCHED SOUND, LISTENING, LOUD-NESS, MUSIC, RESONANCE, RHYTHM, ROLL, SHOUT, SIBILATION, STATEMENT, STRENGTH, VOICE. *Antonyms*—See SILENCE.

---

sour, *adj.* tart, curdled (SOUR-NESS); disagreeable, acid (BAD TEMPER).

source, *n.* origin, spring, deriva-tion (BEGINNING, RIVER).

SOURNESS—*N.* sourness, acer-bity, acidity, astringency, ver-juice, vinegar, acetum (*pharm.*), lemon, lemon juice, acid.

V. sour, acerbate, acidify, acidu-late, turn, curdle, clabber, acetify.

Adj. sour, acid, acidulated, acerb, acidulous, acidulent, tart, rancid, turned (*as milk*), curdled, sourish, green, hard, unripe; as-tringent, austere.

vinegary, acetic, acetous, ace-tose.

bitter, acrid, absinthal, absinth-ian.

See also ANGER, BAD TEMPER, SHARPNESS, UNSAVORINESS. *Anto-nyms*—See SWEETNESS.

---

south, *adj.* southern, southerly, meridional (DIRECTION).

souvenir *n.* memento, token, keep-sake (MEMORY).

sovereign, *adj.* dominant, para-mount, supreme (POWER); rul-ing, regnant, reigning (GOVERN-MENT); independent, autono-mous, self-governing (FREEDOM).

sovereign, *n.* king, monarch, maj-esty (RULER).

sovereignty, *n.* dominion, jurisdic-tion, sway (GOVERNMENT).

sow, *v.* scatter, disseminate (DIS-PERSION); seed, plant (FARMING).

SPACE—*N.* space, extent, territory, tract, expanse, spread, stretch; capacity, accommodation, room; field, margin, area, scope, compass, range, reach, headroom, headway; sphere, arena.

[*unlimited space*] **infinity**, immensity, vastitude, vast (*poetic*), interplanetary (interstellar, intercosmic, *or* intergalactic) space; plenum, ether, heavens; universe, world, wide world.

room, apartment, chamber, rotunda, saloon, casino, hall, alcove, antechamber, anteroom, waiting room; compartment, booth, stall, cubicle, study, studio, den, cuddy, closet, sanctum, carrell, library; kitchen, galley, scullery, pantry, dining room, refectory; nursery, sun porch, solarium, sunroom, vestry; game room, rumpus room.

living room, drawing room, front room, parlor, sitting room.

attic, garret, loft.

cellar, basement, subterrane, vault.

V. space, interspace, interval, arrange, set out, spread out, extend, open up (*or* out), separate.

have room (*or* space), for, accommodate, admit, contain.

Adj. spacious, roomy, commodious, extensive, expansive, immense, capacious, voluminous, ample, large, broad, cavernous, vast, vasty (*poetic*), wide, widespread, world-wide, far-flung, boundless, limitless, endless, infinite; shoreless, trackless, pathless; spatial.

Adv., phrases. spaciously, extensively, etc. (see *Adjectives*); by and large; everywhere, far and near (*or* wide); here, there, and everywhere; from pole to pole, from all points of the compass; to the four winds, to the uttermost parts of the earth.

See also CONTENTS, ENDLESSNESS, HEAVEN, INTERVAL, PLACE, REGION, SLEEP (*bedroom*), SPREAD, WORLD. *Antonyms*—See NARROWNESS, SMALLNESS, THINNESS.

spacious, *adj.* roomy, commodious, extensive (SPACE); voluminous, capacious, comprehensive (SIZE).

spade, *n.* shovel, trowel (DIGGING).

span, *n.* extent, length, stretch (TIME, DISTANCE); extension, wing, bridge (STRETCH, BREAKWATER); arch, arcade, vault (SUPPORT).

span, *v.* bridge, reach, connect, link, cross, subtend (BREAKWATER, STRETCH).

spank, *v.* paddle, flog, cane (HITTING, PUNISHMENT).

spare, *adj.* extra, in store, in reserve (STORE); excess, supererogatory, supernumerary (EXCESS); thin, lean, rangy (THINNESS); meager, bare, poor (INSUFFICIENCY).

spare, *v.* afford, accommodate with (GIVING); have mercy on, relent, give quarter to (PITY, FORGIVENESS).

sparing, *adj.* thrifty, frugal, parsimonious (ECONOMY).

spark, *n.* beam, flicker, gleam (LIGHT, FIRE, SMALLNESS).

sparkle, *n.* flash, glow, glint (LIGHT, FIRE).

sparkle, *v.* glimmer, flicker, scintillate (LIGHT, FIRE).

sparkling, *adj.* bubbly, fizzy, carbonated (FOAM).

sparse, *adj.* scarce, exiguous (FEWNESS); meager, thin, scant (INSUFFICIENCY).

spasm, *n.* paroxysm, convulsion, fit (ATTACK, PAIN).

spasmodic, *adj.* fitful, changeable, erratic (IRREGULARITY).

spat, *n.* set-to, squabble, tiff (DISAGREEMENT).

spats, *n.* gaiters (FOOTWEAR).

spatter, *v.* splash, splatter, spray (EGRESS, WATER); strew, broadcast, sprinkle (THROW); slop, smear (UNCLEANNESS).

speak, *v.* lecture, declaim, recite (TALK); say, utter, pronounce (TALK, VOICE); state, express (STATEMENT).

speakeasy, *n.* blind pig, blind tiger (ALCOHOLIC LIQUOR).

speaker, *n.* talker, spokesman, mouthpiece (TALK); loud-speaker, tweeter, woofer (AMUSEMENT).

spear, *n.* lance, pike, javelin (CUTTING).

spear-shaped, *adv.* hastate (SHARPNESS).

special, *adj.* especial, express; individual, distinctive (DIFFERENCE); sole, specific, unique (UNITY).

specialist, *n.* expert, master (ABILITY).

specialty, *n.* profession, career, major (BUSINESS, LEARNING).

species, *n.* family, genus, breed (CLASS).

specific, *adj.* definite, clear-cut, exact (BOUNDARY); categorical, explicit, precise (CLARITY); sole, special (UNITY).

specific, *n.* item, particular, fact (DETAIL).

specify, *v.* particularize, itemize, individualize (DETAIL); mention, cite, enumerate (TALK, NAME).

specimen, *n.* sample, cross section, example (COPY).

specious, *adj.* plausible, colorable, delusive (FALSENESS); sophistical, captious, casuistic (SOPHISTRY).

speck, *n.* spot, dot, fleck (VARIEGATION, UNCLEANNESS); tittle, tot, trace (SMALLNESS).

speckled, *adj.* dotted, studded, patchy (VARIEGATION).

spectacle, *n.* sight, view, scene (VISION); exhibition, exposition (APPEARANCE); tableau (REPRESENTATION).

spectacles, *n.* eyeglasses, cheaters (*colloq.*), winkers (VISION).

spectacular, *adj.* striking, marvelous, fabulous (SURPRISE).

spectator, *n.* onlooker, bystander, witness (LOOKING, PRESENCE).

specter, *n.* apparition, spirit, spook (GHOST).

speculate, *v.* take a chance, wildcat, plunge (DANGER, CHANCE); guess, surmise, conjecture (SUPPOSITION); theorize, ruminate (THOUGHT).

speech, *n.* parlance, tongue, prose (LANGUAGE); lecture, chalk talk, address (TALK); tone, accents (VOICE).

speech impediment, *n.* stammering, stuttering, dysphonia (SILENCE).

speechless, *adj.* silent, wordless, mute (SILENCE).

SPEED—*N.* speed, rapidity, acceleration, celerity, velocity, expedition, alacrity, dispatch; agility, legerity.

haste, hurry, rush, precipitance, superficiality.

accelerant, accelerator, catalyst, catalytic agent.

[*comparisons*] lightning, greased lightning, flash, light, wildfire; wind, hurricane, cyclone, torrent; cannon ball, bullet, rocket, arrow, dart, quicksilver; thought, split second; eagle, antelope, courser, race horse, gazelle, greyhound, hare, doe.

rate, velocity, speed, pace, tempo; gradient, acceleration.

rate setter, pacemaker, pacer.

speedometer, tachograph, tachometer, tachymeter, velocimeter, accelerometer, decelerometer.

V. speed, fly, hasten, hurry, hustle, spurt, wing one's way, outstrip the wind, skedaddle (*slang*), barrel, tear, tear off, rush; chase, hurtle, plunge, cruise, dartle, flit, flitter, swoop, sweep, shoot, skirr, whisk, whiz, whir, waltz, brush; bolt, arrow, bob, bound, jump, leap, spring; skip, trip, skim, skitter, bicker; rush about, smash, charge, stampede; run, career, course, dart, dash, gallop, lope, pad, trot, race, scamper, scoot, scud, scurry, scutter, scuttle, sprint, squint, whirl.

speed up, quicken, accelerate, gun (*a motor*), hasten, hurry, pick up speed; gain upon, overhaul, overtake, outstrip, beat; shoot through, expedite, precipitate, anticipate, catalyze; hustle off, bundle off, give speed to, lend speed to, speed, give wings to, wing, speed on its (*or* his, etc.) way.

Adj. speedy, rapid, swift, fleet, winged, accelerated, quick, fast, express, velocious, expeditious, alacritous, with dispatch, in full career, quick-fire, rapid-fire; supersonic, transsonic, ultrasonic; agile, brisk, nimble, lissome, lively, volant.

hasty, hurried, rushed, precipitate, precipitant, abrupt, brash, rash, overhasty, headlong; slapdash, superficial, cursory.

fleet-footed, nimble-footed, quick-footed, wing-footed; running, cursive, procursive, cursorial.

fast (*in music*), allegro, prestissimo, presto, veloce, volante (*all It.*).

Adv., phrases. speedily, fast, etc. (see *Adjectives*); amain, apace, presto, full-tilt, headlong, posthaste, pell-mell; with speed, at full speed, chop-chop, at a gallop, on the double, in double-quick time, by leaps and bounds; like wildfire, like lightning, etc. (*see comparisons*); in a hurry, in a rush, in haste.

See also ACTIVITY, CARELESSNESS, FLYING, PROGRESS, VIOLENCE. *Antonyms*—See SLOWNESS.

speedometer, *n.* tachograph, tachometer, tachymeter (SPEED).

speedway, *n.* freeway, thruway, expressway (PASSAGE).

spell, *n.* charm, hex (MAGIC); interval, intermission, interlude (REST); period, term, space (TIME, INTERVAL); turn, tour, hitch (WORK).

spell, *v.* orthographize, trace out (WRITTEN SYMBOL); indicate, connote, signify (MEANING); free, release (RELIEF).

spellbind, *v.* spout, orate, harangue (TALK); palsy, transfix, petrify (MOTIONLESSNESS); enchant, enthrall, ensorcell (MAGIC).

spellbound, *adj.* breathless, agape, openmouthed (SURPRISE); petrified, transfixed (MOTIONLESSNESS).

spelling, n. orthography, phonography (WRITTEN SYMBOL).

spend, v. expend, outlay, disburse (EXPENDITURE).

spendthrift, n. wastrel, prodigal, profligate (WASTEFULNESS).

spent, adj. limp, enervated, exhausted (WEAKNESS).

sperm, n. spermatozoon, seed (MAKE-UP).

spew, v. vomit, disgorge, belch (GIVING, THROW).

sphere, n. ball, globe, orb (ROUNDNESS); earth, planet, terrene (WORLD); realm, orbit, province (POWER, INFLUENCE); zone, ground (REGION); position, station (RANK, SOCIAL CLASS).

spherical, adj. ampullaceous, global, globate (ROUNDNESS).

sphinx, n. androsphinx, criosphinx (MYTHICAL BEINGS); dummy, clam (SILENCE).

spice, n. flavoring, seasoning (TASTE); zest, salt, savor (INTERESTINGNESS).

spice, v. flavor, season, salt (TASTE, INTERESTINGNESS, PLEASURE).

spick-and-span, adj. clean, spotless, immaculate (CLEANNESS); neat, tidy, well-kept (NEATNESS).

spicy, adj. appetizing, piquant, tangy (TASTE); racy, breezy, salty (INTERESTINGNESS); off-color, suggestive, vulgar (OBSCENITY).

spider, n. scorpion, black widow (ANIMAL).

spike, n. point, pike, pricket (SHARPNESS).

spill, v. flow, run, stream (RIVER); splash, spray, slop (WATER).

spill out, v. spurt, squirt, pour (EGRESS).

spin, v. turn, revolve, whirl (ROTATION); weave, knit, crochet (TEXTURE).

spindly, adj. reedy, rangy, stringy (THINNESS, LENGTH).

spine, n. backbone, vertebral column (BONE); quill, spur, needle (SHARPNESS).

spineless, adj. marrowless, nerveless, sapless (WEAKNESS).

spinster, n. bachelor girl, spinstress, old maid (UNMARRIED STATE).

spiny, adj. prickly, barbed, echinated (SHARPNESS).

spiral, adj. helical, whorled, coiled, tortile (CURVE, WINDING).

spiral, n. helix, gyration, coil (CURVE, WINDING); curlicue, flourish, quirk (WRITING).

spire, n. tip, prong, point (END); belfry, steeple (HEIGHT); taper, wedge (SHARPNESS).

spirit, n. liveliness, sparkle, dash (ACTIVITY); bravery, boldness,

daring (COURAGE); élan vital (F.), soul, psyche (LIFE, SPIRITUALITY); specter, apparition, spook (SUPERNATURAL BEINGS, GHOST).

spirit away, v. kidnap, abduct, shanghai (THIEVERY).

spirited, adj. lively, animated, vivacious (ACTIVITY); game, nervy, spunky (COURAGE).

spiritless, adj. slothful, lifeless, inanimate (INACTION).

spiritualism, n. spiritism, occultism, telekinesis (TELEPATHY, SUPERNATURALISM).

SPIRITUALITY—N. spirituality, spirituosity, ethereality, etherealism, rarefaction; spiritual relationship, platonism, platonic love.

immateriality, incorporeity, incorporeality, disembodiment.

soul, spirit, psyche, pneuma, dibbuk (*Jewish folklore*).

reincarnation, transmigration, transmigration of souls, palingenesis, metempsychosis, pre-existence; pre-existentism, infusionism, creationism, traducianism, animism.

V. spiritualize, etherealize, rarefy; discarnate, disembody; immaterialize, incorporealize, dematerialize, dissolve; transmigrate.

Adj. spiritual, spirituel (F.), spirituelle (F., fem.), airy, ethereal, rarefied, supernal, unfleshly, otherworldly; platonic.

bodiless, immaterial, disembodied, discarnate, incorporeal, incorporate, asomatous, unfleshly.

unworldly, supersensible, supersensory, supersensual, unearthly, hyperphysical, superphysical, extramundane, metaphysical, psychic or psychical; unsubstantial, intangible, impalpable.

See also SACREDNESS, SUPERNATURAL BEINGS, SUPERNATURALISM. *Antonyms*—See BODY, IRRELIGION, MATERIALITY, WORLD.

spit, n. spittle, sputum, slaver (SALIVA); skewer, broach, brochette (ROD); mud flat, tideland; neck, isthmus (LAND).

spit, v. expectorate, salivate (SALIVA); sibilate, hiss, sizz (SIBILATION).

spite, n. malice, rancor (HOSTILITY).

spite, v. grudge, begrudge (HOSTILITY); annoy, persecute, beset, harass (ANNOYANCE).

spiteful, adj. spleenful, vicious (*colloq.*), malicious (HOSTILITY).

spitfire, n. brimstone, virago, shrew (BAD TEMPER, VIOLENCE).

spittoon, n. cuspidor (SALIVA).

spit up, *v.* puke, throw up, vomit (NAUSEA).

splash, *n.* dash, drop, splatter (ADDITION).

splash, *v.* spatter, splatter (WATER); strew, broadcast (THROW); swirl, plash, swash (RIVER); spray, sprinkle (EGRESS).

splatter, *v.* splash, spatter, plash (WATER); strew, besprinkle (THROW); spray, sprinkle (EGRESS).

spleen, *n.* rancor, venom, virulence (HOSTILITY).

splendid, *adj.* glorious, lustrous, splendrous (FAME, MAGNIFICENCE); marvelous, prime, superb (GOOD).

splendor, *n.* glory, resplendence, brilliance (MAGNIFICENCE); pomp, pageant (OSTENTATION).

split, *v.* rend, sever, rive (BLOWING, CUTTING, DISJUNCTION); break, crack, snap (BREAKAGE).

split hairs, *v.* sophisticate, paralogize, quibble (SOPHISTRY).

splutter, *v.* spit, slobber, sputter (SALIVA); stammer, stutter, stumble (TALK).

spoil, *v.* injure, hurt, mar (HARM); deface, disfigure (DEFORMITY); decompose, rot, putrefy (DECAY); deteriorate (USELESSNESS); smash, impair (DESTRUCTION, USELESSNESS); indulge, coddle, pamper (MILDNESS); depredate, spoliate, despoil (PLUNDER).

spoils, *n.* booty, loot, prize (PLUNDER, THIEVERY).

spoilsport, *n.* kill-joy, wet blanket (SADNESS).

spoked, *adj.* radiated, starry (ROUNDNESS).

spoken, *adj.* oral, phonic (TALK, STATEMENT).

spokesman, *n.* speaker, mouthpiece, prolocutor (TALK).

sponge, *n.* swab, towel, wiper (RUBBING); parasite, leech (LIFE).

sponge on, *v.* live off, leech on, drone (LIFE).

spongy, *adj.* absorbent, porous, leachy (INTAKE, OPENING); springy, rubbery, resilient (JUMP); poachy, oozy, quaggy (MARSH); pasty, sodden, soggy (SOFTNESS).

sponsor, *v.* answer for, vouch for (LIABILITY).

spontaneous, *adj.* free, unconstrained, voluntary (WILL); impulsive, impetuous (NONPREPARATION); natural, uncontrived (NATURALNESS).

spoof, *n.* quip, jest, joke (WITTINESS).

spook, *n.* apparition, specter, spirit (GHOST).

spool, *n.* reel, bobbin (ROTATION).

spoon, *n.* ladle, dipper, scoop (CONTAINER).

spoor, *n.* trail, track, trace (REMAINDER).

sporadic, *adj.* infrequent, uncommon, rare (FEWNESS).

sport, *n.* fun, frolic, play (MERRIMENT, PLAYFULNESS); pastime, recreation (AMUSEMENT); sportsman, hunter, Nimrod (HUNTING); monstrosity, freak (UNUSUALNESS); derision, mockery; object of ridicule (RIDICULE).

sporting, *adj.* sportsmanlike, sportsmanly, square (IMPARTIALITY).

sportsman, *n.* sport, hobbyist (AMUSEMENT); hunter, Nimrod (HUNTING).

sporty, *adj.* rakish, saucy, smug (FASHION).

spot, *n.* dot, fleck, speck (VARIEGATION); stain, splotch (BLEMISH, UNCLEANNESS, DISREPUTE); locality, site, post (REGION, PLACE, LOCATION, SITUATION).

spot, *v.* dot, fleck, dapple (VARIEGATION); stain, sully, tarnish (UNCLEANNESS); discover, trace (DISCOVERY).

spotless, *adj.* pure, snowy, immaculate (CLEANNESS, PURIFICATION); faultless, stainless (INNOCENCE).

spotter, *n.* patrol, picket, lookout (WARNING).

spotty, *adj.* spotted, flecked, nevose, freckled (VARIEGATION).

spouse, *n.* mate, husband, wife (MARRIAGE).

spout, *n.* faucet, tap, cock (EGRESS, OPENING).

spout, *v.* pour, roll, spill (RIVER); eject, expel (THROW); orate, harangue, gush (TALK).

sprawl, *v.* recline, loll, lounge (REST); stretch, extend (SPREAD).

spray, *v.* sprinkle, squirt, splash (WATER, EGRESS); scatter, shower (THROW); smear, besmear (SPREAD).

spray, *n.* vaporizer, atomizer, sprinkler, sprayer (GAS, WATER).

spread, *n.* extension, stretch (SPREAD); bedspread, bedcover, coverlet (SLEEP).

SPREAD—*N.* spread, extension, extent, stretch, proliferation, ramification; perfusion, circumfusion, suffusion, transfusion, diffusion, radiation.

spreader, spatula, stretcher, rack, extender.

V. spread, sprawl, extend, stretch, mantle, overspread, suffuse, transfuse, overrun, diffuse, bestrew, strew, straggle, proliferate, ramble, blush, ramify, radiate, scatter, splay, deploy (mil.); penetrate, pervade, permeate, stalk through; unfold, unroll, unfurl; broadcast, disseminate, propagate, sow, dissipate.

bespread, smear, besmear, sprinkle, spray, besprinkle, bespray, bedaub, daub, plaster, perfuse, circumfuse.

Adj. spread, sprawly, extensive, overrun, diffuse, straggly; extended, etc. (see Verbs); far-flung, wide-flung, outspread, widespread, patulous, rotate.

See also DISPERSION, DISPLAY, OVERRUNNING, RUBBING, STRETCH, THROW, UNFOLDMENT. Antonyms—See ASSEMBLAGE, COMBINATION, CONVERGENCE, MIXTURE, TRACTION.

sprightly, adj. lively, dashing, vivacious (ACTIVITY).

spring, n. springtime, prime (SEASONS); leap, bound, vault (JUMP); springhead, stock (BEGINNING, STORE); pond, reservoir, tarn (LAKE); hot spring, geyser (RIVER).

spring, v. leap, bound, hop (JUMP); originate, derive (BEGINNING).

springy, adj. rubbery, spongy, resilient (JUMP).

sprinkle, v. scatter, shower, strew (THROW, DISPERSION, POWDERINESS); spatter, splash, squirt (EGRESS, WATER); bespread, spray (SPREAD); rain, drizzle (RAIN).

sprinkler, n. sprayer, atomizer (WATER).

sprinkling, n. scattering, sprinkle, dash (SMALLNESS).

sprint, v. run, scurry, scutter (SPEED).

sprite, n. fairy, fay, pixy (SUPERNATURAL BEINGS).

sprout, v. vegetate, germinate, grow (PLANT LIFE).

spruce, adj. prim, dapper, natty (NEATNESS, CLOTHING).

spruce, v. groom, sleek, prim, slick up (colloq.), primp, prink, titivate (NEATNESS, CLOTHING).

spruce up (colloq.), v. dress up, array, doll up (slang), dress (ORNAMENT).

spry, adj. lithe, agile, nimble (ACTIVITY).

spunky, adj. game, nervy, plucky (COURAGE).

spur, n. stimulus, urge, goad (MOTIVATION); quill, spine, needle (SHARPNESS).

spur, v. urge, exhort, press (URGING).

spurious, adj. false, bogus, fake (FALSENESS).

spurn, v. refuse, reject, scorn (DENIAL); snub, slight (CONTEMPT).

spurt, v. squirt, stream, gush (DEPARTURE, EGRESS, RIVER); hasten, hurry, rush (SPEED).

Sputnik (Russian), n. Explorer (U.S.), Vanguard (U.S.), satellite (WORLD).

sputter, v. spit, slobber, splutter (SALIVA); stammer, stutter, stumble (TALK).

spy, n. scout, lookout, snoop (WARNING, LOOKING); foreign agent, secret agent (CONCEALMENT).

spy, v. see, descry, glimpse (VISION); snoop, pry, peep (LOOKING).

spying, n. espionage, counterintelligence (LOOKING).

squabble, n. set-to, spat, tiff (DISAGREEMENT).

squad, n. force, band, group (ASSEMBLAGE).

squadron, n. regiment, battalion, company (FIGHTER); flotilla, task force (SHIP).

squalid, adj. sordid, slummy (UNCLEANNESS); seedy, shabby, poor (POVERTY); mean, dirty, nasty (MEANNESS).

squall, n. gust, blast, tempest (WIND).

squander, v. dissipate, fritter away, lavish (WASTEFULNESS).

square, adj. rectangular, right-angled, orthogonal (VERTICALITY); sporting, sportsmanly (IMPARTIALITY); equal, even (EQUALITY).

square, n. quadrilateral, rectangle, quadrangle (FOUR); T square (MEASUREMENT); plaza, village green (LAND).

square, v. discharge, liquidate, settle (PAYMENT); true up, regulate (TRUTH).

squash, v. mash, crush, macerate (PRESSURE, PULP); quash, quell, suppress (DEFEAT).

squat, adj. wide, broad, splay (WIDTH); scrub, stocky, dumpy (SHORTNESS).

squat, v. sit, roost, perch (SEAT); pre-empt, settle, colonize (INHABITANT).

squeak, v. cheep, peep, squeal (HIGH-PITCHED SOUND, ANIMAL SOUND).

squeal, v. cheep, peep, squeak (HIGH-PITCHED SOUND); blab, snitch (slang), inform on (DISCLOSURE, INFORMATION).

squeamish, adj. nauseated, sick (NAUSEA); prudish, priggish (PROPRIETY); fastidious, queasy (DISGUST).

squeeze, v. press, compress (PRESSURE, THICKNESS); exact, extort, wrest (FORCE); cuddle, hug, embrace (PRESSURE).

squib, *n.* lampoon, pasquil, pastiche (RIDICULE).

squint, *n.* strabismus, cross-eye (DIM-SIGHTEDNESS).

squire, *n.* landowner, landholder (OWNERSHIP); cavalier, gallant (LOVE); attendant, page (SERVICE).

squirm, *v.* wriggle, skew, twist (WINDING).

squirt, *v.* sprinkle, spray, splash (WATER); spurt, pour out, flow out (EGRESS).

S-shaped, *adj.* sigmate, sigmoid (CURVE).

"S" sound, *n.* sibilance, sibilant, hissing (SIBILATION).

stab, *v.* pierce, thrust, cleave (CUTTING).

STABILITY—*N.* stability, solidity, substantiality, strength.

[*comparisons*] rock, pillar, leopard's spots, law of the Medes and Persians.

stabilizer, brace, ballast, bracket, support.

V. stabilize, steady, brace, firm, stiffen, ballast; ossify.

Adj. stable, steady, firm, solid, substantial, strong, sturdy, stout, tough, stalwart, staunch, stiff, stabile.

See also CONTINUATION, LOYALTY, MOTIONLESSNESS, STRENGTH, SUPPORT, UNIFORMITY. *Antonyms*—See CHANGEABLENESS, IRRESOLUTION, MOTION, OSCILLATION, SHAKE, UNSTEADINESS.

stable, *n.* livery, mews, barn (DOMESTICATION).

stack, *n.* sheaf, bundle, pile (ASSEMBLAGE).

stack, *v.* pile up, heap up, load (STORE).

staff, *n.* cane, pikestaff, stick (WALKING); force, personnel (WORK); teachers, faculty (TEACHER); stave, line (MUSIC).

stage, *n.* platform, scaffold, dais (SUPPORT); point, juncture, moment (TIME); footing, status, standing (SITUATION); scene, theater, arena (ENVIRONMENT); show business (*colloq.*), the theater, the play (DRAMA, ACTOR); coach, stagecoach, diligence (VEHICLE).

stagger, *v.* reel, totter, wobble (UNSTEADINESS, WALKING, OSCILLATION); stun, startle, consternate (SURPRISE).

stagnant, *adj.* still, quiet, standing (INACTION, MOTIONLESSNESS).

stagnate, *v.* stand, stall (MOTIONLESSNESS); vegetate, hibernate (INACTION).

staid, *adj.* demure, earnest, sedate (SOBRIETY).

stain, *n.* blemish, blot, blotch (UNCLEANNESS); spot, taint (DISREPUTE); paint, varnish (COVERING).

stain, *v.* spot, sully, tarnish (UNCLEANNESS); dye, tinge, tint (COLOR).

stainless, *adj.* clean, spotless (CLEANNESS, PURIFICATION); faultless, immaculate (INNOCENCE).

stake, *n.* stick, stave, pole (ROD); prize, award, purse (PAYMENT).

stale, *adj.* stereotyped, banal, hackneyed (COMMONNESS, USE, OLDNESS); zestless, weak, watery (UNSAVORINESS); humdrum, dull, uninteresting (BOREDOM); dry, parched (DRYNESS).

stalemate, *n.* standstill, arrest, deadlock (INACTION); draw, standoff, tie (ATTEMPT, EQUALITY).

stalk, *n.* stem, axis, pedicle (PLANT LIFE, SUPPORT).

stall, *n.* booth, cubicle, compartment (SPACE); pretext, subterfuge, feint (FORGIVENESS, PRETENSE).

stall, *v.* delay, tarry (SLOWNESS); temporize, filibuster (DELAY); stop, arrest, still (MOTIONLESSNESS); fence, quibble (AVOIDANCE).

stallion, *n.* sire, stud, studhorse (HORSE).

stalwart, *adj.* rugged, sturdy, tough (ENERGY, STRENGTH); stout, valiant, valorous (COURAGE).

stamina, *n.* endurance, vitality, vigor (CONTINUATION, STRENGTH).

stammer, *v.* stutter, stumble, falter (TALK).

stamp, *v.* letter, inscribe, mark (WRITTEN SYMBOL); offset, impress, imprint (PRINTING).

stampede, *v.* smash, charge (SPEED).

stamp on, *v.* step on, tramp on, trample (WALKING).

stance, *n.* poise, posture, carriage (POSTURE).

stand, *n.* table, board, counter (SUPPORT); attitude, sentiment, standpoint (CHARACTER); stance, poise, pose (POSTURE).

stand, *v.* cock, erect, poise (VERTICALITY, POSTURE); stand still (MOTIONLESSNESS); tolerate, abide (INEXCITABILITY); endure, last, stay (CONTINUATION); put, locate, dispose (PLACE).

standard, *adj.* normal, regular, stock (COMMONNESS); orthodox, canonical, authoritative (BELIEF).

standard, *n.* yardstick, criterion, gauge (COMPARISON, MEASUREMENT, JUDGMENT, RULE); pattern, ideal, model (COPY, PERFECTION); flag, banner, ensign (INDICATION).

standardize, *v.* homologize, assimilate (SIMILARITY).

stand by, *v.* abide by, back (LOYALTY).

stand-by, *n.* old reliable, old faithful (DEPENDABILITY).

stand for, *v.* symbolize, mean, betoken (REPRESENTATION); represent, appear for (DEPUTY); be a candidate, bid for (OFFER); tolerate, abide (INEXCITABILITY).

stand-in, *n.* substitute, ringer (*colloq.*), dummy (SUBSTITUTION).

standing, *n.* reputation, footing, status (CONDITION, SITUATION).

standoffish, *adj.* aloof, unapproachable (SECLUSION, HOSTILITY).

stand out, *v.* be conspicuous, attract attention (VISIBILITY).

standpoint, *n.* viewpoint, angle (VISION).

standstill, *n.* deadlock, checkmate, stalemate (INACTION, CESSATION).

stanza, *n.* canto, verse, stave (POETRY).

staple, *adj.* important, main, principal (IMPORTANCE); in demand, popular (SALE).

star, *n.* luminary, comet, meteor (WORLD); principal, protagonist (ACTION); hero, lead, headliner (ACTOR).

stare, *v.* gape, gaze (LOOKING).

stargazer, *n.* astronomer, astrophysicist, uranologist (WORLD).

stark, *adj.* chaste, severe, bald (SIMPLICITY); naked, stripped, uncovered, undraped (UNDRESS).

starry, *adj.* stellar, stellary, astral (WORLD).

star-shaped, *adj.* stellate, stellular (SHARPNESS).

start, *n.* commencement, outset, inception (BEGINNING); embarkation, exit, leaving (DEPARTURE); scare, shock, turn (FEAR).

start, *v.* commence, launch, found (BEGINNING); leave, set out (DEPARTURE); propel, set going (PROPULSION); shy, jump, startle (NERVOUSNESS, FEAR).

startle, *v.* frighten, scare, alarm (FEAR); stagger, stun, consternate (SURPRISE).

starve, *v.* famish, raven (HUNGER); want, be poor (POVERTY).

starved, *adj.* emaciated, undernourished, pinched (INSUFFICIENCY, THINNESS).

state, *n.* condition, form (SHAPE); situation, status, position (CONDITION); nation, community (INHABITANT).

state, *v.* say, speak (STATEMENT).

stately, *adj.* impressive, imposing, grand (SIZE, NOBILITY, MAGNIFICENCE, FAME).

statement, *n.* utterance, remark (STATEMENT); bill, account, invoice (DEBT).

STATEMENT—*N.* statement, utterance, mention, comment, account, dictum, manifesto, remark, observation, recitation, pronouncement, exclamation, ejaculation, declaration, assertion; understatement, overstatement; aside, stage whisper.

admission, acknowledgement, concession, allowance, grant, profession, testimony, acceptance, assent; confession, peccavis (*L., pl.*).

saying, adage, proverb, byword, sentiment, toast, posy, saw, wheeze, dictum, apothegm.

maxim, aphorism, axiom, device, gnome, moral, moralism, precept; rule, principle, law, truth.

motto, slogan, shibboleth, war cry, watchword, epigraph.

quip, quirk, epigram, mot (*F.*).

sayings (*collectively*), dicta, gnomology; humorous sayings, facetiae.

V. **state,** say, utter, voice, give voice to, speak, deliver oneself of, vocalize, express, enounce, pronounce; mention, remark, observe, recite, tell, declare, proclaim, announce, enunciate, expound, ejaculate, exclaim; assert, contend, maintain, insist, submit, urge; understate, overstate, exaggerate.

admit, concede, yield, acknowledge, avouch, allow, grant, own, profess; agree, accept, assent; confess, own up, disbosom oneself, get it off one's chest (*colloq.*), make a confession.

Adj. **stated,** said, expressed, verbal, uttered, voiced, vocal, vocalized, spoken, parole, oral; aforementioned, aforesaid.

assertive, dogmatic, positive; self-assertive, aggressive, bumptious.

See also AFFIRMATION, AGREEMENT, EXPRESSION, RULE, TALK, URGING, VOICE, WORD, WORDINESS. *Antonyms*—See SILENCE.

statesmanship, *n.* statecraft, politics (RULER); tact, diplomacy (ABILITY).

static, *adj.* passive, inert (INACTION); changeless, fixed, rigid (UNIFORMITY); standing, stationary (MOTIONLESSNESS).

station, *n.* seat, post, spot (SITUATION, LOCATION); caste, position, level (SOCIAL CLASS, RANK, CONDITION).

station, *v.* establish, plant, install (LOCATION, PLACE).

stationary, *adj.* standing, fixed, immovable (MOTIONLESSNESS).

stationery, *n.* parchment, vellum (PAPER).

statistic, *n.* fact, datum (REALITY); number, figure (NUMBER).

statue, *n.* figure, piece, bust (FINE ARTS).

stature, *n.* altitude, elevation, eminence (HEIGHT).

status, *n.* footing, standing, position (SITUATION).

statute, *n.* act, measure, bill (LAW).

staunch, *adj.* constant, faithful, true (LOYALTY); stable, sturdy, stalwart (STABILITY); firm, inflexible, stiff (STRENGTH).

stave, *n.* stick, stake, pole (ROD); staff, line (MUSIC).

stay, *v.* endure, last, remain (CONTINUATION); respite, reprieve (DELAY); stop, ward off (PREVENTION).

steadfast, *adj.* loyal, tried, true-blue (LOYALTY); unchanging, stable, unvarying (UNIFORMITY); unwavering, intense, single-minded (PURPOSE).

steady, *adj.* firm, solid, substantial (STABILITY); unchanging, unvarying, constant (UNIFORMITY); single-minded, steadfast, unwavering (PURPOSE).

steady, *v.* stabilize, brace, firm, stiffen (STABILITY).

steal (*colloq.*), *n.* buy, bargain, investment (PURCHASE).

steal, *v.* filch, sneak, pilfer; slink (THIEVERY).

stealthy, *adj.* clandestine, furtive, sneaky (CONCEALMENT).

steam, *n.* vapor, effluvium, fog (GAS, CLOUD).

steam, *v.* boil, coddle, parboil, poach (COOKERY).

steed, *n.* equine, Dobbin, mount (HORSE).

steel, *adj.* iron, flinty (STRENGTH, HARDNESS).

steelworker, *n.* ironworker, blacksmith (METAL).

steep, *adj.* abrupt, precipitous, declivitous (HEIGHT, SLOPE, SHARPNESS).

steep, *v.* bathe, soak, souse (INSERTION, WATER).

steeple, *n.* tower, belfry, spire (BUILDING, HEIGHT).

steer, *n.* bullock, taurine (ANIMAL).

steer, *v.* guide, beacon, pilot (GUIDANCE).

stem, *n.* stalk, pedicel, axis (PLANT LIFE, SUPPORT); prow, nose, bow (FRONT); etymon, root (WORD).

stench, *n.* malodor, fetor, stink (ODOR).

stenographer, *n.* tachygrapher, phonographer, stenotypist (WORK, WRITER).

step, *n.* pace, tread, footfall (WALKING); grade, gradation (DEGREE);

measure, maneuver (ACTION).

step, *v.* pace, trip, tiptoe (WALKING).

step in, *v.* negotiate, mediate, intercede (MEDIATION).

step-ins, *n.* underpants, briefs, panties (UNDERWEAR).

step on, *v.* stamp on, tramp on, trample (WALKING).

step up, *v.* raise, boost (INCREASE).

sterile, *adj.* barren, arid (UNPRODUCTIVENESS); futile, vain, fruitless (INEFFECTIVENESS, FAILURE); sanitary, aseptic (CLEANNESS).

sterilize, *v.* emasculate, castrate, caponize (CELIBACY); disinfect, fumigate (CLEANNESS).

sterling, *adj.* valuable, costly, precious (VALUE); excellent, splendid, superb (GOOD).

sterling, *n.* silver, argent (METAL).

stern, *adj.* strict, authoritarian (OBEDIENCE); rigorous, harsh (SEVERITY).

stern, *n.* afterpart, poop, tailpiece (REAR).

stew, *v.* cook, simmer, fricassee (COOKERY); worry, fret, fuss (NERVOUSNESS).

steward, *n.* manager, custodian, caretaker (CONTROL); caterer, quartermaster (QUANTITY); waiter, garçon (*F.*), server (SERVICE).

stick, *n.* stave, stake, pole (ROD); cane, pikestaff, staff (WALKING); club, bludgeon, cudgel (HITTING); board, slat, slab (WOOD).

stick, *v.* lay, put, set (PLACE); adhere, cleave, cling (STICKINESS); pierce, stab (CUTTING).

stick in, *v.* obtrude, thrust in (INSERTION).

STICKINESS—*N.* stickiness, glutinosity, viscidity, viscosity, mucosity, tenacity.

glue, agglutinant, cement, glutinative, gum, paste, plaster, solder, adhesive, mucilage; barnacle, clinger; mucus, slime.

cohesion, coherence, adhesion, adherence, cleavage, conglutination, agglutination.

V. **stick together,** agglutinate, bind, conglutinate, glue, glutinate, gum, paste, plaster, seal; solder, braze, cement, engage; glutinize.

adhere, cleave, cohere, cling, stick.

Adj. **sticky,** adhesive, agglutinative, gluey, glutinous, gummous, gummy, pasty, ropy, stringy, tacky, tenacious, viscid, viscidulous, viscoid, viscous; waxy, doughy, gelatinous; slimy, muculent, mucous, mucid, mucilaginous, clammy.

adhesive, tenacious, clinging,

clingy, coherent, cohesive, adherent, agglutinative, conglutinative.

See also FASTENING, JUNCTION, OIL, SEMILIQUIDITY, THICKNESS. Antonyms—See DISJUNCTION.

stick out, v. jut, project, beetle (VISIBILITY).

stick-to-itive, adj. perseverant, persistent, pertinacious (CONTINUATION).

stick up, v. erect, cock, hump (VERTICALITY, VISIBILITY).

stick-up (slang), n. robbery, holdup (THIEVERY).

sticky, adj. gluey, adhesive (STICKINESS); clammy, muggy (WATER).

stiff, adj. firm, rigid (HARDNESS); set, fixed (THICKNESS); ungainly, gawky, wooden (CLUMSINESS); formal, stilted (FORMALITY); sturdy, stalwart, staunch (STABILITY, STRENGTH); unbending, obstinate, inflexible (STUBBORNNESS).

stiffen, v. stabilize, steady, brace, firm, tense (STABILITY, HARDNESS); set, fix, cake, jell (THICKNESS).

stifle, v. suffocate, asphyxiate, smother (KILLING); restrain, suppress (RESTRAINT); gag, muzzle, muffle (SILENCE).

stifling, adj. close, heavy, stuffy (HEAT).

stigma, n. blemish, blot, brand, (DISREPUTE, DISGRACE); spot, splotch, fleck (VARIEGATION).

stigmatize, v. brand, blemish, besmear, besmirch (DISGRACE, DISREPUTE).

still, adj. noiseless, soundless, hushed (SILENCE); quiet, stagnant, static (MOTIONLESSNESS, INACTION).

still, n. quiet, hush (SILENCE); distillery (ALCOHOLIC LIQUOR).

still, v. quiet, hush, muffle (SILENCE); tranquilize, allay, compose (CALMNESS, PEACE); stop, arrest, stall (MOTIONLESSNESS); slack, lull (INACTION).

stilt, n. pile, post, pole (SUPPORT).

stilted, adj. formal, stiff, angular (FORMALITY).

stimulant, n. motive, stimulus, spur (MOTIVATION, EXCITEMENT); intoxicant, inebriant (ALCOHOLIC LIQUOR); tonic, bracer (STRENGTH).

stimulate, v. spur, urge, prod (MOTIVATION); inspire, provoke, arouse (EXCITEMENT).

stimulus, n. motive, stimulant, spur, urge, sting, prod, whip (MOTIVATION, EXCITEMENT).

sting, v. electrify, inspire (MOTIVATION, EXCITEMENT); prickle, smart, bite (CUTTING, ITCHING); injure, wound (OFFENSE).

STINGINESS—N. stinginess, parsimony, avarice, illiberality, costiveness, etc. (see Adjectives).

miser, niggard, penny pincher, Scrooge, skinflint, tightwad, pinchfist.

V. **be stingy,** pinch, stint, grudge, begrudge, withhold, hold back.

Adj. **stingy,** parsimonious, avaricious, illiberal, costive, closefisted, hardfisted, hardhanded, tightfisted, tight, penurious, penny-pinching, niggardly, miserly, churlish, chary, small-minded, shabby, sordid, scabby, petty, anal (psychoanal.); ungenerous, uncharitable, unchristian.

See also ECONOMY, HOLD, SELFISHNESS, STORE. Antonyms—See CHARITY, GIVING, NOBILITY, RELINQUISHMENT, UNSELFISHNESS.

stink, v. smell, reek, stench (ODOR).

stint, n. task, job, chore (WORK).

stint, v. skimp, scrimp, scrape (ECONOMY); pinch, grudge (STINGINESS).

stipple, v. spot, dot, fleck (VARIEGATION).

stipulate, v. provide, condition, postulate (CONDITION); covenant, contract, agree (PROMISE).

stir, n. hoopla (colloq.), to-do, racket (EXCITEMENT); flurry, fuss, ado (COMMOTION, ACTIVITY).

stir, v. galvanize, electrify (MOTIVATION); move, budge (MOTION, ACTIVITY); waken, arouse (WAKEFULNESS); toss, thrash (NERVOUSNESS); whip, whisk, blend (HITTING, MIXTURE).

stirred, adj. affected, impressed, moved (FEELING).

stirring, adj. moving, touching, emotional (FEELING); exciting, electrifying (EXCITEMENT).

stitch, n. baste, tack, tuck (FASTENING); particle, cantlet, shred (PART); cramp, crick, kink (PAIN).

stitch, v. sew, tack, baste (FASTENING).

stock, adj. regular, set, established (HABIT); typical, normal, standard (COMMONNESS).

stock, n. supply, backlog, reserve (QUANTITY, STORE, ASSEMBLAGE); articles, produce (SALE); livestock, cattle (ANIMAL); strain, species, breed (CLASS, RELATIVE, MANKIND); handle, shank, crop (HOLD).

stock, v. furnish, equip; hoard, reserve (STORE).

stockade, n. prison, bull pen (IMPRISONMENT).

stocking, n. anklet, hose, sock (FOOTWEAR).

stock pile, *n.* stock, reserve, savings, nest egg, hoard, accumulation (STORE, QUANTITY).

stocks, *n.* holdings, bonds, securities (OWNERSHIP, MEANS).

stocky, *adj.* chunky, squat, thickset (SHORTNESS, SIZE, THICKNESS).

stoical, *adj.* unemotional, phlegmatic, impassive (INSENSITIVITY, CALMNESS, UNANXIETY).

stolid, *adj.* unemotional, phlegmatic, stoical (INSENSITIVITY).

stomach, *n.* venter, maw (BELLY); taste, relish, appetite (LIKING).

stomach-ache, *n.* bellyache (*colloq.*), colic, cramps (PAIN).

stone, *n.* boulder, cobblestone, flagstone (ROCK); jewel, gem (JEWELRY).

stoneworker, *n.* mason, stonecutter, lapicide (ROCK).

stool, *n.* campstool, folding stool, footstool (SEAT).

stool pigeon (*slang*), *n.* squealer (*colloq.*), snitcher (*slang*), informer (DISCLOSURE, INFORMATION).

stoop, *v.* bend, crouch (BEND); condescend, deign, patronize (PRIDE); cringe, bow, kneel (SLAVERY).

stooped, *adj.* bent, droopy, slouchy (POSTURE).

stop, *n.* pause, cessation, lull (REST).

stop, *v.* desist, refrain, quit (CESSATION); arrest, stall, still (MOTIONLESSNESS); forestall, ward off, avoid (PREVENTION); restrain, hold back (RESTRAINT).

stopgap, *n.* makeshift, *pis aller* (*F.*), shift (SUBSTITUTION, IMPERMANENCE, USE).

stopper, *n.* bung, cork, plug (CLOSURE, RESTRAINT).

STORE—*N.* store, accumulation, abundance, garner, hoard; stock, supply, reservoir, fund, mine, lode, spring, fount, fountain, well; treasure, reserve, stockpile, savings, nest egg.

crop, harvest, vintage, yield, product, produce, output, gleaning.

storehouse, warehouse, shed, depository *or* depositary, repository, repertory, magazine, depot, cache, garner, granary, grain elevator, crib, silo; bank, vault; armory, arsenal; storeroom, larder, buttery, pantry, bin, cellar; tank, cistern; treasury, treasure house, thesaurus, storage, lazarette, conservatory, conservatoire, humidor.

shop, department store, emporium, chain store, market, supermarket, *boutique* (*F.*), establishment, shopping center; black market.

mart, market place, bazaar, fair,

exposition, stock exchange, Wall Street, bourse, curb, the street (*brokers' cant*); bear market, bull market.

stores, supplies, provisions, furnishings, necessaries, equipment.

V. **store,** store up, store away, save, lay away, lay up, lay by, put by, put by for a rainy day, salt away (*colloq.*), bank, stow away, stock, stockpile, hoard, reserve, garner, treasure, victual, bin, hutch; bottle, pack, can, freeze; cache, hide, bury.

furnish, provide, supply, equip, stock.

accumulate, pile up, heap up, stack, load; garner, harvest.

Adj. **stored,** etc. (see *Verbs*); in store, in reserve, spare, extra.

See also ASSEMBLAGE, CONCEALMENT, CONTAINER, CONTENTS, HOLD, PRESERVING, PRODUCTION, PURCHASE, QUANTITY, SALE, STINGINESS. Antonyms—See EXPENDITURE, WASTEFULNESS.

storehouse, *n.* warehouse, shed, depository (STORE).

storeroom, *n.* larder, buttery, pantry (STORE).

storm, *n.* cyclone, hurricane, tornado (WIND); upheaval, convulsion (COMMOTION); fury, rage, bluster (VIOLENCE).

stormbound, *adj.* snowbound, icebound, weather-bound (IMPRISONMENT).

stormy, *adj.* tempestuous, rugged, turbulent (WIND); boisterous, rampageous, rampant (ROUGHNESS, VIOLENCE).

story, *n.* floor, landing, level (SUPPORT).

STORY—*N.* story, account, narrative, yarn, tale, short story, conte, *nouvelle* (*F.*), anecdote; legend, myth, folk tale, folk story, kickshaw, old wives' tale, fable, allegory, parable, bestiary, apologue; fiction, novel, novelette, *novella* (*It.*), *roman à clef* (*F.*), picaresque novel, romance, love story, saga, serial, sequel, stream-of-consciousness novel; comedy, tragedy, tragicomedy, drama, play, scenario, *succès d'estime* (*F.*); memoirs, reminiscences, autobiography, biography.

stories (*collective*), fiction, drama, legendry, mythology, folklore, anecdotage.

literature, letters, belles-lettres (*F.*), Muses, humanities, classics.

literary person, littérateur (*F.*), bluestocking; author, writer, man of letters.

V. **tell a story,** yarn, spin a yarn

(*or* tale), narrate, describe; fictionize, novelize, serialize, dramatize; allegorize, parabolize; mythicize.

Adj. **narrative,** anecdotal, fictional, fictive, folkloric, mythological, storiological, legendary, allegorical, parabolic.

literary, bookish, belletristic, classical; high-flown, high-sounding; learned, scholarly, well-read, cultured, book-learned.

See also BOOK, DESCRIPTION, DRAMA, LEARNING, MOTION PICTURES, PUBLICATION, TREATISE, WRITER, WRITING.

storyteller, *n.* yarner, author, novelist (WRITER).

stout, *adj.* fat, corpulent, fleshy (SIZE); strong, robust, strapping (STRENGTH); stouthearted, valiant, valorous (COURAGE); sturdy, tough, staunch (STABILITY).

stove, *n.* cookstove, range (COOKERY, HEAT).

straggle, *v.* lag, tarry (DELAY).

straighten, *v.* correct, rectify, even (STRAIGHTNESS).

straightforward, *adj.* open, outspoken, candid (HONESTY, TRUTH).

STRAIGHTNESS—*N.* straightness, rectilinearity, directness.

V. **be straight,** have no turning, go straight, steer for.

straighten, set (*or* put) straight, even, plumb; rectify, correct, put in order.

unwind, untwist, disentangle, disentwine, ravel, unravel, reel out, unbraid, uncurl, unbend, unfold, uncoil, unreel, untangle, untwine, unweave, unwrap, unwreathe.

Adj. **straight,** rectilinear, linear, direct, even, right, horizontal, true; undeviating, unswerving, undistorted, uninterrupted, unbroken, invariable.

erect, upright, upstanding, perpendicular, plumb, vertical.

direct, bald, blunt, categorical, forthright, personal, plump, point-blank, straightforward, summary; frank, candid, truthful.

undiluted, neat, unmixed, unmodified, plain; out-and-out, thoroughgoing, unqualified.

Adv., phrases. **straight,** directly, straightforwardly, lineally, straightly, exactly, in a beeline, in a direct course, point-blank.

See also HONESTY, POSTURE, RULE, UNFOLDMENT, VERTICALITY. *Antonyms*—See BEND, CURVATURE, INDIRECTNESS, PRETENSE, ROUNDNESS, SLOPE, WANDERING, WINDING.

strain, *n.* brunt, tension, stress (PRESSURE, NERVOUSNESS); con-

striction, astriction (TIGHTNESS); stock, species, breed (CLASS, MANKIND); tune, air, melody (MUSIC); streak, suggestion, suspicion (SMALLNESS).

strain, *v.* riddle, sieve, sift (CLEANNESS); tighten, constrict, tense (TIGHTNESS); hug, embrace (PRESSURE); tax, overtask (FATIGUE); struggle, toil, labor (ATTEMPT).

strainer, *n.* colander, riddle, sieve (CLEANNESS).

strait, *n.* sound, narrows (INLET).

straiten, *v.* strap, distress, impoverish (POVERTY).

strait-laced, *adj.* prudish, prim (MODESTY); puritanical, rigid, square-toed (MORALITY, PROPRIETY).

strand, *n.* lock, tress (HAIR); coast, shore, beach (LAND).

strand, *v.* desert, maroon (DESERTION); beach, ground (LAND).

strange, *adj.* extraordinary, bizarre, fantastic (SURPRISE, UNUSUALNESS); foreign, alien, remote (IRRELATION); unseasoned, unpracticed (INEXPERIENCE).

stranger, *n.* foreigner, alien, outsider (IRRELATION).

strangle, *v.* strangulate, bowstring, garrote (KILLING).

strap, *n.* belt, harness (FILAMENT); whip, switch (HITTING).

strap, *v.* belt, birch, flagellate, spank (HITTING); straiten, distress, break (*colloq.*), impoverish (POVERTY).

strapped (*colloq.*), *adj.* straitened, broke (*colloq.*), penniless (POVERTY).

strapping, *adj.* robust, sturdy, stout (HEALTH, STRENGTH); burly, hefty (*colloq.*), husky (SIZE).

stratagem, *n.* subterfuge, trick, shift (DECEPTION, PLAN).

strategy, *n.* tactics, system, scheme (METHOD).

stratum, *n.* caste, station, class (SOCIAL CLASS); course, lap (LAYER).

straw-colored, *adj.* blond, leucous, stramineous, flaxen (YELLOW).

stray, *v.* go astray (LOSS); wander off (WANDERING); do wrong, err, fall (SIN).

streak, *n.* stripe, line, band (VARIEGATION); stroke, bar, rule (LENGTH); ray, beam, stream (LIGHT); strain, suggestion, suspicion (SMALLNESS).

stream, *n.* current, course, flow; waterway (RIVER); run, drift, tide (DIRECTION); ray, beam, streak (LIGHT).

stream, *v.* flow, pour, gush (RIVER, DEPARTURE).

streamer, *n.* bunting, pennant (IN-

DICATION); banner, headline, heading (TITLE).

streamlined, *adj.* modern (NEWNESS); efficient (ABILITY).

street, *n.* avenue, boulevard, terrace (PASSAGE, WALKING).

streetcar, *n.* trolley, cable car (VEHICLE).

street cleaner, *n.* cleaner, scavenger, whitewing (CLEANNESS).

STRENGTH—*N.* **strength,** force, power, might, energy; intensity, concentration, extremity.

vigor, pith, stamina, vim, zip (*colloq.*), virility, vitality, verdure, bloom, prime, heyday.

brawn, sinews, thews, muscle, brute force, physique.

strong man, Atlas, Hercules, Antaeus, Samson, Goliath, Tarzan, Titan; athlete, stalwart, husky (*colloq.*); strong woman, amazon.

strengthener, tonic, stimulant, bracer, roborant.

V. **strengthen,** brace, consolidate, fortify, prop up, buttress, sustain, harden, toughen, steel, set up, sinew; vivify, invigorate, nerve, innerve, vitalize, stimulate, energize, animate, reman, refresh, reinvigorate, regenerate, rejuvenate, rejuvenize, renew, revive, restore; confirm, reinforce, concentrate, condense; heighten, intensify, tone up; stiffen, arm.

[regain strength] **rally,** refresh, rejuvenate, rejuvenesce, revive, brace up.

[grow strong] **bloom,** batten, burgeon, flourish, flower, prosper, thrive.

Adj. **strong,** forceful, forcible, strengthful, rock-ribbed, titanic, withy, powerful, mighty.

brawny, muscular, athletic, able-bodied, burly, sinewy, robust, robustious (*humorous*), stalwart, stocky, stout, sturdy, strapping, wiry, hefty (*colloq.*), husky (*colloq.*), well-knit, bouncing.

vigorous, energetic, rugged, tough, lusty, vibrant, virile, vital, sound; blooming, fresh, youthful.

firm, inflexible, stiff, staunch, stalwart, sturdy, substantial, solid; iron, ironlike, steel, steely; hard, adamant, adamantine.

hardy, rugged, indefatigable, unflagging, inexhaustible.

unweakened, unworn, unexhausted, unspent, unwithered.

irresistible, invincible, unconquerable, indomitable, resistless, impregnable, immovable; overpowering, overwhelming, all-powerful, formidable.

intense, concentrated, keen, acute, vivid, sharp, extreme.

[of language or style] **forceful,** pithy, racy, sinewy, vigorous, virile, vivid, trenchant, striking; violent, vehement, unbridled; abusive, blasphemous.

See also ENERGY, FORCE, HARDNESS, POWER, RESTORATION, RESULT, STABILITY. *Antonyms*—See INEFFECTIVENESS, WEAKNESS.

strenuous, *adj.* arduous, laborious, toilsome (WORK); energetic, aggressive (ENERGY).

stress, *n.* tension, strain, brunt (NERVOUSNESS, PRESSURE); accent, emphasis (IMPORTANCE, VOICE).

stress, *v.* emphasize, accent, accentuate (IMPORTANCE, VOICE).

stretch, *n.* range, reach, spread (STRETCH); extension, extent, proliferation (SPREAD); span, duration, continuance (TIME, LENGTH); sweep, purlieu, region (LAND).

stretch, *v.* extend, mantle (SPREAD, STRETCH); continue, prolong (LENGTH).

STRETCH—*N.* **stretch,** range, reach, spread, span, extent, amplitude, breadth, compass, gamut, purview, scope, overlap; strain, tension; extension, wing, branch, bridge, span.

stretcher, rack, extender, spreader.

V. **stretch,** crane (*the neck*), elongate, extend, spread, prolong (*in time*), rack, strain, tense; bridge, span, subtend, branch out, range, reach, ramble, overrun, overlap; misrepresent, distort, exaggerate.

Adj. **stretchable,** elastic, extendible, extensible, ductile, tensile, tractile, extensile.

extensive, wide, far-ranging, far-reaching, spread out, far-flung, wide-flung, wide-stretched, outspread, wide-spread, outstretched; cyclopedic, encyclopedic.

See also EXAGGERATION, LENGTH, MISREPRESENTATION, OVERRUNNING, PRESENCE, SPREAD, TRACTION, WIDTH. *Antonyms*—See INELASTICITY.

stretcher, *n.* rack, extender (SPREAD, STRETCH); litter, ambulance (VEHICLE).

strew, *v.* scatter, cast, sprinkle (DISPERSION, THROW).

strict, *adj.* rigorous, scrupulous, punctilious (RIGHT); stern, authoritarian (OBEDIENCE); hard, harsh, rigid (SEVERITY); straitlaced, puritanical, prudish (MORALITY).

stride, n. tread, gait, step (WALKING).

stride, v. parade, stalk (WALKING); straddle, bestride (SEAT).

strident, adj. raspy, noisy, clangorous (HARSH SOUND); stridulous, squeaky (HIGH-PITCHED SOUND).

strife, n. conflict, dissension, friction (DISAGREEMENT, FIGHTING).

strike, n. assault, thrust, aggression (ATTACK); contact, blow (TOUCH, HITTING); sit-down strike, walkout (LABOR RELATIONS).

strike, v. slap, smack, beat (TOUCH, HITTING); discover, unearth, uncover (DISCOVERY); ring, peal (BELL).

strikebreaker, n. scab, fink, goon (LABOR RELATIONS).

striking, adj. outstanding, pronounced, signal (VISIBILITY); commanding, lofty, arresting (MAGNIFICENCE); surprising, wonderful, wondrous (SURPRISE).

string, n. cord, rope, twine (FILAMENT); queue, row, line (LENGTH).

stringy, adj. reedy, spindly, gangling (LENGTH, THINNESS).

strip, v. peel, pare, shave (SKIN); take off, withdraw, tear (REMOVAL); expose, uncover; disrobe (UNDRESS); despoil, fleece, rob (TAKING, PLUNDER).

stripe, n. streak, line, band (VARIEGATION); bar, rule, stroke (LENGTH).

stripling, n. boy, lad, shaver, shaveling (YOUTH).

stripped, adj. unclothed, unclad, disrobed (UNDRESS).

stripteaser, n. stripper, ecdysiast (UNDRESS).

strive, v. try, endeavor (ATTEMPT).

stroke, n. blow, impact, shock (HITTING); seizure, fit, convulsion (ATTACK); move, step, measure (ACTION); bar, rule, streak (LENGTH); line, dash, score (INDICATION); peal, chime (BELL).

stroke, v. pet, caress, fondle (TOUCH, CARESS); smooth, comfort, soothe (CALMNESS); massage, rub (RUBBING).

stroll, v. amble, saunter (WALKING); rove, roam (WANDERING).

strong, adj. forceful, forcible rock-ribbed (STRENGTH).

stronghold, n. fortification, garrison, presidio (PROTECTION).

structure, n. edifice, pile, skyscraper (BUILDING); framework, texture, frame (CONDITION); construction, constitution, composition (SHAPE, TEXTURE, MAKE-UP).

struggle, v. battle, grapple,

wrestle (ATTEMPT); toil, labor, work (ENERGY).

strum, v. thrum, drum (MUSICIAN).

strumpet, n. slut, tart (slang), trollop (PROSTITUTE).

strut, n. prop, stay, mainstay (SUPPORT).

strut, v. swagger, parade, prance (WALKING, PRIDE).

stub, n. tail, tag, butt (END); duplicate, tally (INDICATION).

stubble, n. beard, whiskers (HAIR); irregularity, burr (ROUGHNESS).

STUBBORNNESS—N. stubbornness, obstinacy, obstinance, pertinacity, tenacity, persistence, perseverance, resolution, determination, immovability, inflexibility, inexorability, rigidity, obduracy, self-will, perversity.

stubborn person, bullhead, *intransigeant* (F.), intransigent, irreconcilable, mule, pighead, bitter-ender.

V. **be stubborn,** persevere, persist, die hard, not yield an inch, stand firm, hold out.

Adj. **stubborn,** obstinate, determined, resolute, dogged, bulldogged, firm, persevering, persistent, tenacious, pertinacious, tough; bullheaded, pigheaded, mulish, balky, perverse, cussed (colloq.), wayward, untoward, willful, self-willed, wrongheaded, wry, opinionated, opinionative, pervicacious, Procrustean, headstrong, froward, intractable, refractory, unreconstructed, hardbitten.

unyielding, adamant, adamantine, inexorable, unmovable, immovable, inflexible, uncompromising, intransigent, *intransigeant* (F.), irreconcilable, obdurate, relentless, rigid, stiff, unbending, unrelenting, stern, stout, sturdy.

See also CONTINUATION, HARDNESS, PURPOSE, UNWILLINGNESS, WILL. Antonyms—See IRRESOLUTION, RELINQUISHMENT, SUBMISSION.

stuck-up (colloq.), adj. conceited, vain, egoistical (PRIDE).

stud, n. post, beam, truss (WOOD, SUPPORT); sire, stallion (HORSE).

studded, adj. dotted, patchy, speckled (VARIEGATION).

student, n. pupil, scholar, schoolboy (LEARNING).

studied, adj. calculated, premeditated, planned (PURPOSE, WILL); affected, precious, artificial (UNNATURALNESS).

studio, n. study, workshop, atelier (SPACE, WORK).

studious, adj. bookish, scholarly

(LEARNING); thoughtful, reflective, meditative (THOUGHT).

study, n. contemplation, rumination, meditation (THOUGHT); review, inspection, scrutiny (EXAMINATION); subject, course, class (LEARNING); studio, den, library (SPACE, WORK).

study, v. peruse, pore over (READING); brood over, mull over (THOUGHT); scrutinize, inspect (EXAMINATION); tutor in, train in (LEARNING).

stuff, n. fabric, material, goods (TEXTURE, MATERIALITY).

stuff, v. fill, glut, congest (FULLNESS).

stuffing, n. padding, fill, packing (FULLNESS, CONTENTS).

stuffy, adj. close, heavy, stifling (HEAT).

stumble, v. fall down, lose one's balance (DESCENT); stutter, stammer, falter (TALK); err, slip, trip (MISTAKE).

stumbling block, n. obstacle, impediment, hurdle (HINDRANCE).

stump, v. bewilder, perplex, mystify (CONFUSION); barnstorm, troupe (TRAVELING).

stun, v. knock out (INSENSIBILITY); daze, fog, muddle (CONFUSION); overcome, shock, overwhelm (DEFEAT); astonish, astound, stagger (SURPRISE).

stunt, n. exploit, deed, feat (ABILITY, ACTION); antic, dido, caper (MISCHIEF).

stunt, v. check, retard, arrest (SLOWNESS).

stunted, adj. runty, undersized, undergrown (SMALLNESS, SHORTNESS).

stupefy, v. daze, numb, shock (INSENSIBILITY, INSENSITIVITY); awe, astonish, flabbergast (SURPRISE).

stupendous, adj. tremendous, titanic, monster (SIZE).

STUPIDITY—N. stupidity, unintelligence, insipience, incapacity, misintelligence, density, dullardism, duncery, opacity, simplicity, vacancy, vacuity, vapidity, inanity, fatuity, puerility; senility, dotage, second childhood, anility.

feeble-mindedness, amentia, subnormality, mental defectiveness or deficiency, cretinism, Mongolism or Mongolianism; idiocy or idiotism, imbecility, moronism, moronity, moroncy, morosis; hebetude.

[feeble-minded person] idiot, imbecile, moron, high-grade moron; cretin, Mongoloid, Mongoloid idiot, Mongolian, defective, mental defective, subnormal; idiot-savant, idiotic prodigy.

[stupid person] addlebrain, addlehead, addlepate, ass, beetlehead, block, blockhead, bonehead, boob, booby, chucklehead, clod, clodpate, dimwit, dolt, dullard, dumbbell, dummy, dunce, dunderhead, featherbrain, gaby, goose, half-wit, jackass, loggerhead, loon, lunkhead, muddlehead, nitwit, noddy, noodle, numskull, rattlebrain, rattlehead, rattlepate, rattleskull, saphead, sap (slang), silly (colloq.), simpleton, swine, thickhead, thickskull, thickwit, zombie; dotard.

[stupid and clumsy person] lummox, lout, gawk, blunderbuss.

Adj. stupid, unintelligent, insipient, incapacious; addlebrained, addleheaded, addlepated, beefwitted, featherbrained, birdbrained, boneheaded, brainless, mindless, chuckleheaded; emptyheaded, empty-minded, emptypated, empty-skulled; loggerheaded, lunkheaded, rattlebrained, rattleheaded, rattlepated, rattleskulled, muddleheaded, sapheaded; simple, simple-headed, simpleminded, simple-witted; thick, dense, blockheaded, blockish, beetleheaded, clodpated, cloddish, thickbrained, thickheaded, thickpated, thick-witted, numskulled, dunderheaded; duncical, duncish, duncelike; gawky, loutish; senile, anile.

dim-witted, dim, blunt, weakminded, dull, dullard, dull-witted, dumb, doltish, feeble-witted, witless, half-witted; obtuse, imperceptive, opaque, purblind, besotted, lumpish, wooden; asinine, anserine, anserous, bovine, brutish; shallow.

inane, vapid, vacuous, vacant, fatuous, fatuitous, senseless, silly; unthinking, thoughtless, unreasoning, brutish.

feeble-minded, defective, retarded, mentally defective (deficient, or retarded), subnormal; idiot, idiotic, imbecile, imbecilic, moronic, cretinous, Mongolian or Mongoloid.

See also ABSURDITY, FOLLY, IGNORANCE, MISINTERPRETATION. Antonyms—See CLEVERNESS, INTELLIGENCE, WISDOM.

stupor, n. torpor, stupefaction, petrifaction (INSENSIBILITY); inertia, apathy, lethargy (INACTION).

sturdy, adj. hardy, rugged, stalwart (ENERGY); strapping, robust, stout (STRENGTH); staunch, stiff, solid (STABILITY, STRENGTH).

stutter, v. stammer, stumble, falter (TALK).

sty, n. pigsty, Augean stable (UNCLEANNESS).

style, n. mode, vogue (FASHION); manner, way, form (METHOD); type, description, character (CLASS); delicacy, refinement, polish (BEAUTY); phraseology, wording (EXPRESSION); genre (F.), school (FINE ARTS); denomination, term (TITLE).

stylish, adj. smart, à-la-mode (F.), in vogue (FASHION).

SUAVITY—N. suavity, urbanity, unctuosity, unction.

Adj. suave, unctuous, bland, oily, oleaginous, slick, smooth, urbane, smooth-spoken, smooth-tongued, glib.

See also COURTESY, FLATTERY, OIL, PLEASANTNESS, SMOOTHNESS. Antonyms—See CLUMSINESS, NATURALNESS, UNPLEASANTNESS.

subconscious, adj. subliminal, unconscious (INTELLECT).

subdue, v. repress, suppress, tame (DEFEAT); temper, tone down, restrain (SOFTNESS).

subject, adj. liable, open, susceptible (LIABILITY); dependent, subordinate (SLAVERY); conditional, provisional, contingent (CONDITION).

subject, n. content, theme, topic (MEANING, CONTENTS, TOPIC); course, study, class (LEARNING); liege, liege man (SERVICE).

subject, v. subjugate, subordinate (CONTROL); expose, make liable (SLAVERY).

subjection, n. servitude, subjugation, vassalage (SLAVERY).

subjective, adj. introspective, introverted, personal (SELFISHNESS).

subjugate, v. conquer, master, overcome (DEFEAT, SLAVERY); hold sway over, rule over (CONTROL).

subjugation, n. servitude, subjection, vassalage (SLAVERY).

sublimate, v. ennoble, glorify, sublime (NOBILITY).

sublimation, n. inhibition, suppression, repression (CONTROL).

sublime, adj. majestic, noble, grand (MAGNIFICENCE).

submarine, adj. underwater, subaqueous, submersed, suboceanic (WATER).

submarine, n. U-boat (SHIP).

submerge, v. dive, plunge, sound (DIVING); overflow, swamp, whelm (WATER).

SUBMISSION—N. submission, acquiescence, compliance, deference, obedience, subordination, resignation, humility, docility, passivity, passivism, nonresistance; surrender, yielding, indulgence, recreancy, backdown (colloq.); flexibility, malleability, pliability, pliancy, sequacity, tractability, servility, subjection, subservience, appeasement, defeatism; white flag.

submitter, yielder, quitter, defeatist, appeaser, capitulator, truckler, recreant, subject, slave, stooge (slang), puppet.

obeisance, homage, kneeling, genuflection, kowtow, salaam, prostration.

V. **submit,** succumb, yield, defer, bow to, acknowledge, acquiesce, comply, accede, resign oneself, reconcile oneself to, abide, bend, stoop; humor, indulge.

surrender, cede, concede, capitulate, come to terms, lay down one's arms, cry quits, strike one's flag, give way, give ground, give in, relent, truckle, give up, cave in (colloq.), knuckle down (colloq.), knuckle under (colloq.), grin and bear it, appease.

refer, commit, relegate, leave.

offer (as an opinion), put forward, affirm, move, propose, urge, tender, present, advance, proffer, volunteer, state.

Adj. **submissive,** yielding, obedient, pliant, pliable, compliant, compliable, servile, slavish, supine, subordinate, subservient, deferential, concessive, obsequious, supple, obeisant, acquiescent, indulgent, complaisant, amenable, conformable, malleable, flexible, sequacious, tractable, docile, meek, humble, weak-kneed, waxy, recreant; passive, unresisting, unresistant, resistless, resigned, reconciled, unassertive, defeatist.

See also DEFEAT, HUMILITY, OBEDIENCE, SLAVERY, WEAKNESS. Antonyms—See DEFIANCE, FIGHTING, OPPOSITION, RETALIATION, STRENGTH.

submissive, adj. yielding, obedient, pliable, compliant (SUBMISSION); slavish, servile, abject, subservient (SLAVERY).

submit, v. succumb, yield, defer, bow (SUBMISSION); move, propose, offer, advance, put forward, bring forward (SUGGESTION, OFFER).

subnormal, adj. feeble-minded, mentally defective, retarded (STUPIDITY); substandard (UNUSUALNESS).

subordinate, adj. inferior, junior, minor (RANK, LOWNESS); subject, dependent (SLAVERY); subsidiary, accessory, secondary (UNIMPORTANCE).

subordinate, n. junior, inferior (RANK); helper, assistant, underling (WORK).

subpoena, n. summons, process, writ (COURT OF LAW, LAWSUIT, SUMMONS).

subscribe, v. enroll, register; endorse, underwrite, agree (SIGNATURE, COMPACT, ASSENT); give, contribute (GIVING).

subsequent, adj. following, later (FOLLOWING, DELAY).

subservient, adj. slavish, servile, abject (SLAVERY).

subside, v. taper, wane, decline (DECREASE, INACTION).

subsidiary, adj. auxiliary, supplementary (ADDITION); accessory, minor, subordinate (UNIMPORTANCE).

subsidy, n. grant, bounty, award (GIVING, AID); support, pension (PAYMENT).

subsist, v. exist, live (LIFE, EXISTENCE).

subsistence, n. maintenance, upkeep (SUPPORT); nurture, sustenance (FOOD).

substance, n. thing, matter, object (REALITY); essence, stuff (MATERIALITY); marrow, soul (INTERIORITY); riches, assets, means, resources (WEALTH); property, capital (OWNERSHIP); burden, gist, sum (MEANING, IDEA).

substandard, adj. second-rate, shoddy, subnormal (INFERIORITY, UNUSUALNESS).

substantial, adj. steady, firm, sturdy (STABILITY, STRENGTH); large, ample (SIZE, MULTITUDE); physical, concrete, solid (MATERIALITY, TOUCH, REALITY); rich, affluent (WEALTH).

SUBSTITUTION—N. substitution, commutation, subrogation, exchange, interchange, swap, switch, change, supplantation, supersession, supersedure, replacement, displacement, succession (to); representation, symbolism, symbolization; reciprocity, mutuality.

substitute, proxy, alternate, deputy, representative, vicar, delegate, envoy, pinch hitter (colloq.), understudy, replacement, supplanter, ringer (colloq.), dummy, stand-in; successor, succedaneum, locum tenens (L.), surrogate; changeling; symbol, representation; alternative, auxiliary, makeshift, pis aller (F.), stopgap, temporary expedient, shift, apology for, excuse for, postiche (F.), ersatz (Ger.), counterfeit.

scapegoat, fall guy (slang),

whipping boy, goat, patsy (slang).

V. **substitute,** exchange, interchange, swap, switch, commute, subrogate, surrogate, palm off, ring in; take the place of, act for, pinch-hit (colloq.), replace, supersede, supplant, displace, succeed; stand for, represent, symbolize; stand in, fill in for, step into the shoes of, cover for, cover up for, be the goat (slang), take the rap for (slang).

Adj. **substitute,** surrogate, deputy, alternate, acting, temporary, vicarial, vicarious, provisional, tentative, experimental; makeshift, stopgap, ersatz (Ger.), counterfeit, imitation, simulated, pseudo, supposititious, near, artificial; representative, symbolic; substitutive, succedaneous, supersessive, substitutional, substitutionary.

interchangeable, mutual, reciprocal; changeable, exchangeable, replaceable.

See also CHANGE, DEPUTY, EXCHANGE, REPRESENTATION. Antonyms—See REALITY.

---

substructure, n. underbuilding, understructure (BASE).

subterfuge, n. pretext, stratagem, trick (DECEPTION, PLAN).

subtitle, v. entitle, term, style (TITLE).

subtle, adj. tenuous, inconspicuous, indistinct (UNCLEARNESS); dainty, ethereal, exquisite (WEAKNESS); nice, fine, hairsplitting (DIFFERENTIATION); clever, penetrating, perceptive (INTELLIGENCE).

subtract, v. take away, remove (DEDUCTION).

suburb, n. outskirts, outpost, hinterland (DISTANCE); country, village, hamlet (RURAL REGION, CITY).

suburbanite, n. villager, exurbanite (RURAL REGION).

subway, n. underpass, shaft, tunnel (PASSAGE).

succeed, v. prosper, flourish (SUCCESS); follow, go next (FOLLOWING); replace, supersede, supplant (SUBSTITUTION).

SUCCESS—N. success, fruition, prosperity, éclat (F.), succès d'estime (F.); mastery, triumph, victory; easy victory, setup (colloq.), snap (colloq.), walkaway, walkover; costly victory, Pyrrhic victory; accomplishment, achievement, attainment; advance, progress.

successful stroke, master stroke, coup, coup de maitre (F.), coup *d'état* (*F.*), feat, accomplishment, achievement, feather in one's cap.

successful person, victor, master, winner, conqueror, champion; parvenu, *arrivé* (*F.*), arriviste (*F.*), upstart.

V. **succeed,** batten, bloom, blossom, flourish, prevail, prosper, thrive, triumph; accomplish, achieve, attain; prevail against, resist, withstand, weather, triumph over, win, have the last laugh; make it (*colloq.*); bear fruit.

Adj. **successful,** blooming, blossoming, flourishing, fruitful, palmy, prosperous, thrifty, thriving, booming; victorious, triumphant; unbeaten, undefeated, unvanquished; prize-winning, champion.

[*indicating success*] **promising,** auspicious, happy, lucky.

undefeatable, unbeatable, indomitable, unconquerable, unvanquishable, invincible; insurmountable, unsurmountable, unmasterable, impregnable, inexpugnable, ineluctable, insuperable, formidable; unsubduable, untamable, unsuppressible, irrepressible.

Adv., phrases. **successfully,** etc. (see *Adjectives*); with flying colors, in triumph, swimmingly.

See also ASCENT, ELEVATION, PROGRESS. *Antonyms*—See DEFEAT, FAILURE, MISFORTUNE.

---

succession, *n.* series, sequence, chain (FOLLOWING, LENGTH).

successive, *adj.* consecutive, serial (FOLLOWING).

succinct, *adj.* brief, terse, concise (SHORTNESS).

succulent, *adj.* juicy, luscious, mellow (LIQUID).

succumb, *v.* give in, yield (SUBMISSION); die, perish (DEATH).

suck, *v.* absorb, resorb (TRACTION, INTAKE); lick, osculate (TOUCH); drag (*colloq.*), inhale (TOBACCO).

suckle, *v.* nurse, suck, lactate (BREAST).

SUDDENNESS—*N.* **suddenness,** precipitance, impetuosity, impulsivity, impulse.

V. **jerk,** jiggle, wiggle, bob, buck, jump, twitch, vellicate, convulse, hitch, joggle.

Adj. **sudden,** unexpected, swift, abrupt, impulsive, impetuous, spasmodic, acute; precipitous, precipitant.

See also JUMP, NONPREPARATION, PURPOSELESSNESS, SURPRISE. *Anto-*

nyms—See EXPECTATION, PLAN, PREPARATION, SLOWNESS.

---

suffer, *v.* ail, writhe (PAIN); bear, endure, abide (INEXCITABILITY, SUPPORT); undergo, sustain (OCCURRENCE, EXPERIENCE); allow, let (PERMISSION).

suffering, *adj.* in pain, miserable, afflicted, ailing (PAIN).

suffering, *n.* misery, anguish, agony (PAIN).

suffice, *v.* be good enough for, avail, do, serve, satisfy (GOOD, SUFFICIENCY).

SUFFICIENCY—*N.* **sufficiency,** adequacy, enough, plenty, plenitude, *quantum sufficit* (*L.*), competence, abundance, fat of the land, wealth, profusion, shower, affluence, opulence, amplitude, luxuriance, exuberance, reservoir, plethora, superabundance; cornucopia, horn of plenty, horn of Amalthaea.

V. **suffice,** do, be adequate, avail, answer, serve, satisfy, tide over; have enough, have one's fill.

abound, teem, superabound, overabound, exuberate, flow, stream, rain, shower down; pour, pour in; swarm; bristle with, overflow with.

Adj. **enough,** sufficient, adequate, ample, competent, enow (*archaic*), plenty, appreciable.

abundant, ample, copious, plenteous, plentiful, aplenty; abounding, affluent, exuberant, lavish, luxuriant, opulent, overflowing, profuse, rife, superabundant, torrential; replete with, wealthy in.

See also COMPLETENESS, EXCESS, FULLNESS, MULTITUDE, PRESENCE, QUANTITY, SATISFACTION, STORE, WEALTH. *Antonyms*—See ABSENCE, INSUFFICIENCY, POVERTY, THINNESS.

---

sufficient, *adj.* satisfactory, suitable (GOOD); adequate, ample (SUFFICIENCY).

suffix, *n.* affix, postfix, ending (ADDITION, WRITTEN SYMBOL).

suffocate, *v.* smother, stifle, asphyxiate (KILLING).

suffrage, *n.* ballot, franchise (VOTE).

suffuse, *v.* overspread, transfuse, overrun (SPREAD); saturate, impregnate, imbue (FULLNESS); infuse, diffuse (MIXTURE).

sugar, *n.* sucrose, glucose, dextrose (SWEETNESS).

sugar-coat, *v.* sweeten, candy, candy-coat (SWEETNESS).

sugary, *adj.* saccharine, candied, honeyed (SWEETNESS).

suggestible, *adj.* waxen, susceptible, impressionable, sensitive, susceptive (SUGGESTION, INFLUENCE, SENSITIVENESS).

SUGGESTION—*N.* suggestion, tip, advice, exhortation, recommendation, commendation, testimonial; proposition, proposal, motion, resolution, thesis, advancement; implication, overtone, intimation, signification; symbol, symbolization, symbolism, symbology; innuendo, insinuation, insinuendo; self-suggestion, autosuggestion, Couéism; idea, possibility, thought; trace, whisper, breath, hint.

V. suggest, advise, exhort, recommend, commend, tout (*colloq.*); move, propose, offer, submit, advance, broach; imply, intimate, insinuate, signify, symbolize, connote; suggest itself, occur, come to mind, cross the mind.

Adj. suggestive, pregnant, redolent, remindful; insinuative, insinuatory, snide; implicative, symbolic, significant, thought-provoking, provocative; obscene, smutty, sexy, risqué.

suggested, implied, implicit, constructive, tacit, symbolized; recommended, proposed, moved, seconded, on the floor.

suggestible, impressionable, waxy, impressible, susceptible.

See also ADVICE, HINT, IDEA, INFLUENCE, MEANING, MOTION, OBSCENITY, OFFER, SENSITIVENESS.

suggest itself, *v.* present itself, occur to, come into one's head (THOUGHT).

suggestive, *adj.* redolent, remindful (SUGGESTION); off-color, spicy, vulgar (OBSCENITY); tempting, seductive (ATTRACTION).

SUICIDE—*N.* suicide, self-destruction, self-killing, self-murder; self-immolation, self-sacrifice, martyrdom, supreme sacrifice; hara-kiri *or* hari-kari, seppuku (*all Jap.*); sutteeism (*Hindu*).

self-killer, self-destroyer, self-murderer, suicide, *felo-de-se* (*Anglo-Latin, law*); suttee (*Hindu*).

V. commit suicide, destroy oneself, kill oneself, murder oneself, suicide (*colloq.*), do away with oneself, take one's own life.

Adj. suicidal, self-destroying, self-destructive, self-killing.

See also DEATH, KILLING, POISON. *Antonyms*—See BIRTH, LIFE.

suit, *n.* costume, ensemble, wardrobe (CLOTHING); action, case, cause (LAWSUIT); courtship, wooing, court (LOVE); appeal, solicitation (BEGGING).

suit, *v.* satisfy, fulfill, please (SATISFACTION); suffice, serve, (GOOD); adapt, accommodate, adjust (AGREEMENT); fit, befit, beseem (PROPRIETY).

suitable, *adj.* satisfactory, sufficient (GOOD); applicable, appropriate (AGREEMENT); correct, right (PROPRIETY).

suitcase, *n.* satchel, valise, bag (CONTAINER).

suite, *n.* cortege, entourage, retinue (ACCOMPANIMENT, SERVICE), apartment, flat, rooms (HABITATION); succession, series, chain (FOLLOWING).

suitor, *n.* lover, admirer, courter (LOVE); supplicant, suppliant, pleader (BEGGING); litigant, plaintiff, appellant (LAWSUIT).

sulk, *v.* pout, grouch (*colloq.*), lour (ANGER, BAD TEMPER); dummy up, hold one's tongue (SILENCE).

sulky, *adj.* sullen, glum (ANGER, BAD TEMPER, SILENCE); sluggard, sluggish, inert (SLOWNESS).

sully, *v.* pollute, defile, tarnish (UNCLEANNESS); smudge, smirch, begrime (BLACKNESS).

sultry, *adj.* muggy, stifling, close (HEAT); erotic, passionate (SEXUAL DESIRE).

sum, *n.* aggregate, total, whole (ADDITION, COMPLETENESS, MONEY); purport, substance, (IDEA); summary, synopsis (SHORTNESS).

sum, *v.* tot up, total (ADDITION).

summarize, *v.* outline, précis, recapitulate (SHORTNESS).

summary, *n.* synopsis, compendium, précis (SHORTNESS).

summer, *n.* summertime (SEASONS).

summit, *n.* top, vertex, pinnacle (HEIGHT).

summons, *n.* process, subpoena (COURT OF LAW, LAWSUIT).

SUMMONS—*N.* summons, call, calling, command, invitation, subpoena, citation; convocation, convention, assemblage *or* assembly, muster, rally; evocation, invocation, conjuration *or* conjurement; beckon, beck, hail, toll.

V. call, summon, summons, subpoena, cite, beckon, toll, command, invite; call together, rally, muster, convene, convoke, assemble; call forth, invoke, evoke, conjure up; call back, recall; call upon, appeal to; call after, hail.

Adj. calling, vocative, evocative, evocatory, convocational, convocative, invocative, invocatory; recalling, avocatory.

See also ASSEMBLAGE, COMMAND, COURT OF LAW, INDICATION, LAWSUIT. *Antonyms*—See DISPERSION.

sumptuous, *adj.* lavish, munificent, profuse (UNSELFISHNESS).

sun, *n.* orb, fireball, luminary (WORLD).

sunburned, *adj.* bronzed, tan, toasted (BROWN).

Sunday school, *n.* Sabbath school, Bible school (SCHOOL).

sunder, *v.* part, detach, separate (DISJUNCTION).

sundial, *n.* dial, gnomon, hourglass (TIME MEASUREMENT).

sundown, *n.* eve, eventide, sunset (EVENING).

sundry, *adj.* varied, various, divers (DIFFERENCE).

sunlight, *n.* sunshine, sun (LIGHT).

sunny, *adj.* bright, clear, shiny (LIGHT); cheery, beaming (CHEERFULNESS).

sunrise, *n.* dawn, daybreak, daylight (MORNING).

sunset, *n.* eve, eventide, sundown (EVENING).

sunshade, *n.* eyeshade, sunglasses (DARKNESS).

sunshine, *n.* sunlight, sun (LIGHT).

superb, *adj.* excellent, marvelous, unrivaled (GOOD, SUPERIORITY).

supercilious, *adj.* contemptuous, snooty, haughty (CONTEMPT, PRIDE).

superego (*psychoanal.*), *n.* conscience, censor, scruple (PENITENCE).

superficial, *adj.* shallow, depthless, shoal (SURFACE); trivial, empty, silly (SHALLOWNESS); perfunctory, cursory, slapdash (CARELESSNESS, SPEED).

superfluous, *adj.* surplus, *de trop* (*F.*), superabundant (EXCESS); dispensable, expendable, inessential (UNNECESSITY).

superintendent, *n.* supervisor, caretaker, custodian (CONTROL); manager, foreman, straw boss (WORK).

superior, *adj.* better, greater (SUPERIORITY); condescending, patronizing, snobbish (PRIDE); higher, upper, upward (HEIGHT).

SUPERIORITY—*N.* superiority, meliority, predominance, ascendancy, predomination, pre-eminence, lead, preponderance, excellence, eminence, supereminence,

transcendence, prevalence; vantage ground, advantage, drag (*slang*), pull (*slang*), power, influence, authority, prestige; position, rank, nobility.

supremacy, paramountcy, primacy, sovereignty, championship, headship, chieftaincy, captaincy, leadership; maximum, ceiling, record; majority, bulk, greater part (*or* number), plurality.

leader, captain, ruler, *duce* (*It.*), superior, chief, chieftain, head, top sawyer (*colloq.*), *primus inter pares* (*L.*); suzerain, liege, liege lord, lord paramount, prince, overman, superman.

the best, elite, the select, the cream, *crème de la crème* (*F.*); nonpareil, paragon, champion, titleholder, medalist, champ (*slang*).

V. be superior, exceed, excel, transcend, outdo, pass, surpass, better, top, outbalance, overbalance, overtop, outweigh, outrival, outstrip, outrank, out-Herod Herod; cap, beat, beat hollow (*colloq.*), outplay, outpoint, eclipse, throw into the shade, have the upper hand, have the advantage; predominate, prevail; precede, take precedence, come first, rank first, take the cake (*slang*), bear the palm, break the record, put to shame.

best, get the better of, gain an advantage over, circumvent, euchre *or* euchre out (*colloq.*), outgeneral, outmaneuver, outwit, overreach, worst.

Adj. superior, better, higher, greater, major, upper, above, ultra, extreme, exceeding; distinguished.

supreme, highest, greatest, maximal, maximum, utmost, paramount, pre-eminent, foremost, chief, principal, crowning, excellent, superb, peerless, matchless, unrivaled, unparalleled, unapproached, dominant, overruling; second to none, sovereign, incomparable, transcendent.

best, capital, champion, choice, choicest, optimum, prime, superlative, tiptop, top, top-drawer, topflight, top-notch, unequaled, unexcelled, unsurpassed, select.

Adv., phrases. beyond, more, over; in addition to, over and above; at its height.

[*in a superior or supreme degree*] eminently, pre-eminently, superlatively, supremely, principally, especially, particularly, notably, surpassingly, par excellence (*F.*).

See also ADVANTAGE, DEGREE, GOOD, GREATNESS, HEIGHT, IMPORTANCE, INFLUENCE, LEADERSHIP, OVERRUNNING, PERFECTION, POWER, RANK, RULER. *Antonyms*—See INFERIORITY.

superlative, *adj.* best, unexcelled, unsurpassed (SUPERIORITY).
superman, *n.* superior being, prince, overman (SUPERIORITY).

SUPERNATURAL BEINGS—*N.* **spirit,** incorporeal, vision, specter, poltergeist, wraith, apparition, ghost; genie, genius, jinni *or* jinnee (*Moham.*); daemon, daimon, *or* demon (*Gr. rel.*); eudaemon *or* eudemon; sandman; dwarf, gnome, troll, giant; giantry, giantkind; manes (*L.*); spirit world, other world.
evil spirit, demon, fiend, devil, dibbuk (*Jewish*), imp, puck, incubus, nightmare, succubus, cacodemon *or* cacodaemon; lamia, harpy, ghoul, vampire; Mammon; evil genius, bad fairy; bugbear, bugaboo, bogey, bogeyman.
goblin, ouphe, barghest, bogle; rakshasa (*Hindu myth.*).
fairy, brownie, elf, elfin, fay, sprite, pixy *or* pixie; ouphe, nix, leprechaun, hobgoblin, gremlin, sylph, sylphid, undine, puck, spirit; fairyhood, the good folk, the little men, the little people, elfenfolk.
[*belief in spirits*] demonism, demonology, fairyism, vampirism, spiritualism.
Adj. **incorporeal,** immaterial, spiritlike, spectral, wraithlike, wraithy, apparitional, ghostly; daemonic, daimonic, *or* daimonistic; dwarf, dwarfish, gnomelike; giant, gigantic, gigantean, gigantesque.
demonic, demoniac, devilish, puckish, succubine, cacodemoniac, ghoulish, vampiric, vampirish.
fairy, fairylike, elfin, elfish, elflike, elvish, pixyish, sylphy, sylphlike, sylphish.
See also GHOST, GOD, MYTHICAL BEINGS, SPIRITUALITY, SUPERNATURALISM, UNREALITY. *Antonyms*—See BODY, REALITY.

SUPERNATURALISM—*N.* supernaturalism, preternaturalism, transcendentalism, transcendency; eeriness, etc. (see *Adjectives*).
miracle, wonder, wonderwork, wonderment, theurgy, occult.
witchcraft, sorcery, wizardry, theurgy, thaumaturgy, spiritism, occultism; spiritualism, telekinesis.

sorcerer, wizard, thaumaturgist *or* thaumaturge, spiritist, occultist, theurgist; witch, sorceress.
medium, psychic, spiritualist.
Adj. **supernatural,** eerie *or* eery, weird, uncanny, ghostly, unearthly, unworldly, ethereal, otherworldly, transcendent *or* transcendental, superlunary, ultramundane, transmundane, preternatural, occult, psychic *or* psychical; miraculous, wondrous, theurgic *or* theurgical.
See also GHOST, MAGIC, SPIRITUALITY, SUPERNATURAL BEINGS, TELEPATHY, UNREALITY. *Antonyms*—See REALITY.

supersede, *v.* replace, supplant, displace (SUBSTITUTION).
supersonic, *adj.* transsonic, ultrasonic (SPEED).
superstition, *n.* old wives' tale, shibboleth (BELIEF).
supervise, *v.* oversee, superintend, manage (CONTROL, CARE, LOOKING).
supervisor, *n.* superintendent, caretaker, custodian (CONTROL).
supine, *adj.* recumbent, prostrate; sluggish, lymphatic (REST).
supplant, *v.* replace, supersede, displace (SUBSTITUTION).
supple, *adj.* pliant, flexible, lithe (SOFTNESS, BEND).
supplement, *n.* addition, subsidiary, complement, additive (ADDITION).
supplementary, *adj.* auxiliary, subsidiary, additional (ADDITION).
supplication, *n.* appeal, petition, entreaty (BEGGING).
supplier, *n.* provider, furnisher, provisioner, purveyor (QUANTITY).
supplies, *n.* equipment, accouterments, outfit, provisions (QUANTITY).
supply, *n.* stock, backlog, reserve (STORE, QUANTITY).
supply, *v.* furnish, provide, equip (GIVING, STORE, QUANTITY).

SUPPORT—*N.* **support,** maintenance, sustenance, subsistence, sustentation, upkeep.
advocacy, adherence, backing, championship, countenance, espousal, subscription (to), patronage, endorsement, yeoman service; defense, apologia, apology, apologetics; favor, help, aid, encouragement.
base, basis, foundation, groundwork; substruction (*arch.*), substructure, underbuilding; bed, bedding, underpinning, sill, cornerstone, riprap, substratum, ground, terra firma, bottom; footing, foot-

hold, purchase, hold; rest, resting place, fulcrum.

floor, flooring, deck, pavement; landing, level, story *or* storey; entresol, mezzanine.

platform, scaffold, scaffolding, stage, dais, estrade, rostrum, soapbox, stump, podium, pulpit, altar, balcony, gallery, stoop, stand, grandstand.

shelf, ledge, bracket, console; mantelshelf, mantelpiece.

table, board, console, end table, lamp table; trestle, horse, sawhorse, sawbuck, buck; trivet, taboret, sideboard, dresser, tea wagon; dining table, refectory table, sawbuck table; counter, stand.

prop, stay, mainstay, strut, shore, brace, guy, buttress; abutment, rib, splint, truss.

column, pillar, shaft, colonnade, columniation; pile, post, stilt, pole, leg, palisade; stanchion, jamb, stile; mullion, pier, pilaster, colonnette, balustrade, banister, baluster, columella (*tech.*), standard; pediment, pedestal; tripod.

beam, rafter, joist, girder, hurter, lintel, timber, tie, truss, stud, transom, traverse, crossbeam, stringpiece, sleeper.

frame, framework, scaffolding, skeleton, framing, casing, casement, sash, case, rack, yoke, crib; spine, rachis (*anat.*), ridge, backbone, vertebrae (*pl.*), spinal column, vertebral column.

arch, cove (*arch.*), dome, arcade, span, vault, ogive.

stalk, stem, pedicel, pedicle, peduncle, caulis, petiole, caudex, caulicle, cauliculus (*arch.*), shoot, sprout.

maintenance, necessaries, upkeep, sustenance, keep, provisions, food, victuals, nutriment, bread, stores, stock, living, livelihood, grubstake (*slang*).

supporter, upholder, maintainer, sustainer, adherent, advocate, patron, patroness (*fem.*), stand-by (*colloq.*), ally, backer, champion, endorser, espouser, exponent, proponent, second, seconder, subscriber, favorer, pillar, stalwart, defender, devil's advocate.

V. **support,** uphold, upbear, sustain, hold up, bolster up, shore up, shore, bulwark, buoy up, buttress, crutch, poise, strut, brace, truss, stay, prop, underprop, underpin, underset, underlay, underlie, carry, bear, hold; cradle, pillow; bottom, base, found, ground, bed, embed.

endure, tolerate, bear, undergo,

suffer, go through, put up with, abide, submit to.

maintain, sustain, keep, provide for, nourish, nurture, cherish; feed, finance, grubstake (*slang*).

advocate, plead for, champion, patronize, back up, uphold, countenance, back, second, ally (*or* align) oneself with, endorse, espouse, hold a brief for, make common cause with, rally to, range oneself with, side with, subscribe to, take the part of, favor, plump for; recommend, boost (*colloq.*); defend, come to the defense of, take up the cudgels for, justify, vindicate, apologize for.

verify, substantiate, bear out, confirm, establish, clinch (*colloq.*), corroborate.

Adj. **supporting,** supportive, sustentive, alimentary, sustentative; basal, basic, foundational, fundamental.

columnar, columned, columniform, amphistylar; Corinthian, Doric, Ionic, Tuscan, Composite.

arched, arch-shaped, arciform, domed, dome-shaped, domical, testudinate, vaulted.

supportable, bearable, endurable, sufferable, abidable, tolerable.

defensible, maintainable, tenable, justifiable, vindicable, excusable.

See also AID, BASE, FOOD, FRIEND, LOWNESS, PAYMENT, PROTECTION, SEAT, STABILITY, WALL. *Antonyms—* See HINDRANCE.

SUPPOSITION—*N.* **supposition,** assumption, supposal, presupposition, presumption, condition, hypothesis, postulate, theory, thesis, theorem; opinion, belief, view.

guess, guesswork, surmise, conjecture, speculation, suspicion; rough guess, shot, shot in the dark.

theorist, theorizer, speculator, doctrinaire, hypothesist, notionalist, guesser.

V. **suppose,** assume, accept, admit, grant, pretend, take, presuppose, understand, presume, predicate, posit (*logic*), take for granted.

guess, surmise, conjecture, speculate, suspect, hypothesize, theorize, hazard a guess, divine.

imagine, believe, think, deem, conclude, judge, regard, view, consider, dream, fancy, conceive, feel.

propound, propose, set forth, put forth; put a case, submit; move, make a motion; suggest, intimate, allude to, hint.

Adj. **suppositional,** conjectural, presumptive, suppositive, hypothetical, academic, theoretic *or* theoretical, speculatory, speculative; assumed, supposed, reputed, putative, imagined, presumptive; gratuitous; allusive, referential, suggestive.

Adv., conjunctions, phrases. supposedly, theoretically, presumably, hypothetically, as a guess.

if, provided, if so be, in the event, on the supposition that, as if, granting that, supposing that, allowing that, for all one knows; whether, in case.

See also BELIEF, HINT, IMAGINATION, OPINION, PREDICTION, SUGGESTION, THOUGHT. *Antonyms*—See CERTAINTY, KNOWLEDGE.

---

suppress, *v.* hold in, repress, inhibit (RESTRAINT); smother, hush up, cover up (CONCEALMENT).

supreme, *adj.* dominant, paramount, sovereign (POWER); chief, top-drawer, top-flight (HEIGHT); top, highest, greatest (EXTREMENESS, SUPERIORITY); final, terminal, last (END).

sure, *adj.* certain, positive, definite (CERTAINTY).

surely, *adv.* undoubtedly, indubitably, positively (CERTAINTY); assuredly, certainly (ASSENT).

surf, *n.* sea, waves, breakers (RIVER).

SURFACE—*N.* surface, obverse, plane, level, face, facet; area, expanse, stretch; exterior, outside, superficies, periphery; skin, covering, rind, peel; superficiality, exteriority, externality.

V. surface, rise, crop up, crop out, flare up, appear, come up, arise.

Adj. superficial, surface, shallow, depthless, shoal; exterior, external.

See also APPEARANCE, ASCENT, COVERING, EXTERIORITY, SHALLOWNESS, SKIN. *Antonyms*—See CARE, DEPTH, INTERIORITY.

---

surfeit, *n.* glut, plenitude, saturation (SATISFACTION); satiety, repletion (FULLNESS).

surfeit, *v.* glut, jade, pall, satiate, cloy on (SATISFACTION, DISGUST).

surge, *n.* growth, swell, rise (INCREASE).

surge, *v.* billow, swell, rise (RIVER, ASCENT, INCREASE).

SURGERY—*N.* surgery, orthopedics, neurosurgery, prosthetics, plastic surgery, anaplasty, psychosurgery, oral surgery.

surgical operation, operation, the knife; excision, exsection, resec-

tion, section, ablation, surgical removal, biopsy; sacrification, incision.

dissection, prosection, anatomy, autopsy, necrotomy, vivisection.

surgeon, orthopedist, neurosurgeon, plastic surgeon, vivisectionist, sawbones (*slang*), operator.

surgical instrument, knife, scalpel, lancet, trepan, trephine, scarificator, microtome.

V. operate, do (*or* perform) surgery, cut out, remove, amputate, excise, excide, circumcise, exscind, exsect, resect, section; dissect, prosect, vivisect, trepan, trephine; incise, scarify.

Adj. surgical, operative, dissective, dissectional; operable.

See also CUTTING, MEDICAL SCIENCE.

---

surmise, *n.* guess, guesswork, conjecture, speculation, suspicion (SUPPOSITION).

surmise, *v.* guess, conjecture, speculate (SUPPOSITION).

surname, *n.* family name, cognomen (NAME).

surpass, *v.* exceed, transcend, surmount, (EXCESS, OVERRUNNING, ENCROACHMENT, SUPERIORITY).

surplus, *adj.* superfluous, *de trop* (*F.*), superabundant (EXCESS); remaining, left over (REMAINDER).

surplus, *n.* excess, overplus, balance (REMAINDER).

SURPRISE—*N.* amazement, astonishment, astoundment, dumfoundment; awe, stupefaction, shock, consternation, wonder, wonderment.

bombshell, shock, jolt, bolt out of the blue, thunderbolt, thunderclap.

nonexpectation, unforeseen contingency, the unforeseen; disappointment, disillusion, miscalculation; godsend.

marvel, prodigy, miracle, wonder, wonderment, wonderwork, portent, phenomenon, *rara avis* (*L.*), rarity, curiosity.

V. surprise, amaze, astonish, astound, dumfound, awe, stupefy, shock, flabbergast, stagger, stun, startle, consternate.

wonder, marvel at, feel surprise, start, stare, gape, hold one's breath, stand aghast, be taken aback.

be wonderful, etc. (see *Adjectives*); beggar (*or* baffle) description, stagger belief, take away one's breath, strike dumb.

be **unexpected**, come unawares, turn up, burst (*or* flash) upon one; take by surprise, catch unawares, catch napping, spring upon.

Adj. **surprised**, astonished, taken aback, aghast, breathless, agape, openmouthed, thunderstruck, spellbound; lost in amazement, lost in wonder, confused, confounded, blank, dazed, awe-struck, wonderstruck.

surprising, awesome, breathtaking, amazing, etc. (see *Verbs*).

unexpected, sudden, abrupt, unanticipated, unforeseen, unbargained for, unhoped for, uncalculated, uncontemplated, unlooked for; contingent, casual, precipitous.

wonderful, wondrous, striking, marvelous, fabulous, spectacular, mysterious, monstrous, prodigious, stupendous; inconceivable, incredible, strange, extraordinary, remarkable, unprecedented, singular, signal, unwonted, unusual; wonder-working, thaumaturgic, miraculous, magical, supernatural.

Adv., phrases. **unexpectedly**, suddenly, plump, abruptly, unaware, unawares, without notice (*or* warning), like a bolt from the blue.

wonderfully, wondrously, etc. (see *Adjectives*); for a wonder, strange to say (*or* relate), *mirabile dictu* (L.), *mirabile visu* (L.), to one's great surprise; in awe.

See also CONFUSION, MAGIC, MYSTERY, NONPREPARATION, SUDDENNESS, SUPERNATURALISM, UNUSUALNESS. *Antonyms*—See COMMONNESS, EXPECTATION, PLAN, PREPARATION, RULE.

---

surrealist, *n.* abstractionist, nonobjective painter (ARTIST).

surrender, *v.* yield, concede, capitulate (RELINQUISHMENT, SUBMISSION); cede, part with, hand over (GIVING).

surreptitious, *adj.* stealthy, furtive, sneaky (CONCEALMENT).

surrogate, *n.* substitute, proxy, deputy, representative, delegate (SUBSTITUTION).

surround, *v.* encircle, encompass, ring (INCLOSURE, ROUNDNESS); circumfuse, embower, enswathe (ENVIRONMENT).

surroundings, *n.* environs, neighborhood (ENVIRONMENT).

surveillance, *n.* observation, supervision (LOOKING).

survey, *v.* examine, scrutinize, observe (LOOKING, EXAMINATION).

survive, *v.* exist, continue; outlast, outlive (LIFE, EXISTENCE); re-

main, endure (REMAINDER, CONTINUATION).

susceptible, *adj.* susceptive, impressionable (SENSITIVENESS); liable, subject, exposed (LIABILITY); predisposed, prone (TENDENCY).

suspect, *adj.* incredible, questionable (UNBELIEVINGNESS); open to suspicion (GUILT).

suspect, *v.* disbelieve, doubt (UNBELIEVINGNESS); guess, surmise, conjecture (SUPPOSITION); believe, think, hold (BELIEF).

suspend, *v.* stop, interrupt, intermit (CESSATION); inactivate, arrest (INACTION); hang, swing, depend (HANGING).

suspense, *n.* expectancy, anticipation (EXPECTATION).

suspicion, *n.* skepticism, cynicism (UNBELIEVINGNESS); idea, notion, impression (BELIEF); guess, surmise (SUPPOSITION); strain, streak, suggestion (SMALLNESS).

suspicious, *adj.* skeptical, quizzical; farfetched, fishy (*colloq.*), doubtful (UNBELIEVINGNESS).

sustain, *v.* uphold, hold up; maintain, keep (SUPPORT); feed, nourish (FOOD); undergo, suffer, encounter (EXPERIENCE).

sustenance, *n.* maintenance, subsistence, keep (SUPPORT, FOOD).

svelte, *adj.* slim, slender, willowy, sylphlike (THINNESS).

swab, *n.* sponge, towel, mop (RUBBING).

swag (*colloq.*), *n.* booty, loot, spoils (PLUNDER).

swagger, *v.* strut, parade, prance (WALKING, PRIDE); brag, swank, swash (BOASTING).

swain, *n.* young man (*colloq.*), flame (*colloq.*), spark (LOVE).

swallow, *v.* gulp, ingurgitate, consume (RECEIVING); absorb, soak up (INTAKE); fall for, accept (BELIEF).

swan song, *n.* finale, epilogue (END).

swamp, *n.* bog, fen, slough (MARSH).

swamp, *v.* overflow, submerge (WATER); crowd, deluge (MULTITUDE); saturate, surfeit (EXCESS).

swap, *v.* switch, barter, trade (SUBSTITUTION, EXCHANGE).

swarm, *n.* throng, press, horde (MULTITUDE, ASSEMBLAGE).

swarm, *v.* teem, abound; jam, mob, throng (MULTITUDE, ARRIVAL).

swarthy, *adj.* dark, dusky (BLACKNESS).

swat, *v.* wallop (*colloq.*), clout, hit (HITTING).

swathe, *v.* furl, lap, bind (ROLL).

sway, *n.* dominion, regime, empire (GOVERNMENT, RULE); authority, control, command (POWER).

sway, *v.* careen, rock, roll (OSCILLATION); incline, lean (ROLL); wobble, vacillate, waver (UNCERTAINTY); dispose, predispose, govern (INFLUENCE); convince, prevail on, win over (PERSUASION); dominate, rule over (CONTROL).

swear, *v.* vow, warrant, (PROMISE); affirm, attest, testify (TRUTH); curse, damn, blaspheme (MALEDICTION).

swearword, *n.* curse, oath, profanity (MALEDICTION, DISRESPECT).

sweat, *v.* swelter, ooze (PERSPIRATION); spout, exude, eject (THROW); toil, labor, travail (WORK).

sweater, *n.* cardigan, pull-over, slipover (COAT).

sweep, *n.* play, swing, range, (SPACE); stretch, purlieu, region (LAND).

sweep, *v.* brush, vacuum, scrub (CLEANNESS); strut, swagger, parade (WALKING).

sweeping, *adj.* vast, wide, indiscriminate (INCLUSION); comprehensive, exhaustive, all-embracing (COMPLETENESS).

sweetheart, *n.* darling, beloved, truelove (LOVE).

SWEETNESS—*N.* sweetness, mellifluence, saccharinity.

sugar, sucrose, glucose, dextrose, fructose, lactose, cane sugar, beet sugar, burnt sugar, brown sugar, caramel, confectioners' sugar, powdered sugar; syrup, sorghum, molasses, theriaca, treacle (*Brit.*); saccharine; sweet, sweets, dessert, ice cream, custard.

candy, confections, confectionery, sweets, sweetmeats; sweet, confection, confiture, bonbon, sugarplum, chocolate, caramel, butterscotch, cream, fondant, fudge, taffy, toffee, kiss, lollipop, mint, peppermint, nougat, licorice, jujube; candy store, confectioner's.

honey, mel (*pharm.*), hydromel, mead, metheglin.

[*sweet or musical sound*] melody, musicality, harmony, euphony, tune, symphony, pizzicato, chime, coo, purr.

V. **sweeten,** sugar, candy, sugarcoat, candy-coat, saccharize (*tech.*).

Adj. **sweet,** sugary, saccharine, saccharoid, sweetened; candied, honeyed, sugared, syrupy, cloying, luscious, nectareous, candy-coated, sugar-coated.

melodious, melodic, tuneful, sweet-sounding, musical, harmonious, harmonic, canorous, cantabile, Lydian, dulcet, mellow, smooth, soothing, mellifluous, mellifluent, sonorous, rotund, rich, orotund, silvery, euphonious, euphonic.

sweet-tempered, amiable, good-natured, agreeable, charming, gentle, kind, mild, affectionate, lovable.

See also FOOD, HARMONY, MELODY, MUSIC, PLEASANTNESS, PLEASURE. *Antonyms*—See BAD TEMPER, SOURNESS, UNPLEASANTNESS, UNSAVORINESS.

---

sweets, *n.* candy, confections, confectionery (SWEETNESS).

sweet-sounding, *adj.* sweet, mellow, mellifluous, mellifluent (MELODY, SWEETNESS).

sweet-tempered, *adj.* amiable, good-natured, agreeable (SWEETNESS).

swell, *n.* billow, surge; surf, sea, (RIVER); growth, rise (INCREASE); crescendo, increase (LOUDNESS); toff (*Brit.*), fashion plate (FASHION).

swell, *v.* distend, expand (SWELLING); increase, rise (LOUDNESS); grow, surge (INCREASE); exalt, inflate (PRIDE).

SWELLING—*N.* swelling, belly, billow, blister, bulge, fester, inflammation, intumescence, protuberance, puff, tumefaction; bump, knob, knurl, lump, node, nodule, tuberosity, tumor, varicosity; blain, bunion, chilblain, mouse (*slang*), tuber, wheal; swell, surge, wallow, distention, expansion, inflation; swollenness, flatulence, nodosity, torosity, tumescence, tumidity, turgidity, turgor; tympanism, tympany, meteorism, dropsy, edema.

V. **swell,** distend, expand, inflate, blow up, intumesce, tumefy, balloon, belly, bilge, billow, bloat, bulge, bulk, bulk up, puff up, surge, wallow, protuberate; inflame, blister.

Adj. **swollen,** billowy, bulgy, distent, intumescent, protuberant, puffy, surgy; patulous, plethoric, torose, torous, tumescent, tumid, turgid, varicose (*med.*); blubbery, flatulent, tumorous; bumpy, knobby, knobbed, knurled, lumpy, nodous, nodular, tuberous; inflamed, angry.

See also BLOWING, INCREASE, ROUNDNESS. *Antonyms*—See DECREASE, FLATNESS.

swelter, v. sweat, ooze (PERSPIRATION); be hot, broil (HEAT).

swerve, v. shift, veer, swing (CHANGE, TURNING); skew, skid, side-step (SIDE).

swift, adj. quick, rapid, fleet (SPEED); sudden, unexpected, abrupt (SUDDENNESS).

swig, v. swill, toss off (DRINK).

swill, n. refuse, garbage, slops (UNCLEANNESS).

swill, v. swig, toss off (DRINK).

SWIMMING—N. swimming, natation, water sports, nautics, aquacade; breast stroke, crawl, Australian crawl, side stroke, backstroke, dog paddle, side-kick.

swimming pool, natatorium, pool, Olympic swimming pool; diving board, high-diving board.

swimmer, bather, mermaid, naiad, natator, bathing beauty.

swim suit, bathing suit, trunks, Bikini.

V. swim, bathe, wade, go wading, paddle; sound, submerge, dive, high-dive.

Adj. swimming, natant, natatorial, natatory.

See also FLOAT, WATER. Antonyms —See DESCENT.

---

swimmingly, adv. successfully, prosperously (SUCCESS).

swindle, n. extortion, racket, shakedown (slang), fraud, blackmail (THIEVERY).

swindle, v. cheat, defraud, rook (THIEVERY, DECEPTION).

swine, n. pig, hog, boar (ANIMAL); sneak, wretch, cur (CONTEMPT).

swing, n. tempo, meter, lilt (RHYTHM); bop, bebop, boogiewoogie: all slang (MUSIC).

swing, v. dangle, flap (HANGING); lurch, reel, pitch (ROLL); turn, veer, swerve (TURNING).

swipe (slang), v. crib, pinch (slang), purloin (THIEVERY).

swirl, n. curl, crispation (WINDING); twirl, whirl, birl (ROTATION).

swirl, v. curl, wind, snake (WINDING, CURVE).

switch, n. lever, pedal, treadle (CONTROL); whip, strap, belt (HITTING); sprig, offshoot, twig (PLANT LIFE); wig, transformation (HAIR).

switch, v. change, exchange, swap (SUBSTITUTION); convert, turn, shift (CHANGE, TURNING); whip, birch, scourge (HITTING).

swivel, n. pivot, hinge, pin, gudgeon, axis (ROTATION).

swivel, v. pivot, whirl, spin (ROTATION).

swollen, adj. bulgy, distent, puffy (SWELLING); pompous, inflated, pretentious (WORDINESS).

swoon, v. faint, black out (INSENSIBILITY).

sword, n. blade, broadsword, cutlass (CUTTING).

sword-shaped, adj. ensate, ensiform, gladiate (SHARPNESS).

swordsman, n. swashbuckler, duelist, fencer (FIGHTER).

sybarite, n. sensualist, voluptuary (PLEASURE).

sycophant, n. toady, tufthunter, bootlicker (FOLLOWER, SLAVERY).

syllable, n. prefix, suffix, particle (WRITTEN SYMBOL).

syllabus, n. curriculum, content (LEARNING).

symbol, n. letter, character (WRITTEN SYMBOL); numeral, figure (NUMBER); token, mark, emblem (REPRESENTATION, INDICATION).

symbolic, adj. figurative, typical, representative (REPRESENTATION, INDICATION).

symbolism, n. symbology, iconology, totemism (REPRESENTATION).

symbolize, v. denote, show, signify (REPRESENTATION, INDICATION).

symmetrical, adj. regular, shapely, balanced (UNIFORMITY, SHAPE, BEAUTY, WEIGHT).

symmetry, n. regularity, harmony, correspondence, proportion, proportionality, balance (UNIFORMITY, SHAPE).

sympathetic, adj. warm, warmhearted, vicarious (PITY).

sympathize, v. empathize, identify with, understand (PITY).

sympathizer, n. condoler, partisan, champion (PITY).

sympathy, n. warmth, fellow-feeling, empathy (LIKING, PITY).

symphony, n. symphonic poem, tone poem (MUSIC).

symptom, n. prodrome, syndrome; manifestation, evidence, token (INDICATION).

synagogue, n. temple (CHURCH).

synonymous, adj. tantamount, equivalent, equal (MEANING).

synopsis, n. summary, précis, compendium (SHORTNESS).

syntax, n. grammar, accidence (LANGUAGE).

synthetic, adj. man-made, artificial (PRODUCTION); unnatural, factitious, affected (UNNATURALNESS).

syrup, n. sorghum, theriaca, molasses (SWEETNESS).

system, *n.* tactics, scheme, strategy (METHOD, ARRANGEMENT); ideology, philosophy, theory (RULE).

systematic, *adj.* methodical, efficient, orderly (BUSINESS); complete, thoroughgoing (COMPLETENESS).

systematize, *v.* methodize, organize, systemize, arrange (METHOD, ARRANGEMENT).

T

table, *n.* board, console, stand (SUPPORT); catalogue, schedule (LIST); bill of fare, menu (FOOD).

table, *v.* postpone, put aside, shelve (DELAY, SIDE).

tablet, *n.* pill, capsule, lozenge (CURE); pad, quire, ream (PAPER).

tableware, *n.* silver plate, flatware, hollow ware, silverware (METAL).

taboo, *n.* prohibition, proscription (DENIAL); restriction, limitation (RESTRAINT).

tacit, *adj.* unspoken, wordless, implied (SILENCE, INDIRECTNESS, SUGGESTION, MEANING).

taciturn, *adj.* uncommunicative, closemouthed, tight-lipped (SILENCE).

tack, *n.* brad, thumbtack (FASTENING); aim, set, bent (DIRECTION).

tackle, *n.* outfit, appliances, rigging (INSTRUMENT); fishing gear (HUNTING).

tackle (*colloq.*), *v.* attack, take on, accept (ATTEMPT, UNDERTAKING).

tacky (*colloq.*), *adj.* shabby, mangy, seedy (UNTIDINESS).

tact, *n.* diplomacy, delicacy, discretion (ABILITY, WISDOM).

tactful, *adj.* judicious, discreet, politic, diplomatic, statesmanlike (ABILITY, WISDOM).

tactics, *n.* system, scheme, strategy (METHOD, MEANS).

tactless, *adj.* inconsiderate, thoughtless, undiplomatic (INATTENTION, CLUMSINESS).

tadpole, *n.* amphibian, polliwog (ANIMAL).

tag, *n.* slip, label, ticket (INDICATION, NAME); stub, fag end (END).

tag, *v.* heel, shadow, trail (FOLLOWING); label, term, title (NAME); touch, tap (TOUCH).

tail, *n.* dock, caudal appendage; reverse, rump (REAR); stub, tag, fag end (END).

tailor, *n.* *couturier* (*F.*), dressmaker (CLOTHING WORKER).

taint, *v.* contaminate, pollute, defile (IMPURITY, POISON).

take (*slang*), *n.* gate (*colloq.*), returns, proceeds (RECEIVING).

take, *v.* grasp, seize, grab (TAKING).

take after, *v.* look like (SIMILARITY).

take away, *v.* subtract, reduce (DEDUCTION); detach, dislodge (REMOVAL); abduct, kidnap (TAKING).

take back, *v.* retract, recant, backtrack (REVERSION).

take down, *v.* lower, let down (LOWNESS).

take from, *v.* dispossess, tear from (TAKING).

take in, *v.* absorb, assimilate, soak up (INTAKE); receive, get (RECEIVING); shorten, contract, compress (SHORTNESS); deceive, fool, mislead (DECEPTION).

taken aback, *adj.* surprised, astonished, aghast (SURPRISE).

take on, *v.* tackle (*colloq.*), accept (UNDERTAKING).

take prisoner, *v.* take into custody, arrest, seize, apprehend (TAKING).

TAKING—*N.* taking, seizure, capture, apprehension, arrest, abduction, abstraction, removal, appropriation, confiscation, expropriation, attachment, sequestration, usurpation, pre-emption, assumption; adoption, acquisition, reception.

[*device for seizing*] grapple, grappling hook, grapnel, hook, grip, tongs, pliers, pincers, pinchers, tweezers, forceps.

V. take, grasp, seize, grab, grip, clutch, snatch, nab (*colloq.*), clasp, lay hold of; cull, pluck, gather, pick, draw, crop, reap.

[*get control or possession*] capture, catch, collar (*colloq.*), seize, corral, tackle, grapple, bag, net, hook; get, have, gain, win, pocket, secure, acquire, attain, procure, entrap, ensnare; abstract, take away, take off, run away with, abduct, kidnap; steal upon, pounce (*or* spring) upon, swoop down upon, take by storm.

appropriate, adopt, assume, possess oneself of; commandeer, confiscate, expropriate, attach, garnishee, sequestrate, sequester, usurp, pre-empt, impound, help oneself to, make free with; intercept; draft, impress.

dispossess, take from, take away from, tear from, tear away from, wrench (wrest, pry, or wring) from, extort; deprive of, bereave; disinherit; oust, evict, eject, divest; levy, distrain (*law*); disseize (*law*); despoil, strip, fleece, bleed (*colloq.*).

take into custody, take prisoner, arrest, seize, apprehend, pick up (*colloq.*).

Adj. taking, confiscatory, extortionary.

prehensile, prehensive, raptorial.

See also ACQUISITION, BORROWING, DEDUCTION, HOLD, INTAKE, PLUNDER, REMOVAL, SELFISHNESS, TRAP, THIEVERY. *Antonyms*—See GIVING, RECEIVING, RESTORATION.

---

tale, *n.* account, narrative, yarn (STORY).

talebearer, *n.* tattletale, taleteller, tattler (DISCLOSURE, RUMOR).

talent, *n.* knack, gift, genius (ABILITY).

taleteller, *n.* storyteller, yarner, novelist, author (WRITER).

talisman, *n.* charm, amulet, periapt (GOOD LUCK).

talk, *n.* idle rumor, gossip, scandal (RUMOR).

TALK—*N.* talk, speech, soliloquy; somniloquy, somniloquence, ventriloquism; nasalization, rhinolalia.

reference, allusion, advertence, innuendo, insinuation, insinuendo, hint.

conversation, converse, tête-à-tête (*F.*), chat, chitchat, confabulation, commune, causerie (*F.*), colloquy, dialogue, duologue, interlocution, parlance, repartee, pleasantries, small talk; banter, chaff, badinage, persiflage, raillery, *blague* (*F.*).

discussion, argument, conference, consultation, deliberation, negotiation, palaver, parley, panel discussion, ventilation, *Kaffeeklatsch* (*Ger.*), symposium.

discourse, disquisition, monologue, descant, dissertation, expatiation, oration, exhortation, peroration, epilogue, screed, harangue, lecture, chalk talk, speech, address, allocution, prelection, declamation, recitation.

oratory, elocution, expression, eloquence, rhetoric, grandiloquence, magniloquence, multiloquence, command of words (or language), gift of gab (*colloq.*).

talkativeness, garrulity, loquacity, volubility, logorrhea (*med.*).

talker, speaker, spokesman, mouthpiece, prolocutor; soliloquist, somniloquist, ventriloquist; converser, conversationalist.

discusser, discussant, conferee, consultant, deliberator, negotiator, negotiant; chairman, chair, leader, symposiarch; panel, round table.

discourser, public speaker, orator, elocutionist, rhetor, speechmaker, rhetorician, Hermes, Demosthenes, Cicero, spellbinder, lecturer, prelector; monologist or monologuist, interlocutor.

V. talk, speak, say, utter, pronounce, soliloquize, ventriloquize, somniloquize, rhapsodize; drawl, chant, drone, intone, nasalize; talk about, comment on, describe, give voice to, noise of, premise, broach.

mention, cite, enumerate, specify, itemize, recite, recount, rehearse, relate; refer to, advert to, allude to, harp on.

talk to, address, apostrophize, buttonhole, accost, harangue; salute, hail, call to, greet; invoke, appeal to, memorialize.

converse, chat, chitchat, commune, confabulate, cooze.

discuss, talk over, deliberate, argue, canvass, palaver, parley, thrash (or thresh) out, ventilate; confer with, advise with, consult with, negotiate.

chatter, babble, chaffer, drool (*slang*), gab, gabble, gibber, gossip, jabber, jargon, jaw (*slang*), maunder, patter, prate, prattle, rattle on, tattle, tittle-tattle, twaddle, whiffle, yammer, blab, blather, blether, burble, cackle, clack.

discourse, hold forth, descant, dissertate, expatiate, stump (*colloq.*), speechify (*jocose*), spout, orate, perorate, harangue, spellbind; lecture, speak, prelect, declaim, recite; ad-lib, extemporize, improvise; sermonize, moralize, preach, pontificate.

whisper, susurrate, stage-whisper, murmur, mumble, mutter.

spout, gush, slobber, hedge, equivocate, blarney, palter, prevaricate, snuffle, vapor.

growl, grumble, mutter, bark; rant, rave.

stutter, stammer, stumble, falter, lisp, splutter, sputter.

Adj. spoken, oral, unwritten, nuncupative (*chiefly of wills*); phonetic, phonic, voiced, lingual.

eloquent, rhetorical, grandiloquent, magniloquent.

conversational, chatty, colloquial, communicative, conversable.

talkative, loquacious, gabby,

chattering, chatty, garrulous, mouthy, voluble.

See also ABSURDITY, EXPRESSION, GREETING, HINT, INFORMATION, LANGUAGE, RUMOR, STATEMENT, TEASING, VOICE, WORD, WORDINESS. *Antonyms* —See SILENCE.

---

tall, *adj.* towering, alpine; lanky, rangy (HEIGHT); bouncing, vaulting (EXAGGERATION).

tallow, *n.* fat, grease, suet (OIL).

tally, *v.* count, enumerate, reckon (NUMBER).

talon, *n.* claw, pounce, chela (APPENDAGE).

tame, *adj.* domesticated, broken (DOMESTICATION); gentle, feeble, insipid (MILDNESS).

tame, *v.* discipline, train, break in (OBEDIENCE, DOMESTICATION); restrain, subdue, master (MODERATENESS, DEFEAT, SLAVERY).

tame down, *v.* soften, tone down (RELIEF).

tamper with, *v.* interfere with, meddle in (INTERJACENCE); alter, modify (CHANGE); fix, reach (BRIBERY).

tan, *n.* beige, biscuit, khaki (BROWN).

tang, *n.* flavor, savor, smack (TASTE); smell, scent, aroma (ODOR).

tangent, *adj.* contactual, in contact, contingent (TOUCH).

tangible, *adj.* touchable, palpable (TOUCH); perceptible, sensible (SENSITIVENESS, MATERIALITY, REALITY).

tangle, *n.* muss, snarl, rummage (UNTIDINESS).

tangle, *v.* snarl, entangle, embroil (CONFUSION).

tangy, *adj.* appetizing, piquant, spicy, pungent, sharp (TASTE, ODOR).

tank, *n.* cistern, vat (CONTAINER).

tanned, *adj.* sunburned, bronzed (BROWN).

tantrum, *n.* conniption fit (*colloq.*), flare-up (BAD TEMPER, ANGER).

tap, *n.* spout, faucet, cock (EGRESS).

tap, *v.* pat, tip, rap (HITTING); palpate, tag (TOUCH); broach, unstopper (OPENING).

tape, *n.* braid, ribbon (FILAMENT).

taper, *n.* spire, wedge, cusp (SHARPNESS); candle, dip (LIGHT).

taper, *v.* wane, decline, subside (DECREASE, WEAKNESS); reduce, contract (NARROWNESS).

tape recorder, *n.* wire recorder (RECORD).

taps, *n.* reveille (INDICATION).

tar, *n.* pitch, asphalt (RESIN); gob (*colloq.*), salt (*colloq.*), seaman (SAILOR).

tardy, *adj.* late, dilatory, behindhand (DELAY).

target, *n.* aim, ambition, goal (PURPOSE); sport, byword, butt (RIDICULE, CONTEMPT).

tariff, *n.* tax, rate, duty (PAYMENT).

tarnish, *v.* dim, fade, darken (DULLNESS); stain, spot, sully (UNCLEANNESS).

tarry, *v.* loiter, linger (SLOWNESS); delay, stall (DELAY).

tart, *adj.* sour, acid (SOURNESS).

tart (*slang*), *n.* slut, stew, strumpet (PROSTITUTE, SEX).

task, *n.* job, chore, stint (WORK).

TASTE—*N.* taste, gustation, palate; sip, snack, soupçon (*F.*), hint, dash, tinge, trace, tincture, suggestion; aftertaste; foretaste, prelibation.

morsel, bit, sample, drop, mouthful, bite, fragment; delicacy, tidbit, dainty; appetizer, *apéritif* (*F.*), *hors d'oeuvres* (*F.*), *canapé* (*F.*).

flavor, savor, sapor, smack, tang, relish, zest, aroma.

flavoring, seasoning, zest, spice, condiment.

salt; alkali, sodium chloride, brine; saltworks, salina, saltern.

discrimination, discernment, judgment, refinement, distinction, delicacy, cultivation.

V. taste, partake of, savor, sip, sample.

flavor, season, spice, salt, zest, tinge, tincture.

taste of, savor of, smack of.

have taste, appreciate, enjoy; discriminate, distinguish, judge, criticize.

Adj. tasty, flavorful, flavorsome, flavorous, full-flavored, mellow, savory, savorous, aromatic, sapid, saporous, palatable, delicious, delectable, toothsome, dainty, appetizing, piquant, spicy, tangy, sharp, gingery, zestful, pungent, salty, racy, peppery, hot.

tasteful, refined, cultured, aesthetic, artistic, cultivated, graceful; unaffected, pure, chaste, classical, Attic.

salt, saline, salty, briny, brackish, saliferous, salted; alkaline.

See also ELEGANCE, FOOD, IMPROVEMENT, PRESERVING, SHARPNESS. *Antonyms*—See DULLNESS, UNSAVORINESS, VULGARITY.

---

tasteful, *adj.* refined, esthetic, graceful, artistic (ELEGANCE, TASTE).

tasteless, *adj.* flat, flavorless, insipid (UNSAVORINESS).

tatter, *n.* rip, tear, rent (TEARING).

tattle, *v.* blab, babble, gossip (DISCLOSURE, RUMOR).

tattletale, *n.* taleteller, tattler, telltale, talebearer (DISCLOSURE, RUMOR).

tattoo, *n.* rat-a-tat, rub-a-dub, pitter-patter (ROLL).

taught, *adj.* trained, cultivated, cultured, well-bred (TEACHING).

taunt, *v.* scoff at, twit, deride (RIDICULE).

taut, *adj.* tense, high-strung, wiredrawn (NERVOUSNESS); tight, strained, snug (TIGHTNESS).

tavern, *n.* hotel, inn, lodge (HABITATION); taphouse, saloon (ALCOHOLIC LIQUOR).

tawdry, *adj.* gaudy, obtrusive, flashy (VULGARITY, OSTENTATION).

tawny, *adj.* amber, amber-colored, ocherous, ochery (YELLOW).

tax, *n.* assessment, toll, levy (PAYMENT, DUTY).

tax, *v.* impose, levy, assess (EXPENDITURE); accuse, charge (ACCUSATION); overwork, overuse (USE); tire, strain (FATIGUE); load, oppress (WEIGHT).

taxi, *n.* taxicab, jitney (*colloq.*), cab (VEHICLE).

taxi driver, *n.* jehu (*jocose*), cabby (*colloq.*), hacker (VEHICLE).

tea, *n.* social, sociable (SOCIALITY).

TEACHER—*N.* **teacher,** educator, instructor, preceptor, master, tutor, coach, schoolmaster, schoolmistress, schoolma'am, schoolmarm, schoolteacher, schoolman, pedagogue (*often derogatory*), dominie (*Scot.*), don, *Privatdocent* (*Ger.*), professor, lecturer, governess, abecedary, pundit (*often derogatory*), maestro (*It.*), trainer, disciplinarian.

teachers, faculty, staff, professorate.

guide, counselor, adviser, mentor; pastor, preacher, apostle, missionary, catechist; example, pattern, model.

Adj. **teacherly,** teacherish, didactic, donnish, pedagogical, pedagoguish, professorial, schoolmarmish, schoolmistressy.

See also ADVICE, SCHOOL, TEACHING. *Antonyms*—See LEARNING.

TEACHING—*N.* **teaching,** instruction, education, tuition, clinic, tutelage; edification, enlightenment, illumination; catechism, indoctrination, inculcation, implantation, propaganda, doctrine; direction, guidance; preparation, initiation; coeducation, re-education, university extension, chautauqua; self-education, self-improvement, biosophy; pedagogy, pedagogics, didactics.

training, cultivation, discipline, domestication, nurture, qualification, retraining, refresher course, workshop.

lesson, lecture, recitation, exercise, practice, drill, assignment, homework.

V. **teach,** instruct, educate, school, tutor, coach, catechize, give lessons in; lecture, hold forth, preach; propagate, disseminate, sow the seeds of; expound, explain, interpret; edify, enlighten, brief, initiate, inform, guide, direct, show.

train, prepare, groom, ground, prime, qualify, discipline, drill, exercise, practice; cultivate, cradle, nurture; domesticate, tame; break in, show the ropes to (*colloq.*).

instill, implant, plant, inculcate, indoctrinate, infix; imbue, impress, impregnate, infuse, inspire, ingrain, inoculate, infect.

Adj. **educational,** instructional, didactic, preceptive, clinical, cultural, humanistic, pedagogical, tutorial, coeducational; disciplinary, disciplinal, inductive, deductive; homiletic, doctrinal, propagandistic.

scholastic, academic, classical; vocational, pragmatic, practical, utilitarian.

instructive, informative, edifying, educative, enlightening, illuminating.

taught, trained, cultivated, cultured, well-bred, literate, lettered, educated, well-educated, schooled, etc. (see *Verbs*).

See also EXPLANATION, GUIDANCE, INFORMATION, LEARNING, PREACHING, PREPARATION, SCHOOL, TEACHER. *Antonyms*—See MISTEACHING.

---

team, *n.* crew, gang (WORK, ASSEMBLAGE); faction, sect (SIDE); tandem, rig, pair (HORSE).

teamster, *n.* truckman, trucker (VEHICLE).

teamwork, *n.* collaboration, coordination (WORK, CO-OPERATION).

tear, *n.* rip, rent, tatter (TEARING); teardrop, lachryma (WEEPING).

tear, *v.* rip, fray, frazzle, shred (TEARING).

tearful, *adj.* teary, lachrymose (WEEPING).

TEARING—N. tearing, etc. (see *Verbs*); laceration, disjection, divulsion, dilaceration, sunderance, avulsion.

rip, tear, rent, tatter, frazzle, fray.

V. **tear**, rip, fray, frazzle, shred, tatter, lacerate; tear apart, unsolder, sunder, rive, rend, disject, divulse; mangle, dilacerate, discerp.

Adj. **torn**, etc. (see *Verbs*); ragged, shabby, seedy.

See also CUTTING, DISJUNCTION, OPENING, TRACTION. *Antonyms*—See RESTORATION.

TEASING—N. teasing, etc. (see *Verbs*); badinage, banter, chaff, persiflage, raillery.

teaser, tease, hector, baiter, etc. (see *Verbs*).

V. **tease**, bait, devil (*colloq.*), rag (*colloq.*), rib (*colloq.*), badger, needle (*colloq.*), twit, hector, bullyrag, ballyrag; banter, badinage, chaff, guy (*colloq.*), josh (*colloq.*), rally; tantalize.

See also ANNOYANCE, RIDICULE, WITTINESS.

technical, *adj.* occupational, professional, vocational (BUSINESS).

technicality, *n.* particular, specification (DETAIL).

technique, *n.* tactics, usage, procedure (MEANS, METHOD); capability, capacity, skill (ABILITY).

technology, *n.* industry, commerce (BUSINESS); nomenclature, glossology, terminology (NAME).

tedious, *adj.* monotonous, dull, prosaic (BOREDOM); poky, enervating, exhausting (FATIGUE).

tedium, *n.* ennui (*F.*), doldrums (BOREDOM).

teem, *v.* burst, pullulate (FULLNESS); abound, swarm (MULTITUDE); pour, shower (RAIN).

teeming, *adj.* serried, swarming, populous (ASSEMBLAGE).

teen-age, *adj.* adolescent, preadolescent, pubescent, hebetic (YOUTH).

teen-ager, *n.* adolescent, minor, junior (YOUTH).

teens, *n.* youthhood, boyhood, girlhood (YOUTH).

teeny, *adj.* microscopic, tiny, wee (SMALLNESS).

teeter, *v.* lurch, reel (OSCILLATION).

TEETH—N. teeth, deciduous teeth, milk teeth, permanent teeth, buckteeth.

tooth, fang, tusk, denticle, snaggletooth; tine, prong, cog, serration; bicuspid, tricuspid, incisor, canine, cuspid, stomach tooth, premolar, molar, wisdom tooth.

dentition, teething, odontogeny.

false teeth, denture, plate; prosthesis.

filling, inlay, crown, bridge, bridgework.

Adj. **toothed**, saber-toothed, buck-toothed, toothy, snaggletoothed, serrulate, serrate; toothlike, odontoid.

dental, interdental, periodontal, peridental, deciduous, succedaneous.

teetotaler, *n.* ascetic, nephalist, Rechabite (SOBRIETY).

teetotalism, *n.* abstinence, total abstinence, asceticism (SOBRIETY).

telegraph, *n.* cable, wire (*colloq.*), radiotelegraph (MESSENGER).

TELEPATHY—N. telepathy, thought transference; second sight, clairvoyance, clairaudience, extrasensory perception, E.S.P., telesthesia, sixth sense; parapsychology.

spiritualism, spiritism, spirit communication, spirit manifestations; trance; spirit rapping, table tipping (*or* turning), séance, (*F.*), materialization.

automatism, automatic writing, psychography, psychogram; ouija board, planchette.

psychic, medium, seer, clairvoyant, clairaudient; telepathist.

Adj. **telepathic**, extrasensory, psychic, clairvoyant, clairaudient; spiritistic, spiritualistic, mediumistic.

See also SUPERNATURALISM.

telephone, *n.* phone (*colloq.*), radiophone, radiotelephone (MESSENGER).

telescope, *n.* field glass, spyglass (VISION).

television, *n.* TV, audio, video (AMUSEMENT).

tell, *v.* ventilate, voice, advertise (DISCLOSURE); signify, communicate (INFORMATION); speak, express (STATEMENT); ascertain, determine, learn (DISCOVERY); weigh, count (INFLUENCE); tell out (NUMBER).

tell about, *v.* describe, outline, detail (INFORMATION).

teller, *n.* purser, paymaster, cashier (MONEY, RECEIVING).

telling, *adj.* effective, potent, trenchant (RESULT).

telltale, *n.* tattletale, taleteller, tattler, talebearer (DISCLOSURE, RUMOR).

temper, *n.* nature, temperament, disposition (CHARACTER); dander (*colloq.*), bad humor (BAD TEMPER).

temper, *v.* moderate, soften, mitigate (MODERATENESS, RELIEF); keep within reason (REASONABLENESS); harden, anneal, toughen (HARDNESS).

temperament, *n.* nature, make-up, emotions (CHARACTER).

temperamental, *adj.* willful, headstrong, moody (UNRULINESS, BAD TEMPER).

temperance, *n.* uninebriation, moderation (SOBRIETY); conservatism, moderatism (MODERATENESS); austerity, astringency, prudence (CONTROL).

temperate, *adj.* reasonable, conservative (MODERATENESS); sober, abstemious (SOBRIETY); level-headed, composed, collected (INEXCITABILITY); balmy, warm, pleasant (MILDNESS).

temperature, *n.* hotness (HEAT); feverishness, pyrexia (FEVER).

tempest, *n.* storm, squall, bluster (WIND); upheaval, convulsion (COMMOTION).

tempestuous, *adj.* stormy, turbulent, tumultuous (WIND, VIOLENCE, COMMOTION).

temple, *n.* sanctuary, shrine, synagogue (CHURCH).

tempo, *n.* rate, velocity, pace (SPEED); cadence, measure, meter (RHYTHM).

temporal, *adj.* subcelestial, secular, worldly (WORLD); chronological (TIME).

temporarily, *adv.* for the moment, pro tempore (*L.*), for a time (IMPERMANENCE).

temporary, *adj.* fugitive, ephemeral, transient (IMPERMANENCE).

temporize, *v.* stall, filibuster (DELAY).

tempt, *v.* entice, invite, lure (ATTRACTION).

tempting, *adj.* enticing, inviting, seductive, luring, magnetic (ATTRACTION).

TEN—*N.* ten, decade, decuple, decagon (*geom.*), decahedron (*geom.*); decastyle (*arch.*), decasyllable; decennium, decennary; decimal system; one tenth, tithe.

V. multiply by ten, decuple.

Adj. tenfold, denary, decamer-

ous, decimal, decuple; tenth, decuman, tithe.

---

tenable, *adj.* defensible, maintainable, justifiable (SUPPORT).

tenacious, *adj.* bulldogged, persevering, persistent (STUBBORNNESS, CONTINUATION); adhesive, clinging, clingy (STICKINESS); possessive, retentive, pertinacious (HOLD).

tenancy, *n.* possession, occupation, occupancy (OWNERSHIP).

tenant, *n.* occupant, householder, addressee (INHABITANT, OWNERSHIP).

tend, *v.* take care of, mind, watch over (SERVICE, CARE); trend, incline (DIRECTION, TENDENCY).

TENDENCY—*N.* tendency, inclination, mind, impulse, bent, affection, trend, leaning, disposition, proclivity, bias, partiality, slant, set, penchant, turn, propensity; susceptibility, predisposition, addiction, temper.

V. tend, incline, trend, gravitate toward, verge, move toward, lean, turn, bend, predispose, serve, conduce, lead, contribute, influence, dispose, impel; bid fair to, be liable to.

Adj. tending, conducive, working toward, in a fair way to, likely to, calculated to; inclining, inclined, apt, liable, prone, disposed, minded, partial, biased, predisposed, susceptible.

See also CHARACTER, DIRECTION, LIABILITY, LIKELIHOOD, LIKING, PREJUDICE, WILLINGNESS. *Antonyms*—See DISGUST, OPPOSITION, PROPULSION.

---

tender, *adj.* delicate, fragile, frail (SOFTNESS, WEAKNESS); mild, softhearted (PITY, SOFTNESS); affectionate, warmhearted, demonstrative (LOVE); young, vernal (YOUTH); sensitive, thin-skinned, touchy (SENSITIVENESS); painful, aching, sore (PAIN).

tender, *n.* attendant, nurse, handmaid (CARE).

tender, *v.* volunteer, proffer, present (OFFER).

tenderhearted, *adj.* soft, softhearted, sorry (PITY).

tenement, *n.* multiple dwelling (HABITATION).

tenor, *n.* course, trend, tendency (DIRECTION); baritone, alto (SINGING).

tense, *adj.* high-strung, wiredrawn (NERVOUSNESS); strained, taut (TIGHTNESS).

tense, v. string, unstring (NERVOUSNESS); stiffen, firm, brace (HARDNESS); constrict, strain, tauten (TIGHTNESS).

tension, n. strain, stress (NERVOUSNESS); stiffness, rigidity (HARDNESS); constriction, astriction (TIGHTNESS); pressure, brunt (PRESSURE).

tent, n. canvas, tepee, wigwam (HABITATION).

tentative, adj. conditional, provisional, dependent (CONDITION); temporary, experimental (IMPERMANENCE, TEST).

tenure, n. incumbency, administration, regime (TIME).

tepid, adj. warm, lukewarm (HEAT); indifferent, languid (INDIFFERENCE).

term, n. expression, locution, vocable (WORD); denomination, style, appellative (TITLE); period, spell, space (TIME, INTERVAL, CONTINUATION).

term, v. call, tag, title (NAME, TITLE).

terminate, v. stop, cease, discontinue (CESSATION); complete, finish, conclude (END).

terminology, n. wordage, phraseology (WORD); nomenclature, glossology (NAME).

terrace, n. grounds, campus (LAND); bank, embankment (HEIGHT); lawn, grassplot (GRASS); porch, patio, veranda (BUILDING).

terrain, n. territory, terrene, ground (LAND).

terrestrial, adj. mundane, earthly, subsolar (WORLD).

terrible, adj. terrifying, frightening, scary (FEAR); awful, beastly, frightful (INFERIORITY).

terrify, v. frighten, terrorize, petrify (FEAR).

terrifying, adj. fearful, frightening, terrible (FEAR).

territory, n. dominion, enclave, exclave (LAND); domain, quarter (REGION); extent, tract, expanse (SPACE).

terror, n. fright, alarm, panic (FEAR).

terrorism, n. anarchism, anarchy, nihilism (VIOLENCE).

terse, adj. concise, brief, succinct (SHORTNESS).

TEST—N. test, check, trial, tryout, probation, approval, experiment; criterion, standard, plummet, touchstone, yardstick, shibboleth; examination, quiz, investigation, analysis.

acid test, severe test, crucial test, baptism of fire, crucible, furnace, ordeal, aquaregia (for gold).

trial balloon, feeler.

laboratory, testing grounds, proving grounds.

testing, examination, experimentation, trial, validation, investigation, assay, analysis; psychometrics, docimasy, experimentalism, empiricism; docimology.

tests, battery of tests; personality test, psychological test, Rorschach test, inkblot test, Thematic Apperception Test, T.A.T.; achievement test, aptitude test, midterm test, final test, written test, objective-type test, essay test, true-false test, oral test, orals; intelligence test, I.Q. test, Stanford-Binet test, Bellevue-Wechsler test, Army Alpha test, Binet-Simon test, Binet test.

medical test, Aschheim-Zondek test or rabbit test (for pregnancy), Dick test (scarlet fever), Wasserman test (syphilis), Schick test (diphtheria), Ascoli test (anthrax), patch test (allergies), scratch test (allergies), paternity test, basal metabolism test.

V. test, try, try out, make a trial run, put to a test, prove, verify; check, examine, quiz, analyze, assay, validate, experiment, experimentalize; throw out a feeler, send up a pilot (or trial) balloon, feel the pulse, see how the land lies, see how the wind blows.

Adj. testing, trial, probative, pilot, probationary, probational; tentative, provisional, experimental, experimentalish, empirical.

on trial, on (or under) probation, on approval.

untested, untried, virgin, virginal, unproved.

See also ATTEMPT, EXAMINATION, INQUIRY, RULE, SEARCH.

testament, n. legal will, last will and testament, instrument (WILL).

Testament, n. Old Testament, New Testament, Bible (SACRED WRITINGS).

testify, v. affirm, attest, swear (TRUTH, AFFIRMATION); argue, prove, demonstrate (INDICATION, PROOF).

testimonial, n. recommendation, reference, character (APPROVAL); ovation, tribute (RESPECT).

testimony, n. demonstration, evidence, documentation (PROOF); statement, affidavit (AFFIRMATION).

testy, *adj.* irritable, irascible, snappy (BAD TEMPER).

tether, *n.* rope, leash, cord (FILAMENT).

tether, *v.* moor, tie, leash (JUNCTION, LOCATION, FASTENING).

text, *n.* content, matter, context (MEANING, READING, WORD); schoolbook, textbook, manual (SCHOOL).

textile, *adj.* textural, textured, woven (TEXTURE).

textile, *n.* fabric, material, cloth (TEXTURE).

TEXTURE—*N.* texture, weave, composition, make-up, arrangement, disposition, contexture, intertexture, constitution, character, structure, organization; grain, fiber, nap, surface, warp and woof (or weft).

[*that which is woven*] braid, lace, plait, plat, trellis, twine, mesh, lattice, latticework, net, tissue, web, webbing, cobweb, gossamer.

weaving device: loom, spinning wheel.

fabric, textile, material, goods, bolt, cloth, stuff; homespun, frieze, drill, twill, tweed, serge, cheviot, worsted, wool, cotton, orlon, dacron, nylon, etc.

V. texture, weave, knit, crochet, spin, twill; braid, plait, interweave, interknit, intertwine, interlock, interlace, lace, raddle, pleach, plat, twine, wattle, trellis.

Adj. textural, textile, textured, woven; coarse-grained, homespun; fine-grained, fine, delicate, gossamery, filmy.

See also ARRANGEMENT, BODY, CHARACTER, MAKE-UP, SURFACE, WINDING, WOOL.

---

thank, *v.* be grateful, appreciate, acknowledge (GRATITUDE).

thankless, *adj.* ungrateful, unappreciative; unrequited, unrewarded (INGRATITUDE).

thanksgiving, *n.* praise, benediction, grace (WORSHIP).

that is, *id est* (L.), *i.e.,* to wit, namely (EXPLANATION).

thaw, *v.* dissolve, fuse, melt (LIQUID); relax, unbend (FREEDOM).

theater, *n.* playhouse, auditorium (DRAMA); movie house, drive-in (MOTION PICTURES); lecture room, amphitheater (SCHOOL); the stage, dramatics (DRAMA); scene, stage, arena (ENVIRONMENT).

theatergoer, *n.* playgoer, first-nighter (DRAMA).

theatrical, *adj.* histrionic, dramatic, legitimate (ACTOR, DRAMA); affected, stagy, mannered (UNNATURALNESS).

theatricals, *n.* dramatics, acting, theatrics (DRAMA).

theft, *n.* stealing, filchery, pilferage (THIEVERY).

theme, *n.* subject, motif (TOPIC); composition, essay, dissertation (WRITING, TREATISE).

then, *adv.* at that time, on that occasion (TIME); therefore, thence, whence (REASONING).

theologian, *n.* divinity student, seminarian (GOD).

theology, *n.* divinity, hierology (RELIGION).

theorem, *n.* axiom, postulate (RULE); hypothesis, thesis, theory (SUPPOSITION).

theoretical, *adj.* suppositional, hypothetical, academic (SUPPOSITION); impractical, quixotic, abstract (IMAGINATION).

theory, *n.* hypothesis, postulate, assumption (SUPPOSITION, BELIEF); idea, concept (THOUGHT); ideology, philosophy, system (RULE).

therapy, *n.* treatment, medicamentation (CURE); psychiatry, psychoanalysis (PSYCHOTHERAPY).

thereabouts, *adv.* roughly, roundly, generally (NEARNESS, SMALLNESS).

therefore, *adv.* consequently, and so, hence (RESULT, ATTRIBUTION, REASONING).

thermometer, *n.* calorimeter, pyrometer, pyroscope (HEAT).

thesaurus, *n.* dictionary, lexicon, wordbook (WORD); storehouse, treasure house, treasury (STORE).

thesis, *n.* dissertation, essay, theme (TREATISE); theory, hypothesis, postulate (SUPPOSITION).

thick, *adj.* dense, solid (THICKNESS); simple, stupid (STUPIDITY); considerable, great (MULTITUDE).

thicken, *v.* congeal, jelly, jell (THICKNESS).

THICKNESS—*N.* thickness, diameter, bore, ply; viscosity, turbidity; opacity, nontransparency, nontranslucency.

density, body, impenetrability, impermeability, imporosity.

thickening, coagulation, congealment, inspissation; clot, coagulum.

solidity, substantiality; solid, mass, block, lump; concretion, concrete, conglomerate; stone, rock, cake.

V. thicken, congeal, jelly, jell,

stiffen, set, fix, cake, condense, curd, curdle, clabber, inspissate, coagulate, clot.

densen, densify, compress, squeeze, ram down, compact, consolidate, condense; precipitate, deposit; crystallize; solidify, concrete.

Adj. **thick,** viscid, viscous, ropy, grumous, turbid.

thickened, congealed, jellied, jelled, stiff, set, fixed, caked, curdled, coagulated, clotted, solidified, condensed.

dense, compact, close, impenetrable, impermeable, imporous.

thickset, stocky, stubby, stumpy, chunky, pudgy, squat, squatty.

solid, concrete, hard, consolidated, firm.

opaque, nontranslucent, nontransparent.

See also BLOOD, HARDNESS, OIL, PRESSURE, SEMILIQUIDITY, SIZE, STICKINESS. *Antonyms*—See LIQUID, THINNESS, TRANSPARENCY, WATER.

---

thick-skinned, *adj.* insensitive, pachydermatous, imperceptive (INSENSITIVITY).

thick-witted, *adj.* stupid, dense, thick-pated, numskulled (STUPIDITY).

THIEF—*N.* **thief,** pilferer, filcher, purloiner, crook (*slang*), cribber, rifler, shoplifter, kleptomaniac, embezzler, peculator, defalcator; pickpocket, cutpurse, dip (*slang*); plagiarist, pirate.

burglar, housebreaker, second-story thief, picklock, sneak thief, yegg, safebreaker, safecracker, cracksman (*slang*), Raffles.

robber, bandit, brigand, bravo, footpad, highwayman, hijacker, ladrone, latron; rustler, cattle rustler, cattle thief, horse thief.

looter, plunderer, pillager, depredator, depredationist, despoiler, spoiler, rapist.

swindler, sharper, forger, coiner, counterfeiter; racketeer, shakedown artist (*slang*), extortioner, blackmailer.

pirate, corsair, Viking, buccaneer, privateer, filibuster, freebooter, picaroon, rover, sea rover.

pirate flag, black flag, blackjack, Jolly Roger, Roger.

See also THIEVERY.

THIEVERY—*N.* **thievery,** theft, stealing, filchery, pilferage, purloinment, abstraction, burglary,

housebreaking, robbery, brigandage, banditry, larceny, shoplifting; depredation, despoliation, despoilment, spoliation, plunder, pillage, plunderage, rape, rapine; holdup, highway robbery, stick-up (*slang*); kleptomania; piracy, plagiarism; extortion, racket, shakedown, fraud, swindle, blackmail, graft.

embezzlement, misappropriation, peculation, defalcation, appropriation.

kidnaping, abduction, ravishment, snatch (*slang*).

[*that which is stolen*] **loot,** booty, haul (*colloq.*), swag (*colloq.*), score (*slang*), pilferage, plunder, spoils, plunderage, pillage, pelf, defalcation.

V. **steal,** filch, thieve, sneak, palm, pilfer, crib, purloin, cabbage, pinch (*slang*), swipe (*slang*), snitch (*slang*), abstract, appropriate, loot, rifle, burglarize, rob, lift, rustle (*cattle*); depredate, despoil, spoil, plunder, pillage, rape; pirate, plagiarize; hold up, stick up (*slang*), hijack, heist (*slang*); take, make off with.

embezzle, misappropriate, peculate, defalcate.

swindle, cheat, cozen, defraud, victimize, bunco, fleece, trick, rook, bilk; obtain under false pretenses; live by one's wits; shake down, blackmail.

counterfeit, forge, coin, circulate bad money, shove the queer (*slang*).

kidnap, abduct, shanghai, carry off, spirit away, ravish, snatch (*slang*); hold for ransom.

get (*slyly, etc.*), win, allure, alienate, estrange, wean.

[*move secretly or silently*] **creep,** crawl, go stealthily, steal, pass quietly, sneak, slink, withdraw, sidle, pussyfoot (*colloq.*).

Adj. **thievish,** light-fingered, thieving, larcenous, kleptomaniacal, burglarious, abstractive, plunderous, depredatory, spoliative, piratical, plagiaristic.

See also CRAWL, DECEPTION, ILLEGALITY, PLUNDER, TAKING, THIEF. *Antonyms*—See GIVING, RECEIVING, RESTORATION.

---

thin, *adj.* slim, slender, fine (THINNESS, NARROWNESS); unconvincing, filmsy, weak (DISSUASION); dilute, watery, light (WEAKNESS); reedy, penetrating, piercing (HIGH-PITCHED SOUND).

thing, *n.* object, article, commodity (MATERIALITY, VISION).

think, *v.* cogitate, deliberate, contemplate (THOUGHT).

thinker, *n.* solon, pundit, philosopher (WISDOM).

thinking, *adj.* reasoning, thoughtful, rational (REASONING).

think out, *v.* reason out, figure out, conclude (REASONING).

think up, *v.* invent, design, devise (PRODUCTION).

THINNESS—*N.* thinness, gracility, angularity; underweight, emaciation, mere skin and bones; fineness, capillarity, diaphaneity.

thin person, cadaver, scrag, skeleton, spindling, wisp, wraith; slim woman, sylph; slim girl, slip.

thinner, attenuant, diluent.

[*thin or insubstantial thing or substance*] cobweb, froth, vapor, wisp, wraith, film, gauze, gossamer.

V. **thin,** slenderize, slim, reduce, emaciate, skeletonize, macerate, waste, waste away; thin out, prune, trim.

rarefy, attenuate, extenuate, subtilize; dilute, water.

Adj. **thin** (*not fat*), slender, slim, slight, wispy, gracile, lean, spare, willowy, sylphlike, svelte, reedy, weedy (*colloq.*), lathy (*colloq.*), elongated, rangy, spindly, spindling, spindle-legged, spindleshanked, leggy (*colloq.*), gangling, lanky, lank, slab-sided, stringy, wasp-waisted; wiry, withy.

skinny, underweight, bony, angular, rawboned, scrawny, scraggy; drawn, haggard, pinched, starved, underfed, undernourished, peaked, skeletal, skeletonlike, wasted, emaciated, consumptive, cadaverous, wraithlike, shriveled, wizened, withered, macerated; hatchet-faced, lantern-jawed.

[*not thick*] **fine,** delicate, finedrawn, fine-spun, gauzy, gossamer, attenuated, filmy, diaphanous, cobwebby, wispy, sheer, papery, threadlike, hairlike, capillary; ductile, tensile.

insubstantial, airy, aerial, slender, slight, meager, flimsy, sleazy, attenuated, cobwebby, extenuated, frothy, subtile, subtle, tenuous, vaporous, unsubstantial, watery, dilute, diluted, wishy-washy, wraithlike, wispy, shallow, transparent.

[*not dense*] **rare,** rarefied, serous, tenuous, attenuated, extenuated, fine-spun.

[*not full or crowded*] **scanty,** inadequate, insufficient, meager, spare, sparse.

See also CUTTING, DECREASE, FEW-NESS, INSUFFICIENCY, TRANSPARENCY. *Antonyms*—See OIL, ROUGHNESS, SIZE, THICKNESS.

thin-skinned, *adj.* sensitive, touchy, tender (SENSITIVENESS, OFFENSE).

third-degree (*colloq.*), *v.* cross-examine, cross-question, grill (INQUIRY).

thirst, *n.* dryness, dipsosis (*med.*), thirstiness (DRINK).

thirsty, *adj.* dry, parched (DRINK).

thistle, *n.* thorn, barb, prickle (SHARPNESS).

thorn, *n.* thistle, barb, prickle (SHARPNESS).

thorny, *adj.* briery, bristly, bristling (SHARPNESS); difficult, troublesome, severe, baffling (DIFFICULTY).

thorough, *adj.* all-inclusive, sweeping; out-and-out, arrant (COMPLETENESS).

thoroughbred, *n.* blood horse, Arab (HORSE); gentleman, lady (COURTESY).

thoroughfare, *n.* road, artery, highway (PASSAGE).

though, *conj.* although, albeit, even though (OPPOSITION).

THOUGHT—*N.* thought, thinking, reflection, cogitation, consideration, contemplation, rumination, meditation, study, speculation, deliberation, mentation, brainwork, headwork, cerebration; reasoning, ratiocination, deduction, decision, conclusion, analysis, premeditation, attention, debate; theory, idea, supposition, concept; sentiment.

train of thought, association of ideas, stream of consciousness; free association.

abstraction, absorption, preoccupation, engrossment; musing, reverie, dreaminess, bemusement, pensiveness, brown study, self-communing, self-counsel.

second thought (*or* **thoughts**), reconsideration, re-examination, review, retrospection, excogitation, mature thought; afterthought.

V. **think,** reflect, cogitate, deliberate, contemplate, meditate, ponder, puzzle over, muse, dream, ruminate, speculate, theorize, wonder about, fancy, conceive, brood over, mull over, sweat over (*colloq.*), pore over, study, rack (beat *or* cudgel) one's brains, cerebrate, set one's wits to work; reason, analyze, ratiocinate, conclude, deduce, deduct, decide, excogitate;

premeditate, anticipate; introspect, retrospect.

consider, take into consideration, take account of, view, give thought to, mark, advert to, think about, turn one's mind to, attend to, bethink oneself of; suppose, believe, deem, reckon; harbor, cherish, entertain, imagine, bear (*or* keep) in mind, turn over in the mind, weigh, debate; reconsider.

suggest itself, present itself, occur to, come into one's head; strike one, enter (cross, flash across, *or* occupy) the mind; have in one's mind; absorb, occupy, engross, preoccupy.

Adj. **thoughtful,** pensive, attentive, meditative, reflective, contemplative, deliberative, studious, museful, musing, ruminative, ruminant, wistful, introspective, philosophical, speculative, metaphysical; absorbed, rapt, engrossed in, intent, lost in thought, preoccupied, bemused.

thinking, cerebrational, cerebral, intellectual, ideational, conceptual; subjective, objective; abstract, abstruse; resourceful, reasoning, rational, cogitative, analytical, deductive, ratiocinative; theoretical; retrospective.

Phrases. **under consideration,** under advisement, under careful consideration; after due thought, on mature reflection.

See also ATTENTION, IDEA, IMAGINATION, INTELLECT, INTELLIGENCE, OPINION, REASONING, SUPPOSITION. *Antonyms*—See STUPIDITY.

thoughtful, *adj.* pensive, meditative, reflective (THOUGHT); reasoning, thinking, rational (REASONING); considerate, tactful, diplomatic (ATTENTION).

thoughtless, *adj.* heedless, unthinking, inadvertent (INATTENTION, CARELESSNESS); unreasoning, brutish (STUPIDITY); inconsiderate, tactless, indelicate (INATTENTION).

THOUSAND—*N.* **thousand,** chiliad, millenary; millennium; thousandth part, millesimal; ten thousand, myriad.

thousand thousand, million, billion, trillion, quadrillion, quintillion, sextillion, septillion, octillion, nonillion, decillion, undecillion, duodecillion, tredecillion, quattuordecillion, quindecillion, sexdecillion, septendecillion, octodecillion, novemdecillion, vigin-

tillion; centillion, googol, googolplex; zillion (*jocose*).

Adj. **thousand,** millenarian, millenary; thousandth, millesimal; ten thousand, myriad.

thrash, *v.* stir, toss, pitch (NERVOUSNESS, OSCILLATION); whip, whale, flog (HITTING); rush, surge (VIOLENCE).

thread, *n.* yarn, twist, cotton (FILAMENT).

threadbare, *adj.* worn, well-worn, shabby (USE); stale, musty, trite (OLDNESS).

THREAT—*N.* **threat,** threats, menace, intimidation, commination, fulmination, thunder, gathering clouds; omen, portent, impendence, warning; assault (*law*), ramp; blackmail; empty threat, bluff.

V. **threaten,** menace, overhang, portend, impend, loom, forebode; fulminate, comminate, thunder, growl, gnarl, snarl, gnarr, yarr, warn, intimidate, bully; lour, scowl, look daggers; ramp; blackmail; bluff.

Adj. **threatening,** menacing, minacious, minatory; ominous, fateful, overhanging; looming, impending, portentous, sinister, comminatory; ugly, dire, black, scowling, lowering, ill-boding.

See also DANGER, FUTURE, WARNING. *Antonyms*—See FEAR, PROTECTION.

THREE—*N.* **three,** threesome, triplet, trio, ternion, ternary, trine, triple, triune, trey (*cards, dice, or dominoes*), triad, leash, trinomial (*tech.*), cube, triangle, trigon, trigraph, trident, tripod, trireme, triumvirate; trefoil, tribrach; triplication, triplicate.

threeness, triadism, trinity, triplicity, triunity.

trisection, tripartition, trichotomy; trifurcation, triformity.

V. **triplicate,** treble, triple; cube.

trisect, trifurcate, trichotomize, third.

Adj. **three,** triadic, ternary, ternate, triune, cubic, third, tertiary.

threefold, treble, trinal, trinary, trine, triple, triplex, triplicate, three-ply.

trisected, tripartite, trifid, trichotomous; trifurcated, trisulcate, tridentate; three-footed, tripodic, tripodal, tripedal, trilobate, trilobed, tribrachial, trefoil, triform.

triangular, trigonal, trigonous, deltoid.

Adv. **triply,** trebly, threefold, thrice.

three-sided, *adj.* trilateral, triquetrous (SIDE).

thresh, *v.* beat, flail, mash (HITTING).

threshold, *n.* sill, limen (*psychol.*), doorsill (INGRESS); start, starting point (BEGINNING).

thrice, *adv.* triply, trebly, threefold (THREE).

thrifty, *adj.* economical, frugal, careful (ECONOMY); thriving, prosperous (SUCCESS).

thrill, *v.* titillate, tickle; throb, tingle (EXCITEMENT); delight, enrapture (HAPPINESS); tremble, quiver (SHAKE); prickle, creep (ITCHING).

thrive, *v.* prosper, flourish (SUCCESS); bloom, batten, flower (HEALTH, STRENGTH).

THROAT—*N.* **throat,** craw, gorge, gullet, maw, throttle, weasand; larynx; tonsil, amygdala; uvula.

cough, hawk, hack, bark, tussis (*med.*), whoop; [*ailments, etc.*] whooping cough, pertussis, croup; laryngitis, tonsillitis, quinsy, pharyngitis.

V. **cough,** hawk, hack, bark, whoop; cough up, expectorate, vomit.

Adj. **throaty,** guttural, husky, gruff; hoarse, raucous, croaky, roupy, stertorous; jugular, laryngeal, uvular; tussal, tussive; croupous, croupy.

See also HARSH SOUND, HEAD, SALIVA.

throb, *n.* beat, tick, pulse, pulsation (RHYTHM).

throb, *v.* beat, pulsate, palpitate (RHYTHM, SHAKE); tingle, thrill (EXCITEMENT).

throbbing, *adj.* painful, smarting, splitting (PAIN).

throng, *n.* crowd, press, horde (ASSEMBLAGE, MULTITUDE).

throng, *v.* crowd, swarm, troop (MULTITUDE, ARRIVAL).

throttle, *v.* choke, smother, strangle (KILLING).

through, *adj.* done, finished (COMPLETENESS); over, concluded (END).

through, *prep.* via, by way of, by

means of (PASSAGE); throughout, for the period of (TIME).

THROW—*N.* **throw,** etc. (see *Verbs*); throwing, jaculation, ejaculation (*physiol.*), ejection, defenestration, expulsion; gunnery, ballistics.

barrage, volley, discharge, fusillade, shower, beam, dart, missile, pellet, projectile, shot.

bomb, blockbuster, A-bomb, atom bomb; H-bomb, hydrogen bomb, hell bomb; guided missile, intercontinental ballistic missile; fallout, strontium 90.

V. **throw,** cast, fling, heave, hurl, lob, pitch, shy, sling, toss, twirl, chuck, cant, flip, flirt, jerk, bung, catapult, launch, shoot, bombard, barrage, waft; pelt, pellet, pepper, stone, lapidate, pebble; volley, bandy.

throw off, give off, emit, beam, belch, vomit, spew, discharge, ejaculate (*physiol.*), eject, expel, spout, exude, sweat, drop, leave, dump.

scatter, shower, spray, sprinkle, strew, broadcast, besprinkle, bestrew, spatter, splatter, splash.

See also ARMS, ELIMINATION, EXCRETION, PROPULSION, SENDING, SPREAD. *Antonyms*—See TRACTION.

throw away, *v.* eliminate, discard, dispose of (ELIMINATION); dissipate, squander (WASTEFULNESS).

throwback, *n.* atavist, reverter (REVERSION).

throw in, *v.* inject, interpolate (INTERJACENCE).

throw out, *v.* discard, get rid of, scrap (ELIMINATION).

throw up, *v.* puke, vomit (NAUSEA).

thrum, *v.* strum, drum (MUSICIAN).

thrust, *v.* push, shove, jab (PROPULSION).

thrust in, *v.* obtrude, ram in (INSERTION).

thruway, *n.* speedway, freeway, expressway (PASSAGE).

thug, *n.* bruiser, hoodlum, gangster (VIOLENCE).

thumb, *n.* finger, pollex (APPENDAGE).

thumb, *v.* feel, handle, finger (TOUCH).

thumb through, *v.* leaf through, scan, browse (READING).

thump, *v.* beat, pulse, throb (RHYTHM); hit, slap, poke (HITTING).

thunder, *n.* crash, clap, peal (LOUDNESS); boom, cannonade, drumfire (ROLL); threats, menace (THREAT).

thunder, *v.* drum, boom, roar, rumble (ROLL, RESONANCE); growl, gnarl, snarl, utter threats (THREAT).

thus, *adv.* so, accordingly, therefore (REASONING).

thwart, *v.* frustrate, foil, balk (INEFFECTIVENESS, HINDRANCE).

thwarted, *adj.* foiled, frustrated, balked (FAILURE).

tick, *n.* beat, pulse, throb (RHYTHM).

ticket, *n.* tag, slip, label (INDICATION, NAME); ballot, slate (LIST).

tickle, *v.* chuck, brush (TOUCH); tingle, thrill (ITCHING, SENSITIVENESS); titillate, amuse, convulse (LAUGHTER); enchant, gratify, delight (PLEASURE).

ticklish, *adj.* tickly, itchy (ITCHING); delicate, trying, awkward (DIFFICULTY); dangerous, chancy, risky (DANGER).

tidbit, *n.* delicacy, dainty, morsel (TASTE).

tide, *n.* current, stream, drift (DIRECTION); high tide, race, sluice (RIVER); term, duration (TIME).

tidings, *n.* information, intelligence (PUBLICATION).

tidy, *adj.* neat, spick-and-span, well-kept (NEATNESS); ample, substantial (SIZE, MULTITUDE).

tie, *n.* bond, link, connection (FASTENING); necktie, cravat, scarf (NECKWEAR); draw, dead heat, stalemate (EQUALITY, ATTEMPT).

tie, *v.* attach, bind, join (FASTENING, JUNCTION).

tied, *adj.* even, neck-and-neck, drawn (EQUALITY, ATTEMPT).

tiepin, *n.* stickpin (JEWELRY).

tier, *n.* stratum, course (LAYER).

tight, *adj.* strained, taut (TIGHTNESS); closefisted, tightfisted, penurious (STINGINESS); drunk, high (*colloq.*), inebriated (DRUNKENNESS).

tighten, *v.* constrict, strain, tauten, tense (TIGHTNESS).

tightfisted, *adj.* closefisted, tight, penurious (STINGINESS).

TIGHTNESS—*N.* tightness, constriction, astriction, strain, tension, tensity; constrictor, astringent.

V. **tighten,** constrict, constringe, astrict, astringe, strain, tauten, tense, tensify, brace.

Adj. **tight,** braced, constricted, astricted, strained, taut, tense; compact, close, cozy, snug; airtight, hermetic, airproof; watertight, waterproof.

See also STRENGTH. *Antonyms*—See INELASTICITY, LOOSENESS.

tightwad, *n.* pinchfist, skinflint, miser (STINGINESS).

till, *prep.* until, to, up to, as far as (TIME).

tilt, *v.* lean, list, heel (SLOPE).

timber, *n.* lumber, hardwood (WOOD).

timbre, *n.* tone color, quality (MELODY).

TIME—*N.* time, tide, term, duration, date; lifetime, afterlife, eternity; tempo (*music*), tense (*grammar*); chronology.

[*available time*] leisure, freedom, convenience, opportunity, liberty, chance.

endless time, eternity, infinity, perpetuity.

point of time, point, date, juncture, moment, stage.

instant, flash, jiffy (*colloq.*), minute, moment, second, trice, twinkle, twinkling.

period of time, period, term, spell, space, season, span, extent, length, stretch, stage, phase, bout; tenure, incumbency, administration, reign, dynasty, regime.

era, epoch, eon *or* aeon, age, cycle, generation.

[*intermediate time*] interval, interim, meantime, while; interlude, recess, pause, interruption, intermission, interregnum; respite; space, parenthesis.

ages of man: prehistoric period, protolithic period, Stone Age, paleolithic period, eolithic period, neolithic period, Bronze Age, Iron Age, ancient times, antiquity, Middle Ages, *moyen âge* (*F.*), Dark Ages, Renaissance *or* Renascence, modern times.

month, lunar month, lunation, moon (*poetic*); bimester, trimester, semester, quarter; week, seven days, hebdomad; fortnight.

year, twelvemonth; leap year, bissextile; midyear; biennium, quadrennium; quinquennium, quinquenniad, lustrum, pentad; sexennium; septenary, septennate, septennium; decade, decennary, decennium; century, centenary, sexcentenary, millenary, millennium, chiliad.

V. **time,** regulate, measure, adjust, chronologize, synchronize; keep time, harmonize with.

spend time, devote time to, pass time; use (fill, occupy, consume, while away, wile away, *or* take) time; seize a chance, take time by the forelock.

waste time, dally, dawdle, diddle (*colloq.*), boondoggle (*slang*), dillydally, laze, loiter, trifle, idle, loaf; niggle, potter, tinker, putter; dally away (dawdle away, idle away, loiter away, slug away, trifle away, while away, *or* wile away) time.

go on for (*a time*), continue, last, occupy, span, take.

Adj. **chronological**, temporal, junctural, spatiotemporal; periodic, epochal, cyclic, seasonal, phasic.

infinite, eternal, unending, endless.

of geologic time: Archeozoic, Proterozoic, Paleozoic, Mesozoic, Cenozoic, azoic, glacial, postglacial.

monthly, mensal, menstrual, tricenary; bimonthly, bimensal, bimestrial; trimonthly, trimestral, quarterly; quadrimestrial, semestral, semimonthly.

weekly, hebdomadal, septenary; biweekly, fortnightly, triweekly, semiweekly.

yearly, annual; perennial, yearlong; biannual, biyearly, semiannual.

Adv., phrases. **meantime**, meanwhile, in the interim, in the meantime, during the interval; at the same time.

once, formerly, erstwhile (*archaic*).

then, at that time (moment, *or* instant), on that occasion; soon afterward, immediately, hereupon, thereupon, whereupon; at another time, again, later.

when, while, whereas, although; whenever, whensoever, at whatever time, as soon as.

Prep. **during**, until, pending, in the time of; for the period of, over, through, throughout.

till, until, to, up to, as far as, down to, up to the time of.

Conjunctions. **until**, till, to the time when.

while, whilst (*esp. Brit.*), as long as, during the time that, at the same time as; although, whereas.

See also CONTINUATION, ENDLESSNESS, FUTURE, LENGTH, PAST, PRESENT TIME, REST, RULE, SEASONS, TIMELINESS, TIME MEASUREMENT.

---

timeless, *adj.* incessant, interminable (ENDLESSNESS); dateless, antediluvian (OLDNESS).

TIMELINESS—*N.* **timeliness**, fit (suitable, *or* proper) time, high time.

V. **improve the occasion**, seize an opportunity, strike while the iron is hot, make hay while the sun shines.

Adj. **timely**, auspicious, opportune, pat, propitious, providential, seasonable, towardly, well-timed.

Adv., phrases. **opportunely**, seasonably, early, soon; in due time (course *or* season), in good time, in the nick of time, just in time, at the eleventh hour.

See also EARLINESS, EXPEDIENCE, TIME. *Antonyms*—See UNTIMELINESS.

TIME MEASUREMENT—*N.* **time measurement**, chronography, chronology, chronometry, chronoscopy, dendochronology, horology, horometry, horography.

clock, chronometer, chronograph, chronoscope, horologe, watch, timer, stop watch, timepiece, timekeeper, stem-winder (*colloq.*), dial, sundial, gnomon, hourglass, sandglass, isochronon, metronome, water clock, clepsydra, ghurry; chronodeik, photochronograph.

time record, calendar, almanac, menology, chronology, chronogram; diary, journal, annals, chronicle; timetable, schedule.

V. **fix the time**, register, record, date, chronicle, chronologize, measure time, beat time, mark time; synchronize.

See also EVENING, MORNING, RECORD, SEASONS. *Antonyms*—See ENDLESSNESS, MISTIMING.

---

timepiece, *n.* timekeeper, clock, watch (TIME MEASUREMENT).

timetable, *n.* schedule, program, calendar (LIST, TIME MEASUREMENT).

timeworn, *adj.* trite, worm-eaten, moss-grown (OLDNESS).

timid, *adj.* fearful, timorous, diffident (FEAR); mousy, shy, bashful (MODESTY).

tin, *adj.* stannic, stannous (METAL).

tin, *n.* can, canister, cannikin (CONTAINER); stannum, pewter (METAL).

tinder, *n.* combustible, inflammable, kindling (FIRE).

tine, *n.* point, prong, tooth (SHARPNESS, TEETH).

tinge, *n.* tint, cast, shade, tincture (COLOR).

tinge, *v.* tincture, tint, stain (COLOR); infiltrate, saturate, impregnate (MIXTURE).

tingle, *v.* throb, thrill, twitter (EXCITEMENT, SENSITIVENESS); creep, tickle (ITCHING).

tinker, *n.* patcher, mender (RESTORATION).

tinker, *v.* niggle, potter, putter (TIME); boggle, dabble, boondoggle (WORK).

tinkle, *v.* jingle, clink, ring (BELL, RESONANCE).

tinsel, *n.* finery, frippery, trumpery (ORNAMENT, OSTENTATION, WORTHLESSNESS).

tint, *n.* hue, tone, cast, shade (COLOR).

tiny, *adj.* microscopic, teeny, wee (SMALLNESS).

tip, *n.* vertex, peak, apex (HEIGHT, SHARPNESS); point, extremity, edge (END); inside information (INFORMATION); suggestion, inkling (HINT); gratuity, perquisite (PAYMENT).

tip, *v.* lean, list, tilt (SLOPE); turn over, upturn (TURNING).

tip off, *v.* give inside information (INFORMATION); warn, caution (WARNING); prompt, cue (HINT).

tipsy, *adj.* top-heavy, tippy (UNSTEADINESS); rakish, sloping, slanting (SLOPE); drunk, high (*colloq.*), inebriated (DRUNKENNESS).

tiptoe, *v.* step, skip, trip (WALKING).

tiptop (*colloq.*), *adj.* first-rate (*colloq.*), shipshape, sound (GOOD).

tirade, *n.* harangue, screed, diatribe (MALEDICTION).

tire, *v.* weary, bush (*colloq.*), enervate (FATIGUE); bore, pall on (BOREDOM).

tired, *adj.* exhausted, fatigued, weary, all in (FATIGUE).

tireless, *adj.* indefatigable, untiring, unwearied (ENERGY).

tiresome, *adj.* tiring, fatiguing, wearying (FATIGUE); wearisome, tedious, boring (BOREDOM); unrelieved, humdrum, monotonous (UNIFORMITY).

tissue, *n.* net, web, cobweb (TEXTURE); tissue paper, onionskin (PAPER).

titan, *n.* colossus, monster, mammoth (SIZE).

titanic, *adj.* gigantic, stupendous, monster (SIZE).

tit for tat, *n.* quid pro quo (*L.*), blow for blow (EXCHANGE, RETALIATION).

title, *n.* claim, interest, due (RIGHT); name, term (TITLE).

TITLE—*N.* title, name, denomination, style, appellative, term, designation, antonomasia, honorific; address, compellation, salutation, close; right, claim, privilege.

mister, Mr., Master, *monsieur* (*F.*), *Herr* (*Ger.*), *signor* (*It.*), *signore* (*It.*), *signorino* (*It.*), *señor* (*Sp.*), *senhor* (*Pg.*), *sahib* (*India; used after name*).

Mrs., *Madame* or *Mme.* (*F.*), *Doña* (*Sp.*), *Señora* (*Sp.*), *Donna* (*It.*), *Signora* (*It.*), *Frau* (*Ger.*), *Dona* (*Pg.*), *Senhora* (*Pg.*), *Vrouw* (*Dutch*), *Memsahib* (*Hindustani*), *Sahibah* (*India*).

Miss, *Mademoiselle* (*F.*), *Signorina* (*It.*), *Señorita* (*Sp.*), *Fraulein* (*Ger.*), *Senhora, Senhorita* (*Pg.*).

heading, head, caption, rubric, legend, inscription, trope; headline, banner, streamer.

V. **title,** entitle, term, subtitle, style, dub (*archaic or poetic*), denominate, dignify, address; call, name.

Adj. **titular,** denominative, honorific, salutatory; antonomastic; self-titled, self-styled, *soi-disant* (*F.*); titulary; titled, noble, aristocratic.

See also GREETING, NAME, PRIVILEGE, RIGHT, SOCIAL CLASS.

---

titled, *adj.* noble, princely, aristocratic (SOCIAL CLASS, TITLE).

titter, *v.* laugh, snicker, snigger (LAUGHTER).

titular, *adj.* nominal, honorary (NAME); denominative, honorific (TITLE).

to, *prep.* until, up to, as far as (TIME).

toady, *n.* bootlicker, sycophant, tufthunter (FLATTERY, FOLLOWER).

toady, *v.* fawn, crouch, grovel (SLAVERY).

to and fro, back and forth, shuttlewise (OSCILLATION).

toast, *n.* health, pledge (RESPECT, GESTURE, ALCOHOLIC LIQUOR); rye toast, French toast (BREAD).

toastmaster, *n.* chairman, master of ceremonies (BEGINNING).

TOBACCO—*N.* tobacco, Lady Nicotine, nicotine, the weed (*colloq.*), roll, smokes, dottle; chew, snuff.

cigar, Havana, cheroot, stogie, corona, panatela, perfecto, belvedere.

cigarette, fag (*slang*), butt (*colloq.*), cubeb, smoke, tailor-made, weed (*colloq.*), coffin nail (*slang*), filter, cork-tip.

pipe, brier or briar, brierroot, meerschaum, clay pipe, dudeen, churchwarden, calabash, corncob; hookah, narghile (*Persian*), chibouk (*Turkish*); peace pipe, calumet.

tobacco store, cigar store, smoke shop, tobacconist's.

V. smoke, puff, drag (*colloq.*), suck, inhale, exhale.

See also BLOWING, BREATH, GAS.

today, *adv.* at present, now, at this time (PRESENT TIME).

to-do, *n.* hoopla, stir, racket (EXCITEMENT).

toe, *n.* digit, pettitoes (APPENDAGE).

toe hold, *n.* foothold, bridgehead, open-sesame (INGRESS).

together, *adv.* conjointly, collectively (ACCOMPANIMENT); unitedly, jointly (UNITY, JUNCTION); simultaneously, in unison (SIMULTANEOUSNESS).

together with, as well as, along with (ADDITION).

toil, *v.* labor, drudge, struggle (WORK, ATTEMPT, ENERGY).

toilet, *n.* latrine, sanitary, urinal (CLEANNESS).

toils, *n.* snare, pitfall, meshes (TRAP).

token, *adj.* pretended, professed (PRETENSE).

token, *n.* memento, souvenir, keepsake (MEMORY); symbol, denotation, sign (REPRESENTATION); omen, presage (PRECEDENCE).

token, *v.* indicate, show (INDICATION).

tolerable, *adj.* supportable, endurable, bearable (SUPPORT).

tolerant, *adj.* indulgent, lenient, permissive (MILDNESS, PERMISSION); open-minded, broad-minded, liberal (ACCEPTANCE, IMPARTIALITY).

tolerate, *v.* accept, abide, brook (ACCEPTANCE, INEXCITABILITY); bear, endure, undergo (SUPPORT).

toll, *n.* tax, impost, tribute (DUTY, PAYMENT).

toll, *v.* ring, knell, strike (BELL); summon, command, invite (SUMMONS).

tom, *n.* male, he, buck, bull (MAN).

tomb, *n.* grave, vault, mausoleum (BURIAL).

tomboy, *n.* hoyden, romp, chit (YOUTH).

tombstone, *n.* gravestone, marker, headstone (BURIAL).

tome, *n.* volume, album, work (BOOK).

tomfoolery, *n.* mummery, buffoonery, nonsense (ABSURDITY).

tomorrow, *n.* morrow, by-and-by (FUTURE).

tone, *n.* inflection, modulation, pitch (SOUND); hue, cast, shade (COLOR); tonus (HEALTH).

tone down, *v.* subdue, temper, restrain (SOFTNESS).

tongs, *n.* grapple, grapnel, hook (TAKING).

tongue, *n.* language, speech, parlance (LANGUAGE); neck, isthmus, spit (LAND); clapper, cannon (BELL).

tongue-lashing, *n.* comeuppance, dressing-down, censure (SCOLDING).

tongue-tied, *adj.* dumb, inarticulate, mum (SILENCE).

tonic, *n.* bracer, stimulant (STRENGTH).

too, *adv.* furthermore, further, also (ADDITION).

tool, *n.* implement, utensil, machine (INSTRUMENT); puppet, figurehead, cat's-paw (DEPENDABILITY, USE).

too much, excessive, superfluous; glut, overabundance (EXCESS).

tooth, *n.* fang, molar; tine, cog (TEETH); relish, appetite (LIKING).

toothed, *adj.* dentate, serrate, serrated (NOTCH).

toothsome, *adj.* palatable, delicious, delectable (TASTE).

top, *adj.* highest, tiptop, topmost (HEIGHT); maximum, supreme (EXTREMENESS); dominant, paramount (POWER).

top, *n.* pinnacle, peak, summit (HEIGHT); roof, ceiling (COVERING); maximum, limit (EXTREMENESS); lid, cover (COVERING).

top, *v.* command, dominate, transcend (HEIGHT); outdo, surpass, transcend (EXCESS, SUPERIORITY); ream, skim, cream (REMOVAL); cover, face, veneer (COVERING).

topfull, *adj.* brimming, brimful (FULLNESS).

top-heavy, *adj.* unbalanced, lopsided, irregular (INEQUALITY); tipsy, tippy (UNSTEADINESS).

TOPIC—*N.* topic, subject, matter, subject matter, motif, theme, leitmotif, thesis, text, business, affair, matter in hand, question, problem, issue, theorem, proposition, motion, resolution, case, point; moot point, point at issue, debatable point.

Adj. topical, local, limited, restricted, particular.

See also CONTENTS, INQUIRY, MEANING.

---

topknot, *n.* bun, chignon (HAIR).

top-notch, *adj.* unequaled, unexcelled, unsurpassed (SUPERIORITY).

topple, *v.* knock down, overturn; fall, collapse (DESCENT).

topsy-turvy, *adj.* upturned, upended, upside-down (TURNING).

torch, *n.* flambeau, flashlight, spotlight (LIGHT).

torment, *n.* agony, excruciation, rack (PAIN, TORTURE).

torment, *v.* torture, rack, crucify (PAIN, TORTURE); annoy, bedevil, harass (ANNOYANCE).

torn, *adj.* ragged, shabby, seedy (TEARING).

tornado, *n.* cyclone, hurricane, twister (WIND).

torpid, *adj.* inert, numb, stuporous (MOTIONLESSNESS, INSENSIBILITY).

torpor, *n.* stupor, stupefaction, petrifaction (INSENSIBILITY); doldrums, inertia, apathy (INACTION); languor, lassitude, inanition (WEAKNESS).

torrent, *n.* cascade, cataract, waterfall (RIVER); cloudburst, shower, pour (RAIN).

torrid, *adj.* steamy, sweltering, tropical (HEAT).

torso, *n.* trunk (BODY).

torture, *n.* intorsion, deformation, distortion (WINDING).

torture, *v.* deform, distort, gnarl (WINDING).

TORTURE—*N.* **torture,** crucifixion, excruciation, martyrization; impalement, rack, strappado *or* estrapade, torment, third degree.

instrument of torture: rack, boot, Iron Maiden, wheel, torment (*archaic*), scarpines, thumbscrew, strappado.

V. **torture,** crucify, excruciate, rack, martyr, martyrize, boot, strappado, impale, grill.

Adj. **torturous,** torturesome, excruciating

See also PAIN, PUNISHMENT, WINDING.

---

toss, *v.* fling, cast, flip (THROW); stir, thrash (NERVOUSNESS); pitch, lurch, seesaw (ROTATION, OSCILLATION).

tossup (*colloq.*), *n.* chance, odds (CHANCE, POSSIBILITY).

tot, *n.* infant, baby, tyke (CHILD); mite, peewee (SMALLNESS).

total, *n.* whole, entirety, all (COMPLETENESS); aggregate, sum (ADDITION).

total, *v.* add up to, amount to, come to (COMPLETENESS, ADDITION); add up, tot up (ADDITION).

totalitarianism, *n.* dictatorship, fascism, nazism (GOVERNMENT, VIOLENCE).

totemism, *n.* symbolism, symbology, iconology (REPRESENTATION).

totter, *v.* slide, slip, lurch (DESCENT); rock, roll, stagger (UNSTEADINESS, OSCILLATION).

touch, *v.* feel, finger (TOUCH); affect, impress (INFLUENCE); move, tug at the heart (PITY); concern, pertain to (RELATIONSHIP); borrow, make a touch (BORROWING).

TOUCH—*N.* **touch,** feel, taction, grope, manipulation, palpation, percussion (*med.*); tap, etc. (see *Verbs*).

contact, taction, hit, strike, collision, impact, shock, concussion, smashup; carom, etc. (see *Verbs*).

abutment, abuttal, contiguity, adjacency, tangency, tangentiality, contingence.

V. **touch,** feel, grope, handle, manipulate, finger, thumb, paw; palpate, percuss, tag, tap, tip, twiddle, brush, tickle, caress, chuck, stroke, pat, pet, dab, rub, massage; lick, osculate, suck, kiss.

[*come or be in contact*] hit, beat, strike, clank, collide, impinge, crash, ram, smash, carom; brush, glance, graze, kiss, shave; glide over, skim over; lick, lap, patter against, patter on, beat against.

adjoin, abut, meet, border, join.

Adj. **tactual,** tactile, caressive, manipulative, osculatory, palpatory, percussive; touching, approximal (*med.*), impingent, contactual; in contact, contingent, tangent.

contiguous, adjoining, abutting, adjacent, bordering, coterminous.

touchable, tactile, tangible, palpable, perceivable; material, substantial, real, concrete.

See also APPENDAGE, CARESS, FEELING, HITTING, MATERIALITY, NEARNESS, SENSITIVENESS. *Antonyms*—See SPIRITUALITY, SUPERNATURAL BEINGS.

---

touch-and-go, *n.* indeterminacy, pendency, contingency (UNCERTAINTY).

touched, *adj.* nutty (*slang*), pixilated (INSANITY).

touching, *adj.* moving, affecting, emotional (FEELING); pitiful, heartbreaking, heart-rending (PITY).

touchstone, *n.* yardstick, criterion, canon (MEASUREMENT, JUDGMENT).

touch up, *v.* polish, amend (IMPROVEMENT).

touchy, *adj.* thin-skinned, sensitive, tender (SENSITIVENESS, OFFENSE).

tough, *adj.* hard, leathery, planished (HARDNESS); strong, vigorous, rugged (STRENGTH); stout, staunch, sturdy (STABILITY); arduous, uphill (DIFFICULTY); violent, ruffianly, thuggish (VIOLENCE).

tough, n. bruiser, hoodlum, gangster (VIOLENCE).

toughen, v. temper, anneal, planish (HARDNESS); inure, brutalize (INSENSITIVITY).

toupee, n. wig, periwig, peruke (HAIR).

tour, n. trip, journey, jaunt (TRAVELING); shift, hitch, trick (WORK).

tour, v. jaunt, journey, peregrinate, travel (TRAVELING).

tourist, n. traveler, wayfarer, journeyer (TRAVELING).

tournament, n. tourney, tilt, joust (FIGHTING, ATTEMPT).

tousled, adj. disheveled, unkempt (UNTIDINESS).

tow, v. pull, draw, haul (TRACTION).

tower, n. pillar, column, steeple (HEIGHT, BUILDING).

tower, v. soar, dominate, surmount (ASCENT).

tower above, v. overlie, command (REST).

towering, adj. imperial, imposing, stately (MAGNIFICENCE); high, tall, lofty (HEIGHT).

towheaded, adj. blond-haired, platinum, platinum-blond (YELLOW).

to wit, that is, id est (L.), namely, viz (EXPLANATION, NAME).

town, n. municipality, metropolis (CITY).

toxic, adj. venomous, poisonous, virulent (POISON).

toy, n. plaything, gewgaw (AMUSEMENT); miniature, midget (SMALLNESS).

toy, v. trifle, jest, dabble (AMUSEMENT, PLAYFULNESS, FOLLY).

toy with, v. play with, trifle with (PRETENSE).

trace, n. spoor, trail; remains, vestige (REMAINDER); bit, drop, speck (SMALLNESS); whisper, breath, hint (SUGGESTION).

trace, v. pursue, trail, track (FOLLOWING, SEARCH); spot, discern, perceive (DISCOVERY); duplicate, reproduce (COPY).

trachea, n. windpipe, throttle (BREATH).

track, n. path, road, route (DIRECTION); trail, trace, spoor (REMAINDER).

track, v. pursue, dog, trail (FOLLOWING, SEARCH).

track down, v. find, spot, trace (DISCOVERY).

tract, n. area, extent, expanse (REGION, LAND, SPACE); disquisition, exposition (TREATISE).

tractable, adj. manageable, docile, amenable (OBEDIENCE, SUBMISSION); plastic, yielding, malleable (SOFTNESS).

TRACTION—N. traction, draft or draught, haulage, towage; strain, stress, stretch; pull, etc. (see Verbs).

retraction, suction, suck, resorption, absorption; contraction, constriction.

V. pull, draw, haul, lug, rake, trawl, draggle, drag, tug, tow, take in tow, trail, yank (colloq.), jerk, twitch, tweak, twist, twinge, wrench, pluck, thrum; strain, stretch, tear.

pull in, suck, absorb, resorb; pull back, draw back, retract, sheathe (claws), reel in.

draw together, contract, constrict, constringe, clench, tuck.

Adj. tractional, tractive, attrahent, attractive, absorptive, absorbent, suctorial, resorbent; retractive, retractile, retractible.

contractile, contractive, constrictive, constringent.

See also ATTRACTION, INTAKE, REVERSION, STRETCH, TEARING, TRANSFER. Antonyms—See DISPERSION, PROPULSION, SENDING, SPREAD, THROW.

trade, n. occupation, vocation; traffic, commerce (BUSINESS); patronage, custom (PURCHASE).

trade, v. swap, barter (EXCHANGE); buy at, patronize (PURCHASE).

trade in, v. traffic in, truck, deal in (SALE, PURCHASE).

trade-mark, n. mark, brand, emblem (INDICATION).

trader, n. merchant, dealer, marketer (SALE).

tradesman, n. merchant, shopkeeper, retailer (SALE).

tradition, n. custom, usage, convention (HABIT).

traffic, n. movement, transportation (TRANSFER); trade, truck, commerce (BUSINESS).

traffic in, v. trade in, truck, deal in (SALE, PURCHASE).

tragedy, n. calamity, catastrophe, reverse (MISFORTUNE).

tragic, adj. cataclysmic, catastrophic (MISFORTUNE); miserable, wretched; lamentable, deplorable (SADNESS); Thespian, buskined (DRAMA).

trail, n. track, trace, spoor (REMAINDER); wake, train (REAR).

trail, v. track, trace, spoor (FOLLOWING, SEARCH); loiter, lag, draggle (SLOWNESS, FOLLOWING).

train, *n.* car (VEHICLE); following, retinue (FOLLOWER, SERVICE); wake, trail, track (REAR); suite, chain, concatenation (FOLLOWING).

train, *v.* prepare, ground, prime (TEACHING); discipline, tame (OBEDIENCE); aim, slant, point (DIRECTION).

trained, *adj.* experienced, seasoned, practiced (EXPERIENCE); taught, cultivated (TEACHING).

trainer, *n.* breeder, horse trainer (DOMESTICATION).

train in, *v.* study, coach in, tutor in (LEARNING).

training, *n.* seasoning, practice, background (EXPERIENCE); cultivation, discipline (TEACHING).

traipse (*colloq.*), *v.* promenade, saunter, stroll (WALKING).

trait, *n.* characteristic, quality, property (CHARACTER).

traitor, *n.* treasonist, quisling, Judas (DISLOYALTY).

traitorous, *adj.* treacherous, unfaithful, treasonous (DISLOYALTY).

tramp, *n.* wanderer, vagabond, beachcomber (WANDERING); vagrant, hobo, beggar (REST); jaunt, stroll, ramble (WANDERING).

tramp, *v.* stroll, rove, roam, range (WANDERING).

trample, *v.* tread, crush, crunch (WALKING, PRESSURE).

trance, *n.* transfixion, petrifaction (MOTIONLESSNESS).

tranquil, *adj.* serene, calm, placid (CALMNESS, PEACE).

tranquilize, *v.* relax, sedate (CALMNESS); put at rest, still the fears, unruffle (UNANXIETY).

transact, *v.* carry out, discharge, perform (ACTION).

transactions, *n.* dealings, negotiations, intercourse (BUSINESS).

transcend, *v.* exceed, surpass, excel (ENCROACHMENT, SUPERIORITY).

transcribe, *v.* copy, duplicate, reproduce (COPY, WRITING).

transcription, *n.* phonograph record, recording, tape (RECORD); duplicate, carbon copy (COPY).

TRANSFER—*N.* transfer, transference, shift, change, translocation, relegation, assignment, transplantation, deportation, transmittal, transmission, transposal, transposition.

transportation, transport, movement, traffic, cartage, drayage, haulage, transit; truckage, portage, freightage, ferriage; logistics.

carrier, common carrier, carter, conveyer, transporter, bearer, porter, messenger, courier, runner; expressman, freighter, shipper, stevedore; deliveryman, drayman, hauler, coolie; letter carrier, postman, carrier pigeon.

V. transfer, move, hand, hand over, pass, forward; shift, remove, relegate, change, transpose, displace, dislodge, transplant.

send, dispatch, transmit, delegate, consign, mail, post, express.

carry, transport, convey, conduct, bear, wear, bring, fetch, deliver, shoulder, waft, whiff, whirl, whisk; cart, dray, truck, taxi (*colloq.*), ferry, boat, ship, freight, haul, lug, tote.

Adj. transferable, assignable, negotiable, transmissible.

contagious, catching, infectious, communicable.

portable, cartable, movable, conveyable, haulable, transportable; portative, marsupial (*zool.*).

See also CHANGE, CHANNEL, DISPLACEMENT, EXCHANGE, GIVING, MESSENGER, MOTION, SALE, SENDING, SHIP, TRACTION, VEHICLE. *Antonyms*—See HOLD, OWNERSHIP, STINGINESS.

transfix, *v.* palsy, spellbind, petrify (MOTIONLESSNESS).

transform, *v.* transmute, transfigure, revolutionize (CHANGE).

transformation, *n.* metamorphosis, transfiguration (CHANGE); wig, switch (HAIR).

transgress, *v.* encroach, overstep (ENCROACHMENT); disobey, violate, infringe (DISOBEDIENCE); do wrong, trespass (SIN).

transgression, *n.* trespass, wrong, vice (SIN); infraction, violation (ILLEGALITY).

transient, *adj.* passing, migratory (PASSAGE); transitory, evanescent, fleeting (IMPERMANENCE, DEPARTURE).

transition, *n.* change, shift, turn (CHANGE).

transitory, *adj.* fleeting, passing, transient (IMPERMANENCE, DEPARTURE).

translate, *v.* construe, render, reword (EXPLANATION); change, convert, transform (CHANGE).

translation, *n.* rendition, construction, version (EXPLANATION).

translucent, *adj.* transpicuous, luculent, limpid (TRANSPARENCY).

transmit, *v.* dispatch, issue, mail (SENDING, TRANSFER).

transom, *n.* ventilator, window, louver (BLOWING, AIR, OPENING).

TRANSPARENCY—*N.* transparency, transpicuity, translucence, diaphaneity, lucidity, limpidity, pellucidity.

Adj. **transparent**, pellucid, lucid, diaphanous, sheer, gauzy, translucent, transpicuous, luculent, limpid, clear, cloudless, crystal, crystalline, vitreous, glassy, hyaline.

See also CLARITY, SEMITRANSPARENCY, THINNESS, VISIBILITY. *Antonyms*—See THICKNESS, UNCLEARNESS.

---

transparent, *adj.* diaphanous (TRANSPARENCY); clear, plain, unmistakable (VISIBILITY, UNDERSTANDING).

transplant, *v.* transfer, transpose, displace (REMOVAL).

transport, *v.* move, carry, convey (TRANSFER).

transportation, *n.* transport, movement, cartage, transit (TRANSFER).

transpose, *v.* shift, interchange (EXCHANGE, TRANSFER).

transverse, *adj.* crosswise, diagonal (CROSSING).

TRAP—*N.* **trap**, snare, pitfall, booby trap, meshes, noose, toils, quicksand; ambush, ambuscade; catch, decoy, trick, deception; hook, lasso, net, dragnet, seine, snag, trammel; morass, quagmire, rattrap.

V. **snare**, ensnare, entrap, enmesh, entangle, trammel, tangle, ambush, ambuscade, decoy; trick, trip up, deceive, fool.

catch, lasso, hook, net, seine, mesh, snag; catch unprepared, surprise.

catch up to, gain on (*or* upon), overtake, overhaul, reach.

Adj. **entrapping**, ensnaring, enmeshing, entangling, tangling, cobwebby; tricky, deceptive, treacherous, insidious, catchy.

See also CONCEALMENT, DECEPTION, HUNTING, TAKING. *Antonyms*—See DISCLOSURE, FREEDOM, INFORMATION.

---

trappings, *n.* dress, raiment, apparel (CLOTHING); fittings, accouterments, appointments (INSTRUMENT).

trash, *n.* rubbish, debris, rummage (USELESSNESS, UNCLEANNESS); dregs, scum (WORTHLESSNESS).

trashy, *adj.* valueless (WORTHLESSNESS).

TRAVELING—*N.* **traveling**, etc. (see *Verbs*); tourism, globe-trot-

ting, wayfaring, transmigration, emigration; seafaring, navigation; commutation; route, itinerary, track; wanderlust, dromomania.

travel, trip, journey, run, tour, jaunt, circuit, peregrination, outing, excursion, picnic, junket, expedition; pilgrimage, hadj (*Arabic*), migration, voyage, cruise, sail, sailing, crossing; safari, trek; tourism.

traveler, tourist, wayfarer, journeyer, passenger, rider, peregrinator, viator; globe-trotter, excursionist, expeditionist, migrator, migrant, transmigrant, emigrant, émigré (*F.*); voyager, seafarer, navigator, sailor; barnstormer, trouper; commuter; pilgrim, hadji (*Arabic*), caravaneer, trekker, junketer.

V. **travel**, take a trip, tour, jaunt, journey, peregrinate, circuit; migrate, transmigrate, emigrate; voyage, navigate, cruise, sail, cross; go on tour, barnstorm, troupe, stump; commute; caravan, safari, trek, junket; ply, make a circuit of, range over, traverse, travel over.

Adj. **traveling**, migrant, migratory, itinerant, peripatetic; expeditionary, viatorial, globe-trotting, wayfaring; voyaging, cruising, seafaring, seagoing, itinerary, viatic; en route.

See also PASSAGE, SAILOR, VEHICLE, WALKING, WANDERING. *Antonyms*—See REST.

---

traveling bag, *n.* carpetbag, suitcase (CONTAINER).

traverse, *v.* cross, cut across (TRAVELING, CROSSING).

travesty, *n.* caricature, parody (RIDICULE, IMITATION).

tray, *n.* hod, salver, waiter (CONTAINER).

treacherous, *adj.* traitorous, unfaithful, treasonous (DISLOYALTY); tricky, deceptive, insidious (TRAP); untrustworthy, fly-by-night (UNBELIEVINGNESS).

treachery, *n.* perfidy, recreancy, treason, disaffection, infidelity (DISLOYALTY).

tread, *n.* walk, step, stride (WALKING).

tread, *v.* walk, step; step on, trample (WALKING).

treason, *n.* treachery, lese majesty (DISLOYALTY).

treasonable, *adj.* disloyal, traitorous, treacherous (DISLOYALTY).

treasure, *n.* capital, fortune, gold (WEALTH).

treasure, *v.* value, esteem, prize (VALUE).

treasurer, *n.* bursar, controller, cashier (MONEY, RECEIVING).

treasury, *n.* bursary, exchequer (MONEY); thesaurus, storage, lazarette (STORE).

treat, *v.* deal with, handle, manage (ACTION, USE); medicate, doctor (CURE).

TREATISE—*N.* treatise, dissertation, essay, thesis, theme, composition; tract, tractate, disquisition, exposition.

script, typescript, manuscript, article, vignette, sketch, piece, causerie, lucubration, monograph.

biography, autobiography, memoir, vita, profile.

work, autonym, allonym, anonym, epic; pornography, erotica, esoterica, rhyparography; juvenilia, hackwork, potboiler.

commentary, review, critique, criticism, appreciation, editorial.

anthology, compilation, collectanea, miscellany, miscellanea, omnibus, analecta, corpus; mythology, legendry; anecdotage, facetiae.

essayist, dissertator, tractator, writer, author, hack.

commentator, annotator, reviewer, critic, editorialist; editor, compiler, anthologist.

biographer, autobiographer, memoirist, memorialist.

V. write, compose, draft, dissertate, narrate; review, criticize, editorialize; compile, anthologize, collect.

See also BOOK, EXPLANATION, PUBLICATION, STORY, WRITER, WRITING.

treatment, *n.* medication, medicamentation (CURE); therapy, psychoanalysis (PSYCHOTHERAPY).

treaty, *n.* entente (*F.*), concordat, bargain (COMPACT).

treble, *v.* triplicate, triple (THREE).

tree, *n.* sapling, seedling (PLANT LIFE).

trek, *v.* tramp, trudge (WALKING).

trellis, *n.* lattice, fretwork, filigree (CROSSING, TEXTURE).

tremble, *v.* flutter, throb (SHAKE); quiver, shiver, shudder (FEAR).

tremendous, *adj.* huge, immense, enormous (SIZE).

tremor, *n.* flutter, ripple, quiver (AGITATION); temblor, upheaval (EARTHQUAKE).

tremulous, *adj.* trembly, aspen, shaking (SHAKE, AGITATION).

trench, *n.* ditch, dike, gully (PASSAGE, HOLLOW, OPENING).

trend, *n.* course, tenor, tendency (DIRECTION).

trend, *v.* tend, incline (TENDENCY).

trespass, *n.* transgression, offense, wrong (ILLEGALITY, SIN).

trespass, *v.* transgress, infringe, trench on (ENCROACHMENT, OVERRUNNING, IMPROPERNESS).

tresses, *n.* locks, mop, mane (HAIR).

trial, *n.* try, endeavor, effort; testing, experimentation (TEST); ordeal, tribulation (EXPERIENCE); trouble, bother (DIFFICULTY); hearing (LAWSUIT).

triangular, *adj.* trigonal, trigonous, deltoid (THREE).

tribe, *n.* race, clan, stock (RELATIVE); kind, type, ilk (CLASS).

tribunal, *n.* court, court of justice (COURT OF LAW).

tributary, *n.* branch, affluent, confluent (RIVER).

tribute, *n.* tithe, toll, dues (PAYMENT); testimonial, eulogy, encomium (APPROVAL, RESPECT, PRAISE).

trice, *n.* twinkling, second, instant (TIME).

trick, *n.* artifice, subterfuge, stratagem (DECEPTION, PLAN); catch, decoy (TRAP); frolic, joke, lark (MISCHIEF); practical joke, prank (WITTINESS); shift, tour, hitch (WORK).

trick, *v.* deceive, humbug (DECEPTION).

trickery, *n.* chicanery, knavery (CLEVERNESS).

trickle, *v.* leak, ooze, seep (EGRESS).

tricky, *adj.* deceptive, insidious, catchy (AVOIDANCE, TRAP); complicated, intricate (MYSTERY).

trifle, *n.* trinket, picayune, rush (WORTHLESSNESS); bagatelle, fico, fribble (UNIMPORTANCE).

trifle, *v.* toy, dabble, play (PLAYFULNESS, PRETENSE); fool (FOLLY); flirt, philander, coquette (LOVE).

trifling, *adj.* worthless, paltry, petty (WORTHLESSNESS); unimportant, slight (UNIMPORTANCE).

trill, *v.* warble, chirp (SINGING, ANIMAL SOUND).

trim, *adj.* neat, tidy, orderly (NEATNESS).

trim, *v.* prune, clip, crop (CUTTING); pare down, curtail (SHORTNESS); barber, cut (HAIRLESSNESS); adorn, prink, bedizen (ORNAMENT).

trinket, *n.* trifle, picayune, rush (WORTHLESSNESS); bauble, bead (JEWELRY).

trio, *n.* threesome (THREE).

trip, *n.* travel, journey, jaunt (TRAVELING).

trip, *v.* skip, buck, canter (JUMP, WALKING); fall, stumble, slip

(DESCENT); err, blunder (MISTAKE).

tripe, *n.* rubbish, chaff, trash (WORTHLESSNESS); nonsense, poppycock, claptrap (ABSURDITY).

triple, *adj.* threefold, treble (THREE).

trite, *adj.* hackneyed, stereotyped, banal (OLDNESS, COMMONNESS, BOREDOM, USE).

triumph, *n.* conquest, mastery, victory (DEFEAT, SUCCESS).

trivia, *n.* minutiae, fine points, trifles (DETAIL, UNIMPORTANCE).

trivial, *adj.* empty, frivolous (SHALLOWNESS, UNIMPORTANCE).

trolley, *n.* caster, wheel (ROUNDNESS); streetcar, cable car (VEHICLE).

trollop, *n.* strumpet, trull, slut (PROSTITUTE, SEX); draggletail, frump, drab (UNTIDINESS).

trophy, *n.* prize, palm, plume (PAYMENT).

tropical, *adj.* steamy, sweltering, torrid (HEAT).

trot, *v.* canter, run, lope (HORSE, SPEED).

trouble, *n.* trial, bother, inconvenience (DIFFICULTY); affliction, curse (MISFORTUNE); unease, upset (NERVOUSNESS).

trouble, *v.* disquiet, distress, disturb (NERVOUSNESS); afflict, ail (PAIN); annoy, vex, bother (ANNOYANCE); inconvenience, discommode (DIFFICULTY).

troubled, *adj.* anxious, worried (NERVOUSNESS).

troublemaker, *n.* stormy petrel, hellion, firebrand (DIFFICULTY, DISAGREEMENT).

troublesome, *adj.* annoying, bothersome, trying (ANNOYANCE); difficult, painful (DIFFICULTY); disturbing, distressing (NERVOUSNESS); unruly, refractory, ungovernable (UNRULINESS).

TROUSERS—N. trousers, breeches, britches (*colloq.*), pants, jeans; blue jeans, flannels, jodhpurs, Levis, overalls, pedal-pushers, peg tops, plus fours, slacks, striped trousers; knickers, knickerbockers, knee breeches, knee pants, shorts, Bermudas, Jamaicas; bloomers, culottes, trouserettes, pajamas; hose (*hist.*); rompers, jumpers; tights.

loincloth, breechclout, dhoti, G string, pareu, waistcloth, diaper.

belt, sash, waistband, girdle, cummerbund, baldric, Sam Browne belt (*mil.*).

See also APPENDAGE, CLOTHING, COVERING, SKIRT.

trowel, *n.* dredge, shovel, spade, scoop (DIGGING).

truant, *n.* absentee, hooky player (ABSENCE).

truce, *n.* armistice (PEACE); respite, reprieve (REST); lull, halt (CESSATION).

truck, *n.* jeep, pickup; cart, van (VEHICLE).

truck driver, *n.* trucker, teamster (VEHICLE).

truckle to, *v.* bootlick, pander to, court (LIKING, FLATTERY).

trudge, *v.* stumble, trek, wade (WALKING).

true, *adj.* factual, correct (TRUTH, REALITY); loyal, constant, faithful (LOYALTY); unaffected, sincere, genuine (REALITY); straight, even (STRAIGHTNESS).

truly, *adv.* actually, veritably, indeed; truthfully (TRUTH).

trump up, *v.* misrepresent, miscolor (FALSENESS, MISREPRESENTATION).

trunk, *n.* footlocker, wardrobe (CONTAINER); proboscis (NOSE); torso (BODY).

trust, *n.* faith, confidence (BELIEF); monopoly, cartel, syndicate (BUSINESS).

trust, *v.* believe in, have faith in, accredit (BELIEF).

trustworthy, *adj.* believable, credible, plausible (BELIEF); truthful, veracious (TRUTH); trusty, unfailing (DEPENDABILITY).

TRUTH—N. truth, verity, gospel, reality, existence, actuality, fact; naked (plain, honest, sober, unadorned, unvarnished, *or* exact) truth; axiom, principle, truism; verisimilitude, *vraisemblance* (F.).

truthfulness, honesty, veracity, veridicality, candor, sincerity.

trueness, authenticity, accuracy, validity.

V. be truthful, speak the truth, tell the truth; say under oath; make a clean breast, put one's cards on the table, disclose, cross one's heart, show in its true colors; undeceive, disabuse; debunk (*slang*).

hold true, stand the test, hold good; be true, ring true, sound true, hold water (*colloq.*).

true, true up, adjust, regulate, readjust, square, fix, set.

declare true, affirm, attest, testify, authenticate, aver, avouch, certify, confirm, corroborate, maintain, postulate, predicate, substantiate, swear to, validate, verify, vindicate, vouch for, warrant, take one's oath, swear to God, swear on the Bible.

Adj. **true,** actual, factual, accurate, correct, authentic, veritable, genuine, simon-pure, valid, bona fide, axiomatic; unimpeachable, unquestionable, undeniable, irrefutable; verisimilar; rightful, legitimate, orthodox, canonical, official, pure; unvarnished, undisguised, uncolored, undistorted.

truthful, veracious, veridical, truthtelling, honest, reliable, trustworthy, scrupulous, sincere, candid, frank, open, outspoken, straightforward, unreserved, guileless, unfeigned, ingenuous.

Adv., phrases. **truly,** verily (*archaic*), actually, veritably, indeed, in reality; in very truth, in fact, as a matter of fact, beyond doubt, beyond question.

truthfully, etc. (see *Adjectives*); truly, in plain words, honor bright (*colloq.*), honest to God (*colloq.*), in sooth, in earnest, from the bottom of one's heart; openly, straightforwardly.

See also EXISTENCE, HONESTY, PROPRIETY, REALITY, RULE, STRAIGHTNESS. *Antonyms*—See DECEPTION, DISHONESTY, FALSEHOOD, MISTAKE.

try, *n.* trial, endeavor, bid (ATTEMPT).

try, *v.* essay, endeavor, exert oneself (ATTEMPT); test, try out (TEST); hear, arbitrate, referee (LAWSUIT, JUDGE).

trying, *adj.* bothersome, provocative, troublesome (ANNOYANCE).

tryout, *n.* experiment, check, trial (TEST).

tub, *n.* vessel, basin, bowl (CONTAINER).

tubby, *adj.* dumpy, stubby, stocky (SIZE).

tuberculosis, *n.* consumption, white plague (BREATH).

tuck, *v.* plait, pleat, seam (FOLD); contract, constrict (TRACTION).

tuft, *n.* clump, cluster, shock (ASSEMBLAGE); forelock, daglock (HAIR); feathers, plumage, ruff (FEATHER).

tug, *v.* pull, drag, tow (TRACTION).

tumble, *v.* fall, drop, descend; trip, slip (DESCENT).

tumble-down, *adj.* jerry-built, shaky, rickety (WEAKNESS).

tumid, *adj.* swollen, tumescent, turgid (SWELLING).

tumor, *n.* bump, lump (SWELLING).

tumult, *n.* noise, racket, rumpus (LOUDNESS); vociferation, clamor (SHOUT); disorder, riot, turmoil (UNRULINESS, COMMOTION); chaos, anarchy, pandemonium (CONFUSION).

tune, *n.* strain, air, song (MUSIC, MELODY, SINGING).

tune, *v.* adjust, adapt (HARMONY).

tuneful, *adj.* musical, melodic, euphonious (MUSIC, MELODY, SWEETNESS).

tunnel, *n.* underpass, subway, shaft (PASSAGE).

tunnel, *v.* burrow, sap (DIGGING).

turbulence, *n.* tumult, turmoil, disorder (COMMOTION, CONFUSION).

turbulent, *adj.* wild, chaotic (VIOLENCE, CONFUSION, UNRULINESS); stormy, tempestuous, rugged (WIND).

turf, *n.* sod, sward, greensward (GRASS, LAND).

turgid, *adj.* tumescent, tumid (SWELLING).

turmoil, *n.* chaos, pandemonium, tumult (CONFUSION, COMMOTION).

turn, *n.* bend, curve (TURNING); spin, roll (ROTATION); tour, hitch (WORK); scare, shock, start (FEAR).

turn, *v.* incline, yaw (TURNING); rotate, revolve (ROTATION); curdle (SOURNESS).

turnabout, *n.* volte-face (*F.*), reversal, inversion (CHANGE).

turn back, *v.* revert, reverse (TURNING); relapse, backslide, regress (REVERSION).

turned-up, *adj.* pug, retroussé (*F.*), snub (SHORTNESS).

TURNING—*N.* **turning,** turn, bend, curve, quirk, incline, inclination, upturn, downturn, deflection, deflexure; retroflexion, retroversion, reversal, reversion, orientation, pronation, supination.

divergence, branch, fork, crotch, divarication, detour, deviation, digression.

V. **turn,** bend, curve, incline, yaw; veer, swing, swerve, shunt, skew, sheer, dip, tip, deflect, detour, divert, switch, obvert, wheel, whirl, pivot; digress, deviate; retroflex, revert, reverse, turn back; reflect, reflex, retrovert; twist, wriggle, wiggle, wind, writhe, zigzag.

diverge, branch off, fork, divaricate, radiate.

[*turn inside out*] **reverse,** invert, evert, evaginate.

turn over, roll, tip, capsize, upturn, plow; upend, overturn, upset, reverse, invert; turn head over heels, tumble, somersault.

Adj. **turning,** curvy, inclined, inclinatory; wriggly, wiggly, zigzaggy, zigzag, eely, intricate, sinuous, anfractuous; divergent, forked, radial.

turned, bent, curved, askew, awry, splay, pronate, supine.

overturned, upturned, upended, topsy-turvy, upside-down, stern-foremost.

See also BEND, CURVE, OSCILLATION, REVERSION, ROLL, ROTATION, WINDING. *Antonyms*—See STRAIGHTNESS, VERTICALITY.

turning point, *n.* crisis, climax (IMPORTANCE, CHANGE); pivot, hinge, axis (CAUSATION).

turn out, *v.* happen, ensue, eventuate (OCCURRENCE, RESULT); drive out, dispossess, evict (DISMISSAL); appear, visit (ARRIVAL).

turn over, *v.* tip, capsize, upturn (TURNING).

turn round, *v.* revolve, turn, spin (ROTATION).

turret, *n.* tower, steeple, donjon (BUILDING).

turtle, *n.* tortoise, terrapin (ANIMAL).

tusk, *n.* tooth, fang (TEETH).

tussle, *v.* scuffle, contest (FIGHTING); struggle, grapple, wrestle (ATTEMPT).

tutor, *n.* instructor, master (TEACHER).

tutor, *v.* educate, school, coach (TEACHING).

tuxedo, *n.* formal dress (CLOTHING).

tweak, *v.* pinch, squeeze (PRESSURE); twist, twinge (TRACTION).

tweet, *v.* chirp, cheep, peep (ANIMAL SOUND).

tweezers, *n.* nippers, pliers, pincers (HOLD, TAKING).

twelfth, *adj.* dozenth, duodenary, duodecimal (DOZEN).

twelve, *n.* dozen, baker's dozen (DOZEN).

TWENTY—*N.* twenty, score.
Adj. twentieth, vicenary, vigesimal; vicennial.

twig, *n.* offshoot, switch, sprig (PLANT LIFE).

twilight, *adj.* dusky, adusk, crepuscular (DARKNESS, EVENING).

twilight, *n.* dusk, gloaming, nightfall (EVENING).

twin, *adj.* coupled, geminate, paired (TWO); same, identical, duplicate (SIMILARITY).

twin, *n.* identical twin, Siamese twin (CHILD); match, fellow, mate (SIMILARITY).

twine, *n.* cord, string, rope (FILAMENT).

twine, *v.* entwine, weave, twist (CROSSING).

twinge, *n.* ache, pang, throe (PAIN).

twinkle, *v.* gleam, glimmer, glitter (VISIBILITY).

twinkling, *n.* flash, trice, instant (EARLINESS, TIME).

twirl, *v.* revolve, whirl, spin (ROTATION); toss, chuck, cant (THROW).

twist, *n.* ply, torsion, warp (WINDING); curlicue, flourish (WRITING).

twist, *v.* wriggle, wind, writhe (TURNING); warp, contort (WINDING); tweak, wrench (TRACTION); wring, extort (FORCE).

twisted, *adj.* knotted, buckled, wry, awry, askew (DEFORMITY).

twit, *v.* ridicule, taunt (RIDICULE); badger, needle, tax (TEASING, ACCUSATION).

twitch, *v.* jerk, vellicate, jiggle (NERVOUSNESS).

twitter, *v.* tremble, thrill, quiver (SHAKE); twit (RIDICULE).

TWO—*N.* two, couple, couplet, both, twain (*archaic*), brace, pair, mates, deuce (*as in cards*), doubleton, twins, binary, Castor and Pollux, gemini, fellow; yoke, span; distich, binomial (*algebra*); twosome.

duality, twoness, dualism, duplexity, duplicity; bipartisanship; mutuality, reciprocity.

bifurcation, dichotomization, dichotomy, bifidity, bipartition, gemination, duplication.

V. pair, couple, bracket, yoke, match, mate; twin, geminate.

bifurcate, dichotomize, fork.

double, duplify, duplicate, redouble.

Adj. twofold, bifold, binal, binary, dual, dualistic, twin, duple, duplex, duplicate, diploid; bilateral, bipartite, bipartisan; mutual, common, reciprocal.

dichotomous, bifid, biforked, forked, bifurcated, bilobate, bilobed.

coupled, double, geminate, paired, twin.

Phrases. for two, à deux (*F.*), tête-à-tête (*F.*).

See also BISECTION, COPY.

two-faced, *adj.* double-dealing, Janus-faced, mealymouthed (PRETENSE, DECEPTION).

two-sided, *adj.* bilateral, dihedral (*tech.*), bifacial (SIDE).

tycoon, *n.* executive, entrepreneur, industrialist (BUSINESS).

type, *n.* kind, sort (CLASS); original, model, pattern (BEGINNING, COPY); letter, character (WRITTEN SYMBOL).

type, *v.* arrange, class, sort, categorize (ARRANGEMENT); typewrite, write, dash off (WRITING).

typescript, *n.* script, manuscript (WRITING).

typhoon, *n.* cyclone, hurricane, tornado (WIND).

typical, *adj.* regular, stock, unexceptional (COMMONNESS); characteristic, peculiar (CHARACTER); representative, symbolic (REPRESENTATION).

typify, *v.* exemplify, illustrate, epitomize (COPY); symbolize, stand for (REPRESENTATION); characterize, feature (CHARACTER).

typist, *n.* secretary, stenographer, clerk (WORK, WRITER).

tyrannize, *v.* despotize, oppress, bend to one's will (POWER).

tyranny, *n.* absolutism, autocracy, despotism (GOVERNMENT, CONTROL, SEVERITY).

tyrant, *n.* oppressor, dictator (CONTROL, RULER, SEVERITY).

tyro, *n.* beginner, learner, novice (LEARNING, BEGINNING).

U

udder, *n.* mammary glands, dugs (BREAST).

ugly, *adj.* hideous, repulsive, unsightly (DEFORMITY); black, scowling, threatening (THREAT); vinegary, waspish, nasty (BAD TEMPER); scandalous, shocking (UNPLEASANTNESS).

ulcer, *n.* abscess, phagedena (UNCLEANNESS); canker, smutch, virus (IMMORALITY).

ulterior, *adj.* undisclosed, undivulged, unadvertised (CONCEALMENT); farther, more distant, remote (DISTANCE); later, eventual, future (FUTURE).

ultimate, *adj.* farthest, furthermost, lattermost (DISTANCE, END); maximum, supreme (EXTREMENESS).

ultimately, *adv.* eventually, finally (FUTURE).

ultra, *adj.* immoderate, drastic, radical (EXTREMENESS).

umbrella, *n.* parasol, bumbershoot (*jocose*), sunshade (PROTECTION, DARKNESS).

umpire, *n.* arbitrator, arbiter, referee (JUDGE).

unable, *adj.* powerless, helpless, incapable (DISABLEMENT); clumsy, incompetent, inadequate (CLUMSINESS).

unaccented, *adj.* light, unstressed, atonic (WEAKNESS).

unacceptable, *adj.* objectionable, unappealing, repugnant (UNPLEASANTNESS).

unaccommodating, *adj.* unobliging, disobliging, uncheerful (UNWILLINGNESS).

unaccompanied, *adj.* alone, unattended, single (UNITY, SECLUSION).

unaccountable, *adj.* mysterious, unexplainable, inexplicable (MYSTERY).

unaccustomed, *adj.* unwonted, uncustomary, uncommon (UNUSUALNESS); unacquainted, unseasoned (INEXPERIENCE).

unacquainted, *adj.* ignorant, unknowing, unaware (IGNORANCE); unaccustomed, strange (INEXPERIENCE).

unadorned, *adj.* plain, unornate, restrained (SIMPLICITY, SEVERITY); bald, bare, blunt (SIMPLICITY).

unadulterated, *adj.* pure, unalloyed, undebased (SIMPLICITY, PURIFICATION).

unaffected, *adj.* natural, artless, ingenuous (NATURALNESS); sincere, genuine (REALITY); untouched, unruffled, unimpressed (INSENSITIVITY).

unaffectionate, *adj.* cold, unresponsive, uncordial (INSENSITIVITY).

unafraid, *adj.* unalarmed, unapprehensive, undaunted (COURAGE).

unaided, *adj.* alone, unassisted, singlehanded (SECLUSION).

unalarmed, *adj.* nonchalant, insouciant, unperturbed (UNANXIETY, COURAGE).

unalloyed, *adj.* unadulterated, uncontaminated, undebased (PURIFICATION).

unalterable, *adj.* irreversible, unmodifiable, fated (UNIFORMITY).

unanimity, *n.* unison, common consent, consensus (ASSENT, CO-OPERATION).

unanimous, *adj.* agreeing, consentient, like-minded, of the same mind, harmonious, concordant, in accord (ASSENT, UNITY).

unanimously, *adv.* by common consent, to a man, as one man (ASSENT).

unanticipated, *adj.* surprising, unexpected, sudden, abrupt (SURPRISE).

UNANXIETY—*N.* unanxiety, unconcern, unconcernment, insouciance, nonchalance, ease, security, calm, undisturbance, unapprehension.

V. relieve anxiety, relieve the mind of, relieve, ease, calm, soothe, untrouble, comfort, console, put at rest, still the fears, unruffle, tranquilize.

Adj. unanxious, carefree, at ease, easy, secure, unworried, untroubled, undisturbed, unconcerned, unapprehensive, unalarmed, nonchalant, insouciant, undistressed, unperturbed.

calm, cool, unagitated, philosophical, phlegmatic, serene, stoical, unruffled.

See also CALMNESS, RELIEF. *Antonyms*—See FEAR, NERVOUSNESS, PRESSURE.

unappeased, *adj.* unsatisfied, unassuaged, uncontented (DISSATISFACTION).

unappetizing, *adj.* distasteful, uninviting, unpalatable (UNSAVORINESS).

unappreciative, *adj.* ungrateful, thankless (INGRATITUDE).

unapproachable, *adj.* inaccessible, remote (HOSTILITY); standoffish, aloof (SECLUSION).

unashamed, *adj.* impenitent, uncontrite (IMPENITENCE).

unasked, *adj.* unbidden, voluntary (WILLINGNESS).

unassuming, *adj.* modest, diffident, retiring (MODESTY); plain, simple, unpretentious (HUMILITY, MODESTY).

unassured, *adj.* insecure, unconfident, diffident (UNCERTAINTY).

unattached, *adj.* distinct, unconnected, separate (DISJUNCTION); fancy-free, uncommitted, footloose (FREEDOM).

unattainable, *adj.* insurmountable, insuperable, inaccessible (IMPOSSIBILITY).

unattractive, *adj.* uninviting, unappealing (UNPLEASANTNESS); unesthetic, plain, homely (DEFORMITY).

unauthorized, *adj.* unlawful, wrongful, illegitimate (ILLEGALITY); unsanctioned, unwarranted, unjustified (IMPROPERNESS).

unavailing, *adj.* fruitless, futile, bootless (FAILURE, USELESSNESS).

unavoidable, *adj.* ineludible, inevitable, ineluctable (CERTAINTY).

unaware, *adj.* unconscious, unmindful, unheeding (INATTENTION); ignorant, unknowing, unacquainted (IGNORANCE).

unawares, *adv.* by surprise (SURPRISE).

unbalanced, *adj.* top-heavy, lopsided, irregular (INEQUALITY); unhinged, unsettled (INSANITY).

unbearable, *adj.* intolerable, insufferable, insupportable (PAIN).

unbeatable, *adj.* undefeatable, indomitable, invincible (SUCCESS).

unbeaten, *adj.* undefeated, prize-winning, champion (SUCCESS).

unbecoming, *adj.* unbeseeming, unfitting (IMPROPERNESS); unhandsome, unlovely (DEFORMITY).

unbelievable, *adj.* incredible, implausible (UNBELIEVINGNESS).

unbeliever, *n.* skeptic, freethinker, agnostic (IRRELIGION, HETERODOXY); disbeliever, scoffer, doubting Thomas (UNBELIEVINGNESS).

UNBELIEVINGNESS—*N.* unbelievingness, unbelieving, unbelief, nonbelief, incredulity, skepticism, suspicion, Pyrrhonism, quizzicality, cynicism.

distrust, misgiving, mistrust, misdoubt, misdoubts, apprehension.

disbelief, nihilism, rejection, agnosticism, heterodoxy, unorthodoxy, heresy; disillusionment, disillusion, disenchantment.

doubt, dubiety, dubitation, dubiosity, query, question.

disbeliever, scoffer, doubting Thomas, cynic, skeptic, Pyrrhonian, nullifidian, unbeliever, nonbeliever, agnostic, nihilist, unorthodox, heretic, infidel.

V. disbelieve, discredit, reject, scoff at, scout, discount; doubt, misdoubt, suspect, wonder at (or about), distrust, mistrust, skepticize; challenge, query, question, oppugn, impugn, impeach.

discredit, explode, put under suspicion, compromise; disillusion, disillude, disenchant, disabuse.

Adj. unbelieving, incredulous, skeptical, scoffing, Pyrrhonic, suspicious, quizzical, umbrageous, wary, cynical, distrustful, mistrustful, apprehensive, disbelieving, nullifidian, nihilistic, agnostic, heterodox, unorthodox, heretical.

unbelievable, incredible, questionable, suspect, suspicious, far-fetched, fishy (*colloq.*), dubious, doubtful, implausible.

untrustworthy, fly-by-night, shifty, slippery, treacherous, unauthentic, undependable, unreliable.

Adv., phrases. incredulously, etc. (see *Adjectives*); askance, with a

grain of salt, *cum grano salis* (L.).
See also HETERODOXY, IRRELIGION,
UNCERTAINTY. *Antonyms*—See BE-
LIEF, CERTAINTY, DEPENDABILITY, RE-
LIGION.

unbend, *v.* relax, thaw (FREEDOM).
unbending, *adj.* unrelenting, relentless, unyielding (STUBBORN-
NESS, HARDNESS).
unbiased, *adj.* fair, unprejudiced,
objective (IMPARTIALITY).
unbind, *v.* unchain, unfetter, unleash (FREEDOM).
unblemished, *adj.* faultless, flawless, immaculate, pure (PERFEC-
TION).
unblock, *v.* unclog, uncork, unplug (FREEDOM).
unblushing, *adj.* immodest, obscene, shameful (IMMODESTY).
unbolt, *v.* unfasten, unlatch, unlock (OPENING).
unborn, *adj.* uncreated, unconceived, unproduced (NONEXIST-
ENCE).
unbounded, *adj.* immense, infinite,
measureless (ENDLESSNESS); unrestrained, uncircumscribed, unconfined (FREEDOM).
unbridled, *adj.* intemperate, excessive, immoderate (INTEMPER-
ANCE); unrestrained, uncontrolled, uncurbed (FREEDOM).
unbroken, *adj.* whole, intact, indiscrete (COMPLETENESS); endless, perpetual, uninterrupted
(CONTINUATION).
unburdened, *adj.* unencumbered,
unhampered, unhindered (FREE-
DOM).
uncalled-for, *adj.* unnecessary,
needless, gratuitous (UNNECES-
SITY).
uncanny, *adj.* weird, unearthly,
ghastly (SUPERNATURALISM, FEAR,
UNUSUALNESS); mysterious, secret (MYSTERY).
uncared for, *adj.* neglected, unheeded, disregarded (NEGLECT).
unceasing, *adj.* endless, undying,
unending (ENDLESSNESS).
unceremonious, *adj.* informal,
casual (FREEDOM); brusque,
abrupt, curt (BLUNTNESS).

UNCERTAINTY—*N.* uncertainty,
incertitude, indecision, irresolution, vacillation, oscillation, indetermination, shilly-shally; doubt,
question, dubiety, misgiving,
qualm, scruple, hesitation, suspense; insecurity, diffidence, unas-
surance, unconfidence, unself-con-
fidence, unself-assurance; dilemma,
quandary, puzzle.

doubtfulness, disputability, du-
bitability, contestability, question-
ability, controvertibility, impon-
derability, incalculability, indeterminacy, pendency, contingency,
touch-and-go, undependability, unreliability.
vagueness, haze, fog, obscurity,
confusion, ambiguity; pig in a
poke, shot in the dark.
V. feel uncertain, doubt, shilly-
shally, back and fill, vacillate,
wobble, sway, oscillate, waver;
hesitate, scruple, have misgivings,
falter, flounder; wander aimlessly,
not know which way to turn, float
in a sea of doubt, lose one's head.
depend, pend, hang in suspense,
hang, hang (*or* tremble) in the
balance, rest, hinge, be undecided,
be contingent, be dependent.
make uncertain, perplex, puzzle,
confuse, bewilder, muddle, rattle
(*colloq.*), daze, nonplus, throw off
the scent; embarrass, abash, castrate (*psychoanal.*).
Adj. uncertain, unsure, doubtful,
dubious, indefinite, unpositive; insecure, unconfident, unassured, un-
self-confident, unself-assured, diffident, unpoised.
irresolute, undecided, indecisive,
vacillating, vacillatory, willy-nilly,
wobbly, shilly-shally, shilly-shally-
ing, halting, wavering.
vague, indefinite, undefined,
confused, confusing, obscure, indefinable, undefinable, ambiguous.
[*of things or events*] doubtful,
dubious, dubitable, indecisive,
problematical, unassured, pending, pendent, undecided; disputable, questionable, moot, controvertible, controversial, contestable,
debatable; indefinite, indeterminate, undependable, unsure, unreliable, unauthentic, incalculable,
imponderable, indeterminable;
chancy (*colloq.*), precarious,
rocky, contingent, suspenseful,
touch-and-go, changeful, undetermined, in question.
Adv., phrases. uncertainly, etc.
(see *Adj.*); adrift, at sea, at a loss,
at one's wit's end, in a dilemma.
See also AMBIGUITY, CHANCE,
CONFUSION, INACTION, IRREGULARITY,
UNBELIEVINGNESS, UNCLEARNESS. *Antonyms*—See CERTAINTY, CLARITY,
DEPENDABILITY, LIABILITY, LIKELI-
HOOD, STABILITY, UNIFORMITY.

unchain, *v.* unfetter, unhobble, unleash (FREEDOM).
unchangeable, *adj.* immutable, inflexible, invariable (UNIFORMITY).
unchanging, *adj.* fixed, rigid,
static (UNIFORMITY).

uncivil, adj. ill-bred, mannerless, rude (DISCOURTESY).

uncivilized, adj. barbaric, primitive, savage (BARBARIANISM).

unclad, adj. undressed, unclothed, stripped (UNDRESS).

UNCLEANNESS—N. **uncleanness,** impurity, bedragglement; filth, dirt, feculence, dregs, grime, mess, muck, ordure, pollution, slime, smut, soil, dust, soot, squalor.

pus, matter, purulence, suppuration; pus sore, abscess, ulcer, phagedena, fester, canker, chancre; empyema, ulceration, maturation, pyosis.

refuse, waste, waste matter, garbage, slops, swill, sullage, spilth, offal, offscouring, offscum, scouring, dross, draft, dregs, decrement, outscouring, recrement, scoria, slag, scum, sewage, sordes, sordor; cinders, ashes.

rubbish, rubbishry, trash, rummage, rubble, junk (colloq.), riffraff, rejectamenta, shoddy, sweepings, debris; jetsam, jettison, flotsam; scrap, wastements, discard, castoff, reject; slough, exuviae (zool.).

[repositories of filth or refuse] cesspool, sump, septic tank, drain, sewer, cloaca, cloaca maxima; sink, basin, toilet; dunghill, dungheap, dump; dustbin, ash bin, ashpit, ash can, ash barrel, garbage pail, garbage can.

[unclean place] pigsty, sty, lair, den, Augean stable, sink of corruption, cesspool, cesspit; slum, slums, rookery.

dirty language, filth, foulness, ordure, obscenity.

stain, blemish, blot, blotch, blur, discoloration, maculation, macula, macule, smear, smudge, smutch, speck, speckle, splotch, spot, sully, tarnish.

contamination (with germs), infection, insanitation, septicity.

V. **dirty,** soil, besoil, foul, befoul, pollute, defile, sully, filthify, slop, smear, besmear, besmirch, smirch, bespatter, spatter, smudge, besmudge, blur, splash, splatter, plash, bemire, mire, bedraggle, draggle, drabble, bedrabble, grime, begrime, mess, slime, smutch, besmutch, smut, besmut, soot; contaminate, infect.

stain, blot, blotch, blur, discolor, maculate, splotch, spot, sully, tarnish.

become pussy, canker, fester, ulcer, ulcerate, matter, maturate, suppurate.

Adj. **unclean,** impure, dirty, filthy, uncleanly, mucky, nasty, ordurous, feculent, dreggy, foul, grubby, messy, Augean, grimy, collied, smutty, piggish, polluted, slimy, sooty; squalid, sordid, slum, slummy; slovenly, sloppy, dingy, frowzy, mangy, sluttish; soiled, stained, smutched, bedraggled, draggled, draggly, drabbled.

insanitary, unsanitary, contaminated, infected, unhygienic, unsterile, unsterilized.

contaminative, infective, infectious, pythogenic.

stained, blemished, blotted, blotched, blotchy, blurred, discolored, maculate, smeared, smeary, smudged, smudgy, specked, speckled, splotched, splotchy, spotted, spotty, sullied, tarnished.

[using dirty language] **foulmouthed,** filthy, foul, obscene, ordurous, scatological.

pussy, purulent, pyic, abscessed, cankerous, cankered, chancrous, empyemic, festered, phagedenous, ulcerous, ulcerated.

See also IMPURITY, MALEDICTION, OBSCENITY, UNPLEASANTNESS, UNTIDINESS. Antonyms—See CLEANNESS, NEATNESS, PURIFICATION.

UNCLEARNESS—N. **unclearness,** obscurity, obscuration, obscurantism, obfuscation, equivocation, ambiguity.

vagueness, nebulosity, indefiniteness, etc. (see Adjectives).

V. **obscure,** darken, dim, fog, befog, cloud, mist, muddy, roil, blur, confuse, obfuscate, becloud, blot out, enshroud, hide, shadow, shroud; equivocate.

Adj. **unclear,** cloudy, clouded, blurred, blurry, roily, muddy, turbid, hazy, murky, fuzzy, foggy, misty; ambiguous, equivocal, confused, sketchy, unexplicit.

obscure, dark, indistinct, dim, inconspicuous, faint, tenuous, subtle, shadowy, unevident, unobvious.

vague, nebulous, nubilous, casual, transcendental, impalpable, imprecise.

indefinite, undecided, intangible, indeterminate, aoristic, ill-defined.

See also AMBIGUITY, CONFUSION, DARKNESS, MISINTERPRETATION, MYSTERY. Antonyms—See CLARITY, TRANSPARENCY.

---

unclog, v. unblock, uncork, unplug (FREEDOM).

unclothed, adj. unclad, disrobed, stripped (UNDRESS).

unclouded, *adj.* cloudless, azure, serene (CLARITY).

uncluttered, *adj.* orderly, ship-shape, trim (NEATNESS).

uncoil, *v.* unreel, untangle, untwine (STRAIGHTNESS, UNFOLDMENT).

uncolored, *adj.* colorless, hueless (COLORLESSNESS).

uncombed, *adj.* disheveled, tousled, unkempt (UNTIDINESS).

uncomfortable, *adj.* discomfited, ill-at-ease, self-conscious (EMBARRASSMENT); suffering, in pain, sore (PAIN); embarrassing, awkward (EMBARRASSMENT); cheerless, jarring (UNPLEASANTNESS).

uncommon, *adj.* extraordinary, rare, scarce (UNUSUALNESS, FEWNESS).

uncommonly, *adv.* seldom, scarcely ever (FEWNESS).

uncommunicative, *adj.* taciturn, close-mouthed, tight-lipped (SILENCE).

uncompleted, *adj.* incomplete, imperfect, unfinished, fragmentary (INCOMPLETENESS).

uncomplicated, *adj.* simple, uncomplex, uninvolved, uncompounded (SIMPLICITY, EASE).

uncompromising, *adj.* immovable, inflexible, intransigent (STUBBORNNESS).

unconcern, *n.* insouciance, nonchalance (UNANXIETY); tepidity, disinterest (INDIFFERENCE); oblivion, disregard (INATTENTION).

unconcerned, *adj.* unworried, untroubled, undisturbed (UNANXIETY); disinterested, perfunctory, lackadaisical (INDIFFERENCE).

unconditional, *adj.* unqualified, unmitigated, absolute (COMPLETENESS).

unconquerable, *adj.* undefeatable, indomitable, invincible (SUCCESS, STRENGTH).

unconscionable, *adj.* conscience-less, unscrupulous, wanton (DISHONESTY, FREEDOM).

unconscious, *adj.* unmindful, unheeding, unwitting (INATTENTION, IGNORANCE); inadvertent, involuntary (PURPOSELESSNESS); insensible, senseless (INSENSIBILITY); subconscious, subliminal (INTELLECT).

uncontrollable, *adj.* headstrong, ungovernable, unmanageable (VIOLENCE, UNRULINESS).

uncontrolled, *adj.* unrestrained, unchecked, wild (FREEDOM).

unconventional, *adj.* eccentric, irregular, uncommon (UNUSUALNESS); unceremonious, informal (FREEDOM).

unconvincing, *adj.* unpersuasive,

inconclusive, flimsy (DISSUASION).

uncooked, *adj.* underdone, rare, raw (COOKERY).

uncouth, *adj.* unrefined, coarse, crude (VULGARITY); heavyhanded, left-handed (CLUMSINESS); uncourteous, ungentlemanly (DISCOURTESY).

uncover, *v.* uncloak, uncurtain, unshroud (DISCLOSURE); bare, expose, strip (UNDRESS); unearth, dig up, strike (DISCOVERY).

unctuous, *adj.* suave, bland, oily (SUAVITY, OIL).

uncultivated, *adj.* unrefined, unpolished, inelegant (VULGARITY); rough, rude (ROUGHNESS); uneducated, unlearned (IGNORANCE).

uncultured, *adj.* unrefined, unpolished (VULGARITY, ROUGHNESS); uneducated, unlearned (IGNORANCE).

undamaged, *adj.* unbruised, unhurt, uninjured (HEALTH).

undaunted, *adj.* unafraid, unalarmed, unfaltering (COURAGE).

undeceive, *v.* set right, set straight, correct (INFORMATION).

undecided, *adj.* indefinite, pending, doubtful (UNCERTAINTY); wavering, undetermined (IRRESOLUTION).

undecorated, *adj.* unfrilled, untrimmed (SIMPLICITY).

undefeatable, *adj.* indomitable, unconquerable, invincible (SUCCESS).

undefeated, *adj.* unvanquished, prize-winning, champion (SUCCESS).

undemonstrative, *adj.* inhibited, reserved, unaffectionate (INSENSITIVITY).

undeniable, *adj.* irrefutable, unanswerable, indisputable (PROOF, TRUTH).

undependable, *adj.* untrustworthy, treacherous, unreliable (UNBELIEVINGNESS); indefinite, indeterminate, unsure (UNCERTAINTY).

under, *adj.* bottom, lower, nether (BASE, LOWNESS).

under, *adv.* beneath, underneath, below (LOWNESS).

underbrush, *n.* undergrowth, underwood, brush (PLANT LIFE).

underclothes, *n.* underthings, lingerie (UNDERWEAR).

undercover, *adj.* sub rosa (L.), secret, stealthy (CONCEALMENT).

underestimate, *v.* undervalue, underrate, underappraise (DETRACTION).

underfed, *adj.* starved, emaciated, undernourished (INSUFFICIENCY); drawn, haggard, pinched (THINNESS).

undergarments, n. underclothes, underthings, lingerie (UNDER-WEAR).

undergo, v. experience, encounter, sustain (OCCURRENCE, EXPERIENCE); endure, tolerate, bear (SUPPORT, INEXCITABILITY).

undergraduate, n. student, collegian academic (LEARNING).

underground, adj. hush-hush, private, secret (CONCEALMENT); resistant, resistive, unbowed (OPPOSITION); sunken, subterranean (DEPTH).

undergrowth, n. underwood, brush, underbrush (PLANT LIFE).

underhand, adj. secret, sub rosa (L.), stealthy (CONCEALMENT); shabby, unjust (UNFAIRNESS).

underhung, adj. lantern-jawed, underjawed, undershot (HEAD).

underline, v. emphasize, stress, underscore (IMPORTANCE).

underling, n. assistant, subordinate (WORK).

undermine, v. corrode, erode, sap (DESTRUCTION); burrow, tunnel (DIGGING).

underneath, adv. under, beneath, below (LOWNESS).

undernourished, adj. starved, emaciated, underfed (INSUFFICIENCY).

underpants, n. briefs, panties, step-ins (UNDERWEAR).

underpass, n. subway, shaft, tunnel (PASSAGE).

underrate, v. underestimate, undervalue, underappraise (DETRACTION).

underscore, v. emphasize, stress, accentuate, underline (IMPORTANCE).

undersell, v. discount, sell at a discount (SALE).

understandable, adj. intelligible, apprehensible (UNDERSTANDING, CLARITY); readable, clear, legible (READING).

UNDERSTANDING—N. understanding, ken, grasp, grip, mastery; discernment, percipience, perception, perceptivity, perspicacity, penetration, acumen, judgment, wit; impression, notion, conception, inkling; sympathy, catholicity.

comprehension, prehension, apprehension, apperception, assimilation, construction, interpretation, realization, subreption.

insight, intuition, divination; theosophy.

concept, percept; inference, illation, conclusion.

V. understand, grasp, comprehend, apprehend, seize, catch on to, get, follow, fathom, figure out, make out, make head or tail of, assimilate, take in, digest, apperceive, perceive, discern, realize, penetrate, conceive of; gather, conclude, judge, infer, intuit, divine; construe, decipher; master.

Adj. understanding, perceptive, percipient, penetrating, apperceptive, discerning, acute, quick, quick on the uptake (colloq.), perspicacious; sympathetic, catholic.

intelligible, understandable, apprehensible, clear, comprehensible, conceivable, fathomable, lucent, lucid, luculent, luminous, obvious, pellucid, perspicuous, plain, rational, simple, self-explanatory, unmistakable, transparent, exoteric, decipherable.

See also CLARITY, IDEA, INTELLECT, INTELLIGENCE, INTUITION, JUDGMENT, KNOWLEDGE, OPINION, WISDOM. Antonyms—See AMBIGUITY, DIFFICULTY, MISINTERPRETATION, STUPIDITY, UNCLEARNESS.

understood, adj. implied, implicit, inferential (MEANING, SILENCE, INDIRECTNESS).

understudy, n. pinch-hitter (colloq.), stand-in (SUBSTITUTION).

undertaker, n. funeral director, mortician (BURIAL).

UNDERTAKING—N. undertaking, enterprise, endeavor, venture, attempt, task, essay, move, adventure, business, work, project, affair, pursuit.

V. undertake, engage in, embark in, launch (or plunge) into, volunteer, devote oneself to, take up, take on, accept, take in hand, tackle (colloq.), set about; go about, launch forth, attempt, turn one's hand to, enter upon, assume, begin, institute; put one's shoulder to the wheel.

Adj. enterprising, adventurous, venturesome, energetic, aggressive, active, industrious, resourceful.

See also ACTION, ATTEMPT, BEGINNING, BUSINESS. Antonyms—See AVOIDANCE, INACTION.

undertow, n. undercurrent, underset, eddy (RIVER).

undervalue, v. underestimate, underrate, underappraise (DETRACTION).

underwater, adj. subaqueous, submarine (WATER).

UNDERWEAR—N. underwear, balbriggans, union suit, flannels, smallclothes, underclothes, underclothing, underdress, undergarments, underthings, undies (*colloq.*), woollies (*colloq.*); lingerie, unmentionables (*jocose*), bloomers, trouserettes, drawers, shorts, underdrawers, underpants, briefs, pantalettes, panties, step-ins, combination, teddies; brassiere, bra (*colloq.*), bandeau; underbodice, camisole, slip, chemise, shift, shimmy (*colloq.*); shirt, undershirt, undervest, underwaist, waist; corset, corselet, foundation, girdle, stays, corset cover; petticoat, underskirt, crinoline, bustle; corsetry.

See also CLOTHING, TROUSERS, UNDRESS. *Antonyms*—See COAT.

underweight, *adj.* skinny, bony, angular, rawboned, scrawny (THINNESS).

underworld, *n.* Hades, Hell, Tophet (HELL); criminal class, felonry, criminals (ILLEGALITY).

undeserving, *adj.* unworthy, unmerited (WORTHLESSNESS).

undesirable, *adj.* unpleasant, objectionable, unappealing (UNPLEASANTNESS).

undeveloped, *adj.* abortive, embryonic, latent (IMMATURITY).

undignified, *adj.* unseemly, indecorous, unbecoming (VULGARITY).

undiluted, *adj.* neat, unmixed, plain (STRAIGHTNESS).

undisclosed, *adj.* undeclared, untold, hushed-up (CONCEALMENT).

undiscriminating, *adj.* indiscriminate, promiscuous, imperceptive (INDISCRIMINATION).

undisguised, *adj.* unvarnished, uncolored, undistorted (TRUTH); obvious, manifest, apparent (CLARITY).

undistinguished, *adj.* undistinctive, nondescript, mediocre (COMMONNESS).

undisturbed, *adj.* unworried, untroubled, unconcerned (UNANXIETY); calm, smooth, peaceful (CALMNESS).

undivided, *adj.* whole, entire, uncut (COMPLETENESS); united, joined, combined (UNITY).

undo, *v.* free, release, unfasten (LOOSENESS, DISJUNCTION); smash, spoil (DESTRUCTION).

UNDRESS—N. undress, dishabille or deshabille (*F.*), divestment, divesture, negligee.

nakedness, nudity, denudation, exposure, bare skin, the buff (*colloq.*), nudism, strip tease, striptease act.

undresser, disrober, stripper (*slang*), stripteaser, ecdysiast, stripteuse (*neologism*), exotic dancer, burlesque dancer; nude, nudist.

V. undress, disarray, dismantle, divest, unattire, unclothe, ungarment, unlace, untruss; undress oneself, disrobe, peel (*slang*), strip, unbusk, unrobe.

doff, remove, get out of, slip out of, divest oneself of, draw off, take off, get off, pull off, slip off.

bare, denude, denudate, expose, uncover, strip, undrape, lay bare.

molt *or* moult, shed, cast, slough, exuviate.

peel, pare, decorticate, excoriate, skin, scalp, flay, bark, husk, hull, pod, shell, scale, desquamate, exfoliate.

Adj. undressed, unclothed, unclad, disrobed, stripped, unrobed, unpanoplied, uncaparisoned, unappareled, unarrayed, unattired, ungarbed, ungarmented, undraped, untoileted.

naked, nude, bare, bare-skinned, stripped to the buff (*colloq.*), au naturel (*F.*), denuded, denudate, exposed, in the altogether (buff *or* raw), in one's birthday suit (*slang*), stark, stripped, uncovered, undraped, stark-naked, in a state of nature, *in puris naturalibus* (*L.*).

barefoot, barefooted, unshod, discalceate *or* discalced.

unkempt, disheveled, disarrayed; in dishabille, in negligee.

See also HAIRLESSNESS, UNDERWEAR. *Antonyms*—See CLOTHING, COVERING, PROTECTION.

undue, *adj.* excessive, exceeding, unreasonable (EXTREMENESS); unseasonable, untimely, unsuitable (IMPROPERNESS).

undulate, *v.* wave, swell, billow (ROLL); oscillate, pendulate, swing (OSCILLATION).

undulating, *adj.* wavy, undulant, ripply (WINDING).

undying, *adj.* unceasing, never-ending; immortal, eternal (ENDLESSNESS).

unearth, *v.* dig up, uncover, strike (DISCOVERY).

unearthly, *adj.* weird, eerie, uncanny (SUPERNATURALISM, UNUSUALNESS, FEAR); hyperphysical, superphysical, extramundane (SPIRITUALITY).

uneasy, *adj.* upset, apprehensive,

disturbed; restless, fitful (NERV-OUSNESS); uncomfortable, ill-at-ease, self-conscious (EMBARRASS-MENT).

uneducated, *adj.* unlearned, illiterate (IGNORANCE).

unemotional, *adj.* phlegmatic, passionless, marble (INSENSITIVITY).

unemployed, *adj.* leisured, unoccupied, laid off (REST, INACTION); unused, unapplied (DISUSE).

unemployment, *n.* ease, leisure, retirement (INACTION).

unending, *adj.* endless, unceasing, undying (ENDLESSNESS).

unendurable, *adj.* unbearable, insufferable, intolerable (PAIN).

unequal, *adj.* disparate, unequivalent, uneven (INEQUALITY).

unequaled, *adj.* unparalleled, unmatched, peerless (PERFECTION, INEQUALITY).

unerring, *adj.* infallible, inerrable, perfect (RIGHT).

unethical, *adj.* unprincipled, unscrupulous (IMMORALITY).

uneven, *adj.* bumpy, unlevel, humpy (ROUGHNESS, IRREGULARITY); unequal, disparate, unequivalent (INEQUALITY); fitful, spasmodic, changeable (IRREGULARITY).

uneventful, *adj.* inconclusive, indecisive, unfateful (UNIMPORTANCE).

unexcelled, *adj.* top-notch, unsurpassed (SUPERIORITY).

unexcited, *adj.* calm, unagitated, unruffled (CALMNESS).

unexciting, *adj.* unimaginative, unoriginal, banal (COMMONNESS).

unexpected, *adj.* sudden, abrupt, unanticipated (SURPRISE, SUDDENNESS).

unexplainable, *adj.* mysterious, unaccountable, inexplicable (MYSTERY).

unexpressed, *adj.* implied, implicit, tacit (MEANING, INDIRECTNESS).

unfailing, *adj.* unremitting, diligent, constant (CONTINUATION); inexhaustible, unflagging (ENERGY); sure, inevitable (CERTAINTY).

UNFAIRNESS—N. unfairness, discrimination, favoritism, inequity, iniquity, injustice, wrong.

V. **be unfair,** discriminate against, wrong.

Adj. **unfair,** discriminatory, excessive, inequitable, iniquitous, shabby, underhand, underhanded, unjust, unreasonable, unrighteous, unsporting, unsportsmanlike, unsportsmanly, wrongful; arbitrary, despotic, tyrannical.

See also IMPROPERNESS, PREJUDICE, SIDE. *Antonyms*—See IMPARTIALITY, REASONABLENESS.

---

unfaithful, *adj.* false, perfidious, untrue (DISLOYALTY); adulterous (SEX).

unfamiliar, *adj.* unaccustomed, strange, alien (UNUSUALNESS); little-known, obscure, recondite (KNOWLEDGE); incognizant, unacquainted, unversed (IGNORANCE, INEXPERIENCE).

unfashionable, *adj.* outmoded, passé (*F.*), obsolete (OLDNESS).

unfasten, *v.* free, release (FREEDOM, LOOSENESS); unbolt, unlatch, unlock (OPENING); untie, unravel, undo (DISJUNCTION).

unfavorable, *adj.* disadvantageous, inauspicious, unpropitious (MISFORTUNE, HOPELESSNESS, OPPOSITION).

unfeeling, *adj.* cold, callous, stony-hearted (INSENSITIVITY, CRUELTY).

unfetter, *v.* unchain, unhobble, unleash (FREEDOM).

unfinished, *adj.* uncompleted, imperfect, fragmentary (INCOMPLETENESS); immature, unripe, unseasoned (IMMATURITY).

unfit, *adj.* incompetent, inadequate, unqualified (CLUMSINESS).

unfitting, *adj.* improper, unbecoming (IMPROPERNESS).

unflagging, *adj.* unfailing, unrelenting, unremitting (CONTINUATION); energetic, inexhaustible (ENERGY).

UNFOLDMENT—N. unfoldment, expansion, growth, development, maturation, elaboration, evolvement, evolution, inversion.

V. **unfold,** unroll, unwind, uncoil, untwist, unfurl, untwine, unravel, disentangle, open, expand, evolve, develop, ripen, mature; spread out, reveal, disclose, display, make known.

Adj. **evolutional,** evolutionary, evolutive, ontogenic *or* ontogenetic (*biol.*), phylogenic *or* phylogenetic (*biol.*).

See also DISCLOSURE, DISPLAY, INCREASE, MATURITY, ROLL, ROTATION, SPREAD, STRAIGHTNESS. *Antonyms*—See DECREASE, FOLD.

---

unforeseen, *adj.* uncalculated, unexpected, unanticipated (SURPRISE).

unforgettable, *adj.* memorable, rememberable, indelible (MEMORY).

unforgivable, *adj.* inexcusable, indefensible, unpardonable (IM-PROPERNESS).

unforgiving, *adj.* vindictive, grudgeful, vengeful (RETALIA-TION).

unfortunate, *adj.* regrettable, deplorable, lamentable (REGRET); untoward, unpropitious (OPPOSI-TION); adverse, catastrophic, tragic (MISFORTUNE).

unfounded, *adj.* fallacious, illogical, ungrounded (MISTAKE).

unfriendly, *adj.* cool, inimical, antagonistic (HOSTILITY, OPPOSI-TION).

unfruitful, *adj.* sterile, barren (UN-PRODUCTIVENESS); fruitless, unprofitable, futile (USELESSNESS, INEFFECTIVENESS).

unfurl, *v.* unroll, unwind (UNFOLD-MENT); show, spread out (DIS-PLAY).

ungainly, *adj.* ungraceful, gawky, ponderous (CLUMSINESS).

ungentlemanly, *adj.* discourteous, uncouth (DISCOURTESY).

ungodly, *adj.* godless, unholy, irreverent (IRRELIGION, WICKED-NESS); horrid, nasty (INFERIOR-ITY).

ungovernable, *adj.* uncontrollable, headstrong, refractory (VIOLENCE, UNRULINESS).

ungraceful, *adj.* ungainly, gawky, graceless (CLUMSINESS); shapeless, unsymmetrical (DEFORMITY).

ungracious, *adj.* uncivil, unhandsome (DISCOURTESY); inaffable, unamiable (UNPLEASANTNESS).

ungrammatical, *adj.* solecistic, catachrestic, illiterate (MISUSE OF WORDS).

ungrateful, *adj.* thankless, unappreciative (INGRATITUDE).

unhampered, *adj.* unencumbered, unhindered, unimpeded (FREE-DOM).

unhandy, *adj.* awkward, heavy-handed, left-handed (CLUMSI-NESS); bulky, unmanageable (DIFFICULTY).

unhappiness, *n.* melancholy, depression (SADNESS).

unhappy, *adj.* mirthless, blissless, cheerless (SADNESS); unlucky, unfortunate, black (MISFORTUNE); infelicitous, malapropos (IM-PROPERNESS).

unharmed, *adj.* intact, scatheless, scot-free (HEALTH).

unhealthy, *adj.* ill, sick, diseased (DISEASE); harmful, noxious, virulent (HARM).

unheard-of, *adj.* exceptional, unique, unprecedented (UNUSUAL-NESS); unlikely, rare, inconceivable (IMPROBABILITY).

unhinge, *v.* unnerve, uncalm, unsettle (NERVOUSNESS); madden, craze, unbalance (INSANITY).

unholy, *adj.* unhallowed, unsanctified, unblessed (IMPURITY); ungodly, godless, irreverent (IR-RELIGION, WICKEDNESS).

unhurried, *adj.* leisurely, slow, easy (REST).

unhurt, *adj.* unbruised, undamaged, uninjured (HEALTH).

uniform, *n.* livery, habit, robe (CLOTHING).

UNIFORMITY—*N.* uniformity, homogeneity, consistency, constancy, stability, invariability, even tenor; sameness, monotony, treadmill.

periodicity, rhythm, isochronism, alternation, cycle, routine.

regularity, harmony, symmetry, correspondence.

V. **make uniform,** level, smooth, even, grade; stabilize, steady, regularize, routinize, isochronize; symmetrize.

Adj. **uniform,** homogeneous, of a piece, consistent, constant, even, invariable, level, monolithic, stable, steady, undiversified, unchanging, unvarying.

periodic, regular, routine, seasonal, cyclic, isochronous, alternating.

same, colorless, drab, humdrum, monotonous, tiresome, toneless, treadmill, unrelieved.

unchangeable, immutable, inflexible, invariable, irreversible, unalterable, unmodifiable, fated, fateful; incorrigible, irreformable.

regular, symmetrical, well-balanced, well-proportioned, corresponding, harmonious; punctual, regular as clockwork; customary, typical, normal, habitual, usual; methodical, systematic, orderly, steady, reliable.

unchanging, changeless, fixed, rigid, static, steadfast, stable, undeviating, unvarying, unwavering, ossified.

Adv. **uniformly,** etc. (see *Adjectives*); in a rut.

always, ever, evermore, perpetually, forever, eternally, everlastingly, invariably.

See also AGREEMENT, BOREDOM, CONFORMITY, DEPENDABILITY, HABIT, NATURALNESS, RHYTHM, RULE, SEASONS, SHAPE, SIMILARITY, STABILITY. *Antonyms*—See CHANCE, CHANGE, CHANGEABLENESS, DIFFERENCE, MIXTURE.

unify, *v.* unite, fuse, blend (UNITY).

unimaginable, *adj.* inconceivable,

implausible, doubtful (IMPROBABILITY).

unimaginative, *adj.* unoriginal, banal, trite (COMMONNESS).

unimpeachable, *adj.* unquestionable, undeniable, irrefutable (TRUTH).

UNIMPORTANCE—*N.* **unimportance,** immateriality, inconsequentiality, inconsequence, insignificance, nullity, triviality, fribble, frivolity, trivialism, immaterialness, etc. (see *Adjectives*); matter of indifference; nothing, small (or trifling) matter, joke, jest, folderol, mere nothing; flash in the pan, tempest in a teapot, storm in a teacup.

trifle, bagatelle, fico, fribble, frivolity, froth, immateriality, insignificancy, insignificant, nihility, nonentity, nonessential, nullity, picayune, trivialism, triviality; minutiae, trivia, trifles; fig, jot, iota, pin, button, halfpenny, rap, farthing, brass farthing, cent, red cent, damn, tinker's damn (or dam), continental.

[*unimportant person*] **nonentity,** nobody, cipher, insignificancy, nullity, picayune, snip, squirt, whiffet, whippersnapper; small fry (*pl.*).

reduction of importance: anticlimax, bathos.

less important thing: collateral, accessory, subordinate, subsidiary.

V. **be unimportant,** not matter, matter (or signify) little.

[*treat as unimportant*] **ignore,** pooh-pooh, slight, sneeze at, trifle with, make light of, de-emphasize, pay no attention to; subordinate.

Adj. **unimportant,** immaterial, inconsequential, insignificant, null, trivial, frivolous, fribble, frothy, lowly, minute, niggling, nonessential, paltry, peddling, pettifogging, petty, picayune, picayunish, piddling, puny, scrubby, slight, trifling, trumpery, unessential, unnotable, vain, yeasty; noncritical, nonstrategic.

uneventful, inconclusive, indecisive, unfateful, unmomentous.

less important, accessory, accessorial, minor, secondary, subaltern, subordinate, subsidiary, collateral.

falling off in importance, anticlimactic, bathetic.

See also FRIVOLITY, INATTENTION, INDIFFERENCE, UNNECESSITY. *Antonyms*—IMPORTANCE, SOBRIETY.

uninformed, *adj.* unaware, uninitiated (IGNORANCE).

uninhabited, *adj.* unoccupied, empty, vacant (SECLUSION, ABSENCE).

uninhibited, *adj.* expansive, unreserved (FREEDOM).

uninjured, *adj.* unbruised, undamaged, unhurt (HEALTH).

unintelligent, *adj.* moronic, imbecilic, insipient (STUPIDITY).

unintelligible, *adj.* unfathomable, fathomless, incomprehensible (MYSTERY).

unintentional, *n.* accidental, inadvertent, unpremeditated (PURPOSELESSNESS).

uninterested, *adj.* bored, blasé (*F.*), weary (BOREDOM).

uninteresting, *adj.* tedious, monotonous, dull (BOREDOM).

uninterrupted, *adj.* endless, perpetual, unbroken (CONTINUATION).

union, *n.* association, alliance, league (COMBINATION); labor union, trade union (LABOR RELATIONS); fusion, junction (UNITY); blend, compound (MIXTURE, COMBINATION); matrimony, wedlock, alliance (MARRIAGE); coitus, sexual union (SEX).

unique, *adj.* only, exclusive, sole (UNITY); novel, original, atypical (DIFFERENCE); exceptional, *sui generis* (*L.*), unprecedented (UNUSUALNESS); unequaled, unmatched, peerless (INEQUALITY).

unison, *n.* consonance, harmony (AGREEMENT).

unit, *n.* one, ace, integer (UNITY); ingredient, feature; wing, detachment (PART).

unite, *v.* join, conjoin, combine, connect, couple (UNITY, JUNCTION, MIXTURE).

UNITY—*N.* **unity,** oneness, identity; coherence, interconnection, integrality, totality; unification, amalgamation, synthesis, coalescence, fusion, union, junction, coadunation.

harmony, consistency, uniformity; concord, agreement, unanimity.

unit, one, ace, monad (*tech.*), integer, individual, entity, single, singleton.

individuality, individualism, particularity, personality.

V. **unite,** join, combine, connect, couple; merge, fuse, coalesce, blend, cement, weld; centralize, consolidate, solidify, coadunate, unify, concentrate; harmonize, reconcile; federate, ally, confederate, league, associate, band together, conjoin, amalgamate, incorporate.

individualize, individuate, particularize, singularize, specify.

Adj. **one,** sole, alone, lone, single, unaccompanied, odd, individual, unitary, monadic, monolithic, singular.

individual, exclusive, particular, peculiar, personal, respective, each, single, singular, sole, special, specific, unique.

only, exclusive, single, sole, unique.

united, etc. (see *Verbs*); undivided, unitary, indiscrete, homogeneous, coadunate, conjoint, conjunctive, related, allied, cognate, connate; confederate, confederated, leagued, federal, amalgamated, consolidated, unified, corporate, incorporated, unitable, unifiable.

harmonious, concordant, in accord, agreeing, unanimous, friendly, fraternal.

Adv., phrases. **singly,** individually, severally, particularly, respectively, apart, independently, separately, one by one, one at a time; by itself, per se (*L.*).

solely, simply, barely, merely, purely, scarcely, alone, exclusively, only.

unitedly, jointly, conjointly, concordantly, harmoniously, as one man, in unison, together.

See also AGREEMENT, ASSEMBLAGE, COMBINATION, COMPLETENESS, FASTENING, FRIENDLINESS, HARMONY, JUNCTION, MIXTURE, SECLUSION, UNIFORMITY. *Antonyms*—See DISJUNCTION, TWO.

---

universal, *adj.* diffuse, general, catholic (PRESENCE); cosmic, cosmogonal (WORLD).

universe, *n.* creation, nature, cosmos (WORLD).

university, *n.* seminary, college, institute (SCHOOL).

unjust, *adj.* unfair, inequitable, shabby (UNFAIRNESS, IMPROPERNESS); prejudiced, influenced (SIDE).

unjustifiable, *adj.* unreasonable, unwarrantable, inexcusable (IMPROPERNESS).

unkempt, *adj.* uncombed, disheveled, disarrayed (UNTIDINESS, UNDRESS); neglected, dilapidated (NEGLECT).

unkind, *adj.* brutal, inhuman, heartless (CRUELTY, INSENSITIVITY).

unknown, *adj.* unapprehended, unexplained, unascertained (IGNORANCE).

unlatch, *v.* unbolt, unfasten, unlock (OPENING).

unlawful, *adj.* illegal, illicit, lawless (ILLEGALITY).

unleash, *v.* unchain, unfetter, unhobble (FREEDOM).

unlighted, *adj.* dark, sunless, unilluminated (DARKNESS).

unlike, *adj.* dissimilar, unrelated, mismatched (DIFFERENCE).

unlikely, *adj.* improbable, rare, inconceivable (IMPROBABILITY).

unlimited, *adj.* unrestrained, unrestricted, unqualified (FREEDOM).

unload, *v.* disencumber, rid, discharge (FREEDOM, ABSENCE).

unlock, *v.* unbolt, unfasten, unlatch (OPENING).

unloose, *v.* free, let go, release, set loose (FREEDOM).

unlucky, *adj.* unfortunate, black, hapless (MISFORTUNE).

unman, *v.* unnerve, devitalize, effeminize (DISABLEMENT, WEAKNESS); awe, appall (FEAR).

unmanageable, *adj.* disorderly, uncontrollable, ungovernable (UNRULINESS).

unmanly, *adj.* effeminate, womanish, sissy (FEMALE, WEAKNESS).

unmannerly, *adj.* discourteous, impolite (DISCOURTESY).

UNMARRIED STATE—*N.* **unmarried state,** celibacy, singleness, single blessedness; bachelorhood, bachelorship; misogyny, misogamy; maidenhood, old-maidism, spinsterhood, virginity; widowerhood, widowership; widowhood.

unmarried man, bachelor, confirmed bachelor, celibate, celibatory, celibatarian, *célibataire* (*F.*); celibatist; misogamist, misogynist; monk, priest; widower.

unmarried woman, miss, maid, maiden, virgin, celibate, bachelor girl, spinster, spinstress, old maid, feme sole (*law*), single woman; nun, sister, *religieuse* (*F.*), vestal, vestal virgin; widow.

Adj. **unmarried,** unwed, unwedded, single, celibate, spouseless; maiden, virgin, virginal, husbandless; wifeless; widowered, widowed.

bachelorly, bachelorlike, celibatarian, maidenly, old-maidish, old-maidenish, spinsterous, spinsterish, spinsterlike, spinsterly; celibatic, virginal.

See also CELIBACY, DIVORCE. *Antonyms*—See BETROTHAL, MARRIAGE.

---

unmask, *v.* report, betray, expose (INFORMATION).

unmatched, *adj.* unequaled, peerless, unique (INEQUALITY).

unmerciful, *adj.* cruel, merciless, pitiless, unrelenting (CRUELTY, INSENSITIVITY).

unmindful, *adj.* oblivious, unaware, unconscious (INATTENTION).

unmistakable, *adj.* plain, unambiguous, unequivocal (UNDERSTANDING, CLARITY).

unmistaken, *adj.* correct, proper (RIGHT).

unmixed, *adj.* straight, undiluted, neat (STRAIGHTNESS); unadulterated, pure, unalloyed (SIMPLICITY, PURIFICATION).

unmoved, *adj.* unstirred, untouched, unshocked (INSENSITIVITY).

unmusical, *adj.* unmelodious, unharmonious, uneuphonious (HARSH SOUND).

UNNATURALNESS—*N.* **unnaturalness,** artificiality; grotesquery, monstrosity.

abnormality, aberrance, aberration, perversion.

monster, monstrosity, grotesque, gargoyle, freak.

affectation, apery, artificiality, constraint, contrivance, preciosity, sophistication, theatricality, theatricalism.

V. **affect,** act a part, give oneself airs, put on airs, simper, mince, attitudinize, pose, posture, prim, pretend, make believe; overact, overdo.

Adj. **unnatural,** artificial, factitious, synthetic; grotesque, monstrous, freakish; abnormal, aberrant, perverted.

affected, mannered, chichi, airy, apish, artful, artificial, constrained, contrived, factitious, forced, histrionic, labored, mincing, minikin, *postiche* (F.), precious, sophisticated, stagy, studied, theatrical.

See also OSTENTATION, PRETENSE, UNUSUALNESS. *Antonyms*—See MODESTY, NATURALNESS, RESTRAINT, RULE, SIMPLICITY.

UNNECESSITY—*N.* **unnecessity,** superfluity; obviation.

V. **be unnecessary,** etc. (see *Adjectives*); not need, not require, not demand; make unnecessary, obviate.

Adj. **unnecessary,** unneeded, needless, gratuitous, uncalled for, dispensable, expendable, inessential, superfluous, excess, extrinsic, nonstrategic, uncritical, unessential, unneedful, unrequired, undemanded, unincumbent on.

See also EXCESS, UNIMPORTANCE. *Antonyms*—See IMPORTANCE, NECESSITY.

unneeded, *adj.* needless, gratuitous, uncalled for (UNNECESSITY).

unnerve, *v.* unhinge, uncalm, unsettle (NERVOUSNESS).

unobliging, *adj.* disobliging, unaccommodating (UNWILLINGNESS).

unoccupied, *adj.* uninhabited, untenanted, vacant (SECLUSION, ABSENCE); leisured, idle, free (INACTION, REST).

unpack, *v.* unload, unlade, discharge (FREEDOM).

unpaid, *adj.* owing, due, unsettled (DEBT).

unpalatable, *adj.* distasteful, unappetizing, uninviting (UNSAVORINESS, UNPLEASANTNESS).

unparalleled, *adj.* unrivaled, matchless, peerless (INEQUALITY).

unpardonable, *adj.* inexcusable, indefensible, unforgivable (IMPROPERNESS, ACCUSATION).

unplanned, *adj.* extemporized, unprepared, unpremeditated (NONPREPARATION).

UNPLEASANTNESS—*N.* **unpleasantness,** ill nature, uncongeniality, unamiability, inurbanity, inaffability, repellence; disagreeableness, etc. (see *Adjectives*).

offensiveness, blatancy, loudness, etc. (see *Adjectives*).

[*offensive language*] **vulgarity,** obscenity, scurrility, ordure, blasphemy, billingsgate, coprophemia, coprolalia.

displeasure, distaste, repulsion, revolt, repugnance, offense, outrage, objection.

V. **displease,** disoblige, repel, revolt.

offend, outrage, shock, jar, scandalize, affront.

be displeased by, object to, protest, revolt against (from, *or* at); scowl, frown, pout, gloom.

Adj. **unpleasant,** unpleasing, unlikable, disagreeable, displeasing, distasteful, unsavory, unpalatable, objectionable, unacceptable, undesirable, uninviting, unappealing, unattractive; uncheerful, cheerless, uncomfortable, jarring, unagreeable; unlovely, unpresentable, uncomely; ungrateful, unthankful.

unamiable, disobliging, ill-natured, uncongenial, inaffable, inurbane, uncompanionable, uncomplaisant, unconversable, ungracious.

offensive, offending, outrageous, nasty, scandalous, shocking, ugly, fulsome.

repugnant, obnoxious, repulsive, noisome, revolting, repellent, odious, painful.

[*offensive in language*] **blatant,** loudmouthed; vulgar, scurrilous, blasphemous, ordurous, obscene, foulmouthed, thersitical.

offended, displeased, aggrieved, affronted, shocked, outraged, scandalized.

See also DISGUST, DISSATISFACTION, OBSCENITY, OFFENSE, PAIN, UNCLEANNESS, UNSAVORINESS, VULGARITY. *Antonyms*—See ATTRACTION, PLEASANTNESS, SUAVITY, SWEETNESS.

---

unplug, *v.* unseal, unstop, unstopper (OPENING).

unpolished, *adj.* crude, unrefined, uncultivated (LOWNESS, VULGARITY); unvarnished, unwaxed, unglazed (DULLNESS).

unpolluted, *adj.* pure, uncontaminated (PURIFICATION).

unpopular, *adj.* disesteemed, disfavored, disliked (HATRED).

unprecedented, *adj.* singular, exceptional, unique (SURPRISE, UNUSUALNESS).

unprejudiced, *adj.* impartial, unbiased, objective (IMPARTIALITY).

unpremeditated, *adj.* unintended, unmeant, unplanned (PURPOSELESSNESS, NONPREPARATION).

unprepared, *adj.* extemporized, unplanned; unequipped, unprovided (NONPREPARATION).

unpretended, *adj.* sincere, candid, genuine (REALITY).

unpretentious, *adj.* humble, modest, unassuming (LOWNESS, MODESTY, HUMILITY); simple, unelaborate (SIMPLICITY).

unprincipled, *adj.* unethical, unscrupulous, wanton (DISHONESTY, IMMORALITY, FREEDOM).

UNPRODUCTIVENESS—*N.* **unproductiveness,** unproductivity, otiosity, infertility, sterility, infecundity, impotence.

menopause, climacteric, climacterical.

V. **be unproductive,** hang fire, flash in the pan, come to nothing.

render unproductive, sterilize, incapacitate, castrate.

Adj. **unproductive,** unyielding, infertile, unfertile, arid, sterile, barren, otiose, jejune, impotent, unprolific, infecund; issueless, childless; unfruitful, fruitless, useless, fallow; unprofitable, unsuccessful, vain, void, ineffectual; submarginal.

See also FAILURE, INEFFECTIVENESS, USELESSNESS. *Antonyms*—See BIRTH, FERTILITY, PREGNANCY, PRODUCTION, POWER, RESULT, SUCCESS.

unprofessional, *adj.* nonprofessional, nonexpert, amateur (LAITY).

unprofitable, *adj.* unproductive, ill-spent, fruitless (UNPRODUCTIVENESS, USELESSNESS).

unpronounced, *adj.* mute, unsounded (SILENCE).

unpropitious, *adj.* inauspicious, inopportune (UNTIMELINESS); untoward, ill-disposed (OPPOSITION); unpromising, unfavorable (HOPELESSNESS).

unprotected, *adj.* vulnerable, exposed, unguarded (WEAKNESS).

unproved, *adj.* unauthenticated, unsupported (DISPROOF).

unpublicized, *adj.* hushed up, unreported (CONCEALMENT).

unqualified, *adj.* unconditional, absolute, flat, positive (COMPLETENESS, FLATNESS); incompetent, inadequate, unfit (CLUMSINESS); unrestrained, unrestricted, unlimited (FREEDOM).

unquestionable, *adj.* unimpeachable, undeniable, irrefutable (TRUTH, CERTAINTY).

unravel, *v.* unwind, untwist, disentangle (STRAIGHTNESS, UNFOLDMENT); unfasten, untie, undo (DISJUNCTION); fathom, plumb (DISCOVERY).

unreadable, *adj.* illegible, undecipherable, unclear (READING).

UNREALITY—*N.* **unreality,** delusion, hallucination, illusion, optical illusion, mirage; nonentity, shadow, dream, vision, phantom, phantasm, phantasmagory, apparition, ghost, specter, chimera, mare's nest, will-o'-the-wisp, *ignis fatuus* (L.), wisp; fairyland, wonderland.

fiction, fable, myth, legend, fancy, fantasy, invention, fabrication, figment.

V. **imagine,** fantasy, phantasy, fancy; pretend, make up, fabricate, invent.

Adj. **unreal,** imagined, delusive, delusory, illusive, illusory, illusional, hallucinatory; nonexistent, aeriform, notional, insubstantial, shadowy, phantom, phantasmal, phantasmagorical, quasi (*used as a prefix*).

imaginary, legendary, mythical, mythological, fabled, fabulous, fictional, fictitious, fictive, figmental, fabricated, invented; fanciful, romantic, aerial, chimerical, fantastic, visionary.

See also FALSEHOOD, FALSENESS, GHOST, IMAGINATION, MYTHICAL BEINGS, NONEXISTENCE, PRETENSE, SUPERNATURAL BEINGS, SUPERNATURAL-

ISM. *Antonyms*—See EXISTENCE, REALITY.

UNREASONABLENESS—N. unreasonableness, exorbitance, extravagance, illegitimacy, invalidity, irrationality, nonsensicality, unjustifiability, implausibility.

illogicality, illogic, nonsense, *non sequitur* (L.).

Adj. unreasonable, absonant, excessive, exorbitant, extravagant, illegitimate, immoderate, inordinate, intemperate, invalid, irrational, nonsensical, senseless, unconscionable, unjustifiable, unsound.

illogical, farfetched, inconsequential; disconnected, disjointed, incoherent, irrational, skimble-skamble.

See also ABSURDITY, EXCESS, EXTREMENESS, INTEMPERANCE, SOPHISTRY, UNFAIRNESS. *Antonyms*—See MODERATENESS, REASONABLENESS.

unreel, *v.* unfold, uncoil, untwine (STRAIGHTNESS).

unrefined, *adj.* uncultivated, unpolished, inelegant (VULGARITY, LOWNESS); ill-bred, ill-mannered, boorish (DISCOURTESY); crude, raw, coarse (NATURALNESS, ROUGHNESS).

unrelated, *adj.* independent, nongermane, irrelevant (IRRELATION); dissimilar, unlike, mismatched (DIFFERENCE).

unrelenting, *adj.* unbending, rigid, stiff (STUBBORNNESS); persistent, tenacious (CONTINUATION).

unreliable, *adj.* untrustworthy, treacherous, undependable (UNBELIEVINGNESS); indefinite, indeterminate, unsure (UNCERTAINTY); changeful, capricious (APOSTASY).

unrelieved, *adj.* monotonous, tiresome, treadmill (UNIFORMITY); plain, unornamented, unadorned (SIMPLICITY, SEVERITY).

unrequited, *adj.* unreturned, unrewarded, thankless (INGRATITUDE).

unresisting, *adj.* passive, resistless (SUBMISSION).

unresponsive, *adj.* cold, unaffectionate, reserved (INSENSITIVITY).

unrest, *n.* defiance, sedition (DISOBEDIENCE); restlessness, dysphoria (*med.*), uneasiness (NERVOUSNESS).

unrestrained, *adj.* unlimited, uncurbed, extravagant (FREEDOM, INTEMPERANCE).

unrestricted, *adj.* unrestrained, unlimited, unqualified (FREEDOM).

unrewarded, *adj.* unrequited, unreturned, thankless (INGRATITUDE).

unripe, *adj.* callow, unfinished, green (IMMATURITY).

unrivaled, *adj.* unparalleled, matchless, peerless (INEQUALITY).

unroll, *v.* unfold, unwind, unfurl (UNFOLDMENT); show, spread out, unveil (DISPLAY).

unruffled, *adj.* phlegmatic, cool, unexcited (UNANXIETY, CALMNESS).

UNRULINESS—N. unruliness, disorder, commotion, riot, tumult, turbulence, uproar.

Adj. unruly, disorderly, unmanageable, uncontrollable, fractious, intractable, refractory, troublesome, ungovernable, untoward, willful, headstrong, temperamental, froward, incorrigible, irrepressible, restive, resistive, rowdy, rowdyish, stormy, tough; tumultuous, turbulent, wild, uproarious, tempestuous, rambunctious, obstreperous; ugly.

See also COMMOTION, DISOBEDIENCE, ROUGHNESS, VIOLENCE. *Antonyms*—See CALMNESS, OBEDIENCE.

unsafe, *adj.* hazardous, perilous, insecure (DANGER).

unsaid, *adj.* implicit, unuttered, unexpressed (SILENCE).

unsatisfactory, *adj.* unsatisfying, thin, unsuitable (DISSATISFACTION).

unsatisfied, *adj.* unappeased, unassuaged, uncontented (DISSATISFACTION).

UNSAVORINESS—N. unsavoriness, insipidity, vapidity; distastefulness, unpalatability, rancidity.

V. be unsavory, be unpalatable; sicken, disgust, nauseate, pall, cloy, turn the stomach.

Adj. unsavory, tasteless, flat, flavorless, insipid, jejune, namby-pamby, sapidless, savorless, unflavored, vapid, zestless, stale, weak, watery.

distasteful, unappetizing, uninviting, ill-flavored, unpalatable, rancid, rank, bitter, acrid, acid, sharp, vinegary, sour, tart.

See also DISGUST, DISREPUTE, OFFENSE, SHARPNESS, UNPLEASANTNESS. *Antonyms*—See PLEASANTNESS, SWEETNESS, TASTE.

unsavory, *adj.* tasteless, flat (UNSAVORINESS); distasteful, objectionable (UNPLEASANTNESS).

unscrupulous, *adj.* conscienceless,

unprincipled, wanton (DISHONESTY, IMMORALITY, IMPENITENCE, FREEDOM).

unseal, *v.* unplug, unstop, unstopper (OPENING).

unseasonable, *adj.* ill-timed, badly timed, mistimed (UNTIMELINESS).

unseasoned, *adj.* unfinished, immature, green (IMMATURITY); inexperienced, unpracticed, undisciplined (INEXPERIENCE).

unseemly, *adj.* inappropriate, wrong, incorrect (IMPROPERNESS); unbeautiful, unpersonable, uncomely (DEFORMITY).

unseen, *adj.* invisible, out of sight (INVISIBILITY).

UNSELFISHNESS—N. unselfishness, altruism, disinterest; selflessness, etc. (see *Adjectives*).

generosity, free hand, charity, philanthropy, magnanimity, hospitality, beneficence, bigness, etc. (see *Adjectives*); benefaction.

lavishness, munificence, prodigality, profusion, bounty, abundance, extravagance, overgenerosity.

self-denial, self-begrudgment, self-renunciation, self-abnegation, self-sacrifice, self-immolation, martyrdom; abstinence, abstention, asceticism, Spartanism, austerity, temperance, mortification, self-mortification, celibacy.

ascetic, Spartan, celibate, abstainer.

altruist, philanthropist, humanitarian, good Samaritan, benefactor.

V. **be generous,** spend freely, spare no expense, open one's purse strings, give with both hands; lavish, shower upon; keep open house.

Adj. **unselfish,** selfless, uncalculating, ungrudging, altruistic, disinterested, self-forgetful; extroverted, extrospective.

generous, big, bighearted, free, freehanded, giving, liberal, openhanded, openhearted, unstinting, unsparing, ungrudging, handsome, princely; charitable, philanthropic, magnanimous, hospitable, beneficent.

lavish, munificent, prodigal, profuse, sumptuous, bountiful, bounteous, abundant, extravagant, overgenerous.

self-denying, self-begrudging, self-renouncing, self-abnegating, self-sacrificing; abstemious, abstinent, abstentious, austere, ascetic, temperate, celibate.

See also ASCETICISM, AVOIDANCE, CELIBACY, CHARITY, CONTROL, GIVING,

NOBILITY. *Antonyms*—See SELFISHNESS, STINGINESS.

unsettle, *v.* unnerve, unhinge, uncalm (NERVOUSNESS); dement, unbalance, derange (INSANITY); discompose, disturb, upset (UNTIDINESS).

unsex, *v.* unman, emasculate, castrate (CELIBACY).

unshaved, *adj.* bearded, whiskered, stubbled (HAIR).

unsheathe, *v.* whip out, withdraw, pull out (EXTRACTION).

unshined, *adj.* dull, lusterless, unbuffed, unburnished (DULLNESS).

unshown, *adj.* undisclosed, undisplayed, unrevealed (CONCEALMENT).

unsightly, *adj.* ugly, hideous, repulsive (DEFORMITY).

unskillful, *adj.* awkward, inadept, inept (CLUMSINESS).

unsociable, *adj.* withdrawn, nongregarious, retiring (SECLUSION, HOSTILITY).

unsophisticated, *adj.* naïve, unworldly, ingenuous (INNOCENCE, INEXPERIENCE, NATURALNESS).

unsound, *adj.* irrational, nonsensical, senseless (UNREASONABLENESS); groundless, incorrect, specious (SOPHISTRY); defective, impaired (IMPERFECTION); unbalanced, insane (INSANITY); unhealthy, diseased, ill (DISEASE).

unsparing, *adj.* ungrudging, handsome, princely (UNSELFISHNESS).

unspeakable, *adj.* unutterable, indescribable, ineffable (SILENCE).

unspoken, *adj.* tacit, wordless, implied (SILENCE).

unstable, *adj.* inconstant, fickle, changeable (WEAKNESS); shaky, rickety (UNSTEADINESS).

unstained, *adj.* spotless, stainless, unblemished (CLEANNESS, PURIFICATION).

UNSTEADINESS—N. unsteadiness, instability, titubation, reel, stagger, falter, sway, totter, yaw, careen, lurch, waver.

V. **rock,** roll, shake, stagger, reel, totter, teeter, falter, tip, wobble, sway; yaw, bicker, careen, lurch, pitch, waver.

Adj. **unsteady,** unstable, unfirm, shaky, joggly (*colloq.*), ramshackle, loose-jointed, rickety, rocky, wavery, wobbly, wayward, tottery; groggy, reeling, swaying, staggering; top-heavy, tipsy, tippy, ticklish; sandy, shifting.

See also AGITATION, CAPRICE, CHANGEABLENESS, IRRESOLUTION, OSCILLATION, ROLL, SHAKE, WALKING.

Antonyms—See MOTIONLESSNESS, REST, STABILITY.

---

unstressed, *adj.* light, unaccented, atonic (WEAKNESS).

unsuccessful, *adj.* unprosperous, unthriving, unfruitful (FAILURE); unprofitable, vain, ineffectual (UNPRODUCTIVENESS).

unsuitable, *adj.* improper, ill-befitting, inapplicable (IMPROPERNESS); unsatisfying, unsatisfactory (DISSATISFACTION).

unsupported, *adj.* unproved, unattested, unauthenticated (DISPROOF).

unsure, *adj.* doubtful, dubious, unreliable (UNCERTAINTY).

unsuspecting, *adj.* gullible, trusting, unsuspicious (BELIEF).

unsymmetrical, *adj.* shapeless, ungraceful, asymmetrical (DEFORMITY).

unsympathetic, *adj.* uncompassionate, uncommiserating, aloof (INSENSITIVITY).

unsystematic, *adj.* unmethodical, unorderly, disorganized (UNTIDINESS, IRREGULARITY).

untactful, *adj.* unthinking, gauche (*F.*), undiplomatic (INATTENTION, CLUMSINESS).

untangle, *v.* solve, unweave, unsnarl (ANSWER); untwist, disentangle, unravel (STRAIGHTNESS).

untenable, *adj.* vulnerable, indefensible, unprotected (WEAKNESS); unsound, specious, groundless (SOPHISTRY).

untested, *adj.* untried, unproved (TEST).

unthankful, *adj.* ungrateful, unappreciative (INGRATITUDE).

unthinkable, *adj.* absurd, unimaginable, inconceivable (IMPOSSIBILITY).

unthinking, *adj.* thoughtless, unreasoning, brutish (STUPIDITY); unintended, unmeant (PURPOSELESSNESS); careless, inadvertent, napping (CARELESSNESS); indelicate, tactless (INATTENTION, CLUMSINESS).

UNTIDINESS—*N.* untidiness, bedragglement, clutterment, dishevelment.

disarrangement, disorder, disarray, discomposure, disorganization, dislocation, derangement; jumble, litter, clutter; confusion, mix-up, muddle, mess, muss, snarl, tangle, rummage; chaos, bedlam.

[*untidy person*] sloven, slob; ragamuffin, tatterdemalion, scarecrow.

[*untidy woman*] slattern, dowd,

dowdy, slut, drabbletail, draggletail, frump, drab, trollop.

V. [*make untidy*] **dishevel,** rumple, tousle, bedraggle.

disarrange, disorder, disarray, disjoint, dislocate, disorganize; derange, discompose, disturb; unsettle, upset; clutter, litter, jumble, mess up, muss up (*colloq.*); confuse, mix up, muddle, snarl up, tangle, entangle, ruffle.

Adj. **untidy,** disheveled, rumpled, tousled, tously, unkempt, bedraggled, dowdy, dowdyish, poky, tacky, sloppy, slovenly, sluttish, slatternly, draggly, draggletailed, drabbletailed, frowzy, messy, blowzy, disarrayed, grubby, slipshod; untrimmed.

cluttered, littered, jumbled, disarranged, disarrayed, disordered, discomposed, dislocated, disjointed, unordered, unorderly, disorderly; confused, disorganized, mixed up, muddled, snarled, tangled, topsy-turvy; messy, messed up, unsettled, upset.

unsystematic, unmethodical, unorderly, disorderly, disorganized.

shabby, mangy, poky, ratty (*colloq.*), seedy, tacky (*colloq.*), threadbare.

uncombed, bedraggled, blowzy, disheveled, rumpled, tousled, unkempt.

See also CONFUSION, UNCLEANNESS. *Antonyms*—See COMPLETENESS, METHOD.

---

untie, *v.* unfasten, disentangle, undo (DISJUNCTION); free, release (FREEDOM).

until, *prep.* till, to, up to, as far as (TIME).

UNTIMELINESS—*N.* untimeliness, inopportunity, inexpedience, prematurity.

Adj. **untimely,** inauspicious, inopportune, inexpedient, unpropitious, unseasonable, ill-timed, badly timed, mistimed; premature, previous (*colloq.*); immature.

See also IMMATURITY, INEXPEDIENCE, MISTIMING. *Antonyms*—See EXPEDIENCE, TIMELINESS.

---

untiring, *adj.* tireless, indefatigable, unwearied (ENERGY).

untold, *adj.* countless, incalculable, innumerable (MULTITUDE); hushed-up, smothered, suppressed (CONCEALMENT).

untouched, *adj.* fresh, untried, unbeaten (NEWNESS); unmoved, unstirred, unaffected (INSENSI-

TIVITY); unharmed, unscathed, intact (HEALTH).

untoward, *adj.* unfortunate, ill-disposed, unpropitious (OPPOSITION).

untrained, *adj.* callow, green, raw (INEXPERIENCE).

untrimmed, *adj.* unfrilled, undecorated (SIMPLICITY).

untroubled, *adj.* unworried, undisturbed, unconcerned (UNANXIETY).

untrue, *adj.* disloyal, faithless, perfidious (DISLOYALTY); apocryphal, false, fictitious (FALSENESS).

untrustworthy, *adj.* fly-by-night, shifty, slippery (UNBELIEVINGNESS).

untruth, *n.* fib, prevarication, lie (FALSEHOOD); falsity, fraudulence (FALSENESS).

untruthful, *adj.* lying, dishonest, mendacious (FALSEHOOD).

untwist, *v.* unwind, unravel, uncoil (STRAIGHTNESS, UNFOLDMENT).

unusable, *adj.* impracticable, impractical, inapplicable (USELESSNESS).

unused, *adj.* idle, fallow, vacant (DISUSE).

UNUSUALNESS—N. unusualness, scarcity, unfamiliarity, transcendentalism, grotesquery, exoticism, novelty, incongruity; oddity, peculiarity, singularity, curiosity, eccentricity, whimsicality.

abnormality, abnormity, aberrancy, atypicality, exceptionality, irregularity, phenomenality, preternaturalism, unconventionality; subnormality.

(an) oddity, curiosity, singularity, incongruity, drollery, grotesquerie, grotesque, kickshaw; vagary, whimsy, crank, quip.

odd person, eccentric, customer, character (*colloq.*), caution (*colloq.*), punchinello, bird (*slang*).

(a) peculiarity, eccentricity, quirk, kink, foible.

rarity, prodigy, miracle, wonderwork, marvel, phenomenon, portent, *rara avis* (L.), treasure; monotype.

exception, anomaly, irregularity, abnormality, abnormity, aberration, freak, heteroclite.

freak of nature, abnormity, *lusus naturae* (L.), monster, monstrosity, sport, teratism, rogue (*bot.*).

medical science of freaks: teratology.

Adj. **unusual,** uncommon, rare, scarce, infrequent; unwonted, uncustomary, unaccustomed; re-

markable, outstanding, phenomenal, marvelous, prodigious, portentous; out-of-the-ordinary, off the beaten path, extraordinary, out-of-the-way, exceptional, *sui generis* (L.), unique, unprecedented, unheard-of, thundering; novel, fresh, off-beat (*colloq.*).

strange, bizarre, alien, unfamiliar, fantastic, transcendental, baroque, grotesque, outré (F.), peregrine, uncouth, exotic, incongruous.

odd, peculiar, funny, singular, curious, queer, quizzical, quaint, erratic, outlandish, eccentric, droll, whimsical.

weird, eerie *or* eery, supernatural, unearthly, uncanny.

abnormal, aberrant, anomalous, atypical, eccentric, exceptional, freakish *or* freaky, heteroclite, inordinate, irregular, miraculous, monstrous, phenomenal, preternatural, prodigious, supernatural, uncommon, unconventional, unnatural, untypical; subnormal, substandard; supernormal, supranormal.

freakish, freaky, monstrous, teratoid.

See also FEWNESS, IRREGULARITY, NEWNESS, SUPERNATURALISM, SURPRISE, UNNATURALNESS. *Antonyms*—See COMMONNESS, HABIT, NATURALNESS, RULE.

---

unutterable, *adj.* inexpressible, ineffable, unspeakable (SILENCE).

unvarying, *adj.* unchanging, invariable, monotonous (UNIFORMITY).

unveil, *v.* unroll, show, expose (DISPLAY, DISCLOSURE).

unwary, *adj.* reckless, heedless, incautious (CARELESSNESS).

unwavering, *adj.* intense, single-minded, steady (PURPOSE).

unwell, *adj.* sick, ill, disordered, upset (DISEASE).

unwholesome, *adj.* noxious, pestiferous, pestilent (HARM, IMMORALITY); unhealthful, unhygienic, insalubrious (DISEASE).

unwieldy, *adj.* bulky, awkward, cumbersome (CLUMSINESS, SIZE, WEIGHT).

UNWILLINGNESS—N. unwillingness, indisposition, disinclination, aversion, recalcitrance, noncompliance, obstinacy.

reluctance, scruples, hesitation, hesitancy, qualm, shrinking, recoil.

V. **be unwilling,** hesitate, scruple, stickle, demur, stick at, recoil, shrink, refuse, shy at, fight shy of, duck (*slang*); grudge, begrudge.

Adj. **unwilling**, disinclined, uninclined, indisposed, averse, reluctant, loath, recalcitrant, opposed, backward, slow; grudging, begrudging; involuntary, forced, compelled; hesitant, hesitative; unobliging, disobliging, unaccommodating, uncheerful.

Adv., phrases. **unwillingly**, grudgingly, with ill grace; against one's will, *nolens volens* (L.), against the grain, in spite of oneself, with a heavy heart, under compulsion, under protest, involuntarily.

See also DENIAL, OPPOSITION, SLOWNESS, STUBBORNNESS, UNCERTAINTY. *Antonyms*—See EAGERNESS, ENTHUSIASM, SERVICE, WILLINGNESS.

---

unwind, *v.* untwist, unravel, untangle (STRAIGHTNESS, UNFOLDMENT).

unwise, *adj.* inadvisable, ill-advised, silly, senseless (INEXPEDIENCE, FOLLY).

unwitting, *adj.* unintended, unmeant, unthinking, unconscious, unaware (PURPOSELESSNESS, IGNORANCE).

unworldly, *adj.* unsophisticated, innocent, naïve (INEXPERIENCE); spiritual, supersensible, supersensory (SPIRITUALITY).

unworried, *adj.* untroubled, undisturbed, unconcerned (UNANXIETY).

unworthy, *adj.* undeserving, unmerited (WORTHLESSNESS); swinish, wretched, vile (CONTEMPT); unseemly, unsuited, wrong (IMPROPERNESS).

unyielding, *adj.* adamant, inexorable, inflexible (STUBBORNNESS, HARDNESS).

up, *adv.* on high, aloft (HEIGHT, ASCENT).

up, *v.* raise, lift, boost (INCREASE).

upbringing, *n.* breeding, nurture, rearing (CHILD).

upend, *v.* overturn, upset, reverse (TURNING).

upgrade, *n.* acclivity, ascent, helicline (SLOPE).

upgrade, *v.* skip, advance, promote (RANK, ELEVATION).

upheaval, *n.* convulsion, disturbance (COMMOTION); tremor, temblor (EARTHQUAKE).

uphill, *adj.* ascending, rising, acclivous (SLOPE); difficult, hard, tough (DIFFICULTY).

uphold, *v.* sustain, hold up; countenance, endorse (SUPPORT).

upkeep, *n.* maintenance, sustenance (SUPPORT); cost, overhead, budget (EXPENDITURE).

upland, *n.* highland, downs, ridge (LAND).

uplift, *v.* upend, raise, erect (VERTICALITY, ELEVATION); glorify, inspire (ELEVATION).

upper, *adj.* higher, superior (HEIGHT).

upper class, *n.* upper crust, society, four hundred (SOCIAL CLASS).

upper-class, *adj.* aristocratic, patrician, well-born (SOCIAL CLASS).

upper hand, *n.* control, dominance, whip hand (INFLUENCE).

uppity (*colloq.*), *adj.* haughty, cavalier, supercilious (PRIDE).

upright, *adj.* cocked, erect, upstanding (POSTURE); perpendicular, sheer, steep (VERTICALITY); ethical, honorable, moral (RULE, HONESTY).

uproar, *n.* clamor, hubbub, racket (LOUDNESS, CONFUSION); riot, tumult, rumpus (UNRULINESS, COMMOTION).

uproot, *v.* eradicate, weed out, extirpate (ELIMINATION, EXTRACTION, REMOVAL).

upset, *adj.* uneasy, apprehensive, disturbed (NERVOUSNESS).

upset, *v.* perturb, bother, disquiet (NERVOUSNESS, AGITATION); discompose, disturb, unsettle (UNTIDINESS); upend, invert (TURNING); overthrow, overturn, topple (DEFEAT).

upshot, *n.* development, eventuality, conclusion (RESULT).

upside-down, *adj.* overturned, upended, topsy-turvy (TURNING).

upstanding, *adj.* upright, honorable (HONESTY); cocked, erect (POSTURE).

upstart, *n.* parvenu, *nouveau riche* (F.), vulgarian (SOCIAL CLASS, WEALTH).

upsweep, *n.* pompadour, updo (HAIR).

uptilted, *adj.* pug, retroussé (F.), snub (NOSE).

up-to-date, *adj.* modern, up-to-the-minute, neoteric (NEWNESS).

upturn, *v.* turn over, tip, capsize (TURNING).

upturned, *adj.* pug, retroussé (F.), snub (NOSE).

upward, *adv.* above, overhead (HEIGHT).

urban, *adj.* civic, municipal, metropolitan (CITY).

urbane, *adj.* smooth, bland, gracious (SUAVITY, PLEASANTNESS).

urchin, *n.* gamin, street Arab, gutternsipe (YOUTH).

urge, *n.* stimulus, impulse, itch (MOTIVATION, DESIRE, PROPULSION).

urgent, *adj.* pressing, insistent, exigent (IMPORTANCE, DEMAND, NECESSITY, ATTENTION).

URGING—*N.* urging, suasion, exhortation, preachment, admonishment, admonition; incitement, impulsion, precipitation, invitation, encouragement, connivance; prod, goad, spur.

V. urge, exhort, preach, preachify, admonish; press, spur, drive, prod, urge on, prevail upon, precipitate, goad, incite, impel, invite; encourage, countenance, abet, connive with.

Adj. urging, suasive, exhortative, hortative, hortatory, vehement, admonitory .

See also DEMAND, MOTIVATION, OFFER, PERSUASION, PRESSURE, PROPULSION. *Antonyms*—See DISSUASION.

---

urn, *n.* jar, jug, pitcher (CONTAINER).

USE—*N.* use, usage, utilization, employment, service, wear, adoption, application, exploitation, exertion, mobilization, investment, husbandry, practice, exercise.

popularity, prevalence, currency, vulgarity, heyday, reputability.

means, medium, agency, facilities, instrument, instrumentality, expedient, resource; makeshift, stopgap, shift, temporary expedient.

consumption, depletion, exhaustion, expenditure.

utility, function, service, purpose, help, aid, benefit, value, worth, profit, avail; asset, commodity.

usefulness, usability, employability, practicality, practicability, serviceability, exploitability; functionality, utilitarianism, applicability, adequacy, efficacy.

[*repeated practice*] usage, custom, habit, wont, familiarity, practice, mode, method, treatment, way; *modus operandi* (L.), procedure, ritual.

utilitarianism, Benthamism, pragmatism.

user, consumer, purchaser.

[*person used*] cat's-paw, creature, pawn, tool, puppet.

V. use, make use of, turn to use (*or* account), put to use, adopt, utilize, employ, apply, avail oneself of, take advantage of, capitalize on, consume, exploit, make capital of, profit by; put in action, put into operation, set in motion,

set to work, task, put to task; mobilize, bring into play, operate, ply, work, wield, handle, manipulate; exert, exercise, practice; resort to, have recourse to, recur to, take up, try; devote, dedicate, consecrate; invest, husband; overwork, overuse, tax, wear out; scrimp on, skimp on, use sparingly.

be of use, be useful, serve, do, answer the purpose, subserve, avail, boot, bestead, stand one in good stead; profit, bear fruit, help, aid, benefit, advantage; be in use, prevail, obtain.

bring back to use, restore, resurrect, revive; popularize, vulgarize.

treat, behave toward, deal with, handle, manage, act toward.

use up, consume, exhaust, deplete, sap, devour, wear out, spend, expend.

Adj. useful, serviceable, helpful, valuable, invaluable, beneficial, worthy, profitable, advantageous, favorable, good, commodious, convenient, suitable, suited; instrumental; practical, workaday, utile, applied, pragmatical, functional, utilitarian.

usable, practicable, utilizable, adaptable, applicable, employable, exploitable; available, handy, convenient, wieldy; consumable, exhaustible, expendable.

in use, current, popular, prevalent, prevailing, reputable, vulgar, obtaining, employed.

overused, overworked, worn, worn out, sear, shabby, threadbare, well-worn; hackneyed, stale, trite, moth-eaten.

See also ACTION, ADVANTAGE, AGENCY, AID, GOOD, INSTRUMENT, MATERIALITY, RESTORATION, SERVICE, TAKING, VALUE, VULGARITY, WORK. *Antonyms*—See DISUSE, MISUSE, USELESSNESS, WORTHLESSNESS.

---

used to, *adj.* habituated, addicted, accustomed (HABIT).

USELESSNESS—*N.* uselessness, inefficacy, futility; ineptitude, inadequacy, inefficiency, incompetence.

inutility, impracticability, impracticality, inapplicability, unavailability, unemployability.

rubbish, trash, junk (*colloq.*), debris, dross, rubbishry, rubble, scrap, wastements, waste, spoilage, rummage, chaff, jetsam, jettison, litter, lumber; refuse.

impairment, contamination, destruction, deterioration, negation, nullification, ruin, spoilage.

V. be useless, labor in vain, go a-begging, fail; pour water into a sieve, cast pearls before swine, carry coals to Newcastle.

become useless, spoil, deteriorate.

make useless, destroy, ruin, spoil, void, negate, nullify, contaminate, deteriorate, impair.

Adj. useless, rubbishy, scrap, scrubby, trashy, paltry, inutile, waste, worthless; futile, unavailing, bootless, inoperative, inefficacious, inadequate, inept, inefficient, ineffectual, incompetent, unprofitable, unproductive, unfruitful, ill-spent, profitless, gainless, fruitless.

unusable, impracticable, impractical, inapplicable, unavailable, unemployable, unfunctional, unhandy, unserviceable, unwieldy.

See also CLUMSINESS, DESTRUCTION,

DETERIORATION, DISUSE, INEFFECTIVENESS, INSUFFICIENCY, UNPRODUCTIVENESS, WORTHLESSNESS. *Antonyms*—See USE, VALUE.

---

usher, *v.* guide, conduct, direct (GUIDANCE).

usher in, *v.* herald, preface (PRECEDENCE).

usual, *adj.* general, habitual, normal, accustomed, (COMMONNESS).

utensil, *n.* tool, implement (INSTRUMENT).

utility, *n.* usefulness, function, service (USE).

utilize, *v.* employ, apply (USE).

Utopia, *n.* Elysium, Erewhon, paradise (PERFECTION).

utter, *adj.* thorough, out-and-out, arrant (COMPLETENESS).

utter, *v.* speak, deliver, express (STATEMENT, TALK, VOICE).

utterly, *adv.* extremely, to the nth degree (EXTREMENESS).

V

vacant, *adj.* empty, clear; untenanted, unoccupied (ABSENCE); unused, idle (DISUSE); expressionless, blank, vapid (DULLNESS, STUPIDITY).

vacate, *v.* leave, abandon, quit (RELINQUISHMENT, DEPARTURE).

vacation, *n.* holiday, fiesta (REST, AMUSEMENT).

vaccinate, *v.* immunize, variolate (PROTECTION).

vaccine, *n.* inoculant, toxin-antitoxin (PROTECTION).

vacillate, *v.* waver, fluctuate, back and fill (IRRESOLUTION, UNCERTAINTY).

vagabond, *n.* wanderer, vagrant, beachcomber (WANDERING, REST).

vagary, *n.* fancy, conceit, whim (CAPRICE, IDEA).

vagrant, *adj.* vagabond, gypsy, nomadic, migratory (WANDERING).

vagrant, *n.* vagabond, hobo, tramp (WANDERING, REST).

vague, *adj.* nebulous, impalpable, indefinite (UNCLEARNESS, UNCERTAINTY).

vain, *adj.* conceited, vainglorious, egotistical (PRIDE); barren, futile, ineffectual (INEFFECTIVENESS, UNPRODUCTIVENESS, FAILURE); slight, trifling, unessential (UNIMPORTANCE).

vainglorious, *adj.* egotistical, vaunting, conceited (BOASTING, PRIDE).

valet, *v.* *valet de chambre* (*F.*), manservant, man (SERVICE).

valiant, *adj.* brave, stalwart, valorous (COURAGE).

valid, *adj.* bona fide, genuine, authentic (TRUTH); effective, potent, telling (RESULT).

validate, *v.* legalize, legitimize, constitute (LEGALITY); corroborate, substantiate, certify (PROOF, TRUTH).

valise, *n.* bag, satchel, suitcase (CONTAINER).

valley, *n.* canyon, glen, gorge (DEPTH); watershed, river basin, basin (LAND).

valorous, *adj.* stalwart, stouthearted, valiant (COURAGE).

valuable, *adj.* costly, precious, priceless (VALUE); useful, serviceable, helpful (USE).

VALUE—*N.* value, worth, advantage, benefit, account.

worthiness, merit, dignity, caliber, desert, deserts, merits, meed (*poetic*).

asset, commodity, utility; plum, nugget, treasure.

V. value, appreciate, esteem, prize, treasure.

evaluate, appraise, apprize, rate, assess, assay, estimate; transvalue.

rise in value, boom, enhance, appreciate.

overvalue, overappraise, overassess, overestimate, overrate.

be worthy of, deserve, merit, rate, earn.

Adj. valuable, costly, precious, sterling, invaluable, priceless, worth-while.

worthy, deserving, meritorious; deserved, merited, righteous.

See also ADVANTAGE, GOOD, JUDGMENT, OVERESTIMATION, USE. *Antonyms*—See USELESSNESS, WORTHLESSNESS.

valueless, *adj.* trashy, useless, waste (WORTHLESSNESS, MEANNESS).

vampire, *n.* lamia, harpy, ghoul (SUPERNATURAL BEINGS); bloodsucker, plunderer (PLUNDER); flirt, coquette (LOVE).

van, *n.* wagon, cart, truck (VEHICLE); head, vanguard, forefront (FRONT).

vandalism, *n.* damage, malicious mischief, sabotage (HARM, DESTRUCTION).

vane, *n.* weathercock (WIND).

vanguard, *n.* head, *avant-garde* (*F.*), pioneers (FRONT, LEADERSHIP).

vanish, *v.* dissolve, fade, evanesce (DISAPPEARANCE).

vapid, *adj.* insipid, flat, flavorless (WEAKNESS); inane, vacuous, vacant (STUPIDITY).

vapor, *n.* steam, effluvium, miasma (GAS); fog, smog, smaze, smother (CLOUD); moisture, dew, mist (WATER); fancy, caprice, vagary (IDEA).

vaporizer, *n.* atomizer, spray (GAS).

vaporous, *adj.* steamy, miasmal, volatile (GAS); airy, ethereal, shadowy (NONEXISTENCE).

varicolored, *adj.* versicolor, particolored, polychromatic (VARIEGATION).

varied, *adj.* divers, sundry, miscellaneous (DIFFERENCE, CLASS).

VARIEGATION—*N.* variegation, diversification, maculation, striation, marbling; iridescence, opalescence, chatoyancy, play of colors.

check, plaid, tartan, patchwork; marquetry, parquet, parquetry, mosaic, checkerwork; chessboard, checkerboard.

stripe, streak, line, band, cingulum (*zool.*), striation, list; belt, cingulum, ring, cincture, girdle, wave, vein; welt, wheal, weal, wale.

spot, dot, fleck, mote, speck, flyspeck, speckle, mottle, blaze, mackle, macule, patch, splotch, blotch, stigma; freckle, lentigo (*med.*), pock, pockmark, pit, mole; pip (*on a card*).

[*comparisons*] spectrum, rainbow, iris, peacock, chameleon, zebra, leopard; mother-of-pearl, nacre, opal, marble; Joseph's coat; harlequin.

V. variegate, checker, diversify, iridize, opalesce, marble, marbleize, tattoo, inlay, tessellate, water; lace, fret, interlace, embroider, quilt.

stripe, striate, vein, band, belt, girdle.

spot, dot, fleck, dapple, stipple, sprinkle, besprinkle, mottle, speckle, speck, bespot, maculate, blotch, flyspeck, freckle, pock, pockmark, pit, splotch, stigmatize.

Adj. variegated, diversified, multicolor, many-colored, many-hued, divers-colored, varicolored, versicolor, parti-colored, polychromatic, kaleidoscopic.

iridescent, irised, rainbowlike, rainbowy, pavonine, opaline, opalescent, prismatic, pearly, nacreous, chatoyant, nacred, shot, tortoise-shell.

mottled, pied, piebald, skewbald, motley; marbled, marmoreal; pepper-and-salt.

spotted, spotty, flecked, nevose, freckled, lentiginous (*med.*), flecky, brindle, brindled, dappled, dapple, dotted, studded, patchy, punctate, speckled, specked, sprinkled, stippled, blotchy, blotched, splotched, flyspecked, pocked, pock-marked, pitted.

striped, banded, barred, belted, lined, veined; brindle, brindled, tabby; cinctured, cingulate, girdled, streaked, striated, gyrose.

checkered, checked, mosaic, tessellated; plaid, tartan.

See also BLEMISH, COLOR. *Antonyms*—See UNIFORMITY.

variety, *n.* assortment, description, type (CLASS).

various, *adj.* divers, sundry, miscellaneous (DIFFERENCE, CLASS, MULTITUDE).

vary, *v.* alter, modulate, inflect (CHANGE); diversify, assort, variegate; diverge, contrast, deviate (DIFFERENCE); alternate, change (DISCONTINUITY).

vase, *n.* jar, beaker, ewer (CONTAINER).

vassal, *n.* chattel, helot, serf (SLAVERY); minion, henchman, myrmidon (FOLLOWER); feudatory, liegeman (FEUDALISM).

vast, *adj.* great, immense, enormous; boundless, illimitable (GREATNESS, SIZE).

vat, *n.* tank, cistern (CONTAINER).

vaudeville, *n.* variety show, review (DRAMA).

vault, *n.* arch, dome, arcade (SUPPORT, PASSAGE); grave, tomb, mausoleum (BURIAL); crypt, dungeon, cavern (LOWNESS); cellar, basement (SPACE); safe-deposit vault (STORE).

vault, *v.* hurdle, clear, jump over (JUMP).

vaunt, *v.* brag, roister, vapor (BOASTING).

veer, *v.* skew, skid, swerve (SIDE, TURNING, CHANGE).

vegetable, *adj.* vegetative, vegetal, leguminous (PLANT LIFE).

vegetable, *n.* plant, herb (PLANT LIFE).

vegetate, *v.* germinate, sprout, grow (PLANT LIFE); stagnate, hibernate (INACTION).

vegetation, *n.* plants, flora (PLANT LIFE).

vehemence, *n.* passion, fire, heat (VIOLENCE); fervor, fervency, ardor (FEELING).

vehement, *adj.* passionate, impassioned, fiery, hot (VIOLENCE).

vehicle, *n.* car, conveyance (VEHICLE); way, expedient (MEANS).

VEHICLE—*N.* vehicle, conveyance, trundle, car, caravan, gondola, aquaplane.

carriage, chariot, rig, wagonette, brougham, landau, landaulet, sociable, vis-à-vis (*F.*), victoria, barouche, calash, berlin, surrey, stanhope, coupé, phaeton, clarence, buggy, buckboard, runabout; cabriolet, cart, four-in-hand, tandem; chaise, shay (*dial.*), gig, tilbury, dogcart, trap (*colloq.*), sulky.

coach, coach-and-four, tallyho, stagecoach, stage, diligence, mail stage, post chaise.

taxi, taxicab, jitney (*colloq.*), cab, hackney, hack (*slang*); hansom, *fiacre* (*F.*), droshky.

cart, jinrikisha, rickshaw, palanquin, sedan, sedan chair; wheel chair, Bath chair; litter, stretcher, ambulance; dray, dumpcart, tipcart; handcart, pushcart, barrow, wheelbarrow.

baby carriage, bassinet, gocart, perambulator, pram, stroller, coach.

cycle, bicycle, wheel (*colloq.*), tricycle, tandem, velocipede, unicycle, monocycle, hydrocycle, quadricycle, motorcycle.

sled, sledge, sleigh, bob, bobsled, bobsleigh, cutter, double-ripper, double-runner, toboggan; ski, snowshoes, skates.

wagon, buggy, cart, truck, van, moving van, lorry; Conestoga wagon, prairie schooner; caisson.

police car, prowl car, squad car, cruiser; Black Maria, paddy wagon, patrol wagon, police van.

automobile, motorcar, horseless carriage, auto (*colloq.*), motor (*colloq.*), car, machine (*colloq.*), limousine, sedan, coach, brougham, touring car, victoria, cabriolet, convertible coupé, hardtop, landau, phaeton, sports car, station wagon, suburban; rattletrap, jalopy (*colloq.*), hot rod (*slang*).

truck, carryall, jeep, pickup, dump truck, trailer; tractor, caterpillar tractor, tram, half-track; bloodmobile, bookmobile.

omnibus, bus, autobus, motor bus, charabanc.

streetcar, trolley, trolley car, cable car, tram (*Brit.*), electric car.

train, locomotive, express, mail, special, limited, freight train, rolling stock, sleeping car, Pullman, smoker; car, coach, day coach, compartment; baggage car.

driver, chauffeur, autoist, automobilist, motorist; engineer, motorman, conductor; cyclist, bicyclist, velocipedist.

truck driver, truckman, teamster, carter, hauler, wagoner, drayman, mover.

taxi driver, jehu (*jocose*), cabby (*colloq.*), cabdriver, hacker, hackman, hackie (*slang*).

coachman, jehu (*jocose*), coach driver, charioteer, tandemist.

animal driver, drover, camel driver, cameleer, muleteer, mahout (*elephant*); equestrian, equestrienne (*fem.*), horseman, horsewoman, jockey, roughrider.

sledder, bobsledder, bobsleigher, sleigher, tobogganer.

rider, passenger; standee, straphanger.

wagonmaker, wainwright, wagonwright, wheelwright, wagonsmith; mechanic.

gas station, filling station, service station, garage, repair shop.

V. **drive,** ride, ride in, motor, chauffeur, steer; cab (*colloq.*), hack, taxi, trolley (*colloq.*); cycle, bicycle, motorcycle; sled, bobsled, go sleighing, toboggan, coast, bellywhop (*slang*).

Adj. **vehicular,** curricular.

See also MEANS, MOTION, SAILOR, SHIP, TRAVELING. *Antonyms*—See MOTIONLESSNESS.

---

veil, *n.* wimple (HEADGEAR).

veil, *v.* hide, screen, shade (CONCEALMENT, INVISIBILITY, PROTECTION); disguise, cloak, mask (CONCEALMENT).

vein, *n.* wave, stripe, streak (VARIEGATION); blood vessel (BLOOD); mineral, ore, lode (METAL); style, phrasing, wording (EXPRESSION).

velocity, *n.* rate, pace; rapidity, celerity (SPEED).

velvety, *adj.* downy, fluffy, fuzzy (HAIR).

venal, *adj.* bribable, corruptible, rotten (BRIBERY); mercenary, sordid (MONEY).

vend, *v.* sell, market, merchandise (SALE).

veneer, *n.* overlay, facing, leaf (LAYER, COVERING); front, façade (SHALLOWNESS).

veneer, *v.* overlay, face (COVERING, FRONT).

venerable, *adj.* respectable, august, revered (RESPECT, WORSHIP).

venerate, *v.* honor, deify, apotheosize (RESPECT, WORSHIP).

venereal, *adj.* sexual, sensual; aphrodisiac, erotic; copulatory, coital (SEX).

vengeance, *n.* revenge, reprisal, repayment (RETALIATION, PUNISHMENT).

venom, *n.* toxin, virus, venin (POISON); rancor, spleen, virulence, malice (HOSTILITY).

venomous, *adj.* toxic, virulent (POISON); spiteful, malicious (HOSTILITY).

vent, *n.* outlet, exit, spout (EGRESS, OPENING); air hole (AIR OPENING); ventilation, verbalism (EXPRESSION).

vent, *v.* canalize, ventilate (DEPARTURE); express, verbalize (EXPRESSION).

ventilate, *v.* air-cool, aerate, air (BLOWING, AIR); vent, express, verbalize (EXPRESSION).

ventilator, *n.* window, louver, transom (AIR, BLOWING).

venture, *n.* enterprise, endeavor (UNDERTAKING, BUSINESS); plunge, flyer, wager (CHANCE).

venture, *v.* hazard, risk, gamble (CHANCE); dare, make bold (COURAGE).

venturesome, *adj.* enterprising, adventurous, aggressive (UNDERTAKING); hazardous, speculative, venturous (CHANCE).

veracious, *adj.* truthful, honest (TRUTH).

veranda, *n.* porch, patio, piazza (BUILDING).

verbal, *adj.* lexical, vocabular, phrasal (WORD); stated, said, expressed (STATEMENT).

verbatim, *adj.* literal, verbal, exact (MEANING).

verbose, *adj.* wordy, prolix, diffuse (WORDINESS).

verdict, *n.* decree, ruling, finding (COURT OF LAW, JUDGMENT, LAWSUIT, DECISION).

verge, *n.* edge, border, brink (BOUNDARY).

verge, *v.* tend, incline, gravitate toward (TENDENCY); border (BOUNDARY).

verify, *v.* corroborate, substantiate, confirm (PROOF, SUPPORT, TRUTH); test, prove (TEST); find out, authenticate, certify (DISCOVERY, CERTAINTY).

vermin, *n.* blight, pest (ANIMAL); dregs, raff, scum (WORTHLESSNESS).

vernacular, *adj.* colloquial, dialectal, idiomatic (LANGUAGE).

vernacular, *n.* dialect, cant, argot (LANGUAGE).

versatile, *adj.* many-sided, multifaceted (ABILITY).

verse, *n.* poem, rhyme; canto, stanza, stave (POETRY).

versed, *adj.* trained, seasoned, practiced (EXPERIENCE).

version, *n.* account, report, story (DESCRIPTION, INFORMATION); translation, rendition, construction (EXPLANATION).

vertex, *n.* summit, peak, apex (HEIGHT, SHARPNESS).

VERTICALITY—N. verticality, perpendicularity, elevation, erection, right angle.

V. be vertical, stand erect (*or* upright), stand on end, stick up, cock up.

set up, raise up, erect, rear, raise, pitch, uprear, upraise, uplift, upend, upheave.

Adj. vertical, upright, erect, perpendicular, sheer, steep, plumb, bolt upright; rectangular, square, orthogonal, right-angled; rampant (*esp. heraldry*); longitudinal.

Adv., phrases. vertically, etc. (see *Adjectives*); on end, endwise, at right angles.

See also ASCENT, ELEVATION, HEIGHT, POSTURE, SHARPNESS, SLOPE, STRAIGHTNESS. *Antonyms*—See FLATNESS.

verve, *n.* birr, zip, dash (ENERGY).

very, *adv.* extremely, exceedingly, intensely (GREATNESS).

vessel, *n.* basin, bowl, pot (CONTAINER); craft, boat, bottom (SHIP).

vestibule, *n.* lobby, hallway, entry (INGRESS, PASSAGE).

veteran, *adj.* old, experienced, seasoned (OLDNESS, EXPERIENCE).

veteran, *n.* old-timer (*colloq.*), oldster, old soldier (OLDNESS, FIGHTER, EXPERIENCE).

veterinarian, *n.* vet (*colloq.*), horse doctor, farrier (DOMESTICATION, MEDICAL SCIENCE).

veto, *v.* negative, discountenance, disapprove (DENIAL).

vex, *v.* annoy, irk, provoke (ANNOYANCE); disquiet, distress, disturb (NERVOUSNESS).

via, *prep.* through, by way of, by means of (PASSAGE).

viaduct, *n.* bridge, span, overpass (BREAKWATER, PASSAGE).

vial, *n.* bottle, phial (CONTAINER).

vibrant, *adj.* resounding, reverberant, sonorous (RESONANCE); virile, vital (STRENGTH).

vibrate, *v.* tremble, quiver (SHAKE); undulate, ripple (OSCILLATION); beat, flutter, palpitate (RHYTHM); echo, re-echo, redouble (REPETITION).

vicarious, *adj.* indirect, secondary (RESULT); sympathetic, empathetic (PITY).

vice, *n.* evil, maleficence, malignance (WICKEDNESS); offense, transgression, wrong (SIN); degeneracy, depravity, debauchery (IMMORALITY); corruption, lubricity, lechery (SEX); mar, blemish (WEAKNESS).

vichy, *n.* soda, club soda, seltzer (DRINK).

vicinity, *n.* neighborhood, environs, surroundings (NEARNESS, ENVIRONMENT).

vicious, *adj.* wicked, evil, sinful (WICKEDNESS); immoral, vile, corrupt (IMMORALITY); nasty, spiteful, malicious (HOSTILITY); beastly, frightful, horrid (INFERIORITY).

victim, *n.* sacrifice, burnt offering, hecatomb (WORSHIP); sufferer, prey, martyr (PAIN); casualty, basket case (HARM); forfeit, gambit, pawn (RELINQUISHMENT); dupe, gull, easy mark (DECEPTION).

victimize, *v.* swindle, cheat, defraud (THIEVERY).

victor, *n.* conqueror, winner, master (DEFEAT, SUCCESS).

Victorian, *adj.* illiberal, hidebound, bourgeois (PREJUDICE).

Victorian, *n.* prude, Grundyist, Grundyite (MODESTY).

victorious, *adj.* triumphant, winning, champion (SUCCESS).

victory, *n.* conquest, mastery, triumph (SUCCESS, DEFEAT).

victuals, *n.* eatables, viands, edibles (FOOD).

vie, *v.* contest, strive, compete (ATTEMPT).

view, *n.* spectacle, scene; vista, outlook, prospect; sight, eyesight (VISION); landscape, seascape (FINE ARTS); concept, impression (OPINION, IDEA).

view, *v.* see, behold, witness (VISION, LOOKING).

viewpoint, *n.* slant, outlook, angle (CHARACTER, VISION).

vigil, *n.* watch, lookout (CARE).

vigilant, *adj.* watchful, guarded, alert (CARE, WAKEFULNESS, LOOKING).

vigor, *n.* vim, energy, stamina, might (STRENGTH, POWER, FORCE); virility, potency (SEX).

vigorous, *adj.* strong, powerful, energetic (STRENGTH, POWER, FORCE); blooming, bouncing, strapping (HEALTH).

vile, *adj.* low, miserable, wretched (MEANNESS, CONTEMPT); filthy, foul, nasty (OBSCENITY); evil, vicious, nefarious (IMMORALITY, WICKEDNESS).

vilify, *v.* smear, traduce, malign (DETRACTION).

villa, *n.* country house, lodge (HABITATION).

village, *n.* hamlet, suburb (CITY).

villager, *n.* exurbanite, suburbanite, native (RURAL REGION).

villain, *n.* malefactor, evildoer, miscreant (WICKEDNESS); scamp, scapegrace, varlet (DISHONESTY); rascal, rogue (MISCHIEF).

villainy, *n.* deviltry, pranks, knaveries (MISCHIEF, WICKEDNESS).

vim, *n.* vigor, pith, zip (STRENGTH).

vindicate, *v.* excuse, extenuate, whitewash (FORGIVENESS, ACQUITTAL); corroborate, substantiate, defend (PROOF, SUPPORT).

vindictive, *adj.* grudgeful, vengeful, unforgiving (RETALIATION, PUNISHMENT).

vinegary, *adj.* acetic, acetous (SOURNESS); sour-tempered, sour, acid (BAD TEMPER).

violate, *v.* disobey, infringe, transgress (DISOBEDIENCE); oppose, defy, resist (OPPOSITION); profane, desecrate, contaminate (IRRELIGION, DISRESPECT); rape, ravish (SEX).

violation, *n.* infringement, infraction, transgression (ILLEGALITY); outrage, ravishment, rapine (VIOLENCE).

VIOLENCE—*N.* violence, fury, rabidity, rage, rampancy, storm, bluster, brute force; brunt, strain, shock; passion, vehemence, fire, heat.

turbulence, commotion, excitement, disorder, tumult, riot, uproar, frenzy.

fierceness, ferocity, ferity, savagery, truculence, brutality, bestiality.

outrage, violation, ravishment, rapine, profanation, attack, assault.

roughness, hooliganism, rowdyism, ruffianism, thuggery, hoodlumism; roughhouse (*colloq.*), rough-and-tumble.

outbreak, outburst, eruption, explosion, blast, blowup, detonation.

[*political violence*] **anarchism,** anarchy, terrorism, nihilism, coercion; nazism, fascism, dictatorship, totalitarianism; resistance, underground.

[*violent person*] **savage,** wild beast, dragon, tiger, wolf, brute; ruffian, roughneck (*colloq.*), bear, rowdy, hooligan, thug, tough, bruiser, hoodlum, gangster, hood (*slang*); berserker, demon, fiend, hellhound; spitfire, fury, virago, termagant, hellcat, brimstone, harridan, shrew.

terrorist, anarchist, nihilist; nazi, fascist, storm trooper.

V. **be violent,** ferment, effervesce, boil, boil over, fume, foam, rampage.

run wild, run amuck, rage, roar, riot, storm; roughhouse (*colloq.*), ride roughshod, out-Herod Herod.

charge, dash, hurtle, lunge, plunge, rampage, rush, smash, stampede, storm, surge, thrash, whip.

explode, go off, detonate, fulminate, let off, let fly, discharge, blow up, flash, fulgurate, flare, burst, crack, crash, thunder.

Adj. **violent,** furious, rabid, raging, rampageous, rampant, stormy, blustery, blusterous, tempestuous, headlong, rough-and-tumble; vehement, passionate, inflamed, impassioned, fiery, hot, red-hot, white-hot.

turbulent, tumultuous, tumultuary, riotous, boisterous, uproarious; frenzied, frenetic, mad, insane, frantic, berserk, demoniac, demoniacal.

headstrong, ungovernable, uncontrollable, unruly, unbridled, unrestrainable, irrestrainable, wild.

fierce, ferocious, grim, lupine, savage, tigerish, truculent, wolfish, fell.

savage, barbarous, brutal, brute, feral; bestial, wolfish, tigerish.

rough, boisterous, bearish, bear-like, gruff, hooligan, rough-and-ready, rough-and-tumble, rowdy, rowdyish, rude, ruffian, ruffianly, thuggish, tough.

Adv., phrases. **violently,** etc. (see *Adjectives*); hammer and tongs, with a vengeance, tooth and nail, with violence, by force, by storm, *vi et armis* (*L.*), with might and main; headlong, headfirst, headforemost, precipitately.

See also AGITATION, ATTACK, BARBARIANISM, BLOWING, COMMOTION, EXCITEMENT, FEELING, INSANITY, ROUGHNESS, SHARPNESS, UNRULINESS. *Antonyms*—See CALMNESS, MODERATENESS, WEAKNESS.

violet, *adj.* lilac, lilaceous (PURPLE).

violin, *n.* Cremona, Stradivarius, fiddle (MUSICAL INSTRUMENTS).

VIP (*colloq.*), *n.* dignitary, lion, notable (FAME, IMPORTANCE).

virago, *n.* scold, harridan, termagant (SCOLDING, VIOLENCE, DISAGREEMENT).

virgin, *adj.* fresh, untouched, untrod (NEWNESS); untested, untried (TEST); first, initial, maiden (EARLINESS); unused, idle (DISUSE).

virgin, *n.* miss, maid, maiden (CELIBACY, UNMARRIED STATE, YOUTH); greenhorn, babe, colt (INEXPERIENCE).

virginal, *adj.* abstinent, chaste, pure, maiden (CELIBACY, UNMARRIED STATE); untested, untried, unproved (TEST).

virginity, *n.* maidenhood, chastity, purity (CELIBACY).

Virgin Mary, *n.* Holy Virgin, Madonna, Mater Dolorosa (CHRIST).

virile, *adj.* manly, male, masculine (MAN); vigorous, potent (SEX); vibrant, vital (STRENGTH).

virility, *n.* strength, vitality (STRENGTH); potency, vigor (FERTILITY, SEX).

virtue, *n.* goodness, ethicality, honesty (MORALITY); excellence, quality (GOOD); chastity, purity (CELIBACY).

virtuoso, *n.* adept, expert (ABILITY); artist (MUSICIAN).

virtuous, *adj.* chaste, innocent, faithful (PURIFICATION, CELIBACY); ethical, upright (RULE, MORALITY).

virulent, *adj.* harmful, noxious (HARM); poisonous, toxic (POISON); lethal, fatal, deadly (KILLING); venomous, spiteful, malicious (HOSTILITY).

virus, *n.* germ, microbe, pathogen (DISEASE); toxin, toxicant (POISON); canker, smutch, ulcer (IMMORALITY).

vise, *n.* brace, grip, clamp (HOLD, PRESSURE).

VISIBILITY—*N.* **visibility,** noticeability, conspicuity, relief, salience, prominence.

appearance, apparition, dawn, emergence, materialization, occurrence, visualization.

V. **become visible,** visualize, appear, materialize, rise, loom, emerge, dawn, occur, arise, issue, spring, come in sight, show, come into view, burst upon the view, peep out, peer out, crop up (*or* out), present (show, manifest, reveal, expose, *or* betray) itself, stand forth, gleam, glimmer, glitter, glow, twinkle, burst forth, start up, spring up, come out, come forth, come forward; reappear, recur.

be conspicuous, attract attention, catch (*or* strike) the eye, stand out, stare, obtrude, call attention.

stick out, beetle, bulge, extrude, jut, jut out, project, overhang, protrude, protuberate, push out, stand out, stretch out, thrust out; stick up, cock, hump.

make conspicuous, advertise, blaze, feature, mark, point up, show up, signalize.

Adj. **visible,** seeable, visual, perceptible, eidetic (*psychol.*), perceivable, discernible, discoverable, macroscopic, observable; apparent, unhidden, unconcealed, inescapable, limpid, pellucid; open, revealed, in view, in full view, in sight, exposed to view; clinical (*as symptoms*).

conspicuous, noticeable, marked, pointed, outstanding, striking, arresting, eye-catching, pronounced, signal, remarkable, curious, salient, prominent, predominant, preeminent, obvious, bold, in bold (*or* high) relief, manifest, evident; crying, glaring, blatant, protrusive, obtrusive.

distinct, clear, plain, transparent, definite, well-defined, in focus, well-marked, unclouded.

protruding, sticking out, beetle, beetling, bulging, bulgy, bulbous, extrusive, jutting, overhanging, outstanding, outstretched, outthrust, projecting, projective, prominent, salient, protrusive, protuberant, snaggy; cocked.

Adv. **visibly,** etc. (see *Adjectives*); in sight of, before one's very eyes, under one's very nose.

See also APPEARANCE, CLARITY, OCCURRENCE, RELIEF, TRANSPARENCY, VERTICALITY, VISION. *Antonyms*—See

CONCEALMENT, COVERING, INVISIBILITY.

vision, *n.* sight, eyesight (VISION); spirit, specter (SUPERNATURAL BEINGS); dream, nightmare (SLEEP); knockout (*slang*), goddess (BEAUTY).

VISION—*N.* **vision,** sight, eyesight, view; afterimage; stereopsis.

optics, stereoscopy, optometry, ophthalmology.

oculist, ophthalmologist, optometrist, optician.

eyeglasses, spectacles, cheaters (*colloq.*), winkers, glasses, goggles, lorgnette, pince-nez, *lorgnon* (*F.*), bifocals, trifocals, monocle, eyeglass, sunglasses, dark glasses; lens, frame, ear, earpiece.

telescope, field glass, spyglass, field glasses, binoculars, opera glasses.

[*other aids*] periscope, hydroscope, stereoscope, stereopticon, tachistoscope; magnifier, magnifying glass, jeweler's loupe, reading glass; microscope, helioscope, benthoscope.

mirror, glass, looking-glass, reflector, speculum, hand glass, hand mirror.

seeing, descrial, discernment, decernment, discovery, espial, glimpse, notice, observation, penetration, perception, preview.

beholder, discoverer, observer, perceiver, viewer, witness, eyewitness; visionary.

view, vista, outlook, aspect, prospect, panorama, diorama, bird's-eye view, retrospect, glimpse, ken.

viewpoint (*literal or figurative*), point of view, standpoint, angle, aspect, facet, outlook, perspective, retrospect; peephole, sighthole.

observation tower, conning tower, watchtower, crow's-nest, observatory, lookout.

[*that which is seen*] sight, spectacle, view, scene, vision; exhibition, show; object, form, thing, phenomenon.

V. **see,** behold, witness, view, sight, remark, observe, notice, detect, perceive, make out, distinguish, note, discern, decern, discover; descry, espy, glimpse, spy; pierce, penetrate; preview; command a view of.

Adj. **visual,** visional, ocular, optic, optical; audiovisual.

sighted, clear-sighted, clear-eyed, far-sighted, far-seeing, telescopic; sharp-eyed, sharp-sighted, keen-eyed, eagle-eyed, hawk-eyed, lynx-eyed, lyncean; Argus-eyed; observant, perceptive, percipient; stereoscopic, periscopic, photopic, binocular; clairvoyant.

Adv., phrases. **at sight**, at first sight, at a glance, at first blush, prima facie (*L.*), at first view.

See also DISCOVERY, EXAMINATION, EYE, FORESIGHT, GLASSINESS, LOOKING, VISIBILITY. *Antonyms*—See BLINDNESS.

visionary, *adj.* romantic, utopian, quixotic (IMAGINATION).

visionary, *n.* idealist, seer, romancer (IMAGINATION); dreamer, phantast (SLEEP).

visit, *n.* call, visitation (ARRIVAL).

visit, *v.* drop in, call, look in on (ARRIVAL).

visiting card, *n.* calling card, pasteboard (ARRIVAL).

visitor, *n.* caller, guest, habitué (*F.*), transient (ARRIVAL).

vista, *n.* view, outlook, prospect (VISION).

visual, *adj.* visional, ocular, optical (VISION); visible, seeable, perceptible (VISIBILITY).

visualize, *v.* envisage, envision, picture (IDEA, IMAGINATION); appear, materialize (VISIBILITY).

vital, *adj.* essential, critical, indispensable (NECESSITY); vibrant, virile (STRENGTH).

vitality, *n.* animation, being, existence (LIFE); liveliness, vivacity (ACTIVITY); endurance, guts (*slang*), stamina (CONTINUATION); virility, bloom (STRENGTH).

vitalize, *v.* vivify, animate, enliven (LIFE).

vitriolic, *adj.* acid, acrimonious, acerb (SHARPNESS, ANGER).

vituperation, *n.* revilement, abusive language (DETRACTION).

vivacious, *adj.* lively, spirited, breezy (ACTIVITY).

vivid, *adj.* clear, graphic, inescapable (CLARITY); bright, brilliant, resplendent (LIGHT).

vixen, *n.* spitfire, termagant, fury (BAD TEMPER).

vocabulary, *n.* phraseology, terminology; text, context (WORD).

vocal, *adj.* voiced, sonant, uttered (VOICE, STATEMENT); phonetic, phonal, phonic (VOICE); expressive, fluent, articulate (EXPRESSION); choral, lyric, operatic (MUSIC, SINGING).

vocalist, *n.* singer, soloist (SINGING).

vocalize, *v.* sound, say, speak (VOICE, EXPRESSION); sing, warble, yodel (SINGING).

vocation, *n.* occupation, calling, field (BUSINESS).

vogue, *n.* style, mode, popularity (FASHION, LIKING).

VOICE—*N.* voice, lung power, utterance, speech, tongue, tone, accents, inflection, delivery, intonation, modulation, monotone, undertone; vocalism, phonation, vocalization; exclamation, expletive, ejaculation, vociferation, cry; larynx, syrinx.

choice, option, preference, say (*colloq.*), wish, opinion, representation, participation, vote, suffrage, *vox populi* (*L.*), plebiscite, referendum.

pronunciation, diction, articulation, enunciation; orthoëpy, phonetics, phonology, phonemics; accent, brogue, drawl, nasalization, nasality, slurring, elision, synaloepha, synaeresis; trill, roll; sibilance, sibilancy, sibilation, aspiration, hiatus, diaeresis.

accent, accentuation, emphasis, stress.

mispronunciation, misenunciation; lisp, lambdacism, gammacism, lallation.

speech sound, phone, phoneme; vowel, diphthong, aspirate, schwa, triphthong; ablaut, umlaut; tonic, consonant, dental, labial, bilabial, labiodental, velar, fricative, sibilant; phonogram, homophone, digraph, trigraph, thorn.

V. **voice**, give voice to, give tongue to, deliver, utter, express, announce, proclaim.

vocalize, sound, say, speak, intonate, intone, phonate; modulate, inflect.

pronounce, articulate, enunciate; drawl, elide, slur, roll, trill, lisp, mouth, nasalize, sibilate; aspirate, dentalize, diphthongize, labialize; mispronounce, misenunciate.

accentuate, accent, stress, emphasize.

Adj. **voiced**, vocal, sonant, laryngal, pronounced, said, expressed, delivered.

phonetic, phonal, phonic, phonological, phonemic, vocal; accented, emphatic, stressed.

vowel, vocalic, diphthongal, aspirated.

See also CHOICE, EXPRESSION, LANGUAGE, MELODY, MUSIC, OPINION, SIBILATION, SINGING, SOUND, STATEMENT, TALK, VOTE, WILL. *Antonyms*—See SILENCE.

void, *adj.* empty, bare, barren (ABSENCE); ineffective, invalid, inoperative (INEFFECTIVENESS); unprofitable, unsuccessful, vain (UNPRODUCTIVENESS).

void, *n.* nothingness, nullity, nihility (NONEXISTENCE); blank, gap, emptiness (ABSENCE).

volatile, *adj.* fugitive, fugacious, elusive (IMPERMANENCE, DEPARTURE); fickle, giddy, erratic (CAPRICE, CHANGEABLENESS); vaporescent, evaporable (GAS).

volcano, *n.* mountain, alp (HEIGHT).

volition, *n.* conation (*psychol.*), free will, accord (WILL, WILLINGNESS).

volley, *n.* barrage, fusillade, shower (THROW); firing, shooting (ATTACK).

voluble, *adj.* fluent, articulate, glib (EXPRESSION); talkative, loquacious, garrulous (TALK).

volume, *n.* amount, number, figure (QUANTITY); cubic measure (MEASUREMENT); sonority, intensity, power (LOUDNESS); tome, album, edition (BOOK).

voluminous, *adj.* capacious, spacious (SIZE); ample, abundant (GREATNESS).

voluntary, *adj.* willing, unforced, unbidden (WILLINGNESS); free, unconstrained, spontaneous (WILL); deliberate, willful, witting (PURPOSE).

volunteer, *v.* offer, proffer, tender (OFFER, WILLINGNESS).

voluptuary, *n.* sensualist, sybarite (PLEASURE).

voluptuous, *adj.* hedonistic, sybaritic (PLEASURE); fleshly, sensual, carnal (SEX, INTEMPERANCE).

vomit, *v.* spew, disgorge, belch (THROW, GIVING); bring up, heave, retch (NAUSEA).

voracious, *adj.* greedy, ravenous, rapacious (GREED).

VOTE—*N.* **vote,** ballot, suffrage, franchise; referendum, plebiscite; voting, poll, chirotony; primary; affirmative vote, aye, yea; negative vote, nay, blackball; split vote.

voter, elector, constituent, balloter; floater, repeater; electorate, constituency.

suffragism, suffragettism; suffragist, suffragette.

V. **vote,** ballot, poll, plump for; blackball; enfranchise, give the vote to.

See also CHOICE, VOICE.

---

vouch, *v.* vow, warrant, certify (AFFIRMATION).

voucher, *n.* receipt, acknowledgment, acquittance (DEBT, RECEIVING).

vouch for, *v.* answer for, sponsor,

guarantee (LIABILITY, DEBT); attest, verify, confirm (PROOF).

vow, *v.* promise, swear, warrant (PROMISE); affirm, vouch, assure (AFFIRMATION).

vowel, *n.* diphthong, mute, aspirate (VOICE, WRITTEN SYMBOL).

voyage, *n.* journey, cruise, trip (PASSAGE, TRAVELING, SAILOR).

voyage, *v.* sail, cruise, boat, cross, journey, travel (SAILOR, TRAVELING).

vulgar, *adj.* common, plebeian (VULGARITY); off-color, spicy, suggestive (OBSCENITY).

vulgarian, *n.* barbarian, savage (VULGARITY); *nouveau riche* (*F.*), parvenu (*F.*), upstart (WEALTH).

vulgarism, *n.* provincialism, localism, barbarism (WORD).

VULGARITY—*N.* **vulgarity,** plebeianism, ill-breeding, indelicacy, *mauvais ton* (*F.*), bad taste, *mauvais goût* (*F.*), Philistinism, barbarity, provincialism; ostentation.

vulgarism, barbarism, savagism, savagery.

lowness, brutality, rowdyism, ruffianism; ribaldry, obscenity, indecency, filth.

[*excess of ornament*] **gaudiness,** tawdriness, trumpery, frippery, tinsel, clinquant, gingerbread.

vulgarian, barbarian, savage, low-brow (*colloq.*), Philistine, provincial, clodhopper; bear, boor, bounder (*colloq.*); swine, pig, brute; roughneck (*colloq.*), ruffian; loudmouth (*slang*).

V. **be vulgar,** etc. (see *Adjectives*); offend, show poor taste, parade, show off.

vulgarize, coarsen, barbarize, rusticate, plebeianize; popularize.

Adj. **vulgar,** plebeian, common, popular, ordinary, general, public; vernacular, national.

unrefined, uncultivated, unpolished, uncultured, inelegant, in bad taste; uncouth, unkempt, homely, homespun, rustic, countrified, provincial, rough, awkward, clownish, boorish; savage, brutish, wild, barbarous, barbaric, outlandish, rowdy, rowdyish; low-brow (*colloq.*), Philistine, illiberal, crass.

coarse, crude, earthy, lowbred, brutish, indelicate, blatant, gross, low, raffish, vile, base, ribald, obscene, broad, smutty, indecent, offensive, scurrilous, foulmouthed, foul-spoken, abusive.

gaudy, tawdry, meretricious, obtrusive, flaunting, loud, crass, showy, ostentatious, flashy, brummagem, garish, cheap, gimcrack, trumpery, tinsel.

ill-bred, ill-mannered, underbred, uncivil, unmannerly, discourteous, rude, impolite, disrespectful, churlish, ungentlemanly, uncourtly, unladylike, caddish; undignified, unseemly, indecorous, unbecoming, unbeseeming, ungracious.

See also BARBARIANISM, DISCOURTESY, DISRESPECT, MALEDICTION, OBSCENITY, OFFENSE, OSTENTATION, UNCLEANNESS, UNPLEASANTNESS, USE. *Antonyms*—See COURTESY, ELEGANCE.

vulnerable, *adj.* exposed, unprotected, unguarded (WEAKNESS).

W

waddle, *v.* swing, totter, wobble (OSCILLATION, WALKING).

wade, *v.* stumble, trek, trudge (WALKING); bathe (SWIMMING).

wafer, *n.* slice, shaving, paring, (LAYER).

wag, *n.* humorist, wit, jokester (WITTINESS).

wag, *v.* waggle, wiggle, oscillate (OSCILLATION).

wage, *v.* fulfill, carry out, do, engage in (ACTION).

wage earner, *n.* money-maker, breadwinner, provider (MONEY).

wager, *v.* gamble, bet, speculate (CHANCE).

wages, *n.* pay, salary, remuneration (PAYMENT).

waggly, *adj.* waggy, awag, wiggly (OSCILLATION).

wagon, *n.* cart, truck, van (VEHICLE).

wagonmaker, *n.* wainright, wheelwright (VEHICLE).

wail, *v.* sob, whimper, cry (WEEPING); bemoan, bewail, moan (SADNESS).

waist, *n.* blouse, bodice, shirt (COAT); undershirt, undervest (UNDERWEAR).

waistband, *n.* belt, sash, girdle (TROUSERS).

wait, *v.* bide, attend, bide one's time (EXPECTATION).

waiter, *n.* server, carhop, steward (SERVICE); tray, hod, salver (CONTAINER).

wait on, *v.* serve, help, attend (SERVICE).

waitress, *n.* hostess, stewardess (SERVICE).

waive, *v.* disown, disclaim (RELINQUISHMENT).

wake, *n.* train, trail, track (REAR); sitting (SEAT).

WAKEFULNESS—*N.* wakefulness, vigilance, vigil, insomnia.

V. awake, arise, awaken, get up, rise, rouse, arouse, wake, waken, wake up, stir.

Adj. wakeful, wide-awake, vigilant, alert, sleepless, insomniac, astir; hypnagogic, hypnopompic.

See also CARE. *Antonyms*—See SLEEP.

waken, *v.* excite, arouse, rouse (MOTIVATION, WAKEFULNESS).

walkaway, *n.* setup (*colloq.*), snap (SUCCESS).

WALKING—*N.* walking, ambulation, perambulation, traversal, debouchment; noctambulism, somnambulism, somnambulation; tread, stride, gait; constitutional, walk, amble, etc. (see *Verbs*).

step, footstep, footfall, footpace, pace, tread, tramp, skip, trip.

[*place for walking*] walk, alameda, alley, ambulatory, boardwalk, catwalk, cloister, crossing, crosswalk, esplanade, gallery, mall, parade, portico, promenade, sidewalk; road, alleyway, avenue, boulevard, bypath, byroad, bystreet, byway, course, court, footpath, lane, passage, path, pathway, street, terrace, track, trail.

walking stick, cane, pikestaff, staff, stick, Malacca cane.

pedometer, pedograph, odograph.

walker, pedestrian, passer-by, ambler, ambulator, perambulator, trooper, hitchhiker, promenader, saunterer, stroller, toddler, somnambulist, noctambulist, funambulist.

marcher, parader, hiker, patrolman.

parade, march, procession, pageant, motorcade, cavalcade, autocade.

V. walk, amble, ambulate, perambulate, traverse, canter, pad, pat, patter, pitter-patter, promenade, saunter, stroll, traipse (*colloq.*), trip, skip, tread, bend one's steps, wend one's way; stride, strut, swagger, sweep, parade, prance, stalk; limp, hobble; clump, scuff, shamble, shuffle, slog, slouch, stagger, reel, stumble, trek, trudge, wade; toddle, paddle, waddle; lag, trail; mince, tiptoe.

march, debouch, defile, file, pace,

pace up and down, hike, parade, troop, tramp, patrol, file past.

step, skip, trip, tiptoe.

step on, stamp on, tramp on, trample, tread, scotch.

step over, bestride, bestraddle, straddle.

Adj. **walking**, ambulant, ambulatory, perambulatory; afoot, on foot, itinerant, peripatetic; biped, quadruped; pigeon-toed; knock-kneed, valgus; light-footed, nimble-footed, nimble-stepping.

See also ASCENT, DANCE, PASSAGE, ROD, SLOWNESS, TRAVELING, UNSTEADINESS. *Antonyms*—See VEHICLE.

WALL—*N.* **wall**, clerestory, retaining wall, revetment, pier, partition; dado, wainscot; sea wall; paneling, wainscoting.

V. **wall**, protect, partition, panel, wainscot.

Adj. **walled**, fortified, protected, enclosed; mural, extramural, intramural.

See also ENVIRONMENT, INCLOSURE, PROTECTION, SUPPORT.

---

wallet, *n.* purse, billfold; haversack, knapsack (CONTAINER).

wall in, *v.* fence in, rail in, stockade (IMPRISONMENT).

wallop (*colloq.*), *v.* swat, clobber (*slang*), punch (HITTING).

wallow, *v.* welter, loll, sprawl (REST).

wan, *adj.* pale, ashen, pasty (COLORLESSNESS); sickly, peaked, bilious (DISEASE); haggard, tired-looking (FATIGUE).

wand, *n.* baton, scepter, verge (ROD); caduceus, rod, divining rod (MAGIC).

WANDERING—*N.* **wandering**, wander, cruise, jaunt, stroll, tramp, ramble, meander, peregrination, extravagation, noctivagation (*at night*); divagation, digression, excursion; deviation, aberration, deliration.

[*tendency to wander*] **vagabondage**, vagabondism, nomadism, wanderlust, vagrancy, fugitivity, aberrance, deviationism.

wanderer, vagabond, vagrant, tramp, beachcomber, runabout; gadabout, gallivanter, rover, roamer, rambler, meanderer, peregrinator, mooncalf, prowler, stray, straggler; nomad, Bedouin, pilgrim.

gypsy, Romany, *tzigane* (*Hungarian*), *zingaro* (*It.*); Romany rye.

V. **wander**, wander about, cruise, gad, gallivant, jaunt, vagabond, vagabondize, stroll, tramp, rove, roam, range, prowl, ramble, meander, peregrinate, extravagate; wander away, wander off, stray, straggle, divagate, digress, deviate, aberrate.

Adj. **wandering**, vagabond, vagrant, gypsy, nomadic, migratory; errant, erratic, fugitive, planetary; gadabout, strolling, roving, roaming, rambling, skimble-scamble, meandering, meandrous, stray, astray, afield, straggly; delirious, aberrant, deviant, deviate; digressive, digressory, discursive, devious.

See also LOSS, TRAVELING, WALKING, WINDING. *Antonyms*—See MOTIONLESSNESS, STRAIGHTNESS.

---

wanderings, *n.* raving, ravings, deliration (INSANITY).

wanderlust, *n.* dromomania, vagabondage, nomadism (TRAVELING, WANDERING).

wane, *v.* dwindle, abate, fade (WEAKNESS, DECREASE, SMALLNESS).

want, *n.* wish, desire, requirement (DESIRE); lack, need, scarcity (ABSENCE); impoverishment, indigence, destitution (POVERTY).

want, *v.* wish, covet, crave (DESIRE); need, require (NECESSITY); lack, be without, not have (INSUFFICIENCY, ABSENCE); be poor, starve, live from hand to mouth (POVERTY).

wanting, *adj.* deficient, short, lacking (INCOMPLETENESS, ABSENCE).

wanton, *adj.* unprincipled, unconscionable, unscrupulous (FREEDOM); loose, immoral, profligate (SEX); prodigal, spendthrift, profuse (WASTEFULNESS); inconsiderate, outrageous (INATTENTION).

wanton, *n.* libertarian, libertine (FREEDOM); slut, trollop, trull (SEX).

war, *n.* warfare, hostilities, bloodshed (FIGHTING).

war, *v.* disagree, differ, clash (DISAGREEMENT).

warble, *v.* vocalize, yodel, croon (SINGING).

ward, *n.* protégé, dependent, pensioner (PROTECTION, DEPENDABILITY).

warden, *n.* watchman, warder (PROTECTION); jailer, keeper (IMPRISONMENT); guard, convoyer (PROTECTION).

ward off, *v.* forestall, stave off, avert (PREVENTION, AVOIDANCE).

wardrobe, *n.* outfit, costume, ensemble (CLOTHING); trunk, locker, chiffonier (CONTAINER).

warehouse, n. storehouse, shed, depository (STORE).

wares, n. merchandise, commodities, goods (SALE).

warlike, adj. belligerent, bellicose, hostile (FIGHTING, HOSTILITY, DISAGREEMENT).

warm, adj. lukewarm, tepid (HEAT); sympathetic, warmhearted (PITY); fervent, fervid, passionate (FEELING).

warm, v. chafe, toast, bake (HEAT); cook, fix (colloq.), prepare (COOKERY).

warmhearted, adj. affectionate, demonstrative, tender (LOVE); sympathetic, warm (PITY).

warmonger, n. jingoist, jingo, militarist (FIGHTER).

warmth, n. heat, tepidity, temperature (HEAT); ardor, zeal, vehemence, passion (FEELING); sympathy, fellow-feeling (PITY).

WARNING—N. warning, caution, notice, caveat, admonition, admonishment, monition, exhortation; threat, growl; lesson, example; forewarning, foreboding, premonition, handwriting on the wall, Mother Carey's chicken, stormy petrel, bird of ill omen, gathering clouds.

sentinel, sentry, watch, watchman, night watchman, guard, watch and ward; patrol, picket, spotter, vedette (mil.), scout, spy, lookout, flagman, signalman; watchdog, Cerberus, monitor, Cassandra.

warning signal, beacon, alarm, alarum (archaic), alert, tocsin, siren; watchtower, lighthouse, lightship, foghorn.

V. warn, caution, exhort, tip off (colloq.), admonish, monitor, put on one's guard, alert; portend, forebode, premonish, forewarn.

Adj. warning, cautionary, premonitory, admonitory, monitory, exhortatory, monitorial, exemplary.

See also CARE, DISSUASION, INDICATION, PREDICTION, THREAT.

warp, v. twist, contort, intort (WINDING).

warrant, n. assurance, earnest, guarantee (PROMISE); permit, license, authorization (PERMISSION, POWER).

warrant, v. guarantee, certify, assure (CERTAINTY); excuse, justify (FORGIVENESS); permit, empower,

license (PERMISSION); promise, swear, vow (PROMISE).

warrior, n. warfarer, fighting man, soldier (FIGHTER).

warship, n. naval vessel, battleship, dreadnaught (SHIP).

wary, adj. vigilant, alert, cautious (CARE).

wash, v. launder, rinse, shampoo (CLEANNESS); wet, bathe, hose (WATER).

waste, n. extravagance, improvidence, dissipation (WASTEFULNESS); refuse, garbage, slops (UNCLEANNESS); rubble, scrap (USELESSNESS, REMAINDER); excreta, secreta (EXCRETION); wasteland, desert (LAND).

waste, v. dissipate, squander (WASTEFULNESS); wilt, wither, emaciate (WEAKNESS); corrode, erode, eat away (DESTRUCTION).

waste away, v. rot, molder (DECAY); wilt, wither (WEAKNESS).

wasted, adj. emaciated, consumptive, cadaverous (THINNESS).

WASTEFULNESS—N. wastefulness, waste, wastage, extravagance, improvidence, prodigality, profligacy, dissipation.

wastrel, waster, dissipator, prodigal, profligate, scattergood, spendthrift, squanderer.

V. waste, dissipate, fribble away, frivol away, fritter away, lavish, squander, throw away, misspend.

Adj. wasteful, extravagant, improvident, lavish, prodigal, profligate, shiftless, spendthrift, wanton, profuse, penny-wise and pound-foolish, thriftless, unthrifty, dissipative.

See also EXPENDITURE. Antonyms —See ECONOMY, STINGINESS, STORE.

wasteland, n. waste, desert, Sahara (LAND).

waste time, v. dally, diddle (colloq.), dawdle (TIME).

wastrel, n. prodigal, profligate, spendthrift (WASTEFULNESS).

watch, n. timepiece, chronometer, timer (TIME MEASUREMENT); watchfulness, vigilance (CARE); sentinel, sentry, guard (WARNING).

watch, v. eye, inspect (LOOKING); mount guard, patrol (PROTECTION); keep an eye on, look after (CARE); attend, remark, mark (ATTENTION, OBSERVANCE).

watchdog, n. Cerberus, monitor (WARNING).

watchful, adj. vigilant, guarded, wary (CARE); observant, attentive (LOOKING).

watchmaker, *n.* chronologer, chronographer, horologer (TIME MEASUREMENT).

watchman, *n.* sentinel, sentry, guard (WARNING, PROTECTION).

watchtower, *n.* conning tower, observatory, lookout (VISION).

watchword, *n.* password, countersign, shibboleth (WORD, INDICATION).

WATER—*N.* water, H_2O (*chem.*), aqua (L.), aqua pura (L., *pharm.*), eau (F.); fluid, liquid, diluent; hydrosphere; pool, puddle, plash; brine.

moisture, humidity, damp, wet, dew, vapor, mist.

sprinkler, sprayer, spray, atomizer; syringe.

science of water: hydrology, hydrography, geohydrology.

V. water, wet, bathe, imbue, hose, wash; dowse *or* douse, drench, saturate, soak, sodden, sop, souse, steep.

sprinkle, spray, squirt, splash, spatter, splatter, spill, slop, plash, bespatter, besplash, besplatter, bespray, besprinkle.

moisten, dabble, dampen, humidify.

flood, deluge, engulf, inundate, overflow, submerge, submerse, swamp, whelm.

Adj. watery, aqueous, serous, liquid, fluid, hydrous, diluted.

underwater, subaqueous, submersed, suboceanic, submarine, undersea; awash, deluged, flooded, inundated, overflowed, submerged, swamped.

wet, doused *or* dowsed, drenched, dripping, imbued, saturated, soaked, sodden, soggy, sopping, soppy, waterlogged, wringing; marshy, swampy, poachy, rainy.

moist, damp, humid, irriguous, oozy, misty, dewy, vaporous, vapory; clammy, sticky, dank, muggy, soggy.

See also CLEANNESS, LAKE, LIQUID, MARSH, OCEAN, RAIN, RIVER. *Antonyms*—See AIR, DRYNESS.

watercourse, *n.* waterway, canal, stream (PASSAGE, RIVER).

waterfall, *n.* fall, cascade, cataract (RIVER).

waterfront, *n.* beach, bank, sea front (LAND).

waterproof, *adj.* watertight, staunch (DRYNESS, TIGHTNESS).

waterway, *n.* watercourse, canal, stream (PASSAGE, RIVER).

watery, *adj.* aqueous, liquid (WATER); thin, dilute (WEAKNESS, THINNESS); flavorless, flat, stale

(UNSAVORINESS); wet, teary, tearful: *of the eyes* (WEEPING).

wattle, *n.* jowl, dewlap (SKIN).

wave, *n.* sign, high-sign, signal (GESTURE, INDICATION); beachcomber, billow, breaker (RIVER); vein, stripe, streak (VARIEGATION).

wave, *v.* flap, flop, flutter (OSCILLATION); signal, wigwag, semaphore (GESTURE, INDICATION); undulate, swell, billow (ROLL).

waver, *v.* sway, stagger, wobble (OSCILLATION); vacillate, fluctuate, back and fill (IRRESOLUTION, UNCERTAINTY); hesitate, falter (INACTION).

wavering, *adj.* hesitant, faltering, halting, indecisive (INACTION).

wavy, *adj.* ripply, curly, swirly (WINDING); floppy, fluttery (OSCILLATION).

wax, *v.* accumulate, grow, fill out (INCREASE); lubricate, oil, grease (SMOOTHNESS); polish, shine, sleek (RUBBING, WAX).

WAX—*N.* wax, paraffin, ceresin, beeswax, spermaceti, adipocere, earwax, cerumen; ceroplastics.

V. wax, beeswax, paraffin; polish, shine, smooth.

Adj. waxy, waxen, waxlike, ceraceous, ceriferous; waxed, cerated.

See also RUBBING, SMOOTHNESS. *Antonyms*—See ROUGHNESS.

waxy, *adj.* ceraceous, ceriferous (WAX); polished, lustrous (SMOOTHNESS); suggestible, impressionable (SUGGESTION).

way, *n.* technique, procedure, manner (METHOD); vehicle, expedient (MEANS); pathway, lane, road (PASSAGE); usage, practice, habit (USE).

wayfarer, *n.* traveler, tourist, journeyer (TRAVELING).

waylay, *v.* ambush, ambuscade (CONCEALMENT).

wayward, *adj.* fractious, disorderly, uncompliant (DISOBEDIENCE); contrary, froward, perverse (OPPOSITE); aberrant, errant, erring (IMMORALITY); stubborn, willful (STUBBORNNESS).

WEAKNESS—*N.* weakness, infirmity, enfeeblement, debilitation, vitiation, attenuation, devitalization, emasculation, impotence, impuissance (*poetic*), evisceration; wilt, prostration, impairment, decay, deterioration, dilution.

languor, lassitude, inanition, torpor, torpidity, apathy, enervation, debility, exhaustion.

senility, dotage, decrepitude, anility.

delicacy, fragility, frailty, subtlety.

weak point, foible, Achilles' heel; fault, defect, flaw, imperfection, mar, blemish, demerit, delinquency, vice; frailty, infirmity, failing, shortcoming; liking for, inclination for, leaning, propensity.

weakling, feebling, namby-pamby, jellyfish, valetudinarian, dotard, tenderfoot, sissy, pantywaist, mollycoddle, effeminate.

V. weaken, enfeeble, debilitate, devitalize, emasculate, enervate, eviscerate, exhaust, impair, prostrate, sap, undermine, vitiate, waste, waste away, wilt, wither, unnerve; abate, attemper, attenuate, mitigate, moderate, modify, modulate, relax, remit, slacken, slack, subdue, temper; disable, incapacitate, palsy, paralyze, cripple; cushion, deaden, muffle; diminish, extenuate, qualify; effeminate, effeminize, unman; dilute, thin, water; decay, decline, deteriorate, droop, sag, fail, flag, languish; drop, crumble, give way; totter, dodder; dwindle, taper, wane, abate, fade, slack off.

Adj. weak, weakly, feeble, frail, infirm, sheepish, wan, faint, puny.

powerless, helpless, impotent, impuissant (poetic), feckless, prostrate.

flabby, flaccid, flimsy, washy, watery, insubstantial, limp, quaggy, slack.

strengthless, characterless, insipid, namby-pamby; marrowless, nerveless, pithless, sapless, spineless, sinewless.

energyless, languid, languorous, lackadaisical, lassitudinous, listless, lymphatic, supine, moony; sluggish, torpid, apathetic; spent, limp, enervated, debilitated, exhausted.

doddering, doddered, doddery, dotard, infirm, senile, decrepit, anile.

delicate, faint, fragile, frail, slight, tender, papery, papier-mâché (F.), wishy-washy; dainty, ethereal, exquisite, fine, subtle; mincing, minikin, rose-water, minion.

effeminate, unmanly, unvirile, sissy, sissyish, namby-pamby, tender, soft, milky, womanish, effete.

frail, fragile, frangible, shattery, brittle, breakable, flimsy, sleazy, papery, unsubstantial, gimcrack, jerry-built, shaky, rickety, tumbledown.

vulnerable, exposed, unprotected, indefensible, untenable, accessible, assailable, unguarded.

weak-kneed, irresolute, wavering, vacillating, wishy-washy, indecisive; unstable, inconstant, fickle, changeable.

[in health] sickly, wan, valetudinary; asthenic, atonic, adynamic, cachexic, cachectic, hyposthenic (all med.).

[of abstractions] lame, feeble, flabby, flimsy, insubstantial, slight, slim, thin.

[of sound] faint, feeble, gentle, low, soft, small, thin, reedy.

[of liquid] thin, dilute, watery, light, attenuated, insipid, vapid, flat, flavorless.

[in phonetics] light, soft, unstressed, unaccented, atonic, lenis.

See also BLEMISH, BREAKABLENESS, DECREASE, DISEASE, FATIGUE, INEFFECTIVENESS, IRRESOLUTION, LOWNESS, MODERATENESS, RELIEF, SOFTNESS, THINNESS, UNSAVORINESS, UNSTEADINESS. Antonyms—See ENERGY, FORCE, POWER, PROTECTION, STRENGTH.

WEALTH—N. wealth, easy circumstances, opulence, affluence, prosperity, luxury; riches, substance, assets, means, resources, lucre (contemptuous), pelf (contemptuous), capital, fortune, treasure, gold; abundance, luxuriance, profusion, shower.

rich man, millionaire, multimillionaire, billionaire, Croesus, Midas, Dives, nabob, nawab, capitalist, bourgeois, plutocrat, richling, moneybags; nouveau riche (F.), parvenu (F.), arriviste (F.), arrivé (F.), upstart, vulgarian.

rich people, wealthy class, bourgeoisie, nabobery, plutocracy, villadom, society, zaibatsu (Jap.).

source of wealth: bonanza, Golconda, resources.

science of wealth: plutology, plutonomy, economics, political economy.

god of wealth: Plutus, Mammon.

V. be wealthy, roll in wealth, have money to burn (colloq.); afford, well afford.

become wealthy, get rich, make money, fill one's pockets, feather one's nest, make a fortune, make a killing (slang); strike it rich (colloq.); worship Mammon.

make wealthy, etc. (see Adjectives): enrich, endow.

Adj. wealthy, rich, affluent, opulent, prosperous, substantial, well-fixed, well-to-do, well-off, moneyed, flush, pecunious, independent, of independent means, loaded (*slang*), rolling in wealth, born with a silver spoon in one's mouth, well-heeled (*colloq.*).

capitalistic, plutocratic, bourgeois, nabobical, nabobish; *nouveau riche* (*F.*), parvenu (*F.*), upstart, vulgarian.

luxurious, silken, Corinthian, plush, palatial, palatine.

See also ACQUISITION, MONEY, MULTITUDE, OWNERSHIP, SUFFICIENCY. *Antonyms*—See INSUFFICIENCY, POVERTY.

---

weapons, *n.* arms, armament (ARMS).

wear, *n.* use, service (USE).

wear, *v.* dress in, don, draw on (CLOTHING); carry, bear (TRANSFER); endure, last, remain (CONTINUATION); rub, scuff, scrape (RUBBING).

wear away, *v.* abrade, rust, erode (DESTRUCTION).

wearing, *adj.* tiresome, tiring, wearying (FATIGUE).

wearisome, *adj.* weary, weariful, wearing (FATIGUE).

wear out, *v.* overwork, overuse, tax (USE).

weary, *adj.* tired, exhausted; tiresome, wearisome (FATIGUE).

weary, *v.* tire, exhaust, enervate (FATIGUE); bore, pall, stale (BOREDOM).

weather, *n.* climate, clime (AIR); storminess, turbulence (WIND).

weatherglass, *n.* barometer, barograph (AIR).

weather vane, *n.* wind vane, weathercock, vane (WIND).

weave, *n.* composition, make-up, arrangement (TEXTURE).

weave, *v.* braid, cue, complect (WINDING); knit, crochet, spin (TEXTURE); twine, writhe (WINDING).

web, *n.* net, tissue, cobweb, gossamer (TEXTURE); mesh, netting (CROSSING).

wed, *adj.* married, spliced (*colloq.*), coupled (MARRIAGE).

wed, *v.* marry, espouse; join, couple (MARRIAGE).

wedding, *n.* nuptials, espousals, spousals (MARRIAGE).

wedding song, *n.* hymeneal, nuptial ode (MARRIAGE).

wedge, *n.* chock, shim, quoin (INSTRUMENT); spire, taper, cusp (SHARPNESS); entering wedge, opening wedge (INGRESS).

wedlock, *n.* matrimony, alliance, union (MARRIAGE).

wee, *adj.* microscopic, tiny, teeny (SMALLNESS).

weed out, *v.* eradicate, uproot, extirpate (ELIMINATION).

week, *n.* seven days, hebdomad (TIME).

weekly, *adj.* hebdomadal, septenary (TIME).

WEEPING—*N.* weeping, lachrymation, lachrymals; sob, snivel, wail, whimper; cry, howl, yowl, blubber, bawl, squall, vagitus (*med.*); tears.

weeper, crybaby, lachrymist, bawler, etc. (see *Verbs*).

tear, teardrop, tearlet, lachryma; crocodile tears.

V. **weep**, cry, dissolve in tears, break (*or* burst) into tears, shed tears, bawl, blubber, howl, yowl, mewl, pule, snivel, sob, squall, wail, whimper; cry (*or* sob) oneself to sleep; weep; cry (*or* sob) one's heart (*or* eyes) out.

stop weeping, dry one's eyes, dry one's tears.

Adj. **weeping**, wailful, in tears, dissolved in tears; tearful, teary, weepy, lachrymose; crying, etc. (see *Verbs*).

[*of the eyes*] moist, wet, watery, teary, tearful.

[*pert. to tears*] lachrymal, lachrymary, lachrymatory, teary.

tearlike, lachrymiform, teardrop, tearshaped.

See also COMPLAINT, DEJECTION, SADNESS. *Antonyms*—See CHEERFULNESS, HAPPINESS, LAUGHTER, MERRIMENT.

WEIGHT—*N.* weight, gravity, heft (*colloq.*), avoirdupois (*colloq.*), ponderosity, heaviness; tonnage, ballast, pendulum, bob, plumb bob, plummet; specific gravity; troy weight, apothecaries' weight, avoirdupois weight, metric system; flyweight, bantamweight, featherweight, lightweight, welterweight, middleweight, light heavyweight, heavyweight; statics, gravimetry.

balance, counterpoise, equilibrium, equipoise, equiponderance, libration, poise, symmetry; counterbalance, counterweight, offset; equilibrist, tightrope artist.

[*weighing instruments*] **balance**, scale, scales, steelyard, weigh beam, scale beam, beam.

burden, load, millstone, cumber, cumbrance, encumbrance, incubus, onus, oppression, responsibility, charge, tax.

V. **weigh**, press, cumber, bear heavily; heft (*colloq.*), scale, tare; outweigh, overweigh, overbalance.

balance, counterbalance, counterpoise, equilibrate, equipoise, equiponderate, poise, librate; counterweigh, counterweight, offset, redeem; symmetrize.

burden, load down, lade, cumber, encumber, load, oppress, prey on, weigh on, tax, weigh down, task, weight; overburden, overlade, overload.

Adj. weighty, heavy, hefty (colloq.), ponderous, ponderable; cumbersome, cumbrous, leaden, unwieldy, massive, top-heavy, thumping (colloq.), soggy, sodden; burdensome, carking, onerous, oppressive, overburdensome.

burdened, encumbered, cumbered, laden, loaded, loaded down, heavy-laden, oppressed, weighted down; overladen, overloaded, overweighed, overburdened.

balanced, symmetrical, in balance, equipoised, counterbalanced, poised, counterpoised, equilibristic, equiponderant.

See also HINDRANCE, IMPORTANCE, MEASUREMENT, RESPONSIBILITY, RESTRAINT. Antonyms—See LIGHTNESS.

---

weighty, adj. heavy, cumbersome (WEIGHT); important, serious, grave (IMPORTANCE, SOBRIETY).

weird, adj. supernatural, eerie, unearthly (SUPERNATURALISM, UNUSUALNESS); mysterious, secret (MYSTERY); magical, occult (MAGIC).

welcome, adj. pleasing, desirable, grateful (PLEASANTNESS).

welcome, n. greeting, salutation, ovation (SOCIALITY, GREETING).

welcome, v. hail, salute (GREETING); entertain, accept (RECEIVING).

weld, v. join, solder, fuse (JUNCTION, UNITY).

well, adj. robust, hearty, healthy (HEALTH).

well, n. spring, fount, fountain (STORE); pit, shaft (DEPTH).

well, v. issue, ooze, spurt (RIVER, EGRESS).

well-adjusted, adj. well-balanced, sane, unneurotic (SANITY).

well-balanced, adj. levelheaded, coolheaded (WISDOM); well-adjusted, unneurotic (SANITY); uniform, even, proportional (SHAPE).

well-behaved, adj. obedient, orderly, manageable (GOOD, OBEDIENCE); polite, courteous, well-mannered (COURTESY).

well-being, n. euphoria, eudaemonia (HEALTH).

well-bred, adj. courteous, polite (COURTESY); cultivated, cultured (TEACHING).

well-fed, adj. overweight, overfed, overstuffed, rotund (SIZE).

well-groomed, adj. sleek, groomed, trig (NEATNESS).

well-informed, adj. knowledgeable, au fait (F.), well-rounded (KNOWLEDGE); well-read, widely read, well-educated (LEARNING).

well-kept, adj. neat, trim, tidy (NEATNESS).

well-known, adj. common, familiar (KNOWLEDGE); famous, celebrated (FAME).

well-paying, adj. profitable, lucrative, remunerative (PAYMENT).

well-read, adj. learned, scholarly, cultured (STORY, READING, LEARNING).

well-to-do, adj. rich, wealthy, moneyed (WEALTH).

welt, n. bruise, mouse, wale (HARM).

well-worn, adj. hackneyed, stale, trite, moth-eaten (USE).

west, adj. western, westerly, occidental, Hesperian (DIRECTION).

West, n. Western Hemisphere, Occident, Far West (DIRECTION).

wet, adj. drenched, dripping, saturated (WATER); rainy, soppy (RAIN); moist, watery, tearful: of the eyes (WEEPING).

wet, n. moisture, humidity, damp (WATER).

wet, v. bathe, imbue, hose (WATER).

wet blanket, n. kill-joy, spoilsport (SADNESS).

whale, n. cetacean, grampus (ANIMAL).

wharf, n. pier, dock, quay (BREAKWATER).

wheedle, v. blandish, inveigle, seduce (PERSUASION); coax, worm (ACQUISITION).

wheel, n. caster, trolley, roller (ROUNDNESS, ROTATION); cycle, bicycle (VEHICLE).

wheel, v. revolve, swivel, pivot (ROLL, MOTION, ROTATION).

wheelbarrow, n. handcart, pushcart, barrow (VEHICLE).

wheeze, n. snore, râle (F.), murmur (BREATH); saying, adage, saw (STATEMENT); chestnut, old joke (WITTINESS).

when?, adv. at what time? on what occasion? (TIME).

whereabouts, n. site, station, locus (LOCATION); bearings, direction (SITUATION).

whereas, conj. since, because, in as much as (ATTRIBUTION); while, although (TIME).

wherewithal, n. cash, funds, resources (MONEY, MEANS).

whet, v. sharpen, hone, strop (SHARPNESS); excite, pique, stimulate (EXCITEMENT).

whether, *conj.* if, in the event that, in case (SUPPOSITION).

whiff, *n.* puff, breath (WIND); scent, sniff (ODOR).

while, *conj.* as long as, whereas, although (TIME).

while, *n.* interval, interim, meantime (TIME).

whim, *n.* fancy, urge, impulse (CAPRICE, DESIRE).

whimper, *v.* sob, weep, cry (WEEPING); complain, whine, bleat (COMPLAINT).

whimsey, *n.* whimsicality, waggery, drollery (WITTINESS); notion, fancy, conceit (CAPRICE); vagary, crank, quip (UNUSUALNESS).

whimsical, *adj.* amusing, droll, waggish (WITTINESS); fanciful, capricious, crotchety (CAPRICE); quaint, erratic, eccentric (UNUSUALNESS).

whine, *v.* skirl, pipe, whistle (HIGH-PITCHED SOUND); grumble, pule, whimper (COMPLAINT); howl, yowl, wail (ANIMAL SOUND).

whinny, *v.* neigh, whicker (ANIMAL SOUND).

whip, *n.* switch, strap, quirt (HITTING); prod, goad, lash (MOTIVATION); floor leader (LEGISLATURE).

whip, *v.* spank, chastise, flog (PUNISHMENT); switch, knout, swinge (HITTING); stir, whisk, blend (HITTING, MIXTURE); rush, surge, thrash (VIOLENCE); lash out at, blast, rail at (MALEDICTION).

whir, *v.* revolve, rotate, spin (ROTATION); rustle, hum (ROLL).

whirl, *n.* spin, revolution, twirl (ROTATION).

whirl, *v.* revolve, twirl, spin (ROTATION).

whirlpool, *n.* maelstrom, vortex, eddy (RIVER, ROTATION).

whirlwind, *n.* windstorm, cyclone, hurricane (WIND).

whisker, *n.* bristle, vibrissa, feeler (HAIR).

whiskers, *n.* beard, stubble, goatee (HAIR).

whiskey, *n.* liquor, alcohol, spirits (ALCOHOLIC LIQUOR).

whisper, *n.* murmur, mumble (TALK); trace, breath, hint (SUGGESTION).

whisper, *v.* susurrate, murmur, mumble (TALK).

whistle, *n.* pipe, fife, piccolo (HIGH-PITCHED SOUND).

whistle, *v.* skirl, pipe, whine (HIGH-PITCHED SOUND); tootle, toot, blast (BLOWING).

white-haired, *adj.* towheaded, towhaired, albino (HAIR).

white man, *n.* white, Caucasian, paleface (MANKIND).

WHITENESS—*N.* whiteness, pallor, hoar, lactescence, canescence, albescence, albedo; leucoderma (*med.*), albinoism, leucopathy.

white, cream color, flesh color, ivory, off-white.

[*comparisons*] snow, driven snow, sheet, milk, ivory, alabaster.

V. whiten, bleach, blanch, blench, silver, frost, white, grizzle, pale, etiolate (*tech.*).

whitewash, calcimine, white; gloze (*fig.*), gloss over, extenuate, varnish.

Adj. white, snow-white, snowy, niveous, frosted, hoar, hoary, milky, milk-white, lactescent; chalky, cretaceous; silver, silvery, argentine, argent; marble-white, marmoreal, alabaster; leucochroic, leucous, wintry; fleecy.

whitish, creamy, cream, cream-colored, flesh-colored, albescent, off-white, pearly, ivory, fair, blond, ash-blond; blanched, light, light-colored, fair-skinned, pale.

See also CLEANNESS, COLORLESSNESS, GRAY, PURIFICATION. *Antonyms* —See BLACKNESS, DARKNESS.

---

white slaver, *n.* procurer, pimp, panderer (PROSTITUTE).

whitewash, *v.* calcimine, white (WHITENESS); absolve, justify, extenuate (ACQUITTAL).

whittle, *v.* carve, sculpt, form (CUTTING, SHAPE).

whole, *adj.* total, gross, entire; intact, unbroken (COMPLETENESS).

whole, *n.* aggregate, entirety, total (COMPLETENESS).

wholehearted, *adj.* sincere, heartfelt (HONESTY).

wholesaler, *n.* middleman, jobber (SALE).

wholesome, *adj.* healthful, nutritious, salubrious (HEALTH); sane, normal, healthy (SANITY).

wholly, *adv.* altogether, *in toto* (*L.*), totally (COMPLETENESS).

whoop, *v.* scream, yell, bellow (SHOUT); cough, hawk, hack (THROAT).

whore, *n.* trollop, slut, call girl (PROSTITUTE).

whorehouse, *n.* house of ill-fame, house of ill-repute (PROSTITUTE).

WICKEDNESS—*N.* wickedness, enormity, atrocity, infamy, corruption, iniquity, wrong, miscreancy, villainy, devilry, deviltry, devilment: misdeed, misdemeanor.

depravity, abandonment, perversion, immorality, obduracy, unregeneracy.

evil, maleficence, malignancy, malignity, sin, vice, malignities; ill, harm, hurt, injury, mischief.

[*evil or wicked thing*] wrong, atrocity, monster, monstrosity, hydra, curse, cancer, plague, pestilence.

evildoing, malefaction, misdoing, outrage, wrongdoing, wrong, misdeed; misbehavior, misconduct, misdemeanor.

[*place of vice*] den, nest, hotbed, sink of iniquity, cesspool, cesspit, tenderloin.

evildoer, wrongdoer, malefactor, malefactress (*fem.*), misdoer, miscreant, villain, caitiff (*archaic*), sinner, evil worker, mischiefmaker, misdemeanant, monster.

fiend, demon, devil, devil incarnate, Mephistopheles.

V. misbehave, misbehave oneself, misconduct oneself, misdemean oneself; do wrong, do evil, sin.

Adj. wicked, bad, wrong, illbehaved, naughty, atrocious, heinous, flagitious, accursed, cursed, infamous, monstrous, caitiff (*archaic*), corrupt, foul, iniquitous, miscreant, nefarious, pernicious, vile, villainous.

depraved, abandoned, perverted, unnatural, obdurate, immoral; ungodly, godless, unholy, unclean, unrighteous, unregenerate.

evil, sinister, blackhearted, evilminded, baleful, malefic, maleficent, malignant, malign, sinful, piacular, vicious.

satanic, demoniacal, devilish, diabolical, fiendish, fiendlike, Mephistophelian; hellish, infernal, hell-born.

incorrigible, irreclaimable, recidivous, irreformable, obdurate, reprobate.

See also BEHAVIOR, DEVIL, HARM, IMMORALITY, MISCHIEF, SIN. *Antonyms*—See HONESTY, MORALITY, PURIFICATION, RELIGIOUSNESS.

---

wide, *adj.* broad, squat, splay (WIDTH); extensive, far-ranging, far-reaching (STRETCH).

wide-awake, *adj.* vigilant, sleepless, insomniac (WAKEFULNESS); alert, aware, informed (KNOWLEDGE).

widen, *v.* broaden, ream, expand (WIDTH).

widespread, *adj.* prevalent, epidemic, rife (PRESENCE, DISPER-SION); wide-flung, outspread, far-flung (SPREAD).

WIDTH—*N.* width, breadth, amplitude; extent, expanse, stretch, compass, beam (*of a vessel*), tread, span, measure, reach, scope, area.

diameter, bore, caliber; radius.

dilation, dilatation, distention, expansion.

V. widen, broaden, ream; expand, spread, mushroom, open, enlarge, outstretch, stretch, distend, dilate, outspread, deploy (*mil.*), unfold, unfurl.

Adj. wide, broad, squat, squatty, splay; ample, extended, outspread, outstretched, spacious, roomy, capacious, beamy (*naut.*); extensive, comprehensive, general.

See also INCREASE, SIZE, SPACE, SPREAD, STRETCH, THICKNESS, UNFOLDMENT. *Antonyms*—See LENGTH, NARROWNESS.

---

wife, *n.* spouse, better half (*jocose*), helpmate (MARRIAGE).

wig, *n.* periwig, peruke, toupee (HAIR).

wiggle, *v.* twist, wriggle, writhe (TURNING); jiggle, shimmy, shimmer (SHAKE); wag, waggle, wave (OSCILLATION).

wigwag, *v.* signal, wave, semaphore (GESTURE, INDICATION).

wigwam, *n.* tent, tepee (HABITATION).

wild, *adj.* uncivilized, barbaric, savage (BARBARIANISM); unbridled, rampant, abandoned (FREEDOM, VIOLENCE); tumultuous, turbulent, tempestuous (UNRULINESS); rough, choppy, inclement (ROUGHNESS); angry, furious, raging (ANGER); excited, ecstatic, thrilled (EXCITEMENT); lush, luxuriant (PLANT LIFE); self-indulgent, fast (INTEMPERANCE).

wilderness, *n.* barrens, wilds (LAND); confusion, clutter, welter (CONFUSION).

wiles, *n.* deceit, trickery, skulduggery (DECEPTION).

WILL—*N.* will, volition, conation (*psychol.*); free will, accord, volitionality, volitiency; libertarianism, indeterminism, Pelagianism; voluntarism; determinism, necessitarianism, necessarianism, velleity.

will power, force of will, will of one's own, determination, resolution, decision, grit (*colloq.*), strength of character, self-control.

legal will, testament, last will and testament, devise, instrument, codicil.

bequeathal, bequeathment, bequest, devisal, devise; testacy, intestacy.

bequeather, devisor or deviser, legator, testator, testatrix (*fem.*); devisee, legatee; executor, executrix (*fem.*).

legacy, bequest, devise; inheritance, property, patrimony, heritage, estate.

V. will, volitionate; determine, decide, resolve, intend, see fit, choose, think fit, have one's own way, use one's discretion.

bequeath, bequest, legate, leave, devise; disinherit, disherit, cut off, cut out of one's will; probate a will.

Adj. volitional, volitionary, volitive, volitient, free-willed, free, unconstrained, voluntary, spontaneous; optional, discretionary, discretional, facultative.

determined, decided, resolute, resolved, set, bent, strong-willed, purposeful; autocratic, arbitrary, capricious, despotic, bossy (*colloq.*), domineering, dictatorial.

willful, intentional, deliberate, intended, designed, contemplated, purposed, premeditated, studied, planned.

self-willed, obstinate, unyielding, stubborn, perverse, headstrong.

unwilled, involuntary, reflex, reflexive, instinctive.

[*of a legal will*] testamentary, codicillary; testate, intestate; noncupative, oral, unwritten.

Adv., phrases. at will, at pleasure, à volonté (*F.*), as one thinks fit (*or proper*), ad libitum (*L.*).

voluntarily, of one's own accord, spontaneously, freely, intentionally, deliberately, purposely, by choice, of one's own free will.

See also CHOICE, INHERITANCE, PURPOSE, STUBBORNNESS, VOICE, WILLINGNESS. *Antonyms*—See INFLUENCE.

---

willful, *adj.* intentional, deliberate, intended (WILL, PURPOSE); headstrong, temperamental, froward (UNRULINESS); self-willed, wrongheaded, opinionated (STUBBORNNESS).

WILLINGNESS—N. willingness, volition, accord, zeal, enthusiasm, alacrity; disposition, inclination; assent, compliance, acquiescence.

V. be willing, incline, lean to,

not mind; acquiesce, assent, comply with; jump at, snatch at, catch at.

volunteer, offer, proffer.

make willing, dispose, incline.

Adj. willing, ready, game (*colloq.*), prompt, earnest, eager, zealous, enthusiastic; minded, disposed, inclined, prone, agreeable, amenable, well-disposed, favorably inclined, willing-hearted; alacritous, cheerful, obliging, accommodating; voluntary, unforced, unasked, unbidden, unconstrained.

Adv., phrases. willingly, readily, freely, gladly, cheerfully, lief (as in "I would as lief"), with pleasure, of one's own accord, voluntarily, with all one's heart, with alacrity; graciously, with good grace.

See also ASSENT, EAGERNESS, ENTHUSIASM, OFFER, SERVICE, TENDENCY, WILL. *Antonyms*—See DENIAL, UNWILLINGNESS.

---

will-o'-the-wisp, *n.* ignis fatuus (*L.*), jack-o'-lantern, friar's lantern (LIGHT); illusion, mare's-nest, mirage (IMAGINATION, UNREALITY, DECEPTION).

willowy, *adj.* sculpturesque, Junoesque, tall (HEIGHT).

wilt, *v.* waste, waste away, wither (WEAKNESS).

wily, *adj.* cunning, crafty, sly (CLEVERNESS); deceitful, tricky, foxy (DECEPTION).

win, *v.* triumph over, prevail against (SUCCESS); get, gain, secure (TAKING); derive, harvest, reap (ACQUISITION).

wince, *v.* shrink, flinch, cringe (REVERSION, PAIN).

wind, *v.* meander, twist, wiggle (WINDING, TURNING); wrap, envelop, muffle (ROLL).

WIND—N. wind, zephyr, breeze, sea breeze, sea wind, trade wind; northeaster, norther, southwester or sou'wester; gale, bluster; monsoon, mistral, simoon, sirocco; the elements.

[*in classical mythology*] Aeolus or Eolus, cave of Aeolus; Boreas (*north wind*), Eurus (*east wind*), Zephyrus or Favonius (*west wind*), Notus (*south wind*), Caurus (*northwest wind*), Vulturnus or Volturnus (*southwest wind*), Afer (*southwest wind*).

gust, blast, blow, squall, flaw, windflaw, flurry; puff, breath, flatus, waft, whiff.

windstorm, storm, big blow, gale, cyclone, hurricane, tornado, twister, typhoon, squall, north-easter, southwester *or* sou'wester, tempest, bluster, equinoctial, blizzard, whirlwind, dust devil; storminess, turbulence, weather.

wind gauge, anemometer, ventometer, anemograph, anemoscope; wind vane, weathercock, weather vane, vane.

science of wind: anemology, aerodynamics, aerology, pneumatics; cyclonology.

Adj. **windy,** breezy, blowy, blasty, blustery, blusterous, blustering, squally, gusty, flawy; choppy, fluky; wind-swept, exposed, bleak, raw, breeze-swept, wind-blown.

stormy, tempestuous, violent, rugged, wintry, raging, turbulent; cyclonic, typhonic, tornadic; blizzardous, blizzardy.

See also AIR, BLOWING, BREATH, ROUGHNESS, VIOLENCE. *Antonyms—* See CALMNESS.

---

winded, *adj.* short-winded, pursy, breathless (BREATH).

windfall, *n.* fortune, good fortune, fluke (GOOD LUCK).

WINDING—*N.* **winding,** wind, convolution, complication, entanglement, torsion, vermiculation, crook, meander, zigzag, wriggle, squirm; curl, crispation, crispature, crimp, swirl; coil, corkscrew, involution, whorl; spiral, helix, curlicue, gyration; knot, loop, mat, kink; braid, cue, queue (*hair*), plait, wattle; maze, labyrinth, crinkum-crankum.

twist, ply, quirk, torsion, warp, warpage, contortion, intorsion, deformation, distortion, torture.

V. **wind,** crook, meander, slither, snake, zigzag, back and fill, twine, whip around, whip through, weave, writhe, wriggle, skew, squirm; curl, crisp, crimp, friz, swirl, coil, corkscrew, wreathe, convolute, convolve, wrap around, involute, spiral, gyrate; reel; knot, loop, mat, kink.

twist, warp, contort, intort, deform, distort, gnarl, torture; wrench, wrest, wring; tweak, twinge, twiddle.

weave, braid, cue, complect, complicate, plait, raddle, ravel, wattle; entwine, intertwine, interweave, intertwist, interwind, interwreathe, interlace, entangle.

[*curl up in comfort*] **cuddle,** snuggle, nestle.

Adj. **winding,** meandering, meandrous, snaky, serpentine,

sinuous, zigzag; ambagious, circuitous, devious, flexuous, voluminous, convolute, convoluted; wriggly, squirming, eely, vermicular; mazy, labyrinthine, labyrinthian, intricate, involved; reticular, plexiform.

spiral, coiled, tortile, helical, helicoid, whorled, cochleate, cochleous, volute, corkscrew, gyrate, gyratory.

crooked, knurly, tortile, tortuous, wry, awry, askew.

curly, crisp, crispated, crispy, curled, frizzed, frizzled, crimpy, swirly, aswirl, cirrose; kinky, matted, matty, knotted, knotty, looped, loopy.

wavy, undulating, undulant, undulatory, undulated, undulative, ripply.

Adv., phrases. **convolutely,** windingly, etc. (see *Adjectives*); in and out, round and round.

See also BEND, CURVE, DEFORMITY, TEXTURE, TURNING. *Antonyms—*See STRAIGHTNESS, VERTICALITY.

---

window, *n.* casement, skylight, transom (OPENING, BLOWING).

windpipe, *n.* throttle, trachea, weasand (BREATH, AIR OPENING).

windstorm, *n.* gale, cyclone, hurricane (WIND).

wind-swept, *adj.* exposed, bleak, raw (WIND).

windy, *adj.* breezy, blowy, blustery (WIND); wordy, long-winded, lengthy (WORDINESS).

wine, *n. vin ordinaire* (*F.*), champagne (ALCOHOLIC LIQUOR).

wing, *n.* pennon, penna (APPENDAGE); annex, extension (BUILDING); branch, bridge (STRETCH); unit, arm, detachment (PART).

wink, *v.* twinkle, bat, blink (CLOSURE).

wink at, *v.* overlook, blink at, condone (FORGIVENESS, INATTENTION, PERMISSION).

winner, *n.* victor, master, champion (SUCCESS, ATTEMPT, DEFEAT).

winning, *adj.* winsome, charming, engaging (LOVE).

winnow, *v.* select, pick, cull (CHOICE); strain, screen, separate (CLEANNESS).

win over, *v.* convince, prevail on, sway (PERSUASION).

winsome, *adj.* charming, engaging, piquant (PLEASANTNESS, LOVE, ATTRACTION).

winter, *n.* wintertime (SEASONS).

wintery, *adj.* brumal, hiemal (SEASONS).

winy, *adj.* vinous, vinaceous (ALCOHOLIC LIQUOR).

wipe, v. towel, swab, sponge (RUB-BING, CLEANNESS).

WISDOM—N. wisdom, depth, profundity; judgment, acumen, common sense, horse sense (colloq.), practicality, sapience, sagacity, discernment, subtlety, discrimination; omniscience, pansophism; sophistication.

prudence, discretion, expedience, politics, diplomacy, tact.

wise man, sage, Solomon, Nestor, Confucius, solon, pundit, philosopher, thinker; worldling, sophisticate, cosmopolite, pansophist.

goddess of wisdom: Athena, Athene, Pallas or Pallas Athena (Greek); Minerva (Roman).

Adj. wise, deep, profound, Solomonic, philosophical, sensible, shrewd, knowing, astute, sagacious, sage, sapient (often ironical), commonsensical, well-balanced, commonsensible (colloq.), farsighted, levelheaded, coolheaded; discerning, subtle, perceptive, discriminating; all-wise, all-knowing, omniscient, pansophical; worldly-wise, worldly, sophisticated, practical; oracular, Palladian.

prudent, judicious, discreet, expedient, politic, diplomatic, tactful; rational, sound, advisable, well-advised.

See also CARE, DEPTH, FORESIGHT, INTELLIGENCE, JUDGMENT, LEARNING, UNDERSTANDING. Antonyms—See ABSURDITY, FOLLY, STUPIDITY.

wisecrack (slang), n. quip, bon mot (F.), joke (WITTINESS).

wish, n. ambition, aspiration, want, craving, longing (DESIRE).

wish, v. want, crave, desire (DESIRE).

wishbone, n. furculum, merrythought (BONE).

wishful, adj. desirous, wistful, wantful (DESIRE).

wishy-washy, adj. weak-kneed, irresolute, indecisive (WEAKNESS).

wispy, adj. gossamer, filmy, diaphanous (THINNESS).

wistful, adj. desirous, wishful, wantful (DESIRE); melancholy, sad, pensive (SADNESS).

wit, n. pleasantry, levity, repartee; humorist, wag, comic (WITTINESS); brains, sense, mental ability (INTELLIGENCE); penetration, acumen, judgment (UNDERSTANDING).

witch, n. sorceress, enchantress, siren (MAGIC); giglet, minx, hoyden (YOUTH); crone, hag, beldam (OLDNESS).

witchcraft, n. witchery, sorcery, wizardry (MAGIC, SUPERNATURALISM).

witch doctor, n. medicine man, shaman, healer (MAGIC, MEDICAL SCIENCE).

with, prep. together with, along with (ACCOMPANIMENT).

withdraw, v. retreat, retire, secede (DEPARTURE, ABSENCE, RELINQUISHMENT); keep aloof, keep apart (SECLUSION); extract, whip out, unsheathe (EXTRACTION).

withdrawn, adj. unsociable, nongregarious, retiring (SECLUSION).

wither, v. parch, scorch, shrivel (DRYNESS); atrophy, blast, blight (DECAY); waste, waste away, wilt (WEAKNESS); mildew, rust, stale (OLDNESS).

withered, adj. shriveled, wizened, macerated (THINNESS).

withhold, v. keep, keep back, retain (HOLD); reserve, hold back (RESTRAINT); keep from, hide (CONCEALMENT).

within, adj. inside, interior, inner (INTERIORITY).

without, adv. outside, out, out-of-doors (EXTERIORITY).

without, prep. less, minus (ABSENCE).

withstand, v. prevail against, resist, weather (SUCCESS); oppose, violate, defy (OPPOSITION).

witless, adj. half-witted, dull-witted, dumb (STUPIDITY).

witness, n. spectator, onlooker, bystander (LOOKING, VISION); signer, signatory, attestant (SIGNATURE).

witness, v. see, behold, observe (VISION, LOOKING); sign, countersign, attest (SIGNATURE).

witticism, n. joke, squib, sally (WITTINESS).

WITTINESS—N. wittiness, comicality, drollery, jocosity, jocularity, ribaldry, scurrility, whimsicality, pleasantry, levity, wit, repartee, waggery, whimsey, slapstick, farce, esprit (F.).

joke, jest, jape, japery, spoof, quip, wisecrack (slang), gag (colloq.), jocosity, jocularity, bon mot (F.), witticism, squib, sally, quirk, pleasantry, mot (F.), chestnut, wheeze, jokelet, legpull; facetiae (pl.).

practical joke, jape, japery, lark, prank, trick.

humorist, wag, wit, farceur (F.), droll, ribald, comic, comedian, comedienne (F., fem.), reparteeist, first banana or top banana (burlesque comedian—theatrical slang), gag man (*slang*), gagster (*slang*), cartoonist, comic artist.

joker, jokester, jokist, josher, jester, japer, quipster, wisecracker (*slang*), ribald, *farceur* (*F.*), wag, clown, picador.

practical joker, jester, larker, prankster.

V. **be witty,** flash, scintillate, be the life of the party; salt, farce; humorize.

joke, make (*or* crack) a joke, banter, chaff, josh, droll, fool, jest, jape, kid (*slang*), spoof, quip, wisecrack (*slang*), crack wise (*slang*); pull one's leg.

play practical jokes, jape, lark, prank; play a joke on.

Adj. **witty,** humorous, funny, jocose, jocular, waggish, amusing, droll, comical, comic, whimsical, facetious, ribald, Rabelaisian, scurrilous, salty, slapstick; poker-faced, dry; *spirituel* (*F., masc.*), *spirituelle* (*F., fem.*); joking, bantery, jesting, kidding (*slang*), spoofing, quippish, quippy, quipsome.

[*given to practical jokes*] **prank-ish,** larksome, pranksome, pranky, tricksome, tricksy.

See also ABSURDITY, AMUSEMENT, FOLLY, FRIVOLITY, MISCHIEF, RIDI-CULE, TEASING. *Antonyms*—See BOREDOM, DULLNESS, SOBRIETY.

---

wizard, *n.* sorcerer, magician, en-chanter (MAGIC); past master, shark (ABILITY).

wizened, *adj.* shriveled, withered, macerated (THINNESS).

wobble, *v.* sway, reel, totter (UN-STEADINESS, OSCILLATION); waver, vacillate, back and fill (UNCER-TAINTY).

wobbly, *adj.* rickety, rocky, wa-very, tottery (UNSTEADINESS).

woe, *n.* sorrow, grief, grieving (SADNESS).

woebegone, *adj.* miserable, wretched, mournful (SADNESS).

woeful, *adj.* lugubrious, sad, mournful, lamentable (SADNESS).

wolf, *v.* devour, swallow, gobble up (RECEIVING).

woman, *n.* she, lady (FEMALE).

womanish, *adj.* tender, soft, effete (WEAKNESS).

womanly, *adj.* feminine, gentle (FEMALE).

women, *n.* womankind, woman-hood (FEMALE).

wonder, *n.* awe, stupefaction, shock; marvel, prodigy, miracle (SURPRISE).

wonder, *v.* marvel, be amazed (SURPRISE); doubt, disbelieve (UNBELIEVINGNESS).

wonderful, *adj.* marvelous, fabu-lous, spectacular (SURPRISE); ex-cellent, prime, superb (GOOD).

wont, *adj.* habituated, addicted, accustomed (HABIT).

wont, *n.* rule, practice, custom (HABIT, USE).

woo, *v.* make love, spoon, court (LOVE); pursue, seek, solicit (AT-TEMPT).

wood, *n.* lumber, timber (WOOD); forest, woodland, woods (PLANT LIFE).

WOOD—*N.* wood, lumber, timber, hardwood; framing, sheathing, lathing, siding, clapboard, ground-sill, shingle, lath, panel, base-board, woodwork; board, slat, stave, slab, stick, list, wedge, bill-board; plank, pole, stud, post, two-by-four, beam; fagot, brand, cinder.

V. **cover with wood:** plank, board, board up, clapboard, lath, panel, shingle, frame; lignify.

Adj. **wooden,** wood, timbered, frame, woody, ligneous, ligniform.

See also PLANT LIFE, ROD, WOOD-WORKING.

---

woodcraft, *n.* arts and crafts, shop, carpentry (WOODWORKING).

woodcutter, *n.* lumberjack, woods-man, logger (WOODWORKING).

wooden, *adj.* wood, timbered, frame (WOOD); woody, xyloid, ligneous (PLANT LIFE); ungrace-ful, stiff, awkward (CLUMSI-NESS); glassy, glazed (DEATH).

woodland, *n.* forest, woods, wood (PLANT LIFE).

woodsman, *n.* logger, woodcutter, woodchopper, lumberman, lum-berjack (WOODWORKING).

WOODWORKING—*N.* woodwork-ing, woodcraft, arts and crafts, shop, carpentry, cabinetmaking, furniture making, joinery; wood-work; woodcutting, lumbering, logging.

woodworker, carpenter, cabinet-maker, joiner, woodcraftsman.

woodcutter, woodchopper, lum-berman, lumberjack, woodsman, logger.

V. **carpenter,** do carpentry; lum-ber, log, cut, saw, chop.

See also CUTTING, WOOD.

WOOL—*N.* wool, fleece, yarn, shag, fur, coat, pelage; silk, sericulture.

woolliness, flocculence, lanosity, villosity.

Adj. **woolly**, fleecy, floccose, flocculent, flocky, lanate, lanose, villous.

silk, silken, silky, sericeous.

See also HAIR, TEXTURE.

---

woolgathering, *n.* preoccupation, brown study (*colloq.*), reverie (INATTENTION).

woolly, *adj.* fleecy, flocculent (WOOL); hairy, hirsute, shaggy; curly-headed, curly-haired (HAIR).

WORD—*N.* word, expression, locution, term, vocable; blend, portmanteau word, clipped word, contraction, element, enclitic, additive, atonic, abstraction, morpheme, semanteme, usage, epithet, *mot juste* (*F.*); interjection, exclamation, expletive; anagram, acronym, palindrome, spoonerism; euphemism, conceit; Anglicism, Briticism, cockneyism, Hibernicism, Gallicism, Grecism, Atticism; synonym, antonym, cognate, doublet, heteronym, homograph, homonym, homophone, paronym.

catchword, byword, shibboleth, slogan, counterword.

password, watchword, countersign.

colloquialism, vernacularism, idiom, provincialism, localism, barbarism, vulgarism.

new word, neologism, neology, neoterism, coined word, nonce word.

words, wordage, phrase, phraseology, terminology, vocabulary, lexicon, text, context, libretto, lyrics.

word part, element, etymon, stem, root, affix, prefix, suffix, postfix; syllable.

dictionary, lexicon, wordbook, glossary, thesaurus; lexicography, lexicographer.

word game, anagrams, charades, logomachy.

parts of speech: adjective, adverb, conjunction, interjection, noun, preposition, pronoun, verb.

V. word, phrase, express, voice, put into words, give expression to, clothe in words.

Adj. verbal, lexical, vocabular, phrasal, phraseological, terminological, textual; oral, spoken, unwritten.

See also EXPRESSION, LANGUAGE, STATEMENT, TALK, VOICE, WORDINESS.

---

word-for-word, *adj.* literal, verbatim, textual (MEANING).

WORDINESS—*N.* wordiness, verbosity, prolixity, macrology, verbalism, verbiage, diffusion; pleonasm, redundancy, tautology; surplusage, multiloquence, padding; gobbledygook, officialese.

roundaboutness, indirection, circumlocution, circumbendibus, periphrasis.

bombast, fustian, grandiosity, pomposity, tumidity, turgidity, magniloquence, grandiloquence, sesquipedalianism; embellishment, floridity, ornamentation, euphuism, luxuriance, orotundity, flamboyancy.

V. be wordy, expatiate, enlarge, dilate, amplify, descant, expand, inflate, pad; harp upon, dwell on; embellish, ornament.

digress, ramble, wander, beat about the bush.

Adj. **wordy**, long-winded, lengthy, windy, verbose, prolix, diffuse, diffusive, multiloquent, copious; pleonastic, redundant, tautological.

roundabout, indirect, circumlocutory, periphrastic, ambagious; discursive, digressive, wandering, rambling.

grandiloquent, magniloquent, bombastic, fustian, grandiose, pompous, inflated, pretentious, swollen, tumid, turgid, toplofty, sesquipedalian; embellished, florid, flowery, ornate, ornamented, euphuistic, luxuriant, orotund, purple, Corinthian, flamboyant, plethoric, rhetorical, stilted; highfalutin (*colloq.*), high-flown, high-sounding.

See also ORNAMENT, REPETITION, UNCLEARNESS, WANDERING, WORD. *Antonyms*—See CLARITY, SHORTNESS, SIMPLICITY.

---

wording, *n.* style, phraseology, phrasing (EXPRESSION).

wordless, *adj.* speechless, voiceless, mute; unspoken, tacit, implied (SILENCE).

wordy, *adj.* long-winded, lengthy, windy (WORDINESS).

work, *n.* toil, labor (WORK); composition, opus, creation (PRODUCTION).

WORK—*N.* work, labors, endeavors; business, trade, occupation, profession, pursuit; crafts, handicraft, manual work; application, specialization, specialism; operation, manipulation, mechanism, function; craftsmanship, skill, workmanship; *modus operandi* (*L.*).

toil, travail, struggle, drudgery, labor, sweat of one's brow, overwork, slavery, servitude, grind, moil.

co-operation, collaboration, teamwork, synergy, synergism (*physiol.*), connivance, collusion.

task, job, chore, stint, char, boondoggle.

workshop, studio, workroom, study, library, den, atelier, vineyard; shop, plant, factory, mill, laboratory, billet.

shift, tour, hitch, spell, turn, trick, char; night shift, swing shift, graveyard shift (*colloq.*).

employer, boss, taskmaster, master; foreman, straw boss, superintendent, manager.

employee, worker, wage earner, provider, outlier, office worker, white-collar worker, clerk, general factotum, office boy, office girl, secretary, typist, stenographer, executive.

laborer, proletarian, manual worker, day laborer, dayworker, roustabout, stevedore, longshoreman, floater, wetback, coolie, Okie, migratory worker; hand, hired man, handy man, hired girl; workman, workingman, workingwoman, working girl, *grisette* (*F.*).

mechanic, toolman, tooler, operator, manipulator; artisan, craftsman, technician, practitioner, specialist, artificer, artist.

helper, assistant, subordinate, apprentice, journeyman, underling, understrapper, agent; hireling, pensioner, hack (*all derogatory*).

co-worker, teamworker, fellow worker, mate, buddy (*colloq.*), partner, associate, workfellow; co-operator, collaborator, conniver.

toiler, drudge, drudger, grind, grub, plodder, slave, peon; hard worker, hustler, beaver.

potterer, piddler, niggler, tinker, tinkerer, cobbler, dabster, boondoggler, dabbler.

staff, force, office force, personnel, employees, workers, crew, gang, team; proletariat, working people, working class.

V. work, apply oneself, endeavor, try, ply, ply one's trade, pursue, specialize in; co-operate, synergize, collaborate, connive with, collude with; do odd jobs, char, clerk; operate, function; manipulate, manage, run, drive.

toil, labor, sweat, travail, drudge, grind (*colloq.*), plod, grub, moil, struggle, strive, slave, overwork.

tinker, boggle, dabble, boondoggle, niggle, piddle, potter.

Adj. hard-working, industrious, operose, laborious, sedulous, diligent, assiduous.

[*requiring hard work*] strenuous, arduous, laborious, toilsome, toilful, operose.

See also AGENT, AID, ATTEMPT, BUSINESS, CO-OPERATION, SERVICE, SLAVERY, USE. Antonyms—See FRIVOLITY, PLAY, REST.

---

workmanship, *n.* craftsmanship, skill, competence (WORK, ABILITY).

WORLD—*N.* world, creation, nature, universe; earth, terra (*L.; used esp. in phrases*), planet, terrene, globe, sphere, terrestrial globe, wide world; cosmos, macrocosm, microcosm.

heavenly bodies, celestial bodies, luminaries, stars, asteroids, planetoids; Galaxy, Milky Way, galactic circle; constellations, planets, satellites; comet, meteor, falling (*or* shooting) star, meteoroid, aerolite, meteorite; solar system; planets (Mercury, Venus, Earth, Mars, Jupiter, Saturn, Uranus, Neptune, Pluto).

sun, orb *or* orb of day (*poetic*), daystar (*poetic*), fireball, luminary; sun god, Sol (*Roman*), Hyperion (*Gr.*), Helios (*Gr.*), Phoebus *or* Phoebus Apollo (*Gr.*), Phaëthon (*Gr.*), Ra (*Egyptian*), Shamash (*Assyrian*).

moon, satellite, new moon, crescent, increscent moon, decrescent moon, half-moon, demilune, full moon, plenilune (*poetic*), harvest moon, hunter's moon; Queen of Night, moon goddess, Luna (*Roman*), Diana, Phoebe, Cynthia, Artemis, Hecate, Selene (*Gr.*), Astarte (*Phoenician*); Sputnik (*Russian*), Explorer (*U.S.*), Vanguard (*U.S.*).

science of heavenly bodies: astronomy, astrology, astrometry, uranology, astrochemistry, astrophysics, aerology (*Mars*), selenology (*moon*), heliology (*sun*).

cosmology, cosmography, cosmogony.

astronomer, stargazer, astrophysicist, astrochemist, uranologist.

astrologer, astromancer, astroalchemist, Chaldean, soothsayer.

Adj. earthly, global, mundane, planetary, sublunary *or* sublunar, subsolar, subastral, tellurian, telluric, terrene, terrestrial.

worldly, worldly-minded, earthen, earthy, mundane, secular, subcelestial, sublunary *or* sublunar, subsolar, temporal, terrene, terrestrial, unspiritual, profane; carnal, fleshly.

cosmic, universal, cosmogonal, extraterrestrial.

empyrean, empyreal, celestial, heavenly, uranic, astronomical; starry, stellar, astral, sidereal, planetary; solar, heliacal; lunar, Cynthian (*poetic*), lunate, crescent-shaped; planetoidal, asteroidal, nebular; interstellar, intersidereal.

Phrases. in all creation, on the face of the globe, here below, under the sun.

See also HEAVEN, IRRELIGION, LAND, SPACE, SPIRITUALITY, WISDOM.

---

worldly, *adj.* sophisticated, practical (WISDOM); earthy, mundane (WORLD, IRRELIGION).

worm, *n.* angleworm, earthworm (ANIMAL); wretch, cur, sneak (MEANNESS).

worn, *adj.* shabby, well-worn, threadbare (USE).

worried, *adj.* anxious, solicitous, troubled (NERVOUSNESS).

worrier, *n.* fuss-budget (*colloq.*), fusser, fretter (NERVOUSNESS).

worry, *n.* anxiety, worriment, apprehension (NERVOUSNESS).

worry, *v.* bother, disturb, trouble (ANNOYANCE); stew (*colloq.*), fret, fuss (NERVOUSNESS).

worse, *adj.* deteriorated, impaired, regressed (DETERIORATION).

worsen, *v.* deteriorate, degenerate; aggravate, impair (DETERIORATION).

WORSHIP—*N.* worship, adoration, deification, apotheosis, veneration, reverence, glorification, awe; kneeling, genuflection, prostration; misworship, whoredom, Baalism; idolatry, idolism, idolization, idol worship, hero worship, avatar; fetishism.

devotions, service *or* services, chapel, prayer, liturgy, rite *or* rites, ritual.

prayer, invocation, supplication, intercession, petition; collect, miserere, rogation, litany, Lord's prayer, paternoster; Ave, Ave Maria, Hail Mary; complin *or* compline; Mass, Eucharist, Lord's Supper, Holy Communion, Communion; matins, morning prayer, vespers, vigils, lauds (*pl.*).

sacrifice, victim, burnt offering, hecatomb, holocaust, mactation, human sacrifice, immolation, self-immolation, suttee.

offering, oblation, incense, libation; offertory, collection.

praise, laudation, exaltation, magnification, glorification, paean, benediction, grace, thanksgiving, doxology, hosanna, hallelujah, alleluia, *Te Deum* (*L.*), Magnificat (*L.*), Gloria (*L.*); psalm, hymn, chant; response, anthem, motet, antiphon, antiphony.

idol, image, golden calf, graven image, fetish, joss (*Chinese*), false god, heathen deity, Baal, Moloch, Dagon, Juggernaut.

worshiper, adorer, deifier, venerator, reverer, glorifier, hymner, kneeler, genuflector; liturgist; misworshiper, Baalist *or* Baalite; idolater, idolatress (*fem.*), idolizer, idolatrizer, hero-worshiper, fetishist.

science of worship: liturgics, liturgiology.

V. worship, adore, deify, apotheosize, venerate, revere, reverence, glorify; kneel, genuflect, prostrate oneself before, bow down and worship; misworship, whore, Baalize, worship idols; idolize, idolatrize, put on a pedestal.

pray, invoke, supplicate, commune with God, offer up prayers, say one's prayers; tell one's beads, recite the rosary.

praise, laud, glorify, magnify, exalt, celebrate, extol; sing praises, chant, hymn, doxologize; say grace.

Adj. worshipful, etc. (see *Verbs*); deific, reverent, reverential, idolatrous.

[*pert. to worship*] devotional, liturgical, liturgiological, genuflectory, ritual, ritualistic; idolistic, fetishistic, Baalitical.

[*worthy of worship*] reverend, venerable, awful; revered, etc. (see *Verbs*).

See also FORMALITY, KILLING, LOVE, PRAISE, RELIGIOUSNESS, RESPECT, SUICIDE. *Antonyms*—See IRRELIGION.

---

worth, *n.* value, advantage, benefit; merit, dignity, caliber (VALUE).

WORTHLESSNESS—*N.* worthlessness, vanity.

[*worthless person*] good-for-nothing, offscouring, scalawag, scapegrace, scamp, snake, vagabond, vermin; ne'er-do-well, black sheep, cur, bum (*colloq.*); hussy, baggage.

[*worthless people*] trash, dregs, raff, scum, vermin.

rubbish, chaff, trash, tripe, truck, trumpery, waste.

[*worthless thing*] trifle, trinket, picayune, rush; bauble, gewgaw, tinsel, trumpery.

V. lose value, cheapen, decline, depreciate, drop, fall, impair, toboggan.

devaluate, devalue, cheapen, debase, depreciate, depress, impair; adulterate, alloy; minimize.

[*consider unworthy*] disdain, scorn, slight, ignore, disregard.

Adj. worthless, feckless, useless, good-for-nothing, nugatory, picayune *or* picayunish, rubbishy, scummy, trashy, vagabond, vain, valueless, verminous, vile, waste, worm-eaten, wretched; cheap, catchpenny, tinsel, trumpery; base, paltry, petty, trifling, hollow.

unworthy, undeserving; undeserved, unmerited.

See also MEANNESS, UNCLEANNESS, USELESSNESS. *Antonyms*—See USE, VALUE.

---

worth-while, *adj.* valuable, invaluable, priceless (VALUE).

worthy, *adj.* profitable, advantageous, favorable (USE); deserving, meritorious (VALUE).

wound, *n.* injury, lesion, bruise (HARM).

wound, *v.* injure, bruise, contuse (HARM); offend, hurt, cut (OFFENSE).

woven, *adj.* textural, textile, textured (TEXTURE).

wrangle, *v.* quarrel, scrap (*colloq.*), brawl (DISAGREEMENT).

wrap, *n.* cloak, cape, capote (COAT); shawl, stole, fichu (NECKWEAR).

wrap, *v.* envelop, wind, muffle (ROLL); clothe, swaddle, bundle up (CLOTHING); hide, screen, shroud (CONCEALMENT); cover, invest, overspread (COVERING).

wrap around, *v.* coil, corkscrew, convolve (WINDING).

wrapper, *n.* wrapping, jacket, envelope (COVERING); housecoat, duster, kimono (CLOTHING).

wraps, *n.* overclothes, outer dress, outerwear (CLOTHING).

wrath, *n.* rage, ire, fury (ANGER).

wreath, *n.* circle, ring, ringlet (ROUNDNESS); leafage, bouquet (PLANT LIFE); reward, laurel, garland (PAYMENT); belt, girdle, aura (ENVIRONMENT).

wreathe, *v.* twist, swirl, corkscrew (WINDING); encircle, surround, ring (ROUNDNESS); invest, swathe, envelop (ENVIRONMENT).

wreck, *v.* ruin, smash, demolish (DESTRUCTION).

wrench, *v.* tweak, twist, twinge (TRACTION); wrest, wring (WINDING); distort, twist (MISREPRESENTATION).

wrest, *v.* exact, extort, squeeze (FORCE); wrench, wring (WINDING).

wretch, *n.* worm, cur, swine (MEANNESS, CONTEMPT).

wretched, *adj.* miserable, desolate, forlorn (SADNESS); dejected, abject, spiritless (DEJECTION); pitiful, sorry, pathetic (SADNESS, PITY); low, miserable, vile (MEANNESS, CONTEMPT).

wriggle, *v.* twist, wiggle, squirm (TURNING, WINDING).

wring, *v.* squeeze, choke, throttle (PRESSURE); wrench, wrest (WINDING); exact, extort, pry (FORCE).

WRINKLE—*N.* wrinkle, rugosity, crease, cockle, pucker, ruffle, rumple, ruck, seam, crinkle, corrugation, furrow, crumple, crow's-foot; crispation, crispature, contraction (*of the forehead*).

V. wrinkle, crease, cockle, pucker, purse, ruffle, rumple, ruck, seam, wreathe, crinkle, corrugate, furrow, crumple, crisp.

Adj. wrinkled, corrugate, bullate, rugged, rugose, seamy, crinkly, puckery, ruffly, rumply.

See also FOLD, ROUGHNESS. *Antonyms*—See SMOOTHNESS.

---

wrist, *n.* carpus (APPENDAGE).

writ, *n.* summons, process, subpoena (COURT OF LAW); mandate, prescript (COMMAND).

write, *v.* put down, set down, jot down, note; keep in touch, communicate (WRITING, EPISTLE).

WRITER—*N.* writer, scribe, penman, calligraphist, chirographer, yeoman (*U.S. Navy*), clerk, copyist, transcriber, amanuensis, scrivener, secretary, stenographer, tachygrapher, shorthand writer, phonographer, stenotypist, typist; correspondent, drafter, composer, framer, inditer, inscriber, recorder, redactor, registrar, transcriber, autographer.

author, authoress, littérateur (*F.*), free lance, collaborator, coauthor, essayist, pamphleteer, tractator; novelist, fictionist, allegorist, anecdotist, fabulist, folklorist, memorialist, narrator, parabolist, romancer, scenarist, serialist, tale-teller, storyteller, yarner; playwright, dramatist, librettist, poet; contributor, columnist, paragraphist; hack writer, hack.

See also WRITING.

writhe, v. twist, wriggle, wiggle (TURNING, WINDING); suffer, ail, pain (PAIN).

WRITING—N. [act of writing] writing, composition, collaboration, transcription, superscription, inscription, subscription, redaction, endorsement or indorsement, correspondence, expatiation, description; tachygraphy, pseudography, graphorrhea.

[something written, piece of writing, etc.] composition, essay, theme, manuscript, typescript, script, piece, copy, paper, article, thesis, treatise; collaboration; draft, rough draft, sketch, outline; note, marginalia (pl.), jotting, record; transcript, superscript, subscript; postscript, adscript; pseudograph, pseudographia; prose; passage, excerpt, extract, text; chrestomathy.

inscription, epigraph, epitaph, legend, circumscription, dedication, envoy, envoi (F.); autograph.

desire to write, itch to write, creative urge, cacoëthes scribendi (L.), furor scribendi (L.), graphomania.

handwriting, longhand, chirography, manuscription, calligraphy, autograph; text hand, flowing hand, bold hand, cursive writing; macrography, micrography; scrawl, scribble, scrabble, hen tracks (slang), hieroglyphics, cacography, griffonage, illegible writing; hand, penmanship; script, printing, backhand.

[systems] stenography, shorthand, phonography, stenotypy, tachygraphy, speed-writing; logography; ideography, lexigraphy, hieroglyphics, pasigraphy, cuneiform, stylography, cerography, uncial writing; paleography.

writing instrument, pen, fountain pen, stylograph, ball-point pen, pencil, stylus, cymograph, polygraph, micrograph; stationery.

curlicue, flourish, quirk, curl, twist, spiral.

analysis of handwriting: graphology, bibliotics.

secret writing, code, cipher, cryptography, steganography; cryptogram, cryptograph, steganogram.

manuscript, original, author's copy, autograph, holograph; script, typescript, parchment, vellum; palimpsest, opisthograph, paleograph, tachygraph; document, paper, certificate, deed, instrument.

V. write, write down, write out, put down, set down, jot down, note, note down, record, take pen in hand, doodle, typewrite, type, dash off; inscribe, subscribe, superscribe, transcribe, copy, endorse or indorse; correspond, correspond with, write to, keep in touch with; write about, describe, expatiate on (or upon); enroll, register; edit, redact.

compose, draft, indite, frame, draw up, formulate, turn out; collaborate.

write by hand, pen, engross, autograph; scrawl, scribble, scrabble, scratch.

Adj. written, scriptural, superscript, subscript, postscript, adscript, in writing, in black and white.

handwritten, longhand, Spencerian, autographic, chirographic, calligraphic; cursive, running, flowing, legible.

scrawly, scribbly, scrabbly, sprawling, sprawly, cacographic, cramped, illegible, indecipherable.

See also BOOK, DESCRIPTION, DRAMA, EPISTLE, MOTION PICTURES, PAPER, POETRY, PRINTING, PUBLICATION, READING, RECORD, SIGNATURE, STORY, TREATISE, WRITER, WRITTEN SYMBOL.

WRITTEN SYMBOL—N. written symbol, letter, character, symbol, type, hieroglyph, hieroglyphic; capital, big (or large) letter, majuscule, uncial, upper-case letter; small letter, lower-case letter, minuscule; alphabet, ABC; consonant, vowel, diphthong, mute, surd, sonant, liquid, nasal, labial, palatal, dental, guttural; first letter, initial; Z, zed (Brit.), izzard (dial.); italic, cursive, pothook; ideogram, ideograph, pictograph, logogram, phonogram; rune (anc. Teutonic).

code, cryptography, cipher; acrostic, double acrostic; device, monogram, anagram; hieroglyphics, cuneiform, sphenogram; Rosetta stone.

spelling, orthography, phonetic spelling, phonetics, phonography; heterography; notation, ideography, pictography; incorrect spelling, misspelling, pseudography.

syllable, atonic, tonic; antepenult, penult, ultima; prefix, suffix, ending, affix, particle; monosyllable, dissyllable, trisyllable, tetrasyllable, quadrisyllable, pentasyllable, octosyllable, decasyllable, polysyllable.

punctuation mark, period, comma, colon, semicolon, dash, hyphen, question mark, interrogation mark (*or* point), suspension periods (*or* points), parenthesis, braces, bracket, exclamation point (*or* mark), wonder mark, virgule, apostrophe; asterisk, caret, dagger, obelisk, ditto, ditto mark.

diacritical mark, dot, tittle, accent, accent mark, dieresis, umlaut, cedilla, breve, macron.

footnote, *q.v.*, *v.*, *ibid.*, *cf.*, *n.b.*, *sic.*

V. letter, inscribe, stamp, mark, sign, initial.

spell, orthographize, form words, trace out; misspell; alphabetize, syllabify, syllabicate.

punctuate, hyphenate, parenthesize, bracket, apostrophize; accent, asterisk, star, umlaut, italicize, underline, underscore; proofread, copy-edit, correct, revise.

Adj. literal, monoliteral, biliteral, triliteral, quadriliteral; capital, uncial, upper-case, majuscule *or* majuscular; lower-case, minuscular; consonantal, consonant, vowel, vocalic; cursive, italic.

alphabetic, alphabetical, abecedarian; Roman, Cyrillic, runic, hieroglyphic, cuneiform, sphenographic.

See also EPISTLE, SIGNATURE, VOICE, WRITING.

wrong, *adj.* erroneous, inaccurate, incorrect (MISTAKE); improper, inappropriate, unseemly (IMPROPERNESS); bad, ill-behaved, naughty (WICKEDNESS); sinful, piacular, unregenerate (SIN); unethical, unjust, wrongful (IMPROPERNESS).

wrong, *n.* iniquity, miscreancy, villainy; atrocity, monstrosity (WICKEDNESS); offense, transgression, vice (SIN); violence, outrage, grievance (HARM).

wrong, *v.* injure, damage, hurt (HARM, IMPROPERNESS).

wrongdoer, *n.* evildoer, malefactor (WICKEDNESS, ILLEGALITY); sinner, offender, transgressor (SIN).

wrongdoing, *n.* evildoing, malefaction (WICKEDNESS); malfeasance, misfeasance, misdeeds (BEHAVIOR).

wrongheaded, *adj.* willful, self-willed (STUBBORNNESS).

wrought up, *adj.* hysterical, overwrought (EXCITEMENT).

wry, *adj.* crooked, awry, askew (WINDING, DEFORMITY); wrongheaded, willful, self-willed (STUBBORNNESS).

X

X-ray, *v.* fluoroscope, radiograph, skiagraph (PHOTOGRAPH).

X-ray photograph, *n.* roentgenogram, tomogram, radiogram, skiagram (PHOTOGRAPH).

X-ray therapy, *n.* roentgenothera-py, radiotherapy, radium therapy (CURE, PHOTOGRAPH).

x-shaped, *adj.* crossed, decussate, cruciate (CROSSING).

xyloid, *adj.* woody, wooden, ligneous (PLANT LIFE).

Y

yacht, *n.* cruiser, cabin cruiser (SHIP).

yank (*colloq.*), *v.* pull, draw, jerk (TRACTION).

yard, *n.* courtyard, court, quadrangle (INCLOSURE); lawn, terrace (LAND).

yardstick, *n.* criterion, touchstone, standard (TEST, COMPARISON, JUDGMENT, MEASUREMENT).

yarn, *n.* narrative, tale, anecdote (STORY); fleece, shag, pelage (WOOL); thread, twist, linen (FILAMENT).

yaw, *v.* bend, curve, incline (TURNING).

yawn, *v.* gap, gape, yawp (OPENING).

year, *n.* twelvemonth (TIME).

yearly, *adj.* annual, perennial (TIME).

yearn, *v.* long, hanker, hunger (DESIRE).

yell, *v.* scream, screech, shriek (LOUDNESS, SHOUT).

yellow, *adj.* blond, gold (YELLOW); cowardly, afraid, recreant (FEAR).

YELLOW—*N.* **yellow,** blond, lemon, sulphur, brimstone, citrus, topaz, buff, canary, chrome, primrose, cream; brownish yellow, amber, ochre, carbuncle, tawny; reddish yellow, titian, tea rose, rust, orange, peach, apricot, saffron, crocus, citron, citrine, bisque, flesh color, flesh; greenish yellow, olive; gold, aurulence.

V. **yellow,** gild, begild, engild, aureate; jaundice, turn yellow.

Adj. **yellow,** blond, leucous, straw-colored, stramineous, flaxen; lemon-yellow, lemon-colored, citrine, citrean, citreous; topazine, buff, canary, canary-colored, canary-yellow, meline, primrose; cream, creamy, cream-color, cream-colored; luteous, fulvous, flavescent, xanthous, yellowish, flavescent, xanthic, vitelline, lutescent, luteolous (*bot. and zool.*), glaucous; greenish-yellow, olive, olive-colored, olive-drab; sallow, jaundiced.

gold, golden, aureate, aurulent; golden-haired, flaxen-haired, auricomous, blond, blond-haired, platinum, platinum-blond, towheaded, fair-haired.

[*reddish-yellow*] **orange,** peach, peach-colored, apricot, saffron, flesh-color, flesh-colored; titian, tea-rose; rust-colored, lurid, rufous.

[*brownish-yellow*] **amber,** amber-colored, ocherous, ochery, tawny.

See also METAL.

---

yelp, *v.* yip, yap, yawp (HIGH-PITCHED SOUND, ANIMAL SOUND).

yes, *n.* consent, acquiescence, assent (PERMISSION).

yes, *adv.* yea, aye, true (ASSENT); surely, undoubtedly, positively (CERTAINTY).

yesterday, *n.* long ago, bygone days (PAST).

yield, *n.* crop, harvest, product (STORE).

yield, *v.* produce, turn out, provide (PRODUCTION); give off, emit, afford (GIVING); bring in, sell for, cost (SALE); give up, surrender, quit (RELINQUISHMENT); give, relax, sag (SOFTNESS, BEND); submit, defer, bow to (SUBMISSION); admit, concede, grant (GIVING, PERMISSION, STATEMENT).

yielding, *adj.* pliant, pliable, compliant (SUBMISSION); ductile, malleable, plastic (SOFTNESS).

yoke, *v.* join, link, couple (JUNCTION); pair, match (TWO).

yokel, *n.* clodhopper, rube (*slang*), boor (RURAL REGION).

yore, *n.* time gone by, past time (PAST).

young, *adj.* youthful, juvenile (YOUTH).

youngster, *n.* colt, sapling, fledgling (YOUTH).

YOUTH—*N.* **youth,** prime, bloom, juvenility, tender years, dew, springtime of life; immaturity, puerility, green years, salad days, heyday of youth; adolescence, preadolescence, postadolescence, puberty; minority, juniority, nonage; juvenilism (*med.*); rejuvenation, rejuvenescence, juvenescence.

youthhood, boyhood, girlhood, teens, young manhood, young womanhood; childhood, infancy, babyhood, cradle, nursery.

youngster, youngling, colt, sapling, fledgling, sprig, juvenile, kid (*slang*); adolescent, minor, junior, teen-ager, preadolescent.

boy, lad, shaver, shaveling, stripling, hobbledehoy, gossoon, whelp (*contemptuous*) pup (*contemptuous*); gamin, urchin, street Arab, guttersnipe.

girl, maid, maiden, miss, virgin, demoiselle, damsel, damosel, colleen, ingenue, lass, lassie, petticoat, filly (*slang*), houri (*Moham.*), slip, wench, bobby-soxer (*colloq.*); debutante, bud; tomboy, hoyden, romp, chit, flapper (*colloq., used up to 1930*), giglet, minx, midinette (*F.*), witch.

V. **rejuvenate,** rejuvenesce, rejuvenize.

Adj. **young,** youthful, youthlike, youngling, vernal, tender, juvenile; adolescent, preadolescent, pubescent, hebetic, in one's teens, teenage; callow, green, immature, ungrown, underage, unripe, unfledged, puerile, budding, beardless, bread-and-butter, boyish, girlish, coltish; younger, junior, puisne (*law*).

rejuvenescent, juvenescent, revirescent, ageless.

See also CHILD, NEWNESS. *Antonyms*—See OLDNESS.

---

yowl, *v.* howl, wail, whine (ANIMAL SOUND); cry, bawl, blubber (WEEPING).

Z

Z, *n.* zed (*Brit.*), izzard (WRITTEN SYMBOL).

zany, *adj.* nonsensical, crazy, lunatic (ABSURDITY).

zany, *n.* clown, buffoon, jester (FOLLY).

zeal, *n.* ardor, fire, fanaticism (EAGERNESS, ENTHUSIASM, WILLINGNESS); passion, yen (DESIRE).

zealot, *n.* enthusiast, fanatic, monomaniac (ENTHUSIASM); partisan, zealotist (PREJUDICE).

zenith, *n.* climax, tiptop, pinnacle (HEIGHT).

zeppelin, *n.* airship, dirigible, blimp (FLYING).

zero, *n.* cipher, naught, nought (NONEXISTENCE).

zest, *n.* relish, gusto, enjoyment (PLEASURE); savor, flavor, tang; flavoring, seasoning, spice (TASTE, INTERESTINGNESS).

zigzag, *adj.* meandrous, snaky, serpentine, sinuous (WINDING).

zigzag, *v.* wind, crook, snake (WINDING, TURNING).

zincky, *adj.* zincic, zincous, galvanized (METAL).

zither, *n.* harp, lyre, lute (MUSICAL INSTRUMENTS).

zone, *n.* sphere, realm, ground (REGION); belt, zonule, band (ROUNDNESS).

zoo, *n.* menagerie (DOMESTICATION).

ZOOLOGY—N. zoology, natural history.

[*form and structure*] morphology, morphography; anatomy, zootomy; histology (*microscopic anatomy*), cytology (*cells*), embryology; paleontology.

[*development*] etiology, ontogeny, phylogeny, evolution, Darwinism, natural selection, Lamarckism, Neo-Darwinism, Weismannism.

[*habits, environment, etc.*] bionomics, ecology, zoogeography (*distribution*).

[*classification*] taxonomy, systematic zoology; categories: phylum, class, order, family, genus, species, subspecies (*or* variety).

mammalogy (*mammals*), mastology; ornithology (*birds*), entomology (*insects*), herpetology (*reptiles*), ophiology (*snakes*), helminthology (*worms*), ichthyology (*fishes*), cetology (*whales*), malacology (*mollusks*), conchology (*shells or mollusks*), carcinology *or* crustaceology (*crustaceans*).

zoologist, naturalist, morphologist, etc.

See also ANIMAL, DOMESTICATION. *Antonyms*—See BOTANY, MAN, MANKIND, PLANT LIFE.